Contemporary
Literary Criticism

Guide to Gale Literary Criticism Series

For criticism on	Consult these Gale series
Authors now living or who died after December 31, 1959	*CONTEMPORARY LITERARY CRITICISM (CLC)*
Authors who died between 1900 and 1959	*TWENTIETH-CENTURY LITERARY CRITICISM (TCLC)*
Authors who died between 1800 and 1899	*NINETEENTH-CENTURY LITERATURE CRITICISM (NCLC)*
Authors who died between 1400 and 1799	*LITERATURE CRITICISM FROM 1400 TO 1800 (LC)* *SHAKESPEAREAN CRITICISM (SC)*
Authors who died before 1400	*CLASSICAL AND MEDIEVAL LITERATURE CRITICISM (CMLC)*
Black writers of the past two hundred years	*BLACK LITERATURE CRITICISM (BLC)*
Authors of books for children and young adults	*CHILDREN'S LITERATURE REVIEW (CLR)*
Dramatists	*DRAMA CRITICISM (DC)*
Hispanic writers of the late nineteenth and twentieth centuries	*HISPANIC LITERATURE CRITICISM (HLC)*
Native North American writers and orators of the eighteenth, nineteenth, and twentieth centuries	*NATIVE NORTH AMERICAN LITERATURE (NNAL)*
Poets	*POETRY CRITICISM (PC)*
Short story writers	*SHORT STORY CRITICISM (SSC)*
Major authors from the Renaissance to the present	*WORLD LITERATURE CRITICISM, 1500 TO THE PRESENT (WLC)*
Major authors and works from the Bible to the present	*WORLD LITERATURE CRITICISM SUPPLEMENT (WLCS)*

ISSN 0091-3421

Volume 105

Contemporary Literary Criticism

Excerpts from Criticism of the Works
of Today's Novelists, Poets, Playwrights,
Short Story Writers, Scriptwriters, and
Other Creative Writers

Deborah A. Schmitt
EDITOR

Jeffrey W. Hunter
CLC COORDINATOR

Tim Akers
Pamela S. Dear
Daniel Jones
John D. Jorgenson
Jerry Moore
Polly Vedder
Timothy White
Thomas Wiloch
Kathleen Wilson
ASSOCIATE EDITORS

GALE

DETROIT • NEW YORK • TORONTO • LONDON

Library of Congress Catalog Card Number 76-46132
ISBN 0-7876-1195-6
ISSN 0091-3421

Printed in the United States of America
10 9 8 7 6 5 4 3 2 1

Contents

Preface vii

Acknowledgments xi

Preface

A Comprehensive Information Source on Contemporary Literature

Named "one of the twenty-five most distinguished reference titles published during the past twenty-five years" by *Reference Quarterly,* the *Contemporary Literary Criticism (CLC)* series provides readers with critical commentary and general information on more than 2,000 authors now living or who died after December 31, 1959. Previous to the publication of the first volume of *CLC* in 1973, there was no ongoing digest monitoring scholarly and popular sources of critical opinion and explication of modern literature. *CLC,* therefore, has fulfilled an essential need, particularly since the complexity and variety of contemporary literature makes the function of criticism especially important to today's reader.

Scope of the Series

CLC presents significant passages from published criticism of works by creative writers. Since many of the authors covered by *CLC* inspire continual critical commentary, writers are often represented in more than one volume. There is, of course, no duplication of reprinted criticism.

Authors are selected for inclusion for a variety of reasons, among them the publication or dramatic production of a critically acclaimed new work, the reception of a major literary award, revival of interest in past writings, or the adaptation of a literary work to film or television.

Attention is also given to several other groups of writers-authors of considerable public interest—about whose work criticism is often difficult to locate. These include mystery and science fiction writers, literary and social critics, foreign writers, and authors who represent particular ethnic groups within the United States.

Format of the Book

Each *CLC* volume contains about 500 individual excerpts taken from hundreds of book review periodicals, general magazines, scholarly journals, monographs, and books. Entries include critical evaluations spanning from the beginning of an author's career to the most current commentary. Interviews, feature articles, and other published writings that offer insight into the author's works are also presented. Students, teachers, librarians, and researchers will find that the generous excerpts and supplementary material in *CLC* provide them with vital information required to write a term paper, analyze a poem, or lead a book discussion group. In addition, complete bibliographical citations note the original source and all of the information necessary for a term paper footnote or bibliography.

Features

A *CLC* author entry consists of the following elements:

■ The **Author Heading** cites the author's name in the form under which the author has most commonly published, followed by birth date, and death date when applicable. Uncertainty as to a birth or death date is indicated by a question mark.

- A **Portrait** of the author is included when available.

- A brief **Biographical and Critical Introduction** to the author and his or her work precedes the excerpted criticism. The first line of the introduction provides the author's full name, pseudonyms (if applicable), nationality, and a listing of genres in which the author has written. To provide users with easier access to information, the biographical and critical essay included in each author entry is divided into four categories: "Introduction," "Biographical Information," "Major Works," and "Critical Reception." The introductions to single-work entries—entries that focus on well known and frequently studied books, short stories, and poems—are similarly organized to quickly provide readers with information on the plot and major characters of the work being discussed, its major themes, and its critical reception. Previous volumes of *CLC* in which the author has been featured are also listed in the introduction.

- A list of **Principal Works** notes the most important writings by the author. When foreign-language works have been translated into English, the English-language version of the title follows in brackets.

- The **Excerpted Criticism** represents various kinds of critical writing, ranging in form from the brief review to the scholarly exegesis. Essays are selected by the editors to reflect the spectrum of opinion about a specific work or about an author's literary career in general. The excerpts are presented chronologically, adding a useful perspective to the entry. All titles by the author featured in the entry are printed in boldface type, which enables the reader to easily identify the works being discussed. Publication information (such as publisher names and book prices) and parenthetical numerical references (such as footnotes or page and line references to specific editions of a work) have been deleted at the editor's discretion to provide smoother reading of the text.

- Critical essays are prefaced by **Explanatory Notes** as an additional aid to readers. These notes may provide several types of valuable information, including: the reputation of the critic, the importance of the work of criticism, the commentator's approach to the author's work, the purpose of the criticism, and changes in critical trends regarding the author.

- A complete **Bibliographical Citation** designed to help the user find the original essay or book precedes each excerpt.

- Whenever possible, a recent, previously unpublished **Author Interview** accompanies each entry.

- A concise **Further Reading** section appears at the end of entries on authors for whom a significant amount of criticism exists in addition to the pieces reprinted in *CLC*. Each citation in this section is accompanied by a descriptive annotation describing the content of that article. Materials included in this section are grouped under various headings (e.g., Biography, Bibliography, Criticism, and Interviews) to aid users in their search for additional information. Cross-references to other useful sources published by Gale Research in which the author has appeared are also included: *Authors in the News, Black Writers, Children's Literature Review, Contemporary Authors, Dictionary of Literary Biography, DISCovering Authors, Drama Criticism, Hispanic Literature Criticism, Hispanic Writers, Native North American Literature, Poetry Criticism, Something about the Author, Short Story Criticism, Contemporary Authors Autobiography Series,* and *Something about the Author Autobiography Series.*

Other Features

CLC also includes the following features:

- An **Acknowledgments** section lists the copyright holders who have granted permission to reprint material in this volume of *CLC*. It does not, however, list every book or periodical reprinted or consulted during the preparation of the volume.

- Each new volume of *CLC* includes a **Cumulative Topic Index,** which lists all literary topics treated in *CLC, NCLC, TCLC,* and *LC 1400-1800.*

- A **Cumulative Author Index** lists all the authors who have appeared in the various literary criticism series published by Gale Research, with cross-references to Gale's biographical and autobiographical series. A full listing of the series referenced there appears on the first page of the indexes of this volume. Readers will welcome this cumulated author index as a useful tool for locating an author within the various series. The index, which lists birth and death dates when available, will be particularly valuable for those authors who are identified with a certain period but whose death dates cause them to be placed in another, or for those authors whose careers span two periods. For example, Ernest Hemingway is found in *CLC,* yet F. Scott Fitzgerald, a writer often associated with him, is found in *Twentieth-Century Literary Criticism.*

- A **Cumulative Nationality Index** alphabetically lists all authors featured in *CLC* by nationality, followed by numbers corresponding to the volumes in which the authors appear.

- An alphabetical **Title Index** accompanies each volume of *CLC*. Listings are followed by the author's name and the corresponding page numbers where the titles are discussed. English translations of foreign titles and variations of titles are cross-referenced to the title under which a work was originally published. Titles of novels, novellas, dramas, films, record albums, and poetry, short story, and essay collections are printed in italics, while all individual poems, short stories, essays, and songs are printed in roman type within quotation marks; when published separately (e.g., T. S. Eliot's poem *The Waste Land),* the titles of long poems are printed in italics.

- In response to numerous suggestions from librarians, Gale has also produced a **Special Paperbound Edition** of the *CLC* title index. This annual cumulation, which alphabetically lists all titles reviewed in the series, is available to all customers and is typically published with every fifth volume of *CLC.* Additional copies of the index are available upon request. Librarians and patrons will welcome this separate index: it saves shelf space, is easy to use, and is recyclable upon receipt of the next edition.

Citing *Contemporary Literary Criticism*

When writing papers, students who quote directly from any volume in the Literary Criticism Series may use the following general forms to footnote reprinted criticism. The first example pertains to material drawn from periodicals, the second to material reprinted in books:

[1]Alfred Cismaru, "Making the Best of It," *The New Republic,* 207, No. 24, (December 7, 1992), 30, 32; excerpted and reprinted in *Contemporary Literary Criticism,* Vol. 85, ed. Christopher Giroux (Detroit: Gale Research, 1995), pp. 73-4.

[2]Yvor Winters, *The Post-Symbolist Methods* (Allen Swallow, 1967); excerpted and reprinted in *Contemporary Literary Criticism,* Vol. 85, ed. Christopher Giroux (Detroit: Gale Research, 1995), pp. 223-26.

Suggestions Are Welcome

The editors hope that readers will find *CLC* a useful reference tool and welcome comments about the work. Send comments and suggestions to: Editors, *Contemporary Literary Criticism,* Gale Research, Penobscot Building, Detroit, MI 48226-4094.

Acknowledgments

The editors wish to thank the copyright holders of the excerpted criticism included in this volume and the permissions managers of many book and magazine publishing companies for assisting us in securing reproduction rights. We are also grateful to the staffs of the Detroit Public Library, the Library of Congress, the University of Detroit Mercy Library, Wayne State University Purdy/Kresge Library Complex, and the University of Michigan Libraries for making their resources available to us. Following is a list of the copyright holders who have granted us permission to reproduce material in this volume of *CLC*. Every effort has been made to trace copyright, but if omissions have been made, please let us know.

COPYRIGHTED EXCERPTS IN *CLC*, VOLUME 105, WERE REPRODUCED FROM THE FOLLOWING PERIODICALS:

African American Review, Summer, 1992 for "Melvin B. Tolson and the Deterritorialization of Modernism" by Aldon L. Neilsen. Copyright © 1992 by the author. Reproduced by permission of the author.—*Belles Lettres: A Review of Books by Women,* v. 9, Spring, 1994. Reproduced by permission.—*Black American Literature Forum,* v. 18, Fall, 1984 for "Three Artists in Melvin B. Tolson's `Harlem Gallery'" by William H. Hansell. Copyright © 1984 by the author. Reproduced by permission of the publisher and the author.—*Book World--The Washington Post,* June 7, 1992; August 16, 1992; September 12, 1993. © 1992, 1993 Washington Post Book World Service/ Washington Post Writers Group. All reproduced with permission.—*boundary 2,* v. 18, Summer, 1991. Copyright © 1991 by Duke University Press. Reproduced by permission— *The Christian Science Monitor,* May 22, 1988; August 11, 1992. © 1988, 1992 The Christian Science Publishing Society. All rights reserved. Both reproduced by permission from The Christian Science Monitor.—*Cineaste,* v. 18, 1991; v. 19, 1993. Copyright © 1991, 1993 by Cineaste Publishers, Inc. Both reproduced by permission.—*CLA Journal,* December, 1983. Copyright, 1983 The College Language Association. Used by permission of The College Language Association.—*Commentary,* v. 39, June, 1965 for "The Anglo-Indian Theme" by John Mander; v. 94, November, 1992 for "The Critic as Novelist" by Evelyn Toynton. Copyright © 1965, 1992 by the American Jewish Committee. All rights reserved. Both reproduced by permission of the publisher and the authors.—*Commonweal,* v. CXVII, April 6, 1990. Copyright © 1990 Commonweal Publishing Co., Inc. Reproduced by permission of Commonweal Foundation.—*Contemporary Literature,* v. 17, No. 2, Spring, 1976. Reproduced by permission of the University of Wisconsin Press.—*Critique: Studies in Modern Fiction,* v. XVIII, 1976. Copyright © 1976 Helen Dwight Reid Educational Foundation. Reproduced with permission of the Helen Dwight Reid Educational Foundation, published by Heldref Publications, 119 18th Street, N. W., Washington, DC 20036-1802.—*The Economist,* June 25, 1988; August 15, 1992; v. 239, November 6, 1993. © 1988, 1992, 1993 The Economist Newspaper Group, Inc. All reproduced by permission.—*Encounter,* v. XLV, December, 1975 for "The Novelist as Dictator," by John Spurling. © 1975 by the author. Reproduced by permission of the author.—*Essays in Literature,* v. 15, Spring, 1988. Reproduced by permission.—*The Explicator,* v. 51, Fall, 1992; v. 42, Fall, 1983. Copyright © 1992, 1983 Helen Dwight Reid Educational Foundation. Both reproduced with permission of the Helen Dwight Reid Educational Foundation, published by Heldref Publications, 1319 18th Street, NW, Washington, DC 20036-1802.—*Film Comment,* v. 33, January-February, 1997 for "The Invisible Man: Spike Lee" by Kent Jones. Copyright © 1997 by Film Comment Publishing Corporation. Reproduced by permission of the author.—*Film Quarterly,* v. 45, Winter, 1991-92. © 1991 by The Regents of the University of California. Reproduced by permission of The Regents and the author.—*Hudson Review,* v. 18, Summer, 1965; v. XLIV, Winter, 1992; v. XLVII, Winter, 1995. Copyright © 1965, 1992, 1995 by The Hudson Review, Inc. All reproduced by permission.—*The Humanist,* v. 49, July/ August, 1989 for "Dignifying Humanity" by Troy Organ. Copyright 1989 by the American Humanist Association. Reproduced by permission of the author.—*The Journal of American History,* v. 80, December, 1993. Copyright Organization of American Historians, 1993. Reproduced by permission.—*Kirkus Reviews,* v. XLII, June 15, 1974. Reproduced by permission.—*Literature/Film Quarterly,* v. 24, 1996. © copyright 1996 Salisbury State College. Reproduced by permission.—*The Listener,* v. 89, March 22, 1975 for "The Novelist V. S. Naipaul talks about his work to Ronald Bryden" by V. S. Naipaul and Ronald Bryden. © British Broadcasting Corp. 1975. Reproduced by permission of the author.—*London Magazine,* v. 4, 1957; v. 7, May 2, 1985 for "Clytie's Legs" by Daniel Aaron; March 5, 1987 for "In

Brigid Brophy

1929-1995

Irish novelist, critic, essayist, journalist, short story writer, and dramatist.

The following entry presents criticism of Brophy's career through 1995. For further information on her life and works, see *CLC*, Volumes 6, 11, and 29.

INTRODUCTION

A lifelong crusader for multitudinous causes ranging from writers' rights and animals' rights to sexual freedom, women's liberation, and vegetarianism, Brophy produced a varied and extensive body of work. Her best-known novels are *The King of a Rainy Country* (1956), *The Finishing Touch* (1963), and *In Transit* (1969). Admittedly influenced by Sigmund Freud's theories, Ronald Firbank's literary style, and G. B. Shaw's aesthetics, Brophy's writings express unconventional and controversial opinions about modern relationships, religious education in schools, sexual psychology, pornography, and gender issues. Her work often incorporates elements of farce, word play, and witty social satire. While most critics initially responded to Brophy's works quite favorably—finding them consistently clever, lucid, imaginative, and absolutely unique—her books have been neglected for several reasons, although signs of a critical engagement with her oeuvre have begun to emerge. "The neglect of this brilliant woman's work and contributions to contemporary aesthetics is scandalous," remarked Steven Moore. "Those human beings who study contemporary literature never should forget Brophy."

Biographical Information

Born June 12, 1929, the only daughter of Irish novelist John Brophy, Brigid Brophy spent her childhood in London, but she frequently visited Ireland and was raised on Irish ideas. As a child who wrote verse dramas from the age of six onwards, she attended St. Paul's Girls' School and later studied for just four terms at Oxford University, where she excelled as a scholar but was expelled for disciplinary problems. She then took a variety of clerical jobs, published the short story collection *The Crown Princess* (1953), and began work on her first novel, *Hackenfeller's Ape* (1953), which won the Cheltenham Literary Festival first prize for a first novel. Brophy concentrated primarily on writing fiction early in her literary career, most notably the novels *The King of a Rainy Country, Flesh* (1962), *The Finishing Touch, The Snow Ball* (1964), and *In Transit*. She then turned to other forms: *Mozart the Dramatist* (1964), widely

regarded as one of the best books on his operas; *Don't Never Forget* (1966), a well-received collection of her journalism for such English periodicals as *London Magazine* and *New Statesman; Fifty Works of English Literature We Could Do Without* (1967), a controversial attack on such classics as *Beowulf, Hamlet, Jane Eyre,* and *The Scarlet Letter,* written in collaboration with Michael Levey, her husband, and literary critic Charles Osborne; *The Burglar,* a play in which the stage directions and introductory essay mimic the manner of Shaw; *Black and White* (1968), a critical assessment of the works of illustrator Aubrey Beardsley, who also was her subject in the biography *Beardsley and His World* (1976); *The Adventures of God in His Search for the Black Girl* (1973), her second collection of short fiction; and *Prancing Novelist* (1973), a critical biography of novelist Ronald Firbank. In 1974 Brophy joined the Writers Guild of Great Britain as a member of its executive council and the Anti-Vivisection Society of Great Britain, serving as vice-president. She published her last novel, *Palace without Chairs,* in 1978. The next year Brophy was diagnosed with multiple sclerosis, which worsened until she was housebound and confined to a wheelchair; her struggles with the debilitating disease are recounted in the essay collection *Baroque 'n' Roll* (1987). Brophy died on August 7, 1995, in a London nursing home.

Major Works

Brophy's works "evince a continuing emphasis upon art in the broadest sense," according to critic Leslie Dock, and her fiction usually features musical patterns and shifting tempos, cinematic or photographic effects, and architectural images—most notably, baroque—that enrich the narrative texture. *Hackenfeller's Ape* explores a number of themes, among them original sin, the romantic viewpoint, and experimentation on animals for scientific purposes; the novel depicts a scientist whose attempts to civilize an ape result in problems for both himself and the ape. *The King of a Rainy Country,* based largely on Mozart's opera *Le Nozze di Figaro,* focuses on a young boy and girl who embark on a literal and figurative search for a woman who represents their mother. *Black Ship to Hell* (1956), Brophy's first nonfiction work, analyzes the human impulse to violence through Freudianism and rationalism which, combined with her classicism, form the foundation of her critical stance. *Flesh,* Brophy's first popular success and loosely based on Shaw's *Pygmalion,* examines the eccentricities of human sexual behavior by showing the transformation of an introverted young man into a hedonist. *The Finishing Touch,*

Brophy's self-termed "lesbian fantasy," focuses on an English princess's education at a lesbian-run girls's finishing school on the French Riviera. *The Snow Ball*, which derives its plot from Mozart's opera *Don Giovanni*, is a comedy of manners that satirizes middle-class morality and hypocrisy. *In Transit*, widely regarded as Brophy's masterpiece but highly resistant to literary classification, relates the thoughts of an ambiguously gendered narrator, who sits in an international airport lounge waiting for a connecting flight, agonizing over his/her gender confusion while comically trying to determine his/her identity. Finally, *Palace without Chairs* involves an imaginary Eastern European socialist monarchy that eventually crumbles as each heir to the throne dies under unusual circumstances.

Critical Reception

Throughout her career Brophy was recognized as one of the most controversial writers in England, promoting her views in her books and in articles in periodicals as well as on television and radio. For instance, she advocated for and succeeded in the establishment of the British Public Lending Right, which pays royalties to authors whenever their books are checked out of libraries; referred to marriage as "an immoral institution"; exhorted the better treatment of animals long before it was popular; and wrote about gender confusion before a critical context for the topic existed. Many critics have admired Brophy's wit and social criticism, although others have considered her experiments with language, structure, and narrative as major hindrances to comprehending the themes of her fiction. However, Brophy's critical reputation has declined considerably since the early 1980s—the majority of her books remain out of print—despite the freshness and contemporary literary relevance of many of her ideas. A number of scholars have attributed several reasons for this neglect. Moore has suggested that, since her writing career was sharply curtailed by her fifteen-year illness, "few readers under the age of forty recognize her name." Moore also has detected, along with others, that "she was cursed for being too far ahead of her time," exploring topics that only came into vogue during the 1990s. Chris Hopkins has joined the debate by arguing that Brophy's work resists standard literary classifications and categories like realism, modernism, and postmodernism. Yet Hopkins has concluded that Brophy's "books have much to contribute to the current interest in [the postmodern feature of playing with boundaries], as well as to a more various history of twentieth-century literature."

PRINCIPAL WORKS

The Crown Princess, and Other Stories (short stories) 1953
Hackenfeller's Ape (novel) 1953
The King of a Rainy Country (novel) 1956

Black Ship to Hell (nonfiction) 1962
Flesh: A Novel of Indolent Passion (novel) 1962
The Finishing Touch (novel) 1963
Mozart the Dramatist: A New View of Mozart, His Operas and His Age (nonfiction) 1964
The Snow Ball (novel) 1964
Don't Never Forget: Collected Views and Reviews (essays) 1966
*Fifty Works of English Literature We Could Do Without [with Michael Levey and Charles Osborne] (criticism) 1967
Religious Education in State Schools (nonfiction) 1967
Black and White: A Portrait of Aubrey Beardsley (criticism) 1968
The Burglar: A Play and Preface (essay and drama) 1968
In Transit: An Herio-cyclic Novel (novel) 1969
The Longford Threat to Freedom (nonfiction) 1972
The Adventures of God in His Search for the Black Girl (novella and short stories) 1973
Prancing Novelist: A Defence of Fiction in the Form of a Critical Biography of Ronald Firbank (biography) 1973
Beardsley and His World (biography) 1976
Palace without Chairs: A Baroque Novel (novel) 1978
A Guide to Public Lending Right (nonfiction) 1983
Baroque 'n' Roll, and Other Essays (essays) 1987
Reads (essays) 1989

*This work also features American literature.

CRITICISM

Francis Wyndham (review date 1957)

SOURCE: A review of *King of a Rainy Country*, in *London Magazine*, Vol. 4, 1957, p. 69.

[*In the following review, Wyndham praise Brophy's achievement in* The King of a Rainy Country.]

A great deal of fuss is made nowadays about books by young writers and there is certainly no lack of these; young books, however, are more rare, books, that is, in which the quality of youth is a positive feature instead of being an excuse for inexperience or impressively disguised by a precocious maturity. Brigid Brophy is a young writer (under thirty) who has written a book about young people: in **The King of a Rainy Country** she strikes exactly the right note, conveying the gaiety, absurdity and pathos of youth without whimsy, complacency or self-pity. She is witty and observant and has produced, it seems to me, a model light novel. Her ghastly hero, her ruefully romantic heroine, the squalor of their London life, the hilarious account of their career as guides to a coach-load of American tourists in Europe, the culmination of their ridiculous quest at a film festival in Venice, are treated with high-spirited assurance: and when the fantasy of their emotional lives is splintered by a tentative contact with reality, an aching sadness is introduced which the author handles with unsuspected subtlety. This is, in fact, 'more' than the light novel it initially appears to be, but Miss Brophy achieves her serious intention with no sacrifice of readability, economy of style or funniness and although she has written a modern picaresque she shows no trace of the portentousness and implied aggression that this form now suggests.

Jocelyn Brooks (review date 21 March 1963)

SOURCE: "An Anatomy of Violence," in *Punch,* Vol. 242, March 21, 1963, p. 478.

[*In the mixed review below, Brooks suggests that* Black Ship to Hell *"might have been [better] if Miss Brophy had not tried to cover quite so much ground."*]

[*Black Ship to Hell*] is a vast, overloaded rag-bag of a book, in the tradition of Burtons's *Anatomy,* and Miss Brophy, like Burton, is prolific with quotations, recondite allusions and scraps of curious information. The book began, she tells us, as an attempt to psycho-analyse the Greek myth of the Underworld, but grew into a full-scale analysis of violence, aggression and the death-wish. Her attitude is anything but detached: she is a militant atheist, in a refreshingly old-fashioned way, and a militant Freudian as well. She delivers a virulent attack upon Jung, but too often herself falls into Jung's maddening habit of making dogmatic statements unsupported by the least shred of evidence. Apart from Freud, she draws much upon Frazer, and also upon Shaw, whose ideas she considers, rather oddly, to have been as influential as those of Freud himself.

In so far as she comes to any final conclusion, this would seem to be that our aggressive and self-destructive impulses can be overcome only by the release of sexual inhibitions: a theory which, one would have thought, a glance at any newspaper would be enough to disprove. War she considers to be almost entirely the result of repressed homosexuality—a view which, if shared by the Government, would presumably lead to the immediate implementing of the Wolfenden report. Or would it?

This is an interesting, sometimes amusing and often exasperating book; it might have been a better one if Miss Brophy had not tried to cover quite so much ground.

Joseph Kerman (review date 1965)

SOURCE: "Opera Misconstrued," in *The Hudson Review,* Vol. 18, no. 3, Summer, 1965, pp. 309-12.

[*Below, Kerman faults* Mozart the Dramatist *for ignoring Mozart's music and emphasizing a Freudian approach to the musician's operas.*]

I do not think that Miss Brophy knows quite what she is up to in [*Mozart the Dramatist*]. She has some striking and original ideas about the way Mozart's operas reflect his and his century's psychosexuality, but she is constantly shifting ground as to whether this information should be treated as criticism, biography, or sociology. She is as seduced as a sophomore by *Kulturgeschichte*—in her case, by a feminist Freudian *Kulturgeschichte*—but her extended references to Pope, Tiepolo, Jane Austen, Voltaire, *Les Liaisons Dangereuses, Paul et Virginie,* Thomas Love Peacock, Mozart, etc., get hopelessly side-tracked and tangled up. In general she makes herself hard to follow. Some chapters are two pages long, some nearly forty; *The Magic Flute* is analyzed in two practically rigorous long chapters, but one has to hunt for *Così fan tutte* among various obscurely named ones. The writing resembles stream of consciousness more than argument, a great jumble of exhaustingly clever remarks. Miss Brophy may not realize how strong an impression of intellectual exhibitionism her book creates; I am reminded of her own analysis of the role of the virtuoso woman singer in opera. Obviously she is a very bright person and awesomely well read, but unself-critical to an equally awesome degree. She can innocently write.

> Indeed, to my ear, though not, I know, to everyone's, this aria ["Mi tradì" from *Don Giovanni*] is so remarkably Bach-like that I think Mozart must have been musically archaising; and this perhaps is a sign, unconsciously given, that his extramusical thoughts had also gone back in time— to the performance he had witnessed seven years before of an out-of-date play by Shakespeare. Certainly it is in "Mi tradì" that the influence of *Hamlet* expresses itself most strongly: "Mi tradì" is, in fact, an epitome of all Hamlet's soliloquies.

Of course there is nothing in the least Bach-like about "Mi tradì," as, one gathers, Miss Brophy's friends have all been trying to tell her. The innocence consists in assuming that any impression, no matter how private, is worth throwing in pell-mell, as though a book were an analytic session.

The above passage catches the eye as one of extremely few about Mozart's music; Miss Brophy writes so interestingly about his erections and lavatory training that I was looking especially for comments of comparable sensitivity about the music. It is certainly my experience that revealing things can be and have been written about opera by people who are not professional musicians, that indeed the literary sensibility has a great deal to offer music criticism. But can you—ought you—write about Mozart if you can't tell Mozart from Bach? Can you write a book about Tiepolo if you are color-blind? what kind of a book?

Because it will ignore the artistic medium in question, in the deepest sense it will be a superficial book, even though in a superficial sense it may be probing the "deepest" motives. *Mozart the Dramatist* does not engage with Mozart's operas as such, as works of art in their integrity, and it does not even offer an account of the dramatic aspects of Mozart's operas, in spite of its title. No effort is made to isolate and treat all the important dramatic themes or events. So in *Figaro,* Miss Brophy speaks at length (and well) about seduction, but not about the epiphany at the forgiveness scene near the end. In *Don Giovanni* she notices an Oedipal Hamlet situation, but not the fantastic personal integrity of the Don confronted by the Statue. In *Così fan tutte* she draws an arresting parallel between the sisters and the Weber sisters between whom Mozart's affections vacillated, but ignores the feelings expressed by sisters and suitors when they find themselves and the other untrue.

The best one can say is that this book treats the myths or stories underlying the Mozart operas, and then not always fully. But an opera is more than a myth. Miss Brophy sees the distinction (at one time or another she acknowledges almost every facet of the problems she raises, without accepting the responsibility of dealing with them). In the course of an elaborate and even persuasive study of the Pasha Selim, whom she regards as the key figure in *The Abduction from the Seraglio,* she stops to note that he never sings:

> although he is peculiarly detached from the opera because he is not a singing part, the Pasha is much more closely involved with the story than Sarastro, who is a mere figurehead . . .

This is so Irish of Miss Brophy. Since the discourse of the Pasha exists on the colorless level of non-music, far below the imaginative plane of other people in the piece, he has no authority of any kind, whether personal or philosophical, whether as character or observer. As Miss Brophy would put it, he has been effectively castrated by Mozart and the librettist, and Constanze simply makes herself ridiculous by her hysterical reactions to his threats of rape. Miss Brophy does likewise, building everything on aspects of the opera that would remain the same if it had been composed by Handel or Dittersdorf, or if it had never been set to music at all.

It is too bad, intellectually speaking, that Miss Brophy is obsessed with sex; Freudian analysis is a dangerous stimulant for an exuberant and undisciplined mind such as hers.

The idea of hidden motives and their repression allows her to flit licentiously back and forth between any intellectual construction and its opposite. For instance, if the Age of the Enlightenment is characterized by the killing of father-figures, every time someone in an opera is killed that can be a sign of the times, and every time someone isn't that can be evidence of repression. If further we postulate Mozart's basic ambivalence towards his Age, those of his works that cannot be interpreted as pro-Enlightenment can be interpreted as anti. After discovering covert and contradictory sexual motives in every situation, comes the really serious work of discovering a criterion of relevance among them—doubtless as serious in psychoanalysis as in cultural and artistic analysis. In art, at least, a criterion exists in what the artist has chosen to present. Don Giovanni can easily be construed as a parricide, a prevaricating Hamlet who awaits the castration expected by all boys as punishment for Oedipal wishes, but the point is, how, in Mozart's opera, do his actions or his attitudes accord with such a construction? Nothing in the libretto or the music gives support to the idea that Don Giovanni reacts to the Commendatore, dead or alive, as to a father. Unlike Hamlet, he does not go through any "To be or not to be"; but, says Miss Brophy with a quite delightful wriggle, Hamlet's soliloquies are put in the mouth of Donna Elvira, thus illustrating opera's characteristic emphasis on women. "Certainly [that 'certainly'!] it is in 'Mi tradì' that the influence of *Hamlet* expresses itself most strongly . . ."

An opera is both less and more than a myth. If a motive is so far repressed as not to be articulated in the work of art, nothing is gained by bringing it to the surface. Criticism is not psychoanalysis. Art does not need to be healed.

The least Freudian part of the book, indeed, is the solidest, as well as the most closely—or anyhow, the least loosely—argued. In the section entitled, with characteristic aplomb, "'Die Zauberflöte' Solved," Miss Brophy is dealing for once with an overtly allegorical piece with clear mythological underpinnings. She turns from amateur psychoanalysis and amateur criticism to—suddenly—amateur scholarship, offering a new theory to account for the well-known confusions of the libretto. The problem is complex and I would suppose too specialized to discuss in a review—and still far from solution. Still this time the basic argument seems to me persuasive, even though, very interestingly, it assumes much the same form as the surrounding Freudian discourse. The thought is that the original plot had to be changed because, in depicting the initiation ceremonies in hell, it became too overtly Masonic; which cannot be proved because the Masonic rites remain secret. Even in a non-Freudian setting, Miss Brophy finds herself dealing with "repression" of an unknowable.

A strange book, a strange author, and a very strange author's picture on the dust-cover. In the middle ground, soberly clad, sits Miss Brophy, who one can see must clearly be nicer-looking than she appears here with her eyes averted and with the light playing around her mouth in such a way as to make her look older. In center focus is a bright little girl who points with trembling finger at Miss Brophy's lap, the direction also of Miss Brophy's gaze. As though to screen this blunt sexual reference, a plane object is placed edgewise on her knees—doubtless a child's drawing, since to the left another one is displayed, representing three girls dancing in bouffant skirts (repressed Graces?). Court ladies of the Enlightenment would have themselves painted by Nattier or Vigée-Lebrun in the roles of Venus, Hera, Psyche, or Galatea. Miss Brophy has herself photographed as Erda, but as *Urmutter* of artist girl-children only who draw girl-children only. Also as Pallas Athena, perhaps: on the exact level of her ears, a coarse diagonal swings all the way across the back of the photograph—a very heavily-laden bookshelf skewering her brain. Exquisitely, this bookshelf is tilted well off level.

My thoroughly amateur iconographic study has a slightly serious point. A good photograph should presumably show us what Miss Brophy looks like, not distribute clues about her self-image as mind and mother. Consciously or—is it possible?—unconsciously, she has quite misconstrued what photography is about; as she has done with opera.

Times Literary Supplement (review date 1 June 1967)

SOURCE: "Gone with the Wind," in *Times Literary Supplement*, No. 3405, June 1, 1967, p. 485.

[*In the following review, the critic asserts that* Fifty Works of English Literature We Could Do Without *"is little more than a compendium of flaunted smartness."*]

Brigid Brophy has won herself a small reputation in recent years as one of our leading literary shrews. Irascibly well-meaning, intemperately fond of common sense, she is known to have no time for mysteries or maladjustments. Kind to animals, cruel to lettuce, afraid of Virginia Woolf, she is mad about marriage, Mozart, Watteau and champagne. Her tone is hectoringly superior. She knows that sense cannot be all that common, since she has so much of it and others have so little. A lonely, ubiquitous toiler in the weekend graveyards, she has scored some direct hits on massive targets: Kingsley Amis, Henry Miller, Professor Wilson Knight. But she has been compensatingly indulgent to young, up-and-coming female novelists, and a mere whiff of the rococo makes her head spin.

Being right, though, is a solitary calling and for her latest publication B. B. has called in reinforcements, in the shape of Michael Levey (her husband) and Charles Osborne (Assistant Literature Director of the Arts Council). Just as in *Don't Never Forget* she packaged for posterity her merest book reviews, she has now had the idea of immortalizing her after-dinner conversation. Nibbling a nut roast, sipping a last glass of champagne, she has steered the brilliant conversation round to one of her favourite talking points: those Great Books to which the Eng. Lit. operators have persuaded us to pay Dutiful Homage but which, if we were *really honest,* we would admit are pretty second-rate. Neither Mr. Levey (who is Deputy Keeper of the National Gallery) nor Mr. Osborne is noted in his official role for iconoclastic demolition of old, over-rated objets d'art. But they seem to have pitched in with zest and the upshot is yet another volume we would gladly do without.

Fifty Works of English Literature We Could Do Without is little more than a compendium of flaunted smartness. Creaking wit, determined spleen, thin, anxious ironies. All the symptoms of an exhausted social eagerness are on display. The aim is for outrageousness, a superb refusal to be lulled by other people's tepid, idle judgments. The effect is of a damp impertinence. A good number of the chosen (or unchosen) works are easy sport, and a few really do deserve oblivion, but they are hounded with a good deal more ineptness than they can themselves be blamed for. And when this fanged trio set about, say, *Jane Eyre* or *The Scarlet Letter,* we can merely smile. Similarly, when Whitman is written off with a "what is one to say of this garrulous old bore?" (*which* garrulous old bore?) and Hopkins as "a mental cripple", or when we are instructed that "the man must have a heart of stone who could raise a laugh at *Volpone*", or when Defoe and Fielding and Smollett are all found to be as "red-faced as the brick houses of the [Georgian] period, but quite without their elegance and form"—whose mud is in whose eye? A sample of B. L. O.'s intricate textual criticism should put paid to any doubts. Here they are, on Wordsworth's "Daffodils":

> The implication is that to gaze and gaze at them is good for the health or the soul—perhaps even for the income. After all, Wordsworth claimed that gazing has brought him "wealth". Perhaps that's why he called these quintessentially yellow flowers "golden".

What acumen, what rigour! Is nothing sacred? Well, some things are—as a glance at Miss Brophy's old novel reviews will confirm. Janice Elliot, Hortense Calisher, Kathryn Perutz—it is to make room for talents of this magnitude that she would have us ditch the Brontës.

The New York Times Book Review (review date 25 February 1968)

SOURCE: A review of *Fifty Works of English Literature We Could Do Without,* in *The New York Times Book Review,* Vol. 73, February 25, 1968, p. 16.

[*In the following review, the critic wishes that the targets of* Fifty Works of English Literature We Could Do Without *included more of the "beefy sacred cows" of English literature.*]

[***Fifty Works of English* Literature We Could Do Without***] are 50 more or less sanctified old literary birds, habitat Eng. Lit., some still fluttering their wings in the halls of Academe, others so thoroughly fossilized one wonders at the waste of ammunition. They are works of English (*and American) literature the authors could do without, and they largely turn out to be works most of us have been doing without from the moment they were thrust into our unwilling hands early on the road to Graduation Day.

Thus we learn, to our surprise, that *Beowulf* is really a terrible bore and "dreadfully long," that *The Dream of Gerontius* (does anyone remember a word of it?) is dreary doggerel, that Whitman was a repressed(?) homosexual who wrote execrable poetry and that Maugham was a middlebrow. Well, if that were all, we could turn back to our bedside copies of *The Faerie Queene,* but that isn't quite all. This is primarily a blast at the fusty caretakers of the Eng. Lit. syllabus, and as such it is effective. But when the authors let fly at bigger game, notably T. S. Eliot, Hemingway and Faulkner, with some deadly bullets doux, they make one wish they had concentrated on more of these beefy sacred cows instead of all those bedraggled sitting ducks.

Times Literary Supplement (review date 23 November 1973)

SOURCE: "Shavian Shavings," in *Times Literary Supplement,* No. 3742, November 23, 1973, p. 1417.

[*In the review below, the critic admires* The Adventures of God in His Search for the Black Girl, *but dislikes Brophy's "ostentatious" display of her own erudition and "verbal dexterity."*]

It was Brigid Brophy who "devised" that enjoyable literary game in which television viewers could try identifying quotations quicker than the pundits. They would have had fun guessing the author of some items in Miss Brophy's new volume [***The Adventures of God in His Search for the Black Girl***]—a bedside book for the irreverent intellectual. There are some Swiftian fables, a conte or two to please bright kids, and chop-logical conversations such as Lewis Carroll would have appreciated; the title refers to a Socratic dialogue, with echoes of Peacock, a cast that includes Voltaire, Samuel Butler and (of course) "the elderly gentleman with white hair and a white beard" who introduces himself with a page of Irish historical diatribe before delightedly joining the "celestial Fabian Society".

Miss Brophy is always *sui generis,* despite her fondness for playing jokes with her favourite authors, and makes good use of this Shavian bran-tub to provoke, shock or argue the reader into sharing at least some of her preoccupations—vegetarianism, feminism, atheism, and pacifism. A great many bees buzz energetically away, so that the dialogue of the dead is just as likely to include a harangue on characterization in Shakespeare, a plan for public library royalties, and a comparison of the literary merits of Genesis and *Treasure Island* as a metaphysical discussion on human and divine love. There is no doubt that Miss Brophy is exceedingly funny when she is also impassioned—how, for instance, does God reply to "the humble Christian's" ardent prayers? Since the whole debate has arisen because God is determined to demonstrate for good and all that he is a fiction, he merely complains gloomily that his followers are

> like an officious secretary who considers herself a "treasure" because she keeps a pop-up card index that reminds her to remind the boss when his aunt's birthday is coming along . . . only, in my case, it's of my own birthday that they insist on giving me warning weeks in advance.

And it turns out that the Black Girl (who has become one Hector Erasmus Mkolo on a pilgrimage to Rome and Western Success) originated as a female version of *Candide*—a tribute that Voltaire, who appears here as more of an atheist than most historians might accept, receives without comment.

Elysian Fabians may not have been quite what Gibbon, credited with this particular literary game, had in mind. Certainly Shaw's prudish and aseptic ghost would be shocked by Miss Brophy's **"Homage to Back to Methuselah"**, in which Corydon and Co. learn the corruption of materialism by discovering that a ruby lasts longer and shines more brightly than the menstrual blood previously thought of as their greatest treasure. Nor do we all find a ghoulish pastiche of Agatha Christie-ish detection, in which the assembled house-party guests realize that they are accused of murdering kidney, bacon and haddock (not to mention the leather-covered books and desk) quite the witty exposé of our carnivorous customs Miss Brophy intends. The bad taste is, of course, a deliberate challenge to smug indifference. Aspects of society we pretend to deplore invite this kind of satire; Emperors of East and West might one day swim to an ocean chat and agree to total disarmament; it is not altogether preposterous to argue that "poverty is the commonest crime" when the poor suffer very similar deprivations to convicted felons.

Where Miss Brophy tends to lose sympathy—for which this book so entertainingly begs and bullies—is in wearing her "quiz-game" erudition (snippets of half-digested knowledge) and her very considerable verbal dexterity quite so ostentatiously. Far too many puns are of the order of the Minotaur saying he's now a minotaurist attraction, too many good ideas—like the reluctant millionaire who demands amputation of any of his own limbs that contribute nothing to efficiency—are extended just beyond our initial appreciation of the paradox. Like *Fifty Works of English Literature We Could Do Without*, this is Miss Brophy taking the mickey—and if it weren't for the vigour and blarney of her approach, one would be inclined to dismiss her as wasting talent on readers she clearly doesn't much like.

Kirkus Reviews (review date 15 June 1974)

SOURCE: A review of *Adventures of God in His Search for the Black Girl*, in *Kirkus Reviews*, Vol. XLII, No. 12, June 15, 1974, p. 646.

[*Below, the critic briefly describes the content of* Adventures of God in His Search for the Black Girl.]

Brigid Brophy, critic of note and stylist absolutely par excellence, is also a bit of a crazy lady in the classical sense—defender of animals, decrier of hypocrisies, champion of reason and beauty, a sort of solitary, spiritual activist who vaults along by sheer perverse whimsicality and logic. It must be a happy state of existence, judging by these stories, or fables, or whatever you would call the likes of, say, Brahms and Polyhymnia sniping back and forth about Sir Edward Elgar—in which Brophy provides herself with arrestingly choice occasions for the airing of her views which might not hold up so well in a more usual form of exposition. Instead, a frequent ploy is to invent a couple of types or invoke historical personages and let them bat out restricted segments of the argument. Voltaire, Gibbon and God, plus a psychiatrist and a couple of academic specialists and an assortment from the general populace, cover a good many topics in the course of a ramble across the Elysian fields, God proving to be a quite sophisticated, reflective sort of being, modest, and profoundly cognizant of his existential nature as a fictional character. (He has a striking rapport with Voltaire, who is less modest and posthumously addicted to psychoanalysis.) The topics they debate

would interest the parties involved, probably, and the quality of the argument will delight anyone with a suitably literary turn of mind, but these are crotchets that will be shared or not. What everyone can enjoy in Brophy is style and wit nearly always adequate to the burdens she puts upon them. The few real fables are acid and lovely, just as such.

Brigid Brophy with Leslie Dock (interview date 17 July 1975)

SOURCE: "An Interview with Brigid Brophy," in *Contemporary Literature*, Vol. 17, Spring, 1976, pp. 151-70.

[*In the following interview conducted on July 17, 1975, Brophy discusses her early career, the influence of psychoanalysis, Sigmund Freud, Ronald Firbank, and Mozart on her works, her position as a feminist, and her association with the Writers' Action Group.*]

Novelist, playwright, critic, and essayist, Brigid Brophy is an Anglo-Irishwoman who lives in England. Her childhood was spent in London, yet, since her father, the novelist John Brophy, was fervently Irish, she visited Ireland frequently and was brought up on Irish ideas. As a child she appeared briefly in a film, was bathed by T.E. Lawrence, and wrote verse dramas from the age of six onwards. After attending Oxford for four terms, Brophy was, in effect, expelled for indiscretions. She then took a variety of clerical jobs, published a volume of short stories, and began work on her first novel, *Hackenfeller's Ape* (1953). While writing it she met Michael Levey, who is now her husband and director of the National Gallery. With their daughter Kate, Levey and Brophy live in an elegant four-room flat on the Old Brompton Road in London, where the interview took place on July 17, 1975.

Since 1953, when her first volume was published, Brophy's output has been extensive: six novels, two collections of short prose fiction, one play, four nonfiction works, a critical collection written in collaboration with Michael Levey and Charles Osborne, and numerous articles. Her best-known novels are *The King of a Rainy Country* (1962), *The Finishing Touch* (1963), and *In Transit* (1969). *Black Ship to Hell* (1956), her first nonfiction work, is a lengthy treatment of Freudianism and rationalism which, combined with her classicism, are the underpinnings of her critical stance.

Her essays, both topical and critical, treat issues and the arts from a psychological and rational standpoint. In England Brophy is known both for her fiction and as a proponent of human and animal rights who writes and speaks out in favor of vegetarianism, birth control for animals and birds, prison reform, freedom from censorship, and a change in attitudes toward marriage and divorce. Her essays are both whimsical and penetrating: she has analyzed Mickey Mouse as a modern folk-hero and animated phallic symbol.

What Brophy considers to be the best, or most representative, of her articles are collected in the nonfiction volume, *Don't Never Forget* (1966). An allusion to a phrase in one of Mozart's letters (written, in broken English, to an English-speaking friend), the title reflects Brophy's love for Mozart's music and her eclecticism. To varying degrees, her works all evince a continuing emphasis upon art, in the broadest sense. She uses musical patterns and shifting tempos, cinematic or photographic effects, and architectural images—most notably, baroque—to enrich the texture of her fiction.

Although her approach to fiction and concern with human and animal rights have remained fairly constant, her works are not all of a piece, which, she thinks, may be one reason for her not being well-known, especially in the United States. *Hackenfeller's Ape* explores a number of themes, among them original sin, the romantic viewpoint, and experimentation on animals for scientific purposes; *The Burglar* (1968) treats sexual puritanism and society's attitudes toward criminals; *The King of a Rainy Country* concerns a young boy and girl who undertake a literal and figurative search for a woman who represents their mother; and so on. Her most recent work, *The Adventures of God in His Search for the Black Girl*, subtitled *A Novel and Some Fables* (1968), indicates her debt to Shaw, as do the preface to, and stage directions for, *The Burglar*. Equally influential on Brophy's style and aesthetics is Ronald Firbank, the subject of her nonfiction work, *Prancing Novelist* (1973), and the stylistic model for *The Finishing Touch*.

Although she claims not to be totally Irish and, like Yeats, has lost faith with the Irish revolutionary movement, she retains an Irish drollness of expression and speech. Unfortunately, an interview such as this diminishes the satiric force of her diction in phrases such as "The British Museum has not made me an offer." Her voice, although soft, is musical. She sits very still, thinks about a question, utters a characteristic "ahh" or "ummm," then plunges into a complex sentence structure.

[Dock:] *Having read your article, "My Mother," I have a fairly clear impression of her personality. About your father, I know little other than that he was a "middlebrow novelist."*

[Brophy:] I was so fond of him that, although ten years have passed since his death, I still don't find it very easy to talk about him. I got on with him, by nature, very much better than with my mother. We had in common the fact that, ob-

viously, the arts meant more to us than anything else. He was a very generous, very easygoing person. We argued and disagreed furiously about literature the whole time, but, as I say, had this in common, that it mattered desperately to us both. What else ought I to say about him?
If you don't want to say more, fine.

He was a very remarkable person in very many ways and a lot of people have asked me why I have never written about him, but I don't think this would be emotionally possible.

In the story "Fordie," which is in **Crown Princess,** *a collection of your early stories, are any of the characters— Fordie, Philip, or Elgin—based on real persons?*

I shouldn't think so. I think it's probably true to say that, with one exception, I have never written anything based on a real person, though obviously little pieces of real experience get used. But I have certainly never attempted to put— and I don't think I have ever even inadvertently succeeded in putting—a real person into a book.

What would that one exception be?

I wrote a novel called **The King of a Rainy Country,** in which there is a young man called Neale; that was a deliberate, close attempt—definitely, though with all his externals disguised—to make a portrait of somebody I had been involved with.

Was he the "Jungian"? You said in an essay that you were once attached to a Jungian, and that later the relationship ended with your disliking both the Jungian and Jung.

That is very shrewd of you. Yes, indeed, he was, or is, the character on whom Neale is based.

Would you care to tell his name, or not?

It is probably better that I shouldn't; he is in no way famous, but I wouldn't care to suffer his return into my life after all these years, in the form of a libel action.

You published an article entitled "The Rococo Seducer" two years before **The Snow Ball** *appeared in print. How long do you usually work on each novel?*

I have no idea how long the ideas for a novel germinate: probably a very, very long time. The actual writing I usually do very quickly, but one of the stories in that first collection—the stories that you spoke of, which I published when I was twenty-two or twenty-three—I can remember writing an early version of when I was fifteen, during my Latin class in school. So, things do go on for a very long time in the mind. But they don't for me go on for very long on paper.

Do you remember which story that was?

It was a story called **"The Late Afternoon of a Faun."**

Ah, yes. I can see how it could be an escape from Latin class, in a way.

It was, indeed, classically inspired. I was a person who read Latin and Greek at Oxford, because of a passionate love of Greek. At that time I disliked Latin very much indeed, but one couldn't do Greek without Latin, so I had to struggle through it. And, indeed, through exploring the nonclassical periods of Latin literature, I came to have much more respect for the Latin language than I set out with.

*How long did it take you to write **Black Ship to Hell**? The reason I ask is that I was wondering if you had those ideas in mind when you wrote **The King of a Rainy Country**.*

Yes, I think I probably did quite consciously have the ideas in mind; I certainly did unconsciously. It took me a long time to write. I wrote a complete version of it first in a completely undramatized manner, just as if I had been writing a statistical report, or something. I had difficulty finding a publisher for it, and so on, and came to see that this escape wouldn't do, that if one were going to write nonfiction, one couldn't just write it as though one were concocting a report. So then I rewrote the whole book, at a time when I had a very young child around; thus it was a very happy book to write, but it was very fraught, physically, because I had this thing crawling around on the desk at the time!

*Yes, there is that gap between 1956 and 1962, between **The King of a Rainy Country** and **Black Ship to Hell**; were you more or less taking care of Kate the whole time and working on the book when you could?*

Yes. I had a gap, a sort of emotional gap, anyway—a thing I used to have in those days about writing—I no longer do. And then, in that intermittent gap I had the child, and this proved to be sufficient occupation for the time being.

Do you type, or do you write rough drafts longhand? How many drafts do you write?

I write the whole thing in longhand, meticulously. I can't actually even write a letter straight onto the typewriter, partly because I touch-type. I earned my living as a typist and therefore the eye constantly seeks the copy to copy from, so I have to have one, as I say, to write a letter.

*In your article **"Sex-'n'-Violence"** you say that psycho-analysis, by advancing the concept of normality, has hindered the advance of sexual tolerance. Have your attitudes toward psychoanalysis changed significantly since the publication of **Black Ship to Hell**?*

I don't think so. I think that, as Freud himself recedes in history, it becomes easier to pick on the things which were incidental (and a lot of what he said about women comes under that heading) and to, as it were, write them off. At the same time I think my impression of the absolutely vital, Aristotelian-sized importance of what he discovered just grows stronger and stronger; hardly a day goes by without some incident which simply makes one say over and over again, "He was right! He was right!" If one goes to a committee meeting somebody will betray what he is really thinking by a slip of the tongue.

So, then, your contention is with psychoanalysis, and not with Freud; your contention is with his practitioners?

I differ from Freud; he was superman, but he wasn't super-superman. He couldn't instantly distinguish between where he'd picked up the accepted ideas of his time and where the truth was: so, once or twice, he went wrong. But I think it was, to revert to this normality thing, inevitable that he should take over that concept of normality from medicine— he was a doctor—and take over the concept of, "If it's normal, it's healthy, it functions," and this is not an adequate concept to deal with human beings in society, because one has to take in "what it ought to be," as well. I think he wasn't always altogether clear about this, but he was so good at clearing through the undergrowth, that one is not accusing him.

*In **Black Ship to Hell** you observe that the eighteenth century failed to produce a "penetrating literary aesthetic because it lacked a free and vital theater." You have also said that you began writing plays at the age of six. Why is it, then, that you have written many more novels than plays?*

Oh, because nobody would put the plays on, as simple as that. They put one on, and it was a gross commercial failure.

The Burglar?

Yes. There have been quasi-bites ever since, towards later ones, with the stipulation to me, "If you rewrote the whole of Act Two, and changed all the male characters into female characters, and moved the whole setting from Sweden to Australia, then. . . ." But nothing serious. I feel very attracted by the theater, but I know now, what I didn't know at the time of *The Burglar,* that the author's responsibility extends all the way. You've got to go to every rehearsal; you've got to teach the actors how to act in the style you want; when they say, "I can't say the line," you've got to explain to them the idea of the line as it's written; you've got to tell the director the pace at which it should go; you've got to do everything in the theater. And I'm not very good at doing these personal things in personal relationships to people I don't know very well. Therefore, I prefer to dodge out of this responsibility.

It would be easier, then, if you did a movie because, once done, it would be forever on film, as your books are forever on paper.

It would be very nice to do a movie, I must say!

You mentioned in the preface to **The Burglar** *that you had written a play, or were about to write a play, called "Libretto" or "The Libretto." Was it ever published, and if so, where? I haven't been able to find it.*

No, it was never published, because it was never performed. In England one can't publish a play that hasn't been performed.

How early did you begin reading Ronald Firbank? Do you remember when it was?

No. I read one novel, *The Artificial Princess,* as a child; I guess there was a copy in my home. I don't know at what age, because I began reading everything at the age of about five.

Part Two of the preface to **The Burglar** *begins with your describing the writer of your works as a "masochistically-inclined non-narcissist." In other articles, as well, you speak of your masochism. Could you please elaborate: do you see writing as a masochistic act?*

No, except insofar as it's very painful, but then creating a work in any medium is very painful, I imagine. No, I don't think writing is, in itself, masochistic. I think that one might guess the masochism in my personality from the fact that I practice criticism as well as creative writing, which would suggest that the critical faculty was very sharpened and was always ready to turn on the creator.

Have you read Simon Raven's insulting article, "Brophy and Brigid," in which he maintains that the "intelligent writer of clear masculine prose is Brophy," whereas Brigid is the "faddy and finicking" female? That review was in the Spectator, 1966.

I may have read it, yes; it doesn't sound unfamiliar.

I ask because, in **In Transit,** *there are those constant flagellation scenes where "he" is flagellating or whipping*

"her." And I was wondering if, perhaps, you were parodying Raven's comment at that point.

Not consciously, but I recognize it; obviously, I've read it. So you could be right.

I wondered if you were, perhaps, parodying his views entirely, parodying the idea that the male is the dominant type. It wouldn't necessarily be that you would have read his review, but I thought you might be splitting yourself into the "he" and the "she," with the masochistic writer being beaten by this ascendant, logical type?

It would be amusing! But I don't think that I would sufficiently accept that the male is the logical one, the female illogical and subservient.

Of course, I meant that the split would be a parody, because you've said in your essays that women are men's equals.

Well, it may be an unconscious parody; you may well be right, but I was certainly not aware of it.

Hunter Davies conducted a personal interview with you in your home in March, 1974, and from that I gathered several facts about your life, about your relationship with your husband, and so forth. My question is, superficially, **Flesh** *and* **The Snow Ball** *seem to be based on your experiences: the lovers' meeting each other at a New Year's Eve party in* **The Snow Ball***; Marcus' sense of being lost, then "finding himself" in marriage in* **Flesh,** *and so on. You have said that you once worked for a firm which sold pornographic books, as does Susan in* **The King of a Rainy Country.** *Did you ever guide a tour of Americans through the Continent, as does Susan?*

No, the guided tour was pure fiction. I once worked for a firm which sold "remaindered" books, some of which were pornographic, but it wasn't exactly a pornographic bookseller, as it were. The whole of *Flesh* is pure fiction. Marcus bears no resemblance whatever to my husband, and I trust I bear none to Marcus' wife.

The meeting at a New Year's Eve party in *The Snow Ball* was a case of entirely unconscious autobiography, because that was a very grand party in fancy dress, and part of the point of the book was that these were two not-rich people, in among rich people. The party where I, in fact, met my husband, was very far from grand, and nobody was in fancy dress, and so on. But obviously, there was an element of autobiography in it; it was entirely unconscious until a man that we both knew remarked on it to me one evening, and I said "My God!" So I was actually unaware of that.

Their meeting at a New Year's Eve party is convenient

from a classical point of view; New Year's Eve marks the changing of the year, the time of upheaval, and so forth, so I can see why, structurally, you'd want to do it that way.

Yes, it had many determinants, and my relationship to my husband has not been so fleeting and unhappy as that relationship was, thank God.

Fordie, in the story of the same name, is womanish (he wears a shawl and is termed "dear mother"); the professor in **Hackenfeller's Ape** *sings the Countess' song; the narrator of* **In Transit** *is confused about his or her sexual identity; and the choral pitches in* **In Transit** *are such that males sing soprano, women bass. Could you please comment on your purpose in merging, reversing, or reworking sexual stereotypes so frequently? for blending male and female stereotypic characteristics?*

Yes, first, a simple Freudian recognition of the basic bisexuality of everybody. Second, a conscious desire to counteract the mythology of literary criticism at the moment, which so often cries that only women can write about women, and only men can write about men. One constantly reads that there are no good parts for women in the theater, because there aren't enough women dramatists. The point is, that Hedda Gabler and Cleopatra were not created by women dramatists. I have a feeling that this is not only a mistaken approach to sex, but also a mistaken mythology of basic mental differences between the sexes, which I don't accept exists. I feel that that mythology is a denial of imagination, which I think one has to counter.

The whole purpose of fiction is that the writer (and thereby the reader) is transported into some form of life which is absolutely different from his own; and to be transported, if one is female, to a male character, and vice versa, is a terribly light transposition: this is a very small flight, compared to what the imagination can do. Consequently, I feel a certain obligation to insist on the mental interchangeability of the sexes, as well as believing that this is basically true.

Yes, Virginia Woolf's conception of androgyny. You don't like her novels, though, do you, as a rule?

No, I don't, I'm afraid. I wish I could; I think she was ever-so-right about ever-so-many things, but she just doesn't, for me, take off as a novelist.

In a 1965 essay, "The Unmentionable Subject," you said that the subject on which you had written and about which you had thought the most, was art; second, human and animal rights; and third, sex. Since then, has the order changed at all?

No, all that has happened is that the first has slightly blended in my life with the second, in that the last three years of my life have very largely been given to a struggle for authors' rights.

With Maureen Duffy and the Writers' Action Group?

Yes. We are still very deeply engaged in a campaign for Public Lending Right, and we are also engaged in a trade union for writers, and in generally insisting on authors' rights, so this, I would say, is a practical merging of the first and the second. A trade union for writers is not a very sexy occasion, so to that extent, the third has had to recede.

I see the first and the third as part of each other, actually; in **In Transit,** *sex and art are interwoven; the book continually weaves in the pornographic "sub-art" form.*

Yes. Would you say that human rights are involved for or against pornography?

Human rights would be for pornography.

Yes.

At times you have expressed a fascination with "American" as a language. Yet you have also said that the American language is "licking the brains out of [your] native civilisation." Would you elaborate, please?

I think the threat to the English language from the southern section of the United States has slightly receded. There was a time, which obviously began during the war, when, I think, there was a genuine danger that English-English was going to be replaced by United States-English. You will note how pedantically I call it "United States-English," not "American-English," which shows a simple, Gore Vidal-like objection to United States imperialism. I have always wanted to make some public reference to Castro as the American president, to show that he's an American too.

I think that the danger to our language from United States-English is probably now past, but there's a whole spectrum of bureaucratese which issues from the European economic community, which is not a language at all; it's not the idiom of any of the countries in Europe: this is the new danger.

We call it "duckspeak."

"Duckspeak." I don't know, I think ducks are perhaps more articulate. At least, I don't think they make their noises in order to obscure thought.

If you were thinking about commenting on Castro as an American president, and if you were going to step into that *arena, I was wondering why you have never said much about the political situation in Ireland. In the article, **"Am I an Irishwoman?"** you do discuss the Irishman's feeling of being a second-class citizen, his feeling about taking on English, which is not quite his own language, and yet not being an Irishman; yet I wonder why you have never commented on the situation in Northern Ireland in an article?*

I *have* commented on it, in fiction, actually, though in a very disguised way, in a book called *The Adventures of God in His Search for the Black Girl.*

Since I wrote that essay about being quasi-Irish, I have, emotionally, withdrawn totally from Ireland, and I was amused to notice that certain self-reproaches still happen about this. The last twenty-third of April we of the Writers' Action Group staged a demonstration of writers outside the Ministry of the Arts, in Belgrave Square, demanding PLR [Public Lending Right]. We chose to do this on the twenty-third of April because it's both the putative birthday of Shakespeare and St. George's Day, and St. George is the patron saint of England. We asked two actors to dress up as St. George and the dragon; we took a bunch of red roses (red roses for England) to the Minister of the Arts, and said, "Would you please rescue English literature?" The speakers at this rally each wore a red rose, for England, on St. George's Day. And as I stood on the platform, a sudden terrible arrow went through me: "You are not English; you shouldn't be wearing a red rose; St. George's Day is nothing to you; you were brought up to celebrate St. Patrick's Day." And I was very amused that this feeling could still, from one's childhood, reach out and affect me.

Juliet Mitchell, in Psychoanalysis and Feminism, *discusses Freud's using the Zeus-Kronos-Uranus myth to "supplement the Oedipal legend" in Freud's "recreation of man's phylogenetic and ontogenetic history." In **Black Ship to Hell** you discuss the Diana Triformis myth. The three women in **The King of a Rainy Country**—Cynthia, Helena, and Susan—seem to embody the Diana trinity, and Neale and Susan both seem to be working through Oedipal conflicts. Could you please comment on your reasons for using a mythical framework or pattern for **The King of a Rainy Country**?*

I think the reasons are practical. One has only the furniture of one's own mind, and I am, as I say, a classical scholar (or I was) and a Freudian; given that each layer of furniture is reinforced by the other, I had no alternative. I don't think that it is very insisted-on; but you were absolutely right to detect it.

Part of my question concerns the fact that some writers have criticized Freud for not analyzing sufficiently women's myths. Were you trying to add on to the body of Freudian

myth-analysis by presenting, in novel form, a working-out of the women's part of the Zeus-Kronos-Uranus myth? There are very few characters in that novel. There's Neale, of course, yet he's actually another facet of Susan (this is my impression); he says he has her past; they have pasts in common; both are looking for a mother. Then there's Philip, and he seems to be a mere appendage to Helena.

Yes, he's not there. I think that this effect may be the result of, in me, the egotism of youth. Or, if I were lucky, it might be an attempt to actually depict the egotism of youth. It is a first-person novel; it's the only one that contains any consciously, deliberately, autobiographical material. It was probably a rather belated attempt on my part to outgrow that material and distance it. Whether it was consciously an attempt to add an Electra side to the Oedipus, I don't know. However, whether it was conscious or unconscious, you were right in detecting that that's what it does.

*You describe the style, the idiom, of **The Finishing Touch** as "superficially Firbankian." Yet the content and plot, to me, seem to owe something also to Colette, specifically* Claudine at School. *Would you agree?*

Certainly, I think the plot does, and the atmosphere. This is another interesting example of how hard it is for people to believe that one's work is entirely nonautobiographical. The number of people, starting with the publisher of the book, who asked which finishing school I had been at, you would hardly believe.

The publisher was terribly worried, because he took it for an absolutely straightforward account of the finishing school I had been at; he was terribly worried about libel. I assured him I had never been at a finishing school in my life, and had no idea, even, what they were like. He found this very hard to believe, and indeed sent somebody to the South of France to search for finishing schools that might take an action against him.

Yes, it might well owe a lot to Colette, and to the *Claudine* books in particular, which I am curiously fond of, absurd as they are, in a way. They contain, I think, some of her most directly autobiographical, in an emotional sense, material.

*But when you wrote the book you weren't consciously saying, "*Claudine at School *depicts events when the two headmistresses were young; let's see what happens when they're a bit older and when the weaker one has the upper hand." In other words, you weren't consciously reworking Colette's material and taking the book one step further, from a different perspective?*

I don't think so, because what I consciously had in mind

was a real-life situation which concerned an educational institution in London (which I will not name), but a very much higher educational institution than the one in the book, in London, which had a male director and a female vice-director who was terribly gone on him. He was extremely elegant and fey, and as queer as a coot. And this extremely tweedy, down-to-earth lady, his deputy, was romantically so absolutely besotted by him, that this situation had for a long time amused Michael and me very much. This was, as it were, the germ of the book. Michael caught chicken pox from our daughter, had to stay at home for three weeks, and was very bored. He felt terribly ill for the first twenty-four hours, and then felt better, but he couldn't go out, for fear of infecting people. So I produced something to amuse him.

But, of course, in the process you changed the characters from a woman and a man to two women. I think that makes quite a difference to the reader.

Yes. It would have been very hard to create a scandal from a woman and a man; therefore it had to be changed.

You have criticized Simone de Beauvoir for her pedantry, for being a plodder, for her deficient style and content—specifically, for missing Freud's point. Are there any feminists, other than de Beauvoir, that you do admire or favor?

What is a feminist? I mean, there are many women writers that I admire, and I certainly admire any woman who gets on with the job as though she were not a woman. I may have a very slight dislike for, and contempt for, women who make a profession out of being women, as indeed I have for Frenchmen living in England who make a profession out of being Frenchmen, or anything of that kind. I am a feminist, of course, but there is no sense in which I would accept that women are anything but the total equals of men. Perhaps I have the feeling that, if one has no subject matter except feminism, then one is trading on nothing, as though one were to make a career out of proclaiming that grass is green.

You don't think, then, that Greer's The Female Eunuch, *which you seem not to mind, in* "Everybody's Lib," *has any validity for the women or men who haven't had their "consciousnesses raised," as the cliché has it?*

This is always a difficult matter: should one pick out these things that need liberation? Something in me half-believes that it is better to exemplify than to preach. No, this is unfair, perhaps. But the world has Jane Austen and George Eliot, two minds which will demonstrate to anybody who is open to demonstration that a female mind is not necessarily inferior to a male mind. I basically think that the point of Women's Lib is better made by having more Jane Austens and George Eliots, and high-powered civil servants

and so on, than by constantly reiterating a truism when you have nothing else to say. There are a number of reputations which are open to the question, "Suppose you'd been born a man?" Would we ever have heard of them? Suppose she or he had been born heterosexual; would we ever have heard of heard or him? And this can beg the very question that they're trying to preach.

Still, I'm not sure about this one; I may be being unfair. And indeed, I think one has to say that feminism, and indeed Gay Lib, have done things that were not done simply by people simply living their lives and being talented. Therefore I am being unfair, though it may turn out that the journalists' fashion for Women's Lib—and, to some extent, for Gay Lib—may suddenly pass, leaving us exactly where we were before. Journalists are incredibly without memory, and without historical sense. For example, when Arthur Ashe won Wimbledon, they announced that this was the first black person who'd ever won Wimbledon; this was not true.

Yes, I read your letter to the Times *the other day.*

I made a feminist point about it in the *Times,* which was unfair, but I wanted them to print it. In fact, the real point to be made is against journalists, because journalists have only just heard of black power; this is an "in" thing. And they believe it has happened only in the past three years. (Journalists' memories never go back beyond three years.) This is untrue, because, in fact, when Althea Gibson won Wimbledon, it was an enormous feat; it was very much greeted by black people as being a great victory for them. And of course there was a movement for the liberation of black people 'way back in 1956. It's just that, as I say, journalists believe that black power, Women's Lib, Gay Lib, are entirely new phenomena! and this strange absence of historical sense in journalists could mean that, when they suddenly start thinking of Women's Lib as old hat, we will find that it hasn't advanced things, socially.

In your essay, "The Importance of Mozart's Operas," you say that, in Don Giovanni, *Mozart produced "one of the world's imperfect masterpieces . . . an eternal enigma," as a result of using, unconsciously, autobiographical material.* **In Transit** *is, for me, somewhat of an enigma. I can pick out some of the elements: pornography, musical tempos, confusion about oneself in relation to others, plus a parody of detective fiction, but the pattern or design is unclear. Could you please explain your intent and, if possible, comment on the autobiographical material, the circumstances that pushed you into writing it? In an essay you say that it depicts the "impulse to fiction," but I have no idea of how the pattern works.*

The pattern is about disintegration of accepted routines. We "intellectually structure our world" (I'm sorry about the jargon) by certain received truths which we think to be true, in various moods. So when the "I" character in *In Transit* deliberately decides to miss the plane for which she or he has a ticket, the timetable is disrupted, and this is the first disintegration of the rulebook.

In Transit is about a series of disintegrations of rulebooks, including the sexual stereotypes, ending with the question of whether Aristotelian logic might disintegrate, whether we are mistaken in thinking that a thing cannot be both X and not-X, whether we are mistaken in thinking that the syllogistic argument is valid. There are a good many passages referring to Aristotelian logic in the book. And then, going from the logical proposition to the sentence, the book poses the question of whether the accepted Western sentence structure (subject-verb-object) is also disintegrating. When I say that these rules are disintegrating, I mean that what is being questioned is, do they reflect any necessary truths, or are they entirely arbitrary?

> **In Transit is an attempt to write in four movements, and with a more complicated development of each theme within each movement. I don't know that it succeeds.**
> —Brigid Brophy

The structure of the book, to express these disintegrations or questionings, is the first instance of my trying to write in symphonic form. Everything else I have written (and I think this would probably be true, even if I write an article of 2000 words) is structured on the concerto, in three movements, with a one, two, one-A structure within each movement. *In Transit* is an attempt to write in four movements, and with a more complicated development of each theme within each movement. I don't know that it succeeds.

The symphonic structure I had in mind was Brahms's. I don't know; some days I think he was a very great composer, and other days I think he was just a windy old Victorian. But he certainly is a composer who affects me very strongly, whether for good or for bad. And he also is a composer whom one sees as having had the ability to create disintegration: sometimes he builds toward an orchestral climax, and what is structurally a climax, but you have the impression that it's also about falling apart. It's lost faith, and he's questioning, "Is this a tune? Is it the same as the other tune, or is it different?" I feel he was full of self-doubt, and that is why he was my model for the structure of *In Transit*.

*Weren't you more or less trying to create that same sort of disintegration of rhythm in **The Snow Ball**, where most of the descriptions start out as neutral, if not positive (I am*

thinking of the cherubs all over the house), and gradually, within the passage, the description becomes quite negative— or was that not your intent?

Yes, this is true, but I didn't attempt, in *The Snow Ball,* to disintegrate the actual structures of thought. I only disintegrated one person's thought, with a few persons peripheral to her emotional structures. That was the main fact, the fact that people die, which, I would agree, is the ultimate in disintegration. But in *The Snow Ball* there is not the disintegration of an actual intellectual world, as distinct from one person's world.

*Yes, it seems to me that in **The Snow Ball** the furnishings were disintegrating. One character makes the comment that the antique furniture probably looked better two hundred years ago.*

I think this disintegration is there; my fear about civilization is that, if we can no longer make beautiful furniture— and, more to the point, beautiful buildings—which we hardly can, nowadays, the few beautiful ones that we haven't knocked down are not going to last us very much longer.

*In **Prancing Novelist** you maintain that, today, private incomes are drying up in Western countries, thus decreasing the chances of a great artist's having income sufficient to support himself or herself. The answer is, you say, "greater generosity, spreading the money more widely." Given England's economic situation, how would you propose this be done?*

Firstly, obviously, by paying authors for the lending of their books in public libraries, which is more important in this country than in any other Western country, for the simple reason that we have a larger public library service than anybody else. Not even proportionately to our population, but absolutely, we have a larger one. Therefore the loss to authors is even greater in this country than anywhere else. By adding four million pounds to the central government's budget per year, you could spread the money around perfectly justly to authors whose books are borrowed. Some of them are authors who also sell well, but a lot of them are not, because 73 percent of all adult borrowing in British public libraries is borrowing of fiction, but the number of novelists who are best sellers, and make a lot of money from sales, is very small. Therefore there are a great number of novelists who make very little money, but are heavily borrowed. To pay a Public Lending Right to them, would make an enormous difference, especially for fiction, but not only for fiction.

That is the first method. The other method is an increase in state patronage; of all the money spent on the arts in this country, only 1 percent goes to literature. So an increase in state patronage to writers would make quite a lot of difference.

Would it extend to dead writers? Sometimes a writer doesn't make any money during her or his lifetime; would it extend to a widower or widow?

This is our intention, that it shouldn't extend for the full fifty years after death of the copyright period, because if you are, as this country is, short of money, it is perfectly legitimate to say, should we support grandchildren or ninth cousins? But we certainly intend, the writers intend, or the government intends, that it should be applicable to widowers and widows and to children under twenty-one.

Are there any works of yours which, now, you wish you hadn't published?

Yes. My first book, a volume of short stories, **The Crown Princess,** which I do not mention in any reference books, and have to that extent suppressed. I would like the opportunity to rewrite and improve them all, but no, I'm not positively ashamed of any of them, except that.

Why that?

I think it was a book written by a little girl trying to be good, producing what was expected, and the only story I would except is the one called **"The Late Afternoon of a Faun,"** which was, as I said earlier, the earliest story in it, and which is the only one, it seems to me, to have anything. The others seem to me manufactured, written for a certain middlebrow market, to be life imposed on me, not me on life.

You describe your father as a "middlebrow novelist"; would you say you are high, middle, or lowbrow, as a novelist?

I would say that I try to write to the top of my intellectual ability, and I try never to baffle readers deliberately, because that is simply pretentiousness. But if, when I have put it as clearly as I can, it baffles them or puts them off, that is too bad; it isn't they that will suffer, it is I, because they won't buy my books. To that extent, I suppose one has, using the word I don't very much like, to say "highbrow."

Are you working on a novel right now?

No, alas. In intervals I've been bludgeoning the British government. I'm rewriting a book about Aubrey Beardsley, whom I've already written about. It's taking a rather long time, partly to write, and partly because there's quite a lot of new material, new facts. I've discovered the true version of previously wrongly accepted facts, which is nice, but I wish I had more leisure to do it in.

I am also about to publish my first excursion into writing for children. There are two stories which are to be published in a volume in the spring of 1976 and which will at the same time be read on BBC television. They are for children, but not, I hope, exclusively for children. They concern a very nasty and self-regarding character called Pussy Owl.

Do you save your manuscripts or give them to the British Museum?

The British Museum has not made me an offer. I keep them in a plastic box underneath the bed, which prevents them from cluttering the place up. It also prevents Maureen Duffy's dog, who spends a lot of time here (because Maureen is here a great deal of the time, running Writers' Action Group with me), from getting under the bed, which used to be her chief delight during the days that she spent here. She got under once, and couldn't get out again; she and I had quite a half-an-hour's struggle. She scrabbled at my manuscripts, I scrabbled at her; eventually we got her out.

What do you think of Norman Mailer?

It is always very necessary to protest masculinity in the United States. There has always to be a figure: there was Hemingway, and now there is Norman Mailer, whose very name is so very amusing in that connection. I think this is something which is missing from English literary life, unless one says that the thirties tradition of cricket and poets is an assertion of the same thing, which it may be.

What about the nonliterary life? Do you think that English men are more advanced in terms of treating women as equals, than are American men?

I haven't been in the United States for a long time, though, obviously, I have met a lot of people from the United States over here. I think—very slightly, yes. If one goes about one's own affairs or business in this country, I don't think that most men will particularly notice that one is a woman. Obviously, they notice, but I think they got over the fact of this a long time ago, and I don't think these descriptions apply in the United States, although I may be wrong.

Peter Keating (review date 28 January 1977)

SOURCE: "Outline Is All," in *Times Literary Supplement,* No. 3907, January 28, 1977, p. 108.

[In the following review, Keating highly commends
Beardsley and His World.*]*

"I am anxious to say something somewhere, on the subject of lines and line drawing", Aubrey Beardsley wrote to his former school teacher A. W. King on Christmas Day 1891, and added: "How little the importance of outline is understood even by some of the best painters." At this time Beardsley was nineteen years old; he had recently been told by Burne-Jones that he would one day "assuredly paint very great and beautiful pictures", and, on Burne-Jones's advice, he was attending evening classes at the Westminster School of Art.

As Brigid Brophy points out in this excellent book [*Beardsley and His World*], Burne-Jones had "recognised the existence but not the nature of Beardsley's genius", this being to "create drawings which were completed pictures in themselves". At the moment when he rejected the advice that his future lay in painting and stressed instead the "importance of outline", Beardsley had less than seven years to live, and he seems to have understood this as well. "I shall not live longer than did Keats", he proclaimed, and reinforcing both the truth of, and the reason for, this prophecy is the moving painting by Sickert, which is reproduced here, of Beardsley leaving Hampstead Church in 1894 after attending the ceremonial unveiling of a bust of Keats. Elegantly dressed, gaunt, and appallingly thin, Beardsley seems to be dragging himself away from the gravestones. It is a picture, as Brigid Brophy says, "terrifying in the nakedness of its symbolism".

The format of the Thames and Hudson series in which *Beardsley and His World* is published depends for its success on a skilful blending of pictures and text, and here again this is managed superbly. There are photographs of Beardsley at various moments in his life, and of his relatives, homes, and lodgings, and examples of his work from the juvenile "Kate Greenaway" sketches; through the drawings published in *The Studio, The Yellow Book,* and *The Savoy,* to the highly ornate illustrations for an edition of *Volpone* on which Beardsley was working when he died. Among the less familiar drawings are those illustrating Poe's *Tales of Mystery and Imagination,* and, just as sinister in every respect, there is a welcome reproduction of one of Beardsley's two surrealistic oil paintings.

The only curious omissions are the openly erotic illustrations of *Lysistrata.* Curious because one of them was reproduced in Brigid Brophy's earlier study of Beardsley, *Black and White* (1968). It is described here, in almost the same words, as a picture "aching with an explicit sexual frustration that was probably Beardsley's own", but without the drawing itself. It is tempting to ask why? Brigid Brophy is so insistent, and perceptive, on the generally erotic nature of Beardsley's art (especially phallic tassels and erections, which she finds everywhere) that the absence of the gigan-

tic "aching" phalluses from *Lysistrata* seems almost wilful or imposed.

In *Black and White* Brigid Brophy largely restricted herself to a critical examination of Beardsley's work: here, a far stronger emphasis is given to his life. Brighton, where Beardsley was born and spent many of his early years, is discussed as a major formative influence upon his imagination; the misleading reminiscences and exaggerated claims of his mother, Ellen Beardsley, are firmly corrected; some basic biographical facts are established for the first time; and throughout, there are illuminating conjectures on the relationship between Beardsley's brief, intense life, and the amazing emergence and fruition of his genius. *Beardsley and His World* is an exceptionally attractive book and, at today's prices, a real bargain.

Gabriele Annan (review date 28 April 1978)

SOURCE: "A Romp among the Royals," in *Times Literary Supplement,* No. 3969, April 28, 1978, p. 463.

[*In the review below, Annan praises the satiric tone of* Palace without Chairs.]

The crown prince's name is Ulrich; his brothers, the archdukes, are called Balthasar, Sempronius, and Urban; the youngest child is the Archduchess Heather, a butch seventeen-year-old; their father rules the modern kingdom of Evarchia. All this, with the subtitle "a baroque novel", suggests a Firbankian romp, or something like Muriel Spark's *The Abbess of Crewe.* That was a send-up of politics and the media; they are sent up here too, but fundamentally [*Palace without Chairs*] is a moral fable in a pretty and entertaining guise: poetic descriptions of animals, landscape, and the weather relieve a steady flow of wit and humour, and passionate convictions lie beneath.

The plot is ten-little-nigger-boys: the whole royal family (except for one member) is gradually eliminated. The dropping out and dying does not seem unduly sad when it starts, and gets blackly funnier by accumulation. All the same, there is an undertone of sadness: "tout passe, tout lasse, tout casse", as one of the characters observes. The story begins with Ulrich hastening home from his mistress, Clara, to the bedside of his dying father. The king gets better: the person who dies is the charmer Sempronius, shot during the thanksgiving celebrations for the royal recovery by a lunatic who mistakes him for the crown prince. The crown prince, meanwhile, renounces his right of succession and goes into exile. That gets rid of him, and Balthasar succeeds him as heir to the throne and Clara's lover: her affair with Ulrich is over.

> [*Palace without Chairs*] is a moral fable in a
> pretty and entertaining guise: poetic
> descriptions of animals, landscape, and the
> weather relieve a steady flow of wit and
> humour, and passionate convictions lie
> beneath.
> —*Gabriele Annan*

The king falls dangerously ill a second time, but again it is others who die. Balthasar is accidentally killed in the Brophyan pursuit of rescuing a wounded bird from a cliff top; Clara topples after; the queen, a gentle, dotty intellectual, dies unexpectedly and painlessly during her siesta; and her death frees the slightly autistic Urban to do what he has always longed to do—commit suicide; and he does it with glee. The king recovers a second time. Heather is now the heir apparent. She has always been unsympathetic towards her father, and it turns out she was right: he is revealed as a pious, selfish fraud: even his illnesses were at least partly sham. Nevertheless, a third bout carries him off: Heather promptly renounces the throne and thunders off to England accompanied by the young English governess—once her lover and now her friend. The book ends cheerfully with Heather embarking on a new lesbian affair in London, while the governess catches the tube home to her family, and a military dictatorship takes over in Evarchia.

The chairs of the title are the subject of a sub-plot. There are not enough chairs in the palace and none at all in the royal nursery. The archdukes have to take it in turn to sit on the old rocking-horse until it finally and symbolically gives way under Heather's colossal weight. Balthasar decides to ask for chairs, and what follows is a lampoon on red tape and officialdom: a committee is set up to consider the whole matter, right down to the possible definitions of a chair, because, as the comptroller of the royal household says to the exasperated Balthasar, "his Highness wouldn't want to endorse sloppy thinking". News of the committee leaks into the press and a columnist attacks the archduke and the whole institution of royalty:

> Not content with living at public expense in the lap of luxury, Archduke B. is trying, it seems, to get the whole interior of the Winter Palace made over. . . . The country's foreign exchange problems evidently don't weigh with the man who's always had everything. Prince Charming, did I hear you say? Or was it Prince Greedy?

This kind of satire is not new, but it is funny if it is good and good if it is funny, and Brigid Brophy's is both. Among her targets are Iron Curtain espionage, the security services, communism in capitalist countries, trade unions, strikes,

court-room procedure, and public holidays with the time they waste. She also rides her familiar hobby horses with style: animals' rights, homosexuals' rights, writers' rights (PLR), language rights (i.e. the right of languages to be properly spoken and written), vegetarianism, atheism, and so on. She is not at all savage this time: a Shavian good temper prevails.

Her favourite device is to lead the reader up a garden path which appears to be bordered with clichés, and then to clobber him when he bends down to enjoy their scent. For instance, the opening scene with the lonely figure of Ulrich riding through the snow is full of potential pathos: if his father dies, as one assumes he will, Ulrich will be forced to give up Clara. But it is not really sad at all: not because the king recovers, but because Ulrich is no longer in love.

Love, especially romantic love, and conventional ideas of honour are among the values that get devalued: Ulrich explains to Heather that if he renounces the throne he will have to marry Clara, otherwise it would be dishonourable. "Your concept of honour is ludicrous", says Heather. "It's so punitive. . . . Is it an act of honour to put [Clara] in the role of the person who makes you miserable?" Ulrich agrees, but is unhappy because "to pass from one seeming true love to another was to devalue them all, since it was to admit that one's love had been founded on illusion". The anti-idealist Heather has accepted that long ago. She is the one with the motto "tout passe, tout lasse, etc." This crucial conversation comes about halfway through the book and is the first indication that Heather may turn out to be its heroine (which she does). Up till then she has seemed the least attractive of the royal children: hoydenish, insensitive, and crude. Could it be a wicked self-caricature? Certainly Heather's seem to be the author's.

All the chief characters have enough attributes and idiosyncrasies ingeniously and unexpectedly assembled to make them engaging; they are not totally real, but that would be than you could expect in an allegorical comedy of this kind. They also have—a very difficult thing to bring off—a lot of charm. It comes from the way they talk. In Heather's case the charm is only unveiled by degrees, because her transformation from ugly duckling to swan—or rather, from what would, by conventional standards, be an ugly duckling, but is, in the Brophy scale of values, a swan from the beginning—has to come as a surprise.

What is the scale of values? Aesthetic and intellectual fastidiousness come quite high up, love nowhere much, reason, friendship, compassion, and tenderness right at the top; "the passionate affection" between Heather and the governess, for instance, or the bond between Ulrich and his mother. As these two wait to open a court ball together, they look embarrassed. "But as a matter of fact, Ulrich and the queen were seldom so conscious of the tenderness between them as when each felt compassion towards the other's public embarrassments." Brigid Brophy used to be a bit Voltairean in her Weltanschauung and attack; now her sensibility seems mellower and her views more akin to Montaigne's.

Edmund White (review date 16 July 1978)

SOURCE: "Gradations of Silliness," in *The New York Times Book Review,* July 16, 1978, pp. 8, 27.

[*Below, White favorably compares Brophy's "silliness" in* Palace without Chairs *to Ronald Firbank's literary style, but concludes that "the book doesn't work."*]

Through the sturdy homespun of English fiction runs a single thread of silver silliness. It is a filament drawn from an art that may seem snobbish and arch but that in fact affects attitudes only for the sake of the imagination. For that reason it must not be regarded as satire, for the foolish, delicate creatures it pokes fun at have, alas, never existed save in the tented gossamer daydreams of a few writers. I'm thinking of a tradition that begins with Pope's *Rape of the Lock* and extends through Thomas Love Peacock, Oscar Wilde, Ronald Firbank and Henry Green and that ends, implausibly enough, in America with W. M. Spackman and his splendid, recently published *An Armful of Warm Girl.* The distinguishing characteristics of the style of sublime silliness are its atmosphere of innocent romance and gorgeous effects, its tight design and economy of expression played off against an almost total absence of content. There is also, usually, a coiled, edgy quality to the writing, as though the author were trying to transcribe a humor that eludes language.

> *Palace Without Chairs* can be read as a homage to Firbank's 1923 novella, *The Flower Beneath the Foot.* Both books are set in fairytale kingdoms that maintain pretensions to power and culture but have actually gone to seed.
> —*Edmund White*

Brigid Brophy is an intelligent admirer of the tradition and has written an enormous biography of Ronald Firbank, *Prancing Novelist.* Her new novel, *Palace Without Chairs,* exhibits the stigmata of her devotion. She has adopted many of Firbank's mannerisms, including: his scraps of unassigned dialogue overheard at parties; his use of droll place names and proper names; his affectionate regard for elegant Art Deco natives; his insertion of shockingly *mondaine*

slang into stuffy contexts; his raillery against the church (Firbank is the inventor of Catholic Camp); his appreciation of the teasing and sumptuous amorality of nature; his deadpan reports of human sexual ambiguity; even his habit of composing one-sentence paragraphs. Like Firbank, Miss Brophy throws seemingly ordinary words into unsettling italics or between insinuating quotation marks until the familiar begins to seem alien. And like Firbank she observes the ways in which the serious moments are invariably undermined by trivial, irrelevant thoughts.

In fact, *Palace Without Chairs* can be read as a homage to Firbank's 1923 novella, *The Flower Beneath the Foot.* Both books are set in fairytale kingdoms that maintain pretensions to power and culture but have actually gone to seed. In both books the tutor to the royal children is a bogus Englishwoman (in Firbank she is a Cockney teaching her charges to drop their h's; in Brophy, a woman who speaks English well enough but learned it not in England, as she claims, but in her native Beirut and Alexandria). In both books the ludicrousness of protocol is lampooned, and in both the anachronism inherent in modern monarchy is sent up. In both there are alfresco scenes of lesbian love. And in both the plot meanders quirkily along, stopping often for attractive but gratuitous tableaux.

These resemblances, however, do not detract from the originality of Miss Brophy's fable. Her story is quite her own. The long-suffering King of Evarchia is ailing, and the officials are concerned about the succession. The Crown Prince renounces his claim to the throne. The son next in line is assassinated by a madman. Soon the other sons meet grotesque ends and the heir becomes an amiable lesbian daughter. But she, too, refuses her historic role—and the kingdom is seized by an unappetizing military dictator. A full fleet of secondary characters—Communists, gossip columnists, minor nobility—are skillfully traffic-directed down the narrative lanes.

Interesting as all this may sound, the book doesn't work. The style of silliness is not suited to Miss Brophy's true concerns. Disguised by the ornaments of her technique are her passionately held convictions against the double-talk of Communism, the cruelty of most people toward animals, the eerie heartlessness of fascism, and society's mistreatment of writers. In themselves, of course, these convictions are laudable, but they are not well served by whimsy. What has happened is that the style belittles the content and the content torpedoes the style. I am not saying that these are illegitimate subjects for fiction, much less for comic fiction. What I am asserting is that Brigid Brophy's fey mannerisms betray her message and her message sinks her showy technique; what should be all restless chatoyancy becomes a fixed light blinking code.

Worse, Miss Brophy's writing, looked at line by line, does not compare well with her mentor's. In Firbank every sentence is shapely, terse and surprising, whereas Miss Brophy is quite capable of writing: "Almost every village contained some recently built but already tumble-down structure, its grandiose nameplate surviving intact, as if to exacerbate the sore, though its roof had probably fallen in and its walls had succumbed to an invasion of bougainvillea and wild hydrangeas, that had been set up, on mainland capital and initiative, as a co-operative, intended to provide the Islanders with employment and incentive, and that had failed." Obviously she has no ear and only an impressionistic sense of grammar.

Brigid Brophy would, in my opinion, be better served by the straightforward, sometimes lackluster but always dignified manner of, say, Doris Lessing, whose prose merely delivers her thoughts. Silliness, it seems, is the province not of philosophers but of inspired artists.

A. S. Byatt (review date 13 January 1987)

SOURCE: "An Explosive Embrace," in *Times Literary Supplement*, No. 4380, January 13, 1987, p. 269.

[*In the following review, Byatt calls* Baroque 'n' Roll *"a celebration of life and thought."*]

The English perceive Brigid Brophy as a maverick. They do not know where to have her. She writes athwart our traditions of understatement and mild social comment. Her novels are witty and artificial, and irritate the tidy categorizer, since they resemble each other only in the intellectual sensuality of their construction. Her enthusiasms are also disparate, but have in common a tendency to combine precision of expression, a certain extravagance, and formal or logical rigour pushed as far as it will decently go. Shaw, Wilde, Mozart, Jane Austen, Purcell, Firbank, the vegetarian cause, the art of lawn tennis, the baroque in its multitude of forms. She is, of course, not an English humorist but a member of that Celtic school in which, as she points out, Shaw and Wilde were briefly (and uneasily) linked. She is an Irish wit, and also a remorseless moralist.

Baroque 'n' Roll gathers up various essays: offering new insights into *Edwin Drood* and *As You Like It,* praising Freud and Navratilova, making us appallingly sensible of the pain we cause to our fellow-creatures, fish. The title essay, last in the book, is a six-part demonstration or definition (like Marvell's *Definition of Love*) of what she means by baroque. The essay itself is an example of the formal movements it attempts to define. It opens with the assertion that "form is

constant throughout the arts" and examines the order and irregularities of poetry (Marvell, metaphysical verse, Milton), sculpture (Bernini), painting (a marvellous disquisition on Titian's Actaeon paintings and their possible influence on Shakespeare), music (Purcell and Dryden) and architecture. "A structure can be transposed from one art into another", Brophy says, and argues that Marvell's poem "To His Coy Mistress" resembles an Aristotelian syllogism, that English explores relationships through metaphor and Greek through the modulations of its very syntax. (Tennis, too, is a baroque form: it has its geometry, its orderly sequence of rules and scores, its asymmetrical, dissimilar, extravagant gestures. John McEnroe is, "if not an angel at least a baroque putto".)

> **All writers in this country are in debt to Brigid Brophy for her pertinacity, pugnacity and vision in the battle for Public Lending Right. There is nobody like her, no one who sees the world quite in her original way.**
> —*A. S. Byatt*

Perhaps the centre of this complex construction is the Bernini sculpture of Saint Teresa, ecstatically and ambivalently pierced by the angel. "Baroque", Brophy tells us, "is an open, sometimes an explosive embrace of contradictions and oppositions, intellectual and of feeling". She goes on:

> In sculpture, as often in architecture, the quintessential substance of the baroque is marble, a material likely, like some types of cheese, to be veined by a countercolour. When it is pure white, it can, at the working of a master, simulate the various softnesses of hair, lace and flesh, and yet it remains hard and cold. A natural rendering of the baroque ambivalence, it renders flesh at once more desirable and in the clutch of *rigor mortis.*

Which brings us to Brophy's account of the invasion of her own life by the progressive disabling of multiple sclerosis. These autobiographical pages have a matter-of-fact authority and a kind of nakedness not found elsewhere in the book. They are also wholly gripping as narrative: her situation is terrible, and yet she makes us curious about the detail of her experience, the nature of the insensitivity of doctors, and of the unnatural numbness in her legs, which "does not preclude pain or even the further numbness of cold but makes one inhabit a surrealist world". The illness is susceptible to her baroque vision; she considers its metaphorical relation to an earlier experience of emotional violence, and notices its elements of absurdity—arresting us with the vision, imagined through other eyes, of "that eccentric Lady Levey, crawling across the hall". She has the right, in her position, to tell us that no other creature should suffer in the process of finding a cure. "It is not my personal stake that makes my anti-vivisectionist argument correct", she points out, but claims "the authority of a person with a personal stake in the matter."

All writers in this country are in debt to Brigid Brophy for her pertinacity, pugnacity and vision in the battle for Public Lending Right. There is nobody like her, no one who sees the world quite in her original way. *Baroque 'n' Roll* is, despite the fearful events of the "case-historical fragment", a celebration of life and thought.

John Bayley (review date 5 March 1987)

SOURCE: "In Praise of Brigid Brophy," in *London Review of Books,* March 5, 1978, pp. 11-12.

[*In the following positive review, Bayley defines "baroque" as portrayed in* Baroque 'n' Roll.]

In his recent book *Reasons and Persons* the Oxford philosopher Derek Parfit is inclined to decide that persons have no existence, and that the motives to morality are for that reason clearer and more cogent. So-called personality is a matter of self-interest: bees in a hive have no moral problems. Examining their own world and using their own vocabulary, empirical and linguistic philosophers quite naturally and rightly come to such conclusions. Hume could perceive only a bundle of sensations, and Parfit finds in himself only a quantity of experiences. Death is that much easier to accept, because it is simply a matter of there being 'no future experiences which will be related in certain ways to these present experiences', and personal self-interest easily becomes 'rational altruism'.

Such conclusions have been reached, though less consciously, ever since churches and parties were invented; and, further back still, the Parfit state is the natural life of the tribe. The Japanese, with their concept of *amae,* still live it: for them, the idea of personal identity is virtually meaningless. Most religions, secular or spiritual, tend to go along with this, though Christianity, by a remarkable balancing act, stresses that love does the trick: by losing yourself in it, you find yourself. Perhaps this is because the Christian religion is based on a story, a work of art, a novel subject to many interpretations. Could it be that personal identity is only discovered by means of stories and novels, and that this is why philosophers, who seldom or never read them, have been unable to find it?

We read therefore we are. The idea is suggested to me by Brigid Brophy's essays [in *Baroque 'n' Roll*], which constitute one of the strongest proofs of personal identity I have ever come across. If a real person is not here, where is a person to be found? She writes therefore she is, and to receive such an impression, so clearly, is very uncommon indeed. The style is the man is not the kind of observation that would fit into the Parfit thesis, and can indeed appear fatally ambiguous. Mozart has style, and Shakespeare has style, but where is Mozart, where is Shakespeare? The same applies to much great art, and perhaps particularly to the baroque art to which Brigid Brophy is so greatly drawn. With their amiable curlicue pun for a title, the linked essays on baroque which conclude her book are as fascinating as they are informed, and every sentence creates the author, on the one hand, while illuminating the spirit of baroque, on the other. The combination is rare, in every sense, and reveals what all its most devoted clients know by instinct: that art is both communal and personal; that it tells us we are individuals at the same time that it transcends individuality. Art encourages us to become ourselves while reminding us it is something else.

The paradox is brilliantly explored in Brigid Brophy's reflections on a picture story of Titian and Shakespeare. The play on personality here, and its metamorphosis, is shown to be literally enchanting. Titian's *Venus and Adonis,* painted by him with the Danae as a pair of *poesie* for Philip II of Spain, was sent to England in preparation for his marriage with Mary Tudor. Could Shakespeare have later seen engravings of it? Very possibly. More significant still, however, is the probability that he knew, either by report or in engraving, of Titian's two superb Diana paintings, also done for Philip—*The Trial of Callisto,* and *Diana surprised by Actaeon*—now on loan from the Duke of Sutherland to the National Gallery of Scotland.

> **We read therefore we are. The idea is suggested to me by Brigid Brophy's essays [in *Baroque 'n' Roll*], which constitute one of the strongest proofs of personal identity I have ever come across.**
> **—*John Bayley***

Brigid Brophy engagingly observes that Titian 'had several times before been on the verge of inventing the baroque, most notably in Bacchus's great joyful and athletic leap from his chariot in the Bacchus and Ariadne in the National Gallery'. She is sure that the two Diana paintings show Titian's final accomplishment of the style 'as an idiom for the visual arts', and specifically as a means of representing the architecture of bodies or of buildings, exploding in dramatic collapse or subjected to the slow processes of time.

There is certainly something both explosive and exceptionally deliberative about Shakespeare's *Venus and Adonis,* as if the poet were following out, and almost too conscientiously in terms of verbal syntax, what is essentially a pictorial style. But Titian's Dianas, in conjunction with Ovid, may have offered a challenge to Shakespeare in terms of the goddess's personality. According to Ovid, poor Callisto was betrayed by the very sexual tastes which Diana, 'a kind of lesbian gym-teacher', encouraged in her following, for cunning Jupiter had disguised himself as Diana when he made his advances to her.

Jealous Juno turned Callisto into a bear and her son by Jupiter hunted her when he grew up, but the father of the gods forestalled matricide by turning mother and son into constellations, the Great and Little Bear. Yet perhaps Diana herself did not get away with it? At the beginning of the passage in *Metamorphoses* where Actaeon blunders onto the bathing scene (a scene, as Brigid Brophy points out, which Titian represents as a stage, with players and properties), Ovid gives Diana one of her rarer titles, Titania—a reference to her Titan-born ancestry. In Shakespeare's Titania Diana reappears as a different personality, the cruel gym mistress changed into a sulky spouse, jealous of her husband's amours. Shakespeare knew well what metamorphoses occur in daily life, and how unexpected and incongruous fates lie in wait for touch-me-not persons. Diana-Titania falls helplessly in love with a comic version of the very young man whom she had cruelly enchanted with the stag's head and horns. Bully Bottom, monster of the comic baroque, becomes the creature she dotes upon.

Thus the baroque acts both to fantasise the personal and explore, in the most searchingly realistic way, the human personality. How could the Church have permitted the Cornaro chapel, in Santa Maria della Vittoria at Rome, to have become metamorphosed in the 1650s 'into a silent opera house permanently displaying a spectacle which, in a symbolism too transparent to be refused or refuted by the most non- or anti-Freudian, consists of sexual intercourse'? The answer, as Brigid Brophy says, is that the baroque literary imagination had an extraordinary power of penetrating religion with the humanly personal, just as it could penetrate mythology with the psychological. The literary imagination not only gives no offence but can only be understood in terms of its own intuitive underlife. In our depersonalised age a statue—no doubt non-representational—representing a figure in rapture being penetrated by another figure, could only mean one thing. Parfit man, that assemblage of experiences, can only experience one thing at a time, because he has no personality in which to conjoin them.

Personality, in other words, can move simultaneously in many dimensions, and baroque does the same. On the vaulted ceiling of the Cornaro chapel the painted figures of angels disport themselves in clouds composed of plaster. Quoting Howard Hibbard's Penguin book on Bernini, Brigid Brophy remarks that the appearance is exactly as if one of them had descended to the altar and there become a three-dimensional marble figure who, holding his lance 'as fastidiously as a fork at a buffet supper', thrusts it into a rapturous St. Teresa. 'Bernini's baroque lack of fear of the literal import of religious imagery' raises the question of St. Teresa's own realisation of the matter. Her description of the moment of bliss is just as explicit as Bernini's tableau, and confirms the suspicion that sexual awareness is born in the head and in literature, not in physical experience. 'In disguise from both herself and the church St. Teresa's autobiography was not the pattern of saintliness it passed for, but a classic account of the pattern of the developing literary imagination.' Forbidden by her father to read novels, and later by a father confessor to read anything but Latin, Teresa took to conversing with God, who, in a delphic observation she did not understand when he first made it, promised her 'a living book'. From then on, she began to experience rapturous visions, and indeed made a book. Her visions, as Brigid Brophy shrewdly says, were the result 'not of sexual but of literary frustration'. Charlotte Brontë and *Jane Eyre* were to come out from under her cloak in time, as Dostoevsky says that Russian literature came from under Gogol's overcoat.

The section on baroque is a little—indeed not so little—masterpiece, packed with insights and concluding with the happy suggestion that the song from Purcell and Dryden's *King Arthur, or the British Worthy: A Dramatick Opera* would be the most acceptable substitute for our present National Anthem.

> Fairest Isle, all Isles Excelling,
>   Seat of Pleasures, and of Loves;
> Venus, here, will chuse her Dwelling,
>   And forsake her *Cyprian* Groves.

Of course the government of Cyprus might be less than pleased by the change. And Brigid Brophy may not know that the Church of England has in some degree adopted her suggestion: 'Love divine, all love excelling', composed by a Victorian bishop to Purcell's tune, is one of its most spirited hymns. As a personal critic, in the best sense, she would be content to share a patriotic baroque fantasia with a cheerful ecclesiastical song of praise. No lover of the baroque would grudge St. Teresa her visions, her belief, and her glorious sense of divinity; as well as the literary imagination that went with them. The baroque personality, like the Irish bird, can easily be in two places at once.

The shorter pieces in this book are equally fascinating. There is Mozart as a letter-writer, and Mozart with Da Ponte and with Jane Austen; an essay **'In Praise of Ms Navratilova'**, and another doing the same for Lodge and Shakespeare. These 'Reflections and Reviews', some of which appeared in the *London Review of Books,* include a brilliant piece on Murasaki and Fanny Burney, and an analysis of *The Mystery of Edwin Drood,* and its conclusion by Leon Garfield, coming up with the intriguing suggestion that Dickens— who can tell what the unconscious of that great novelist may have got up to?—made John Jasper more in love with Edwin than he is with Rosa. I also much enjoyed the essay on Lady Morgan, known as 'Glorvina' and author of *The Wild Irish Girl* (the title is ironic—the girl was an animated and cultivated bluestocking), and its guess that Jane Austen, who thought poorly of the novel, may have had Glorvina in mind when she created Mary Crawford a few years later in *Mansfield Park.* Byron thought Glorvina 'fearless', which Mary Crawford certainly is. Mary, like Glorvina, is a notable harp performer and full of charm, even of 'warmth', qualities much in vogue in Regency circles and associated with Tom Moore and the fashion for Irishness—sedulously cultivated by Lady Morgan—as for Scotchness. Jane Austen was impressed by neither Glorvina nor Robert Burns, championing instead that model of quiet English moral sobriety Fanny Price.

Brigid Brophy's funniest piece is on fish, that silent persecuted majority, whom even hostesses who are delighted to provide a vegetarian meal ('Oh, by the way, you do eat fish don't you?') persist in regarding as a vegetable. A member and strong supporter of the Labour Party, Brigid Brophy none the less cannot help being amused, and indignant, at a section of its campaign document, 'The New Hope for Britain', which assures us that 'Labour will also provide for wider use of the countryside for recreational purposes, such as angling.' 'What has destruction to do with any form of creation, including recreation?' she pertinently observes. The matter of foxes and fishes (coarse fishes, that is) is, of course, one of divisiveness. It may seem natural and proper to take it from the fox killers and give it to the fish killers, although the ordinary working person on the canal bank is surrounded by almost as much elaborate and expensive equipment as the class enemy on horseback. But in politics style is all.

The most moving essay is the **'Fragment of Autobiography'** which opens the collection. To observe one's symptoms—in this case, the advance of multiple sclerosis—and one's medical experiences for the benefit of others is a service rarely performed. Brigid Brophy does it with humour and stoicism, and in addition performs the almost impossible feat of thanking her husband and friends for all they have done for her, without seeming to be going through the routine motions. That is as much a personal triumph as is her always creative criticism.

Sheryl Stevenson (essay date 1991)

SOURCE: "Language and Gender in Transit: Feminist Extensions of Bakhtin," in *Feminism, Bakhtin, and the Dialogic,* edited by Dale M. Bauer and Susan Janet Mckinstry, State University of New York Press, 1991, pp. 181-98.

[*In the following essay, Stevenson discusses parallels between Mikhail Bakhtin's theory of language and* In Transit, *focusing on the connections the novel makes between the mutability of language, conceptions of gender, modernist fiction, and individual identities.*]

Tracing an Orlando-like figure through shifting guises of femininity and masculinity, Brigid Brophy's *In Transit* lends support to Sandra Gilbert's idea that modernist writers envision gender identities as transiently assumed roles, "costumes of the mind." An Anglo-Irish iconoclast with decidedly modernist affiliations, Brophy operates in the tradition of Woolf and Joyce, particularly in using parody to unsettle inherited notions of gender. But her 1969 novel places a distinctive emphasis on connections between gender and language, which Brophy reinforces by exploiting conventions of allegory. *In Transit* thus concentrates its actions in a single symbolic setting, an international airport, which distills the highly mixed, transient quality of modern culture. As a representative citizen of such a culture, the novel's dubious Everyman (or woman) is barraged by languages and surrounded by gaudy images of social unrest: a student revolution, a lesbian putsch, an assault by parachuting nuns—each aimed at the Control Tower of masculine authority. This environment of intense linguistic and social conflict seems fraught with occupational hazards, especially apparent in the dual disease or paired afflictions which utterly undo Brophy's protagonist: "linguistic leprosy," a deterioration of the character's language, and gender-amnesia, the ultimate identity crisis.

By suggesting that individual identity is tied to language, and by presenting both in an unstable condition, *In Transit* draws attention to a juncture between feminist studies of gender and Mikhail Bakhtin's theory of language. Like Bakhtin, Brophy emphasizes that human consciousness is a social phenomenon, constituted by widely shared, ideologically charged discourses. Yet by concentrating on the social nature of *gender* identity, her novel also anticipates a major focus of the seventies and eighties feminist scholarship. Feminism and dialogism meet and illuminate each other in Brophy's text.

Devices of modernist fiction facilitate this mutual exchange between feminism and Bakhtin, by making language, as Brophy's narrative itself proclaims, "one of the hero(in)es immolated throughout these pages." This ritualized sacrifice takes place in the novel's exuberantly fantastic, allegorical plot, as Language plays the part of the female victim relished by pornography. Yet the mutilation of language also occurs in portmanteau words, multilingual puns, stylistic parodies, and a disjunctive narrative structure, shifting from an initial first-person narrative to various third-person accounts mixed with "authorial" digressions. Paying explicit tribute to Joyce ("the old pun gent himself"), Brophy's self-consciously modernist narrative graphically renders the mutability of language which Bakhtin stresses, while also highlighting the problematics of gender explored by contemporary feminists. The following discussion will therefore approach Bakhtin's theory of language through parallels in Brophy, while moving toward connections *In Transit* makes among language, gender, and the novel itself as an art form. Brophy's synthesis of these three areas suggest extensions of Bakhtin's ideas in two directions he has been criticized for not considering: modernist fiction and feminist issues.

By suggesting that individual identity is tied to language, and by presenting both in an unstable condition, *In Transit* draws attention to a juncture between feminist studies of gender and Mikhail Bakhtin's theory of language.
—Sheryl Stevenson

A path into Bakhtin's theory can be charted through qualities he ascribes to language—as dialogic, ideological, "heteroglot," and anti-systematic. These qualities take startling, wacky forms as *In Transit* defamiliarizes this subject which literally becomes one of the text's "hero(in)es."

Brophy embodies her concept of language in an allegorical dream-quest undertaken by the novel's initial first-person narrator and protagonist, later identified as Evelyn Hilary O'Rooley (nicknamed "Pat"). The plot springs from the protagonist-narrator's decision to forego flight and remain "in transit," in the unrooted, culturally mixed state which the narrator presents as the twentieth-century frame of mind. Encompassed by a Babel-like confusion of tongues, the narrator dramatizes how languages pervade the subjective consciousness. These languages are, first of all, the national tongues which mix and collide within the narrator's perceptions and punning thoughts. Yet the airport's environment of many languages seems itself symbolic of proliferating forms of discourse which the narrator ingests—magazines, TV, postcards, signs, as well as various literary forms. (For example, the airport's public address system broadcasts a wildly camp, gender-inverted Italian opera, appropriately named for the airline, *Alitalia*.) A hodgepodge of voices, the first-person narrative conveys a psyche so permeated by social discourses that it seems, as Bakhtin says, a "*border-*

line" phenomenon, merging self and society and so having "extraterritoriality status." In both Bakhtin and Brophy this metaphor of extraterritoriality (of being in transit, between states) reflects a notion of language as the constituting element of a radically social psyche.

Peculiar features of Brophy's protagonist-narrator further fill out her novel's Bakhtinian conception of language. The decision "to live in in-transit" marks one such peculiarity. This move is apparently motivated by egalitarian "internationalism," a radical *linguistic* politics summed up in the narrator's citizenship oath: "I adopt the international airport idiom for my native." Pat O'Rooley seems predisposed to this "ideological gesture," having been transported as a child from Ireland to England and hence deprived of a "native language." "Extraterritoriality" is George Steiner's term for this condition, a lack of "at-homeness" in any national tongue which he sees as characteristic of multilingual artists like Nabokov and Beckett. Bakhtin finds a similar "linguistic consciousness" endemic to multilingual cultures, where contact with alternative languages breeds a disease with any one formulation. An emblematic citizen of the twentieth century, Brophy's deracinated narrator seems to embody Bakhtin's idea and, indeed, claims that in the airport (an internationally mixed, modern culture) "no one is native. We are all in transients."

Along with acute awareness of languages and their limits, the first-person narrative reveals a second eccentricity in Brophy's protagonist: obsessive concern with locating and addressing various interlocutors. This obsession is articulated in the novel's opening paragraphs, as the narrator focuses not on Barthes's characteristic question, "Who is speaking?" (*S/Z*), but on the question of the addressee of the narrative discourse:

> Ce qui m'étonnait c'était qu'it was my French that disintegrated first.
>
> Thus I expounded my affliction, an instant after I noticed its onset. My words went, of course, unvoiced . . .
>
> Obviously, it wasn't myself I was informing I had contracted linguistic leprosy. I'd already known for a good split second.
>
> I was addressing the imaginary interlocutor who is entertained, I surmise, by all self-conscious beings—short of, possibly, the dumb and, probably, infants (in the radical sense of the word).

If we take the protagonist-narrator as a representative figure, then the novel suggests that inner speech as well as spoken discourse is always directed to someone, even if the interlocutor is ultimately imagined, a projection. *In Transit* plays up this idea when the narrator briefly takes the p.a. system as an interlocutor:

> The phantom faces of the interlocutor are less troubling than the question of *where* he is. I am beset by an insidious compulsion to locate him . . .

> The problem was the more acute because I was alone in a concourse of people. After a moment I noticed that my situation had driven me to think my thoughts to the public-address system, which had, for the last hour, been addressing me—inter aliens—with commands (couched as requests), admonitions (a tumble of negative subjunctives) and simple brief loud-hails, not one of which had I elected to act on.

Brophy's extremely other-oriented protagonist closely resembles Dostoevsky's narrator in "Notes from Underground," as analyzed by Bakhtin: "The discourse of the underground Man is entirely a discourse-address. To speak, for him means to address someone." Both apparent monologuists are actually dialoguists, revealing one of the ways in which all discourse is "dialogic": "every word is directed toward an answer and cannot escape the profound influence of the answering word that it anticipates."

Dostoevsky's Underground Man begins his narrative in this way: "I am a sick man . . . I am a spiteful man. I am an unpleasant man. I think my liver is diseased. However, I don't know beans about my disease, and I am not sure what is bothering me" (Dostoevsky's ellipsis). Similarly, *In Transit* immediately confronts us with a diseased narrator, but in this case the sickness is one of language, "linguistic leprosy," the third oddity of Brophy's peculiar Everyone. The narrator thus complains of foreign tongues atrophying and "fall[ing] off," like the fingers and toes which can be lost through leprosy. Yet the narrative mixes and compares Greek, Latin, Gaelic, Italian, and French, commenting on the "idiomsyncrasy" of each. Gripped by "compunsion," Brophy's intensely multilingual protagonist-narrator playfully illustrates the "crossing" of languages which Bakhtin sees as fundamental to their evolution. Exaggerating this condition of languages within the narrator's consciousness, *In Transit* dramatizes how language itself is "in transit"—ever in a process of change as languages mix, mutate, "die."

I see this idea fleshed out in Brophy's comic Story of Oc—that is, "O" with a "c" or "ch" added. Providing a great example of female parody-pornography, the narrative incorporates substantial excerpts of a porno-novel, purchased by Pat from the airport bookstall and entitled, "L'HISTOIRE DE LA LANGUE D'OC" (which is translated, "THE STORY OF OC'S TONGUE"). As a student

at a girls' school of pleasure, the bondage fanatic Oc undergoes various exquisite tortures, during which she finally dies. Along the way, in an offhand reference, the narrative reminds us that the *langue d'oc* was the language of Southern France, replaced by the northern *langue d'öil* (the alternative terms referring to each area's pronunciation of the word for "yes"). In Brophy's kinky allegory, the porn-heroine Oc represents the specific, transient language—subject to a process of mutilation and death which parallels the narrator's linguistic leprosy. The novel then makes this parallel explicit when the first-person narrator goes through a scene of linguistic torture, a dismemberment of the narrative's language, which is sandwiched between the final binding of Och and the announcement of her death.

The parallel stories of Oc and Pat foreground the radically transient status of language and of human consciousness, while also pointing toward ties between changes in each. As a masochist whose name recalls inter-language conflict, the mutable Oc/Och illuminates Bakhtin's notion of language as "a continuous process of becoming," a dynamic struggle of tongues. On one level, this conflict occurs between "centripetal" and "centrifugal" tendencies in language. Hence, groups and institutions seeking political and ideological centralization posit a "correct," unifying language, which is constantly undermined by heterogeneous social usage (or "heteroglossia"), the ceaseless stratification of any national language by countless social groups, each of which has a "language" of its own, with meanings and inflections reflecting the group's world view. As each word is imbued with values and associations, fraught with conflicting connotations acquired in the course of "its socially charged life," the word itself "exists in continuous generation and change." Bakhtin's "anti-linguistics," as Susan Stewart calls it, thus presents language as antisystematic, "ideologically saturated," and ever in transit.

Matching Brophy's paired transients, Oc and Pat, Bakhtin sees human consciousness as strongly tied to the shifting languages (and ideologies) of society: "Language lights up the inner personality and its consciousness; language creates them . . . Personality is itself generated through language." Brophy joins Bakhtin in stressing that the subjective consciousness is formed in a responsive, dialogic relationship with the words and world views of others. To see how *In Transit* brings out the implications of this position for current gender theory, we need to consider the ultimate peculiarity of Brophy's protagonist, the uncertain gender of Evelyn Hilary O'Rooley. By studying this final trait in some detail, we can see how the novel ties the formation of gender identity to a larger process of linguistic and cultural change.

Following Pat's decision to put off departure and stay in the Transit Lounge, the narrative discourse is filled with enthusiastic apostrophes, elaborating the benefits and egalitarian politics of choosing a nonstatic, nondefined state of becoming. But while Pat O'Rooley gaily rejects "arbitrary" categories, like those of nation and class, which artificially limit human self-definition, the state of in-transience also seems to entail loss of gender distinctions: in other words, the narrator can no longer remember whether he or she is male or female.

From this point, the novel's fragmented, zany plot highlights Pat's romance-quest in search of a fixed sense of gender identity. While virtually the whole of *In Transit* can be seen as a series of parodic discourses, some of the most marked and swiftly changing parodies occur after the onset of Pat's gender-amnesia. Pursuing Pat in his/her shifting sense of gender, the narrative indicates each shift with a new parody. Two examples can suggest how each parodied discourse is imbued with conceptions of masculinity or femininity which Pat tries on and is tested by—romance adventures in which the styles Pat takes on are tested notions of gender.

> **While virtually the whole of *In Transit* can be seen as a series of parodic discourses, some of the most marked and swiftly changing parodies occur after the onset of Pat's gender-amnesia.**
> —*Sheryl Stevenson*

When first convinced of being female, Patricia descends into the airport's basement, a "lesbian underworld" of female porters, and then is whisked onto the panel of a television game show, *WHAT'S MY KINK?* Addressed as a man, under the intense glare of public attention, Pat faces the moment when the cameras will focus on him? her? with an accession to the language of popular adventure stories:

> Time ponderously raced: a count-down of seconds passed at fever-speed and yet in the detail of slow-motion. This was an experience of time with enlarged pores.

> When the moment came, would he/she be able to utter a syllable?

> It was a clenching pressure of dread, in which a soul might crack: and he publicly exposed . . . A count-down of seconds, it was, until the very second when this individual, Pat, should have one second to make or mar: and if it was a second of shame, there was no revoking it, ever.

Given the implicit macho of this passage, it is hardly surprising that at the crucial (reiterated, expanded) *second*, "Pat

resolved to be Patrick" and "coolly and decisively" fires his winning answer.

In a later sequence, when Pat decides she is instead a lesbian, her choice of an exclusively female self-definition is reflected by the narrative, which mimics the super-"feminine" genre of popular romance. A woman of quiet dignity, pop-romance heroine Patricia is approached and wooed by an aristocratic stranger, an aging Byronic roué equipped with military bearing and a face distinguished by a duelling scar. Queenly Patricia rejects this self-confessed "Don Juan," yet as she accompanies him to his departure gate her fears of his possible death in flight are expressed in a sentimental, metaphor-enriched style which presumably expresses her chastely "feminine" sense of self (that is, as a lesbian). This wacky parody undermines, even as it exposes, assumptions about men and women which saturate the gush of popular romance, with its darkly attractive, sexualized males and vascillatingly attracted, sentimental females. The sexual ideology implicit here—one of absolute differences between the sexes—is exploded by the scene's camp termination:

> "Kiss my hand," she said, letting fall the separate words like queen's pearls or tears.

> "My dear," he said, letting the tones of a roué cynic curl the edges of his words like autumn-leaf mustachios tobacco-cured in an irony against himself, "I know we are said not to live in a permissive society. But I would not risk exposing you to the comment and disapproval which, I very strongly suspect, would ensue were a middle-aged man to be seen, in so public a place as this, to kiss the hand, be it never so beautiful, of a boy."

This scene exemplifies a pattern of the novel's gender adventures, since from this encounter "Patricia" (now in quotes, a gay male) spins off to try out another distinct, yet finally inadequate, conception of his masculinity (or "her" femininity). In this unsettling of the protagonist's gender identity, Pat's story resembles Joyce's Nighttown episode in *Ulysses,* which takes Bloom through fantasized metamorphoses of himself, as he experiences the ambiguities of his gender, the multiformity of his desires. And Pat's quest also recalls another fantasy-shaped underworld descent, that of Lewis Carroll's Alice. Changing sex as often as Alice changes size, Pat undergoes a series of Wonderland transformations, which can be explained as fantasies and which mainly differ from Alice's similar dream-quest for self-definition in that Pat, unlike Alice, does not become a queen (of either sex). Trying on numerous styles of manliness or femininity—like that of Slim, the sleazy detective, or Oruleus, the Spenserian knight—Pat seems impelled by the limits of each gender-conception and each parodied discourse to move on to another style, another conception, in a never completed process. Hence, at the novel's close, Patricia's and Patrick's simultaneous but contrasting deaths are depicted in adjacent columns, a vast improvement on John Fowles's double-ending of *The French Lieutenant's Woman* in that it exhibits even more clearly the ambiguous, indeed contradictory, nature of the protagonist.

Commenting on this aspect of *In Transit,* David Lodge suggests that contradiction is a primary structural principle of postmodern novels, which often focus on "sexually ambivalent" characters or other central, unresolved paradoxes. While Lodge's perspective is illuminating, his brief analysis seems to miss a crucial effect of Brophy's unresolved representations of gender. Rather than simply presenting a metaphysical paradox (Pat is and is not male, is and is not female), her parodies draw attention to the process of self-definition through language, and more specifically, through widely shared discourses. By shifting styles with every fleeting notion of Pat's gender, the narrative implies that Pat O'Rooley can only become "feminine" or "masculine" through transient cultural conceptions, expressed in specific, often contradictory, texts or discourses. The problem of gender becomes a matter of cultural change and social (rather than metaphysical) contradiction. Brophy's androgynous protagonist then represents something more than a Freudian-based conception, indicating the ubiquity of human sexual desire and the ability of people to identify with models of either sex (psychoanalytic tenets which *In Transit* flaunts with much glee). Going further, much like Virginia Woolf's *Orlando,* Brophy's novel ties notions of masculinity and femininity to specific periods and discourses, implying that the individual's sense of his or her gender—and of what constitutes femininity or masculinity—will alter along with broader shifts in intellectual and literary fashion.

While clearly linked to other modernist explorations of gender, Brophy's novel also intersects with more recent feminist studies from diverse disciplinary perspectives. Since the early seventies, anthropologists have increasingly focused on "meanings" or "interpretations" of sexuality and gender which they trace to highly specific factors of society and culture. Linguistics further specifies the role of language in the social formation of gender identity. Sally McConnell-Ginet explains this thrust of linguistics: "The major challenge that feminist scholarship on language poses is to explain how there could be any interaction at all between language and an individual's thought, on the one hand, and the social and cultural contexts in which language is used, on the other." In meeting this challenge, feminist inquiry has spurred linguistics itself toward what can be seen as a Bakhtinian view of language, turning from emphasis on universal structures toward study of conflicting, and possibly liberating, language use: "Indeterminacy and multiple meanings are not the exception but important features of linguistic

systems that underlie the role of language in changing society, culture, and personal consciousness."

The role of ideologically charged language in shaping both social institutions and individual consciousness has especially been central to feminist studies of gender influenced by French historian Michel Foucault. Rosalind Coward, for example, stresses the value of Foucault's *History of Sexuality* in showing how sexuality and identity are "discursively constructed." Offering more resistance to Foucault (by way of Bakhtin), historian Carroll Smith-Rosenberg details the place of nineteenth-century women's writing on prostitution and gender. Foucault lies behind Smith-Rosenberg's notion that "[w]e construct our sense of self out of words" which are themselves "cultural constructs." Yet she agrees with other feminist historians who "challenge Foucault's understanding of the constraining force of 'discourse.'" Wishing to complicate his model by accounting for women's transformations of dominant discourses, Smith-Rosenberg uses Bakhtin's idea that society's languages tend toward diversity and disruption as well as unification and hegemony. Film theorist Teresa de Lauretis makes a similar move in her assertion that "the construction of gender" takes place not only in the media, schools, and courts, but also "in avant-garde artistic practices and radical theories," including feminism. Hence this construction is "also affected by its deconstruction" through competing, alternative discourses.

Repeatedly approaching gender as "construct," "interpretation," "discourse," or "representation," contemporary feminist scholarship suggests both the constructing role and the disruptive possibilities of language. Feminist inquiry can further benefit from connections Bakhtin makes between the heterogeneity of language and specific literary forms: the novel, carnivalesque discourse, and parody. American scholars have widely admired and discussed Bakhtin's view that the novel's multiplicity of discourses and styles presents a dialogue between ways of conceiving the world, an aesthetic representation of the many-voiced, "dialogic" nature of language itself, which undermines any singular, monologic "truth." "Centrifugal" dialogism opposes "centripetal" monologism in literature as well as in language, as Bakhtin finds the epic and poetry tending toward a restrictive, unified viewpoint while the novel heroically promotes creative diversity.

How can the novel's many-voiced dialogism contribute to the construction (and deconstruction) of gender? *In Transit* illuminates this question by combining conceptions of language and the novel which, like Bakhtin's, highlight the decentralizing tendencies of each. The antisystematic nature of language especially emerges in exchanges between "Och" and a linguistics professor, who act out the "centrifugal" and "centripetal" roles that Bakhtin ascribes to language and modern linguistics (a recurring theme of "Discourse in the Novel" and *Marxism and the Philosophy of Language*). While the highly rational linguist resists radical changes, Och is essentially anarchic, as she suggests in the following comments:

> "To be absolutely frank, what I should most like to resemble is a small but powerful and concentrated bomb. My ambition is to explode and shatter the rules . . . "

> "And yet for all my creative energy I feel impotent," Och sadly said.
> "I can't find anyone who will teach me the rules. So how can I make sure of breaking them?"

The kind of bomb Och wishes to emulate does, however, explode, starting an avalanche of printed matter from the airport bookstand, during which Linguistics tries (with dubious success) to teach Language its rules:

> O'Rooley and the professor at once linked themselves into a protective canopy over Och; and so it was about their two heads alone that a gently, scarcely more than ticklingly absurd world began to cave in. A soft fall of newsprint bombed them, a structural collapse not violent but slipshod.

> The professor was most heavily struck by blunders of form, especially the formula "he was x, y and had a z."

> "Well, tell me the rule, then," Och implored, tugging from underneath at the professor's raincoat.

> "'X, y and z,'" the professor began to explain, "can legitimately be thus strung together only if you suspend them from one verb . . . "

> She was cut off by a large fall of things this big and persons not that bad . . . "It should be 'so big' or 'thus big' or 'as big as this,'" she was panting when she was almost done for by the editorial of the *Evening Standard* of 6 June, 1968, which spoke of "every mass media."

Though O'Rooley joins the professor in trying to shield language from "error," he suggests that they may be "swimming against the grain of the living language." Within Pat's livingly mixed "Irishidiomism," Brophy incorporates one of Bakhtin's favorite phrases, "living" language. This intersection between the views and even phrases of Brophy and Bakhtin points to their mutual conception of language as a dynamic, conflictive process rather than a restrictive, internalized system. For both, the rule-bound system is over-whelmed by anarchic usages, which include (in Brophy's zany scene) William Faulkner's novels—a final onslaught of deviance which is fatal to the system-protecting linguist.

Brophy's allegory aligns the syntactically deviant, experimental novel—here represented by Faulkner—with the "erring," centrifugal impulses of language itself. It is not surprising, then, that *In Transit* renders this dynamism of language not only in the comic explosion of printed "errors," but also in its own narrative discourse. Increasingly fragmented by parodies, interpolated texts, diagrams, and "authorial" digressions, the modernistic narrative graphically conveys an "in transit" protagonist, dissolving into a series of voices and possible selves.

Yet *In Transit* also explicitly considers how fiction might contribute to this dynamic condition of both self and language. Just as Bakhtin foregrounds the novel's dialogic potential through contrasts with epic and poetry, so Brophy juxtaposes Pat O'Rooley's reader-response evaluations of several literary forms. Where the dialogic-monologic polarity serves as Bakhtin's touchstone, erotic pleasure functions in *In Transit,* as in Barthes's *Pleasure of the Text,* to assess various experiences of reading. Calling upon erotic analogues, Brophy's protagonist thus finds that the unsatisfying characterization within mystery novels leads the reader into "lust-hunting-down the characters who are increasingly not there," yielding an experience similar to that of pornography, a "literary masturbation."

Through its interludes, *In Transit* presents the novel itself as a dialogue between writer and reader (Kermode calls Brophy's work "a phenomenological fantasia"). Yet this dialogue takes place "inter aliens"— between mutually unknown, hence mutually "fictitious," participants.
—*Sheryl Stevenson*

Distinctive characterization results in Pat's greater pleasure from *Alitalia*, Brophy's parodic representative of the "furthest-fetched of all forms of fiction": "Sweet monster opera, I am in your whirlpool kiss. You have sucked me deep into your contralto throat, drawn me down into identification with your characters by your sheer liquid expressiveness of their emotions." Printed in dual columns (Italian text, English translation), with "transvocites" (Frank Kermode's term for the work's male sopranos and female baritone), this parody-opera stresses the implausible characters audiences can be led to identify with, the fictions of identity to which readers are drawn. Yet because of the opera's tonality (because its hero Orestes is "bereaved in tune"), the narrator can be whirled and pulled to extremes, and still be left reassured—self-assured and reinforced. *Alitalia* is not, in other words, one of those musical compositions the narrator earlier defends: "Not that it's unfairplay to play on our expectations of key and, instead of playing in key, dispense with it. The object is to unstring us: one of the psycho-tortures self-inflicted, by way of pleasure, in masophisticated societies." Instead of masochistic "psycho-torture," *Alitalia* produces a self-complacent "euphoria" in Pat O'Rooley. Brophy's screwy opera thus illustrates, oddly enough, Barthes's tame "text of pleasure": "the text that contents, fills, grants euphoria; the text that comes from culture and does not break with it, is linked to a comfortable practice of reading." By implicitly opposing her tonal opera with music that "unstring[s] us," Brophy matches Barthes's greater admiration for the "text of bliss," "the text that imposes a state of loss, the text that discomforts . . . , unsettles the reader's historical, cultural, psychological assumptions, the consistency of his tastes, values, memories, brings to a crisis his relation with language."

In Transit forthrightly discusses and pursues such discomforting effects through a series of "interludes," entitled variantly "Interludibrium," "Interlugubre," "INTERLEWD," "INTERLOO." In these digressions, the reader is directly addressed by an authorial first-person narrator, who signs one such "Open-Letter" with the initials "(p.p.B.B.)" over "E.H.(P.)O'R.," a playful identification of Brophy with her "HERO," as Leslie A. Dock observes, noting the anagram formed by the protagonist's initials. Foregrounding techniques and ambiguities of the narrative's "machinery," these ludic addresses seek to unstring both reader and writer by calling into question the status of each. Hence in one such interjection (just after the onset of Pat's gender-amnesia), the authorial narrator asserts that "relations between us are by no means so straightforward" as some may assume:

> Suppose for the sake of argument that I am a fictitious character or at least one who appears so to you. I have invited from you a certain temporary identification. I am prepared to be taken over, possessed, by you. In your own eyes, I don't doubt, you are a very real part of the real world. But please remember that, to me it is you who are the fictitious—the, indeed, entirely notional—character. To be engulfed by you into an identification must be like being nibbled at, ticklingly, by a void. I have to summon my weightiest resources of gravity to take you seriously. I don't even know, for example, what sex you are.

Through its interludes, *In Transit* presents the novel itself as a dialogue between writer and reader (Kermode calls Brophy's work "a phenomenological fantasia"). Yet this dialogue takes place "inter aliens"—between mutually unknown, hence mutually "fictitious," participants. The

protagonist-narrator's weird interlocution with the public address system thus becomes a model for the dialogic text, illuminating Bakhtin's ideas by dramatizing how the reader's and writer's interlocutor is always a fiction. Further, these interludes teasingly flaunt uncertainties of gender identity by reinforcing ties between "Brigid Brophy," as a fictitious character in her own novel, and Patricia-Patrick, potential selves the author explores and (in their simultaneous deaths) abandons, with the summary comment "Explicit fiction." If this inconclusive ending leaves "Brigid Brophy's" gender both fictitious and unresolved, a similar effect is achieved by the authorial narrator's final address to the reader as "both of You," imputing an analogous androgyny, or at least ambiguity, to the reader. This last authorial address is then followed by the word "FIN," inscribed on the fin of a fish. Foreclosing closure with a typical verbal-ideographic pun, the novel invites the reader to pursue the implications of "both of You" toward an ambiguous, unfixed gender identity, a fictitious, multiple self which each individual authors as "Brophy" has, dialogically, in response to the words of others, the discourses of society.

Bakhtin emphasizes the novel's devices for representing an unsettled dialogue between ideas and voices, along with a many-voiced, "dialogic" consciousness. *In Transit* conveys this dialogism and multiplicity by drawing on specific devices of modernist fiction. As the narrative disintegrates into a multitude of texts, set apart by point of view, style, spacing, typography, and inserted diagrams, the novel fully exploits possibilities of the printed word for rendering distinct languages and viewpoints. Hence, it is appropriate that, besides language, Brophy's other proclaimed "unsung, unstrung heroine" is "Miss Print." Yet through the ambiguity of this pun, *In Transit* sings (or is it unsings?) both the printed text and its tendency toward error, exemplified by *L'histoire de la Langue d'Oc,* the sole novel lengthily examined within Brophy's novel. Filled with misprints and ambiguous cases of possible error, *Oc* is made even more unstable when Pat detaches one of its pages, causing the loss of a paired page that apparently would have been critical in his/her "sexegesis." The repeated direction "Déchirez" then reiterates the entropic, tear-out status of the material text, countering any notion that written language affords an escape from transience or an exegetical key to gender.

In Transit highlights the mutability of texts, languages, conceptions of gender, and individual identities. In Brophy's allegory of interacting transients, language appears as a disruptive element, not a prison-house; rather than determining gender identity, it offers a surplus of conflicting meanings for femininity and masculinity. This conception of language—a meeting ground between Bakhtin and feminism—spawns the parodies of Brophy's novel. As they juxtapose numerous "official" and popular versions of woman and man, these parodies convey a carnivalesque stance toward the "social construction of gender," as a limited, highly conflictual, shifting process. Dramatizing how gender is socially determined and indeterminate, historically situated and fluid, *In Transit* richly illustrates the novel's power in promoting an open-ended "sexegesis."

Sarah Lyall (essay date 9 August 1995)

SOURCE: "Brigid Brophy Is Dead at 66; Novelist, Critic and Crusader," in *The New York Times,* August 9, 1995, p. D20.

[*In the following obituary, Lyall summarizes Brophy's life and career achievements.*]

Brigid Brophy, a novelist, critic, essayist and crusader for myriad causes ranging from better royalty payments for writers to better treatment for animals, died on Monday at a nursing home in Lincolnshire, England. She was 66 and had been suffering from multiple sclerosis for many years.

Miss Brophy was the author of 4 plays, 7 novels and 14 other books, but she is just as well known for her most successful campaign, for landing rights for authors. In 1979, her efforts resulted in a law that for the first time allowed authors to receive royalty payments from the British Government every time their books were checked out of a public library.

But Miss Brophy also campaigned—even from her sickbed—for the rights of women, of prisoners and of animals. She was a vice president of the National Anti-Vivisection Society, and no animal escaped her sympathy. She even became active in an anti-angling campaign; and at one point sent a letter to the fishing correspondent of *The Daily Telegraph* in which she compared anglers to "thugs who beat up old-age pensioners for fun" and quoted Lord Byron's remark that fishing was "the stupidest of pretended sports."

Brigid Antonia Brophy was born in 1929 in London, the only daughter of the Anglo-Irish novelist John Brophy. She was educated at St. Paul's Girls' School and later at Oxford, where she excelled as a scholar but was soon expelled because of drunken, raucous behavior. She was acting, she later wrote, in the belief that I had more to learn by pursuing my personal life than from textual emendation, with the result that the authorities could put up with me for only just over a year.

"I came down at the age of 19 without a degree and with a consequent sense of nudity which I have never quite overcome."

In 1954, before she was even 30, she burst onto the literary scene when her novel *Hackenfeller's Ape,* about an ape at the London Zoo and its increasingly close relationship to the professor observing its mating habits, won the Cheltenham Literary Festival First Prize for a first novel. Her novels are known for their imagination and acerbic wit, and include *The Snow Ball,* in which the characters attend a ball dressed as figures from *Don Giovanni; Flesh,* which she described as "an almost distressingly cold-blooded little story," and *In Transit,* set, claustrophobically, in an airport transit lounge.

But she also developed a reputation as a sharp thinker and fierce intellectual who liked a good fight, and her nonfiction books tended to have provocative, often mischievous points of view. In 1967 for instance, she was one of the authors of *Fifty Works of English Literature We Could Do Without,* an attack on a number of classic books including *Jane Eyre,* which was likened by the authors to "gobbling a jar-full of school-girl stick-jaw." She also championed the writing of Ronald Firbank in *Prancing Novelist* (1973), subtitled *A Defense of Fiction in the Form of a Critical Biography in Praise of Ronald Firbank.*

Miss Brophy, who spoke freely in her early years about her bisexuality and often referred to marriage as "an immoral institution," nonetheless married in 1954. Her husband, the art historian Michael Levey, shared her delight in literature and the arts. He became director of the National Gallery in 1973 and was knighted eight years later.

In a tribute to Miss Brophy in *The Independent* on Tuesday, her literary agent, Giles Gordon, described her as a "deeply shy, courteous woman" who wrote delightful thank you letters and kept to rigorous standards in her work. "Woe betide the 'editor' who tried to rewrite her fastidious, logical, exact prose, change a colon to a semi-color (or vice-versa), or try to spell 'show' other than 'shew,' slavish Shavian that Brophy was," Mr. Gordon wrote.

In 1979, Miss Brophy's physical problem was diagnosed as multiple sclerosis, which steadily worsened until she was housebound and had to use a wheelchair. She remained at home, looked after by paid companions, friends, and her husband, who in 1987 quit his job to help care for her. But she continued to work with all the energy her illness would allow. In 1987 she published *Baroque 'n' Roll,* a collection of essays in which she outlined, with lucidity and detail, the debilitating toll her condition had taken on her. Eventually, her condition deteriorated so badly that she had to move into the nursing home where she died.

She is survived by her husband and a daughter, Kate.

Steven Moore (essay date Fall 1995)

SOURCE: "Brigid Brophy: An Introduction and Checklist," in *Review of Contemporary Fiction,* Vol. 15, No. 3, Fall, 1995, pp. 7-11.

[*In the following essay, Moore provides an overview of Brophy's literary career.*]

There was a time, in the sixties and early seventies, when no one needed an introduction to Brigid Brophy. She was one of the most controversial writers in England—occupying a position somewhat like Camille Paglia's today—and here in the States her books were published by the best New York houses and widely reviewed. Now, unfortunately, most of her books are out of print on both sides of the Atlantic and few readers under forty recognize the name. Some of the reasons for this neglect are understandable: she didn't publish a novel after 1978, and a debilitating struggle with multiple sclerosis over the last fifteen years of her life sharply curtailed her writing career. Also, she was cursed for being too far ahead of her time: in her 1953 novel *Hackenfeller's Ape* she was writing about animal rights long before the cause became popular, and in 1969 wrote the definitive novel about gender confusion (*In Transit*) long before there was a critical context for the topic. But any informed reckoning of twentieth-century literature must take Brophy's work into account: not only her nine books of fiction, but a career's worth of sharp, intelligent essays (most gathered into three collections), books on Mozart, Freud, and Beardsley, and a 600-page tour de force "defence of fiction in the form of a critical biography of Ronald Firbank," *Prancing Novelist.*

Her literary career began early. Born in 1929, she was reading authors like Firbank at the age of five (as she reports in an excellent interview with Leslie Dock in *Contemporary Literature*) and from age six onwards was writing verse dramas. When she was fifteen she wrote an early version of **"The Late Afternoon of a Faun,"** which appeared in her first book, *The Crown Princess and Other Stories,* published in 1953 when she was twenty-four. Later that same year she published her first novel, *Hackenfeller's Ape,* which won the Cheltenham Literary Festival prize for best first novel. Brophy later dismissed *The Crown Princess* as too mainstream—I think it's better than that—but *Hackenfeller's Ape,* as Mark Axelrod shows in his essay, demonstrated her ability at an early stage to integrate a variety of themes and concerns (Mozart, original sin, vivisection) in a form owing as much to music as to literature. (Baroque architecture would become an additional model

for her novels.) Mozart and musical (specifically operatic) form dominates many of her early works: her charming second novel, *The King of a Rainy Country* (1956), relies heavily on Mozart's *Le Nozze di Figaro* (as Patricia Juliana Smith notes in her insightful essay in [*Review of Contemporary Literature*]) just as her dazzling fifth novel, *The Snow Ball* (1964), relies on his *Don Giovanni*. (In the same year she published her nonfiction study *Mozart the Dramatist,* widely hailed as one of the best books on his operas, and recently reprinted both in Britain and the U.S.)

Brophy's third novel, *Flesh* (1962), is an unusual novel about the effect of marriage on an awkward, unsociable man that plays against the Pygmalion theme. Dedicated to Iris Murdoch, this story of north London Jews was her first popular success. It was followed by her fourth and most elliptical book of fiction, *The Finishing Touch* (1963), a wickedly clever novella—half Firbank, half Colette—about a lesbian-run girls' finishing school on the French Riviera. Corinne E. Blackmer explores its literary heritage in detail in [*Review of Contemporary Literature*] and correctly praises it as "an important milestone in the history of lesbian and, more broadly, antihomophobic literature."

Brophy was in her element in the iconoclastic sixties. She became notorious for her views on vegetarianism, sexual freedom, animal rights, writers' rights (she played a major role in Britain's current Public Lending Right, by which authors are paid a royalty whenever their books are checked out of libraries), women's rights, pornography (pro), and educational reform (contra religion in school, pro Greek), promoting her views on television and radio as well as in print. The same year she published *Flesh* (1962) she published a long nonfiction work entitled *Black Ship to Hell,* a rigorous Freudian reading of the dynamics of hate, compared by the *London Telegraph* to Norman O. Brown's *Life against Death.* The best of her essays and reviews were published in book form in 1966 under the title *Don't Never Forget,* and have lost none of their bite, wit, and lightly worn erudition thirty years later. With her husband Michael Levey and friend Charles Osborne she collaborated on the cheeky *Fifty Works of English and American Literature We Could Do Without* (1967), and the following year she wrote the first of two books on the 1890s artist Aubrey Beardsley. Also in 1968 she published a book version of her 1967 play, *The Burglar,* with a long, Shavian introduction (she has written other, unproduced, plays).

The decade came to an explosive climax in 1969 with her masterpiece, *In Transit.* Several essays [in *Review of Contemporary Literature*] deal with this extraordinary novel, and several more would be needed to encompass its achievement. As the ambiguously named narrator sits in an international airport waiting for a connecting flight, he/she suffers a kind of gender amnesia and goes through a series of comic attempts to discover his/her sex. The novel is a riot of multilingual puns, parodies, opera allusions, typographical high jinks (one thinks of roughly contemporary books like William H. Gass's *Willie Masters' Lonesome Wife* and Christine Brooke-Rose's *Thru*), and should be a *locus classicus* for today's gender critics and advocates of experimental fiction.

The next few years were spent researching and writing her massive book on Firbank, which was met largely by uncomprehending reviews, most questioning the wisdom of using Firbank, of all people, on whom to erect a theory of creative fiction. Once again, Brophy was years ahead of the pack, for only now in the nineties is Firbank becoming recognized for the subversively innovative writer he is. In 1973 she also published her second collection of short fiction, *The Adventures of God in His Search for the Black Girl;* it's a lively if somewhat miscellaneous collection, some of the pieces a mere page, the title fable novella-length. Then in 1978 she published her final novel, *Palace without Chairs,* an oddly muted fairy tale set in an imaginary Eastern European socialist monarchy, somewhat in the vein of Firbank's *Flower beneath the Foot.* After that, Brophy wrote very little; two collections of her essays were published in the 1980s, supplementing (and in some cases reprinting) those in her 1966 collection *Don't Never Forget.* She died on 7 August 1995, a few weeks before this issue went to press.

The neglect of this brilliant woman's work and contributions to contemporary aesthetics is scandalous, and I hope the essays in this issue begin a long-running critical engagement with her body of work. In the afterward to *Reads,* Brophy says she took the title of her first essay collection from Mozart's attempt at English in a friend's album—"Don't never forget your faithfull friend"—because "I consider it vital that human beings never should forget Mozart." Those human beings who study contemporary literature never should forget Brophy.

Chris Hopkins (essay date Fall 1995)

SOURCE: "The Neglect of Brigid Brophy," in *Review of Contemporary Fiction,* Vol. 15, No. 3, Fall, 1995, pp. 12-17.

[*In the following essay, Hopkins explains why Brophy's fiction resists generic classification and academic characterization, concluding that her manipulation of multiple literary conventions, often within a single work, deserves a wider audience.*]

Brigid Brophy has been neglected not only in the academy but also outside it: neither my university library in England nor the local public libraries possess any of her novels, and they are now equally unobtainable in bookshops. Neglect (and ultimately obscurity) is, of course, the fate of many authors, but there are perhaps specific reasons in this case—reasons that are paradoxically also very much part of what is interesting about Brophy's work. A main reason for this neglect seems to be that her work is not easily categorized or characterized. Though uniqueness, originality, and creativity are recognized as distinct literary qualities, it is nevertheless essential for readers to be able to place those qualities within some kind of framework. Association of an author with a particular kind of novel or a particular kind of writing is, for example, a helpful starting point for reading a text by an author and a shorthand way of keeping in mind what an author/author's books are like.

Simple as such kinds of categorization may seem, they are central to the ways in which literary texts are, or are not, kept in circulation. This is as true of the academy as outside it, and although the selection of material read in literature departments ("the canon") may sometimes seem to bear an odd relation to the selection of a wider reading public (even a "literary" one), there is a relationship there that can affect which authors remain in print. This is particularly critical in the transition for an author from being a contemporary novelist (reviewed in newspapers and widely circulated literary journals) to being an academically read author (which can in turn help to keep him or her alive as a "public" writer).

Brigid Brophy has not, I think, retained her position as an author still being widely read, and she has not made a transition into the academy (either in England or the U.S.). This transition is, of course, one for which there is tremendous competition: there are always too many authors (particularly recent ones) and too few opportunities to study a complete range. Selection is made by means of the ways in which literature courses are organized around particular topics. Thus most university literature departments will have some general courses on "Twentieth-Century Literature" and a variety of more narrowly defined courses on "The Modernists" or "Writing between the World Wars" or "Contemporary Writing" and so on. In either case the processes of selection make it hard for an author like Brophy to be included. Her writing is not clearly associated with a specific period (her work has not particularly been seen as representing the sixties, for example), nor is it associated with a specific novelistic genre or kind of writing. In this her work is not unique—other British women novelists, such as Doris Lessing, Iris Murdoch, and Muriel Spark, do not occupy clearly defined niches either—but Brophy is more neglected, and the variety and sheer oddness of her work may play a role in this, together with features of academic literary study itself.

None of the obvious critical labels seems helpful; terms such as modernism, realism, and postmodernism can each be helpful up to a point, but none seems easily attached to all of her work. Part of the problem is that the first and last of these terms tend to suggest not only stylistic matters but also particular periods. Brophy seems too late for modernism and too early for postmodernism. That would seem to leave the long-enduring and central novelistic tradition of realism, but, as I shall argue, that too is helpful only up to a point (besides the fact that realism as a contemporary mode is generally not privileged in the academy and thus gives little force to a claim for Brophy's significance). A major part of this failure of Brophy's fiction to be characterized or canonized stems indeed from the way in which twentieth-century literature has been "periodized" or fitted into a historical framework. Up to the seventies, modernism (particularly Joyce, Lawrence, Woolf, and Hemingway) dominated literature courses. In the eighties contemporary literature began to be studied, especially new women writers, and by the middle of the decade, notions of the postmodern novel became widespread. None of these focuses helped Brophy much: she fitted none of them very exactly.

What I wish to do then is to introduce some of the variety of Brophy's work in order first to show some of the reasons for its lack of obvious classification and, more important, to suggest why it is of interest. Having said that Brophy's novels are not classified as postmodern, it should nevertheless be said that part of their variety does come from their being written after modernism (and several decades of reaction to modernism) and hence from a sense of a large vocabulary of possible novelistic kinds. Though this is part of a definition of postmodernism, most of Brophy's novels are not only not considered postmodern but are indeed not postmodern, for she does not usually foreground the mixing of this vocabulary within a single novel but draws variously and creatively on different tendencies in the novelistic tradition in different books. I will illustrate this variety and its interest in three Brophy novels written between the early sixties and the late seventies.

Flesh: A Novel of Indolent Passion (1962) looks initially as if it is a reasonably traditional (in terms of its technique), realist novel. The inside cover of the second edition (Corgi Books, 1965) certainly draws attention to content more than style, though with some suggestion that the novel is not a simple one: "this brilliant enigmatic novel tells the story of a contemporary Pygmalion and Galatea." The "enigmatic" here implies that some things in the novel are not easily explained, while the description of it as a rewriting suggests a ready-made model for interpreting the story. In fact, apposite as the Pygmalion model is, the question of interpretation is exactly one of the features of the novel that prevents it from being traditional in any straight-forward sense.

For though there are many clues in the narrative that seem to provide ways of thematizing the story, there never is any clear sense given of how to read it. Thus the issue of the weight of the male Galatea figure, Marcus, is signaled as important (he is painfully thin before Nancy cultivates and marries him but becomes suddenly and deliberately obese at a certain point in their marriage), yet the text never establishes a clear attitude towards it. It is not, of course, that traditional novels make everything clear, but the building up of clues that are never pushed into an interpretation easily available to the reader does seem a distinctive and perhaps particularly modern quality.

This effect principally depends on the novel's use of narration and characterization. Jennifer Plastow in an entry on Brophy in *A Dictionary of British Women Writers* (1989) writes that one of the later novels "fulfils the observational function of earlier fiction without distancing the reader." This is a very useful comment on the curious relationship created among characters, narrators, and readers in *Flesh* (and other Brophy novels). The narrator of *Flesh* mixes total knowledge of characters with great detachment and neutrality:

> Nancy quite accepted the responsibility. But to Marcus's surprise she said that, on thinking it over, she had decided the job was not right for him, and that he should wait for one that was. Marcus had expected her to take the brisk therapeutic line that in a case as bad as his any job was better than no job. Now that she did not, but at the same time did not dismiss him as hopeless, he felt cherished.

The way in which the omniscient narrator here can move in and out of different minds is nothing new, but what is new is that the omniscience really is equally applied. There are no subtexts (except those the narrator identifies the characters as already knowing about themselves) and no suggestion that one of the two minds being described is more sympathetic, superior, more central, or more authentic. This is not an isolated effect but is sustained throughout the novel. We can enter into characters' minds but on a basis of strict equality. We therefore cannot engage very closely with any one character nor discriminate between characters. Hence at the end of the novel, we cannot readily interpret the significance of the events of which we (apparently) know so much. While the book cover may claim that Nancy "comes to regard her creation with some alarm," it is not actually clear at the end of the novel that this is the story of a reversal of roles or attitudes. Certainly, our attitudes toward the two main characters seem to have undergone no reversal, because they have remained static in terms of emotional commitment to them. Equality of treatment is maintained right to the end: "Perhaps her body was too nice to be pained. Anyway, he was too nice, and too lazy, to pain her."

The overall effect of this is perplexing—and for that reason worthy of more attention. If realism is (at least partly) defined as the creation of a recognizable world shared by character, narrator, and reader, then this novel could be described as realist: nothing inexplicable happens, and we therefore all share a common understanding of emotions and events. However, in a more fundamental sense of *share* we share nothing with the world of the characters and the novel: we understand the sequence of the characters' experiences, but we do not have any illusion of sharing the experience itself. Yet neither are we invited—or tempted—to judge in a completely external fashion.

Palace without Chairs: A Baroque Novel (1978) shares some of these features (an omniscient and neutral but less distanced narrator), while working in a very different genre. It is the story of the royal family of Evarchia, particularly Prince Ulrich, and of the end of monarchical rule in Evarchia. As the names may suggest, the novel is based on a Ruritanian fantasy type of novel. More specifically, it is clearly influenced by the playful novels of Ronald Firbank (about whom Brophy wrote a study called *Prancing Novelist,* published in 1973). This does not sound a very promising subgenre for serious novelistic achievement, but in many ways the novel writes against the reader's expectations of the genre while also using them. Thus Jennifer Plastow has used this novel as an example of the way in which Brophy's later fiction is "more substantial and developed" than her earlier.

The novel is undoubtedly comic to a degree, particularly in its use of odd juxtapositions and jumps: between reader expectations of the genre and its actual characterization, between formal and colloquial language, between a sense of the modern and the traditional in Evarchia itself. However, surprisingly, these unexpected features are not merely comic: it does matter what happens to these characters, and the events in Evarchia are made serious for the reader (paradoxically, it is easier to sympathize with the problems of the Evarchian royal family, eccentric as these problems sometimes are, than with the much more familiar ones of the characters of *Flesh*).

The first feature one notices about the novel is that these fantasy characters have complex consciousnesses:

> He could overcome Clara's objections by the simplest (so it seemed as his mind sketched it) of acts, the renunciation of his inheritance. And if he embraced his true love after his affection had in fact ceased, the abnegation of the rest of his life was no more than the perpetual martyrdom he owed to all

the other true loves he had slid past among the stones. . . .

> A nostalgia took him for his own feelings as they had been before his father's illness, when love, lust and honour had all (or so it seemed to him now) been plaited into a single silken bond.

Though there is an ironic-comic element to this complexity (that is, we may suspect that the complexity merely dresses up simpler desires), this does not fully explain the complexity, which remains instead as partly a sign of real complication and nuances of feeling in the character. Just as *Flesh* seems to be a novel that pushes realist devices in an unusual direction, it could be said that *Palace without Chairs* draws on aspects of modernism in unexpected ways (given its comic aspects and apparent genre). While the characters in *Flesh* know themselves completely, the characters here, though highly self-conscious, have a much more provisional sense of themselves: they continually try to explain themselves to themselves via a series of complicated but never finished attempts.

As in some kinds of modernism (that of Virginia Woolf, for example), there is a great interest in language itself in the novel and the capacity or incapacity of language accurately to render the self. Ulrich's reflection on an attempted letter to his (ex)beloved Clara may refer not only to his own sense of how hard it is to express himself but also to the distinctive style of the novel:

> his exposition became repetitive, self-contradictory and full of inverted constructions he could see no way of wrenching to a syntactical conclusion. Eventually, there was no letter and not even a draft. They had disappeared into their own maze of arrows and loops signifying insertions and transpositions.

The novel, indeed, again like *Flesh,* comes to no very clearly thematized conclusion. While the several royal deaths suggest tragedy, Ulrich and his lesbian sister Heather (the only survivors of the family in fact) may find escape from the entrapment of their roles in Evarchia (though exactly what they have escaped to is not clear).

Finally, Brophy's *In Transit* (1970) offers yet another kind of fiction. Here the model is clearly James Joyce (perhaps with a touch of Samuel Beckett), but the text has games of its own to play, in particular with gender. For while *In Transit* is as interested as any Joyce text in multilingual punning, its most striking feature is that its first-person narrator has no idea of her own identity. The speaking I knows that it is in an airport (a suitable symbol of the dislocations of modernity) and hence "in transit" and seems to have a capacity for generating language, but that is all. Thus the voice has a great consciousness of the culture embodied in language, but no knowledge of how it relates to the discourses it refers to so promiscuously. The novel opens:

> Ce qui m'étonnait c'était qu'it was my French that disintegrated first.

> Thus I expounded my affliction, an instant after I noticed its onset. My words went, of course, unvoiced. A comic-strippist would balloon them under the heading THINKS—a pretty convention, but a convention just the same. For instance, is the "THINKS" part of the thought, implying the thinker is aware of thinking?

> Moreover—and this is a much more important omission—comic strips don't shew whom the thoughts are thought to. . . .

> Consciousness: a nigger minstrel show in which you are forever grabbing a disembodied buttonhole and gabbling "Pardon me, Mister Interlocutor."

The self-consciousness within the narrating voice of the problems of stream of consciousness narration is striking and an index of the novel's obsession with narration and language. Indeed, this metafictive quality (an awareness of fiction as an issue to be explicitly emphasized within the fiction itself) and the simultaneous self-awareness and fragmentation of the narrator over numerous different kinds of discourse take this novel towards postmodernism in a more obvious sense than that suggested earlier as applicable to Brophy. So too does the sense that, as Margeret Atwood's *A Handmaid's Tale* says, "Context is all." The I's sense of itself switches startlingly as it suspects it is one gender or another and as it fits into language in different ways, none of which seems definitive ("unmanned Patricia reeled out of earshot").

Jennifer Plastow comments that a nonfiction work by Brigid Brophy called **Black Ship to Hell** (1962) has a "'feminine' refusal to acknowledge conventional boundaries." This seems true—in a variety of ways—of all of Brophy's oeuvre, both within individual texts and across her whole output. The fact that her work is not easy to characterize (and her characterization is an important part of the difficulty) may partly account for its neglect but can also suggest how interesting that work is and how it can challenge both academic and nonacademic readers.

Her work is an example of the fact that there is no single kind of realism or modernism or postmodernism and that such categories can be overlapped and challenged and oddly used within a single author's work (indeed within single novels). Moreover, her interest in playing with boundaries

suggests that her books have much to contribute to the current interest in that feature of postmodernism, as well as to a more various history of twentieth-century literature.

Patricia Juliana Smith (essay date Fall 1995)

SOURCE: "Desperately Seeking Susan[na]: Closeted Queens and Mozartean Gender Bending in Brigid Brophy's *The King of a Rainy Country,*" in *Review of Contemporary Fiction,* Vol. 15, No. 3, Fall, 1995, pp. 23-31.

[*In the following essay, Smith examines the latent homosexuality and postponed heterosexuality in* The King of a Rainy Country, *relating these themes to various narrative plot conventions that structure Brophy's novel.*]

At first glance (and perhaps second and subsequent glances) Brigid Brophy's second novel, **The King of a Rainy Country,** might not seem an Ur-text of lesbian postmodernity. Like many of its earliest critics, Charles J. Rolo found it merely "a curious sort of comedy" concerned with "the romantic temperament" and "youthfulness of spirit." Indeed, in the midfifties, long before postmodernity was consciously defined as a mode of "playful irony, parody, parataxis, self-consciousness, [and] fragmentation," Brophy's slippage-ridden text must have seemed to many readers (if not most) little more than a diverting and slightly risqué book that ultimately falls short of the mark, one that, in Rolo's words, is "as a whole . . . far from being a success: it is somewhat disjointed, lacking in coherence, and at times not sufficiently convincing." But I would argue that with the critical hindsight of nearly four decades we can readily perceive **The King of a Rainy Country** as an example of early postmodernity, a metafiction that tries on and discards a variety of conventional generic plots which, because of their deeply ingrained heterosexual narrative ideologies, offer no viable solutions or means of closure to the protagonists. Ultimately, Brophy indicates, when all other plots fail, there is always opera. And opera, not coincidentally, has long been one of the few "respectable" art forms in which women *en travesti* can switch their gender and make love to other women with impunity.

The tripartite structure of **The King of a Rainy Country,** while recalling that of the superannuated Victorian tripledecker, in fact delineates the shifts from one master narrative to another. These transitions are not only carefully manipulated on Brophy's part, but are also self-consciously metafictive on the part of her literarily aware protagonists, who, given a lack of conventional, established fictions by which to plot their own desires, attempt to "normalize" themselves, hopelessly, through conformity to available narratives. Thus Brophy begins with an offbeat courtship plot *à la vie de Bohème* in the novel's present, backgrounded with a homoerotic girls' school narrative. Once the protagonists push the conflicts of those modes to their logical points of climax without achieving the prerequisites for any resolution to ensue, they embark on a new plot, a picaresque travelogue qua quest narrative. When this strategy also fails in achieving the socially and narratively prescribed outcome of heterosexual consummation, the main characters, now expanded in number from two to four, attempt to enact and, ironically, come to varying levels of self-knowledge about their desires through the adoption of a plot from opera, in this case Wolfgang Amadeus Mozart's *Le Nozze di Figaro*. Through this most self-consciously artificial mode of fictional representation, the characters are able to perform their irreconcilable forms of otherness and achieve various degrees of closure that, perhaps inevitably, fall somewhat short of absolute or even satisfactory resolution—at least to readers with conventional expectations.

> **We can readily perceive *The King of a Rainy Country* as an example of early postmodernity, a metafiction that tries on and discards a variety of conventional generic plots which, because of their deeply ingrained heterosexual narrative ideologies, offer no viable solutions or means of closure to the protagonists.**
> **—*Patricia Juliana Smith***

Until its highly original denouement, ***The King of a Rainy Country*** chronicles the unsuccessful courtship of Susan and Neale, a young couple who are ostensibly "in love" and, without any formal declaration of intention, assume that they will eventually marry. Although both are the products of a relatively privileged educational background, they assume a Bohemian lifestyle of voluntary poverty, with Neale working as a dishwasher and Susan as the secretary to Mr. Finkelheim, a pornographer functioning under the guise of a rare book dealer, a Gentile pawning himself off in the business world as Jewish. Finkelheim's disreputable game of appearances versus reality serves not only as a reflection of the couple's own naive game of passing, but as a conduit for the subtle expression of the troubling reality behind their facade of acceptable—even, in its historical context, avant-garde—heterosexuality. For while Susan and Neale do in fact share a bed, they do not do so simultaneously. Their shared fiction that they are prevented from consummating their relationship by the exigencies of work schedules (Susan works during the day, Neale late nights and early mornings) could potentially provide the foundation for a comedy of manners and a series of jests revolving around the familiar bed trick. Yet in the context of Brophy's novel (in which the couple does contrive, despite the demands of their em-

ployment, to spend a significant amount of time together), sleeping separately in the same bed provides not the basis of endless jokes but rather a shield to deflect suspicion. When Susan balks at the idea of having any of her old school friends "snooping round our flat," Neale inquires if she is "afraid they'll think we go to bed together"; instead she fears that "they'll guess we don't." For Susan, the raised eyebrows that might result from this simulacrum of an unsanctioned and therefore daring heterosexuality are preferable to a revelation of the celibate condition that in fact attains.

Ironically, the trappings of Finkelheim's shop, where Neale regularly visits in the proprietor's absence, provide the means by which the inexplicable obstacles to consummation become clarified. Susan, while uninterested in the volumes of male nudes in stock, discovers in her perusal of a striptease picture book the likeness of her schoolmate Cynthia Bewley, the obsessional object of the girls' school narrative constantly present in Susan's memory. Homosocial school fictions, though given relatively little attention as a serious novelistic mode, have their own particular conventions and narrative expectations. Usually focused on the *bildung* of one particular and often troubled girl, they feature the highly emotive attachments and conflicts of adolescent female psyche in an atmosphere of ubiquitous sexual awakening. Separated from the world of men and boys, the students conduct themselves in a type of lesbian utopia, minimally aware of but generally oblivious to social disapprobation of same-sex love until discovery or intervention, usually by an authority figure, exposes the "inappropriateness" of the affection. This disruption of an Edenic situation, which generally precipitates the separation of lovers, ends, at worst, in tragic consequences. At very least, as in Susan's case, the result is one of unresolved and ongoing hurt and shame.

As the events of Susan's day-to-day life with Neale plod on, the narrative of the past surfaces in nonsequential and fragmentary fashion. As she is in Neale's presence when she discovers Cynthia's picture, some explanation of her visceral response is required. Thus it is revealed that, some years past, the adolescent Susan was enamored of the slightly older Cynthia, and, over the course of a fall term, the two entered into a close romantic friendship that culminated, on the last night before the winter break, in a passionate kiss during a performance of *As You Like It*. While the cross-dressed Rosalind makes her speech to her "pretty little coz," Cynthia, sent with Susan into the storage space beneath the stage to retrieve, suggestively, "Hymen's crown," finds a faded silk rose among the old props and, placing the flower in Susan's lapel, suddenly kisses her friend. Before Susan can realize her desire "to kiss again," the girls are interrupted by an importuning school-mistress, leaving Susan yearning and "dissimulating in an entirely new way." Susan's complete understanding of the extent of this dissimulation must, however, be deferred; she must endure the separation of the winter break, anticipating the results of this awakening. We discover from another fragment of Susan's recollections that what subsequently transpires is not fulfillment but rather an inexplicable aloofness and alienation on the part of Cynthia, who refuses to communicate further. Subsequently, she publicly rejects and humiliates Susan and enters into a superficial attachment of dispassionate sex play with Susan's erstwhile friend Gill, leaving Susan alone without either solace or an explanation of a series of events that, because of their unspeakability, must stand unexamined.

Under more usual circumstances Neale might be expected to become jealous or suspicious of a past female love who continues to hold so strong an attraction for his presumed intended; yet he not only encourages Susan's apparent obsession but joins in it himself. He encourages Susan to find the "lost" girl, urging her to call all the Bewleys in the London telephone directory, to contact other former schoolmates for information, and to visit the art school where she was last known to model. The absent Cynthia not only becomes one more example of what Terry Castle calls the "ghosted lesbian" but also the erotic connection between Neale and Susan in lieu of a heterosexual relationship—and yet another excuse for delaying what would seem the inevitable in this relationship. Indeed, Neale, whose interest in sex and marriage seems primarily a matter of discourse, is as undefined in his orientation as Susan. This is readily apparent early in the novel when Susan returns home to discover François, a mysterious French houseguest with whom, at Neale's invitation, she is to share a room for the night. Affronted by this unwanted bedfellow, Susan balks; but François, in the course of an episode rendered almost entirely in French (contributing even further to the slippage that permeates the novel) informs her she need not fear for her virtue: "Pas impuissant, non. Pas impuissant—comment dit-on en anglais? C'est un des mots que je connais—*quair*." But while Neale's "quair" friend soon vanishes, in effect, from the text, this interlude, along with his interest in Finkelheim's male nudes and his distaste for the shop's "marriage manuals," indicates the extent of Neale's own dissimulation and suggests that what brings Susan and Neale together is nothing more or less than their shared latent homosexuality.

Susan and Neale could, conceivably, continue their game of deceptive appearances and shared obsessive fantasies of Cynthia interminably; but such a scenario would soon become static and, accordingly, nonnarratable, the avoidance of conflict ultimately allowing no hope of resolution. Accordingly, two events put an end to the stagnant courtship plot. A police raid of Finkelheim's shop leaves Susan bereft of employer and employment, and a missive from Gill (in response to Susan's letter at Neale's instigation) brings a newspaper clipping announcing that the aspiring actress "Cynthia Beaulieu" will be attending a film festival in Venice—along with the warning "Don't ever write to me again." Given these motivations, the pair falsify their qualifications, obtain employment as tour guides conducting American tourists from Nice to Venice, and exchange their exhausted narrative for a new one, that of the travelogue; but what is found in this journey is merely a variety of means by which heterosexuality can be postponed.

The exigencies of travel almost inevitably give rise in the picaresque to numerous and various occasions for illicit sexual encounters. If the restraints of British middle-class mores were all that had prevented carnal knowledge between Neale and Susan, surely the context of another country would allow for a release from these inhibitions. But, as we have seen, this is only the case ostensibly; and, ironically, exposure to the boorishly libidinous Americans only reinforces the pair's stereotypically English reticence, an attitude that seems to grow in proportion to the Americans' expectations. Sexual union becomes, for Susan and Neale, a highly articulated (and thus artificial) fantasy that can only occur at an optimal moment. The very real possibility of rape—which, in the minds of the young American men of the traveling party, is merely a matter of fulfilling social expectation—serves the purpose of minimizing the likelihood of this moment for Susan; yet Neale persists in seeking, presumably for no purpose other than to provoke rejection and thus continue to postpone the seeming inevitability of heterosexual consummation.

Once they have arrived in Venice and are relieved of their charges, however, there seems little excuse for deferral left. Outside the hotel lobby, as Neale badgers her with a series of tired poetic clichés, Susan reluctantly assents to the moment, distracted all the while by scene around her: "Out of the corner of my eye, I saw a cotton dress move in the hotel foyer. I turned. So did Neale. . . . Inside the hotel, Cynthia was facing us, but not looking out: we were the direction, not the object of her gaze." Although Neale whispers "Let her go," as soon as Cynthia turns her back toward them, both burst through the door in pursuit of her. In this interrupted moment of possibility Susan and Neale find the dea ex machina Cynthia and thus in a sense fulfill their quest; but then they must face what they hoped to achieve in doing so. Conventional literary wisdom dictates that the end of the quest narrative must result in some sort of self-knowledge or completion for the seeker. Would the resolution of an earlier interrupted moment (and the apparent sexual panic that arose from it) clear the path for heterosexuality in the present? Would it offer an explanation of Neale's problematic sexuality as well? Or was the fantasy, as Neale later suggests, in itself more pleasurable than its fulfillment? As the end of this journey results, in any case, in merely one more reason to defer consummation, yet another generic plot fails the characters—and so a new one begins.

Part 3 commences with Cynthia's arrival for her reunion with Susan. Neither woman seems willing or able to face this meeting alone; just as Susan is accompanied by Neale, so Cynthia too brings a friend: the fading operatic soprano Helena Buchan. As Cynthia proves herself the stereotypical starlet, a form virtually devoid of content, Helena comes to the fore. Once known for her portrayals of the tragic Tosca and the betrayed Donna Elvira in *Don Giovanni,* Helena, who deems herself "not feminine enough," has over time settled into the role of the Countess Almaviva in Mozart's *The Marriage of Figaro*—a woman, like Helena, for whom romantic love and marriage have proved disappointing. Accordingly, the other three assume various operatic demeanors as the plot shifts into a miscast version of Mozart's opera, a *Marriage of Figaro* without a Figaro to regulate (and manipulate) the excesses and foolishness of the other characters. The result is a romantic rectangle in which all parties are sexually ambivalent and thus unsure of their own desires.

Cynthia, with her childish dreams of fame and glory, has become little more than ancillary to the grand diva; as such, she functions as the page Cherubino to Helena's Countess Almaviva. Neale, for his part, becomes churlishly aggressive as the sole male in this ensemble. He would assert his "right" to dominance over the women, suggesting that Helena run away with him, in much the same manner that Count Almaviva in the opera would reassert the traditional *droit du seigneur*. But as he is thoroughly lacking affluence and power—and really desires an erotically tinged mother-son relationship with the diva—so does he too become Cherubino. In her critical study of Mozart's operas Brophy makes a point of explaining **"Who is Cherubino, What is He?"** (*Mozart the Dramatist* 103). But she omits one salient point about this character: while Cherubino is literally a sexually overwrought adolescent male and figuratively, according to Brophy, an eighteenth-century manifestation of Cupid (Eros), he is performed, both in Mozart's opera and historically in Beaumarchais's original play, by a woman. Thus while the staged "reality" of the opera presents a boy attempting to seduce a woman, the overriding appearance of what transpires on stage is a simulacrum of lesbianism.

But with a Countess, no Figaro or Count, and two Cherubinos, Susan's part in this opera remains vague. The adulation around the ever-present Helena not only prevents Susan from obtaining any explanation from or resolution with Cynthia—who seems to have acquired a highly selective amnesia about the past—but results in an alienation of Neale's affections. Only after Helena kindly but resolutely declines Neale's proposition can Susan assume her designated role, that of her operatic namesake Susanna, the Countess's confidante. Intuiting Susan's resentment, Helena invites her, alone, on a day trip to Padua, where the diva is

to have a publicity photograph taken. While en route, they discuss the intimate details of their lives. Helena tells of her failed marriage, in which she "wasn't really the girl," "wasn't the type," and simply "gave a performance"; and, dropping all inhibition, Susan explains "about Neale. And Cynthia." Just *what* she explains, however, is a matter of critical interpretation; Brophy provides only a white space in lieu of direct discourse.

In the wake of this confession Brophy departs from the Mozartean plot in order to restage the novel's foundational narrative. As Helena waits for the photographer, she and Susan rummage through the studio props and find a wreath of silk roses; Helena takes one and places it in Susan's lapel, thus replacing Cynthia's rose, which Susan had preserved and Neale had since appropriated as his own. In this case, however, the photographer does not intervene, nor is there panic and dissimulation; rather, the two women acknowledge their mutual "sympathy." Subsequently, they stay the night at a local inn, where Helena pays a curious visit to Susan's room. Terry Castle calls the episode "a tender lesbian scene between diva and female fan." Indeed, the encounter is suggestive, taking place as Susan lies naked in bed and Helena speaks of her own recent nakedness, proscribed only by her need to traverse the corridor. But while no sexual act is directly represented, the symbolic resonances serve their purpose: the women exchange acknowledgments of their otherwise covert sexuality. In achieving this self-knowledge, Susan can effectively put closure to all her previous and abortive plots.

Upon her return to Venice, Susan discovers that Neale and Cynthia have mutually succumbed to their own form of sexual panic. Cynthia, having failed her much-sought screen test, and Neale, stung by Helena's rejection and seeming "conspiracy" with Susan, turn to each other. At Cynthia's demand, Neale beds her, immediately becomes engaged to her, and makes plans to go into business and assume an appropriately middle-class existence—with Cynthia as housewife—upon their return to England. Thus in a moment with Cynthia he accomplishes what could never occur with Susan. While this final plot is a *Marriage of Figaro* without a Figaro, it will not lack for a wedding, the conventional ending to a comedy. He explains to Susan that he is not really in love with Cynthia, but "at the back of my mind I have the faintest feeling—as if I had, once, been in love with her." Unable or unwilling to take the risks that male homosexual existence entails (the law that sent Oscar Wilde to prison was, lest we forget, still in effect in the 1950s), Neale opts for a simulation of lesbianism instead, appropriating Susan's past so as to become her and thus write a happy ending to her earlier narrative. Yet because it lacks the self-knowledge inherent in Susan's revision of the interrupted moment, Neale's conclusion can offer little in the way of resolution or closure.

Back in England to begin a new plot, Susan places the rose from Helena in a drawer for safekeeping. Her friend Tanya, who helps her set up new housekeeping arrangements, remarks that she has "brought back" Cynthia's old rose. She replies, "No. It's a replacement." In the end, Helena—quite literally—replaces Cynthia as the lesbian ghost. Susan, having earlier declined an invitation to join Helena in her travels, finds in the older woman a conclusion rather than a continuing narrative; as Helena, unknown to Susan, is terminally ill, little in terms of continuance would be possible. Susan returns home to chart a new course for herself, only to discover that Helena has died en route to Vienna—and that a parcel from the diva awaits her: Helena's own wedding dress, a fulfillment of her promise of a gift "You may have a use for. . . . Or you may not. It doesn't matter if not." Countess Almaviva does, after all, oversee the preparations for Susanna's wedding to Figaro. A conventional interpretation might assert that this gesture symbolizes a mother-daughter bond between the two women, a passing-on from generation to generation. But this overlooks that the dress is itself the symbol of a failed marriage plot—and that the figure of Figaro is conspicuously absent from the opera plot of part 3. Rather, the dress is a symbol of shared knowledge and a union, metaphysical if not physical, between Helena and Susan; it is a *memento mori,* a reminder to keep alive the moment in Padua that has obviated the earlier painful one, a reminder of the "temporary shelter" that the marriage plot, if embarked upon falsely, provides.

Thus Brophy's opera buffa makes one last generic plot shift to opera semiseria. Susan, once more, will have to find a new plot by which to live; but it will be a plot to which the reader will not be privy and, we may assume, one for which there is not a preordained narrative convention. As for girls who want to be Cherubino, however, Brophy returns to that trope in *The Snow Ball* (1964) through the character of Ruth Blumenbaum. Dressed as the Mozartean page for a costume ball, Ruth intermittently obsesses about Anna K. as her potential Countess figure; but Anna K. is far too busy to notice, for she is in the throes of playing Donna Anna, pursued by—and pursuing—a suitor disguised as Don Giovanni. And that is another opera—and another novel—altogether.

Corinne E. Blackmer (essay date Fall 1995)

SOURCE: "*The Finishing Touch* and the Tradition of Homoerotic Girls' School Fiction," in *Review of Contemporary Fiction,* Vol. 15, No. 3, Fall, 1995, pp. 32-9.

[*In the following essay, Blackmer situates* The Finishing Touch *in the tradition of homoerotic pedagogical fiction, suggesting that the novel* "*represents an important milestone in the history of lesbian and, more broadly, antihomophobic literature.*"]

Upon her death, the British novelist Sarah Scott (1732-1795) requested that her personal papers, including her intimate correspondence with her longtime companion Barbara Montagu, be destroyed. Yet given the suave, bravura skill with which, two hundred years later, Miss Antonia Mount, the headmistress in Brigid Brophy's comic masterpiece of girls' school homoeroticism *The Finishing Touch* (1963), negotiates the differences between the appearance of innocently platonic "romantic friendship" and the reality of lesbian sexuality, we might surmise that she has read the occlusions and absences in the tradition of her predecessors as signposts of the "love that dare not speak its name." This literary tradition of female homosocial passion and idealism in women's schools dates as far back as Scott's *A Description of Millenium Hall* (1762), which portrays a conventlike community of happily *un*married women preserving their independence and contentment while pursuing their love of aesthetics and learning in a pastoral Greco-Roman-style country house. Scott's work comes near the beginning of a long series of homoerotic fictions in all-women schools that include, most prominently, Colette's *Claudine at School* (1900), Gertrude Stein's *Fernhurst* (1904), Ivy Compton-Burnett's *More Women than Men* (1933), Christa Winsloe's *The Child Manuela* (1933), Dorothy Strachey's *Olivia* (1949), Muriel Spark's *The Prime of Miss Jean Brodie* (1961), and Brophy's *The Finishing Touch.*

> *The Finishing Touch,* which affectionately parodies and outs the lesbian desires of its literary predecessors, depends on readers' acquaintance with this tradition for much of its subtle meanings.
>
> —*Corinne E. Blackmer*

While originary historical moments are difficult to pinpoint with accuracy—indeed, Sappho's school for girls on Lesbos may represent the beginnings in Western culture of this homoerotic pedagogical tradition—lesbian social historians such as Lillian Faderman have argued that modern lesbian identity dates from the so-called Scotch Verdict Trial of 1811, in which two teachers in an all-girls school, Miss Woods and Miss Pirie, were accused of engaging in "improper" displays of affection in front of their charges and therefore of corrupting the morals of children. After much tribulation, the two women were exonerated, in large part because the judges were more terrified of admitting the reality of female-female sexual passion than in prosecuting those involved in the supposed crime.

In the wake of this ambivalent acquittal—which was subsequently transformed into a tragic lesbian melodrama ending in suicide in Lillian Hellman's *The Children's Hour* (1934)—an atmosphere of suspicion, arousal, and possibility clung to the institution of the girls' school. Indeed, *The Finishing Touch,* the title of which puns on both the act of masturbation and transformative erotic "touch" of lesbian culture transmitted to the girls in this "finishing" school, provides the comic metafictive "finish" to the tradition of girls' school fictions governed by what Martha Vicinus terms the dynamic of "distance and desire," in which self-control and academic discipline are manifestations of sublimated erotic desire for an admired teacher or older student. *The Finishing Touch,* which affectionately parodies and outs the lesbian desires of its literary predecessors, depends on readers' acquaintance with this tradition for much of its subtle meanings. Because the aptly named Miss Antonia Mount knows how to employ covert metaphor, textual allusion, and double entendre to transform her students into subversive readers of literature, she succeeds in transcending or "mounting" the cultural prohibitions against lesbian passion, thus ensuring the continued existence of her *école*—or, in the words of the early twentieth century lesbian writer Liane de Pougy, her *idylle—Sapphique*. Moreover, Brophy grafts the highly stylized camp aesthetics of her beloved literary forebear Ronald Firbank—who himself wrote frequently about lesbians—onto the tradition of homoerotic pedagogical fictions; thus, her finishing school becomes a doubly queer site in which learning and female bonding are linked with eros and eloquence as the students (and readers) are given charming lessons in the arts of manipulating the cultural semiotics of the (in)significance of lesbian love for their own significant pleasures.

The oblique Firbankian plot of this novella turns on the arrival of the English royal daughter, otherwise known simply as "royalty" or "H.R.H.", to the school. While Miss Mount and her closeted lesbian partner Miss Hettie Braid interpret her enrollment as a sign of the growing fame of their school and Miss Mount even anticipates that she will be made a "Dame," in the flesh H.R.H. proves both an aesthetic disappointment and a considerable pedagogical challenge. Ironically, Miss Mount's success as a teacher has depended on her talent for acculturating her students by transforming them into sophisticated interpreters of the homoerotic subtexts of the ostensibly straight world. H.R.H., whose outward deportment ironically coincides with stereotypes of female "inverts" as *hommes manqués,* is, in reality, completely devoid of queer sensibility. Indeed, she seems to have walked (straight) off the pages of Radclyffe Hall's sentimental medical sexologist apologia for female "inversion," *The Well of Loneliness* (1928). Soon after she disembarks from her British destroyer (which Miss Mount calls "The last flicker . . of gunboat diplomacy"), she greets the headmistresses by saying, "'Smashing trip! Smashing to

see you! Smashing . . . ,' then, in her bumptuous manner, proceeds to smash an antique hydrangea pot. Later, she boisterously inquires after the "playing fields . . . For rounders," blissfully unaware that the school gardens, with their "secluded corners, sunken spots, grottoes one would never guess were there," are designed for more private lesbian erotic sports. In attempting to fill the empty brains of this royal "head" of British society, Miss Mount, who understandably feels more languidly world-weary than ever in the face of such purblind ignorance, confronts her greatest challenge in her career as a queer pedagogue.

Before the impromptu arrival of royalty, Miss Mount, with the unsuspecting assistance of Miss Braid—who seems not altogether cognizant of the lesbian nature of her own adoration of Miss Mount—had run their school on the French Riviera—which openly advertises itself in its prospectus for the "*Personal attention and care of the joint head mistresses for each girl*"—as a covert sapphic utopia whose international cast of students recalls the habitués of the health resort in Firbank's *Valmouth*. The lovely Regina Outre-Mer provides, in her role (as her name suggests) as the "Overseas Queen" of the finishing school, an enchanting French homoerotic counterpart to the bovine asexuality of English royalty. Regina, an especially promising scholar, is so enamored of Miss Mount that she tears her embossed name from a piece of the school's stationery and "wriggle[s] the die-stamped words in such a way as surreptitiously to caress them against the flesh of her bosom." La Badessa di Poggibonsi, a "secular Abbess" who inherited the title from her proto-Renaissance female forebears, walks about in a pair of stiletto sandals fastened with a "large white plastic daisy." Fraise du Bois, a nineteen-year-old registered drug addict "already well advanced down the slope pioneered by her cousin Blanche"—the latter whom readers will recognize as Tennessee Williams's fictionalized self-portrait as the heroine of *A Streetcar Named Desire*—provides fewer disciplinary problems than the rest of the pupils combined, "droguée," as Miss Mount observes, "as the poor creature is from dawn to dusk." The Monacan heiress Miss Jones disports herself in a bikini, while the Lebanese (read Lesbian) princess, evidently something of a dildo fancier, obligingly tosses out her "exotic" and "one or two erotic" objects in deference to the "discretion" Miss Mount asks the girls to practice in the presence of H.R.H. The aristocratic President's daughter of a "dark republic" inspires Miss Mount to conduct eroticized imaginative "experiments" with her appearance because her "bloomy skin" is a "natural show-case . . . for jewels." At last, the Plash sisters, Sylvie and Eugénie, whose surnames recall both the slang term for homosexual schoolgirl "crushes" (i.e., "pashes") and the dualistic character of the relentlessly fatalistic, documentary style, and (alas and at last) hopelessly heterosexual American poet Sylvia Plath, eventually prove the occasion for near tragedy.

The new discretion Miss Mount asks her pupils to display before royalty has the ironic effect of forcing consciousness of lesbianism to the surface. Before the advent of H.R.H., Miss Mount's more encoded social references to sapphic "knowledge" are evident in her dealings with the Catholic Church and reveal how readily lesbianism can slip between the cracks of traditional moral injunctions against birth control and prenuptial heterosexual sex. Miss Mount, annoyed that she must conduct her Catholic girls not only to church on Sunday mornings but also to confession on Saturday evenings, informs the parish priest that "none of her girls had anything to confess," which echoes almost verbatim the words of Una Troubridge, the lover of the British lesbian novelist Radclyffe Hall, who, when asked how she and "John" reconciled their lesbianism with their Catholicism replied, "There was nothing to confess." Since the Catholic Church opposes precautionary steps and "rhythm seemed not to be in the nature of girls," Miss Mount fears that "we shall one day find ourselves trapped between the two kinds of irregularity to which girls are prone." In other words, parents might blame *her* for the heterosexual and homosexual irregularities of her charges, an anxiety that the Cardinal alleviates by allowing that the girls might confess only during their vacations. Nonetheless, to remain on the safe side, Miss Mount is more "insistent with the Catholic girls than the others in bidding them, if they should by chance have that capacity, satisfy themselves with the company of their own sex." Thus Catholicism, in its doctrinal incoherencies, proves (as Firbank himself well knew) quite friendly to the conversion of religious into lesbian meanings as long as the actual state of affairs is not made *too* explicit.

This somewhat comfortable (if enervating) state of quasi-closeted, quasi-encoded lesbian meaning, so common in earlier homoerotic girls' school fictions, is transformed by the revolutionary disequilibrium introduced into this social microcosm by royalty. Determined simultaneously to amend and expose the privileged obtuseness of H.R.H. (who seems beyond the need for intelligence) and, moreover, to pursue her erotic interest in Eugénie Plash and Regina Outre-Mer, Miss Mount decides to start one of the earlier informal course offerings in lesbian studies, "a special Literature group." It begins, appropriately enough, with the poems of Renée Vivien, an early twentieth-century expatriate American lesbian poet who wrote homoerotic verse in French inspired by Sappho. In the face of this unmistakable and explicit queer knowledge, Eugénie "pouts," Regina "blushes," the President's daughter "seem[s] not to care," and H.R.H. remains "deep-puzzled," thus confirming each of them in, respectively, their aversion, desire, indifference, or incomprehension vis-à-vis lesbian passion. The conspiratorial Plash sisters begin to deride Regina, who cannot understand why *anyone* would not love Miss Mount, for her worship of the headmistress and tell various mean-spirited inside jokes about the engrained block-headedness of

H.R.H. and the "drinking habits" (another code for lesbian habits) of Miss Mount. In the meantime, Miss Mount, who now aches with desire for Regina, must convince her partner that she persists in these classes from her pure educational motive of vanquishing the ignorance of royalty and thus combating the "doom" of talented people, as Miss Braid herself conveniently expresses it, of being "misunderstood." Thus the class proceeds with Proust's classic of torrid lesbian desire *Albertine Disparue,* which, while met with blankness by H.R.H., inspires in Miss Mount an almost uncontrollable urge to kiss Regina, if only she could "rely on [royalty's] uncomprehension—of everything." Now desperate for Regina (a state she once again presents to Miss Braid as a heroic struggle against the intellectual doltishness of H.R.H.), Miss Mount decides to "force" clear understanding on her pupils by having them read Colette's *Claudine à l'école.* This is a potentially perilous choice for the adored *authoritative* teacher in her still delicate situation with Regina, for this book portrays the rambunctiously aggressive adolescent schoolgirl Claudine as a ready and willing seducer of her older teacher. Fortunately, the book makes Regina laugh, a sign that she welcomes (and will eventually act upon) the sexual component of her love for Miss Mount.

The erotic possibilities between adored teacher and desired pupil are developing beautifully according to pedagogical plan when an accidental act of nature, in collusion with the machinations of the Plash sisters, who have been looking for incontestable documentary evidence of Miss Mount's lesbianism, intervenes. H.R.H. is stung by the fatal "guêpe du midi," or the midday wasp, an occurrence which provides both the climactic turning point and the quasi-naturalized dea ex machina of the plot. Miss Mount, wishing all the while that she might thus have permission to kiss "innocently" the bosom of Regina, overcomes her considerable aversion for the person of H.R.H. and sucks the venom of the wasp bite from the "royal décolletage." Yet while Miss Mount can remove the *literal* poison, she cannot completely innoculate herself against the far more insidious *social* venom produced by the persistent obtuseness of royalty or the homophobic malice of the Plash sisters. Indeed, the sisters, who have been observing this scene of rescue from their window, furnish the local newspaper with a photograph which shows Miss Mount in the apparent act of kissing Royalty on the bosom. That Miss Mount feels *no* attraction for H.R.H. does not prevent the Plash sisters from interpreting her action as an attempt to curry favor in high places (and subvert British social authority) by converting royalty to lesbianism, nor does it prevent the newspaper from reprinting the photograph along with a scandalous headline: "Étrange Affection entre Professeur et Elève."

This false public outing, the result of both an idiotic failure to discern the differences between appearances and realities and the false social ambitions and snobberies introduced by royalty, is, in some measure, propelled by the convoluted dynamics of erotic jealousy that is a staple of girls' school fictions such as *Olivia* and *The Prime of Miss Jean Brodie*. If Miss Mount, the evident favorite among the pupils of the two officially "co-equal, co-eval, co-proprietors," has a tragic flaw (or, alternately, a redeeming grace) it is her marked preference for beautiful young women. She directs all her attention toward her attractive and talented lesbian-leaning students such as Regina Outre-Mer and Eugénie Plash, leaving her partner Miss Braid to deal with less fetching heterosexual-leaning girls such as Sylvie Plash, whom the deep-voiced Miss Braid upbraids for receiving letters from a "coarse" sailor by informing her that "men are coarse." This moralistic pedagogy (although a matter of sexual and aesthetic taste for Miss Mount and physical aversion and self-closeting for Miss Braid) fails, and, combined with the destabilizing presence of H.R.H., the subtle competition between Eugénie Plash and Regina Outre-Mer for the affection of Miss Mount, the growing conspiratorial designs of the Plash sisters, and, most important, the exposure to lesbian-themed literature (which can either infect students with or innoculate them against the poison of homophobia) leads to the infamous venom-sucking scene, in which Miss Mount comes close to losing her career by heroically saving the life of royalty.

Originally published in 1963, *The Finishing Touch* represents an important milestone in the history of lesbian and, more broadly, antihomophobic literature.
—*Corinne E. Blackmer*

Although an ostensibly lighthearted novel, *The Finishing Touch* contains an important message about the need for constant watchfulness among queers, inasmuch as the venom of homophobia and its antidote spring from similar sources and depend on how individuals respond to the power conferred on them by sexual knowledge. Indeed, the headmistresses eventually succeed in innoculating themselves against the various poisons that inevitably accompany queer life, from the comical vagaries of role playing through the politics of religion and public scandal. Through the quasi-operatic distinction between the soprano voice of Miss Mount and the baritone of Miss Braid, the two women are initially established as a prototypical femme-butch couple. But these appearances prove misleading, all the more so as Miss Braid is far more reticent to acknowledge or recognize her lesbianism than Miss Mount. In the beginning the ever solicitous and "masculine" Miss Braid spends her time anticipating the needs and alleviating the distresses of the "feminine" Miss Mount. After the arrival of H.R.H., however, their positions are reversed. Miss Mount must soothe

the persistent apprehensions of Miss Braid, who fears (accurately, as it turns out) that some bizarre and unforseen catastrophe will befall H.R.H. and, therefore, them. In the end Miss Mount must once again act heroically to save the school from disrepute by seducing Commander Curl, a closeted homosexual British naval officer who has been sent to determine whether intelligence reports that the women are running a sapphic school for scandal are true. In this early exploration of the duplicities inherent in the policy of "don't ask, don't tell," Miss Mount succeeds in vanquishing her political opponents by deploying their own weapons against them. Moreover, Miss Mount *uses* the Commander to relieve what she refers to as "the tensions, the hysteria, the really at times too insupportable emotional *fraught*-ness, of these all-female institutions," which, of course, alludes to her frustrated sexual longings for Regina Outre-Mer.

As in her earlier dealings with the Catholic Church, in her confrontations with British Intelligence Miss Mount is aided in large measure by the unspeakability of lesbianism. For example, when the intelligence officers ask for background information on "this Mount woman" to determine whether she's "*that kind of woman*," one officer thinks this means "communist" (an accusation frequently launched at queers), and another fears he cannot "*write . . . down*" the "salient facts in memorandum form." While Miss Mount and Miss Braid lose most of their pupils, including Regina Outre-Mer and even the droguée Fraise du Bois, in the wake of the newspaper scandal, they almost immediately receive "several new applications." Although Miss Braid wonders whether the new students will be "quite the type of girl we want," Miss Mount (in yet another reversal of type) confidently replies that "they will be in some ways even *more* the . . . ." Although Miss Mount trails off before substituting the word "lesbian" for "girl," her conception of the mission of her finishing school has clearly undergone a radical transformation. By forcing what Virginia Woolf termed "this very queer knowledge" to new levels of awareness, the scandal caused by the collision of social snobbery and envious malice with idealistic love and passionate desire ultimately *strengthens* the hand of queer education and helps to fulfill the ambition, expressed by Miss Mount near the beginning of the text, that her school might encourage lesbianism as an adult way of life rather than a mere adolescent passing phase: "We are supposed to send them away *finished*. Though in some cases . . . I prefer to think I've sent them away just *begun*."

Originally published in 1963, *The Finishing Touch* represents an important milestone in the history of lesbian and, more broadly, antihomophobic literature. Affectionately sophisticated in its treatment of its predecessors in Firbankian, French homosexual, and homoerotic girls' school fiction, Brophy's metafictional comic masterpiece in the end both accompanies and acknowledges a new and more explicit brand of lesbian *bildungsroman* as represented by, among others, Maureen Duffy's moving depiction of a working-class lesbian child's fight to receive an education in *That's How It Was* (1962), Rosemary Manning's autobiographical treatment of lesbianism, hypocrisy, and betrayal in a girls' boarding school in *The Chinese Garden* (1962), and Monique Wittig's innovative *nouveau roman* of the early development of lesbian consciousness in *The Opoponax* (1957; trans. 1964). Unlike these fictions, *The Finishing Touch* is not, as Brophy herself has repeatedly pointed out, either semiautobiographical or documentary. This does not, however, lessen this book's authority or importance as an imaginative metafictive comedy of manners that reveals that the roots of homophobia rest precisely in the inability to *play* with language and a dour insistence on the literality of meaning, both of which, finally, prove fatal to all erotic joyousness, imaginative empathy, and creative liberty.

FURTHER READING

Criticism

Brophy, Brigid. "The Great Celtic/Hibernian School." *Performance & Reality: Essays from Grand Street,* edited by Ben Sonnenberg, pp. 118-25. New Brunswick, NJ: Rutgers University Press, 1989.

> Details the consequences of Oscar Wilde's morality trail and its consequences in relation to his thematic concerns in some of his works.

Miller, Karl. "Brigid Brophy: A Memoir." *Raritan* 15 (Spring 1996): 38-52.

> Reminisces about Brophy's writings contributed to the *New Statesman,* where Miller was editor, and the various critical reactions they prompted.

Review of *Palace without Chairs,* by Brigid Brophy. *Washington Post Book World* IX, No. 9 (7 October 1979): 15.

> Briefly comments that the novel "is told in a verbally dexterous style, with dialogue that is alternately silly and sharp."

Additional coverage of Brophy's life and career is contained in the following sources published by Gale: *Contemporary Authors,* **Vol. 149;** *Contemporary Authors Autobiography Series,* **Vol. 4;** *Contemporary Authors First Revision Series,* **Vols. 5-8;** *Contemporary Authors New Revision Series,* **Vol. 25;** *Dictionary of Literary Biography,* **Vol. 14; and** *Major Twentieth Century Writers.*

Stephen Hawking
1942-

(Full name Stephen William Hawking) English cosmologist, mathematician, author, and editor.

The following entry presents an overview of Hawking's career through 1997. For further information on his life and works, see *CLC*, Volume 63.

INTRODUCTION

Hawking is considered one of the most influential and important theoretical physicists of the twentieth century. His theories on black holes and his search for a grand unification theory, which would link the theories of relativity with those of quantum mechanics, have propelled him into the scientific ranks of Sir Isaac Newton and Albert Einstein. He has attracted widespread public interest through his best-selling work *A Brief History of Time* (1988).

Biographical Information

Hawking was born on the 300th anniversary of Galileo's death, January 8, 1942, in Oxford, England. His father was a research scientist specializing in tropical diseases and his mother was a secretary; Hawking was the first of four children. He received a first-class honors degree from Oxford in 1962 and proceeded to Cambridge University to pursue graduate studies in cosmology. In 1965, he completed his dissertation on black holes and received his Ph.D. He received a fellowship in theoretical physics at Cambridge and continued his work on black holes. At the age of thirty-two, Hawking was named a fellow of the Royal Society and in 1978 he received the Albert Einstein award of the Lewis and Rose Strauss Memorial Fund, the most prestigious award in theoretical physics. The next year he was named Lucasian Professor of Mathematics at Cambridge, a position he continues to hold and one which was once occupied by Newton. While a student, Hawking was diagnosed with amyotrophic lateral sclerosis (ALS), commonly referred to as "Lou Gehrig's Disease," a degenerative disease of the nerve cells that control muscular movement. Hawking eventually became unable to move except for his fingers, and in the early 1980s he also lost the ability to speak; he now communicates with the aid of a talking computer. Hawking married linguist Jane Wilde in 1965; the two later divorced and he has since remarried. Hawking has three children from his first marriage.

Major Works

Hawking first gained recognition for his doctoral thesis concerning black holes, on which he collaborated with Roger Penrose, a mathematician. Hawking and Penrose demonstrated the validity of black holes, which scientists had previously been reluctant to acknowledge due to a lack of empirical evidence or mathematical proof. Hawking later suggested that some subatomic particles and radiation could escape from a black hole, summarized in his famous statement, "black holes ain't so black." In his most popular work, *A Brief History of Time*, which reached the best-seller list in both America and Britain, Hawking related the discoveries and implications of his lifetime of work. Written for the layman, *A Brief History of Time* offers a survey of historical and modern developments in physics, addresses various cosmological theories, and relates Hawking's quest for the unification of physics. Hawking followed *A Brief History of Time* with *Black Holes and Baby Universes and Other Essays* (1993), a collection of essays and speeches which provide an overview of his scholarship as well as insight into his physical disability. *The Nature of Space and*

Time (1996), which explores general relativity quantization, is drawn from a series of lectures Hawking and Penrose presented in Cambridge in 1994.

Critical Reception

Most of Hawking's writings are highly technical and understandable only to a small, highly specialized audience. Accordingly, general-readership reviewers have reacted most strongly to his works aimed at a popular audience. *A Brief History of Time* has been widely acclaimed as a clear, informative, and entertaining introduction to complex ideas that have significantly challenged traditional scientific and metaphysical views of the cosmos. Jeremy Bernstin stated, "The most original parts of Hawking's book consist of the descriptions of his own work. Since this has been of such great importance in modern cosmological theory, and since he describes it so lucidly, this gives the general reader an opportunity to learn some deep science directly from the scientist." Hawking's overall scholarship and theories also receive praise from his peers, but some debate certain elements of his work. Some philosophers have criticized Hawking's cosmology—his interpretations of the impact that his scientific theories have on religion and the origins of the universe. John Leslie defended *A Brief History of Time*, arguing that "the book's central ideas made it of greater philosophical interest than almost all the volumes ever written by philosophers," but conceded that Hawking's arguments "are highly oracular." Michael Rowan-Robinson, however, said of *The Nature of Time and Space*, "This elegant little volume provides a clear account of two approaches to some of the greatest unsolved problems of gravitation and cosmology."

PRINCIPAL WORKS

The Large Scale Structure of Space-Time [with G. F. R. Ellis] (nonfiction) 1973
General Relativity: An Einstein Centenary Survey [editor; with Werner Israel] (essays) 1979
Three Hundred Years of Gravitation [editor; with Israel] (essays) 1987
A Brief History of Time: From the Big Bang to Black Holes (nonfiction) 1988
Stephen Hawking's A Brief History of Time: A Reader's Companion [editor] (nonfiction) 1992
Black Holes and Baby Universes and Other Essays (essays) 1993
The Nature of Space and Time [with Roger Penrose] (nonfiction) 1996

CRITICISM

Bryce DeWitt (review date 16 November 1973)

SOURCE: "Much-Esteemed Theory," in *Science*, Vol. 182, No. 4113, November 16, 1973, pp. 705-06.

[*In the following review, DeWitt states that* The Large Scale Structure of Space-Time *is a masterpiece but laments that it is primarily for mathematicians and not physicists.*]

Ask a prospective graduate student in theoretical physics what area he hopes to work in, and the chances today are better than 50-50 that he will reply "gravitation theory." This has caused problems for some physics departments, but it shows where the action is—or at least where many students think the action is. This prejudiced reviewer happens to think the students are right—in that the theory of gravity poses some of the most challenging conceptual problems in physics, problems that touch the foundations of nearly all physical theories. The students are simply expressing a gut awareness of the fact.

The theoretical framework for gravitational research has remained unaltered for nearly 60 years. Although proper attention, both experimental and theoretical, has been given to alternative theories, *the* theory is still Einstein's general relativity, as it was in 1916. The remarkable stability of this theory may fairly be attributed to the extreme practical difficulties one encounters in attempting to devise crucial experiments to challenge it. The challenges it faces today have mostly been devised from within, slowly and with many false starts, by men and women who were willing to gamble (and in some cases throw away) their professional careers by studying the internal consistency of general relativity and elucidating, with pencil, paper, and computer its many fantastic predictions, most of which Einstein himself never knew.

[*The Large Scale Structure of Space-Time*] by Hawking and Ellis contains a canonical sampling of these fantastic predictions, as well as a full and rigorous account of the chinks in the armor of the theory, which have been uncovered in the past decade. As a fundamental physical theory general relativity is a failure. It is a failure because it predicts that, under very general conditions, singularities must occur in space-time, beyond which the theory is incapable of saying anything. That is, the theory predicts that it cannot predict. It is not fundamental enough. It must eventually be superseded by something more universal.

This is an old story in physics: Classical electrodynamics, hydrodynamics, statistical mechanics, and quantum field theory are all examples of theories whose incompleteness can be shown on internal grounds alone. (Think of point charges, shock waves, phase transitions, and quantum field theoretical divergences) But these theories by virtue of their overwhelming utility and beauty are still part of our standard curriculum, and we think none the less of them for their failings. Neither do we demote general relativity in our esteem. On the contrary, we see in the problems it presents to us only wonderful adventures for the future. The student who wishes to share in these adventures must master the material that Hawking and Ellis cover.

> [*The Large Scale Structure of Space-Time*]
> is a masterpiece, written by sure hands.
> But it is a flawed masterpiece. The student
> who conquers it will be richly rewarded.
> But he will have to work unnecessarily
> hard.
> —*Bryce DeWitt*

Beginning with a 50-page résumé of differential geometry in modern notation and a 20-page statement of general relativity theory as a set of postulates about a mathematical model for space-time, the book proceeds briskly to the construction of the tools needed for proving the main theorems. These tools include the theory of geodesics and conjugate points, Raychauduri's equation, energy conditions, the conformal definition of "infinity," topological constructs necessary for analyzing the causal structure of space-time, precise statements of various more or less physically reasonable causality conditions, and the definitions of Cauchy surfaces, Cauchy horizons, global hyperbolicity, and asymptotic simplicity. These tools are then applied in successive chapters to the Cauchy problem in general relativity, to the proofs of the great singularity theorems, to the prediction and analysis of black holes, and to the implications of general relativity for the cosmos as a whole (a singularity in our past).

Except for the black-hole theorems of Israel and Carter, which are stated without proof, all of the major theorems of the book (the majority of which were given in original form by Choquet-Bruhat, Geroch, Hawking, and Penrose) are proved in full in their most general forms. Utmost attention is given throughout to precision of statement, including statement of the minimum differentiability or continuity conditions that must be imposed on the metric. Chapter 5 contains an excellent collection of exact solutions of Einstein's equation together with descriptions of their causal structures. These structures range the gamut of known behaviors and motivate many of the later definitions: Cauchy horizons, event horizons, trapped surfaces, imprisoned curves, incomplete geodesics, and the Schmidt b-boundary.

[*The Large Scale Structure of Space-Time*] is a masterpiece, written by sure hands. But it is a flawed masterpiece.

The student who conquers it will be richly rewarded. But he will have to work unnecessarily hard. This is because the authors are unable to decide who their audience is. The weight of internal evidence suggests that they are writing for mathematicians and not for physicists. Certainly the authors make few concessions to the nonmathematician. Too often lemma follows lemma and proposition follows proposition in a way that only those who believe a theorem is its own reward will find stimulating. Too often, especially in the crucial sixth and eighth chapters (causal structure and singularities), the running commentary is held to an absolute minimum, with the significance of a given proposition being discussed after its proof rather than before. A happy exception to this rule is the third section of chapter 9 (gravitational collapse), where all proofs are postponed to the end. Why this felicitous procedure could not have been adopted throughout is a mystery.

That the authors must occasionally have believed they were writing for physicists is clear from the 50-page introduction to differential geometry and from the material on stellar collapse and the expansion of the universe that prefaces chapters 9 and 10. The latter material surely could not have been intended for the average mathematician. It assumes far too much knowledge of graduate-level physics and is too condensed. The authors even lapse on one occasion into that awful sin of astrophysicists: giving formulas containing observational numbers but without stating the units.

The book should be about 100 pages longer. The discussions preceding the difficult theorems should be greatly expanded. At least a dozen more examples and counter examples should be given, motivating the introduction of technical machinery. And many more diagrams could profitably be included. What a great book for students it would then be!

The book contains a few eccentricities: use of "data" as a singular noun; references to "measurements" in general relativity (for example, physical determination of a $Cr+1$ atlas!) that would mystify an experimental physicist; and calling the founder of black-hole theory (in an appended translation of his original paper on the subject) by the name Peter Simon Laplace. One is reminded of those famous ghosts of Westminster Abbey: Michel Faraday and Jacques Maxwell.

The book also contains one failure to distinguish between mathematics and physics that is actually serious. This is in the proof of the main theorem of chapter 7, that given a set of Cauchy data on a smooth space-like hypersurface there exists a unique maximal development therefrom of Einstein's empty-space equations. The proof, essentially due to Choquet-Bruhat and Geroch, makes use of the axiom of choice, in the guise of Zorn's lemma. Now mathematicians may use this axiom if they wish, but it has no place in physics. Physicists are already stretching things, from an operational stand-point, in using the axiom of infinity. It is not a question here of resurrecting an old and out-of-date mathematical controversy. The simple fact is that the axiom of choice never is really needed except when dealing with sets and relations in nonconstructible ways. Many remarkable and beautiful theorems can be proved only with its aid. But its irrelevance to physics should be evident from the fact that its denial, as Paul Cohen has shown us, is equally consistent with the other axioms of set theory. And these other axioms suffice for the construction of the real numbers, Hilbert spaces, C algebras, and pseudo-Riemannian manifolds—that is, of all the paraphernalia of theoretical physics.

In "proving" the global Cauchy development theorem with the aid of Zorn's lemma what one is actually doing is assuming that a "choice function" exists for every set of developments extending a given Cauchy development. This, of course, is begging the question. The physicist's job is not done until he can show, by an explicit algorithm or construction, how one could in principle always select a member from every such set of developments. Failing this he has proved nothing.

Happily, every other theorem in the book is as sound as a rock, and students could not ask for better navigators through space-time than Hawking and Ellis.

Dennis W. Sciama (review date 8 February 1980)

SOURCE: "General Relativity since Einstein," in *Science*, Vol. 207, No. 4431, February 8, 1980, pp. 631-32.

[*In the review below, Sciama remarks favorably on the essays collected in* General Relativity: An Einstein Centenary Survey.]

To celebrate the centenary of Albert Einstein Stephen Hawking and Werner Israel have gathered together 16 papers by leading authorities on general relativity. Their total impact is overwhelmingly powerful. Together they provide an outstanding modern account that covers all the important aspects: observational, mathematical, astrophysical, cosmological, and quantum mechanical. It shows very clearly that general relativity has come of age and is now part of the mainstream of science, rich in concepts and techniques and in consequences for the rest of physics and for astronomy.

The history behind this development is an interesting one. It took Einstein ten years of painful and essentially lonely effort to pass from special relativity to the general theory. Almost immediately thereafter some of the main conse-

quences of thetheory were established: the Schwarzschild solution, the three crucial tests, the cosmological models, gravitational waves. This was succeeded by a fallow period (which Einstein, sadly, did not outlive), resulting partly from the paucity of observations and partly from the rapid growth of quantum mechanics.

Then in the late '50's began the renaissance of general relativity. This was partly the consequence of a series of successful conferences, beginning with one held in Berne in 1955 to celebrate the 50th anniversary of the discovery of special relativity and continuing with the Chapel Hill conference of 1957 and the Texas conferences on relativistic astrophysics. But it was mainly the result of a series of spectacular discoveries in astronomy that were widely linked with cosmology and with general relativity: radio galaxies, quasars, x-ray sources, the $3°K$ background, and pulsars. In the '60's and '70's cosmology was transformed and black holes came into their own. Finally in 1974 Hawking discovered that quantum mechanical processes lead to thermal emission by black holes. This great discovery showed that there are deep, hitherto unsuspected, links between general relativity, quantum field theory, and thermodynamics. The discovery has led to a flood of new work on the connections between quantum field theory and general relativity and to renewed hope that a consistent quantum theory of gravity may be constructible.

[*General Relativity: An Einstein Centenary Survey*] itself begins with a survey by the editors that describes this history in detail. Then follows a discussion of the observational situation by C.M. Will based on the PPN (parametrized post-Newtonian) formalism. The paper is essentially complete up to 1977, but it is a testimony to the present rate of change of observations in gravitational physics that the possible evidence for damping of the orbit of the binary pulsar by the emission of gravitational radiation had to be inserted at the proof stage and that there was no opportunity for discussion of this potentially key result. For the same reason there is no mention of the newly discovered binary pulsar, of the two close quasars that may result from the action of a gravitational lens, or of the possibility that linear polarization of the x-rays from Cygnus X-1 may soon provide definite evidence of the presence of a black hole in this system and at the same time a strong field test of general relativity. In addition, neither in this paper nor in those on cosmology was there the opportunity to discuss recent work using grand unified theories to account for the baryon asymmetry of the universe, work that has at least two potential links with observation, namely the observed ratio of thermal photons to baryons in the universe ($\sim 10^9$) and the predicted half-life of the proton ($\sim 10^{32}$ years).

The next paper, by D. H. Douglass and V.B. Braginsky, should also be of wide interest to physicists and astronomers. It is an account of likely astronomical sources of gravitational radiation and of the basic principles underlying the design of the currentgeneration of detectors. The pioneering work of J. Weber has certainly borne fruit; there are at least 14 experimental groups attempting to improve the sensitivity of detectors. I share the confidence of the authors that gravitational wave astronomy will one day be an observational science.

The style of the book changes abruptly at this point, becoming highly mathematical. There is a paper by A.E. Fischer and J.E. Marsden on the initial value problem, which is intended for specialists. Unfortunately it was written just too early to record the significant progress achieved by R. Schoen and S.-T. Yau, who have gone far toward proving the fundamental conjecture that a physically realistic system cannot evolve toward such a tightly bound gravitational state that its total energy becomes negative.

Another mathematical paper, by R. Geroch and G. T. Horowitz, is on the global structure of space-times. It makes a real attempt to convey modern topological studies in general relativity to the uninitiated. In view of the importance of these studies I would urge non-mathematicians to tackle the paper. I believe that they would find it difficult but rewarding.

Lovers of black holes will need no urging to study the chapters by B. Carter, S. Chandrasekhar, and R.D. Blandford and K.S. Thorne. Carter describes the general theory of the mechanical, electro-magnetic, and thermodynamic properties of black holes, and chandrasekhar gives a detailed account of the Kerr metric and its perturbations. By contrast Blandford and Thorne discuss the astrophysical aspects of black holes. These papers are written in the characteristic (and characteristically different) styles of their authors and together provide an excellent contemporary introduction to the subject.

We are still hardly more than halfway through the book, and now cosmology receives attention. First come two rather personal statements of point of view by leading cosmologists, one by R. H. Dicke and P. J. E. Peebles and the other by Ya. B. Zeldovich. These are followed by a more objective and technical account of anisotropic and inhomogeneous cosmological models by M.A.H. MacCallum. A paper by R. Penrose on singularities and time asymmetry is another personal account. Penrose makes the intriguing proposal that one should impose on the initial singularity of the universe a time-asymmetric initial condition (namely the vanishing of the Weyl tensor) and that this is related to the second law of thermodynamics via the gravitational field's contribution to the total entropy density of the universe.

The last set of papers concern the relation between quantum field theory and general relativity. G.W. Gibbons describes the "halfway house" in which one attempts to construct a quantum field theory in a curved but classical background space-time. There are still some unsolved problems here, but Gibbons takesthe discussion as far as it can be taken at the present time. The other papers concern the full quantum theory of gravity. In fact a satisfactory theory of this kind does not yet exist, partly because when gravity is coupled to matter the usual quantization procedures lead to a nonrenormalizable theory. B.S. DeWitt reviews the present status of these problems, and Hawking and S. Weinberg offer accounts of their own proposals for solving them (Hawking using path integrals in a space-time with positive-definite metric, which he believes may be dominated by gravitational instantons, and Weinberg using renormalization group arguments in terms of which he proposes that the requirement of renormalizability may be adequately replaced by a weaker one of asymptotic safety).

[*General Relativity: An Einstein Centenary Survey*] is remarkably varied and the papers are of a consistently high quality and interest. Indeed, in their power and comprehensiveness they constitute a unique monument to the genius of Einstein, and, may I add, to the brilliant and profound work of the contemporary generation of relativists, many of whom are at once the creators of the present state of the subject and, in the pages of this marvelous book, its masterly expositors.

Michael Harwood (essay date 23 January 1983)

SOURCE: "The Universe and Dr. Hawking," in *New York Times Magazine*, January 23, 1983, pp. 16-19, 53-9, 64.

[*In the essay below, Harwood provides an overview of Hawking's life and works.*]

The theoretical physicist, although he deals in such arcane, modern concepts as curved time and space, is part of a philosophical and spiritual tradition older than recorded history. He seeks to know not just life as he experiences it but how the hidden parts of the universe work and fit together. Ultimately he hopes to learn if and how and why the universe began and if and how and why it will end.

These questions and the new knowledge to which they lead are so far from our daily round of getting, spending, surviving and reproducing that they demand a special language and symbolism in which to discuss them. That isolates the theoretical physicist from the intellectual mainstream, yet the rewards may be cosmic in scope, for the physicist seeks grand answers that will affect the lives of everyone—on spiritual and practical levels—forever after.

The seeking requires a certain amount of visible action—the communication of ideas with colleagues, the publication of papers. Mostly, however, it requires that the physicist *think*. "There's no other way to put it," says William Press, chairman of the astronomy department at Harvard. "He also thinks about the thinking process. If he has an idea that's not fully formed he has to try to isolate the idea in particular examples and then do detailed calculations to see whether those examples are self-consistent. It's a process of trying to build a large arch, where you work brick by brick, holding it up with a scaffolding, and you really don't know until you finally put in the keystone whether it's all going to support itself, or if when you take the scaffolding away it's all going to come crumbling down.

The art [of theoretical physics] demands an exceptional ability to concentrate, to remember, to make connections between ideas. It is perhaps significant, then, that Stephen W. Hawking . . . should have attained his intellectual stature while his body was failing him, atrophying, shaping him increasingly into a cerebral being.
—Michael Harwood

"This must have its equivalent in most artistic endeavors, where the struggle is with technique and detail but is in service of some grander plan, and you don't know whether it will all come together until all the pieces are together. Science really is art at this level, but it's art in service of finding objective truths about the universe."

The art demands an exceptional ability to concentrate, to remember, to make connections between ideas. It is perhaps significant, then, that Stephen W. Hawking, a physicist whose insights about gravity and matter are changing the way we look at the universe, should have attained his intellectual stature while his body was failing him, atrophying, shaping him increasingly into a cerebral being.

Hawking is attempting to unify two great theoretical breakthroughs in 20th-century physics, seeking whether there is one bigger law from which all the other laws can be derived. The first, general relativity, deals with predictable events and huge objects, such as stars and planets. The other, quantum mechanics, deals with minute details inside the atom, an arena where we have not learned—and may never learn—to predict events precisely. He is trying to forge the links between this odd couple while at the same time try-

ing to discover how the universe worked at its very beginning.

He has already provided strong proof that if Einstein's general relativity theory is correct the universe had a beginning—the "big bang." Since then, he has extensively explored a theoretical concept known as black holes, because black holes seem to contain clues to the nature of the big bang. Although astronomers are still only on the verge of proving by observation the existence of black holes in space, the theoreticians have drawn an increasingly detailed picture of what black holes ought to be like. Among Hawking's key contributions to this process was his finding that they are not simply black holes, cold and dead collections of invisible matter, with gravitational power so strong that nothing radiates from them, but have temperature and some can be extremely active, bright and hot. As he has made his discoveries about them, he has on occasion managed to surprise even himself.

The Cambridge University building where Hawking has his office stands along Silver Street—an ancient, winding English byway about wide enough for three horses abreast, just off King's Parade in Cambridge. If you don't look sharp, you'll miss the entrance, an alley marked—apparently as an afterthought—by an unobtrusive sign over a mail slot on the brick building: DEPT of APPLIED MATHEMATICS AND THEORETICAL PHYSICS.

This leads into a homely courtyard and parking lot. At one end is a bright blue door with a glass window, alongside a brass nameplate identifying the place in a somewhat more distinguished fashion, but the atmosphere of the building within is again vaguely anonymous and haphazard. A zigzag hallway with closed doors on both sides leads to a large, high-ceilinged, scruffily furnished common room, off which are a few more offices—one of them Hawking's. The style is Universal Academic, I suppose, but it seems at first an unfitting arena for a man believed by many of his peers to be one of the most important theoreticians of this generation, whose intellect is sometimes compared to Albert Einstein's. Now 41 years old, Hawking holds the Lucasian professorship of mathematics at Cambridge—the very chair once held by Isaac Newton.

He is several minutes late for our first meeting. These past few months have been exceptionally hectic for him. He has organized and acted as host of a three week conference on the very early universe, has been to the United States three times to accept four honorary degrees (Princeton, Notre Dame, University of Chicago and New York University) and will leave with his wife in a few days on another visit to the United States to attend a conference at Santa Barbara, Calif. Before they go, they will give a party for a daughter—one of their three children—so the Hawking household is at sixes and sevens.

He comes around a corner into the common room—a slight figure folded into an electric wheelchair, left arm crossed over right to grip the control dial. He appears to be of medium height; at a guess, he doesn't weigh as much as 120 pounds. For virtually all his professional life, Stephen Hawking has been afflicted with a progressive and incurable motor-neuron disease, and although his mental capacities have obviously not been affected by the illness, driving his wheelchair is one of the few physical things he can still do for himself.

He has grown so weak that his speech—for many years difficult to understand—can now be interpreted only by those closest to him; to a stranger's ears it sounds like a soft, gravelly tenor hum sprinkled with m's and n's. So for the purposes of ourinterviews, he has arranged for a "translator," Don N. Page, an American physicist, a former post doctoral researcher in his department and now an assistant professor at the Pennsylvania State University, who returns each summer to visit and work with Hawking.

Page lets us into Hawking's office, which looks like the office of any busy university scholar—shelves bearing books and journals and stacks of papers, a desk heaped with work in progress. Hawking is a prolific author of papers and editor of conference proceedings. Without such production he would be anonymous, of course; publish or *vanish* is the operative law of scholarly success. Even so, his production seems remarkable. The manner in which something is done, the proper method for bringing off a solution, is a central problem in a theoretical physicist's intellectual existence, but Hawking has to struggle, at even the most basic level of getting things accomplished.

That sort of struggle, however, is not as important to him as it might appear at first. The face of his illness tends to mask him from the outsider; one sees the physical man virtually paralyzed and while trying to cope with that image, may fail to see beyond it. Most of us who remain upright and mobile are by instinct—empathy—frightened by what has happened to Hawking and inclined to think that his disability either somehow detracts from his effectiveness or makes him miserable. But neither seems to be the case, and after reading a draft of this article he remarked that I'd made too much of his physical condition. That was reminiscent of a remark by Einstein: "The essential in the being of a man of my type lies precisely in what he thinks and how he thinks, not in what he does or suffers."

Furthermore, Hawking travels all over the world by plane to attend conferences and visit universities, although he cannot go on such expeditions without one or two companions to help him manage the traveling and to feed and dress him. He and his wife, Jane, maintain a busy social life, giving parties and going out. And in terms of earthbound man in relation to the huge universe, there is virtually no difference between the restrictions on his mobility and the restrictions on anyone else's.

But to produce results he has certainly had to adapt to his circumstances. As we talk in his office, I ask, for instance, about his use of sources—the accessibility of other people's work. Most of us can take a book down from a shelf, flip through it, put it back, and try another one. That isn't possible for him. He can't hold a book, never mind rise to take it from a shelf. He does have a bookstand with an automatic page-turner, but someone has to fetch the book for him and put it in the stand. He doesn't use the page-turner much, anyway, he says, because he reads mostly papers from scientific journals. In that case, he has the paper he wants photocopied and spread out on the desk in front of him. His desk, as a result, is awash with papers, and from my own experience as a one-way correspondentwith Hawking, things quickly become buried there. He is unable to do something as simple as clean up his desk, or even to burrow in the pile after an article or a letter he read last week.

He can't take notes for himself, either. I ask him if he has a photographic memory for the material he reads. "Not a photographic memory, no I don't remember all the details, but I can remember the basic ideas." (Hawking's head rests against the back of the wheel chair. Don Page, sitting beside him, leans close to hear the indistinct words, mouths each phrase to be certain he has caught it, often pauses and asks for a repetition, speaks a phrase back to Hawking sometimes to make certain, corrects himself.)

But I have the impression, I tell him, based on various articles about him, that as he does experiments in his head—I am about to say he is alleged to do reams of computations, comparable to "Mozart composing an entire symphony in his head"—but he interrupts me, laughing: "I think you shouldn't believe what you read." He takes a deep breath to laugh, and his face, which at rest often appears pained and weary, is suddenly lighted by an enormous grin. His laughter is much muted by the paralysis—no ha-ha-ha, just a single long note sung on the exhalation of breath, yet it conveys so much delight one is propelled into laughing with him.

At some point, I ask him if he mustn't run through chains of equations or numerical proofs in his head. "I tend to avoid equations as much as possible," he replies. "I simply can't manage very complicated equations, so I have developed geometrical ways of thinking, instead. I choose to concentrate on problems that can be given a geometrical, diagrammatic interpretation. I can manage equations so long as they don't involve too many terms." Ten would be too many for me, I tell him. He laughs again. "And too many for me. Often I work in collaboration with someone else, and that is a great help, because they can do all the equations."

To be sure, such routine activities as eating go very slowly for Hawking and take up a great deal of his time. But no one asks him to chauffeur the children somewhere or to mow the lawn. He cannot be seduced into taking an afternoon off to play golf. His responsibilities to his department at the university are limited: He administers the small "relativity group," and he advises four or five students. The physicist Kip S. Thorne of the California Institute of Technology, one of Hawking's closest friends, once asked him what the effect of his illness had been on his career, and Hawking said that "he thought it had enhanced his career . . . because he was not expected to give lectures on a regular basis—to teach courses. He had that much more time free simply to think about physics."

Hawking's affliction seems to have a beneficent effect on the distillation and expression of ideas. He writes by dictation, andhe does very little rewriting. "It's just too difficult," he says. "I have to impose on people enough just to dictate once, so to do a lot of revision would involve too much of other people." The pace of his delivery—the fact that he often has to repeat himself for listeners and that he must in any event dictate phrase by phrase, at the most a sentence at a time—may make his thoughts seem fragmented on first hearing. Yet as I transcribed, for example, my taped interviews with Hawking, I was struck by the clarity and precision of his sentences.

Later, I asked Don Page about this. "I found it very good training," Page told me, "during the three years I was a postdoc here. I lived with the Hawking family, and a lot of times I'd walk back and forth with him." Now as then, Hawking "commutes" by wheelchair from his home about half a mile away. "Of course, I couldn't write while I was walking, and sometimes he'd ask me something, and I'd try to think it out in my head. When you have to do it in your head, you have to get really to the heart of the matter and try to eliminate the inessential details." This, said Page, gives Hawking's papers "a great deal of elegance and beauty, because they really speak of the essential things, although sometimes it does have the unfortunate aspect that those of us who don't understand all the details may find some connecting arguments missing."

Attention to detail is not crucial to Hawking's contribution, as Page would be the first to agree. Harvard's William Press explains that at the frontiers of theoretical physics what is needed is not precision but "key overview ideas—great organizational principles, from which the details can follow. And then, of course, working out those details, ultimately to compare them with experiment, with reality—*that* involves technique and calculation and so forth. That's what Stephen leaves, by both necessity and choice, to his collaborators, and Stephen is the one who tries to come up with the great ideas that make these calculations possible. His track record on that is not just superb, it makes him one of the greatest physicists of our age."

One wonders where these key overview ideas come from. Are they produced like spiritual revelations? That's the way it seems when the public learns of a great breakthrough Hawking agrees there is "a certain similarity, in that there is no prescribed route to follow to arrive at a new idea You have to make an intuitive leap. But the difference is that once you've made the intuitive leap you have to justify it by filling in the intermediate steps in my case, it often happens that I have an idea, but then I try to fill in the intermediate steps and find that they don't work, so I have to give it up."

. . . . .

Hawking once told an interviewer that he wanted to know why the universe exists at all and why it is as it is. I quote that back to him and ask if his search has a religious component. "Isuppose so. But I would have thought that everyone would want to know that." Is the search in competition with religion? "If one took that attitude," he replies, "then Newton"—a very religious man—"would not have discovered the law of gravity.

"The whole history of human thought has been to try to understand what the universe was like. I think you can do that without prejudice as to the idea that God exists. Even if God created the universe, we want to know what it is like." I start to ask a clarifying question, but he interrupts me. "One attitude would be that God set up the universe in a completely arbitrary way, with all that anyone can say about anything is that it is just the will of God. But in fact, the more we examine the universe, we find it is not arbitrary at all but obeys certain well-defined laws that operate in different areas. It seems very reasonable to suppose that there may be some unifying principles, so that all laws are part of some bigger law. So what we are trying to find out is whether there is some bigger law from which all other laws can be derived. I think you can ask that question whether or not you believe in God."

For some people, I remind him, the existence of God is a satisfactory answer to all the questions he is dealing with. "Yes, but it is certainly not to me. I don't think that it answers anything. Whether you say that God created the universe does not really make any difference. I would regard it as a very meaningless statement, unless you're going to attach some other attributes to God. I'm not sure that I believe anything else about God. If that is the only attribute, then it is an unnecessary concept, because it doesn't have any consequences."

Yet man does need to explain the Beginning, the First Cause. How did it all start—and what existed to make a start possible? Science has not achieved that explanation, and the theoretical physicists are still searching. "I have an idea that people would feel happier with the idea of a big bang than of a universe that existed forever and ever," says Hawking. "The big bang may not be very like Genesis, but at least you can regard it as a creation, and you can invoke God as the creator. But if you had a universe that existed forever, people might feel there was not much room for God. I was at a conference on cosmology at the Vatican last year, and the Roman Catholic Church seems to be very happy with the idea of the big bang."

Does he himself think of time as having had a start? "The point is, the very meaning of time becomes very uncertain, very badly defined, when you go back to those very early times. I do think that you cannot have the ordinary concept of time going back indefinitely. So in that sense, time had a beginning. You might just say that time earlier than about 20,000 million years ago is simply not defined."

The search for the Beginning, be believes, will not be complete until we are able to understand the "boundary conditions," orwhat "preceded" the Beginning—what matter, what space, what time. "By the boundary conditions I mean the question of whether time had a beginning, and if so what the universe was like at the beginning of time, and if time does not have a beginning, what does determine the condition of matter in the universe."

. . . . .

In search of the answer to these questions, Hawking has followed a path marked by signposts that so far are invisible except to the imagination—ideas proposed by theoreticians but not yet supported by direct observation. One of these is black holes. Nearly two centuries ago, an English astronomer, John Michell, pointed out that a heavy star, if sufficiently compact, would have a gravitational field so strong that not even particles of light would have enough velocity to escape. In this century theoreticians have shown that the same effect would be produced by the collapse of a large celestial body—its density would become increasingly great as it fell in upon itself—and, further, that large stars *must* collapse when most of their nuclear fuel is spent.

In 1968, the American John A. Wheeler applied the term "black hole" to this idea of a self-hiding body. For some time, it was thought that the presence of a black hole could be discerned only through its gravitational effects on other bodies.

The effect on nearby objects can be fatal, as the black hole attracts and swallows more and more matter and grows in mass and size. In the heart of a black hole lies the second of the main signposts along Hawking's path, something known as a "singularity"—a point that might be fantastically, infinitely small, a theoretical edge of space and time. Toward that edge, that minuscule point, races at unimaginable speed all the matter sucked into the black hole, all the matter of a star or even a universe, to be crushed into a region of infinite density from which nothing escapes and where none of the known laws of physics apply.

Hawking's first major contribution to our picture of the universe was his demonstration with a colleague, Roger Penrose, that the big bang began with a singularity. (Then the space in which the big bang started, I asked him, was at first no bigger than the proverbial head of the pin? "Yes," he said, "that's about right. We're not sure whether it came from absolute zero size, but we know that it must have been very small indeed.")

We can apparently never see a singularity. It gives off no information whatever to an observer outside. But through Hawking's work we now know that a black hole emits particles from the region around the entrance to the hole, and that makes some black holes theoretically visible. One might even watch a black hole explode and thus learn something about the big bang.

The belief in theoretical concepts, such as black holes, which cannot be observed at the time, has a long and honorable history in physics. Often a theoretician predicts the existence of something that is not found for years or decades. In one sense, however, this approach through the invisible has been elevated recently to become the center line of a major avenue along which physicists now search for the Beginning.

It represents a leap forward from Einstein's work, and the springboard for that leap is quantum theory, which describes the behavior of elementary particles—the component parts of the atom. Einstein, made major contributions to quantum theory, but he didn't really like the theory—he viewed it as a stepping stone to some better theory—because it depends on something called the "uncertainty principle." That principle says that an observer cannot precisely predict at any moment both the location and the speed of a particle within an atom. He can do one or the other; or he can predict both with poor precision. This introduces an element of chance for the human observer. He can know only half of what he wants to know about a particle; the other half is hidden. In classical physics—including. Newtonian theory and Einstein's theory of general relativity, which describes gravity—the observer can reliably predict both location and speed of an object in space at the same time. There is no apparent uncertainty, which is one of classical physics' attractive qualities. Einstein preferred that sureness, and complained of quantum theory: "I shall never believe that God plays dice with the world."

But quantum theory "works." It often does so in situations where classical physics does not, and an acceptance of uncertainty may prove necessary to a complete understanding of the way the universe operates. Hawking has used quantum theory to study black holes, and he found that in the vicinity of a black hole the uncertainty is particularly bad. There is no way to predict *either* the position or the speed of the particles emitted by a black hole. One can only predict "the probabilities that certain particles will be emitted." Hawking says this suggests "that God not only plays dice but also sometimes throws them where they cannot be seen."

Moreover, connecting links have been proven between quantum theory and every known physical field of force except gravity, so, as Hawking has said, consistency seems to require that general relativity theory be brought in under the tent of quantum theory. This is known as "quantizing gravity," and it is the knottiest problem in physics today. It has resisted solution for more than half a century.

The solution is important to an understanding of the Beginning. "The thing is," explains Hawking, "that in the very early stages of the universe"—by which he means a split second after the big bang began—"the length scales were all very small: Therefore, they were of particle physics dimensions, or less. So tounderstand the beginning of the universe, you have to understand how particle physics and gravity interact."

And that is what he is working on today.

. . . . .

Stephen Hawking grew up in London and in St. Albans, 20 miles north of the city, and prepared for university at St. Albans School. Some commentators have given the impression that he was an indifferent student then, rather as Einstein is said to have been, but according to Hawking, that picture has been over-drawn. "I wasn't at the top of my form," he concedes, "but it was a very high-powered-form." His father was a doctor who did research in tropical medicine, "so I always had a strong interest in science. I reacted against my father to the extent that I did not go into medi-

cine. I felt that biology and medicine were too descriptive, not exact enough. Had I known about molecular biology I might have felt differently I wanted to specialize just in mathematics and physics, and my father was very unhappy about that, because he did not think there would be any jobs for mathematicians."

In British education such career choices are made when the student is 14 or 15. Hawking applied for admission to University College at Oxford, where he would read mathematics and physics.

"His father was an old member of the college," said Robert Berman, who was to be young Hawking's physics tutor, "and was rather anxious that Stephen should get in. I am always rather wary in such instances. People shouldn't get in because they're old members' sons. But he took the entrance examinations. There were two papers in physics, and he got alpha on both of those. The math wasn't so good. Then he had a general interview." Berman referred to the notes he had taken on that occasion. "It just says, 'A—no other comment. Impressed us all.'"

Hawking began his studies at Oxford in 1959. "The first year, he read mathematics," said Berman. "There was an exam at the end of the year. He didn't do especially well. I mean, it was all right, but it wasn't sensational. He then took up physics, and he did very little work, really because anything that was doable he could do. It was only necessary for him to know that something could be done, and he could do it without looking to see how other people did it. Whether he had any books I don't know, but he didn't have very many, and he didn't take notes.

"Of course, his mind was completely different from all his contemporaries', and he did, I think, positively make an effort to sort of come down to their level and, you know, be one of the boys. If you didn't know about his physics and to some extent his mathematical ability, he wouldn't have told you. He coxed the college second eight, and he was very popular."

However he achieved the effect, naturally or consciously, the "common hearsay" about Hawking among his colleagues today is that he was a free spirit with a wide range of interests as an undergraduate.

His independent and casual method of working at Oxford had its drawbacks, Berman noted, because "he didn't do all that well in the final examination, and he was on the borderline between first and second-class honors." Anyone in such a situation took an oral exam, "and of course the examiners then were intelligent enough to realize they were talking to someone far cleverer than most of themselves."

By the time he was 20, Hawking had decided to become a cosmologist—literally, a student of the universe. Physicists in that discipline attempt to construct principles and images of the cosmos.

Hawking said he did consider other specialties in physics, "but it just seemed that cosmology was more exciting, because it really did seem to involve the big question: Where did the universe come from?

"At the time I entered it, cosmology was a very undeveloped field"—it is now well populated. "I didn't realize that when I chose to work in it, but it turned out there were lots and lots of problems that were waiting to be solved."

The first two years, however, were to be bad ones. Just as he started graduate work at Cambridge, he began to show symptoms of motor-neuron disease. The illness was diagnosed as amyotrophic lateral sclerosis, which is usually fatal within a short time. "It seemed to be developing very rapidly at first," he said, "and I was very depressed. I didn't think there was any point in doing any research, because I didn't feel I would live long enough to get my Ph.D."

But he did not, in fact, quit, nor did he go to pieces. For one thing, he had good resources to draw on—the buoyancy (call it adaptability, if you wish) for which he had been noted at Oxford and, more important, his engagement in a life of intellectual challenge, in an existence nourished by what happens in the mind. The disease was not the only thing distressing him in those first two years of research, because he was struggling with his studies. It appears from his present recollection that he spent as much energy and concentration on the intellectual difficulties he confronted as he did on the possible proximity of death. I asked him why he kept going at all after he became ill, and he replied, "I didn't really. At first, I was doing very little work. I had very little mathematical background, so that made it difficult to make any progress For the first two years as a research student, I got very little research accomplished."

That must be characteristic of theoretical physicists as aspecies. Hawking's thesis supervisor at Cambridge, Dennis Sciama, who is now at Oxford, reflected the same focus. I had remarked on Hawking's feelings of depression at the time he started his research—meaning as he faced imminent decline and death, and Sciama received the thought on another level. "That's probably true," he said, "because it's very difficult in these advanced fields to find a good thesis topic. Cosmology at that time was a bit fragmentary. It was not easy to say, 'Well, here's a problem. It will take you three years; now go on and do it.' So indeed he looked around for quite a bit. While he did quite interesting things, the real measure of his ability was hardly emerging yet, and I can imagine it was a bit frustrating for him."

But "then things seemed to become more hopeful," Hawking told me. "The disease wasn't progressing so rapidly, and I got engaged to be married. So that was really the turning point. I realized that if I was going to get married, I would have to do some work—I'd have to get a job. About that time, I began to understand what I was doing as a mathematician."

This turning point, which Hawking describes in such a flat, cursory way, involved rather momentous developments. One was his falling in love with Jane Wilde, then an undergraduate in London, who now has a Ph.D. in languages. She proved willing to tie herself to a man whose future might be very short and difficult. He has said that she gave him "the will to live," and she was to do far more than that.

Jane Hawking is soft-voiced and affectionate, small and pretty, with straight dark brown hair. She is "very outgoing . . . a great professional asset" to her husband as a hostess, said Don Page. Hawking's Oxford tutor, Robert Berman, calls her "a remarkable woman. She sees that he does everything that a healthy person would to. They go everywhere and do everything."

At the same time that she came into Hawking's life, his thesis was rounding into shape, and one guesses he was beginning to sense his power. Dennis Sciama identified the academic turning point as having been the publication of an important paper by the theoretician Roger Penrose, now a professor at Oxford. The subject of the paper was singularities.

. . . . .

It had long been considered theoretically possible that when a dying star collapsed inward it could continue falling in on itself until all its mass was concentrated in a very small space that would have infinite density and therefore a gravitational field from which nothing could escape. Until Penrose wrote his paper, however, theoretical physicists had believed that—based on Newtonian principles—such a collapse to infinite density could not occur in the real universe, because the collapse of the star would have to be perfectly smooth, spherically symmetrical, and have no irregularities. Penrose showed, as Sciama put it,that in general relativity—the theory developed by Einstein to describe gravity—"new factors come into play, which guarantee that despite irregularities a singularity can occur."

Hawking took fire from that paper. "He conceived the idea," said Sciama, "that similar methods, suitably adapted, could be applied to the whole universe." Hawking knew that one theorist had shown that a universe could begin in a singularity, but only if it were a perfectly smooth universe, which ours is not. But our slightly asymmetric universe was observably expanding. If one ran the cosmic clock backward, one could demonstrate that, according to the principles of general relativity, the universe began with a singularity—a particle of infinite density.

In the last chapter of his thesis, and then in papers written as he began to move up the academic ladder at Cambridge, Hawking developed his singularity theorems of the universe and variations on the theorems—"which require very high-brow methods," said Dennis Sciama, "at least by the standards of theoretical physicists."

Theoretical physics is at one level a matter of methods, of approaches, of perspectives. If a given method seems to provide a useful way of solving a problem, it—or some part of it—may prove to be applicable to an allied or similar problem. Hawking had taken Penrose's approach to one question and adapted it for new purposes. Now he began to apply these new methods he had developed to an examination of the properties of black holes.

Perhaps this was not strictly "cosmology," though the exploration would shed light on the origins of the universe. One characteristic that sets Hawking apart from the main body of theoretical physicists is his readiness and ability to take up problems in a variety of specialties. I asked him if he would describe himself as a "cosmologist" now, and he answered, "That's partly right. That's one of the things I'd like to be. I'd call myself a theoretical physicist primarily interested in gravity—on all scales."

To say the least, that is a job description of considerable scope. The approaches in the different branches of physics, Don Page said, "are often quite a bit different. Stephen is certainly very good at understanding the principles behind the different ways of doing things. He may not know all the details of how particle physicists calculate certain complicated things. But he'll know the principles involved and be able to relate them to principles of another area. And he'll be able to take perhaps a part of a formula—say, from particle physics—and apply it in a different context—say, in cosmology or gravitation—in a way that persons working just in particle physics wouldn't be able to do."

So Hawking applied to the investigation of black holes the methods he used in his singularity theorems, and showed that asthe black hole swallows matter it can only get bigger—that when examining black holes with the tools provided by general relativity theory, there is no way to get a black hole to diminish in size, nor to have one black hole fission into two black holes. "That was just a fantastic result," said William Press. Until then, it would have been considered impossible to demonstrate that a black hole could not become two black holes, because the proof would be far too complicated. "Stephen's genius," said Press, "is in

piercing through to the solution without having to calculate nonessential pieces. And, in fact, that theorem now can be taught to first-year graduate students."

Hawking began to turn his attention to the question of *little* black holes that might have been formed in the birth of the universe. Big black holes can be described using general relativity theory, but little black holes cannot. The scale of little black holes puts them in the domain of the elementary particles, the domain where general relativity does not apply and where quantum mechanics—particle physics—takes over.

He was interested in work on black holes being done by the Russian theorist Yakov B. Zeldovich, who suggested that if a black hole is not stationary but rotates it should radiate its rotational energy and thus emit particles. According to Don Page, who had also been working on the same question, Hawking "liked the idea, but he didn't like the way it was derived, so he was going to derive it correctly."

The results surprised and dismayed Hawking. If his approach was right, when one examined black holes at the quantum-mechanical level they emitted particles even without rotating. In other words, black holes could lose mass and diminish in size. Eventually they could even evaporate. But Hawking's own relativity theorems of black holes forbade all that. Because he had characteristically reached this result by attacking the problem in a broad-brush way, perhaps some of the details he had left out were important and would wreck the quantum mechanical solution if they were added. He added them, but he got the same results. "It's a little bit unusual for Stephen," said Don Page, "in that this was a case where he didn't guess the correct answer beforehand and then work out the justification for it."

So Hawking had developed two very important and apparently contradictory ways of looking at black holes. In the regime of relativity or gravity theory, large black holes can only grow; in the regime of quantum theory, they can shrink.

The apparent contradiction did not mean either set of statements about black holes was useless. Indeed, the discovery of the apparent contradiction itself provided what may be a crucial clue in the quantum-gravity mystery. Hawking quickly realized, as Kip Thorne put it, that the supposedly contradictory results only reflected "two different aspects of a thermodynamic behavior of black holes, so they weren't contradictory at all. They were thesame thing. In fact, in different regimes." Thorne believes "they were the seeds of a great new insight about a unified law that applies in both regimes."

. . . . .

Colleagues expect that if anyone is to succeed at "quantizing gravity"—finding that fully unified law of gravity and quantum mechanics—Hawking will.

However, the possibility of failure is a key part of the enterprise.

"We're all risk takers," Kip Thorne told me. Part of the risk is that the theoretician can head off in an entirely wrong direction, a long blind alley, while others are solving the problem with different approaches. Physics is a very lively field at this moment, and there are more than a few brilliant individuals seeking insights about unifying laws and about the beginning and end of the universe. Not all of them agree that Hawking will lead the way to further important insights or is even on the right track.

What are Hawking's chances of solving the quantum gravity problem, bringing gravity in under the quantum tent with the rest of physics, and thereby producing (or at least inducing) a great theory that explains the behavior of all matter? Judging from his career to date, William Press suspects that Hawking will actually "come up with nothing so simple as the mere answer to that problem," but will go beyond it somehow, find a revolutionary way of restating or looking at it, and once again open previously unseen doors in theoretical physics, leading to new understanding of our universe.

One might wonder, of course, whether his disease puts him in a race against time now. I asked him about it, and his reaction seemed to typify his strikingly good-natured attitude toward the human condition, a characteristic that lifts him above the ordinary as much as his accomplishments in theoretical physics do. "I don't think of it that way at all," he says. "Any theoretical physicist is in a race against time, because as he gets older he gets less able to come up with new ideas. It's all a matter of mental agility. I think I'm probably over the hill anyway at 40. My supervisor, Dennis Sciama, held a party when he was 30 to celebrate being finished as a theoretical physicist."

I reminded him of the barracks song about old soldiers never dying, just fading away, and I asked what old physicists do. He laughed the long, sung, one-note laugh: "They try to quantize gravity."

Leonard Parker (review date 20 May 1988)

SOURCE: "Newton Tercentenary," in *Science,* Vol. 240, No. 4855, May 20, 1988, pp. 1069-70.

[*In the review below, Parker discusses the essays contained in* Three Hundred Years of Gravitation.]

[*Three Hundred Years of Gravitation*] is a collection of 16 solicited contributions published in association with a Newton Tercentenary Conference held last summer at Trinity College, Cambridge, and summarizing the state of gravitation 300 years after the publication of Isaac Newton's *Principia.* The initial essays by Stephen W. Hawking and Steven Weinberg discuss Newton's greatest achievements. These include his development of the laws of mechanics, the universal inverse square law of gravitation, and the calculus. Weinberg feels that at the heart of the greatness of the Newtonian achievement is the fact that "mankind for the first time saw the glimpse of a possibility of a comprehensive quantitative understanding of all of nature." Hawking points out that the Newtonian universal law of gravitation is inconsistent with the idea held in Newton's time that the universe is filled with a static and nearly uniform distribution of stars extending infinitely in all directions. As Hawking shows, Newton used a fallacious argument to justify a static universe. When Einstein first published his theory of general relativity (which includes Newtonian gravitation as an important limit), his equations did not permit a static universe. In order to allow a static universe, Einstein in 1917 modified them by introducing the cosmological constant. He later called this modification his worst blunder. It is remarkable that two such great minds as Newton and Einstein missed an opportunity to predict a nonstatic universe.

Roger Penrose's essay is interesting because of his unconventional view of why Newton doggedly maintained his belief in his corpuscular theory of light and because of Penrose's conviction that the gravitational field is instrumental in the reduction of the wave packet—a profound idea. In any volume purporting to survey research in gravitation, a review of experiments is essential. A.H. Cook and Clifford M. Will admirably survey the status of current experimental and observational tests of theories of gravitation. Cook concentrates mainly on laboratory experiments, whereas Will's discussion also ranges over the motion of the planets, the moon, light, and stars in binary systems. One of the most important systems for testing general relativity is the binary pulsar PSR 1913 + 16, which consists of a pulsar in close orbit about an unseen companion. General relativity is essential for determining the orbital parameters of this system. As Will points out, the rate of loss of orbital energy can be attributed to gravitational radiation and is consistent with the quadrupole formula of general relativity and inconsistent with dipole formulas predicted by a class of alternative metric theories of gravitation. The discovery of the binary pulsar has encouraged much recenttheoretical work on the general relativistic two-body problem. Thibault Damour reviews the current status of this problem.

Werner Israel gives a carefully researched and readable historical sketch of the development of the idea of black holes. He starts with the work of John Michell, who speculated in

1783 on the possibility that there might exist bodies so dense that "their light could not arrive at us," continues through the history of white dwarfs and neutron stars, the final states of gravitational collapse, and the thermodynamics of black holes, and ends with the discovery in 1974 by Hawking that black holes produce blackbody radiation through gravitational effects. This historical sketch is particularly good because of the author's insight as an important contributor to the field. He states that as the narrative "moves nearer to the present, the perspective inevitably becomes more subjective. Others, located at diverse research centres around the globe, will have experienced the events recounted here in their own very different ways." This reviewer is one case in point. The quantum field theoretical method of treating particle production in gravitational fields, which was applied in deriving the black-hole radiation, was originally developed by me in the 1960s to investigate particle production by the expanding universe. The method was further applied in 1971-72 by Stephen Fulling in his Ph.D. dissertation to a situation involving event horizons. My work and the work of Fulling played an important role in the development of the ideas that led to Hawking's definitive calculation of the spectrum of particles created by a black hole, although it is not included in this historical sketch. Furthermore, the assertion that skepticism about Hawking's 1974 paper was "prolonged and virtually unanimous" is not entirely correct. (I, for one, immediately recognized the result as correct.)

Astrophysical black holes occurring as the end state of stellar gravitational collapse are sufficiently massive that their temperature is negligible. However, they act as sources of energy through the heating of infalling matter, which radiates as it spirals gradually inward. R.D. Blandford gives an up-to-date survey of astrophysical black holes, including a good discussion of observational evidence for their existence, which appears strong in at least three cases. In the next one or two decades gravitational wave astronomy will open up a key new window on the universe. One of the most important contributions in this volume is a complete review of gravitational radiation research by Kip S. Thorne. This includes a particularly good discussion of astrophysical sources of gravitational waves and methods for detecting them. The Newtonian dynamics of bound groups of galaxies seems to imply that much of the matter in the universe is in a nonluminous, unobserved form. An interesting discussion of dark matter and the large-scale structure of the universe is given by Martin J. Rees. Alexander Vilenkin gives a clear exposition of the basic physics involved in deriving the gravitational properties of cosmic strings, one of the candidates for explaining the large-scale structure of the universe.

The cosmological constant introduced by Einstein has regained significance in recent work. Certain elementary particle theories imply that at very early times there may have been a large cosmological constant caused by vacuum energy, which would have produced a very rapid early expansion of the universe. These "inflationary" models are of considerable interest because they offer a possible explanation of several observed facts, such as the homogeneity of the cosmic background radiation and the near spatial flatness of the universe. Steven K. Blau and Alan H. Guth offer a well-written, comprehensive review of inflationary models. This is followed by Andrei Linde's discussion of chaotic inflation, in which inflation is produced by an initial nonequilibrium distribution of a scalar field. Some of the deepest issues in cosmology are addressed in the essay by Hawking on quantum cosmology. These include the choice of the initial quantum state of the universe and the question why the observed universe shows an asymmetry between the future and the past. The leading candidate for a unified theory that includes gravitation is superstring theory, in which the elementary constituents are strings rather than point particles. John H. Schwarz, one of the key developers of the theory, gives an overview. Finally, Cedomir Crnkovi and Edward Written in a clearly written essay show how to express the foundations of the canonical formalism of Yang-Mills theory and general relativity in a manifestly covariant way.

This volume is unusual because of the clarity with which many of the essays are written. The less technical contributions may be read with enjoyment by nonspecialists and students interested in learning about the state of gravitation 300 years after the *Principia*. They will see that gravitation is a healthy and vital area of research, which may yet hold the answers to many of the unsolved fundamental problems of physics. Many of the more technical contributions will be of value to advanced students and researchers in the field. I heartily recommend this volume.

Robert C. Cowen (review date 22 May 1988)

SOURCE: "The Cosmic Questions," in *Christian Science Monitor*, Vol. 80, No. 103, May 22, 1988, pp. 19-20.

[*In the following review, Cowen praises* A Brief History of Time *but warns that understanding its ideas will require some effort on the part of the reader.*]

"Where have we come from? What are we? Where are we going?" These fundamental questions, which inspired Gauguin's famous picture, also give Stephen Hawking his theme. Gauguin expressed them in the imagery of painting. Dr. Hawking explores them through the concepts of physical science.

The great problem of being—its source, nature, and destiny

or(to put it in physical terms) the origin, evolution, and fate of our universe—that's what [*A Brief History of Time: From the Big Bang to Black Holes*] is about. Time, which figures so prominently in the title, comes into it only because time and our universe are inseparable. Our universe evolves through time. Time has no meaning apart from our universe, nor do the laws of physics that Hawking uses to think incisively about his baffling subject.

Gauguin posed his questions with a sense of despair at getting any answer. Hawking writes with the physicist's faith that scientific exploration can at least put the enigma into new and unexpected perspective. People, he says, "yearn to know why we are here and where we came from . . . [this] is justification enough for our continuing quest. And our goal is nothing less than a complete description of the universe we live in."

His book recounts how far we have come toward that goal—further than one might have expected three decades ago when Einstein's lifelong quest for a unifying theory of nature ended in failure. But physicists are still only exploring the foothills at the base of the mountain from whose summit they hope to find the unifying perspective they seek.

Even Hawking—who optimistically predicts we'll find the elusive unity within a generation—admits he doesn't really know how steep the ascent will be.

This is one of the best books for laymen on this subject that has appeared in recent years. Hawking is one of the greatest theoretical cosmologists of our time. He is greater, by consensus among his colleagues, than other expert authors who have written good popular books on the subject recently. And he is greater, by far, than the "experts" who have "explained" quantum physics and cosmology in terms that support a religious agenda.

There are no dancing Zen masters or hidden faces of deity here. When Hawking mentions God, he, like Einstein, tends to use the term metaphorically. He discusses cosmic science imaginatively, even at times poetically. He leads readers to share his delight in its mysteries, but without descent into mysticism.

Einstein made little progress toward a single underlying physical theory because knowledge he needed simply did not exist in his day. Physicists work with the concept on four basic forces—gravity, electromagnetism, the weak force of radioactivity, and the strong force holding an atomic nucleus together.

This is a convenient classification for theorists, which, as Hawking notes, "may not correspond to anything deeper."

A unified theory seeks to explain these four forces as aspects of a single underlying force.

By the mid-1970s, physicists had a theory linking the weak and electromagnetic forces that experiments support. They now havetheories uniting the electro-weak and strong forces—the so-called Grand Unified Theories—for which there is as yet no experimental evidence. And theorists are playing with super-theories that would achieve the ultimate unity that Einstein sought. They don't know which, if any, of these schemes may be correct. But they at least believe they now know what such a theory should probably contain.

Yet, even though the more advanced theories may still be speculative, cosmic scientists can use them to gain new insight into the ultimate nature of our universe. For example, Hawking, who is a leader in such thought, explains how the new physics allows one to speculate meaningfully about the possibility that our universe appeared virtually from nothing.

This would not violate the law that energy can't be created from nothing, since the new universe would appear with equal amounts of positive and negative energy whose total would be zero. Hawking explains this and other arcane physical concepts well, allowing laymen interested enough to make the effort to think along with him.

And there is an effort involved. This is Hawking's first book for general readers. It has one possibly serious flaw—if indeed it can be called a flaw. It is neither technical nor academically obscure. But it is written in a scientist's mode of thought.

This can be an impediment to understanding for laymen unfamiliar with the way scientists habitually use seemingly common terms in uncommon ways—terms such as time, force, work, energy, principle. When these are used technically in connection with specific phenomena or specific theories, the use of such terms can be clear. But when a scientist moves from such specifics to general comments or conclusions about cosmic origins and reality, laymen can become confused.

This might happen, for example, when Hawking uses real and imaginary time—a quite definite mathematical concept—to track our universe's history. But readers who make the not-too-demanding effort to think along with Hawking should soon catch on.

While Hawking, the optimistic physicist, can show how physics has put the fundamental cosmic questions into a new perspective, its practitioners may be no closer to definitive answers than are Gauguin's Tahitians.

Hawking notes that while "we already know the laws that govern the behavior of matter under all but the most extreme conditions [such as the birth of the universe] . . . we have, as yet, had little success in predicting human behavior from mathematical equations!"

Thus, Hawking explains, "A complete, consistent, unified theory[of the basic forces] is only a first step: our goal is a complete *understanding* of the events around us, and of our own existence." If Hawking's optimism is justified, we may indeed unify the forces within a generation. But no one knows when-if ever-physical science will give us such understanding.

Jerry Adler (essay date 13 June 1988)

SOURCE: "Reading God's Mind," in *Newsweek*, June 13, 1988, pp. 56-9.

[*In the following essay, Adler juxtaposes Hawking's brilliant career with his debilitating illness.*]

Like light from a collapsing star, exhausted by the struggle against gravity, the thoughts of Stephen Hawking reach us as if from a vast distance, a quantum at a time. Unable to speak, paralyzed by a progressive, incurable disease, the 46-year-old British physicist communicates with the world by a barely perceptible twitch of his fingers, generating one computer-synthesized word approximately every six seconds, consuming an entire day in composing a 10-page lecture. And the world awaits the words, for the same reason that astronomers search the heavens for the precious photons from remote galaxies, or that Newton spent his last years consumed by Biblical prophecy: Hawking is trying to read the mind of God.

He believes he is as close as man has ever come. It is difficult, of course, to assess the career of a great scientist while he is still relatively young and productive, but Hawking is not above giving us some hints. The jacket copy on his best-selling survey of modern cosmology, *A Brief History of Time*, observes that Hawking "was born on the anniversary of Galileo's death, holds Newton's chair as Lucasian Professor of Mathematics at Cambridge University and is widely regarded as the most brilliant theoretical physicist since Einstein." So that no one misses the point, Hawking wrote an appendix consisting of brief biographical essays on these three, each beyond a doubt the greatest scientist of his era. He is obsessed with their hardships: Einstein's persecution as a pacifist and a Jew, Galileo's heresy trial, Newton's campaign to keep Leibniz from grabbing the credit for inventing calculus. All together, of course, those difficulties don't measure up to Hawking's 26-year losing

battle with amyotrophic lateral sclerosis, better known as Lou Gehrig's disease. Hawking, who is known to have a sense of humor about himself, might appreciate the irony that he managed to contract not just any terminal illness but one named after the greatest first baseman of his age.

Specifically, Hawking is one of a number of scientists searching for the magnificently named Grand Unification, a theory linking the two greatest intellectual achievements of the 20th century,relativity and quantum mechanics. The former deals with the large-scale structure of the universe, as determined essentially by gravity; the latter is concerned with the forces that operate at the atomic scale and below. Reconciling these two theories, a goal that eluded even Einstein, might hold the key to understanding how the universe came into being. A grand-unification theory would deserve not just a Nobel Prize but the last Nobel Prize; as Hawking puts it, "There would still be lots to do [in physics], but it would be like mountaineering after Everest."

Necessarily, Hawking pursues these questions on a purely cerebral level. But also by choice: he is a theoretical physicist, a discipline that in recent years has far outstripped the ability of scientists to make observations. In his book Hawking quotes a description applied to the great theoretical physicist Wolfgang Pauli, of whom it was said that "even his presence in the same town would make experiments go wrong." But, after all, experimenters deal in mere data; it would be a puny sort of God who let himself be seen in a radio telescope or trapped in a particle accelerator. Hawking prefers to stalk him on what he considers the higher plane of human intellect, armed only with the language he is confident they both speak, mathematics.

Hawking's most famous work has been on the nature of black holes. These are regions of extremely dense matter in which gravity is so strong that nothing, not even light, can escape. Astrophysicists believe a black hole might form when a burned-out star collapses. Surrounding a black hole is a surface known as the event horizon, a kind of trapdoor through which matter could pass in only one direction—inward—sealing off the hole from the rest of the universe. The existence of black holes was first posited in the 18th century (by a Cambridge don, Hawking notes smugly). They have been written about and studied and cited so often that it comes as a bit of a shock when Hawking observes that there is still no conclusive physical evidence that they exist. Hawking has a wager riding on the question with the physicist Kip Thorne at Caltech. Hawking bet *against* the existence of black holes; if he wins, much of his life's work will be wasted, but he will get a four-year subscription to Private Eye, a British satirical magazine. If black holes do exist, Thorne gets a year of Penthouse and, conceivably, Hawking gets the Nobel Prize.

In 1974, at a conference near Oxford, Hawking set out to show that it was possible for black holes to emit radiation. His calculations were based on the principle of quantum mechanics that at the subatomic level particles do not obey the same laws that we see in material objects around us. They lead a strange kind of contingent existence, in which their position and momentum are usually uncertain, subject to random fluctuations over infinitesimal fractions of a second. Particles can even be created out of empty space—with the proviso that they are created in pairs of "virtual particles" that must instantlycollide and annihilate one another. What would happen if such a pair were to come into existence right at the event horizon? Hawking demonstrated that it was possible for one of the particles to be sucked into the black hole and the other to escape into space. This was such a revolutionary assertion that the chairman of the conference stood up to denounce it on the spot, but it has gained considerable acceptance since then, and the radiation that would result from this process has come to be called Hawking radiation. Of course, no one has ever found it in nature, either. The real significance of Hawking's paper was that it married quantum mechanics—the source of virtual particles—to relativity, the theory that predicts black holes. He had taken the first step on the road to a Grand Unification.

Legendary Courage

A step on the road: it is instructive to realize how inadequate even simple metaphors are in dealing with someone like Hawking. He can't take a step any longer, but his courage in facing his affliction is legendary. His collaborator on black-hole theory, the great Oxford physicist Roger Penrose, remembers visiting Hawking when he could still maneuver on crutches, and watching him spend a quarter of an hour going up the steps to bed, declining all help. Even now he travels the world extensively, attended by three nurses working round-the-clock shifts and by graduate student Nick Phillips, who looks after his elaborate array of computerized communications gear. Just this past spring Hawking visited California, recalls Berkeley cosmologist Joseph Silk, "going up and down the state, giving more than a dozen talks, on a schedule that any fit person would find exhausting."

He was not always such a paradigm of energy. As an undergraduate at Oxford, he worked just hard enough to let his professors know how brilliant he was. He was the sort of student, recalls his physics tutor Pat Sandars, who preferred picking out the mistakes in his textbooks to doing the problems at the end of the chapter. For the next couple of years, which he spent at Cambridge, he barely bothered even to do that. Symptoms that he had first noted at Oxford—slurred speech, difficulty tying his shoes—had become worse, and doctors told him he had what the English call motor neuron disease. His time was spent in his room listening to Wagner, reading science fiction—and drinking. There was another problem as well, recalls Dennis Sciama, who supervised Hawking's graduate work: "There weren't a lot of problems lying around suitable for someone of his ability." When he finally found one, in a paper by Penrose on black holes, things began to change quickly. He began working hard for the first time in his life, the progress of his disease inexplicably slowed—and he fell in love with a language student named Jane Wilde. They were married in 1965 and they now have three children, two boys and a girl, the youngest born in 1979. Through disease and the potentially more distracting peril of fame, Hawking has managed to maintain a decent, happy family life. "Stephen doesn't make any concessions to his illness, and I don't make any concessions to him," Janehas said.

Taking Tea

For a successor to the mantle of Newton and Einstein, Hawking seems not to rate many perks. His office is a narrow, cluttered cubicle in the Department of Applied Mathematics and Theoretical Physics, which occupies a building as charmless and functional as its name. He spends his days there writing, seeing students or taking tea with them in the drab common room. He usually rolls up in his motorized wheelchair, which he steers with a joy stick on the half-mile ride from home in late morning, and works until around 7 in the evening. On a typical Friday last month, he began his day at the lunchtime meeting of a relativity seminar he leads. Two dozen students filled the room, sharing boxes of cookies and packages of luncheon meat, as Hawking wheeled quietly in and surveyed the scene.

His fingers twitched and the screen mounted on his wheelchair flickered. "Like old times," came a metallic voice from a speaker behind his seat.

Hawking's computers are cleverly designed for someone who can make only one movement. On the screen before him, the cursor flicks among letters of the alphabet, stopping at one when he squeezes his switch; this calls up a screen full of pre-programmed words beginning with the chosen letter. There are 2,600 such words, mingling the esoteric language of his field with the mundane nouns a man needs to get around in the world—thermal, theory, topology; thanks, Thursday, tea. The cursor scrolls down the lists until Hawking makes his choice, and the word is added to a sentence at the bottom of the screen, ready to be pronounced—or, in a formal interview, displayed on a desk monitor for precise note-taking. He can also spell out new words, which he does with no short-cuts or abbreviations. Anyone trying to finish his sentences for him feels the silent scorn of that imperturbably flicking finger.

The seminar consisted of a research fellow, Peter Ruback, reading a paper on "New Uniqueness Theorems for Charged Black Holes." As Ruback filled the blackboard with equations, Hawking watched, swallowing a few forkfuls of lunch fed to him by his nurse. At the end of an hour and a half, there was a brief burst of applause, followed by silence, and Hawking's ominous clicking. "I would be interested if you could find a different wormhole," came the voice, "—with a different topology."

Asked later what he thought of Hawking's reaction, Ruback shrugged: "I think he thought it was rather obvious—which it may be, to him."

Self-righteous

To anyone dependent on Hawking's approval, his handicap can be maddening, because his synthetic voice is completely devoid of expression and his one change of facial expression—a slightly slack-jawed grin—serves for a wide variety of emotions. His terse remarks take on an oracular quality that can preclude disagreement. "Students have to take what he says and go away and figure it out," Penrose observes. He recalls one heroic three-day argument over black holes that was never fully resolved: "If [Hawking] wanted to speak, he made a noise. I would have to stop and listen and I'd lose the train of my argument. It was very frustrating."

And there is a self-righteous streak in Hawking that some colleagues find nettlesome. In his book, he recounts discussing an unpublished theory of the Russian physicist Andrei Linde at a lecture in Philadelphia in 1981. Paul Steinhardt, a young assistant professor at the University of Pennsylvania, was in the audience and later published a paper, with Andreas Albrecht, proposing "something very similar to Linde's idea . . . ," Hawking wrote. He added, "[Steinhardt] later told me he didn't remember me describing Linde's ideas. . . ." The implications of a remark like this, from a world-famous scientist about a lesser-

known colleague, can be devastating. Steinhardt—who says he had already corrected Hawking on the point—was disturbed enough when the story reappeared in the book to dig up a videotape of Hawking's lecture, which he says supports his assertion that Hawking never mentioned Linde's work. "Hawking is an outstanding physicist," said Steinhardt, now a full professor, "but he's not a god, he's a human being." Steinhardt sent the tape to Hawking, and—after *Newsweek* raised the question—Hawking announced, through his U.S. publisher, that the account will be expunged from future editions.

To be sure, Hawking wasn't seeking credit for himself but for his friend Linde. And, already living on borrowed time, he can perhaps be forgiven for his impatience in correcting what he sees as injustice. Has a similar attitude of impatience affected his scientific work? Penrose believes that Hawking's condition has forced him to work more creatively, to take imaginative leaps where someone with a less uncertain future might want to cogitate a little longer. Hawking himself dismisses that notion utterly. The only effect of ALS on his work he is willing to concede is that "I avoid problems with a lot of equations, because I cannot manage to do them in my head. But," he adds, "those are the most boring problems."

There is really only one interesting problem, which is the problem of everything. "My goal," Hawking has said, "is a complete understanding of the universe, why it is as it is and why it exists at all." And slowly, painfully, he has advanced on that goal. The journey has taken some surprising turns. Hawking, together with Penrose, was a leader in postulating a property of black holes known as singularities. As predicted by relativity, these are points at which matter is not merely tremendously dense but *infinitely* dense—the remnants of a star collapsed to a point of zero size. Since the laws of physics, in their mathematical expression, cannot accommodate infinite quantities, the logical conclusion was that these laws no longer apply at a singularity—and *literally anything can happen*. (We never see the laws break down because it happens inside the event horizon, from which nothing can escape.) The universe, according to some models, began with a singularity, which erupted into the Big Bang. Many physicists are satisfied with some version of this account. But Hawking realized you could never completely understand a universe that began at a point where anything could happen.

Imaginary Time

His journey, therefore, has taken him away from singularities, toward a theory that modifies the stark predictions of relativity through the application of quantum mechanics. He achieved this result in a totally abstract and mathematical form, by postulating a different kind of time, "imaginary" time as distinct from the "real" time that measures our days and years. ("Imaginary" is used here in a technical mathematical sense—meaning the square root of a negative number—it does not have its common-sense meaning of "illusory." And it is impossible to discuss it in ordinary physical terms; the question "How long is an imaginary year?" is meaningless.) In imaginary time, there are no singularities; the universe is finite, but without the boundaries that singularities imply, in the way the surface of the earth is finite but unbounded. In an hourlong interview, Hawking rises to the level of a paragraph on only one subject, this "no-boundary proposal": "I think that it really underlies science because it is really the statement that the laws of science hold everywhere. Once you allow that there could be exceptions to the laws of science, you couldn't predict anything. . . . If the laws of science broke down at the beginning of the universe, they could break down anywhere."

And is this, then, the key that will unlock the true secret of the universe? The next two decades, Hawking has said, should hold the answer. Project Hawking's intellectual growth over the next 20 years and the possibilities are almost limitless; do the same with his physical deterioration and. . . . There is a phenomenon of relativity known as time dilation, in which time appears to slow down almost to a stop for bodies that approach the speed of light. Hawking alludes, in his book, to what it might be like for an astronaut as he accelerates toward a black hole, as all eternity passes by outside in an instant of his time. There is a sense in which Hawking himself has experienced a kind of time dilation, an inexplicable slowing of a natural process that has added decades to his expected life span. The answer he seeks may be almost within his sight. But so, perhaps, is the event horizon.

Economist (review date 25 June 1988)

SOURCE: "Putting Infinite Space into a Nutshell," in *Economist*, Vol. 307, June 25, 1988, pp. 91-2.

[*In the following review of* A Brief History of Time, *the critic states that while Hawking's theories are mind-boggling, his presentation is disappointing.*]

When Stephen Hawking was diagnosed as having amyotrophic lateral sclerosis, a progressive wasting-away of the nerves that control body movements, his doctors gave him two years. Understandably, he stopped working on his PhD thesis. But at the end of two years, the disease had not progressed very far, and Mr Hawking had become engaged. He needed a job, so he needed a doctorate. That was 23 years ago.

The topic which he picked then was one which has engaged him ever since—the similarities between black holes and the big bang. His work on these subjects has made him one of the most respected physicists in the world, rising to be Lucasian professor of mathematics at Cambridge, a post once held by Newton. But his wider fame is not due to his position, or the exact nature of his theories. It is the contrast between the body trapped in a wheelchair, able to speak only through a computer system, and the mind that ranges the cosmos which has caught the public imagination: the king of infinite space, bounded in a nutshell.

Mr Hawking's book [*A Brief History of Time*] is his not-altogether satisfactory explanation, to the layman, of the ideas that have earned him so much respect among his colleagues. He talks about the marriage of ideas from different fields—relativity, dealing with stars and galaxies, and quantum mechanics, dealing with the vagaries of tiny particles—which led to the success of his work on black holes. And he describes how similar techniques may be leading to an explanation of the creation—or lack of it—of the universe.

The theory of general relativity is the best explanation so far of the force of gravity, which determines the way the universe works on large scales. By considering time as being like one of the three dimensions of space, Einstein managed to explain the force of gravity as resulting from the shape of four dimensional "space-time".

The idea runs into trouble when gravity gets particularly strong and space-time is thoroughly bent and mangled. Things can get so twisted that a point occurs where the force of gravity is infinite—a "singularity". Singularities are bad news for physicists. Because they are unique points, a theory which depends on shapes cannot deal with them—so Einstein's theories break down.

Black holes, formed when a massive star dies, contain singularities. But these riddles are wrapped in other mysteries—the "event horizons". Anything that happens within these horizons is unknowable to the outside cosmos; they mark the bourne from which no traveller, even light, can return, because of the intense gravity. So it is possible for physicists to accept singularities by invoking a "Principle of Cosmic Censorship" to explain why the conceptually indecent singularities are never seen by those who are impressed by the laws of physics.

Mr Hawking, though, found a way to get rid of the singularities altogether. According to quantum mechanics, there are always some random events going on in a vacuum. If these take place just next to an event horizon, they will result in negative energy falling into the black hole. That means less energy in the hole, which means less mass and thus a smaller hole. Eventually, the hole evaporates completely and the singularity vanishes in a puff of radiation.

So much for black holes. But the biggest singularity still remains. The fact that the universe is expanding, with every point in it getting farther away from every other point, implies that there was a time when everything was in one place. The force of gravity there would have been infinite—it would be outside the ken of relativity. There, beyond the laws of physics, one might be seeing the point—or, indeed, the act—of creation.

Even this singularity is not Hawking-proof. Early on in the

universe, gravity has to be explained in terms of quantum effects, rather than space-time geometry, because of the tiny distances involved. That can be done by "summing histories": considering all the places something could have been, and all the ways it could have got here from there, and then adding up the possibilities.

To do the sum, you have to introduce "imaginary" time. (Imaginary in the technical sense of numbers which produce a negative number when multiplied together, not in the sense of made-up.) And if the universe is considered as having three dimensions plus imaginary, rather than real, time, it has no singularities at all, in much the same way as the surface of a sphere has no beginning. That suggests that theories of quantum gravity—none is finished yet—may one day get rid of the one singularity left for a creator outside the laws of physics to hide in.

This is all mind-boggling stuff. But Mr Hawking's presentation is disappointing. There is not much sense of the process of physics. The history mentioned in the title is a rather perfunctory list of the achievements of great men—Galileo, Newton, Einstein and Hawking—not an analysis of how different ages foster different ideas. Contemporary physicists turn up in the book as names attached to ideas, rather than as people. There is a smattering of anecdote, but there is little sense of how and why people chose to ask the questions to which the book provides simplified answers. Hamlet blamed his bad dreams for his inability to reign over infinite space; it would be nice to know what dreams haveled to Stephen Hawking's deserved enthronement as a king of four-dimensional space-time.

Hubert Reeves (review date 21 October 1988)

SOURCE: "Universal Models," in *Times Literary Supplement*, No. 4464, October 21-27, 1988, p. 1167.

[*In the excerpt below, Reeves argues that while* A Brief History of Time *is well-written, Hawking fails to communicate that his ideas are based on assumptions which have yet to be proven.*]

A Brief History of Time is a document, both scientific and human, about a man who has fought against a terrible illness (motor neurone disease) to become one of the leading figures in contemporary astrophysics. Stephen W. Hawking is well on his way to matching the popularity of Einstein among the general public. The book tells us about the evolution of his thinking, which has deeply influenced the face of contemporary cosmology. It should be read by everybody interested in physics and astronomy. It is also highly readable, the style being brisk, sharp and often witty. The argu-

ments, reduced to the essential, are clearly made and convincing, and Hawking's comparisons and analogies are very much to the point. He reveals himself here as a master of scientific popularization. He asks, too, the fundamental question of cosmology: "Even if there is only one possible unified theory [of the universe], it is just a set of rules and equations. What is it that breathes fire into the equations and makes a universe for them to describe?"

After presenting a summary of contemporary cosmology, Hawking introduces us to his own contribution to the physics of black holes. Quantum mechanics has reversed the diktats of General Relativity; after Hawking, "Black holes ain't so black" any more. Could it play the same trick on the classical "singularity" of the Big Bang? Hawking and his collaborators hope that it can. Their programme is grandiose, being nothing less than to give a complete theory of the universe, without a singularity and without any beginning to time.

Physical theories are made of two essential ingredients: a set of laws and a set of "arbitrary initial conditions". But, in the case of the universe, what can we say about the initial conditions? How were they chosen? Do we have to appeal to a divinity? Hawking's dream is to show that these initial conditions are not arbitrary but can themselves be derived from his cosmological model. Interesting results have already been published on the subject. But the model is still at an early stage. No one knows how far these fascinating views will be taken. Hawking warns us that the final results are still far away, but the warning is perhaps not expressed strongly enough. I have asked a number of unscientific readers of the book and they, generally, were under the impression that Stephen Hawking's views already were the new cosmology, that we need no initial singularity and no beginning to time.

Both the cosmologies advanced here are based on an assumption, which is not mentioned in either book and which may well turn out to be wrong: the assumption that the universe has just the so-called "critical" density, between an ever-expanding universe and a later, contracting one. This assumption (which, as far as I can see, is essential to both models) is not supported by observations. The present best estimates of universal density yield a value of 10 to 20 per cent only of this critical density, so despite the wishes of many theorists, and despite the efforts of many observers, there is no sign that the universe has the critical density. This should have been stated clearly in both books. "I hate it when I see beautiful theories trampled down by ugly facts", said Mark Twain. "Trampled" may be too strong here, "threatened" would be more appropriate.

Troy Organ (essay date July-August 1989)

SOURCE: "Dignifying Humanity," in *Humanist*, Vol. 49, No. 4, July-August 1989, pp. 29-30, 50.

[*In the following essay, Organ considers the humor in Hawking's writing.*]

Stephen Hawking dignifies our humanity. He was born in 1942, exactly three hundred years after the death of Galileo—as he likes to note. When he was diagnosed as having the illness commonly known as Lou Gehrig's disease, he dropped his graduate studies to consider what to do. Insights into life and its possibilities came with meeting and marrying Jane and in begetting three children—Robert, Lucy, and Timmy. For the past twenty years, he has been confined to his wheelchair. He has little control over his muscles, and he can no longer speak. Yet, he writes, "Apart from being unlucky enough to get ALS, or motor neuron disease, I have been fortunate in almost every other respect." He is the Lucasian Professor of Medicine at Cambridge University, a post once held by Newton. He is a fellow of the Royal Society of London and is widely acclaimed as the most brilliant physicist since Einstein. The unified field theory to which Einstein unsuccessfully devoted the last twenty years of his life is now within reach of Hawking—at least, so many think. Hawking, however, has recently said that this theory will require the work of younger and more adventurous minds.

In 1982, Hawking decided to write a popular book about space and time. The result is *A Brief History of Time: From the Big Bang to Black Holes*. Carl Sagan says it is "a book about God . . . or perhaps about the absence of God . . . [since] a universe with no edge in space, no beginning or end in time, [has] nothing for aCreator to do." Sagan also describes the book as "lucid revelations on the frontiers of physics, astronomy, cosmology, and courage." I want to note another aspect of the book. Hawking's illness could understandably have produced Diogenean cynicism or Schopenhaurean pessimism. But it did not. I, as one of the philosophers whom Hawking says "have not been able to keep up with the advance of scientific theories," wish to indicate my appreciation of Hawking and his book by noting the humor in his writing. I wish to call attention to Hawking's humorous observations about five subjects: Hawking himself, human beings in general, physicists, physics, and the universe.

Hawking says he chose to study theoretical physics because it is "all in the mind." No muscles are needed. "So my disability has not been a serious handicap." In 1985, he caught pneumonia and had to have a tracheostomy operation. Now he speaks by means of a communications program, a speech synthesizer, and a small personal computer. The result, he says, is "I can communicate better now than before I lost my voice."

Physical movement for him is a slow, painful process. But that gives him more time to think. He reports that "one evening in November that year [1970], shortly after the birth of my daughter, Lucy, I started to think about black holes as I was getting into bed. My disability makes this rather a slow process, so I had plenty of time."

There is a delightful puckishness about Hawking's humor. When someone told him that each equation could halve the sale of the book, he "resolved not to have any equations at all." Well, almost none at all; he could not leave out E=mc2. "I hope that this will not scare off half my potential readers," he noted.

He has a bet with Kip Thorne of the California Institute of Technology that Cygnus X-1 has a black hole. If it does, Thorne must send Hawking a four-year subscription to *Private Eye*. If it does not, Hawking owes Thorne a year of *Penthouse*. The image of two world-famous astronomers betting on the absence or presence of a black hole in a star is bathos.

In my opinion, the most humorous observation of Hawking on Hawking is his description of a conference on cosmology which was organized by the Jesuits in the Vatican in 1981. At the close of the conference, the participants were granted an audience with the pope. Hawking reports:

> He told us that it was all right to study the evolution of the universe after the big bang, but we should not inquire into the big bang itself because that was the moment of Creation and therefore the work of God. I was glad then that he did not know the subject of the talk I had given at the conference—the possibility that space-time was finite but had no boundary, which means that it had no beginning, no moment of Creation. I had no desire to share the fate of Galileo, with whom I feel a strongsense of identity, partly because of the coincidence of having been born exactly 300 years after his death.

In some places in his book, Hawking be-littles human beings. For example:

> In an expanding universe in which the density of matter varied slightly from place to place, gravity would have caused the denser regions to slow down their expansion and start contracting. This would lead to the formation of galaxies, stars, and eventually even insignificant creatures like ourselves.

After all, human beings evolved from a macro-molecular error. Earth, he writes, was initially very hot and without an atmosphere. An atmosphere developed from the emission of gases from the rocks. But there was no oxygen. All that appeared were a lot of other gases, such as hydrogen sulfide, the gas of rotten eggs. Some atoms formed into structures called macromolecules, and these reproduced themselves. Some reproductions were "errors," which were forms of macromolecules that were better at reproducing themselves. These "errors" and their offspring consumed hydrogen sulfide and released oxygen, and this allowed the development of higher forms of life such as "fish, reptiles, mammals, and ultimately the human race."

Hawking, like many astronomers, seems to delight in reminding laypersons that the universe is not eternal. It began with a big bang, and it will end with a big crunch. The big bang occurred about ten thousand million years ago, and the big crunch will take place about that far into the future. Hawking advises that the end of the universe should not unduly worry us, since "by that time, unless we have colonized beyond the Solar System, mankind will long since have died out, extinguished along with our sun." So, do not worry about the big crunch; we shall not be around to witness it.

Hawking's final evaluation of humans is far from belittlement. He does not forget that we are "beings who investigate the laws of the universe and ask about the nature of God."

Hawking enjoys calling attention to humor in his fellow physicists. For example, he notes that physicists say that quarks have six "flavors" (up, down, strange, charmed, bottom, top) and that each "flavor" comes in three "colors" (red, green, blue). However, "flavor" does not denote flavor, and "color" does not denote color. Quarks have neither color nor flavor. Hawking comments—with tongue in cheek—that this demonstrates that modern physicists have more imaginative ways of naming new particles than by seeking a proper term in the Greek language.

In his discussion of the indeterminacy principle, Hawking says that Wolfgang Pauli was "the archetypal theoretical physicist." His presence in the same town was sufficient to make experiments go wrong.

He reports that in 1948 George Gamow and his student, Ralph Alpher, coauthored a paper. Then Gamow persuaded nuclear scientist Has Behte to add his name to the paper so that the list of authors would be Alpher, Behte, Gamow. This similarity to the first three letters of the Greek alphabet—alpha, beta, gamma—was fitting, says Hawking, since the paper was about the beginning of the universe.

The science of theoretical physics may not seem to be an object of humor, but it is for Hawking. He enjoys inserting an obliquitous phrase at the end of an important sentence. For example, ". . . a theory is just a model of the uni-

verse. . . . It [the theory] exists in our minds and does not have any other reality (whatever that may mean)." Sometimes, the obliquity is an entire sentence. For example, after conjecturing that if one took all the heavy water in all the oceans one could build a hydrogen bomb that would create a black hole where Earth is, he adds, "Of course, there would be no one left to observe it."

Shifts from physics to psychology are found throughout the book. In a discussion of antiparticles, Hawking writes, "There could be antiworlds and antipeople made out of antiparticles. However, if you meet your antiself, don't shake hands! You would both vanish in a great flash of light." The boundary of a black hole, he says, is formed by paths in space-time of rays of light that just fail to get away from the black hole. He comments, "It is a bit like running away from the police and just managing to keep one step ahead but not being able to get clear away."

Why are there so many more quarks than antiquarks, asks Hawking. Why not an equal number of each? He answers, "It is certainly fortunate for us that the numbers are unequal because, if they had been the same, nearly all the quarks and antiquarks would have annihilated each other in the early universe and left a universe filled with radiation but hardly any matter."

The book contains two chapters on black holes. Chapter six is entitled "Black Holes"; chapter seven is entitled "Black Holes Ain't So Black." Only a scholar on top of his subject matter with a fine sense of humor would risk a title like that.

The behavior of black holes, according to Hawking, is much like entropy. Lest the reader fail to grasp his meaning, Hawking adds, "It is a matter of common experience that disorder will tend to increase if things are left to themselves. One has only to stop making repairs around the house to see that."

Hawking's evaluation of what is and is not important in cosmic evolution is puzzling and humorous:

> Within only a few hours of the big bang, the production of helium and other elements would have stopped. And after that, for the next few million years or so, the universe would have just continued expanding, without anything much happening.

His references to God often have curious twists. In one place, he wonders why God chose to start the universe "in such an incomprehensible way" and then let it "evolve according to laws that we could understand."

If we can ever develop a "complete, consistent, unified theory"—a theory that accounts for gravitational force, electromagnetic force, the weak nuclear force that is responsible for radioactivity, and the strong nuclear force that holds the quarks together in the proton and neutron—concludes Hawking, that is "only the first step." Our goal is *a complete understanding* of the events around us, and of our own existence." For Hawking, the ultimate question is: "Why does the universe go to all the bother of existing?"

Scientific American (essay date October 1989)

SOURCE: "Cosmic Quarrel," in *Scientific American,* Vol. 261, October, 1989, pp. 22, 26.

[*In the following essay, the critic discusses the theoretical disagreement between Hawking and philosopher Huw Price.*]

Theoretical physicists, equipped with counterintuitive perceptions and a formidable mathematical armory, are considered by philosophers to be armed and dangerous. Their turf—however interesting—is usually avoided. Huw Price, a philosopher from the University of Sidney, belongs to a different breed. He has taken on Stephen W. Hawking of the University of Cambridge, one of the world's leading cosmologists. The rift developed over whether Hawking has, as he claims, found a possible explanation for the arrow of time.

Time occupies a strange place in the cosmological scheme of things. Most physical laws would allow the universe to run equally well forward or backward. The major exception is a relentless tendency for the extent of disorder in the universe, or entropy, to increase. In his best-selling book *A Brief History of Time,* Hawking argues that the tendency toward entropy underlies the psychological experience that we know as time. He makes the connection by observing that living things can exist and record memories, thus gaining a sense of time, only by overcoming the rising tide of entropy within a local region. To do so, they have to use energy supplied by the sun. So, according to Hawking, the deeper question underlying our perception of time is: Why does the universe at this stage of its evolution contain ordered structures such as the sun rather than just total disorder—random radiation?

Like most cosmologists, Hawking believes the known forces of nature can account for galaxies, stars and other ordered systemsonly if there was a big bang that started the universe expanding rapidly from a very hot, dense and relatively organized state. Hawking and his supporters also think disorder will spread until the universe becomes a bland void that may eventually contract in a big crunch. Hence, for Hawking, the really deep mystery about time is: Why is the universe ordered at one pole of time (the one we call the big bang) but disordered at the big crunch? Why won't nature's epic film run backward?

Hawking finds his answer in a quantum-gravity model of the universe, a theoretical hybrid that combines relativity and quantum physics. He has proposed that cosmologists should focus their efforts on a particular type of quantum-gravity model, one in which the history of the universe is finite in extent and in time but has no boundary. Such a universe lacks an edge or wall because space-time is curved; a straight line eventually meets itself. Hawking calculates that this "no boundary" proposal, together with some other assumptions, leads to the grand conclusion that the real universe is by far the most probable type: ordered at one end of time, expanding to a maximum extent and then, aeons hence, contracting once more, yet becoming more disordered all the while.

At this point Price charges into Hawking's cosmological briar patch. Writing affably in the pages of *Nature,* he suggests that *A Brief History of Time* fails to explain how Hawking finds the arrow of time embedded in his no-boundary proposal. The book, according to Price, teases the reader with a mystery that lacks a denouement. "It is as if we are assured that the butler did it, without being told how he overcame the evident obstacles (that he was incarcerated in Wormwood Scrubs at the time, for example)," he writes.

Price argues that Hawking's explanation for the arrow of time assumes what it sets out to show: that one end of time is different from the other. Price maintains that in a discussion about time, external final conditions are just as valid as initial conditions: any explanation for the high state of order at the moment of the big bang that is built into Hawking's model should, he suggests, apply equally to the big crunch. And if Hawking's model assumes some kind of temporal asymmetry, Price says, then it does not explain the arrow of time.

Hawking sticks to his guns. He writes to *Scientific American* that the no-boundary proposal does indeed explain the arrow of time because it predicts, essentially, that a universe of any given size has two distinct, highly probable degrees of disorder. In the low-disorder state, entropy increases as the universe expands; in the high-disorder state, disorder increases as the universe contracts. Hawking interprets the low-disorder state as belonging to the early history of the universe and the high-disorder state as coming after the universe has started to contract. "He does not have to assume time," one Hawking sympathizer comments. "If he is right, this answers thequestion."

Other cosmologists are not quite so sure. Don N. Page of Pennsylvania State University, who collaborates with Hawking, observes that "it's not clear what fraction of simple models of universes have an arrow of time." If the property of being simple itself predicted an arrow of time, then Hawking's no-boundary proposal might not explain very much.

Nevertheless, Page is confident that further work will clarify the situation. "It may be that Hawking's argument is wrong for other reasons, but I don't think it's because he's smuggling the arrow of time in there," he says. In fact, Page thinks, Hawking may have come on a truly profound insight. "If the time asymmetry is borne out by more complicated models, this would seem to be an amazing fact about the universe that this model might explain. . . . I know of no previous explanation for the arrow of time."

Chet Raymo (review date 6 April 1990)

SOURCE: "Stephen Hawking and the Mind of God," in *Commonweal*, Vol. CXVII, No. 7, April 6, 1990, p. 218.

[*In the following review, Raymo suggests why* A Brief History of Time *has enjoyed such popular success.*]

The longevity of Stephen Hawking's *A Brief History of Time: From the Big Bang to Black Holes* on international best-seller lists is itself a phenomenon worthy of scientific investigation. As I write, the book has been on the American list for more than ninety weeks. For a work on relativity and quantum physics to achieve this distinction is unprecedented.

Hawking is a physicist with a particular interest in cosmology. He has achieved theoretical insights of remarkable originality, particularly with regard to the quantum physics of black holes. In *A Brief History of Time* he describes his personal discoveries within the context of our current understanding of the origin, evolution, and ultimate fate of the universe.

Hawking interprets modern cosmology with admirable clarity, but his book is hardly a "gripping" read. So what accounts for the book's extraordinary popular appeal? Some uncharitable critics have suggested that *A Brief History of Time* is more a publicity event than a book, that it is bought but not read, and that its main value is as a coffee-table status symbol. Best sellers do have a way of generating their own aura of irresistibility, but, in the case of Hawking's book, this can hardly be the whole story.

I would suggest several reasons for the popularity of *A Brief History of Time*. The first and most obvious is Hawking himself. Stephen Hawking suffers from ALS, or motor neu-

ron disease, commonly known as Lou Gehrig's disease. His body is almost totally disabled. He is confined to a wheelchair and speaks and writes with the help of a computer and voice synthesizer. Within this incapacitated body is contained a remarkably capacitated mind, some would say the most brilliant theoretical mind since Einstein. Hawking was born on the anniversary of Galileo's death and holds Isaac Newton's chair as Lucasian Professor of Mathematics at Cambridge University. He is a fitting successor to those illustrious explorers of the cosmos.

For many people, Hawking's physical trial and intellectual triumph confirms the primacy of mind over matter, of optimistic spirit over debilitating misfortune. (Hawking himself might merely use the words "lucky" and "unlucky.") Purchasing Hawking's book may be a conscious or unconscious way of paying homage to the inspiring courage of the man.

But there is more. Professor Hawking's reputation has exploded beyond his physics to make him a revered icon of our time. We are seduced by his achievement into believing that whatever he has to say on any topic must be worth listening to—even as Newton was pressed into public service as Master of the Mint and Einstein was sought out to be Israel's head of state.

In this regard, I am put in mind of an anecdote described by New Age guru Shirley MacLaine in her book *Going Within: A Guide to Inner Transformation*. MacLaine goes on pilgrimage to Cambridge to interview Stephen Hawking. She seeks wisdom. Hawking, characteristically, asks for a kiss. After some chatty preliminaries, MacLaine asks if the harmonic energy of the universe is "loving".

"I don't know that there is anything loving about energy," says the wheelchair-bound professor, via his computerized voice-synthesizer. "I don't think loving is a word I could ascribe to the universe."

"What is a word you could use?" wonders MacLaine.

"Order," replies Hawking. "The universe is well-defined order."

Gregory Benford (review date 7 June 1992)

SOURCE: "Master of the Universe," in *Washington Post Book World*, Vol. XXII, No. 23, June 7, 1992, p. 11.

[*In the following review, Benford surveys Hawking's life and work.*]

When I first came to know Stephen Hawking in the 1970s,

his speech was already nearly unintelligible to all but hisintimates. Yet with laconic humor he soon showed himself to be a complex man who refused to be treated condescendingly because of his slowly worsening "Lou Gehrig's disease." He could be funny, arrogant, pensive, unafraid to bluntly tell others they were wrong, speculative one moment and intricately precise the next.

This is the Hawking who shines through both these books [*Stephen Hawking's A Brief History of Time: A Reader's Companion* and *Stephen Hawking: A Life in Science,* by Michael White and John Gribbin]. *The Reader's Companion* in fact spotlights his companions, with anecdotes related by friends and colleagues. It touches on some of Hawking's startling ideas, with elegantly simple illustrations. White and Gribbin's casually effective biography gives much more of the story, plus thumbnail sketches of how scientists work, think and argue. Their portrait of science as a lived experience in our time is telling and savvy.

Hawking himself rightly scoffs at references to himself as the "new Einstein." He is certainly one of the most influential—and more important, most imaginative—of living scientists. But his stature is not monumental on the scale of Newton, and I suspect that his personal drama transfixes the public more than his insights. As with Einstein, the public lingers long on his life, quickly sliding past the difficult science.

And then there is that metaphor which springs so readily to mind. Like those of a physicist drawn into a black hole, his signals come to us more weakly, pulsing slower, the swallowing darkness sluggishly robbing us of his fine intelligence. Kip Thorne of Caltech remarks on the middle stages of Hawking's disease, when he would make his way up to bed by grabbing hold of the pillars of the stairway, pulling himself up by the strength of his arms alone. It served as physical therapy, "yet at first, when you're a stranger to it, you're really taken aback and you see him through very different emotional eyes than after you've come to know him well."

Resolute, stoic energy became a signature. As Hawking says, in what White and Gribbin suggest would well stand as his epitaph, "One has to be grown up enough to realize that life is not fair. You just have to do the best you can in the situation you are in." Enduring would suffice for most, but Hawking soared.

His slow, descending gyre led him to develop geometrical methods of studying black holes, techniques that did not require writing down long equations. These were intuitive tools others did not have, giving him advantages, a habit of coming at problems with an odd twist. This led to a memorable episode in the early 1970s, when Hawking used the idea that black holes always get larger as they absorb matter, suggesting that the area of a hole is related to the disorder created in enlarging it. Disorder in physics is entropy, which relates to temperature. Following his intuitive nose, Hawking showed that holes do have a temperature, even though it took months for him to convince himself; at first hehad dismissed the idea, which had been introduced by a mere graduate student, Jacob Beckenstein. Slowly Hawking realized that the implied temperature was indeed real and that, like any other object, a black hole with a temperature would radiate. **"Black Holes Aren't Black,"** as the title of his award-winning essay put it, and the discovery rocked the world of physics.

Hawking's mother believes that his affliction has made him concentrate on physics far more, compensating for dwindling physical mastery by building intellectual edifices—"he can so much live in his head." From this internal terrain sprang growing originality. In the last decade he has streamlined his methods still further, speeding toward his goal of understanding, as Einstein put it, whether God had any choice when He made the universe. Rigor slows, so Hawking uses his geometrical intuitions and physical, qualitative arguments to hasten results. "I would rather be right than rigorous," he says. This approach has led him to question whether our idea of time itself is the correct way to regard the origin of the universe—indeed, whether origins mean anything in a deeper picture.

There are compelling glimpses of vast intellectual landscapes in these books, but they share a warmer aspect—science as joy and rivalry, work and awe. We understand the surprise as his Oxford undergraduate friends discover that lazy Stephen has done 10 tough homework problems while they've struggled with one. We can nod, a bit dazed, when Anthony Hewish, a Nobel Laureate, remarks that in his early career, "we didn't even know whether the universe was evolving or steady state," and "the most fantastic thing about the last twenty years is that you can now argue about what went on before a millionth of a second after the beginning of time."

Questions of origin naturally bring in God. Hawking has rather cannily implied that, properly considered, the universe did not do something extra to get started. It could simply exist in its own self-made matrix, needing no God. Do such comments venture unnecessarily beyond physics? Hawking smiles enigmatically. His early agnostic stance has veered toward atheism, and this appears to have contributed to his separation from his wife of 25 years. Yet such severe emotional costs do not deflect him any more than infirmity did. His children remark on his strength of purpose with both wonder and concern.

To the credit of these books, they show Hawking as a whole

man, by turns both stubborn and lofty, both comical and re-mote. They do service to him and to the great intellectual movement of outward discovery he represents.

Stanley Kauffmann (review date 28 September 1992)

SOURCE: "State of Mind," in *New Republic,* Vol. 207, No. 14,September 28, 1992, pp. 28, 30.

[*In the review below, Kauffmann praises* A Reader's Companion *and the film inspired by Hawking's* A Brief History of Time.]

Bantam has recently published *A Reader's Companion to A Brief History of Time*, edited by Stephen Hawking, and a companion it is—not to the book but to the documentary film of that title just released here. Hawking says in his fore-word that "this is The Book of The Film of The Book. I don't know if they are planning a Film of The Book of The Film of The Book."

He can well be jocular: his joke is about a useful book about a completely fascinating film, itself occasioned by a book on theoretical physics that has sold five-and-a-half million copies in thirty languages, written—as many more millions know—by a shrunken and paralyzed Englishman, bound to a wheel-chair, who can communicate only with a "clicker" that connects with a voice synthesizer. (This, he complains, has given him an American accent. I thought it more Irish myself.)

The film, gently and empathically made, is more about the man than the work. It consists principally of interviews: with mother, sister, numerous friends, teachers, students. (Wife and children are absent; there are family difficulties.) These are interwoven with "voice"-overs by Hawking and, inevi-tably, poignant photographs from the healthy past. The *Reader's Companion* prints all the spoken material in the film, plus much that was cut, together with biographical notes on the speakers. I wish the film had identified the speakers: they are listed at the end, but that isn't much help.

The director was Errol Morris, whose *The Thin Blue Line* (1988) I egregiously omitted to review. That picture, which was about a man wrongly convicted of murder in Dallas and which got him exonerated, was made in an intricate, idio-syncratic style. The Hawking film is not. It is a straight T.V. documentary (sponsored by American, British, and Japanese networks), done with skill and warm lighting, principally by John Bailey. Only two matters are unconventional. In the midst of a subject's remarks, the camera often "blinks" as the film cuts to a later part of his/her interview. Presumably

these blinks are left visible like a touch of dissonance in con-ventional music—to keep us alert. And the score by Philip Glass, who also did the score for the earlier Morris film, has an apt spacy feeling.

About Hawking's work at Cambridge, I, along with a few million other purchasers of his book, am incompetent to speak. All the talk of the Black Hole, the Big Bang, and the inevitable Big Crunch sounds like dinner-chat concessions to those with my grip of science; still, they are welcome. Bernard Shaw says somewhere that there is a law of the con-servation of credulity. At one time, people believed that a million angels could dance on the head of a pin. We scoff at them, yet we believe that the Sun is93 million miles from the Earth. Most of us have as much reason of our own to believe one proposition as the other: we take the word of experts. I and millions of others are quite willing, and pre-sumably quite right, to believe that Hawking has a giant mind, that he is rightly placed in a professorial chair once held by Newton.

But Hawking's personal story is within the grasp of all, and grasp is the right word: it grips. He was a bright boy and youth, keen on mathematical problems and on dancing. He was bright, too, at Oxford but, he says, lazy:

> I was on the borderline between a first-and second-class degree. I had to be interviewed to determine which I should get. They asked me about my fu-ture plans. I replied that I wanted to do research. If they gave me a first, I would go to Cambridge. If they gave me a second, I would stay in Oxford. They gave me a first.

Hawking suffers from amyotrophic lateral sclerosis—Lou Gehrig's disease. The onset of the sclerosis, his marriage, and the arrival of his three children, in that order, are shown; further developments in his private life are not. We get a clear view of his present state and his mode of contending with his condition in order to get on with his work. Nurses are constantly in attendance. His office—a replica made for filming—is decorated with two large photos of Marilyn Monroe. (The closing credits thank the photographer Philippe Halsman for the right of reproduction here—a nicely anomalous touch for a film about a scientist.)

Hawking is not religious. The central question of his think-ing, as put by a friend, is: "Why does the universe go to all the bother of existing?" It's not a question that would plague a religious person—at least, not phrased that way. Hawk-ing, according to Michael White and John Gribbin in their biography, "is not an atheist; he simply finds the idea of faith something he cannot absorb into his view of the Uni-verse." Perhaps it's as well for physics and the world that he (dis)believes as he does.

But more persists in this film than the fervor of a rationalist trying to move toward an explanation of everything—of more than everything. His very life apostrophizes the work being done in that life. Here is a scientist saved for science by science. Before the invention and development of computer technology and all the other sophisticated devices that make his being possible, he would long since have been merely a sad case, a mute prisoner within a useless body. He stands (figuratively, alas) in the forefront of science because other scientists have made it possible—almost a science-fiction figure, a nearly disembodied brain.

Within that empowerment by science, something seems to be happening for which scientific thought and research areultimately only the medium. When we hear the deaf Beethoven's music or look at the maimed Renoir's paintings, we mutter about courage, physical and moral, about the fire of genius overcoming handicaps. Beneath that fire, however, there is another: the fire of self, the refusal of the ego, sheer ego, to be slighted by fate.

Few of us can judge Hawking's intellect, but any of us can sense that fire, that insistence of self on self. Stephen Hawking (thinks Stephen Hawking) is going to have only one chance, one time around, and before he slips into infinity, Hawking wants Hawking to make that chance the fullest one possible. He is the sole guardian of his particular collection of brain cells and curiosities, and illness or not, he seems amiably imperious in his intent to make the most of them. For this reason, along with several others, Morris's film about him is viscerally and intellectually thrilling.

Curt Suplee (review date 12 September 1993)

SOURCE: A review of *Black Holes and Baby Universes and Other Essays*, in *Washington Post Book World*, Vol. XXIII, No. 37, September 12, 1993, p. 6.

[*In the excerpt below, Suplee contends that while* Black Holes and Baby Universes *is interesting, it adds nothing new to Hawking's theories in* A Brief History of Time.]

If asked to list the cruelest disappointments of modern life, most folks will cite their first date, latest paycheck and page 134 of Stephen Hawking's *A Brief History of Time*.

That is the point at which the fabled Cambridge physicist is just about to reveal his theory on the shape and fate of the whole confounded cosmos—and then notes that, of course, it can only be understood in terms of "imaginary time" whose values produce negative numbers when squared. Make that simple adjustment and presto: "The dis-

tinction between time and space disappears completely." So, alas, does comprehension.

Even brand-name brains boggle at imaginary time, and many a reader reluctantly abandoned the book in intellectual despair. But now, five years later, a new Hawking volume has arrived. And naturally expectations are high that *Black Holes and Baby Universes and Other Essays* will fill the very considerable explanatory gaps left by *Brief History*.

But no. The new book is merely a collection of Hawking's various speeches and writings (including a Scientific American article 16 years old!) that have never been published together—for the excellent reason that there is no particular need to do so. The 14 short pieces range from reminiscences about his childhood to athoroughly conventional plea for greater public understanding of science to various lectures on astrophysics to the transcript of a BBC interview broadcast last Christmas.

The autobiographical material is pretty familiar. Born in 1942 to a somewhat eccentric research physician and his wife, Hawking was the eldest of four children. He went to such a progressive school that he was 8 years old before he learned to read. He was fascinated with toy trains, and eventually chose to study physics because it was the "most fundamental science" even though it was demonstrably "the most boring subject at school because it was so easy and obvious. Chemistry was much more fun because unexpected things, like explosions, kept happening."

At 17 he went to Oxford, where he detected the first premonitory signs of Lou Gehrig's disease, a progressive motor-nerve disorder that would eventually confine him to a wheelchair and require 24-hour nursing care. After a period of depression ("I took to listening to Wagner, but reports . . . that I drank heavily are an exaggeration"), his engagement to "a girl called Jane Wilde" "gave me something to live for." Apparently so: He finished his doctorate at Cambridge, fathered three children and became one of the most distinguished theoreticians in modern memory. This despite a tracheostomy that left him able to speak only through a computer voice synthesizer. Hawking has never been interested in revealing personal details of his illness or how he coped with it, and continues that reticence here.

He wrote the phenomenally successful *Brief History* in part to pay his daughter's school bills, chose Bantam as the publisher because "I wanted it to be the sort of book that would sell in airport book stalls," and vigorously disputes the idea that "Bantam shamefully exploited my illness and that I cooperated with this by allowing my picture to appear on the cover. In fact, under my contract I had no control over the cover."

In the BBC interview, he reveals a keen fondness for music, and a surprisingly eclectic taste. Asked what records he would want if marooned on a desert island, he cites Poulenc's "Gloria," Brahms' Violin Concerto, Beethoven's String Quartet (Op. 132), Act One of "The Valkyrie," The Beatles' "Please Please Me" and Edith Piaf singing "*Je Ne Regrette Rien*" among others. The last, he writes, "just about sums up my life."

The eight scientific pieces, though interesting, are largely a restatement of material treated at more commodious length in *Brief History*. Seven of them are texts of speeches that contain a great deal of overlap, including repetition of some of the same jokes. People curious about Hawking's mind-stretching insights into cosmology will be better served by returning to the original 1988 volume, which still offers the biggest cerebral bang for the buck.

Economist (review date 6 November 1993)

SOURCE: "The Mind of Stephen Hawking," in *Economist*, Vol. 329, November 6, 1993, pp. 120-21.

[*In the following review of* Black Holes and Baby Universes and Other Essays, *the critic states that the essays are repetitive and provide little insight about the author.*]

Histories of 20th-century physics will surely have a place for Professor Stephen Hawking. So will histories of publishing. His work on the nature of black holes and the origin of the universe earned him the respect of other cosmologists. The descriptions of that work in *A Brief History of Time* earned him fame, record-breaking bestsellerdom, and stacks of money.

His new book is a collection of essays and speeches. The two forms are in large part indistinguishable for Mr Hawking. Before his tracheostomy, the degenerative nerve disease that confines him to a wheel-chair had so slurred his speech that his talks had to be delivered by an interpreter. Since his tracheostomy in 1985, he has used a computerised speech synthesiser, and it has given him a new lease of life as a public speaker. The pre-programmed words can be delivered to a lecture hall direct from the chair. As the man who made a film devoted to his ideas remarked, Mr Hawking, mute and immobile, has become the ultimate non-talking head.

With his condition, it has been easy to cast him as the disembodied mind of man. His intellectual quarry is, he would claim, the essence of the universe: the natural laws which say why the universe is the way that it is, and is not—cannot be—any other way. He believes this complete theory

to be near at hand and he imbues it with phenomenal qualities. In the hyperbolic conclusion of the *Brief History*, he spoke of the "how" of the complete theory as a basis for divining the "why" of "the mind of God".

The essays in the current slim volume will not provide any reader of the *Brief History* with much further enlightenment on the mind of God or the science of cosmology. Much that is new in cosmology is not covered. In 1992, for example, hints of the structure of the very early universe were revealed by a satellite survey of the cosmic microwave background. Mr Hawking described it then as: "The most important scientific discovery of the century, perhaps of all time." That might lead you to expect that he would write about it—if only to apologise for saying something so silly. But there is nothing about it in the book at all.

The fact that the essays repeat each other, as well as the *Brief History*, is not necessarily the weakness it might appear. These are difficult topics, and to see them presented slightly differently from piece to piece may allow the reader to develop a better picture of the subject as a whole. One of the fascinating things about Mr Hawking's work is how many different pictures can be used to evoke its mathematical truths. The radiation that comes from black holes can, for instance, be seen as travelling backwards in time or faster than light, depending on your preference—or can be seen as a temperature thrust on the hole by the laws of thermodynamics. Given that the travellers in Mr Hawking's universe are blind without sophisticated mathematics and the concepts of higher physics, it is a good idea for them to be given as many chances to touch the elephant as possible.

Some themes, though, are simply confused by repetition. Take the mind of God. In these essays, Mr Hawking admits the point that he finessed in the other book.

> Although science may solve the problem of how the universe began, it cannot answer the question: Why does the universe bother to exist? I don't know the answer to that.

At another point, he suggests that the initial conditions of the universe may have been chosen by God, or may have been determined by the laws of science. By presenting the two as alternatives he appears to allow a place for God; in fact, though, he relegates God to a position of no more profound significance than that of the physics—an explanation of how, not why. No reader of this book could come away imagining that Stephen Hawking really knows, or feels he needs to know, anything about God.

Steven Weinberg, a physicist as eminent as Mr Hawking and a far better writer, ended his "The First Three Minutes" with the bleak insight that "the more the universe seems comprehensible, the more it also seems pointless." It is hard not to feel that Mr Hawking's position must, at heart, be something similar. That is fine: there is no reason why the universe should have any intrinsic point, or, if it does, why anybody should expect physicists to be able to reveal it. But if Mr Hawking is not really employed in an effort to read the mind of God, what is the feeling that animates him so strongly?

Mr Weinberg suggests that the search itself is a source of solace for the searchers, "one of the very few things that lifts human life a little above the level of farce." Yet this process is not one about which Mr Hawking is forthcoming. He explains ideas as they are in his mind, rather than as they came to be—he is not interested in explaining the workings of his mind or of his discipline. His autobiographical sketches are curiously distant; the only time at which he begins to intrigue the reader as a person is in the transcript of an interview on the BBC's "Desert Island Discs", broadcast in 1992. Here there are glimpses of a fully rounded figure, one who listens to the slow movement of a Beethoven's string quartet, Opus 132 (which thanks God for the end of an illness), while associating it with suicide, one who reaches the heights of pleasure through mental exertion. How much more interesting it would be to read that man's book.

Sara Maitland (review date 20 November 1993)

SOURCE: "The Art of Giving," in *New Scientist,* Vol. 140, No. 1900, November 20, 1993, pp. 40-1.

[*In the excerpt below, Maitland writes that* Black Holes and Baby Universes *is patronising and not rigorous enough in its explanation of science.*]

About five years ago, partly because I wanted to write about dinosaurs in a novel, partly because of some theological questions, and partly because I had a curious child, I decided to learn more about science. It was not easy to find helpful books: a quick tribute here to Stephen Hawking (*A Brief History of Time*), Paul Davies (for *inter alia, The Mind of God*), Keith Devlin (*Mathematics; The New Golden Age*) and many others.

Apart from learning all sorts of things to expand the mind and the imagination, I have also been forced to consider a major cultural problem that we have in Britain: while science students are supposed to be "well-rounded", arts students are not. Coming from a decidedly arts background myself, I feel deprived.

I am not alone in feeling there is something amiss here. In the 1950s C.P. Snow was writing with concern about "the two cultures". In his new book about genetics, Colin Tudge analyses the problem:

"Quite simply science [is] not in the public domain . . . this is far more true in Britain than in many other countries. In Britain indeed educated people take pride in not knowing any science. We live in a society dominated by science and technology, but we do not live in a science 'culture'. Science and technology are not treated as a flowering of human creativeness . . . . I want to describe the new science of genetics largely to show just how interesting it is. . . . Science is not a penance. It contains some of the greatest excitements that any pursuit has to offer: aesthetic as well as intellectual."

Presumably *New Scientist* is not the most important place to raise this concern as its existence is a major challenge to the dominant culture, but as readers you might consider doing your bit for a new culture by giving science books to your less scientific friends and relatives for Christmas. They must, of course, be the right books.

I have been thinking a good deal recently about what sort of books these are. I think the clue may lie in two words in Tudge's last sentence: "excitements" and "aesthetic". Arts-oriented people really do want to know, really are interested, but we are scared. No one likes feeling stupid; and we feel stupid if the text is inaccessible or we feel we are being patronised. To take two negative examples: Gianfranco Vidali's *Superconductivity: TheNext Revolution* is scary. Some of this is Cambridge's fault: it is packaged like a textbook, not like a good read. But some of it, however, is Vidali's he uses the royal "we" throughout (bad mistake—scientists are distant enough without them avoiding the first person). On the second page he writes: "We require only some background in high school or introductory college physics." Do we indeed? Then I don't measure up. On a quick skim through the pages there are far too many complicated-looking diagrams, which convey no immediate information. I did struggle through and learn a great deal, but I would not have done so if I had not been invited to review it.

Stephen Hawking's new collection of essays, ***Black Holes and Baby Universes,*** errs in the opposite direction: a good deal of it seems extremely patronising. Apart from giving almost everyone a nannyish ticking off (TV producers, philosophers and the public are all apparently acting irresponsibly) Hawking reiterates his conviction that "each equation I included would halve the sales". I am sure that this is untrue . . . and it lets the writer off too easily. This is a slight and irritating volume: mostly not about science at all, but about Hawking's low opinion of the rest of us.

John Leslie (review date 12 May 1994)

SOURCE: "The Absolute Now," in *London Review of Books,* May 12, 1994, pp. 15-16.

[*In the following excerpt, Leslie reviews* Black Holes and Baby Universes *and asserts that while he admires Hawking's work, the essays make contradictory arguments.*]

After the enormous press coverage of *A Brief History of Time,* all the world knows that Stephen Hawking has motor neurone disease, can speak only with a computer-synthesised voice controlled by the few fingers that he can move, and fills the same Cambridge chair as Newton did. The 14 essays of the new book, together with a Christmas Day radio interview of 1992, form a very mixed bunch. They cover Hawking's early years, his experiences with slowly progressing paralysis, his views about the human race and its probable future, and some of his physical and cosmological ideas. These are introduced at levels varying from the elementary to the fairly advanced: one of the essays is his Inaugural Lecture of 1980. Mathematical formulas are avoided.

Hawking's essay number five, **"A Brief History of *A Brief History,"*** tells us that despite dust-jacket photographs—not, he emphasises, a matter under his control—of the severely crippled author, the huge sales of the earlier book came as a big surprise both to him and to his publishers. I find this hard to understand. Hawking's personal history was scarcely mentioned in the book itself, but journalists would scarcely have been likelyto overlook it. His unremarkable performance at school (he was nearly demoted to a 'B' stream); his managing to get a first at Oxford despite working at physics for only about an hour a day; his later sudden energy, inspired by his wife and by the idea that he was unlikely to live much longer; his rapid rise to the Lucasian Professorship as his health continued to crumble; his unwillingness to allow his condition to end scientific work of first-rate importance although at one stage his only means of communication was by waggling his eyebrows; his probing of the cosmos from the depths of a wheelchair; what journalist worth his salt would disregard these things? The sales figures were not surprising.

It so happens that the book was very well worth reading. People in universities, and philosophers in particular, tended to complain about its obscurities, but popular writing almost never escapes that kind of reaction. And the book's central ideas made it of greater philosophical interest than almost all the volumes ever written by philosophers.

Black Holes and Baby Universes will help those eager to learn more about Hawking's stubborn war against his paralysed condition. It will also be certain to upset the same philosophers as before; not entirely unwarrantably. Hawking's ideas are often very exciting. One would love to understand them. But often this is no easy task-and not always just because physics and cosmology are difficult subjects. At many crucial points his explanations are highly oracular. Quite often their obscurity is recognised good-humouredly, apologetically; sometimes, though, it is defended in words which can easily sound too bellicose. Hawking is a warrior through and through—a great contrast with David Bohm.

Take one of the book's chief ideas: that all the details of the universe, including the workings of our minds, could be explained by a Theory of Everything-some fairly simple set of laws dictating events right back to the beginning of time. These laws might actually be discovered within our lifetimes, Hawking thinks. What form would a Theory of Everything take? The Inaugural Lecture bets fairly heavily on a theory called 'N=8 Extended Supergravity'. In the book's later essays attention centres on something else. In the Sixties, Hawking and Roger Penrose seemed to have shown that any universe beginning in a state of infinite density, a 'singularity', which is how our universe was thought to have begun, would necessarily begin unpredictably. All Theories of Everything would fail at the very earliest times. But Hawking later came to believe that quantum physics allowed the beginning—at least as modelled in 'imaginary time', which is in some ways more like space than like ordinary time—to be entirely free of singularities. All of the universe's events, from start to finish, might then be dictated by a few fairly simple mathematical equations. And although the universe wouldn't have existed eternally, there would have been no time before it began, just as there is no place on Earth to the northof the North Pole. There would thus have been no need for a divine being to make things spring into existence at one moment rather than another.

Hawking admits that he cannot explain why the universe began: what it is that, as he puts it, 'breathes fire into the equations'. Again, he points to evidence which could well show that the universe is fine-tuned to life's requirements. Very small changes in such things as the strength of electromagnetism, or the mass difference between the neutron and the proton, could well have made it a universe in which life would never have evolved. As he remarks, this might suggest that there exist hugely many universes, their characters varying randomly. Necessarily, we living beings would then find ourselves in one of the universes which just happened to be life-permitting. But when you talk of this or that 'just happening' to be so, a Theory of Everything is of course in difficulty.

There are two other important problems for any such theory. The first comes from Hawking's most famous discovery: that black holes aren't completely black. A black hole was traditionally described as a system whose gravitational pull was so strong that light itself couldn't escape from it. To everybody's surprise, Hawking showed that light—together with particles of all kinds, including (on very, very rare occasions) particles which simply chanced to form television sets or the works of Proust in ten leatherbound volumes—could tunnel out of black holes by exploiting quantum theory's Uncertainty Principle. Black holes would therefore 'evaporate', at first very slowly but eventually with extreme violence. Their final explosions might release energies equivalent to those of ten-million-megaton H-bombs. One strong possibility is that black holes would give rise to separate 'baby universes' which would later rejoin our universe—as black holes evaporating into it—at unpredictable times and places. Here would be a reason why a Theory of Everything could fail.

The second problem is still more interesting-and highlights the difference between the warriorship of Stephen Hawking and the quieter advocacy of David Bohm. The fact is that Hawking's model of the universe incorporates many-worlds quantum theory. The key ideas of this theory were formulated by Hugh Everett nearly forty years ago. Quantum physics appears to tell us that the universe is intrinsically unpredictable. Events keep developing in fuzzy ways. The fuzziness then 'collapses' into something definite, but one never can say just what a collapse will lead to. Look at an electron at one moment. Nobody can tell precisely when and where this particular electron will next be seen. Everett suggested, however, that collapses never really occur. Instead, the universe continually streams into branches which develop differently. Observers branch like everything else. Thus you can never say exactly what you—'you' being just one branch of the you of a moment ago—will see until you actually look. The big question is, whether Hawking really believes any of this. He answersoracularly but with no apologies—even, indeed, a little aggressively.

I teach philosophy for a living. I can see why other philosophers, including those who admire Hawking's work as greatly as I do, can often read him only with sighs of frustration. Look at his essay number twelve. This discusses human freedom against the background of his belief that the world is fully deterministic-so that if it could somehow be rewound and started off again precisely as before, then everyone would do precisely what they did on the first occasion. Hawking ties himself in knots. He could be expected to opt for the 'compatibilist' view, defended by philosophers in their thousands, that even such decision-making machines as advanced computers, while remaining fully deterministic, could still really make decisions, in which case they should be described as free. However, it seems never to have entered his head that freedom and deterministic decision-making might be compatible. He declares that, because we are fully deterministic, we cannot be free. Yet he then goes

on to say—in maddening disregard of the fact that one *ought* to do something only if *free* to do it or not do it—that we all *ought* to pretend to ourselves that we are free, although we aren't. What a tangle! Yet why, after all, should a philosopher expect Hawking to discuss freedom expertly? Does it matter if he gets tangled up? Surely not. It is, however, immensely frustrating that one can't make out where he stands on such philosophically fascinating questions as whether many-worlds quantum theory is right. Does Hawking's universe actually branch, or doesn't it?

He appears to reply in two flatly contradictory ways. He tells us firmly that there isn't just a single history of the universe. Instead there is a collection of all physically possible histories. One and the same cat can die of old age in one history, while dying much earlier by violence in another. These branches are equally real. People who refuse to believe this have missed 'the whole point of quantum mechanics'. And yet, virtually in the same breath, Hawking says that all this concerns 'just a mathematical model' and that it makes no sense to ask whether any theory of physics 'corresponds to reality'. He also says that philosophers (and while he avoids spelling it out, many top-flight physicists too) are tediously out of date when they keep puzzling over the foundations of quantum mechanics.

It would be nice to think that in other equally real universe branches, Hawking has written just as interestingly but a little less oracularly and a little more mildly.

Michael Rowan-Robinson (review date 25 January 1996)

SOURCE: "On the Wilder Shores of Cosmology," in *Nature*, Vol. 379, No. 6563, January 25, 1996, pp. 309-10.

[*In the following excerpt, Rowan-Robinson remarks favorably on* The Nature of Space and Time.]

Stephen Hawking and Roger Penrose are well-known both for their work on the nature of black holes and for successful books for the general public. ***The Nature of Space and Time*** has its origin in a series of lectures that they gave at a study programme in 1994 at the Isaac Newton Institute in Cambridge. They outline their past and current work on the global causal structure of space-time, singularity theorems, cosmic censorship, the laws of blackhole dynamics, quantum black holes, Schrödinger's cat paradox, the no-boundary proposal, the arrow of time, and the twistor view of space-time. This is an extremely demanding book, with many equations, and requires some knowledge of general relativity and quantum theory. The main theme of the lectures is the quantization of general relativity. Hawking's work on quantum effects near black holes and Penrose's on twistor theory have proved enormously illuminating, but few physicists, I think, believe that a full quantization of general relativity will be achieved along these paths. A better bet, surely, is string theory, despite the difficulty of developing this to the state of testable predictions. The claims made for the no-boundary proposal seem overstated. The 'prediction' of the microwave background fluctuations detected by COBE is a success also claimed by the whole generic class of inflationary theories. The debate between the positivist Hawking and the platonist Penrose on how the paradox of Schrödinger's cat should be understood is enjoyable, though the comparison with the classic debate between Einstein and Bohr in the 1920s on the correct interpretation of quantum theory, made by Michael Atiyah in his introduction, seems a bit grandiose.

John Barrow (review date 16 March 1996)

SOURCE: "Battle of the Giants," in *New Scientist,* Vol. 149, No. 2021, March 16, 1996, pp. 48-9.

[*In the following review of* The Nature of Time and Space, *Barrow states that the book's debate format works well and the author's theories are clearly explained.*]

General relativity and quantum theory have always held a special fascination for physicists. They govern empires that appear superficially disjoint and rule their separate dominions with a precision unmatched by any other products of the human mind. The accuracy of Einstein's general theory of relativity, for example, is demonstrated by the spectacular observations of a pulsar engaged in a gravitational pas de deux with a dead star. Einstein's expectations are born out by observations—accurate to one part in 10 14. Almost as impressive is the accuracy of the quantum theory: agreeing with experiment at one part in 10 11.

The quantum world deviates strongly from those of Newton when things are very small. By contrast, general relativity only changes Newton's predictions when gravitational fields are strong and masses are very large. These conditions rarely overlap except in the cosmological problem of the Universe's first expansive moments.

Over the past thirty years, Stephen Hawking and Roger Penrose have done more than anyone to further our understanding of the nature of gravitation and cosmology. Both have developed new approaches to these problems that differ from the mainstream work by particle physicists (and from each other). *The Nature of Space and Time* is the result of their attempt to stage a structured dialogue about these problems, to isolate points of disagreement, and stimu-

late further investigation of these problems. Alternate lectures are presented by the two protagonists, culminating in a final debate where they summarise their points of agreement and disagreement. The level of argument is highly technical, but you can skip the equations and still get a feel for what is going on.

Generally, great debates in science don't work. Science is not a democratic activity in which the idea that gains the most popular votes wins. Politicians need not apply. Nonetheless, this volume shows that this adversarial style can be extremely valuable—at least at a textual level. Both authors are well acquainted with each others' ideas and write with great clarity. They agree on much and have to struggle a bit to play up points of disagreement over the interpretation of quantum mechanics, irreversibility, violation of CPT in gravitational collapse, the equivalence of black and white holes.

The opening two lectures introduce the minimum collection of ideas from differential topology needed to understand what a singularity is (an edge of space-time found, for example in a black hole, where all laws of physics break down), and the conditions under which it would be inevitable in our past. Then they move on to quantum effects and gravity with Hawking discussing black hole thermodynamics and introducing Euclidean methods. Penrose lets the cat out of the bag (and into a box) introducing the problems of interpreting quantum measurement, even proposing a simple formula for the time duration of wave function collapse.

The final pair of lectures is about quantum cosmology. Hawking argues for the inevitability of the Hartle-Hawking "no-boundary" condition as a way of describing the initial state of the Universe which uses quantum mechanics to explain how time originates at the big bang. Penrose, on the other hand, argues for some measure of gravitational entropy. In this picture the second law of thermodynamics implies that a low value for gravitational entropy at the initial state would be natural. So the Universe would be almost isotropic and homogeneous initially, but chaotically irregular at any final singularity.

If you cast a critical cosmological eye over the proceedings, then several things are evident. Neither author is very impressed by superstring theory (to the exasperation of at least one questioner at the end of the lecture), both have wonderful geometrical intuitions and their taste in theories is strongly influenced by that penchant. Neither believes that inflation—the fashionable idea that the Universe underwent a phase of accelerated expansion in the first moment of its existence—is the whole answer to the problem of why the Universe is so isotropic and homogeneous today. And neither adequately considers the impact of cosmological inflation upon their viewpoint.

Hawking argues that superstring theories make no observable predictions that are not those of general relativity, to which superstrings reduce when gravity is weak. By contrast, he also claims that the no-boundary condition of quantum cosmology makes two successful predictions: the amplitude and spectrum of fluctuations in the microwave background. This claim is surely a piece of gamesmanship. These two predictions come from inflation, not from the no-boundary condition. The no-boundary condition allows inflation to occur but only by adding extra matter called a scalar field. This leads to the observed spectral slope of the fluctuations in microwave background radiations, but I could just as well have inserted a different scalar field into the early Universe which would give fluctuations in conflict with the observations, even though the no-boundary condition still holds.

The "correct" fluctuations come in all cases from an arbitrary choice of the scalar field, rather than from any prediction of the no-boundary condition itself.

Another important aspect of the picture of an inflationary Universe that both authors ignore is that observation requires only the "beginning" of the Universe be uniform over a tiny region. Inflation can enlarge that uniform region so that now it is almost uniform over a region larger than our entire visible Universe. Beyond our horizon, however, the Universe could be quite different. The global structure of the Universe today may be extremely irregular: parts may be collapsing, rotating or possess huge variations in density. This possibility arises naturally from general initial conditions.

The possibility of such initial conditions cuts through many of the assumptions made by both protagonists in this debate. They both maintain that current observations require a high level of uniformity in the initial stages of the Universe, using this to justify their own strong theories about cosmological initial conditions. But the observations do not require this and the initial state may have been globally highly irregular, contrary to Penrose's claim that the initial Weyl curvature was very small or Hawking's claim that the Universe began in a ground state defined by the no-boundary condition.

Considering this possibility is vital because, if allowed, it changes the entire nature of the Universe. It removes the evidence for any initial state of low "gravitational entropy" or the need to distinguish fundamentally between initial and final singularities. Indeed, there need be neither a global initial singularity nor any quantum tunnelling of the Universe out of nothing. It shows how cosmology is unlike any other physical problem: the causal horizon structure of the Universe forbids us access to the information that we require to test a theory of cosmological initial conditions.

The debate between Hawking and Penrose is a live one between brilliant scientists that covers far more ground than their seven cameo lectures can encompass. This elegant little volume provides a clear account of two approaches to some of the greatest unsolved problems of gravitation and cosmology. It is recommended to critical readers who should not forget that there are other more widely supported views about these cosmological problems. Which, if any, view is true? At present only God knows—or maybe not.

Robert M. Wald (review date 7 June 1996)

SOURCE: "Quantum Gravitationists," in *Science*, Vol. 272, June 7, 1996, p. 1445.

[*In the following review, Wald remarks that although* The Nature of Space and Time *may be "too technical for a layperson," most readers "should be able to enjoy the flavor of much of the discussion."*]

The theory of general relativity was formulated in a mathematically complete form 80 years ago, and the basic principles of quantum theory were laid out about 70 years ago. Nevertheless, only within the past few decades have major efforts been under way to merge these theories into a mathematically consistent and complete quantum theory of gravitation. Despite these efforts, research in quantum gravity remains highly speculative, with very few solidly established results and with wide disagreements among researchers not only about the best approach to take but even about what unresolved issues deserve the most attention.

Stephen Hawking and Roger Penrose are, without question, the leading developers of our modern view of the structure of space and time. In particular, their singularity theorems and their contributions to the theory of black holes have provided us with major new insights. Both Hawking and Penrose have given considerable thought to the relationship between quantum theory and gravitation. In view of the situation noted in the paragraph above, it is not surprising that they differ widely in their views.

[*The Nature of Space and Time*] is based on a series of public lectures by Hawking and Penrose and is described as a debate between them. This characterization is accurate only if one understands the term "debate" in the sense used in American Presidential campaigns. Both Hawking and Penrose do an excellent job of expounding their own views and perspectives on fundamental issues related to space-time structure and quantum theory. Although they make some criticisms of each other's views as well as some criticisms of other alternative approaches (including some "one line zingers" on string theory), most of the criticisms and responses are of a "sound bite" nature; there is relatively little direct engagement at a deep level between them in the book.

The first two chapters (one each by Hawking and Penrose) discuss some key concepts and results in modern general relativity. Almost all of these results are solidly grounded, and there is little or no disagreement between Hawking and Penrose here. Chapter 3, by Hawking, describes his work on particle creation by black holes and some related (somewhat more speculative) ideas in Euclidean quantum gravity. Chapter 4, by Penrose, primarily introduces his concerns about quantum measurement theory. Chapter 5, by Hawking, presents his (much more speculative) views on quantum cosmology, while chapter 6, by Penrose, contains a very brief discussion of twistor theory and his views on how it may related to quantum gravity. The final chapter, entitled "debate," contains some direct engagement between Hawking and Penrose on issues such as "Schrodinger's cat," Euclidean methods in quantum gravity, and the equivalence or inequivalence of black holes and white holes. All of the main ideas in the book have appeared in previous scientific writings by the authors (and, indeed, their views do not seem to have evolved significantly in the past decade or so), but the discussion here is much more lively and informal than can be found elsewhere.

Most of the details of the arguments given in [*The Nature of Space and Time*] are far too technical for a layperson to follow—or even a physicist not specializing in general relativity or related areas. Nevertheless, even readers without much technical background should be able to enjoy the flavor of much of the discussion. This is an interesting book to read now, but it promises to become an even more interesting book for future generations of physicists, after it becomes more clear which present-day ideas lie on the path toward the development of a quantum theory of gravity.

John Preskill (review date July 1996)

SOURCE: A review of *The Nature of Space and Time*, in *Physics Today*, July, 1996, pp. 60-1.

[*In the review below, Preskill describes* The Nature of Space and Time *as "a succinct and clear technical account of the penetrating work and thought of two of our most brilliant and eloquent scientists."*]

The clash between Niels Bohr and Albert Einstein over the meaning of quantum theory greatly clarified some fundamental issues, but to this day it is widely felt that their differences have never been satisfactorily resolved. It seems most appropriate, then, for two leading physicists of the current era to carry on the debate, and who could be better

qualified than Stephen Hawking and Roger Penrose? Arguably, the two most profound developments in general relativity since Einstein were the introduction of the global analysis of causal structure by Penrose an the discovery of black-hole radiance by Hawking. Furthermore, both men are justly admired for their lucidity of their writings and lectures, and they disagree sharply on some fundamental questions.

The Nature of Space and Time is based on a Hawking-Penrose debate that took place in England, at the University of Cambridge, in the spring of 1994; the "debate" consisted of alternating lectures (three by each author) followed by a final joint discussion. The lectures revealed that there is much on which Hawking and Penrose agree. Both believe that black holes destroy information and hence undermine the foundations of quantum theory. Both argue that the origin of the second law of thermodynamics can be traced back to the extremely homogeneous conditions that reigned in the very early universe and that it is ultimately the task of quantum gravity to explain these initial conditions. They also seem to agree that general relativity, a beautiful and highly successful fundamental theory, sometimes fails to get the respect it deserves from the particle physicists.

Various points of disagreement are mentioned at least in passing. Hawking advocated the Euclidean path-integral approach to the fundamental issues of quantum gravity; Penrose is skeptical. Hawking offers the "no boundary proposal" (rooted in the Euclidean formalism to account for the initial conditions in the Big Bang; Penrose prefers the more phenomenological Weyl-curvature hypothesis. Hawking believes that the universe must be closed (as seems to be required by the no-boundary proposal); Penrose favors an open universe (which meshes more easily with his idea that quantum gravity should be formulated in terms of "twistors"). Hawking is an enthusiast of the inflationary-universe; Penrose is not.

There are two important issues over which the disagreements are more profound and more interesting. First, there is disagreement about the time-reversal invariance (or more precisely, *CPT* invariance) of the microscopic laws of nature. Hawking has a strong conviction that *CPT* is an inviolable symmetry. But Penrose believes that the quantum behavior of black holes shows otherwise; he argues that the laws of quantum gravity must make a fundamental distinction between past and future singularities. Further, they disagree about the measurement problem of quantum theory; Penrose insists that there must be a genuine physical mechanism underlying the "reduction of the state vector" in the measurement process, and he further proposes that quantum gravity plays an essential role in this reduction; Hawking rejects these ideas.

These are certainly fascinating questions, so it is rather disappointing that the authors do not flesh out their positions more fully. To understand Penrose's views clearly, I needed to reread his previous books, especially chapters 6-8 of *The Emperor's New Mind* and chapter 6 of *Shadows of the Mind*. The key problem repeatedly stressed by Penrose in *The Nature of Space and Time* is that we never perceive macroscopic superpositions—the famous conundrum of Schrodinger's cat. This emphasis surprises me. While the modern theory of decoherence is surely incomplete—it is largely based on heuristic arguments and oversimplified models—I think that there is a plausible explanation, within conventional quantum theory, for the fact that superpositions of macroscopically distinct states decohere very rapidly. Penrose thinks otherwise. There may be other more serious objections to the foundations of quantum theory, some of which are mentioned in Penrose's other books, but these receive scant attention here. Hawking, for his part, defends the status quo, but in so sketchy a manner as to provide little guidance for the perplexed.

I should not give the impression that this is a book about the measurement problem in quantum theory; the lectures largely address other issues: Hawking's three lectures concern global methods and singularity theorems; quantum black holes and information loss; and quantum cosmology, inflation and the origin of the anisotropy of the cosmic background radiation. These lectures are unapologetically mathematical, at an appropriate level for a graduate student in theoretical physics but quite beyond the grasp of the typical lay reader. Penrose's lectures on cosmic censorship, the measurement problem and twistors are less demanding than Hawking's (and about half as long), but they are also intended for a mathematically sophisticated audience. Advanced students and even some experts will appreciate, for example, Hawking's succinct summary of the ideas underlying the singularity theorems or Penrose's overview of the ideas motivating the twistor program.

There is much to savor in this slim volume, but as a dialogue on fundamental issues in quantum theory, it falls well short of expectations. A reader seeking an exposition of Penrose's unconventional views will do better to read his other books. For a well-presented defense of the conventional wisdom, I would recommend *The Interpretation of Quantum Mechanics* by Roland Omnes. Still, we should appreciate this little book for what it is—a succinct and clear technical account of the penetrating work and thought of two of our most brilliant and eloquent scientists.

FURTHER READING

Biographies

Hawking, Stephen. "Handicapped People and Science." *Science Digest* 92, No. 9 (September 1984): 92.

Discusses his physical handicap and encourages others to make the best of their situation.

Criticism

Drees, Willem B. "Stephen Hawking: Timeless Quantum Cosmology." *Zygon* 26 (September 1991): 378-96.

Explores the implications Hawking's cosmology has for theology.

Lovejoy, Derek. "The Dialectics of the Tenth Dimension: Some Recent Writings on Science, Philosophy and the Cosmos." *Science & Society* 59 (Summer 1995): 206-22.

Discusses recent work in the area of physics and society, including Hawking's *A Brief History of Time*.

Lovell, Bernard. "Friedmann's Expanding Universe." *Times Literary Supplement*, No. 4743 (25 February 1994): 5-6.

Surveys recent works on cosmology, including Hawking's *Black Holes and Baby Universes*.

Pollard, B. R. Review of *Superspace and Supergravity*, edited by Stephen Hawking and M. Rocek. *British Book News* (September 1981): 541.

Considers the collection a timely review of the work being done on supergravity.

Interviews

Sampson, Russ. "Two Hours with Stephen Hawking." *Astronomy* 21, No. 3 (March 1993): 13, 16.

Remarks on a press conference with Hawking at the University of Alberta.

Additional coverage of Hawking's life and career is contained in the following sources published by Gale: *Authors and Artists for Young Adults*, Vol. 13; *Bestsellers 1989*, No. 1; *Contemporary Authors*, Vols. 126, 129; and *Contemporary Authors New Revision Series*, Vol. 48.

Spike Lee
1957-

(Full name Shelton Jackson Lee) American director, producer, screenwriter, nonfiction writer, and actor.

The following entry presents an overview of Lee's career through 1996.

INTRODUCTION

Spike Lee has become a cultural icon in America. Known for his outspokenness as well as for his films, Lee has attracted both controversy and critical attention. Tackling such topics as racism, the life of slain African-American activist Malcolm X, interracial relationships, phone sex, and the world of drug dealing, Lee's work has met with mixed reviews. His greatest impact in the realm of film has been the presentation of a different picture of African Americans to the moviegoing public, and his success has created opportunities for other African-American directors.

Biographical Information

Lee was born on March 20, 1957, in Atlanta, Georgia, to William and Jacqueline Lee. His father was a musician and composer, and his mother was a teacher. While he was still a baby, Lee's mother nicknamed him Spike for his toughness. His family moved to Chicago and then to Brooklyn when he was very young, and many of his films are set in Brooklyn neighborhoods similar to the ones in which he spent his youth. His mother died in 1977, and his father later remarried a Jewish woman. From the beginning of his career, Lee has involved his family in his film productions. Lee's father scored several of his films, and his sister has acted in many of the movies as well. Lee attended his grandfather's and father's alma mater, Morehouse College, where he received his B.A. in 1979. He first became interested in filmmaking during college, and after graduation he attended New York University film school. His first film was a short parody of D. W. Griffith's *The Birth of a Nation,* which was not well-received by the faculty. In the film he criticized Griffith's condescending portrayal of African Americans. He went on to win the Student Director's Award from the Academy of Motion Picture Arts and Sciences for *Joe's Bed-Stuy Barber Shop: We Cut Heads* (1982). To make ends meet after film school, Lee worked at a movie distribution house cleaning and shipping film. His first film after N.Y.U. was the low budget *She's Gotta Have It* (1986), which won the Prix de Jeunesse from the Cannes Film Festival and the New Generation Award from the Los Angeles Film Critics. After the success of his first film, Hollywood's

interest in Lee enabled him to make bigger budget pictures, but he still operated with considerably less money than most Hollywood movies. Even with help from Hollywood, Lee remains an independent filmmaker who has had to provide his own financing for most of his films. He started his own production company, Forty Acres and a Mule, named for the unfulfilled promise of what would be given to every African American at the end of slavery. Lee also acts as his own manager and agent. He has managed to retain creative control over the final cuts of his movies because he does not rely solely on financial backing from studios.

Major Works

Lee's films focus on various aspects of contemporary African-American life. *She's Gotta Have It* centers on the life of Nola Darling, a young woman with strong sexual desires who does not believe in restricting herself to one man to fulfill them. Nola represents a modern, independent woman who makes her own choices about her sexuality, yet in the end she discovers she loves the man who rapes her. Lee's second major film was *School Daze* (1988), a musical which parodies the conflict between light-skinned and dark-skinned African Americans at an all-black college in the South. Lee's *Do the Right Thing* (1989) follows a day in the Bedford-Stuyvesant section of Brooklyn on the hottest day of the summer. Racial tensions rise, culminating in the murder of a young African-American man by the police and the burning of a local pizzeria. In *Mo' Better Blues* (1990), Lee explores the world of a jazz musician and the conflicts between his creative life and his love life. Lee's next project, *Jungle Fever* (1991), centers on an interracial affair between an African-American architect and his Italian-American secretary. The relationship is met with scorn and violence from the families and members of the neighborhood. "Jungle fever" describes the phenomenon of sexual attraction between the races based on sexual myths, and the film explores this aspect of interracial relationships as opposed to relationships based on love and culminating in marriage. *Malcolm X* (1992) was one of Lee's most ambitious projects and covers the life of African-American activist Malcolm X. *Crooklyn* (1994) is a semi-autobiographical movie that Lee wrote with his sister and brother. The story follows a few months in the life of a family in the 1970s. The Carmichael family lives in Brooklyn; the father is a musician, the mother a teacher. The film is told from the perspective of the 10-year-old daughter and follows her as she deals with the death of her mother and her journey to adulthood. In *Clockers* (1995) Lee tells the story of an African-American teenager who becomes a drug dealer. The character is able to rationalize his decision to deal crack until he sees the murder and black-on-black violence that drugs bring about. With *Girl 6* (1996) Lee returned to a female protagonist. The heroine is an actress who becomes disenchanted when a director asks her to take her top off during a reading. She turns to the phone sex business to make a living and is quite successful. When a sadistic customer reveals that he knows where she lives, Girl 6 decides to leave the business, move to California, and resume her acting career. The film closes as it began, with a director asking her to take off her top, but this time she calmly finishes her monologue and leaves.

Critical Reception

Critics who review Lee's work often digress into discussions of Lee's persona in addition to or instead of his films. Some assert that Lee is a keen commentator on contemporary society and a cinematic innovator. Others describe him as an untalented commercial sellout. Lee is typically criticized for his lack of technical virtuosity. Reviewers point to his use of a moving screen behind two still characters to make them appear to be walking as a sign of his amateurish preoccupation with cinematic gadgetry. Feminists often complain about Lee's portrayal of women. bell hooks states that "Like many females in Lee's audience, I have found his representation of women in general, and black women in particu-

lar, to be consistently stereotypical and one-dimensional." The female protagonist of *She's Gotta Have It* came closest to a portrait of a modern, independent woman, but critics assert that the rape scene subverted the character Lee had created. Reviewers point to Nola's rape as a punishment for her sexual independence, and the scene has caused many reviewers to accuse Lee of sexism and misogyny. Lee is sometimes compared to Woody Allen because New York City plays such a pivotal role in both directors' films and both directors act in their own movies. Lee resists the comparison, however, citing the lack of African Americans in Allen's films as an unrealistic portrayal of the racial makeup of New York. Some reviewers complain that Lee's work is superficial and that his plots lack focus. Bert Cardullo, writing in *The Hudson Review*, asserts that Lee "prefers to do the easier thing: cram his film with incident rather than exploration, with texture rather than subtext." Most critics mention the ambiguity in Lee's films, including the question of what the right thing is in his *Do the Right Thing*. Reviewers are divided on the success of the ambiguity. Some praise Lee for refusing to give his audience simple Hollywood answers, while others complain that his films are unstructured with unfocused plots. Despite the controversy surrounding the filmmaker, most critics agree that Lee's portrayal of the everyday lives of African Americans is new and refreshing, and his success will make it possible for other African-American directors to make further contributions.

---

*PRINCIPAL WORKS

Joe's Bed-Stuy Barbershop: We Cut Heads (film) 1983
She's Gotta Have It (film) 1986
Spike Lee's "Gotta Have It": Inside Guerilla Filmmaking (nonfiction) 1987
School Daze (film) 1988
Uplift the Race: The Construction of "School Daze" [with Lisa Jones] (nonfiction) 1988
Do the Right Thing (film) 1989
"Do the Right Thing": The New Spike Lee Joint [with Lisa Jones] (nonfiction) 1989
Mo' Better Blues (film) 1990
"Mo' Better Blues" [with Lisa Jones] (nonfiction) 1990
Jungle Fever (film) 1991
Malcolm X [with Arnold Perl and (uncredited) James Baldwin; based on the book *The Autobiography of Malcolm X*, written by Alex Haley] (film) 1992
By Any Means Necessary: The Trials and Tribulations of the Making of "Malcolm X" [with Ralph Wiley] (nonfiction) 1992
Crooklyn [with Joie Lee and Cinqué Lee] (film) 1994
Clockers [with Richard Price; based on Price's novel of the same title] (film) 1995

Girl 6 [written by Suzan-Lori Parks] (film) 1996
Get on the Bus [written by Reggie Rock Bythewood] (film) 1996
Best Seat in the House: A Basketball Memoir [with Ralph Wiley] (nonfiction) 1997
4 Little Girls (documentary film) 1997

*In addition to directing the films listed here, Lee has also directed numerous television commercials and music videos. Bracketed information refers to screenwriting credit only.

CRITICISM

Stuart Mieher (essay date 9 August 1987)

SOURCE: "Spike Lee's Gotta Have It," in *The New York Times Magazine*, August 9, 1987, pp. 26-9, 39, 41.

[*In the following essay, Mieher discusses the making of Lee's* School Daze *and his emerging success as a film-maker.*]

The scene is an old fairgrounds building in Atlanta, now Madame Re-Re's Beauty Salon, a surreal creation of plywood, plaster and paint. The set has been packed with a score of dancers, a film crew and the director Spike Lee, all of them sweating under 140,000 watts of lighting to piece together a production number. Now the crew is taking a break. The dancers, overheated, head for cooler air outside.

Lee wanders out too, a short, spindly figure in black trousers, black sneakers and a Mets baseball cap. He is looking for an audience, and he finds one, a visitor. He asks, "Did you hear we got kicked off campus?" The campus in question is that of Morehouse College, Lee's alma mater and the main location for his second feature film, about student life at an all-black college. Things are not working out as planned. Lee tells of how the school's president, Hugh Morris Gloster, "thought this would be a negative portrayal of black colleges." The director pauses at a snack table to stuff a few orange slices into his mouth, then adopts a mocking, presidential tone: "He said, 'We have information that actors in the movie use an obscene word, and parents wouldn't want to send their children here if they heard that.' Sure, we're using the word. And so are the parents of those kids."

(Gloster, the Morehouse president, says: "They came in shooting on the campus and we began to get reports about things that were going on," such as some football cheers with decidedly off-color references. Parents, he feared, "would judge the school on what they see in this film.")

Lee devours a few more slices of orange, then continues: "We were going to do a premiere in Atlanta. Now we'll do it in New York. We need a warm reception, and there are too many people, powerful people in Atlanta who wish we'd never come here."

This is Spike Lee, talking wise, disrespectful of authority, a bit paranoid, hungry. As a first year graduate-school film student, he had the audacity to parody the cinematic classic *The Birth of a Nation*. As director, writer, star and producer of his first feature-length film, he became a phenomenon. *She's Gotta Have It* was the tale of a young black woman who felt no need to choose among her three lovers. She was, says Lee, "living her life like a man." Lee played Mars Blackmon, a rapping street kid who joked his way into her bed and stole scene after scene. The film, made in 1985 for less than $175,000, pulled in $7 million at the box office. For an independent, shoestring production, this was remarkable. For an independent shoestring production by a black man about black people, it was astounding.

Since then, Lee has emerged as a nexus of black culture. Stevie Wonder wrote a song for his new film. Jesse Jackson delivered a prayer on the set for the project's success. In Atlanta, clean-cut Morehouse students beseeched Lee for autographs, seeing in him a new role model. One, grasping a copy of Black Enterprise magazine that featured an article about Lee, asked, "Should brothers and sisters go to an entrepreneurial mode and struggle it out, or go to white corporations?" Lee's advice: "It's always better to have your own thing going."

Still only 30 years old, Lee has gained a degree of respect and freedom accorded few independent film makers at any age. "I consider him, forget black and white, one of the most original young film makers in the world," says David Picker, president of Columbia Pictures. Lee's current project, which Columbia plans to distribute next February, is a musical with the punnish title *School Daze*. Its budget of about $6 million is small by Hollywood's standards, but three dozen times larger than Lee has had before.

With an audience or an interviewer, Lee is animated, opinionated, gloriously quotable. He rails against black celebrities who "have a vicious crossover mentality." According to Lee, "They want to get on the cover of *Rolling Stone*. That's when you start seeing the symptoms—the nose jobs, the cleft chins, the blue and green contact lenses."

He takes the film establishment to task for producing shallow, misleading portrayals of black society. "I'm tired of people who know nothing about us defining our lives," he says. He trumpets a grand ambition: to present a new view of black life to the mass audience.

But on the set of *School Daze,* a different Spike Lee emerges, one with little of his shoot-from-the-lip arrogance. He is a thoughtful, organized and silent presence, focused on the task at hand, giving an occasional direction but welcoming no interruption. One friend calls him "a pot at continuous simmer," and the description seems apt.

The director, all 125 pounds of him, is sitting in a college auditorium, a black pork-pie hat perched on his head. His sweatshirt this evening says on the front "Mission," the name of the fictitious black coed school where the film takes place. On the back, a motto: "Uplift the Race." Lee's high-top basketball shoes are secured with orange Day-Glo laces. His socks droop around his skinny ankles. He is a minor spectacle.

It is three months before the Madame Re-Re scene, the first day of casting calls in Atlanta. The site is Spelman College, the black women's school across the road from Morehouse. Lee is cracking jokes, filling the short breaks between auditions by swaying to music swelling out of a tape player. He recognizes a young woman who wants one of the minor roles Lee has reserved for student talent. "Miss Wannabee, the prototype," he says teasingly. The term is short for "wannabee white," and it describes one of the opposing groups of students in the film, whose plot revolves around the clash between well-to-do, light-skinned students—wannabees—and poorer, darker students, whom the script calls "jigaboos."

Morehouse and Spelman form one of those bastions of the black middle class about which the rest of America knows little. Blacks seeking to communicate the schools' preeminence call them the black Harvard and Radcliffe. Their students have included Martin Luther King Jr., the novelist Alice Walker and not only Spike Lee but his father and grandfather.

Shelton Jackson Lee, nicknamed Spike by his mother, was born in Atlanta shortly before his family moved to Brooklyn. His mother, who died in 1977, taught art and black literature. His father, Bill Lee, is a jazz musician and composer. Spike had been indifferent to guitar and piano lessons. But in 1976, during his sophomore year at Morehouse College, he began playing around with another instrument, an eight-millimeter camera. Lee made his first short film during a summer in New York, interposing footage of the 1977 blackout with shots of disco dancers.

If Morehouse was an education, it was also an inspiration. As at many colleges, students built their social lives around fraternities and football rivalries. Lee helped direct the Coronation pageants, the highlight of homecoming weekends, huge productions, the size of a Broadway musical.

At Morehouse, Lee says, as in black culture generally, there were signs that blacks discriminated on the basis of color, that light-skinned blacks had an easier time reaching the upper levels of society. Yet even the thought of such color lines is controversial, and Lee's new film is already cause for grumbling. "This just isn't true, and it's never been true," says Hugh Gloster. "I don't see anyone around here wanting to be white."

Lee says that while his film may exaggerate a bit, it speaks an essential truth. "The people with the money, most of them have light skin. They have the Porsches, the BMW's, the quote good hair unquote," he explains. "The others, the kids from the rural South, have bad, kinky hair. When I was in school, we saw all this going on." He grins wickedly. "I remember saying. 'Some of this stuff has to be in a movie.'"

After his graduation from Morehouse, Lee enrolled in the film program at New York University's Tisch School of the Arts, where he was one of only a handful of black students. His first-year project was a cheeky film portraying a black scriptwriter assigned to a remake of D.W. Griffith's *The Birth of a Nation,* and it included some digs at the classic director's portrayals of blacks in the Old South. The short bombed with Lee's instructors—he suspects they didn't like his criticism of the great Griffith—and he barely made the cut for the second year. Eleanor Harnerow, the film program's director, says that Lee was simply too ambitious: "You make 10-minute films in your first year, and it's hard to redo *Birth of a Nation* in 10 minutes."

Lee went on to win a student director's academy award, given by the Academy of Motion Picture Arts and Sciences, for a 45-minute film about a barbershop-cum-numbers-joint in Brooklyn's Bedford-Stuyvesant section. But the prize produced no work. Lee made ends meet by cleaning and shipping film at a movie distribution house for $200 a week, all the while trying to line up film projects. He networked feverishly in New York's artistic community. Larry Fishburne, who plays one of the two pivotal male roles in *School Daze,* remembers he was watching a comic in Washington Square Park one evening when he felt a tap on his shoulder. "It was this little guy who said, 'You're Larry Fishburne, you're a great actor.' I said, 'Thanks.' Then he said, 'I'm Spike Lee, and I make films.'"

She's Gotta Have It came about almost by accident. In the summer of 1964, Lee was set to begin a family drama about a young black bicycle messenger coming of age. Then, shortly before shooting was to begin, part of the financing fell through. So Lee wrote a different script for a smaller project, used some of the same actors and rounded up a crew of friends. He began filming with $18,000 in grant money from the New York State Council on the Arts. Most of the film's eventual cost of $175,000 was financed by I.O.U.'s.

The effort was to Hollywood what a street bazaar is to Tiffany's. Cast and crew sweated their way through 12 days of summer shooting in a poorly ventilated restaurant attic. The film, shot in black and white, was edited in Lee's studio apartment, with a rented editing machine wedged between Lee's bed and his huge record collection. By the end, Lee was so behind on his bills that his film lab threatened to auction off the finished product.

Lee eventually ransomed the film, found a distributor, Island Pictures, and had his hit. Investments in the film paid off handsomely, and Island Pictures offered Lee a production deal.

Lee went to work recasting a three-year-old script into a musical, *School Daze*. The project grew into a family enterprise. An aunt, pianist Consuela Lee Morehead, was named assistant music director. Spike's sister, Joie, was cast as one of the "jigaboos." Two brothers, David, and Cinque, were assigned jobs on the crew. And to write much of the music, Lee turned to his father, Bill Lee, who had done the lush score for *She's Gotta Have It*. By November, Lee had cast many of the principal roles.

Then, on Jan. 19, a Monday, Lee was awakened after midnight by a phone call from Island's California office. The small production and distribution company likes to keep its projects below $4 million, and *School Daze* was beginning to look more expensive. Island wanted out. "The picture got a little rich for us," explains Laura Parker, Island's vice president of production. "We really wanted to do the movie, but we didn't want to cramp Spike's style," she explains. Without backing, the project would have to fold.

Lee remained calm. The next morning, Tuesday, he began calling studios. That afternoon, he hopped a subway to Manhattan and delivered a script to Columbia's president, David Picker. On Wednesday, Lee cut a deal with Columbia, and on Thursday, he flew to Los Angeles for a round of meetings.

That weekend, Lee went to the Super Bowl and had a taste of what life could be like Hollywood-style—the studio, he says, had found him some great seats.

It is a brilliant afternoon, perfect for shooting one of the film's big scenes, the homecoming football game. The two teams run through their drills in a borrowed football stadium. A band plays some jazzy tunes under the direction of Bill Lee, his hips swaying, sweat beating on his brow. More than a thousand extras pack the stands. They have been working all day for free, and they are tired and disgruntled. The Columbia deal raised the budget by $2 million but *School Daze* still has to scrimp.

Lee has been in motion all day, shuttling among the three cameras, loping up and down the field with a pigeontoed gait. Now and then he directs himself in his role as Half Pint, a "pledgee" with Mission College's most powerful fraternity, Gamma Phi Gamma. He tends toward the "jigaboo" in color and background, but he has "wannabee" aspirations.

One crew member says Half Pint is "a kid who doesn't have a romantic interest and is very inept at finding one." Lee says nothing at all, perhaps fearing that talk of the role will lead to one of his pet peeves, his label as the "black Woody Allen." There are some similarities. Both directors are from New York. Both write and direct ethnic films that transcend their ethnicity. But most of all, both act in their films, playing frail, fast-talking lovers whose sex appeal lies in their wit.

The comparison angers Lee. He says his cinematic role models are directors like Akira Kurosawa, Martin Scorsese and Gordon Parks.

"Woody Allen, he can do a film about Manhattan—it's about one-half black and Hispanic—and he doesn't have a single black person in the film," Lee says. "And they ask me. 'When are you going to have some white people in your films?' Nobody asks Kurosawa, 'When are you going to have non-Japanese?' But a black film maker, they say he's racist, he's separatist, because he doesn't have any white people."

The comment points to one of Lee's paradoxes as a film maker, that he both affirms and challenges America's view of itself as an integrated society. The affirmation comes from his talent: *She's Gotta Have It* eloquently communicates black culture to a broader audience. The challenge comes from Lee's desire to make films that highlight the uniqueness of black society.

In the early 1970's, Hollywood wooed black audiences with so-called "blaxploitation" films. Artistically, the results were uneven, but the best of the films, such as the *Shaft* detective series, made millions for the studios, employed black directors and gave black actors big roles that challenged negative stereotypes. The genre soon petered out. Recently Hollywood has shown new interest in films about blacks, including *A Soldier's Story* and *The Color Purple*. The industry has also begun to appreciate films by black directors. Earlier this year, *Hollywood Shuffle*, Robert Townsend's comedy about the travails of black film actors, was received warmly by both critics and audiences. But it disturbs Lee that he might be part of another passing fad. "We don't want to have two or three films, and then wait 10 years again," he says.

Good films, Lee says, should be able to cross cultural lines.

But he also has a message. "We want to show we're not all hanging around in the ghetto, shooting up, selling crack," he says. "We want to look at the black middle class, at some of the success stories."

Yet Lee and those who know him say his agenda is artistic, not political. "I think that when ideas first come to Spike, it's because there's something intrinsically right about transforming them into films," says Barry Brown, Lee's film editor for *School Daze,* who co-directed a documentary about the Vietnam era that won him an Academy Award nomination. "Spike was just in love with the cinema," Brown explains, recalling his first encounter with Lee. "He was the only one I knew who wouldn't look down his nose at a musical, for instance. Everyone else thinks that isn't serious film making."

Lee thinks cinematically, conceiving his films in visual as well as verbal terms, and this is one reason he insists on controlling the film from scripting through editing. "I have the original vision, and I see the film in its finished form before one frame is shot," he says. "When you get people dickering with your stuff, it distorts the vision and it's not what you set it out to be."

Lee started to plan the major shots for *School Daze* last fall, with Ernest Dickerson, a friend from N.Y.U.'s film school. To prepare for the dance scenes, they watched old M-G-M musicals and *West Side Story,* observing the bright colors, the intense lighting, the way the dancers were photographed.

"We didn't want the dance to be edited into motion," says Dickerson. "And we wanted to film the dance in full figure, the way an audience would see it on stage." To plan the actual shots, they drew storyboards, diagrams of how certain shots should look through the camera. As a result, when shooting began, the pace moved quickly enough to cram all the shots into an eight-week schedule.

Watching Lee on the set gives few clues to his methods. One day he is filming a scene with Larry Fishburne, who plays the campus radical, head of the anti-wannabee faction. In this scene, Fishburne's task is to ring an antique bell. Lee watches silently for a take or two. Then he gives his most conspicuous direction of the day: "Larry, the way you did it the first time was really better."

Dickerson says this is the height of extroversion. "Sometimes" he says, "Spike has his back turned and his eyes closed. He will just listen."

Much of Lee's direction takes place off the set, in small groups. And he encouraged the actors whose characters belonged to different factions—the fraternity men, the wannabees, Fishburne's rabble-rousers—to become friends with their on-screen friends and avoid their on-screen enemies. "It was brilliant," says Fishburne. "He knew a director just cannot tell a group of eight actors, 'I want you all to be as one.' So he sets you up in a situation where you're going to be together 24 hours a day."

On the set, says Fishburne, "Spike really doesn't communicate verbally with actors a lot. I'll look at him like I'm wondering, 'Hey, am I doing O.K.?' And he nods."

Fishburne says this is, in part, the silence of inexperience. "I don't think he's developed all the skills he might need to communicate with actors." But it might imply the silence of sheer inscrutability. "When he gets behind the camera, there are other things at work," Fishburne says. "And what they are, I have no idea."

If Lee loves film more than basketball, perhaps it is only because, at 5-foot-6, he is too short to play. Even so, he hopes one of the perks of success will be a pair of season tickets behind the bench at Madison Square Garden. His passion for the game found its way into the character of Mars Blackmon in *She's Gotta Have It.* During an argument, Mars describes the star forward of the Boston Celtics, Larry Bird, who is white, as the ugliest so-and-so in the National Basketball Association. The line has since echoed off locker room walls throughout professional basketball.

So it was probably inevitable that Lee's and Bird's paths would cross. It happened one night last January, when the Celtics were playing the Knicks. "I had great seats," Lee says. "I could see what they were saying on the bench." Conner Henry, a Celtics guard, who was sitting next to Bird, spied Lee. "He pokes Bird, and he points to me and says, 'Look at him, the guy in the hat, he's the guy who made the movie.' And when Bird looks around, he isn't laughing."

"All the guys in the N.B.A. have seen the movie," Lee says, "and that line is their biggest laugh."

Lee seems pleased by such celebrity, and he relishes the chance to make films with real money. These days, he says, $4 million, the original budget for *School Daze,* is too small. "If you do that you end up with two people talking in a closet," he says.

Lee's production company, Forty Acres and a Mule Filmworks now operates out of a stylish converted firehouse in Brooklyn where he is polishing *School Daze* into its finished form. Otherwise, aside from his notoriety in the N.B.A., success has had few detectable effects on his life. When in New York, he still rides the subway; he doesn't own a car, and he doesn't drive one. He is already preparing himself for the time when he is no longer a novelty. He volunteers that: "On your first film, people will fall all over you. With your second film, the audience and critics can be laying for you. They're ready to put you to the firing squad." Lee now has a chance for a bigger success, or for his first big failure. But the prospect doesn't seem to worry him. "I feel that I'm a very good film maker, and this film's going to make money, regardless," he says. "I think I will be making films for the rest of my life. And I'm just going to get better."

David Handelman (essay date 13-27 July 1989)

SOURCE: "Insight to Riot," in *Rolling Stone*, No. 556/557, July 13-27, 1989, pp. 104-9, 174-5.

[*In the following essay, Handelman discusses the making of Lee's* Do the Right Thing *and its reception at the Cannes Film Festival.*]

"I don't need this shit!" says *USA Today* gossip columnist Jeannie Williams. It's the morning of May 19th, and Williams has just seen the breakfast press screening of *Do the Right Thing* at the Cannes film festival. Tonight, the film will have its black-tie, red-carpet gala première at the Palais des Festivals, on the Côte d'Azur beach, where it will be competing with films from around the world for the coveted Palm d'Or prize. This morning, the more modest Palais press-conference room is abuzz with a few hundred international journalists and photographers waiting for the arrival of the film's director, Spike Lee.

"I live in New York," Williams says, her eyes flashing. "I don't need this movie in New York this summer. I don't know what they're thinking!" The ghetto in the movie is "too clean," Williams complains to a colleague, its inhabitants are "too nice," and there's too much violence.

Williams's diatribe is interrupted by Roger Ebert, the *Chicago Sun-Times* critic and TV personality, the only journalist ever called on by name at these conferences. He sweeps into the room and declares, "It's a great film, a great film. If this doesn't win the grand prize, I'm not coming back next year." (In the back of the room is Tom Pollock, the head of Universal Pictures, which is releasing *Do the Right Thing* on June 30th; Pollock later says Ebert's threat may hurt the film's chances of winning.)

Williams, who clearly values Ebert's upward thumb, is horrified. "How can you say that? What's going to happen when they *release* this?"

Ebert smiles and says, "How long has it been since you saw a film you thought would cause people to do *anything?*"

Ebert moves on, leaving Williams to bluster. "I can't believe Roger liked it!" she says.

Without even entering the room, Spike Lee has rocked it. *Do the Right Thing* portrays a block in Brooklyn's predominantly black Bedford-Stuyvesant neighborhood during the hottest day of the summer. The day starts peacefully and ends in a racial brawl, the murder of a black youth by a white cop and an ensuing riot. Lee's impressive, upsetting movie is inspired by—and pointedly dedicated to—black victims of white violence in New York City, like Eleanor Bumpurs, an elderly woman who was killed by police after she wielded a knife; Michael Griffith, who was chased onto a highway by white youths in Howard Beach, Queens, and killed by a car; and graffiti artist Michael Stewart, who was killed while in police custody. As complex and insistent as its title, the film is designed to spark controversy from its opening song—Public Enemy's discordant, militant rap "Fight the Power"—to the quotes that scroll before its end credits: Martin Luther King Jr. decrying violence, then Malcolm X claiming that violence used in self-defense is "intelligence."

When the wiry, poker-faced Lee, 32, enters the press-conference room, he is wearing a T-shirt that says MALCOLM X: NO SELLOUT. He sits at a table with cast members Ossie Davis, Joie Lee (his sister) and Richard Edson; he announces that today would have been Malcolm X's sixty-fourth birthday and that Davis gave the eulogy at the 1965 funeral.

This leads a journalist to ask Lee about the movie's two end quotes. "The quotes complete the thread of Malcolm and Martin that has been woven throughout the film," Lee says patiently. "In certain times, both philosophies can be appropriate, but in this day and age, the year of our Lord 1989, I'm leaning more toward the philosophies of Malcolm X. . . . Nonviolence and all that stuff had its time, and there are times when it's still appropriate, but when you're being hit upside the head with a brick, I don't think young black America is just going to turn the other cheek and say, 'Thank you, Jesus.'"

Someone asks why drugs are never mentioned in the film. "This film is not about drugs," says Lee. "It's about people and racism. Drugs are at every level of society today in America. How many of you went and saw *Working Girl* or *Rain Man* and asked, 'Where are the drugs?' Nobody. But the minute we have a black film that takes place in the ghetto, people want to know where the drugs are . . . because that's the way you think of black people. I mean, let's be honest."

Another journalist says, "I'm a Canadian living in New York, and it's my sense that it's all going to come down this summer, it's going to be a mess. A lot of people are going to get hurt. Your film seems to be anticipating that and speaking to that. What is your impression?"

Lee smiles and says, "I see Mr. Pollock getting fidgety back there. . . . We wanted to come out this summer [because] in November there's going to be an election for mayor of New York, and [current mayor Edward] Koch has divided the city into black and white. . . . If anything happens, it'll be because the cops killed somebody else with no reason, but it won't be because of *Do the Right Thing.*"

"This film," another journalist says, "takes a very despairing view of the possibility of an amicable relationship between the races."

"I think there's some hope at the end, a shaky truce," says Lee. "But on the other hand, I think it'd be very dishonest to have a kind of Steven Spielberg ending where we all hold hands and sing 'We Are the World.'"

In many ways, the same could be said about Spike Lee's relationship with Hollywood.

> **Spike Lee sees himself as a man with a mission: to shake down the creeping resurgence of racism in post-Reagan America, to inform, entertain and motivate—all the while operating in an industry entirely controlled by whites.**
> **—David Handelman**

The question that really gets Spike Lee going is "What do you think of *Mississippi Burning?*" The Academy-Award-nominated film—which recast the civil-rights movement as the triumph of a white FBI agent—came up during many of the constant interviews at Cannes, being one of the few recent Hollywood films that is even about blacks, and it symbolizes everything Lee thinks is wrong with Hollywood today. Like *Cry Freedom* and *The Cotton Club,* Lee says and says again, *Mississippi Burning* distorted history, exploiting blacks to turn whites into heroes. "*Hated* it," Lee says. "They should have had the guts to have at least one central black character."

Lee speaks in measured tones, every now and then unleashing a wild "Ha!" or a quieter "Ch-ch-ch-ch" laugh. But he mostly goes about the tedious business of answering for his movies with a deadly seriousness. Lee calls his production company Forty Acres and a Mule Filmworks (after the never-realized proposal following the Civil War to give land and a mule to each freed slave); he's published a book about the making of each of his films. In the one about *Do the*

Right Thing, he writes: "I've been blessed with the opportunity to express the views of Black people who otherwise don't have access to power and the media. I have to take advantage of this while I'm still bankable."

Spike Lee sees himself as a man with a mission: to shake down the creeping resurgence of racism in post-Reagan America, to inform, entertain and motivate—all the while operating in an industry entirely controlled by whites. It is a tall order for a man who stands five feet six in Air Jordans.

His path to Hollywood, Lee says, has been pitted with racist potholes. After growing up in various racially mixed Brooklyn neighborhoods and graduating from all-black Morehouse College in 1979, he went to New York University's film school and found himself in a "hostile situation."

"I had to prove whether I belonged," Lee says, "or was just another quota." When NYU professors criticized his first student film, *The Answer,* he attributed it to "cultural arrogance," because his film took D.W. Griffith's classic *The Birth of a Nation* to task for its condescending portrayal of blacks.

Lee's 1982 senior thesis, *Joe's Bed-Stuy Barbershop: We Cut Heads,* was shot by Ernest Dickerson, the only other black to complete NYU's three-year program while Lee was there. (Dickerson has gone on to shoot all of Lee's films.) The movie won the student Academy Award. Two years later, Lee got a grant to start filming a script called *Messenger,* but the Screen Actors Guild refused to grant him a low-budget waiver of its union wages, Lee says, on the grounds that his script was "too commercial." According to Lee, white directors with larger budgets are regularly granted the waiver. "It was a definite case of racism," he says.

Lee quickly wrote the serious and saucy comedy *She's Gotta Have It,* which takes place mostly in a woman's bed, and filmed it for $175,000 in the summer of 1985. (His hilarious performance as bike messenger Mars Blackmon stole the film.) In order to keep *She's Gotta Have It* from getting an X rating, he had to shorten one of the film's sex scenes; he insists that white sex scenes in films like the R-rated *9 1/2 Weeks* were much more deserving of an X rating than what he had to cut.

She's Gotta Have It won the Prix de la Jeunesse at Cannes in 1986 for Best New Director, was released by Island Pictures and earned $8 million. This enabled Lee to get Columbia to finance his second feature, *School Daze,* a $6 million musical about activism and intraracial divisions at a black college. *School Daze* also did well at the box office, grossing $18 million despite no advertising support from Columbia Pictures after its chairman David Puttnam was deposed. *School Daze* was ambitious, if problematic—suffering from overlong dance numbers, wandering plot lines and an insider tone. Lee didn't take the criticism well, particularly the pan from *New York Times* critic Janet Maslin, who questioned Lee's technical abilities. Believing her comments "dangerous; like the same Al Campanis shit that black people don't have the capabilities to be baseball managers," Lee wrote a petulant letter to the *Times,* demanding that Maslin never review his films again and ending with the line "I bet she can't even dance, does she have rhythm?"

Is this reaction racist? "I don't think blacks can be racist," Lee says. "Racism is where you put laws into effect, structures that affect you socially. What can black people do to harm Jewish people as a people? Set up laws in Congress, stop them from voting? That's what racism is.

"We still have people in America who say that racism ended when Lyndon Johnson signed the Civil Rights Act and black people were allowed to vote," he continues. "And because Michael Jackson's the number-one rock star, Eddie Murphy's the biggest box-office draw in the world, Bill Cosby is the number-one TV star, Mike Tyson is the world heavyweight champion, Michael Jordan is the greatest basketball player in the world, that black people have arrived, and everything is all right. But the black underclass in America now is larger than it's ever been. So you can't be lulled to sleep just because Eddie Murphy's huge."

In fact, Lee has been an outspoken critic of celebrities like Murphy and Whoopi Goldberg, who he feels have not asserted their black identities and have not flexed their money muscle to get blacks hired.

According to the *Los Angeles Times,* while twelve percent of Americans are black and blacks make up twenty-five percent of the moviegoing audience, minority membership in the Writers Guild is a paltry 1.6 percent. Furthermore, there are no black film executives with the power to approve a movie, and although Lee has helped open the door for black directors like Robert Townsend (*Hollywood Shuffle*) and Keenen Ivory Wayans (*I'm Gonna Git You Sucka*), blacks directed fewer than one percent of Hollywood's releases last year.

Against these odds, Lee has gotten his movies made, adopting Malcolm X's credo "By any means necessary." He works without an agent, a manager, a publicist or membership in the Writers and Directors guilds, supervising every aspect of his films down to the logos, soundtracks and videos. He's scraped around for studio "pickup deal" financing that guarantees him the final cut. Both onscreen and off, he has tried to employ as many blacks as possible, found-

ing a minority-student scholarship at the NYU film school and a Forty Acres film-training program at Long Island University. He has also been able to make some pocket money from being an ad clotheshorse for both the Gap and Barneys and from directing a series of jump-cut commercials for Nike starring Michael Jordan.

But the necessary means were hard to come by for *Do the Right Thing,* even though its final budget was $6.5 million, one-third that of the average Hollywood film. The first studio Lee approached, Paramount, balked at the ending, and Disney also passed. When Universal approved the script, the executives there hadn't yet experienced the uproar over the studio's release of Martin Scorsese's *Last Temptation of Christ.* And when Lee's finished film seemed harsher than the script, some were troubled; there were nervous murmurs that it could be a second coming of *Christ.*

The film is being released in one of the most competitive movie summers ever, against *Batman* and sure-fire sequels like *Ghostbusters II* and *Indiana Jones and the Last Crusade.* Though Universal would like it to earn $30 million, vice-president of production and acquisitions Jim Jacks says, "It deals with emotional issues, and when you make movies like that, you never know what's going to happen."

All Lee hopes is that the controversy doesn't dampen the receipts, because his license seems short-term. "Hollywood will overlook subject matter in my case," he says, "because my films [so far] make money. Universal did not make this movie because they're in love with me."

"I loved your movie," a man says, approaching Spike Lee at the outdoor-terrace bar at the stately Carlton Hotel, in Cannes. "I run this film festival on the West Coast. We'd love to have you out there." He hands over a pamphlet.

Lee looks at it and reads, "Wine Country Film Festival? When is it?"

The man tells him it's in mid-July, two weeks after *Do the Right Thing* opens. "Maybe next film," Lee says kindly.

He's sitting with Jim Jacks, and, leafing through the latest copy of *Variety,* he stops at the ad for *See No Evil, Hear No Evil.* "How does Gene Wilder keep getting top billing over Richard Pryor?" Lee asks Jacks. "Folks are not going to see *him.*"

Lee turns to the chart of grosses. "*Mississippi Burning* made only $34 million? What happened, backlash?"

"It'd be great if we made more than them," says Jacks. "Hey, imagine what kind of file J. Edgar Hoover'd have on you if he were around today."

Lee doesn't smile. "My phone was bugged, you know. The line was dead, then came back on two days later. I had it checked, they didn't find anything, but that doesn't mean anything."

"What are you doing?" asks Jacks, skeptical.

"Film is a very powerful medium," Lee says soberly.

"Don't make it any more powerful," says Jacks with a laugh. "I don't think I could take it!"

The official screening of **Do the Right Thing** is tomorrow night. Jacks asks Lee if he's nervous about the Cannes competition, which pits him against much-ballyhooed films such as Denys Arcand's *Jesus of Montreal,* Shohei Imamura's *Black Rain,* Jim Jarmusch's *Mystery Train* and Steve Soderbergh's *sex, lies and videotape.* Lee shakes his head. "This man is *ice!*" Jacks exclaims.

Lee puts down *Variety,* stands up and pantomimes dribbling a basketball on the terrace floor. "On the line," he says, taking aim at an invisible hoop. "One second to go, one point down." He mimes two shots and makes two *whoosh!* sounds and sits down again, smiling.

Do the Right Thing was stirring things up even before it got to film. Lee showed up last July 12th at its first cast read-through with T-shirts emblazoned with the film's title and flags of Africa, America, Italy and Puerto Rico, and he distributed them to the cast he had assembled from wildly varied backgrounds: Bronx street-kid-turned-actor Danny Aiello as pizzeria owner Sal; Lee himself as pizza deliveryman Mookie; stage veterans Ossie Davis and Ruby Dee as neighborhood stalwarts Da Mayor and Mother Sister; stand-up comic Robin Harris as one of three lay-about "corner men"; legal secretary Rosie Perez as Mookie's Puerto Rican girlfriend Tina; and Yale School of Drama graduate John Turturro as Sal's racist son, Pino. Turturro mumbled his scripted slurs, thinking, "God, what have I got myself into?"

After the reading, Lee opened the floor for discussion, and Paul Benjamin, who plays a corner man, complained that the script showed nothing but lazy, shiftless blacks.

This sent Rosie Perez—who grew up in Bedford-Stuyvesant and whom Lee discovered dancing at an L.A. disco—on a ten-minute tirade about how people like the corner men exist and that the cast should go to Bed-Stuy and take a look. Lee explained that he wanted to deal with the realities of the neighborhood but treat the people with dignity and humor.

Today, Lee says that he doesn't agree with those who think that only positive black images should be portrayed. "I think

people still look very good in this movie," he says. "You can accent the positive or talk about the problems. My approach has been to talk about the problems."

Yet after the read-through, the cast of this movie about racial issues never really discussed those issues. "It's an indication of how divided the races are that you can't even talk about racism on a personal level," says Richard Edson, who plays Sal's more sympathetic son, Vito. "There's too much distrust, too historical a thing to be able to relax. To even bring it up is a threat, to both blacks and whites."

The turning point in the movie is a fight between Sal and a neighborhood agitator named Buggin' Out (Giancarlo Esposito). And while the scene was being shot, the improvisation that Lee encourages on his sets tapped something deep. Esposito's real-life mother is black and his father is Italian; off-camera, he had gotten chummy with Aiello, and the two talked in Italian. But when the cameras rolled, Aiello, ad-libbing, suddenly called Buggin' Out "nigger," and Esposito went wild, flinging back epithets like "guinea bastard."

"It was a sense of pride," says Aiello. "Giancarlo and I have an audience out there watching—neither of us wanted the other guy to get one over on us. So we started using words like the roughest truck drivers you ever seen."

"It was very shocking to me," says Esposito. "When Danny said, 'Nigger,' I freaked. It finally came up for him. I knew that at some point in his life, he'd called somebody a nigger, and I went crazy because he was someone I liked. Danny was upset with himself, I was really upset with myself, and Spike was gleaming, because he'd gotten the scene."

Filming took place on location in Bedford-Stuyvesant. Members of Louis Farrakhan's Fruit of Islam were employed as suit-and-bow-tie security men; they closed down three crack houses on the block, nailing them shut. Lee used locals on the production and set up a scholarship fund for the neighborhood high school. (He also commissioned black filmmaker St. Clair Bourne to make a documentary about the filming.)

Filming the riot took weeks. "It was frightening," says Joie Lee, 26, who plays Mookie's sister, Jade. "Once the cameras were rolling, you didn't know what to do—there was water, flames. There was one time I looked at the monitor and I saw film, but the rest of the time, I believed it."

"You'd stop and see the pizza parlor burning," says Edson, "200 extras running out in the street, and you'd think, 'This could be the real thing, this is the *shit.*' The question is, why do these things keep happening? Who's gonna do the right thing? Would I? And what is the right thing, at the moment of truth?"

"Can I get a dessert?" Spike Lee asks the waiter. He's back at the bustling Carlton Hotel bar.

"*Non,*" the waiter replies, "only drinks on ze terrace."

Lee, a near teetotaler, disappears a few seconds later, then returns in his slightly pigeon-toed, speedy gait, carrying a fruit-and-cream confection. "That guy didn't know what he was talking about," he says and digs in.

Asked to name his influences, Lee says, "I would say my parents more than any filmmaker." Bill, a jazz musician who has scored all of Spike's films, and Jacquelyn, a teacher (she died in 1977), took Spike and his four younger siblings to dance and jazz performances and Broadway shows. (Besides Joie, there is David, 28, a still photographer on Spike's films, and Cinque, 24, also a filmmaker, who appears in Jarmusch's *Mystery Train.* Another brother, Chris, lives in Washington, D.C.) "I think that's what everything's about, exposure."

The first films Lee recalls going to are *Bye Bye Birdie* at Radio City Music Hall and a double feature of *Dr. No* and *A Hard Day's Night.* But his favorites are searing *cinéma vérité* like Hector Babenco's *Pixote* and Martin Scorsese's *Mean Streets* and fantasies like *The Wizard of Oz* and *West Side Story.*

As a kid, Shelton Jackson Lee (his mother nicknamed him Spike as a baby) was more of a sports fan, organizing games on the block, sending baseball cards away for autographs, fighting to watch Knicks games on TV when his sister wanted to watch *The Brady Bunch.* Today, his main reading is the daily sports pages; he has Knicks season tickets, he says, "but not as good as Woody Allen's."

Until graduating from high school, says David Lee, Spike had a "massive Tito Jackson 'fro," and Lee himself says he looked like a kid until halfway through college. The only one of the Lees to attend Morehouse, Bill Lee's alma mater, Spike got involved there with writing, directing and producing the gown-and-float homecoming coronation, a spectacle on the order of an MGM musical, which served as the inspiration for *School Daze.* He began to dabble in 8-mm movies, and after graduating in 1979 he went to NYU film school. "I went knowing that I wasn't going to learn anything from the faculty," he says. "I just wanted the equipment to make films, because I knew that's how I'd become a filmmaker."

When rookie Spike Lee was in Cannes in 1986 touting *She's Gotta Have It,* he was one of eight people sharing a cramped apartment. This year, his photo is up on a billboard on the palm-tree-lined main drag alongside those of Woody Allen, Francis Coppola and Wim Wenders, and with Universal's money, he has a two-room suite at the Carlton to himself. (He doesn't have a steady girlfriend but would like to some-day get married and have five kids.)

He walks around the hotel in sneakers, athletic socks, a T-shirt, stone-washed jeans, a leather-thong Public Enemy me-dallion, a baseball cap and a Knicks windbreaker. He spends much of his time giving interviews to the international press, which often puts him in the dicey position of being the spokesman for Black America. He is quick to remind re-porters that the movie applies not just to New York or America but to racism everywhere. Because of his intro-verted, aloof manner, at least one journalist departs saying, "I think he thought my questions were stupid."

One interviewer asks about the grandstanding of the Rev-erend Al Sharpton, the New York black activist. "By focus-ing on him, the press ignores the issue," Lee says. "Any time there's a movement, people tend to focus on personalities, instead of what's being fought for. Whether people think Sharpton's a clown or not has nothing to do with what hap-pened to Tawana Brawley."

One scene in *Do the Right Thing* takes place in front of a brick wall sprayed with the graffiti TAWANA TOLD THE TRUTH! Despite overwhelming evidence that the upstate-New York black teenager's story was fabricated, Lee says, "I find it unbelievable that a fifteen-year-old girl would smear herself with feces and throw herself in a plastic bag. The truth still hasn't come out yet."

Asked about black-separatist leader Louis Farrakhan, Lee says, "I don't agree with everything he says. But anything the media says about him has been distorted. Time and time again, the press has tried to have me come out and blast him, but I won't do it."

Certain questions pop up in nearly every interview:

What's "the right thing"?

"I don't know. I know what the wrong thing is: racism."

Will Sal be able to reopen his pizzeria after the riot?

"I don't know. The movie's not about that. It's about rac-ism. The white critics identify with Sal, but the movie's not about him. You cannot equate a human life with the destruc-tion of a pizzeria. Why does no one ask me if the cops are going to be tried for the murder?"

What can be done about racism?

"People cannot expect me to have answers. That is not my goal or agenda. What I have to do as a filmmaker is present the problem so that discussion can start. If America was thinking about racism, *Do the Right Thing* wouldn't be the first film about it."

Spike Lee still lives in the same spartan Brooklyn basement apartment he did before making *She's Gotta Have It,* works out of the same converted firehouse, travels by subway. Forty Acres vice-president (and Lee's Morehouse classmate) Monty Ross explains, "If people who're going to make a difference leave the black community, how is the standard there ever going to be raised? Spike wants to make a difference. Hanging out in Brooklyn, you tend to stay involved and committed, instead of out in a mansion in Hollywood."

Lee only started to vote in 1984, when Jesse Jackson ran for president; he directed a commercial for Jackson's '88 campaign and has offered to do the same for David Dinkins, a black candidate for mayor of New York City.

Next, Lee says, "I want to do a less antagonistic, less confrontational film." He has already written the script, *Love Supreme,* named after a John Coltrane song. It's a contemporary tale of a jazz musician trying to balance his work and his love life. Lee, who will play the jazz band's manager, is reportedly seeking a $12 million budget.

Also in the planning stages is a movie about drugs and their effect on young kids. "We can't have art for art's sake," says Monty Ross. "There's so much of black life that needs so much work. Forty Acres will always do movies that are entertaining and give people something to talk about. It won't be movies in the south of France with people running around talking about a cherry moon. Our agenda has to include education."

Lee himself has few illusions about the educational impact of his movies. "The only time I've seen a film take real effect was *The Thin Blue Line*—that got a guy out of jail. Something like that only happens once in a blue moon. I don't think I'm gonna be able to walk through Bensonhurst or Howard Beach because of *Do the Right Thing:* 'Let's not crack him on the head with a bat because we saw his movie and we're all brothers and sisters.'"

On May 23rd, the Cannes Film Festival awards were announced: The Palm d'Or went to *sex, lies and videotape,* the first feature by Steven Soderbergh, a twenty-six-year-old American. Many films won prizes, but *Do the Right Thing* was shut out. The *New York Times* reported that the film's only supporters among the judges were director Hector Babenco and actress Sally Field. "We got robbed," Lee says back in Brooklyn. "I guess they really wanted to stick the knife. [Cannes jury president and film director] Wim

Wenders was quoted as saying, '*Sex, lies and videotape* shows there's a future for cinema,' so I guess we're not the future."

That same week, an unemployed construction worker named Richard Luke, twenty-five and black, died in a New York City jail after a struggle with city-housing police. His family had called the police because he was having difficulty breathing. But after his death, his mother was quoted saying, "My son was beaten. . . . They had a nightstick right up under his throat." The Reverend Al Sharpton held another demonstration. The medical examiner ruled the death was drug related. A grand jury said it would investigate.

And the summer hadn't even begun.

Jim Merod (essay date Summer 1991)

SOURCE: "A World without Whole Notes: The Intellectual Subtext of Spike Lee's *Blues,*" in *Boundary 2,* Vol. 18, No. 2, Summer, 1991, pp. 238-51.

[*In the following essay, Merod analyzes Lee's portrayal of jazz in his* Mo' Better Blues, *and includes a discussion with other scholars about the importance of jazz in the film.*]

The depiction of jazz musicians and of jazz-related subjects in the history of North American film has suffered from the chronic neglect and misunderstanding that still marks this culture's pathological abuse of creative energy. The inventory of that abuse is poised to expand with another dramatic adventure in applied techno-sadism as computer-operated tanks and planes prepare to fertilize the Saudi desert with human blood. In the history of North American cinema, war, murder, violence, and destruction of every imaginable kind have archetypal predominance above the ordinary uses of human capacities. When we turn to a film that explores the risks and joys of artistic development, we hope for an enlargement of our understanding about the ways that creativity thrives or lingers against harassment. Spike Lee's recent film, *Mo' Better Blues,* promises to reward such hope. If it defers the task of giving the jazz musician a place and a voice appropriate to the magnificent accomplishments carved from endless (and seemingly unending) struggles—accomplishments and struggles specific to the constant re-emergence of jazz in North American culture—that deferral no doubt reflects several forms of ambivalence.

One of them is certainly Spike Lee's own uncertainty about the importance of jazz in twentieth-century North American culture. *Mo' Better Blues* displays a weak interest in capturing, in representing, the fire and dignity (the indomitable beauty) embedded within each genre of the jazz archive. Put bluntly, *Mo' Better Blues* does not portray the world of the jazz musician convincingly or compellingly. When Bleek Gilliam, the film's ambitious trumpet "star," gets his bell rung savagely in a back alley pounding by the cudgels and ferocious punches of street thugs sent to discipline his errant gambling manager, Spike Lee escapes from the perplexity of his own central subject. Bleek no longer has the embouchure adequate to continue as a trumpeter. Lee's film, then, is free to stalk on as an exercise of moral anxiety.

The major premise of Lee's film is a minutely drawn—in truth, an overblown—awareness of the danger of artistic commitment. Lee's moral fable pursues the ambivalent love life of its brooding trumpeter as a contemporary black incarnation of a Faustian wager. Bleek Gilliam sells his imaginative life and his emotional soul to the devil of his own artistic inspiration. The film's romance with the archetype of romantic self-dissolution inscribes the theme of creative isolation on the remarkably public and inherently communal world of jazz musicians as if the fundamental forging of the jazz musician's identity, knowledge, talent, and self-confidence were developed privately and at a protected distance from human relationships. Bleek Gilliam is shown to defend himself from the commitments and responsibilities of ongoing mature heterosexuality by dividing his sexual energy between two women—each talented, each attractive, each fascinated by his macho self-absorption. But that ambivalence is depicted as a defense from the obligation to sublimate self-concern and artistic narcissism.

Spike Lee is simultaneously tempted by the seductiveness of artistic self-possession, of creative narcissism, and alarmed by it. *Mo' Better Blues* works itself out as a moral tale giving the prideful place of public and personal success to Bleek Gilliam's companion-rival, Shadow Henderson, a crafty and aggressive musician/businessman/lover. Shadow steals one of Bleek's two women, gives her the artistic support her own musical ambitions require, and develops an apparently relaxed capacity to express himself as a lover, as a partner, and as a jazz musician. When Bleek, attempting a comeback from his wounds and his layoff after the beating he took, joins Shadow's gig—a gig that features Bleek's beautiful former lover, Clarke Betancourt (played to stunning effect by Cynda Williams)—he is thwarted by three startling events: Shadow's generosity, Clarke's talent, and his own musical incapacity. The entanglement of so much personal significance within a public moment of embarrassment compels Bleek to retire. *Mo' Better Blues* works its way to a thumpingly banal conclusion that fulfills its predictable subtext. Bleek returns to the second of his two previous lovers, summons her late at night, after a year's neglectful leave, to accept his need for her healing warmth. The name Indigo suggests, metaphori-

cally, the very uncertainty, confusion, and ambivalence that Indigo's character (played with saucy tolerance by Spike Lee's sister, Joie) suffers from Bleek's inconstant attention. Indigo's overly submissive acceptance of Bleek's amorous reversal suggests that a deeper code is at stake in her name and in the film.

The bottom line of Lee's celebratory wedding scene is the assertion of happy family-hood and the virtues of well-earned monogamy. As a safe haven from the torments of artistic insecurity, marriage takes on the dim glow of any booby prize. *Mo' Better* begins as an exploration of a supposedly dedicated young musician's struggle to find and express the soulful fire that jazz has always carried in its rich and unpredictable ninety-year heritage. It ends as a dull, comic portrait of the artist as a patient father giving his son just that extra measure of understanding, in the face of a scolding mother, that Bleek may have wanted or needed as a child. Sports, the neighborhood gang, and the riotous, amorphous pleasures of hanging out in Brooklyn's tree-shaded autumn light supplant the father's relentless youthful pursuit of the right note, a semblance of perfect pitch. The son will carry on his father's dream with the difference that playground experience lends.

A reading of *Mo' Better* as a filtered study of the black family is plausible, more plausible perhaps if it is pursued as an affirmative tale that quarrels with Oedipal relationships. Lee has claimed that his film is "about" relationships. One of them may be the archetype of family romance, the relationship of parental authority in the symbiotic gestation of erotic and artistic energies. Such a reading would have to accommodate the strange evasion that defines *Mo' Better Blues*. How can a filmmaker, whose avowed ambition is to construct a film that does justice to jazz, its people, and its heritage, produce such an embarrassed representation, one that miscasts and misunderstands its central purposes? How can it be that the black cultural context sketched in vaguely—and wholly sifted through the brooding, if also beautiful, foreground of frustrated and compensatory romance entanglements—is left to blur into stereotypes of artistic and erotic hopes unfulfilled?

The hopes most unfulfilled are those carried by the viewer who wants to see a film worthy of the music called *jazz,* a body of deeply engaging music that is revered everywhere the spirit of Afro-American creative intelligence resides. Lee's film joins a slowly growing list of films that nod toward the Afro-American musical heritage. That nod takes on ever new forms of disavowal. The nod turns into a perplexed gaze. In *Mo' Better Blues,* jazz is the excuse to explore dramatic camera angles, lovely canvases of color, even more beautiful surfaces of lovemaking, and no less gorgeous sound tracks filled with the masterful blowing of John Coltrane and Miles Davis and Wayne Shorter as well as that mountainous index of saxophone purity, Julian "Cannonball" Adderly.

When Spike Lee writes midway through the book he wrote with Lisa Jones, *Mo' Better Blues,* "Jazz has been an integral part of all my movies. My father has scored every film I've done since my second year at film school, and all these scores have been jazz-based," he cops a plea.

The plea is a reach for authority mediated by filial lineage and repeated experience. Like most pleas, it is an appeal for understanding and leniency. In Lee's collaborative book, the chapter "Mo' Better Music" addresses the sound track, as well as the "philosophy" of jazz, that are meant to undergird the film. That chapter reads as an apology for limited conceptual depth:

> I knew that the average moviegoing audience is not the same audience that frequents jazz clubs, and they won't come to a theatre to sit through a fifteen minute musical number. . . . I didn't make this film out of some lofty mission to bring jazz to the masses. If people are exposed to jazz through this film, that's wonderful. I hope that [John Coltrane's] *A Love Supreme* sells two hundred thousand more copies because of *Mo' Better Blues,* but ultimately that's not the reason I made this film. This was simply the film I had in me at the time.

Unlike Clint Eastwood's *Bird* and Bertrand Tavernier's *Round Midnight,* Spike Lee's treatment of Bleek Gilliam is not an attempt to portray a legendary jazz musician or a luminous composite figure. *Bird* circles low over the dark incarnation of Charlie Parker, while *Round Midnight* treks wearily through a smaller-than-life depiction of an American expatriate "star," part Bud Powell (the innovative bop pianist), part Lester Young (the appealing and understated, if also somewhat enigmatic, tenor saxophonist). The failure of those two films in the face of biographical and cultural contexts that deserve careful rendering leaves a viewer to forage among the images of passionate personal and artistic neglect that each tale offers. One comes away from them with the bitter leavings of lives obliterated by drugs and sickness. As cinematic statements, *Round Midnight* and *Bird* clarify almost nothing about the force and the dignity of the music. They evade both the life struggles and the creative achievements of their putative subjects. *Mo' Better Blues* avoids the burden of biographical accuracy, but it executes its fictional search for individual musical distinction in a setting filled with rivalries and sophomoric quests for middle-class satisfaction. The film that Lee had "in" him appropriates the world of the jazz musician in order to weave an Oedipal tale of entrepreneurial failure.

Bleek Gilliam does not fall short of his artistic destiny. His misspent act of heroic intervention provides the premise for the film's aggressive moralizing to thwart his self-absorption. Bleek, deftly fleshed out on screen by Denzel Washington, is a half-hip urban Quixote whose sensitivity is reserved for studied moments of lovemaking with his two women and for brief moments of exasperated patience with his parodic Sancho Panza side-kick/manager, Giant. The predominant feature of *Mo' Better Blues,* beyond its brilliant color and its fluid sound track, past the self-conscious pursuit of dense meaning among half-rendered artistic and erotic relationships, is the vivid absence of any insight into the extremely variable (richly annotated) world of jazz. The primary contribution of Spike Lee's film, from that perspective, is its paradigmatic pretense to explore jazz as a scene of sustained and explicable creative interactions between divergent, but wholly engaging, temperaments. This paradigm—of promises subverted, of one art form (jazz) lost in the fumblings of another (cinema)—constitutes an almost Dostoevskian theme of betrayal. One thinks of the Karamazov family as the adequate representation of so much squandered energy. Motives, in Dostoevsky, are always explicable in the consequences of their indirect destinations. The occasion to paint jazz, the jazz musician, and the jazz subject as powerful instances of secret wisdom (of the public display of private reckonings too forceful for routine knowledge) is too tempting for witnesses like Lee and Eastwood and Tavernier to turn down. What becomes indirect but without destination is their treatment of the jazz artist as an empty site to be filled in with somber clichés and dramatic caricatures.

The largest emptiness called up by these filmic gestures is the perfect zero of the jazz legacy in the history of film. Lee, Tavernier, and Eastwood merely call attention to the longstanding incapacity of filmmakers and the film industry to penetrate the fatuous imagery of self-destruction and self-involvement that confuses the popular representation of jazz. One might expect a black filmmaker, who celebrates his pride in the music and in his father's contributions to the music, to deliver a greater degree of nuanced understanding. But then, something about the art form seems to elude each approach to cinematic capture.

With the remarkable exception of a single film, *Straight No Chaser,* which focuses closely on the music and personality of a stunningly brilliant and stunningly eccentric innovator, Thelonious Monk, jazz has received no adequate embodiment as a cultural archive or a musical universe with its own special depths and stories and human features. That this should be the case as jazz enters its tenth decade of formal self-manufacture is nearly, but not completely, inexplicable.

The absence of mature explorations of what can only be thought of as North America's most powerful indigenous art form expresses the studied neglect and the active demotion attending black cultural life in the United States. When we see that Spike Lee, an energetic and clearly alert black filmmaker, fluffs his own attempt to portray jazz as a cultural phenomenon that cannot be reduced to drug-driven inspiration, a larger issue than the failure of a single film emerges. Lee's film carries out the predicament of any filmmaker to render adequately a heritage, and a richly woven complex art, that has accumulated the full of its considerable force against the predominant values of a majority cultural apparatus. On one side, jazz has enjoyed haphazard success as a distinctly black art form given refuge in the crevices of popular commercial culture. On the other side, as jazz has grown older, more accepted by established interests and tastes, it has suffered an increasingly indifferent reception from black audiences. Surrounding both receptions—perhaps, more accurately, suffused within or beneath hostility and insouciance—the long-enforced and well-calculated decision by large capital interests (record companies, television networks, school systems) to treat jazz first as "race music" and then as an explosive and seductive, but altogether inferior, embodiment of incomprehensible excitation has maintained the cultural, if not so fully the financial, marginality of the music.

In the case of Spike Lee's misrepresentation of jazz as a world of enigmatic inspiration marked by personal rivalries and predominant egos, the failure to capture the simple dignity of the music's immediate force and elegance can be looked at as a consequence of the black intellectual's plight—a difficulty that my esteemed colleague Cornel West has described as "a grim predicament." To frame his important essay of 1985, "The Dilemma of the Black Intellectual," West uses the following epigraph from Harold Cruse's *Crisis of the Negro Intellectual:*

> The peculiarities of the American social structure, and the position of the intellectual class within it, make the functional role of the negro intellectual a special one. The negro intellectual must deal intimately with the white power structure and cultural apparatus, and the inner realities of the black world at one and the same time. But in order to function successfully in this role, he has to be acutely aware of the nature of the American social dynamic and how it monitors the ingredients of class stratifications in American society. . . . Therefore the functional role of the negro intellectual demands that he cannot be absolutely separated from either the black or white world.

West immediately acknowledges that the circumstances Cruse accounts for "has little to do with the motives and intentions of black intellectuals; rather it is an objective situation created by circumstances not of their own choosing. Those objective conditions can be thought of as massively material conditions—of conditions inhabiting and surrounding black intellectual work that are specifically institutional in their placement, culturally perfected and reinforced, commercially routinized, legally sanctioned, and socially dispersed in ways that reenact (and constantly reenact) the internal stratification of clans, neighborhoods, interest blocs, political assemblages, and families, not to mention the organizations of people construed by that most amorphous and deceptive designation, "race."

One of the stratifications that can be lifted from the layering of differences at work in the ensemble of black intellectual identities is the "choice of becoming a black intellectual" in the first instance—a choice (if in fact such a submersion within the crevice of double self-identification can be, after all, an act essentially of will) that is necessarily "an act of self-imposed marginality." One becomes, in a professionally marked culture, an "intellectual" by considerable effort of initial subordination. Such subordination to mentors, curricula, schools, local production protocols, and the like is endured for the sake of mastery to come: mastery and the opportunities for analytic differentiation and ideological discrimination. I nudge the term "discrimination" forward along with Paul Bové's memory of R.P. Blackmur calling up the root sense of discrimination as an operation with criminal implications. Such resonances of the inexpungible baggage of criminality—of our inevitable self-incrimination in the unself-conscious expenditures of intellectual effort—are echoes of Blackmur's (and Bové's) labyrinthine techniques of unsystematic critical suspicion.

The notion of a crime endured as well as a crime to be administered haunts the understanding that Cornel West brings to his careful reading of the black intellectual's plight. The crime suffered most painfully may well be "the inability of black intellectuals to gain respect and support from the black community." A number of forces create that condition, the most problematic is "the widespread refusal of black intellectuals to remain, in some way, organically linked with Afro-American cultural life."

Of the most immediate means of access for black intellectuals to reach a close working relationship to ongoing and long-standing traditions that define black life in North America, two are inherently rich enough and historically elaborated enough to warrant West's belief that they are genuinely "organic intellectual traditions in Afro-American life: *The Black Christian Tradition of Preaching and The Black Musical Tradition of Performance.*"

> Both traditions, though undoubtedly linked to the life of the mind, are oral, improvisational, and histrionic. Both traditions are rooted in black life and

possess precisely what the literate forms of black intellectual activity lack: institutional matrices over time and space within which there are accepted rules of procedure, criteria for judgement, canons for assessing performance, models of past achievement and present emulation, and an acknowledged succession and accumulation of superb accomplishments.

One of the troubling elements of Spike Lee's *Mo' Better Blues* is its inability to step within the self-conscious understanding of the jazz heritage that is ever more enticingly, always probingly active in the work of just those musicians that his film claims to honor by way of cinematic remembrance—by way of sound track reproduction, script, dialogue, visual, if nonetheless frequently fleeting, images, and most of all a somewhat proud engagement of narrative/dramatic performances. The spirit of John Coltrane is invoked repeatedly, only to dissolve in a facile gesture: his name is presented, his legacy beckoned, and his music put on display without the careful, calm exploration of artistic structures that in fact marked the whole of Coltrane's musical life. Coltrane was a restless, but always quiet and innovative, artist. His life's work is used cheaply if its exemplary energy—the enigmatic clarity of an undisruptable musician—is misappropriated.

One might assume without much difficulty that the concept of intellectual work engaged by Spike Lee, across his efforts in *Do the Right Thing* and *Mo' Better Blues,* is at some distance from the notions of intellectual identity that inform "traditional" intellectuals who define themselves within norms set up by white humanistic paradigms. But Marxist and Foucauldian intellectual frameworks are inappropriate for the consciousness-raising effort apparently under way in Lee's films. I do not know Lee's first two films, but in his two most recent "texts" something akin to an "insurgency model" of black intellectual activity, an effort constructed within a set of very specific social circumstances, is at work. West believes that "the uniqueness of the black intellectual predicament" demands for filmmakers like Lee to "articulate a new 'regime of truth' linked to, yet not confined by, indigenous institutional practices permeated by the kinetic orality and emotional physicality, the rhythmic syncopation, the protean improvisation, and the religious, rhetorical, and antiphonal repetition of Afro-American life."

This sense, coupled with a demand, may miss the gesture of accommodation to a distinctly hip and cryptic model of knowledge on display in Lee's flirtation with the jazz heritage. Although I am uncomfortable with the characterization of black life in West's snapshot definition, his tentative conclusions about the black intellectual's embeddedness in traditions that are remarkable for their melodic and poetic power deserve the attention of white and black intellectu-

als, of critics of every persuasion and interest, without evasion:

> The distinctive Afro-American cultural forms such as the black sermonic and prayer styles, gospels, blues, and jazz should inspire, but not constrain, future black intellectual production; that is, the process by which they came to be should provide valuable insights, but they should serve as models to neither imitate nor emulate. Needless to say, these forms thrive on incessant critical innovation and concomitant insurgency.

The following discussion took place immediately after this paper was presented and involved Jim Merod, Andrew Ross, Sharon Willis, Stephen Crofts, Patricia Mellencamp, and Rob Wilson.

Ross: It seems to me that there's a very interesting debate and it is where the historical exploitation on the part of club owners runs right up against the grain of white romanticizations of jazz in the Nat Hentoff tradition, so I'm wondering where your reading of those characters [in Lee's film] and your opinions about that debate fall in the general context of exploitation.

Merod: My sense is that Spike Lee has trivialized the aggression and the exploitation of the two Jewish club owners. First, most club owners aren't Jewish; second, to make them Jewish is another form of stereotyping that is not going to advance a critique, and it will not help him embody the kind of historical significance about the place of jazz in North American culture that the film is apparently concerned with. If anything is at stake there, I'd say that the depiction of the exploitation is so sketchy, so trivial, that it dismisses the ways that exploitation of musicians really takes place. That rip-off occurs on so many levels that it cannot be, except metaphorically, located at the intersection of the club owner who pays bills and the jazz artist who gives up time and energy. Frankly, the greatest exploitation takes place between the jazz musician and the record companies and the media. That squeeze has been going on, as you know, for sometime—I've seen references in your work to knowledge of this, which I've got to congratulate you for since critics of jazz often overlook this completely. An example [of this squeeze] is the breaking of the musicians' strike in the late forties, which created a contractual situation in which instrumentalists were subordinated to star singers. Musicians were thereby relegated to the sideman's role and paid maybe a hundred bucks for a record session without any credit at all or an acknowledgment much diminished. And no percentage of the profits. This has been going on with little deviance unless a lucky "heavyweight" musician, like Miles Davis or Wynton Marsalis, signs with a major record company and has the added benefit of good legal advice. Otherwise, even for the musician with a promise of a percentage take of profits, the control of how much that musician receives remains in the record executive's closet. This is the exploitation that has demoted the jazz musician more than any other kind. It is a matter, also, of the jazz artist not having much say in the representation of jazz as an art form. One notices, for example, how seldom, over the forty-plus years of the television age, jazz has been given large-scale national exposure. You can attribute that malign neglect to several indigenous cultural sources. It is another form, larger than exploitation by club owners, of white cultural hegemony of the sort Spike Lee points to, yet misses, in his film. Jazz musicians are quite aware of the power that record company advertising holds over their working lives, but none that I am aware of has a strategy to counteract it or turn it to their own control. How could they, since the representational manipulation of powerful capital formations plays heavily throughout the entertainment industry? This is a subject of much attention and considerable discussion among the musicians. There are two attitudes that seem to have taken hold among the main cadre of working jazz artists. Frequently the older, more traveled musician says "What the hell can you do? I just try to figure out a way to keep playing and meeting ends." Younger musicians, with recent examples of high-profile contracts and the lionizing of peers like Branford and Wynton Marsalis, Roy Hargrove, Marcus Roberts, and now Mark Whitfield, are often less tolerant.

Ross: Given what you say, why do you think Spike made a movie like this one?

Willis: He's confused.

Merod: That's the best reason I can come up with. If there's a strategic reason, where he believes his film is somehow presenting a kind of culturally rich tactical gesture that reaches into the black community, I'd have to say that I think he's got that wrong, too, for reasons that are mapped out in Cornel West's understanding of forces and opportunities at work on organic black intellectual activity.

Crofts: I agree with you along the lines of the reading you've set out. I think, at the same time, that we have to look at the conditions under which the film industry offers possibilities to make films about jazz. My comment would be to have us think a bit about the history of Hollywood cinema and so I'm thinking here of, is it *Straight No Chaser*, the movie about Chet Baker.

Merod: Let's Get Lost, a film where the same thing happens. Chet is romanticized for fifteen minutes, everyone falls in love with his incredible James Dean good looks and with the beautiful sound track underscoring the idealized jazz scene. But from that point on you go through a tour of his

self-ravaging decomposition without any real sense of the world that brings jazz creativity into being and without an accurate portrayal of Chet's own personal struggles—how he got so far as an artist despite his problematic, drug-riddled life.

Crofts: I'm struck by the fact that *'Round Midnight* is the first full-length feature about jazz with any depth and detail. The first thing we encounter there is a relaxation of racism sufficient to allow a black or a group of blacks to be central figures. The second thing is the yuppification of jazz, certainly, I think, on the East Coast. I don't know about the West Coast. Jazz has seemed to move from clubs to something like chamber music halls. One of the signs of that is Wynton Marsalis as a jazz star who is also a classical musician, where the classical cache is important for the promotion of jazz and Marsalis. I remember a night in 1986 when I saw Art Blakey at Sweet Basil's in New York, and I heard a group of listeners wondering out loud who this guy Blakey was, after all. I think such comments reflect the new respectability based on the yuppification of jazz. Another concern is the kind of aesthetic that the film industry concocts around jazz. There seems to be no way to deal with it directly but in terms of "couple formation," which gets jazz into, for example, Spike Lee's film. Maybe we can say that, given the constraints working against jazz, people with jazz projects have to operate with the industry's standards and limitations in force.

Mellencamp: You know, much the same thing happened with rock in the Hollywood film, since all the film studios signed contracts with the white upper-middle class union. Rock did not enter into American movies until the seventies, and, in a way, it's the same phenomenon. No rock music is offered as scoring for sound tracks, for example.

Willis: In terms of what irks you so completely about Spike Lee's film, the fact that it's a lie about the actual jazz scene, isn't it possible to say that the film isn't at all "about" jazz? It is sort of an apology to Spike Lee's father, since Spike has been so much more successful in his own career. But, more than anything, it feels like a film about Spike's ambivalence about his own class position and his relation to an audience.

Merod: There's a lot to be said about that.

Willis: One of the reasons why the film keeps collapsing just as you've shown is because it can't seem to make its mind up about whether it is concerned most with Bleek or Giant. That is made all the more confusing for me because Giant happens to have Spike Lee's face, but the film seems to want to say that the real "Spike Lee" figure is Bleek—whose ambivalence finally is demonstrated at its most banal level when he argues with Shadow about their audiences.

Merod: Exactly. But even that argument is skewed because Shadow is depicted earlier as taking long Coltrane-like solos that go on forever, and yet later he pugnaciously insists that he intends to play for the masses. He accuses Bleek of being a somewhat dysfunctional purist. The flip-flops in their rivalry blur the sense of what it would mean to address both the hip jazz cognoscenti and a wider, general audience that just loves good music. But I think you're no doubt right. This is not a movie about jazz in any essential way despite the fact that Spike Lee wanted it to be called *A Love Supreme,* which is the title of one of the three or four most important recordings John Coltrane made and probably the one recording most centrally identified with his legacy. You may know that Alice Coltrane, his wife, would not give Lee the rights to that title—mostly on the ground that the film was filled with profane words she objected to. Nonetheless, Lee truly did want his film to have an even more overt and resonant relationship to the high jazz tradition than he was able to create.

Wilson: I want to come back to the theme of the film's attempt to make an intervention into the Afro-American community. You've pointed out that something about jazz as an art form seems to "elude each approach to cinematic capture." I'm wondering here about the idea of "capture"—capture for whom? There is you, who has an archival understanding of jazz in its many versions and transformations as well as how it functions in the black community. But how many people know that history? In a way, you've portrayed jazz as if it is uncapturable: that is to say, it is a nomadic, improvisational form that eludes any sort of capture.

Merod: No, jazz is not merely or essentially an instance of the sublime.

Wilson: Well, my more vulgar point here is my sense that the affirmation of the bourgeois family and the polarization of the two women create a kind of vulgar politics in the film itself. And yet, I see that as an affirmation of the black family being decimated. It makes a very stark attempt to recuperate black family life. And, looking at the film's preoccupation with the Jewish club owners, we find such a broad, reductive statement about New York City politics that I can only read it as a surprisingly clichéd and vulgar form of nationalistic political thinking.

Merod: This is no doubt in part what Andrew [Ross] had in mind at the outset of our discussion. While I agree with the points you're after here, I find both of those themes rendered so sketchily in the film as to make an unconscious code that is deeply puzzling. On one hand, Spike Lee has a political agenda that he is quite unembarrassed to develop from film to film. On the other hand, he has not yet found

the narrative and cinematic resources of his fellow filmmaker, Charles Burnett, whose remarkable film, *To Sleep with Anger,* constructs a grand fable of upper-middle class black family life on a scale (and with a leisurely pacing) capable of confronting just those racial stereotypes that undermine, from either side, the cultural common ground that jazz—perhaps more than any art—has placed among frequently miscast, sometimes unendurable, forms of diversity.

Spike Lee with Janice Mosier Richolson (interview date 1991)

SOURCE: "He's Gotta Have It: An Interview with Spike Lee," in *Cineaste,* Vol. 18, No. 4, 1991, pp. 12-15.

[*In the following interview, Lee discusses his film* Jungle Fever *and his approach to filmmaking.*]

Spike Lee is a filmmaker with a vision and an agenda. He makes no bones about it: his purpose is to hold his cinematic mirror up to reflect African-American reality as experienced by his generation. These are the young blacks who grew up after the civil rights movement and the assassinations of Martin Luther King, Jr. and Malcolm X. They have seen the dream of a Great Society and Affirmative Action crumble into crackhouses and quota-babble.

*Not yet thirty-five, Lee has directed five feature films since 1986—***She's Gotta Have It, School Daze, Do the Right Thing, Mo' Better Blues,*** and ***Jungle Fever***—which have earned him a controversial reputation for interpreting contemporary black America to itself and to society at large. He's a man with a commitment and credentials, working in the right medium for the times.*

Born in Atlanta into an educated, culturally stimulating family environment—his father is an accomplished jazz musician—Lee moved as a child with his family to New York City, where he lived in middle class Brooklyn neighborhoods. He returned to Atlanta to become a third generation graduate of Morehouse College. After a summer internship at Columbia Pictures, Lee enrolled at New York University's film school where he and friends from Morehouse formed a creative team that has stayed together.

Cultural advantages, solid education, old school ties . . . sounds like upscale America. But it's the middle class family and the college campus that often incubate American liberal reformers. A shrewd businessman, adept at marketing and public relations, Lee talks freely and concisely about the controversial subjects portrayed in his films. He knows how to work the press, how to take control of an interview and make it serve his own ends. At the same time, he main-

tains a pose of professional detachment, projecting the high seriousness of an artist and social critic. He directs his gaze slightly away from the questioner, but drops his mask when irritated or amused, replying sharply or bursting into hearty laughter, and sometimes revealing adolescent-like petulance or impish charm. It's hard to tell the public persona from the man and best to take Lee at face value on his own terms. He continues to live and work in Brooklyn as an independent filmmaker at his own company, 40 Acres and a Mule Filmworks, and is currently at work on a feature film on Malcolm X.

The following interview, which took place at the 1991 Cannes Film Festival after the screening of **Jungle Fever,** *also incorporates Lee's responses to questions posed at a general press conference and at a panel discussion of American directors.*

[*Mosier Richolson:*] *What is the primary purpose of your films?*

[Lee:] I try to show African-American culture on screen. Every group, every culture and ethnic group needs to see itself on screen. What black filmmakers can do is show our culture on screen the same way Fellini's done for Italians and Kurosawa's done for the Japanese.

You describe your films as "litmus tests" that measure the pulse of public opinion on issues of social concern. Do you believe that the cinema has significant social power to help eliminate racism and prejudice?

I don't think my films are going to get rid of racism or prejudice. I think the best thing my films can do is provoke discussion. In my films, I try to show that there's a very serious problem. Racism is such a broad subject. I think conditions are the same as they've always been. There is still prejudice in the United States and Europe. To me prejudice is based on ignorance. A lot of times, racism is tied directly to exploitation and money. I think the biggest lie that's ever been perpetrated on the American people is 'If you're American, it doesn't matter what race, nationality, religion, or creed you are—you're American, and that's all that matters.' That's a lie and it's always been a lie. The United States is built on the Constitution of the United States. In that Constitution, it says that black people are three-fifths of a human being and could be sold as property . . . as cattle. Black people have been trained and taught to hate themselves. We've been taught that everything black is negative or derogatory. We've been taught that Africa, our homeland, which is a cradle of civilization, is a place where cannibals run around naked, swinging on trees.

You've made two films about confrontation between Afri-

can-Americans and Italian-Americans. Why did you pick these ethnic groups?

New York City is made up of many different ethnic groups. That is not to say that the only conflicts between ethnic groups there are those between blacks and Italians, but these are the most violent ones in my mind. I don't know what it is, but when blacks and Italian-Americans get together, a lot of times you have a conflict. Take the murder of Yusuf Hawkins as an example. One day he wanted to check out a used car and ventured into a neighborhood which happened to be a predominantly Italian-American neighborhood and he was shot.

You dedicated **Jungle Fever** *to Hawkins. Does that mean there is revenge in the air?*

No. I don't think there is any revenge in the air. What happened in 1989 happened then. It's two years later. I'm a kinder, gentler person.

In your film, you use the term "jungle fever" for the sexual attraction some whites and blacks feel for each other. Have you ever felt jungle fever?

No. I've never had a relationship with a white woman.

What kind of research did you do? Was the film based on personal experience or invention?

Both. A lot of my films are based on personal experience. My mother died in 1977 when I was twenty. My father remarried a white woman. That probably had something to do with it.

Did the marriage work?

Yes, they're in love. They had a child. I have a little brother.

Do you like the woman?

We don't get along, but it's not because she's white. I was my mother's first child, so my stepmother's never going to be my mother.

What do your father and stepmother think of the film?

They haven't seen it yet. It might be hard for him to look at. She ain't gonna like it.

Do you think she'll take the issues of the film as a personal slight?

What's she gonna do—beat me? I'm a grown man.

What are you trying to show in the film?

I think what we're trying to do with this film is to show sexual myths. What's important about this film is that the characters Flipper and Angie, played by Wesley Snipes and Annabella Sciorra, are not drawn to each other by love but by sexual myths. When you're a black person in this country, you're constantly bombarded with the myth of the white woman as the epitome of beauty—again and again and again—in TV, movies, magazines. It's blond hair, fair skin, blue eyes, thin nose. If you're black, you never see yourself portrayed in that way—you don't fit that image, you're not beautiful. So we cut away our noses to get a thinner nose . . . we'll cut away our lips . . . wear blue and green contact lenses. Why do we do that? Because that's what's pounded into us constantly. Annabella Sciorra's character bought into the myth that the black male is a stud, a sexual superman with a penis that's two feet long. So those are the two sexual myths that bring these two people together.

Are you saying that they wanted to explore the sexual myths—that they were curious about each other's flesh?

That was the basis of their relationship. One thing a lot of people aren't picking up on is that the film is not just about interracial marriages and relationships. It's about identity. There are people in the film who are *products* of mixed marriages. My character's wife in the film has a black father and a white mother. The same is true for Flipper's wife. The people in the film are constantly talking about their identity, where they belong. They make a distinction between mulattoes, quadroons, and octoroons. And not just the blacks. In the candy store, the Italian-Americans have the same concern. There are a lot of dark Italians. Sicily is very close to Africa. The character Frankie says, "I'm not black. My mother's a dark Italian. I'm as white as anybody here."

In one scene, the black women characters speak frankly and openly about sexuality and color. Was it scripted?

It was completely improvisational. We did between twenty and twenty-five takes. I find the more you talk the more honest you get.

How do you feel about interracial relationships?

Interracial relationships and marriages have been going on since we were brought over here as slaves. We're not trying to condemn interracial relationships. People have to realize that this film does not represent every single interracial couple in the world. We're not saying that a black man with a white woman won't work. I think if two people love each other, that's great. There's another interracial couple in the film. The John Turturro character named Paulie and the

character Orin. I think they have a chance of having a better relationship because they have a real foundation of friendship, whereas Flipper and Angie's was based on myth. They didn't really love each other. I think if they had, love would have enabled them to withstand the onslaught of abuse they were getting from their family and friends and the two neighborhoods they live in—Harlem and Bensonhurst. In the end, Angie comes to love Flipper, but he still loves his wife.

When Angie's Italian-American father finds out that she's been with a black man, did he have to beat her up so badly?

He feels he does.

Would he have done the same if she'd gotten involved with any other man who wasn't Italian-American?

No. If Angie had gotten involved with an Irish or Jewish man, her father might have been upset, but the fact that he's black—that's the ass-whipper.

She seems to get the worst of it. Her family's reaction seems much more violent than the one Flipper gets.

It's been my experience—I'm not going to say both communities welcome interracial relationships—but it's very rare that black people disown a relative if they marry somebody white. They might not talk to you for a week or so, but they're not going to lock their door. I know several cases where white people with black partners were thrown out of the family and the family hasn't spoken to them since. They're cut out of the will and all types of stuff. That's the difference.

When Flipper's wife discovers that her husband is unfaithful to her, she seemed more upset that her husband was with a white woman than with the fact that he was unfaithful.

I think that regardless of whether the other woman was white or black, Flipper's wife would be throwing his stuff out of the window. The fact that he was having an affair with a white woman made it that much worse of an offense.

Flipper is a very well-heeled, upwardly mobile professional African-American. Is there a point being made there?

Yes. We're saying that one should not lose himself—who they are—while striving to be successful. There are other things more important than success.

Why did you wait so long to tackle the issue of the drug problem?

I felt that drugs should be a big part of this film. It was right for *Jungle Fever*. I had to be the one to determine when drugs would be in my films. I wanted to show the drug problem as a main theme in a film, not just stick it in because the drug topic is trendy, chic, or faddish. In *Do the Right Thing,* drugs would have been a bogus sub-plot. The main thrust of that film was racism. In *Mo' Better Blues,* I did not want to make another typical story of a jazz musician who's an alcoholic or who's hooked on heroin.

Religion is a big theme in this film. In your portrayals of the characters Gator and the Good Reverend Doctor—Ossie Davis's character—you seem to imply a relationship between religion and drugs.

That implication's not there for me. Gator's on crack for a lot of reasons. One is the relationship with his father, who's a reverend. The Good Reverend Doctor is out of touch. He goes overboard, and I think religion really had a bad effect on Gator in the film. But I don't think religion is what turned Gator into a crackhead. His brother Flipper isn't on drugs. I really think people are responsible for their own actions. Gator likes getting high.

Where did you get the idea for the characters of Gator and the Good Reverend Doctor?

The whole idea of the Good Reverend Doctor killing his son is based on Marvin Gaye Sr. shooting Marvin Gaye Jr., who was a cokehead at the time.

You definitely say 'no' to drugs in the film. You show Flipper wandering through a crackhouse looking for Gator, then crying 'no' as he holds a young addict close to him. Is that your 'no' or the 'no' of the character.

Me and him. Flipper's going crazy. He just spent the last two hours in hell.

Is your portrayal of a crackhouse realistic?

Crackhouses aren't that big. It was artistic license. I wanted to show how crack is totally wiping out generations of African-Americans.

Do you think of yourself as a role model for black filmmakers?

No, I don't think of myself like that. I think from the beginning, I never, ever wanted to think of myself as 'king of the hill' of African-Americans who make films.

How did you get started as a filmmaker?

When I went to film school, I knew I did not want to have my films shown only during Black History Month in February or at libraries. I wanted them to have a wide distribu-

tion. And I did not want to spend four or five years trying to piecemeal together the money for my films. I did my first film, *She's Gotta Have It,* independently for $175,000. We had a grant from the New York State Council on the Arts and were raising money the whole time we were shooting. We shot the film in twelve days. The next stage was to get it out of the lab. Then, the most critical part was when I had to hole up in my little studio apartment to get it cut. I took about two months to do that. I had no money coming in, so I had to hold off the debtors because I knew if I had enough time to at least get it in good enough shape to show, we could have some investor screenings, and that's what happened. We got it blown up to 35mm for a film festival. What you have to do is to try to get a distributor. You enter as many film festivals as you can. *She's Gotta Have It* was picked up for $475,000 after a lot of distributors saw it at a festival.

Your name is often mentioned today as a milestone in black filmmaking. How do you feel about that?

It's very encouraging. But even though I might be the one who's getting the publicity, there were a lot of people before me who made it happen. If Melvin Van Peebles didn't do *Sweet Sweetback's Baadasssss Song,* none of this would have been possible. And there's Gordon Parks, Ossie Davis—all these people and others put up with a whole lot of stuff. So the people following them twenty or thirty years later are able to do what we're doing now. Because of my success, it's going to make it easier for the next generation that comes up behind us.

Do you think you've opened the door for black filmmakers?

I try to make the best films I can, good films that make money to enable things to open up. I'm not saying the door's wide open . . . it's not wide open. But the fact is that blacks are making films instead of the door being shut. I think there were nineteen films by black filmmakers released last year, and that's more than the whole previous decade combined. I think what's important is that we not get too high and start doing cartwheels and say that happy days are here, that Hollywood's in love with black people. That's not the case. We're not getting the same treatment as general market films, which means films for white moviegoers. And this is something we continue to fight. We want to raise the ceiling of how much Hollywood will spend to make and promote our films.

As your films get bigger, as you get more success, do you find that you're getting intervention from the moneymen? Do they try to persuade you to do the film their way?

They're always going to tell you what they think. If their suggestions are good, I use them. If they're not, I don't. I think I have the best of both worlds because I'm an independent filmmaker with complete creative control of my films. I hire who I want. I have final cut. But at the same time, I go directly to Hollywood for financing and distribution. I find it's best for me to work within the Hollywood system. It's an individual choice, and you have to make up your mind. I have a classmate from NYU who hates Hollywood. He's found his financing with Japanese money.

Music is an important component in your films. How much of that is your input?

I start thinking about the music for my films at the same moment I'm writing the script. It's part of my creative process. I pay as much attention to the music as I do to the cinematography, casting, and production design. I'm the son of a great jazz musician, Bill Lee. He's done the scores for all of my films before *Jungle Fever.* I was raised with jazz. It was played in the house all the time.

Stevie Wonder did the music for **Jungle Fever.** *You also used some Frank Sinatra songs. Why was that?*

For juxtaposition. We had three songs by Frank Sinatra at the candy store in Bensonhurst, representing the Italian-American community. We also had four songs by Mahalia Jackson for the scenes with the Good Reverend Doctor and his wife.

You often use music and dialog at the same time.

A lot of people say you shouldn't do that. I don't agree. If it's the right music, you can play it behind dialog. We had a great ten week mix to make sure we had the right balance, that the music never overrides the dialog.

What's your next project?

I hope to make a film on an epic scale about Malcolm X. I want it to be on a David Lean scale. The Malcolm X project has been trying to get made for twenty years. There were several directors . . . scripts were written. I thought the first script—James Baldwin's—was the best.

When it comes to race relations, would you say that you're an optimist or a pessimist?

I think I'm a realist. In my films, I'm not saying, "Throw up your hands, there's no hope," or that black and white people will never get together. Even though some people say my films have a bleak outlook, I think my films are optimistic. I still think there's hope.

Do you think the problems of racism and prejudice can change in your lifetime?

I don't think racism can be eliminated in my lifetime . . . or my children's or grandchildren's. But I think it's something we have to strive for. I'm going to keep working toward that day coming.

Benjamin Saltman (review date Winter 1991-92)

SOURCE: A review of *Jungle Fever,* in *Film Quarterly,* Vol. 45, No. 2, Winter, 1991-92, pp. 37-41.

[*In the following review, Saltman discusses Lee's* Jungle Fever, *asserting that 'Amid his pop sociology and artistic excesses, Lee demonstrates a thoroughly contemporary consciousness and the ability to put it on film.'*]

Spike Lee developed his skills in independent movie making and music videos, working his way up to become an American *auteur*—perhaps not quite ready to be an artistic successor to Woody Allen, but ready to enter the social and political space left by Costa-Gavras and Godard, and in racial issues to locate himself somewhere between Eddie Murphy and Malcolm X. In other words, Lee is hard to pin down. Perhaps of all his work so far *Jungle Fever* is the hardest to locate. Lee's filmic style is a kind of slowed-down MTV, an assemblage of fragments which present his social concerns broadly and unanalytically. As an entertainer he mastered the attack language of pop music and night-club comedy and adapted it with persistence and ambition to interracial and intraracial issues. Some serious reviewers have rejected *Jungle Fever,* first for Lee's apparent scorn for integration, second for his misreading of black-white relationships, and third for his creation of bad art. They find the love relationship in the film to be superficial: the interracial affair between a black man and a white woman is dismissive, and the whole issue of interracial relationships is treated too harshly. Because the affair doesn't work out and the two lovers split at the end of the film to go back to their neighborhoods (Bensonhurst and Harlem) Lee seems despairing and separatist, and in fact appears to attack integration in the manner of the black nationalists of the sixties—but without their heroism.

> **The real theme of *Jungle Fever* is, in fact, the power and persistence of racial oppression; the film argues that the chief issue for blacks is the amelioration of their condition, to which other issues must be subordinated.**
> **—*Benjamin Saltman***

The answer to this criticism may lie in Lee's use of social

types from the African-American and white worlds. Neither Lee's talent nor interest point toward character in depth; in flat panels he raises the racial and ethnic types who make up his story. The audience can hardly help but notice that the plot in *Jungle Fever* is a mockup of *Romeo and Juliet* by way of *West Side Story;* in this case culture-and-race-crossed lovers represent not some Renaissance notion of the individual creative romantic self but racial and ethnic stances. There is no lyric here but rather a desultory passionate moment, an experiment in cross-race sex, followed by confusion and regret. Without the intensity or complexity of their literary ancestors, the lovers play an ensemble role together with others in the film who also make a strong claim upon our attention and are portrayed just as sharply and just as superficially.

In this context the film would therefore seem to fail. But my point is that the love story is a pseudo-theme designed to present race relationships and stereotypes, a cleverly ironic frame designed to dismiss traditional romance, to point out its irrelevance. The real theme of *Jungle Fever* is, in fact, the power and persistence of racial oppression; the film argues that the chief issue for blacks is the amelioration of their condition, to which other issues must be subordinated. This theme is distributed in the film in curious ways: it does not move toward a single overwhelming point, nor does it unify a variety of interrelated points. The love story plays no better or more unifying part than any other story within the film. Lee's concern transcends "romance"; he has little use for idealized sexual relationships in the face of vital economic and political needs—his crude verb for sexual intercourse is "to bone." This cynical attitude about romance is certainly not new for him; it was thoroughly developed in *She's Gotta Have It,* where it was a form of domination.

It is a mistake to accuse Lee of failing to develop the love story in *Jungle Fever* or even give it time to mature; he even rejects the tradition of secrecy between lovers. The affair is almost immediately evident to both the black and the white families and friends of the lovers. The social matrix takes precedence over intimate romance, making the sexual affair a localized social disaster and not a personal event. The lovers only succeed in dramatizing the incommensurability of the white and black worlds of New York, typified by white Bensonhurst and black Harlem. And Lee wants it that way. He could have chosen Greenwich Village as the scene of an affair with which to examine the subtle personal pressures that touch mixed-race couples; but that was not his story. The subjects of this decentered film are instead the black condition, the drug-riddled poor, the continuing economic disaster of a devastated Harlem, and the problems of the black middle class, whose confused and uneasy black professionals (the hero is a talented architect) are inescapably caught up in the realities of racism. Flipper Purify,

played by Wesley Snipes, works for a glitzy white firm while in Harlem the houses are falling down. He is disassociated from his surroundings even though he chooses to live in Harlem. His romance with an Italian-American temp-secretary is halfhearted, hardly a challenge to his marriage. The film opens with a highly charged sex scene between Flipper and his wife, played by Lonette McKee, and in its heat there is no implication that the hero is jaded, or suffering a midlife crisis—he is clearly happily married, and the subsequent "boning" of the white woman performed upon his architect's drafting table becomes an act of curiosity for both characters and of cynical social commentary on Lee's part. In setting up this situation Lee is not critical of black professionals only; the social and economic background of the affair is part of its foreground. He is insisting that the black condition takes precedence at this time and place over personal issues.

Yet Lee's obvious manipulative traits, his conceit, his MTV personality, his money-making commercials with Michael Jordan, his presuming to be a spokesman for blacks, distort the perception of his movie. He neither analyzes the black condition with care, nor does he reveal much compassion for it. He appears to lack the high seriousness that characterized earlier spokesmen for African-American causes; writers like Amiri Baraka, James Baldwin, and Eldridge Cleaver were intensely analytic, and presented the issues in sharply focused works. Lee's world is cool, eclectic, and despairing, its focus wanders; it suggests a cynical yet dismayed withdrawal from situation similar to television commercials that show young African Americans playing basketball on brick courts in city ghettos wearing impossibly expensive Nikes.

Lee's cynicism, his lack of focus, of unity, is the key to his special effect as film-maker. He is often under attack for not doing what he does not intend to do, while what he does achieve is misunderstood. Unlike Woody Allen, he does not focus upon a single complicated protagonist who represents contemporary dilemmas. Allen's strongly centered, highly unified work reflects the modernist traditions of Bergman and Fellini, but Lee's work celebrates the despair and pleasure attendant upon disunity. *Jungle Fever* is loosely connected, decentered; it portrays the black condition in one anecdote after another containing characters who surface and disappear like offshore rocks. An example is Flipper's family: his brother, played beautifully by Samuel Jackson, is a drug addict who will do virtually anything short of murder to find his fix; but the incidents which lead to his death at the hands of his father have virtually nothing to do with the hero's interracial fling. The father is also a story in himself (in a perhaps too easy performance by Ossie Davis): a rigidly religious preacher bitter over the black condition but unable to do anything about it. The tentative romantic subplot involving the secretary's ex-boyfriend and an intellectual black woman comments on the difficulty encountered by successful black women—they turn to white men rather than "ordinary" black men, since there aren't enough successful black males to go around and since black males are intimidated by successful black women. Thus another offfocus aspect of the film explores the plight of black women of achievement who feel emotionally, sexually isolated—a gathering in which black women unload their complaints is perhaps the film's funniest scene. Lee's anecdotal method differs here from the multiple-story form familiar to us in movies and on TV, in films like *Towering Inferno* or *Airport* (one may call it "The *Grand Hotel* Method"), because this form is designed to explore character, as superficial and stereotyped as that character might be. Lee's point is social and not individual, and his loose structure is a mockery of plot. The final incident, a stereotypical freeze frame, depicts the hero embracing in anguish a black teenage junkie hooker, confronting the black condition from which he has been escaping through personal ambition and cross-racial dalliance. The hero has passed the hooker at various points in the film, so the final shot comes as no great shock in itself—what is shocking is that the hero's sudden tortured outburst completely shatters any notion of his character we may have gleaned from the film. This scene cannot be explained logically by the glimmer of plot which supports it; although Flipper has witnessed the failure of his interracial affair and the murder of his dope-addict brother by his father, he has given no hint of the emotional resources needed for his explosive reaction.

Lee seems incapable of making a straightforward statement about the social and political issues he depicts. His juxtaposition of anecdotes defines no particular stance, no unified vision. Those who want a definite statement such as "Fight the power" will not find it, because Lee is himself divided about the nature of the struggle. He will not and perhaps cannot embrace an ideology. He inhabits an aimless political space. As Robert Chrisman says of *Do the Right Thing:* "Lee's inability to present a coherent value system in the replication of black life in his films raises the question, indeed, what is the right thing?" It is too easy to claim that *Jungle Fever* raises significant questions; questions must be asked in coherent and significant ways. Lee's assemblage of anecdotes prevents him from entering deeply into any one of them. The very structure of his work is against analysis and for surfaces. With an entertainer's despair of depth and delight in types and observation, he gives us sketches of men and women in the context of a racist society. These are types but not, with the exception of a few misses here and there (Flipper's bosses and his mother), stereotypes. Flipper and his wife are not stereotypes; Flipper's brother transcends stereotype as a drug addict like a virtuoso musician transcends a night-club hack.

Essentially, then, the film is episodic, a combination of bur-

lesque and street theater brought into the multi-million dollar milieu of a nineties film. It is relentlessly popular in its quest for effects, in its shtick. Incidents in the film stand out and apart from each other as if they were culled from different films. The astounding scene in the Taj Mahal crack house is dreamlike and expressionistic; the scenes between the bible-thumping father and his family are melodramatic family drama; the scenes involving the Italian fathers (who are comically similar, though Anthony Quinn's portrait is more accomplished) are farcical; the scene in which the hero's wife throws his possessions from the window of their apartment is an adaptation of Lee's communal street scenes in *Do the Right Thing. Jungle Fever* is decentered in plot, in filmic style, and ultimately in tone.

The film's tone—comic, angry, cynical, turgid, ridiculous, melodramatic, despairing—is its most vital aspect. This tone is decentered in the sense that it neither knows itself nor proceeds from a unified authorial identity; it is not so much ambiguous as it is vaporized in the multiple stories and styles of the film. The special quality that distinguishes *Jungle Fever* from other postmodern films like *Blue Velvet* or *Crimes and Misdemeanors* in which the tone is at bottom despairing is the film's socio-political message, which ultimately cannot permit the wry, cynical helplessness of Lynch's and Allen's films. There is always a reformer's hope in even the darkest political films, and this is true of *Jungle Fever.* Lee's achievement is to combine an unfocused construction of contingencies with serious political satire. His work cannot be characterized as a monolith but rather as a sprawling and varied city. Such combinations would seem to be self-canceling, but in this case the result is an unsettling comedy which demands that Americans make room for diversity, for the multiplicity of otherness. Amid his pop sociology and artistic excesses, Lee demonstrates a thoroughly contemporary consciousness and the ability to put it on film.

Bert Cardullo (review date Winter 1992)

SOURCE: "Law of the Jungle," in *The Hudson Review*, Vol. XLIV, No. 4, Winter, 1992, pp. 642-7.

[*In the following excerpt, Cardullo discusses Lee's* Jungle Fever *and suggests that Lee watch African films to "discover something not only about artistic economy, about the virtue (and resonance) of a simple tale straightforwardly told, but also about the culture of his Mother Africa."*]

. . . Spike Lee's *Jungle Fever* is about villagers of a different kind: those of New York City, which, with the possible exception of upper Manhattan, is America's most parochial city. (My mother, who spent the first forty years of her life in Brooklyn, rarely felt the need to venture outside Flatbush, let alone the borough itself.) Lee's "villagers" are all played by professionals, and it shows in the unevenness of their work, in the absence from all but a few scenes of an ensemble feeling. For every subtly inflected performance, like that of John Turturro or Annabella Sciorra, there is a forced or wooden one, like that of Wesley Snipes or Lee himself. For every powerfully affecting piece of acting, like Samuel L. Jackson's, there is a slackly maudlin one, like Anthony Quinn's. Even the cinematography of *Jungle Fever*—by Ernest Dickerson, who has shot all of Lee's features—is uneven, in that it combines realistic or on-location interiors— in a Bensonhurst candy store, an uptown architectural firm, a Harlem restaurant, a Greenwich Village apartment—with prettified or doctored exteriors, with outdoor scenes whose visual effects are so calculated that they seem to have been shot on sound stages. This has been a problem in all of Lee's color films, and I can only conclude that his time spent in film school (at New York University) has addicted him to cinematic trickery, to the legerdemain of the studio over the reality of the street. How else can one explain his outrageous use—twice!—of a traveling matte behind two characters in conversation, which creates the illusion that they are taking a walk when in fact they're standing still?

Jungle Fever is Spike Lee's fifth feature film (he has made one documentary, his thesis project at NYU's Tisch School of the Arts in 1982: *Joe's Bed-Stuy Barbershop: We Cut Heads*), which, as usual, he wrote as well as directed, and it comes amidst a plethora of films by blacks, about blacks—that is, about blacks more as they relate to one another than as they relate to whites. But Lee is the only one among the new wave of black directors who's even close to being an artist, and, despite its failings, his *Jungle Fever* is easily the best of the current crop of films about black America. It is far more sophisticated in its exploration of interracial relationships than his *School Daze* was in its treatment of the intraracial clash between light-skinned and dark-skinned blacks at an all-black college, and it deserves to be taken as seriously as *Do the Right Thing,* Lee's serious but fatally flawed examination of racism and economic exploitation in the Bedford-Stuyvesant section of Brooklyn. Certainly *Jungle Fever* is something of a return to form for the thirty-four-year-old Lee after the disastrous *Mo' Better Blues,* which thought it was telling the story of a black jazz musician from a black filmmaker's point of view, but was only retelling the formulaic, melodramatic story of countless jazz films, substituting a black trumpeter for the young white man with a horn, and throwing in a little anti-Semitism (in the person of two grossly caricatured Jewish club owners) for bad measure.

"Jungle fever" is the movie's description for interracial love—or lust—in the urban jungle of New York. Flipper

Purify (Wesley Snipes)—God knows why Lee gave him this ridiculous name—is a successful young architect who lives on Striver's Row in the Sugar Hill section of Harlem with his light-skinned black wife, Drew (Lonette McKee), a buyer at Bloomingdale's, and his adoring little daughter, Ming. Angela Tucci (Annabella Sciorra) is a temp secretary with only a (Catholic) high-school education who lives in the Bensonhurst district of Brooklyn with her widowed father and two brothers, Jimmy and Charlie—the same Bensonhurst where in 1989 a gang of young Italians killed a black teenager, Yusuf Hawkins (to whom *Jungle Fever* is dedicated, and whose murder, says Lee, sparked the making of the film), because they thought he was dating a local white girl. Flipper and Angie meet when she takes the place of his former secretary at the architectural firm in Manhattan where he works, and which he eventually quits to go into business for himself (he says, but we never see this happen) because his two white bosses will not elevate him— their best, most productive architect—to partner. Flipper and Angie get along, despite the fact that he had demanded a black secretary, and after a few late-night work sessions topped off with heartfelt conversation over Chinese takeout, they copulate on a drafting table. Here's Lee on the nature of Flipper and Angie's relationship: "She's attracted to him because she's been told that black men know how to fuck. He's attracted to her because all his life he's been bombarded with images of white women being the epitome of beauty and the standard that everything else must be measured against."

I beg your pardon, Spike, but your film reveals that Angie falls in love with Flipper (although Lee rushes the blossoming of that love), rejects her longtime boyfriend, Paulie Carbone (John Turturro), for him, and endures a beating from her father as well as the ostracism of her Bensonhurst neighbors—who learn of her affair from a girlfriend to whom she had entrusted her secret—in order to remain with her black lover. Flipper, by contrast, never commits himself to Angie, never has what can be called a complex relationship with her, despite his description of it as such. He moves into a Greenwich Village apartment with her only because his wife, to whom he has never before been unfaithful, throws him out of their place (after learning of his affair with a "low-class white bitch" from her best friend, Vera, who learned of it from her husband, Cyrus [Spike Lee], to whom Flipper had entrusted *his* secret); he insists to Drew that he loves her, not Angie; and he leaves his white lover the moment he has an excuse to: after his father, a defrocked Baptist preacher (Ossie Davis), delivers a racist tirade against miscegenation that culminates in his calling his son a whoremonger in front of Angie—a tirade that is followed by an incident on the street in which Flipper is accosted by two white cops for attempted rape, merely for playfully returning a punch that Angie threw at him to break the tension. When Flipper tells Angie that he doesn't love her and questions her motivation in getting together with him, she responds, "Speak for yourself, not for me."

So Flipper pursued Angie merely out of sexual curiosity, as he finally admits, but by not having this character fall in love with his white girlfriend, Lee missed the opportunity to explore an interracial relationship, perhaps an interracial marriage, in depth—a marriage that Drew herself is the product of, and whose mixed race has drawn her the abuse of some blacks together with the adoration of others, like Flipper, as well as instilled in her the paradoxical belief that blacks should stop diluting their blood by procreating with whites. The closest we get to a genuine interracial relationship is in the tender moments between Paulie and a middle-class black woman who comes into his candy store every morning to buy the *New York Times,* but must settle for the *Post* or the *Daily News* instead, since Carbone's won't stock a newspaper that doesn't sell to its mostly working-class clientele. Paulie pursues this woman, Orin Good, after Angie breaks up with him, despite protests and beatings from his domineering father (Anthony Quinn) and loutish friends. Toward the end of the film, he has his first date with Orin, for which he arrives to the accompaniment of Sinatra's "Hello, Young Lovers" on the soundtrack. But although Lee has asserted that "their initial attraction is based on genuine feelings," he doesn't develop that attraction; we leave Orin and Paulie at her front door, never to see them again. (As in the Flipper-Angie relationship, the black in this one is educated and the white Italian is not, though he talks of applying to Brooklyn College; Lee doesn't seem to realize that, after race, differences in education—and thus in social class as well as earning power—keep people apart more than anything else.)

Instead of spending more time on the relationship between Orin and Paulie, why did Lee base *Jungle Fever* on the short-lived affair between Flipper and Angie, a couple that, according to the director, "came together because of sexual mythology"? Because, as he did in *Do the Right Thing,* he prefers to do the easier thing: cram his film with incident rather than exploration, with texture rather than subtext. It isn't as if he didn't have examples to draw from: there were 211,000 interracial marriages in the United States in 1990, of which 71 percent were between black men and white women, while 29 percent paired white men with black women. Lee's texture is sometimes very good: he gets exactly right, for example, the atmosphere of Carbone's Candy Store and the behavioral rhythms of the young men and old-timers who hang out there; and, with the help of Ernest Dickerson, he visually complicates the relationship between Flipper and Angie where his screenplay has tended to simplify or reduce it—during this couple's penultimate scene together in their sparsely furnished Greenwich Village apartment, for instance, she poignantly asks, "Are we together?" as they look off in opposite directions and are photographed

in separate frames, with white light shining on Flipper in silhouette and low-key lighting on Angie in a black dress off one shoulder.

But texture of this kind is not enough, and incident alone is too much, as in the case of Flipper's strained relationship with his crack-addicted brother, Gator (Samuel L. Jackson), whose sad story takes up a significant portion of the film. Lee seems to be responding here to the criticism that he unrealistically omitted the drug culture from the jazz world of *Mo' Better Blues* and the Bedford-Stuyvesant ghetto of *Do the Right Thing.* In *Jungle Fever,* however, the drug culture is superfluous: what does Gator's addiction have to do with Flipper and Angie's affair, with the response of the Good Reverend Doctor (the title by which his wife and sons always address him, despite his having been defrocked, apparently for sexual misconduct) and Mrs. Purify (Ruby Dee) to that affair? What does the Reverend's murder of Gator—for his addiction, for stealing from his own family, for tormenting his mother—have to do with Mr. Tucci's beating of Angie for "fucking a nigger"? And what does Flipper's anguished embrace, in the film's very last shot (during which the camera hyperbolically zooms in on him), of a drug-crazed black hooker have to do with his rejection of Angie? The answer to all of these questions is, of course, "nothing." Spike Lee has yet to learn that merely to juxtapose disparate narrative strands—something that film can do almost too easily—is not to connect them, to link them with a central theme. Two narrative strands that he could handily and fruitfully have merged, he fails to do: Flipper's starting his own business, beginning a career as a black architectural entrepreneur, with his committing himself to an interracial relationship in which Angie is his partner in work as well as in love.

By the end of *Jungle Fever,* Angie has returned home to the father who had banished her, while Flipper has returned home to the wife who had banished him and who banishes him again for his infidelity—but only after this black stud has satisfied her sexual needs as no white man ever could (this is the film talking, not your film critic!). Lee prefaces the bedroom scene between Flipper and Drew with a crane shot down to the street to pick up the delivery of the *New York Times* to the Purifys' doorstep, then up to and through their bedroom window. This sequence is a reprise of the one that opened the film and is testimony to little more than Lee's addiction to circularity and the use of his Louma crane—he used a similar shot to open and close both *Do the Right Thing* and *Mo' Better Blues.* Circularity here serves no purpose: it's thematically bankrupt, as it was not in *Tilaï,* and all the more so since it does not end the film, but is followed instead by Flipper's commiserative embrace of the black hooker after she has solicited him on the street.

Neither does much of Stevie Wonder's music serve a purpose: his eleven songs may make a new album for him (his first in four years), but most of them seem laid on the film; they combined with three Frank Sinatra recordings, a few tunes from Mahalia Jackson (heard during scenes in the home of Flipper's parents), a little rap music, and even some conventional movie scoring (by Terence Blanchard) to give this viewer a case of sensory overload. Again, contrast this heavy dependence on music with *Tilaï*'s discreet application of it: the title song is the only song, sung (by Abdullah Ibrahim, its author) over the opening and closing credits, and the instrumental music in-between never competes for attention with events on the screen. I suggest that Spike Lee take a look at *Tilaï* and other African films like it: he might discover something not only about artistic economy, about the virtue (and resonance) of a simple tale straightforwardly told, but also about the culture of his Mother Africa—an Africa that he and his fellow black artists routinely trumpet as their ultimate place of origin, but about which they know so very little.

Spike Lee with Gary Crowdus and Dan Georgakas (interview date December 1992)

SOURCE: "Our Film Is Only a Starting Point: An Interview with Spike Lee," in *Cineaste*, Vol. 19, No. 4, 1993, pp. 20-4.

[*In the following interview, which took place in December, 1992, Lee discusses the making of the film* Malcolm X, *and explains his reasons for excluding certain material.*]

In addition to our Critical Symposium on **Malcolm X,** Cineaste *felt it was important to talk to Spike Lee and incorporate his comments in our overall perspective on the film. In the following interview, Lee explains his primary desire to introduce Malcolm X to young viewers and his awareness that the time limits of even a nearly three and a half hour movie prevented him from producing anything more than a "primer" on one of America's most charismatic black leaders. His additional comments about the difficulties of attempting to produce an epic political film within the budgetary constraints imposed by Warner Bros. and in light of the many other pragmatic and political considerations involved are important aspects in arriving at a fully informed appraisal of the artistic achievement and political significance of* **Malcolm X.** *Spike Lee spoke to* Cineaste *Editors Gary Crowdus and Dan Georgakas in mid-December 1992, just three weeks after the film's nationwide premiere.*

[*Cineaste:*] *What sort of research did you do for the film? And what was the role of your Historical Consultant Paul Lee?*

[Lee:] I read everything that I could, including a new book by Zak Kondo about the assassination that was very important in helping us re-create the assassination in the film. Paul Lee was a great help because he's someone who's really devoted his life to Malcolm X. Paul, who lives in Detroit, was in the Nation, I think, when he was twelve years old. As far as scholars go, I don't think there's anyone who knows more about Malcolm X than Paul Lee.

I also talked to a lot of people, including Benjamin Karim, who's Benjamin 2X in the film, Malcolm's brothers—Wilfred, Omar Azziz, and Robert—his sister Yvonne, Malcolm's widow, Betty Shabazz, and Malcolm Jarvis, who's Shorty in the film. I also went to Chicago and talked to Minister Farrakhan. That's where a lot of the good stuff came from, going around the country and talking to people who knew Malcolm. Not just his relatives, but people who were in the Nation with him, in the OAAU, and so on.

Have you had any dealings with the Socialist Workers Party? They got to Malcolm early, gave him podiums numerous times, and published a lot of his speeches.

Pathfinder Press? No, I just used their books, because they're fine documents.

Of the various screenplay adaptations of The Autobiography *that had been written, why did you feel that the James Baldwin/Arnold Perl script was the best?*

I read 'em all—the David Mamet script, Charles Fuller's two drafts, Calder Willingham's script, and David Bradley's script—but the Baldwin/Perl script was the best. James Baldwin was a great writer and he really captured Harlem and that whole period. He was a friend of Malcolm's.

What did your rewrite of the Baldwin/Perl script involve?

What was lacking, I felt, in the Baldwin/Perl script was the third act—what happens during the split between Malcolm and the Nation, between Malcolm and Elijah Muhammad. A lot of stuff about the assassination had not come out then. William Kunstler was a great help on that. He represented Talmadge Hayer and gave me a copy of Hayer's affidavit where he 'fessed up to the assassination. I mean, if you look at the credits of the movie, we name the five assassins, we *name* those guys—Ben Thomas, William X, Wilbur Kinley, Leon Davis, and Thomas Hayer.

I also wanted to tie the film into today. I did not want this film just to be a historical document. That's why we open the film with the Rodney King footage and the American flag burning, and end the film with the classrooms, from Harlem to Soweto.

The speeches in the Baldwin/Perl script were not really Malcolm's best speeches, they did not really show the growth politically of Malcolm's mind, so we threw them all out. With the help of Paul Lee, who gave us copies of every single speech that Malcolm gave, Denzel and I chose and inserted speeches. Baldwin had stuff out of order. He had Malcolm giving speeches at the beginning of the movie that didn't really come until 1963 or 1964, so we had to get rid of those.

So Denzel was involved somewhat in working on the script?

Yeah, Denzel was very involved. He has a good story sense. We both knew a lot was riding on this film. We did not want to live in another country the rest of our lives. We could not go anywhere without being reminded by black folks, "Don't fuck up Malcolm, don't mess this one up." We were under tremendous pressure on this film. We can laugh about it now, but it was no joke while we were doing the film.

Given the difficulty of portraying about forty years of a man's life in any film, even one nearly three and a half hours long, are there some aspects of Malcolm's life you felt you weren't able to do justice to?

No, this is it, this is the movie I wanted to make. Our first cut was about four hours and ten minutes, I forget exactly, and we had more speeches and stuff, but this is the best shape the film can be. Of course, people say, "Why did you leave this out and why did you leave that out?," but you cannot put a man's whole life in a film.

People have told us, "The most important year in Malcolm's life was his final year," and "Why didn't you show his whole pan-Africanism thing?" But it's limited. We've never said that anyone who sees this film doesn't need to know anything else about Malcolm X. I mean, the man had four or five different lives, so the film is really only a primer, a starting point.

But don't you think that showing him meeting heads of state in Africa would have added to his dimension at the end, especially for people who don't know?

But people don't know who Kwame Nkrumah is anyway. Besides, we didn't have the money. I mean, we just barely got to Egypt. We shot in the U.S. from September 16, 1991, up to the Christmas holiday and after the holidays we did what we had to do in Cairo and then we went to South Africa. But I don't think we would have gained anything by showing him meeting with Nkrumah or others. Besides, at that point in the film, we're trying to build some momentum.

Cassius Clay/Muhammad Ali is sort of dropped from the film, too.

What, and get someone to impersonate him? I think it was important to have Muhammad Ali in the movie, but we show him in a newsreel clip in the montage at the end.

You don't think it dissipates some of the anti-Vietnam War feeling that was in the Nation?

They weren't really anti-Vietnam. Malcolm was, but Elijah Muhammad never said anything about the Vietnam War. And by the time Malcolm spoke out against the Vietnam War, he had already been kicked out of the Nation.

Do you feel a film of this financial scale has built-in 'crossover' requirements in terms of its audience?

We felt so. We felt that everybody would want to see the film and we've received a large white audience to date. This is my first PG film—the previous five have all been rated R—because we wanted to get a young audience. We feel this is an important piece of American history and people, especially young kids, need to see this.

Is that why the few sex scenes in the film are considerably milder than those in the published screenplay?

Yes, because we made the decision for a PG-13 rating. We did not want to give teachers, schools, or parents an excuse why they could not take their children to see this film. I think when you weigh it, it's much more important for young kids to be exposed to Malcolm X than to see that other shit. We're preparing a classroom study guide on the film that'll be out in January.

It's amazing, I've seen this film with ten, eleven, and twelve-year-olds and they're just riveted in their seats. You know the attention span of young people at that age—they're usually throwing popcorn at the screen—but there's not a sound, they're riveted for three hours and twenty-one minutes. A whole generation of young people are being introduced to Malcolm X and people who've heard of him or had limited views of him are having their views expanded. Above all, we hope that black folks will come out of the theater inspired and moved to do something positive.

What sort of message would you like white viewers to come away with from the film?

I think that, as with any film I've done, people will take away their own message. For a large part of the white audience, however, I think we're helping to redefine Malcolm X because for the most part their view of Malcolm came from the white media which portrayed him as anti-white, anti-Semitic, and pro-violence. It's funny, when we had the national press junket for this film, many of the white journalists said they felt they'd been robbed, that they'd been cheated, because they'd never been taught about Malcolm X in school or they had only been told that he was anti-white and violent. A great miseducation has gone on about this man.

In that regard, we heard that Warner Bros., presumably concerned about defusing any controversy about potential violence at screenings, held advance showings of the film for police departments around the country.

That was Barry Reardon's decision. I did not agree with that. I thought it was inappropriate. I mean, if they do that to us, they should do it to *Terminator*. How many cops got killed in those films? Actually, it was the exhibitors. Before the film came out, exhibitors were calling Warner Bros., they were scared shitless, they were requesting extra police protection. One theater in Chicago even installed metal detectors!

What was the response at the police screenings?

Oh, the cops loved it. In Los Angeles, they showed it to Willie Williams, the new Police Commissioner there. It was the exhibitors and also the press who were waiting for that violence so they could destroy the movie. **Do the Right Thing** was really hurt at the box office when the press—people like David Denby, Joe Klein, and Jack Mathews—predicted that the film was going to create riots. In Westwood, in Los Angeles, for example, nine police were at the theater on the opening weekend, some mounted on horseback.

What's interesting for me now in reading a lot of the reviews of **Malcolm X** is how so many critics had predetermined that the film was going to be inflammatory.

To a great extent that's because of their unfamiliarity with Malcolm X other than what they've read in the mainstream press.

And with me, with the combination of Malcolm X and Spike Lee. They were expecting a film that for three hours and twenty-one minutes would be saying, "C'mon, black folks, let's get some guns and kill every single white person in America," but in the end the critics were saying, "This film is *mild*."

In the published screenplay, there are two sort of 'dramatic bookends' scenes. In the first scene, Malcolm brushes off the well-intentioned young white woman outside Harvard who asks how she might be of help in his struggle. The second scene, which occurs later at the Hilton Hotel in New York, involves the same type of encounter but this time Malcolm has a completely different response. The two scenes emphasizes Malcolm's evolution on this question, but only the first scene appears in the film. Why?

We shot that other scene, but the acting just didn't work. Anyone who's read the book knows that Malcolm's response to that young woman was one of his biggest regrets. I wanted to give Malcolm a chance to make up for it, so I wrote the scene where he could answer that same question again, but it just didn't work.

Are you concerned with how the dramatic weight has now shifted to that first scene? At the two screenings we've attended, that scene always gets a big laugh.

Who's laughing? Black viewers or white viewers?

They've been mixed audiences.

White people don't laugh at that because for the white audience that young white woman is *them*. We shot the second scene, but it just didn't work, so what were we supposed to do? In any case, I think we see Malcolm change when he comes back from Mecca.

In terms of The Autobiography's *portrayal of Malcolm's youthful criminal career and the extent of his drug abuse, Malcolm was much more critical of himself in the book than the film is. Do you think that aspect of the book is exaggerated?*

I've talked to Malcolm's brothers and they said that he was not that big of a criminal. He was a street hustler and not even a pimp, just a steerer. I think he was a wannabe, a wannabe big-time gangster, but he wasn't. The description in the book was not so much to build himself up but to lower the depths from which he rises. That's OK, but I don't buy this Bruce Perry bullshit that Malcolm was a homosexual, that he used to crossdress, or that Malcolm's father burned down their house in Omaha or that Malcolm fire-bombed his own house in Queens. That's bullshit! He did a lot of research, and some of the interviews were good, but Bruce Perry's book reads like *The National Enquirer*.

Many feminists are critical of the Nation of Islam's sexist attitudes towards women. In fact, one of their well-intentioned slogans refers to women as "property."

We didn't make that up. That was an actual banner.

No, we understand that was historically accurate, but since you've taken so much heat from feminists in the past. . .

Hey, you know who should be taking more heat than me? Oliver Stone!

Oh, he has taken a lot of heat.

Not as much as me, though, about women.

In a historical film like this, the dilemma seems to be whether one can—or should even attempt to—deal with such an issue by presenting an anachronistic, retroactive 'politically correct' perspective on the Nation's attitude towards women.

We just showed it the way it was.

We thought you dealt with this issue well in at least one scene where you intercut Elijah Muhammad's various strictures against women with Malcolm's conversation with Betty where he parrots pretty much the same line.

Yeah, he's a mouthpiece. [*Lee at this point does a pretty good impersonation of Al Freeman as Elijah Muhammad*] "She should be half the man's age plus seven. She must cook, sew, stay out of trouble." [*Laughs*] Sure, I've been at some screenings where women go, "Ugh!," but, look, those are not my views.

You often have scenes where there's no obvious interpretation, you leave it up to the viewer.

A lot of my work has been done that way. Some things I'll slant, but a lot of time I let people make up their own minds.

We're thinking especially of the scene where Denzel is watching television, and you intercut newsreel footage of police repression of civil rights demonstrations with a slow zoom into his face.

Yeah, and with John Coltrane's "Alabama" on the soundtrack.

There are a couple of different levels of interpretation there. You can think that he's despising Martin Luther King, Jr. and his nonviolent approach, or you can think that he's regretting that he's not involved in action like that. In this regard, we also wondered about the little smile you see briefly on Malcolm's face just before he's shot.

That was Denzel's idea.

I guess that's also open to interpretation.

Well, Denzel and I felt that he just got tired of being hounded. In actuality, you know, there were several assassination attempts. The CIA tried to poison him in Cairo, and the Nation tried to kill him numerous times. There was a big assassination attempt in Los Angeles, another in Chicago, and one night he had to run into his house because guys with knives were chasing him. So he was hounded for a year, the last year of his life, and Denzel and I thought about it and just felt that, you know, he was happy to go. It was Denzel's idea to smile right before he gets the shotgun blast—like, "You finally got me," and it was over.

Malcolm knew that he was going to die—even in the book he says, "I'll be dead before this comes out"—and that idea is played through that montage where Malcolm, his aides, and the assassins are all driving in separate cars to the Audubon Ballroom—an idea we got from *The Godfather*, by the way ('props' to Francis)—accompanied by the Sam Cooke song, "A Change Is Gonna Come."

In terms of FBI and CIA involvement in the assassination, do you think it was more a case of them letting it happen rather than actually doing it?

In my opinion they definitely stirred things up between Malcolm and the Nation. The FBI's COINTELPRO operation had infiltrated the Nation and was writing letters back and forth. Then I think they just stood back and let it happen. I don't think the FBI or CIA needed to assassinate Malcolm because, if you read *Muhammad Speaks* at that time, the Nation was going to do it themselves.

The FBI did the same thing on the West Coast, fomenting a rift between the Black Panthers and Ron Karenga.

Oh yeah, they're great at that. A very important book in this regard is *Malcolm X: The FBI File*. Two new books coming out—*The Judas Factor: The Plot to Kill Malcolm X* by Karl Evanzz and *Conspiracys: Unravelling the Assassination of Malcolm X* by Zak Kondo—both say the Nation was responsible. Of course, Amiri Baraka's saying that I'm part of some great government conspiracy and that the reason the studio let me make the film is because I was going to pin the assassination on black people. That's bullshit!

The five assassins were from Temple No. 25 in Newark, New Jersey, and the orders came from Chicago. I don't know if they came from the Honorable Elijah Muhammad, but it was from somewhere high up. That's the truth. I mean, Baraka should talk to Betty Shabazz, he should ask her who killed her husband. She told me the same thing. I'm not part of some conspiracy to turn black folks against the Nation of Islam. That's bullshit!

Has the Nation had a response to the film yet?

The Thursday before the movie opened we had a special screening in Chicago for Minister Farrakhan.

How did that go?

He was there, and I got a note from his secretary saying he was going to respond by letter, but we haven't heard from him since. But Minister Farrakhan has been supportive. While we were shooting the film, he said, "Look, Spike, I support your right as an artist." That's been it.

Do you think they'll make an official pronouncement, one way or another?

I think they'll just let it blow over.

In making this film, did you arrive at a more sympathetic understanding or appreciation of Islam?

Yeah, I mean you had to have respect. Denzel and I were reading the Koran before we began to shoot. We *had* to. If we didn't have a sympathetic attitude toward Islam, why would the Saudi government allow us to bring cameras into Mecca to shoot the holy rite of *hajj?* You have to be a Muslim to enter Mecca, so we had two second units, Islamic crews, who in May 1990 and June 1991 were permitted, for the first time ever in history, to film in Mecca.

I think the Saudi government realized this film could be good publicity for Islam. I mean, Islam and the Arabs in general have been taking a bashing in the West—what with Khomeini and the Gulf War and everything—and in Islam Malcolm is considered a martyr. That's why they let us bring cameras in.

Will the Islamic countries be an important overseas market for the film?

Yeah, we're going to try. We've got to be careful, though, because the same people who gave us the stamp of approval, the Islamic Court, are the same cats who sentenced Salman Rushdie to die, so we don't want to fuck around.

Some felt that the film's Mecca scenes were a little saccharine, somewhat like Christian movies of Jerusalem.

If the man says this was a deeply religious experience, you have to be true to that, no matter how you feel personally about religion. I mean, if up until that point the man felt that every single white person was a blue-eyed, grafted devil, and he no longer believed that after his visit to Mecca, something must have happened.

A very powerful scene in the film is when the young man, after seeing Malcolm and other members of the Nation con-

front the police, approaches Malcolm and says he wants to become a Muslim. It showed the power of the Nation to influence people and change their behavior.

People can talk about Elijah Muhammad all they want, but there's never been a better program in America for black folks to convert drug addicts, alcoholics, criminals, whatever. Elijah Muhammad straightened those guys out and, once they were clean, that was that.

A lot of people felt Malcolm would have left Islam, but we always thought he was as devout a Muslim as King was a Christian.

No, he would never have left Islam. He would have moved on to other stuff, but he would have remained a Muslim. He would not have made it a requirement to join his organization because he saw it was too regimented. He wanted to include as many people as possible. People wanted to follow him but they weren't willing to give up pork, or sex, or whatever.

There was always this tension between Malcolm and King which some people saw as a contradiction but which we saw as more of a dynamic tension.

I agree. At the end of **Do the Right Thing,** when I use the statements from Malcolm and King, I wasn't saying it's either one or the other. I think one can form a synthesis of both. When Malcolm was assassinated, I think they were trying to find a common ground, a plan they could both work on.

Some people felt I took a low blow at King in the film in the scene where John Sayles, as an FBI agent listening in on a phone tap on Malcolm, cracks, "Compared to King, this guy is a monk." I don't think that's low blow. J. Edgar Hoover had made tapes of King with other women and he confronted King with them, saying, "If you don't commit suicide, I'm going to send these tapes to Coretta," and he did. Afterwards things weren't the same between Coretta and Dr. King, but I'm not taking a low blow at King. The low blow was the FBI doing this to Dr. King. But some black people told me, "Spike, you know, you shouldn't have done that."

They have a hard time dealing with King as a sexual being. Baldwin also thought that there was this dynamic, this dialectical tension, between Malcolm and King. Toward the end, Malcolm seemed to be saying, "You'd better deal with King, because, if you don't, you'll have to deal with me." It's the Ballot or the Bullet.

He said that all the time. He told King, "I'm good for you."

Some people would have liked for you to have included the

scene where Malcolm went down to Selma and spoke to Coretta King. Did you think of putting that in?

[*Covers his head in a defensive manner and laughs uproariously*] We couldn't do everything! We knew going in that, at best, we'd just get the essence of the man, that's the most we'd be able to do. Besides, Henry Hampton of Blackside—you know, the guy who did *Eyes on the Prize*—he's preparing an eight hour series on Malcolm. They'll be able to do a lot more than we did, and I'm glad.

We've also heard that there are plans to re-release, at least on video, the 1972 feature documentary on Malcolm.

Marvin Worth's film. It's good. I think if more people can learn about Malcolm X, that's cool.

We thought you might have done more with Ossie Davis's eulogy.

What, you mean see him delivering it? Then we'd have to restage the funeral and I didn't want to see Denzel in a casket. Besides, by that time we show footage of the real Malcolm X. I gotta give my props here to Oliver Stone. Barry Brown [*the editor who cut* **School Daze** *and* **Do the Right Thing**] and I saw Oliver Stone's *JFK* the first day it came out, and I said, "Barry, man, look what they're doing. C'mon!" That film gave us great inspiration.

You remember the opening newsreel montage in *JFK*? Well, we tried to do the same thing, or better it, with our montage at the end where Ossie Davis delivers the eulogy. We also had some of the black and white thing going, like newsreel footage.

So you were directly influenced by JFK?

Yes. There are other similarities between *Malcolm X* and *JFK* but what makes our film stand out is the performance of the lead actor. I think Kevin Costner is an OK actor, and I know that's probably the only way Oliver could have gotten the film made with the amount of money he wanted to, but I love that film *despite* Kevin Costner's performance. In *Malcolm X,* Denzel is the film, he's in every single scene. I hope he gets nominated for the Academy Award and I hope he wins.

Another thing we're really proud of with this film is the craft. Far too often with my films the craft is overlooked, but I think everything here—Barry Brown's editing, Ruth Carter's costume design, Terence Blanchard's score, plus the source music we used, and Ernest Dickerson's cinematography—is outstanding.

The cameo appearances in your film are another similarity

to JFK. *In some ways they're amusing, and people love them, but, on the other hand, they seem to disrupt the dramatic intensity, because people are saying, "Hey, that's Al Sharpton," or "There's Bill Kunstler," or "Did you see Bobby Seale?"*

Not that many viewers know who these people are, and for me it just added weight to the stuff. I don't think I was making jokes or trying to make it campy or funny. I actually wanted Clint Eastwood to play the cop in the Peter Boyle scene, but he was shooting *Unforgiven.*

Has Warner Bros. been supportive in terms of the advertising campaign and the national release?

Yes, ever since they saw the rough cut. I mean, for a while there during production we went at it toe to toe, but since they've seen it they've been behind the film. We're on 1600 screens nationwide. I have no complaints.

In terms of the highly publicized dispute during production between yourself, Warner Bros., and the Completion Bond Company, to what extent do you feel racism was involved?

Racism is part of the fabric of American society, so why should the film industry be exempt? I think it's a racist assumption that white America will not go to see a black film that's not a comedy, or that doesn't have singing and dancing, or that doesn't star Eddie Murphy. I think there are racist tendencies that keep this glass ceiling on the amount of money that is spent on black films, to produce them or to market and promote them. I mean, how is it that Dan Aykroyd, a first-time director, can get $45 million to do *Nothing But Trouble?* $45 million! They're willing to give more money to these white boys right out of film school than they are to accomplished black directors.

In terms of the controversy, films go over budget all the time. so why I am on the front page? I wasn't calling up these newspapers and saying, "I'm over budget and the Completion Bond Company is taking the film over."

Wasn't there some sort of misunderstanding about the delivery date of the film?

No. Here's what happened. Any time a director and the lead actor are shooting, that is first unit, that is principal photography. The Completion Bond Company tried to say that what we did in Africa was second unit. But Denzel and I were shooting, so that's principal photography. We finished shooting in Soweto in late January 1992, and five weeks later they wanted a first rough cut!

The Bond Company was mad because they were getting stuck by Warner Bros. and were having to deal with a

$5,000,000 overage. Usually the studio will help out the bond company, but in this case Warner Bros. said, "Fuck you. We paid you a fee and this is your job." So the Bond Company said to us, "Look, until we work this agreement out with Warner Bros., we're not paying you anything." So they fired all our editors. We had no money coming in to complete the film, so that's when I made the phone calls to these prominent African-Americans—Oprah Winfrey, Bill Cosby, Magic Johnson, Michael Jordan, and others.

And their contributions were gifts.

These were gifts—not loans, not investments. So for two months we continued to work and neither the Bond Company nor Warner Bros., knew where the money was coming from. That really fucked 'em up. I chose to announce what we had been able to do on May 19th, Malcolm's birthday, at a press conference at the Schomburg Center. *Miraculously,* two days later, the Bond Company and Warner Bros. worked it out. They say it was just a coincidence, that it would have happened anyway. I say bullshit.

But I hope this will be a precedent. Next time, maybe myself or some other filmmaker will bypass Hollywood altogether for financing and go directly to people like Oprah or Bill or Magic or Michael who'll finance the production, and then just go to Hollywood for distribution once the film is done. There are plenty of black people with money, plenty of black entrepreneurs. It can be done.

Are there other major black historical figures that you'd like to do films on?

Yeah, Walter Yetnikoff and I are working to acquire the rights to Miles Davis's life story. I heard that Robert Townsend may direct and star in a film on Duke Ellington. Right now, Touchstone is getting ready to do the Tina Turner story, with Angela Bassett, who plays Betty Shabazz in *Malcolm X,* as Tina and Larry Fishburne as Ike Turner. What we hope, what we're praying for, is that with the success of *Malcolm X,* you'll be able to eventually see films about Miles Davis, Paul Robeson, Harriet Tubman, Sojourner Truth . . . you can go right on down the line.

bell hooks (essay date 1993)

SOURCE: "Male Heroes and Female Sex Objects: Sexism in Spike Lee's *Malcolm X,*" in *Cineaste,* Vol. 19, No. 4, 1993, pp. 13-5.

[*In the following essay, hooks discusses Lee's treatment of women in his films, and asserts that by leaving out the title* character's half sister from Malcolm X, *"Lee continues Hollywood's devaluation of black womanhood."*]

In all Spike Lee's films, he is at his creative best in scenes highlighting black males. Portraying black masculinity through a spectrum of complex and diverse portraits, he does not allow audiences to hold a stereotypical image. For that reason alone, I imagined *Malcolm X* would be a major work, one of his best films. At last, I thought, Spike's finally going to just do it—make a film that will allow him to focus almost exclusively on black men, since women were always at the periphery of Malcolm's life. Thinking that the film would not focus centrally on females, I was relieved. Like many females in Lee's audience, I have found his representation of women in general, and black women in particular, to be consistently stereotypical and one-dimensional.

Ironically, Nola Darling in *She's Gotta Have It* remains one of Lee's most compelling representations of black womanhood. Though a failed portrait of a liberated woman, Darling is infinitely more complex than any of the women who follow her in Lee's work. *She's Gotta Have It* showed an awareness on Lee's part that there has indeed been a Women's Liberation movement that converged with the so-called 'sexual revolution.' Nola Darling was not obsessed with conventional heterosexist politics. Throughout much of the film she seemed to be trying to forge a sexual practice that would meet her needs. This film shows that Lee is capable of thinking critically about representations of black women, even though he ends the film by placing Nola Darling in a misogynist, sexist framework that ultimately punishes her for daring to oppose sexist norms of female sexual behavior. Rape is the punishment that puts her back in her place. And it is this scene in the film that ruptures what began as a transgressive narrative and makes it humdrum, commonplace.

Just as Lee abandons Nola Darling, undermining the one representation of black womanhood that breaks new cinematic ground, from that moment on he apparently abandoned all desire to give viewing audiences new and different representations of black females. Lee's desire to reach a larger, mainstream audience may account for the shift in perspective. Once he moved out of the world of independent filmmaking into mainstream cinema, he was seeking to acquire an audience not necessarily interested in challenging, unfamiliar representations. No matter how daring his films, how transgressive their subject matter, to have a predictable success he provided viewers with stock images. Uncompromising in his commitment to create images of black males that challenge shallow perceptions and bring the issue of racism to the screen, he conforms to the status quo when it comes to images of females. Sexism is the familiar construction that links his films to all the other Hollywood dramas folks see. Just when the viewer might possibly be alienated by the radical take on issues in a Spike Lee film, some basic sexist nonsense will appear on the screen to entertain, to provide comic relief, to comfort audiences by letting them know that the normal way of doing things is not being fully challenged.

Certainly the female role that most conformed to this pattern was the character of Tina played by Rosie Perez in *Do the Right Thing*. She is the nagging, bitchified, seductive female who is great to bone (not to be taken seriously, mind you). No matter how bitchified she is, in the final analysis her man, played by Spike, has her under control. This same misogynist message is played out all the more graphically in *School Daze* where the collective humiliation of black females enhances black male bonding. Yet it is *Mo' Better Blues* that sets paradigms for black gender relations. Black females are neatly divided into two categories—ho' or mammy/madonna. The ho' is out for what she can get, using her pussy to seduce, conquer, and exploit the male. The mammy/madonna nurtures, forgives, provides unconditional love. Black men, mired in sexism and misogyny, tolerate the strong, 'bitchified,' tell-it-like-it-is black woman but also seek to escape her. In *Mo' Better Blues* the black woman who gets her man in the end does so by surrendering her will to challenge and confront. She simply understands and accepts. It's a bleak picture. In the final analysis, mo' better is mo' bitter.

Jungle Fever plays out the same tired patterns, only the principal black woman character, Drew (Lonette McKee), is a combination of bitch/ho' and mammy/madonna. The film begins with scenes of lovemaking, where she is busy pleasuring her man. We see her later in the film cooking and cleaning. Even her job is mainly about looking good. Her most bitchified, 'intense' read of Flipper (Wesley Snipes) occurs when he comes to her workplace. As with all of Spike Lee's representations of black heterosexuality, men and women never really communicate. Portrayals of white female characters are equally stereotypical. They are sex objects, spoils in the war between white males and black males over which group will dominate the planet.

> **In Lee's version, relationships between black men and white women never transcend the sexual. Indeed, in Lee's cinematic world, every relationship between a black man and a woman, whether white or black, is mediated by his constant sexualization of the female.**
> **—*bell hooks***

In *Jungle Fever* white and black women never meet, they exist in a world apart. This media construction is a fiction which belies the reality that the vast majority of working black women encounter white women daily on the job, encounters that are charged with tension, power struggles fueled by racism and sexism. These aspects of white and black female interactions are only hinted at in *Jungle Fever* in the one improvised scene where black women gather to discuss Drew's situation and their collective obsession with getting and keeping a man.

Within the cultural marketplace, *Jungle Fever* courted viewers by claiming to address the taboo subject of interracial sex and desire, highlighting black male interactions with white females. Despite the shallowness of the film, this focus drew crowds. Overall, however, the film had nothing new or revelatory to share about race, gender, or desire. No doubt the crowd-drawing appeal of such material accounts for the fact that Spike Lee's cinematic reconstruction of Malcolm X's life begins with a sorry remake of *Jungle Fever*. Anyone who has studied Malcolm X's life and work knows that no one has considered his involvement with white women as the high point of his career as small time pimp and hustler. Yet it is this involvement that most captures Spike's imagination, so much so that almost half of the film focuses on Malcolm's relationship with a white woman named Sophia.

The young Malcolm X was sexist and misogynist, and, in fact, made a point of treating women badly. Yet Lee ignores the sexism that shaped and determined Malcolm's attitude towards women and makes it appear that his lust for Sophia is solely a response to racism, that having the white man's woman is a way to rebel and assert power. Like the younger Malcolm, the real-life Sophia was a hustler, not the portrait of an innocent little girl trapped in a woman's body which Lee gives viewers. It was disturbing to see Lee's version of Malcolm's life begin with and focus centrally on his lust for white female bodies, but it was even more disturbing that this relationship was portrayed as yet another example of 'jungle fever.' Spike Lee refuses to allow for the possibility that there could be meaningful affectional ties between a black man and a white woman which transcend the sexual. The film does not show that Malcolm maintained contact with Sophia long after their sexual relationship ended. In Lee's version, relationships between black men and white women never transcend the sexual. Indeed, in Lee's cinematic world, every relationship between a black man and a woman, whether white or black, is mediated by his constant sexualization of the female.

Fictively recreating the relationship between Malcolm X and Betty Shabazz provided an opportunity for Spike Lee to bring to Hollywood cinema a different representation of black womanhood and black heterosexuality. Lee did not rise to the challenge. All his films show darker skinned men choosing lighter skinned black female partners. Malcolm X should have been different. By his choice as a fair-skinned black male of a darker skinned partner, Malcolm was disrupting a black politics of desire which reflected internalized racism. Rather than honoring through his representations the significance of this choice, Lee reinscribes the same color caste conventions he exploits in all his films. Though a madonna figure in *Malcolm X,* Shabazz is portrayed as an advocate of 'women's rights' challenging Malcolm's sexism and misogyny. This portrait falsely constructs an image of black womanhood that would not have been acceptable for female initiates in the Nation of Islam, who were taught not to be manipulative or seductive, to be obedient to male authority. Lee's fictive Shabazz seduces and traps. She 'reads' her man in the bitchified manner that is Lee's trademark representation of heterosexual black coupling. Even though the real-life Shabazz shared with her that she did not argue with Malcolm, no doubt because she was conforming to the Nation of Islam codes of behavior which were informed by sexist notions of appropriate female behavior, Lee's film portrays them as fighting. Indeed, the most intense scene in the film is their near violent argument. As with all good nanny/madonna figures, the fictional Shabazz fights with her man because she has his best interests at heart. This image is consistent with the way Spike Lee's films depict black marriage; couples are either fucking or fighting. Like other female characters in *Malcolm X,* Shabazz must be molded and shaped by Lee so that her character mirrors prevailing stereotypes. Lee's film conforms to racist/sexist iconography that depicts white women as innocent and therefore desirable and black woman as controlling-domineering therefore undesirable. Had Lee chosen to represent Shabazz as submissive, his film would have challenged Hollywood's stereotypical portrayal of black women as always domineering—or as always sexual.

One of the most serious gaps in Lee's fictive portrayal of Malcolm's life is the fictive erasure of Malcolm's half sister (whom he referred to as his sister), Ella Little. She is not present in the film and their relationship is never discussed by other characters. A major influence in Malcolm's life, Ella, along with their brother, Reginald, converted him to Islam, helped educate him for critical consciousness. By not portraying Ella or referring to her influence, Spike creates a fictive world of black heterosexuality in which all interaction between black women and men is overdetermined by sexuality, always negotiated by lust and desire. Conveniently, this allows the film to reinscribe and perpetually affirm male domination of females, making it appear natural.

By not portraying Ella, Lee is able to create a film that does not break with Hollywood conventions and stereotypes. In Hollywood films the super-masculine hero is most often portrayed as a loner, an outlaw, a cultural orphan estranged from family and society. To have shown the bonds between Ella and Malcolm which were sustained throughout his life,

Lee would have needed both to break with Hollywood representations of the male hero as well as provide an image of black womanhood never before imagined on the Hollywood screen. The character of Ella would have been a powerful, politically conscious black woman who could not be portrayed as a sex object. Lee's portraits of black women in *Malcolm X* mirror the usual stereotypes found in films by white directors. Ella was radical in her thinking about blackness, more of a leader than a follower. To represent her fictively, Lee would have had to disrupt the fiction that politics is a male realm, that the fight to end racism is really a struggle between white and black men.

It reveals much about the nature of sexism and misogyny that the erased, symbolically murdered figure of Ella is replaced by a fictional, older black male character, Baines, who initiates Malcolm into the political realm. The invention of this make-believe character allows Lee to fictively create a hierarchical world of male power that conforms to popular, black nationalist, sexist insistence that males are best taught by males. Scenes of black male homosocial bonding in the prison context reaffirm the patriarchal assumption that it is only the actions of men that matter. This creates a version of black political struggle where the actions of dedicated, powerful, black female activists are systematically devalued and erased. By writing Ella out of Malcolm's history, Spike Lee continues Hollywood's devaluation of black womanhood.

Bill Nasson (essay date December 1993)

SOURCE: "A 'Whiteout': Malcolm X in South Africa," in *The Journal of American History,* Vol. 80, No. 3, December, 1993, pp. 1199-1201.

[*In the following essay, Nasson discusses the reception of Lee's* Malcolm X *in South Africa.*]

In Spike Lee's modest contribution to method writing, *By Any Means Necessary,* a high-octane account of the making of *Malcolm X,* we learn that on the Johannesburg shoot to capture Nelson Mandela as a Soweto teacher for the film's final clip, "there was a whiteout of our activities, like we were never there, according to the news organizations of South Africa." There is a nice whiff of radical audacity to this, but it is quite preposterous. With the shooting of *Malcolm X* no particular danger to the already crumbling fabric of South African society, white English-language papers took rather positive notice of filmmaker and subject. In fact, the only unsporting notes appeared in the country's leading liberal weekly, *Johannesburg Weekly Mail,* and in the black *Johannesburg Sowetan.* These reported grumbling amongst local black crew over working conditions under the visiting director, adoringly identified by his production assistant as "a brother who had come home to visit."

What have we here? What we have is not just a filmmaking chronicle that is somewhat economical with the truth, but a film with an equally rough-and-ready grasp of historical logic. Inserting Mandela into *Malcolm X* may have made it natural for the film to have its April 1993 South African premiere at the African National Congress (ANC) Culture and Development Conference. But the ANC president, with his multiracial populism, is surely not the most appropriate symbolic figure to link the legacy of black struggle in America associated with Malcolm X to black liberation politics in South Africa. The more obvious historical symbol is Steve Biko, murdered in security police detention in 1977. The martyred Biko was the best-known proponent of the separatist black consciousness that, in the 1960s and 1970s, drew a good measure of its intellectual, cultural, and political inspiration from the Black Power movement in the United States, with the contraband speeches and autobiography of Malcolm X then a prominent *samizdat* source. Still, Spike Lee's purpose is a "brothers-in-the-struggle" historical biography for the 1990s. After all, finding apt historical analogies can be complicated, if a little more even-handed toward both past and present.

With the current "rediscovery" of Malcolm X through this film, the brother has already been appropriated in some fairly novel South African ways, including the mock-heroic. Thus, the university teacher who heads a fringe Coloured National Liberation Front that seeks a post-apartheid transition to an autarkic homeland for people of mixed black and white ancestry has been dubbed "the Coloured People's answer to Malcolm X." Moreover, Chris Hani, the recently assassinated South African Communist party leader and ANC guerrilla commander, haunted several reviews of the movie as the embodiment of Malcolm X, in that "he died preaching peace," or owed his political consciousness in part to the African-American racial experience as articulated by Malcolm X, Huey Newton, and Stokely Carmichael. This last flatulence, aired by the ANC journal, *Mayibuye,* is silly.

Malcolm X is the third of Spike Lee's movies to be shown in desegregated South African cinemas. *Do the Right Thing* was favorably reviewed by liberal white critics, while screened mostly in cinemas in black areas. Similarly, *Jungle Fever* was acclaimed for its relevance "to life in a multiracial society such as ours" and was shown to mixed, middle-class cinema audiences mainly in white areas.

The ease with which these supposedly incendiary African-American films have been absorbed by South African political culture makes the reception of *Malcolm X* not just interesting, but intriguingly so. It is, for instance, mistaken to imagine that poor and marginalized township youths have swarmed into cinemas to view this brash portrait of black nationalism; inflated seat prices generally restrict movie going to the middle class and better-off working-class minor-

ity. There were, of course, black audiences. Promoted as a "civil rights" biography, *Malcolm X* saw service in fundraising showings for ANC branches, community organizations, and both colored and African high schools. And despite tart criticism of Lee's historical representations of Islamic life from local Muslim publications, *Malcolm X* as *El Hajj Malik El Shabazz* had popular benefit screenings for Muslim educational and welfare projects. Yet, by and large, the commercial showings were to ethnically mixed audiences in mostly white venues. In short, actual viewing was a fairly low-key business. Attendance was accompanied by nothing like the boisterous black crowd activity that used to accompany South African screening of *Scarface* or *El Cid* in urban working class areas such as District Six in Cape Town during the peak 1930s-1960s decades of cheap cinema. Then, thanks to frenzied fans in surging ticket lines, Hollywood entertainments were an occasional threat to civic sobriety or even public order in white cities.

None of this is to suggest that *Malcolm X* failed, as Americans say, to go down big. None other than Betty Shabazz, Malcolm's widow, while on a promotional tout in South Africa, was warmly interviewed at peak time on the state-controlled South African Broadcasting Corporation. Breathless black and white journalists were assured of an ultimate common cause between Malcolm X and Martin Luther King, Jr., in the history of America's antiracist struggle. The English-language white press heaped considerable praise on the production, typified by the headline "Lee's Winner." The national *Sunday Times* observed, "Whereas King offered his followers comfort and hope, Malcolm X offered anger and action." Indeed, major Afrikaans papers provided positive reviews, with the influential Cape Town newspaper, *Die Burger,* declaring Malcolm X the hero of young, black South Africa. But, whereas English reviews neatly assimilated Malcolm X to the nonracialism of South African political correctness, Afrikaner critics were less sanguine about the film's radical black nationalism, suggesting that its extremism could be likened to the current antiwhite rancor of the Pan-Africanist Congress, with its "One Settler, One Bullet" slogan.

On the left, the *Socialist* (affiliated with the International Socialist Organization, based in the United States) criticized Lee for muffling Malcolm's hostility to capitalism and for glossing over Central Intelligence Agency (CIA) meddling in Africa but praised the film's portrait "of a tradition of uncompromising black struggle." On the other hand, ANC-supporting black papers and periodicals, such as the *Johannesburg New Nation*, carried the black role-model image as a strong theme, with the consumerist *Tribute* peddling Malcolm X goods in its March issue; Denzel Washington adorned the cover over the slogan, "VOTE for a New Government."

But the popular story is not all glitter. One unifying thread in responses to *Malcolm X* was skepticism, ranging from mild to caustic, about Lee's handling of historical facts and contingencies. Another was that dragging in Mandela to signify global black struggle was labored or trite. A third, coming, ironically enough, from the Afrikaans magazine *Vrye Weekblad,* was annoyance at the idea of Malcolm X as a torchbearer for South African resistance, on the grounds that local liberation movements have no need of imported heroes. A final reaction was that the saintly iconography of X was ultimately merely another Hollywood marketing opportunity, what one perceptive critic called "buy any means necessary."

This year, for the first time, demonstrating black students at the liberal University of the Witwatersrand in Johannesburg have hoisted a banner or two declaring, "By any means necessary." Perhaps more important, though, are the larger and longer cultural connections, many of which are not so politically comprehending. After all, *Malcolm X* entered a country whose youth, predominantly black but including whites, are in abject enchantment with American popular culture, be it rap or the Raiders. And, predictably perhaps, the film may find its true niche as the ideological equivalent of Cabbage Patch Kids dolls. Black street stalls sell X clothing and caps, stores in largely white shopping malls stock X merchandise from local manufacturers—all invariably without any reference to the source. Numbers of college students are under the quaint impression that X is the New York Giants or Chicago White Sox logo. A final South African irony for *Malcolm X,* the movie, is that the symbol of an oppressed people that had forgotten its surname may already be on the way to losing its first name too.

bell hooks (essay date August 1994)

SOURCE: "Sorrowful Black Death Is Not a Hot Ticket," in *Sight and Sound,* Vol. 4, No. 8, August, 1994, pp. 10-14.

[*In the following essay, hooks asserts that Lee's* Crooklyn *presents an "anti-woman, anti-feminist vision of black family life."*]

Hollywood is not into plain old sorrowful death. The death that captures the public imagination in movies, the death that sells, is passionate, sexualised, glamorised and violent. Films like *One False Move, True Romance, Reservoir Dogs, Menace II Society, A Perfect World* bring us the sensational heat of relentless dying. It's fierce—intense—and there is no time to mourn. Dying that makes audiences contemplative, sad, mindful of the transitory nature of human life has little ap-

peal. When portrayed in the contemporary Hollywood film, such deaths are swift, romanticised by soft lighting and elegiac soundtracks. The sights and sounds of death do not linger long enough to disturb the senses, to remind us in any way that sorrow for the dying may be sustained and unrelenting. When Hollywood films depict sorrowful death, audiences come prepared to cry. Films like *Philadelphia* advertise the pathos so that even before tickets are bought and seats are taken, everyone knows that tears are in order, but that the crying time will not last long.

The racial politics of Hollywood is such that there can be no serious representations of death and dying when the characters are African-Americans. Sorrowful black death is not a hot ticket. In the financially successful film *The Bodyguard,* the sister of Rachel Marron (Whitney Houston) is accidentally assassinated by the killer she has hired. There is no grief, no remembrance. In most Hollywood movies, black death is violent. It is often trivialised and mocked—as in that viciously homophobic moment in *Menace II Society* when a young black male crack addict holding a fast-food hamburger while seeking drugs tells the powerful drug dealer, "I'll suck your dick", only to be blown away for daring to suggest that the hard gangsta mack would be at all interested. Pleased with the killing, he laughingly offers the hamburger to onlookers, a gesture that defines the value of black life. It's worth nothing. It's dead meat.

Even black children cannot be spared Hollywood's cruelty. Audiences watching the film *Paris Trout* witness the prolonged, brutal slaughter of a gifted southern black girl by a powerful, sadistic, racist white man. The black males who are her relatives are depicted as utterly indifferent. Too cowardly to save or avenge her life, for a few coins they willingly show the lawyer who will defend her killer the blood stains left by her dragging body, the bullet holes in the walls. Her life is worth nothing.

Violent slaughter

Audiences are so accustomed to representations of the brutal death of black folks in Hollywood films that no one is outraged when our bodies are violently slaughtered. I could find no Hollywood movie where a white child is the object of a prolonged, brutal murder by a powerful white male—no image comparable to that of *Paris Trout.* Yet no group in the United States publicly protests against this image—even though the film is shown regularly on Home Box Office, reaching an audience far wider than the moviegoing public, finding its way into the intimate spaces of home life and the private world of family values. Apparently the graphic representation of the murder of a little black girl does not shock, does not engender grief or protest. There is collective cultural agreement that black death is inevitable, meaningless, not worth much. That there is nothing to mourn.

This is the culture Spike Lee confronts with his new film *Crooklyn*. On the surface, the movie appears to represent issues of death and dying in black life as though our survival matters, as though our living bodies count, yet in the end the usual Hollywood message about black death is reaffirmed. Lee has made a film that is both provocative and controversial. To introduce it to consumers who do not take black life seriously, advertisements give little indication of its content. Huge billboards tell consumers "The Smart Choice is Spike Lee's hilarious *Crooklyn*", suggesting that the film is a comedy. The seriousness of the subject matter must be downplayed, denied.

Lee's magic as a film-maker has been best expressed by his construction of an aesthetic space wherein decolonised images (familiar representations of blackness that oppose racist stereotypes) are lovingly presented. But this radical intervention is most often framed by a conventional narrative and structure of representations that reinscribes stereotypical norms.
—bell hooks

Expecting to see a comedy, moviegoers I talked to were not so much disappointed as puzzled by the fact that the comedic elements were overshadowed by the serious representation of a family in crisis that culminates with the mother's death. When the movie ended, the folks standing around the theatre in Greenwich Village were mostly saying: "It wasn't what I expected. It wasn't like his other films." But *Crooklyn* differs from Lee's previous work primarily because the major protagonist is a ten-year-old-girl, Troy (Zelda Harris). Positively radical in this regard—rarely do we see Hollywood films with black female stars, not to mention child stars—*Crooklyn* invites audiences to look at black experience through Troy's eyes, to enter the spaces of her emotional universe, the intimate world of family and friends that grounds her being and gives her life meaning.

Lee's magic as a film-maker has been best expressed by his construction of an aesthetic space wherein decolonised images (familiar representations of blackness that oppose racist stereotypes) are lovingly presented. But this radical intervention is most often framed by a conventional narrative and structure of representations that reinscribes stereotypical norms. The laughing darky family portrait that advertises *Crooklyn* is just one example. Moviegoers want to see this image rather than those that challenge it. This

contradictory stance tends to undermine Lee's ability to subvert dominant representations of blackness. His radical images are usually overshadowed by stock characterisations and can be easily overlooked, particularly by audiences who are more accustomed to stereotypes. Even progressive, aware viewers may be so fascinated by the funky, funny 'otherness' of typical Spike Lee black images that they refuse to 'see' representations that challenge conventional ways of looking at blackness.

J. Hoberman's review of *Crooklyn* in *Village Voice* is a perfect example of the way our standpoint can determine how we see what we see. Hoberman did not see a film that highlights issues of death and dying—to his mind's eye, "the grittier specifics of the Lee family drama" are exemplified by arguments at family dinners and witty disagreements over television programmes. Indeed, he saw the movie as having "no particular plot"; never mentioning the mother's death, he did not see the film as constructing a context in which this event, more than any other, leads to a ten-year-old black girl's coming of age. Hoberman is more engaged with the comedic aspects of the film, especially those that centre on the eldest child in this family of four boys and one girl, Clinton (Carlton Williams), the character who most resembles Lee himself. Not unlike other moviegoers I talked to, Hoberman seems more fascinated with the antics of Spike Lee, controversial film-maker, than with the content of his film. By deflecting attention away from *Crooklyn* and on to Lee, Hoberman and others do not have to interrogate the film on its own terms. To do that would require looking at *Crooklyn*'s treatment of death and dying, and the way this aspect of the film fails to excite and challenge our imagination.

Play and pleasure

Crooklyn is most compelling in those moments when it offers fictive representations of black subjectivity rarely seen in mainstream cinema, depictions that counter both racist stereotypes and facile notions of positive images. The property-owning, artistic, progressive 70s black family portrayed is one that dares to be different. The Carmichaels in no way represent the conventional black bourgeoisie: they are not obsessed with being upwardly mobile, with the material trappings of success. Counter-cultural—a mixture of the nationalist movement for racial uplift and a bohemian artistic subculture—they represent an alternative to the bourgeois norm.

The father Woody (Delroy Lindo) is an aspiring jazz musician and composer, the mother Carolyn (Alfre Woodard) a non-traditional schoolteacher. Their five children are all encouraged by progressive, hands-off parenting to be individuals with their own interests, passions and obsessions. These are not your average kids: they take a democratic vote to see which television show will be watched and are made to participate equally in household chores. Though black nationalist thinking shapes the family politics, the world they live in is multicultural and multi-ethnic—Italians, Latinos, gays and straights, young and old, the haves and have nots are all part of the mix. This is the world of cultural hybridity and border crossing extolled by progressive contemporary critics. And much of the film depicts that world 'as is', not framed by the will to present images that are artificially positive or unduly negative.

Beginning in the style of a fictive documentary (enhanced initially by the cinematography of Arthur Jafa), the film's opening scene offers a panorama of visual images of black community that disrupts prevailing one-dimensional portrayals of urban black life. Highlighting scenes of play and pleasure, the beauty of black bodies, the faces of children and old men, we see joy in living as opposed to the usual depictions of racial dehumanisation and deprivation. These representations signal heightened creativity, an unbridled imagination that creates splendour in a world of lack, that makes elegance and grace so common a part of the everyday as to render them regular expressions of natural communion with the universe.

Northerners in drag

This opening sequence acts like a phototext, calling us to be resisting readers able to embrace a vision of blackness that challenges the norm. Lee engages a politics of representation which cultural critic Saidiya Hartman describes in 'Roots and Romance', an essay on black photography, as "a critical labor of reconstruction". She explains: "It is a resolutely counterhegemonic labor that has as its aim the establishment of other standards of aesthetic value and visual possibility. The intention of the work is corrective representation." At rare moments through the film this strategy is realised. And it is marvellous to follow where the camera leads—to catch sight of such empowering images. Seduced by this initial moment of radical intervention—by the way it shifts paradigms and requires new ways of seeing—the enthralled viewer can sit in a daze of delight through the rest of the movie, failing to experience how the cinematic direction and narrative structure counteract the initial subversive representations.

A distinction must be made between oppositional representations and romantically glorifying images of blackness which white supremacist thinking as it informs movie-making may have rendered invisible. Visibility does not mean that images are inherently radical or progressive. Hartman urges cultural critics to interrogate this distinction, to ask necessary questions: "Simply put, how are redemptive narratives of blackness shaped and informed by romantic racialism, the pastoral and sentimental representation of black

life? How is the discourse of black cultural authenticity and Afrocentrism shaped and informed by this construction of Africanism and do they too maintain and normalise white cultural hegemony?" *Crooklyn* is offered as a redemptive narrative. The counterhegemonic images we see at the beginning serve to mask all that is 'wrong' with this picture.

From the moment we encounter the Carmichaels at their dinner table, we are offered a non-critical representation of their family life. Shot like docu-drama, these early scenes appear innocent and neutral; the ethnographic day-in-a-life style of presentation demands that the viewer see nothing wrong with this picture. The camera aggressively normalises. These family scenes are presented unproblematically and so appear to be positive representations, fulfilling Lee's quest to bring to the big screen 'authentic' black aesthetic subjects.

Since Spike Lee's cinematic genius is best revealed during those moments when he documents familiar aspects of a rich black cultural legacy wherein collective internal codes and references that may or may not be known to outsiders converge, it is easy to overlook the fact that these counterhegemonic representations are constantly countered in his work by stock stereotypical images. When these are coupled with Lee's use of 'animal house' type humour appropriated from mainstream white culture, a carnivalesque atmosphere emerges that seems directed towards mainstream, largely white, viewers. This cultural borrowing, which gives the movie cross-over appeal, is most evident in the scenes where Troy travels south to stay with relatives in a Virginia suburb. Though the cinematography didactically demands that the audience detach from a notion of the 'real' and engage the 'ridiculous and absurd', these scenes appear stupid, especially the mysterious, not really comical, death of the pet dog Troy's aunt dotes on. Lee works overtime to create a comedic atmosphere to contrast with the seriousness of the Carmichael household, but it does not work; the switch to an anamorphic lens confuses (no doubt that is why signs were placed at ticket booths telling viewers that this change did not indicate a problem with the projector). In these scenes Lee mockingly caricatures the southern black middle class (who appear more like northerners in drag doing the classic Hollywood comedic rendition of southern life). Lee gives it to us in black face. It is predictable and you can't wait to return home to the Carmichael family. However, while he strategically constructs images to normalise the dysfunctions of the Carmichael family, he insists on making this family pathological. This attempt at counterhegemonic representation fails.

Anyone who sees the Carmichael family without the rose-coloured glasses the film offers will realise that they are seriously dysfunctional. The recurrent eating disorders (one of the children is coercively forced by verbal harassment to eat to the point where on one occasion he vomits in his plate); an excessive addiction to sugar (dad's pouring half a bag of the white stuff into a pitcher of lemonade, his cake and ice-cream forays, his candy-buying all hint that he may be addicted to more than sugar, though he is not overtly shown to be a drug-user); the lack of economic stability, signified by the absence of money for food choice, shutting off the electricity, as well as dad's mismanagement of funds, are all indications that there are serious problems. By normalising the family image, Lee refuses to engage with the issue of psychological abuse; all interactions are made to appear natural, ordinary, comedic, not tragic. The autobiographical roots of *Crooklyn* may account for Lee's inability to take any stance other than that of 'objective' reporter; working with a screenplay written collaboratively with his sister Joie and brother Cinqué, he may have felt the need to distance himself from the material. Certainly emotional detachment characterises the interaction between family members in the film.

Joie Lee stated that to write the screenplay she "drew from the few memories I have of my mother", who died of cancer when she was 14. Yet the children in *Crooklyn* are much younger than this and are clearly deeply ambivalent about their mother. Portrayed as a modern-day Sapphire with direct lineage to the *Amos n' Andy* character, Carolyn responds to economic crisis by constantly nagging and erupting into irrational states of anger and outrage that lead her to be mean and at times abusive. Even though the problems the family faces are caused by Woody's unemployment, he is depicted compassionately—an aspiring artist who just wants to be left alone to compose music, always laid-back and calm.

Sexist/racist stereotypes of gender identity in black experience are evident in the construction of these two characters. Although Carolyn is glamorous, beautiful in her Afrocentric style, she is portrayed as a bitch goddess. Her physical allure seduces, even as her unpredictable rage alienates. In keeping with sexist stereotypes of the emasculating black matriarch, Carolyn usurps her husband's authority by insisting that as the primary breadwinner she has the right to dominate, shaming Woody in front of the children. These aspects encourage us to see her unsympathetically and to empathise with him. His irresponsibility and misuse of resources is given legitimacy by the suggestion that his is an artistic, non-patriarchal mindset; he cannot be held accountable. Since Carolyn's rage is often over-reactive, it is easy to forget that she has concrete reasons to be angry. Portrayed as vengeful, anti-pleasure, dangerous and threatening, her moments of tenderness are not sustained enough to counter the negatives. Even her sweetness is depicted as manipulative, whereas Woody's 'sweet' demeanour is a mark of his artistic sensibility, one that enhances his value.

As the artist, he embodies the pleasure principle, the will to transgress. His mild-mannered response to life is infinitely more compelling than the work-hard-to-meet-your-responsibilities ethic by which Carolyn lives. Being responsible seems to make her 'crazy'. In one scene the children are watching a basketball game when she encourages them to turn off the television to do schoolwork. They refuse to obey and she goes berserk. Woody intervenes, not to offer reinforcement, but rather to take sides. Carolyn becomes the bad guy, who wants to curtail the children's freedom to indulge in pleasure without responsibility. Woody responds to her rage by being physically coercive. Domestic violence in black life is sugarcoated—portrayed as a family affair, one where there are no victims or abusers. In fact, Carolyn has been humiliated and physically assaulted. But her demand that Woody leave makes him appear the victim and the children first attend to him, pleading with him not to go. Her pain is unattended by her male children; it is Troy who assumes the traditional feminine role of caretaker.

In contrast to Carolyn, the ten-year-old Troy is concerned with traditional notions of womanhood. Her mother expresses rage at not being able to "take a piss without six people hanging off my tits", repudiating sexist thinking about the woman's role. Flirtatious and cute, Troy manipulates with practised charm. It is she who advises her dad to take Carolyn on a date to make up. Troy embodies all the desirable elements of sexist-defined femininity. Indeed, it is her capacity to escape into a world of romantic fantasy that makes her and everyone else ignore her internal anguish. When she lies, steals and cheats, her acts of defiance have no consequences. As the little princess, she has privileges denied her brothers; when her mother is sick, it is only Troy who is sheltered from this painful reality and sent down south.

In the home of her southern relatives, Troy meets a fair-skinned cousin who is portrayed as conventionally feminine in her concerns, though she is eager to bond with her guest. By contrast Troy assumes a 'bitchified role'. She is hostile, suspicious, until charmed. Representing the light-skinned female as 'good' and Troy as 'bad', *Crooklyn,* like all Lee's films, perpetuates stereotypes of darker-skinned females as evil. While her cousin is loving, Troy is narcissistic and indifferent. When she decides to return home, it is her cousin who runs alongside the car that carries Troy away, waving tenderly, while Troy appears unconcerned. This encounter prepares us for her transformation from princess to mini-matriarch.

Taken to the hospital to see her mother, Troy is given instructions as to how she must assume the caretaker role. Contemporary feminist thinkers are calling attention to girlhood as a time when females have access to greater power than that offered us in womanhood. No one in the film is concerned about the loss of Troy's girlhood, though her brothers remain free to maintain their spirit of play. Clinton, the eldest boy, does not have to relinquish his passion for sports to become responsible; he can still be a child. But becoming a mini-matriarch because her mother is sick and dying requires of Troy that she relinquish all concern with pleasure and play, that she repress desire. Sexist/racist thinking about black female identity leads to cultural acceptance of the exploitation and denigration of black girlhood. Commenting on the way black girls are often forced to assume adult roles in *In the Company of My Sisters: Black Women and Self-Esteem*, Julia Boyd asserts: "Without fully understanding the adult tasks we were expected to perform, we filled shoes that were much too big for our small feet. Again, we did not have a choice and we weren't allowed to experience the full developmental process of girlhood." Lee romanticises this violation by making it appear a 'natural' progression for Troy rather than sexist gender politics coercively imposing a matriarchal role via a process of socialisation.

Television times

Carolyn did not make gender distinctions about household chores when she was well, and the movie fails to indicate why she now has an unconvincing shift in attitude. As if to highlight patriarchal thinking that females are interchangeable, undifferentiated, the film in no way suggests that there is anything wrong with a ten-year-old girl assuming an adult role. Indeed, this is affirmed, and the mother's dying is upstaged by the passing of the torch to Troy. The seriousness of her illness is announced to the children by their father, who commands them to turn away from their gleeful watching of *Soul Train* to hear the news (even in her absence, the mother/matriarch spoils their pleasure). Throughout *Crooklyn* Lee shows the importance of television in shaping the children's identities, their sense of self. While the boys panic emotionally when they hear the news, bursting into tears, Troy's feelings are hidden by a mask of indifference. That the children obey their father in their mother's absence (not complaining when he tells them to turn off the television) suggests that he is better able to assume an authoritative parental role when she is no longer present. Woody's transformation into a responsible adult reinscribes the sexist/racist thinking that the presence of a 'strong' black female emasculates the male. Carolyn's death is treated in a matter-of-fact manner; we learn about it as the children casually discuss the funeral. We never see the family grieve. Troy, who is emotionally numb, only confronts the reality of this death when she is jolted from sleep by what she imagines is her mother's raging voice. Bonding with her father in the kitchen, her suppressed grief does not unleash tears; instead she vomits. This ritual cathartic cleansing is

the rite of passage that signals her movement away from girlhood.

Taking her mother's place, Troy is no longer adventurous. She no longer roams the streets, discovering, but is bound to the house, to domestic life. While the male children and grown-up dad continue to lead autonomous lives, to express their creativity and will to explore, Troy is confined, her creativity stifled. Since she is always and only a mother substitute, her power is more symbolic than real. We see her tending to the needs of her brothers, being the 'little woman'. Gone is the vulnerable, emotionally open girl who expressed a range of feelings; in her place is a hard impenetrable mask. Just as no one mourns the mother's death, no one mourns the erasure of Troy's adolescence. In their book *Failing at Fairness: How America's Schools Cheat Girls*, Myra and David Sadker document the pervasiveness of a "curricular sexism" that turns girls into "spectators instead of players". Troy becomes a spectator, standing behind the gate looking out at life, a stern expression on her face.

Silent losses

Though dead, Carolyn reappears to reassure and affirm her daughter. This reappearance is yet another rejection of loss. The controlling, dominating mother remains present even when dead, visible only to her girl child, now the guardian of patriarchy who gives approval to Troy's subjugation. Powerful black mothers, who work outside the home, the film suggests, 'fail' their families. Their punishment is death. When she is dying Carolyn gives lessons in sexism to her daughter in a way that runs counter to the values she has expressed throughout the film (she does, however, encourage her daughter to think about a work future, if only because it is her own career that ensured the family's economic survival).

The Sadkers conclude their introductory chapter, which exposes the way sexist socialisation robs girls of their potential, with a section called 'Silent Losses' that ends with the declaration: "If the cure for cancer is forming in the mind of one of our daughters, it is less likely to become a reality than if it is forming in the mind of one of our sons." Whereas *Crooklyn* attempts to counter racist assumptions about black identity, it upholds sexist and misogynist thinking about gender roles. Order is restored in the Carmichael house when the dominating mother-figure dies. The emergence of patriarchy is celebrated, marked by the subjugating of Troy, and all the household's problems 'magically' disappear. Life not only goes on without the matriarch, but is more harmonious.

Crooklyn constructs a redemptive fictive narrative for black life where the subjugation of the black female body is celebrated as a rite of passage which is restorative, which ensures family survival. Whether it is the grown woman's body erased by death or the little girl's body erased by violent interruption of her girlhood, the sexist politics embedded in this movie has often gone unnoticed by viewers whose attention is riveted by the exploits of the male characters. In failing to identify with the female characters or to bring any critical perspective to these representations, audiences tacitly condone the patriarchal devaluation and erasure of rebellious black female subjectivity the film depicts. Oppositional representations of blackness deflect attention away from the sexist politics that surfaces when race and gender converge. The naturalistic style of *Crooklyn* gives the sense of life-as-is rather than life as fictive construction.

Lee is indeed fictively re-imagining the 70s in this film and not merely providing a nostalgic portrait of the way things were. In his ahistorical narrative there is no meaningful convergence of black liberation and feminist politics, whereas in reality black women active in nationalist black power groups were challenging sexism and insisting on a feminist agenda. In *Crooklyn* Lee's aggressively masculinist vision is diffused by excessive sentimentality and by the use of Troy as the central embodiment of his message. Writing about the dangers that arise when excessive emotionality is used as a cover-up for a different agenda, James Baldwin reminds us that: "Sentimentality is the ostentatious parading of excessive and spurious emotion. It is the mark of dishonesty, the inability to feel." Such emotional dishonesty emerges full force in *Crooklyn*. The focus on Troy's coming of age and her mother's death is a non-threatening cover for the more insidious anti-woman, anti-feminist vision of black family life that is the film's dominant theme.

It is used to mask the repressive patriarchal valorisation of black family life, in which the reinscription of sexist idealised femininity symbolically rescues the family from dissolution. Death and dying are merely a subtext in *Crooklyn,* a diversionary ploy that creates a passive emotional backdrop on to which Lee imposes a vision of the black family that is conservative and in no way opposed to the beliefs of white mainstream culture. The aspects of the film that are rooted in Lee's own life-story are the most interesting; it is when he exploits those memories to create a counter-worldview that will advance patriarchal thinking that the narrative loses its appeal.

Women's work

Testifying that writing this script was cathartic, that it enabled her to confront the past, Joie Lee declares: "The emotional things that happen to you as a child, they're timeless, they stay with you until you deal with them. I definitely cleaned up some areas in my life that I hadn't dealt with before—like death." But the film Spike Lee has made does not confront death. In *Crooklyn,* death and dying are realities males escape from. There is no redemptive healing of a gendered split between mind and body; instead, *Crooklyn* echoes the patriarchal vision celebrated in Norman O. Brown's *Life Against Death,* where the hope is that "unrepressed man" "would be rid of the nightmares . . . haunting civilization" and that "freedom from those fantasies would also mean freedom from that disorder in the human body."

The messiness of death is women's work in *Crooklyn*. Expressing creativity, engaging pleasure and play is the way men escape from the reality of death and dying. In the space of imaginative fantasy, Lee can resurrect the dead female mothering body and create a world where there is never any need to confront the limitations of the flesh and therefore no place for loss. In such a world there is no need for grief, since death has no meaning.

Manohla Dargis (review date December 1994)

SOURCE: A review of *Crooklyn,* in *Sight and Sound,* December, 1994, pp. 44-5.

[*In the following review, Dargis praises Lee's* Crooklyn *citing the camera work, the music, and the fact that the film is presented through the eyes of a nine-year-old African-American girl.*]

For a number of years now, Spike Lee has made more of a name for himself as an ideologue and entrepreneur than as a film-maker. Although he's one of the busiest of directors—six features, in addition to TV commercials, music videos, a production company, a record business, retail stores—his off-screen words and deeds have often commanded as much if not more attention than his work in film. Whatever the personal gain, Lee's extra-curricular activities have cost him dearly. Acclaimed by the black community (at least publicly), patronised, condemned and fetishised by the white media, the artist has been swamped by his own creation, a phenomenon otherwise known as Spike Lee.

Crooklyn is Lee's most personal work since his startling debut eight years ago with *She's Gotta Have It,* and decidedly his best to date. The semi-autobiographical film, which Lee co-wrote with his sister Joie and younger brother Cinqué, traces the emotional arc of the fictional Carmichael family over a few crucial months during the early 70s, a sentimental interlude that closes in tragedy. Amy Taubin has called the film "operatic", and it's not for nothing that in one scene the clan's patriarch and resident tortured artist Woody proclaims that he's writing a folk opera. Some 20 years after the fact, Lee has done just that.

Woody is a purist under siege. A composer and jazz musician, he's pressured by his wife Carolyn to compromise his art to put food on the table. Although clearly adoring, Carolyn is weary of playing the heavy for both her kids and husband. When Woody complains about her lack of support (he's just bounced his fifth cheque of the month), she reacts with fury, storming, "I can't even take a piss without six people hanging off my tits," and pointedly counting him into the equation.

Bristling with passion, Carolyn is by turns nurturing and punishing, a woman whose frustrations with her family are tempered by overwhelming love. She's also Lee's most complicated female character since his first feature, and her eventual departure goes a long way toward explaining the general failings of his other cinematic women. While Woody sneaks the kids sweets and spins out promises, Carolyn is the one who rises at dawn, conjures the meals, and does time from nine to five. Tougher than Woody, and demonstrably less sympathetic, she's the only parent who's keeping it together.

For all that *Crooklyn* is a family melodrama, nearly as much time is devoted to the outside action as that rolling about inside the Carmichael brownstone. Lee launches his film with one of his characteristic flourishes, the camera sweeping over a riot of sounds and images, rushing to keep pace with all the children running, jumping and hurtling through these less than mean streets. This is Brooklyn as it used to be, a place where gossiping neighbours outnumber jiving glue sniffers, and racial unease simmers but rarely burns. More to the point, this is Brooklyn as remembered by its children.

One of the remarkable things about this remarkable film is that much of it is seen though the eyes of a nine-year-old African American girl. Troy is both the film's conduit and its wellspring, the one for whom the world either slows down to a sensuous crawl, or squeezes together for a surreal kink. Devoted to her mother, enamoured with her daddy, Troy's gender makes her an outsider within the litter as well as, the script suggests, a keener witness to the family romance. For all that the boys of the Carmichael Five struggle to rock their world, it's Troy who signifies the loudest.

Shaped more by sensation than by narrative thrust, *Crooklyn* unfolds through a succession of shifting scenes, some little more than snapshots. With one striking exception (Troy's trip south, a sequence lasting roughly 20 minutes and related entirely through the use of an anamorphic lens), the mood is familiar, intimate, soulful. Arthur Jafa's camera keeps close to characters but doesn't crowd them, while the extraordinary soundtrack, as lush as that in *GoodFellas*, eases everyone on their way.

The original definition of melodrama is drama with music, and there's scarcely a moment in *Crooklyn* that isn't punctuated by either Terence Blanchard's plangent score or the wild style of over three dozen hot licks, pop hits, ballads, lamentations and sundry witless ditties. As much as the dialogue or lighting, it's music that shapes the film, filling in texture and building density. From Curtis Mayfield to the Partridge Family, the Carmichaels are awash in music, a fact that has as much to do with Woody's calling as with the cultural moment in which the director himself came of age. Long before he found his voice in film, Lee had discovered the pulse and pleasures of Brooklyn, New York.

Amy Taubin (review date October 1995)

SOURCE: A review of *Clockers*, in *Sight and Sound*, October, 1995, p. 45.

[*In the following review, Taubin asserts that "In terms of form and content* [Clockers *is*] *easily Lee's riskiest and most accomplished film to date," but argues that the film does have flaws.*]

In a drug-ridden Brooklyn housing project, Strike is a 16-year-old-clocker (lowest level drug dealer). Troubled by ulcers so severe they cause him to spit blood, he is nevertheless the favourite of Rodney Little, the local crack kingpin. Rodney asks Strike to prove his loyalty by killing Darryl, a young pusher that Rodney claims has been cheating him.

Strike heads for Ahab's, a fast food joint where Darryl does his dealing. Trying to work up his nerve, he goes to the bar next door where he meets his older brother Victor, a model African-American citizen. Strike babbles some story about how Darryl deserves to die because he beat up a 14-year-old girl. When Victor says that he might know someone who could kill Darryl, Strike realises that his brother is drunk and splits. A short while later, someone pumps four bullets into Darryl.

The next day, Victor turns himself in, claiming he killed Darryl in self-defence. Veteran homicide detective Rocco Klein thinks Victor is protecting Strike. Rocco begins pursuing Strike with a vengeance. For Strike, Rocco is one too many among the people—narcotics cops, his mother, local black cop Andre and bright, idolising 12-year-old Tyrone—who hassle him on a daily basis. Rocco arrests Rodney, suggesting that it's Strike who ratted on him. Strike realises he'd better get out of town. While packing his gear, he realises his gun is missing. He gives Victor's wife the money for Victor's bail but Strike's mother refuses to make peace with him.

Errol, a stone killer in the last stages of AIDS dementia and Rodney's right hand man, comes gunning for Strike. Tyrone sees him before Strike does, pulls out the gun he's 'borrowed' from Strike and shoots Errol dead. At the police station, Andre begs Rocco to help Tyrone get off with a minimum sentence. He then beats up Strike for getting Tyrone involved. Strike barely makes it back to his car when he spots Rodney coming after him. He takes refuge in the police station where Rocco presses him to confess to murdering Darryl. Suddenly, Strike's mother appears and tells Rocco that Victor came home that night acting crazy and that his story is true. Strike is set free but, finding his car has been trashed by Rodney, he leaves on a train heading west.

Adapted from the Richard Price novel of the same name, Spike Lee's *Clockers* is about black-on-black violence. Lee shifts the focus from Price's central character Rocco Klein (a middle-aged white cop having an identity crisis) to Strike, the African-American teenage crack dealer who makes what he believes is a rational choice—to earn his living selling a product people want even though it kills them—and finds himself torn apart by the violence of the drug world and the unexpected revolt of his own conscience. The film shows that there are no positive choices for black men born into the underclass. Attempting to live an upstanding life, Strike's brother Victor is also driven crazy.

Clockers opens with a title sequence that's bravura even for Lee. The camera travels over a succession of grisly police photos of murder scenes—black male bodies torn apart by bullets. Behind a yellow police tape, crowds of black faces watch a nightly spectacle of bloodletting that's both too immediate and too removed to be comprehensible. At once didactic and operatic, this opening positions us for the film that follows. What's most startling about *Clockers* is its intimacy. Lee puts us inside the skin of a kid who seems morally reprehensible at the outset, making the agony of his experience inescapable.

Lee's choice of camera placement and movement has never been more brilliant. The camera's erratic rhythms and circular patterns articulate the extreme confinement of Strike's world and his panicky sense of being held in a vice. Similarly, the narrative, though dense with incident, seems to turn in on itself, covering the same ground over and over again. Everything in Strike's world—the repetitive riffs of rap music, the claustrophobic space of video games, his fetishised electric trains that circle a single track even as they testify to the existence of unknown and distant places—reinforces the feeling of confinement.

Given everything that comes before it, the final sequence—Strike's face pressed against the train window as it crosses a desert landscape that must seem to him as vast and charged with possibility as outer space—is, for a moment, wildly liberating. But Lee undercuts this feeling with a cutaway to one of Strike's crew, lying dead in a pool of blood on the concrete platform where we first saw Strike. Already the crowd is gathering around the corpse. Strike has escaped but he carries his past with him. Given what we know of American society today, why would we think there's place for him that's different from where he's been?

In terms of form and content easily Lee's riskiest and most accomplished film to date, *Clockers* is not without its flaws. In focusing so much on Strike, Lee makes the other characters one-dimensional. Newcomer Mekhi Phifer makes an amazing Strike, so much like an ordinary kid it's hard to remember that he's acting. Yet such extraordinary actors as Isaiah Washington, Delroy Lindo, Harvey Keitel and John Turturro are strait-jacketed by the script and direction.

Lee encourages cinematographer Malik Sayeed to extend the experiments with the cutting together of various types of film stock begun by Arthur Jaffa in Lee's *Crooklyn*. Sometimes this method yields expressive results, as in the flashback sequences which have the texture of over-saturated 16mm Kodachrome. Just as often, the effect is purely decorative, as in the burnt-up look of the police interrogation scenes which seem borrowed from Oliver Stone's *J.F.K.*

The director's most serious mistake, however, is to toy with a whodunnit structure until the climactic and hopelessly stagy interrogation of Strike by Rocco reveals the truth about Darryl's death. Viewers who have read the novel will know that Strike is not a murderer (Price puts that issue to rest early on in his narrative) but newcomers will be led down paths that are irrelevant, if not downright destructive, to the sense of subjectivity that Lee wants to convey.

With the mystery out of the way, the film seems infinitely more powerful on the second viewing, and even more so on the third. Desolate, hallucinatory and fearlessly heartfelt, it is the 'hood movie to end all 'hood movies. In its violence, there is neither glamour, nor pleasure, nor release.

Leslie Felperin (review date June 1996)

SOURCE: A review of *Girl 6*, in *Sight and Sound*, June, 1996, pp. 43-4.

[*In the following review, Felperin analyzes Lee's* Girl 6 *as a response to criticism of Lee's treatment of female characters and in terms of its relationship to his earlier film* She's Gotta Have It.]

New York City. The present. A young actress goes for an audition with a famous director, but when he insists she take her top off, she walks out, upset and humiliated. Her agent is furious with her, but her upstairs neighbour, Jimmy, offers sympathy. Fed up with low-paying jobs, she speaks to a woman who runs a 'phone-sex' business, but because she hasn't got her own line she has to look elsewhere for work. Eventually, she lands a job doing phone sex at an office-based company, where she is trained by supervisor Lil, introduced to her co-workers and renamed Girl 6.

Before long, Girl 6 is drawing in regular customers and proving to be highly proficient at her new career. One night she sees a news report about a little girl, named Angela King, who has been injured falling down a lift shaft and the news story of her recovery is tracked closely by her. At work, Girl 6 starts to get disturbing phone calls from Mr Snuff, a client who likes to talk about his sadistic fantasies. Girl 6 agrees to meet a client she likes but is stood up by him. She meets with her ex-husband and demonstrates how she talks on the phone but she refuses his sexual advances.

Getting too involved with her work, Girl 6 starts to have a breakdown. Lil recommends she take some time off. Through the agency of the woman she met earlier, Girl 6 sets up business at home. However, after an especially disturbing phone call from Mr Snuff who reveals that he knows where she lives, Girl 6 decides to quit working in phone sex and move to California to resume her acting career. She gives some money to Angela King and says goodbye to her ex-husband, who calls her by her real name, Judy. In California, Judy goes for a reading with a director who asks her to take her top off. She refuses and calmly walks out, but not before she finishes giving the monologue she started during the first reading at the beginning of the film.

Girl 6 opens with it's unnamed heroine trying out for a part by reciting a monologue which originally opened director Spike Lee's first feature, *She's Gotta Have It*. In the speech, Nola Darling explains that she only agreed to take part in this film because she wishes to "defend herself" in the face of others' distortions. The defensive note is significant. It's an obvious in-joke, but on a brute level of realism, it's not inconceivable that an aspiring black actress would audition with these lines. (As the film points out, there are precious few good parts written for black women.)

On another level though, Lee alludes here to his earlier film because *Girl 6* seems to constitute a response to a persistent criticism levelled at him—that he doesn't pay enough attention to black women's experiences. Through this monologue, Lee reminds us that not only has he explored this territory before, but also he declaims his intention to go further this time. In other words, for Lee, Nola Darling in *She's Gotta Have It* was the audition, while this is the 'real thing'.

Yet, despite their dissimilar plots and the fact that the screenplay for *Girl 6* was written by Suzan-Lori Parks, the two films seem to be in some kind of dialogue with one another. Where *She's Gotta Have It* concerned Nola's refusal to settle for one man in favour of sexual freedom, *Girl 6* features a largely celibate central character, but one no less interested in being in control of the sexual relationships, conducted almost entirely over the phone, that she is involved in.

An adventurous inclination to explore unconventional visual styles is displayed in both films: *She's Gotta Have It* had its documentary, to-camera scenes, while *Girl 6* features odd pastiches of older black genres and texts, including *Carmen Jones,* blaxploitation films and *The Jeffersons,* (none of which further the plot but are rather fun). Within both films, the central characters act as screens on which other characters project idealised notions of femininity. This is very effectively figured in *Girl 6* when, during the course of a single conversation, the protagonist changes with the flick of an edit into all the different guises—blonde bimbo, afro-haired 70s chick, smooth besuited lady—we've already seen her as throughout the film. Both women are presented as strong and attractive, empowered by their sexuality, yet limits are brutally imposed on them by their respective narratives. Crucial to both films is the moment when their respective characters lose control: Nola eventually decides to settle down with Jamie only after he rapes her, while Girl 6 chooses to abandon phone sex when Mr Snuff, the sadistic client, gets literally too close for comfort.

This last plot twist in *Girl 6* symbolises one of the film's major problems—it can't seem to make up its mind what it thinks of phone sex. It starts out by appearing to celebrate it by making the office Girl 6 works in a happy, matriarchal utopia, offering kindly lady bosses and sisterly colleagues, good money and a measure of sexual liberation. Then, just when Girl 6 seems to have become a success at it, she's shown to have become "too close" to the job, goes a little off her head and eventually chooses to reject it. In the end, she gives away most of the money she's earned to a little girl damaged in a lift-shaft accident, a plummeting downwards that is explicitly matched with Girl 6's descent into the world of phone sex. The result is not complexity and productive ambivalence, but just a sense of bafflement as to what point the filmmakers are trying to make.

A similar feeling of perplexity is produced by the film's capricious games with realism and fantasy. I have already mentioned the film's odd pastiche interludes, but the most puzzling thing about them is that you have no idea whether these are meant to be Girl 6's own fantasies or her customers', or filmic non sequiturs tied to no one's consciousness in particular. The third option is that they are meant to work as Brechtian distanciation devices. In that case, they are certainly effective frustrations to involvement, working well with the distancing apparatus of phone sex itself.

Girl 6 is shot in such a highly expressionist manner anyway—cinematographer Malik Hassan Sayeed uses a rich palette of hot reds and electric blues and features many striking tracking shots and other lovely visual flourishes—that one starts to wonder whether this all might be a fantasy. This feeling is particularly acute when weird things happen in the 'real' world of the story, such as telephones raining down from the sky when Girl 6 kisses her ex goodbye. A similar disjunctiveness is achieved by the use of largely old songs by the artist formerly known as Prince while, though evocative, often bear no lyrical relation to the action on screen.

At one point, Mr Snuff mentions that he saw an Oprah Winfrey programme about phone sex and that it revealed that most the women who worked the lines were "ugly". Even though his remark is meant to reflect his misogyny, it does make you think about how phoney this version of phone sex work we've seen so far probably is, featuring a cast of almost all beautiful girls, including Naomi Campbell, Debi Mazar and Madonna as Boss 3. The reality is probably much closer to the conditions shown in *Short Cuts,* where poor working-class women in K-Mart clothes jiggle babies on their knees or cut their toe nails at home while lazily describing blow jobs over the phone.

In the end, you get the impression that Lee wants to acquire a few feminists credentials and eat his cheesecake too. When *She's Gotta Have It* was originally released, many critics and viewers felt thrilled by its energy and visual inventiveness, but its treatment of women, especially given its rape scene, divided many viewers. *Girl 6* is equally as inventive, comes with many amusing moments and a fine central performance (in a sketchy role) by the protean Theresa Randle. However, its script is much weaker than its direction, and ultimately it is a poor defence against the accusations about Lee's clumsy handling of female characters that are obliquely invoked in its opening monologue.

Colette Lindroth (essay date 1996)

SOURCE: "Spike Lee and the American Tradition," in *Literature/Film Quarterly,* Vol. 24, No. 1, 1996, pp. 26-31.

[*In the following review, Lindroth discusses Lee's* Do the Right Thing *as an American narrative in the tradition of* Huckleberry Finn.]

From the moment it opened, Spike Lee's movie *Do the Right Thing* has raised questions and aroused controversy among critics and ordinary moviegoers alike. From its initial success at the Cannes Film Festival to its almost complete exclusion from the Academy Award nominations, the film has provoked heated response from both defenders and attackers, and publications as disparate as *Vogue, The New Yorker, American Film,* and *Mother Jones* reviewed, interviewed, and often second-guessed Lee. The film was praised for its "unclichéd, antiheroic vision of . . . contemporary racial tension," and for "asking questions about the country's racial chasm that few artists, or even political leaders, are willing to broach." So much of the focus has been on the political message of the film, however, that much of its real artistry, and nearly all of its relevance to the tradition of American literature as a whole, has been overlooked. Even a review that considered it necessary viewing, for example, praising its "easy, colloquial vivacity" and "sensational look," also dismissed most of its characters as being "there to represent something or to move the plot along" and complained that its style is a "belligerent, in-your-face mode of discourse" that "winds up bullying the audience." In focusing on the message and condescending to the style, *The New Yorker* critic, like many others, missed much of the movie's power and most of its subtle, apparently offhand artistry.

Viewed more analytically, ***Do the Right Thing*** is a worthy addition to a central tradition of American literature, the tradition dealing with difficult moral choices. While Lee does not dwell on the fact, his characters occupy the same moral landscape that American heroes from Natty Bumppo to Huck Finn have always occupied. Faced squarely with moral choice, the American hero has always tried to "do the right thing," and has usually succeeded. Lee's movie is a particularly somber entry in this tradition, however. Despite its deceptively simple title—what could be easier than doing the right thing?—the events of the movie suggest that, in the modern world, it may no longer be possible to make the right choice, no longer possible to recognize the right thing.

In this respect the movie resonates most strongly with *Huckleberry Finn*, and their differences and similarities illustrate the complexity of Lee's vision of America. During the course of his journey, Huck frequently finds himself challenged to do the right thing, most significantly in racial terms. He is nagged by guilt over his complicity in the escape of the runaway slave, Jim. His Southern social conscience, very much imposed from without, tells him he should turn Jim over to the authorities; his growing sense of self, however, knows he will do no such thing. Confronting these conflicting demands in the moral climax of the novel, he rejects this "conscience" shouting, "All right then, I'll *go* to Hell!" In choosing Hell, paradoxically, he does the right—the truly moral—thing. As he shucks off the false "conscience" of a slave-owning society, he frees himself to become an independent individual. The rightness of the choice has resounded throughout American literature ever since it was made.

Things refuse to work out this way in the Brooklyn of 1989, however; hence the unsettling quality of Lee's movie, and the strength of audience response to it. Lee focuses strongly on the ironic possibilities of his title. Between an early admonition to "do the right thing" and a final scene in which Sal, standing in front of his burned-out pizzeria, repeats those exact words with heavy irony, much has happened. A community in Brooklyn has survived the hottest day of the summer, a variety of racial and ethnic hatreds has been expressed, a young Black man has been killed, and a neighborhood landmark has been burned down. Clearly, the right thing has not been done. Even more ominously, none of the things that did happen were intended. Events have gone out of control.

Lee, like Twain, makes it clear that he is dealing with a microcosm of America in his work. Twain is characteristically elliptical in making this suggestion. In his "explanatory note," for example, he specifies the variety of dialects he uses in his novel: "the Missouri negro dialect; the extremest form of the back-woods Southern dialect; the ordinary 'Pike County' dialect; and four modified varieties of this last." Despite its apparent lightheartedness, this note and countless references in the novel make it clear that he is presenting a careful cross section of the world he knows. Similarly, Lee's Journal reveals his concern that his movie be truly representative, a valid and accurate cross section of the modern urban landscape: "The neighborhood will have a feel of the different cultures that make up the city, specifically Black American, Puerto Rican, West Indian, Korean and Italian American. Unlike Woody Allen's portraits of New York." Twain insists that his presentation of the South, with its slavery, hypocrisy and materialism, is nineteenth-century reality. Lee insists that his picture of racially torn Brooklyn, with its volatile variety of races, is a true cross section of twentieth-century reality. Woody Allen and other filmmakers might present more attractive, commercial portraits; his he promises, will be a true one.

Lee's intention to present an objective picture of "race relations, . . . America's biggest problem . . . since we got off the boat"—without letting it become "just a diatribe"—reveals the significance of the film's frequent reminders that these events are part of the fabric of American life. In response to Buggin' Out's demand that the "Italian Wall of Fame" in Sal's Famous Pizzeria include "some brothers . . . Malcolm X, Angela Davis, Michael Jordan," Sal flatly refuses. "You want brothers up on the Wall of Fame, you open up your own business, then you can do what you wanna do," he says. "This is America," he adds proudly, making it clear that the individual's right to free expression is an important part of America's meaning for him.

Faced with a second, stronger challenge, this time from his son Pino, who desperately wants to sell the business and move to their "own neighborhood," Sal is equally adamant: "So what if this is a Black neighborhood, so what if we're a minority," he says. "I've never had trouble with these people, don't want none either, so don't start none. This is America. Sal's Famous Pizzeria is here for good." The American dream of self-determination is clearly part of Sal's ethical makeup, as is a strong sense of fair play: We don't bother them, they don't bother us. "This is America."

In America as elsewhere, however, being right does not prevent one from doing wrong, and good intentions frequently count for nothing. Part of the irony in *Do the Right Thing* is that no one means the tragedy to happen; neither, however, does anyone do anything to prevent it, and together everyone blunders into violence. Six characters find themselves on a collision course. Each thinks himself to be in the right; to some extent each is in the right; no one can clearly communicate his feelings and disaster results.

Buggin' Out is a forceful example of an uncommunicated desire. In demanding room for the brothers on the Wall of Fame, he is making a reasonable request; unfortunately, his disposition and demeanor are so intense, his demands so heated, that they are never couched in reasonable terms. His words pour out in torrents, overwhelming his audience, drowning his meaning and infuriating Sal. Offended by the stridency of Buggin' Out's demands, Sal rejects his ideas; yet Sal, too, is within his rights. Buggin' Out has a reasonable request, which he communicates with unreasonable force; Sal has a reasonable reservation, which he communicates with contemptuous dismissal. No one is entirely wrong here; two rights block each other. Sal is right in feeling free to put his own heroes in his own walls; Buggin' Out is right in feeling that, in a Black community, a Black face or two among those heroes isn't too much to ask. Unfortunately, feelings, instead of reason, speak.

A second figure on this collision course is an equally forceful symbol of communication blocked or misdirected. Radio Raheem communicates at once too much and too little. His beloved "boom box," the radio so huge one wonders how he can lug it around, blares an unmistakable and certainly understandable message: "FIGHT THE POWER!" It's the only song he wants to hear. He himself, however, is almost totally inarticulate, and when he does speak his words seem to belie his music. His size, his blaring radio, his formidable demeanor all shriek "FIGHT!" Yet his first words, uttered to a group of neighborhood children, are a disarming "Peace, y'all." For the most part, Raheem's demeanor communicates for him. Everyone in the neighborhood, whether willingly or reluctantly, gives him the space his size and his noise demand, and there is no violence. His radio is his identity, however, and when that is destroyed his only means of communication is physical.

Yet a third character whose blocked communication puts him on a collision course with tragedy is Smiley, the ironically named character who almost never smiles. Smiley, who constantly listens to the speeches of Malcolm X on a Walkman, stammers so severely as to be literally incomprehensible. Incessantly referring to "Martin" [Luther King] and "Malcolm" [X], Smiley accosts everyone he meets, trying to involve them with these heroes of the Black American experience. His incoherence, however, coupled with his insistence, turns people off instead of involving them. Ironically, none of these Black Americans want to hear much about Martin or Malcolm on this hot summer day. Smiley only adds to the tensions of the neighborhood when he interrupts Sal and Pino as they clash over Sal's refusal to sell the pizzeria. Infuriated, Pino leaps to his feet, cursing Smiley and threatening him and his heroes. Smiley, accustomed to gentler treatment than this even from the bigoted Pino, backs off in anger and resentment, stammering incomprehensively. Eventually, this rebuff and those of Buggin' Out and Radio Raheem become the combined links in the chain of events leading to violence.

Countering these three Black characters are Sal and his sons, Pino and Vito. Their motivations, too, are understandable and they are not entirely in the wrong. Even Pino, the most furiously bigoted man in the movie, is not simply one-dimensional. More weak than evil, he detests the neighborhood, detests its residents, detests his customers, and detests his own embarrassment in front of his friends who taunt him for his "demeaning" job. In his frustration, he, too, has become uncommunicative; his main avenues of expression are through racial insults to Mookie, whom he is constantly calling "nigger," and punches for his brother, whom he bullies endlessly. But although he remains a bigot, Pino is a complex character. Mookie challenges him to name his favorite athlete—Magic Johnson; his favorite comedian—Eddie Murphy; and his favorite rock star—Prince. Trying to explain these loyalties in one who hates Blacks, Pino fumbles for reason: "It's different. Magic, Eddie, Prince, are not niggers. I mean are not Black. I mean they're Black, but not really Black. They're more than Black. It's different." As Lee's screen directions wryly reveal, "With each word Pino is hanging himself even further." Pino, fumbling for a rationale for his contradictory feelings, becomes as incomprehensible as Smiley.

Pino's contrast to Huck Finn is telling here. Like Huck, Pino has grown up with a set of unquestioned attitudes imposed from without, attitudes that tell him Blacks are inferior. His own tastes, however, tell him that Black individuals—Magic Johnson, Eddie Murphy, Prince—are admirable. Unlike Huck, Pino fails to resolve this tangle of inner and outer at-

titudes. Instead of managing to think for himself, he resorts to hatred and invective, hurrying the movie's tragic confrontation along.

If anyone is to manage to do the right thing it should be Vito, Sal's second son. Vito feels no hatred for his neighbors and is genuinely fond of Mookie, who treats him with more brotherly affection than does his bullying brother Pino. But Vito fails to bridge the gaps of hatred around him. Challenged by Mookie to stand up to Pino just once, he tries to do so, but fails. He cannot break the habit of years any more than anyone else in the movie. Unable to articulate his feelings, he fails himself, his family, and his friends. He doesn't hurt anyone; he simply does nothing.

It is Sal's characterization, however, that is most complex. As played by Danny Aiello, he is full of contradictions. On one hand he is affectionate, generous, proud of his sons, proud of his business and generally pleased that the kids in the neighborhood have literally grown up on his food. After the fire, he violently rejects Mookie's suggestion that the insurance money will solve his problems. It's not the money, he roars; it's his sweat, his effort, his very life that was destroyed with the building he put together with his own hands. Sal is also obstinate and irascible, however, and not immune to feelings of racial superiority. The pride represented by his Wall of Fame is admirable but his blunt refusal to add "some brothers" is condescending, and his highhanded ejection of Buggin' Out is insulting. His demand that Radio Raheem turn down the volume is understandable—the noise level is painful and Sal has to scream to be heard at all—but his contemptuous dismissal of the music itself is an affront to Raheem's racial identity. Although he may feel the right thing—regard for at least some of his neighbors, affection for Mookie, and a strong senses of fair play—he fails to communicate these feelings. Instead he communicates condescension toward Black cultural pride and hatred of both the noise and the message of Raheem's radio.

Resentment, hostility, misunderstanding, and flaring tempers conspire to produce tragedy. Ironically, the violence almost does not happen; an accident of timing brings it about. The long day is over; exhausted by the heat, Sal and his son are closing their doors for the night. The neighborhood kids, however, suddenly gather at the door, begging for one last slice. Feeling generous at the end of a profitable day, Sal good-heartedly gives in. At this point, however, Buggin' Out, Radio Raheem, and Smiley suddenly appear, joined in their resentment of Sal's earlier brusqueness. Buggin' Out demands a boycott until Sal grants his requests; Smiley shakes his pictures and stammers about Martin and Malcolm; Raheem turns his radio up to full volume. Exhausted and enraged, Sal loses control. Screaming over the noise, he grabs a baseball bat and attacks, demolishing

Raheem's radio with a brutality that suggests that his real target is Raheem himself.

Raheem, his identity smashed, attacks Sal. He in turn is attacked by Sal's sons; Buggin' Out and Smiley join in and the whole mass spills over onto the sidewalk. The crowd gathers; the police arrive, and as violence and chaos escalate, they "put a choke hold on Radio Raheem to restrain him"—and instead kill him, in a scene whose physical details make it clear that this is to be seen as another kind of lynching. Now it is too late. Whatever the right thing might have been, it can no longer be done.

For a long, tension-filled moment, the onlookers—now described in the screen directions as a "mob"—stare in mute rage at Sal and his sons, blaming them for yet another outrage against a Black man. Suddenly, but with actions clearly thought out, Mookie seizes a garbage can, carefully removes the lid, and—screaming "HATE!!!"—hurls it through the pizzeria window. As the screen directions phrase it, "*All hell breaks loose. The dam has been unplugged, broke. The rage of a people has been unleashed, a fury.*" The pizzeria is looted, fire is set, the building is destroyed—an event no one intended has occurred.

Yet Lee does not end his movie with this moment of hatred, frustration, and destruction. Rather he ends it with an uneasy, tentative rapprochement between Sal and Mookie on the next morning, in a final scene whose delicate balance between hostility and understanding reveals how effectively *Do the Right Thing* and *Huckleberry Finn* illuminate each other.

Much of the contrast between movie and novel lies in the relative freedom of their characters. For all his narrow escapes, Huck is essentially a free spirit from the moment he gets away from Pap. His developing conscience depends on his physical freedom. After rejecting the social conscience of his environment, whether he understands it or not, Huck can never retrace his steps. When he lights out for the territory at the end of the novel, Huck is establishing his freedom of conscience along with his freedom of movement. It is essential that he do so. The Huck who would "*go to Hell*" rather than betray a friend will hardly be welcome in the communities of the slaveowning South. But no such physical freedom exists for the residents of Bedford-Stuyvesant in Brooklyn. The economic realities of the modern world limit the personal freedom of Whites and Blacks alike. They are bound together, like it or not, and must face each other on the morning after violence, just as Sal and Mookie face each other, resentful and uneasy, in the movie's final scenes.

The fact that they can face each other at all gives cause for

some hope, and the movie ends with balance, stasis, rather than in action. It is a balance which has been present throughout the movie, though never as strongly as in the final scenes. Earlier, forces in conflict have balanced each other: Old balances young, passive balances active, White balances Black, male balances female. Above all, the elements of comedy, which dominate the earlier scenes in the movie, balance the possibility for tragedy. The accidents of timing which precipitate the tragedy upset this balance, but Sal and Mookie reestablish it as they regard each other in front of the remains of the previous night's violence. They face each other uneasily, aware that last night made them enemies: Sal's destruction of the radio was the first step on the road to Raheem's death, and Mookie's hurling of the garbage can was the first step on the road to the pizzeria's destruction.

Yet they can put that behind them and regard each other as individuals. After Sal's impassioned explanation of what his business meant to him, Mookie understands him more clearly than he had before. And Sal surely understands the feelings of this community with more clarity and compassion than he had previously felt. They face each other awkwardly, still resentful, but with more openness and less artificiality than they have previously shown. The chance to do the right thing is still there. It will be more difficult for Sal and Mookie than for Huck, since there is no free territory for them to light out to; it is not impossible, however. Both novel and movie end in openness.

One of the most intriguing statements in T.S. Eliot's essay "Tradition and the Individual Talent" is his assertion that "what happens when a new work of art is created is something that happens simultaneously to all the works of art which preceded it . . . it is not preposterous that the past should be altered by the present as much as the present is directed by the past." At first glance, it seems impossible that a new representative of a tradition could change something created a century earlier. Consideration of *Do the Right Thing* in conjunction with Huckleberry Finn, however, illuminates Eliot's remark at the same time that it affirms Lee's artistry and Twain's centrality to American literature, current as well as past. Mookie's and Sal's uneasy truce, together with their awareness of their shared future, illuminate once again the rightness of Huck's choice. His freedom to make that choice and then "light out" illuminates the reality of life in contemporary America. This sense of balance and openness, the idea that important choices are still to be made, is soberly emphasized by the quotes from Martin Luther King and Malcolm X that follow the last scene of the movie. As Lee concludes in his Journal, "In the end, justice will prevail, one way or another. There are two paths to that. The way of King, or the way of Malcolm."

Kent Jones (essay date January/February 1997)

SOURCE: "The Invisible Man: Spike Lee," in *Film Comment,* Vol. 33, No. 1, January/February, 1997, pp. 42-7.

[In the following essay, Jones discusses Lee's body of work.]

The proof of Spike Lee's insight is the clamor of opposing rash positions around his films—how difficult is it to imagine a scene from a Lee movie in which a gaggle of film critics scream their opinions about the relative worth of a young African-American filmmaker's oeuvre in each other's faces, shot in contrasting off-angles and perfectly sculpted light? His less sophisticated admirers, in other words those who are unwilling to apply the same sort of hardworking analysis to his work that he applies to American society, have never done him any favors by pushing him as an "innovator." (Some innovator: his actor-on-the-dolly move, cribbed from *Mean Streets* and monotonously reprised in every film from *Mo' Better Blues* through *Girl 6,* is numbingly off-key and gives the impression to the unsuspecting viewer that certain sidewalks in the New York area are equipped with conveyor belts.) Then there are those who claim that he is basically reheating old-fashioned social consciousness in a rock video microwave. But the classic social consciousness of, say, *To Kill a Mockingbird* begins with an abstraction—Racism, and How It Can Be Overcome—and structures its narrative accordingly: a racist malefactor and a good and righteous man square off against the backdrop of an amorphously indifferent populace that could be swayed either way and finally listens to reason. Lee, on the other hand, always starts from the specifics that make up the fractured consciousness of African-American males. "Hey daddy, I'll suck your big black dick for two dollars!" drawls the teenaged whore to Wesley Snipes's Flipper Purify before he screams with indignation and takes her in his arms at the end of *Jungle Fever.* It's one of the few sweepingly rhetorical moments in modern cinema that earns its weight and self-importance because it's the culmination of a whole battery of anxieties, horrors, disappointments, and subterfuges that have all been laid out by Lee with his typical block-by-block, hard plastic clarity.

There is also the overgrown-film-student charge, somewhat easier to fathom but essentially wrong and recklessly dismissive. What I understand people to mean by this is that Lee is a showoff, which is true enough. His camera never gets comfortable, and no stroll down the block is complete without at least six changes of angle. He is also constantly throwing aesthetic blankets over large chunks of his movies: changes of film stock for different locales in *Clockers* and *Get On the Bus,* high-def video for the images of the phantom callers in *Girl 6,* the infamous (and truly maddening) squeezed anamorphic image for the Southern section of *Crooklyn.* That's not to mention the liberal application of pop songs ladled over large portions of his films. There are few filmmakers whose work seems less organic and more the sum of their aesthetic choices.

Moreover, there are few filmmakers who are less interested in (or less adept at?) giving us the rhythms of quotidian existence. The world of Spike Lee is almost completely devoid of the everyday tasks and actions that make up the backbone of most films. When he does have a go at everyday life, it is often editorialized to a level beyond absurdity. Annabella Sciorra's family in *Jungle Fever* is so heavily singularized and lacking in nuance that "Italian Family" seems to be a new flavor of salad dressing. The opening scenes of *Malcolm X* are the most embarrassing, a fifth-hand evocation of zoot-suit culture. Lee's relentless, never-ending control leaves you with the feeling that when his good actors (Snipes, Denzel Washington, Angela Bassett, Alfre Woodard, Giancarlo Esposito) score a few points, they're getting one over on their director.

The fact is that legibility and visibility are more important to Spike Lee than anything else. Every film has its own eye-catching design and every moment is held only as long as it takes to register as a sign; everything beyond that feels like a holding action. Lee is a completely arrhythmic filmmaker in this sense: tempo and nuance are always sacrificed for clarity. It's fascinating to watch one of his attempts to render abandon because of his complete unwillingness to surrender his lock on the visuals. (Image and sound often seem like two separate categories with their own energies: while the visuals feel uptight, cramped, and fixated on the center, the soundtrack is always a mighty river of words and music.) When Denzel Washington's Bleek is composing a tune in *Mo' Better Blues,* Lee puts his poor actor on the dolly and spins the room around him. It's very similar to Troy's dream of a glue-induced flight over the block in *Crooklyn* because of the way that both actors are all but stapled to the camera. What is supposed to play as a sense of flight, artistic in the first instance and psychosexual in the second, is instead tidy and tight as a drum. On close inspection, though (and close inspection of Lee's cinema is always rewarding), there's something conceptually right about the *Mo' Better* scene, since the story deals with the way that artistic expression can be the unhealthy result of a transferral of guarded aggression from mother to son, a mask of mastery to wear in a racist world.

Which is pretty close to a self-portrait, at least based on the evidence of Lee's films (and his acting: in all of Lee's performances his voice and his body seem to be going in two different directions, which plays like a bizarre and quite intriguing evasion technique). His detractors make an enormous leap when they lazily insist that there's nothing but a vacuum behind all that "style." How ridiculous: what other filmmaker has been more adept at delineating the process of American racism and treating it as a living organism rather than a frozen entity? It's no small achievement, even when the film is as artistically pallid and mushy as *School Daze* or *Mo' Better Blues*. The insistence on leaving nothing to chance, which often flattens out his representations of jazz clubs, city blocks, and middle-class homes to the point that they feel like computer art, has a painful, extracinematic edge. You can feel Lee's desire to loosen up, but it's always checked by his fear of making a move without the protection of his agile mind. His films are personal in the strangest sense: the artist is revealed by the many ways with which he chooses to constantly camouflage his personality.

The film school complaint is the other side of the coin from the more absurd charges of "reverse racism," divisiveness, and separatism, all of which are hogwash, and all of which start from the wrongheaded assumption that Lee is some kind of "special interest" filmmaker. Aside from the fact that people are constantly attributing sentiments voiced by Lee's warring characters to Lee himself, what's so striking about the frequent criticisms and judgments of his work is their eagerness to reduce it to a lowest "cinematic" denominator and sweep it under the rug. The idea that Lee is a propagandist grows out of what can only be understood as fear of encroachment on the sacred territory of American cinema and its myths. It's the same kind of fear that once prompted a friend of mine to make the following remark to an acquaintance on the neighboring barstool who said he was afraid to go to Harlem: "Let me get this straight— you're afraid to be a white man in America?"

Lee goes against the grain of the model well-rounded filmmaker, balanced between the thematic and the organic, between action and emotion. As an artist, he has firmly positioned himself midway between didacticism and dialectics. The didactic side is his tireless effort to keep the desires, frustrations, looming terrors, and class diversity among African-American men visible and viable within mainstream, i.e. white, i.e. racist American culture. (He is less interested in women but willing to keep his films democratically open to their viewpoints, as in the interminable but informative improvised discussion in *Jungle Fever*.) The dialectical side is the rigorous manner in which he breaks down and presents the warring components of American society, a pot in which nothing melts and everything congeals (he has never been interested in the currently fashionable Hollywood idea of "positive images of black people," in which Wesley Snipes or Samuel L. Jackson is afforded the same golden opportunity as Bruce Willis or Harrison Ford to play the lead in idiotic action movies). The ensuing tension, which catches characters in a grid between the personal and the societal, is palpable in every one of his films, from the throwaway *Girl 6* to the hymnlike *Get On the Bus,* from the synthetically delicate *She's Gotta Have It* to the

grandiose *Malcolm X,* from the awful yet shaggily lovable *School Daze* to the magnificent *Do the Right Thing* and *Jungle Fever*. And that tension makes something odd but undeniably beautiful out of *Crooklyn,* an autobiographical reminiscence filtered through his sister Joie (he co-authored the script with her and brother Cinqué) that all but denies the possibility of Proustian reverie in favor of a systematic and seemingly exhaustive survey of the focal points, obsessions, and imagery of an early-Seventies African-American childhood. ·It's a haunting film in which the action is interestingly dispersed across a more delicate visual palette than the burnished tones of Ernest Dickerson would have allowed (courtesy of *Daughters of the Dust* cinematographer Arthur Jafa), suggestive of public-school mural art.

Placing Lee as a filmmaker rather than as a public figure or a provocateur has been somewhat set aside over the years. An instructive comparison would be Claire Denis, another essentially cold and precise filmmaker intent on rendering the multicultural makeup of modern life, who also strategically casts her films in warm, convivial tones and atmospheres. Denis is also a filmmaker of choices: a handheld camera for *S'en fout la mort,* interlocking narratives in *J'ai pas sommeil,* extreme closeup sensuality spread dolloped all over *Nénette et Boni*. But there are moments of comfort and reflection for her characters, and none whatsoever for Lee's—the people in his films are just as guarded and wary as their creator, who may never be relaxed enough to make a spontaneously generated autobiographical work like *U.S. Go Home*. A better precedent for Lee in world cinema is Nagisa Oshima, in whose films the patient accumulation of dry detail and opposing forces bursts open with an emblematic action at the film's climax. The ending of *Jungle Fever* or Mookie's garbage can in the window at the end of *Do the Right Thing* are kissing cousins to culminating moments like the eating of the apple in *Cruel Story of Youth* or the moment in *Dear Summer Sister* when the girl says, "They should never have given Okinawa back to the Japanese." Oshima is a more naturally elegant and economical filmmaker than Lee—more than he would probably have cared to admit in his angrier days—but they are both children of Brecht with a shared obsession with clarity, specificity, and the abandonment of personal concerns in favor of political directness. An interesting cultural divide: where one might say that Lee "likes" all of his characters, one might in turn say that Oshima "hates" all of his, at least in early films like *The Sun's Burial* (perhaps it's more correct to say that he equalizes them to a uniform unpleasantness). In any case, the net effect is virtually identical.

Lee may be even bleaker than his relentlessly tough Japanese cousin. There is always a lot of high spirits, Fifties-style sentimentality, and verbal jazz in Lee's work. But they hide what is in the end a despairing vision of existence, in which the backdrop of divisiveness and polarization not only never gives way to transcendent action and understanding (the way it does with the kiss at the end of Oshima's *Merry Christmas, Mr. Lawrence*) but shadows his characters mercilessly. When it's not felt in the restless visuals or through the neurotically inert characters—Lee's people, like Fassbinder's, are forever making small, tightly circumscribed movements across a limited selection of folkways that make them look like rats in a maze—it's there in the oppressively heavy atmosphere, a side effect of turning every field of action (Morehouse College, a movieish jazz club located in some unimaginably bland netherworld, the life of Malcolm X, a project courtyard, a Brooklyn block) into a metaphorically charged space. There's an uncharacteristic moment in *Jungle Fever* when Lee suddenly cuts to Flipper standing on a bad corner of Harlem a split second before he consorts with some unsavory characters in search of his crackhead brother (Samuel L. Jackson). You can feel his tension, distaste, and angry confusion in the way he mills around, his body tight. It's an unusual moment because it hands over the reins to an actor, no matter how short the duration. The entire Harlem—swanky-architectural-firm—Bensonhurst social grid that Lee has set up seems to be pressing down on Flipper.

There are appalling things in *Jungle Fever,* but it remains his most devastating film, perhaps for the crazy reason that it's the one most packed with interlocking thematic material. That's the paradox of Lee as an artist: the more linear and streamlined his films are, the duller they get and the more they flounder. The Tim Robbins-Brad Dourif yuppie tag team, the Italian family scenes (Anthony Quinn's performance as a supposedly prototypical Italian father—"Your mother was a *real woman!*"—is like an industrial disaster in an olive oil factory), the floating conversations between Lee and Snipes all just sit there, but their place in the grid that Lee sets up, the way they counterpoint, amplify, and bruise one another, give the film a remarkable fullness and social three-dimensionality. As in *Do the Right Thing* (which has some similarly awful moments that are nonetheless vital cogs in the machinery, like Lee and Turturro's conversation about niggers), Lee achieves something rare in American cinema, which is an illustration of the degree to which people are products of their environment, a far cry from the bogus individualism of so much American cinema. Flipper and Angie (Sciorra) are ciphers at the center of *Jungle Fever,* surrounded by a range of far more vivid characters: Ossie Davis's terrifyingly stern, separatist, Old Testament father and Ruby Dee's pathologically genteel mother, John Turturro's haloed candy store proprietor, and Samuel L. Jackson's horrifying crackhead. And on reflection what seems like an artistic miscalculation turns out to be a dialectical strategy. Lee is speaking to middle-class people like Flipper (and himself, presumably) who keep things status quo by avoiding the cacophony of warring voices in their ears, just as in *Do the Right Thing* he is

speaking to layabouts like Mookie who try to float through the world and eventually act out of sheer psychic exhaustion. When Mookie throws that garbage can through the window, he is egged on by his neighborhood friends, as Jonathan Rosenbaum has correctly pointed out, but he is also making a fruitless and mindless gesture that is the result of so much heat, aggravation, and sloganeering. It seems appropriate that the characters are diminished by the confusion that makes up their world (was this the reason Wim Wenders made his insane and now legendary comment that Mookie was not enough of a hero?) and that they have no time or room to analyze calmly.

In his less successful work, the striking moments come unmoored in a sea of heady aesthetic choices. Since Lee films every moment with equal weight and at an unvarying rhythm, his hyperbolic clarity can backfire on him when the focal points are reduced in number. *Clockers* is an unsatisfying film because the sheer immersion technique of Richard Price's novel is antithetical to Lee's aesthetic strengths. If any of his films does actually follow the old social-consciousness model it's this one, in which every character represents not a societal force but a different symbolic aspect of The Drug Problem In The Ghetto. (Lee is about as good a candidate for an in-depth study of life in the projects as Richard Attenborough.) But there are impassioned moments, particularly the montage in which a slow track away from Strike (Mekhi Phifer) playing with his trains is intercut with terrifyingly immediate shots of real crackheads scoring and getting high. There's nothing terribly wrong with *Malcolm X* beyond the fact that it drains a lot of the flashfire anger and drama out of the autobiography to give us a good, sturdy, dignified tour through the subject's life (the most striking passages of the film move with the slow and stately rhythm of Washington and Angela Bassett's immaculately acted mutual respect). *Girl 6,* which seems to enter a more playful mode, devolves into nothing much by the end (although it does have one of Lee's most physically frank moments: Isaiah Washington's shoplifter sweet-talks ex-wife Theresa Randle into an alley and shoves her hand down his pants).

Get On the Bus marks a turning point for Lee, a move towards a valid, tempered feeling of uplift and more faith in his actors and away from so much fanatical control. Lee finds myriad ways of exploring the faces of his uniformly magnificent actors in worried contemplation, to the point where his film takes on a singing beauty and a simple closeup of the great Charles Dutton carries real weight. There have been some ridiculous things written about this buoyant, defiantly old-fashioned movie, far from a song of praise to Louis Farrakhan. The Million Man March does not take on ideological but symbolic import: the simple and joyous fact of one million African-American men congregating in one place is what motivates everyone to get on the

Spotted Owl to Washington, and the feeling is echoed by the actors as they bite into their meaty roles. The makeup is standard WWII bomber crew stuff: an old failure, a young upstart actor, a gentle cop, a reformed gangbanger, a homosexual couple, a silent Muslim, a Republican businessman, an estranged father reunited with his gangbanger son and chained to him by court order, a Jewish relief driver, an aspiring filmmaker/witness ("Spike Lee Jr.," as one of the characters calls him), and the bus driver-spokesman hash out what seems like every conflict that currently besets the African-American community in a more musical version of vintage Rod Serling or Reginald Rose. But as always, Lee short-circuits any answers beyond a lonely self-respect. There is a painfully beautiful moment midfilm when the cop, whose father has been killed by gang members and whose beat is the ghetto, listens to the murder confession of the former gangbanger-turned-counselor, a moment made possible by the fellowship of the bus ride. And the cop suddenly turns the tables and tells him he'll have to arrest him when they get back to L.A. Lee cuts away from the standoff to a shot of the moon seen from the front window. This is presumably one of the moments in the film that's been called a cop-out, but is it a cop-out to illustrate a hopelessly divisive issue and refuse to put a Band-Aid on it? Lee isn't turning away from the conflict but turning towards the sad flow of time.

Get On the Bus may be his most heart-felt movie, but it still has the protective coating of every other Lee film—its materials are just more human. As he slowly loses his audience in the increasingly foul atmosphere of corporate culture (*Bus* disappeared from theaters with ruthless speed), it's puzzling to imagine how Lee will evolve. As a filmmaker he is caught between a rock and a hard place: he is too resolutely anti-American for the self-satisfaction of the current political climate, and he is too tightly coiled an artist to generate new enthusiasms now that the first flush has been over for some time. As much as I admire his abilities as a dialectician, the most penetrating moments in his enormously complex cinema are the small, instinctive ones. There is a moment at the end of *Crooklyn* when three of the children are walking up a public staircase, two of them holding hands and the other straggling behind, and they are lackadaisically singing a song that is gently echoed by a harmonica in Terence Blanchard's score. When they stop they wonder what they'll be wearing to their mother's funeral. The heartbreak—and the moment is heartbreaking like few moments in recent cinema—is in the high oblique angle that places the kids in a vast expanse of concrete, a detail that feels as if it comes straight from the filmmaker's memory. And it's in the stoic trudge up the steps, the sense of a burden that must be shouldered with dignity at all costs.

And then there are two moments in *Jungle Fever* and *Get On the Bus,* almost identical. In *Jungle Fever,* during the

crushing scene where Snipes and Sciorra are fooling around on the hood of a car, Lee makes a brief cut to a shot from the point of view of an apartment window looking down on them. We never see the inhabitant and the shot is over quickly, but once Lee cuts back to his interracial couple we just wait for the sirens to start blaring. And in *Get On the Bus,* amidst the guarded but real camaraderie of a Memphis bar (exemplified by a lovely moment in which Davis and the proprietor bridge their racial divide with a shared passion for rodeo, reminiscent of the scene in Powell's *A Canterbury Tale* in which the Oregonian G.I. and the Kentish carpenter talk woodworking), Lee makes an almost subliminal cut to a shot of a random white face staring. We don't see what he's staring at, but we don't have to. In both instances, a whole range of anger and fear is shot right into the heart of the film. It's during moments like these that I feel another, more vulnerable Spike Lee lurking beneath the quicksilver intelligence and stoic demeanor of the one we know. The question is: does he really want to reveal himself to those staring faces and open windows, positioned throughout American culture, even in the supposedly generous world of cinephilia?

FURTHER READING

Criticism

Baker, Houston A., Jr. "Spike Lee and the Commerce of Culture." *Black American Cinema,* edited by Manthia Diawara, New York: Routledge, 1993, 154-76.
  Discusses the cinematic critique Lee has developed throughout his career, and laments the absence of a Black feminist critique in the director's work.

Burgess, Dana L. "Vergilian Modes in Spike Lee's *Do the Right Thing.*" *Classical and Modern Literature: A Quarterly* 11, No. 4 (Summer 1991): 313-16.
  Asserts that Lee employs Vergilian modes in his *Do the Right Thing* and discusses the ambiguity of the film's ending.

Christensen, Jerome. "Spike Lee's Corporatist Art." *The Delegated Intellect: Emersonian Essays on Literature, Science, and Art in Honor of Don Gifford,* edited by Donald E. Morse, New York: Peter Lang, 1995, 89-106.
  Asserts that Lee is a corporate populist who takes no responsibility for the effect his products have.

Horvath, Brooke and Melissa Prunty Kemp. "All Things to All People: Opposing Agendas and Ambiguous Purpose in the Films of Spike Lee." *The Hollins Critic* XXXI, No. 4 (October 1994): 1-17.
  Analyzes the progression in the political and artistic agenda of Lee's films throughout his career.

Jones, Jacquie. "Spike Lee Presents Malcolm X: The New Black Nationalism." *Cineaste* 19, No. 4 (1993): 9-11.

Favorably reviews Lee's *Malcolm X,* but complains that the film contains some of Lee's typical problems.

Lee, Spike. "Class Act." *American Film* XIII, No. 4 (January/February 1988): 57, 59.

Discusses the making of his film *School Daze* and the difficult reception he expects the film to have from critics.

Lester, Julius. "Black Supremacy and Anti-Semitism: Religion in *Malcolm X*." *Cineaste* 19, No. 4 (1993): 16-7.

Asserts that Lee's *Malcolm X* is anti-Semitic and an irresponsible distortion of history.

Locke, John. "Adapting the Autobiography: The Transformation of Malcolm X." *Cineaste* 19, No. 4 (1993): 5-7.

Discusses how Lee transformed the history of Malcolm X's life to conform to the commercial needs of directing a film.

Lubiano, Wahneema. "But Compared to What?: Reading Realism, Representation, and Essentialism in *School Daze, Do the Right Thing,* and the Spike Lee Discourse." *Black American Literature Forum* 25, No. 2 (Summer 1991): 253-82.

Attempts to contextualize the discourse of Lee's films in the current cultural and political climate.

New, Elisa. "Film and the Flattening of Jewish-American Fiction: Bernard Malamud, Woody Allen, and Spike Lee in the City." *Contemporary Literature* 34, No. 3 (Fall 1993): 425-50.

Analyzes the work of Bernard Malamud, Woody Allen, and Spike Lee, and the place of the city in their work.

Scott, Matthew S. "Are You Ready to Invest in the Film Industry?" *Black Enterprise* 27, No. 5 (December 1996): 66-73.

Discusses the private funding of Lee's *Get on the Bus.*

Sklar, Robert. "What Is the Right Thing?" *Cineaste* 17, No. 4 (1990): 32-9.

Discusses the problem of critically assessing Lee's *Do the Right Thing.*

Thompson, Andrew O. "Magic *Bus.*" *American Cinematographer* 77, No. 11 (November 1996): 56-60, 62, 64-6.

Discusses the cinematography of Lee's *Get on the Bus.*

Additional coverage of Lee's life and career is contained in the following sources published by Gale: *Authors and Artists for Young Adults,* Vol. 4; *Black Writers,* Vol. 2; *Contemporary Authors,* Vol. 125; *Contemporary Authors New Revision Series,* Vol. 42; and *DISCovering Authors Modules: Multicultural Authors.*

V. S. Naipaul

1932-

Trinidadian-born English novelist, short story writer, essayist, journalist, and nonfiction writer.

The following entry presents criticism of Naipaul's work through 1995. For further information on his life and career, see *CLC*, Volumes 4, 7, 9, 13, 18, and 37.

INTRODUCTION

Often referred to as "the world's writer," Naipaul is both one of the most highly regarded and one of the most controversial of contemporary writers. His ironic accounts of colonial and postcolonial Third World societies have drawn acclaim from North America and Europe, but they generally have not met with the same favor in Africa, Asia, and the Caribbean for their negative portrayal of the peoples of those regions. Much of Naipaul's work deals with individuals who feel estranged from the societies they are supposedly a part of and who are desperately seeking a way "to belong."

Biographical Information

Naipaul was born in Trinidad in 1932 to Seepersad and Dropatie Capildeo Naipaul, the descendants of Hindu immigrants from northern India. After attending Queens Royal College, Trinidad's leading secondary school, he was awarded a government scholarship to study abroad, which led him to University College, Oxford, in 1950. After leaving Oxford in 1954, Naipaul worked briefly in the cataloguing department of the National Portrait Gallery in London before taking a position with the British Broadcasting Corporation, writing and editing for the program *Caribbean Voices*. It was during this period that he began to write stories for what was eventually to become *Miguel Street* (1959). By 1961, Naipaul's reputation in Britain was already considerable; he was the author of three successful books, two of which had won prizes (the 1958 John Llewellyn Rhys Memorial Prize for *The Mystic Masseur* [1959] and the 1961 Somerset Maugham Award for *Miguel Street*). Naipaul spent much of the 1960's traveling abroad, visiting India, a number of African nations, and his native Trinidad. These travels provided Naipaul with a wealth of material and served as the motivation for works such as *The Middle Passage* (1962) and *An Area of Darkness* (1964). By 1971, Naipaul had won all of Britain's leading literary awards, including the 1971 Booker Prize for *In a Free State* (1971). During the 1970s, Naipaul continued to travel for his literary inspiration. His book of essays, *The Return of Eva*

Perón; with The Killings in Trinidad (1980), is drawn from his visits to Trinidad, Zaire, and Argentina and focuses on the dangers of charismatic political leadership. *Among the Believers* (1981) is based on Naipaul's journeys in the Middle and Far East, in which he recounts his personal attempt to explain the "Islamic revival." Most of Naipaul's work during the late 1980s and 1990s has consisted of similar material garnered from his travels; *A Turn in the South* (1989) describes his travels in "the old slave states of the American southeast," and *India* (1991) explores the character of the people of India. Naipaul's most recent work, *A Way in the World* (1994), is a collection of partly autobiographical, partly fictional character sketches that are linked in some way to the Caribbean region. Naipaul and his wife, Patricia Hale, live in London, England.

Major Works

Critics generally agree that Naipaul's finest work is *A House for Mr. Biswas* (1961). Set in Trinidad, the novel is both a minutely circumstantial account of an individual's life and an allegory of the East Indian's situation in Trinidad, or of the colonial predicament more generally. Mr. Biswas, the main character, is Naipaul's Third World "Everyman," in search of his role in the world—more specifically, a home he can call his own. This sense of "rootlessness" is a recurrent theme in Naipaul's work and stems from his unique background: he was born in Trinidad to the descendants of Hindu immigrants from northern India and educated at England's Oxford University. Another convention of Naipaul's work, one for which he has drawn the ire of many Third World nations, including his native Trinidad, is his depiction of the peoples of these nations as culturally inferior. In *The Middle Passage,* for instance, Naipaul refers to the people of Port of Spain, Trinidad's capital, as "monkeys pleading for evolution, each claiming to be better than the other, Indians and Negroes appeal to the unacknowledged white audience to see how much they despise each other."

Critical Reception

Naipaul is widely considered one of the world's finest authors. His prose exhibits narrative skill and command of language, especially dialect. Many critics consider his early fiction (*The Mystic Masseur, Miguel Street, A House for Mr. Biswas*) superior to his later work, but it is generally agreed upon that the social awareness displayed early in his career has become more prominent in his more recent books. His negative appraisal of life in the Third World has met with a great deal of controversy, especially in novels such as *In a Free State, Guerrillas* (1975), and *A Bend in the River* (1979). Each of these works contain elements of sexual and political violence within an atmosphere of impending chaos, prompting reviewers to conclude that Naipaul finds Third World societies essentially hopeless. *Among the Believers* intensified the controversy surrounding Naipaul's work; his scathing portrait of civil and social disorder attributed to Islamic fanaticism in Iran, Pakistan, Malaysia, and Indonesia prompted some critics to accuse Naipaul of merely confirming preconceived notions about his subject rather than attempting a deeper analysis of Islam. Naipaul's work continues to draw mixed reviews, due mainly to his subjective approach rather than his prose.

PRINCIPAL WORKS

The Suffrage of Elvira (novel) 1958
The Mystic Masseur (novel) 1959
Miguel Street (novel) 1959
A House for Mr. Biswas (novel) 1961
The Middle Passage: Impressions of Five Societies—British, French and Dutch—in the West Indies and South America (nonfiction) 1962
An Area of Darkness (nonfiction) 1964
In a Free State (novel) 1971
Guerillas (novel) 1975

A Bend in the River (novel) 1979
The Return of Eva Perón; with The Killings in Trinidad (essays) 1980
Among the Believers: An Islamic Journey (nonfiction) 1981
Finding the Centre (nonfiction) 1984
The Enigma of Arrival (novel) 1987
A Turn in the South (nonfiction) 1989
India: A Million Mutinies (nonfiction) 1990
A Way in the World (novel) 1994

CRITICISM

John Mander (review date June 1965)

SOURCE: "The Anglo-Indian Theme," in *Commentary*, Vol. 39, No. 6, June, 1965, pp. 94-7.

[*In the following review, Mander praises Naipaul's descriptive powers, but notes that* An Area of Darkness *is similar to other novels that explore British influence in colonial India.*]

From their duration, their intimacy, and intensity, an outsider might take Anglo-Indian relations to be one of the richest and most fascinating of historical themes. The British, after all, ruled India for some two centuries—sending out, not the riffraff of their cities, but many of their finest minds and wisest spirits. And India was not always unresponsive. The great Bengali reformers of the 19th century were equally determined to revive India's traditions and to bring India the best in modern European thinking—which tended to mean Bentham and the two Mills (the elder Mill, of course, was one of the greatest of all British servants of India). Yet, by the end of the century, the mood had gone sour. It was in Bengal that the first anti-British terrorist campaign was to break out. In Kipling's *Kim* there is an affection and respect for India and the ways of its natives—though not for the new, Western-educated "native"—that reflected the experience of many a British District Collector in the 1880's. How much of this was left by the 1920's may be judged from E.M. Forster's *A Passage to India*—an accurate book in this (though not in every) respect. Again, the powerful impress of British institutions on contemporary India can mislead, as the Englishness of a Nehru misled. Nehru's successor—and his possible successors—are distinctly less English, less Western, distinctly more traditional, more Hindu. The course of Anglo-Indian relations has its bursts of grandeur; but on the whole it is a wretched story. It never was a marriage of true minds; to many it seems in retrospect more like a squalid *mésalliance*.

That this is a sad, indeed a tragic, outcome for both Britain and India hardly needs to be stressed. And there are wider implications. After all, if India and Britain, with their long historical intimacy, understood one another so little, what of those other, briefer colonial relationships between the West and the Third World? Was each bedeviled by the same mutual misunderstanding? Will the outcome, mutual resentment and repudiation, prove to be the same? Perhaps it is still too early to say. It is perfectly arguable that each colonial relationship should be considered for itself. What Oscar Mannoni, in his *Prospero and Caliban,* says of French-Malagassy relations may, or may not, be true of French-Guinean relations, or of relations between Australians and aborigines, Dutchmen and Indonesians. India, in other words, may be a special case: the tragedy of the Anglo-Indian encounter may prove nothing. My own inclinations are toward the position taken up by Mannoni: that there are useful generalizations to be made about the colonial relationship. Prospero and Caliban can never be made equal partners by political decree—if only because, in Mannoni's psychological terms, Prospero has willed Caliban into being, and Caliban Prospero. What, even now, can be said with some assurance is that the act of independence does not put an end to the unequal relationship. Even the comparatively innocent American has to live with the psychological burden of colonialism bequeathed to him by his white brother-nations. Even for him, therefore, the question of whether or not India is a special case assumes some importance.

Yet this potentially rich and fascinating field has been surprisingly little explored. In Britain, the generation under forty knows almost nothing of India, and cares less. For those over forty who once lived and labored in India, the Raj is a fading dream: there are still strong sentimental ties, especially among military men, but they will hardly survive their generation. In India itself, Britain might appear to loom large: the image of the Raj is still powerful, perhaps more powerful in the glow of retrospective emulation than in the days of its actual glory. But the Britain the new Hindu Raj emulates is not the Britain of Harold Wilson, Kingsley Amis, and the Beatles. The living link has snapped. The Britain that is admired is an abstraction—a textbook model of jurisprudential wisdom, welfare-state economics, and parliamentary etiquette. Thus the Anglophilia of educated Indians is both embarrassingly flattering, and finally shallow—because it refers to an England that does not, and indeed never did, exist. A charming Indian lady once assured me over the lunch-table, after her guest had told a particularly scarifying tale of corruption in high places, "You will find this hard to understand, I believe, we know that such things cannot happen in your country." I did not like to disillusion her (this was about the time of the Profumo scandals). But in any case it would have done no good. What Indian editorials picked out was the fact that Mr. Profumo had actually got up in Parliament and *confessed.* How many Indian ministers, it was slyly suggested, would have been prepared to do a thing like that! And how much more, it

was insinuated, would some of *our* ministers have to confess! How could one protest? Should one have insisted that these doings shed a rather murky light on the England of 1963? That would have been resented, and almost certainly not believed. These educated Indians were confident that they knew what the real England was: for them, whatever might happen, the real England would keep breaking through.

Since Independence there have been, I think, only three books which have done justice to the Anglo-Indian theme. The first, in point of time, was Nirad C. Chaudhuri's great *Autobiography of an Unknown Indian,* perhaps the best book in the English language ever written by an Indian. The second was *The Men Who Ruled India,* by Philip "Woodruff," an eloquent, erudite, romantic monument to the British administrators of imperial India—perhaps the most convincing apologia for imperialism (though its author, Philip Mason, is no "imperialist" in the contemporary, pejorative sense) that has ever been composed. V. S. Naipaul's new book, **An Area of Darkness,** deserves to take its place as the third in this pantheon. It differs from its predecessors, each written shortly after Independence, in that it records a contemporary India, the India of Nehru's last years, of the Sino-Indian border dispute. But it differs also in the quality of the author's involvement. Both Mr. Chaudhuri and Mr. Mason were children of the British Raj—indeed their books may prove, with Kipling's and Forster's, its most enduring monuments. Mr. Naipaul, too, is a child of British imperialism, but in rather more indirect fashion. He is the grandson of a Brahmin from the Benares region who went to Trinidad in the 19th century as an indentured laborer. But his education is British and he confesses that he lacks sympathy with much that is deeply Indian—he has no religious sense, no liking for metaphysics. Nevertheless, admirers of his earlier books must have hoped that he would one day write about India. They have been richly rewarded.

The strengths of Mr. Naipaul's book lie, then, where one would expect them to lie—in his novelist's ear for talk, in his shrewd, observant eye for detail. The descriptions of that lakeside hotel in Kashmir where he stayed, of that first agonized encounter with the sights and smells of the Orient in Bombay and Alexandria, are done with a sureness that is equal to anything in his fiction. But it is above all Mr. Naipaul's account of his return to the ancestral village ("the Village of the Dubes") that seems certain of a high place in any anthology of English writing about India. Until the very end of his journey, the author seems to cling to the illusion that somewhere, somehow, he will discover what it is that connects him, through his Brahmin forebears, with this sprawling, defecating, inchoate India of today. Arrived in the village, he finds the shrines erected by his grandfather, with money sent from Trinidad, still standing. But the village and its Brahmin community are not quite as he and his Trinidad family had been brought up to believe. A traditional welcome is laid on: but it is soon apparent that this prodigal's return is seen as a financial opportunity not to be missed. It is the final humiliation. The shameless beggary of India—as it must appear to a Westerner—could not be more cruelly brought home. Mr. Naipaul, who is nothing if not candid, admits that he panicked: from that moment he wanted only to get out of India as fast as he could.

In the best of his descriptive episodes Mr. Naipaul—and there is no higher praise—is not far inferior to Kipling. But the book has the defects of its virtues; it is interested largely in the immediacy, the accidents of life. Now that, in an Indian context, is very strange. For the Hindu sets little store by appearances—the world of *maya*. To the Hindu, essence is all. That is why most reportage, most descriptive writing in modern India, is so bad. In other words, the average Indian writer is weak precisely where Mr. Naipaul is strong. (Whether he is always strong where Mr. Naipaul is comparatively weak—in historical speculation, in philosophical contemplation—I would not care to say: though these gifts are certainly generously developed in Mr. Chaudhuri's books.) But it does seem that Mr. Naipaul is deaf to a good deal in the complex music of India—think, for instance, of the breathtaking aesthetic appeal of Satyajit Ray's films—because his own gifts lie in quite another direction. For all his Brahmin ancestry, Mr. Naipaul is very English in his sensibility (he is primarily a comic writer). In one sense, then, his book is intensely personal. It is the record of an attempt to clear that "area of darkness" which India, since childhood, had represented in the author's mind. The attempt succeeded, disastrously well: the darkness of ignorance yielded to the more painful darkness of knowledge. In that sense, Mr. Naipaul's journey was justified: he will hardly need to go back. But there is more to it than that. It is not chance that Mr. Naipaul's personal Odyssey conforms to the pattern of so many other attempted explorations, so many other passages to India, both in its high expectations, and in its final humiliation and rejection. Indeed, it appears to echo the tragedy of the British Raj itself. Mr. Naipaul's book is the latest, but not the last, nail in the coffin of that brave, but ill-favored endeavor.

Ronald Bryden (interview date 22 March 1973)

SOURCE: "The Novelist V. S. Naipaul Talks about His Work to Ronald Bryden," in *The Listener*, Vol. 89, March 22, 1973, pp. 367-70.

[*In the following interview, Naipaul discusses various aspects of his work, including the development of his book,* The Loss of El Dorado.]

I wrote in one of my early articles that London was for me a good place to work in. I suppose one was always aware of other minds. London was a place where one encountered a generous reaction—from publishers, critics, newspapers—and so one had constant stimulus, minds brushing against minds. But fairly early on I felt that I had to get out and look at the world, otherwise I was just going to shrivel up as a writer and have nothing more to say. One of the difficulties about coming from a background like my own, a fairly simple, barbarous and limited background, was that I found that I couldn't do the kind of novel which I'd set out to do. I wanted to be a writer because I had read a certain kind of writer. I assumed that I, too, had the kind of society that those writers had. You know, Balzac paints a picture of an entire society, Maupassaint a picture of a great peasant society, and of Paris as well. I quickly found that I didn't have that kind of society. This was one of my first halts. It occurred quite early on, the decision to look much more closely at the narrow world I had, to see what I could do with it and to abandon all previous patterns.

But one of the things that you seem to have decided, looking at the society of Trinidad, of the West Indies and of many of the other places that you have visited and described in **The Overcrowded Barracoon,** *is that a society has got to have sufficient coherence and authenticity of its own. It doesn't derive from elsewhere. It has to be sufficiently settled and traditional to provide the people in it with some sense of purpose and value, it has to be a culture in order to produce a culture. But there you are, producing, as your publishers have said, a kind of autobiography—because a writer's autobiography is all he has written—with no settled place. You seem to be saying one can't write without roots, and yet you've uprooted yourself to find somewhere to write and you've chosen the whole world.*

I don't know whether I've got the figures absolutely right, but they say that in a place like Mauritius, there are, shall we say, eighty types of job, and in a place like England or France you have perhaps about ten thousand kinds of job. I feel that the simple society cannot lend itself to extended imaginative treatment. The possibility of adventure is always limited, and this brings about a kind of limitation as well in one's imaginative handling of the material. Again and again, as a writer trying to devise a story which is a symbol for what one feels, one has to decide what to do with the main character. What kind of job will you give him? How will he go through this particular passage of time? What will he do? How will he occupy himself? And again and again, with simple societies, you're landed with the same thing. A man becomes a teacher or a professional man, or he becomes a lorry-driver. I had to face the barrenness of this, I also had to face—and this is why my career, which appears from the outside to have a kind of inevitability about it, has really been full of stops and starts—I had to face the fact that I was heir to a type of education which came from a much more developed world, that I was practising my career as a writer in a city like London, and I had to do something to reconcile these two worlds. I couldn't pretend the one world excluded the other. All my work is really one. I'm really writing one big book. I came to the conclusion that, considering the nature of the society I come from, considering the world I have stepped into and the world which I have to look at, I could not be a professional novelist in the old sense. I realised then that my response to the world could be expressed equally imaginatively in nonfiction, in journalism: and I take my journalism extremely seriously because I think it's a very fair response to my world. It's very personal and very particular. It's something that can't be converted into fiction. It is almost too private. I went to India for a year in 1962 just to have a look, and I was so full of this thing of being the novelist, the man who invented, the man who converted experience into something else, that when I came back from India I tried to convert my experience into a novel and actually spent about six or seven weeks pretending to write a novel. It failed because the experience was far too particular. Someone like myself, coming from Trinidad, living in England, being a writer, then going to India to have a look—that was too particular an experience, and the correct form for that was non-fiction.

I feel that the simple society cannot lend itself to extended imaginative treatment. The possibility of adventure is always limited, and this brings about a kind of limitation as well in one's imaginative handling of the material.
—V. S. Naipaul

Yes, I can see that your journalism has become more and more important to you, and it does all interlock with the novels. The curious thing to me is that although you've written one novel about England and English characters, **Mr Stone and the Knights Companion,** *there's very little English journalism. Do you find England not a culture that you are a journalist in?*

I've been living in England, but really I think it's truer to say that I've been attached to London, these few square miles which make an international city, a great metropolis. As soon as I move out of that little enchanted area, I'm in a foreign country in which I'm not terribly interested.

Is it that London is a synthetic society almost as much as any other now?

I suppose it draws people together from many parts of the

world and many parts of the country, for all kinds of reasons: in a way, it's artificial, and one isn't violating anybody's society by being in London, whereas to try to impose myself on a smaller society—in the provinces, say— would be really quite ridiculous. I couldn't even do it in an Indian village or town.

I was astonished, reading **The Overcrowded Barracoon,** *at the extent to which the whole world seemed to fit this analysis. The whole world is in a state of flux. Your characters are 'in a free state': the old novel, the novel about the chambered organic society, just isn't possible any more. Your one great book is turning into the novel of the new synthetic world.*

I don't think it is possible any longer for people to write those novels where you could say, 'They lived happily ever afterwards,' because we no longer have this assurance of the world going on. Societies everywhere have been fractured by all kinds of change: technological, social, political. We can no longer regard the action of a novel as covering a little crisis, a little curve on the graph which will then revert to the nice, flat, straight, ordered life: and I think this is one reason why, as you say, the traditional novel is just no longer possible. It is also one reason why people find it very hard nowadays to read fiction, and why people go back to what they call the old masters. I think there's an element of nostalgia in reading Hardy, and even in reading Dickens or George Eliot. There is narrative there, the slow development of character, and people are longing for this vanished, ordered world. Today, every man's experience of dislocation is so private that unless a writer absolutely matches that particular man's experience the writer seems very private and obscure. So I think the art of fiction is becoming a curious, shattered thing. It's one reason why there are so few young writers about. The complaint of publishers and literary agents is that the talent that should be going into the writing of fiction is going elsewhere. People say it's television that's taken it away. I think it may be that the whole world now requires another kind of imaginative interpretation.

When you think of it, there can't have been a generation of European writers that wasn't interrupted by war.

The war's always been such a blessing to older writers in this country: six years of rest in which they were able to recover and look at themselves again. Writers today, those who are in my position, are compelled to go on, and it's very daunting for young persons who say: 'I'm going to be a writer.' You know, I'm only 40, but I'm at another curious stage, one of those stop periods in my career. I have committed myself to the profession. There's nothing else I can do or want to do, and yet the years stretch ahead of me and I wonder how I'm going to fill them. The world abrades one, one comes to certain resolutions and then one devises by instinct and through dreams and all kinds of senses a story that is a symbol for all this. But one can't do it all the time.

But isn't it possible that because of this pattern of peace and war—with the writer having his subject given him on a plate in that way—that a kind of artificial division has grown up? I mean, the archetypal novel is War and Peace. *Novels seem to divide themselves into the great peaceful 19th-century ones and 20th-century masterpieces like Evelyn Waugh's* Men at Arms: *you seem to have found the territory between the two because there hasn't been an overt war in quite the same sense. You seem to have been able to look more closely at societies and see that there never was, in many of them, this organic ordered peacefulness, that the violence was there, the disorder, the wrong patterning which produces contradiction, Perhaps this is the new career?*

Well, I don't know. I think all my writing has issued from a kind of personal panic, panic to do with what I've just been talking about, the sense of having come to a stop— and then political panic, perhaps, at one's position in the world. One has always tried to reach some kind of personal balance, so you don't go quite unhinged.

It seemed to me that you reached the turning-point with **The Loss of El Dorado,** *your book about the history of Trinidad, where you looked below the surface of that society we both came out of and dug up things that were certainly new to me. Were they as new to you when you found them?*

Absolutely. I'll tell you about that book. That book was to be a simple bit of journalism which I was going to write for the Americans and make a lot of money. I was going to make 10,000 dollars. I thought the place had no history. I thought I would swiftly look at the records and produce something, and then I discovered this appalling history that hadn't been ignored but had just somehow dropped out because the place itself had ceased to be important, so that all the history books were wrong. The discovery, the colonisation, the extermination of the Indians, the emptiness then, the use of that island as a base for South American revolution—this recurring dream of Europe—then the revolution going wrong, the base of the revolution becoming a slave island, the further corruption, the slaves that were abandoned, desolation, the colonial past which we knew: I thought this was an immense story. It was especially alarming to me to see that if you were unimportant all that had happened to you could be ignored. I still feel so about some of the subjects I write on, that perhaps unimportant people are profoundly unimportant and what happens to them is, really, of no great moment in the world. When I went to Mauritius and wrote the article which is the title-piece of the new book, it was a terrible experience for me. I actu-

ally fell ill on the way back from Mauritius, and I think that the two things were linked. I wrote that piece in illness and the illness was partly made up of my distress at what I'd seen, that lost, abandoned people, and so I wrote this article out of great pain, and offered it to the magazine which had sent me out there as news which I thought would be very moving. But it was about ten months before the piece was printed in the paper, because the place is not an important place.

But, good heavens, it symbolises two-thirds of the earth, all the abandoned places, just as it seemed to me **The Loss of El Dorado** *symbolised the whole imperial process: what had been done to places by having the imperial idea imposed on them from outside. It seems to me that there and in the pieces you've written since then you have discovered the great new subject.*

I think one reason why the world is not interested in these places is that the world has got too many received ideas. I think that this whole thing about Right and Left gives such a distorted view of the world, and so many people now have rather settled ideas about the way it's all going, that investigation seems to have become unnecessary. I think that one reason why my journalism can last is because I never had any such ideas about Left and Right. One just looked at what had happened. There are no principles involved in one's vision. One doesn't try to fit what one sees into the kind of pattern which would suit some political dogma, but, with all these received ideas floating about, it seems to people that the world has really been settled, organised. There is nothing more to do, so they have ideas of racial apocalypse, which I think is nonsense, or Communist apocalypse which is equally nonsense—and the people who are the victims, and are deficient because of their past, themselves contribute to this simplification of their problems.

As you say in **The Overcrowded Barracoon,** *politics are the opium of the people because the problems are not those that politics try to deal with.*

They're the problems of people who are powerless. They're the politics of people who have no power, and it has become a kind of game. It is an opium for them.

You've become a kind of unstitcher of systems for yourself and for your readers. Do you find that this unstitches you as a novelist?

Put like that, it sounds as though I've decided to look after myself and to try to preserve my own calm and happiness— as though I'm shutting out the distress. To some extent, this may be so, but I also think I have an understanding of what is possible in our world: that the oppressed or depressed cultures of the world have really to look after themselves. I'm comforted by two people. There's Josephus, who was able to retire from Jerusalem to Rome to write his history of the Jewish war which the Romans conducted in AD 70, if I get the facts right. And there's that marvellous story which is told about the Inca, Garcilaso de la Vega. Garcilaso was the son of a Peruvian princess and a Spanish Conquistador. He decided when he was quite a young man that history was flowing in the direction of Europe and Spain, so he went to Spain. One day, when he was very old, Bartolomé de Las Casas, the apostle of the Indians, a great friend of the Indians, saw a man across a room who was clearly an Indian from the New World, and went across to him and said very friendlily: 'You're from Mexico, aren't you?' Garcilaso, recognising Las Casas, said, 'No, I'm from Peru,' and both men at once knew that in a most ridiculous and grotesque way they were on opposite sides. I'm comforted by that because I think that Garcilaso made the correct decision—understanding that, the way the current was flowing, it was very silly for one man to try to pretend it wasn't flowing in that direction.

Do you still think that there's a current flowing in the direction of the 'important' world?

I think so. Let us take a very highly industrialised country of the poor world. India, which has a very considerable industrial base now, and where there's an awful lot of talent. I think the gap between a country like India and, shall we say, Europe is not only a money gap or a technological gap now: I think it is also an intellectual gap. It's a gap of sensibility. I think that men, responding to all the terrible changes that technology brings about in the world, do, in some ways, become sharper and more acute. They're always responding to new challenges, and the mind is always at work: they're feeding the world, intellectually, in a way that I think that India will never feed the world. To try to be a writer in Argentina, for example, is extremely difficult. The only thing you can do is to be like Borges. You can delude yourself that you have a country that's already been created, a fatherland that has fought its battles and has built its great city and whose culture is flourishing: but that is delusion. The point about the future synthetic cultures, and people like ourselves who come from them, seems to be that we still need the support of the others.

I suppose South America is the oldest of the synthetic societies. No hope there either?

Well, Argentina, to me, was very interesting because it's a colonial society and it's entirely European, so that what one was talking about, what one had discovered about the world, could be seen not to be a purely racial matter. Here, the people who'd come over at the turn of the century to service the great *estancias,* on land that had been won from the pampas Indians, have become a rather lost people. They

have not been able to create an organic society. Few things are more distressing when you're in a small pampas town than to see Italians living in this very desolate landscape, a lost people. One felt about them the way one feels about people in the other territories of the New World. They're people who've been cut of from the source of their culture. They've been cut off from all the things that bound their old culture together. These were individuals like the rest of us, and somehow their society—on a much bigger scale, there are 23 million of them—wasn't working. There were no internal reverences any longer. There were no shared ideals, and the country was just cracking up. One saw it very, very clearly there, and the big thing, as I say, was the discovery that the artificial society perhaps isn't always a product of empire or colonial oppression, but simply, perhaps, of migration. Societies that were doomed to remain half-made.

Do you still think Britain is the country where to be a writer means most?

Well, I come back to England because I have all my friends here now, in London. It's the place where I operate, and my publishers are here, the magazines for which I write are here. But again I must make the point that it's not a place where I can flourish completely. It doesn't feed me.

Which is the place which has fed you most? You said, in **The Middle Passage,** *that nothing was made in the West Indies. You were made in the West Indies.*

I wonder how much I was made in Trinidad? I've often thought that if I'd started in another country I would have started from a higher base. I remember how low my sights were when I began to write, how deliberately I restricted myself, and I wonder whether, if I had begun in a more developed place, with my inclinations and tenacity and aptitudes, I really wouldn't have been a much more, as it were, important writer than I am now. A good and rather tragic example is Jean Rhys. Jean Rhys is like us. She's really the pioneer. She came over here at the turn of the century. She was from the West Indies, and had very high principles as a writer. She wouldn't falsify her experiences. Her experiences were those of an uprooted person adrift in the world. Now she has been revived. She does enjoy a reputation, quite justifiably. But she will never become really popular. She'll never feed a culture or alter sensibility, and I think if you're a writer these are the things you want to do. You want to operate at the top. You don't just want to turn your books out and make a living, if you have a respect for your craft.

It seems to me that you yourself are moving toward a readership much wider than any you could hope for in this country, in the West Indies or in America. Because you are writing about the problems of the unimportant, of places like the West Indies, Mauritius, India, you've uncovered something which represents almost everybody. Is a universal audience impossible?

I certainly am aware of my books falling into a kind of void. That I find very heartbreaking. When I was younger it didn't seem to matter. I've often said that when I was younger and thought of being a writer, I thought I was serving a thing called art, and that art was somehow divinely judged, and what was good would be rewarded. I very quickly found that it wasn't so, that I was always being judged politically. It was said that I was looking down on the people I wrote about, on the land of my birth. That is something that would never have been said about Evelyn Waugh, or any other writer from a more developed culture. What a labour it has been to ignore this and break out of it.

But isn't this, perhaps, a writer's fantasy: that once upon a time in ancient Athens Euripides, Aeschylus and the rest of them were as popular as footballers, or the kings of the carnival bends in Trinidad, or their champion cricketers? Browning, I think wrote a couple of poems imagining this kind of life for a poet. In fact, has it ever happened? Shakespeare was always being put down by Ben Jonson.

Perhaps one is asking for the impossible. But one needs to have some kind of conversation with a society. One cannot write in a total vacuum.

That's suggesting a new kind of career, the writer as a culture hero. I suppose Mailer has gone further than anyone in that direction. You accompanied Mailer around New York when he stood for mayor. How did that work out?

I thought it worked out very well. I'm much more sympathetic towards Mailer than many people. I liked the way his mind worked. I liked his gift of language. I liked the way he was always ordering experience and fitting everything that occurred very, very swiftly into experience, making a whole of it, so that any moment he could present you with a very ordered, total philosophy. That was so impressive. I was overwhelmed by Mailer—and I found him a very shy man, oddly enough.

But is it possible for a writer to turn himself and his writing, as one unit, into a product unless he is in some way a source of scandal, like Byron? Mailer, to some extent, has made himself a scandal.

Yes, but probably this is what will happen to writers more and more. It seems to me quite a legitimate thing to happen to writers. I can't do it myself, but to be in conversation with your society seems to me very, very marvellous and desirable for a writer.

Benjamin DeMott (review date 15 November 1975)

SOURCE: "Lost Worlds, Lost Heroes," in *Saturday Review*, Vol. 3, No. 4, November 15, 1975, pp. 24-5.

[*In the following review, DeMott calls* Guerillas *"continuously interesting," but argues that its protagonist lacks "substance," due more to changes in the socio-political climate of the day than Naipaul's skills as a writer.*]

A political novel, *Guerillas* takes for its hero an Orwellian Englishman named Peter Roche, who endures imprisonment and torture while serving the anti-apartheid cause in South Africa, and then moves on to Trinidad, obsessed now as before by the suffering of black people. For a time his tropical service as an anti-racist seems tame, even suburban. Roche has a house on Rich Folks' Ridge, a maid, a slot in the corporate structure, an identity among local establishmentarians both black and white, who see him as some kind of buffoon. ("He was not a professional man or businessman; he had none of the skills that were considered important. He was a doer of good works, with results that never showed, someone who went among the poor on behalf of his firm and tried to organize boys' clubs and sporting events, gave this cup here and offered a gift of cricket equipment there.") Roche has, in addition, Jane, a London dollybird impressed with his courage and hungry for religious vision, who flies out from home to live with him.

At length, though, his life-texture roughens. The precipitant is a weirdo black-power leader named Jimmy Ahmed, homo-heterosexual, would-be novelist, and "organizer" of a pitifully unorganized guerilla youth force/commune. Personally corrupt and politically inept, Ahmed seems a mediocre revolutionary at best—until a boy recruited by Roche for the youth force/commune dies, triggering a local political explosion. Ahmed steps forth at this moment as a ferocious orator, a whipper-on of mass demonstrations, block-burnings, and the like. (The summit of violence is a sex slaying—a brilliant stretch of writing, terrifying yet absolutely without lubricity.) By the book's close the Establishment is back in command, having crushed the "revolution." Jimmy Ahmed is once again powerless, and Roche is once again on the road, in search (as it seems) of yet another front on which to struggle for his cause.

Black-power issues in the islands—St. Croix, St. Thomas, St. Lucia, elsewhere—haven't lacked for chroniclers in recent years, but few living writers appear better qualified to deal with them than V.S. Naipaul. Himself a Trinidadian, this writer has to his credit a superb analytical history of his homeland, *The Loss of El Dorado* (1969), a book that provides an extraordinarily rich context for understanding black-white encounters everywhere in the New World. His authority as an interpreter of present-day realities has been further confirmed by a half-dozen novels dense with feeling for Caribbean landscape, sensations, rhythms of speech. Part Chinese, part black, Naipaul has more than once shown conversancy with the surfacing of ethnic rivalries in Caribbean political conflict—see his early comic novel *The Suffrage of Elvira* (1958). And, as D.A.N. Jones helpfully noted in a *London Times Literary Supplement* notice of *Guerillas,* the novelist had at hand for this book an easily adaptable "real life" political situation and hero. The life of his Jimmy Ahmed directly parallels that of a young rogue-comic black-power leader called Michael Abdul Malik, who, in the late Sixties, was taken up by English literary liberals, was encouraged to write, was made a "plaything-playboy," and was then dropped and banished to his homeland, where he was subsequently hanged for murder.

Devotees of Naipaul will find in this newest book many reminders of golden pages in his earlier novels. An account of a Trinidad youngster's evening at the movies watching Sidney Poitier in *For the Love of Ivy* is an entirely original and touching invention—as fond and kind, and very nearly as relaxed, as the best chapters of *A House for Mr. Biswas* (1961). Comic turns issuing from an American evangelist's visit to the island, comic monologues spoken by a duped husband named Harry de Tunja, recall zany moments in several other Naipaul fables composed in more innocent, if not happier, political hours. And because this writer has a penetrating mind as well as an exceptionally pure and elegant style, he offers perspectives on the psychology of race tension, details of inner response, that have uncommon value. He's especially shrewd about black suspicion—the disposition to test the liberal, a skepticism of the liberal's "impersonal" concern:

> [Blacks] could be tense and combative with Roche. They knew his South African history; they felt safe with him. But it was as if they wished to test him further, as if each man, meeting Roche for the first time, wished to get some personal statement from him, some personal declaration of love. Such a man might begin by attributing racialist views to Roche or by appearing to hold Roche responsible for all the humiliations he, the islander, had endured in other countries. . . .

But while *Guerillas* is a continuously interesting book, it is something less than a successful novel. The problem lies with the point-of-view character, Roche himself, and seems susceptible at first glance to conventional explanation: the character "lacks substance," has no stable, knowable interior core. Roche's dollybird comes to this conclusion about him. So, too, more or less, does Jimmy Ahmed. So, too, do a number of relatively objective observers. Toward the end of the book, Roche is pressed by a radio interviewer for some account of his concern for the exploited, some descrip-

tion of what goes on inside him as he works at his political task. Frustrated by the Englishman's evasive responses, the interviewer charges that "there seems to be no framework of political belief" in him. He proposes that Roche's activism has nothing behind it but the desire to "make a gesture." Insultingly, he asserts that Roche is actually the servant of The Selfish—that he is a safety valve, a means by which the complacent and the uncaring can avoid confronting their own guilt. The prober is intelligent and persistent, determined to find the center of Roche's commitment—but, as it turns out, the center can't be reached. Peter Roche sidesteps, defends the oblivious folk around him, claims his only motive is securing personal ease, an escape from personal pain; his aim, he insists, is simply to do "a job of work."

The silence and the evasions suggest a hero unfleshed, an unfinished man. And the relative emptiness of the characterization leaves the book centerless, without adequate human focus. But the silence in question signifies more, in the end, than a mere novelistic failure at characterization; it signifies the death of a language. The reason why Peter Roche is shadow, not substance, the reason why neither he nor we can touch his commitment, is that the terms necessary for the dramatization of that commitment are no longer utterable. Like many another writer on political subjects nowadays, V.S. Naipaul has been victimized by the withering away of the language of altruism; convention dictates that the selflessly giving political man must present himself as an enigma, must declare himself inexplicable, must discover no expressible reason for his being. Incapable of naming his "virtue," he stands before his own decency in puzzlement and ultimately vanishes as a person, devoured by profound—and profoundly inexpressible—embarrassment. There are novels whose failure tells us more about where we are, what we've cut loose from, and what the cutting-loose costs, than do a hundred formally successful works. Looked at as political fiction, *Guerillas* is one of them.

John Spurling (essay date December 1975)

SOURCE: "The Novelist as Dictator," in *Encounter,* Vol. XLV, No. 6, December, 1975, pp. 73-6.

[*In the following excerpt, Spurling argues that Naipaul does not permit his readers to form their own impressions of his characters and their surroundings; instead, he imposes his outlook "dictatorially."*]

Reviewing a book in *The Times* [London] early last year, Richard Holmes wrote of "that frontal advance of the biographic form . . . which now surely promises to make the biography, as a genre, the most fruitful in contemporary English writing." His own special interest in it being so was revealed a few months later when he published a weighty reappraisal of Shelley. All the same it is noticeable that biographies are generally given greater prominence than novels on review pages and that one's acquaintances, even if they haven't read them, are more aware of the latest biography than of the latest novel.

The phenomenon is not as new as all that. In the epilogue to *The Characters of Love,* published in 1960, John Bayley writes:

> I think we are already beginning to see a great revulsion in the reading public against the whole idea of the writer's consciousness. Memoirs, biographies, accounts of war and travel in which other people have a real existence, are coming more and more to the fore.

Bayley is not of course arguing against fiction. The purpose and achievement of his book is precisely to examine how three masters of fiction "can liberate the inner life of their characters", can create characters that, beyond speaking to us, simply "are." But his epilogue is an attack, though a characteristically well-mannered one, on "most modern novels."

The attack centres on the pursuit of "meanings" at the expense of character: "we more and more assume that the novelist . . . need not start out by making his characters like 'real life', but will subordinate their individuality to the general atmosphere and purpose of the work." Bayley distinguishes those traditional writers who take Nature for granted from those more modern ones who hold an attitude towards the Human Condition. He suggests that our heightened awareness of ourselves and of the changes in the world beyond ourselves leads to novels which concentrate on the individual consciousness, which explore the "exceptional" rather than the habitual world, which attempt to pin down the peculiar significance of "our time." "The fatal drawback" is that "the writer, like some self-devouring pelican, is really feeding the audience on his own consciousness, not on that of his characters" and "the commonest and most dangerous assumption the modern novelist can make is that his world—just because it *is* his world—must fascinate other readers."

I paraphrase arguments from a very well-known book only because, 15 years later, the sort of novels Bayley is attacking are so much the general rule that we are perhaps in danger of forgetting there is any alternative. If we are all reading biographies, is it perhaps less the fault of the Novel than of the novelists?

V.S. Naipaul's *Guerrillas* begins with an evocation of a Caribbean island on the verge of revolution. The method is familiar enough, might indeed be borrowed from the title sequence of innumerable films: two of the central characters are put into a car and driven out of town. They pass slogans: *Basic Black. Don't Vote. Birth Control is a Plot Against the Negro Race.* The scenery is described with detailed care:

> The sea smelled of swamp . . . after the rubbish dump burning in the remnant of mangrove swamp, with black carrion corbeaux squatting hunched on fence-posts . . . after the new housing estates, rows of unpainted boxes of concrete and corrugated iron already returning to the shanty towns that had been knocked down for this redevelopment . . . the land cleared a little.

Next factories, then "what remained of an industrial estate, one of the failed projects of the earliest days of independence." In this "waste land" of bush, secondary forest, paved areas of concrete and asphalt is a place, surrounded by forest, where the land has been cleared. But the land, though ploughed, is full of weeds and there is an abandoned tractor "half into the forest." The car stops beside a concrete and corrugated iron hut. This is the "People's Commune" run by the third central character of the book and called Thrushcross Grange.

The point about this opening is that, although the two people in the car—a white South African liberal called Roche (Rochester?) and his white mistress called Jane (Eyre?)—are given a few snatches of dialogue, the scenic description is presented directly by the writer to the reader and for all its apparent objectivity conveys a strong sense of distaste. Furthermore the characters are from the outset brushed into it. They are wholly subordinate to the author's consciousness, with its powerful implication of desolation and decay. Jane is given the line: "I used to think that England was in a state of decay." Her consciousness is not only not separate from the author's, it is being used by him to open a further line of meaning in the novel, the comparison between the state of England and the state of this Caribbean island, just as the name Thrushcross Grange for a people's commune must at least suggest the idea of comparing the black revolutionary Jimmy Ahmed with Heathcliff.

In fact, of course, he has more in common with Naipaul's fellow-Trinidadian, Michael X or Abdul Malik. Like Malik, Ahmed has been first raised up, then abruptly dropped by trendy revolutionary circles in England; like Malik, he is dropping still further in his native island; like Malik, he murders. But this comparison, though it must so soon after Malik's execution be present to most readers' minds, is not intrinsic to the novel. Ahmed, whatever his original basis in a real person, is fully integrated into Naipaul's scheme of things. He is, like the scenery, the atmosphere and the other characters, an element in the significance of the novel. Since Naipaul is an outstandingly skilful novelist, all these elements start off the page with seemingly independent life, but like the three-dimensional models which stand up from inside children's books, they are all ready to lie down again as soon as the writer's meaning demands it.

> **The pessimism of Naipaul's outlook [in *Guerillas*], the unlikability of his characters would not in themselves make the novel seem unreal, if they were not imposed so dictatorially. The reader is at no point permitted to form his own impressions of this gloomy island or have private words with its inhabitants.**
> **—*John Spurling***

The book, in its own terms, is hardly open to criticism. Naipaul's materials—his characters, white and black, political or apolitical, his city, his island, his commune, his background story of an abortive revolution overcome by the local authorities with the help of American helicopters, his foreground story of the complex sexual and political relationships between Ahmed, Roche and Jane—obey his lightest whim. So in a sense does the reader, slipping along the greased rails of the writer's purpose.

To take a single example, there is this description of a secondary character at his first entrance:

> Meredith was short and walked with a spring. He was slender but his body looked hard: he was heavier than he looked. He wore a white shirt with a button-down collar; it was unbuttoned at the neck but not too open, and it didn't suggest holiday dress. The shirt was too tight over his solid shoulders, the collar was too close to the neck: a tie seemed to be missing.

Meredith's background has already been placed before the reader. He is an ex-politician, has been one of the island's ministers, but is now a successful lawyer with another career as a radio personality. The two white people, Jane and Roche, resenting his apparent contentment as a "political drop-out" and his happy home life, have come to consider him somewhat "suburban." He is meeting them again on a Sunday at a house by the beach. The description above is direct authorial intervention, not filtered through the consciousness of any particular character. Why does it dwell so much on the shirt collar? The reader registers a slight disturbance and passes smoothly on.

Only much later do we learn that in the crisis of the ap-

proaching attempt at revolution Meredith has been called back into politics. Unknown to the other characters as well as to the reader he was already a minister again when he appeared in that holiday setting. His collar is a tiny signal, a typically deft touch on Naipaul's part, but one which operates independently of any of the characters involved and which, almost unnoticeably, reduces their independence.

If one is dissatisfied at the end of the novel it is certainly not with the machinery, nor even with Naipaul's reading of a contemporary *malaise*, which he makes clear enough by extracting a quotation from his own text and putting it at the front of the book: "When everybody wants to fight there's nothing to fight for. Everybody wants to fight his own little war, everybody is a guerrilla." This is Ahmed speaking. The white girl Jane is given the knowledge "that she had come to a place at the end of the world, to a place that had exhausted its possibilities." Her lover Roche says: "Oh my God, why is anyone of us allowed to live at all?" The pessimism of Naipaul's outlook, the unlikability of his characters would not in themselves make the novel seem unreal, if they were not imposed so dictatorially. The reader is at no point permitted to form his own impressions of this gloomy island or have private words with its inhabitants. The writer's consciousness is for ever at his elbow and it is his only human contact.

Anthony Boxill (essay date 1976)

SOURCE: "The Paradox of Freedom: V. S. Naipaul's *In a Free State*," in *Critique: Studies in Modern Fiction*, Vol. XVIII, No. 1, pp. 81-91.

[*In the following essay, Boxill discusses the paradoxical nature of freedom and the symbolic "prisons" in Naipaul's* In a Free State.]

Prison is an important presence in V.S. Naipaul's first-written book, *Miguel Street*, and it is, if anything, more central in his recent *In A Free State*. Although the characters in *Miguel Street* live in the shadow of an actual jail, Naipaul suggests that Miguel Street and Trinidad itself are both so limiting as to deserve to be seen as wider prisons in which the characters find themselves trapped. In spite of its universal resonances, especially in the author's ability to create characters that live, *Miguel Street* implies that Trinidad is like a prison because of its remoteness and its past of colonialism and slavery. Its characters, many of whom are creative, are frustrated because they live in a community which lacks standards and does not value creativity. The book implies that freedom can be achieved by escaping to a country which has not been stunted by colonialism, for its narrator accomplishes such an escape.

No actual prison appears in *In A Free State.* Such a place is quite unnecessary in its world, because Naipaul manages to suggest that the whole world and, indeed, freedom itself function as the perfect prison from which escape is not possible, except possibly in death. The characters of the book are not artists—they are not frustrated creators. The book does not solicit sympathy for a select few; it concerns itself with all mankind, even the insane and the perverted; it does not try to pinpoint the oppressor of mankind. The enemy is not simply slavery or colonialism; it is life itself, mankind itself.

A sign of Naipaul's growing maturity is that he shies away more and more from categoric answers to human problems. *In A Free State* is an extremely provocative book because, while it draws attention to human problems and human suffering, it makes no pretense of identifying the enemy or of producing a simple scapegoat. Instead, it illustrates the innumerable facets of the human personality and the physical world with which humanity has to cope, and which contribute to the range of problems confronting mankind. Most of the serious problems of humanity have been created by man himself; since man is extraordinarily complex, one must expect his problems to reflect that complexity.

All of the important characters in *In A Free State* possess or achieve a greater degree of freedom than Naipaul has allowed any of his characters previously. His main characters up to now, from Ganesh to Mr. Stone, have been pinned down by historical, environmental, economic, and social stakes. Now these considerations take second place to the bonds imposed by freedom. In the Prologue, "The Tramp at Piraeus," the tramp on the steamer says, "What's nationality these days? I myself, I think of myself as a citizen of the world." The freedom of which the tramp boasts makes him the most vulnerable man on the boat. Being completely without attachment, he has no one to whom to turn when the rest of the world joins ranks against him. The wide cross section of nationalities represented on the ship makes it both a microcosm of the real world and a world of its own. Naipaul loses no time in introducing the tensions of the Middle-East—the ship is travelling to Egypt—into the community on the ship. On board is a group of Egyptian Greeks who have been expelled from Greece and are being sent back to Egypt, a country with which they have lost touch. The various nationalities on the ship quickly split into factions: the Arabs and the Germans gang up; the tramp remains an outsider. The pressures of living in a disrupted and tense world clearly affect the people on the ship. The hostility they feel toward each other is thinly disguised and accentuated by the ship's cramped passenger accommodations. A scapegoat must be found, someone to vent their hostility on. And who better than the tramp, the citizen of the world, the wandering Jew, everybody's victim and no one's responsibility? After sharing a cabin with the tramp for a night,

the Lebanese businessman says, "I will kill him," identifying his enemy and resolving how to deal with him. The insane Trinidadian of the book's third section is more admirable than the Lebanese because, although he realizes that an act of violence against one's enemy might be purgating and liberating, he also realizes the impossibility of pinpointing a single enemy. His plea, "Tell me who to kill," is heartfelt and honest. No such honesty or scrupulousness marks the Lebanese and those who join him in baiting the tramp. They want a scapegoat and preferably a vulnerable one. To escape their national prejudices and hostilities, the tramp has to lock himself first in a toilet, then in his cabin. Actual prisons can prove more protective than freedom in a world which does not understand freedom.

After the passion of the Lebanese, the reader is left to ask himself of what possible use would have been the identifying and killing of such an "enemy." What liberation could result from the destroying of a man so weak, so tattered, so insecure, and so lonely that he "wanted only the camouflage and protection of company"? The answer is, of course, none; but man, wanting always simple answers and easy scapegoats, has ceased to wish to find the real enemy and has settled for sacrificing the handiest victim. The very notion of sacrifice has become meaningless.

Santosh, the narrator of "One out of Many," the second section of the book, after disentangling himself from the restrictions of his Indian nationalism, finds that America has not yet come to recognize citizens of the world. To be a free man in America he must become an American citizen: "Marry the *hubshi*. That will automatically make you a citizen. Then you will be a free man." When we first meet Santosh, he is a poor man who sleeps on the sidewalks of Bombay "although in our chambers a whole cupboard below the staircase was reserved for my personal use." He has friends, a regular job, a position in a rudimentary system. It does not seem to be much, but Santosh is proud of his achievements since he has started from very little in a remote Indian village. His sense of achievement in having liberated himself from the crippling destitution of his village, no doubt, urges him to pressure his employer to take him to America. He cannot go back to the limitations of his village, and the freedom of America beckons.

He is hardly on the plane which will take him from Bombay to Washington before he realizes that the freedom he has achieved is now threatened. He begins to feel claustrophobic: "From the aeroplane to the airport building to the motor car to the apartment block to the elevator to the corridor to the apartment itself, I was forever enclosed." In Bombay he had slept under the real sky, but "below that imitation sky" of his apartment in America he "felt like a prisoner." He also discovers that his new quarters are to be in another cupboard, this time more prison-like because he has no side-walk to escape to.

The freedom Santosh achieves in America—being without friends or attachments, having no real point of contact with the life going on around him—is not what he had bargained for. "This isn't Bombay. Nobody looks at you when you walk down the street. Nobody cares what you do." With the isolation that Santosh's new freedom has brought, he is no better off than in prison. Having achieved it, having ceased to see himself as part of his employer's or anyone else's presence, having graduated from a cupboard to a real room, to a drab house, he cannot easily renounce his free state. By further advancing his freedom by increasing his isolation, he comes to the dismal conclusion that "all that my freedom has brought me is the knowledge that I have a face and have a body, that I must feed this body and clothe this body for a certain number of years. Then it will be over."

While Santosh is moving to the freedom of his isolation, the *hubshi* (his word for the American Blacks) are seeking their freedom by acts of violence against their enemy. After they have burned a considerable portion of Washington, Santosh comments: "Happiness was on the faces of the *hubshi*. They were like people amazed they could do so much, that so much lay in their power." As with all violence, the freedom that it brings must be short lived and ultimately futile because the whole enemy has not been destroyed—nor can it ever be, since much of the enemy is within. Santosh helps prove it: he marries a *hubshi* woman to help him gain American citizenship, and the *hubshi* scrawl "Soul Brother" outside his house to protect it from new burnings. Santosh says that, though he understands the words, he feels no sense of brotherhood to anyone—and identifies himself to the reader as part of the enemy which has not been identified by the *hubshi*. His freedom has led him to want to dissociate himself from the brotherhood of man. The *hubshi*, too, are guilty for stressing a racial rather than a human brotherhood.

The narrator of the third section, "Tell Me Who to Kill," is free from even the direction of his mind. His story consists of the distraught interior monologue of a madman who senses that he is like a ship without a rudder which must go in whatever direction the stream of life takes it. His thoughts go through his mind, apparently without direction, as he makes a trip to attend his brother's wedding: "But I don't know what bus we will take when we get to the station, or what other train, what street we will walk down, what gate we will go through, and what door we will open into what room." The loss of control over his life is emphasized by the fact that he seems to be on a day's release from a mental hospital in the charge of an attendant, Frank. Frank, we feel, is in control, knows where they are going, and has decided how they are to get there. Even though he is kind

to his charge, his watchfulness makes him somehow sinister.

These relationships prove richly complex and ironic for him since he can present the reader with an individual who has been freed by his illness from making decisions and from taking responsibility for his actions. Ironically, such an individual needs a jailer to make decisions for him and to control his actions. Not even the freedom which mental breakdown imparts is absolute.

The monologue of the narrator also makes clear that the freedom of the madman is paradoxical: while his thoughts are free, their very obsessiveness controls him very effectively. Their obsessiveness gives the monologue coherence and direction, for the madness of the narrator becomes evident not because his thoughts occur to him helter-skelter, but because they come to seem more and more inevitable as we pursue them. One becomes aware that his words reveal pent-up hatred and frustration which have driven him to breakdown since he has been unable to find release for these emotions.

His story begins with his memory of deprivation in rural Trinidad. Naipaul's description of the dreary, ugly, hopeless environment is executed with a precision he has demonstrated in his earlier works. Here again the house is used as a reminder of the sordidness of the characters' lives and as a symbol of their dreams. Surrounded by so much that is ugly, the narrator resolves to dedicate his life to preserving and developing the only thing of beauty that is close to him, his younger brother: "He is so pretty. If he grow up he will be like a star-boy, like Errol Flim or Fairley Granger. The beauty in that room is like a wonder to me, and I can't bear the thought of losing it." Unfortunately, physical beauty is finite; Dayo, the younger brother, does not possess the inner beauty which might have justified the self-effacement which his brother undertakes on his behalf.

Naipaul makes clear that to deny oneself completely, to be content as a part of someone else's presence, is to accept slavery, to condemn oneself to prison. As he has indicated frequently, Naipaul considers such denial an especially West-Indian tendency, encouraged by history and environment. The narrator, too cowardly to discover his own personal beauty, continually seeks to identify with other people; with film stars, such as Flynn and Granger; with a rich man of whom he says, "I worship this man"; with his uncle, Stephen, whom he adored when small. Like his brother, these men prove unworthy of his slavery, but his disillusionment does not prevent him from accepting Frank as his jailer and new master. Again, the awareness that he has willingly surrendered the conduct of his life disturbs him sometimes: "You are just going where the ship is going, you will never be a free man again." Instead of trying to take control, however, he wishes that he will be relieved forever from responsibility for himself: "I don't want the ship to stop, I don't want to touch land again."

The narrator's attempt to liberate himself from himself by sacrificing himself to others, achieved in a way by his mental breakdown, is as extreme as Santosh's attempt to isolate himself completely. Self-effacement proves ultimately to be as imprisoning as its opposite, complete isolation. The narrator of the third section, however, is more perceptive than Santosh, since he senses that something is wrong with his position: "O God, show me the enemy. Once you find out who the enemy is, you can kill him. But these people here they confuse me. Who hurt me? Who spoil my life?" That the section ends with these questions underlines its narrator's difference from Santosh who, having taken refuge in his isolation, ceases to question. Santosh never comes close to recognizing that he is his own worst enemy; the narrator of this section senses that he is himself most to blame, but he cannot understand why. Neither he nor Santosh understand that self-love prevents them from seeing the value of their own individuality and that of others.

The characters of "In a Free State," the fourth section, are never in any doubt about who the enemy is or that they must kill him. The story is set in a newly independent country in Africa. Political independence has its limitations, because the Africans, whose loyalties are tribal rather than national, have had little to do with creating the state they now possess. Inheritors of a way of life they have not developed for themselves, they are foreigners in their own country:

> the capital, which, in spite of the white exodus to South Africa and in spite of deportations, remained an English-Indian creation in the African wilderness. It owed nothing to African skill; it required none.... It was still a colonial city, with a colonial glamour. Everyone in it was far from home.

Naipaul gives us glimpses of Africans whose lives have been unaffected by the West: two naked men covered with chalk who run along the road, and people seen tilling the soil with simple implements and living "the immemorial life of the forest." For such people political independence has no meaning; they are free of the burdens of independence that oppress the educated African, but they are the prisoners of their ignorance and poverty. The paths they have created and which they follow are "simple forest paths, leading to nothing else." Incongruous as they might seem in a modern independent state, these people have integrity and an identity of their own.

The Africans into whose hands the free state has been entrusted certainly lack these. Like the narrator in "Tell Me Who to Kill," they have attempted to efface their own iden-

tities to assume European ones, to cope with their new nation which they correctly recognize as European in design. They wear European suits which they have not paid for; their hair style is known among city Africans as "the English style"; they frequent the night clubs from which they had been barred before independence. Their incongruity is emphasized by the fact that Bobby, the Englishman in the story, wears a "native" shirt made of phony native fabric, designed and woven in Holland. Both of these dishonest styles of dress are contrasted with that of real Africans:

> On a path on the wooden hillside just above the road about a dozen Africans in bright new cotton gowns were walking one behind the other in the rain, covering their heads with leaves. With the bright colours of their cottons, and the leaves over their heads, they were very nearly camouflaged.

Further on, two men run into the road:

> They were naked, and chalked white from head to toe, white as the rocks, white as the knotted, scaly lower half of the tall cactus plants, white as the dead branches of trees whose roots were loose in the crumbling soil.

These two passages describe people who are so much a part of their environment that they are almost indistinguishable from it. The narrator seems to be saying, as Conrad did, that "they wanted no excuse for being there." These are the only free people in the book, though ironically they are probably unaware of and uninterested in the political status of their country. The political turmoil, the heritage of the political freedom that the novel describes, seems far away from them.

The city Africans, on the other hand, exchange their natural freedom for one they have not earned and which, being foreign, enslaves them. Like slaves, and like the narrator of the preceding section, they try to find fulfillment by assuming the identity of their masters who, ironically, have just liberated them politically. Of course, the Africans feel uneasy in their new positions. They sense that they can never feel free until they have the strength to assert their own identities and purge themselves of their European ones.

Violence is an important theme in the book, and it contributes considerably to the mounting tone of terror as the stories progress. Bobby and Linda, an English pair, are driving from the capital of the state to the compound in the collectorate in another part of the country. In the compound, the Europeans who have remained to help run the country preserve something of their old style of life. As Bobby and Linda progress in their long drive, one becomes aware that they are seriously threatened by the tribal hostility between the king and the President. As individuals, they are innocent of blame for the turmoil of the country, but they are obvious reminders of the colonial past. Since neither is especially intelligent, they are not sure how to handle the hostility and menace they sense in the attitude of the Africans they meet. Linda takes refuge in aggressiveness and in the prejudices of colonial Europeans towards Africa. Bobby, on the other hand, wears an "African" shirt, makes passes at African boys, wishes that his skin was black, and delights in announcing that his boss is an African. His attempts to free himself from himself fail miserably since his weakness and masochism are readily identified and violently dealt with by Africans seeking a stability which their freedom has denied them. The African continent quickly converts the little pockets of Europe which the whites had created into forest, a recurring image which Naipaul associates with Africa. The forest, relentless and foreboding, suggests the depth of the African past and emphasizes the superficiality of the changes which the Europeans have wrought on it. The image allows Naipaul to contrast those Africans who have remained close to the forest with those who have emerged freshly from it. Clothing, an important motif in the section, is used to illustrate the differences between these two groups. Those Africans who are just beginning to feel the influence of Europe are described as wearing "cast-off European clothes," "fighting the encumbrance of [their] dungarees," and, most incongruous of all, "in jodhpurs and riding boots, red caps and jackets." No doubt many readers will feel that these descriptions are unkind, snobbish, and used to ridicule. In the context of the novel, however, these pictures reveal the distress of the narrator who finds so much evidence of the enslaved mentality in a country which wants to think of itself as free. He seems to suggest that the African freshly emerged from the bush must have other alternatives than to turn himself into a pathetic mimic of the European. The African himself is not so much to blame for his mimicry as his former colonizers and his neo-colonizers, the liberal European and the citified African.

Such mimicry can ultimately bring only self-disgust and pathetic, futile attempts to purge through violence the revulsion at what the Africans have become. They choose Bobby as their sacrificial lamb, but Bobby, another version of the tramp in the first section, is quite incapable of bearing the burden of guilt they wish to impose on him. A homosexual, he is rejected and ridiculed in both England and Africa; he has severed relations with England but finds a relationship with Africa impossible to fuse. His homosexuality and his race make him truly free, but free in a way which renders him a casualty. He is not, like Santosh, one who takes pride in his complete detachment. He yearns for some lasting attachment but is repulsed and abused because he is vulnerable.

The acts of violence which he suffers, therefore, strike terror in the reader and bring no release for their perpetrators.

In many ways the story seems to illustrate the shortcomings of Frantz Fanon's theory that the way for the colonized to rid themselves of their colonizers is by violence. The kind of violence implied to be effective is the violence of brutal self-appraisal. Without it, mimicry will continue to compound itself, and self-revulsion will continue to demand meaningless sacrifices, like the beating of Bobby. Free, unattached, and vulnerable people like Bobby will continue to be victimized by people seeking to liberate themselves from pressures—psychological, cultural, economic—that bind them.

The book concludes with "The Circus at Luxor," an Epilogue taken, like the Prologue, from a journal—but no journal in the ordinary sense. The careful selection of word and incident, the provocative and illuminating juxtaposition of superficially incongruous and unrelated scenes, suggests the same artistry and intensity as the fictional sections. In the Epilogue the narrator is more central to the action than he had been in the Prologue. A tourist in Egypt, he sees some children being treated in an inhuman way, and he takes steps to put an end to it. The narrator's action has been seen as an expression of "anger and a sense of injustice" with which callousness and inhumanity should be met. No doubt it is, but even the freedom to act in a humane way is compromised by the attention which the action calls to itself. "I felt exposed, futile," says the narrator after his gesture. Naipaul ends by suggesting that in this world no time has ever been pure and, consequently, absolute freedom can never exist. Purity and freedom are fabrications, illusions, causes for yearning, things for the tomb. Put this way the ending sounds trite, futile, and pessimistic in an adolescent way, but that is far from the truth. If man would recognize the impossibility and, indeed, the immorality of absolute freedom, then he would assume his responsibilities to vulnerable creatures, such as the tramp, Bobby, and the Egyptian children, whose freedoms he jeopardizes in his selfish search for his own. Yet the illusion of purity and freedom must be maintained as a safeguard against man's selfishness and ambition, which Naipaul symbolizes ominously with the image of the Chinese Empire announcing itself.

Man should neither reject completely or embrace fully the notion of freedom. *In A Free State* illustrates superbly that to be meaningful freedom must be understood to be paradoxical.

Gordon Rohlehr (essay date 1977)

SOURCE: "The Ironic Approach: The Novels of V. S. Naipaul," in *Critical Perspectives on V. S. Naipaul*, Heinemann Educational Books, 1977, pp. 178-93.

[In the following essay, Rohlehr discusses Naipaul's ironic approach toward and "sympathetic rejection" of Trinidadian culture.]

About Naipaul's first three novels George Lamming writes in *The Pleasures of Exile:*

> *His books can't move beyond a castrated satire; and although satire may be a useful element in fiction, no important work comparable to Selvon's can rest safely on satire alone. When such a writer is a colonial, ashamed of his cultural background and striving like mad to prove himself through promotion to the peaks of a 'superior' culture whose values are gravely in doubt, then satire, like the charge of philistinism, is for me nothing more than a refuge. And it is too small a refuge for a writer who wishes to be taken seriously.*

This is an important and damaging criticism which merits examination. Lamming, Selvon and Naipaul are equally preoccupied with the West Indian social scene and with what it means to them, as individuals, to be West Indians. Yet Lamming criticizes Naipaul's presentation of the West Indian experience and the nature of his personal quest to discover where he stands. There is the assertion that mere irony is irrelevant to West Indian society at this stage. Thus satire is a means of running away from the sordid truth, by seeking refuge in laughter, whose basis is an assumption of one's own cultural superiority to the world one ridicules.

Yet Naipaul's 'Englishness' does not manifest itself, as Lamming suggests in a crude and overt striving to attain the dubious standards of the metropolis. In fact, his ironic awareness uncovers all that is drab, petty and humourless in English life, as we see in *Mr Stone and the Knight's Companion.* It manifests itself, rather, in his unconscious acceptance of a typical European view of Third World inferiority, a view which is now being attacked from several quarters. It shows itself in his contemptuous rejection of all things West Indian, which at times breaks through even the geniality of *The Mystic Masseur* (1957). The conviction of an anarchic society which the author must reject lies also behind *Miguel Street.* Here, however, the rejection is not done in contempt, but with considerable sympathy. This book, like *A House for Mr Biswas* (1961), forces one to reconsider Lamming's criticism to see what it misses of Naipaul's subtlety, and to see what it does not say about the complexity of his situation.

Naipaul is a Trinidad East Indian who has not come to terms with the Negro-Creole world in Trinidad, or with the East Indian world in Trinidad, or with the greyness of English life, or with life in India itself, where he went in search of his roots. After these two books Naipaul wrote *The Middle*

Passage (1962), which manifests all the new depth and astringency which his irony has assumed, and at the same time demonstrates all the superficiality which one thought he had left far behind. This book makes one feel again the justice of Lamming's criticism, and realize how true a comment it is on one very real aspect of Naipaul's attitude, as it appears in some of his books.

The position of the ironist in colonial society is indeed a delicate one. Lamming can see little that is risible in a society whose history is one of underprivilege. One appreciates his point. The early Naipaul is at times the irresponsible ironist, subtle, but lacking in a sensitive participation in the life he anatomizes. If one says that the exercise of irony precludes sympathy, one is merely defining the limitations of irony, and the limitations of any of Naipaul's work which depends solely on irony. So far one agrees with Lamming.

Satire is the sensitive measure of a society's departure from a norm inherent in itself. Since Naipaul starts with the conviction that such a norm is absent from his society, his task as satirist becomes doubly difficult. Not only must he recreate experience, but also simultaneously create the standards against which this experience is to be judged. This explains the mixture of farce and social consciousness which occurs in the two early novels. In 1957 Naipaul's first novel, *The Mystic Masseur,* was published. It is about an Indian, Ganesh Ramsummair, who begins his career as a secondary school teacher and then becomes a masseur. He only achieves success, however, when he becomes a 'mystic', and attends to Trinidad's spiritual problems. His brilliance as a mystic helps him to become a successful author, politician, diplomat and eventually gains him an M.B.E. In 1958 followed Naipaul's second novel, *The Suffrage of Elvira.* It deals with the farce of elections in an unsophisticated part of Trinidad, beset by superstition and ignorance, where everyone is conscious only of the profit he can make out of this new game.

The tone of these two books is almost the same. A situation of superstition, ignorance, absurdity, knavery and self-interest, is presented as the reality in Trinidad social and political life. Naipaul consciously presents his real world as farcical. The reader is invited simultaneously to recognize the degree of distortion and to share in the author's grin as he insists that the situation is perfectly normal. 'I myself believe that the history of Ganesh is, in a way, the history of our times.' It is the Chaucerian pose; the genial elevation of the absurd and the constant pretence on the part of the satirist that he fully condones the behaviour of the rogues he satirizes. Chaucer's rascals are always the best fellows in the land. 'Ganesh elevated the profession by putting the charlatans out of business.' Naipaul's humour here awakens Chaucerian echoes.

It is only when one reads *The Middle Passage* that one realizes how completely Naipaul has accepted anarchy and absurdity as the norms of his society. If in the early farces an absurd world is presented as real, in *The Middle Passage* a real world is presented as tragically futile and absurd. The deeper implication of the first two books is that West Indian society, emerging from ignorance and superstition, is peculiarly susceptible to depredation by the fraud and the politician, and by all opportunists who are prepared to exploit the social unease for their personal ends. That Ganesh and Harbans are treated so genially conceals Naipaul's seriousness of purpose. Ganesh, who poses as the defender of Hinduism while it is politic and profitable to do so, completely rejects Indian dress and changes his name to G Ramsay Muir once he becomes a successful politician. This change of name and dress is always used by Naipaul to symbolize the acculturation of the East Indian to pseudo-western patterns of life, which is something he writes of with bitterness, despair and regret. One should not be misled by his genial tone to overestimate his admiration for Ganesh, the successful fraud.

Yet even in a book of the geniality of *The Mystic Masseur* Naipaul can lack sympathy. His hero approaches his nadir in such scenes as the dinner at Government House, where Naipaul depicts an imaginary confrontation between the most unsophisticated members of Creole and Indian society, and the hypercivilized governor's wife. All that Naipaul finds ridiculous in Creole society is paraded here: the bad grammar, lack of taste or social grace, complete unawareness and the struggle to be white. A black man, of whose blackness Naipaul makes a special point, is dressed in a blue suit, with yellow gloves and a monocle, which eventually falls into the soup. Several of the guests have some difficulty in manipulating their knives and forks. One can accept this as farce intended, in its distorted way, to show the Creole and Indian on the painful and ridiculous road to whiteness. But the suspicion persists that Naipaul himself regards these people with more contempt than compassion. These are the same people whom he describes in *The Middle Passage* as being 'like monkeys pleading for evolution'. The incongruity of his position here, as Lamming points out, is that while he laughs at his Creoles crudely aping standards of pseudo whiteness, he can only do so assuming these very norms himself.

In 1959 came *Miguel Street,* a series of short stories about an urban slum in Trinidad, told by a boy who speaks in the first person. The 'I' in this book is not merely an autobiographical 'I'. To discover Naipaul, one must get past the voice that tells the tale to the narrator behind the narrator. One must appreciate all the nuances and shifts of irony, of which the boy could not possibly be conscious. The boy-narrator is not Naipaul, but a device exploited by Naipaul the artist who operates in detachment. If these stories are autobiography, they are autobiography set at a distance through irony.

Early on a theme of futility is established.

> *Popo's workshop no longer sounded with hammering and sawing. The sawdust no longer smelled fresh, and became black, almost like dirt. Popo began drinking a lot, and I didn't like him when he was drunk. He smelled of rum, and he used to cry and then grow angry and want to beat up everybody. That made him an accepted member of the gang.*

It is such a careful selection of detail that makes these stories less slight than appears on the surface. The whole pattern of the book is to depict the inevitable movement from freshness to dirt, and from laughter to tears. Moreover, at every point the boy judges and measures this degradation, until he finally rejects a society which reduces everyone to its own level of amorality. But while the boy hints at a norm by saying that he does not like Popo drunk, Miguel Street accepts him fully. So that when Popo goes to jail, the mecca of Miguel Street, the verdict of the street is, 'We was wrong about Popo. He is a man like any of we.'

The statement serves two functions. It links the world of *Miguel Street* to the world of *The Mystic Masseur* by suggesting the distortion of accepted moral values as the norm. At the same time the claim is being made that all the eccentrics of Miguel Street are men 'like any of we', that Yahoo-land is a real place. As I have suggested, in a society which is seen as having no true standards, irony is bound to operate in reverse, the ironist starting with an abnormal situation and hinting at a sanity which is absent from his world. However, if the impulse behind *Miguel Street* is similar to that behind *The Mystic Masseur,* the whole tone is more serious. The farce has become a nightmare. Here one finds it difficult to accept Lamming's description of Naipaul's satire as a refuge and escape from experience. If satire is a means of running away, it is equally a means of fighting; an act of bravery, not cowardice; the confrontation of a nightmare, not the seeking of a refuge.

This passage is an example of how Naipaul's larger ironic awareness controls the boy's naive account of the facts:

> *And once Hat said, 'Every day Big Foot father, the policeman, giving Big Foot blows. Like medicine. Three times a day after meals. And hear Big Foot talk afterwards. He used to say, "When I get big and have children, I go beat them, beat them.".. .'*
>
> *I asked Hat, 'And Big Foot mother? She used to beat him too?'*

*Hat said, 'Oh God! That would kill him. Big Foot
didn't have any mother. His father didn't married,
thank God!'*

What Naipaul is aware of here is a lack of family life and a
heritage of brutality passed on from father to son. Miguel
Street accepts this as normal and ideal.

One of the main themes of these stories is the nature and
complexity of laughter in Miguel Street. Hat constantly
points out how apparent laughter conceals tears. The laughter of Miguel Street is sometimes crude and cynical. But
whenever this occurs, the boy points out the need for a
greater sensitivity. 'And all of us from Miguel Street
laughed at Big Foot. All except me. For I knew how he felt.'
At most other times, however, there is propriety about the
street's laughter. It is silent when Laura cries 'all the cry
she had tried to cover up with her laughter.' Contemptuous
laughter is always frowned upon, limits are placed on cynicism. This is why Nathaniel can never belong to the street,
and Hat relegates him to a lower world. '"I don't know why
he don't go back to the Dry River where he come from.
They ain't have any culture there and he would be happier."'
There are the several occasions when Hat threatens to thrash
Boysie if he dares laugh at the latest Miguel Street misfortune. Because of Naipaul's sympathy, Miguel Street comes
across to the reader not merely as a jungle, but as a place
where people in the face of insuperable frustration still preserve an intimacy and humour which is almost a new type
of maturity.

In 1960 Naipaul revisited Trinidad after an absence of ten
years. Born in Trinidad in 1932, he had left at the age of
eighteen for England, where he went to Oxford and has lived
ever since. In **The Middle Passage,** a travel-book written
about his return to the West Indies, he attempts to assess
his relation to the world which he has been treating in his
fiction. Although this book was published in 1962, one year
after *A House for Mr Biswas,* one feels justified in considering it first, since in the latter book Naipaul presents his
experience with a completeness and conclusiveness which
is absent from **The Middle Passage.** Naipaul shows in his
direct examination of Trinidad a superficiality which he has
outgrown in his novels.

It has been pointed out that **The Middle Passage** is not written from the standpoint of a professional historian or soci-
ologist and that Naipaul's reactions are those of imaginative
sensibility. This is true and this is where the difficulty lies.
To this author's sensibility, Trinidad represents a nightmare,
and one has constantly to differentiate between his sensitive examination of history and his honest expression of hysteria. He confesses a pathological dislike for Trinidad.

I had never wanted to stay in Trinidad. When I was

*in the fourth form I wrote a vow on the endpaper
of my Kennedy's Revised Latin Primer to leave
within five years. I left after six; and for many years
afterwards in England, falling asleep in bed-sitters
with the electric fire on, I had been awakened by
the nightmare that I was back in tropical Trinidad.*

It is a nightmare which, nurtured through a decade of absence, and reinforced by the literature which Naipaul has
read about the West Indies, has now become an obsession.
'As soon as the *Francisco Bobadilla* had touched the quay
. . . I began to feel all my old fear of Trinidad. I did not want
to stay.'

**Naipaul uses Trinidad as an example of all
that is degrading in the West Indian
experience and, because of this, is in a
sense not writing about Trinidad at all. He
is writing an essay on the horrors of
acculturation, and an explanation of why
he had to escape.**
—*Gordon Rohlehr*

The book, however, is written with a conscious nobility of
purpose. It purports to be an assessment of Naipaul's West
Indian experience and an apology for his self-chosen exile.
The important first two chapters of the book are carefully
written. One notes, for example, the appropriateness of all
the quotations which Naipaul uses as epigrams to these
chapters. First there is the general epigram to the book, a
quotation from Anthony Froude's *The English in the West
Indies.*

*They were valued only for the wealth which they
yielded, and society there has never assumed any
particularly noble aspect . . . There are no people
there in the true sense of the word, with a character and purpose of their own.*

Or one may consider the two quotations from Thomas Mann
and Tacitus, at the beginning of the chapter on Trinidad. The
quotation from Mann is particularly apt. What one notices
is that these three quotations are about three entirely different peoples: West Indians, Israelites and Britons. The impression conveyed is one of the timelessness of the process
which Naipaul observes at work in the West Indies today.
It is to his credit that he chooses his epigrams from three
different sources, and thus places the West Indian experience against a backcloth of universal experience. It is re-
grettable that this impression of universality could not be
maintained.

The name 'Middle Passage' is a symbol at many levels. It

is symbolic of that original journey which was the beginning of a slavery and which Naipaul sees existing in spirit. At the same time it is a symbol of the West Indies today in that transitional middle stage between the cultures which her people lost and the new sense of cultural identity which they have not yet gained. Like Thomas Mann's Israelites, they are seen to be 'in a transitional land, pitching their tents between the houses of their fathers and the real Egypt . . . unanchored souls wavering in spirit and without a secure doctrine'. Like the Britons under Roman rule, they are seen to speak to 'such novelties as "civilization" when really they are only a feature of enslavement'.

The name 'Middle Passage' also refers to the new journey which the West Indian emigrant makes to England. The first chapter is a sensitive record of certain very real aspects of West Indian life. There is the emigrant who abandons a perfectly good job to go to a land of which he is completely ignorant, but which even as a child he has known to be the Mother Country. There are the tourist-class petty bourgeois West Indians with their values of colour and money, who demonstrate every feature of insularity, ignorance, vulgarity and self-contempt in their society. These people refer to the immigrants as the 'wild cows' and the 'orangoutangs'. But as is suggested by the sentence beginning, 'Like monkeys pleading for evolution', Naipaul is himself capable of the denigratory comparison. His contempt is the result of superior intellectual awareness; the tourists' contempt is self-contempt, the result of ignorance. It is difficult to say which is worse. There is also the Englishwoman, completely perplexed at it all, an apt representative of the society towards which the emigrants travel.

One of the questions which the book poses is, 'What explains the West Indian emigrant?' The answer which it suggests can be found in the themes on which it is written. Those themes are stated in the epigrams. West Indian history has bred 'no people in the true sense of the word, with a character and purpose of their own'. The West Indian experience, as Naipaul has expressed it, is not a fusion or coalition of cultures to enhance their separate excellences, but their degradation to a new norm of anarchy. Naipaul uses Trinidad as an example of all that is degrading in the West Indian experience and, because of this, is in a sense not writing about Trinidad at all. He is writing an essay on the horrors of acculturation, and an explanation of why he had to escape. He sees only what was destroyed in the West Indies.

> *How can the history of this West Indian futility be written? . . . The history of these islands can never be satisfactorily told . . . History is built around achievement and creation; and nothing was created in the West Indies.*

Naipaul sees the West Indies as a rubbish-heap. It is a de-spairing image to choose. This explains the sublimated bitterness which lies behind his laughter whenever he observes the East Indian conforming to the pattern of West Indian history; joining the Negro-Creoles in their quest for 'whiteness'. Perhaps the most delicate and ruthless of his stories is the **"Christmas Story,"** where an East Indian is made to describe the process of his acculturation and, supremely ignorant of the fact, becomes the mouthpiece of his own degradation. He is a teacher who adopts the Christian faith when he realizes that this is the only way to gain promotion in a school managed by the Church. He is not given the cynical awareness of a Ganesh as he outlines the stages of his acculturation, but naively declares that he has buried his East Indian past, and refers to other Indians as 'these people' or 'the others'. Behind the **"Christmas Story"** and *The Middle Passage* is a bitter despair of the whole colonial process and an implicit rejection of the colonial experience, which expresses itself in irony and in contempt for all things West Indian.

> *The city throbbed with steel-bands. A good opening line for a novelist or travel writer, but the steel-band had long been regarded as a high manifestation of West Indian culture, and it was a sound I detested.*
>
> *The land of the Calypso is not a copy-writer's phrase. It is one side of the truth, and it was this gaiety, so inexplicable to the tourist who sees the shacks of Shanty Town and the corbeaux patrolling the modern highway, and inexplicable to me who had remembered it as the land of failures, which now, on my return, assaulted me.*

It is apparently beyond Naipaul to be able to understand why there is music in spite of the rubbish-heap, and to recognize in such merry-making not merely cynical indifference to the dunghill, but evidence of an affirmation and vibrancy of life, however crude. Such recognition requires not brutality and subtlety, which he points out as the special gifts of the satirist, but the entirely different talents of delicacy, tenderness and a quality of intimacy. In *Miguel Street,* in spite of the fact that the boy eventually rejects the rubbish-heap, there is a sympathy for its inhabitants, and an implicit recognition of the positives of this world. This is why parts of *The Middle Passage* strike one as superficial, and a retrogression in sensibility.

Sometimes one wonders at Naipaul's hypersensitivity and asks oneself whether the neurosis is completely controlled by the irony. Is not this complete acquiescence with Froude that there are 'No people there in the true sense of the word', a formula for evading the complex sympathy which the West Indian experience seems to demand? I stated above that what appears to Lamming as a conscious struggle on

Naipaul's part to adopt the standards of a 'superior' metropolitan culture, is explicable as a too easy acquiescence with European historians; they assumed that the 'native' was an inferior animal and consequently failed to look for positives in his society. Perhaps it is easier to see Trinidad as an historical rubbish-heap and a sociological abstraction; easier to see evidence in every observed and carefully chosen detail of some deep-seated social malaise which justifies one's neurosis; easier than to see the country as a vast Miguel Street of individuals, people in a truer sense of the word than Froude seems to have been aware of, each making demands on one's imaginative sympathy, because of the unique history which each has endured.

Naipaul's hatred of the steel band and all it indicates is no mere rejection of West Indian culture, but a rejection of the single common ground where Trinidadians of all races meet on a basis of equality. Carnival in Trinidad, dominated by steel-band, calypso and costume, is more than a time of general merry-making. One can, without naively propounding a West Indian version of the myth of the happy Negro, recognize Carnival as one of the few symbols, however tenuous, of a oneness in the Trinidadian people. Naipaul can show us how both Indians and Negroes despise each other in a monkey-like struggle to ape standards of pseudo-whiteness. But he rejects as crude, noisy and unsophisticated the sole symbol of their miscibility, the one sign that the people themselves are reconstructing something to take the place of the personality which history destroyed.

A similar shortcoming manifests itself in what Naipaul has to say about the Negro. He is able to recognize Negro self-contempt as a product of history, to see the historical inferiority complex as the central dilemma of Creole culture. But he does not understand the Negro's attempt at reconstructing something to take the place of his lost dignity.

> *The involvement of the Negro with the white world is one of the limitations of West Indian writing, as it is the destruction of American Negro writing. The American Negro's subject is his blackness. This cannot be the basis of any serious literature, and it has happened again and again that once the American Negro has made his statement, his profitable protest, he has nothing to say.*

The obvious comment is that where one's blackness means something very definite, it can become the basis of the most serious literature. And much as one accepts Naipaul's point that protest literature can become a sterile and stereotyped posturing in the name of blackness, one also realizes that protest against the past is a vital transitional stage in the reconstruction of a sense of personality. Naipaul does not realize that in treating the theme of East Indian acculturation, and the reconstruction of the Indian personality in the New World, he is at one with Negro writers who are also trying to reconstruct personality, and is writing a most vital portion of the sensitive history of the West Indies. Naipaul's Mr Biswas rebels because his society denies him personality and forces him to live with an inferiority complex and a sense of nonentity. Negro writers, in the Caribbean or America, protest because their society annihilated identity. Both in the case of Mr Biswas and the negro of the New World, underprivilege is struggling to build its symbolic house against overwhelming odds.

A House for Mr Biswas is more profound than anything else Naipaul has written because, for the first time, he is able to feel his own history not merely as a squalid farce, but as an adventure in sensibility. Mr Biswas has nothing to recommend him except a talent for sign-painting, and the fact that he is a Brahmin and therefore an accessible target for Hindu snobbery. These qualities together land him in trouble. For it is while he is painting decorations at the Tulsi store, that he is detected passing a love note to one of the Tulsi daughters. When summoned before Mrs Tulsi and her right-hand man Seth, he allows himself to be brow-beaten into marriage and spends the rest of his life fighting to be independent of the Tulsis. His ambition is to build a house of his own.

The book can be interpreted on several levels. There is the obvious surface level where Biswas can be seen as a second-generation Indian who, although rebelling against his own decaying Hindu world, cannot come to a meaningful compromise with the Creole world of Trinidad. This Creole world comes in only by implication and allusion. The Tulsis refer to it with contempt, although Biswas is quick to point out to them just how degrading a concession they make to it by sending their sons to a Roman Catholic school. Naipaul himself is aware of acculturation in the bilingualism which is now imposed on the East Indian. Hindi remains the language of intimacy but, by the end of the book, Mr Biswas has for years been a journalist writing in English, and the readers and learners all speak Creole.

In *An Area of Darkness* Naipaul writes thus of the East Indian confrontation with the Creole world:

> *Into this alienness we daily ventured, and at length we were absorbed into it. But we knew that there had been change, gain, loss. We knew that something which was once whole had been washed away. What was whole was the idea of India.*

The Hindu world soon becomes the world Naipaul describes in *The Middle Passage:*

> *an enclosing self-sufficient world absorbed with its quarrels and jealousies, as difficult for the outsider*

*to penetrate as for one of its own members to es-
cape. It protected and imprisoned, a static world,
awaiting decay.*

Since the society offers him two equally terrible nightmares,
isolation and non-identification are the only alternatives left
to Biswas. The two houses which he builds and has to abandon are built in inhospitable waste-lands far from society.
'He had built his own house in a place as wild and out of
the way as he could have wished . . . not seeming to invite
habitation so much as decay.' But rejection of his Hindu
roots proves a formidable task, and the Biswas who, as a
boy contemptuously spurns this dead ritualistic life, mutters
'Rama, Rama, Sita, Rama' during the storm. At the most
acute moment of crisis, the old ritual is what reasserts itself. It is a sign of Naipaul's complete control that even in
this little detail he is not found wanting. *A House for Mr
Biswas* moves far beyond preoccupations with race or the
Hindu world in Trinidad, and depicts a classic struggle for
personality against a society that denies it. But the book is
only able to do so because this narrow, enclosed Hindu
world has been established with such fidelity and completeness.

Naipaul establishes this world with such consistency that it
becomes symbolic of darkness, stagnation and decay.
Hanuman House, the home of the Tulsis, is an

> *alien white fortress, bulky, impregnable and blank
> . . . windowless . . . slightly sinister. . . . The kitchen
> . . . was lower than the hall and completely with-
> out light. The doorway gaped black . . . blackness
> seemed to fill the kitchen like a solid substance.*

Every other Tulsi home is like this. There is the shop at The
Chase where 'the walls were black and fluffy with soot as
though a new species of spider had been bred there', the
barracks at Green Vale, 'The trees darkened the road, their
rotting leaves choked the grass gutters. The trees surrounded
the barracks'. The Tulsis soon reduce the house at Shorthills
to a ramshackle decay; round the house in Port-of-Spain
they build a symbolic wall.

The term 'barracks' suggests the regimentation of life which
Biswas fights until he builds a house of his own. Biswas's
rebellion can be read as the rebellion of an individual against
a communal way of life. Hanuman House, symbolically presided over by the monkey-god, is described as a 'communal organization' whose maintenance depends on a
recognition of authority by, and a denial of personality to
the ruled. As soon as Tulsi autocracy becomes weak, the
whole system disintegrates, and one has the anarchy of the
Shorthills episode, where the naked self-interest behind
Tulsi ritual manifests itself, and life returns to the law of

the jungle as the beauty and luxuriance of the land are wan-
tonly despoiled.

In this decaying paradise of totalitarianism, Biswas the individualist is described as 'serpent' and 'spy'. As he appears
before 'the family tribunal' Seth describes the nature of the
crime which he has committed. 'This house is like a republic already.' The argument which the Tulsis employ against
him is the eternal argument of totalitarianism; namely, that
the individual is meaningless if he tries to be independent
of the system. The Tulsis try to make Biswas aware of the
fact that he has come to them with no material possessions
and argue that he is therefore a nonentity who can only gain
significance if he surrenders to them. Tulsidom depends for
its existence on the psychic emasculation of the men and
on the maintenance of their sense of inferiority. At the most
humiliating moments of his struggle, Biswas nearly surrenders to this sense of inferiority. It is seen by Naipaul as a
surrender to darkness and chaos.

It is worth pointing out that the traditional Hindu custom
requires the bride to join her husband's household and become almost a servant of her mother-in-law. The complete
humiliation of Biswas's position is that he has to assume
the ritualistic role of the newly married Hindu girl. Thus his
is a rebellion against complete humiliation in the eyes of
society, and against nonentity in an entire and comprehensive sense. It is interesting to note the honesty and care with
which this rebellion is depicted. Initially Biswas enjoys it.
It exhilarates him. But it soon becomes a vicious and bitter
struggle, fought with invective, saliva and scorn. Indeed,
Biswas is at times petty, cowardly and contemptible, and
part of the book's triumph is that Naipaul has been able to
present a hero in all his littleness, and still preserve a sense
of the man's inner dignity.

As the rebellion progresses, Biswas finds that 'All his joy
had turned into disgust at his condition'. This happens one
morning as he realizes his irrelevance to the Tulsi scene. If
he were to disappear, the ritual would still go on. He therefore realizes that rebellion for rebellion's sake is not enough,
and must coincide with the positive act of constructing
something new to take the place of the old life one repudiates.

For the present, however, he merely seeks to emancipate
himself from Hanuman House, and is sent to The Chase, a
Tulsi outpost in a remote area. But when, for the first time
since marriage, he confronts life outside Hanuman House,
Biswas finds himself afraid of the freedom which his rebellion has won him. Like so many protest politicians, he fails
initially when required to be constructive—'How lonely the
shop was! And how frightening! . . . afraid to disturb the
silence, afraid to open the door of the shop, to step into the
light. . . .' *A House for Mr Biswas* can be read as a book

which probes the relationship between rebellion and independence. True independence, it is revealed, does not immediately follow rebellion; true personality does not immediately follow emancipation, but must be constructed in a lifetime of painful struggle and retrogression. What does follow emancipation is a dark 'void' which Biswas must learn to face before he can 'step into the light'. It takes him all his life to fight the void and whatever graciousness life has to offer comes late, when he has almost lost the capacity to enjoy it. His victory lies in the fact that he has remained himself.

The house, which Mr Biswas determines to build as soon as he sees the Tulsi barracks at Green Vale, is more than a place where he can live. It is his personality symbolized, the private individuality which he must both build and maintain against the rest of the world. The development in Mr Biswas's house parallels at all points his development as a person. We are reminded of the destructive power of the Tulsis in the scene where Shama, acting as the agent of their malice, smashes the doll's house which Biswas buys for his daughter. It is described as if it were a body torn apart.

> *None of its parts was whole. Its delicate joints were*
> *exposed and useless. Below the torn skin of paint*
> *. . . the hacked and splintered wood was white and*
> *raw.*

> *'O God!'*

The scene is rendered with complete naturalness and sensitive force and its point is clear. Anything which manifests individuality and difference causes dread, envy and hostility in Hanuman House. The reaction of the Tulsis to the doll's house is a measure of the terrible revenge which this 'communal organization' can take on one who dares to be individual.

The book can be interpreted on a metaphysical level, since it questions the basis and meaning of personality. An interesting ambivalence emerges from the book. Firstly there is the dependence of the individual upon society for his sense of being; where by society one means not only other people, but a whole concrete world with which the consciousness establishes some deep intimacy, and claims as its own. As soon as Biswas 'stepped out of the yard, he returned to nonentity'. Outside Tulsi society he is lost. Secondly there is the necessary rebellion which the individual must make against society and the void which must be confronted. In the void are meaninglessness, nonentity, fear, lunacy and chaos, the storm within and the storm without. It is out of this confrontation that the new personality grows.

In many ways Biswas is an archetypal figure. He is described as stranger, visitor and wanderer. Weak, and frequently absurd, he is recognized in Hanuman House as a buffoon, and the role of fool is one which he at times accepts in humiliation and at others rejects with bitterness. But Biswas the clown is also Biswas the rebel. He is also man the artist, and his art is the only aspect of him that the Tulsis really admire, not realizing that it is an expression of the very personality they detest. Whenever Biswas is attacked by the sense of life as meaningless void, he immediately turns to his paint brushes and tries to create something against the emptiness. Perhaps he himself gives the best definition of his significance. To his bewildered son who asks him, 'Who are you?' he replies, 'I am just somebody. Nobody at all. I am just a man you know.' Biswas is Everyman, wavering between identity and nonentity, and claiming his acquaintance with the rest of men.

The book is powerfully symbolic, but it is never crudely or obtrusively so. If Biswas represents all the things I feel he does, it is because he is fully presented as a person whose every quirk and idiosyncracy we know, in a world whose every sight, sound and smell is recorded with fidelity and precision. Whatever is suggested of the numinous and universal, is conveyed through a fidelity to the concrete and particular. Landscape and life are not treated as isolated, but both conform to the artist's unity of purpose. Description is organically employed to reinforce theme. In the end, nature which, when associated with the Tulsis, took the form of jungle, nettle and weed surrounding The Chase, or decaying leaves on half-dead trees surrounding Green Vale, or the landslide at Shorthills, manifests itself in the coolness of the laburnum, and the scent of the lily in Mr Biswas's yard. His house may be dangerously cracked in places, but because it is his own, there is grace in its grotesqueness.

Ostensibly preoccupied with the present, Naipaul observes acculturation as a timeless feature of the West Indian experience which he never really accepts. Like the boy in *Miguel Street,* he rejects the rubbish-heap. Like Mr Biswas, he rejects Hanuman House. Rejecting Hanuman House and Miguel Street as two sides of the greater nightmare of being an Indian in Trinidad, he seeks the freedom of the independent personality, and makes the difficult choice of exile and dispossession. There are few pleasures in his exile. Yet out of it grow irony and a necessary detachment from the nightmare.

> *So later, and very slowly, in securer times of dif-*
> *ferent stresses, when the memories had lost the*
> *power to hurt, with pain or joy, they would fall into*
> *place and give back the past.*

> *How can the history of this West Indian futility be*
> *written?*

This finally is the question which Naipaul, and which perhaps every serious West Indian writer, asks, as he wonders what qualities of mind and feeling are necessary in order to face the West Indian experience. The answer which Naipaul ventures in *The Middle Passage* relates to the problem of West Indian creative writing, as well as to the writing of West Indian history as an academic pursuit. West Indian history can never be satisfactorily told, he says, because nothing was created in the West Indies, where there is neither achievement, nor a tradition of accepted values. Yet in *Miguel Street* and *A House for Mr Biswas* he tells a vital part of West Indian history, for the books are a sensitive presentation of the history of underprivilege. The worth of his irony is that it enables him to examine his past without any sentimental self-indulgence. We see Biswas as a full human being who is as weak and contemptible as he is forceful and admirable. Irony enables Naipaul to get down to the bare humanity beneath his history. Because he is dealing with his own personal past, his irony does not preclude sympathy but reinforces it. He is able to answer in terms of creative sensibility a question to which he could find no satisfactory academic answer.

John L. Brown (essay date Spring 1983)

SOURCE: "V. S. Naipaul: A Wager on the Triumph of Darkness," in *World Literature Today,* Vol. 57, No. 2, Spring, 1983, pp. 223-27.

[*In the following essay, Brown praises Naipaul's skill as a novelist, focusing on his "dark" vision of the world.*]

V.S. Naipaul has traveled far since his Trinidad beginnings. He was born there in 1932, a third-generation West Indian of Hindu ancestry. His father, a reporter with literary ambitions, encouraged his son to study and write. Even as a very young man Naipaul was determined to get away from the narrow, neocolonial world of his birth. At eighteen he left for England, took an Oxford degree, worked for the BBC, began to write. With his early stories of West Indian life he received immediate recognition from British critics as the most talented of contemporary Caribbean writers. He was covered with prestigious English literary prizes, four of them in a little more than ten years. Lately he has begun to pick them up in the United States as well, winning in 1980 the Bennett Award, given to a "writer of literary achievement" who is considered to "have received insufficient attention"—which, to tell the truth, is not really Naipaul's case. In the opinion of some of his disgruntled West Indian colleagues he became a prize exhibit of the London intellectual establishment, living proof of the generous recognition of colonial talents in the capital. He has often been accused, in judgments motivated, it would seem,

more by envy than by justice, of "looking down his long Oxonian nose" at the trivialities, the pretensions and the provincialism of the West Indies. One Trinidadian official indeed informed me that "Naipaul is certainly not our favorite native son"—something of an understatement. Naipaul seemed to have adapted swiftly to English life. He married a young English woman, acquired a prose style hailed as masterly. His eye was unerring in observing English scenes, as he demonstrated in *The Mimic Men* and in *Mr Stone and the Knights Companion.*

But it was clear that Britain wasn't "home" any more than Trinidad had been. Like every other place, it was a place to get out of. Naipaul early recognized in himself that sense of placelessness and of universal insecurity which afflicts the characters of his later novels. He began to travel, more perhaps to prove to himself that he didn't belong anywhere than to find a permanent haven. In 1960 he returned to the Caribbean, a sobering and bitter experience recounted in *The Middle Passage* (1962), which mingles history and sharp, personal observations. He visits Trinidad, British Guiana, Surinam, Martinique and Jamaica, all of them "borrowed cultures." He has few illusions about the future of the entire region, now largely freed from that colonialism which had been so often blamed for its misfortunes. Many of the issues discussed in this volume reappear in *The Mimic Men.* A close relation exists between Naipaul's travel books and his fiction, the travel books often serving as raw material for the novels.

He returns to the West Indies once again in *The Loss of El Dorado* (1969), a historical work in which he explores the origins of modern Trinidad. He highlights two key events: the founding of Port of Spain in 1592 by Antonio de Berrio, a belated conquistador obsessed by the legend of El Dorado and the capture of the island by the British in 1797. Berrio, quite out of his mind, spent the last years of his life in a mad search for the golden city. And the first British governor, a deranged sadist, reveled in hangings and floggings and was finally brought to trial for torturing a young mulatto girl. But by that time the West Indies were already rapidly becoming the backwaters of the empire. Naipaul handles these events with a novelist's skill and sense of drama, but he also exhibits that vital feeling for history which is apparent throughout his later work. Using unpublished archival material, he vividly evokes what Walter Allen has called "the contradictions and the tragic absurdities, the whole inheritance of cruelty and chaos" which marks the history of the Caribbean.

In 1962 Naipaul went to India for a year, traveling widely: south to Madras, east to Calcutta, north to Kashmir, where he spent several months. He accompanied a crowd of pilgrims to a holy cave high in the Himalayas and visited his grandfather's desolate native village in Uttar Pradesh. He records his impressions in *An Area of Darkness* (1964), which, on its appearance, provoked cries of protest from Indian intellectuals. H.B. Singh branded Naipaul as "a despicable lackey of neo-colonialism" who deserves "utter contempt." Another critic claimed that "the area of darkness" is within Naipaul himself. In 1977 came *India: A Wounded Civilization*. For Naipaul, India is "a difficult country." It isn't his home, but he cannot reject it because of his family background. On this second visit he wished to investigate the "Emergency" of 1976, when Indira Gandhi had in effect seized absolute power. He reaches the conclusion that with this suppression of democratic institutions and "with no foreign conqueror to impose a new order," India is now forced to face alone "the blankness of its decayed civilization."

The Return of Eva Perón (1980) contains four essays written between 1972 and 1975: **"Michael X and the Black Power Killings in Trinidad," "The Return of Eva Perón," "A New King for the Congo: Mobutu and the Nihilism of Africa"** and **"Conrad's Darkness."** These essays have close links with the novels. The "Author's Note" states: "These pieces . . . bridged a creative gap; from the end of 1970 to the end of 1973, no novel offered itself to me. . . . Out of these journeys and these writings, novels did in the end come to me." Many of Naipaul's articles and some of the more important of his numerous book reviews are included in *The Overcrowded Barracoon* (1972). They include **"*Cannery Row* Revisited,"** a particularly interesting piece, since Steinbeck's book has sometimes been mentioned as a forerunner of *Miguel Street.*

Among the Believers: An Islamic Journey, the most recent (1981) and the least well-received of Naipaul's nonfiction books, contains observations on his seven-month trip to four countries—Iran, Pakistan, Malaysia and Indonesia—which are all undergoing Islamic revolutions. It has been pointed out that, curiously, the volume has nothing to say about any Arab state. Specialists have noted that Naipaul seems inadequately prepared to deal accurately with a complex phenomenon which varies from country to country. And his fondness for anecdote and personal narrative often leads him to pay relatively little attention to crucial events taking place in the Islamic world during his trip: the storming of the American Embassy in Teheran; the violent incidents in the Great Mosque in Mecca; the Russian invasion of Afghanistan; the reign of martial law in Pakistan. In the section on Pakistan there is a chapter titled "Killing History," deploring the violence with which Islam "tramples on the past." Islam's kind of "selective history" fuels the rage that Naipaul encountered wherever he went, the rage to kill and to destroy, a love of violence masquerading as faith ("Islam sanctified rage"). But sometimes he has the fleeting impression that Islam can give people a kind of serenity, a feeling of completeness—if only the world outside, the

world of Western technology which the "Believers" hate but without which they cannot get along, could only be cast away.

But remarkable as Naipaul's travel books may be, he is essentially a novelist, and it is as a novelist that his achievement must be evaluated. In the field of fiction he is certainly no innovator. He has mastered the craft of traditional narrative and shows little interest in technical experiment. He is closer to Dickens or Balzac than he is to Joyce or *le nouveau roman;* his concern is to tell a story and also to discuss ideas. He would never subscribe to Flaubert's ideal to "write a book about nothing." *Miguel Street*—the first of his Trinidad stories to be written, although it was published in 1959, after *The Mystic Masseur* and *The Suffrage of Elvira*—consists of a series of sketches about a lower-class neighborhood in Port of Spain. There is the vivacious Laura, mother of eight children by as many fathers, "whose shouts and curses were the richest things I ever heard. She like Shakespeare when it comes to using words." There we also encounter B. Wordsworth, the poet who had never written poetry but who lived it; Man-man, who thought he was the Messiah and who sent out invitations for his crucifixion; Eddoes, "one of the aristocrats of the street" because he drove the garbage truck and only had to work mornings.

Miguel Street differs from most West Indian writing about the poor in that it expresses no overt social protest, but rather a humorous delight in these colorful characters, apparently happy in spite of their poverty. These vignettes, with their mix of sentimentality and irony (and perhaps with a dash of condescension as well), are always charming and occasionally even somewhat coy. The leading character of *The Mystic Masseur* (1957), Ganesh, already appears in *Miguel Street* no longer as a pundit in a dhoti but as a rising politician in "an expensive looking lounge suit." Pundit Ganesh Ramsummmari, after having failed in a series of undertakings, finally gains a reputation as a learned man and a mystic. He then embarks on a political career, is elected to the Trinidad Legislative Council, becomes more and more British and finally assumes the name of G. Ramsay Muir, M.B.E.

> **After *Biswas* the novelist's vision of the world grows darker. He will never be able to find his way back to the innocence of *Miguel Street*. The years in England had confirmed his feelings about the secondhand quality of his place of birth.**
> **—John L. Brown**

The Suffrage of Elvira (1958) also treats of Trinidad politics. A rich Hindu, Harbans, is seeking election to the Legislative Council from the Elvira district. Democracy "had taken everybody by surprise" when it had come to Elvira after the war, and no one is very sure how it should work. So here, as elsewhere, Elvira apes the world outside. Harbans hires a truck with a loudspeaker and a brash young campaign manager to drive it and blat out the campaign slogans. He passes out free "rum vouchers" so that prospective supporters can get drunk free and democratically in the local rumshop. However, success finally depends on buying up the votes. Harbans wins the election, but it has cost him a lot of money. As he leaves Elvira, he shakes his fist at the countryside he is now representing and shouts: "Elvira, you is a bitch." As usual in these Trinidad stories, Naipaul shows an enviable command of local language: "you talking arseness"; "you suckastic and insultive in my pussonal." These electoral antics in Elvira are marvelously entertaining. But Naipaul is also expressing concern about the degradation of democracy in many emerging countries. Only in the emerging countries? Harban's comment, as he is forced to bribe more and more, has an uncomfortably familiar ring: "'They should pass some sort of law to prevent candidates from spending so much money, . . .' But then he pulled out his wallet."

The last of the Trinidad novels, *A House for Mr Biswas* (1961), goes beyond local color to embrace a universal theme: the desire of a man to have a home of his own, to "be somebody" in his own right. Looking back on his early years, Naipaul has created a "remembrance of things past," a large-scale chronicle teeming with life and rich in feeling. It retraces the history of a tentacular Hindu family, the Tulsis, into which the poor orphan Mr Biswas marries nearly by accident, admitted only because he is a Brahmin and the Tulsis are of an inferior caste with many daughters to provide for. But they are prosperous. They own a store, a sugar plantation and a big house, where all the tribe live in stifling proximity. The sons-in-law are expected to work on the family properties. As a man who knows how to read, Biswas refuses to work in the fields; so he is assigned to manage a small grocery shop the family owns. But he has no business sense and is given another job as an assistant overseer on the sugar plantation, where he and his family are forced to live in one room in the barracks. Unable to stand it, he manages to build a cheap house on a nearby site. A house of his own! But a tropical storm wrecks it, and he is forced to return to tribal life with the Tulsis. He takes refuge in reading: "He discovered the solace of Dickens." He finds pleasure in transferring Dickens's characters and settings "to people and places that he knew," as perhaps Naipaul himself did in writing *Mr Biswas*. By a stroke of luck, Biswas gets a newspaper job, and although he is still under the roof (and the thumb!) of the Tulsis, his prestige as a journalist makes life more tolerable. He also derives comfort from his children, especially his only son, a bright boy who eventually wins a scholarship to study abroad.

Conventional, romantic love has little place in Naipaul's world. Biswas's relations with his wife seem without affection. Her deepest loyalties are to the tribe rather than to her husband. Only with his son does Biswas exhibit any real tenderness. Finally, he manages to borrow money to buy a rundown dwelling. After a heart attack he loses his job but is able to take refuge in "a home of his own," and soon afterward he dies there, under his own roof, content in spite of all the disappointments and frustrations of his life. Naipaul, so often lacking in emotional warmth, clearly has a special affection for Biswas. He succeeds admirably in communicating this affection to the reader. Of all his novels, this is perhaps the most appealingly human.

After *Biswas* the novelist's vision of the world grows darker. He will never be able to find his way back to the innocence of *Miguel Street*. The years in England had confirmed his feelings about the secondhand quality of his place of birth. Determined to avoid being categorized as a "West Indian writer," he set out in his next book, *Mr Stone and the Knights Companion* (1963), to write of British life and proved himself an expert craftsman who could do it extremely well. The protagonist, Mr Stone, has spent his obscure career as a clerk in a large London firm. On the eve of his retirement he dreams up a program by which the pensioned employees will get together to assist the less fortunate retirees. Management backs the scheme, and Stone hopes that it means he will acquire a prestige he never enjoyed before. But a brash public-relations man takes over, and Stone is once again relegated to obscurity.

The Mimic Men (1967) is set largely in Trinidad (here called "Isabella"), although the opening and closing sections take place in London, where the narrator Ralph Singh studied as a young man and to which he has now returned as an ex-minister in disgrace. He is only forty, but he knows that he is washed up: "The career of a colonial politician is short and ends brutally." Back home from England, he has embarked on a profitable real-estate operation and has become involved in politics. But the exercise of power cannot conceal from him the void of his "bastard world." He and others like him "in Isabella and in 20 other countries" are all "mimic men." Some readers branded the novel as reactionary, and many of Singh's opinions would seem to justify the accusation. He describes Isabella in the colonial period as "a benevolently administered dependency." He has a nostalgia for "the good old days" on the great cocoa plantations. But the old regime was not as benevolent as that and was marked, as *The Loss of El Dorado* makes clear, by horrifying brutality. Still, it would be an error to label Singh (or his creator) simplistically as neocolonialist. Both "write from both sides." Singh "hates oppression and fears the oppressed." He is aware, like many disillusioned liberals, that the oppressed, once delivered from oppression, are swift to become oppressors in their turn. Singh shares

Naipaul's interest in history, deplores that "there is no such thing as history nowadays . . . only the pamphleteering of churls." In both of them there lurks more than a hint of snobbishness, of Brahmin superiority. (Naipaul has written an essay, **"What's Wrong with Being a Snob?"**) And as the exiled Singh meditates on the history of Isabella, with "its hunters and hunted, rulers and ruled," he realizes that its message is cruelly clear: nothing is secure. So, alone in London, he settles down to accept "the final emptiness" which, it is implied, awaits us all.

The short stories in *A Flag on the Island* (1967) restate familiar themes: placelessness, alienation, meaninglessness, the illusion of "progress." The title novella deals with the return to a Caribbean island by an American soldier who had been there during the war and who is saddened at the devastation wrought by tourism and by the vulgarity of a gadget civilization.

In a Free State (1971) consists of the two journal entries **"The Tramp at Piraeus"** and **"The Circus at Luxor,"** and two short stories—**"One Out of Many,"** about an East Indian trying to adjust to life in Washington, D.C., and **"Tell Me Who to Kill,"** an account of a West Indian and his brother adrift in London—as well as the novella **"In a Free State,"** one of Naipaul's outstanding achievements. All the characters in this last-named work have in one fashion or another escaped the constraints of their own culture to live in a "free state," only to discover that they don't belong anywhere. Geographically, the "free state" is a recently independent African country, torn by civil war between the new president and the old tribal king, who is in flight before the government forces and who is finally murdered by them. The protagonist Bobby, a neurotic, homosexual Englishman, works for the government as a foreign expert. He longs to be a part of African society. He wears native-style shirts, attempts to speak the patois of the region, seeks friendship (and love) among the natives. During his stay in the capital for professional meetings he attempts to pick up a young Zulu, who disdainfully rejects him and spits in his face. The next morning he sets out to drive back to his work in "the Southern Collectorate," accompanied by Linda, the wife of one of his colleagues. During the long trip the two keep talking randomly away, but they have little to say to each other, since Linda does not share Bobby's enthusiasm for Africa.

Naipaul masterfully conveys the feel of the country they are driving through, in all its vastness, emptiness and menace. They stop for the night in a run-down inn, once a tourist attraction, now unfrequented because of civil disorder. The proprietor, a crusty old colonial, reveals in a confrontation with one of the black servants all the hatred that exists between the few whites remaining in the area and the natives bent on taking over. The next day Bobby and Linda press on through the empty land, occasionally surprised by bizarre

sights: "Two men ran out into the road . . . they were naked and chalked white from head to toe, white as the rocks." When Bobby stops to inquire about a rumored curfew, he is seized and beaten (for no clear-cut reason) by a group of soldiers and is then permitted to go on his way. On their arrival in the compound, Luke, the houseboy, begins to laugh at the battered Bobby, and Bobby knows that he must "sack" him in order to preserve his own dignity. This unsettling narrative, for all its strangeness, gives an impression of a frightening authenticity, and as we read contemporary African history, we sense that Naipaul's view of things may be uncomfortably close to the unreal reality.

Before the appearance of *Guerrillas* (1975) Naipaul was relatively little known in the U.S. Of course his earlier fiction, even that dealing with revolutionary situations in newly independent countries, had avoided sensationalism, had appealed mostly to a literate minority. *Guerrillas,* on the other hand, struck a new note with its emphasis on brutality and on the explicit treatment of morbid sexuality. A deliberately bleak and nihilistic work, it made nevertheless a greater impact here than anything he had previously written, was extravagantly praised, even overpraised as "the masterpiece of the best novelist now writing." All the characters—from Jimmy Ahmed, the confused, self-dramatizing Black Power leader; to Jane, the Anglo-Canadian victim of his sadistic hate; to Roche, the South African dissident; to Bryant, Jimmy's slum-boy lover—are at once pitiful and repulsive, minimonsters smelling of "rotten meat" (one of Jimmy's frequently used expressions). The novel itself, however, is no more macabre than the events on which it is based, recounted in the essay **"Michael X and the Black Power Killings."**

Peter Roche, banned from South Africa after having suffered torture and imprisonment, arrives on a West Indian island as a public-relations man for a foreign company bent on improving its image and also on counteracting any incipient revolutionary disturbances. He is accompanied by his mistress Jane, who (like her real-life counterpart in **"Michael X"**) is looking for thrills and for the excitement she identifies with Black Power. Roche becomes associated with Jimmy Ahmed, half black, half Chinese, who, after having been deported from England where he had achieved a certain notoriety in "radical chic" circles as "the black Pekinese" of salon revolutionaries, has founded an agricultural commune "for the land and for the Revolution." The enterprise is financed in part by Roche's company, who see in it a possible means of defusing certain potentially dangerous elements in the island's urban youth gangs. Jane, bored with Roche, no longer the heroic figure she imagined him to be, takes Jimmy to bed, although it is difficult to see what either one finds attractive in the other. Meanwhile, the slaying by the police of Stephens, a young black gang leader who had briefly belonged to Jimmy's commune, provokes an abortive popular uprising. Houses are burned, stores looted. But soon the government, with the support of "Americans" in helicopters, restores order of a sort. These events persuade Jane that it is time to get out, but, drawn by the odor of "rotten meat," she goes to pay a last visit to Jimmy. Their final sexual encounter, at once savage and absurd (in these matters Naipaul is at his least convincing), ends with Jimmy's offering Jane as a victim to his young lover ("Bryant, the rat, kill the rat"); the hysterical, hate-crazed boy hacks her gruesomely to death with his cutlass. Roche, probably aware that Jane has been done away with, destroys her papers so that there will be no evidence that she ever existed, and, fearful for his own life, prepares ingloriously to flee.

Africa evidently made a deep impression on Naipaul, as *A Bend in the River* (1979) testifies. One of his major achievements, much larger in scale than *In a Free State* and rich in Conradian resonances, it merits the comparison sometimes made to *Heart of Darkness*. Naipaul's characters, however, lack the tragic dimensions of Conrad's Kurtz, who had, at least in the beginning, nourished the hope that humane concern might bring light into the darkness. In Naipaul's work, on the contrary, the characters have long since renounced such an illusion—if indeed they ever had it at all. For its subject matter, *A Bend in the River* draws largely on the essay **"A New King for the Congo: Mobutu and the Nihilism of Africa"** but demonstrates once again how a novelist of Naipaul's gifts can convey a new density, a deeper significance to "facts," can absorb and transform the document.

Naipaul's preoccupation with history and with historical change is everywhere apparent. Early in the story the narrator Salim, the son of an Indian Moslem family installed for generations on the African coast, realizes that with the rise of revolutionary movements "another tide of history was coming to wash us away." He decides to strike out on his own and acquires a store in a small city in Zaire, on "a bend in the river." He finds the town in shambles after the disorders which followed the departure of the Belgians: "You were in a place where the future had come and gone." But soon the new president, backed up with tough white mercenaries, succeeds in imposing order of a sort, and the town comes to life again. The little foreign colony draws a breath of relief and settles down to make money. Naipaul hates the greed of the Europeans, but he is swift to point out that the Africans are just as greedy. The native officials, gathered in the newly opened Bigburger, "wore as much gold as possible—gold-rimmed glasses, gold rings, gold pen and pencil sets, gold watches."

On the outskirts of the town, the president ("the Big Man") creates a showy institute for the training of young officials and for international meetings to which Western experts on African affairs, picturesquely clad in native costumes, are invited. The director of the center, a middle-aged Belgian professor, had been "the Big Man's white man," but he is aware that he is on the skids, that his boss has no further need of him. Salim engages in a rather absentminded liaison with the director's young wife. Their couplings are marked by sadistic violence; on one occasion she falls to the floor under Salim's blows: "Then I used my feet on her." Soon conditions again grow worse for the foreign colony. The Big Man nationalizes all foreign property and distributes it to the "people." Salim becomes the manager of his own store, now the property of an illiterate native called Citoyen Théotime. Anxious to make money in order to get out, he engages in illegal traffic in ivory, is flung into jail and later gains release only through the intervention of Ferdinand, a young native whom he had befriended in the past and who had risen to be "a commissioner." But in spite of his official position, Ferdinand too is deathly afraid. He foresees mass killings when the Big Man arrives to conduct a purge: "They're going to kill and kill and kill." Salim manages to get on the steamer—perhaps the last one for some time—that is leaving the next morning. But we know as well as he does that there is nowhere for him to go.

These works of his maturity reveal that Naipaul is far more than "the most gifted West Indian novelist of his generation," more indeed than the most compelling and troubling of the writers who have confronted the tragic contradictions of the Third World. He implies that their problems—placelessness, disorder, violence, racial hatred, irrational frenzy, self-destroying greed—may be ours as well. We can certainly accept the validity of his grim premonitions. It is more difficult, however, to accept the bleak and intransigent hopelessness with which he views the human situation. Throughout his work he has always insisted that he refuses to take a position "for" or "against." But, on a deeper level, he is a partisan, indeed a fierce partisan of an apocalyptic conception of history whose dogmatic blackness betrays a romantic immaturity. His knowledge of the past should have shown him that every ending is also a beginning, that neither men or events are inexorably predestined, that the human adventure is an eternally disconcerting mixture of good and evil, of darkness and light—even though the light may often seem very faint and flickering indeed. But so far he has wagered consistently on the triumph of darkness, insufficiently aware that prophets announcing the end of the world have appeared in every generation in the past and that, in spite of their prophecies, new worlds have arisen to take the place of those which have passed away. But of course these past cultures were unprovided with nuclear playthings.

James Atlas (interview date March 1987)

SOURCE: "V. S. vs. The Rest," in *Vanity Fair*, Vol. 50, March, 1987, pp. 64-8.

[In the following interview, Atlas offers insight into Naipaul's methods and motivations.]

"Whatever the labor of any piece of writing, whatever its creative challenges and satisfactions, time had always taken me away from it," recalls V.S. Naipaul in *The Enigma of Arrival,* out this month from Knopf. "And, with time passing, I felt mocked by what I had already done; it seemed to belong to a time of vigor, now past for good. Emptiness, restlessness built up again; and it was necessary once more, out of my internal resources alone, to start on another book, to commit myself to that consuming process again."

From this process has come Naipaul's most self-revealing book, the chronicle of an inward journey that proved more harrowing than his travels in darkest Africa. *The Enigma of Arrival* marks a culmination in Naipaul's career; an autobiography in the form of a novel, it explains with ardor and eloquence what drove him to produce a body of work that makes him the rival of anyone writing in English.

Naipaul's books are fiercely candid, but he detests publicity and rarely sits for interviews. He's known to be proud, imperious, even rude. "His contempt is severe," notes Paul Theroux. His widely quoted opinion of the publishing scene: "an extraordinarily shoddy, dirty, dingy world" dominated by men with "the morality and the culture of barrow boys—street sellers, people pushing rotten apples." The people of his native Trinidad were "Monkeys," he once said, for whom "drumbeating is a higher activity." Every culture was primitive in its own way, even Oxford—"a very second-rate provincial university." On the way to see Naipaul, I remembered David Hare's portrait of Victor Mehta, the haughty Indian writer (based on Naipaul) in *A Map of the World,* whose books include a novel about journalists entitled *The Vermin Class.*

Naipaul's flat was on a quiet residential street of tidy redbrick apartments that had a newly renovated look. He led me down the hall past several sparsely furnished rooms and ushered me into the dining room. I asked if he had just moved in. "Yes, but I'm leaving," he said tersely. "The walls are too thin."

I wasn't surprised. Naipaul's characters are forever pulling up stakes, establishing themselves in seedy boarding-houses, then departing without a trace. Over the years, he has lived in India, Africa, South America, the Middle East. The Wiltshire village described so lovingly in his new book is the only permanent home he's ever had. Naipaul has lived there—first in a modest rented cottage, then in a house he bought and restored—for seventeen years.

Small, fastidious, precise in his gestures, Naipaul wears a plain gray sport coat and a blue tie. His hair is ebony black. Now fifty-four, he looks weary but fit; he's vegetarian, drinks sparingly, does yogic exercises every morning. His features are delicate, austere; his expression is often pained.

In the dining room a woman, white-haired but with a handsome, youthful face—a character out of Iris Murdoch—brings us tea and slips away. It can only be Naipaul's wife, Patricia Hale, who for many years has closely edited his work. They met at Oxford and married in 1955. Yet no reader of Naipaul could presume him married; in twenty books, the only intimation of anyone else in the picture occurs in *An Area of Darkness,* where he refers—once—to his "companion." When he taught at Wesleyan, his wife remained in England. In the Wiltshire cottage, where he writes his books, he lives alone.

I ask him about *The Enigma of Arrival.* Why did he decide to write about England? "I've only been here thirty-six years," he says with a laugh. "It takes time to adjust." And why has he chosen to call the book a novel when it's so obviously autobiographical? "It has an autobiographical *crust,*" he concedes, "but it's not an autobiography in the usual sense. It's impersonal. The man has no qualities of his own. He's anonymous, an observer. No detail of his own life ever intrudes."

Naipaul talks about himself with an eerie detachment: "One was lost in London." "One had no idea who one was." "One was alone." More than any other writer I know, he has invented himself, pieced together a coherent identity out of a multifarious past. Trinidad, where he was born in 1932, was "a dot on the map," he's often complained, "a ridiculous little island." A place—if you had ambition—to escape. "When I was in the fourth form," he recalled in *The Middle Passage,* "I wrote a vow on the endpaper of my Kennedy's *Revised Latin Primer* to leave within five years. I left after six; and for many years afterwards in England, falling asleep in bedsitters with the electric fire on, I had been awakened by the nightmare that I was back in tropical Trinidad." Why nightmare? I ask. "If you're from Trinidad, you want to get away," he says grimly. "You can't write if you're from the bush."

In 1950, Naipaul took up residence at Oxford on a government scholarship, but he's made no literary use of the experience (unlike just about every other writer who ever put in time there), and he's reluctant to discuss those years. "It was a difficult time," he says softly. "There was lack of money, uncertainty, great worry about my family. I was very isolated. My studies were of no importance. They didn't interest me." Hadn't there been some kind of emotional crisis at Oxford? "I had a mental disturbance owing to the strangeness of where I was, to loneliness. One was so far from home," he says. "So far from what one knew. It was an alien world, Oxford." He pauses. "It was clear one would remain a stranger."

It wasn't until he arrived in London at the age of twenty-one that his life as a writer began in earnest. "It was the most artificial thing for me to be a writer," he says now. "As a boy in Trinidad, I wanted to be a scientist, then a painter, but I couldn't buy a tube of paint." Installed at a desk in the typing room of the BBC, where he worked as a broadcaster for the Caribbean Service, he wrote a novel that was never published, began another, then a third. It was an arduous apprenticeship. "I was confined to a smaller world than I had ever known. I became my flat, my desk, my name." To have emerged out of Trinidad by way of India—his grandfather arrived from the province of Uttar Pradesh in the 1880s—was to have been doubly exiled from the start. To become a novelist in the stratified, class-conscious world of literary London was yet another form of exile. In a piece entitled **"London"** that appeared in the *T.L.S.* in 1958, Naipaul complained that he had written three books and made £300. "The Americans do not want me because I am too British. The public here do not want me because I am too foreign."

Still, three books—what strikes anyone is how precocious he was. Two of those books had appeared in print by the time he was twenty-six; they won prizes and got excellent reviews (from, among others, Kingsley Amis). By the time he published his masterpiece, *A House for Mr. Biswas,* he was an established writer in England, with a small but loyal following. He was a year shy of thirty. A triumph? Naipaul didn't see it that way. "I had dreamed of coming to England," he writes in *The Enigma of Arrival.* "But my life in England had been savorless, and much of it mean."

The main event of this novel-autobiography is a second nervous breakdown, suffered when Naipaul was in his late thirties, a "grief, too deep for tears or rage," brought on by the failure of a book. For two years he'd been working on a history of Trinidad (*The Loss of El Dorado*). In the midst of his research he resolved to leave England and go back to the New World. "The house I had bought and renovated in stages I sold; and my furniture and books and papers went to the warehouse." Four months later, a "calamity" occurred. The book was turned down; the publisher who'd commissioned it "wanted only a book for tourists." Naipaul was forced to return to England. Broke, exhausted, in need of a refuge, he retreated to a Wiltshire cottage on the grounds of a manor inhabited by a reclusive landlord, and it was there, "in that unlikely setting, in the ancient heart of England, a place where I was truly an alien, [that] I found I was given a second chance, a new life, richer and fuller than any I had had anywhere else."

These days Naipaul seems utterly at home in England. His clothes are tweedy, his shirts bespoke; his accent is unswervingly "U"; until a few years ago he ordered snuff from Fribourg & Treyer and dipped it with a silver spoon. He carries a British passport and thinks of himself as a British writer. (One publisher who made the mistake of advertising Naipaul as "a West Indian writer" was quickly dropped.) Yet he's often had bitter things to say about his adopted land. A decade ago he described England as "a country of second-rate people—bum politicians, scruffy writers and crooked aristocrats."

When I remind Naipaul of this observation, he questions me closely about my sources. "I wouldn't make big remarks about England now," he says mildly. "It's a very humane place." What about the racism he encountered? The wrong word, I discover. "That is an eighties word," he says, slapping the table. "Don't oversimplify. We must not use anachronistic words." His dark, hooded eyes are bright with anger. "People come from all over; they have all kinds of roots. There's nothing strange about it. If you're an Eskimo, you want to define yourself." The humiliations he recalled with such agonized fervor in his work—the sense of excludedness, of marginality, that afflicts so many of his early characters transplanted from the West Indies to London—have given way to a sense of "racial pride." The crisis is over. England has become that green and pleasant land.

In *The Enigma of Arrival,* Naipaul surveys the gardens and valleys and farms of rural Wiltshire, the manor and its decaying grounds, the cottage where he writes his books, with a naturalist's penetrating eye. Beneath the picturesque surface, the shady lanes and meandering streams so beloved of urban exiles, is an aura of ominous change. In the course of the book, barbed-wire fences appear; the roads are paved over; buildings vanish overnight, leveled and replaced by new ones. Naipaul's Wiltshire is about as idyllic as Hardy's. No, he says, it wasn't the landscape that attracted him; it was the community, his neighbors—the gardener, the servants in the manor house, the owner of the local car service. "One was dealing with people," he says with obvious feeling. "One was brought closer to others. They were available to one. It's the most benign place I've ever known."

A virtual recluse when he's working, Naipaul seldom answers letters from people he doesn't know, and insists that he hardly ever sees anyone. "I know fewer and fewer people," he says. Yet somehow when a name comes up—Theroux, Anthony Powell—it's someone Naipaul has talked to lately. "Very social people like Antonia Fraser—people who could lend him a cottage for the weekend—were onto him from the start," recalls the critic John Gross of Naipaul's early days in London. In New York, there are dinner parties given by his publisher at Lutèce; there's the New York literary-dinner-party circuit. When he does go out, he goes out in style.

In the same way, he shrugs off references to his reputation. Routinely acknowledged as one of the pre-eminent writers of our day, frequently mentioned as a candidate for the Nobel Prize, he still maintains that he's largely ignored. "One never knows where one stands." He doesn't read the *Sunday Times,* not even when his own books are reviewed. Only once, in 1971, did he monitor the reception of a book he'd published. And what book was that? "I don't like to speak the names of my books," he says. Back in my room, I discover that it was *In a Free State,* for which he won England's prestigious Booker Prize, worth £12,000. Was he caught up in the speculation about its chances? For all his asceticism, Naipaul is keenly interested in money. "The capitalistic streak in him runs very deep," confirms one of his friends. He likes to know how much things cost. (He once asked a journalist if his wristwatch was a genuine Cartier.) He's reputed to be merciless in negotiating contracts. Last year, after he'd turned in *The Enigma of Arrival,* publishing circles in New York were full of talk about a proposal Naipaul's agent had circulated to several publishers for a new book, tentatively entitled *Slave States: A Journey Through the American South.* The asking price was said to be $300,000. Eventually, according to one source, there was a much lower offer. The project was shelved. "In the beginning, one was badly represented," he recalls. "I was a great believer in the adage that virtue would look after itself. Nowadays one is more clear-sighted." A few months ago, he stunned his London publisher, André Deutsch, by leaving for another house—Viking. Deutsch had handled Naipaul for twenty-nine years; he had published every one of Naipaul's books. "He never even thought it appropriate to send a postcard," says a bewildered Deutsch.

That is Naipaul: abrupt, easily slighted, wary of allegiances. "My vocation made me a free man," he declares. "I never had to stay in a job, never had to work for anybody. The peasant doesn't work for anyone else." He likes to say that he has no enemies, no rivals, no masters. "I fear no one." Perhaps not. But his books simmer with scarcely suppressed rage—the refugees gunned down on a barge in *A Bend in the River,* the rape-murder that ends *Guerrillas.* "Hate oppression; fear the oppressed," writes Naipaul's exiled Caribbean minister Ralph Singh in *The Mimic Men.* Once, on a visit to New York, he became so antagonistic about the people he saw on the street that a publisher cautioned him, "I wouldn't go around talking like that. You can get killed."

Yet he's capable of incredible tenderness and empathy. Think of the "Traveller's Prelude" to *An Area of Darkness*—to me the most powerful scene in all of Naipaul's work. It describes, in charged, hallucinatory prose, the night

of a cruise ship's arrival at the dock in Alexandria, the passengers besieged by horse-drawn cabs jostling for a fare.

> Not far away, below a lamp standard stood a lone cab. It had been there since the late afternoon; it had withdrawn early from the turmoil around the terminal. It had had no fares, and there could be no fares for it now. The cab-lamp burned low; the horse was eating grass from a shallow pile on the road. The driver, wrapped against the wind, was polishing the dully gleaming hood of his cab with a large rag. The polishing over, he dusted; then he gave the horse a brief, brisk rub down. Less than a minute later he was out of his cab again, polishing, dusting, brushing. He went in; he came out. His actions were compulsive. The animal chewed; his coat shone; the cab gleamed. And there were no fares.

The obscure, the expendable, the unmourned: these are the ones who haunt Naipaul. His books on India especially are chronicles of a nation he's likened to hell. What he saw there—men reduced to objects, men starving in the dust—appalled him. His critics have claimed that Naipaul is an enemy of the Third World, that he condescends to it. "The condescension is in those who don't notice," he responds. "You've got to be awfully liberal not to be moved by distress. When you see human degradation on that scale, you can never be the same again."

Reading Naipaul, you feel the powerful urgency that impels his talent. His genius is a genius lashed on by the sheer will to write. "One was so driven by ambition for so long," he says, "endlessly able to pick oneself up. There was always something over the hill." He writes his books in tremendous bursts of concentration. "I can't *be* with a book for more than thirteen or fourteen months," he says. "It's in one's head. You're absorbed with it all the living day. I've written each book as if it was the last book I was going to write." Writing for Naipaul is a desperate act; he once described the process as "a sickening." No, he replies sharply when I mention having read this: it's more a feeling of uncertainty. Does he still find writing difficult? "Not *difficult*," he snaps. "*Uncertain* is the word I used: full of stops and starts." But again and again he persists to the end, "fighting the Monkey side of my nature," as he once put it.

In the closing pages of *The Enigma of Arrival,* Naipaul recounts the sudden death of his younger sister and his journey back to Trinidad for her funeral. The book is dedicated to his brother, Shiva, who died eighteen months ago of a heart attack in London at the age of forty. If the new book is in some ways more benign, less despairing than his others, it's still a book about death. Jack the gardener dies, Mr. Phillips the caretaker dies, the handyman murders his wife. The landscape itself begins to die, changed beyond recognition. What is the lesson of this book? "I know that we all die, that books date very, very quickly now," Naipaul says wearily, shielding his eyes. "The book culture is fading. Books are no longer important."

Naipaul's talk on this darkening afternoon is dominated by death. "I'm close to the end of creativity." "Death is very, very final." "I've put all my affairs in order." But isn't this simply the exhaustion of finishing a project? "Writing isn't a young man's game," he acknowledges. "It's for the mature, the suffering, the wounded—for people who need elucidation." He used to say he was old at thirty-four; at fifty-four, he has written more, seen more, lived more than most of his contemporaries. But he's still only middle-aged, I point out. He fixes me with his black, penetrating eyes. "I'm telling you how I feel." He hesitates. "There are no children . . . Perhaps that would have made it easier."

Our interview done, Naipaul is suddenly relaxed, affable, even gay. To my utter astonishment, I hear us talking about a subject so incongruous that I actually begin to blush. How much money do you need to live in New York? Naipaul interrogates me intently: $100,000? $150,000? $200,000? And how much does a journalist make? I laugh in disbelief and shrug. Do I own my apartment? he presses me. Does one hear people overhead? How much are co-ops going for these days? Under prompting, I offer a figure. He shakes his head: "Unbelievable."

Out on the street, walking among the twilight crowd, I glance back at Naipaul's window, a square of light in the dark, and think of the cabman alone on the dock.

Patrick Parrinder (essay date 1987)

SOURCE: "A Novel for Our Time: V. S. Naipaul's *Guerrillas*," in *The Failure of Theory: Essays on Criticism and Contemporary Fiction*, The Harvester Press, 1987, pp. 185-206.

[*In the following essay, Parrinder addresses a number of themes in* Guerrillas, *including the notion of the "Noble Robber" and sexual violation.*]

I

I think there's an element of nostalgia in reading Hardy, and even in reading Dickens or George Eliot. There is narrative there, the slow development of character, and people are longing for this vanished, ordered world. Today, every man's experience of dislocation is so private that unless a writer absolutely matches that particular man's experience

the writer seems very private and obscure. So I think the art of fiction is becoming a curious, shattered thing. . . . I think it may be that the world now requires another kind of imaginative interpretation.

An autobiography can distort; facts can be realigned. But fiction never lies: it reveals the writer totally.

Of the five contemporary novelists considered in Part II of this book, Anthony Burgess, Muriel Spark and Doris Lessing were born in 1917, 1918, and 1919 respectively. V. S. Naipaul and B. S. Johnson belong to a younger generation, having been born in 1932 and 1933. These novelists are 'English' in the sense that their life and work has been centred in Britain and the Commonwealth rather than the United States. For all that, two are resident in Mediterranean countries, one (Muriel Spark) is of Scottish-Jewish descent, and both Muriel Spark and Doris Lessing spent much of their childhood in Southern Africa. V. S. Naipaul is a Trinidad East Indian. Several of the five (like most successful English writers of the century) probably derive a large proportion of their income from the United States. Only Johnson, a Londoner and a London novelist, satisfies *all* the standard criteria of 'Englishness'—or did so, that is, at the time of his suicide in 1973.

V. S. Naipaul's characters are, as often as not, homeless expatriates. Like them, their creator has no fixed audience or close-knit community to which he belongs. He is not even a 'novelist's novelist' in the Jamesian or Conradian sense, having shown himself to be as uneasy about the inherited traditions of the novel as any of his contemporaries. His novels do not seem to have been written according to predetermined patterns or preconceived theories, and they have appeared at irregular and increasingly lengthy intervals. He has spoken of writing as an instinctive, unconscious process: 'The world abrades one, one comes to certain resolutions and then one devises by instinct and through dreams and all kinds of senses a story that is a symbol for all this'. Novels and stories are offered to him (as he once put it) from time to time, though in the last dozen years he has published only two of them, *Guerrillas* (1975) and *A Bend in the River* (1979). Meanwhile, his writing and his occasional interviews have emphasised the contemporary novelist's idiosyncrasy, his determined isolation and cherished independence of his fellow-writers, groups and movements.

The belief that a writer's identity lies in his or her unpredictability and independence is a defining characteristic of the culture in which Lessing, Spark and Burgess, as well as Naipaul, are significant names. B. S. Johnson was another dedicated individualist, the leader, as it were, of a literary movement that was never permitted to attract more than one member. Almost any other contemporary English novelist of repute could be chosen to illustrate the same qualities of pluralism and idiosyncrasy. Literary theory would argue, however, that the individualism of these writers is simply one of the delusions of bourgeois liberalism.

It is curious that two of the opposing literary dogmas of the age—the creed of authorial independence and the structuralist theory of the 'death of the author'—should particularly attach themselves to the writing of novels. (Roland Barthes' seminal essay 'The Death of the Author', for instance, begins and ends with the question of whether Balzac was an 'Author'). Naipaul has described the novel as a literary form 'born at the same time as the spirit of rebellion', which 'expresses, on the aesthetic plane, the same ambition'. The concept of 'rebellion', which Naipaul derives from Albert Camus' *The Rebel*, refers in the first instance not to collective upheaval but to the action of an individual, which is 'representative' to the extent that it comes to be seen as focal and symbolic. The novel also is an act of individual, not of collective, creation. Unlike works for the cinema, the theatre and the concert hall, it is not dependent on the dynamics of group performance for its realisation. At the same time, novels are composed of time-honoured structures and devices whose function it is to disguise and dissipate their origins in the work of named individual producers. These devices, such as the fictitious narrator, the multiplication of internal discourses and the artificiality of the narrative situation have understandably been emphasised by formalist and poststructuralist criticism.

In the past, many novels not only had a fictitious narrator but remained anonymous or pseudonymous on their first appearance. Yet the novel as Naipaul has defined it—as an expression of the spirit of rebellion—cannot forever remain anonymous. The fact that anonymous or pseudonymous novels have often been presented as 'authentic' and 'nonfictional' documents before their authorship was revealed suggests that a novel, like an act of rebellion, may be constituted as such at the moment when somebody claims the responsibility for it. A hold-up or a bomb explosion requires the signature of an individual or an organisation in order to be construed as an act of rebellion or sabotage; and much the same may be said of the way that we recognise a novel. But the author remains invisible, 'underground', even though he has put his name to the text; all we know for certain is that the visible fictive structure is his handiwork. To recognise the author behind the fiction requires an inductive leap comparable to the leap we make when we come to see a crime or a display of intransigence as an intelligible act of rebellion.

This argument suggests that, if the 'death of the author' proclaimed by literary theory had indeed taken place, the novel could survive only as a 'curious, shattered thing', a feeble anachronism. On the other hand, if the novel remains healthy it is surely because the inductive leap which converts literary structures into forms of individual expression is still everywhere capable of being made. The two epigraphs to this chapter (which both date from the early 1970s) show how Naipaul, for one, has oscillated between the paralysis of doubt and the energy of faith. Both the moment of doubt and the moment of renewed energy are implicit in the dialectics of the novel as an act of self-assertive rebellion. As for Naipaul's expressed belief that fiction 'never lies', that it 'reveals the writer totally'—these statements are no less true for being, on the face of it, outrageous paradoxes. It is as if he were calmly declaring that the ideal of a morally transparent art of fiction—the ideal towards which B. S. Johnson had so valiantly and yet so laboriously striven—was attainable, as it were, by default: that fiction always reveals the author (just as the deed reveals its perpetrator) whether he likes it or not. This belief bespeaks a confidence in liberal humanism which Johnson, for one, could not feel. But Naipaul's liberalism is not of a traditional sort, any more than his fiction belongs to such crude theoretical categories as 'classic realism' or the 'conventional novel'. To make this case we must turn to *Guerrillas,* a major novel which I shall interpret as Naipaul's answer, given in the mid-1970s, to the question of the 'kind of imaginative interpretation' which the world now requires.

II

Does fiction 'never lie'? Does it 'reveal the writer totally'? The cliché of 'imaginative interpretation' is a reminder that the novel occupies a middle ground between journalism (which almost inevitably lies as it attempts to tell the truth) and fantasy (which reveals the writer even in the act of concealing him). The plot of *Guerrillas* shows marked similarities with a series of actual events in Naipaul's native Trinidad in 1971-2—events which he has outlined in a penetrating journalistic essay, **'Michael X and the Black Power Killings in Trinidad'** (1980). When *Guerrillas* first appeared some reviewers, aware of these events, mistook it for a documentary novel rather than a work of imaginative invention. It is not a documentary, as comparison with Naipaul's essay makes clear. Yet the essay also argues that the 'actual events' in Trinidad represented a horrifying and revealing acting-out of the fantasies of those responsible for them; and Naipaul in turn has fantasised about the events and has used his fantasy to explore the revelatory relations of the real and the fantastic. If the result is to be classed as fictional 'realism' then it is the realistic fiction of a fantasy age.

Even the title is a fantasy, for in *Guerrillas* no one is a guerrilla (though there is one disillusioned ex-guerrilla) and yet everyone fantasises about guerrillas. On the unnamed Caribbean island in which the novel is set 'the newspaper, the radio and the television spoke of guerrillas', but nobody really knows why they do so. The crimes and acts of violence that occur could be the manifestations of an organised revolutionary group, but it seems far more likely that they are the work of isolated bandits, fanatical sects, and criminal gangs. The government, however, has an interest in proving that the 'guerrillas' exist, and can be defeated, once it is confident of putting an end to the disturbances. The world-wide cult of the guerrilla which has inflamed the imaginations of many people on the island is responsible both for the spread of this collective fantasy and for the possibility of exploiting it.

Naipaul's most distinctive contribution to the 'terrorist novel' . . . is his exploration of the symbiotic relations between revolutionary violence and literary fantasy.
—*James Atlas*

A guerrilla is an irregular soldier. However, there are many other activities which overlap with guerrilla warfare to some extent, so that bandits, outlaws, terrorists, assassins, rebellious peasants, and agrarian revolutionaries all came to be associated with the cult of the guerrilla (which reached its height at the time of the killing of Che Guevara in Bolivia in 1967). *Guerrillas* is constructed around the figure of Jimmy Ahmed, a would-be revolutionary leader whose 'agricultural commune' on a disued colonial plantation is looked upon by the authorities as a 'cover for the guerrillas'. Although some parallels could be drawn with events in Jamaica and Grenada as well as Trinidad, the model for Jimmy Ahmed is Michael Abdul Malik, the former Black Power leader known as 'Michael X' who was hanged in Trinidad in 1975. Four years earlier, Michael X had returned to his and Naipaul's native island, where he started a commune on a suburban plot near Port of Spain. The produce of the 1 1/2-acre strip of land was to be sold at a 'People's Store'. Far from becoming a base for agrarian reform, the commune was soon torn apart by the murder of two of its own members.

It is a reflection of the well-publicised spread of guerrilla and terrorist activities in the last twenty years that there has grown up a genre of 'terrorist novels', comparable perhaps to the industrial novels of the 1840s and to the anarchist novels of the 1880s and '90s. In addition to *Guerrillas,* Doris Lessing's *The Good Terrorist,* Muriel Spark's *The Only Problem,* Brian Moore's *The Revolution Script,* Angus Wilson's *Setting the World on Fire,* and Raymond Williams's *The Volunteers* may be mentioned as examples of the form. Closely related to it are novels of violent social revolution, such as Nadine Gordimer's *July's People,* and novels of state terrorism and social upheaval such as Margaret Atwood's *Bodily Harm* and Naipaul's own *In a*

Free State. Many of these novels portray political violence from a 'middle-class' standpoint, but its handling in *Guerrillas* is unusually indirect: we do not even get an eye-witness account of the riots in which Jimmy Ahmed briefly emerges as a popular leader. Naipaul's most distinctive contribution to the 'terrorist novel', however, is his exploration of the symbiotic relations between revolutionary violence and literary fantasy. He has quoted a witness of the urban guerrillas in Argentina in the early 1970s as saying that 'They see themselves as a kind of comic-book hero. Clark Kent in the office by day, Superman at night, with a gun'. Of the murder of the Englishwoman Gale Benson, planned by Michael Abdul Malik and Hakim Jamal (an American Black Power campaigner) in Trinidad in 1971, Naipaul has written as follows:

> This was a literary murder, if ever there was one. Writing led both men there: for both of them, uneducated, but clever, hustlers with the black cause always to hand, operating always among the converted or half-converted, writing had for too long been a public relations exercise, a form of applauded lie, fantasy. And in Arima it was a fantasy of power that led both men to contemplate, from their different standpoints, the act of murder. . . . Benson, English and middle class, was just the victim Malik needed: his novel began to come to life.

Naipaul is probably unique among commentators on the Malik case in focussing on Michael X's unfinished novel, a primitive narrative which nevertheless serves as a 'pattern book, a guide to later events'. In it he was 'settling scores with the English middle class'. *Guerrillas,* like '**Michael X and the Black Power Killings in Trinidad',** tells the story of a literary murder, and in a certain sense both works are extended pieces of literary criticism.

Jimmy Ahmed's public statements, such as his *'Communique No 1'* and his noticeboard advertising the 'PEOPLE'S COMMUNE/ FOR THE LAND AND THE REVOLUTION', are themselves a species of fiction. In addition, *Guerrillas* offers lengthy extracts from Ahmed's correspondence and from the novel he is trying to write. Both Naipaul's novel and his essay on Michael X can be read as the work of a genuine novelist relentlessly exposing a bad and bogus one. In the essay, Michael X is portrayed as the creator of an elaborate murder plot: 'When he transferred his fantasy to real life', Naipaul observes, 'he went to work like the kind of novelist he would have liked to be'. Whether or not Jimmy Ahmed's involvement in murder is premeditated to this extent is hard to determine; on the whole it seems unlikely. The murder in *Guerrillas* is felt as inevitable and is the outcome of a powerful literary logic—but the 'author' of this particular plot is V. S. Naipaul, not one of his characters.

Jimmy Ahmed has named his commune 'Thrushcross Grange'. In the opening paragraphs Jane, an Englishwoman, and Roche, a politically exiled white South African, are on their way to visit the Grange. Jimmy, Roche explains, 'took a writing course', and *Wuthering Heights* was one of the books he had to read. 'I think he just likes the name', Roche adds. But Jimmy, a half-breed who claims to have been born in a Chinese grocery, identifies with Heathcliff, to whom Catherine Earnshaw once said that 'Your mother was an Indian princess and your father was the Emperor of China'. Jimmy's self-projection as Heathcliff makes him one of the line of literary fantasists—including Ganesh Ransumair, the mystic masseur, B. (for Black) Wordsworth, the poet of Miguel Street, and Mr Biswas, sign-painter and journalist—who had been the central figures of Naipaul's early fictions. The comic innocence of those earlier books is summed up in the figure of Elias, the slum boy in *Miguel Street* (1959) who pronounces 'literature' as 'litricher' ('it sounded like something to eat, something rich like chocolate'). But Jimmy's mispronunciations, such as 'T' rush-cross Grange' and 'Wur-thering Heights', have a more sinister sound.

Guerrillas makes other references to the Victorian novel. Naipaul has mentioned Jean Rhys as the pioneer of West Indian fiction, and *Guerrillas,* like Rhys's *Wide Sargasso Sea,* has some crucial echoes of *Jane Eyre.* The heroine is called Jane, she is English, and she is associated with air travel, flying in near the beginning of the novel and being on the verge of using her return air ticket to the end; finally the fiction of her departure by air is used to cover up the fact of her murder. Jane, whose mind is a morass of borrowed notions and half-baked radical opinions, might be called Jane Air (she has no other surname). She is torn between two lovers—Roche, who has come to the island to work in public relations for one of the old colonial trading companies, and Jimmy—a choice faintly reminiscent of Jane Eyre's choice between St John Rivers and Mr Rochester, especially as Jimmy has a prior commitment in the form of his homosexual relationship with the psychopathic slum-boy Bryant. Socially the situations of Jane and her Mr Rochester have been reversed: he is the orphan, she is the 'blanche' or white lady. Yet her status cannot protect her from the series of violations foreshadowed when Bryant, aware that she is beginning her liaison with Jimmy, calls her the 'white rat'. (Jane Eyre, it will be remembered, was called a 'rat' by her arch-enemy John Reed.)

The tragedy of *Guerrillas* takes the form it does because Jimmy's affair with Jane arouses Bryant's latent fury. Jimmy has been described as a 'succubus', a word that Jane is forced to look up; this may mean that he has a demonic nature like Heathcliff, or it may be a codeword for homosexuality. Jimmy's ambitions are not confined to being the leader of an agricultural commune, 'buggering a couple of slum boys' in the bush. But despite the bravado of his public statements, in private he is a lost and disillusioned man in whose eyes the 'revolution' has become devalued to endless, anarchic and pointless struggle. As he writes to an English friend,

> *Things are desperate Roy, when the leader himself begins to yield to despair, things are bad. The whole place is going to blow up, I cannot see how I can control the revolution now. When everybody wants to fight there's nothing to fight for. Everybody wants to fight his own little war, everybody is a guerrilla.*

(The last two sentences here supply Naipaul with his title and epigraph.) Many strands in Jimmy's make-up, including fear and something one can only describe as generosity, go into the promise he makes, immediately after writing these words, to pacify Bryant (who has just seen the 'white rat'):

> He went and put his hands on Bryant's shoulders. His fingers pressed against the gritty jersey and the damp skin below. He took his face close to Bryant's and said, 'I'll give her to you'.

The 'gift' of Jane to Bryant cannot be paralleled in *Jane Eyre* or *Wuthering Heights;* on the contrary, love is fiercely possessive in the Brontë novels. We are in the presence of an older literary stereotype, to which a slender clue may be given by Jane's reading-matter shortly before she is murdered. For why should Jane, a representative of a section of the middle class which Naipaul has described as 'the people who keep up with "revolution" as with the theatre, the revolutionaries who visit centres of revolution, but with return air tickets, the people for whom Malik's kind of Black Power was an exotic but safe brothel'—why should Jane with her fate hanging over her be found indulging in such 'safe' reading as a copy of Hardy's *The Woodlanders*? Is it coincidence that the idea of the greenwood—the forest in which men struggle to maintain their independence and comradeship in defiance of the state apparatus—is subtly connected with Jimmy's 'agricultural commune'?

The Thrushcross Grange communiqué, a 'fairy story, a school composition, ungrammatical and confused, about life in the forest', begins as follows:

> *All revolutions begin with the land, Men are born on the earth, every man has his one spot, it is his birth right, and men must claim their portion of the earth in brotherhood and harmony. In this spirit we came an intrepid band to virgin forest, it is the life style and philosophy of Thrushcross Grange.*

Thrushcross Grange is not 'virgin forest' but an abandoned

plantation originally developed in the days of slavery. Jimmy, whose personal slogan is *'I'm Nobody's Slave or Stallion, I'm a Warrior and Torch Bearer'*, ironically refers to Roche, the agent of the trading company which helps him with supplies, as 'Massa'. Fear of Jimmy and the power he might exert over the dispossessed has caused the leading capitalists of the island to subsidise the commune, which is ostensibly serving a useful purpose by rescuing slum-boys from a life of unemployment and gang warfare. Jimmy's description of his commune as an 'intrepid band' makes him a Robin Hood figure, and, since his threats have produced a small amount of charitable redistribution, he might actually claim to be robbing the rich and giving to the poor. The historian E. J. Hobsbawm has described Robin Hood as 'the quintessence of bandit legend', and Jimmy Ahmed's self-image corresponds, at most points, with Hobsbawm's analysis of the image of the Noble Robber which forms part of the world-wide mythology of peasant societies. Jimmy, that is, sees himself as a victim of injustice and persecution whose mission it is to right wrongs, to take from the rich and give to the poor, and to kill only in self-defence or just revenge ('I have no gun, I'm no guerrilla', he says). Jimmy relies on getting popular support, and for a brief moment when the poor quarters of the city erupt into rioting he becomes their leader. In all this he seems to be a twentieth-century radical intellectual playing at the role of Noble Robber or primitive rebel. At the end he is waiting to be hunted down by the authorities. Naipaul certainly does not glamorise the Noble Robber, but he takes this figure seriously, in a way that (for example) Muriel Spark in her recent novel *The Only Problem* singularly refuses to do. (To the extent that *The Only Problem* contains a subsidiary Robin Hood theme, Spark's sympathies lie unambiguously with the Sheriff of Nottingham.) Spark's international terrorist and bank robber, Effie, embarks on her career as a result of stealing two bars of chocolate from a petrol station. Her rich travelling companions are merely embarrassed by this woman who 'ate her chocolate inveighing, meanwhile against the capitalist system'. It is the companions, not Effie, who arouse Spark's curiosity and interest. *The Only Problem* is the work of a novelist who can only caricature and trivialise the issue which is fundamental to any prospect of real social justice and equality: the issue of forcible redistribution.

In Naipaul, redistribution and the circulation of commodities become the subject of a profoundly disturbing series of actions. Jane, the revolutionary tourist, is theoretically committed to political, economic and sexual redistribution. Politically, she has come to the Caribbean because she had subscribed, in London, to the theory that 'the future of the world was being shaped in places like this, by people like these'. But she has learned instead that 'she had come to a place at the end of the world, to a place that had exhausted its possibilities'—and she hangs on to her return air ticket.

Sexually, Jane has a history of mild promiscuity and she measures up every new man as a 'candidate' or competitor for her sexual favours. In a novel in which sexual relations can be construed as commodity relations she is herself a prime example of the fetishism of commodities. When she arrives at the all-male commune of Thrushcross Grange she fails to respond when Bryant first addresses her, calling her 'sister'. The name to which she does respond, however, is 'white lady'—and she responds by giving Bryant a dollar. At the Grange, partly through her own choice, she becomes a priced and labelled commodity—first the 'white lady', later the 'white rat'. On two occasions Jimmy will lure her back to the Grange with the claim that Bryant wants to give her back her dollar. Bryant, however, actually spends the dollar on going to see a Sidney Poitier movie, which merely intensifies his sense of deprivation. Money in the novel circulates within a closed system: the advanced countries exploiting the Third World by holding out the lure of consumer gratifications. With sex, however, it is different. By telling the story of Jane, Naipaul means to bring home to his readers that redistribution can only be accomplished with violence, and that redistribution involves violation.

The central image of violation in the novel is sexual: rape and sexual degradation leading to murder. The sexual politics of *Guerrillas* will probably not meet with universal approval: both men and women are shown as being complicit in the sexual violence and commodification. Men are the consumers of pornography, the sexual aggressors, and the projectors of an agrarian communism in which (apparently) there is no place for women. Jimmy treats Jane as if she were a commodity, although his fantasies—revealed in the Mills-and-Boon style romance he is writing—convert her image into a fetish. Jane's sex life, however, has always been a process of violation, with which she has more or less willingly complied. It is she who reaches out for her neighbour's pornographic book in order to while away the time during her flight from London. When Jimmy goes to bed with her he perceives that 'without knowing it, she had developed the bad temper, and the manners of a prostitute'. And with Jimmy she realises that she is 'playing with fire', and yet she goes on playing with it, just as Jimmy himself goes on playing with the idea of revolution. Both seem destined to die in the knowledge that they have been fooling themselves.

Guerrillas is the most sexually explicit of Naipaul's novels, with an explicitness which only the social currency of pornography in today's world has made possible for the writer. The meaning of the sexual acts Naipaul describes is that, through them, his protagonists find themselves working out the symbolic conflicts inscribed in the history of the Caribbean—a history of slavery. The men reading pornography on the plane are executives of the American bauxite company which, as Roche puts it, 'owns the island'; in earlier days they would have got their kicks from exploiting the 'niggers'. Both Jimmy and Bryant, as Jane's murderers, are acting out fantasies based on the role of the rebellious slave—the slave who cannot get at his real aggressors, such as the bauxite company's shareholders or the American soldiers whose arrival at the airfield is sufficient to quell the city riots. The circuit of sexual redistribution is thus not only violent but wholly ineffectual, symbolic; but this is the case with almost all the actions of primitive rebels.

Of Jane we are told that 'she was indifferent, perhaps blind, to the contradiction between what she said and what she was so secure of being'; and this faculty of saying one thing and being another is, according to Naipaul, a characteristic of European duplicity. Nevertheless, every figure in *Guerrillas* has a split personality, and each of them is guilty to a greater or lesser extent of Orwellian 'doublethink'. On several occasions we see one person inflicting humiliation by exposing the contradictions of another; yet Jane, having been humiliated by Jimmy, is eventually killed by the one character who is more helpless and vulnerable than she is. The split in Bryant is represented by the irreconcilable dualism of his taste in films: on the one hand, Sidney Poitier movies and, on the other, 'interracial-sex films with Negro men as star-boys', which he comes to believe are wicked. Bryant's split personality gives rise to an intense self-hatred, which can only find an outlet in spasms of uncontrollable symbolic hatred of others. Together with Jimmy he kills Jane, and (if the authorities do not get there first) he will probably end up by killing Jimmy as well.

Jane's sexual value as a 'white lady' and Bryant's murderousness are, in a sense, the givens of the novel, the barbarous and unexamined results of a history of colonialism and slavery. Jimmy's behaviour and emotions are more elaborately fantastic, more of a deliberate narcissistic creation. He writes a novel in which Jane is the narrator, and in which Jane sees him as the incarnation of the Noble Robber:

> *He lives in his own rare world, his head is full of big things, he is carrying the burden of all the suffering people in the world, all the people who live in shacks and grow up in dirty little back rooms.... He is an enemy to all privilege and I am middle class born and bred and I know that in spite of his great civility and urbane charm he must hate people like me. I only have to look in his eyes to understand the meaning of hate.*

The extent to which Jimmy's self-consciousness is a fictional artifice is revealed when we learn that, in England, a female journalist had written of him that to look into his eyes was to understand the meaning of hate. In Jimmy's novel, in Mills-and-Boon style, 'Jane' reflects that *'he's the man who controls this hate I see around me and he's the only*

man who can turn this hate into love'. In place of self-reflection Jimmy has substituted the fetishisation of a fetishisation.

The presence of Jimmy's debased romantic narrative within Naipaul's novel is an exemplification of Harry Levin's view of the realist novel as a dialectic of 'fabulation and debunking', a synthesis of the 'imposition of reality upon romance' and the 'transposition of reality into romance'. Unusually, we see the progress of Jimmy's fictionalisation of Jane and of his actual attempt to start an affair with her side by side. The fictionalisation feeds his behaviour; at one moment early in the seduction he even tells Jane that 'I thought my imagination might have been playing tricks'. Jane is aware of what this might mean, but she is trapped because she 'yet allowed herself to play with the images he had set floating in her mind'.

III

We say that Jane is trapped *because* . . .—and in that judgment, and in judgments of a similar kind that we might make about many other characters and incidents, lies the whole force of *Guerrillas*. In other words, Naipaul's novel stands or falls by its mimetic evocation of the Aristotelian processes of probability and necessity. The novel for Naipaul is a supremely rational imaginative medium, an inquiry into human action and the reciprocal relationships of fantasy and action. Like a juridical process, the inquiry itself is open to inquiry, and that is why Naipaul could later claim that 'fiction never lies': to the extent that it did lie, it would be found out. Perhaps it is inevitable that fiction of this sort would come down harshly on the spectacle of the imagination playing tricks on itself. Finally—as in a law-court—'truth' and 'fantasy' have to be distinguished from one another. If my reading of *Guerrillas* is found to be persuasive, then Naipaul's fundamental opposition to the sort of nihilism which is endemic in deconstructionist thinking will be evident; indeed, I would say that *Guerrillas* poses a challenge to contemporary literary theory of a kind that theory, as at present constituted, could only meet by misreading or belittling Naipaul's work. After all, to a rigorous conventionalist the idea that there is some external moral standard against which hallucination, or the imagination 'playing tricks', could be weighed and found wanting is meaningless. All that matters to the conventionalist is, so to speak, winning tricks in the game that the imagination plays. And this is why poststructuralist 'textuality' tends to exalt comic fiction, with its self-delighting virtuosity and witty reflexivity, and (by the same token) to call in question the gravity of tragic fictions which, so often, turn on what we must call the 'fact' of murder. Tragic novels cannot *force* our acceptance of the deaths or murders, with which they conclude, as 'facts'—for they are after all fictions—but unless we accept these deaths as truths in the Aristotelian sense (that is, as probable and necessary outcomes) tragic gravity will seem to be no more than a device and the impact of the fiction will be much diminished.

> **Where the modern tragic novel such as *Guerrillas* differs from its nineteenth-century predecessors is chiefly in the narrative restraint that it shows, presenting a delicate and arduous case and inviting the reader to serve as juror.**
> —*James Atlas*

Jane views her sex life as a form of compulsive play; but play that is a 'continuing violation'. 'She spoke as though she had never exercised choice. Events, society, the nature of men, her own needs as a woman, had sent her out into the sexual jungle, to play perilously with the unknown'. Her 'needs as a woman', as she sees them, are principally a need for the 'little delirium', the adventure of sexual excitement. Naipaul views this need without compassion, revealing it rather as one of the phenomena of cultural decadence: his characters are conscious of decay and corruption all around them, of a sense of desolation learnt in England but enhanced by the squalor of the Third World and the tropics. This shared vision of a 'world running down' and coming to an end stands in the novel for a version of truth; a truth against which the characters' addiction to various forms of play is to be judged. But there seem to be other forms of truth in *Guerrillas,* manifestations more specific and local, and perhaps more absolute. These are truths that appear in the form of momentary insights or pronouncements, 'sentences' which are unforeseen, involuntary, and apprehended privately. In *Guerrillas,* then, we find a contrast between the discourse of imaginative play and literary invention—a poetic mode of perception, moulded by fantasy, whether in the narrative voice or attributed to a particular character—and a discourse of revelation or annunciation: a perception, later to be authenticated by the unravelling of probability and necessity, which is said to be visited on the individual from an unknown source.

Jimmy Ahmed, for example, finds his equivalent to Jane's 'little delirium' in the act of writing sub-pornographic fiction; but once he has lost the 'writing excitement' he sees that 'The words on the page were again just like words, false'. The words are a screen intended to blot out his 'vision of darkness, of the world lost forever, and his own life ending on that bit of waste land'—a prophetic vision which by the end of *Guerrillas* seems very likely to be fulfilled. Jane's momentary intimation of danger after she lets Jimmy seduce her is more explicitly invested with prophetic authority:

She looked at the driver's mirror: his red eyes were considering her, and they held her return stare. She looked out at the fields; the junked motor-cars beside the road; the men far away, small and busy, stuffing grass into the boots of motor-cars to take home to their animals; the smoking hills, yellow in the mid-afternoon light. But she was aware of the driver's intermittent stare; and whenever she looked at the mirror she saw his red, assessing eyes. A whole sentence ran through her head, at first meaningless, and then, as she examined it, alarming. She thought: I've been playing with fire. Strange words, to have come so suddenly and so completely to her: something given, unasked for, like an intimation of the truth, breaking into the sense of safety, of distance being put between her and the desolation of that house.

We can, of course, discount this if we wish: the taxi-driver's eyes are a familiar figure for the Protestant conscience— Big Brother is watching—and, the 'little delirium' over, Jane feels as if she has been naughty and has been found out. But the narrative will confirm that this was indeed an intimation of the truth. Roche, arriving at Thrushcross just after the murder and also aware of someone else's gaze, has a comparable moment of insight:

> He thought: This place has become a slaughter-ground. The words seemed to have been given to him, and he thought: I've just done the bravest thing in my life. He concentrated on Jimmy and addressed him mentally: You wouldn't do anything to me. You wouldn't dare.

The moment is not without its irony: Roche's 'courage' does not consist in denouncing the crime that has been brought home to him, but in saving his skin by turning his back on it and walking away. The words which are 'given to him' and which convey an intuitive knowledge do not in any way guarantee a proper or heroic response. If language in Naipaul sometimes acquires a mysterious authority—as if it were the very voice of reality—his characters are destined to be judged by the reader not to have listened to it. But the novel itself does not enact such a judgment—it is left entirely to the reader. Where the modern tragic novel such as *Guerrillas* differs from its nineteenth-century predecessors is chiefly in the narrative restraint that it shows, presenting a delicate and arduous case and inviting the reader to serve as juror.

The central difficulty of moral judgment in *Guerrillas* is provided by the figure of Roche. At first sight he seems something of a cliché, an embodiment of the pathos of the defeated liberal. He seems to attract more narrative sympathy than either Jane or Jimmy, and his perceptions are made to seem more authoritative than theirs. Roche is a former guerrilla fighter who was involved in amateurish acts of sabotage in South Africa, and was subsequently imprisoned and tortured. He was exiled to England, wrote a book, and acquired something of a martyr's halo. But, like Jimmy's, his English reputation was bogus: he had lost his political vision, and left England for the Caribbean not under the sway of idealism but because he had been frightened away by the South African secret police. Torture and humiliation have entered his soul; to what extent, we do not fully realise until after the riots when official disapproval has descended on Thrushcross Grange, and Meredith Herbert, a politician and media personality, subjects Roche to a devastating radio interview. Roche has a propensity for walking into traps: in South Africa, in his Caribbean job of organising support for a commune which could not conceivably have fulfilled its promises, and in the interview—given when the government is in need of a scapegoat—which effectively undermines his position on the island. He does not fight back against the people who trap him, preferring to escape from their clutches and move somewhere else. There is something abject and sterile about his passivity, which Meredith (who would have made a passable torturer) cunningly exposes on the radio. Roche's intelligence and rationality are made to seem futile. Like Winston Smith, though much less sensationally, he bears an unacknowledged responsibility for his own victimisation. None of this, however, prepares us for the ending which robs him of the last vestige of moral heroism.

It is Jane's intuitions about Roche which add up to a different story. In the opening chapter, we read that 'Roche laughed, and Jane saw his molars: widely spaced, black at the roots, the gums high: like a glimpse of the skull'. No explanation is offered for this detail, but we later become accustomed to Jane's perception of Roche as a split personality, divided between his 'saint's manner' and the 'satyr's smile' which appears when he reveals the roots of his molars. What is Jane, and what are we, to make of these glimpses of a 'grotesque stranger'? 'In these relationships some warning, some little hint, always was given, some little sign that foreshadowed the future', the narrator tells us (we are not quite sure whether or not to attribute this superstitious awareness to Jane). If we follow the logic of intimations such as these, we shall come to see all three of Naipaul's main characters as based on primitive archetypes: Jimmy the succubus, Jane the prostitute, and Roche the satyr. But Jane cannot deal with the 'little sign', and neither for the time being can the reader. The narrative foreshadowing is not obtrusive, and the ending, which shows Roche to be a personality as crippled as Jimmy or Jane, comes to us like a new and shocking revaluation.

Guerrillas is formally open-ended: Jimmy, Bryant and Roche are still apparently free agents, even if Jane is dead.

There is not even the likelihood of the discovery of the murdered body and of a trial and a hanging such as closed the case of Michael Abdul Malik. Nevertheless, a burden of judgment is, as we have seen, laid upon the reader (though a poststructuralist interpreter would doubtless emphasise, not the nature of this judgment, but its deferral). The imagined evidence that Naipaul puts before us—though a good deal more complex than a necessarily simplifying and foreshortened account such as the present one can indicate—is not 'undecidable': it admits of a verdict. The narrative is one of circulation, a redistributive cycle in which a human being is violated by being turned into a commodity, but finally the circulation comes to a stop: Jane's violation is terminal. At this point we can pass moral judgments on those who took part in it. But the judgments are of a different sort from those implied or stated by more traditional 'liberal-humanist' fictions.

In an essay on 'Character Change and the Drama', Harold Rosenberg draws a distinction between the 'biological/historical' and the 'legal' views of character. According to the biological or historical view, character is the expression of a psychological condition, a developing organic identity. Action or behaviour, in this view, is 'a mere attribute of, and clue to, a being who can be known only through an intuition'. The organic view of personality as based on 'continuity of being' is expressed in biography and, for the most part, in the modern novel; and this is the view which is normally associated with liberal humanism. The legal view, by contrast, defines the human individual as an actor, whose identity arises from the 'coherence of his acts with a fact in which they have terminated (the crime or the contract) and by nothing else'. Individuals are 'conceived as identities in systems whose subject matter is action and the judgement of actions. In this realm the multiple incidents in the life of an individual may be synthesised, by the choice of the individual himself or by the decision of others, into a scheme that pivots on a single fact central to the individual's existence and which, controlling his behaviour and deciding his fate, becomes his visible definition'. This mode of identity is represented in tragic drama, even though, from a traditional liberal-humanist perspective, the identification of a person with a single, terminal act (say, as a murderer or an accomplice after the fact of murder) may be no more than a 'legal fiction'. The legal identity of the individual is determined not solely by his own actions but by the judgment that is passed upon them.

The contrast between 'organic personality' and 'legal identity' is likely to be present in all major novels and plays: Rosenberg himself applies it to the analysis of *Hamlet*. My claim is that in *Guerrillas* Naipaul exploits it in a way that is quite different from nineteenth-century fiction, where a delayed revelation of legal identity is normally used to endorse organic identity. In his interview with Meredith

Herbert, Roche is trying desperately to preserve and justify his own sense of organic identity in the face of Meredith's indictment of his actions. Roche is, in effect, arguing for forgiveness, for the right to make mistakes, the right to be judged on the purity of his intentions. He would like to plead that he is someone apart from his actions. Meredith, a harsh prosecuting counsel, denies this, mocking what he takes as Roche's self-indulgence: 'what a nice world you inhabit, Peter. You have so much room for error'. Inhabiting such a 'nice world' is, Meredith implies, one of the privileges reserved for 'white people'. The interview, however, is not fought to a finish, and the question of its moral outcome is something Naipaul is careful to leave suspended.

In nineteenth-century novels the commonest way of uncovering a character's organic identity is to look into his or her face: the face serving as a window allowing us to read off what is written in the soul, or the heart. Jane, we have noted, has moments of recognition in which, looking at Roche's sinister smile, she intuits the 'inner man'. But the value of these moments is left uncertain, and what is revealed is so shockingly different from Roche's own sense of his 'inner man' that the intuition can only be taken as a parody of comparable moments in nineteenth-century novels. Jane does not see anything that liberal individualism would recognise as an organic identity. Instead, she sees a satyr, a being that is irreducible and inhuman: an alien. (In this, *Guerrillas* perhaps resembles *Wuthering Heights,* where the protagonists also invest one another with non-human characteristics. Both novels break with liberal individualism by invoking archaic and demonic notions of identity.) The significance of Jane's vision is that, arguably, it foreshadows the true 'legal identity' of Roche, as it appears from his terminal actions at the end of the novel. But we can scarcely maintain that Roche 'is' the satyr—we see him in all his complexity as a represented character—a character, however, who eludes our attempts to reduce him to organic coherence.

We can ask: who or what are Roche, Jimmy, Jane?—but finally our questions will turn to the novelist who animates these fictions with such originality and truth of observation. In *Guerrillas* Naipaul has furthered a technique of impartiality which is, more or less, constitutive of serious modern fiction. It is the technique of 'perpetual shifting of the standpoint' and of the 'artifice of seeing through the eyes of characters' which, as long ago as 1895, H. G. Wells observed in the novels of George Meredith. What Wells added on that occasion is also relevant: 'It may be that Mr Meredith sometimes carries his indirect method to excess, and puzzles a decent public, nourished on good healthy straightforward marionettes'. There is no 'revolutionary' break between the fiction of writers such as Meredith and Conrad and that of Naipaul, but the degree of indirection achieved by the latter would, surely, have puzzled Meredith's most ardent readers. Naipaul's ostentatious, even fastidious, detachment is the most difficult element in the novel that we must unravel: a detachment which implies disinterestedness, but scarcely impartiality, for it 'reveals the writer totally'. Our sense of Naipaul's detachment comprehends a number of factors. There is, for example, a tension between the novelist's almost vindictive exposure of his characters' inadequacies and self-contradictions, and his shafts of surprising sympathy and generosity towards the least lovable of them. There is Naipaul's palpable irritation with the more rootless of his characters (those uncommitted to life on the island), and his, or the narrator's, rather unquestioning respect for the 'authorities' who have the task of making a continuing orderly life possible there. There is the curious and disturbing feature that, in such a mordant study of contemporary racial and sexual confusions, Naipaul has eliminated characters of his own race and has tied his characters' 'revolutionary' hopes to the success of a homosexual commune, a foundation on which (by definition) the future cannot be built.

The quality of detachment in *Guerrillas* is linked to the fact that, alone among Naipaul's novels, it does not contain a single character of Indian descent. (In real life Michael X's entourage included two Trinidad Indians, one of whom gave himself up to the police and was eventually sentenced to life imprisonment.) Naipaul's early novels, *The Mystic Masseur* and *A House for Mr Biswas,* portrayed the Trinidad Hindu as comic epic hero. His two other major novels, *The Mimic Men* and *A Bend in the River,* are first-person narratives told by Indian settlers (the former in London and the Caribbean, the latter in East and Central Africa). Even **'In a Free State',** his novella-length study of Europeans in a politically turbulent African state, includes the image of an ordinary, 'decent' Hindu trader. In these books detachment coexists with an open warmth and partisanship; the characters' success in engaging our attention is also the author's, even when he mocks them. *Guerrillas,* however, is set not in Trinidad but on a fictional Caribbean island inhabited by Negroes, creoles, Europeans, and Chinese, but not apparently by East Indians. Is that why the island is so unremittingly condemned as a lost and fallen world, in which—though good order and restraint are still felt as virtues—'When everybody wants to fight there's nothing to fight for'? Can it be that in *Guerrillas* Naipaul has constructed for himself a way of playing with fire without getting burnt?

If so, that is his privilege. The weaknesses so fully exposed in Roche, Jane, and Jimmy, are human weaknesses, which in some way must reflect the weaknesses of their creator. If the figure of Jane, the murdered and violated woman, is offered as the embodiment of circulation as violation, the novelist is a circulator who can share the viewpoints of all his characters and yet remain inviolable. For example, in an unforgettable passage, Naipaul allows us to enter into

Bryant's consciousness. Bryant, stunted, poverty-stricken and starved of affection, symbolises the moral injustice of the distribution of the world's resources which leads to the perennial, and misleading, legend of the Noble Robber. Bryant is doomed: whatever charitable gifts are made to him—his place in the commune, his dollar, his 'rat'—are only aids to his destruction. Bryant is rooted on the island, while the novelist, like his principal characters, is free of such roots: the slum-boy is, so to speak, the human material which Naipaul, as traveller and journalist, goes to investigate. And from this we may conclude that Naipaul, like Roche (his 'satyr') is an escape-artist, and that his art is the art of the survivor who pieces together a tale which could only be 'authentically' voiced by people who have been silenced, who have suffered violent deaths or who languish imprisoned by their own inarticulacy, if not by the law. Naipaul's art is, inevitably, fabricated, speaking not through revealed truths but through the constructions of fantasy and the 'legal fictions' of probability and necessity. Its significance lies not only in its intricate construction and imaginative play but in its wisdom. Writers, whom Naipaul has rather wistfully compared to tribal wise men, must, he has said, 'know more, have felt more and thought more than others, offering us some point of rest'. They must also address the tribe on matters on which the rest of the tribe is silent.

Ian Buruma (review date 14 February 1991)

SOURCE: "Signs of Life," in *New York Review of Books,* February 14, 1991, pp. 3-5.

[*In the following review, Buruma praises Naipaul for his depiction of India and its people as they struggle to achieve what Naipaul calls "universal civilization."*]

Near the end of V.S. Naipaul's first book about India, *An Area of Darkness,* there is an unforgettable piece of writing. It is a description of his visit to the village of the Dubes. It was from there that Naipaul's grandfather left for Trinidad around the turn of the century as an indentured laborer. Naipaul, "content to be a colonial, without a past, without ancestors," visits his ancestral village with a feeling of dread.

In fact, the village is not as bad as he had expected. An old woman who had known Naipaul's grandfather is produced. She tells him a family story. Naipaul gives her some money. Then the wife of a man named Ramachandra wishes to see him. She bows before him, seizes his feet, "in all their Veldtschoen" (a wonderful Naipaulian detail, this), and weeps. She refuses to relax her grip on his *Veldtschoen.* Naipaul, horrified, asks his guide what he should do.

The next day, in a nearby town where Naipaul is staying, Ramachandra himself turns up. Ramachandra is the present head of Naipaul's grandfather's branch of the Dubes. He is a physical and mental wreck: "His effort at a smile did not make his expression warmer. Spittle, white and viscous, gathered at the corners of his mouth." He too, clings to Naipaul, wanting to talk, to invite him to his hut, offer him food. Again, Naipaul is horrified, asks for help, tells him to go away, draws the curtains in his hotel room. He can hear Ramachandra scratching at the window.

When they meet again, in the village, Ramachandra still refuses to let go. He speaks of his plan to start some litigation over a piece of land. Naipaul was sent by God. Naipaul must help him. Another man slips Naipaul a letter. Naipaul is followed around by a crowd of men and boys. It is all too much. Naipaul wants to escape. He gets in his jeep. A young boy, freshly bathed, asks for a lift to town. "No," says Naipaul, "let the idler walk." And: "So it ended, in futility and impatience, a gratuitous act of cruelty, self-reproach and flight."

I wish to recall this passage at some length because it says a great deal about the writer; above all about his pride, and his horror at the lack of it in others. The clutch of the *Veldtschoen,* the inertia of poverty, the abjectness of Ramachandra, these are what make Naipaul take flight. He is an expert on humiliation, sensitive to every nuance of indignity—see his novel *Guerrillas,* see his analysis of Argentine *machismo* in *The Return of Eva Perón,* see pretty much everything he has written on India.

But when Naipaul behaves badly, as he undoubtedly does in the village of the Dubes, it is without the blinkered contempt that Blimpish colonials display. Nor is he like Kipling, whose fear of the tarbrush was perhaps one reason for his desire to keep the people at the Club amused with cutting descriptions of the natives. This is however precisely the way many so-called third world intellectuals see Naipaul, as a dark man mimicking the prejudices of the white imperialists. This view is not only superficial, it is wrong. Naipaul's rage is not the result of being unable to feel the native's plight; on the contrary, he is angry because he feels it so keenly.

Pride and rage: they go together, and they are at the heart of Naipaul's work, of his latest book on India, no less than of his earlier, younger, more ill-tempered books. Pride is what enables him to empathize with people whose politics or religious views, or social customs, may be alien to him, even abhorrent. Naipaul, the fastidious aesthete and connoisseur of good wines and Elizabethan sonnets, is rather far removed from the average southern redneck, yet he senses in him a pride, an aesthetic, a feeling of independence.

Rednecks may also be racists, but that, in this instance, is rather beside the point.

Nor is there reason to believe that Naipaul has any sympathy with militant Sikhs, Hindu nationalists, or Bengali Maoists; yet he describes them with a kind of tenderness, and a rare understanding, which is neither patronizing nor sentimental. This is because, as he wrote in the introduction to his masterly little book *Finding the Center,* "The people I found, the people I was attracted to, were not unlike myself. They too were trying to find order in their world, looking for the center; and my discovery of these people is as much part of the story as the unfolding of the West African background." In this case he was writing about people on the Ivory Coast.

This empathy with people struggling with their fate, trying to find their center, people who, as Naipaul puts it somewhere, reject rejection, who try to escape, however naively, clumsily, or even violently, from the darkness and poverty of their past, the empathy with such people is what explains Naipaul's relative optimism about India.

Optimism might strike people who read about India in the newspapers as perverse. Just after I received Naipaul's book I read a description in a London paper of Hindu holy men storming a mosque at a time of day deemed auspicious by astrologers for destroying the Muslim shrine. They believed that the Hindu god Rama was born on the site and were prepared to die for the sake of reinstating their idol there. The ensuing riots caused hundreds of deaths. The holy men were supported by the party, the BJP, that might one day form the government of India. One of its leaders had been touring through northern India in a Rama chariot, fanning Hindu hatred. One of his colleagues threatened to destroy three thousand other mosques occupying Hindu sites. The present government is headed by a thuggish opportunist, not averse to having an irksome opponent beaten up by his boys.

It is all a far cry from the civilized secularism and Old Harrovian rectitude of Jawaharlal Nehru. And yet Naipaul's optimism is not ill-considered. For it is based on a deep truth about India: even thuggish opportunists, however much they might end up undermining it, are still part of a remarkably resilient political process, which is Indian democracy. In describing a Sikh militant whose head is in some ways still buried in the darkness of myths and holy wars, Naipaul is struck by how much he takes for granted—the constitution, the law, the centers of education, the civil service, etc. Naipaul is right to say that in India "power came from the people. The people were poor; but the power they gave was intoxicating. As high as a man could be taken up, so low, when he lost power, he could be cast down." The rascals, in India, can still be voted out, which is more than you can

say of almost any other country in Asia—even, in practice, of Japan.

Naipaul likes to say that he has no views. As he put it to Andrew Robinson in the *Literary Review* (London): "My ideas are just responses to human situations." Here, I think, he is being a little coy. Of course he has views. He presented them beautifully in his recent talk to the Manhattan Institute, published in this journal. It is a liberal view in the classical sense of the word. Naipaul's view of what he calls universal civilization is one where people have escaped from the world of myths and ritual and instinct and worship of ancestors and gods. Universal civilization "implies a certain kind of society, a certain kind of awakened spirit. I don't imagine my father's parents would have been able to understand the idea. So much is contained in it: the idea of the individual, responsibility, choice, the life of the intellect, the idea of vocation and perfectibility and achievement."

Many of the people Naipaul describes in his books are awakening to this idea, which does not mean that their responses are not often muddled, to say the least. Again and again Naipaul applies his view to India:

> To awaken to history was to cease to live instinctively. It was to begin to see oneself and one's group the way the outside world saw one; and it was to know a kind of rage. India was now full of this rage. There had been a general awakening. But everyone awakened first to his own group or community; every group thought itself unique in its awakening; and every group sought to separate its rage from the rage of other groups.

The million mutinies of Naipaul's title are to be seen as signs of life, of India kicking itself out of its old inertia, the inertia of poverty, which was perpetuated in a vicious circle of karma, gods, and holiness. Here, then, is the pride of the low caste Dravidian politician dedicating his life to the struggle against Brahmin supremacy:

> In this small dark man were locked up generations of grief and rage. He was the first in his line to have felt the affront; and, from what he had said, he was still the only one in his family to have taken up the cause. His passion was very great; it had to be respected.

And here, in one of the best passages in the book, is Gurtej Singh, the young Sikh militant, mentioned above, who resigned from the Indian civil service to fight for the cause of "my people." Gurtej was highly educated, had awakened, as Naipaul would say, and yet he had turned back to the gods, the myths, and the holy men. Just as pride comes with rage, confusion comes with awakening:

> Like Papu the Jain stockbroker in Bombay, who lived on the edge of the great slum of Dharavi and was tormented by the idea of social upheaval, Gurtej had a vision of chaos about to come. Papu had turned to good works, in the penitential Jain fashion. Gurtej had turned to millenarian politics. It had happened with other religions when they turned fundamentalist; it threatened to bring the chaos Gurtej feared.

Democracy is always a messy process. In India it is bound to be messier than anywhere else. And as the thuggish politicians, pushed up by the poor and the no longer quite so poor, do their best to remove the Old Harrovian legacy of Nehru, many people in India fear this mess. Naipaul fears it, too. He is an orderly man. But he does not make a fetish of order. Disorder is an inescapable consequence of India's awakening. It is why he can respect the passion of men whom most Western liberals would regard with, shall I say, Blimpish disdain: the religious radicals, the Indian rednecks, so to speak. This may be another reason why so many "progressive" third world intellectuals see Naipaul as a reactionary figure; for it is they, the admirers of Mao and Kim Il Sung, who make a fetish of order, and it is Naipaul who has the deeper understanding of the social forces which progressives claim to despise—perhaps because they are themselves still in the grip of those forces.

The fetish of order is something many progressives, in East and West (or if you prefer, North and South), have in common with many conservatives. Mao was much admired by European leaders, such as Edward Heath and Georges Pompidou. Like so many intellectual Sinophiles—Henry Kissinger is another—they were impressed by the discipline Mao imposed, and were ready to defend the order reimposed on Tiananmen Square (even if they didn't like the methods). Many saw a unified society of busy bees, all expressing great confidence in their leaders, all working in serried ranks toward a glorious collective future. Some even saw the regimentation of China as a mark of superior civilization, so unlike our own disorderly world. Left-wing Indian intellectuals admired China so much that they developed an inferiority complex about messy, chaotic India. Nehru himself was deeply exercised about the question why the Chinese achieved such wonderful unity, whereas India was forever on the brink of collapse and disunity. It was always India that had to take a leaf from China's book.

What all these admirers chose (and, alas, often still choose) to overlook was that China's order was the order of a slave state. It is said that Mao, however much blood still sticks to his waxy hands, restored pride to the Chinese people. If

so, it was only to the People, and not to people that he gave this pride. The price for Mao's proud banners was the virtually complete destruction of Naipaul's universal civilization, which did exist in China: the individual, responsibility, choice, the life of the intellect, and so on. In this respect, despite all the subcontinent's problems, China should take a leaf from India's book.

What makes Naipaul one of the world's most civilized writers is his refusal to be engaged by the People, and his insistence on listening to people, individuals, with their own language and their own stories. To this extent he is right when he claims to have no view; he is impatient with all abstractions. He is interested in how individual people see themselves and the world in which they live. He has recorded their histories, their dreams, their stories, their words. As we know, the first thing that leaders or worshippers of the People do is to rob people of their words, by enforcing a language of wood.

Naipaul's characters, most of whom talk at considerable length, never speak a language of wood. In his interviews, Naipaul insists on details; he wants to know how things smelled, felt, sounded, looked, especially looked. And where it concerns ideas, he wants to be told how they were arrived at; not just what people think, but how they think. This is also the method of his own writing. Naipaul, in *Finding the Center:*

> Narrative was my aim. Within that, my traveling method was intended to be transparent. The reader will see how the material was gathered; he will also see how the material could have served fiction or political journalism or a travelogue. But the material here serves itself alone. . . . All that was added later was understanding. Out of that understanding the narrative came. However creatively one travels, however deep an experience in childhood or middle age, it takes thought (a sifting of impulses, ideas, and references that become more multifarious as one grows older) to understand what one has lived through or where one has been.

The extraordinary achievement of Naipaul's latest book is that we can see his characters; more than that, we can see how they see, and how they, in turn, are seen by the author: Amir, the melancholy son of a raja in Lucknow, Cambridge-educated, a Marxist, a devout Muslim; Namdeo, the outcast poet, whose "ideas of untouchability and brothel-area sex, childbirth and rags, all coming together, were like an assault"; and many, many more. This is what makes the book a work of art. At this level it ceases to matter whether the writer is engaged in fiction or nonfiction, or whether you call a book such as *The Enigma of Arrival* a novel. Whatever his literary form, Naipaul is a master. The people in

India: A Million Mutinies Now are so alive they could have sprung from a great writer's imagination.

There is, however, one thing that sets such a book apart from fiction, and that is the language itself. Whereas the writer controls every word in a work of invention, this cannot be the case in a factual account. Here there is a slight problem: the language of Naipaul's characters inevitably tends to sound flat, compared to the author's own literary prose. This is particularly true when Naipaul has to go through an interpreter to hear the person's story. Because the stories are so interesting, it is not a major problem, but I must admit nonetheless that here and there I felt a certain relief when a long quotation ended and Naipaul's words began.

And what words! The few paragraphs describing the decrepitude of Calcutta are among the best things ever written in English about that sad, wonderful, dying place. Naipaul writes like a painter. Small, visual details tell you all: the buzzards hovering over the grubby little street market behind the Grand Hotel, where people go about their minute tasks, one man walking by "carrying a single, limber, dancing sheet of plywood on his head." Or the "pink-walled room" of the Hindu activist in Bombay, who worships at the shrine of Ganpati in Pali: "On the wall at the back of the Sony television there was a colour photograph or picture of this image at Pali: the broad, spreading belly of the deity a violent, arresting red, not altogether benign."

Referring to himself, Nirad Chaudhuri, the cosmopolitan Bengali writer, now living in Britain, once wrote: "To be *deraciné*, is to be on the road forever." This could serve nicely as V. S. Naipaul's motto, too. Naipaul, the grandson of uprooted Indians, uprooted himself to come to England. He is a man continuously on the road, and continuously fretting about roots, his own and those of the people he meets. One sometimes has the impression of a man traveling through the dark and rainy night, stopping at houses on the way, pressing his nose against the windows. Peering at the people inside, cosily sitting around the family hearth, he is reminded of his own rootlessness. The assumption is that those others, seen through the window, are at home, rooted, and whatever the opposite is of *deraciné*.

This must account for Naipaul's nostalgia for what he has called "whole and single societies." He has often used such words as "damaged" or "wounded" for societies that are fragmented and apparently rootless. Gandhi, the Mahatma, he told Andrew Robinson, "is a man, whose life, when I contemplate it, makes me cry. I am moved to tears. . . ." This is, as always, largely a matter of pride, of dignity: Gandhi's own sense of dignity, which he imparted to the Indian masses. But it is also a question of Naipaul's admiration for Gandhi's vision of one single India, a racial vision, a vi-

sion of wholeness. Nehru had the same vision, albeit in a more secular way. So did Naipaul on his first visit to India. It was an idea of India, which, as Naipaul writes, incorporated the independence movement, the great civilization, the great names, the classical past. "It was," Naipaul writes in his latest book,

> an aspect of our identity, the community identity we had developed, which in multi-racial Trinidad, had become more like a racial identity.

> This was the identity I took to India on my first visit in 1962. And when I got there I found it had no meaning in India. The idea of an Indian community—in effect, a continental idea of our Indian identity—made sense only when the community was very small, a minority, and isolated.

And now, on his last trip, Naipaul believes he has found the makings of this all-Indian community. He calls it "a central will, a central intellect, a national idea." The Indian Union, he writes, "was greater than the sum of its parts; and many of these movements of excess strengthened the Indian state, defining it as the source of law and civility and reasonableness." This may be right, even though the present bunch in power seems excessive rather than civil, and the latest wave of Hindu chauvinism poses a serious threat to the secular state of India. But this focus on the whole, the single, the central also reflects Naipaul's own state of mind, his nostalgia for an orderly identity. He has remarked elsewhere, quite convincingly, that Gandhi's all-Indian vision was shaped in South Africa, just as Nehru's was formed at Harrow. It is the old dream of the deracinated, a regret about things past.

But a dream is all it is. One senses the same nostalgia in most of the people Naipaul meets on his Indian trip. As Naipaul himself has pointed out so many times, a common desire of those who have escaped the dark embrace of the tribe is to find the way back; nostalgia is the concomitant of change; the educated Sikh who dreams of restoring Ranjit Singh's nineteenth-century kingdom; the urban intellectual in Calcutta dreaming of pastoral purity; Dravidian politicians in Madras dreaming of medieval emperors who preceded the rule of the Brahmins. Whether or not they know it, the millions of mutineers, wrestling with their fates, are all on the road forever. That is the truth of Naipaul's excellent book.

Richard Eder (review date 22 May 1994)

SOURCE: "The Root of Rootlessness," in *Los Angeles Times Book Review*, May 22, 1994, pp. 3, 11.

[In the following review, Eder argues that by "refusing to conceal or temper his own crabby vision," Naipaul achieves a "unique authenticity" in his A Way in the World.]

The word *Caribbean* may conjure up all kinds of vivid colors, but to V. S. Naipaul it suggests gray: a land and seascape bleached out by unmediated sun and a counterfeit history. It is the gray in the face of a professional entertainer the morning after a late night.

The displacing and alienating effects of a colonial past on today's post-colonial peoples has been Naipaul's leading theme ever since, once past his early Trinidad novels, he broke through the colors to the gray underneath. He has pursued it in his fiction and nonfiction, set in Britain, Africa, South America and India, the home of his forebears.

> **He is one of literature's great travelers and also one of its oddest. He seeks not roots but rootlessness. He travels not for acquaintance but for alienation.**
> —*Richard Eder*

He is one of literature's great travelers and also one of its oddest. He seeks not roots but rootlessness. He travels not for acquaintance but for alienation. Paul Theroux does that, to an extent, but the difference is very large. For one thing, Naipaul, who can be petty, vain and cruel, both uses and transcends his defects. His theme is the terrible inauthenticity that history has imposed on the heirs of colonialism's subjects. But by refusing to conceal or temper his own crabby vision—a walleyed sensibility that tends to swivel inward—he achieves at his best moments a unique authenticity.

His nightmare Argentina, for example, can be unrecognizable but there is no question about the nightmares that it produces in Naipaul. When he is not displaying a certain haste and roughness (on purpose, perhaps, like a musician asserting his freedom to play sour), he is a great writer. In a magical and redeeming phrase he will suddenly link up the particular estrangements he acquires, wherever he goes, to the estranged wanderer in all of us.

A Way in the World is a series of partly autobiographical and partly fictional variations on his theme. Each centers on a different personage, and Naipaul himself appears in many of them. The principal characters differ widely. There is a Trinidadian who uses his color sense as both a funeral parlor cosmetician and a cake decorator; and a conservative Port of Spain lawyer who unexpectedly reveals his flaming commitment to black power. There is a supercilious English writer who helps and patronizes the narrator;

an itinerant Caribbean radical—"an impresario of revolution"—who is lionized by the radically chic in London and New York, and an enterprising Venezuelan who has submerged his identity as a Trinidadian Hindu.

Some of the figures are historical. Naipaul writes a vivid fictionalized account of Sir Walter Raleigh, aged and desperate, seeking to discover El Dorado as a way out of his political troubles at home. He paints a poignantly imagined portrait of the early Venezuelan revolutionary, Francisco de Miranda, lifted up and let down by his British patrons and finally, betrayed by the supporters of Bolivar, dying in a Spanish prison.

At first glance there seems to be little connection among the real, part-real and fictional characters he writes of. The styles differ considerably too: from factual documentary to a first-person combination of memoir and commentary to poetic evocation. In fact all of the protagonists are linked by their passage through the world of the Caribbean. It is a world that, instead of evolving gradually through slow migrations and evolution, was created in a kind of cataclysm.

In the space of a few years, the Spanish, the French and the British landed, fought each other, and shoved aside the Native Americans as unfit for their purpose. Their purpose was sugar plantations; and to accomplish it they brought over slaves from Africa and indentured laborers from India. And then, after a couple of centuries, they were gone; leaving behind a fragmented culture resting on a jumbled, conflicting, half-dreamed past. Naipaul doesn't draw the comparison, but one thinks of Prince Sigismund in Calderon's "Life Is a Dream." Arbitrarily immured in a tower from infancy, he suddenly finds himself—arbitrarily released and royal once more—in a wide and terrifying universe.

Sigismund went temporarily mad. Naipaul's characters are put together out of pieces that don't fit. Though not usually mad, they maneuver hybrid and uncertain identities through a world constructed of misapprehensions and are visited by undissolved bits of a heritage they are unconscious of.

In his gentle corpse-and-cake decorator, Naipaul sees an ancestral ghost of "the dancing groups of Lucknow, lewd men who painted their faces and tried to live like women." He adds: "He frightened me because I felt his feeling for beauty was like an illness; as though some unfamiliar deforming virus had passed through his simple mother to him and was even then . . . something neither of them had begun to understand." The lawyer, Evander, a properly British-mannered black professional in a still-colonial Trinidad, receives a courtesy visit from young Naipaul, about to depart for London on a prized scholarship. There is a starchy moment or two; then, startlingly, Evander raises his fist, smiles, and says: "The race! The race, man!"

It was meant as a secret, confraternal sign to a youth who was off to learn from the enemy and come back to fight. Except that Naipaul wasn't. He was off to gather the rewards that the British colonial authorities had implied would be his when he reached London with his prize. Instead there were years of misery, condescension and the grinding struggle to find himself as a writer. In his portrait of Foster Morris, an established author who helps him generously and then mortally offends him, Naipaul vents with gleeful malice his feelings toward the grip of British attitudes, not only on his country but also on his own divided nature.

But Evander mistook young Naipaul in another respect, as well. As a member of Trinidad's Indian minority, he felt no kinship with the black nationalist current that was to accompany independence in Trinidad and other parts of the Caribbean. On the contrary, he felt his own identity threatened; as he would years later in Africa, where the Indian middle class was a particular target of black politics.

Doubly rootless, doubly colonized, Naipaul draws his most blistering portrait when he writes of Lebrun. A cultivated, brilliant black Communist, Lebrun was adviser to a number of nationalist leaders in the independence days. Once in power, they had no use for him; his ideology was good for building up their strength but they had no intention of actually setting up a Marxist regime.

Still, he remained much in demand among left-wing circles in Britain and the United States. A penetrating review of Naipaul's early work—Lebrun saw a political and social significance that the author himself was unaware of—led to a short-lived friendship. Soon, Naipaul felt he was being colonized once more and broke away. The fashionable '60s formula for the Caribbean—socialism—was just as much an imperial imposition as anything the British had devised. In any case, like black nationalism, it took no account of Naipaul. His pursuit of Lebrun through a later career advising African dictators is perceptive, cruel and, like one or two other pieces, far too long.

Naipaul's angers can be useful as well as shrill, and usually directed at those—British and black—who exercise power. The finest portraits are of figures torn and fluttering through their lives and identities. His Miranda is one of the best things he has done, and he writes of the deluded Raleigh with unusual compassion. And there is the Indian whom Raleigh, assuming he comes from El Dorado, takes back to London to make up for the gold he couldn't find. In fact, Don Jose comes from the well-settled province of Nueva Granada (Colombia). His reflections on Raleigh and on European dreams have a haunting simplicity. Asked

years later what difference he finds between the Europeans and the Indians, he answers with an irony that points up what Naipaul is after:

> "I've thought a lot about that. And I think, Father, that the difference between us, who are Indians, or half Indians, and people like the Spaniards and the English and the Dutch and the French, people who know how to go where they are going, I think that for them the world is a safer place."

Brent Staples (review date 22 May 1994)

SOURCE: "Con Men and Conquerors," in *The New York Times Book Review*, May 22, 1994, pp. 1, 42-3.

[*In the following review, Staples praises* A Way in the World, *calling it a "probing meditation on the relationships among personal, national and world histories."*]

Few writers of V. S. Naipaul's stature have been so consistently and aggressively misread on account of ethnic and racial literary politics. Much of the criticism stems not from what Mr. Naipaul writes but from expectations about what he *ought* to write given that he is a brown man (of Indian descent) born into the brown and black society that is Trinidad. Alas, after a 40-year voyage as a writer, Mr. Naipaul has arrived at a time when his work is too often viewed through the filter of race. This would be an impoverished way of seeing in any case. In V. S. Naipaul's case, a strictly racial reading amounts to no reading at all.

Mr. Naipaul typically takes his readers into the farthest reaches of the third world—Africa, the Caribbean, Asia, the Middle East—to pursue one or both of his twin obsessions: what it means to become and finally to be a writer; what happens in postcolonial societies when foreign power recedes, leaving cruelty and chaos to fill the breach. The second obsession has provoked far more drama than the first. The news from newly free societies—as conveyed through novels like *Guerrillas, A Bend in the River* and *In a Free State,* or in nonfiction books like *Among the Believers: An Islamic Journey, India: A Wounded Civilization* and *The Return of Eva Perón*—has been deeply and unremittingly grim. Corruption, brutality and tribal hostilities, like those driving the slaughters in Rwanda and Bosnia, flower bloodily and unchecked. Time and again, Mr. Naipaul's readers encounter "half-made societies that seemed doomed to remain half-made."

V. S. Naipaul has 22 books to his credit, many of them displaying the coolest literary eye and the most lucid prose we have. His 11th novel, *A Way in the World,* is a distinguished book even by Naipaulian standards, a bewitching piece of work by a mind at the peak of its abilities. The book can only loosely be termed a "novel" and is well outside the limits of what one expects from a traditional work of fiction. The narrative is made from nine linked and complementary narratives—some personal, some historical, some traditionally novelistic. Though fewer than 400 pages long, *A Way in the World* is epic in scope: Columbus, Sir Walter Raleigh, Simon Bolivar and his fellow Venezuelan revolutionary Francisco Miranda all appear in the book, though in ways one could hardly have predicted. At its heart, this novel is a probing meditation on the relationships among personal, national and world histories. The themes—inheritance, immortality—are timeless ones.

The V. S. Naipaul one encounters in the press is a snappish little man whose contempt for interviews and interviewers is frequently evident. At times, the harshness seems a performance, a way of cutting short his encounters with pesky reporters. Performance or no, Mr. Naipaul has ample reason to be snappish. Knighthood notwithstanding, the response to both the public Naipaul and to his work has often been caustic and personal, especially in the third world. The Palestinian scholar Edward W. Said has characterized Mr. Naipaul's posture as that of "a white man's nigger," always "looking down." The poet and Nobel laureate Derek Walcott, born in St. Lucia, not far from Mr. Naipaul's native Trinidad, has derided his fellow West Indian for an alleged "abhorrence of Negroes" and for revering England, once Trinidad's colonial mistress, over the Afro-Caribbean heritage that Mr. Walcott mythologizes in his epic poem, "Omeros."

It has become a matter of reflex for Mr. Naipaul's reviewers to say: "What marvelous writing. But why doesn't he write about the shortcomings of white folks in the West?" That's as absurd as asking why Proust didn't set *Remembrance of Things Past* in, say, the American Midwest. It's the writer's story; he can set it where he wants.

Mr. Naipaul's first-world defenders have been just as fixed on race, and just as colonialist and condescending, as his third-world critics. Often these defenders characterize him as "brave" for telling "the truth," despite all those colored folks who want him to paint a sunnier portrait. (The writer Jane Kramer has called him "the Solzhenitsyn of the third world.") Two years ago, The Guardian in Britain suggested that V. S. Naipaul had been passed over for the Nobel Prize because of "reservations" about his "suitability to represent the Caribbean." In place of "represent," read "celebrate." But since when is a celebratory view of one's home ground a mark of great literature? If history teaches us anything, it's that the darker view (Dostoyevsky, Saul Bellow, fill in the others yourself) is by far the most penetrating and literary. Keep in mind as well that the Caribbean, despite its

swaying palm trees and glistening beaches, is historically a place of slaughter, slavery and indentured servitude as nasty as any in the world.

A Way in the World opens upon the Caribbean of modern times—late-colonial Trinidad in the 1940's, specifically Port of Spain, the city of Mr. Naipaul's youth and the one to which he often returns in fiction. Here we encounter again the questions about himself that Mr. Naipaul has often tried to answer: how he became a writer; how he grew from a cloistered island person into the wanderer and voice of exile he finally became. We join the narrator at 17, filling the summer between high school and college with work as a clerk in a stuffy government office. About him are the human remnants of colonialism: angry, distrustful men constantly aware of the doors that were barred to them because they entered civil service at a time when the best jobs were reserved for whites from England.

One of those angry men is Blair, a black senior clerk who has done well, but less well than he might have, had the best schools not been closed to him. A narrator who seems to be Mr. Naipaul goes off to England to study and write. The years pass. Back at home, proselytizers preach racial politics and revolution in the town square as Trinidad hurtles headlong toward independence. Some of these proselytizers are confidence men who will spend the rest of their lives in orbit from nation to nation, living on their wits. Blair is a different sort. He gives himself, body and soul, to the new politics and develops an international career as a financial adviser for newly independent third world governments. In the end, his commitment kills him. A corrupt east African regime retains him to straighten out its affairs. Government officials have him murdered when he threatens their gold and ivory smuggling.

The story of people flung to the far corners of the globe by the collapse of colonial empires would make an absorbing novel on its own. But Mr. Naipaul intends something far deeper. Musing over Trinidad's landscape, he writes:

> "I can tell you . . . the Amerindian name for that land. . . . I can look at the vegetation and tell you what was there when Columbus came and what was imported later. I can reconstruct the plantations that were laid out. . . . While the documents last we can hunt up the story of every strip of occupied land.

> "I can give you that historical bird's eye view. But I cannot really explain the mystery of . . . inheritance. Most of us know the parents or grandparents we come from. But we go back and back, forever, we go back all of us to the very beginning: in our blood and bone and brain we carry the memories of thousands of beings. . . . We cannot understand

all the traits we have inherited. Sometimes we can be strangers to ourselves."

With this passage Mr. Naipaul announces what he's about here: an archeology of the colonial impulse, the thing that spun Columbus, Raleigh and countless others out of their easy chairs into the great dark unknown, on missions of discovery to the New World. Partly it was the myth of El Dorado, the city of gold that Raleigh and Columbus never found and the quest for which was partly responsible for ruining both of them. Partly it was a certain "madness and self-deception" that permitted these men to cause and endure horrendous suffering, even when it was apparent that they'd mischarted the course. But beneath these forces, Mr. Naipaul writes, lay the simple urge of these men to create themselves anew. Often the exercise had universally dramatic consequences.

Toward the end of the novel, we find ourselves in the Gulf of Desolation, between Trinidad and Venezuela, witnessing the final journeys of three agents of empire: Columbus (1451-1506), Raleigh (1554-1618) and the failed Venezuelan revolutionist Miranda (1750-1816). Columbus's final voyage—one racked by mutinies, illness and bad luck—is his most catastrophic, and Columbus returns to the Spanish court in chains. Raleigh, in 1618, is a sick old man waiting in the gulf for scouts who have gone to find El Dorado. The news of El Dorado never arrives. Raleigh returns to England and is beheaded.

Least known and most central to the plot—and most similar to Mr. Naipaul himself—is Francisco Miranda, a Venezuelan aristocrat who leaves his home at the age of 21 to seek his fortune in Europe. Of Miranda Mr. Naipaul writes:

> "I saw him as a very early colonial, someone with a feeling of incompleteness, with very little at home to fall back on, with an idea of a great world out there, someone who, when he was out in this world, had to reinvent himself. I saw in him some of my own early promptings (and the promptings of other people I knew)."

To help cover his expenses in Europe, Miranda takes to Spain 450 pounds of cocoa beans (no doubt grown, at the cost of great suffering, on the family's slave estates). The cocoa fetches 115 pesos. Miranda spends the entire sum on a silk handkerchief and a silk umbrella, artifacts that symbolize his wish to move as soon as possible among Europe's rich and famous. Miranda becomes a swindler and world-class confidence man. Still, he is welcomed all over Europe. As the only South American of culture most Europeans have ever seen, he is free to present himself as whoever he wishes to be. Introductions continue, onward and upward; in Rus-

sia, Catherine the Great makes him an officer and showers him with favors.

Miranda keeps a journal of his adventures. It is through this journal that he makes himself anew. Wandering and writing, wandering and writing. Miranda the mountebank, Miranda the dilettante, convinces himself that he is Miranda the sovereign, "a government in waiting," entitled to assume leadership of the South America from which he has been absent for 35 years. He invades Venezuela, fails to rout the Spaniards and spends the rest of his life in dungeons.

The principal brilliance of this book is the way it situates its present-day characters—Blair, the revolutionaries and Naipaul himself—squarely in the historical currents of the colonial age. Writers scribbling themselves into being are not unlike the so-called "great men" of history who re-created themselves from spit and myth, in hopes of playing larger and longer on the world stage. In the hands of a lesser writer these comparisons of writers and the "great men" of history would seem forced, even pretentious. Mr. Naipaul embraces Miranda's days and nights, and his inner demons, in a way that is both plausible and moving. We are all of us confidence men (and women), making ourselves up as we go along.

William H. Pritchard (essay date Winter 1995)

SOURCE: "Naipaul's Written World," in *The Hudson Review,* Vol. XLVII, No. 4, Winter, 1995, pp. 587-96.

[*In the following essay, Pritchard argues that Naipaul's "decline as a novelist" can be attributed to his "banishment" of irony and humor in his later works.*]

V. S. Naipaul's twenty-second book is an occasion for looking over his extraordinary career and considering how much it weighs and what parts of it weigh most. That he hasn't yet won the Nobel Prize is continuing matter for speculation and doubtless has to do with his outspoken airings of prejudices that are insufficiently liberal. Reviewing the new book's predecessor, *The Enigma of Arrival* (1987), Derek Walcott—a Nobel winner—both praised it as writing and deplored Naipaul's disdainful attitudes toward black people and the West Indian world. Even so, said Walcott, Trinidadians had large enough hearts to forgive him for choosing England as the place of authority and tradition from which other places were judged and found wanting. One has the sense, then, of Naipaul as a politically incorrect figure whose views on things political count more than does his art as a writer (though everybody says he "writes well"), to the extent that the art has not been properly examined and evaluated.

In particular one wants to ask about the sort of novelist we have on our hands. *A Way in the World,* like *The Enigma of Arrival,* insists on its title page that it is a novel. Yet by no stretch of my imagination can either book be called a novel in any but the loosest and most unhelpful sense. Randall Jarrell's witty definition of the genre as a prose work of some length that has something wrong with it, will hardly do to characterize *A Way in the World.* Unlike *Enigma,* which concentrated obsessively and minutely on the narrator's life in a Wiltshire cottage over a period of years, the new book has no unifying thread of time or place; nor is its nine-part scheme of biographical reminiscence, historical fable, and portraiture of imaginary-real figures, consistently "voiced" in such a way as to assure us we can trust the narrator. Sink or swim, is more like it, and a number of times I sank.

You could say that Naipaul began as a writer of novels and late in his career has become a writer of "novels." (The English edition of *A Way in the World* calls it a "sequence," which is safe enough.) In what to my taste was the most engaging section of this sequence, "Passenger: A Figure from the Thirties," Naipaul recounts his relationship with an English writer he calls Foster Morris, who encouraged Naipaul at the beginning of his career as a novelist. In 1937 Morris had written a book about Trinidad centering on a strike in the oilfields and on the leader of the strike, a preacher named Tubal Uriah Buzz Butler. In "Passenger," Naipaul (we scarcely need to call him "the narrator") praises Morris' book for the way it depicted Trinidad people "with the utmost seriousness," treating them without irony, as if they were English. But, adds Naipaul, well-intentioned as *The Shadowed Livery* was it was also wrong, since it suppressed "the sense of the absurd, the idea of comedy"—the "preserver," Naipaul calls it. His own earliest efforts at fiction, in which he attempted to use English settings and people encountered after he settled in London in 1956 were, he soon decided, misconceived, since they suppressed his comic inheritance. The comedy inherited was a double one, from his story-telling Hindu family and from the street life in Port of Spain. More than once he has described how his true direction became apparent to him one afternoon when, sitting in the offices of the BBC for whom he was an occasional worker, he wrote the opening paragraphs of the opening story in what would be *Miguel Street* (his third published book, though the first to be written):

> Every morning when he got up Hat would sit on the banister of his back verandah and shout across, "What happening there, Bogart?"

> Bogart would turn in his bed and mumble softly, so that no one heard, "What happening there, Hat?"

In Naipaul's "Prologue to an Autobiography" (in *Finding the Center,* 1984) he writes about this opening that

> The first sentence was true, the second was invention. But together—to me, the writer—they had done something extraordinary. Though they had left out everything—the setting, the historical time, the racial and social complexities of the people of the street—they had suggested it all; they had created the world of the street. And together, as sentences, words, they had set up a rhythm, a speed, which dictated all that was to follow.

Of note in this portrait of the artist by himself, is Naipaul's confident assumption that the difference between truth and invention is perfectly clear, and that the account given here of his beginnings as a writer is obviously true, not invented.

Naipaul's emphasis on the pace and idiom of comedy, with its roots in local observation and its dependence on artfully combined sentences and words, surely characterizes with accuracy the feel of the stories in *Miguel Street* and—even more satisfying—his first two novels, *The Mystic Masseur* (1957) and *The Suffrage of Elvira* (1958). In *The Mystic Masseur,* Ganesh—the struggling masseur who turns himself into a famous writer and healer—observes a shop notice written by Leela, his bride-to-be, who is being recommended to Ganesh by her father, Ramlogan:

> "Is Leela self who write that," Ramlogan said. "I didn't ask she to write it, mind you. She just sit down quiet quiet one morning after tea and write it off."

> It read:

> NOTICE:

> Notice, is. Hereby; provided: That, Seats!
> Are, Provided. For; Female: Shop, Assistants!

> Ganesh said, "Leela know a lot of punctuation marks."

> "That is it, sahib. All day the girl just sitting down and talking about these punctuation marks. She is like that, sahib."

Later, to the surprise of those around him, Ganesh writes his first book, titled *A Hundred and One Questions and Answers on the Hindu Religion,* which contains sticklers such as number 46, "Who is the greatest modern Hindu?" (Ans. Mahatma Gandhi) and 47, "Who is the second greatest modern Hindu?" (Ans. Pandit Jawaharlal Nehru) and 48, "Who is the third greatest modern Hindu?" (Ans. not revealed to us). Ramlogan is delighted: "Is the sort of book, sahib, they should give to children in school and make them learn it by heart."

The idiom is as memorable as the inventive comedy it conveys: Ganesh's aunt is known by him as "The Great Belcher" for reasons of her expressive dyspepsia; Ramlogan says that having to look after himself since he was five years old has given him "cha'acter and sensa values, sahib. That's what it gives me. Cha'acter and sensa values." In *The Suffrage of Elvira,* about a political campaign in one of Trinidad's first free elections, the tone is even broader and more farcical, with many fine scenes, one of which involves a dead chicken that someone lays squarely in the middle of Ramlogan's doorway, just after he has luxuriously rubbed himself with Canadian Healing Oil (the "Canadian" touch is especially good in this Caribbean venue). When one of the characters is told by his son that the son will no longer support his father's candidate in the election, the older man doesn't attempt to argue with him since "You is a big man. Your pee making froth." Many further examples of a living idiom could be adduced as proof of the way, in Naipaul's retrospective phrase about it, "the world of the street" has been created.

The "Passenger" section from Naipaul's new work throws interesting light on how he sees the relation between his first three "street" books and what is generally acknowledged to be his masterwork, *A House for Mr. Biswas* (1961), by any standards among the major novels of our century. Naipaul tells us that though his early way of writing had given him confidence and gotten him started, by 1960 or thereabouts he had begun to be bothered by its "jokeyness," a humor that seemed to lie "on the other side of hysteria," just as did the colonial society he had written about. He says—it must be in reference to *Mr. Biswas,* though he doesn't name it directly—that he was "absolutely secure in this new book" which was taking him much longer to finish than the previous ones. And although the six hundred pages of *Biswas* contain much comedy—especially in the verbal inventiveness of the protagonist's name-calling of his Tulsi in-laws—and much fiercely sardonic humor in Mr. Biswas' struggle with the world's stupidities and follies, the novel frequently takes on a deeper note. Mr. Biswas could be said to exist, like the comedy Naipaul had become adept at creating, on the other side of hysteria or anxiety, that "deeper root of comedy" that had become this novelist's subject. Biswas suffers a major nervous collapse during the book as well as countless smaller defeats and depressions; so when Naipaul provides him with a momentary vision of self-possession, of peace, the effect on a reader is strong and satisfying, as in this memory of morning in Port of Spain:

> The newspaper, delivered free, still warm, the ink still wet, sprawled on the concrete steps down

which the sun was moving. Dew lay on trees and roofs; the empty street, freshly swept and washed, was in cool shadow, and water ran clear in the gutters whose green bases had been scratched and striped by the sweepers' harsh brooms.

Or this moment, in his final dwelling place two weeks before he dies:

> He thought of the house as his own, though for years it had been irretrievably mortgaged. And during these months of illness and despair, he was struck again and again by the wonder of being in his own house, the audacity of it; to walk in through his own front gate, to bar entry to whoever he wished, to close his doors and windows every night, to hear no noises except those of his family, to wander freely from room to room, and about his yard . . .

A House for Mr. Biswas is invariably called "Dickensian" by critics, as I suppose any big book teeming with characters (many of them caricatures), disdaining economy of effort and moving always toward expansion, determined to leave nothing out, could be so called. But except for the reflective gravity of some of the narrative in *Great Expectations,* Dickens, whose "jokeyness" is always cropping up, contains little of the sustained depths and glooms that lie not very far beneath Mohun Biswas' story.

Having published, at age twenty-nine, a novel containing as much life as did *Mr. Biswas,* what was Naipaul to do next? A possibility, frequently made use of by English novelists of this century, was to travel, then write up your travels: accordingly Naipaul went back to the Caribbean, then to India, and produced absorbing accounts of these places in *The Middle Passage* (1962) and *An Area of Darkness* (1964). But while in India he also wrote, one presumes fairly rapidly, the oddest and in some ways most delightful book of his career, *Mr. Stone and the Knights' Companion,* the one novel of his set wholly in England and with English characters. To those familiar with Naipaul's other fiction, both early and late, *Mr. Stone* reads like a ventriloquist's performance, as if Muriel Spark or Elizabeth Taylor were at the controls. The tone and irony of the novel is delicate and mischievous, with yearning and melancholy in it as well. It was if Naipaul were saying, if you think I'm merely a regionalist entertainer, let me show you what I can do as well or better than any contemporary English novelist. By the same token, it was something only to be done once.

Naipaul's decline as a novelist—or at least his metamorphosis into a very different, and to my eyes less appealing, one—began with the award-winning *The Mimic Men* (1967). His first novel in the first person, it is an example of what Henry James, speaking of that mode, called "the terrible fluidity of self-revelation." Whether we are meant to identify the narrator, one Ralph Singh, with Naipaul, or whether Singh is the object of authorial irony, is impossible to determine. What is damagingly evident is that comedy has been thoroughly laid aside in favor of Singh's largely toneless recitation of his career in London, his childhood in the Caribbean, his marriage and its dissolution, his decision to write a memoir. Instead of comedy, we have endless assertion and declaration (the book is only 250 pages long but feels much longer). Nothing is dramatized; the mode of presentation is as flat and uninflected as Singh's life seems to have been. Here for the first time we see Naipaul—as he characterized himself in a recent *New Yorker* profile—as a hater of "style" in prose: "I want the writer not to be there . . . In my writing there's no self-consciousness, there's no beauty." He says in the profile he is against "smoothness," against rhythm, against Santayana and Gibbon and the King James Bible ("Unbearable—*unbearable*"); he is against plot (Trollope would be all right if he weren't always plotting); he is in favor of Richard Jeffries and William Cobbett as admirable nineteenth-century writers, rather than Jane Austen and Henry James. Although these prejudices don't express themselves fully in his writing until the last two "novels," they begin to be felt in ***The Mimic Men*** and in the three political novels of the 1970s which followed.

In 1974, the year before the second of these books, ***Guerillas,*** was published (***In a Free State*** appeared in 1971, ***A Bend in the River*** in 1979), Naipaul wrote an essay about Joseph Conrad in which, rather tortuously, he delineated his relation to that writer. As criticism, it is a curious performance: "An Outpost of Progress," an early Conrad story, is designated "the finest thing Conrad wrote," while "The Lagoon" (also an early story) provided Naipaul with something "strong and direct" that he was never again to find in Conrad. By contrast, *Lord Jim, The Secret Agent, Under Western Eyes,* and *Victory* are in their different ways unsatisfactory, and he couldn't finish *Nostromo.* Yet, and this is the burden of the essay, Naipaul eventually discovers that Conrad has been there before him: that Naipaul's desire to make a romantic career for himself as a writer was doomed to fail, since the world had changed:

> The new politics, the curious reliance of men on institutions they were yet working to undermine, the simplicity of belief and the hideous simplicity of actions, the corruption of causes, half-made societies that seemed doomed to remain half-made: these were the things that began to preoccupy me.

This had been Conrad's experience, and Naipaul attempted to match it, he says, by losing "one's preconceptions of what the novel should do and, above all, to rid oneself of the

subtle corruptions of the novel or comedy of manners." These words are extremely revealing: the corruption of causes, of half-made societies, of "politics," necessitates something different from the subtle corruptions of fiction. If "novel" equals "comedy of manners," then it can't relevantly deal with politics. Perhaps Naipaul believes that Conrad's austerity and lack of comedy were also to be emulated; yet *The Secret Agent* and *Under Western Eyes* are full of a sardonic humor directed at institutions and at "the hideous simplicity of actions." Indeed you might even say that in them Conrad came closest to writing the comedy of manners, and they are perhaps the novels of his that wear best.

What I find disturbing in Naipaul's political novels from the 1970s is a tonelessness at their center; an absence of narrative performance—of "style" if you will—that novels have not often tried to do without. Bent on displaying the corruption of causes in African and Caribbean "half-made societies," these books do so at the price of readerly pleasure. Even admirers of them might admit that they're not much fun to read; for Naipaul has deliberately moved beyond the "fun" that was so importantly a part of his pre-*Mimic Men* fiction. Taking the long view, we see that this was the way he had to go—to "develop": yet such development exacts its price. ***Mr. Biswas*** will be read when ***Guerillas*** is barely remembered, because the earlier book is art, the later one closer to a cautionary tale told in icy, noncommittal prose that doesn't admit any mixed feelings.

With ***The Enigma of Arrival*** and ***A Way in the World,*** Naipaul has ceased to write novels in favor of densely meditative prose excursions, linked together through something other than story ("Yes, oh, dear, yes, the novel tells a story," squeaked E. M. Forster). Or put it that the story has been internalized and historicized into something presumably deeper and more profound than a mere piece of fiction. In the *New Yorker* interview, Naipaul spoke of himself as a man who weighs his words, doesn't just say what comes into his head, and that therefore his books demand special treatment: "My paragraphs are very rich—they have to be read. Many things are happening in the paragraph. If you miss a paragraph—if you miss a page—it's hard to get back into it." He thinks that "twenty good pages" at a stretch is about as much as a careful reader of him can manage. ***The Enigma of Arrival*** contains a hundred or so rich pages ("The Journey") describing Naipaul's leaving Trinidad and early sojourn in England. But the rest of the book, centered on the manor-cottage life he lived in Wiltshire, is not so rich as it is labored. The assumption behind his remark about weighing words carefully is that a writer who does so will be neither vain nor prolix. Yet the minutiae of observation and speculation, the teasing out of the people and places that surround him—done without humor, largely without irony in ***Enigma***—constitute an obstacle course that can be traversed only with much effort and frequent stops along the way.

Naipaul's power and authority as a writer is such that to admit to failure on a reader's part, to lapse into inattention or boredom, makes for a guilty sense of inadequacy. Isn't there something really *deep* here that, if I were a better reader, I could discover?

On the basis of *A Way in the World,* I'd have to say—not necessarily. As with *Enigma,* the best parts of it are distinctly autobiographical: early memories ("A Smell of Fishglue") of administrative work in the Red House in Port of Spain; the aforementioned sequence with Foster Morris; and at least part of the section about the revolutionary Lebrun (a C. L. R. James-like figure). But much of the book is devoted to what Naipaul calls "unwritten stories," three of them, one of which is about Sir Walter Raleigh in his old age coming back to Trinidad, still occupied with the fading possibility of an El Dorado to be discovered up the Orinoco; another, even longer, story is about the career of the Venezuelan revolutionary, Francisco Miranda, a late eighteenth-century precursor of Simon Bolivar. By calling them unwritten stories, Naipaul, it seems to me, bids to disarm us by deconstructing the business of writing fiction (these are not "stories," you understand, not "written" in the usual sense), then taking the liberty to spin out at some length combinations of imaginative-historical embroidery. But their power to make us ask the crucial narrative question—what happened next?—is too often absent, with the effect that they feel, in the main, contrived and willed—interesting ideas that end up being overwritten rather than unwritten.

A Way in the World is a strange book, and though it has been called (along with *Enigma*) Proustian, there seems to me a huge difference between the densely psychological, often playful-painful exploration Proust gives his narrator, and what Naipaul does to the "I" in the presumably more autobiographical sections of the new work. A single instance will have to do to show what I mean and why it's a problem. In the section dealing with the revolutionary Lebrun ("On the Road"), Naipaul is invited to a dinner in London for the man at which West Indian food is served—a dish called "coo-coo" or "foo-foo" consisting of "a heavy glistening mound" of yams and green bananas and peppers. Repelled by it, Naipaul leaves it on his plate (no one noticed, he tells us). Eight pages later he is in New York City, again at dinner with friends of Lebrun with whom he has been put in touch. The host has promised him that gefilte fish will be served, a "special dish," which Naipaul says he's never had. When it appears this is what happens:

> I didn't like the way it looked, and have no memory of it. The idea of something pounded to paste, then spiced or oiled, worked on by fingers, brought to mind something of hand lotions and other things. I became fearful of smelling it. I couldn't eat it. With the coo-coo or foo-foo in the Maida Vale flat I had

been able to hide what I did to the things on my plate. That couldn't be done here; everyone knew that the gefilte fish had been specially prepared for Lebrun's friend from London.

> Manners never frayed. Conversation revived. But the embarrassment that began in the dining room lasted until I was taken back to the Manhattan hotel.

This is as much as we are told. What is the meaning of it and why should it be presented as imaginatively significant? We know that Naipaul is an extremely fastidious man, a strict vegetarian, prey to disgust at certain kinds of culinary treats. And that he is as fastidious about what he writes (he weighs the words) as about what he eats. But for the life of me I can't see anything more to this passage than that gefilte fish didn't pass his scrutiny and embarrassment ensued. What does this have to do with Lebrun, or with the world about which Naipaul moves with such deliberate complication? By banishing irony and humor, the staple of comedy of manners and of a certain kind of novel, Naipaul has put himself out there on a limb with little besides his righteous, proud sense of himself as a man of integrity. Too often, in *A Way in the World,* that's all we're left with, and it feels flat, merely asserted. This is by way of saying that the new book (a strong bid for the Nobel?) is not the crown, but a curious outgrowth rather, of his distinguished writing life.

FURTHER READING

Criticism

Chauhan, P. S. "V. S. Naipaul: History as Cosmic Irony." In *Reworlding: The Literature of the Indian Diaspora,* edited by Emmanuel S. Nelson, pp. 13-23. New York: Greenwood Press, 1992.
    Examines Naipaul's development as a writer, focusing on his ironic perspective.

Derrick, A. C. "Naipaul's Technique as a Novelist." In *Critical Perspectives on V. S. Naipaul,* edited by Robert D. Hamner, pp. 194-207. London: Heinemann, 1977.
    Studies major thematic strands in Naipaul's work.

Miller, Karl. "Elephant Head." *London Review of Books* 12, No. 18 (27 September 1990): 11-13.
    In-depth review of *India: A Million Mutinies Now.*

Murdoch, David. "The Riches of Empire: Postcolonialism in Literature and Criticism." *Choice* 32, No. 7 (March 1995): 1059-69.

Examines the lasting effects of colonization as it appears in literature and criticism.

Ramraj, Victor J. "V. S. Naipaul: The Irrelevance of Nationalism." *World Literature Written in English* 23, No. 1 (1984): 187-96.

Studies Naipaul's literary approach to politics and the manner in which he de-emphasizes political conflict as a primary motivating force for fiction.

Roy, Ashish. "Race and Figures of History in Naipaul's *An Area of Darkness.*" *Critique—Studies in Contemporary Fiction* XXXII, No. 4 (Summer 1991): 235-57.

Argues that *An Area of Darkness* reflects a global strategy to present subjective observation in the guise of realistic documentary.

Ware, Tracy. "V. S. Naipaul's *The Return of Eva Perón* and the Loss of 'True Wonder'." *ARIEL: A Review of International English Literature* 24, No. 2 (April 1993): 101-12.

Discusses the influence of Joseph Conrad present in Naipaul's *The Return of Eva Perón*.

Interviews

Gussow, Mel. "V. S. Naipaul: 'It Is Out of This Violence I've Always Written'." *The New York Times Book Review* (16 September 1984): 45-6.

Naipaul discusses a number of issues, including the role of the editor and his attitude toward emerging nations.

Additional coverage of Naipaul's life and career is contained in the following sources published by Gale: *Concise Dictionary of British Literary Bibliography,* **1960 to Present;** *Contemporary Authors,* **Vol. 1-4R;** *Contemporary Authors New Revision Series,* **Vols. 1, 33, 51;** *Dictionary of Literary Biography,* **Vol. 125;** *Dictionary of Literary Biography Yearbook, 1985; DISCovering Authors: British; DISCovering Authors: Canadian; DISCovering Authors Modules: Most-Studied* **and** *Novelists;* **and** *Major Twentieth Century Writers.*

Susan Sontag

1933-

American essayist, critic, novelist, short story writer, editor, screenwriter, dramatist, and film director.

The following entry presents an overview of Sontag's career through 1997. For further information on her life and works, see *CLC*, Volumes 1, 2, 10, 13, and 31.

INTRODUCTION

Sontag is one of the most influential contemporary American critics. Considered a popular icon for her role in the development of modern culture and intellectual thought, Sontag addresses issues of interpretation and has exposed Americans to the works of modern European intellectuals.

Biographical Information

Sontag was born January 16, 1933, in New York City, but spent her youth in Tucson and Los Angeles. She graduated from high school at the age of fifteen and entered the University of California, Berkeley, transferring after one year to the University of Chicago, from which she received a B.A. in philosophy in 1951. While at the University of Chicago, Sontag met Philip Rieff, a social psychologist; the couple married in 1950 and had a son, David, two years later, but divorced in 1959. Sontag pursued graduate studies at Harvard from 1951 to 1957, earning master's degrees in English (1954) and philosophy (1955). She continued her graduate studies at St. Anne's College, Oxford, and the University of Paris. After several years of teaching at various universities, Sontag began writing full-time; her first collection of critical essays was published in 1966. In the early 1970s Sontag was diagnosed with breast cancer, which contributed to her writing of *Illness as Metaphor* (1978.)

Major Works

In her first collection of critical essays, *Against Interpretation and Other Essays* (1966), Sontag eschewed standard methods of critical analysis that rely on content and various levels of meaning, asserting instead that the function of criticism is to show "how it is what it is, even that it is what it is, rather than show what it means." Included in this collection is the famous essay "Notes on Camp" in which Sontag defends "camp" as a serious art form. *Styles of Radical Will* (1969) contains the essay "The Pornographic Imagination" in which Sontag argues that pornography is a valid literary genre. *Illness as Metaphor* (1978) and *AIDS and Its Metaphors* (1989) both deal with the way in which western

society interprets and creates cultural myths about disease. Sontag has also written several works of fiction, including *The Benefactor* (1963), *Death Kit* (1967), and a collection of short stories entitled *I, etcetera* (1978). Most noted among her fiction is *The Volcano Lover* (1992), an unusual account of Emma Hamilton and Horatio Nelson told from the point of view of Hamilton's husband, Sir William Hamilton. This novel provides a sweeping look at society and culture in Naples from 1764 to 1780, with which the author contrasts contemporary culture. Sontag has also written a play, *Alice in Bed* (1993), about the life of Alice James, the sister of Henry and William James.

Critical Reception

Sontag's work has generated much criticism. While some reviewers have praised her for providing a new interpretation of modern culture and for exposing Americans to modern European writers and intellectuals, others contend that Sontag's arguments are not supported adequately and that she diverges too much from her central themes. Bruce Bower writes, "It sometimes seems as if Sontag's chief priority as an essayist is not to clarify, persuade, or illuminate, but to demonstrate to the world that she is the highest of the highbrows, an intellectual, a breed apart from the lesser scribblers." Some critics have made similar assessments of her fiction. Richard Jenkyns states that Sontag has put too much of her own voice in *The Volcano Lover:* "Her characters are squeezed out to make room for her own insistent voice." Most critics, however, are united in their praise of Sontag's descriptive narrative and her depiction of historical trends and settings.

PRINCIPAL WORKS

The Benefactor (novel) 1963
Against Interpretation and Other Essays (essays) 1966
Death Kit (novel) 1967
*Duet for Cannibals (screenplay) 1969
Styles of Radical Will (essays) 1969
Trip to Hanoi (essay) 1969
*Brother Carl: A Filmscript (screenplay) 1971
*Promised Lands (screenplay) 1974
On Photography (nonfiction) 1977
I, etcetera (short stories) 1978
Illness as Metaphor (nonfiction) 1978
Under the Sign of Saturn (essays) 1980
A Susan Sontag Reader (collection) 1982
*Unguided Tour (screenplay) 1983
AIDS and Its Metaphors (nonfiction) 1989
The Way We Live Now (novel) 1991
The Volcano Lover: A Romance (novel) 1992
Alice in Bed: A Play in Eight Scenes (drama) 1993

*Sontag also directed these films.

CRITICISM

Merle Rubin (review date 11 August 1992)

SOURCE: "Susan Sontag's Cavalier Cavaliere," in *The Christian Science Monitor*, August 11, 1992, p. 11.

[*In the following review of* The Volcano Lover, *Rubin writes that Sontag provides a fresh approach to the story of Admiral Horatio Nelson and his lover Emma Hamilton.*]

A diplomat by vocation, a collector by avocation, the eponymous "volcano lover" of Susan Sontag's meditative, unconventional, historical romance [*The Volcano Lover*] is a typical man of the Enlightenment. As the British envoy from 1764 to 1800 to the court of Naples (capital of the Kingdom of the Two Sicilies), Sir William Hamilton—or, as

Sontag dubs him, "the Cavaliere,"—divides his time between attending upon the outrageously uncouth Bourbon king and attending to his own special passions: collecting antique vases and other objets d'art and exploring the famous, still-active volcano of Mt. Vesuvius.

The Cavaliere is urbane, aristocratic, and possessed of a keenly inquiring mind. He has cultivated an attitude of detached superiority that allows him to take pleasure in life's diversity and vicissitudes. Interested in everything, but disturbed by almost nothing, he is the quintessential expatriate: "Where those stunned by the horror of the famine and the brutality and incompetence of the government's response saw unending inertia, lethargy, and a hardened lava of ignorance, the Cavaliere saw a flow. The expatriate's dancing city is often the local reformer's or revolutionary's immobilized one, ill-governed, committed to injustice. Different distance, different cities."

Volcanoes, too, look better from a safe distance. But the Cavaliere's boundless curiosity drives him to venture up the mountain again and again to peer into the smoldering crater. It is almost as if his familiarity with the volcano, combined with his aristocratic detachment, has left him feeling immune to its dangers.

"To love volcanoes," the narrator elsewhere observes, "was to put the revolution in its place." The Cavaliere's sense of disengagement, his ability to take the long view, helps him to view with equanimity the massive social upheaval that will shake Europe during his tenure as envoy.

The Cavaliere's wife, Catherine, a devoted, musically gifted woman, does not share his enthusiasm—either for volcanoes or for the vulgar, corrupt Neapolitan court. Yet her gentle and loving presence has been very important to him, so much so that when she dies, still in her early 40s, he loses his zest for life. But then, his life is changed again when a beautiful, vibrant, young woman—the former mistress of his nephew—arrives in Naples to stay with him. Although she is of humble background, a blacksmith's daughter, she is bright, affectionate, quick to learn, and gifted with a rare ability to enter into other people's feelings. She becomes the Cavaliere's mistress and later—to his family's consternation—his wife. Her married name is one that will become famous and notorious: Emma Hamilton.

The love affair of Emma Hamilton and the great British Admiral Horatio Nelson was a scandal in its time and has been a source of material for novelists, dramatists, and filmmakers ever since—from well-known retellings like Terence Rattigan's play "A Bequest to the Nation" and the Laurence Olivier-Vivien Leigh film of "That Hamilton Woman" to the kind of informal parodies that made the subject of Lord Nelson and Emma Hamilton a staple of after-dinner charades and tableaux vivants. It has been viewed as a grand love story; it has also been viewed as an outbreak of foolish passion that led a great hero (and otherwise honorable married man) to lose his judgment over a blowsy, no-longer-beautiful, reputedly vulgar, married woman.

In attempting a fresh look at this story in *The Volcano Lover: A Romance*, Sontag is resourceful. Her first defense against triteness is to shift the bulk of attention to the neglected figure of Emma's husband, William—"the Cavaliere." In addition to putting a somewhat overshadowed figure into the limelight, this enables the author to portray Emma's charms—and Nelson's charisma—as seen through the eyes of a seasoned diplomat, who feels love and admiration both for his wife and their distinguished friend. Sontag also combats the reader's sense of over-familiarity by almost never referring to the characters by their all-too-well-known names: thus, Hamilton becomes "the Cavaliere" or "the collector," Emma, "the Cavaliere's wife," and Nelson, "the hero." In the same vein, Goethe, who makes a cameo appearance visiting Naples in the course of his famous "Italian journey," is identified simply as "the poet."

Narrating most of the story in her own voice, with plenty of opportunities for essayistic asides, Sontag surveys the salient features of the age. "The collector" and "the poet" are seen as epitomizing the contrast between the old-fashioned Enlightenment desire to add to the sum of knowledge and the "modern" (or Romantic) lust to understand the secrets of nature and human nature in order to be able to transform the world and oneself. Nelson, "the hero," emerges as a figure like his great foe Napoleon: concentrated, dynamic, and single-minded. He is also sincerely devoted to the idea of attaining glory through military bravery. He wants to be admired and "understood."

Some of Sontag's generalizations are surprisingly shopworn, as when she observes that the difference between an age that idealized its heroes and our own preference for seeing them "warts and all" is the result of our democratic dislike of "feeling inferior."

Perhaps Sontag's most impressive achievement is the way she places events in context: from the intimate drama of a love affair to the world-shaking crises of human—and natural—history. Before she is through, we have heard from everyone from the Cavaliere's first wife to Emma's doting mother, not to mention an unwittingly self-incriminating self-defense by Emma. Sontag gives the last word to Eleanora de Fonseca Pimentel, one of the band of brave, gifted, and truly cultivated Neapolitan patriots condemned to death by Nelson—who is in league with the vengeful Bourbon monarchy—for their part in the short-lived Neapolitan Republic.

What are we to think of a "civilized" Cavaliere who allows some of his own friends and fellow-naturalists to perish? And what of the warm-hearted, ever-sympathetic Emma, who cannot be bothered to think of anyone beyond her immediate circle? Sontag's penetrating, insightful portrayal of these people and their times is a devastating illustration of how seemingly minor moral blindness can lead to major moral catastrophes.

Gabriele Annan (review date 13 August 1992)

SOURCE: "A Moral Tale," in *New York Review of Books*, Vol. 39, No. 14, August 13, 1992, pp. 3, 4, 6.

[*Below, Annan offers a positive review of* The Volcano Lover.]

The Volcano Lover is the story of Nelson and Emma and William Hamilton. Susan Sontag calls it "a romance" and is intrepid enough to describe the first kiss between Nelson and Emma, "the fat lady and the short man with one arm." A *frisson* of ecstasy comes across; the scene works. And so does the pathos of the whole familiar saga. All the same, I should not call Sontag's book a romance so much as a moral tale, with reflections on many different topics coming out of it like balloons from a cartoon strip. The range of topics is extraordinary: travel, melancholy, painting portraits, telling jokes, the neoclassical versus the modern ideal in art, changes in conceptions of greatness, changes in attitudes to women, environmental pollution, the nature of performance, irony, revolution, mobs, liberal intellectuals and how they don't understand the masses, and collecting.

Sir William Hamilton is the "Volcano Lover." He was a collector of art, antiquities, and natural specimens and wrote a book on volcanology. He bought the late Roman Portland vase and resold it to the Duchess of Portland who allowed it to be copied by the Wedgwood factory; which prompts a reflection on mass production. And that is not all, by any means, *even with the* many reflections erupting from Vesuvius itself. A volcano is almost too perfect a metaphor for almost too many things. Not that this one is an abstract idea; there are many—perhaps just a few too many—virtuoso takes of it heaving, churning, thundering, oozing, and belching sulphurous fumes.

> I should not call Sontag's book a romance so much as a moral tale, with reflections on many different topics coming out of it like balloons from a cartoon strip.
> —*Gabriele Annan*

The reflections, in their turn, are punctuated by maxims: "Living abroad facilitates treating life as a spectacle—it is one of the reasons that people of means move abroad"; "the zero point of pleasure [is] where pleasure consists in being able to put unpleasant thoughts out of one's mind." One thinks of La Rochefoucauld, and because Sontag generally refers to her three principal characters as "the hero," "the beauty," and "the Cavaliere," one also thinks of La Bruyère. And this seems appropriate, because her psychology is not the psychology of Freud and after, but of an earlier, more severe age. She is not interested, in how people get to be the way they are, but in their motives.

There are many versions of the Nelson/Emma story. In the most traditional one, Nelson is a hero caught in the toils of a vulgar, boozy trollop, and Sir William is a bloodless elderly cuckold. Recent writers (Tom Pocock, for instance, in his popular biography of Nelson published five years ago) acknowledge Hamilton's dignity and decency, and Emma's affectionate and enthusiastic nature. The most romantic version is Alexander Korda's film *That Hamilton Woman*. It was made in 1941 as a piece of patriotic propaganda, stars Laurence Olivier and Vivien Leigh, and is a regular performer on midnight TV. Napoleon is the off-screen Hitler look-alike: Nelson, of course, a super-hero, Sir William sometimes inhuman and sometimes quite humane; Emma not only irresistible, but selfless and self-sacrificing. And *thin:* even in the opening flash-forward to her last days in Calais, when she had become a helpless mountain of flesh. Leigh remains a genteel wraith. To Sontag, Emma's fatness is what comes closest to making her—but doesn't quite—into a feminist martyr: "for nothing was she judged more harshly than her failure at what is deemed a woman's greatest most feminine accomplishment; the maintenance and proper care of a no longer youthful body.... Though it was still several decades before the Romantics inaugurated the modern cult of thinness ... *she* was not to be pardoned for becoming fat."

The version of history that Sontag seems to favor is to be found in an extraordinary book called *Naples in* 1799 and published in London in 1903. It is by Constance Giglioli ("née Stocker," it says on the title page), and is a passionate indictment of the behavior of the Bourbons, the Hamiltons, and Nelson toward the defeated Neapolitan republicans. Even some of Sontag's descriptions of tortures and executions seem closely based on Giglioli or on her sources. Still, Sontag is very taken with Emma to begin with (and before she got fat): with her stunning looks, her spontaneity, her sympathy and compassion, her courage, her quick intelligence, her eagerness to improve herself, her unpretentiousness, her gift for languages (in Naples she soon made herself fluent in French and Italian), her musical talent. Sontag's Emma sings ravishingly; Pocock's merely sings loud. Sontag even takes-seriously Emma's famous "attitudes"—the poses she struck at parties in imitation of scenes from classical history and mythology. In her book, they are not the half-absurd, half-erotic, and probably a bit embarrassing posturings most people imagine, but inspired performances offering their audience unique aesthetic insights. She calls in Goethe as a witness. But Goethe will have to wait until later.

Sir William gets the first quarter of the book to himself and it is clear that Sontag likes him a lot too. He is handsome, affectionate though not passionate, civilized, well-behaved, and his strategy for living his life is admirable. "He ferried himself past one vortex of melancholy after another, by means of an astonishing spread of enthusiasms." Besides, he comes truly to love Emma. As she grows less careful about behaving like a lady, more drunk, noisy, and vulgar, he does nothing to restrain her. He has stopped "minding: he loved her." As for Nelson, "the thirty-five-year-old captain was undoubtedly a star—like the Cavaliere's wife"; and like Olivier and Leigh. Later in the book Emma will describe stardom as experienced from the inside: "Wherever I went, I felt chosen. I do not know from where I drew such confidence. I could not have been *that* extraordinary, and yet I was." In order to drum up sympathy for Nelson—her own included—Sontag has much to say about his gruesome mutilations and the unimaginable courage with which he bore them. But she does not truly admire him:

> The hero wants to be understood—which for him means being praised and sympathized with and encouraged. And the hero is romantic: that is, his vanity matched by an inordinate capacity for humility when his affections were engaged. He felt so honored by the Cavaliere's friendship, by the friendship and then the love (he dared call it love) of his wife. If I am loved by people of this quality, then I know I am worth while.

There is surely a hint of contempt here and the word "romantic" is not a complimentary one: in fact, if it weren't about so many other things as well, Sontag might have called her book *Against Romanticism.*

She dwells on the great admiration and affection between all three of her principal characters both before and after Nelson and Emma become lovers, and right up until Sir William's death. He admired Nelson because he was a hero; and Nelson admired him because he was civilized, learned, and grand. It was a good *ménage à trois.* What disgraced the trio was not adultery and its condonement, but their behavior in 1799 toward the defeated Neapolitan republic after the British Navy under Nelson put the Bourbons back on their throne. Not only Republicans, but even mere suspected sympathizers, some of them from leading Neapolitan families, were publicly hanged or beheaded, and often tortured first—and that in spite of a treaty promising them a free passage into exile. Nelson could not distinguish between justice (as he saw it) and punishment. Self-righteously, he ordered the brutal and unjust executions. Emma exulted in them and Sir William did nothing to stop them. Sir William finished his life in reduced circumstances, Emma in poverty and disgrace, and Nelson, as Sontag tells the story, very nearly in disgrace as well. What could be more of a morality tale?

She makes much of contemporary disapproval of Nelson: first because of his ridiculously public affair with the by now very fat and noisy Emma, which caused him to disobey Vice-Admiral Lord Keith's orders to move his ships from the Bay of Naples; and secondly because of his gratuitous vindictiveness toward the defeated Republicans. People accused Emma of egging him on, and the Queen of Naples (Marie Antoinette's sister) of influencing Emma, who had become her best friend. (Here Sontag has it both ways. She deplores the behavior of the two women, while complaining that it's always the women who get the blame.) The battles of Copenhagen and Trafalgar reestablished Nelson's heroic stature with the public, though not with Sontag. "Eternal shame on the hero!" He has become a villain. Even his death, according to Emma's mother, was not so very admirable: "Why go about the boat in his admiral's frock coat and his stars so a French sharpshooter could find him easy and kill him, if he wanted to stay alive to come back to her. Men are so foolish. Women may be vain, but when a man is vain it is beyond believing, for a man is willing to die for his vanity."

Emma's mother, who called herself Mrs. Cadogan, is speaking from beyond the grave. *The Volcano Lover* ends with four posthumous monologues, spoken by four women. They are Sir William Hamilton's first wife, Catherine; Emma's adoring mother; Emma herself; and Eleanora Fonseca di Pimental, a liberal aristocrat and poet who edited a Republican paper in Naples and was hanged for it. The first three loved greatly: Catherine loved Sir William and lived only to please him, Emma's mother never left her side, and Emma wanted her there. She saw her daughter through her early vicissitudes as an unmarried mother and London call girl, and when the young man she loved wanted to get rid of her and posted her to Naples as a mistress for his widowed uncle, Sir William Hamilton, Mrs. Cadogan went with her. She was an uneducated country woman with a rackety past: unlike her beautiful child, she made no attempt to improve herself. So she lived in her daughter's shadow, sitting at the back of the audience when Emma sang or performed her attitudes. People thought she was a paid companion or a poor relation, and from that position she dispensed admiration and comfort until she died. A good and selfless life.

The four posthumous monologues are all written with great feeling and without the irony that puts a cool sheen on much of the book. Eleanora Fonseca is the odd woman out: love does not come into her story. She is an intellectual, and a proto-feminist who despises women who live by love. Emma, she says, "was an enthusiast, and would have enlisted herself with the same ardor in the cause of whomever she loved. I can easily imagine Emma Hamilton, had her nationality been different, as a republican heroine, who might have ended most courageously at the foot of the gallows. That is the nullity of women like her." Still, Eleanora is not quite satisfied with her own performance either: "Sometimes I had to forget I was a woman to accomplish the best of which I was capable. Or I would lie to myself about how complicated it is to be a woman. Thus do all women, including the author of this book." This is *seconde vague* feminism, thoughtful, self-aware, and self-ironizing in its use of Mozart's opera title *Cosí fan tutte*. The quote is a reprise; the first time round it is applied with sharper feminist sarcasm to explain the huge success of Emma's "attitudes": "It seems the ultimate feminine gift, to be able to pass effortlessly, instantly, from one emotion to another. How men wanted women to be, and what they scorned in women. One minute this. The next minute that. Of course. Thus do all women."

Emma's attitudes generally: represented tragic heroines—Niobe, Medea, Iphigenia, Dido—on the point of undergoing their various ordeals: i.e., just before their sufferings become unbearable to witness. This is where Goethe comes in. Emma's performances conformed to the classical ideal he was formulating (under the influence of Winkelmann's *Laocoön*, which is also discussed) at the time he turned up in Naples on his *Italian Journey*. So when Emma brings up his early ur-Romantic best seller *Werther,* she doesn't get very far with him. Her attitudes, on the other hand, are his thing exactly: "The significant moment!. . . . That is what great art must render. The moment that is most humane, most typical, most affecting. My compliments. . . ." Goethe's famous slogan "the significant moment" gets a grisly reprise later on when Sontag is describing the republicans on their way to the scaffold. "They, too, saw themselves as future citizens of the world of history painting, of the didactic art of the significant moment. . . . What people admired then was an art (whose model was the classical one) that minimized the pain of pain. It showed people able to maintain decorum and composure, even in monumental suffering."

"We admire, in the name of truthfulness, an art that exhibits the maximum amount of trauma, violence, physical indignity. (The question is: do we feel it?) For us, the significant moment is the one that disturbs us most." Sontag herself belongs to the modern school: her book is full of unbearable moments, from Nelson having his arm amputated without an anesthetic (and there are frequent mentions of his stump afterwards) to Eleanora Fonseca being jumped on to break her neck as she hangs alive from the gallows. Sontag does her utmost to make us "feel it."

The most painful episode is the murder by slow torture of an elderly duke and his mad brother at the hands of the royalist Neapolitan mob. The scene is watched with glee by Baron Scarpia, who has wandered in from Puccini's *Tosca*. Sontag demonstrates her freedom as a writer of romance by moving out of history into opera. It is not much extra trouble to change the scene from Rome to Naples: "So this is the man before whom all Naples trembled," says Sontag's Tosca, altering just one word of the most famous line from Illica's libretto. But the vital link between the Nelson-Hamilton saga and *Tosca* is to be found not in the opera but in the play by Sardou upon which it is based. In the opera, the painter Cavaradossi gives his picnic lunch to the republican fugitive Angelotti and helps him escape from the church of Sant'Andrea della Valle where Act I is set. In Act II Scarpia has Cavaradossi captured to get him to reveal Angelotti's new hiding place; Angelotti himself never appears again. Sardou gives him more of a part and the opportunity to explain why he is being hounded by the police: on a visit to London as a very young man, he says, he picked up a prostitute in Vauxhall Gardens. Many years later he sees her again at a dinner given by the British ambassador in Naples: she has become the ambassador's wife, and is gloating noisily over British reprisals against the defeated Neapolitan republicans. Angelotti is so enraged that he tells the assembled company about his first meeting with Lady Hamilton. In revenge, she sets Scarpia on him. Sontag uses the story of Tosca and her lover to prove that "emotional women who don't have power, real power, usually end up by being victims." The prima donna and the painter live only for their art and each other; and that is not enough.

Scarpia is a monster, but Sontag has an extra reason for loathing him: she is an elitist and he a jumped-up vulgarian, uneducated and only recently ennobled. Her Scarpia hates the aristocracy and the intelligentsia from whose ranks the Neapolitan republicans were drawn. The mob is on Scarpia's side. They resent the rich and cultured but love the king. The distance between their wretched state and the glamour of the court is a kind of drama to them, and they enjoy it. They also enjoy the drama of aristo-bashing. But their sadism is not as refined as Scarpia's: "The crowd is no less gratified if the person being tormented is already unconscious. It is the action of bodies on bodies, not bodies on minds, which the crowd enjoys."

Scarpia is pure opera and pure evil, a gift to Sontag. In a world governed by a post-Freudian view of life he couldn't exist. He'd be depraved on account of he was deprived, or had suffered a childhood trauma. The post-Freudian view

has forgiveness built into it. The classical view with its insistence on noble behavior needs something else to temper its severity. What it needs is mercy.

> Mercy is what takes us beyond nature, beyond our natures, which are always stocked with cruel feelings. Mercy, which is not forgiveness, means not doing what nature, and self-interest, tells us we have a right to do. And perhaps we do have the right, as well as the power. How sublime not to, anyway. Nothing is more admirable than mercy.

This passage illustrates the unique combination of high moral tone and throw-away chic in Sontag's writing. And it sounds as though it might be the key to her book.

But which, if any, of the four posthumous voices at the end belongs to its heroine? Not Emma's, who even after death deceives herself about her part in the executions—or at any rate about her failure to prevent, in particular, the execution of her former doctor, Cirillo. She is harsh to her daughter by Nelson, and refuses even on her deathbed to tell the girl who her father was: "Why should I have consoled her when there was no one to console me?" Eleanora Fonseca dies with a curse on the Hamiltons and Nelson: "I cannot forgive those who did not care about more than their own glory or well-being. They thought they were civilized. They were despicable. Damn them all." There is no forgiveness here, let alone mercy. So that leaves Catherine Hamilton and Mrs. Cadogan, meek women who subordinated themselves to those they loved. Certainly not feminist heroines.

In her prologue Sontag makes it clear that she is not to be pinned down. She describes herself hovering at the entrance to a New York flea market: "Why enter? Only to play. A game of recognitions. To know what, and to know how much it was, how much it ought to be, how much it will be. But perhaps not to bid, haggle, not to acquire. Just to look. Just to wander. I'm feeling lighthearted. I don't have anything in mind." History, literature, art, and opera are her flea market, and she shops around in it.

For instance, having got Goethe to the Hamiltons' party in order to reflect on Classical and Romantic canons of art, she begins, in her seventeenth-century French mode, to outline and compare the characters of the thinker poet and the collector dilettante (Sir William). The latter wants to admire and acquire, the former to gain insight, to be transformed by the impact of new sights and objects. Sir William bores Goethe with his "simpleminded" epicureanism; and Goethe bores Sir William and unsettles his guests because "He can't help . . . bringing along his higher idea, his better standards. He, the stony guest, reminds the revelers of the existence of another, more serious way of experiencing. And this, of course, will interfere with their pleasures." So now she has wandered off to the stall selling bits from Don Juan, and Goethe is cast as the Commendatore: "He shakes your hand. It's chilling. You settle back. The music is louder. What a relief. You like your life. You're not going to change. He is pretentious, overbearing, humorless, aggressive, condescending. A monster of egotism. Alas, he's also the real thing." The Don Juan myth has been an irresistible metaphor to writers over the ages. It seems just possible that Sontag catches a glimpse of her own doppelgänger in the stony guest. But in any case the myth doesn't quite work here: not just because at the time of his Italian journey Goethe had not yet petrified into the alarming Olympian figure he was to become, but simply because it's too far-fetched.

Being far-fetched is the defect of Sontag's merits. She stops at the consideration of nothing (except religion, which is briefly recommended by Scarpia as a means of keeping order; as a private experience or motive for behavior, it never gets a mention, which seems odd). Her book is unconventional—almost a new genre. So she is taking risks. The most obvious risk, with all those cultural quotes, is to be thought pretentious. The bigger risk is to be full of moral fervor, passionate and preachy. The risks pay off because she moves so fast and has such a light and casual touch with language; and also because she keeps her promise to write a romance and combines her unconventional concept and structure with bouts of character drawing and storytelling so conventionally skillful and engaging that any romantic novelist might be jealous.

Economist (review date 15 August 1992)

SOURCE: "Cuckholded by Nelson," in *Economist*, Vol. 324, No. 7772, August 15, 1992, p. 77.

[*In the review below, the critic argues that, in* The Volcano Lover, *Sontag "employs the techniques of an essayist and a social historian better than those of a story-teller in her version of the lives of William Hamilton, his wives Catherine and Emma, and Lord Nelson."*]

Set mostly in Naples in the last 30 years of the 18th century, Susan Sontag's **The Volcano Lover** follows the career of the British ambassador to the court of the Kingdom of the Two Sicilies. At the beginning of the narrative, this figure, dubbed "Il Cavaliere" by "polite Naples", is already well known for his passion for collecting: paintings, books, scientific instruments and, from his earlier days in Naples, classical artefacts discovered by the continuing excavations at Herculaneum and Pompeii.

More unusually, he also "collects" Vesuvius, the still active

volcano that in AD79 buried the two Roman cities. He visits it night and day, he commissions paintings of it, he gathers rocks and lava samples and writes of his findings to the Royal Society; he becomes known back in England as "the volcano lover" (hence the book's title). The ambassador's private life is also described: his first marriage to the asthmatic and retiring Catherine, who is good on the harpsichord, and, after her death, his second marriage to the humbly born former mistress of his nephew.

His second wife is 37 years his junior but, though the marriage is frowned upon by society, it works reasonably well for both parties for a decade. Then an English naval officer, soon to become a national hero in the struggle against Napoleon, visits Naples and he and the ambassador's wife fall in love. As anybody with a smattering of history knows, it ended in tears.

For 30 years Ms Sontag has been a critic; unsurprisingly, she employs the techniques of an essayist and a social historian better than those of a story-teller in her version of the lives of William Hamilton, his wives Catherine and Emma, and Lord Nelson. At the end of an often slow-moving novel the reader may have little sense of the four principals as individuals, but he will be well acquainted with the look and feel of the place and the period as experienced by a particular national and social set.

The novel is ingenious at finding ways to plop the modern reader into the 18th century. Mozart's career, and the tragic plot of Puccini's opera "Tosca", are set side by side with the Cavaliere's story. The Neapolitan king's hunting forays are described in all their disgusting detail. And whether or not the incident occurred exactly as she portrays it, Ms Sontag's recreation of the assault by a Neapolitan mob on a local "collector" brilliantly illustrates what can happen when an abyss is fixed between sophisticated rich and ignorant poor.

A. S. Byatt (review date 16 August 1992)

SOURCE: "Love and Death in the Shadow of Vesuvius," in *Washington Post Book World*, August 16, 1992, pp. 1-2.

[*Below, Byatt praises* The Volcano Lover *as intelligent and provocative.*]

It is difficult to imagine anything more resolutely anti-romantic than Susan Sontag's "Romance," **The Volcano Lover**. It is set in late 18th-century Naples, in the shadow of Vesuvius. Its main characters are the Cavaliere, an English diplomat, his beautiful second wife, and the Hero, a visiting admiral who becomes the lover of the wife. They are, of course, Sir William Hamilton; Emma, Lady Hamilton and Lord Nelson, perhaps always slightly absurd as romantic figures, but here so remorselessly cut down to size that Sontag's icy irony becomes a kind of passion that in turn generates a strange affection for her struggling manikins.

The world of the novel is constructed of glittering descriptions of people, events and things, all considered with the same detached, energetic curiosity. The court of the Bourbon King of the Two Sicilies, and his wife, sister of Marie Antoinette, is loathsome and lively. The king likes bloody killing, infantile jokes and entertaining whilst defecating. The queen is brighter, but rattled into cruelty by the French Revolution. The Cavaliere is imperturbable and ineffective. His two passions, before the arrival of Emma, at that stage his nephew's mistress, are collecting, and observing the volcano, another form of collecting. Other notables make brief appearances: Goethe; the Gothic novelist and collector William Beckford, in pursuit of beautiful boys, but ready to appreciate the unconsidered musical talent of the first Lady Hamilton; the young Mozart. When the French Revolution comes, there is a brief rising in Naples, and the doomed establishment of an enlightened Republic, based on Reason, and brutally suppressed by the English admiral. This episode introduces the nearest thing to a heroine found in the novel—the revolutionary Fonseca de Pimentel, who believes in Justice and does not understand human unreason and cruelty. She is executed by hanging.

This Romance is written in the stench and shadow of Death. The fear of death, its inevitability, the fact that the reader knows from start to finish that the actors are all long dead and judged, makes the narrative into a kind of gruesome puppetplay, and also gives it a kind of tragic dignity, beyond the absurd. An early set piece is the king's construction of an artificial mountain, laden with food, for his starving people. The mountain is 40 feet high, and live animals are tethered to it, to be torn apart and bloodily eaten by the crowd that is loosed on it, prefiguring the brutal acts of both sides in the later political upheaval and its suppression.

This mountain is part of the subtle and savage use of the image of the volcano of the title. This represents Love, in one way, with its cliched images of hot red clefts and smoldering fires. The finicky and detachedly observant Cavaliere tries to turn it into an object to be collected, makes careful tours of observation, records facts of its behavior and history. Susan Sontag herself likes to describe its eruptions in terms of "mushrooming" clouds, our own pervasive image for cataclysm. But it is also a symbol for the fascination of violence and defiance, and thus associated at a distance with revolution, too. She writes:

"Maybe it is not the destructiveness of the volcano

that pleases most, though everyone loves a conflagration, but its defiance of the law of gravity. . . . What pleases first at the sight of the plant world is its vertical upward direction. That is why we love trees. Perhaps we attend to a volcano for its elevation, like ballet. How high the molten rocks soar, how far above the mushrooming cloud. . . ."

This image is at the beginning of the book, which closes with a downward drag just as emphatic, Fonseca de Pimentel's prevision of her own hanging, (accurate, we are told) where the hangman jumps onto the hanging body to make sure it is weighted down.

The image of the collector, too, has been used by other novelists to describe the peculiarly modern interest in narrating and recuperating the past. I think of Brian Moore's *The Great Victorian Collection,* or the excellent use made of the Great Exhibition by J.G. Farrell in *The Siege of Krishnapur.* Sontag's narrative voice compares her own activity to the Cavaliere's collecting and list-making. Hamilton sold the Portland Vase to the Duchess of Portland and lost a priceless collection of vases at sea, trying to send them to England to save them from the revolution. Sontag's narrator in her prologue wanders into a flea market in Manhattan in the spring of 1992, "checking on what's in the world. What's left. What's discarded. What's no longer cherished. . . . But something I would want. Want to rescue. . . ." And moves straight into the sale of Hamilton's "Correggio" Venus in 1772. The past is bric-a-brac that might speak to individual desires or predispositions.

And what finally counts in this book, what makes it piquant on a first reading, and I suspect, stronger and more complex on every re-reading, is Sontag's own atmosphere of interest, her own peculiar mixture of fire and ice. She has an interesting meditation, late in the novel, on the difference between 18th-century art and our own. She describes the "fixed" agony of classical images of the strangling of Laocoon by serpents, or the flaying of Marsyas, and says (not quite lightly in my view):

"Whatever art shows it is not going to get any worse." And, "What people admired then was an art that minimized the pain of pain. It showed people able to maintain decorum and composure, even in monumental suffering.

"We admire, in the name of truthfulness, an art that exhibits the maximum amount of trauma, violence, physical indignity. (The question is: do we feel it?) For us, the significant moment is one that disturbs us most."

Sontag's art here reconciles the virtues of the two modes,

and makes something new of them. At the opening of the story the Cavaliere is reading *Candide*, a text those cool fury Sontag has used elsewhere for her own purposes. She has learned from 18th-century satire, and yet when she chooses to be modern, and exhibit trauma, she makes sure we go through it, she makes sure, precisely, that we *do* feel. She sees all her people through their deaths, clinically and passionately, and makes us imagine what we would rather not imagine. *The Volcano Lover* is a slippery, intelligent, provocative and gripping book, and a very good one.

Richard Eder (review date 16 August 1992)

SOURCE: "That Hamilton Woman," in *Los Angeles Times Book Review,* August 16, 1992, pp. 3, 7.

[*In the following review of* The Volcano Lover, *Eder states that although Sontag digresses and provides commentary, she tells her story well.*]

Susan Sontag at play. That is not remarkable in itself. Double-domes make their stabs at levity: George Will writing about baseball; Chief Justice William Rehnquist capering solemnly—I saw him—in an amateur production of "Patience"; John Kenneth Galbraith trying his hand at an academic novel.

What sets *The Volcano Lover* apart from such heavy-footed exercises is not just that it is light-footed but also that, as play, it is both great fun and serious fun. Writing what I suppose could be called a historical novel about the celebrated and sloppy triangle of Admiral Horatio Nelson, Lady Emma Hamilton and her celery-stalk husband, Sir William Hamilton, Sontag condescends not at all.

The cross-country impetus of her thinking is as nervy as ever. But it is transmogrified. It is ideas as a game—real ideas and real game—as sentient and agile as a choreography of Michael Jordan's sneakers.

Sontag tells a story and tells it extremely well, with speculative digressions and comment that serve, as in "Tristram Shandy," to open the picaresque mental landscape through which the collecting is essentially a masculine activity. It stems from a man's innate and oddly isolating assurance that he has a place in the world and, conversely, that the world belongs to him. Women, paradoxically, are too close to the world and too responsive to it to command such gassy assurance. Similarly—the connection is arcane but inveigling—it is only men who can tell a joke properly.

Emma the volcano can be collected no more than Vesuvius can. When young Nelson sails in, to protect Naples from Napoleon and to prop up the dissolute Bourbon king and his ferocious Ilapahurg wife, the grand passion ignites. It sustains itself through Nelson's triumphant comings and goings, and through a brief *ménage d trois* residence in England. (Having lost ownership of his prize collectible, Sir William stays on as a kind of curator; there is a splendid image of him and Nelson fussing together over the household accounts.) After the husband's death and Nelson's own death at Trafalgar, Emma perishes in destitution despite the hero's dying plea to his countrymen—grateful, but only just—to look after her and their child.

Nelson is an imp of fame; willful, avid, innocent and cruel. He is not quite real. Reality is a burden that rather hampers history's great achievers, and Sontag's Nelson is all the more effective in his will-o'-the-wisp character of a sanguinary Peter Pan. I sense a wry suggestion in Sontag's sunny feminism, which manages to be both stirring and mocking, that male reality can also be a burden to the passions of a Real Woman.

Certainly Emma is a Real Woman. A ravishing milkmaid beauty when she narrative marches. When the digressions are a trifle long-winded, it almost seems like human respect; a witty person may be long-winded but this can be an amiable trait, like corpulence; you don't just shut it off.

She also respects her story. It is a vehicle to say things about women and their mismanaged fires—the volcano of the title, which nicely arranges to be Mt. Vesuvius as well. It speaks about men and their vulnerable outrages, about the English character, about the frailty of revolutions and the deadly power of counterrevolutions, about the inhuman aspects of art and power, and the richly decomposing stew of history that is Naples, where the book is set.

But it is an invigorating story in its own right. Sir William Hamilton, distantly connected to the king, finds himself Minister to the Court of Naples at the time of the French Revolution. (He had hoped for Madrid, but his connection was too puny.) He is a chilly egotist whose ruling passion is collecting art, antiquities and scientific specimens; notably, fresh lava scooped up at personal risk from the perpetually rumbling Vesuvius.

A depth in Sir William responds to the volcano's own churning depths, but his ingrained response to being moved is to collect. Thus, when his seemingly complaisant wife dies, and his nephew sends over a discarded mistress to get her out of the way, Sir William is smitten to the point of making a scandalously unsuitable marriage.

Emma is a former artist's model who worked—just how, is left to the imagination—for a doctor specializing in the cure of impotence. She is vulgar, ravishing and a vital force; she ravishes Sir William. Imprisoned in his overbred nature, he can only treat her as an objet d'art.

Among Sontag's many bravura interjections is the argument that comes out from England, she stops Neapolitan passers-by in their tracks. She brings her cheerfully Hogarthian mother with her and the latter's dryly disenchanted account in one of the book's several epilogues is shrewd and terribly moving.

Emma's vitality is unquenchable, and so is her redoubtable determination to fly upward like the sparks. Her vulgarity is one of her most appealing qualities, the polar opposite of camp. She is a great success at the Neapolitan court, where spontaneity seems exotic. Her looks soon go, and she grows fat; but she never doubts her right to a grand passion. Fortunately, neither does Nelson. He finds her magnificent, and that may be his most endearing quality.

It is Hamilton, though, who is the most remarkably rendered of the characters. Never has a frozen sensibility been so suggestive. Before he meets Emma, he acquires a pet monkey. The monkey loves him but Sir William wants a jester, not a child, Sontag writes. He spurns the monkey's snuggle and teaches it tricks instead. Obediently, it performs. The Englishman has turned a loving thing into a collected thing. With Emma, of course, he fails. She never does manage more than affection with him; at the end, it is he who is collected.

The portrait is devastating, yet lightened with humor and understanding. There is a wonderful confrontation between Sir William and Goethe, who admires the Minister's collection as a means to understand the principles of nature. For his pragmatic host, it exists for its own sake. In a shrewd evocation of her very male and very English protagonist, so lordly and so impotent, Sontag writes:

> "His is the hyperactivity of the heroic depressive. He ferried himself past one vortex of melancholy after another by means of an astonishing spread of enthusiasms."

There are other suggestive figures, among them Hamilton's first wife, whom we come to recognize as a dormant version of Emma's spurting volcano. There is the decadent greed of Naples' Bourbon king who eats and fornicates prodigiously, kills great quantities of game, butchers it himself, and sells the meat to his soldiers.

There is a fascinating portrayal of the short-lived Vesuvian Republic, set up by intellectuals and aristocratic idealists after the example of the French Revolution; and with Napoleon's fickle protection, its repression is brutally managed by the king and queen from their refuge in Sicily, im-

placably enforced by Nelson in England's interest and haplessly abetted by the Hamiltons. It is a wonderful reflection on the relative, strengths of idealism, bloody reaction and a Great Power's chilly reasons of state. With one of the executed revolutionaries the poet Eleonora de Fonseca, Sontag makes a brief proxy appearance, much as Hitchcock used to do but with more charm.

We require stories. We can do without them for a while. We can read stories about the impossibility of telling stories, or stories that caution us against imagining that there is anything to them but our own arbitrary readings. But eventually, we require them.

It is a problem for a contemporary writer who wants to do more than retail personal sensibility, regional color or besieged childhoods. Stories imply a pattern to life; perhaps our lives have none.

History, on the other hand indubitably does have a pattern, even if it is imposed contemporaneously and handed down. A number of writers have tried to use historical pattern to provide a story upon which to explore their insights and sensibilities. Sontag satirizes the process at the start of the book. She writes of a figure—we recognize her in her jeans and white silk blouse—meandering through a flea market and picking something out almost at random.

The story she has picked out she writes with entire fidelity and with all of a novelist's art. Her contemporary interjections—digressions, questions, exclamations—in no way dilute or deflect the narrative. They do not weaken its three dimensions; they add a fourth which, without removing it from its time brings it into ours.

R. Z. Sheppard (review date 17 August 1992)

SOURCE: "Lava Soap," in *Time*, Vol. 140, No. 7, August 17, 1992, pp. 66-7.

[*In the following review of* The Volcano Lover, *Sheppard argues that Sontag uses the novel as a vehicle for discussions of feminism and class.*]

Long before the U.S. lost its trade balance, it was lopsided with intellectual goods from Europe. Marx, Freud, Sartre and Lévi-Strauss were required cribbing. Books translated from the French and German were best sellers and their authors culture heroes. So were their interpreters. As a critic and novelist, Susan Sontag handled European ideas and forms with brilliance and style. The camera loved her dark good looks, and she became an American knockoff of the Continental intellectual as gravely seductive celebrity. The brain, she said on at least one occasion, is an erogenous zone.

The Volcano Lover, her fifth work of fiction, is a mild cerebral aphrodisiac. It is the sort of book that Sontag would probably call determinedly middlebrow. Her publisher, eager to start a buzz, compares it to "the postmodern potboilers of Umberto Eco and A.S. Byatt."

The subject is the scandalous romance of the late 18th century's hottest couple: Lord Nelson, Britain's greatest naval hero, and Lady Emma Hamilton, the empire's most luscious pinup—and wife of diplomat Sir William Hamilton.

The story has usually been told from the straightforward missionary—not to say colonial—position. The Alexander Korda version, *That Hamilton Woman,* starring Vivien Leigh and Laurence Oliver, was Winston Churchill's favorite movie.

As a critic and novelist, Susan Sontag handled European ideas and forms with brilliance and style.
—*R. Z. Sheppard*

Sontag creamily shifts perspective. The hero and his mistress are egoists gone on fame and oblivious to the welfare of the masses. Off the poop deck, Nelson is an unimposing shrimp. Without her billowing satins, Emma the society swan is grossly overstuffed. Most of the action takes place in Naples, where nearby Mount Vesuvius huffs and puffs. It is a natural wonder, but also an unavoidable symbol of molten passion and the republican revolution that erupts in France and spreads south.

Royalty and privilege are threatened. So too is a genteel culture represented by Sir William, British envoy to the decadent Neapolitan court. A collector of antiquities and an amateur scientist, he occasions Sontag's heavier musings. Unfortunately, he is too underpowered to be the principal vehicle in a historical tour de force. Making a cameo appearance, Goethe dismisses him as "a simple-minded epicurean."

Eventually Sontag also sours on Sir William's detachment and bloodless pleasures. In fact, all three members of this famous love triangle are abruptly damned in an operatic epilogue about male-dominated class structures and the challenges of feminism. The message is unexceptionable but jarring. Perhaps Sontag, like Vesuvius, simply blew her top. More likely, the outburst was calculated to amplify an otherwise low-key narrative and convince readers that the author is not only postmodern but also politically correct.

John Simon (review date 31 August 1992)

SOURCE: "The Valkyrie of Lava," in *The National Review,* Vol. 44, No. 17, August 31, 1992, pp. 63-5.

[*In the review below, Simon questions whether* The Volcano Lover *is a romance and argues that Sontag focuses too much on her opinions and not enough on her characters.*]

Two of the most arresting things about Susan Sontag's new book, *The Volcano Lover: A Romance,* are the title and the subtitle. Why "romance," when to all intents and purposes it looks like a novel? In an interview, Miss Sontag declared that, "to find the courage to write this book," she needed "a label that allowed me to go over the top," as if novelists since Proust, Kafka, and Joyce had done anything less than that. Also, she said, "the novel becomes such a self-conscious enterprise for people who read a lot." Does that mean that habitual novel readers lose their ability to read un-self-consciously? Or that, when they turn authors, they cannot write an un-self-conscious novel?

None of this makes sense, especially if you look closely at her chosen genre, from medieval tales to Harlequin romances. Actually, in telling the story of Sir William Hamilton, the British ambassador to the court of Naples, his wife, Emma, and her lover, Lord Nelson, Miss Sontag has written nothing like a romance, which, by definition, is something uncomplex. Did she, then, try to disarm criticism by mock-ingenuously pretending to offer it a love story and bodice ripper?

In truth, Miss Sontag undertook to write an anti-romance, and went about it studiously and systematically. Though her point of view is until near the very end that of the omniscient narrator, she carefully positions herself much closer to the noble cuckold she graciously keeps referring to as "the Cavaliere" than to the victorious admiral and world-famous beauty who complete the triangle. And not only does she pick the least dashing player to exalt, she also deglamorizes the other two. Her Emma is, for the most part, not the supermodel to famed painters, dazzling performer of Attitudes (as she called her impersonations of heroines from mythology and art), but the prematurely aging, overweight, gone-to-seed adulteress, whose vulgarity is no longer mitigated by world-class beauty, and who remains lovely only to her uxorious husband and purblind lover. As for Nelson, he is vainglorious, tyrannical, and short of stature, as well as short one eye, one arm, and quite a few teeth.

Furthermore, Emma is always only "the Cavaliere's wife," and Nelson "the hero," which, lower-cased, sounds both mundane and slightly ironic. To be sure, history is on Miss Sontag's side: the cuckold was civilized and fastidious; whereas Horatio and Emma, by the time they became lovers, made unlikely figures of romance. So the subtitle must be a subterfuge to lure those who fear Miss Sontag's vaunted intellect or, worse yet, haven't heard of Susan Sontag at all.

But what about the title, *The Volcano Lover*? It refers to Sir William's documented interest in Vesuvius in particular, and volcanoes in general. For besides being a tireless and influential art collector, he was fascinated by science and by the fierceness, unpredictability, danger of those firespewers throughout history. Clearly, Miss Sontag intends the volcano to symbolize—what? Passion, sex, revolution, destruction, beauty and its risks, artistic creation, the spasmodicity and evanescence of life itself. To this end, she peppers her prose with words and tropes that spell out or suggest the volcanic, the eruptive and disruptive, the thrill of fireworks and devastation of lava. Both are dispensed by that great symbol, which, to cap it all, is both male (erection, emission) and female (crater, hole).

Be it said in her favor, Miss Sontag has mastered (mistressed?) the historical background. Her Kingdom of the Two Sicilies, Habsburgs and Bourbons, Nelson and Napoleon (the latter merely a shadow), revolutionaries and counterrevolutionaries, vignettes of daily life in southern Italy's *sette-cento* and England's early nineteenth century, ring fresh and true. When she chooses to get inside her characters, she does so easefully and evocatively. Yet the surest way of getting into them and getting them down—dialogue—is rarely used. She keeps talk to the second-barest minimum; and further de-emphasizes it by dispensing with quotation marks. Thus printed, dialogue tends to merge into narrative, description, digression.

Ah, digression! There is little in her story that does not engender digressions. We are not allowed to forget the author for more than a page or two before she has elbowed her way back in—expatiating, explaining, editorializing, and philosophizing. These digressions may be playfully contemplative. When the revolution forces the court to leave Naples for Palermo, we get an excursus on "the south of the south." "Every culture has its southerners—people who work as little as they can, preferring to dance, drink, sing, brawl, kill their unfaithful spouses," she begins, and before you know it, "Hanoi has Saigon, São Paulo has Rio, Delhi has Calcutta, Rome has Naples, and Naples [to shorten a long sentence] Palermo." Or they may be philosophical-elitist: "We like to stress the commonness of heroes. Essences seem undemocratic. We feel oppressed by the call to greatness. We regard an interest in glory or perfection as a sign of mental unhealthiness, and have decided that high achievers, who are called overachievers, owe their surplus of ambition to a defect of mothering (either too little or too much)" etc.

More unsettling are divagations thrown in for sheer bravura. Thus the scene of Marie Antoinette's beheading, dragged

in, as it were, by the hair; thus the fictitious Scarpia made police chief of Naples, and the story of *Tosca* retold with additional, quite gratuitous, embellishments. In a similarly operatic vein, Goethe's stay with the Hamiltons is mythicized (unsuccessfully) into the coming of Mozart's Commendatore. Miss Sontag is an opera lover; even that lengthy visit (ten pages!) to Bomarzo may have been prompted by Ginastera's opera; it certainly isn't intrinsic to her story.

Celebrities make their appearances: Goethe; William Beckford, the misanthropic author of *Vathek;* the famous painters for whom Emma sat. Miss Sontag manipulates them tendentiously. Though she mentions Goethe's general coolness toward Emma, she doesn't quote his calling her a "dull creature," an "inexpressive speaker," and a "disagreeable singer." Sir William, on the other hand, she builds up beyond her sources. He appeals to her by being the nearest thing to an artist and critic: a connoisseur and collector. Indeed, most of the fine pages of the book—and there are some very fine ones—concern collecting, which is to say the nature and value of art as it impinges on life.

One could cite many examples. The collector as heroic toiler—when, having spent all his money on his collection, he must sell it and start all over again. The collector as tragic hero "with a divided consciousness. No one is more naturally allied with the, forces . . . that preserve and conserve. But every collector is also an accomplice of the ideal of destruction. For the very excessiveness of the collecting passion makes a collector also a self-despiser" etc. The collector as great lover: "Like sexual feelings, when they . . . are actually lived out in all their vehemence and addictiveness . . . the feeling for art (or beauty) can, after a while, only be experienced as excess, as something that strains to surpass itself, to be annihilated. To really love something is to wish to die for it. Or to live only in it, which is the same thing." Finally, the collector as humanitarian; Sir William muses on his deathbed: "While there are more exalted destinies . . . to discover what is beautiful and share that with others is also a worthy employment for a life."

True, but, as so often, Miss Sontag contradicts herself. If her collector wants to die into his passion, or keep starting from scratch, how come that "Every collector feels menaced by all the imponderables that can bring disaster"? And if "like the impostor, [he] has no existence unless he goes public. . . . Unless he puts his passions on display," how can he be the hard-bitten loner? "Most unnatural to be a co-collector. One wants to possess (and be possessed) alone." And how can he resemble the lover? "The soul of the lover is the opposite of the collector's. The defect or blemish is part of the charm."

The collector is a true admirer—of art, volcanoes, women's

beauty. Yet, we learn, "A man who has to admire in order to desire is likely to have led a modest sexual life." Contradictions are everywhere, but there is also the neat epigrammatic conclusion, as in "What a deft antidote to anxiety or grief one's own erudition can be."

Impressive as the stylistic pyrotechnics become—such as telling a bit of the story in Q&A format, or switching to narration in the second-person singular (though Michel Butor beat Miss Sontag to that one), or frequently playing with the hypnotic refrain of "here" and "there"—from all that over-reaching (not overachieving) the result is surfeit. Especially as Miss Sontag can fall off her high horse into the bathos of, "She seemed to admire him so much, and he enjoyed that."

The delirious use of anachronism, anachorism, prolepsis, hortatory analogy is likewise wearying. We tire of these foreshadowings, flashbacks, parallels, asides; we are blinded by such pennant-waving erudition, particularly when gross errors undercut our faith in the author's omniscience. Thus the word is sherbet, not sher-bert; the god (as opposed to the tyrant) is Dionysus, not Dionysius; the subjunctive is wrong in "the Cavaliere asked if she were tired"; a hotel room, unlike a person, can't be raffish; destruction of a city, fancifully put, would be urbicide, not urbanicide; the nominative is called for in "the cousin whom the Cavaliere had told her was very eccentric"; you don't interpose something with something else, you intersperse it; you are racked, not wracked, by spasms; you avoid tautologies such as "one cannot help but see"; and avoid even more stringently such danglers as "With his grey face and long beard and the peasant clothes he wore to disguise himself, the Cavaliere hardly recognized the 47-year-old Neapolitan admiral"; and so on.

But the costliest mistake is the very concept of "the volcano lover." It should infuse and animate the work, make it come into relevant focus. When Empedocles, according to legend, jumped into Etna, the image reverberated—see Hölderlin, Meredith, Matthew Arnold. But when the Cavaliere concludes his dying monologue with "Far from punishing me for my devotion, [Vesuvius] brought me only pleasure," nothing falls into place with a satisfying click. The governing symbol misfires, remains dormant.

And it's no use when Miss Sontag—as a feminist pleading for one of her characters, a hanged woman journalist—talks of women having to delude themselves: "Thus do all women, including the author of this book." What? Miss Sontag forced to lie to herself? Miss Sontag, the winner of prizes, a martyr? She who has long been the media's favorite firebrand, the dauntless valkyrie spouting her private brand of lava? The mother of all eruptors, our very own Crater Mater? Say it isn't so!

Bruce Bawer (essay date September 1992)

SOURCE: "That Sontag Woman," in *The New Criterion*, Vol. 11, No. 1, September, 1992, pp. 30-7.

[*In the essay below, Bawer discusses cultural elitism in Sontag's works, focusing on her novel* The Volcano Lover.]

In these times when charges of cultural elitism are routinely hurled by East Village poets at their formalist rivals, by *au courant* English professors at champions of the literary canon, and by the vice president of the United States at Hollywood producers, it seems particularly appropriate to ponder the career of Susan Sontag, who has for decades been the very apotheosis of a certain kind of cultural elitist. To be sure, the cultural elitist—if by those words one simply means a lover and defender of high culture—is at present perhaps the most precious and imperiled species in the artistic and intellectual bestiary. But Susan Sontag is the sort of cultural elitist for whom the term often seems primarily to designate not selfless devotion to certain valued things that exist apart from oneself but, rather, membership in a select class of people, an aristocracy of the mind. It sometimes seems as if Sontag's chief priority as an essayist is not to clarify, persuade, or illuminate, but to demonstrate to the world that she is the highest of the highbrows, an intellectual's intellectual, a breed apart from lesser scribblers.

How does she do this? Mostly by writing essays chockablock with provocative-sounding assertions about a subject—some of them genuinely perceptive but many of them dubious, pretentious, self-evident, and/or irreconcilable—and supporting few of them at length, but instead leaping briskly from one to another. What's more, she gratuitously sprinkles these essays with quotations from European intellectuals, references to obscure filmmakers, etc.—the purpose being not only to introduce relevant ideas but, even more important, to say "This is the company in which my mind moves," and to imply that if you're in her intellectual league you'll recognize the reference or the quotation. She has said herself, by way of accounting for her essays' discontinuity, that she doesn't have the patience to develop an argument from *a* to *b* to *c*. Another explanation might be that she is by nature less an originator or assimilator of ideas than a collector of them, a hero-worshiper; to read many a Sontag essay is to find undigested and discrepant fragments of her intellectual gods poking out all over the place—a bit of Roland Barthes here, a chunk of Walter Benjamin there.

Yet her critical method has proven, over the years, to have several strategic advantages for Sontag: (1) it keeps many readers constantly off-balance and thus intimidated at the thought that Sontag, bounding around inside a topic like a toddler in a playroom, is at home with all the esoteric material that she has managed to include; (2) it makes Sontag look as though her intellect is bursting with so many ideas that she can't spare much time for any given one of them; and (3) it moves so quickly past each of her contentions that the reader isn't encouraged to mull any of them over, to ask: "Is this true? Does that make sense? Is this consistent with that?" To read her alongside someone like Guy Davenport, whose essays bear a superficial resemblance to hers in many respects (e.g., the formal discontinuity, the frequent highbrow name-dropping and quoting, the attraction to demanding and obscure literary works and to extreme political and sexual phenomena), is to appreciate more than ever Davenport's captivating and elegant prose, his eagerness to comprehend and clarify, his lack of interest in obscuring or making an impression. While Sontag is all over the place, strip-mining the intellectual landscape, Davenport is sinking a shaft. Reigning over the New York intellectual scene, plugged into every trend, Sontag is a writer very much of the moment, whose essays read like self-conscious footnotes to the history of the time in which they were written; Davenport is a writer for the ages. Her temperament is essentially romantic, postmodern; his is classical, modern.

It sometimes seems as if Sontag's chief priority as an essayist is not to clarify, persuade, or illuminate, but to demonstrate to the world that she is the highest of the highbrows, an intellectual's intellectual, a breed apart from lesser scribblers.
                                        —*Bruce Bawer*

"Taste is context," she insisted in a 1974 essay, **"Fascinating Fascism."** The remark is elucidated by a passage in her new novel, *The Volcano Lover*, in which the narrator, describing Josiah Wedgwood's late eighteenth-century mass production of copies of the Portland Vase, asks: "Who can really love the Portland Vase now?"—the point being that manufacturing thousands of replicas of a beautiful object destroys its beauty, not because such copies are aesthetically inferior, but because an essential ingredient of the object's appeal is its *exclusiveness,* its status as a unique object esteemed by a coterie of connoisseurs. Implicit here is that the essence of the Church of High Culture abides not in the inherent qualities of the objects of worship but in the inherent qualities of the worshipers. This view of things, I would submit, lies at the heart of Sontag's brand of elitism; and the notion, following logically upon such a view, that anything that happens to interest highbrow minds, even as a diversion, should necessarily be taken seriously as art or idea, goes a long way toward explaining Sontag's attempts

to certify pornography and Camp as legitimate objects of serious critical inquiry.

It is difficult to find in Sontag's fiction any indication that she has ever given a moment's thought to what life might be like for someone other than an artist or intellectual. Her 1963 novel *The Benefactor* (whose solemnly cerebral tone and stark Continental *mise en scène* recall Camus and Canetti, among others) centers on a young Paris intellectual, and draws a hilarious contrast between his earnest, sophomoric hyper-intellectuality and his complete lack of common sense, human sympathy, and emotional self-knowledge. (The novel's major problem is that one cannot be sure that Sontag actually meant for the book to be funny.) Her other novel, the labored, humorless *Death Kit* (1967), is so entirely derivative of the New Novel of Nathalie Sarraute and Alain Robbe-Grillet that even to speak of it as taking place in the world (as opposed to the author's mind) is rather to miss the point. In the self-consciously avant-garde bits and pieces collected in *I, etcetera* (1978), the only characters who aren't intellectual types are the cleaning ladies and other peripheral underlings. And the effective story **"The Way We Live Now"** (which appeared last year as a book) concerns a circle of highbrows with names like Tanya, Orson, Quentin, and Yvonne, whose lives are touched by the AIDS epidemic; when the narrator mentions on the first page that "Stephen . . . was back from the conference in Helsinki," it's clear who the "we" of Sontag's title are—and who they aren't.

A seminal document in the history of Sontag's cultural elitism, of course, is her notorious 1968 essay *Trip to Hanoi,* in which she managed to be taken in by North Vietnamese propaganda crude enough to make an eighth grader wince. How did this happen? As the essay makes clear, part of the explanation is that Sontag's interest in Ho Chi Minh's revolution had less to do with her concern for the masses than with her enthusiasm for new experiences, her vulnerability to flattery, her love of glamour, and her desire to be where the action was. Apropos of her Hanoi visit, she observes that "[a]n event that makes new feelings conscious is always the most important experience a person can have": in other words, what ultimately mattered most to her about the Vietnam conflict was not its potential consequences for the people of Indochina or America or the world but its effect upon her own psychic development. "The aesthete's radicalism," she writes in a 1981 essay on Roland Barthes, "is the radicalism of a privileged, even a replete, consciousness—but a genuine radicalism nonetheless. . . . The aesthete's radicalism: to be multiple, to make multiple identifications; to assume fully the privilege of the personal." Indeed, a reader of *Trip to Hanoi* cannot help feeling that for Sontag, circa 1968, the ordeals and emotions of American servicemen, South Vietnamese civilians, and others with whom she could not readily identify had no more reality or urgency than her theories about them; to express it a bit differently, she emulates Barthes in viewing the world around her as if it were a text. (As Alfred Kazin once put it, Sontag "sees the world as a series of propositions *about* the world.")

Sontag has been castigated for proclaiming that "the white race is the cancer of human history," but given her nearly slavish reverence for European life and culture, one can only imagine that, on some level, this proclamation is to be understood as a disguised compliment; perhaps it was informed by a notion that culture and "cancer" are two sides of the same coin—that you can't produce great works of art or architecture or scholarship without also spawning imperial ambitions and aggressiveness. Could it be that she was so easily taken in by North Vietnamese propaganda because she simply didn't think a people with such modest cultural and intellectual attainments could be capable of lies and atrocities that would dwarf those of the American government?

If I have dwelt at some length on the subject of Sontag's particular brand of cultural elitism, it is because it plays an important role in **The Volcano Lover**. At the center of this historical novel—or, to use Sontag's word, this "romance"—is Sir William Hamilton, the English ambassador to Naples from 1764 to 1800, who is known to posterity as the husband of Horatio Nelson's mistress, Lady Emma Hamilton. The book chronicles the last years of Hamilton's first marriage, to a plain, devoted pianist named Catherine, and the whole of his marriage to Emma, during which the chief dramatic interest is provided by her involvement with Nelson and the English-aided struggle against French-backed republican rebels for control of the Kingdom of Naples, whose rulers, King Ferdinand II and Queen Maria Carolina, are close friends of the Hamiltons.

At first blush, the story of Nelson and the Hamiltons hardly seems like the sort of thing you'd expect to find retold in a Susan Sontag novel. After all, this is vintage romance-novel territory; it was even the subject of a movie with Laurence Olivier and Vivien Leigh—and not an obscure French film of the sort that *cinéaste* Sontag adores, but a stiff costume drama, released in America under the title *That Hamilton Woman*, that one can imagine her gagging over (though in earlier days, come to think of it, she might have celebrated it as Camp). The costume-drama stereotypes implicit in the material are deliberately underscored by Sontag's habit of referring to Nelson as "the hero," to Hamilton as "the Cavaliere," to Emma as "the Cavaliere's wife," and to the Neapolitan sovereigns as "the king" and "the queen." (Nelson's name is never mentioned, nor are those of the royal couple; Hamilton isn't named until the last two pages.) But Sontag's purpose in using these fanciful labels is ironic; for her characters are like nothing out of a romance novel or a prestige picture by Alexander Korda. Only the suave,

cultivated Cavaliere—who gets his thrills by hiking to the summit of Vesuvius and his aesthetic pleasures from the *objets d'art* of which he is a famous collector—comes close.

This is a very discursive novel, full of narratorial opinions about one thing and another, notably about collecting (a pet topic of Walter Benjamin's). In tone and perspective the narrator's remarks on the subject are entirely reminiscent of Sontag's essays; as in her essays, moreover, the remarks add up not to an argument but to a sort of inventory of provocative-sounding observations that are, by turns, dubious, pretentious, self-evident, and irreconcilable. Page 70: "There are so many objects. There is no such thing as a monogamous collector. Sight is a promiscuous sense. The avid gaze always wants more." Page 106: "Collectors and curators of collections often admit without too much prodding to misanthropic feelings. They confirm that, yes, they have cared more for inanimate things than for people."

Gradually it becomes clear that these seemingly random observations about collecting point to what Sontag apparently perceives as the connoisseur's ultimate dilemma: namely, that to love and collect beautiful things can place one in a problematic relationship with most of human-kind. Napoleon, we are reminded, was a collector, stealing art from all over the Continent. Page 72: "Every collector is potentially (if not actually) a thief." For the Cavaliere's rich, eccentric nephew William, collecting is a way of excluding the world; for the Cavaliere, it is a means of connection to it. Page 245: "[T]he Cavaliere, like all great collectors, wished to say with objects: look at all the beauty and interest there is in the world." But the pieces in a Sicilian prince's grotesque collection, which the Cavaliere examines after he and Emma and the royal party have been forced by republican revolutionaries to flee Naples for Palermo, are different. "They said: the world is mad. Ordinary life is ridiculous, if you take some distance from it. Anything can turn into anything else, anything can be dangerous, anything can collapse, give way." Collecting, we are meant to understand, is of particularly urgent sociopolitical significance in an age of revolution:

> Collectors have a divided consciousness. No one is more naturally allied with the forces in a society that preserve and conserve. But every collector is also an accomplice of the ideal of destruction. For the very excessiveness of the collecting passion makes a collector also a self-despiser. Every collector-passion contains within it the fantasy of its own self-abolition. Worn down by the disparity between the collector's need to idealize and all that is base, purely materialistic, in the soul of a lover of beautiful objects and trophies of the glorious past, he may long to be purged by a consuming fire.

Which apparently helps to account for the Cavaliere's fascination with Vesuvius. He is, we are told, a "connoisseur of disaster" who is "ill-prepared . . . for the real thing" (i.e., revolution). He is also fascinated by Emma, who enters his life when his nephew Charles, whose mistress she was, tires of her company. Wondrously sensitive and empathic, this humbly born young woman becomes to the aging Cavaliere something of an artwork, a cherished part of his collection, famous for her beauty and for the *tableaux vivants* of classical scenes that she offers up regularly to dinner guests. Yet she is also big, loud, and vulgar, and has a checkered past; by the time Nelson enters her life, moreover, she is getting a bit long in the tooth and is "thickened by drink." Nelson, for his part, is even less of a stereotypical romance-novel protagonist than she is. Napoleon's nemesis, "*the* hero to the rulers of Naples," is "maimed, toothless, worn, underweight," and considerably shorter than Emma. ("It was," Sontag writes, "a time for concentrated men of preposterous ambition and small stature who needed no more than four hours of sleep a night.")

> **Skillful as Sontag can be at delineating her characters' psychology, . . . she only rarely attempts to convey a sense of them through dramatic action; instead of showing, she tells.**
>
> **—Bruce Bawer**

On the whole, Sontag's prose here is less than fastidious—by turns slack and frantic, deft and clumsy. Emma is "engulfed in the ecstasy of being alive"; the Cavaliere, visiting Paestum, "avowed himself irritated by the stumpy, conically shaped Doric columns." Confused, overwrought metaphors abound: "He ferried himself past one vortex of melancholy after another, by means of an astonishing spread of enthusiasms." There are even grammatical errors: "If she could have, if he would have permitted it, she would have gladly gone, booted and bundled up in furs, on the boar hunt with the Cavaliere." Elisabeth Vigée-Lebrun is introduced to the reader as "one of the few professional painters who was [!] a woman." A description of a flea-market crowd as "Vulpine, larking"—a seeming contradiction—suggests that even on the rare occasion when Sontag endeavors to set a picture before the reader, she doesn't really see it herself. But then this is a novel whose chief purpose is manifestly not to capture the sights and sounds of eighteenth-century Naples but to serve as a framework for the author's cerebrations; it is an act of will rather than of visionary compulsion, a work crowded with ideas rather than with life.

To be sure, there are many forceful passages here, including graphic descriptions of battle casualties, mob rioting and its consequences, and the punishments meted out to republican revolutionaries. Sontag is good, too, at rendering the Cavaliere's state of mind: when Emma tells a lie at dinner, the rapid succession of emotions with which he reacts to it is convincing and sensitively evoked. Skillful as Sontag can be at delineating her characters' psychology, however, she only rarely attempts to convey a sense of them through dramatic action; instead of showing, she tells. Thus we don't feel as if we know them in the way a friend would, even if at times we feel as if we have a pretty good idea of what it is like to *be* them.

This novel is set, Sontag's narrator tells us, in a time "when all ethical obligations were first put up for scrutiny, the beginning of the time we call modern . . . the beginning of the age of revolutions." For Sontag, the Cavaliere's collecting becomes the quintessential symbol of pre-revolutionary civilization ("To collect is, by definition, to collect the past—while to make a revolution is to condemn what is now called the past"), and the Cavaliere a prototypical pre-modern figure: "Everything should be understood, and anything can be transformed—that is the modern view. . . . The Cavaliere was not trying to understand more than he already did. The collector's impulse does not encourage the lust to understand or to transform. Collecting is a form of union. The collector is acknowledging. He is adding. He is learning. He is noting." It is only appropriate that when Goethe, the poet of the new sensibility, meets the Cavaliere, he condemns him in his thoughts as "a simpleminded epicurean . . . a man incapable of delving deeply into what interested him."

It seems significant that Sontag calls **The Volcano Lover** not a novel but a romance—a word that Hawthorne used to describe works of fiction that, as he wrote in the preface to *The House of the Seven Gables,* depart from the novel's "very minute fidelity . . . to the probable and ordinary course of man's experience." In writing a romance, Hawthorne explained, the author "may so manage his atmospherical medium as to bring out or mellow the lights and deepen and enrich the shadows of the picture"; what made *The House of the Seven Gables* a romance was "the attempt to connect a bygone time with the very present that is flitting away from us." All this seems germane to Sontag's purposes in **The Volcano Lover.** There may be several reasons why she has chosen to call her book a romance: first, it's set in the Romantic Era; second, she may want to set it apart from her first two novels, to signal that this time around she isn't operating under the influence of the French *nouveau roman* or trying to win a prize for most avant-garde novel of the year; third, like Hawthorne, she offers a decidedly colored version of the past, with some things emphasized and others downplayed; fourth, the book is about a romance, or rather several romances: Hamilton's romance with Emma, with his collection, and with his volcano; Emma's with Nelson; and (yes) Sontag's own long-standing romances with those two incompatible phenomena that figure significantly in these pages—high culture and populist revolution.

Presumably it is Sontag's desire to "connect a bygone time with the present" that accounts for the abundance of contemporary allusions in **The Volcano Lover**. The narrator uses words like "overachiever" and "dumbed down"; she refers to the "rain-in-Spain" lessons given Emma by the Cavaliere, notes the "strobe-like succession" of Emma's *tableaux vivants,* and labels one passage a "flash-forward." There are references to Nagasaki, Isadora Duncan, Las Vegas, and a collector in Florida who stores his acquisitions in a castle in Genoa; and we're told that suicide would be more widespread if it were made easy by the digging of a hole "at the corner of Seventeenth and Fifth Avenue in Manhattan. Where the Frick Collection is. (Or a prole-ier address?)" As a rule, these deliberate anachronisms strike one as self-conscious, intrusive, and aesthetically ill-advised. Even more unattractive and bewildering are the frequent shifts between past and present tense, which sometimes occur twice within a single sentence.

One way in which Sontag contrasts the period of her novel with our own day is by discussing attitudes toward heroism, then and now. When painting heroic figures, she notes, Napoleonic-era artists sought to "preserve the larger truth of a subject from the claims of a literal, that is, inferior truth." Apostles had to be noble-looking; Alexander the Great must be tall. By contrast, we of the twentieth century

> like to stress the commonness of heroes. Essences seem undemocratic. We feel oppressed by the call to greatness. We regard an interest in glory or perfection as a sign of mental unhealthiness, and have decided that high achievers, who are called overachievers, owe their surplus of ambition to a defect in mothering (either too little or too much). We want to admire but think we have a right not to be intimidated. We dislike feeling inferior to an ideal. So, away with ideals, with essences! The only ideals allowed are healthy ones—those everyone may aspire to, or comfortably imagine oneself possessing.

These observations are valid and well worth making. Yet if Sontag mocks the modern distaste for heroes, she also scorns Nelson's heroism. After he drives the French-backed revolutionaries out of Naples, crushing their short-lived republic, his merciless punishment of the rebels—and, in particular, his insistence upon the execution of eminent poets, scholars, and scientists—makes the word "hero" sound increasingly ironic. He is, the narrator notes, "not chivalrous, high-minded, but vindictive, self-righteous. . . . Eternal shame upon the hero!" In their support of Nelson's violations of international law, the Cavaliere proves to be "not

benevolent, detached, but spiritless, passive," and Emma "not merely exuberant and vulgar, but cunning, cruel, bloodthirsty. All three giving themselves over to a terrible crime."

These narratorial verdicts on the protagonists are not an isolated instance. An anecdote illustrating the queen's vindictiveness concludes: "Nothing is more hateful than revenge." A few pages later there is a lecture on mercy: "Mercy is what takes us beyond nature, beyond our natures, which are always stocked with cruel feelings. . . . Nothing is more admirable than mercy." At the close of the novel—after several brief sections consisting of the deathbed musings of the Cavaliere and of posthumous reflections by Emma, Emma's mother, and the Cavaliere's first wife, Catherine (whose romantic friendship with his rich nephew, William, presages the Emma-Nelson affair)—we are offered the posthumous testament of Eleanora Fonseca di Pimental, a poetry-writing noblewoman who was executed for her pro-revolutionary activities. Fonseca, whose status as a female literary figure and activist makes it hard not to identify her with Sontag, devotes her final pages—which are the final pages of the book—to a fierce condemnation of Nelson, of the Neapolitan royals, of Sir William Hamilton ("an upperclass dilettante. . . . Did he ever have an original thought, or subject himself to the discipline of writing a poem, or discover or invent something useful to humanity, or burn with zeal for anything except his own pleasures and the privileges annexed to his station?"), and of Emma, who she pronounces an "enthusiast" with "no genuine convictions. . . . I can easily imagine Emma Hamilton, had her nationality been different, as a republican heroine, who might have ended most courageously at the foot of some gallows. That is the nullity of women like her." Implicitly contrasted with Emma is Fonseca herself:

> I was earnest, I was ecstatic, I did not understand cynicism, I wanted things to be better for more than a few. I was willing to give up my privileges. I was not nostalgic about the past. I believed in the future. I sang my song and my throat was cut. I saw beauty and my eyes were put out. Perhaps I was naïve. . . . Sometimes I had to forget that I was a woman to accomplish the best of which I was capable. Or I would lie to myself about how complicated it is to be a woman. Thus do all women, including the author of this book. But I cannot forgive those who did not care about more than their own glory or well-being. They thought they were civilized. They were despicable. Damn them all.

What are we to make of these blunt verdicts by the narrator and by a character who doesn't even appear until the last few pages and connects herself explicitly with Sontag? Could these last pages be intended as Sontag's own *apologia pro vita sua*? If earlier in the novel her sympathies appear to be very much with the Cavaliere, here she manifestly wants us to identify this woman with her, which would seem to demand that we further identify the chaos of the Napoleonic wars with the tumult of the Vietnam era, revolutionary France with the Soviet Union, the Neapolitan republic with North Vietnam, and the British Empire with the United States. This is not the only place in *The Volcano Lover* in which Sontag suggests such parallels. Her reference, elsewhere in the novel, to the English military in Naples as "agents of a world empire . . . in a far-off southern satrapy rich in traditions of corruption and indolence, where they are trying to inculcate martial virtues and the necessity of resisting the opposing superpower," is an obvious jab at America's involvement in Vietnam. (Whatever one may think of the conduct of the war, to suggest in 1992 that Vietnam was a U.S. "satrapy" and the war a manifestation of American imperial ambitions is disgraceful; though Sontag did get around to condemning Communism a few years back, she would still seem to have trouble accepting that the imperial ambitions underlying the war in Vietnam were those not of America but of the Soviet Union.)

Likewise, Sontag would appear to be trying to put the best possible face on her own Vietnam-era naïveté and idealism when she has her narrator say that the Neapolitan revolution "doesn't have a chance. Indeed, it is the classic design, confected in that decade, reused many times since, for a revolution that doesn't have a chance. And will go down in history as naïve. Well-intentioned. Idealistic. Premature. The sort of revolution that gives, to some, a good name to revolution." At the end, it's hard not to read Fonseca's attack on the Hamiltons as a surrogate attack by Sontag on the artists, intellectuals, and other privileged folk who failed to mount the 1960s barricades alongside her—and as a suggestion that she is as noble as Fonseca because she gave a damn, that the only difference between her and the intellectual types who weren't taken in by the likes of Ho Chi Minh and Castro was that her colleagues were less bighearted than she was, and that her only flaw was an excess of benevolence with which the world has yet to catch up. "You can always count," the narrator complains, "on the naïveté and gullibility of the benevolent. They go along, marching ahead, thinking they have people behind them, and then they turn around and . . . nobody there. The mob has peeled off, looking for food or wine or sex or a nap or a good brawl. The mob is unwilling to be high-minded." Could this possibly mean that when Sontag reflects upon her behavior during the Vietnam War she believes that if the American public failed to be sold on socialist revolution, it was because they weren't as capable as she is of devotion to a moral ideal?

If so, Sontag deserves some kind of award for chutzpah. For even the remotest suggestion of a parallel between her and Fonseca is outrageous. Fonseca cares about the commonfolk; Sontag, whose *dramatis personae* doesn't include one full-bodied member of the proletariat, continues to exhibit only the most pro forma interest in and concern for the lower orders. Fonseca willingly sacrifices her comfort and security to support a republican government; Sontag, sacrificing nothing, traveled to North Vietnam and Cuba as a guest of totalitarian dictators and praised their murderous, repressive regimes while condemning American democracy. Fonseca ends up on the gallows; Sontag ended up with a MacArthur grant. Of course; one could argue that Sontag, by painting a largely sympathetic portrait of the Cavaliere, Emma, and "the hero" and then having a character attack them, means to represent her own internal conflict between, on the one hand, her own connoisseurship, her sense of identification with a creative, attractive woman, and her tendency toward hero-worship, and, on the other, her sense of obligation to feel solidarity with the masses. She has, after all, written that "[l]ike all great aesthetes, Barthes was an expert at having it both ways"; perhaps she, who surely considers herself a great aesthete, wants to have it both ways too: to assert at once the rectitude and pointlessness of populist revolution and the joy and moral equivocality of connoisseurship, creativity, and heroism, and thereby to draw our attention to the problematic nexus between ethics and aesthetics, virtue and valor, morality and epicurism. To put it differently, one could argue that Sontag embraces both the Cavaliere and Fonseca, the pre-Revolutionary and the modern, the conserver and the destroyer, the involved and the detached, the lover of beautiful things and the lover of people—that she contradicts herself, in short, because she contains multitudes.

Or perhaps we're meant to understand that Sontag is playing some kind of postmodern game here—a game with the idea of narratorial assertion, old-fashioned moralizing, authorial intrusion. This is, after all, the woman who wrote in **"On Style"** that a critic should not treat a work of art "*as a statement being made in the form of a work of art.*" And: "A work of art is a thing *in* the world, not just a text or commentary on the world." And: "A work of art, so far as it is a work of art, cannot—whatever the artist's personal intention—advocate anything at all." By incorporating in *The Volcano Lover* several references to the unreliability of art and the use of literature as a means of escape, Sontag would seem to be cautioning us not to read her autobiographically.

Yet even as she does this, she would also seem to be compelling us to relate the novel's closing pages to her own personal history. Perhaps the fundamental problem here is that the controlling sensibility of this book ultimately seems less that of Sontag the artist than that of Sontag the author of "commentary on the world." Instead of gently coaxing local truths out of her characters, Sontag too often thrusts upon them ready-made, generalized notions about connoisseurship, heroism, etc.; instead of seeking to comprehend the mystery of motivation—how a poor English girl ends up supporting a tyrannical monarchy and a noble-woman ends up a populist rebel—Sontag too often uses her story as an excuse to toss off axioms and air prejudices. Now, had Fonseca been a well-rounded character who figured throughout much of the novel, and about whom we knew enough to be able to believe in her devotion to rebellion and care about her fate—and had we seen enough, moreover, of Neapolitan peasant life to appreciate the reasons for that devotion—her posthumous tirade might have worked, and Sontag might have managed to engender a potent, credible, and dramatically effective tension between this woman's *Weltanschauung* and that of the Cavaliere and company. As it is, alas, Sontag's closing pages simply come off as one more instance of the lamentable self-centeredness—and, yes, the peculiarly constructed cultural elitism—with which her readers have become all too familiar.

Richard Jenkyns (review date 7 September 1992)

SOURCE: "Eruptions," in *New Republic,* Vol. 207, Nos. 11-12, September 7-14, 1992, pp. 46-9.

[*Below, Jenkyns offers a negative assessment of* The Volcano Lover.]

Sir William Hamilton, the principal character of Susan Sontag's new novel [*The Volcano Lover*], was what the eighteenth century called a virtuoso, a cultivated aristocrat with an amateur interest in art and science. As British ambassador to the court of Naples from 1764 to 1800, he became what passed for a vulcanologist, making more than twenty ascents of Vesuvius, and collected antiquities, especially Greek vases. His enduring fame, however, is as one of history's most notorious cuckolds.

Hamilton's second wife, Emma, of the humblest origins, was celebrated first as the great beauty of her day, then for her "Attitudes" tableaux, in which she posed in the roles of the heroines of classical myth. ("People are mad about her wonderful expression," Horace Walpole observed, "which I do not conceive, so few antique statues having any expression at all, nor being designed to have it.") But finally, and most lastingly, she was celebrated as Lord Nelson's mistress. Nor was Nelson the only spectacular visitor to Naples: Goethe passed through, and described his encounter with Emma in his *Italian Journey,* and a more exotic bird of passage was William Beckford, soon to be notorious for *Vathek,* a lurid tale of Oriental cruelty and sensuality, and later for creating a fabulous palace at Fonthill in Wiltshire, with a gothic tower nearly 300 feet high. It is quite a cast; and it is something of an achievement for Sontag to have made these people so dull.

The Volcano Lover is being launched with more than the usual fanfare of promotional trumpets, but the din cannot disguise that it is a big disappointment. What went wrong? A part of the answer, perhaps, is that Sontag seems to have had no clear notion of what sort of book this was to be. Maybe the idea was to produce a "baggy monster," to borrow Henry James's description of the Victorian novel, a treasure house sparkling with precious and fascinating objects. In a recent interview Sontag is quoted as saying that "it's a historical novel, but it's written from a modern point of view and it's a book that speaks in many voices. . . . The point is, I don't want just to write only a historical novel, but I do want it to be historical." Of course, many voices can make a rich and harmonious polyphony—or they can be babel. The fluctuation of tone in *The Volcano Lover* usually suggests not depth or complexity, but uncertainty and a lack of control. Perhaps the problem originated in Sontag's feeling that it would not be good enough to write only a historical novel. In any event, for most of the time her novel is more historical in its way than most historical novels. We are given a great deal of factual information. The tone is almost professional. What Sontag says of Hamilton could be applied to herself: "He wanted to make sure that their amusement was as saturated with knowledge as his own. Wherever he was, the Cavaliere was prone to cast himself in the role of guide or mentor."

Sometimes the little lectures are absurdly prosy:

> Then as now an ascent had several stages. The road, in our own century turned into a motorway, did not exist then. But there was already a trail on which one came about two-thirds of the way, as far as the natural trough between the central cone and Mount Somma.

And at moments the lecturer turns into the schoolmarm, with a priggish shaking of the head over Hamilton's political incorrectness, and a superiority too easily won. When Madame Vigée-Lebrun paints Emma, "Probably, he [Hamilton] did not give any thought to the fact that this would be the first portrait of her by one of the few professional painters who was a woman." Tsk, tsk.

Often the book reads more like a chronicle or a biography than a novel, and in fact Sontag has a considerable talent for descriptive narrative. Scenes such as the arrival of Nelson or the riot of the mob in the Neapolitan counter-revolution are excellently done. But there is no consistency of style or approach. Odd bits of the author's own stream of consciousness intrude for no discernable reason, and the characters reflect sometimes in an eighteenth-century manner, sometimes in a modern one. Thus, when Hamilton visits a fortuneteller, we have a naturalistic scene of Italian low life, when suddenly the fortuneteller is given magical powers and foresees tarmac, the disappearance of horse-drawn traffic, mass tourism, the century of the common man, and "even the American professor will be interested in me."

> **Great novelists can elevate the everyday—Austen can make a scene between a dull young man and a straight-laced young woman seem endlessly absorbing—but Sontag does the reverse. Given extraordinary people, she makes them commonplace.**
> **—*Richard Jenkyns***

It is a serious weakness that Sontag shows little ability, with one minor but welcome exception, for creating character. She has one or two sporadic ideas about Hamilton—that he is an aristocratic cold fish, that he is an obsessive collector—but these are not developed or made to fit together into a coherent picture. And so there is a hole at the heart of the novel. Until a page from the end Hamilton is never named, but referred to as "the Cavaliere," even when we are seeing him through the eyes of his wife or his family. Emma, we are told, "was not born to that kind of snobbery which prides itself on an indirect expression," and it is a pity that Sontag could not learn from her. The tiresome mannerism of periphrasis, one of the many affectations with which the book is littered, is symptomatic: Sontag seems less interested in her characters than in striking attitudes toward them.

Emma must be a problem for a novelist, because her quality seems to be irrecoverable. One gets little sense of her beauty or her charm from the vapid portraits of her. Sontag depicts her as a sort of hearty barmaid, and perhaps that will do, more or less. But again there is infirmity of purpose. Sontag blunders in quoting from Emma's authentic letters. "Oh Charles on that day you always smiled on me & staid at home & was kind to me & now I am so far away.... But I will not no I will not rage. If I was with you I wood murder you and myself boath." Suddenly Emma has become touchingly alive—and how painfully we feel the contrast when Sontag returns to the flatness of her own invention: "It is impossible to describe how much I miss you, Charles, wrote the girl. Impossible to describe how angry I am."

If Emma's magnetism is lost to us, the problem with Nelson is the reverse: we know too much about him. His fierce suppression of the revolution in Naples may well have been the darkest episode in his career. You may, if you choose, be repelled by him, but he undeniably had what now we call charisma and was then described simply as the Nelson touch. Not since Alexander the Great was there a commander in whom iron will was so bound up with the romance of personality; and on top of that, he was the greatest

naval genius in history. What will not do, then, is to depict this astonishing figure as a pathetic little man, which is how Sontag depicts him. When Nelson enters Naples in triumph, the best that she can imagine is him wishing that his wife and father were there to see him. We may not know how it felt to be Nelson, but it surely cannot have been *that*. And she comments repeatedly on the grotesqueness of the lovemaking between Nelson and Emma, a small man with one arm and a large woman running to fat. This is merely vulgar, a failure of human understanding.

Great novelists can elevate the everyday—Austen can make a scene between a dull young man and a straight-laced young woman seem endlessly absorbing—but Sontag does the reverse. Given extraordinary people, she makes them commonplace. Goethe meets Lady Hamilton, and all he can manage is cocktail-party conversation. With Beckford, however, Sontag does better, inventing a platonic tendresse between him and Hamilton's first wife. This *amitié amoureuse* between a middle-aged woman and an insecure young homosexual is conventional enough, and it hardly does justice to a character of bizarre flamboyance, but at least it has some life to it.

A good deal of Sontag's prose is bad in a creative writing way. Consider this sentence, about Beckford's arrival in Naples: "A restless, abbreviated version of the Grand Tour (he left England only two months earlier) had brought him to its southernmost station with record speed, casting him on the shore of the Cavaliere's hospitality just in time for the hot wind, one of the great winds of southern Europe (mistral, Föhn, sirocco, tramontana) that are used, like the days leading up to menstruation, to explain restlessness, neurasthenia, emotional fragility: a collective PMS that comes on seasonally."

Or consider the ship *Colossus* "plodding nervily" across the Mediterranean. What motion is less like a ship's than plodding? And "nervily" is pseudopicturesque and means nothing. The ship is then seen "clinging to the western ledge of Europe," a poor description of a passage up the flatlands of the French Atlantic coast, before running into "a merciless, protean storm." The first of these adjectives is lazily sentimental, the second shows that Sontag may not know what "protean" means. Throughout the book, with a grim sense of the inevitable, we discover that Vesuvius is to be loaded with a mass of labored symbolism—molten passions seething beneath the apparently hard surface, that sort of thing—and the less said of this the better. And there is plenty of cultural self-advertisement, too. Sontag lets us know that she knows about Heian Japan, say, or about opera—though any reader who can pick up the allusions does not need to be taken through the plot of *Don Giovanni* or—for seven pages!—of *Tosca*. (Scarpia is also introduced into the narrative of the novel itself, appearing as a fee-fi-fo-fum sadist who makes Puccini's own figure seem understated.)

Above all, the book is thick with authorial comment and portentous aphorism. At its worst, this is tastelessly facetious. Thus, on Pompeii and Herculaneum: "Like a more recent double urbanicide, one murdered city is much more famous worldwide than the other. (As one wag put it, Nagasaki had a bad press agent.)" Or there is word play so feeble that one marvels at the lack of self-criticism: "The sleep of reason engenders mothers." (No, it does not make much better sense in context.) More often banality is endlessly elaborated as though it were a dazzling new perception. So the obvious thought that when you are haggling you should not seem too keen is spun out into a whole slack paragraph:

> That tremor when you spot it. But you don't say anything. You don't want to make the present owner aware of its value to you; you don't want to drive the price up, or make him decide not to sell at all. So you keep cool, you examine something else, you move on or you go out, saying you'll be back. You perform a whole theater of being a little interested, but not immoderately; intrigued, yes, even tempted; but not seduced, bewitched. Not ready to pay even more than is being asked, because you must have it.

And so on and on.

Too often the Great Thoughts are simply wrong or silly. The collector's strategy, we are informed, "is one of passionate self-effacement. Don't look at me, says the collector. I'm nothing. Look at what I have. Isn't it, aren't they, beautiful." One has only to think of Getty or Thyssen or what S.N. Behrman called Duveen's "brisk trade in immortality" to see that this is nonsense. The lover, says Sontag, is the opposite of the collector: "The lover's relation to objects annihilates all but the world of the lovers. This world. My world. My beauty, my glory, my fame." Again, this is deficient in emotional truth. Love has sometimes been called an *égoïsme à deux*, but Sontag makes it into an *égoïsme tout court*. Is being in love really a self-congratulatory narcissism of this kind?

Sontag's understanding of grief and bereavement is similarly skewed. Suppose, she says, that someone you love has died on the other side of the world. The fact that this person may have been dead for some months "makes a mockery of the finality of death. Death is reduced to news. And news is always a little unreal—which is why we can bear to take in so much of it." Think about it: your beloved is dead, far away; therefore you feel that death is mocked, not final. What person of decent feeling has ever reacted like

that? In such passages especially, Sontag is much too busy being smart.

The last part of the novel turns in a new direction. Sontag abandons naturalism, and four women in succession address us from beyond the grave. This is a fully self-conscious scheme to shift the book into a different mode; and the offering of a new perspective, in a way involved, in a way detached, is attractive, though it might have been more successful if the preceding naturalistic tone had been maintained more steadily. In one instance the late shift works especially well. The second of these women is a character who has played little part in the story so far, Emma's mother, Mrs. Cadogan. She is Sontag's most successful creation. Sontag brings vividly to life the garrulous old lady, disillusioned but warmhearted; with a rough peasant wisdom. Mrs. Cadogan is an unpretending character, and for once Sontag can forget to be pretentious. Yet even here she lacks consistency of purpose: Emma's mother is made to use the rural eighteenth-century vernacular (a good piece of impersonation), but when Emma herself returns to the stage as the third of these voices from the dead, she speaks in the tone of a twentieth-century sensibility.

The last of these women is Eleonora Pimentel, poet and journalist, who was hanged for her part in the Neapolitan revolution. There are lots of executions and tortures in *The Volcano Lover*, too many, and rashly Sontag lets Eleonora offer us one more of these, telling us what it is like to be hanged in public: "Then it was my turn—and, yes, it was exactly as I had imagined it." Oh, like *that*, was it? This means, of course, only that Sontag has not been able to imagine it. Near the end, moreover, Eleonora turns to some pious feminist sentiments: "Sometimes I had to forget that I was a woman to accomplish the best of which I was capable. Or I would lie to myself about how complicated it is to be a woman. Thus do all women, including the author of this book." The idea that this revolutionary heroine, dying horribly for the sake of liberty, should spend some of her last words to us on the hardship of being Susan Sontag provides the book, in its final paragraph, with its most ripely comic moment.

Great novelists may be intolerable in their private lives, but in their work they show a certain reticence. Tolstoy was a raging egoist, but in his fiction he deferred to the autonomy of his creations. Sontag may be the soul of modesty in herself, but her literary persona is much too self-important. Her characters are squeezed out to make room for her own insistent voice. The novelist needs to know where he or she is, what ground he or she is standing upon, but this Sontag does not quite know. A failure of imaginative engagement with her story is suggested, for example, by the frequent slippage of tenses. One small example (italics added): "Catherine *does* not think he will ever become devout (and he *did* not)." Such things jar in the reading, not because they feel grammatically odd, but because the writer does not seem to have her feet planted firmly in either of her centuries.

It is interesting to compare *The Volcano Lover* with the triumph a few years ago of A.S. Byatt's *Possession*—both books have the subtitle "A Romance" and both measure a past era, in Byatt's case the Victorian age, against the values of today—and to wonder why the one novel should succeed so much better than the other. One answer is that Byatt plunges exuberantly into her chosen period with love and admiration, while Sontag rises superior to hers. Byatt is ready to learn; Sontag sets out to teach. She has Eleonora Pimentel conclude that the Hamiltons were worthless people, greatly pleased with themselves but devoid of originality, generosity, or convictions. "They thought they were civilized. They were despicable. Damn them all." These are the last words of the book. Perhaps we should not assume that Eleonora's sweeping contempt is the author's own, but it does seem uncomfortably close. To be sure, a satirist may write a novel about worthless people (though it should not be necessary to explain that they are worthless), but Sontag has not written a satire.

Sontag reveals her attitude of lordly insouciance, in fact, right at the beginning of her book. There is more heavy symbolism. She depicts herself as lingering at the edge of a flea market, condescending to the vulgar populace ("Sloppy crowds. Vulpine, larking.") and wondering whether she will bother to enter:

> Why enter? Only to play. A game of recognitions. To know that, and to know how much it was, how much it ought to be, how much it will be. But perhaps not to bid, haggle, not to acquire. Just to look. Just to wander. I'm feeling lighthearted. I don't have anything in mind.

Nothing in mind—well, maybe not nothing, but the admission seems still too true.

Jonathan Keates (review date 25 September 1992)

SOURCE: "The Antique Collector's Guide," in *Times Literary Supplement*, No. 4669, September 25, 1992, p. 24.

[*In the review below, Keates finds* The Volcano Lover *brilliant at its core but lacking in consistency and discipline.*]

The historical events, characters and contexts explored by this remarkable book [*The Volcano Lover*] constitute the richest of rewards to any novelist. There is something in-

stantly enviable in the prospect of being able to embark on a story which, in addition to its exotic setting beneath the minatory shadow of Vesuvius, will embrace Lord Nelson, Lady Hamilton, Goethe, Beckford, and that copper-bottomed harpy, Queen Maria Carolina of Naples, as well as throwing in, with a certain cheeky self-assurance, the figures of Angelotti, Scarpia and Floria Tosca from Sardou via Puccini. Who, after all, would not wish to have taken some part, as actor or witness, in these lives, against the background of so sublimely irrational a moment in the annals of modern Europe?

Confronted with such profusion, spread promiscuously like a buffet supper, Susan Sontag is both epicure and glutton. Contemporary fiction often seems short of any sense that novelists genuinely enjoy their own creations, relishing those acts of revival, animation and mimicry in which they indulge and sharing this pardonable vanity with the reader. The conviction of *The Volcano Lover* is that of an author who has had a good time.

In more than one sense, she is profoundly identified with her subjects. Indeed it is hard to think of a recent novel, more especially a historical novel, which so emphatically reflects this symbiosis between writer and theme. Her central figure, Sir William Hamilton (referred to throughout, for whatever reason, as "the Cavaliere") is a collector, at ease amid a scatter of terracottas, intaglios, cameos and vases, the swiftly hidden loot of excavations, adding, as a grace-note to the ensemble, the ultimate collectable in the form of Emma Hart, the scouse coryphée whose whole life has awaited fulfilment as a gallery of living statuary, the antique brought to life in a sequence of shawl-draped attitudes.

"Beauty surrounded me. I surrounded myself with beauty. Each new enthusiasm a new crater of an old volcano." By the same token, Sontag herself becomes, in the archaic sense of each term, a virtuoso and a dilettante, seizing hold of whatever happens to catch her fancy in the cultural vitrines of the late Enlightenment and proto-Romanticism. The things that ought to take place in a novel of this kind—war, revolution, feasting, love affairs and death-beds—are interspersed with episodes more blatantly linked with the author's personal concerns. A visit, for example, by Nelson and the Hamiltons to a Sicilian villa adorned with grotesque statuary affords an opportunity for Sir William to read in these leering marble freaks a satirical commentary on the nature and purpose of collecting, and allows the author to incorporate her own marmoreal eighteenth-century generalizations within the narrative flow.

If Sontag is her own William Hamilton, the book more dangerously becomes its own volcano, complete with lava streams and fumaroles, probably less by intention than as a result of sheer unrestrained inventiveness. Up to a point, we can be happy that it never assumes any sort of consistency, reading like the unedited materials of a novel whose final polishing has for whatever reason been abandoned. As with most active volcanoes, however, we spend much time irritably wondering which of its considerable range of tricks it will choose to spring next.

Many of these relate to the author's determined, often positively obsessive interventionism. She favours the mode initiated by John Fowles in *The French Lieutenant's Woman* and given added sophistication by writers like Patrick Süsskind in *Perfume,* whereby the writer acts as interpreter, offering the occasional gloss on the quirks and foibles of the age evoked and keeping the reader carefully alienated by means of a post-modern tricksiness with tenses and spasmodic references to events still to happen or to concepts yet unhatched.

The effect of this is an unwelcome leadenness, a text stifled by its own volubility, pestered by little bursts of inopportune rhetorical musing and embarrassed by the nakedly thrilling or entertaining potential of the various incidents it describes. Or rather doesn't describe, since at its most maddeningly wayward, the narrative, at such moments as the butchery of the Neapolitan Jacobins by Cardinal Ruffo's Sanfedisti, possesses the indoorness, the armchairness, of historiography rather than fiction.

Formally, the novel has only the linear cohesion of chronological sequence on which to rely for structure. Otherwise what urge us forward are the solemn, candid beauty of Sontag's prose and the casual enchantments of her detailing, from the paintings of Thomas Jones to the wreck of the vase-laden Colossus. We must make what we can of the closing monologues by four women whose lives interlocked with Hamilton's, including Emma's mother, Mrs Cadogan, and the Neapolitan revolutionary Eleonora de Fonseca Pimentel. The dignity and authenticity of their utterances are worth waiting for, but, juxtaposed with so much else in *The Volcano Lover* that appears either undisciplined or else too fastidious, they merely enhance the air of smothered brilliance in this literary Herculaneum, this noble ruin of a novel.

Alexandra Johnson (review date 5 October 1992)

SOURCE: "Romance as Metaphor," in *The Nation,* Vol. 255, No. 10, October 5, 1992, pp. 365-68.

[*In the following review, Johnson describes Sontag as a skilled storyteller and* The Volcano Lover *as an insightful novel.*]

"Collecting," muses Susan Sontag in her latest novel, "is a succession of desires. . . . To collect is to rescue things, valuable things, from neglect, from oblivion, or simply from the ignoble destiny of being in someone else's collection rather than one's own."

In *The Volcano Lover,* Sontag has rescued a story locked in many a biographer's prized collection: the tangled fortunes of Lady Hamilton and Lord Nelson, whose notorious liaison scandalized eighteenth-century Naples. In a sense, though, Sontag's observations about collecting apply more slyly to herself as a writer. In her revisionist retelling of the Hamilton saga, she's found the ideal forum to display her own succession of desires. For *The Volcano Lover* is no less than a Grand Tour of ideas that have animated Sontag's fiction and nonfiction these past three decades: the primacy of aesthetics, the totalitarian impulse to sacrifice intellectuals, the moral role of art in history. Sontag's passion for ideas channels itself into the arenas of passion—political, amorous, aesthetic—all played out on a vast cultural stage, the ill-fated republican struggle for Naples.

A historical romance by Susan Sontag? Is this the ultimate literary oxymoron? A tempting parody by our premier intellectual voice, whose essays on Canetti, Barthes, Benjamin and Bresson are classics in avant-garde criticism? Surely if two words define Sontag, they are "Against Interpretation," not "A Romance," the subtitle of her new novel. If we know anything about the author of *On Photography* and *Illness as Metaphor,* it is Sontag's capacity to surprise, to challenge our received opinions. With *The Volcano Lover,* it is the writer herself who has most skillfully resisted interpretation.

Sontag's foray into historical romance parallels that of another sophisticated theorist, A.S. Byatt, whose 1990 Booker Prize-winning novel *Possession* rocketed her to bestsellerdom. Fittingly, Byatt's literary scholar protagonists are entangled in the area often associated with Sontag: the thicket of critical theory. Sontag's quarry, as Elizabeth Hardwick has noted, is "the wide, elusive, variegated sensibility of modernism." If, most recently, she's explored it with elegiac precision in *AIDS and Its Metaphors* (1989) and its fictional counterpart, *The Way We Live Now* (1991), her most successful statement is the novel at hand. *The Volcano Lover* is a literary conceit: an eighteenth-century story within which Sontag illuminates the inexorable pull of the past on modern life.

The germ for the novel has long resided in one of her strongest stories, **"Unguided Tour."** Collected in *I, etcetera* (1978) (and also the subject of her fourth film), it's a spare conversational duet between lovers wandering the ruins of Italy and their own relationship. Travel as consumption: objects, scenery, monuments. Travel as repetition: language, memory, history. Taking her cue from one of the lovers,

Sontag sets herself a dare as an author: "Say to yourself fifty times a day: I am not a connoisseur, I am not a romantic wanderer, I am not a pilgrim." That single line gives *The Volcano Lover* its theme and its literary license.

Style, as Sontag notes in **"Against Interpretation,"** "is the principle of decision in a work of art, the signature of the artist's will." How remarkable and radical a departure this new fiction is from those willfully opaque puzzle novels *The Benefactor* (1963) and *Death Kit* (1967). In *The Volcano Lover,* Sontag finally achieves the "transparence" she cites as the hallmark of all true art. Gone are the artful elisions of Barthes. In their place are the thunder and props of narrative, the very narrative she's banished in previous fiction. And how skilled a story-teller she is. Like Byatt, who ingeniously mimics the moral spaciousness of the nineteenth-century novel to reflect on our own century, so Sontag has found her ideal counterpart in the eighteenth century's elegantly aphoristic novel of ideas.

What more fitting setting than Naples, "capital of natural disaster," to serve as the backdrop for "the telluric forces" of the late eighteenth century? Rocked by revolutionary upheaval, it is the age of royalists and republicans; art and artifice; romanticism and rationalism. An age that crackles with change: Franklin's experiments with electricity; Marat's incendiary Jacobinism; Europe's gleam of the guillotine blade. Yet it's Vesuvius, volcano as entertainment and apocalypse, that provides Sontag with the ideal metaphor for the century's explosive energies. Shimmering on the Bay of Naples is the "emblem of all the forms of wholesale death: the deluge, the great conflagration . . . but also of survival, of human persistence." Seeking "their ration of apocalypse," visitors from Goethe to Archduke Joseph scale Vesuvius to stare into the active abyss. Naples, nestled beneath the shadow of death, "had been added to the Grand Tour."

Congregating under these skies are gentlemen tourists, sexual exiles, volcano pilgrims, an opera house replete with a "continual ravishment of castrati," and a King of the Two Sicilies who doesn't speak Italian. In this third-largest city in Europe, courtly love takes on new meaning. Sexual excess, domestic spying and sport as bloodbath amuse the Bourbon monarch and his wife, sister of Marie Antoinette. Attending them is the "envoy of decorum and reason," Sir William Hamilton, British Ambassador to Naples. Scholar, courtier, aesthete, "Il Cavaliere" is a familiar Sontag saturnine personality. (Betraying "the hyperactivity of the heroic depressive," he "ferried himself past one vortex of melancholy after another by means of an astonishing spread of enthusiasms.") Thanks to his wife, an asthmatic, harpsichord-playing heiress, he collects treasures. Etruscan vases, cameos, intaglios, shards of lava from nearby Pompeii are sold to the British Museum.

Long mistaking his "capacity for detachment . . . with his temperament," the Cavaliere civilizes his passions into inanimate objects. At home after his wife's death, though, he meets the 19-year-old, auburn-haired mistress of his nephew Charles. A favorite of the painter Romney, Emma has a less decorous past as a model, including a semiclad stint for a doctor curing couples of impotence. Charles, in need of his own heiress, offers Emma to his widowed uncle, some thirty years her senior. He studies the artifact of his desire. The "small receding chin, the blush of eczema on her elbows . . . the stretchmarks of pregnancy" are all overlooked. For the true collector, "an object is not sullied. . . . What counts is that it has reached its destination, been locked into the circle of possessions of the one who most deserved to own it." Emma is shipped to Naples.

Nowhere is Sontag's ironic eye more merciless than in viewing the sexual politics of instruction. Dispatching a battery of tutors to his household, the Cavaliere admires Emma's nimble intelligence as she quickly masters French, Italian, botany and music. Like his pet monkey, Jack, she displays a keen talent for pleasing, one of the many strategies of charm Sontag inveighs against as the social destiny of women. Yet in playing Galatea to his Pygmalion, Emma upends the myth: From her niche in his "gallery of living statues," she steals the limelight. Donning white tunic costumes, she assumes a succession of theatrical poses—Niobe, Medea, Dido, Ariadne. These "Attitudes" soon make her a court favorite, indispensable confidante to the queen. The volcano lover marries his demimondaine. He collects, she performs. Together, their lives affect "poses that excited the greatest admiration."

The collector's public need to admire and be admired is what fatefully links the Hamiltons and Lord Nelson. When the commander of the British fleet arrives for the naval blockade of Naples, the trio find themselves "united in feeling themselves actors in a great historical drama; saving England, and Europe, from French conquest and from republicanism." Three's not a crowd; it's a collection. An "ideal enabler," the Cavaliere lends the hero of the Battle of the Nile his friendship and, ultimately, his wife. As the Cavaliere hoards his treasures, Nelson his honors and Emma her pleasures, each becomes locked in the curio cabinet of the other's vanity and affections. Vesuvius erupts. Jacobins conspire in Naples. The court watches Emma perform her antique Attitudes.

Sontag's considerable achievement in *The Volcano Lover* is that she's managed to create real characters, not Ideas in eighteenth-century button-and-muslin dress. As admirable, she's made history itself a living character. The first half of the novel is leisurely devoted to the Cavaliere and Emma. The second is a fast-paced, compulsively readable roll call of history: the fall of the Bastille, the Terror of 1794, the

1799 Bourbon exile negotiated by the Hamiltons and Nelson. The trio's fate is intertwined with the Continent's historical destiny. As French troops storm Naples, Nelson commandeers the British fleet, squiring the royal exiles to Sicily. The "Kingdom of cinders" is set ablaze, not by the volcano but by the wholesale slaughter of artists, intellectuals and political sympathizers. Offshore, adrift from history, the trio fiddle while Naples burns.

It was the time, we are told, when "all ethical obligations were first put up for scrutiny, the beginning of the time we call modern." While Sontag rues the spirited naïveté of the enlightened republicans, *The Volcano Lover* scorns the tyrannies of mob rule, even if that mob is only three lovers. Sontag locates the political in the telling specifics of character. The Cavaliere waits out the French menace by reading his favorite author, Voltaire. With Gallic disinterest, he evacuates his priceless collection with the skill of Napoleon. When his cargo of antiquities is sunk, the only box salvaged is a coffined admiral en route to England for burial. This ironic event, of course, foreshadows Nelson's recall to England, chastised for being private yacht captain to the royal exiles.

In Naples, the restored Bourbon queen erects a Greek temple in gratitude. Entombed inside are smiling wax effigies of the trio. In the highest tradition of historical romance, Sontag has breathed life into these waxworks. Her skill as a novelist is in evoking both our sympathy and our horror at her protagonists' monstrous self-absorption. Each is culpable. Identity, she implies, is never co-authored. For this, Sontag deprives them of their names (throughout, Hamilton is referred to as "the Cavaliere"; Emma, "the Cavaliere's wife"; Nelson, "the hero"). Public scorn singles Emma out as scapegoat. Like Eleanora de Fonseca, unsung heroine of the republic, and even the queen herself, Sontag sees each as punished for having stepped outside the spheres of feminine influence. (Perhaps most treasonous for a woman, Emma gets fat and loses her famous beauty.)

Yet history is effaced to anecdote—Hamilton remembered as the complicit cuckold; Nelson as the vengeful tyrant, wreaking final terror on Naples; Emma as court favorite dying destitute in France after Nelson's death at Trafalgar—and Sontag underlines this with an idea from *On Photography:* how the mass proliferation of objects helps fragment existence and erode meaning. In suggesting the collector's and lover's acquisitive relationship to the world, she exploits fine narrative details: Emma wearing Nelson's name sewn into her hem; the Cavaliere, first owner of the priceless Portland vase, allowing Josiah Wedgwood to mass-reproduce it; Nelson lending his profile for "candelabra, vases, medallions, brooches."

Sontag's meditations on objects extend to those of erotic desire. Is the love affair a work of art? An original? Or do the repetitions of body and spirit mass-produce emotions, therefore rendering them subject to cliché? "The soul of the lover," she writes, "is the opposite of the collector's. The defect or blemish is part of the charm." Literally. Among the novel's more memorable scenes is Emma kissing the stump of Nelson's right arm; him lovingly viewing her bloated body with his only good eye. In a Sicilian garden of grotesqueries, Nelson plays Mars to Emma's Venus. Alone in a nearby chapel, the Cavaliere is grateful for being in the orbit of their friendship. While the novel is a rich conjugation of connoisseurship—art, women, politics, relationships—at its core is the lesson of **"Against Interpretation"**: the ultimate uniqueness of an object, feeling or person.

With the Cavaliere as the novel's sympathetic lens, *The Volcano Lover* also plays with the shifting nature of perceptions, the constant, perhaps inevitable, disjunction between experience and memory. Sontag opines: "You project onto the volcano the amount of rage, of complicity with destructiveness, of anxiety about your ability to feel already in your head." Inner peace, like the volcano itself, cannot be collected. Like Pliny the Elder, to whom he compares himself, the Cavaliere is obsessed by the image of Vesuvius erupting in 79 A.D.: "the fearsome noise, the cloud in the shape of an umbrella pine, the death of the sun, the mountain burst open . . . the rat-grey ash." It is this image that haunts him as he observes the final eruption of the self, his own death.

In grappling with what constitutes the heroic ("And strange, too, seeing the hero in reverse. From another view, the view of history"), Sontag probes its contradictory images in painting. Romney loves Emma's cockney gusto; Elizabeth Vigée-Lebrun loathes it. Reynolds prefers the scholarly Cavaliere as *idea* of hero to the bony angularity of Nelson. And so she probes how each age, classical and modern, needs to see itself through art. In the eighteenth century, "it showed people able to maintain decorum and composure, even in monumental suffering." Yet today, "the significant moment is the one that disturbs us most."

To that end, Sontag uses a cool cinematic lens to show—and make us feel—moments of ultimate suffering. Chief among those is the gallows scene in which Eleanora de Fonseca is jumped upon, her neck broken, as she hangs alive. Suffering is often best shown in the novel's cameo roles: Baron Scarpia, the black-cloaked police spy of Tosca ("To the wicked, a person understood is a person manipulated"); the Neapolitan duke who is savagely tortured, his collection of Titians and rare books burned by a mob suspecting him of Jacobinism.

One finishes *The Volcano Lover* certain of its inevitability. It seems a novel Susan Sontag was destined to write, a shift from the moral intelligence of the essayist to the intelligent heart of the novelist. To her admirers, the novel will only confirm her originality, and perhaps win over a whole new set of readers. For *The Volcano Lover* is not just a thinking woman's (or man's) historical romance but a sly, luminously insightful, provocative novel.

Like Henry James in that other novel on collecting, *The Portrait of a Lady,* Sontag works the connections between travel, place and desire. In that same sundrenched landscape of southern Italy in which he set Isabel Archer reflecting on art, marriage, women and fate, James asked:

> Where, in all this . . . was the element of "horror". . . . What obsession that was not charming could find a place in that splendid light, out of which the long summer squeezes every secret and shadow? I'm afraid I'm driven to plead that these evils were exactly in one's imagination, a predestined victim always of the cruel, the fatal historic sense. To make so much distinction, how much history had been needed! So that the whole air still throbbed and ached with it, as with an accumulation of ghosts.

In *The Volcano Lover,* Susan Sontag illuminates that fatal historic sense, its secrets, its shadows, through the ghosts she's brought back to life.

Evelyn Toynton (review date November 1992)

SOURCE: "The Critic as Novelist," in *Commentary,* Vol. 94, No. 5, November, 1992, pp. 62-4.

[*In the following review, Toynton argues that* The Volcano Lover *leaves readers with Sontag's opinions but not with an understanding of the characters.*]

Susan Sontag arrived at her present intellectual eminence with the publication of her first collection of essays, *Against Interpretation* (1966), a consideration of such chic cultural phenomena as happenings, the *nouveau roman,* French movies, and camp. In the title essay of that book, she argued for a radical new approach to art, one in which the emphasis would be on form rather than content. Interpretation, she declared, was "reactionary, impertinent, cowardly, stifling" (note the list of adjectives, a characteristic mannerism); the important thing was to "recover our senses . . . to see more, to hear more, to feel more."

At the time, this essay, like the book as a whole, was seen as a liberating force, a romantic rallying cry for the avantgarde to emancipate art from the shackles of fusty mean-ing. But for all its surface glitter, there was something peculiarly sterile in the kind of romanticism Sontag espoused. In its way, it was a debased reworking of the *esthétique précieuse* of Walter Pater, that guru of the English Decadence, and like Pater's exhortation to "burn always with [a] hard, gem-like flame," it proved to be something of a dead end.

Yet in her criticism over the years, Sontag has remained largely faithful to that early creed, in the sense that she does not perceive her function as one of uncovering meaning; her essays do not plunge into the depths so much as skate imperiously over the surface. The work of interpreting, with its connotation of a journey toward revelation, obliges the critic to pursue a line of reasoning, construct an argument; this Sontag has never done. She proceeds, in her criticism, not by argument but by assertion, delivering a series of judgments and pronouncements to which the reader is expected to submit without question. For all her defense of various types of freedom, hers is a curiously dictatorial voice.

Now, however, [in *The Volcano Lover*] Sontag has written a novel that would appear to be a grand departure from all her earlier work—her stylized experimental fiction as well as her acclaimed nonfiction. Not only does she call it a romance, but she was at some pains to make clear, in an adulatory article about her in the New York *Times Magazine,* that writing this book was an act of pure love—no sort of intellectual exercise whatsoever. Certainly, those reviewers who have enthused over the novel in the pages of *Vanity Fair* and elsewhere have expressed delight at the incongruity of her subject: the famously scandalous, early-19th-century romance between Lady Emma Hamilton, flamboyant young wife of the elderly British envoy to the Court of the Two Sicilies, and Lord Horatio Nelson, England's greatest naval hero. We are meant to understand that there is something particularly endearing about such a rigorously postmodern intellectual expending her talents on this old-fashioned historical subject.

And the story is indeed a colorful one, rich in comedy as well as pathos. Emma, the exuberant daughter of a village blacksmith, was originally sent to Sir William Hamilton in Naples as a bribe, or so it was said: a profligate nephew of Sir William's, unable to pay his debts to his uncle, shipped off his pretty young mistress instead. When she arrived in Naples, accompanied by her illiterate mother, Sir William— a widower thirty-six years her senior, a fastidious aesthete and art collector, as well as the volcano lover of Sontag's title (he made over twenty ascents of Mount Vesuvius while in Italy)—set about having her tutored in gentlewomanly subjects like music and Italian and art. She would dance and sing for his guests, dress up in elaborate costumes and strike "attitudes" based on mythological figures; a shameless flatterer, a bit of a drunk, she was endlessly gossiped about by the visiting English, while the normally reticent William openly adored her.

> **The technique [Sontag] employs in [*The Volcano Lover*] is curiously similar to that of her criticism: despite the inherent drama of the narrative, the book proceeds less as a series of events and encounters than as a string of verdicts and summations, observations and pronouncements.**
> **—*Evelyn Toynton***

Twelve years after Emma's arrival, Nelson showed up in Naples, ill and exhausted, having just lost his arm and suffered a head wound in battle; Lady Emma and her mother nursed him back to health, and he began going about everywhere with the Hamiltons, the three of them singing one another's praises. It was the only time that Nelson neglected his duties, or his wife at home. According to the hand-wringing English version of the story (at least until the revisionist movie of 1941, *That Hamilton Woman,* starring Laurence Olivier and Vivian Leigh), Emma was a sorceress who bewitched the great man, and was to blame both for his idleness and for the uncharacteristic ferocity with which he put down a republican uprising in Naples. (The normally kindly Nelson issued summary orders for the execution of the aristocratic republicans.)

The Hamiltons and Nelson then returned to England together; after Nelson's final break with his wife, the three even shared a house, from which Emma's and Nelson's daughter was spirited away hours after her birth, in order to spare Sir William's feelings. The lovers presided jointly over Sir William's deathbed, and then lived together openly in the rare intervals when Nelson was not off at sea battling Napoleon's navy. On the eve of the Battle of Trafalgar, he wrote a will pleading with his king and countrymen to look after his dear Emma and their daughter in the event of his death—a request they conspicuously ignored, while erecting countless monuments to his memory.

This is the story Susan Sontag tells—a romance, indeed. But the technique she employs in the novel is curiously similar to that of her criticism: despite the inherent drama of the narrative, the book proceeds less as a series of events and encounters than as a string of verdicts and summations, observations and pronouncements. And again, there is no attempt to plumb the depths, to reveal the characters' inner lives.

Indeed, the characters remain amalgams of superficial mental traits, occasions for aphorism: "A star, unlike an actress,

always wants to be recognized." "A hero is one who knows how to leave, to break ties." But unlike Montaigne's epigrams, or even Oscar Wilde's, Sontag's have no ring of truth; they are maxims in search of a meaning. (Would it not sound just as convincing to say, "A hero is one who *never* breaks ties, who always returns home"?) This is minimalist fiction presented in maximalist fashion, elaborating endlessly on its themes without ever heading for the interior.

In dealing with Sir William, for example—and the first third of the book is largely taken up with describing "the Cavaliere's" daily life before the arrival of Emma in Naples—we get dozens of passages like this:

> The collector's impulse does not encourage the lust to understand or transform. Collecting is a form of union. The collector is acknowledging. He is adding. He is learning. He is noting.

For all the rhetorical flourishes, the wisdom-dispensing tone, this is just portentous hot air. (Indeed, it sounds less like Proust than like Joan Didion on a bad day. "Boca Grande is. Boca Grande was. Boca Grande shall be." Etc.) And nowhere do we get a depiction of Hamilton's immediate sensations as he makes an acquisition—the one thing that might have brought us to empathize with this figure at least briefly, to feel something toward him other than supercilious detachment.

But if Sontag never allows Sir William to breathe, she is infinitely kinder to him than to Nelson—always referred to in the book as "the Hero." So in fact he was known in England, where even today pubs all over his native Norfolk still carry signs of him bearing that legend. Sontag, however, uses the epithet in a purely sarcastic sense. Of all the judgments rendered in this novel, none is more righteous or more final than the condemnation of Nelson's conduct during the Neapolitan revolt—if there is one thing bound to provoke Sontag's leftist ire, it is the suppression of a republican uprising. Yet her portrayal seems tinged with a certain personal spite as well.

Perhaps Sontag is affronted by the sheer roast-beef Englishness of Nelson (she is a great lover of all things French), or perhaps the virtues he possessed—fierce courage, a high degree of independence—are simply outside her sphere of interest. There are no elegant discriminations to be made about physical bravery; one can only feel a certain humility before it, and that Sontag is incapable of—just as she is incapable of showing us what might have gone on in the mind of someone like Nelson when he was standing on deck with cannonballs whizzing around him; or climbing into a ship unaided, his shattered arm dangling at his side, after stopping his small boat to pick up wounded crew members floating in the water.

Emma fares much better here. Not only does Sontag seem to approve of her more than she does of the others—presenting her as a generous spirit rather than the slut of English morality tales, and as a victim of various injustices perpetrated on females in a male society—but, toward the end of the book, she even gives us a glimpse into Emma's consciousness, unmediated by the narrator's insistently knowing voice. In a brief, moving scene, as Emma is dancing in a drunken frenzy before Sir William's horrified guests, Sontag suddenly gives her a voice of her own—wild with sorrow and defiance, ardent in just the way Emma ought to be. For almost the first time, the novel comes alive. Later still, Emma's ignorant, doting mother takes over briefly to tell the story in her own words, and once again we actually feel the presence of a live human being.

But in the end, apart from some vivid images of street scenes in Naples, of a rampaging mob, of Sir William's pathetic pet monkey, and of Emma dancing, the strongest impression one takes away from this book is of the suffocatingly humorless presence of Susan Sontag.

She has become by now a virtual icon of Mind, the ultimate "glamorous intellectual," as *Vanity Fair* puts it. Yet her chief strength may lie in nothing much more than the ability to assume a voice of authority at all times. In the case of *The Volcano Lover*, what this produces is a solemn rather than a serious novel, in which portentous observations are made in the tone of someone offering a glimpse of the Holy Grail.

Linda Colley (review date 3 December 1992)

SOURCE: "Elitism," in *London Review of Books*, Vol. 14, No. 23, December 3, 1992, p. 18.

[*In the following review, Colley ponders Sontag's reasons for writing* The Volcano Lover.]

Why did Susan Sontag write [*The Volcano Lover*]? Essayist and cultural critic, interpreter of Aids, cancer, the cinema, Fascism and pornography, recipient of Jonathan Miller's burdensome accolade 'probably the most intelligent woman in America', why should she want to attempt a historical novel? It's been a success of course. There have been the entries into the best-seller lists, the interviews and profiles in the right magazines, the respectful and often rapturous reviews. Only the occasional still small voice has risked pointing out—what is almost certainly true—that the bulk of those who have purchased this book have wanted the latest high-cultural artefact for their glass-topped tables,

not ideas or literature. It is easy to read. It is even entertaining. But why did she write it?

It concerns, apparently, one of the two best-known British ménages à trois of the late 18th and early 19th centuries: the relationship between the Ambassador to Naples, Sir William Hamilton, the one-time prostitute who became his mistress and eventual second wife, Emma Lyon, and the naval hero and victim of Trafalgar, Horatio Nelson. The other famous trio of this time, William Cavendish, fifth Duke of Devonshire, his wife Georgiana and Lady Elizabeth Foster, concealed their goings-on and their miscellaneous progeny in the grand seclusion of Chatsworth and Devonshire House. Less socially-exalted, the Hamiltons and Nelson were at once more notorious and far more vulnerable.

All three were outsiders of a kind. Hamilton was only the fourth son of a Scottish nobleman, and his posting at the Court of the repulsive King Ferdinand of Naples and his clever, fecund Queen, Maria Carolina, placed him very much in the outer circle of British diplomacy. Emma was a blacksmith's daughter who never lost her Lancashire accent. She went to London, as so many did, and saved herself from the streets by intelligence, beauty, a capacity to attract successive wealthy protectors, and a willingness to discard her love-children, both an early mistake and—perhaps—one of a set of twins she had by Nelson. And the sailor-hero, what of him? Again, he was a marginal figure, the son of a minor Norfolk clergyman, with relations who were shopkeepers, as well as a few with noble blood and lofty positions in the state. All three had to work hard at inventing themselves anew when ambition and accident brought them to prominence; all three—as Sontag seldom fails to point out—were capable of vulgarity, all three were ardent collectors, of objects, people, victories, medals, praise, anything that might increase their value in the eyes of others.

Just what the business of collecting means is a subject that Sontag has discussed before, and her frequent discursions on it in this book are sharp and predictably intelligent. Sir William Hamilton, the Cavaliere as he is called here, was a Fellow of the Royal Society, a bibliophile, a connoisseur of ruins, and a dealer in paintings and Greek vases (including the recently-mended Portland Vase). He was also volcano-mad, one version of the volcano lover of Sontag's title. For him, she suggests, collecting art objects, like the bits and view of Vesuvius he risked his life for, were defences against official neglect, local squalor, the limits of his first wife, an 'amiable, not-too-plain, harpsichord-playing heiress', and his own essential emptiness of involvement: 'The Cavaliere was not looking. He was looking away.' Then, with bereavement, came his chance to emulate Pygmalion, and collect something new. His nephew, Charles Greville, handed over his luscious and unaware mistress, Emma, on the tacit agreement that Hamilton would not re-marry and cut him out of his will.

Greville and an earlier protector had already pruned Emma of some of her original rusticity, teaching her how to pour tea and how to ride a horse. Now, Hamilton added Italian, French, singing, art appreciation, even a sprinkling of the Classics. And he had her perform her famous 'attitudes'. First in a specially constructed frame; then with the addition of some diaphanous shawls, she learnt how to freeze herself into different Classical postures. She was Dido, or Ariadne, or Medea, or any other heroine from Hamilton's books and vases, not just Pygmalion's statue come to life, but a creature who could revert to a tasteful immobility whenever it pleased her keeper and his guests. Just what Emma herself thought of all this is a question that has perplexed her recent biographers. Used to monitoring and catering to the whims of men as the only way to survive, she was rarely self-reflective on paper, so we can only guess what went on in her mind. Sontag presents her as a woman of enthusiastic plasticity, torn from her roots and avidly collecting love and the lifestyles of her lovers as a means of giving herself shape and purpose. The only rebellions that Emma permitted herself, in this version, were alcoholism, extra-vagance, and putting on weight.

Yet I suspect that in reality she was a much harder woman than this, if no less masochistic. She succeeded, after all, in getting Hamilton to marry her in 1791, when he was 60 and she 26 years old. Seven years later, she demoted him to a kindly-treated cuckold. And she took Nelson away from his wife, Fanny, apparently without any qualms at all. 'Mrs Tom Tit' was Emma's name for her pleasant, bird-like rival. Though there could be no real rivalry... Nelson had lost his mother when he was nine, an arm, an eye, most of his teeth, and much of his health subsequently. He was an indisputable, incandescent and frequently immature hero who was desperate to collect battle honours, gongs, promotions, influential friends, approval and love. In 1798, the Hamiltons welcomed him to Naples after the splendours and hardships of the Battle of the Nile. And soon Emma had adopted another attitude, playing Cleopatra to his Antony, Dido to his Aeneas, a by now rather pneumatic enchantress distracting the warrior from his duty. 'My Lord Thunder', she called him, with just a touch of mockery. The lava in Mount Etna, he wrote, was no warmer than his passion. So Nelson, too, is the volcano lover of the title.

Sontag claims that her characters are the doubles of the 'real' historical figures, fictional creations 'on whose behalf I have taken what liberties' seemed appropriate to their natures. Yet she follows recent biographies of Nelson and Emma Hamilton very closely indeed, and only lets her imagination flow in the slightly embarrassing sex-scenes, and in her acute characterisation of Hamilton himself about

whom rather less is known. In general, though, Sontag does her homework thoroughly: and this may well point to one very basic reason why she has selected the apparently bizarre literary form of a historical novel. As Balzac put it, characters in ordinary novels have to be roused to life by their inventors. But historical characters have already lived, and are consequently easier to flesh out in words. Sontag has turned to the historical novel because she needs this crutch, because she is not—despite all of her enormous gifts, and perhaps because of them—a natural novelist. She cannot write dialogue. Her powers of storytelling are limited. Her characters soliloquise in Sontag's own voice.

This indeed is primarily why one should read *The Volcano Lover,* not for its rehearsal of an already well-documented relationship between two men and a woman, but for the snippets it contains of Sontag herself. There are the brilliant plays on words, which only occasionally go wrong ('The sleep of reason engenders mothers'). There are the acid comments on human relationships and deceptions, the predictable division of roles among couples, the weight of male egos and the extent of female compliance in them: 'Talking with him,' Hamilton's first wife muses sadly, 'was like talking with someone on a horse.' Most of all, there are the signposts to the state of Sontag's mind and politics.

Historical novels tend to get written by those in search of an escape from the pressures of the present, or by those who want to use a version of the past to comment on the present. Initially, Sontag seems an escapist. The novel opens with a shudder at contemporary popular consumerism, a New York street market cluttered with 'Navajo rugs ... World War II bomber jackets ... model cars', then jumps back to Sir William's rather more austere bargaining in Classical knick-knacks in the London of 1772. When the story reaches Naples, there is the same revulsion at modern squalor. An unlikely fortune-teller imagines a future Mount Etna covered in souvenir shops 'scarves or plates with pictures of the mountain. . . . The future is a hole.' Whatever the devastation of the French Revolutionary era, we are told, 'people then did not know what ruin could be!' Sontag leaves us in no doubt of her distaste for much of the present, and in particular of her revulsion at its masses.

On the other hand, she dislikes most of her quasi-historical characters almost as much. She is skilful at introducing each member of the famous trio to us in turn in a sympathetic light, then, after a while, exposing ruthlessly their various failings and cruelties. Hamilton dwindles from his first appearance as a reserved and rational scholar-diplomat and kind if distant husband into a selfish dilettante who refuses to feel. Emma, by contrast, is at the beginning the woman of feeling who clambers gamely over every social obstacle. By the end of the book, though, she seems an empty space, awash with sentiment, but with few scruples. As for Nelson,

Sontag barely troubles to conceal her contempt. Of course he is a hero and desperately courageous. But, then, the 1790s were a time for 'concentrated men of preposterous ambition and small stature'.

Sontag could scarcely have come to any other conclusion since events at Naples and off its shores between 1798 and 1800 formed indisputably the nadir of Nelson's career. The old, unreconstructed history books attributed his actions at this time to the malign influence of his seductress Emma Hamilton: newer accounts refer to the effects of his recent concussion at the Battle of the Nile, combined with intermittent malaria, plus the shock of unprecedented sexual bliss. Either way, the record is black. Nelson first helped the King and Queen of Naples to escape from local republicans. He then used the might of his fleet to blockade the short-lived Neapolitan Republic, and presided distantly but effectively over the show-trials and summary executions of its leaders and supporters. 'Eternal shame on the hero!' declares Sontag, and labels him the Bourbon executioner, an instrument of British imperialism.

One suspects that few aficionados of either naval or imperial history will be much drawn to this book, but the record should still be set straight. The British establishment, in fact, disapproved mightily of Nelson's antics off Naples, not so much because of the inhumanity, as because naval officers were not expected to involve themselves in the politics of foreign states. As for Nelson, he seems to have acted as he did because he was ill, because—like Emma—he had a parvenu's romantic attachment to monarchy, and because he believed that a Neapolitan republic organised on the new French principles of government might give Napoleon control of the Mediterranean. Moreover, the Italians were not just foreign, they were Papist to boot, the lot of them not worth the life of a single British seaman, as one of his crew remarked. But, in truth, it is not Nelson's motives that interest Sontag, but his victims, and in particular a woman called Eleonora de Fonseca Pimentel.

[*The Volcano Lover*] is a historical novel slanted to the conflicts of the present, far more than it is nostalgic about the past.
—Linda Colley

She was Portuguese by birth, an intellectual prodigy who wrote poetry, plays, economic treatises and mathematical equations. Separated from her husband, she lived on the bounty of the Neapolitan Court, a fashionable representative of its local Enlightenment. Then came the French Revolution and her conversion to republicanism. During the five brief months in which a new regime was able to cling to power in Naples, she presided over its principal newspaper, arguing for liberty, toleration, reform, and an end to the old superstitions. She too, loved the volcano, and like so many others, was hanged for her pains, one executioner pulling at her feet, another cavorting on her shoulders. Sontag makes her the subject of her entire last chapter, and has claimed that writing it made her weep.

It is not, in fact, all that good or moving a chapter, but it does serve to confirm that Sontag wrote this book partly as an exercise in autobiography, and partly to vindicate certain ideas about what is important now. Hers is a historical novel slanted to the conflicts of the present, far more than it is nostalgic about the past. In particular, it is an argument for élitism. At one level, she demands that we defer to genius, even if it takes the form of Nelson's genius for killing the enemy stylishly and in large numbers: 'We like to stress the commonness of heroes. . . . We want to admire but think we have a right not to be intimidated. . . . The only ideals allowed are healthy ones—those everyone may aspire to, or comfortably imagine oneself possessing. 'She will have none of this tepid democracy that drags distinction down. And makes the same point still more energetically (because now it is intellectual genius that is involved) when she has Goethe act the crashing bore at one of the Hamiltons' cultural evenings:

> How superior he had felt to these people. And how superior he was. . . . He is pretentious, overbearing, humourless, aggressive, condescending. A monster of egotism. Alas, he's also the real thing.

The masses will not acknowledge this of course. Like the Neapolitan peasants, they hang Eleonora Pimentel and her sort, the intelligent liberals who offer them reform, and opt instead for the tinsel, superstition and tyranny of King Ferdinand. 'The mob is unwilling to be high-minded,' she writes. 'Smite, stomp, throttle, clobber, stone, impale, hang, burn, dismember, drown': that's what the mob do. It's an uncompromising position, but very much in line with some of Sontag's expressed views in the past. She is reputedly often supercilious, an unabashed intellectual who takes herself seriously and has no taste at all for what the British tend to view as the virtue of ironic self-deprecation. This is one reason her books are little read here. But even in the States, she is often now attacked for her cosmopolitanism and neglect of popular culture—by Camille Paglia, for instance, who lays into her regularly with the pure and simple aim of rising on her ashes. So perhaps in [*The Volcano Lover*] Sontag is getting her own back. For what could be more piquant than for an author to insert statements of the most unbridled élitism and intellectualism into a book that appears on the surface to be the most populist that she has ever written, a mere historical novel?

Marie Olesen Urbanski (review date 10 October 1993)

SOURCE: "A Festering Rage," in *Los Angeles Times Book Review*, October 10, 1993, p. 8.

[*In the following review, Urbanski writes that the subject matter of* Alice in Bed *is challenging and interesting but the play suffers from numerous limitations.*]

How do you write a play about emptiness, about a woman whose "career choice" was to be an invalid? Who retreated from life to her bed with recurrent, undefined—perhaps imaginary—illnesses? Who read a lot, had a few friends and kept a journal, but never held a job or took a lover? This is the difficult subject Susan Sontag has chosen to dramatize in *Alice in Bed*, her new play about Alice James, who lived from 1848 to 1892.

If known at all today, James is remembered for being the sister of the famous novelist Henry James and the renowned psychologist William James. In literary circles, she first attracted attention for the strange diary she kept the last three years of her life. First published in 1934, the journal is admired today for its austere and acerbic social commentary, but it first caused a stir for her expression of "enormous relief" upon receiving a diagnosis of cancer at the age of 42.

James' startling reaction to the news of her premature demise surely attracted Sontag's attention, perhaps in part due to her own diagnosis of breast cancer at around the same age. Although in *Illness as Metaphor*, Sontag considered tuberculosis as the disease for 19th-Century romantics, she suggests that James's retreat into her "mental prison" of illness was the Victorian lady's archetypal response to anger and grief.

Much of the success of the theatrical production of *Alice in Bed*—which has been produced in Germany and Austria but not yet in the United States—would depend on the shock value of seeing the crippled character pinned under 10 mattresses and in watching a supposed victim manipulate her able-bodied nurses, relatives and even a burglar. The play sizzles as the young thief, puzzled by the insouciance of his chatty victim as he ransacks her drawers implores: "Why don't you scream?"

After the stark, post-modernist manner of Samuel Beckett, Sontag creates muted dialogue, showing Alice pitting her passive aggression against her nurses, brothers and father. In one scene, she introduces historical personages Margaret Fuller and Emily Dickinson having tea with Alice while stage directions indicate that she is shrinking like Alice in "Wonderland."

Feminist activist Fuller is the perfect foil to the invalid, but instead of showing Fuller as the accomplished and charismatic woman that she was, Sontag perpetuates an outdated stereotype by depicting her as intimidating and insensitive. Though this transgression might seem surprising coming from the feminist Sontag, such slipshod characterization is doubtless due to the two-week period she devoted to writing the play rather than any literary malice of forethought. To her credit, Sontag does better by Emily Dickinson, whose characterization lacks the trivial treatment given the poet by William Luce in his popular play, "Belle of Amherst."

The essayist in Sontag often overwhelms the dramatist as throughout *Alice in Bed* she substitutes intellectual concept for pure dramatization. She falters in a scene showing James' fantasy life in Italy: "[I]n my mind I can go as far as I want, I can do what I can't do, what I shouldn't do, in my mind." In this monologue, Sontag's Alice lacks the emotive power of Tennessee Williams's heartsick heroines who declaim their losses, not by repeating words, but by high poetry.

It would have been much easier for Sontag to create a modern Medea who could rave against the man who had betrayed her and enact a terrifying revenge, than to create a protagonist paralyzed by internal conflict. Given the difficulties of dramatizing that special weakness of women in this century and the last—psychological self-immolation—Sontag was brave to attempt so challenging a subject.

Despite its limitations, readers and theatergoers will surely be exposed to a rare but little-explored reality, from the female experience: a festering rage that causes depression, and perhaps illness—ultimately the "life force" turned on itself.

Marcie Frank (essay date 1993)

SOURCE: "The Critic as Performance Artist: Susan Sontag's Writing and Gay Cultures," in *Camp Grounds: Style and Homosexuality,* edited by David Bergman, University of Massachusetts Press, 1993, pp. 173-84.

[*In the following essay, Frank explores the relationship between camp and gay culture in Sontag's writing.*]

—I think the main question people have is, creature, what is it you want?

—Fred, what we want, I think, what everyone wants, is what you and your viewers have—civilization.

—But what sort of civilization are you speaking of, creature?

—The niceties, the fine points, diplomacy, standards, tradition—that's what we're reaching toward. We may stumble along the way but, civilization, yes, the Geneva Convention, chamber music, Susan Sontag, yes, civilization. Everything your society has worked so hard to accomplish over the centuries—that's what we aspire to. We want to be civilized.

[In *Gremlins* 2: *The New Batch* (dir. Joe Dante, 1990), one of the creatures drinks brain hormone and is interviewed as the spokesperson for the species. His voice is done by Tony Randall.]

D.A. Miller begins his review of Susan Sontag's *AIDS and Its Metaphors* with a telling citation of Sontag, who, in an interview, expressed her disappointment at the book's reception by scientists and AIDS experts. She would have preferred it to have been recognized as a "literary *performance* [having] more to do with Emerson than with Randy Shilts" (emphasis added). Miller explains what he calls "the phobic quality of Sontag's writing" in her book on AIDS by characterizing it, rightly, as a consequence of the status she gives to her writing. Sontag's book concentrates on the metaphors of AIDS at the expense of people with AIDS. She is interested in demystifying the metaphors used to discuss AIDS even as she claims that her writing is, itself, immune—if not from metaphor, then from the disease. Sontag's writing is "phobic," Miller argues, because writing obviously is not subject to disease. Sontag's attitude betrays panic in the privilege it proclaims for the purity of writing. But the status that Sontag claims for her writing, that it is a "literary performance," is not new to the AIDS book.

Sontag has claimed performative status for her writing from the beginning of her career. In the note to the paperback edition of *Against Interpretation,* published in 1967, Sontag presents herself as a novelist rather than a critic, thereby highlighting her "literary performance[s]": "The articles and reviews collected here make up a good part of the criticism I wrote between 1962 and 1965, a sharply defined period in my life. In early 1962 I finished my first novel, *The Benefactor*. In late 1965 I began a second novel. The energy, and the anxiety, that spilled over into the criticism had a beginning and an end." Defining her critical achievements as an interlude between novelistic endeavors, Sontag states that the value her essays may possess lies in "the extent to which they are more than just case studies in [her] own evolving sensibility" (*Against Interpretation*). However, this claim is about her "evolving sensibilities." Insofar as she implies that the value of her essays increases because she is a novelist, Sontag is being disingenuous. Moreover, the essays generally have been regarded more highly than the novels, which may lead us to reject her attempt to evaluate her es-

says. Nevertheless, we need to investigate her underlying assumption: that there is a relation between her sensibility and her goals as a critic. This relation pervades her critical writings; to elucidate it is also to describe how her writing constitutes a performance.

Perhaps the most memorable intersection of Sontag's sensibility and her "literary performance" occurs in the **"Notes on Camp"** where she describes her critical goal: "to name a sensibility, to draw its contours and recount its history" (*Against Interpretation* 276). In the five paragraphs that introduce the **"Notes on Camp,"** Sontag reflects on the task she has assumed and sketches a justification of the form her writing takes: "To snare a sensibility in words, especially one that is alive and powerful, one must be tentative and nimble. The form of jottings, rather than an essay (with its claim to a linear, consecutive argument), seemed more appropriate for getting down something of this particular fugitive sensibility" (*Against Interpretation* 277). Her introductory remarks end in a dedicatory flourish that establishes both her aspirations and her high standards. "It's embarrassing to be solemn and treatise-like about Camp. One runs the risk of having, oneself, produced a very inferior piece of Camp. These notes are for Oscar Wilde" (*Against Interpretation* 277). Inferior or not, Sontag acknowledges that in the service of analyzing it, she has herself become a producer of camp. In fact, the essay ends as it begins, with Sontag recognizing that to describe the conditions for appreciating camp is to produce camp. In the fifty-eighth and final note, Sontag summarizes her accomplishments. She identifies "the ultimate Camp statement: it's good because it's awful. . . . Of course, one can't always say that. Only under certain conditions, those which I've tried to sketch in these notes" (*Against Interpretation* 292). It is telling, however, that her acknowledgment of her production or performance of camp is ambivalent. Although her essay attempts to identify the analysis of camp with its performance, this production carries with it no guarantee of aesthetic excellence. As we will see, trying to supply the missing guarantee drives Sontag's critical career in the directions it takes.

In her study of Sontag, Elizabeth Bruss makes a crucial observation about the shape of Sontag's career: she notices that the early concern with "sensibility" is displaced in *On Photography* and *Illness as Metaphor* by more impersonal terms like "photographic seeing" and "Ideology" (*Beautiful Theories*). But how do we get from one to the other? Elizabeth Hardwick suggests that the shift in Sontag's career from "sensibility" to "ideology" is measured in the shift from "spiritual" to "fascist." Her apparently neutral summary of Sontag's familiar claims characterizes the range of Sontag's interests: from the "spiritual style" of the films of Robert Bresson, which is "cool, impersonal and reserved," to the "fascist style" of Leni Riefenstahl, which is "dramatic, grandiose, orderly, communal and tribal." Hardwick's point is that Sontag's interest in style proposes this symmetry between "spiritual" and "fascist": both are styles of filmmaking; both are modified by a series of evocative adjectives. In fact, in a later essay, **"Fascinating Fascism"** (1975), Sontag returns to the question of camp; in the context of discussing Riefenstahl, she repudiates it.

In this essay, I argue that the linchpin in Sontag's shift from sensibility to ideology is camp. In note #37 of **"Notes on Camp,"** Sontag describes three sensibilities: "The first sensibility, that of high culture, is basically moralistic. The second sensibility, that of extreme states of feeling, represented in much contemporary 'avant-garde' art, gains power by a tension between moral and aesthetic passion. The third, Camp, is wholly aesthetic" (*Against Interpretation* 287). In 1975, Sontag renounces the high valuation of the "wholly aesthetic," condemning it as dangerously porous because it can be injected with politically abhorrent meanings. But her repudiation is less a contradiction of her earlier position than it might appear. In fact, the two attitudes are consistent. Sontag's shift from "sensibility" to "ideology" is structured by her understanding that criticism is a "literary performance." She expresses her idea of performance paradigmatically in **"Notes on Camp,"** where it has an explicit relation to gay subcultures. Sontag's desire to give her writing the status of a "literary performance" remains constant throughout her career and this critical stance derives from a (disavowed) relation to gay subcultures; in both the instances that she embraces camp and those in which she repudiates it, she assumes that there is a special relation between gayness or gay culture and performativity.

Sontag's dedication of **"Notes on Camp"** to Oscar Wilde and her interspersing of some of Wilde's epigrams among her own numbered entries, a gesture Elizabeth Hardwick characterizes as an audacious "incorporation" of Wilde (*A Sontag Reader*), suggest that a comparison between Sontag's and Wilde's understanding of the role of the critic would elucidate Sontag's complicated attitude toward criticism as a "literary performance."

In "The Critic as Artist," Oscar Wilde explodes the false dichotomy between a "critical" faculty and a "creative" one when he proposes that criticism is autobiography. As Wilde's speaker, Gilbert puts it, "the highest criticism really is the record of one's own soul. It is more fascinating than history, as it is concerned simply with oneself. It is more delightful than philosophy, as its subject is concrete and not abstract, real and not vague. It is the only civilised form of autobiography" ("The Critic as Artist" 68). Wilde's understanding of criticism seems to offer a model for Sontag. Indeed, Sontag's statement, "A sensibility (as distinct from an idea) is one of the hardest things to talk about" (*Against Interpretation* 275), is reminiscent of Gilbert's

more forceful assertion, "It is very much more difficult to talk about a thing than to do it" ("The Critic as Artist" 60). But Sontag appropriates Wilde selectively.

If she seems to adopt Wilde's blithe sublation of the opposition between objective observation and subjective investment or participation, Sontag also retreats from a full embrace of the autobiographical, offering in its place coy gestures that intensify her personality. She adopts Gilbert's critical watchword: "It is only by intensifying his personality that the critic can interpret the personality and works of others" ("The Critic as Artist" 78). She thereby replaces Wilde's understanding of critical practice by a notion of "literary performance."

The paradoxical terms by which Sontag characterizes her position as a critic in her introduction to **"Notes on Camp"** illustrate her misappropriations of Wilde. On the one hand, she represents herself as an intrepid investigator, embarking on a difficult, and therefore rewarding, task: "A sensibility (as distinct from an idea) is one of the hardest things to talk about; but there are special reasons why Camp, in particular, has never been discussed. . . . Camp is esoteric—something of a private code, a badge of identity even, among small urban cliques" (*Against Interpretation* 275). On the other hand, she is significantly less detached than her anthropological tone might suggest. Commenting on the dearth of discussions about camp, she declares. "To talk about Camp is therefore to betray it" (*Against Interpretation* 275). How can the discussion of a sensibility constitute a betrayal? The affect of the term, "betray[al]," illustrates, but does not explicate, Sontag's investment in camp.

Sontag quickly transforms her contradictory position into the famous announcement of her critical qualifications:

> I am strongly drawn to Camp, and almost as strongly offended by it. That is why I want to talk about it, and why I can. For no one who wholeheartedly shares in a given sensibility can analyze it; he can only, whatever his intentions, exhibit it. To name a sensibility, to draw its contours and recount its history, requires a deep sympathy modified by revulsion. (*Against Interpretation* 276)

Initially, her claim to critical expertise seems to overcome the opposition between the critic as objective observer and the critic as participant in terms that are similar to Wilde's. However, the contrast Sontag draws between analyzing and exhibiting a sensibility reinscribes the polarity and privileges analytical detachment. Furthermore, initially, it seems that her contradictory reactions to camp—being both attracted and repelled—enable her as a critic. But a closer look reveals that while her attraction to camp may give her the knowledge to talk about it, it is her revulsion that qualifies her as a critic.

Even more paradoxically, Sontag's critical position expresses her ambivalence about performance. She wants to limit the performance of sensibility even though her own writing is the performance of her sensibility. She suggests that the acceptability of performance is a matter of degree: if an unspecified degree of involvement in a sensibility is necessary, "wholehearted sharing" disables analysis. Significantly, the terms she chooses to limit performance are moral: "no one who wholeheartedly shares in a given sensibility can analyze it; he can only, *whatever his intentions,* exhibit it" (emphasis added). Too much participation in a sensibility turns one into an inadvertent exhibitionist. Both betrayal and exhibition are overloaded terms whose moral resonances measure the distance between Sontag and Wilde.

Rejecting the autobiographical mode as exhibitionism, Sontag does not identify the characteristics that allow her to know camp. Instead, she produces her revulsion as a badge of the average, which offers the reader grounds for identifying with her. Her statement, "To talk about Camp is therefore to betray it" (*Against Interpretation* 275), constitutes readerly curiosity as voyeurism, but both our voyeurism and her betrayal are transvalued by averageness. Sontag supplies information about camp that is both ostensibly not otherwise available and appropriately "modified by revulsion"; this supply yields the moral gain of self-edification: "If the betrayal can be defended, it will be for the edification it provides, or the dignity of the conflict it resolves. For myself, I plead the goal of self-edification" (*Against Interpretation* 276). "Our" identification with her revulsion allows us to be edified by proxy.

Sontag's motives for evading the autobiographical are now perhaps clearer: the autobiographical mode would stymie the moral transvaluation of betrayal and voyeurism into edification because it would explain Sontag's investment in camp in other terms. Evasion grounds Sontag's critical position as a moralist. The hip knowingness that her writing exudes results from an intensification of personality, but her retreat from the autobiographical means that the sources of this knowledge are mystified even as she purports to analyze them.

By criticizing Sontag's desire to produce "literary performances," I am not advocating antitheatricalism; I am noting a paradoxically antitheatrical slant in Sontag's endorsement of the theatrical. After all, it is Sontag's understanding of performance that allows her to write her groundbreaking essay on camp. Furthermore, by holding Wilde's definition of criticism as autobiography over Sontag's head, I do not mean to suggest that what is missing from Sontag's writing is information of a private na-

ture. When Wilde has Gilbert say that criticism is autobiography, I do not take him to mean "private" or "personal." The fact that Gilbert is a character dramatized by Wilde in "The Critic as Artist" both invites and complicates taking him as an autobiographical figure. Nevertheless, Wilde's wholehearted embrace of the theatrical means that his practice of criticism as autobiography works in the following way: when Wilde talks about himself, he can talk through himself (or through Gilbert's talking about himself) about issues of aesthetic valuation and meaning. What I would require of Sontag, then, is not a confession about her investments in camp, but rather a fuller embrace of critical practice instead of performance, that is to say, a fuller embrace of autobiography. By ostensibly suppressing herself in order to talk about "other things," by acting on an antitheatrical valuation of "detachment" or "impersonality," all she manages to do, paradoxically, is to draw attention to her desires to be a "literary performer."

In taking camp as the paradigm of performance, Sontag transforms Wilde's depiction of the critic as artist into the critic as performance artist. The position of the critic as a performance artist allows Sontag to equate the analysis of camp with the production of it at the same time that it also provides her with a covert position of morality from which she can supply the otherwise absent guarantee that her productions will be of aesthetic quality. In **"Fascinating Fascism,"** Sontag turns to the political register in order to enforce that guarantee by explicitly moral means.

Whatever we may want to make of the claim from **"Notes on Camp"** that "Camp taste, is above all, a mode of enjoyment, of appreciation—not judgment" (*Against Interpretation* 291), we need to see the continuities with the pronouncement Sontag makes in **"Fascinating Fascism"**: "Art which evokes the themes of fascist aesthetics is popular now, and for most people it is probably no more than a variant of camp" (*A Sontag Reader*). "Most people," she seems to be saying, currently can't recognize fascism because they (mis)take it for camp.

> Fascism may be merely fashionable, and perhaps fashion with its irresistible promiscuity of taste will save us. But the judgments of taste themselves seem less innocent. Art that seemed eminently worth defending ten years ago, as a minority or adversary taste, no longer seems defensible today, because the ethical and cultural issues it raises have become serious, even dangerous, in a way they were not then. (*A Sontag Reader*).

What has changed so substantially between 1964 and 1975 to raise such an alarm? In note #2 of **"Notes on Camp,"** Sontag had claimed that "it goes without saying that the Camp sensibility is disengaged, depoliticized—or at least apolitical" (*Against Interpretation* 277). In 1975, however, Sontag seeks to recuperate the political valences of what, in 1964, she depicted as resolutely "apolitical." The paragraph from **"Fascinating Fascism"** that I just cited continues: "The hard truth is that what may be acceptable in elite culture may not be acceptable in mass culture, that tastes which pose only innocuous ethical issues as the property of the minority become corrupting when they become more established. Taste is context, and the context has changed" (*A Sontag Reader*). Could the critical change between 1964 and 1975 be the politicization, after Stonewall, of what had seemed to Sontag to be a purely aesthetic phenomenon, namely, camp? If so, then perhaps Eve Kosofsky Sedgwick's recent description of Allan Bloom's defense of the canon is relevant: in defending "that curious space that is both internal and marginal to the culture"—the bohemian elite—Bloom offers "an unapologetic protection of the sanctity of the closet."

> The modern, normalizing, minoritizing equal rights movement for people of varying sexual identities is a grave falling-off, in Bloom's view, from the more precarious cultural *privilege* of a past in which "there was a respectable place for marginality, bohemia. But it had to justify its unorthodox practice by intellectual and artistic achievement."

Like Bloom, Sontag wants to protect a bohemian elite, but her desire to do so operates only as long as the aesthetic and apolitical "quality" of its artistic productions can be guaranteed. In **"Notes on Camp,"** camp was "at least apolitical" (*Against Interpretation* 277); in **"Fascinating Fascism,"** Sontag brings a full-blown moral vocabulary masquerading as politics to ensure that if gay culture won't stay apolitical, it is guaranteed to be marginalized, or worse.

Interestingly, Sontag's "political" solution is already apparent in **"Notes on Camp."** In entry #51, Sontag makes explicit the relation between gay culture and camp:

> The *peculiar* relation between Camp taste and homosexuality has to be explained. While it's not true that Camp taste is homosexual taste, there is no doubt a *peculiar* affinity and overlap. Not all liberals are Jews, but Jews have shown a *particular* affinity for liberal and reformist causes. So, not all homosexuals have camp taste. But homosexuals, by and large, constitute the vanguard—and the most articulate audience—of Camp. (*Against Interpretation* 290, emphasis added)

In parenthesis, Sontag explains the analogy between the peculiarity of homosexual taste and the particularity of Jewish morality.

> (The analogy is not frivolously chosen. Jews and homosexuals are the outstanding creative minorities in contemporary urban culture. Creative, that is, in the truest sense: they are creators of sensibilities. The two pioneering forces of modern sensibility are Jewish moral seriousness and homosexual aestheticism and irony.) (*Against Interpretation* 290)

In entry #52, Sontag asserts that the social marginalization of both homosexuals and Jews is what makes them more creative; both groups are motivated by their search for legitimation and acceptance by society: "The Jews pinned their hopes for integrating into modern society on promoting the moral sense. Homosexuals have pinned their integration into society on promoting the aesthetic sense. Camp is a solvent of morality. It neutralizes moral indignation, sponsors playfulness" (*Against Interpretation* 290). After Stonewall, it would no longer have been possible for Sontag to characterize homosexuals' sociopolitical interest as primarily to sponsor playfulness nor to propose "integration" as their goal. It could no longer be said of a gay movement agitating for legal and political recognition that it advocated a purely aesthetic sense.

But Sontag is not the only one, who, in 1975, sought to recuperate the political valences of the things she had described in purely aesthetic terms in 1964. Like Bloom, Sontag's use of political terms to protect the bohemian elites should be seen in the context of a general reaction to the 1960s. It is instructive to consider Sontag's always slightly avant-garde development alongside the shift in the literary academy from the sixties to the eighties from formalist to political criticism of all stripes. We now know that it probably was never possible to call any phenomenon "purely aesthetic." What then becomes salient is the inadequacy of the political terms Sontag chooses.

In **"Fascinating Fascism,"** Sontag seeks to identify the features of a fascist aesthetic. On the one hand, she presents the fascist aesthetic as no different than a sensibility, but on the other hand, she relies on the term "fascism" to produce the moral outrage that will differentiate sensibility from ideology. Sontag turns from sensibility to ideology on ostensibly moral grounds. Under-writing the morality, unfortunately, is homophobia. Whereas in **"Notes on Camp,"** camp reveals "a mostly unacknowledged truth of taste: [that] the most refined form of sexual attractiveness consists in going against the grain of one's sex. . . ." (*Against Interpretation*), in **"Fascinating Fascism,"** "once sex becomes a taste, it is perhaps already on its way to becoming a self-conscious form of theater, which is what sadomasochism is about" (*A Sontag Reader*). Here is the same antitheatrical bent that constitutes Sontag's ambivalence toward performance in **"Notes on Camp"**; the terms are simply more explicit.

In **"Fascinating Fascism,"** after discussing the rehabilitation of Reifenstahl, which she calls "First Exhibit," Sontag turns to "Second Exhibit," a book of photos called *SS Regalia* that she uses as the point of departure to decry the erotic uses to which Nazi paraphernalia have been put. In the closing line, Sontag offers the most memorable instance of the essay's hysterical rhetoric: "The color is black, the material is leather, the seduction is beauty, the justification is honesty, the aim is ecstasy, the fantasy is death" (*A Sontag Reader*). Each clause repeats the structure of the previous one, but instead of providing clarification, each equation merely increases the vehemence of tone. The scene she unfolds before the reader can only become spectacular, however, after Sontag has affiliated sadomasochism with homosexuality. Notice the progression in this paragraph:

> In pornographic literature, films and gadgetry throughout the world, especially in the United States, England, France, Japan, Scandinavia, Holland and Germany, the SS has become a referent of sexual adventurism. Much of the imagery of far-out sex has been placed under the sign of Nazism. Boots, leather, chains, Iron Crosses on gleaming torsos, swastikas, along with meathooks and heavy motorcycles, have become the secret and most lucrative paraphernalia of eroticism. In the sex shops, the baths, the leather bars, the brothels, people are dragging out their gear. But why? Why has Nazi Germany, which was a sexually repressive society, become erotic? How could a regime which persecuted homosexuals become a gay turn-on? (*A Sontag Reader*)

How did we get from meathooks and motorcycles to gay turn-ons? Through Nazi paraphernalia, of course! Moreover, the insinuating logic of the list of locations in which we might find erotic gear—"sex shops, baths, leather bars, brothels"—makes it clear that the "people dragging [it] out" are gay men. Sontag equates gay male sexuality with sadomasochism, and, more damagingly, sadomasochism with an imputed "fascism" that is equivalent to Nazism.

Sontag's attempt to repoliticize what she had placed in the domain of the purely aesthetic founders on two substitutions: the confusion of moral for political categories (notable especially in her use of the term "fascist"), and the substitution of her own literary or critical performance for the phenomenon she discusses, and ultimately, for a critical practice.

Like D.A. Miller, Elizabeth Hardwick recognizes the ways in which Sontag's writing promotes the assimilation of her subject matter to her own sensibility. Unlike Miller, however, Hardwick has nothing but praise for this tendency: "The camp sensibility is not a text to be held in the hand.

The only text is finally this essay [of Sontag's] . . . [with] its incorporation of the exemplar of the camp mode—the epigrams of Oscar Wilde." At its most extreme, Sontag's writing involves the replacement of camp as a phenomenon by Susan Sontag herself. As Miller points out in the review I cited at the beginning, although Sontag at first affiliates camp with gay performance, she almost immediately repudiates the connection, severing camp from homosexuality, and putting "the claim to camp's origination . . . up for grabs. Someone else could invent Camp, and who better than the author of this manifestly inventive and authoritative essay?"

Sontag's statement that the value of her essays lies in the extent to which they are more than case studies in her own evolving sensibilities to the contrary, we need to recognize that her description of the modern sensibility is no more and no less than a description of her own development.

> Somewhere, of course, everyone knows that more than beauty is at stake in art like Reifenstahl's. . . . Backing up the solemn choosy formalist appreciations lies a larger reserve of appreciation, the sensibility of Camp, which is unfettered by the scruples of high seriousness: and the modern sensibility relies on continuing trade-offs between the formalist approach and Camp taste. (*A Sontag Reader*)

This characterization recapitulates the moves Sontag has made from **"Notes on Camp"** to **"Fascinating Fascism."** It is Sontag herself who blurs the boundary between Reifenstahl's Nazi propaganda and the leather paraphernalia of sadomasochism. The main claim of **"Fascinating Fascism,"** that camp lacks the moral seriousness necessary to prevent the resurgence of fascism, only makes sense, if it does *at all,* in the context of Sontag's earlier claims about camp. And from this point of view, we can see that Sontag's descriptions of camp have more relevance to her own career than to any other phenomena.

"Sensibility," the key term in her writings of the sixties, is the conceptual grid through which Sontag poses the problem that most sustains her interest to this day: how to connect "culture" to tradition and history. From the perspective offered on **"Notes on Camp,"** first by **"Fascinating Fascism,"** and later, by *AIDS and Its Metaphors,* we can see that by sensibility, Sontag means gay performance—one that first needs to be rehabilitated by her imitation of it in **"Notes on Camp,"** and then requires the ideological correction by moral inoculation she attempts to give it in **"Fascinating Fascism."**

Susan Sontag with Erika Munk (interview date 19 August 1993)

SOURCE: "Only the Possible: An Interview with Susan Sontag," in *Theater,* Vol. 24, No. 3, 1993, pp. 31-6.

[*In the following interview, Sontag discusses her production of Samuel Beckett's* Waiting for Godot *in Sarajevo.*]

[*Munk*]: *What did you hope to achieve, coming here?*

[Sontag]: My original motivation was to work with professionals living here and produce for this audience. Had I made a film this would not have been possible. I could have used local people for lighting, etc., but the final work would be for an international audience—Sarajevans would get to see it if I gave them a print, but it wouldn't be for them, as it couldn't be by them. I don't know what they know: that's why the choice of theater seemed obvious. I can't just be here as a visitor or as an onlooker, I'm not gathering information to write an essay or a book. So I had the idea of theater—for want of a better word, an ethical idea. And then once I had decided to work in the theater, it was obvious to me that this was the play to do.

Did it ever occur to you that you'd be the only notable intellectual from the West to come to Sarajevo?

Yes. It was already obvious to me as a fact. What amazed me was that nobody else was coming and that it didn't occur to anybody else. So I hoped as a side effect—it certainly wasn't a principle intention—my coming here to work would make it clear that this was possible.

Possible, or desirable?

It's only the possible that I can show. Many people in the outside world asked, how do you get there?, because it isn't very real what or how serious a siege is, or what the bureaucratic routes are to enter the city. I could get journalist credentials, any writer can get journalist credentials. So I would say, get a press card. And they looked at me with astonishment. It's not a problem to get here.

The real failure is of imagination, abetted by ignorance of history. When people are astonished that there's theater in Sarajevo, I remind them that there was theater in Berlin, in 1945, under a much worse bombardment. People are so ill-informed. One person will say he's going to send me something express mail to Sarajevo, as if there's mail service, and another will ask whether I see a lot of bodies in the street, as if no one rescued the injured or took the dead away for burial.

Why did you decide to do just the first act of Godot, *and to have three Gogos and Didis?*

It's an absolutely unorthodox but, I think, valid reading because of the play's unique construction. The second act is formally—though not substantively—identical with the first act. Vladimir and Estragon are there, Pozzo and Lucky arrive, Pozzo and Lucky leave, Vladimir and Estragon are alone again, the messenger comes with the same message, and they are alone again. This is repeated. There are two endings, two departures, so they are tremendously deflated. Since it's the only play in world literature that's constructed this way, it's the only play you could do this with. I would not take the last two acts off *Hamlet* and say that by doing the first three I'd done *Hamlet.* But I think there is an argument to be made that you can do the whole of *Waiting for Godot* by doing only the words of the first act. You can—what's the right image?—you can pump it up, you can expand it, you can vary it so that you have a total experience.

I don't consider this a truncated production, I consider it first of all a production conceived for Sarajevo. You have to remember that I began the production process five weeks ago [July 1993], with the build-up of hope for another intervention, and that was going on for three of the five weeks we rehearsed. It seemed to me that it was more passionate, and crueler in a way, to have only the text of the first act but to expand it, so that you have three pairs of Vladimirs and Estragons. They do three variations on the theme of the couple, formally in terms of gender identity and gender behavior, and emotionally because they are very, very different, so I'm putting much more into the first act.

I wouldn't be surprised, you know—I have no evidence for this—if Beckett originally conceived the play as one act. I wouldn't be surprised to find that he started out thinking this was going to be only one day, and somewhere toward the end of writing the first act he thought, oh, I'll have the second day or the day after. The second act is, of course, much darker than the first. I regretted sacrificing Vladimir's speech at the end of the second act, and I thought of putting Iso back up on stage to give it—"the air is full of our cries"—but I thought, I really have done it, I've done it by tripling the Vladimirs/Estragons.

The staging also does something interesting to the play, with Pozzo and Lucky never moving down from the upper level although the Vladimirs and Estragons come on and off. Pozzo and Lucky, though they're only played by one actor each, become something like Lear and the Fool or a 70-year-old Clytemnestra and her, you know, apprentice character, and the Vladimirs and Estragons become at moments a Chorus, in the Greek sense, because except at the beginning and the end, da capo, they don't all say the same lines, the text is simply passed from one group to another. There was a lot of thought, as you can imagine, given to which segments of the text went to which couple and where to break, where to cut.

How did you decide what to give to whom?

I had an enlarged copy of the Grove Press edition, and I wrote the Bosnian above each line so I could learn what they were saying in relation to the English and vice versa. I also had a Bosnian script, and wrote the English above it. I watched them for a couple of days and I went chronologically. You could see my script, but even that wouldn't really tell you much. It was a musical thing, completely intuitive, depending on my sense of the balance. Though I tended to move serially from one couple to another, the moment in which I shifted was the one I sensed gave energy. It was like a piano score. At the very beginning and end, when each couple said the dialogue, I began with pair one, then two, then three, and ended in the reverse order, three-two-one.

Every two days I'd give the three couples more divisions, I didn't know up to the end who said what, because I was feeling their capacities and their emotional impact, imagining myself as spectator. I didn't come to the first rehearsal and say, on page three, the seventh line down, this goes to the two women, and then on page five, the fourth line from the top it goes to the other woman—I did it day by day, out of the rehearsal process. But it wasn't just done in relation to the actors, it was done in relation to the meaning of the text. There are certain things only men can say, most obvious being "oh an erection" and jumping up on the stage. But most of the other time it was those characters as they developed in relation to the text.

We worked up to Pozzo and Lucky—that's something like the first 20-25 minutes of the play—in the first two weeks, while I spent a few hours in the morning with Atko on Lucky's speech. I told him, in every version I'd seen of the play—I've only seen it in English, French, and German—I didn't understand the speech, I didn't hear the speech, it's said like nonsense, I want you to say it as if it makes perfect sense. I divided it into five parts, and I subdivided the parts and we talked about everything from stones to apotheia. And I said you must say this with great sincerity, not too fast, and we worked and we worked and worked on that speech. That was quite separate.

When the Vladimirs and Estragons watch Lucky dancing, they are his audience, but we are their audience. . . .

And they turn their backs to us, exactly! Then it's divided into an A part, with Pozzo alone giving, as only Ines can do it, her signs of distress, the six being very attentive and silent, and a B part where they join in but at a lower vocal register—there was a tendency for a while in rehearsals for them to start outshouting each other though she always outshouts them—then there's this C, where they become silent again but she's going up, up, up, and then D, where

they start to express their discomfort and distress and knock Lucky over, and Velibor crawls between his legs so that he can fall on Velibor's back. That actor weighs only 50 kilos and he has a hard time with the suitcase, which is empty but heavy.

And how did he manage his extraordinary dance?

Iso is trained in ballet and I tried for a long time to work out a ballet thing that started with him doing the five positions, then doing some elementary steps, and ending with—he was going to do 32 feuilletées like the Black Swan and Ines would count them and the others would start counting them, the way the audience always does at *Swan Lake*. But it didn't work. The stage is just a makeshift platform rather badly constructed without an absolutely flat floor. I've spent a lot of time with dancers, so I'm sympathetic to dancers' anxieties, and he could have really injured himself. I thought of bringing him down to the lower level of the stage but that didn't accord with the visual conception, so all that remains is those few turns at the end.

What was the actors' part in the interpretation? There were so many little things immediate to this situation— the Marlboros out of the hat, etc.—where did they come from?

It was absolutely a traditional rehearsal process, we read the script through about seven times around a table, discussed my idea of what the words meant and the intention of the play. All were very silent except Ines, and read their lines in an absolute monotone the way actors usually do because they don't want to give you anything, they want you to pull it out of them. But Ines was acting up a storm from day one—she's the grand dame of Sarajevo theater, a real star here, I picked her for those qualities. I didn't worry that she'd be over the top because Pozzo is over the top.

Occasionally the actors had little bits of business to suggest. Milijana, the junior of the two-women pair, teaches physical movement at the Academy and one day I saw her in the corner doing a headstand, and I thought, oh I have to put that in. Simply in their behavior they were suggesting things to me all the time. The only real idea that came from an actor was that Vladimir Number One would be a pickpocket, and I thought it was brilliant. What is Pozzo's distress? It's always about losing objects. And these objects do disappear one by one. He suggested it—fabulous! Then he developed it. Ends up taking a pair of pink underpants from Nada's pocket. Was there enough light to catch this the first time you saw it?

Yes. You had the solar lamps, for the opening.

Did you have trouble today?

No, but I already knew it was there.

We needed more candles. We expected to have electric light today and weren't fully prepared. The light failed on the tree on the left immediately. Anyway, you can do that sort of thing only if you have multiple Vladimirs and Estragons, with one set I wouldn't have done it but with three Vladimirs, why couldn't one of them be a pickpocket?

In a conventionally cast production, it would have been hopelessly over-topical.

Exactly.

Literal, local readings tend to take over in this situation. Do you think that's good thing?

I think people like to see a play which reflects their situation. For example, I could have had a child play the messenger, but I knew I wanted to use an adult because I wanted the others to be able to express rage. You can't be aggressive or manhandle a small child, so you end up with quite another meaning when this messenger is a sturdy handsome young man in shorts. I wanted to get their anger at him, people are so angry here.

This is not like any other staging of Beckett—I didn't want to do it in a Beckett style, whatever a Beckett style would be. I wanted to treat it as a passionate play, in which the actors would say their lines passionately. First of all that's what they're good at, this is the Eastern European style, and second it seems to me appropriate, there's no reason to do this play in any sense minimalistically, it would absolutely be wrong for here.

I saw Beckett's staging of *Godot* in Berlin, and read the notes that he took and the diary of his assistant. I was actually quite shocked by his production. To my surprise—I knew he thought this but I didn't realize as a director he would do it—its sources in silent film comedy dominated the reading of the characters. There were all sorts of Charlie-Chaplin-like routines, and it was clearly rooted in silent film comedy acts and characterizations, Laurel and Hardy, Keaton and Chaplin—archetypes—it was very funny, it was very fast, as if someone had taken literally Chekhov's declaration that *Three Sisters* was a comedy. I found it in short much too amusing.

Yours is the least amusing Godot *I've ever seen.*

Yes, this is the anti-Beckett-as-director *Godot*. I don't presume to judge Beckett as a director but he is someone who has only directed his own work. Clearly this is how he saw the play and he got exactly what he wanted from the German actors but it's not the way I saw *Godot*. I wanted to

direct it for all the emotions the play inspires in me, which are very passionate.

Won't the Beckett purists be furious?

I don't know how anyone can be furious. I didn't receive a penny, I paid all my own expenses, I volunteered a month and a half of my life, the actors are working for nothing as is every person on the staff, the tickets are free, and it's Sarajevo. How can they object? This is a very extreme case of a not-for-profit production. I should think they'd be proud. I venture to say that there are more people in this besieged, mutilated city who have heard of *Waiting for Godot* than there are in Paris and London and New York. I'm stopped by children in the street who say to me in Bosnian, "Waiting for Godot!"—it's become a legend in this city. It's to the glory of this play that it should be played here.

Could you conceive of a similar Godot *production in any other city right now?*

No. Absolutely, it was done for here. I'd like to come back and do *The Three Sisters,* I think a lot of plays would work here.

Besides Three Sisters, *what?*

Trojan Women. Want more? I'm just going to depress you. Feydeau doesn't apply.

When I was in Zagreb a week ago a leading intellectual who shall remain nameless said to me, whatever possessed her to do Godot? *People need to be entertained!*

Only people who don't live here say that, and some of the journalists in the Holiday Inn. "Won't they find it depressing?" And I said, on the contrary, people are enthralled by something that mirrors life. If you were—it's a different art form, but let's say if you were in Theriesienstadt and you had permission to form a little ensemble and you wanted to play Beethoven quartets, would people say do a Strauss operetta? No, people want something that affirms the depth of their feelings. I didn't have any hesitation, I didn't have a thought that it would be redundant. That was suggested to me only by journalists. I'm confident that not one single person in Sarajevo feels that. I know the mood of the city.

What's so interesting about your production is that it has a political function, and a morale-building function, and a community-building function, all without being agitprop. . . .

I've also done gender-blind casting in a country where the feminist agenda is barely visible—without ever making the point, but also without ever encountering any opposition.

No one ever said, why is Pozzo played by a woman? That is absolutely innovative here. And I didn't want Pozzo to be played by a woman—I found one actor and one actor only who could play Pozzo and that actor happened to be a woman.

I read meaning beyond gender-blind casting into what you did with the three Vladimir-Estragon pairs, however. I thought, there's straight couple and two gay couples, one male and one female.

I didn't think it was necessary or interesting for the same-sex couples to be gay. I did try, however, to get the mixed couple to behave a little more like a heterosexual couple who might have been involved with each other, like a married pair. I'd tell them, you like each other, you're a married couple, you can touch each other, and the man would say, yeah, but it's an unhappy marriage. We'd have these crazy conversations, these very primitive conversations you have with actors. I'd say, yeah, but you still make love, and he'd say, we haven't made love for years, and I'd say, but you want to make love, so you can touch each other with a certain familiarity as people do who were once physically intimate. I got Irena to put her foot on his thigh, it was a struggle. But I didn't try very hard, because I don't think sexual input would add anything to the play. It's not that I'm shying away from it, it's just that basically these are bereft people who have banded together.

Why did you label the male couple Number One?

It was a kind of joke. A costume choice, and a joke. The actors used to say, *I'm* Estragon Number One, right? The real reason is, because they're the best.

That's why the two men are in the center?

You bet. If the mixed couple were the best actors I would have put them in the center. But I found myself, despite my original intentions, reaffirming something in Beckett's text by making the two men the main couple.

In October, after Sontag had made a return visit to Sarajevo, we spoke briefly on the phone: How did the performance look when you saw it again after being gone a month?

A big success—they're doing it four to five times a week, occasionally two performances a day. The actors are faster now and it's more energetic. In theater, the director is sent away and power goes to the actors—the opposite of film, where the actors are sent away and everything is done in the editing room.

If you do your Godot *outside Sarajevo will you include the second act?*

Yes. The primary reason not to do it was always that the performance would be too long. Nothing in that situation should be longer than an hour and a half, it's too much to ask. But doing the second act with only one Vladimir and one Estragon would fit the circumstances beautifully: the image of the shrunken world, Pozzo and Lucky reduced. The shape would be more narrative. I can imagine a narrower stage, the whole thing darker, just one spotlight, or one lit place in the center.

Do you think theater in Sarajevo is any use?

Don't ask the question of usefulness. I believe in right actions. Theater is what they do and I admire them for doing it, for always finding the feeling and expressing it.

Do you think the arts' community's efforts to maintain a transethnic culture have any chance of success?

Multicultural society will not survive. It is too much to ask the people of Bosnia to stick to this ideal when they are under attack by groups composed of single ethnicities, Serb or Croat. The people we like and admire won't turn into something else, they will leave and be replaced.

What did you do during your most recent visit?

I taught some classes at the Drama Academy. We also auditioned 20 17- and 18-year-olds for the entering class, ending up with five. You know, the rest of the University is shut down, but they're going on.

Tess Lewis (review date Spring 1994)

SOURCE: "Wild Fancies," *Belles Lettres,* Vol. 9, No. 3, Spring, 1994, pp. 25-6.

[*In the following review of* Alice in Bed, *Lewis argues that Sontag fails to bring her characters to life and concludes that the best part of the book is the afterword in which Sontag explains her intent.*]

"How wild can be the fancies of the unimaginative female!" the bedridden Alice James wrote in her diary in 1891. Unfortunately, wild, self-indulgent fancy rather than quickening imagination is the guiding spirit of *Alice in Bed,* Susan Sontag's play based on Henry and William James's invalid sister. Intended as a play "about women, about women's anguish and women's consciousness" and about the imagination, *Alice in Bed* is in fact little more than a procession of emblematic figures uttering portentous, clipped sentences at one another. Rather than bring the historical and fictional figures to life on stage, Sontag exploits them for all the sociocultural atmosphere they are worth, leaving the intellectual heavy lifting to the spectator. Alice, for example, informs Emily Dickinson, "I think your interest in death is more interesting than mine." That may well be, but how, and why, and what difference does it make? Such pronouncements as the fictional Dickinson's "Death is the lining. The lines." hardly clear things up.

Sontag's emblematic use of historical and literary figures was far more successful in her recent novel *The Volcano Lover*, in which the main characters—Sir William Hamilton; his wife, Emma; and Lord Nelson—are not referred to by name, but as the Cavaliere, the Cavaliere's wife, and the hero. Goethe; William Beckford, the notorious collector, amateur architect, and author of *Vathek*—the scandalous tale of a sadistic sultan; and the Baron Scarpia from *Tosca* also make their appearances. But whereas *The Volcano Lover*'s elaborate settings and dramatic action bring most of the characters convincingly to life, *Alice in Bed*'s intellectual scaffolding remains woefully bare.

Alice in Bed opens in 1890 with a 40-ish Alice in bed under several thin mattresses bickering with her nurse about whether she can, will, or even wants to get up. She eventually does, smokes opium, delivers a monologue, and gets back into bed. Throughout the play, the mattresses—social pressures, family expectations, etc.—are piled upon her or taken away by a man and a woman in sailor outfits. In the central scene, inspired by a fusion of Alice James with the heroine of Lewis Carroll's *Alice in Wonderland*, Alice is joined for a mad tea party by Margaret Fuller; Emily Dickinson; Alice's mother; Kundry from Wagner's *Parsifal*, who wishes to sleep away her adulterous guilt; and Myrtha, the Queen of the Wilis—a group of women in Adolphe Adam's ballet *Giselle* who died before their wedding days and returned to torment unfaithful lovers. Utterly devoid of humor, this scene reduces such eloquent, passionate women as Fuller and Dickinson to mouthing superficial banalities. For example, Sontag has Dickinson say, "I trust that my flowers have the good grace to be seared by our shouts," and Margaret Fuller, "Women despair differently. I've observed that. We can be very stoical."

Rather than bring the historical and fictional figures to life on stage, Sontag exploits them for all the sociocultural atmosphere they are worth, leaving the intellectual heavy lifting to the spectator.
—Tess Lewis

Henry James makes an appearance, quoting from Alice's diary and from his own writings about her. In another scene a younger Alice asks her father's permission to commit suicide, a request the senior Henry James did in fact grant his then 30-year old daughter. However, that he should then remove his wooden leg and beat it with a hammer is dramatically, not to mention historically, implausible.

A touch of *nostalgie de la boue* enters in the form of a gentle, bumbling young thief with "a Cockney or Irish accent." Assured that Alice was ill and would not wake up, he agrees, despite his inexperience, to break into her room only to find a suddenly energetic Alice who drinks his gin, points out the choice pieces he should steal, and reveals her dark visions.

Intended as proof of Alice's victorious imagination as well as the imaginative climax of the play, Scene 6 consists of a monologue delivered by a shrunken Alice in an oversized bed. She describes her mental flight to Rome but fails to draw the reader in. Her constant repetition of the qualifier "in my mind" not only ensures that the imagined scene remains Alice's alone, but also prevents us from believing that she herself is wholly caught up in her imaginative displacement. Alice has, it seems here, constructed an insurmountable barrier between her self and her imagination. Moreover, if this monologue reflects Sontag's view of the limitations and advantages of the mental defense mechanisms of 19th-century women, why does she not illustrate her view at greater length and with greater subtlety? We are offered no insight into the suffering and invalidism prevalent among intelligent women in the 19th century, into the pressures suffered by such women as James, Fuller, and Dickinson, or into their very different reactions to these pressures.

The best thing about the book is the afterword, lumbering though it is. In this "Note on the Play" Sontag explains what she has tried to accomplish. In fact, she explains her intentions so thoroughly that there is no real need for the play at all. Sontag ends her afterword with the rallying cry: "But the victories of the imagination are not enough." Yes, and how dismal are its failures.

Henry James, himself a surprisingly unsuccessful playwright, wrote that "the dramatist only wants more liberties than he can really take." Sontag has clearly taken far too many here.

Boyd Tonkin (review date 2 October 1994)

SOURCE: "Suffering in Silence," in *Manchester Guardian Weekly*, Vol. 151, No. 14, October 2, 1994, p. 29.

[*In the review below, Tonkin suggests how themes in Sontag's career contributed to her writing* Alice in Bed.]

Last year, Susan Sontag defied Serbian gunnery and media mockery to direct *Waiting For Godot* in Sarajevo. This wasn't just a show of solidarity with a people under siege whose rescuers had failed to turn up. Right at the start of her 30-year career as writer and critic, Sontag argued that the "strenuous modesty" of Beckett and his ilk was more than a fugitive trend. She insisted that their austerity—"the pursuit of silence"—caught the temper of the times as chattier art never could.

Vietnam, fascism, Bosnia, Aids: Sontag has fought the public monsters of our age with conspicuous gallantry. Yet through all her work, in essays and in fiction, persists the figure of a suffering and often silent body. This reduced self lingers on in pain, in despair, or in the spiritual deadlock of Beckett's Vladimir and Estragon. In 1992, readers seized on *The Volcano Lover*, her frolicsome romance of Nelson and the Hamiltons, as welcome proof that the sibyl of Manhattan had lightened up at last. Perhaps; but that novel's most poignant creation was surely Lady Catherine, Sir William Hamilton's valetudinarian first wife, whose "repressed rage" leaves her "ailing for decades".

Alice In Bed, a dramatic fantasy written in 1990, resuscitates another "career invalid". Alice James, the learned sister of novelist Henry and philosopher William, sank into illness as a refuge from—or revenge on—her "brilliant talkative family". After 24 years of vague ailments, cancer killed her at 43. Did she fall, or was she pushed? Sontag stresses that her exemplary Victorian plight embodies the "grief and anger" of thwarted women.

But Sontag erases one crucial fact about the real Alice. For 20 years, her emotional lifeline was a companion called Katherine Loring. Why? It could be that the idea of Alice abed—a mute reproach to power and lies—has plagued Sontag too long for mere history to dilute it. In her author's note to the play, she admits that "I have been preparing to write *Alice In Bed* all my life". Return to her 1967 novel *Death Kit*, and you find a tormented soul whose guilt over a random killing renders him "entirely bedridden and debilitated".

Styles Of Radical Will—her critical pieces from the same period—includes not only her minimalist manifesto but also a famous essay on **"The Pornographic Imagination"**. Sontag views erotic frenzy as one route to the "loss of self". Madness, mysticism, orgasm, even revolutionary zeal: all can lead from breakdown to breakthrough. Very New York; very sixties.

Sontag grew and changed, of course. Her brave texts on cancer (which she overcame) and then Aids reaffirmed the sheer arbitrariness of disease. Yet even this dauntless good sense failed to exorcise the silent sufferer. The brisk Margaret

Fuller, high-achieving New England feminist, tells Alice to "let those hard griefs slither away like curds turned out of their dish".

Sontag's life has been like Fuller's, not like Alice James's. But those "hard griefs" refuse to slide away. The Couch Potato still shadows Action Woman.

Larissa MacFarquhar (review date 16 October 1995)

SOURCE: "Premature Postmodern," *Nation*, Vol. 261, No. 12, October 16, 1995, pp. 432-34, 436.

[*Below, MacFarquhar reviews Liam Kennedy's* Susan Sontag: Mind as Passion, *a study of Sontag's writings and their historical context.*]

There are certain poignant little facts sprinkled around us by that novelist in the sky that convey with especial vividness the gulf between past and present. One of these facts is that in the sixties some people considered Susan Sontag to be lacking in seriousness. Listen to Irving Howe writing in *Commentary* in 1968:

> We are confronting, then, a new phase in our culture, which in motive and spring represents a wish to shake off the bleeding heritage of modernism and reinstate one of those periods of the collective naif which seem endemic to American experience. . . . The new American sensibility does something no other culture could have aspired to: it makes nihilism seem casual, good-natured, even innocent. . . . Alienation has been transformed from a serious and revolutionary concept into a motif of mass culture, and the content of modernism into the decor of *kitsch*. . . . [This new sensibility] is reinforced with critical exegesis by Susan Sontag, a publicist able to make brilliant quilts from grandmother's patches.

In 1968, at 35, Sontag was both a popular icon and one of the country's most respected critics. She wrote for *Partisan Review* and *Esquire*, for *Mademoiselle* and *The New York Review of Books*. She had published her first novel, *The Benefactor*, in 1963, her second, *Death Kit*, in 1967 and her first essay collection, *Against Interpretation*, in 1966. Reading it now, you can sense how exciting it must have been to pick up *Against Interpretation* in 1966, when it was unexpected: those luscious sentences, those enticing paragraphs and that curious, appreciative, calm, intelligent, *innocent* voice, without a trace of knowingness or sarcasm, that skipped so easily between flirtatious epigrams and earnest reasoning.

At the time, compared with Stalin-era types like Howe, Sontag was indeed a girl of the *Zeitgeist*. She had railed against traditional, Howe-style literary interpretation and condemned it as "reactionary," "cowardly" and "stifling." She had resuscitated Antonin Artaud by favoring spectacle over psychologizing in art, and proclaimed the "new sensibility" to be exemplified by visual arts like cinema, dance and painting—not novels. Rejecting Clement Greenberg's and Dwight Macdonald's efforts to put a *cordon sanitaire* around the avant-garde, she had attached quotation marks to "high" and "low" culture and declared the distinction practically meaningless ("The feeling . . . given off by a Rauschenberg painting might be like that of a song by the Supremes"). She had infamously declared the white race to be "the cancer of human history" and concluded that "Mozart, Pascal, Boolean algebra, Shakespeare, parliamentary government, baroque churches, Newton, the emancipation of women, Kant, Marx and the Balanchine ballets don't redeem what this particular civilization has wrought upon the world."

It was clear even then that Sontag did not reject everything Howe's generation had stood for, but she gave it all a new, impertinent, sixties twist. She agreed with Lionel Trilling, for instance, that art could and should have a moral effect on consciousness, but she thought that that effect could be derived from the most disengaged, aesthetic kinds of experience. She looked for self-transcendence, yes, but she found it in pornography (though only of the most highbrow sort).

She still believed in the unity of political and cultural radicalism, that signature of Howe's generation, but was too fond of her anti-interpretive ideas to conceive of an easy connection. She loved pop culture, but for high-culture reasons: Every bit as formalist as Greenberg, she argued that the business of contemporary art should be the "analysis of and extension of sensations," for which purpose a Supremes song might indeed be as useful as a Rauschenberg painting. All of this made for a peculiar, ambivalent style: She was a rigorous sensualist, an optimistic modernist, an earnest advocate of irony, a serious champion of playfulness. She had a sophisticated understanding of the comic but no sense of humor.

As far as Howe was concerned, this ambivalence—what he saw as Sontag's pseudo-modernist trappings—made her all the more insidious. Modernism, he had concluded gloomily in another late-sixties essay, "will not die [but] live on . . . through vulgar reincarnation and parodic mimesis. . . . Not the hostility of those who came before but the patronage of those who come later—that is the torment of modernism." Sontag was one of those who came later. Howe was ludicrously wrong, of course, to suspect Sontag of lacking seriousness, or even of valuing the modernist legacy any

less than he did. But he may have understood better than she where her theories were leading.

Reading Sontag now, her essays seem less to be refining ways of thinking about modernism, as she thought they were, than presaging postmodern developments. Howe predicted the mutation of modernism into postmodernism, but reading Sontag you can actually see it happening. In **"Notes on 'Camp,'"** you can see her vacillate between her proto-postmodern attraction to camp—its unapologetic aestheticism, its generous playfulness, its style—and her instinctive, modernist revulsion from its frivolous amorality ("I am strongly drawn to Camp, and almost as strongly offended by it"). In **"On Style"** you can see her championing formalism, surfaces and materiality against the notion of "content," but still for the old-fashioned moral reason of educating the senses: "For it is sensibility that nourishes our capacity for moral choice, and prompts our readiness to act . . . the qualities which are intrinsic to the aesthetic experience (disinterestedness, contemplativeness, attentiveness, the awakening of the feelings) . . . are also fundamental constituents of a moral response to life."

In a 1980 essay on Elias Canetti, Sontag distinguished between "ear culture" and "eye culture"—Hebrew versus Greek, as she put it, moral versus aesthetic. "The ear," she wrote, "is the attentive sense, humbler, more passive, more immediate, less discriminating than the eye [which] . . . affirms the pleasures and the wisdom of . . . surfaces." In the sixties, it was eye culture that captured Sontag's attention. Howe worried, more than she did, that ear culture was in danger of disappearing altogether.

By the late seventies and early eighties, though, Sontag's perspective had shifted. By the time she began writing the essays that would constitute *On Photography* (1977), she had become much warier of the dehumanizing, morally neutralizing quality of the sensuous-formalist ways of thinking that she had relished before. Thinking about photography, she became suspicious of its tendency to depersonalize, to flatten value systems, to encourage satisfaction with the status quo, to fracture the wholeness of the world. In 1974 she wrote:

> Art that seemed eminently worth defending ten years ago, as a minority or adversary taste, no longer seems defensible today, because the ethical and cultural issues it raises have become serious, even dangerous, in a way they were not then. The hard truth is that what may be acceptable in elite culture may not be acceptable in mass culture, that tastes which pose only innocuous ethical issues as the property of a minority become corrupting when they become more established. Taste is context, and the context has changed.

By 1979 Sontag had decided that Howe's worst nightmare had indeed come true. "There is really quite a close fit between avant-garde art and the values of the consumer society which needs products, constant turnover, diversity, outrage and so on," she admitted in an interview. "The consumer society is so sophisticated and so complex that it has broken down the lines between high and mass taste, between the conventional sensibility and the subversive sensibility."

The context *has* changed. And at this point, although most of Sontag's essays seem as brilliant and relevant as they ever did, others seem hopelessly quaint. The camp sensibility that in 1964 she considered so esoteric, so private that "to talk about [it was] therefore to betray it" has of course become thoroughly mainstream—indeed irritatingly omni-present. In the wake of deconstruction, Sontag's old formalist theories seem antiquated. It's telling, though, that that wild excess of hers she later regretted—calling the white race "the cancer of human history"—today sounds more banal than anything else, coming from a white person.

In *Susan Sontag: Mind as Passion,* Liam Kennedy sets out to describe Sontag's work and the context within which it appeared. It's Kennedy's first book; he's a lecturer in American and Canadian Studies at the University of Birmingham in England. Most of the book is summary—unfortunately, since Sontag does an excellent job of explaining herself. As an exegesis, though, it's nicely done, and Kennedy traces Sontag's main themes deftly along tortuous paths through both essays and fiction. Her metasubject, Kennedy quotes Sontag as saying, is "what it means to be modern." And then there are her various demi-metasubjects: Sontag exploring extreme states of consciousness, Sontag thinking about artistic isolation, Sontag pondering the ethics of connoisseurship, etc.

Unfortunately, Kennedy writes as though Sontag were dead. He compares her work only to that of her predecessors, with the result that you have little sense, upon finishing the book, of what effect (if any) she is having on younger writers. Her generalism, her polemical essay style, her Europhilia and her political engagement Kennedy links, naturally, to the New York intellectuals: to the generalism of Edmund Wilson, Paul Goodman and Harold Rosenberg, and to the *engagé* literary criticism of Trilling, Philip Rahv and Mary McCarthy. The let's-think-about-me mode she employs in *Trip to Hanoi* and elsewhere he connects to the Mailer-style new journalism of the sixties. Periodically he discusses her in relation to the dead-or-not-dead debate over the public intellectual.

Since Sontag herself spends so much time detailing her relationship to her antecedents, I regret not hearing more about the aspects of her *oeuvre* she *doesn't* talk about. With a publication history as eclectic as hers, her omissions are as telling as her subjects. Why, for instance, after vacuuming up more or less everything written in French in the fifties, from Camus to Barthes to Cioran, did she not write about anyone from the generation that followed? These questions are left hanging.

"My aim," Kennedy states at the outset, "is not to incorporate Sontag into academic frames of thinking." Insofar as that means he's resolved not to use jargon, fair enough, but a dogmatic exclusion of academic reference points seems silly, though certainly Sontagian. One would think it would follow from Kennedy's (and everyone's) conclusion that the public-intellectual tradition has mostly withered away that academic debates are precisely the most interesting ones to include her in these days. Especially the literary-theoretical ones of the seventies and eighties that took up the thread of French thought where Sontag appears to have dropped it.

This is a particularly frustrating omission since Sontag has always been more or less ignored by academia. Kennedy's explanation for this is only somewhat plausible: He claims academics are threatened by her refusal to specialize. Angela McRobbie, a British cultural studies theorist, is more pointed: "In many circles she is viewed with suspicion as at best an elitist, Eurocentric aesthete." McRobbie's view seems to have been borne out by the reception of Sontag's 1989 book, *AIDS and Its Metaphors*. Intruding as she was on a particular academic turf, Sontag suddenly received lots of professorial attention, much of it negative. D.A. Miller wrote a particularly hostile review in which he accused her of homophobia. Much of what he was reacting to, though, was her perhaps willful ignorance of academic politics: her use of the word "homosexual," for instance, and her aggressive assertion of her right to talk about AIDS with the prefatory sentence, "Rereading *Illness as Metaphor* now, I thought. . . ."

Kennedy offers only a few critiques. Boringly, he faults her for restricting her discussion of pornography to the literary variety, thus "bracket[ing] off many of the socio-moral questions central to the pornography debate." Boringly, he reproves her for the cultural elitism that is at the heart of her enterprise. At a very late stage in the book he suddenly comes out as an antimodernist and begins to take Sontag to task for her "perverse, private effort to keep the dead alive." Still, he does defend her against accusations that she has turned to the right, correctly ascribing some of these to a facile equation of her retro universalist rhetoric with neoconservatism.

Shortcomings aside, the mere fact that Kennedy's book exists is interesting. Sontag, as *Partisan Review* editor William Phillips observed in 1969, has always "suffered from bad criticism and good publicity"; she's underrated by the right people and overrated by the wrong people. As a result she is frequently gossiped about but rarely discussed in writing. The only other book-length study of her work—Sohnya Sayres's *Susan Sontag: The Elegiac Modernist* (1990)—is out of print. She's in neither of two recent essay anthologies—Phillip Lopate's *The Art of the Personal Essay* and *The Oxford Book of Essays.*

I would like to read a book that situated Sontag in the present as well as the past, and that analyzed her from the point of view of sensibility—as a writer and appreciator, rather than primarily as a theorist (though of course the two are inextricable). This approach might go some way toward explaining, for one, why her essays are so much better than her novels—why her writing seems too sweet without the salt of information. And it would be an appropriately Sontagian approach, since so much of her writing consists of, as she has put it, "case studies of [her own] evolving sensibility." After all, as she wrote admiringly of fellow-generalist Roland Barthes on his death in 1980, "It was not a question of knowledge . . . but of alertness, a fastidious transcription of what *could* be thought about something, once it swam into the stream of attention."

FURTHER READING

Criticism

Gingrass, Lynn. "Marked by Contrariness." *American Book Review* 15, No. 3 (August-September 1993): 28.
  Reviews *The Volcano Lover* and claims that the novel is admirable despite its disparate elements.

Olster, Stacey. "Remakes, Outtakes, and Updates in Susan Sontag's *The Volcano Lover.*" *Modern Fiction Studies* 41, No. 1 (Spring 1995): 117-39.
  Discusses modernism and post-modernism in Sontag's novel.

Interviews

Poague, Leland, ed. *Conversations with Susan Sontag.* University Press of Mississippi, 1995, 270 p.
  Collection of more than twenty interviews with Sontag.

Additional coverage of Sontag's life and career is contained in the following sources published by Gale: *Contemporary Authors,* Vols. 17-20R; *Contemporary Authors New Revision Series,* Vols. 25 and 51; *Dictionary of Literary Biography,* Vols. 2 and 67; *DISCovering Authors Modules: Popular Fiction;* and *Major 20th-Century Writers.*

Melvin B. Tolson
1898-1966

(Full name Melvin Beaunorus Tolson) American poet, journalist, and dramatist.

The following entry presents an overview of Tolson's career. For further information on his life and works, see *CLC*, Volume 36.

INTRODUCTION

Tolson's highly allusive poetry celebrates the African-American spirit. Although his work eventually received scholarly study and praise, Tolson spent much of his career in a no-man's-land between the world of the white literati and that of African-American audiences. Much of his work is devoted to the unusual position of the African-American artist and his attempt to make his work relevant to a diverse audience.

Biographical Information

Tolson was born in Moberly, Missouri, in 1898. His father was a Methodist minister; the influence of the oral history of preaching is evident in Tolson's later poetry. Tolson's family moved from parish to parish in Missouri and Iowa during his childhood. Tolson demonstrated an early interest in poetry, publishing his first poem, "The Wreck of the *Titanic*," in an Iowa newspaper in 1912, and continued to write poetry throughout high school. He attended Lincoln University and graduated in 1923, then moved to Marshall, Texas, where he taught English at Wiley College. While at Wiley, Tolson directed a number of dramatic productions, coached the school's debate team to an impressive success record, and became known as a gifted raconteur and orator. Tolson received a Rockefeller fellowship which allowed him to pursue a master's degree in comparative literature at Columbia University in the early 1930s. During this time he lived in Harlem and mixed closely with the writers of the Harlem Renaissance. Tolson composed *A Gallery of Harlem Portraits* based on his time in Harlem, but was unable to find a publisher for the work; it was published posthumously in 1979, almost forty years later. After returning to Wiley, Tolson began writing a column for the *Washington Tribune* in addition to his teaching and extracurricular activities. The column was called *Caviar and Cabbage,* and in it he discussed a variety of social issues. The columns, which ran from 1937 to 1944, were collected and published as a book of the same title in 1982. In 1940 Tolson wrote "Dark Symphony" for a poetry contest sponsored by the American Negro Exposition in Chicago. He won first prize,

and after the poem appeared in *Atlantic Monthly,* a publisher approached Tolson about putting together a collection which he titled *Rendezvous with America* (1944). In 1947 Tolson left Wiley for Langston University, where he worked as professor of creative literature. Tolson was named Poet Laureate of the Republic of Liberia, for which he wrote *Libretto for the Republic of Liberia* (1953). At this time he also served four terms as mayor of Langston, Oklahoma. In the 1960s, Tolson retired from Langston University and occupied a chair in humanities at Tuskegee Institute, teaching only one class. Tolson won the National Institute of Arts and Letters Award in 1966. He was working on the second volume of his projected five-volume work, *Harlem Gallery* (1965), when he died in 1966.

Major Works

Tolson's *A Gallery of Harlem Portraits* represents a cross-section of Harlem life in all of its diversity. The poems in *Gallery* also address the class divisions created by economic disparity. Tolson believed that class was more of an issue than race in the problem of inequality, but his work retains the hope that racial equality is a possibility when economic equality is addressed. He often uses the rhythm and language of blues music in his poetry. In *Gallery,* Tolson uses blues lyrics to introduce his poetic portraits. In *Rendezvous with America,* Tolson continues to celebrate diversity, but expands his setting from Harlem to include the entire country. In it he uses a variety of poetic forms, including sonnets and free verse. Tolson wrote *Libretto for the Republic of Liberia* to commemorate that nation's centennial, taking as his topic the whole of African history. *Harlem Gallery: Book I, The Curator* studies the dichotomies that exist in man's social roles. The central character, the Curator, has trouble fitting into any accepted notion of identity. He is neither black nor white, poor nor rich. He inhabits two different worlds, trying to bring the art of "high" culture to the poverty-stricken streets of Harlem. Although the action is filtered through the consciousness of the Curator, it revolves around three artists: the painter, John Laugart; the composer, Mister Starks; and the poet, Hideho Heights. Each of these artists struggles with his inner self as expressed through his art and public reaction to it. Two of the artists die and the third's death seems imminent. The Curator is left shaken about the way art affects the African-American artist, but the work ends with a recognition that dichotomies are a part of life.

Critical Reception

Tolson's work, especially his early work, has not received much critical attention. Tolson himself insisted that he began as a mediocre poet and that he learned and developed a better technique through the years. Dolphin G. Thompson asserts that "in addition to mastering poetical techniques, he has initiated a style of dramatically lifting the Negro experience to classical grace." Tolson's poetry is highly allusive, and can be difficult to comprehend for the average reader. Many critics point to the difficulty of Tolson's poetry as the reason his work has been critically neglected. Reviewers often cite Walt Whitman as one of Tolson's influences. The most striking example is Tolson's own "Song of Myself," from his *Rendezvous with America,* but reviewers also point to Whitmanesque qualities in *Libretto for the Republic of Liberia.* Dan McCall notes, "In the *Libretto* Whitman continues to be abundantly influential . . . in the enormous catalogues, the wry asides, the self-conscious displays of learning, and the prose-paragraphs of the final section." Reviewers also mention the influence of T. S. Eliot and Ezra Pound, some complaining that Tolson's work was overly imitative. Some reviewers faulted *Libretto* for its traditional structure, asserting that it should have been written in Negro dialect. Tolson addressed this issue in *Harlem Gallery: Book I, The Curator,* adding African-American dialect to the traditional style of his earlier poetry. Tolson's intentions as a writer reached beyond his life's experiences: As Robert M. Farnsworth remarked, "Tolson developed a

poetic style which he hoped would enable him to project the needs and interests of black people into the imaginations of a still developing audience of the future."

PRINCIPAL WORKS

Rendezvous with America (poetry) 1944
Libretto for the Republic of Liberia (poetry) 1953
Harlem Gallery: Book One, The Curator (poetry) 1965
A Gallery of Harlem Portraits (poetry) 1979
Caviar and Cabbage: Selected Columns by Melvin B. Tolson from the Washington Tribune, 1937-1944 (articles) 1982

CRITICISM

Roy P. Basler (essay date March 1973)

SOURCE: "The Heart of Blackness—M. B. Tolson's Poetry," in *New Letters,* Vol. 39, No. 3, March, 1973, pp. 63-76.

[*In the following essay, Basler recommends Tolson's poetry for a general readership as opposed to an exclusively African-American audience.*]

What American poet will symbolize and represent our milieu to readers in the future, as Shakespeare represents the Elizabethan, Milton the Puritan, or, to come closer, Whitman the Civil War era? Will it be Eliot? Pound? Sandburg? Frost? William Carlos Williams? Time may tell, perhaps is already telling, that although they spoke to us in a special voice, none knew us in our latitudinal-longitudinal complexity, or used quite our whole language with the love and imagination of a master. Will it be one of the younger generation of Roberts—Lowell, Duncan, Creeley, or—? I think not.

Even in our current concern with ecology, Eliot's *The Waste Land* seems something less than symbolic or representative of our age, though better than any other poem it suggests the spiritual vacuum of what has seemed to some the fading of the Christian era. Pound's *Cantos,* while brilliantly projecting the intellectual disillusion and aesthetic discord of a civilization gone rationally mad, are at best a schizoid satire, to be read obliquely. Sandburg's *The People, Yes,* like all his poetic work, so subtly musical and complex in the pagan mysticism with which it conveys the fluidity of hard "reality," to me appears an inadequate reflection of the spirit of the age. And so on.

In thus dropping, one by one, these great contemporaries, I

must admit that to some extent I am conditioned by a view of American tradition and history which may be held by the cynical to be merely a vestige of our eighteenth century origins—what the historian Henry Commager has characterized as Thomas Jefferson's "prospective," as opposed to John Adams' "retrospective," concept of history and culture. With this confessed bias in mind, the reader may consider what follows, and its implications for literary study.

I suppose even those who read a great deal of modern poetry are inadequately prepared for reading a truly great poem for the first time. One's first reaction must be put off. Let's be careful, *nil admirari* as Cicero said, even when the poem comes most highly "introduced" by a scholar-poet-critic whom one respects, Allen Tate. Such was my reaction to M. B. Tolson's *Libretto for the Republic of Liberia* in 1953. Since then, things have been happening on the literary scene which make appreciation of poetry even more of a self-conscious quiddity. Remembering how M. Carl Holman's autobiographical, "The Afternoon of a Young Poet" recorded his suspicion that the white audience gave "the dancing bear . . . higher marks than a man might get for the same performance," my WASP appreciation of Tolson has had to survive some peculiar inner resistances to its own convictions, which a black critic may find it difficult to comprehend. Yet one must face the fact that literary study today is affected willy-nilly by the racial febricity in our sick society, whose antibodies seem hopefully to be overcoming the toxins, even those infecting the literary establishment.

My "appreciation," however, refuses to be squelched by the possibilities of either exaggeration or mitigation, in the view that Tolson is perhaps the poet of our era who best represents, or comes nearest to representing, in his comprehensive humanity, the broadest expanse of the American character, phrased in the richest poetic idiom of our time. Better than his contemporary peers, he knew the span from low-brow to high-brow in both life and literature, and he loved the American English language, from gutter to ivory tower, better than any of them. His poetic diction is a natural blend of home words and hall words, where *hearth* and *bema* sing side by side. He is the natural poet who cultivated his nature, both root and branch, for the flower and the seed, for it was the seed even more than the flower, Ruskin to the contrary, that Tolson the poet believed art grew for—yes, the "yellow wasps of the sun swarm down," but when Tolson's "New Negro" speaks for "his America," the word is more American perhaps than any of his great contemporaries have spoken.

In his first book, *Rendezvous with America* Tolson established his lyric strength and a relatively simple but frequently incisive diction. Most simply put his message reads:

A man

Is what
He saves
From rot.

The success of Tolson's metaphor is its appropriateness to the poem in which it grows. In a simple poem about a great teacher whose community "struck him down" it is "the gallows of ignorance that hanged the little town." One of his best early poems, **"The Ballad of the Rattlesnake,"** apparently the only ballad he ever wrote, epitomizes with simplicity the brutal tragedy of the sharecropper's lot, whether black or white, in the image of an Apache Indian mode of torturing a prisoner:

The desert holds
In its frying pan
The bones of a snake
And the bones of a man.

And many a thing
With a rock on its tail
Kills the nearest thing
And dies by the trail.

On the other hand, in one of his most complex and allusive later poems—more allusive even than Eliot or Pound or Hart Crane—he begins in sarcastic good humor at the expense of learning and poetry, with a metaphor that only a great poet with a great sense of humor could devise to laugh off the pomp of his proud occasion as Poet Laureate of Liberia, and follows it immediately and miraculously with magical reversal of image to exalt the living truth which escapes not only his occasion, but all occasions, and all words.

Liberia?
No Micro-footnote in a bunioned book
Homed by a pedant
With a gelded look:
You are
The ladder of survival dawn men saw
In the quicksilver sparrow that slips
The eagle's claw!

Reading the author's footnotes to such a marvelously complex poetic tapestry as the *Libretto for the Republic of Liberia* is almost as much of a literary adventure as reading the poem, and the impulse to add notes of one's own for their own sake is all but irresistible, in spite of the poet's serio-comic warning in the opening lines just quoted. How humorously serious in poetics this heroic ode waxes in its flamboyance seems to have escaped even the admiration in which Allen Tate wrote his introduction. Perhaps Tate did not approve Tolson's laughing about a technique Tate's masters, Eliot and Pound, had created all too seriously as the hallmark of modern poetry. To appreciate fully Tolson's aesthetic one must abandon the humorless restraints of the "new criticism" and revel in the sheer delight of a superbly scholarly Negro artist at work with words, on a rostrum and with a message, more exalted than any ever afforded even James Weldon Johnson's preacher. No other American— one almost said no other poet—has ever blended the comic and heroic as well as the comic and tragic in a flight so high. Perhaps only a scholar-poet of a downtrodden race could have dared it. In any event, the only "creation" I have ever heard or read that even suggests viable comparison was the sermon of a well-educated Negro "holiness" preacher, many years ago, delivered to a black congregation, black except for two white college students who had slipped in and whose presence in no way inhibited, but I am inclined to think may even have further inspired, the improvisation of extempore poetry distilled by an American Negro's imagination from Hebrew sources that were our common cultural heritage. Who's afraid of big words, arcane words, low-down words, any words of any kind that are possible to poetry? Not M. B. Tolson, when he sings the meaning of Liberia and the hope of humanity.

The *Libretto for the Republic of Liberia* is not only one of the great odes in the English language, it is in many respects one of the finest poems of any kind published in the English language during the twentieth century, so far as my acquaintance goes. Allen Tate's minor caveats are meaningless to me in the presence of Tolson's afflatus and Jovian humor. I get carried away. And the "irony," which Tate comments on, that an American government has never, could never have, commissioned such an official poem to be read in Washington, only reminds me that I agree with Tolson that "these truths," of which Jefferson wrote, are bearing and will bear fruits for which white Americans must yet acquire the taste. Imagine if you can the humor of this black Pindar of a Mark Twain celebrating the dignity of the small African republic founded by American ex-slaves with a poem at once so everyday American and yet so arcane, abstruse, and allusive that even with the author's notes it flies largely over the highbrow heads, not merely in his Liberian audience but of his fellow countrymen, white or black, literati suckled on Eliot and Pound for a quarter century! To imagine one of the less difficult but enormously pregnant passages marching across the years with heavy tread is to appreciate what Tolson will be when his black and white kinfolk come up to him:

> Like some gray ghoul from Alcatraz,
> old Profit, the bald rake *paseq,* wipes the bar,
> polishes the goblet vanity,
> leers at the tigress Avarice
> as
> she harlots roués from afar:
> swallowtails unsaved by loincloths,
> famed enterprises prophesying war,

> hearts of rags (Hanorish tharah sharinas) souls of
> chalk
> laureates with sugary grace in zinc buckets of
> verse,
> myths rattled by the blue print's talk,
> ists potted and pitted by a feast,
> Red Ruin's skeleton horsemen, four
> abreast
> . . . galloping . . .
> Marx, the exalter, would not know his
> East
> . . . galloping . . .
> Nor Christ, the Leveler, His West.
> *Selah!*

For one who cut his literary eyeteeth explicating the civilized soul of T. S. Eliot's eunuch Prufrock, not to mention assorted passages depicting psychotic brunettes fiddling "whisper music" on their long black hair, *et cetera, et cetera,* this kind of poetry is "a fun thing," as the "mod" collegians like to describe their own "bag" today. Half a page of poetry with half a page of notes to explain it, notes which themselves frequently challenge the reader no less than does the poetry. And all for the fun of it. For example, here is Tolson's note on the line "old Profit, the bald rake *paseq,* wipes the bar."

> *Paseq:* "divider." This is the vertical line that occurs about 480 times in our Hebrew Bible. Although first mentioned in the *Midrash Rabba* in the eleventh century, it is still the most mysterious sign in the literature.

How abstrusely appropriate a "visual" word can a poet find to name his personification of the motive most extolled in the gospel of capitalism by Chamber of Commerce evangelists? Not merely as a "vertical" dispenser of intoxicants to the habitués of this whore house, but also, something Tolson's note does not tell us, the not-at-all mysterious use of the *paseq* in the Hebrew Bible, namely to call the tune, so that the reader will not read two words together that should properly stand apart.

What Tolson undertook, I think, with great success, was to liberate the allusive, scholarly poetry Eliot created from the service of Eliot's sterile tradition and philosophy, and, while embellishing it with large humor, to put it to use as a vehicle for his own "prospective" view of human history.

Such is the fantastic poem published in 1953 by the poet who in 1962, nearly a decade later, was not invited to participate in "the National Poetry Festival" held at the Library of Congress, along with some thirty established poets, because he was not well enough known among the literati who had adulated Eliot and Pound for a generation. One wonders, was it the music or the theme of Tolson's song that put them off?

Anecdote of a committee of poets. "What about Tolson?" "Who?" "M. B. Tolson, you know—*Libretto for the Republic of Liberia.*" "Oh, well, Langston Hughes and Gwendolyn Brooks are much better established."

That the committee was all white was not the trouble, for even if it had been a committee of all black poets the verdict would probably have been the same, for "'tis true 'tis pity / And pity 'tis 'tis true" that even yet black studies scholars seem not much better acquainted with Tolson's work than are the white scholars across the hall from them. One of our most distinguished black men of letters told me recently of reviewing for a leading publisher the manuscript of an anthology of the allegedly "best" Negro writers, which omitted M. B. Tolson but gave considerable space to Leroi Jones. It is indeed time, not only to begin revising the curricula of our schools so that the black man's contribution to American civilization may be honestly appreciated, but also to begin improving the literary judgment of the people who are revising the curricula.

It has been said by recent black writers that the black writer today must write primarily for black readers. It has also been said that the black writer must also write for white readers, or have few readers. Tolson recognized in his blood and bones as well as in his head that such statements are partial truths, and he set about writing for any reader who would take as much trouble to enjoy the reading as he took to enjoy the writing of poetry. Karl Shapiro has said that Tolson "writes Negro." True perhaps to some extent, but what does it mean when Tolson sounds to me more like Tolson (as Whitman sounds like Whitman) than he sounds like a Negro and more like a man than a member of any race? It happens he was Negro-Irish-Cherokee, with as much or little as any of us to be proud of in the matter of ancestry. And intellectually he was more a Jeffersonian of the basic Jeffersonian tradition than most white Americans have ever been since Jefferson himself. For he believed in equality of "the man inside," which is the title of his tribute to his friendship with a white writer, V. F. Calverton:

> They told me—the voices of hates in the land—
> They told me that White is White and Black is Black;
> That the children of Africa are scarred with a brand
> Ineradicable as the spots on the leopard's back.

> They told me that gulfs unbridgeable lie
> In the no man's seascapes of unlike hues,
> As wide as the vertical of earth and sky,
> As ancient as the grief in the seagull's news.

> They told me that Black is an isle with a ban
> Beyond the pilgrim's Continent of Man.

> I yearned for the mainland where my brothers live.
> The cancerous isolation behind, I swam
> Into the deeps, a naked fugitive,
> Defying tribal fetishes that maim and damn.

> And when the typhoon of jeers smote me and hope
> Died like a burnt-out world and on the shore
> The hates beat savage breasts, you threw the rope
> And drew me into the catholic Evermore.

> We stood on common ground, in transfiguring light,
> Where the man inside is neither Black nor White.

Typical of the young black intellectuals today espousing a "Black Aesthetic" is the critic Don Lee, who in a review of Robert Hayden's *Kaleidescope,* an anthology of Afro-American poetry, dismisses Tolson because of "his capacity to lose the people that may read him," namely, the black reader. It is Lee's belief that "Afro-Americans are better prepared to pass judgment" on black writers than are white critics. The shibboleth on which black aesthetes are choking is "relevance." If Tolson is not "relevant," it is because his reader, black or white, has not measured intelligence with him. Where black phrase-makers of the last instant are telling both black and white people that "violence is as American as cherry pie," Tolson would still remind us that

> . . . on the Courthouse Square
> A statue of the Lost Cause bayonets
> Contemporary air.

And, he hoped, black or white may be wise and kind as well as beautiful:

> Time
> Speaks in pantomime
> In spite of mimic clocks
> And dirty voices on the soapless box.
> Time
> Saints the unity of blood and clime
> Martyred by Caesars of the Undersoul
> Who rape the freedoms and their crimes extoll.

It is such wisdom and kindness that Tolson, somewhat atypically among midcentury black intellectuals, recognized as the essence of Abraham Lincoln's humanity. His appreciation of Lincoln as a man, attested in a remarkable piece published in the column *Caviar and Cabbage* which Tolson contributed during 1938 to the *Washington Tribune,* was further evidenced in his long poem **"Abraham Lincoln of Rock Spring Farm,"** published in Herbert Hill's anthology

Soon, One Morning. In my judgment, this is one of the finest poems written about Lincoln since Whitman, and certainly the outstanding poem about Lincoln's genesis. It is, however, a deliberately plain, if heroic, poem, where the **Libretto** is a polyphonic and syncopated fugue. Perhaps his recognition of a certain kinship of spirit, as well as his respect for Lincoln's genius, ran close to the river bed of Tolson's frequently turbulent current of words.

Tolson's unfinished masterpiece, *The Harlem Gallery,* was planned to be a major epical work, of which only the prologue, "**Book I: The Curator,**" was published in 1965, the year before his death, with a brilliant introduction by Karl Shapiro. Although one can only speculate about the overall plan, which called for four books—Egypt Land, The Red Sea, The Wilderness, and The Promised Land—to follow "**Book I: The Curator;**" the latter stands alone as a unique work for which traditional poetic terminology has no entirely adequate word. It is not an ode, as was the **Libretto,** though in some respects like it, but rather a kind of lyric-dramatic narrative sermon in verse. In any event it is as carefully and often as intricately structured as a Tantric mandala, but swinging with Harlem rhythm and sublimely mingling the idiom of bedroom, street slang, scholarly diction, Shakespearean metaphor, and foreign tongues with a controlled abandon that only a poet who had observed all levels of life and touched all aspects of language could command.

Perhaps the one other fine poem with which *The Harlem Gallery* may be compared best is Langston Hughes' *Montage of A Dream Deferred.* Both poems are deeply moving and highly charged with emotion for any reader whose humanity spans more than one extreme of the color spectrum. Both poems are distillations of American English, but Hughes writes quite legitimately as a folk poet, with no particular obeisance to or love for either the matter or the manner of literary tradition, whereas Tolson employs very nearly the entire art and learning, not merely of the Hebraic-Christian-Classical tradition, but Oriental and African literary lore as well. Comparing Hughes and Tolson, however, is like comparing Robert Burns and John Milton, either useful or useless, depending on whether one really knows both—and the difference.

Consider as illustration the section "**Theta,**" which states Tolson's aesthetic in richly allusive, but colloquial, fashion and clinches the bitter truth of art from Harlem to Paris, or Rome—that pleasure and happiness are not one and the same:

> No guinea pig of a spouse
>   to be cuckolded in a mood indigo,
>   no gilded in-and-out beau
>   to crackle a *jen de mots* about the house—

> Art, the woman Pleasure, makes no blind dates,
>   but keeps the end of the tryst with one:
>   she is a distant cousin of aeried Happiness
> the love bird seeks against the eye-wrying sun,
>   in spite of her fame;
>   dubious as Galen's sight
>   of a human body dissected,
>   in spite of the *hap* in her name,
>   ominous as a red light.

>   The claw-thrust
>   of a rutting tigress,
>   the must
>   of a rogue elephant—
>   these con the bull of predictability,
>   like Happiness
>   a *capriccio* bastard-daughter of Tyche.
>   KKK, the beatnik guitarist, used to say
>   to High Yellah Baby
>   (before he decided to rub
>   out the light of his eyes
> in the alley of Hinnom behind the Haw-Haw Club):
> "The *belle dame*—Happiness—the goofy dream of
>   is a bitch who plays with crooked dice
>   the game of love."

It is not *The Waste Land* or *Four Quartets,* I think, which limn the present or light the future with the past so well that scholars salvaging libraries of this era may someday guess what manner of men were we. Nor is it even Sandburg's *The People, Yes,* nor William Carlos Williams' *Paterson,* but Tolson's *The Harlem Gallery,* rather, where the heart of blackness with the heart of whiteness lies revealed. Man, *what* do you think you are is not the white man's question but the black man's rhetorical answer to the white man's question. No poet in the English language, I think, has brought larger scope of mind to greater depth of heart than Melvin Tolson in his unfinished song to the soul of humanity.

Tolson's learning makes a mockery of the proud ignorance of a John C. Calhoun, who was quoted that "if he could find a Negro who knew Greek syntax, he would believe that the Negro was a human being." What it makes of the utterances of some of Calhoun's latter-day disciples is difficult to choose a word for. But more than his learning and intelligence, it is his art that makes a mockery of all racial pride or prejudice.

The message of *The Harlem Gallery* is that art, like humanity, knows no single race or peculiar color of its own. Art is human rather than Negro, Caucasian, or whatever, and the terms African art, or European art, or Afro-American art are named for the artist's immediate audience, not for his craft or his imagination, each of which is his and not his country's or his people's except by his largesse. So "English poetry" is a meaningless term except as it means "in English language," but "Shakespeare's poetry" or "Keats' poetry" means, as "Homer's poetry" or "Tolson's poetry," the unmistakable creation of its maker. This is a lesson that the study of any artist will teach, but that Tolson can teach with especial power, today and tomorrow.

And yet, granting the unique stamp of the creator on his matter, there is also the indubitable representation of his milieu, with which his culture has outfitted him, no less than the snake's or the fawn's, "nature" has outfitted him, so that he "belongs". Only the intellectually and culturally deprived, especially those unaware of their deprivation, can any longer fail to see that American culture, as Albert Murray has pointed out in *The Omni-Americans,* is neither white nor black, but mulatto. And what is true of American culture in general is particularly true of American language and is becoming more and more true of American literature. However Eliotic the retrospective tradition may seem to those who understand only what they have been taught, the Tolsonian prospect lies certainly, and I think clearly, ahead.

Poetry provided for M. B. Tolson what research, teaching, writing, and publication failed to provide for his black counterparts in the world of science, education, and learning—an opportunity to employ his intellect and project his identity as a man in a realm where skin color was nonsignificant. Classical scholarship of the highest order might not permit William S. Scarborough to move and mingle on the level of his peers in WASP universities or learned societies any more than historical scholarship would permit Carter G. Woodson, or scientific discovery and accomplishment would permit William A. Hinton, to receive the respect and rewards that would have been showered upon a white man with their respective accomplishments; but classical and historical scholarship of high order accompanied by anthropological knowledge of wide expanse could blend with the art of poetry to transcend the intellectual, scientific, and religious poverty of human relationships in a society and a culture still bound by a myth of white superiority. One might find himself forced to be a Negro historian, but not a Negro poet. One could be a man, and proudly a Negro, and especially a poet, without specializing in being primarily the Negro on the one hand, or apologizing for being one on the other. This M. B. Tolson felt, believed, declared, and demonstrated. To my mind, this is a supreme accomplishment of an individual human spirit in America in our day, to which moon-walking as the supreme collective accomplishment of our engineering know-how shines like a candle in broad daylight, Tolson refused the fate of what he termed

> the white and not-white dichotomy
> the Afroamerican dilemma in the Arts—
> the dialectic of

> to be or not to be
>
> a Negro

Art was the means by which he believed not only an individual poet but also mankind could transcend, in some measure, both the past and the present in the future, if mankind put art to its highest use in recreating human life. So his prospective view, like Jefferson's, saw the imagined passing into the real, rather than the reverse, as taught by a sterile school of letters, that art merely imitates. And he addressed his concluding question and answer in *The Harlem Gallery* thus:

> White Boy
> Black Boy,
> What if this Harlem Exhibition becomes
> a *cause célèbre?* . . . .
>
> . . . .
> Our public may possess in Art
> a Mantegna figure's arctic rigidity;
> yet—I hazard—yet,
> this allegro of the Harlem Gallery
> is not a chippy fire,
> for here, in focus, are paintings that chronicle
> a people's New World odyssey
> from chattel to Esquire!

Tolson has written of American life as it is and will be. He has taken our white-black culture and imagined it into a new thing more representative of the modern human condition than any of his contemporary peers among poets has managed to create, and it is not "negritude," although he has plenty of that, but "humanitude" that enabled him to accomplish the feat. I do not expect anyone to accept this judgment until he has read and appreciated Tolson's poetry for himself, and I do not expect professors of American literature to accept it generally for perhaps a quarter century, but Tolson's recognition will come as surely as has Whitman's.

Robert M. Farnsworth (essay date Summer 1981)

SOURCE: "Preface to Melvin B. Tolson's *Caviar and Cabbage* Columns," in *New Letters,* Summer, 1981, pp. 101-02.

[*In the following essay, Farnsworth discusses Tolson's* Caviar and Cabbage *columns.*]

Melvin B. Tolson's last two books of poetry, *The Libretto for the Liberian Republic* and *Harlem Gallery* won him deservedly strong critical acclaim. But those who know his work only by these rewarding, but bristlingly demanding, major poems are cut off from the roots of his writing experience.

From November 13, 1937, until June 24, 1944, Tolson wrote a weekly column, *Caviar and Cabbage,* for the Washington *Tribune.* These years included the closing years of the great depression and the United States' entry into World War II. These two events were a major influence on Tolson's writing career, and they also strongly influenced the terms by which black Americans then defined their cultural role in national and international communities. The social ravages of the great depression during the thirties increasingly caused black leaders and intellectuals to stress class rather than race as the determining factor in the plight of black people. The events of World War II made the linkage between racism and colonialism publicly visible. Black Americans increasingly recognized that the drama of their lives was being played on an international, not just a national, stage.

By 1937 Tolson had earned a notable reputation as an outspoken public speaker and an extraordinarily successful debate coach at Wiley College. This was probably the basis for the invitation to write *Caviar and Cabbage.* That same year his first published poems began to appear. He wrote his column, taught a full load at Wiley, coached the debate team, helped to organize the Southern Association of Dramatic and Speech Arts, directed college dramatic performances, spoke on platforms across the country, and still managed to begin two novels, to continue writing dramas, and to write most of the poems which were to appear in his first book, **Rendezvous with America,** published in 1944, all concurrently. Obviously *Caviar and Cabbage* was often written hastily and under considerable pressure. As a consequence, however, these columns frequently reveal Tolson's thought and feelings much more directly and immediately than does his more carefully wrought poetry.

Melvin Tolson is no highbrow. Kids from the cottonfields like him. Cowpunchers understand him. He is a great teacher of the kind of which any college might be proud. It is not just English he teaches, but character, and manhood, and womanhood, and love, and courage, and pride.
—Langston Hughes

The columns published here make clear Tolson's primary concern with those black people, for whom, "color is a birthmark and poverty a birthright," a concern which never wavered even after Tolson began to win critical acclaim for writing increasingly esoteric poetry. Tolson saw the depression as affording an opportunity for black workers and white workers to recognize their mutual class interest and to organize to achieve them. He saw the racial barrier between these two groups as of less importance than the class barrier between black workers and the black middle class. Paul Robeson's ambition to make a film based on the life of Oliver Law seemed to Tolson to offer possibilities of introducing substantially different proletarian values into film making.

Tolson's father was a Methodist minister, and the poet taught at Wiley College, a Methodist school. He often couched his appeal to "the little Negro" in the caring paternalism of the pulpit: "Tomorrow belongs to the little people. The Big Boys are through. He who is greatest among you, let him be the servant of all. We used to think a big house, a big car, a big salary, a big position—made a big man. Those days are gone forever. A big man now is a big servant of little people." In middle age he often remembered the working experiences of his youth with self-critical irony. Intense social ambition screened his youthful perceptions. Working in the stockyards of Kansas City, he was initiated to the economic conditions which caused workers to bond together, but it was only in retrospect that the message reached him fully and clearly.

In 1945, Langston Hughes described Tolson in the Chicago *Defender* as "The most famous Negro professor in the Southwest. Students all over that part of the world speak of him, revere him, remember him, and love him, . . . But Melvin Tolson is no highbrow. Kids from the cottonfields like him. Cowpunchers understand him. He is a great teacher of the kind of which any college might be proud. It is not just English he teaches, but character, and manhood, and womanhood, and love, and courage, and pride."

Robert M. Farnsworth (essay date Fall 1981)

SOURCE: "What Can a Poet Do? Langston Hughes and M. B. Tolson," in *New Letters*, Vol. 48, No. 1, Fall, 1981, pp. 19-29.

[*In the following essay, Farnsworth traces Tolson's relationship with fellow poet Langston Hughes.*]

The academic year 1931-1932 was in retrospect probably the most crucial year of Melvin B. Tolson's writing career. He was thirty-four years old. He had a wife and four children. He had been teaching in the English Department of Wiley College since 1923. And he had been writing poetry and fiction at least since the age of fourteen when he published a poem about the wreck of the Titanic in a local newspaper in Oskaloosa, Iowa. The poetry and fiction which can be gleaned from Tolson's high school and college publications and a later story which appeared in a Wiley College yearbook all lend credence to the self-evaluation Tolson wrote late in the 1930's: "In 1932 I was a Negro poet writing Anglo-Saxon sonnets. As a graduate student in an Eastern university, I moved in a world of twilight haunted by the ghosts of a dead classicism."

In 1931-1932 Tolson, with the aid of a Rockefeller fellowship, was able to arrange for his family to live with his parents in Kansas City, while he moved to Harlem to enroll at Columbia University in a Master's program in Comparative Literature. For his M.A. he wrote a thesis on "The Harlem Group of Negro Writers." Living in Harlem, coming into extended personal contact with the writers of Harlem, and studying their work caused Tolson to begin his first ambitious poetic project, *A Gallery of Harlem Portraits,* a collection of approximately 200 brashly vivid poetic portraits, which by their great variety was meant to give an epic cross-section of the city of Harlem. Tolson began writing *A Gallery* while he was still writing his M.A. thesis on the Renaissance writers. A first draft of *A Gallery* probably was not completed until 1935, but the first poem published from this manuscript, **"Hamuel Gutterman,"** appeared in V. F. Calverton's *Modern Monthly* only in April, 1937.

In his thesis Tolson devotes individual chapters to these writers: Countee Cullen, Langston Hughes, Claude McKay, Walter White, Eric Walrond, Rudolph Fisher, Jessie Fauset, George Schuyler, W. E. B. DuBois, James Weldon Johnson, and Wallace Thurman. He begins his chapter on Langston Hughes by observing: "Countee Cullen and Langston Hughes represent the antipodes of the Harlem Renaissance. The former is a classicist and conservative; the latter, an experimentalist and a radical." While Tolson's thesis strives for academic neutrality, there is never much doubt with which of these two antipodes Tolson's own literary sympathies lie. With a tinge of envy Tolson observes: "With a biography that reads like a page from the *Arabian Nights,* Langston Hughes, the idealistic wanderer and defender of the proletariat, is the most glamorous figure in Negro literature."

Tolson, well aware of the restraints of his own professional and family responsibilities, envied Hughes' travel opportunities in Mexico and several countries in Europe and Africa, and he admired his staunch and sincere proletarian commitment. To be a Bohemian traveler voicing the concerns of the peoples of the world seemed a marvelous vocation. The quotation Tolson chooses from Hughes' poetry to preface his thesis suggests that in Tolson's imagination Hughes also had preceded him in discovering a more vivid and vivifying world in the streets of Harlem:

> Strange,
> That in this nigger place

> I should meet life face to face;
> When for years, I had been seeking
> Life in places gentler-speaking,
> Until I came to this vile street
> And found life stepping on my feet.

Tolson apparently completed an initial draft of his thesis before he left Harlem to return to his teaching position in Marshall, Texas, in the fall of 1932, but he didn't turn in a final draft until nearly eight years later. Meanwhile another event triggered a revealing literary statement by Tolson. That was the publication late in 1932 of Hughes' poem, "Good-Bye Christ," and the righteous attacks by clergymen and others which it provoked while Hughes was still in Russia.

Tolson chose to reply to an attack on both Hughes and his poem made by the Reverend Mr. J. Raymond Henderson in the Pittsburgh *Courier.* Tolson's reply, his first significant literary statement to be published, appeared in two parts in the January 26 and February 2, 1933, issues of the *Courier.* Tolson initially defends the poet against the clergyman's charge that the poem was not worthy of serious consideration, that it was a cheaply sensational means of attracting public attention: "Langston Hughes is a Catholic, a rebel, and a proletarian in his personal life and in his poetry and criticism. These he has always been. . . . Nobody who knows Langston Hughes intimately can doubt his sincerity. He has always stood for the man lowest down and has sought to show his essential fineness of soul to those who were too high up—by the accident of fortune—to understand." Then Tolson insists that Hughes' poem is not the real issue. The real issue is the challenge that it makes to present-day Christianity:

> The world is in a terrible condition today, and, if Christianity does not do something to solve the problems of humanity, it will have hurled at it repeatedly such challenges as "Good-Bye Christ" . . . . The disciples of Karl Marx carry his teachings forward with a verve and a courage that are admirable; the followers of Christ, on the other hand, enter into bootless denunciations. The leaders of Communism starve for hunger and die to put over the teachings of Marx; the leaders of Christianity live in comfortable homes and ride around in big cars and collect the pennies of washer-women. Magnificent edifices are erected, while people go hungry and naked and shelterless. Preachers uphold or see not the ravages of "big business." "Good-Bye Christ" is the outgrowth of tragic modern conditions.

Some paragraphs later Tolson concludes:

> The point is: Men are concerned with present-day

Christianity. Christianity must come down from the pulpit and solve the problems of today. Men will no longer listen to the echo of that beautiful, but illogical, spiritual of long ago:

> *You may have all this world,*
> *Give me Jesus.*

In fact, Jesus Christ would not have sung a song like that. He was a radical, a Socialist, if you will. His guns were turned on Big Business and religionists. He heralded the dawn of a new economic, social, and political order. That is the challenge to all.

Tolson actively organized both white and black sharecroppers in the thirties in Southeast Texas. His proletarian commitment probably preceded his residence in Harlem. Similarly since his father was a Methodist minister and a strong model in Tolson's life, his Christian views were certainly shaped before he met and knew Hughes. But the deep similarity in their positions provided the means for Tolson to empathize strongly with Hughes. Both believed in a revolutionary Christ who represents the poor and the powerless. To both writers during the Great Depression the teachings of Marx seemed to follow within this Christian prophetic tradition. For both Tolson and Hughes, Marx was far closer to the authentic Christ than the "mouth-Christians" who failed to address the cruel economic injustices of the thirties.

Many years later in a weekly column, *Caviar and Cabbage,* which Tolson was to write for the Washington *Tribune,* he remembered an incident with Hughes which also marked in his mind the year 1932, although the incident probably actually occurred in 1931. The scene is set in "an elegant parlor on Sugar Hill." Hughes and the hostess are discussing his proposed tour through the South. Suddenly Hughes remembers a rally to collect money for the Scottsboro boys. His hostess tries to persuade him that it is raining too hard:

> There is a tenseness, an agony in the Poet's face. It seems that his life depends on getting to that meeting in time. We hasten downstairs and catch a taxicab. The rain is now torrential. The Poet leans forward, tells the driver to put on speed. The Poet talks passionately about the Scottsboro boys. They are innocent. They must go free. It'll take money.
>
> The car stops. It skids. Before us looms the great, aristocratic church. It is dark. In front of the church is a milling multitude. We learn that the church would not let the rally be held in the House of God. People said it was just Communist propaganda. The Poet asks me to come with him. I tell him I have a previous engagement.

> Langston Hughes looks at me with a sad half-smile. He says goodnight. I see him pushing through the crowd in the rain. His face looks tired and old and pain-ridden. I start to get out. Then I tell the driver to step on the gas. But I am to feel a hundred times that I doublecrossed the Scottsboro boys!
> (June 29, 1940)

In the conclusion to his M.A. thesis, Tolson credits the Harlem Renaissance with making Negro America "conscious of the inflowing of a powerful verve. . . . The Harlem Renaissance was not a fad," but it "has been followed by a proletarian literature of Negro life, wider in scope, deeper in significance, and better in stylistic methods." It is clear, however, that Tolson saw Hughes, more than any other writer of the Renaissance, as anticipating the later deeper proletarian concerns of Black writing which were to characterize the thirties.

The particular characteristic of Hughes' poetry which most effectively demonstrated his profound social commitment, and which later inspirited Tolson's own poetic ambition, was the power of the Blues. According to Tolson, Hughes "catches the undercurrent of philosophy that pulses through the soul of the Blues singer and brings the Blues rhythms into American versification." After quoting from "Po' Boy Blues," Tolson comments:

> If one has that sympathetic imagination which Mr. Mencken likes to talk about, one can, through identification of feeling, experience the utter physical and mental fatigue of the Negro after the cruel sleeplessness of the night-hours, facing the desolate flatness of another day. Langston Hughes understands that tragedy of the dark masses whose laughter is a dark laughter.

Tolson notes that the colored bourgeoisie criticize Hughes' poems for being "just like the nigger blues," but then he adds ironically that they are "unmindful that this is the highest tribute they can pay to these artistic creations."

The impact of Hughes' achievement on Tolson's imagination is made clear in the introductory poem of *A Gallery of Harlem Portraits,* where he uses a variety of Blues lyrics to introduce the poetic portraits which are to follow. He prefaces these lyrics, however, with a comment which suggests a distinction between his own and Hughes' experience which will become of increasing importance as Tolson's own poetic career ripens and flourishes. Tolson's writing is much more rooted in the academic world, in the world of esoteric scholarship, and speculative theorizing about the nature of the world and of mankind. Thus he writes:

Dusky Bards,

Heirs of eons of Comedy and Tragedy,
Pass along the streets and alleys of Harlem
Singing ballads of the Dark World:

He follows that, however, with a series of Blues beginning with the classic lament of a woman:

When a man has lost his taste fer you,
    Jest leave dat man alone.
Says I . . . a dawg won't eat a bone
    If he don't want de bone.

Tolson follows that with a verse which implies the contemporary relevance of the Blues, the Blues as a continuing adaptive tradition:

Happy days are here again
Dat's sho' one great big lie.
Ain't had a beefsteak in so long
My belly wants to cry.

He continues then to alternate classic Blues with more pointed contemporary social comment:

Preacher called to bless my home
An keep it free from strife.
Preacher called to bless my home
An keep it free from strife.
Now I's got a peaceful home
An' de preacher's got my wife.

Rather be a hobo, Lawd,
Wid a stinkin' breath
Dan live in de Big House
Workin' folks to death.

A Gallery of Harlem Portraits shows evidence of multiple literary influences, yet Tolson's first book of poems is remarkable as a very personal poetic celebration, the celebration of his discovery of Harlem as a community that made the dreams and dilemmas of black Americans vivid, and the celebration of his discovery of a literary heritage which enabled him to link his strongly felt personal and social experiences to direct, yet subtle, and imaginative, literary expression. In this process the example of Langston Hughes was one of the more vivid presences which helped Tolson to exorcise "the ghosts of a dead classicism" from his imagination.

The story of the relation between Tolson and Hughes from this point on is held together by a thread of biographical anecdotes. Tolson could not find a publisher for *A Gallery of Harlem Portraits*. Eventually he wrote an article telling the story of how his first book came to be written and the difficulties he had in finding a publisher. He called it **"The Odyssey of a Manuscript."** But he had no more success finding a publisher for his article than he had for his book. In the article, however, he tells of trying to enlist the support of several prominent literary figures, including Langston Hughes, in his effort to get his manuscript published. He showed Hughes his poems in Los Angeles in 1935. Tolson was there in two roles, as a representative of the state of Texas to the San Diego International Exposition and as coach of a crack Wiley debate team which challenged and defeated the team of the University of Southern California, who were then national champions.

If Hughes was too preoccupied with his personal problems on this occasion to be of much help to Tolson, he was soon to be involved in other key moments of Tolson's developing writing career. In 1939 Hughes, along with Arna Bontemps and Horace Cayton, named Tolson's **"Dark Symphony"** the prize poem for the American Negro Exposition held in Chicago. The later publication of **"Dark Symphony"** in *Atlantic Monthly* proved to be the key factor in Tolson's first successful book publication, *Rendezvous with America*. On December 15, 1945, in "Here to Yonder" in the Chicago *Defender*, Hughes paid tribute to both Tolson and his new book:

That Texas is some State! I was down there once or twice myself. And I have found some very amazing things—including Melvin Tolson.

Melvin Tolson is the most famous Negro professor in the Southwest. Students all over that part of the world speak of him, revere him, remember him, and love him. He is a character. He once turned out a debate team that beat Oxford, England. He is a great talker himself. He teaches English at Wiley College, Marshall, Texas, but he is known far and wide. He is a poet of no mean ability, and his book of poems, *Rendezvous with America,* is a recent fine contribution to American literature. The title poem appeared in that most literate of literary of publications, the *Atlantic Monthly.*

But Melvin Tolson is no highbrow. Kids from the cottonfields like him. Cowpunchers understand him. He is a great teacher of the kind any college might be proud. It is not just English he teaches, but character, and manhood, and womanhood, and love, and courage, and pride. And the likes of him is found no where else but in the great State of Texas—because there is only one Tolson!

The recently published collection of letters between Arna Bontemps and Langston Hughes have several references to Tolson in them, frequently referring to both writers' hopes that Tolson will be of help in arranging for a performance of one of their plays or in the arranging of an appearance at Wiley College. But two other incidents are particularly notable. Hughes, on June 22, 1949, tells Bontemps of the progress he is making in editing a special issue of *Voices* featuring black writers. It "is coming along fine, lots of poets have responded with good stuff, Tolson with his BEST poem yet." The "best" poem of Tolson's is **"African China,"** still one of Tolson's most frequently anthologized poems. **"African China"** is a slightly rewritten amalgam of two poems originally part of *A Gallery of Harlem Portraits*. At the time Hughes wrote these remarks Tolson was also hard at work on the revisions for **Libretto for the Republic of Liberia,** a poem Hughes could admire only with distant irony. Thus the poem Hughes admires is predictably enough the poem which is rooted in that part of Tolson's career when Hughes himself was such a vivid presence.

> **In the late 40's and early 50's Tolson developed a poetic style which he hoped would enable him to project the needs and interests of black people into the imaginations of a still developing audience of the future.**
> **—*Robert M. Farnsworth***

In this same letter Hughes asks Bontemps: "Do you know any nice gentle old Negro who could play the lead in *Cry the Beloved Country* which I've been trying to help Maxwell Anderson and Kurt Weill to cast?" Bontemps replies on June 26:

> A person you should have Mamoulian-Anderson-Weill consider for *Cry the Beloved Country* is none other than M. B. Tolson. His hair is gray, he has the gentleness, etc., and moreover he has been a director of little theatres and debating teams for years. He is at home on a stage. I think he would love it, that he could easily get a leave from Langston U. for this purpose, and that he would be a stomping success. And he is very much the Roland type! Tell Reuben I send this nomination with my warm regards and best wishes for the success of his new production.

Hughes makes the suggestion. Weill asks him to phone Tolson. Tolson is enthusiastic about the project. There is a question about Tolson's singing voice. Then for some reason not clear in the letters someone else gets the part.

In the spring of 1965 Hughes introduced Tolson at a poetry reading for AMSAC in New York City. In his introduction Hughes recounts a funny but pointed adventure that he and Tolson had when they were in Jackson, Mississippi,

in 1952, as part of an impressive gathering of black writers celebrating Jackson State College's 75th Diamond Jubilee. Hughes had heard that the crack Panama Limited which stopped at Jackson on its way from Chicago to New Orleans was very reluctant "to haul coal." Even Charles S. Johnson of the Urban League complained he was unable to get a ticket on this train in Chicago. Since Tolson was wiser in the ways of the South, he took the initiative. The two bought tickets for New Orleans days in advance, arrived at the depot an hour ahead of schedule, but boarded only at the last minute. The conductor then held up the train while he called down the line of cars searching for an empty drawing room to avoid seating them with the white passengers, and they finally ended up riding in the most elegant drawing room on the train, although after the rigors of the conference and considering the early hour in the morning, they both slept most of the way to New Orleans.

In the late 40's and early 50's Tolson developed a poetic style which he hoped would enable him to project the needs and interests of black people into the imaginations of a still developing audience of the future. He based his experiment on the self-conscious modernism of such poets as Pound, Eliot, Williams and Stevens. Tolson's stylistic experiment, particularly in **Libretto for the Republic of Liberia,** took him, at least ostensibly, further and further away from Hughes as a poetic model or mentor. I say ostensibly because Tolson was delighted when Stanley Edgar Hyman noted that although Tolson's technique of juxtaposition could easily be identified with Eliot's *Waste Land* and Pound's *Cantos,* its kinship to the associative organization of the blues is also obvious. And while Tolson may have borrowed many poetic techniques from T. S. Eliot, the radical, international, democratic revolution he prophetically visions in **Libretto** is a world in which Langston Hughes and William Carlos Williams would be far more comfortable than would T. S. Eliot.

And certainly in Tolson's final book, **Harlem Gallery,** he comes full circle. Even though this final book is placed in the consciousness of the Curator who thinks of himself as an artist manqué and who reportedly speculates on the nature of art and of man, there are still many of the same vivid characteristics of the earlier Harlem which meant so much to both Hughes and Tolson. The Curator ironically acknowledges at the outset that while ready to deliver "a full / rich Indies' cargo," he often hears "a dry husk-of-locust blues / descend the tone ladder of a laughing goose, / syncopating between / the faggot and the noose." John Laugart's painterly attack on the Black Bourgeoisie, Hideho Heights' entertaining the Zulu Club wits, and Mister Starks' penetrating poetic portraits all intensely imply a Harlem which still represents the dreams of a people whose dreams have been too long deferred.

Patricia R. Schroeder (essay date December 1983)

SOURCE: "Point and Counterpoint in *Harlem Gallery*," in *CLA Journal,* Vol. XXVII, No. 2, December, 1983, pp. 152-68.

[*In the following essay, Schroeder discusses Tolson's* Harlem Gallery *and asserts that "the character of the Curator and the central dilemma in which he is placed provide a perfect vehicle for an examination of social divisions and conflicting roles."*]

Although first published in 1965, Melvin B. Tolson's highly allusive poem *Harlem Gallery* has yet to attract much critical recognition. With the exception of an unpublished dissertation, a rather general critical biography, a handful of reviews, and some widely scattered articles, the poem has been virtually ignored; as Robert M. Farnsworth has recently expressed it, "Critics and scholars have been ducking the challenge of his [Tolson's] work for years." The reasons for this neglect of a modern masterpiece undoubtedly stem from the difficulties of the poem itself; the density of its allusions and the erudite perplexities of its language. Until a much-needed annotated edition of the poem is published, however, we can begin to penetrate its ornate facade by isolating important clusters of imagery and significant movements in its narrative structure, thereby locating the focal points for subsequent critical investigations of its provocative thematic complexities.

In a brief note on T. S. Eliot, Tolson himself has given us a clue to one such focal point in *Harlem Gallery*. He says, "Eliot antithesizes in order to synthesize—that is the root of thinking—which is establishing a definite relation between ideas and groups of ideas." This movement from thesis to antithesis, from point to counterpoint in a dialectic interplay, produces a central impulse in *Harlem Gallery,* directing the flow of its narrative and informing much of its imagery. Midway through the poem this issue is explicitly invoked, as Dr. Obi Nkomo says to the troubled Curator of the Harlem Gallery:

> Dialectics?
> The midwife of reality.
> The cream separator of life.
> The sieve, Curator, of wheat and chaff.

Such images of bifurcation, clearly recognized as significant by the wise and flexible Nkomo, recur constantly throughout the poem and explain much of its action and language. Through the controlling consciousness of the Curator, himself suffering from a number of social and emotional ruptures and lacking Nkomo's cheerful equilibrium, the poet explores some seemingly irreconcilable points and counterpoints of life in Harlem and the world of the modern artist, including the oppositions inherent in all structures founded on democratic compromise, and the confusion about personality which often accompanies a split in social roles. But as we follow the Curator's wanderings (both mental and physical) through the twenty-four sections of the poem, from alpha to omega, through blackness and whiteness, through highbrow and lowbrow, from the public functions of art to the private ones, and from lofty philosophical abstractions to dismal ghetto reality, we come to share his growing acceptance of the constant interplay of opposites which defines life. With the Curator, we learn that an awareness of the disparate elements of existence and a conscious personal attempt to maintain equanimity can be in itself a balance between polarities.

The character of the Curator and the central dilemma in which he is placed provide a perfect vehicle for an examination of social divisions and conflicting roles. Both raceless (his "Afroirishjewish" heritage has left him with a fair skin which belies his sense of belonging to the Negro community) and classless (he exists in a sort of limbo between the opulence of the gallery Regents and the poverty of his Lenox Avenue familiars), the Curator furnishes us with an educated, bipolar intelligence with which to view the different worlds he inhabits.

In the theoretical treatise **"Alpha"** through **"Epsilon"** which begins (or perhaps introduces) the poem, the Curator attempts to define his function as caretaker of the fine arts and to establish in his own mind the nature and functions of art, both in the gallery and in the Harlem community. Mister Starks' characterization of the Harlem Gallery as "the creek that connects the island and the mainland" is painfully, if ironically, apt; the Curator's task is to bridge that creek which in reality *separates* the lives of the Harlemites from the world of art. For the Curator, art should be essentially wedded to life; it is "not barrel copper easily separated / from the matrix"; it is part of a creative process as human and as necessary as the sexual instinct. In order that art remain a living organism, however, each generation of artists must reshape in its own idiom the materials it inherits; unfortunately, the stratification of society has paralyzed this creative process and arrested intercultural advancement. The artist's need to choose between God and Caesar for patronage has torn art away from the people who most need its succor, and at the same time denied the enrichment of popular culture to the fine arts themselves. The Curator deplores the academic, the commercial, and the political uses of art. He seeks to present a kind of art in the Harlem Gallery which will speak to all men on all sides of social barricades and which will connect the island with the mainland; he believes and hopes to demonstrate that art is the medium which can integrate opposites. The Curator's immediate, agonizing dilemma, then—and a large problem for one who "in the drama *Art,* / with eye and tongue, / . . . play[s] a minor vocative part"—is to reconcile the best of the active, personal world of popular tastes to the financial interests of the gallery Regents. In effect, he must harmonize the demands of God with those of Caesar.

The Curator must thus wear a variety of masks, and his awareness of the prescribed social roles he must play is underscored by his constant use of dramatic imagery and stage directions. His confusion as to the suitability of his masks is evident from the inversions with which he describes himself: "Sometimes a Roscius as tragedian, sometimes a Kean as clown." Perhaps the essential conflicts he feels between his two primary roles (Negro and Curator) as well as his inhibitions about his ability to play them allows him greater sensitivity to the plight of the artist who "endures / —like Everyman— / alone." Like the artist, the Curator is denied unequivocal acceptance in any of the social spheres in which he moves; his refusal to separate his world of art from the general tenor of ghetto life partially excludes him from both.

The Curator's constant efforts to incorporate diametric opposites into an integrated whole are manifest on every level of the poem, from basic setting and structure to character and language. Even his linguistic habits reflect his desperate attempts to seek out the similarities between things, to somehow make his life a work of art. The richly metaphoric texture of his rather baroque, conceited language displays both his interest in artistic form and the underlying pattern of his thoughts: the very structure of metaphor indicates a tension, an attempt to literalize abstraction by analogy and comparison. The selection and combination of two patently unlike objects based on some minor likeness between them (that is, the construction of a metaphor or simile) indicates the Curator's inability to appreciate the contexts which bind things and reflects his desire to establish internal points of connection. His continual battle to reconcile unlike worlds causes the Curator to discuss his situation in deliberately pretentious analogies; for him, the interplay of "Heart and Hand and Soul" renders man's experience "Like Caesar's Gaul, / like the papal tiara, tripartite," and the Zulu Club wits when drunk become

> absent
> like the similes in the first book of the *Iliad,*
> or
> ugly
> like the idiom the Nazarene spoke,
> or
> tight
> like ski pants at the ankle.

The Curator's extensive use of puns likewise exhibits his dilemma; based on a single structure with several sharply diverse meanings, a pun can express linguistically the Curator's awareness of his own multiplicity of roles. The

very tone of his voice is divided, presenting us with a simultaneous sense of comic and tragic. As we shall see, however, the poem ends with a comic acceptance of the polarities of life and with an affirmation of the probable— that life will continue, that man and his art will both endure, and that the tension between the poles of the Curator's life is finally the element which gives it shape and meaning.

The entire movement of *Harlem Gallery* is paradoxical. The poem achieves a linear progression in that the Curator, through his ponderings, his experiences, and his relationships with the other characters, comes to a fuller understanding of himself and the roles he must play. The poem also proceeds dialectically, however, working in terms, characters, and events paired by their fluid and interacting distinctions rather than by strict and inviolable oppositions. The first five sections of general theory can stand alone (and have, in *Prarie Schooner*); they present the set of assumptions which motivate the Curator throughout the action which follows. As the drama ensues, we are presented (in **"Zeta"** through **"Xi"**) with a variety of scenes counterpointing the inhabitants and the art of the Gallery coterie with those of the Zulu Club, and emphasizing the Curator's attempts to define his place in each world. In **"Omicron"** and **"Pi"** the Curator returns to the realm of abstract speculation, but now incorporates his new experiences into his philosophy. For example, Dr. Nkomo intrudes into the speaker's consciousness several times here, whereas the earlier theoretical sections included no characters. Likewise, the Curator's previous awareness that the age determines its art is buttressed (after his meeting with John Laugart) by his new, bitter understanding that the artist must bow to the predominating powers if he hopes for survival. In language deflated from the Latin "O Tempora / . . . O Mores" of the early **"Beta"** chapter which it echoes, he wonders how art can survive in an age motivated by political expediency:

> O Time, O Customs,
> how can an artist make merry
> in the tenderloin's maw,
> unless he add a head and a wing and a claw
> to the salamander of Gerry?

These two sections occur roughly at the midpoint of the poem's action and divide it into two contrasting halves; the second part, however, moves in the same dialectic fashion. The Curator returns to street scenes in Harlem with his new experiences absorbed into his philosophic framework, but the discovery of Hideho Heights' secret poem, coupled with the objective view of his own actions afforded him by Mister Starks' *Harlem Vignettes,* causes the Curator a serious psychic shock; he must once again reevaluate himself and reassess his position. This constant oscillation between abstract theory and concrete reality produces a repetition that somehow progresses, and is understood best in the Curator's own metaphor: he has moved "across the dialectic Alps from Do to Do"; he has returned to the note on which he began, but with the improved vantage point of a higher octave and a clearer appreciation of the pattern.

The dramatic action of the poem revolves around three Harlem artists—each of whom is torn between his private reality and his publicly accepted art—and the effects of their works on the Curator. Immediately following the theoretical prologue to the drama, we meet John Laugart, a half-blind, half-dressed "castaway talent" who is more than half-afraid of the controversy his painting may engender. In a deliberate parody of the symbolic diction which characterized the five theoretical sections of the poem, **"Zeta"** opens with the alert squeakings of a "Hamletian" tenement rat (hardly the Afric pepper bird which awakened the Curator to his cause) and the grumblings of an ancient toilet. We have clearly deserted the spheres of aesthetic theory and entered the world of Harlem reality. Laugart, however, a physical manifestation of the Curator's theories, is unwilling to divorce his art from ghetto experiences. As its title implies, his *Black Bourgeoisie* apparently satirizes the black elite who have divorced themselves from their cultural heritage and have "accepted unconditionally the values of the white bourgeois world: its morals and its canons of respectability, its standards of beauty and consumption." The Curator sees the painting as a potential cross-cultural bridge, a vehicle for bringing the "babbitted souls" of the Regents back in touch with their folk backgrounds, and art back in touch with life. He says of the painting, "*[T]his,* somehow, [is] a synthesis / (savage—sensitive) / of Daumier and Gropper and Picasso"—all artists, like Laugart, noted for the social concerns of their work. After some prodding by the Curator, Laugart rises to the challenge of the tight-fisted Regents—"the doges in the Harlem manger"—and refuses to misrepresent or undervalue his work. His final heroic statement is undercut by his imminent death at the hands of a Harlem burglar, but his words linger on in the Curator's mind:

> "It matters not a tinker's dam
>   on the hither or thither side of the Acheron
>   how many rivers you cross
>   if you fail to cross the Rubicon!"

All that remains for Laugart himself is "infamy, / the Siamese twin / of fame," but like his prophetic words, his *Black Bourgeoisie* remains alive and important in the mind of the Curator. As a central point of interest and contention in the gallery's latest exhibit, by the end of the poem *Black Bourgeoisie* has become a *bête noire* for the Regents and a test of the Curator's ability to cross his own Rubicon.

In contrast to John Laugart, whose defiance of the Regents

emphasizes the hitherto private world of art he inhabited, is Mister Starks, whose death in the second half of the poem counterpoints that of Laugart in the first. Different from Laugart in his public success as a composer, Starks, too, bequeaths a painful legacy to the Curator in the penetrating candor of his private manuscript, *Harlem Vignettes.* Mister Starks is aware of the disjunction that has occurred in his life, allowing him to produce both barroom successes—*Rhapsody in Black and White*—and classical compositions—*Black Orchid Suite;* he says of himself, "My talent was an Uptown whore; my wit a Downtown pimp." He also recognizes the similarities between his predicament and that of the painter Laugart: in the first stanza of his *Vignettes* he mentions Laugart, then continues with a bitter question:

> Am I not a Negro, a Harlemite, an artist—
>   a trinity that stinks the ermine robes
>   of the class-conscious seraphs?

Like Laugart's painting, Starks' manuscript becomes "the birth-after-the-father-is-buried / [which] will doubtless fetch no white laurel of joys, / no black crepe of regrets"; however, the poem helps the Curator acknowledge the possibilities of his position, and encourages him to defend *Black Bourgeoisie* in the face of his own Hamletian fears.

Despite the tremendous impact on the Curator of both *Black Bourgeoisie* and *Harlem Vignettes,* the artist-character who exerts the strongest influence on him is the complex Hideho Heights. A chameleon-like figure in all respects, in his bifurcated existence Hideho also reiterates the personal and aesthetic problems set forth by the Curator. Often described in images of American Indians, Hideho evidently comes from a mixed racial ancestry which emphasizes the internal division produced by

> the bifacial nature of his poetry:
> the racial ballad in the public domain
> and the private poem in the modern vein.

A former expatriate "bistro habitué," Hideho moves comfortably in all realms of the poem, from the elegant gallery opening to the neighborhood dives; his existence, unlike that of Laugart or Starks, spans both halves of the work. Unfortunately, Hideho Heights makes no attempt to reconcile the worlds in which he lives. He maintains a private poetic existence apart from his public role as Poet Laureate of Lenox Avenue, and thereby violates his own understanding of the nature of art:

> "A work of art is a two-way street,
>   not a dead end,
>   where an artist and a hipster meet."

Recapitulating the fates of both Laugart and Starks, Heights will eventually be destroyed by his bipolar existence. In him, we see the entire process of dislocation, which we glimpsed only briefly in Laugart and Starks, completed and personified.

We first meet Hideho Heights at the opening of the new gallery exhibit, against a background of "Blakean tigers and lambs on the wall"; we soon realize that his split psyche reflects *The Marriage of Heaven and Hell* and that both the tiger and the lamb reside, unassimilated, within him. It is here that we first sample Hideho's work, as he recites for the Curator his tribute to Satchmo. This poem provides many clues to the source of the rift in Hideho's talents and recalls the peculiar juxtapositions within **Harlem Gallery** itself. He delivers the poem in a public place, but to a limited audience of one; the poem itself, ostensibly a hymn of praise to Louis Armstrong, can also be interpreted as an ironic expression of disgust at the stereotypical Uncle Tom image Armstrong preserved. The work exudes the simple faith of a Negro spiritual (ending, as it does, with Gabriel's trumpet), but contains allusions to academic literature as well (Villon's "Ballad of Ladies of Times Gone By" is thematically and rhythmically echoed in the second stanza). Despite the popular appeal of Hideho's work, then, he is apparently an educated man, capable of describing the Curator in Shakespearean terms and recognizing the rattle of "Eliotic bones." The very subject of the poem at hand indicates the division within the poet; by celebrating the power of Satchmo's horn to "syncopate the heart and mind," Hideho emphasizes both the jazz rhythms which permeate his own poetry and his inability to integrate his talents or reconcile his roles.

We next encounter a truly public version of Hideho in performance at the Zulu Club, playing his part as the people's bard; he is now as much rhetorician as poet, gearing the themes and forms of his poetry to the audience at hand and painfully suppressing his personal poetic interests. In these Zulu Club performances art is indeed a two-way street, as the audience's lively response interrupts the recitation and reshapes the poem in the telling:

> The Zulu Club patrons whoop and stomp,
> clap thighs and backs and knees:
> the poet and the audience one,
> each gears itself to please.

Before the Club regulars, the "vagabond bard" loses all pretension to modernist art as he celebrates a mythic Negro hero in standard folk rhythms. "The Birth of John Henry" reverberates with a traditional comic affirmation of the strength of the individual and belies the pain of the poet as his art plays pander to his spiritual needs.

In "E.&O.E.," however, we discover a very different Hideho

Heights. The fragments of the poem with which we are presented exhibit a profound sense of fatality; the poet speaks in a personal idiom about alienation and obscurity, about the frustration of a black artist who, in order to communicate with his own people, must allow his audience to dictate the forms his art will take:

> Why place a dry pail
> before a well
> of dry bones?

The hopelessness evinced by the poem is a function of Hideho's Janus role. Riven by his desire to appeal to an audience that is unable to appreciate contemporary poetic forms, he feels that the tension between his conflicting identities has squeezed him into

> the white and non-white dichotomy,
> the Afroamerican dilemma in the Arts—
> the dialectic of
> to be or not to be
> a Negro.

Hideho's belief that "a man's conscience is home-bred" is at odds with his modernist talent, and his failure to reconcile theory with reality causes his dissipation. Just as John Laugart was destroyed by his tenement situation and Mister Starks was a victim of the corrupt upper echelons into which he had moved, Hideho Heights gives us the fully realized portrait of a man who fails in his attempt to inhabit two distinct spheres, a man incapable of incorporating his many avatars into a single identity. As the Curator says:

> These Lion Hearts (then) are unsynchronized
> opposites,
> gentlemen and galoots
> from Afroamerica.

Hideho Heights' unwitting personal revelations, combined with the Curator's previous experiences with Laugart and Starks, have an immeasurable effect on the Curator's conscience; he becomes increasingly aware that the agony of the artist is augmented terribly by the added pain—and seeming contradiction—of also being black. He begins to understand that in his capacity as Curator, he may somehow be able to alleviate that pain and prove the contradiction false. Through Starks' *Vignettes* he attains an honest evaluation of his lack of courage; through Heights' "E.&O.E." he comes to understand that personal apathy and feelings of hopelessness only widen the gap and further the dilemma; and in Laugart's *Black Bourgeoisie* he finds a cause.

The split in personal identity manifest by the Curator and the artist characters of the poem is apparent on much broader levels as well; as we saw in the case of Laugart and Starks, many characters are presented contrapuntally. Mr. and Mrs. Guy Delaporte III are described as

> mismatched oddlegs:
> he,
> with a frown like curd;
> she,
> with a smile like whey.

Likewise, the activities of the impoverished would-be intellectuals—the Zulu Club Wits, "dusky vestiges of the University Wits"—are seen in bitter contrast to those of the "Cadillac Philistines" who patronize the gallery. Even within these seemingly cohesive groups contention exists and internal discord presides: the Regents' meetings are described as "bull rings of pros and cons," and the Zulu Club discussions revolve around picky literary debates.

A figure central to both these forums of debate (and necessary for a clear understanding of the Curator) is Dr. Obi Nkomo, "the alter-ego of the Harlem Gallery," and in many respects the alter-ego of the Curator: "Perhaps we are twin colors in a crystal," the Doctor says. Like a negative version of the fair-skinned Curator, Nkomo is an outsider—a Bantu expatriate and not a native Harlemite; both his background and inclinations equip the Doctor with a cynical philosophy which allows him to view Harlem activities with a detachment completely lacking in the Curator. Nkomo appreciates the emotional distance from life he has developed, and his guru-like tranquility renders him an apt foil for the troubled Curator. "Aeons separate my native veld / and your peaks of philosophy," he declares. But Nkomo, too, has confronted internal tensions and a variety of roles:

> His psyche was a half-breed,
> a bastard of Barbarus and Cultura;
> and the twain shall never meet
> on the D-Day dreaded by the Scholar-Gypsy.

Despite (or perhaps because of) the dialectic of his Afro/ American nature, Nkomo has learned to accept with equanimity the pluralities of existence; he is able to maintain the objectivity to understand the paradoxes and complexities which define life.

From the moment the gallery opens we see Nkomo and the Curator in "counter-poise beside / the ebony doors of the Harlem Gallery." The relationship between these two "oddest hipsters on the new horizon of Harlem" partially determines the shape and development of the poem, while personifying its theme of the necessity of conflict. Nkomo's covert advice and his direct verbal challenges to the Curator prove, in Blake's phrase, that "Opposition is true friend-

ship," as his proverbial wisdom helps the Curator come to terms with his bipartite roles.

In *Harlem Vignettes* Mister Starks remarks:

> I used to say that if I knew the difference between
> The Curator and Doctor Nkomo,
> I'd know the ebb and flow of tides of color.

This essential dissimilarity between the Curator and the Doctor is exemplified by their differing uses of language. Seen through the controlling consciousness of the Curator, Nkomo's speech necessarily partakes of that heavily allusive, metaphorical style which characterizes the Curator. Nkomo, however, as an objective observer of the goings-on around him, is more aware of the connections between things; therefore, he often speaks epigrammatically, spounting proverbs and aphorisms with commonsense morals that indicate a realistic turn of mind. For Obi Nkomo, a metaphorical discussion of the role of the Afroamerican results in a bold prose maxim: "The little python would not let go the ass of the frog—so the big python swallowed both." Furthermore, his quick retorts to the gibes of Hideho and the Club Wits reveal a calculating shrewdness that the Curator lacks; the Doctor immediately recognizes Hideho as "an Aristotelian metaphorist," indicating his suspicions about the true poetical talents of the Lenox Avenue bard.

Perhaps because of his poet's sensitivity to language, Mister Starks finally discovers for himself the difference between Nkomo and the Curator, and reports it in his *Vignettes.* The distinction becomes clear to him during a philosophical debate on the art of "cream-skimming," an image central to **Harlem Gallery,** Starks watches the interplay of character:

> While the Curator sipped his cream
> and Doctor Nkomo swigged his homogenized
> milk
> I tried to gin the secret of
> the mutuality of minds
> that moved independently of each other—
> like the eyeballs of a chameleon.

For Nkomo, the image of the cream rising up above the milk implies a belief in that "stinking skeleton," the theory of white racial superiority. The Curator's weak retort indicates his refusal, at this point, to accept responsibility for unequal social or artistic conditions, and in effect repudiates his role as caretaker of the arts: "Since cream rises to the top," he says, "blame Omniscience— / not me." Nkomo and Starks both see that the dialectic shuffle of the Curator's mind has not yet resolved itself and that his constant vacillation functions only to support the *status quo* and allow the cream of culture to be skimmed off the milk of the people. The

Curator's failure to conciliate the Regents and the Harlem artists, and his inability to turn his idealistic theories into purposeful actions indicate his lack of personal courage. His continual meanderings have not yet resulted in that synthesis which is the aim of dialectics.

> "*Mens sibit conscia recti*,"
> said Doctor Nkomo
> —definitively—
> "is not a hollow man who dares not peddle
> the homogenized milk of multiculture,
> in dead ends and on boulevards,
> in green pastures and across valleys of dry bones."

The Curator's indecisiveness has contributed nothing towards the intermingling of cultures necessary for a true, thoroughly human understanding between men, and he must now strive for the incorporation of the point and counterpoint of his otherwise futile dialectic.

Starks' perceptive rendering of the cream-skimming incident has a permanent effect on the Curator; the poet-pianist has discovered him

> the failure of nerve
> Harlem would never see—
> the charact in the African
> that made
> him the better man.

The Curator had imagined himself inexorably trapped, like the "pig in the boa's coils"; from his contacts with Nkomo, Starks, Heights, and Laugart he comes to believe instead that he and his kind must not "die like hogs."

In the two concluding sections of the poem, the Curator returns to the theoretical gropings with which the poem began. Now that he has become more intimately aware of the effects of artistic creation on the artist (he has witnessed two deaths and senses the imminence of yet another), his original dogmas about the function of art and his concept of his own role in its preservation are somewhat shaken. In these final sections, however, we see the hopes of the Curator beginning to supersede his fears; we see the butterfly slowly and carefully shedding the protective chrysalis which had until now insulated him. Despite the psychic shocks he has suffered, the Curator is starting to formulate an affirmative statement of continued existence for artists and men of every class and color.

In his final attempt at self-definition, the Curator strives to isolate "Negroness," which in his case is merely "a state of mind conjured up by Sterotypus." The dialectic struggle of the entire poem is here repeated in the Curator's language; his alternation of the phrase "White Boy" and "Black Boy" is in address to himself as well as to the world at large. Throughout his philosophical ramblings, the Curator has become aware that in him, as in all living things, bipolarities exist and must be somehow connected, despite the fact that

> Just as the Chinese lack
> an ideogram for "to be,"
> our lexicon has no definition
> for an ethnic amalgam like Black Boy and me.

For the Curator, finally, the problem of racial definition resolves itself into a forced, conscious acceptance of both his innate identities, and into the creation of a personal lexicon to define them.

The resolution of this dialectic of race allows the Curator a starting "point" with which to begin to solve his next dilemma—that of his role of Curator. This final mental process underlines a theme crucial to *Harlem Gallery*—that opposites will always exist and must be integrated before one can progress to the next dialectic. The Curator can now ask:

> Should he
> skim the milk of culture for the elite
> and give the "lesser breeds"
> a popular latex brand?

The speaker's newfound sense of personal integrity provides an answer to the question as he realizes that his latest Harlem Gallery exhibit—the potential *cause célèbre*—may prefigure "a people's New World odyssey / from chattel to Esquire." He comes to realize that the eternal "phoenix riddle" of the black/white controversy in art, as well as in life, can never be solved except by a balanced assimilation of elements from both cultures. The dialectic structure and the counterpoint of characters which pervade the poem now prove to be thematically profound as well: the Curator discovers that the controversy which the gallery exhibit provokes will begin a new process of synthesis, and that, to borrow from Blake once again, "Without Contraries is no progression." The war between contradictory truths is, finally, the truth which brings forth new life.

William H. Hansell (essay date Fall 1984)

SOURCE: "Three Artists in Melvin B. Tolson's *Harlem Gallery*," in *Black American Literature Forum*, Vol. 18, No. 3, Fall, 1984, pp. 122-27.

[*In the following essay, Hansell analyzes the roles of the three artists in Tolson's* Harlem Gallery.]

The first and final chapters of Melvin B. Tolson's *Harlem Gallery,* **"Alpha"** and **"Omega,"** serve many purposes, the most important of which is to introduce or recapitulate aesthetic principles exemplified and developed throughout the poem. My summary here of the crucial chapters is designed to serve as the introduction to a study of three characters, John Laugart, Hideho Heights, and Mister Starks, each of whom is an artist and contributes substantially to the dramatic embodiment of the aesthetic principles underlying the volume.

Beginning my study of three major characters with the discursive, ode-like chapters seems appropriate also because Tolson's poem opens with several chapters that focus on subjects, race and art in particular, which later become the subjects of dramatic exchanges among a number of characters. The three artists portrayed in the poem itself create the kinds of works which illustrate the new art announced in **"Alpha":** Laugart in painting; Starks in music, classical and popular; and Heights in poetry. There is, however, some overlapping. Mister Starks, for example, is also a poet, and his "Harlem Vignettes" is made up of short poems given in their entirety in *Harlem Gallery;* Starks sketches several characters and provides a self-portrait as well. But his greatest creations are musical compositions.

"Alpha," which opens with the optimistic announcement of a new art, contains, in Ronald Walcott's words, "a statement of the poet's intention to invigorate modern poetry with the Black Americans' idioms and sense of life." Fully aware that bourgeois attitudes and tastes—"the Great White World"— will be alarmed, the narrator remains confident a new age, "a people's dusk of dawn," is being born:

> In Africa, in Asia, on the Day
> of Barricades, alarm birds bedevil the Great White
> World,
> a Buridan's ass—not Balaam's—between no oats
> and hay.

Like the legendary ass that starved because of an inability to choose between "oats and hay," the Great White World is helpless in the confrontation with the forces bringing about political and aesthetic revolutions.

That the narrator has searched widely for an aesthetic which includes tragic and comic components is revealed in the short second stanza:

> Sometimes a Roscius as tragedian,
> sometimes a Kean as clown,
> without Sir Henry's flap to shield my neck,
> I travel, from oasis to oasis, man's Saharic up-and-
> down.

In reversing the typical roles of the great comic actor Roscius and of Edmund Kean, the great Shakespearean tragedian, Tolson complicates the role of the artist who must often draw upon comedy for serious ends. There is the implication, too, that traditional forms and labels must not restrict the new art forms. Or to put it another way, the narrator believes that the artist, although influenced by traditional genres, must adapt them to his own ends, creating new forms in the process.

The new art will absorb existing forms and cultural influences in the creation of a truly universal and eclectic aesthetic. From the image of himself as a nomad, wandering from "oasis to oasis," the narrator presents himself returning with "a full/rich Indies cargo." Nonetheless, the single doubt nagging at him, as a black man, is whether the search has been worth it:

> "Black Boy, O Black Boy,
> is the port worth the cruise?"

That is, he knows that the myth which alleges that Afro-Americans have no enduring cultural heritage has convinced many that they are inferior: "Sometimes the spirit wears away / in the dust bowl of abuse." He, however, is confident of his personal, universal, and racial identity: his "I-ness . . . humanness and Negroness." Although conceding there are differences among races, Tolson affirms that humanity, like art, is universal.

In **"Omega,"** complex and esoteric art forms, even if they require expounders, intermediaries between the work of art and most audiences, are emphatically defended. In fact, it seems almost the duty of those who understand to convey it to others:

> Those in the upper drawer give a child
> the open sesame to the unknown
> What and How and Why;
> that's *that* which curators, as Pelagians, try
> to do[.]

The Curator is probably the volume's most important character, and he often serves as the narrator; but he is not an artist. "Curators, as Pelagians," would seem to emphasize the belief in the basic freedom of the will and perhaps, too, the natural goodness of men, both of which are implied in Pelagius's rejection of the doctrine of original sin and in his affirmation of the capacity for goodness in the unaided human will. Art, therefore, if carefully studied, can bring men to truth. Since the labor may be great and the truth painful, the narrator recommends suitably measured doses:

> Sometimes a work of art is bitter crystalline
> alkaloid

> to be doled out
> at intervals, between the laugh and flout
> of an Admirable Doctor; but, if taken too much
> at a time, it delivers the cocainizing punch
> of a Jack Dempsey nonesuch.

The artist's sensibility and aesthetic standards, moreover, must not be compromised because of ignorance, illiteracy, or the stultified sensibilities of an audience habituated to certain art forms:

> Should he
> (to increase digestibility)
> break up
> the fat globules and vitamins and casein shreds?

More important to the artist than simplicity and popularity is the need to reflect the varied materials on which he may draw. The eclectic nature of art is likened to a river fed by many streams, a source of vital renewal in even the most sterile of circumstances to all who bathe in it:

> Many mouths empty their waters
> into the Godavari of Art—
> a river that flows
> across the Decan trap of the age
> with its lava-scarred plateaux;
> and, in the selfheal of the river,
> pilgrims lave the bruises of the Rain of woes.

A "dream" of another character (Dr. Nkomo) declares the need to create a "dusky Everyman," someone, like Monet or Matisse, who can convey the mystery and beauty of Harlem and, in effect, be a true heir of the Harlem Renaissance. In any event, a new black art is taking shape and will profoundly influence America's destiny. Whatever else, there is more of vitality and optimism in Harlem than elsewhere:

> In the black ghetto
> the white heather
> and the white almond grow,
> but the hyacinth
> an asphodel blow
> in the white metropolis!

Tolson himself has interpreted the symbolism: "I say that the flowers representing decay and death are found in the white metropolis, but the flowers of hope grow in the black belt. I speak here of the masses of poor people. They are on the move. Most American writers are cynical. But even in the violence of a Richard Wright there is something that lifts you. There is no despair." Both in the poem and in the note, Tolson intends *white* to symbolize bourgeois values and attitudes; throughout the poem, parochialism, racism, and elitism, considered at great length, are rejected by each of the major characters.

The new art, finally, will triumph—and these are the final lines of *Harlem Gallery*—because it embodies the entire history of Afro-Americans:

> this allegro of the Harlem Gallery
> is not a chippy fire,
> for here, in focus, are paintings that chronicle
> a people's New World odyssey
> from chattel to Esquire!

The three artists portrayed in *Harlem Gallery* are discussed in the approximate order in which they are introduced in the poem, because that order is climactic; that is, the final artist, Hideho Heights is presented last and developed more fully in the poem. Heights most clearly dramatizes that art is universal. His audience is largely the common man. But the Curator, in his seemingly random movement through Harlem, first encounters a painter.

John Laugart immediately impresses the Curator as an artist with the qualities of greatness, a neglected genius with unshakeable integrity, preferring poverty to popularity. His masterpiece, *Black Bourgeoisie*, enthrals and delights the Curator. Laugart, a "half-blind painter," has an almost regal air, but in a melodramatic outburst, he cries that he feels neglected and misunderstood, that "No man cares for [his] soul!"

The Curator, who is on a search for items to exhibit in the Harlem Gallery, after briefly glimpsing the painting, speculates grandiosely that Laugart's room might be the modern counterpart of Patmos, where St. John is supposed to have written the Apocalypse, thereby evoking associations with a profoundly symbolic religious work at the beginning of the Christian era. (Possibly the era whose demise is declared in **"Alpha"**?) In the Curator's eyes, Laugart's painting marks the beginning of a new aesthetic and combines the artistry of the greatest painters of our century. Equally important, Laugart has combined aesthetic excellence with social protest, something the Curator previously believed impossible, which is the reason that his astonishment at the masterpiece created by Laugart is likened to several moments in ancient and modern times, which were also marked by shock and delight at the moment of discovery, an experience both rending and curative:

> colors detonating
> fog signals on a railroad track,
> lights and shadows rhythming
> fog images in a negative pack:
> *this,* somehow, a synthesis
> (savage—sanative)

> of Daumier and Gropper and Picasso.
> As a Californian, I thought *Eureka;*
> but as Ulfilas to the dusky Philistines I said,
> "Oh!"

This is sketchy and impressionistic, but it is the most detailed description of the painting in *Harlem Gallery.* Subsequently, only effects are described.

The visual imagery of fog and shadow combine with the sound imagery, a piercing train whistle in a fog. And there is the rhythm of the colors dynamically playing against one another, overlapping and interweaving, to give the impression of blurring. There seem to be no hard edges, no simple or pure colors. Laugart's social intention, given the context of the painting, would seem to be quite clear. Middle-class blacks lack definition and identity. Behaving and thinking like middle-class whites, they have become a composite of both races, succeeding only in obliterating their true identity. Of course an important assumption is that all middle-class people have corrupt values and attitudes. Elsewhere in *Harlem Gallery,* the Curator and Dr. Nkomo, for example, repeatedly comment on the necessity of rejecting bourgeois values. Similarly, the art and artists celebrated in the poem, the work of Laugart, Starks, and Heights, arouse the masses, but stir fear and trembling in the middle-class characters.

The aesthetic intention, just as important, seems also self-evident. Masterpieces are eclectic; great artists combine traditional styles from disparate sources in the effort to forge an original style. In a sense, Laugart accomplished in paint what Tolson did in words. Tolson consciously adapted the styles of many great poets, most notably Harte Crane, T. S. Eliot, and Ezra Pound; he obviously drew on a great variety of traditions and cultures; and he wanted to improve the human condition.

The Curator is convinced immediately that most viewers of Laugart's work will not understand it, yet will howl with outrage at what they suspect they see; *Black Bourgeoisie* "will wring from their babbitted souls a Jeremian cry!" Laugart, too, anticipates hysterical resentment, but confidently observes,

> "A work of art
> is an everlasting flower
> in kind or unkind hands;
> dried out,
> it does not lose its form and color
> in native or in alien lands."

For Laugart, the artist's dedication must be to excellence, even at the risk of failure: "'It matters not a tinker's dam /

... how many rivers you cross / if you fail to cross the Rubicon!'"

Laugart and his painting are, in fact, vigorously rejected by "the Regents of the Harlem Gallery," which is to say everyone with middle-class values. For the Regents, Laugart is a "castaway talent." In a rather abstruse reflection on those ("the half-alive") who misunderstand and deride works like *Black Bourgeoisie,* the Curator stresses that successful irony often has a positive effect. That is, art can have a positive influence even when misinterpreted. Painting a fantastic picture of the ordeal of the Regents' attempting to understand the painting, the Curator pictures them in comic bafflement: They "confuse / the T-shape of the gibbet with the T-shape of the cross." They so completely misconstrue the painting that they see symbols of salvation instead of symbols of death. But again, the Curator reminds himself that great art may unconsciously penetrate the most insensitive psyches:

> —a Jacob that wrestles Tribus and sunders
> bonds—
> discovers, in the art of the issues
> of Art, our prose, as well as our cons,
> fused like silver nitrate used
> to destroy dead tissues.

The pain of the Regents may be a sign that some of their moribund attitudes are giving way; perhaps they are even beginning to understand that great art and social criticism are compatible. After we are told of his lonely death, the most important of subsequent references to Laugart appear in a series of poems, *Harlem Vignettes,* included in **"Upsilon"** and composed by another Harlem artist. The world's neglect of Laugart is likened to its neglect of another great artist; its betrayal is likened to the selling of Christ.

Mister Starks, composer, pianist, conductor, and poet, is credited with a popular song, "Pot Belly Papa," which made a great deal of money; two major classical works, *Black Orchid Suite* and *Rhapsody in Black and White;* and the ten poems collected under the title *Harlem Vignettes.* These last have marked parallels to Tolson's *A Gallery of Harlem Portraits,* poems written by 1935, but not published until 1979. A dominant influence on Starks (and on Tolson's early work) is the Edgar Lee Masters of *The Spoon River Anthology.* The poems are character sketches, sometimes very brief, in free verse. Starks' style, in the *Vignettes,* on the other hand, reflects Tolson's mature style in its dense allusiveness and imagery.

In **"Mister Starks: A Self-Portrait,"** the narrator initially disparages his own talents and behavior, feeling he has compromised his aesthetic principles for money, and he announces his intentions:

I etch, here and now, a few
of the everybodies and somebodies and nobodies
in Harlem's *comédie larmoyante.*

After quoting John Laugart on the immortality of art, Starks stresses that his career, if not a great success, was freely chosen. With a brief, harsh slant at those who have failed to appreciate his art, he adds,

Am I not a Negro, a Harlemite, an artist—
a trinity that stinks the ermine robes
of the class-conscious seraphs?

He tells also of a time in Europe when he was influenced by the works of jazz musicians and by great composers of classical music. But his final revelation is of absolute confidence in the greatness of his composition *Black Orchid Suite,* even though it never received public acclaim. We are dramatically informed about the creation of the *Suite,* the first creation in his "new" style. This discovery immediately caused profound changes in Starks and another major character, convincing them that they had to abandon all ideas of absolute racial or aesthetic distinctions. That is, they continue to believe that individuals, societies, and nations in every age contribute distinctive and valuable elements to art, but they now believe that those diverse components can be brought harmoniously together.

In the final part of **"Upsilon,"** Starks tells of a night on which he played the piano more or less with the intention of ignoring a self-pitying and maudlin white man, a petty criminal, whom Starks, to himself, calls a "Derby," possibly because he and his counterparts wear them. Somewhat absentmindedly, then, Starks let his fingers wander into "a corny polka style / reminiscent of Kid Ory's trombone in *Sweet Little Papa.*" After some bitter reflections on the inattentive audience and racism, Starks suddenly discovered something original in the music he had been playing:

As I explored the theme phrase,
a new rhythm and melody vistaed before me:
the tones feathered into chords
and leafed and interlaced
in fluxing chromatic figures.

With his love of music and its revelations about the human condition, Starks cannot but believe that, if such intricate and new harmonies are possible in music, they may also be possible in life. His thoughts turn to Doctor Obi Nkomo, a character who speculates elsewhere in **Harlem Gallery** at great length on the subjects of art and race. Starks remembers Nkomo's image of the ideal world as being like the necessary black and white keys of a piano, "blended in the majestic *tempo di marcia* of Man." Tolson might very well have intended an illusion to Langston Hughes's "Daybreak

in Alabama," in which a similar metaphor of man in a harmonious society appears. Asked what he is playing, Starks explains,

Then I magicked an arpeggio of syncopated colors
(my left hand, like Fats', suggesting a bass fiddle)
and said with a flourish, *"Rhapsody in Black and White."*

He is not certain of his success, but, as he expresses it, every artist must risk everything in choosing between "Caesar or God." He is not overly concerned that his immediate audience does not understand his new work. Obviously embittered by the neglect of his masterpiece, and even by the monetary success of his popular works, Starks does not believe himself an utter failure because he remains confident of the greatness of his classical compositions.

Hideho Heights, the third artist portrayed in **Harlem Gallery,** is a poet; he enters with a satirical jibe, in "a voice like a / ferry horn in a river of fog," at the expense of the bourgeois tastes of the others:

"Hey, man, when you gonna close this dump?
etch highbrow stuff for the middlebrows who
don't give a damn and the lowbrows who ain't
hip!
Think you're a little high-yellow Jesus?"

Later, Heights is alluded to as "a crab louse / on the pubic region of Afroamerica." As if we needed to be told, we are informed that satire is one reason for his renown. After a brief glance at the art displayed in the Harlem Gallery, he observes, "'In the beginning was the Word . . . not the Brush!'"

Heights next reveals he's been listening to Louis Armstrong and been so inspired as to improvise a tribute: "'I'm just one step from heaven / with the blues a-percolating in my head.'" Immediately, he produces the manuscript dedicated to "old Satchmo." It is of the nature of jazz, we learn from Heights' poem, *"to syncopate the heart and mind"*; and he ranks Armstrong with the greatest musicians, singers, and folk heroes: King Oliver, Bessie Smith, Jelly Roll Morton, Papa Handy, Leadbelly, and John Henry. A calculated interracial point is made, moreover, with the further comparison of Armstrong's importance to *"Wyatt Earp's legend."*

The narrative continues to be dominated by Heights in the next chapter, **"Mu,"** in which everything and everyone in the nightclub is at fever pitch. Like many poems by Langston Hughes, these scenes are accompanied by jazz, blues, and booze. In fact, that the roots of jazz—therefore of all art—lies in man's sensual nature is nowhere more emphatically portrayed in **Harlem Gallery** than in these scenes. Still, it is a very unlikely atmosphere for a form of discussion which clearly parallels the Socratic dialogues. (There is some value, I believe, in reminding ourselves that Socrates also asserted that everything of importance should be discussed twice, once when drunk, again when sober.)

After a brief flirtation with a woman whose provocative dress and movements are highly erotic, Heights reveals to the Curator:

> "She's a willow,"
> "a willow by a cesspool."
> Hideho mused aloud,
> "Do I hear The Curator rattle Eliotic bones?"

With this allusion to Eliot, Heights begins to reveal his rejection of the belief that modern man is doomed because of the corruption of Christianity. But there is no reply from the Curator, whose attention turns to the jazz played in the Zulu Club:

> Out of the Indigo Combo
> flowed rich and complex polyrhythms.
> Like surfacing bass,
> exotic swells and softenings
> of the veld vibrato
> emerged.

Heights describes the dancing which begins as "'the penis act in the Garden of Eden,'" and the Curator thinks of it as "a prismatic-hued python / in the throes of copulation." Further, the Curator sees in the dancing an epitome of jazz performers and styles:

> In the *ostinato*
> of stamping feet and clapping hands,
> the Promethean bard of Lenox Avenue became a
> lost loose-leaf
> as memory vignetted
> Rabelaisian I's of the Boogie-Woogie dynasty
> in barrel houses, at rent parties,
> on riverboats, at wakes:
> The Toothpick, Funky Five, and Tippling Tom!
> Ma Rainey, Countess Willie V., and Aunt Harriet!
> Speckled Red, Skinny Head Pete, and Stormy
> Weather!

In complete agreement with the Curator, Heights extends the musical example of a rich and varied tradition into an argument that Gertrude Stein was wrong in saying "'The Negro suffers from nothingness.'" Heights' next observation seems at first glance to denounce jazz as nothing but escapism ("'Jazz is the marijuana of the Blacks'"), but Robert J. Huot argues correctly that Tolson almost certainly alludes to ancient rituals in which part of the initiation

ceremony was a mind-expanding preparation for a visionary climax. In this sense, obviously, drugs, including alcohol, aren't escapist, but rather ceremonial agents. Jazz, then, for Heights, is important as the embodiment of a rich cultural heritage and as a form of vital communal ritual.

The Curator agrees with Heights and turns from the meaning of music for blacks to its meaning for whites: "'Jazz is the philosophers' egg of the Whites.'" I take this to be, in part, a humorous distortion of the frequently asked question, "Which came first, the chicken or the egg?" Whites who believe blacks have no history are confronted with the dilemma of explaining the African components in jazz.

The necessity of musical accompaniment for a wide range of activities—secular and religious—informs the third stanza from the last, while the Curator insists further that jazz is as natural a music for blacks as "Liszt in the court at Weimar." **"Mu"** closes on a muted note of anticlimax:

> With a dissonance
> from the Weird Sisters,
> the jazz diablerie
> boiled down and away
> in the vacuum pan. . . .

Calling up images of witches, boiling cauldrons, and demons to describe the atmosphere created by the jazz, Tolson satirically exaggerates the accusations of its harshest critics, who often condemn the inducement to sensual indulgence.

Rufino Laughlin, master-of-ceremonies in the Zulu Club, believes absolutely in the immortality of Heights and declares this to the audience, when introducing the poet (in **"Mu"**). A prostitute, "a tipsy Lena," also seeking the immortality of poetry, offers herself free and forever if he will promise to write about her. Heights sends her off giggling with the observation, "'Sister, you and I belong to the people.'" Meanwhile, the Curator has been much impressed by the intimate relationship between Heights and habitués of the Club: "My thoughts wandered and wondered / . . . *the poet is no Crusoe in the Zulu Club.* . . ." When Heights reads (in **"Xi"**), the attention of the audience is religious, and they respond enthusiastically, very much in the way some black congregations enter into call-and-response exchanges with ministers. Heights' opening words are

> "Only kings and fortunetellers,
> poets and preachers,
> are born to be."

The Curator underscores the priestly, even messianic, aura given off by Heights. In addition to the priestly function, the artist is said to have prophetic or mystical powers with

which to "see and hear / when our own faculties fail."
Heights' ballad, a source of intense delight for the audience,
also owes much to the "tall-tale" tradition:

> *John Henry—he says to his Ma and Pa:*
> "Get a gallon of barleycorn.
> *I want to start right, like a he-man child,*
> *the night that I am born!*"

Also striking to the Curator in the performance is the mutual inspiration which occurs between poet and musicians,
and the evidence that both draw on traditional European and
folk forms:

> The creative impulse in the Zulu Club
> leaps from Hideho's lips to Frog Legs' fingers,
> like the electric fire from the clouds
> . . . that blued the gap between
> Franklin's key and his Leyden jar.

This "poet's feast" the Curator calls a "counterpoint / [of]
protest and pride." His attention focuses, next, on the relationship among diverse musical forms, and he alludes to one
French writer's intense study of black music:

> O spiritual, work song, ragtime, blues jazz—
> consorts of
> the march, quadrille, polka, and waltz!
> *Witness to a miracle*
> —I muse—
> *the birth of a blues,*
> *the flesh*
> *made André Gide's*
> *musique nègrel.*

Heights' recital ends with John Henry's rueful discovery that
racism and its effects exist everywhere in America: "*'I came
to Lenox Avenue, / but I find up here a Bitchville, too!*'" An
elaborate exchange of views on racism and on some personal problems follows. Heights is made almost desperate
by what he interprets as defeatism, or at the very least as
an unhealthy preoccupation with the problems of being
black. His final comment, "'My people, / *my* people— / they
know not what they do,'" obviously echoes Christ's outcry
just before his death. Clearly, they have not understood
Heights in the sense he intended, desiring, almost certainly,
that John Henry's story be an inspirational model of endurance and personal integrity.

Heights is the subject of a markedly eulogistic poem-within-
a-poem ("**Upsilon**"), one of a series of character sketches
called the *Harlem Vignettes* and attributed to Mister Starks.
Countering Plato's exclusion of poets from the ideal state,
Starks asserts that the poet, in particular Heights, is absolutely essential to any state:

> Plato's bias will not banish,
> from his Republic,
> the post laureate of Lenox Avenue. . . .

Starks admiringly quotes Heights' rejection of the idea that
artists are absolutely alienated from society's values and attitudes:

> "A work of art is a two-way street,
> not a dead end,
> where an artist and a hipster meet."

Heights is praised for believing in dynamic and communal
art forms, for his "tragic-comic" range, his humor and pride,
and his belief that form and content are inseparable:

> "The form and content in a picture or a song
> should blend like the vowels in a dipthong."

Heights, who later decides he has heard enough of cynicism
and despair, intends to write a poem that will have powerful social consequences:

> "The Centennial of the Emancipation Proclama-
> tion
> Ye Muses!
> As the People's Poet,
> I shall Homerize a theme that will rock the Nation!
> And every damned Un-American will know it!"

Drolly prodding Heights on, the Curator, possibly echoing
W. H. Auden, cautions him to "'remember / a tribal anthem
/ is the yankee-doodle diddle of a tittle.' Heights, contemptuous of further cynicism, prepares to recite "The Sea-Turtle
and the Shark," a ballad describing the way a sea turtle,
when swallowed alive, can claw and tear at the shark's
stomach until he makes

> "*his* way to freedom,
> beyond the vomiting dark,
> beyond the stomach walls
> of the shark."

Such triumphant defiance reminds at least one man of
Claude McKay's "If We Must Die," and the use Prime Minister Churchill made of it in his effort to harden British determination at a low point in World War II. The poem he
recites and the reference to McKay's "If We Must Die" are
Heights' way of asserting his belief that poetry is vital to
mankind in all times; Heights thereby refutes the Curator's
assertion. The Curator observes that Heights had never before allowed others to share in the creation of a poem, never
before "left the cellar door / of his art ajar." Heights, moreover, in an attempt to explain the process and product of
creation, compares them to

> ". . . a whore giving birth
> to a pimp's son, Curator, on a filthy quilt.
> (In travail a woman shows no sign of guilt.)"

He insists that all art is basically the product of *"élan vital,"* the sensibility's response to uncertainty and torment:

> "Maybe, yes, maybe,
> an artist's travail is like
> a woman's; and her baby is like
> a poem, a picture, a symphony—
> an issue of the *élan vital* in sweat and blood,
> born on a brazen
> sea and swaddled
> on a raft of life and shaped like a question mark."

The emphasis in the description on pain and a natural process which must run the full course probably refers to the demand that the artist master essential technical skills before attempting to create. The emphasis on illegitimacy and squalor affirms that beauty can come from the basest seeming things. And perhaps the originality of all true masterpieces makes them "bastards" in the sense that they combine existing traditions into a new object.

Each of the artists in *Harlem Gallery* dramatically embodies the principles introduced in "Alpha" and recapitulated in "Omega."
—*William H. Hansell*

Artists who do not endure entirely the creative ordeal are harshly attacked by Heights. Those artists who resort to "'midwives'" produce "'abortions.'" The lines "'the new-born sun-gods snatched / from cradles on the sly'" seem to castigate young poets who write in free verse. With at least some self-satire, he launches out at poets who read to jazz accompaniment:

> "consider the abortions
> of the *howl-howl-with-the-combo* quacks;
> the little Eddie Jests and Shortfellows. . . ."

For so short a passage, Tolson has loaded it with allusions, some fairly obvious and serious, some almost certainly tongue-in-cheek. Allen Ginsberg, echoically associated with this group, may be the most well-known Beat poet, and, elsewhere in *Harlem Gallery,* Beat poets are praised for originality, independence, and most importantly, for their defiance of conventional ideas about art. Langston Hughes is famous for his experiments with jazz accompaniment for public readings throughout his career of over forty years. Tolson had the highest regard for Hughes and for his work.

Finally, Heights scolds famous poets who renounce their early work,

> "who abandon the little
> hybrid bastards of their youth
> without
> saying
> 'Good-by!'"

Tolson himself abandoned his early style very deliberately, on the urging of Allen Tate and under the influence of Harte Crane, T. S. Eliot, Ezra Pound, and James Joyce. And even if we weren't told so in the opening lines of **"Chi,"** we would understand that Heights deeply loves all legitimate art and would not attack what he considered valid experimentation or innovation. After all, he has defended *Black Bourgeoisie,* scathingly criticized by the Regents, although a transcendent experience for the Curator.

Each of the artists in ***Harlem Gallery*** dramatically embodies the principles introduced in **"Alpha"** and recapitulated in **"Omega."** Whatever evils they identify, each is fundamentally optimistic. Their works, for the most part, are innovative, eclectic, and often esoteric. The artists derive their materials and forms in part from the immediate environment, but they also acknowledge a wide diversity of influences on their work. These artists, therefore, like Tolson himself, created original art forms to explore and portray the black experience in both its particular and its universal significance. As Nathan A. Scott, Jr., has recently argued, Tolson, Ralph Ellison, James Baldwin, Gwendolyn Brooks, and some others *"belong* not just to a special ethnic tradition but to the integrally American achievement in the literature of the present time."

Rita Dove (review date Autumn 1985)

SOURCE: "Telling It Like It I-S 'IS': Narrative Techniques in Melvin Tolson's 'Harlem Gallery,'" in *New England Review and Bread Loaf Quarterly,* Vol. VIII, No. 1, Autumn, 1985, pp. 109-17.

[*In the following review, Dove traces Tolson's* Harlem Gallery *and its reception among African-American intellectuals.*]

When Melvin B. Tolson published part I of his projected epic poem, *Harlem Gallery,* in 1965, critical response was immediate and controversial. Whereas the mainstream literati (read: white) were enthusiastic, proclaiming Tolson's piece as the lyrical successor of *The Waste Land, The Bridge,* and *Paterson,* proponents of the rapidly solidifying Black Aesthetic were less impressed. Part of the controversy was sparked by Karl Shapiro's well-meaning Foreword. "Tolson writes and thinks in Negro," Shapiro pronounced, prompting poet and essayist Sarah Webster Fabio to remark:

> Melvin Tolson's language is most certainly not "Negro" to any significant degree. The weight of that vast, bizarre, pseudo-literary diction is to be placed back into the American mainstream where it rightfully and wrongmindedly belongs.

Shapiro describes *Gallery* as "a narrative work so fantastically stylized that the mind balks at comparisons." Divided into 24 sections corresponding to the letters in the Greek alphabet, *Harlem Gallery* contains allusions to Vedic Gods, Tintoretto, and Pre-Cambrian pottery, as well as snippets in Latin and French. No wonder some of his black contemporaries thought he was "showing off."

To be sure, the timing was bad for such a complex piece. The Civil Rights movement was at its peak, and Black Consciousness had permeated every aspect of Afro-American life, including its literature. Black writers rejected white literary standards, proclaiming their own Black Aesthetic which extolled literature written for the common people, a literature that was distinctly oral, using the language patterns and vocabulary of the street to arouse feelings of solidarity and pride among Afro-Americans.

Although Shapiro prefaced his precocious linguistic analysis with a righteous outburst against the "liberal" politics of American tokenism, the suspicion had already been raised that M. B. Tolson was the white critics' flunky. "A great poet has been living in our midst for decades and is almost totally unknown . . ." Shapiro exclaimed; Paul Breman, however, in his contribution to *Poetry and Drama, The Black American Writer* (vol. II), declared "[Tolson] postured for a white audience, and with a wicked sense of humour gave it just what it wanted: an entertaining darkey using almost comically big words as the best wasp tradition demands of its educated house-niggers."

Who *was* this Tolson? Could he be the same man appointed Poet Laureate of Liberia and commissioned to write the *Libretto for the Republic of Liberia* in celebration of Liberia's Centennial? Allen Tate had written a patronizing introduction to this piece; conversely, William Carlos Williams salutes the *Libretto* in *Paterson*. Could the "white man's darkie" be the same man who taught at black colleges all his life, the teacher who gleefully watched his debate students defeat the debate team at Oxford? Could he be the same poet who said, "I will visit a place T. S. Eliot never visited"? And is this that most "unNegro-like" voice that Fabio protested:

> but often I hear a dry husk-of-locust blues

> descend the tone ladder of a laughing goose,
> syncopating between
> the faggot and the noose:
> "Black Boy, O Black Boy,
> is the port worth the cruise?"

Tolson's virtuoso use of folk talk and street jive was forgotten whenever the readers stumbled across more "literary" allusions like "a mute swan not at Coole." In the controversy over racial loyalties and author's intent, nobody bothered to read *Harlem Gallery* on its own terms. The poem—and the story it tries to tell—got lost in the crossfire.

Harlem Gallery, Book I: The Curator is the first part of a proposed five-part poem delineating the odyssey of the black man in America. . . . In *Book I: The Curator* (the only book Tolson completed before his death in 1966), the role of the black artist is examined on several levels. The narrator, a Mulatto of "afroirishjewish origins" and ex-Professor of Art, is curator of the Harlem Gallery. His gallery allows him ample opportunity to observe the shenanigans of the black bourgeoisie; his dealings with starving artists such as John Laugart, as well as his friendship with other black cultural figures, give him glimpses into all strata of black life. The Curator's alter ego, Dr. Nkomo, is his stronger, more prideful counterpart; taken together, their observations form a dialectic of the position of blacks—and most specifically, the black artist—in white America.

The Curator muses on the predicament of being black and an artist in America. "O Tempora, / *what* is man?" he asks in **"Beta"**; "O Mores, / what *manner* of man is this?" Spliced into this highly stylized ode are little stories—dramatic monologues, vignettes—which serve to illustrate the philosophical stance of the more discursive parts. These stories exhibit classical narrative techniques, as well as several storytelling "riffs" which are rooted in the Afro-American oral tradition.

The lives of three black artists are limned. The first, the half-blind, destitute painter John Laugart, we first meet in **"Zeta."** In his search for new work to show, the Curator visits Laugart in his "catacomb Harlem flat." The character sketch of Laugart is as gritty and muscular as anything in Dickens:

> His sheaf of merino hair
> an agitated ambush,
> he bottomed upon the hazard of a bed—
> sighing:
> "The eagle's wings,
> as well as the wren's,
> grow weary of flying."
> His vanity was a fast-day soup—thin, cold.

Laugart has just finished his masterpiece, *Black Bourgeoisie*, a painting the Curator feels is certain to arouse the ire of the patrons of his gallery. Yet Laugart refuses to compromise his art in order to pay the rent. The consequences—related in a dry postscript—"He was robbed and murdered in his flat, / and the only witness was a Hamletian rat."

John Laugart's tragic fate is sandwiched between the shimmering overture of the first five sections and the underworld glimmer of the Harlem of the Thirties. The Curator leaves Laugart to his chill vigil and stops in at Aunt Grindle's Elite Chitterling Shop to shoot the philosophic bull with his ace boon coon, Doctor Obi Nkomo. They are next seen at a *Vernissage* at the Harlem Gallery, where sublimated versions of black history and its heroes hanging on the wall provide ironic contrast to the ignominious private lives of the prospective buyers, exemplified by Mr. Guy Delaporte III, "the symbol / of Churchianity" to the "Sugar Hill elite."

"Hey man, when you gonna close this dump?" cries Hideho Heights as he bursts into the hushed gallery. Our second black Artist, the "poet laureate of Harlem," is boisterous and irreverent. He stops his good-natured ribbing only long enough to declaim his latest poem, a tribute to "Satchmo" Armstrong. Those sections of **Harlem Gallery** devoted to Hideho Heights display a virtuoso rendering of narrative layers—a tribute, perhaps, to Heights's own extravagant linguistic paeans. In the section **"Mu,"** the scene at the Zulu Club provides a backdrop to Hideho's recitation of his rather militant version of the John Henry ballad. This story-within-a-story, however, is interrupted by the anecdotes of the "Zulu Club Wits," whose tableside conversation ranges from an anecdote about service in a Jim Crow restaurant to an animal fable reminiscent of Brer Rabbit (which draws its spirit from Africa) about the mistreated minorities in America: Hideho relates the "strange but true" story of the sea-turtle and the shark. Driven by hunger to swallow the sea-turtle whole, the shark is utterly helpless as the "sly reptilian marine" gnaws / . . . and gnaws . . . and gnaws . . . / *his* way to freedom."

The dialogues in the Zulu Club scenes show how close Tolson's baroque surface mirrors typical black street speech. When Heights pinches a "fox," she whirls around and "signifies" on him:

> "*What* you smell isn't cooking," she said.
> Hideho sniffed.
> "Chanel No. 5," he scoffed,
> "from Sugar Hill."

Hideho Heights's John Henry poem ("The night John Henry is born an ax / of lightning splits the sky, / and a hammer of thunder pounds the earth, / and the eagles and panthers cry!") is right in the tradition of great black ballads, as well as incorporating the bawdiness ("Poor Boy Blue! Poor Boy Blue! / I came to Lenox Avenue, / but I find up here a Bitchville, too!") of a "toast." In her excellent study on black speech patterns, *Talkin and Testifyin: The Language of Black America*, Geneva Smitherman describes the toast:

> Toasts represent a form of black verbal art requiring memory and linguistic fluency from the narrators. Akin to grand epics in the Graeco-Roman style, the movement of the Toast is episodic, lengthy and detailed. . . . Since the overall narrative structure is loose and episodic, there is both room and necessity for individual rhetorical embellishments and fresh imaginative imagery. . . . the material is simply an extension of black folk narrative in the oral tradition.

In fact, the whole of **Harlem Gallery** is very much like the Toasts to Shine and Stag-o-lee, those mythic "bad-men" heroes in black oral tradition. In Tolson's case, however, his hero is the archetypal Black Artist.

Many of Tolson's narrative techniques are based on devices exclusively rooted in the Afro-American tradition. "Metaphors and symbols in Spirituals and Blues / have been the Negro's manna in the Great White World," sighs one Zulu Club wit; perhaps the most vivid declaration of this appears in **"Iota":**

> In the Harlem Gallery, pepper birds
> clarion in the dusk of dawn
> the flats and sharps of pigment-words—
> quake the walls of Mr Rockefeller's Jericho
> with the new New Order of things,
> as the ambivalence of dark dark laughter
> rings
> in Harlem's immemorial winter.

The third Harlem artist is Mister Starks, conductor of the Harlem Symphony orchestra. Mister (his mother gave him the first name "Mister" so that whites would have to address him with respect) appears in sections **"Rho,"** **"Sigma,"** **"Tau"** and **"Upsilon."** To relate the circumstances of Starks's mysterious death, Tolson uses all the devices of the criminal drama, right down to the Smoking Gun and the Deep Dark Secret Revealed in the Secret Papers.

"Rho" begins with a phone call from the police station. "O sweet Jesus, / make the bastard leave me alone!" a hysterical Heddy Starks screams. The Curator recalls how Mister Starks met Heddy, then a striptease dancer called "Black Orchid," and how she used "The intelligentsia of Mister's bent" as "steps on the aerial ladder / of the black and tan bourgeosie."

Next comes a flashback to the day of Starks's death. He has sent a copy of his Last Will and Testament to his friend Ma'am Shears, owner of the Angelus Funeral Home. Fearing the worst, she phones to discourage him: "It's not like Black folks to commit suicide," she pleads. Starks's only response is a dry repartee: "Aren't we civilized yet? The Will contains explicit instructions for Starks's funeral, as well as an admonishment to his wife to turn over to the Curator the manuscript she has "possessed / with malice aforethought." Seven pages after Heddy's hysterical phone call, we learn why she is phoning: "arrested at a marijuana party / and haunted in her cell," she has decided to give the manuscript to the Curator and make "her peace with God."

Starks is found with a bullet in his heart; the gun is found in the toilet bowl of a character named Crazy Cain. Now we know "who-dun-it," but we don't know anything about the murderer. For that information we need to read the manuscript, a collection of poetical portraits written by Starks and titled *Harlem Vignettes*.

The section **"Upsilon"** is comprised entirely of these vignettes, which begin with a painfully honest self-portrait. Starks is aware that he has compromised his talents, writing boogie-woogie records when he should have been pursuing the excellence of his one triumph, the *Black Orchid Suite*. The *Harlem Vignettes* are incisive thumbnail sketches of many of the characters already encountered in **Harlem Gallery,** including John Laugart, Hideho Heights, and the inscrutable Curator. In Crazy Cain's sketch we learn that Mister Starks had fired him from the Harlem Symphony; he was also the illegitimate son of Black Orchid and Mr. Guy Delaporte III.

Can I get a Witness? Because what Tolson has been doing all along is testifying, which is nothing more than to "tell the truth through story." The *Vignettes* are important not only as an advancement of the plot, but for their function as narrative history—in designing them, Tolson is a sort of literary counterpart to the African griot, the elder assigned the task of memorizing tribal history.

There are a host of other characteristics typical of black speech which appear in **Harlem Gallery**—mimicry, exaggerated language, spontaneity, bragadoccio. There is one narrative technique, however, which informs the overall structure of Tolson's piece. Smitherman calls this mode of presentation "narrative sequencing" and observes that many Afro-American stories are actually abstract observations about the larger questions of life rendered into concrete narratives:

> The relating of events (real or hypothetical) becomes a black rhetorical strategy to explain a point, to persuade holders of opposing views to one's own

point of view. . . . This meandering away from the "point" takes the listener on episodic journeys and over tributary rhetorical routes, but like the flow of nature's rivers and streams, it all eventually leads back to the source. Though highly applauded by blacks, this narrative linguistic style is exasperating to whites who wish you'd be direct and hurry up and get to the point.

Tolson doesn't stop there, but employs another important technique of black/African storytelling—what Smitherman calls "tonal semantics": using rhythm and inflection to carry the *implication* of a statement. "Oh yes, it *bees* that way sometimes," an old blues lyric goes; Tolson syncopates his passages by erratic line lengths strung on a central axis, thus propelling our eye down the page while stopping us up on short lines:

> The school of the artist
> is
> the circle of wild horses,
> heads centered,
> as they present to the wolves
> a battery of heels . . .

Harlem Gallery is composed according to Tolson's **"S-Trinity of Parnassus"**—the melding of sound, sight and sense. Sound refers to the oral nature of the poem—"Just as sound, / not spelling, / is the white magic of rhyming in the poet's feat. . . ." Tolson meant for his lines to be read aloud; the visual impact of the centered lines contributes to the forward thrust that a lively oral recitation would possess. "Sense" refers to both meaning and the sensory aspect of language.

Tolson's extravagant verbiage pays homage to the essence of "style"—he mixes colloquial and literary references as well as diction; irony and pathos, slapstick and pontification sit side-by-side. And if we look closely at **Harlem Gallery's** dazzling array of allusions—one component of what Sarah Webster Fabio calls Tolson's "vast, bizarre, pseudo-literary diction,"—we find no favoritism for any social or cultural group. . . . If anything, Tolson is deliberately complicating our pre-conceived notions of cultural—and, by further implication, existential—order.

Even the title of Tolson's poem can be taken a thousand different ways. Its primary meaning—the art gallery in Harlem which the Curator runs—is embellished by a host of secondary connotations: 1) the peanut gallery (cheaper balcony seats in a movie theater, where blacks were relegated in segregated establishments); 2) the art gallery as symbol, suggesting a reading of the poem as a series of *portraits* (an earlier Tolson work, *A Gallery of Harlem Portraits,* is similar to Mister Starks's *Harlem Vignettes* in that it is more a collection of portraits than a tale); 3) the sense of gallery as a promenade; Tolson's characters certainly "exhibit" themselves, and Tolson makes a case for the hero as stylist; for Hideho Heights, Mister Starks, the Curator and Doctor Nkomo, style *is* being. This importance of "style" finds its more popular counterparts in the lyrics of James Brown and the hot "cool" image of Prince; you make do with what you got, you take an inch and run with it. As Ronald Walcott says in his essay "Ellison, Gordone and Tolson: Some Notes on the Blues, Style and Space":

> For Melvin Tolson, the victories attainable through style are not only real, considerable and worthy of record, but they are indicative as well of his people's invincible sense of the possible. . . ; style, if one takes it seriously as an expression of vision, *is* substance, insofar as it reflects and determines one's experience, assessment and response being what experience, after all, is about.

Harlem Gallery is not merely a showcase for Tolson's linguistic and lyrical virtuosity; neither is it a hodge-podge of anecdotes and small lives set like cameos in the heavy silver of philosophical discourse. It is to be viewed *not* as the superficial "Sugar Hill elite" inspect the art works hanging at the exhibition in the Curator's gallery. Rather, the lives of John Laugart, Hideho Heights and Mister Starks should be seen as illustrations of the three possibilities/alternatives for the black artist. One can embrace the Bitch-Goddess Success (personified by Hedda Stark/"Black Orchid"), as did Mister Starks: "My talent was an Uptown whore," he says of himself, "my wit a Downtown pimp." One can, like Laugart, remain uncompromising and be spurned by one's own. Or one can lead a double life, producing crowd-pleasers (which don't necessarily have to lack aesthetic principles) while creating in secrecy the works one hopes will last. The Curator discovers Hideho's double life one night when he takes the poet home, dead-drunk in a taxi; on the table the Curator discovers a poem "in the modern idiom" called *E. and O.E.*—which happens to be the title of a psychological poem for which Tolson received *Poetry* magazine's Bess Hokin award in 1952.

Where does Tolson place himself in this "trinity that stinks the ermine robes"? Certainly not with Mister Starks, although he is sympathetic to Starks's weakness. And, similarities notwithstanding, he does not identify himself with the Poet Laureate of Harlem. Although he admires Hideho's flair and to a great extent believes in Heights's aesthetic manifesto ("A work of art is a two-way street, / not a dead end, / where an artist and a hipster meet. / The form and content in a picture or a song / should blend like the vowels in a diphthong . . .") Tolson certainly didn't hide his "difficult" poems from the public.

Tolson's meditation on the plight of the black American artist emerges most vividly in **"Psi."** The Curator sees his place in America quite clearly. "Black Boy," he begins, "let me get up from the white man's Table of Fifty Sounds / in the kitchen; let me gather the crumbs and cracklings / of this autobio-fragment / before the curtain with the skull and bones descends." The kitchen is the place for servants, but it is also the place where scraps of song and gossip blend to become a marvellous "kitchen talk."

Paradoxically it is John Laugart, the artist given least space in *Harlem Gallery,* who most exemplifies Tolson's own sense of artistic responsibility. And though Tolson didn't die destitute and anonymous—in fact, he received the annual poetry award of the American Academy of Arts and Letters a few months before his death in 1966—he was misunderstood by many of those he loved most, by those to whom he dedicated his energies in the creation of his last work—the black intellectuals. No one understood this predicament better than Tolson himself. As he has the Curator say near the end of *Harlem Gallery:*

> Poor Boy Blue,
> the Great White World
> and the Black Bourgeoisie
> have shoved the Negro Artist into
> the white and non-white dichotomy,
> the Afroamerican dilemma in the Arts—
> the dialectic of
> to be or not to be
> a Negro.

Mariann B. Russell (essay date 1986)

SOURCE: "Evolution of Style in the Poetry of Melvin B. Tolson," in *Black American Poets Between Worlds, 1940-1960,* edited by R. Baxter Miller, University of Tennessee Press, 1986, pp. 1-18.

[*In the following essay, Russell analyzes the progression of Tolson's thought and style throughout his career.*]

The consideration of Melvin Tolson's evolving style concerns the maturation of his thought. Here I concentrate on his epic form and his developing perspective. I shall first generalize about his worldview and then trace the development of the hero figure, for both processes set into relief the stylistic growth. The examination includes less the discussion of metrics and figurative language than the concern for poetics in the deepest sense.

Tolson writes: "A great preacher is a great artist. Words are his tubes of paint. Verse, his brush." These sentences go far to explain the poetics of the speaker. He does not belong to that stream of Anglo-American poetry which is purely lyric, expressing directly and mellifluously the poet's own emotions. He concerns himself, on the contrary, with social issues as the barebones of life. His style comes closer to oratorical rhetoric than to song, and his poem is generally public rather than confessional.

The son of a "fighting preacher"—"I used to watch my Dad in the pulpit and feel proud . . ."—Tolson was himself a great speaker and debate coach as well as a director of theater. Concerned with the underdog in general and with the Black underdog in particular, he saw words as weapons in the war against social ills. Closely linked to the Afro-American oral tradition and the personal commitment to fighting injustice, he shaped a Christo-Marxist worldview. As in the poetry of others during the thirties, his lyric encompassed a social, metaphysical, and communal burden.

> **The immediate model for *Portraits* is the *Spoon River Anthology* volume, which attempts to tell "the story of an American country town so as to make it the story of the world."**
> **—*Mariann B. Russell***

Over the years he had four books of poetry published. The first, written about 1934, was brought out posthumously. *A Gallery of Harlem Portraits,* as it was called, contained verses about Harlemites. His next book was *Rendezvous with America,* a collection somewhat influenced by World War II; his third volume, *Libretto for the Republic of Liberia,* was written after he had been chosen the poet-laureate of the country so named. In "academic" style the booklength ode celebrates the African nation. His final volume, *Harlem Gallery,* was another booklength ode, intended as the beginning of an epic about the American Black.

Before undertaking any discussion of the first book, it would be helpful to outline Tolson's cultural theory. His poetry begins with his life experience, which he mulls over, talks over, and subsumes into his phenomenally eclectic reading. Then he transmutes the whole into verse. For the talented and intellectually probing college professor in the Southwest and West from 1923 to 1965, racial discrimination and prejudice were abiding concerns. A Jim Crow existence provoked direct protest and probing into human nature. The Marxist interpretation became a focal point of his thought.

Tolson's epic intention persists in varying forms. In a world that is class-divided and economically determined, the exploited masses become crucial. The underdog, the despised, the poor appear heroic now and foreshadow even greater heroism after the establishment of a new society. Tolson, sometimes ironically, celebrates the human potential embodied in the voiceless majority of the underprivileged.

The masses, in their human potential, become an abstract ideal, a generic hero. But Tolson finds individual nations such as America and Liberia heroic in the present promise and in the future apocalypse. Individual characters who are heroic include persons like Crispus Attucks and Paul Bunyan as well as the poet-prophet, the "ape of God." In one way or another, such various heroes inform his epics.

But Tolson is not merely an epic poet looking for an epic hero. His perspective encourages the epic search, since he proposes the great man theory of history. In his newspaper columns he asserts that geniuses improve humanity's lot. He cites poets, prophets, and scholars as specific types through whose efforts humankind comes to understand and ultimately reform its condition. His early books portray many political and social reformers as well as folk heroes as appropriate instruments. In the last book, he shifts to the poet-prophet, the true artist in any mode, as the necessary means to social equality.

The first book, *Portraits,* responds to the remark by a fellow student, himself German-American: "Say, we've never had a Negro epic." Tolson finds precedent for the genre in the Anglo-American literary heritage. His models are, among others, Longfellow, Whittier, Milton, Tennyson, and Poe. His Tennyson is not the melancholy lyricist, but the poet who envisages "the Parliament of man." Tolson emphasizes the Donne of "no man is an island" rather than the metaphysical poet. Edwin Markham and Langston Hughes, mentors and friends, embody the American populist tradition in white and Black. Literature as well as life fostered his epic intention.

The immediate model for *Portraits* is the *Spoon River Anthology* volume, which attempts to tell "the story of an American country town so as to make it the story of the world." Tolson wants to fashion the story of Harlem into a metaphor for the Afro-American. The technique, an extended synecdoche, "gives . . . Negro America its comedy and tragedy in prismatic epitome" ("Notebooks"). His Harlem becomes metonymically the "mecca," "city of refuse," "Nigger-Heaven," "City of Refuge," and "Capital of the Negro world."

When Tolson presents in *Portraits* approximately two hundred characters significant of the Black community, his worldview becomes clear. The tragicomic tone emanates from the assumption that "the basis of racial prejudice in the United States is economic." He sees the Harlem community, with its great variety of types, classes, and colors, not as the exotic area of "jungle-bunny" fame but as the subject of an "earthy, unromantic and sociological literature." Throughout the book, indirectly and sometimes directly, Tolson advocates the union of the masses, poor white and poor Black, as the solution to racial and class discrimination. The final goal of proletarian unity is an apocalyptic democracy—classless, multiracial, multicultural—an attainable utopia.

The hero of *Portraits* is the "underdog," who might some day understand and assume his own destiny. Those Harlemites who already have such knowledge are more directly heroic. The group includes Big Jim Casey and Zip Lightner, proletarian heroes who live for the union of Black and white workers. But the particularly flawed hero is Vergil Ragsdale who, as his name suggests, is the poet of the people. He shares their exploited condition. Though there are more effective artists, he appears at greatest length. His perspective may most approximate Tolson's view then:

> "Harlem, O Harlem,
> City of the Big Niggers,
> Graveyard of the Dark Masses,
> Soapbox of the Red Apocalypse. . . ."

Sustained by gin and cocaine, Vergil, the dishwasher at Manto's cafe, dreams of completing his epic poem to Harlem. Although he truly foresees his own pathetic death from tuberculosis, he does not predict the real tragedy: an ignorant landlady will burn the poem, his raison d'être, as trash. Still, this character articulates and represents his people's condition as well as imagines their retribution. His life is ambiguous, as is his heroism.

The style of these poems suits Tolson's epic intention. Characters, presented in short vignettes of about a page, represent the great variety of Harlem humanity, from Peg Leg Snelson to Mrs. Alpha Devine to the Black Moses. As with the poems in *Spoon River,* each of these short ones ends with a climax, a dramatic event, a revelation, a statement, or, in many instances, a blues verse. Tolson, influenced by the imagists, relies on presentation more than on commentary. The larger poetic structure of the entire book, however, lacks variety as poem after poem is introduced mechanically. The diction characterizes occasionally the people in dialect and blues, but the larger voice is the narrator's. The latter speaks of the "little man" as victim but assumes an appreciative tone. The poem presents nobly the techniques of survival in a blues style.

Tolson's next book, *Rendezvous with America,* continues the epic intention in a different vein. As the author broadens his thematic concerns from Harlem to various places in America and to the world at large, the social concerns deepen. The subject here is man—Black and white—as re-

vealed through economics, sociology, and psychology. But the heroes are still political and artistic. Such poets as Sandburg and Whitman set precedents for Tolson's celebration of human potential, despite the actual corruption, inequality, and injustice in still flawed America. Democracy, true justice, and multiculture continue to engage him: "These States breed freedom in and in my bone: / I hymn their virtues and their sins atone."

The epic strain here is less obvious than in *Portraits.* Under the impetus of World Ward II, Tolson sees good and evil written large in human affairs. Celebration of American promise and human potential go hand in hand with the praise of such historical figures as Nat Turner, Frederick Douglass, and Harriet Tubman. The book is replete with heroic figures (and some villains) who become symbolic in the literary context—Daniel Boone, Joe Dimaggio, Thomas Paine, Abraham Lincoln, and many more.

How then do these hymns to America and humanity differ from the art in Rockefeller Center during the 1930s or from Fourth of July oratory? Although the poetry emphasizes American ideals, it escapes from being merely patriotic encomia. The poetry is skillfully grounded in realistic observation. In many poems from **"Ex-Judge at the Bar"** to **"Vesuvius,"** Tolson illustrates the "idols of the tribe"—those deliberately fostered myths of race, caste, and class that separate mankind. His optimism takes root in the faith that the masses will eventually see through the snares, shams, and hypocrisies to a republican ideal. His ironic—sometimes satiric—tone works against any blind faith in the American dream; he reveals frequently through incident, character, or animal imagery the gulf between the dream and reality.

By now he has worked out for himself a poetic ideal. He refers to the "'3 S's of Parnassus'—Sight, Sound, and Sense." Sight concerns the look of a poem on a page. He experiments frequently with centered placement, especially of short lines, to emphasize his point. At other times he works a short line against a longer one for visual effect. His second "S" refers to sound. Sensitive to the ear, he writes poetry to be read aloud—he seldom uses an eye-rhyme. His frequent use of parallelism encompasses both sound and sight. The last "S" means "sense," meaning and imagination—chiefly the use of figurative language. Tolson's tropes depend on often startling associations or similarities, frequently using personifications and synechdoche to link seemingly opposed realities in a kind of imaginative dialectic.

Some examples of Tolson's figurative language appear in the long title poem, **"Rendezvous with America":** "his bat cuts a vacuum," "surfed in white acclaim," "scaling the Alpine ranges of drama with the staff of song," "blue-printing the cabala of the airways," "imprisoning the magic of symphonies with a baton," "enwombing the multiple soul of the New World." Although some of these metaphors are not entirely satisfactory, they do illustrate the quality and kind of Tolson's imagery.

To see the effect of this aesthetic ideal—the sight, sound, meaning, and language of a poem beautifully meshed—I shall consider another of *Rendezvous'* long poems, **"Dark Symphony,"** in detail. On the surface, Tolson's theme merely transforms the cliché of the melting pot into the ono-matopoeia of symphonic movement. Called an ode by Joy Flasch, the poem has six sections, each with a different musical direction. The first part, three quatrains long, *Allegro Moderato,* moves visually down the page like a series of "s's." The long line, the short line to the left, and the long line, short line to the right, play against each other. While the metric scheme has the long lines in each stanza and the short lines rhyming, the initial line of each stanza does not do so. There is some alliteration.

In such a poem the names Crispus Attucks and Patrick Henry are expected but not so the lines, "the vertical / Transmitting cry," and "No Banquo's ghost can rise / Against us now." Such obvious metaphors as "the juggernauts of despotism" and "hobnailed Man" and "thorns of greed / On Labor's brow" are offset by "dust is purged to create brotherhood." The stanzas are controlled through their parallel structure and by the musical movement.

The next section, *"Lento Grave,"* details the pathos of those who perform spirituals emblematic of their condition:

> Black slaves singing *One More River to Cross*
> In the torture tombs of slave-ships,
> Black slaves singing *Steal Away to Jesus*
> In jungle swamps.

Here again Tolson controls rhythm through the musical direction and the parallel structure, as one line of each couplet, the "Black slaves," ends with the title of a spiritual; the following line indicates the symbolic place where it is sung.

The third section, *"Andante Sostenuto,"* counterpoints the previous stanza's slave songs to Psalm 136 (137 in Protestant bibles), which calls to mind the Jewish Babylonian captivity. Each of the three stanzas opens and closes with a repetend, the first two with "They tell us to forget," and the third with "Oh, how can we forget?" Here the expected indictment of racial discrimination in America occurs, but the effective Biblical echo and analogue transcend mere cliché; "They who have shackled us / Require of us a song" recalls Psalm 136. The climactic, "Oh, how can we forget" recalls

the Psalmist's "How could we sing a song of the Lord in a foreign land?"

The fourth part, with the direction *"Tempo Primo,"* turns to the New Negro, "Hard-muscled, Fascist-hating, Democracy ensouled," who becomes an ideal of Democracy through his identification with Afro-American heroes. This generic Black signifies his race's contribution by referring to the work done by the slave and free Black masses throughout American history. Their contributions appear in the parallel structure which controls the Whitmanesque categories of Black labor. The section ends with the inevitable stanza showing the New Negro's striding toward the Promised Land of Tomorrow.

"Larghetto," the fifth section, returns to the first section's satire on white lip service to Democracy. The repetend in each of the four sestets exempts Blacks from particular hypocrisies: "None in the Land can say / To us black men Today."

The final section's *March Tempo* works well through the stanzas of iambic tetrameter and the oft-repeated short line, "We advance!" recalling **"The Underdog"** in the call to unite. In **"Dark Symphony,"** with the irregular rhyme schemes, varied meters, repetitions, and word placements on the page, Tolson illuminates the stock subjects, at least for Black poets during the twenties and thirties. For him, such topics shape themselves into the art epic.

Throughout **Rendezvous,** with few exceptions (there are very few private poems), Tolson practices oratorical rhetoric and evinces social concern. Here the reader encounters a variety of styles in the four long poems, **"Rendezvous with America," "Dark Symphony," "Of Men and Cities,"** and **"Tapestries of Time."** There is still greater experimentation in the short poems grouped in sections including free verse, Shakespearean sonnet, ballad, and ballade. One poem in iambic monometer, **"Song for Myself,"** is a poetic tour de force, as the diversity in poetic forms increases.

Even where there may be a dramatic incident, or a striking character in the short poems, it has a parabolic effect in building to a climax. The effective **"Ballad of the Rattlesnake"** is framed by another poem which portrays Black and white sharecroppers. Although they extend now beyond the specific Harlem community, Tolson's concerns remain now in the deeper structure, the same as those in *Portraits* earlier, but they take shape in both conventional and unconventional metrics. In the long and more complex poems, he uses devices that are both poetic and oratorical, including repetition with variation, striking metaphors, and wide-ranging allusions. He subsumes the Black sermon into the artistic voice, and it readdresses the cultural concern. The rhetorical triangle which binds the folk source, the independent imagination, and the appreciative audience continues unbroken.

Besides the American promise and the proletarian expectation, there is another heroic element. Here appears the figure of the bard. "The Poet" portrays a generalized figure who, though largely disregarded in his time, looks uncaringly into the nature of things:

> An Ishmaelite
> He breaks the icons of the Old and New
> . . . .
> The poet's lien exempts the Many nor the Few

and

> A champion of the People versus Kings—
> His only martyrdom is poetry:
> A hater of the hierarchy of things—
> Freedom's need is his necessity.

The proud "Ishmaelite" and "anchoret" intuits a "bright new world." Heroic in insight, he dedicates himself to the communication of his vision, which penetrates custom. He reincarnates the Vergil Ragsdale figure, but without the same locale and pathetic circumstances. In *Rendezvous* the Ethiopian Bard of Addis Ababa is equally a kind of prophet. From insight into contemporaneity, he foresees the "bright new world." Lyric vision and social celebration merge.

> His name is an emblem of justice
> Greater than *lumot* of priest
> . . . .
> The seven league boots of his images
> Stir the palace and marketplace.

These two, poet and prophet, fuse in Tolson's great man or genius. Tolson saw heroes and villains as representative of human potential for greatness and evil. To serve this social vision, his style evolved with many of the characteristics of oratorical rhetoric.

During his time spent at Columbia University (1931-32) and Greenwich Village (1930s), Tolson became acquainted with the first wave of the moderns represented by Sandburg, Hughes, and Masters. On his own he discovered Eliot's *The Waste Land* and later Crane's *The Bridge* which, according to Mrs. Tolson, "showed her husband that he was 'on the wrong road.'" He therefore set out, still on his own, to come to terms with this academic style:

> Imitation must be in technique only. We have a rich heritage of folklore and history. We are a part of America. We are a part of the world. Our native symbols must be lifted into the universal. Yes, we

must study the techniques of Robert Lowell, Dylan Thomas, Carlos Williams, Ezra Pound, Karl Shapiro, W. H. Auden. The greatest revolution has not been in science but in poetry. We must study such magazines as *Partisan Review,* the *Sewanee Review, Accent,* the *Virginia Quarterly.* We must read such critics as Crowe Ransom, Allen Tate, Stephen Spender, George Dillon and Kenneth Burke.

In the period between the publication of *Rendezvous* and the writing of *Libretto,* Tolson included in his eclectic reading the moderns who set the tone of the two decades between the world wars. The reading and the public occasion of Liberia's centenary resulted in the style and content of *Libretto.* In the poem packed with Eliotic notes, we have Tolson's venture in a style aimed at the literary caviar.

Here his view extends from Liberia and Africa to the world. The hero is, symbolically, Liberia, one of only two uncolonized nations in Africa then. Tolson reflects on this historical fact, on Liberia's contribution to Allied efforts in World War II, and on the history of this republic founded by American Blacks freed from slavery; he therefore celebrates its national identity. The epic qualities from *Portraits* and *Rendezvous* reappear here in a different context. Liberia, historically exploited by France and England, aids these two countries by supplying rubber and providing airports during the war. The campaign against "fascists" becomes almost a holy war. Liberia, the name and motto signifying freedom, emerges as both real and symbolic. Transcending racial and economic biases, it foreshadows Africa's triumph in the world. Tolson thus fuses epic material and "academic" style.

The poem is either an ode or a series of eight odes. The titles of metrically varying sections range the diatonic scale from "Do" to "Do." The sections are thematically and symbolically interconnected in the ode form:

> Metrically, the term ode usually implies considerable freedom in the introduction of varied rhythmic movements and irregularities of verse-length and rhyme-distribution. There is something "oratorical" about a true ode; and its irregularities may be conceived of as produced by its adaptation to choric rendition or to public declamation, either actual or imagined. . . . Primarily, it [ode] refers to the content and spirit of a poem, implying a certain largeness of thought, continuity of theme, and exalted feeling.

Tolson, faced with the problem of writing an occasional poem about a little-known nation, turns deliberately to the ancient form.

Besides the real and symbolic Liberia, there is a lesser heroic image in the poet-visionary. Because for Tolson man complexly fuses the biological, the sociological, and the psychological, only the Ishmaelite poet knows him deeply. Knowing humanity, historical and contemporary, the poet-prophet discerns the future. Tolson embodies human history in the ferris wheel symbol, which subsumes empires and nations. They rise and fall, alternating decadence and "bright new beginnings." To escape the cyclic nature of power, Tolson asserts through the protagonist that humankind must advance teleologically to a classless utopia. Liberia therefore marks the vanguard, the poet-prophet being instrumental to the movement.

The style reveals a formal polish and philosophical weight in a broad reference which requires pages of notes. Some elements descend directly from earlier techniques, such as Tolson's love of word play, his use of neologism, and his extensive allusions. Once more he uses parallel structure to control the verse. Such elements, all subject to the "3 S's," mark the Tolsonian style.

The first and final "Do" illuminate the manner. The first sets out the principal themes in the attempt to define the meaning of Liberia. A centered question, "Liberia?" highlights the dominant image. In each eight-line stanza, there follows a negation of some cliché: "microfootnote," "barker's bio-accident," "pimple on the chin of Africa," "caricature with a mimic flag," and "wasteland" (Europe) or "destooled elite" (Africa). After a denial, the fifth line in each stanza recenters the definition around the repetend "You are." In regular rhyme-schemes the metrically irregular verses relate Liberia to Europe as lightning rod and Canaan's key and "The rope across the abyss. . . ." Images abound as definition proceeds; Liberia is a metonym spatially to "The Orient of Colors everywhere," philosophically to *"Liberatas* flayed and naked by the road," mythically to "Black Lazarus risen from the White Man's grave," and nationally to "American genius uncrowned in Europe's charnel-house." The final two lines indicate how the nation eludes logical definition: "Liberia and not Liberia, / A moment of the conscience of mankind!"

The poem, unlike earlier ones, minimizes direct, hortatory rhetoric. Allusions help structure and codify meanings. Here the tagends of quotation as well as infusions from different languages including Spanish, French, German, Italian, Latin, Russian, Greek, Turkish, and Hebrew, complicate a line already abstruse. So do the African languages. Symbols like the *Hohere,* the ferris wheel, the merry-go-round, and the tiny republic enrich the verse.

The first section reveals the tone and many of the poetic devices which recur throughout the verse. Liberia has survived the exploitation of Western colonizers. Although its freedom is "flayed and naked," the ideal lives on in promise.

"Liberia and not Liberia," the dialectic, the tension of opposites plays throughout the ode. It leads from the initial poem of definition through those which describe the nation's founding (**"Mi," "Sol," "La,"**) to the relationship to France, Britain, and the United States (**"Fa," "Ti"**). Finally, it widens to classic African civilization (**"Re"**) and the masses everywhere (**"Ti"** and *passim*). Tolson resolves the tension in "Africa-To-Be" (second **"Do"** and *passim*).

In the long last section (**"Do"**), Tolson crafts languages and symbols into a vision of Africa's bright future. Through the metaphors of the automobile, train, and ship, as well as the airplane, he aesthetically transports Liberia, Africa, and the world to an apocalyptic Pluralism. Africa saves itself as well as Europe, America, and Australia. Africa achieves the cosmopolis, *Hohere,* through the United African Nations' cooperation in "polygenetic metropolises polychromatic." The Parliament of African Peoples redeems both the elite and the masses.

The final **"Do"** sums up the significance of the Liberian experience. It evokes the future in verse that changes from sestet through staggered unrhymed couplets, to centered patterns and finally to prose poetry. The final **"Do"** thickens with fragments in different languages, references to African as well as European and American thought. Why does the ode, despite the chillingly simple poem, **"Fa"** (ominous in its simplicity), end in prose paragraphs? Possibly, oratory and Tolson's notion of climax coincide here.

The entire ode moves to a climax as each of the eight sections achieves a minor affirmation. While the first **"Do"** climaxes in the symbolic definition ("A moment of the conscience of mankind"), the final **"Do"** declares a new beginning ("the Rosh Hashana of the Africa calends"). And it silences doubters: *"'Honi soit qui mal y pense!'"* Yet Tolson does not deny the corruption in society and the individual. While "profit" and "avarice" continue, the masses are on a merry-go-round of the "unparadised" who have nowhere to go. The gorged snake, the bird of prey, and the tiger wait in a false peace to strike again. And African nations still wear "Nessus shirts from Europe on their backs."

Tolson's last book of poetry, *Harlem Gallery,* fuses the early subject matter of *Portraits* with his later techniques. Although he presents mechanically more than two hundred Harlemites in *Portraits,* he abandons the strategy here in favor of a much more dynamic one. A number of poems are thematically integrated into the one irregular ode. A different letter of the Greek alphabet labels each of the twenty-four poems in order, just as the names of notes mark *Libretto.* Both poems work toward a signed and structured climax.

The ode incorporates Tolson's epic principle. He has viewed

Harlem Gallery: Book I, the Curator as the first of five works that would delineate Afro-American history from the African origins to the contemporary world. He has intended to "analogize the history of the Hebrew people in the episodes of the Old Testament as regards persons, places, and events. The dominant idea of the *Harlem Gallery* will be manifest." According to the plan, Book II, Egypt Land, is to be an analogue for the Slave Trade and Southern Bondage; Book III, the Red Sea, an analogue for the Civil War; Book IV, The Wilderness, an analogue for Reconstruction, and Book V, The Promised Land, an analogue for the race's present existence: "a gallery of highbrows and middlebrows and lowbrows against the ethnological panorama of contemporary America."

In *Portraits* the once-mentioned Curator places the book's characters on his gallery walls. His voice is unheard throughout the book. The protagonist in *Libretto* speaks in the two **"Do's"** and possibly throughout the entire ode, but the primary text does not develop him. In *Harlem Gallery* the Curator is continually present. Here, too, he has his gallery, though his paintings do not represent the characters in the ode.

While the protagonist in *Libretto* is undramatized throughout the ode, the Curator is a real persona, appearing in significant places like the Zulu Club, meditating on art and life, and interacting with various others. His gallery, though symbolic, is real with regents, gallery-goers, pictures on the four walls, and real curators. The last ones include himself and his alter-ego, Dr. Obi Nkomo. Tolson combines the Curator in *Portraits,* a speaker who is scarcely even a framing device, and the protagonist in *Libretto,* possibly the consciousness through which the poem is played. This evolution marks the current curator.

The Harlem Gallery is a firmer and more centralized metaphor than was Liberia. Harlem appears less now through representation than through evocation. As with Liberia and America in the earlier books, the area is both place and symbol. It maintains historicity but assumes a larger meaning. Although the numbers of characters are fewer, major figures are more deeply probed. Harlem the social place becomes Harlem the human type.

The figures of Vergil Ragsdale (*Portraits*), the poet, Good Grey Bard (*Rendezvous*), and the Bard of Timbuktu (*Libretto*) become fused and enlarged here. The artists evoke both their personal and public lives. The division between private failure and public assurance in the aesthetic vocation, evident even in Ragsdale, appears uniquely human. Harlem, a nexus of Afro-American artist-heroes, shares the inhabitants' ambivalent and tragicomic blues. The inhabitants suit well the modern epic:

in this race, at this time, in this place,
   to be a Negro artist is to be
a flower of the gods, whose growth
   is dwarfed at an early stage—
     a Brazilian owl moth,
a giant among his own in an acreage
   dark with the darkman's designs,
where the milieu moves back downward like the
sloth.

Tolson even maintains the abstract hero and symbolizes Art itself, but the hero no longer strides with the masses toward an apocalyptic new earth. Tolson has his concept of an economically determined world transmuted by true art. The true artist foreshadows the new world not as the "Futurafrique" (*Libretto*), but as the "dusk of dawn." The artistic subsumes the political. Art, like John Laugart's "Black Bourgeoisie," so long as authentic, becomes sanative.

The style of the ode is more dynamic than that in *Libretto.* The new mode, with allusiveness and complexity of metaphor, image and symbol, excludes verbiage. Here emerge greater mastery and flexibility. The poems project their themes through a flux of character, interaction, and talk. The peripatetic Curator goes to Laugart's apartment, Aunt Grindle's Chitterling Shop, the Harlem Gallery, and the Zulu Club. He hears or knows about the happenings at the police station, the Haha Club, and the Angelus Funeral Home. His wanderings focus the geography of Harlem. His thoughts about the characters, life, and art are projected in both discursive and narrative cantos. At once a dramatic persona and an undramatized prophet like Eliot's Tiresias, he represents the consciousness through which the ode is played. In a sense he "makes" the "autobio-fragment"—the ode itself—literally humanize intellect and oratory. The poem ends then with the achievement of the metonym:

The allegro of the Harlem Gallery
   is not a chippy fire,
for here, in focus, are paintings that chronicle
   a people's New World odyssey
     from chattel to Esquire!

Some indication of how Tolson's poem works can be seen in the first canto. In **"Alpha,"** one hears the voice of the Curator for the first time. The basic symbols appear in the first two lines:

The Harlem Gallery, an Afric pepper bird,
   awakes me at a people's dusk of dawn.

The Harlem Gallery, like the pepper bird native to Africa, stirs the Curator to action. He must envision the ode, the "autobio-fragment," at a people's dusk of dawn, the transition between night and morning symbolically figuring a new socio-economic age. Here the Afro-American will attain his full stature. The ode itself will both prophetically and aesthetically help to usher this in.

Perhaps *Harlem Gallery* is not exclusively for the elite. Here one reads and enjoys with persistence more than with erudition.
—*Mariann B. Russell*

Then the poem evokes some Third World challenges to the "Great White World," the former being the social equivalent to the Curator's craft. Introspectively, the Curator turns to himself, faces the task, and sees himself as flawed, being comic where seriousness is called for, being serious when comedy is required. He shares humankind's meandering approach to the necessary search for true freedom. He envisions the task again, now hearing "a dry husk-of-locust" blues asking "Black Boy, O Black Boy, / is the port worth the cruise?" Inhibitions based on self-doubt harden the task; to maintain the integrity of self, humanity, and race proves nearly too much. The "clockbird's jackass laughter" haunts his effort. Challenged by the pepper bird, but mocked by the clockbird, he reveals the spirit of transitional man in a transitional world.

As in **"Alpha"** the entire ode centers in irregular rhyme, internal rhyme, alliteration, assonance, and consonance. Major symbols in the ode, such as Harlem Gallery, African pepper bird, Dusk of Dawn, and clockbird, recur now. The Buridan's ass and "the gaffing *To ti*" have appeared earlier in different genres, but images of the Hambletonian gathering for a leap, the apples of Cain, and barrel cactus are fresh. Here closes the decade long evolution in his worldview as an Afro-American, for his craft subsumes and perfects his oratory.

But with an epic intention, why does he abandon the folk model for the academic one? Why, if so committed to the Black and white masses, does he write in the style of the literary elite?

Perhaps *Harlem Gallery* is not exclusively for the elite. Here one reads and enjoys with persistence more than with erudition. Or, maybe Tolson regards the style as a criterion of excellence. Perhaps he wants to master the technique but to maintain his Afro-American experience. A final answer comes from Tolson, himself one of the "crafty masters of social conscience":

> Today
> The Few
> Yield Poets
> Their due;

> Tomorrow
> The Mass
> Judgment
> Shall Pass.

Michael Bérubé (essay date January 1990)

SOURCE: "Masks, Margins, and African American Modernism: Melvin Tolson's *Harlem Gallery*," in *PMLA*, Vol. 105, No. 1, January, 1990, pp. 57-69.

[*In the following essay, Bérubé discusses Tolson's work in relation to African-American modernism.*]

Harlem Gallery has been alternately celebrated and castigated for its formal difficulty—when, that is, it has been read at all. Yet although the poem is as formidable as any hypertextual text produced by the throes of modernism—saving *Finnegans Wake*—there seems something amiss in the idea that its difficulty should be a significant issue in itself; surely, by now, allusive, elliptical poetry should not be grounds for controversy. Still, even if the grounds are questionable, they are by no means powerless. Readers have apparently found the poem so generally inaccessible that publishers have followed suit and rendered it literally inaccessible, for even in the midst of the current revolution in African American letters, *Harlem Gallery* has quietly gone out of print.

More to the point, however, Tolson's poetic technique *has* been controversial, appropriately or not, insofar as it has been taken as evidence of Tolson's wrongheaded emulation of T. S. Eliot. And on this count, to be sure, some of the confusion can be traced directly to Tolson: he himself spoke repeatedly of Eliot's poetry as if it were somehow historically inevitable, as if its "revolution" were at once totalizing and irreversible. He writes, for example, in a 1955 book review that "when T. S. Eliot published *The Waste Land* in 1922, it sounded the death knell of Victorianism, Romanticism, and Didacticism. When Eliot was awarded the Nobel Prize in Literature, the victory of the moderns was complete. The modern idiom is here to stay—like modern physics." The curious terms of Tolson's certainty are worth noting—poetry and physics are construed here as analogously developmental disciplines whose paradigm shifts obliterate all that has gone before—but even more curious is the focus on Eliot's Nobel Prize as the sign of modernism's "victory." It is small wonder, therefore, that *Harlem Gallery*'s more hostile critics read Tolson as if he were simply out of touch, a late modernist writing in the midst of the black aesthetic of the sixties. Only after the Nobel Prize was awarded to Eliot, apparently, did Tolson decide that modernism would leave behind the poets who did not confront and assimilate it. Accordingly, his reaction, self-consciously belated, seems something of an overcompensation: witness his declaration, in a 1948 commencement address at a small black college in Kentucky, that

> [n]ow the time has come for a New Negro Poetry for the New Negro. The most difficult thing to do today is to write modern poetry. Why? It is the acme of the intellectual. Longfellow, Whittier, Milton, Tennyson, and Poe are no longer the poets held in high repute. The standard of poetry has changed completely. Negroes must become aware of this. This is the age of T. S. Eliot who has just won the Nobel Prize in Literature.

This speech seems to me at least as striking as his review of seven years later—not only for its commitment to the politics and poetics of assimilation but for the thoroughness of its adoption of modernist polemics; his dismissal of Milton and Tennyson is an especially accurate touch. And sure enough, in his "New Negro Poetry"—"E. & O.E." in 1951 and *Libretto for the Republic of Liberia* in 1953—he deliberately and pedantically suggests his affiliation with *The Waste Land* by appending to each poem pages of footnotes, like Eliot's both explanatory and obscure. But despite such testimony, I intend to show that the crux of the work lies not in whether it is an artifact of African American modernism but in what it has to say about modernism's relation to African American literature. And if we read the poem in this way, we find that, for all its vaunted "modernism," its central argument turns on—of all things—a parable. That "argument," as we will see, seeks to demonstrate that resistance to modernism, in the form of a black separatist poetics, is a cultural stance impossible to maintain; and the "parable" is the extempore ballad of the sea turtle and the shark recited by Hideho Heights, the populist "poet laureate of Lenox Avenue" in **"Phi,"** the twenty-first of the poem's twenty-four irregular odes, each entitled a letter of the Greek alphabet.

I

Before I turn to the parable, however, I want to sketch out its position in the poem; for if we are to retrieve the subversive force of Hideho's ballad, we need first to retrieve the dominant discourse and ideology his ballad threatens to subvert. In *Harlem Gallery,* the predominant voice is that of the Curator, whose romantic/modernist vision of art holds not only that an authentic art must disturb and thereby transform its immediate audience but also that art's value lies in resistance to and concomitant transcendence of history, ideology, and the material base that creates or enables various conditions of reception—including, in one representative passage, the passing parade of PhDs:

> In Chronos Park
> the Ars-powered ferris wheel revolves
> through golden age and dark
> as historied isms rise and fall
> and the purple of the doctor's robe
> (ephemeral as the flesh color of the fame flower)
> is translated into the coffin's pall.

Thus, in his moments of crisis as the gallery's curator—when he feels torn from his ideally disinterested role by the demands of the gallery's audience or its regents—he consoles himself with a version of Yeats's tragic gaiety; and the weight of his argument falls, specifically, on the work of the French avant-garde of the late nineteenth and early twentieth centuries:

> Then O then, O ruins,
> I remember
> the alien hobnails
> of that cross-nailing Second of September
> did not crush like a mollusk's shell,
> in café and studio,
> the *élan* of Courbet, Cézanne, and Monet,
> nor did the self-deadfall of the Maginot
> palsy the hand of Chagall,
> Matisse,
> and Picasso.

Such is the Curator's cultural position: he is a champion of art, especially experimental art, for the reason that art is a profound affirmation and consolation, a basso continuo in the threnody of human history. It is a theory of art—and of art's relation to history—with which we are, no doubt, thoroughly familiar.

> *Harlem Gallery* **has been alternately celebrated and castigated for its formal difficulty—when, that is, it has been read at all.**
> —*Michael Bérubé*

But the Curator is able to maintain this "cultural position," and eventually to use it to critique Hideho Heights, only by refusing to specify his *historical* position. Of course, given the Curator's commitment to the transhistorical—or ahistorical—element in art, which defines for him the value of the "masterpiece," his refusal to locate himself temporally may be ideologically appropriate. Yet much has been made of *Harlem Gallery's* stylistic ambiguities; it is odd, then, that no critic has seen fit to question the purpose of the ambiguity of the poem's present tense, its time of narration. The question is not simply critical pedantry; in a poem whose "central" problematic concerns the ultimate place of the "marginal" artist, it is necessarily a central issue.

Does the poem take place, then, in the twenties, the forties, the sixties, or an amalgam of temporal loci scattered over this span? And if the last, what are the ramifications of this temporal "dispersion" for the poem's invocation of great artists? When the Curator alludes to Matisse, for example, is he invoking the turn-of-the-century Fauvist Matisse or the mid-century Matisse of paper cutouts who said he wanted to create art the tired businessman could come home to? And to what end in either case? To put the question another way, if the poem wants to narrate, in its allusive subtext, the story of how the impressionists of Paris garrets became the impressionists we see in coffee-table tomes, then is the poem celebrating the process by which revolutions in aesthetics eventually make their way into the cultural lingua franca, or is it alerting us to the historical process by which the avant-garde is transmuted into kitsch and thus calling us to carry on the revolutions of the avant-garde?

We cannot answer these questions—not because we do not have enough textual evidence but because the textual evidence itself will not allow the questions to be answered. In the matter of narrative time, indeterminacy is inscribed in the poem at every turn; it is as if the poem, like the electron in Heisenberg's principle, cannot say where it is—its position can be specified only in terms of probability and range. And Tolson has apparently been careful to cover his tracks: in **"Beta"** the Curator writes of "Young Men labeled by their decades / The Lost, The Bright, The Angry, The Beat"; but in **"Eta"** we hear that Rommel has just died. In the Zulu Club, despite the reference Hideho Heights makes to improvisatory jazz poetry, we find him sneaking alcohol under the table as if Prohibition were in effect; and at one point, the Curator's good friend, the Bantu expatriate Dr. Nkomo, brings the poem into the sixties, as he urges

> the artists
> of the Market Place Gallery in Harlem:
> "Remember
> the Venerable Yankee Poet
> on the unfamiliar red carpet of the Capitol
> as he visaed the gospel of the Founding Fathers
> . . . *Novus Ordo Seclorum* . . .
> spieled by every dollar bill."

Indeed, we may find this temporal ambiguity even in the poem's opening quatrain:

> The Harlem Gallery, an Afric pepper bird,
> Awakes me at a people's dusk of dawn.
> The age altars its image, a dog's hind leg,
> And hazards the moment of truth in pawn.

For even given the oblique allusion, in line 2, to W. E. B. Du Bois's 1940 *Dusk of Dawn,* it is unclear when this dusk of dawn takes place. It may be, for example, as one critic has it, that "Harlem Gallery" refers metonymically "to the artists who contribute to the gallery; in which case, this may also be a topical allusion to a cultural revolution brought about by the Harlem Renaissance"; it may as well be, on a similar principle, that the "people's dusk of dawn" occurs not in the 1920s but in the early 1940s, during the first of the wartime Harlem riots, or, for that matter, during the dawn of the civil rights movement of the 1960s. Lines 3 and 4 compound the uncertainty. The objects of "altars" in line 3—"image" and "dog's hind leg"—parallel the appositive noun phrases in line 1, and line 4 closes the quatrain on a rhyme. Pattern is evoked by repetition and completion, and yet the metrical pattern of the first line's symmetrical trochees and dactyls ("Harlem Gallery," "Afric pepper bird") is broken, in line 3, on "altars," just as the fourth line, constructed of two anapests flanked by iambs, disrupts the iambic pentameter of the second. Indeed, if we try to read line 4 against the second line's norm, we find that the most heavily accented words turn out to be "hazards," "moment," and "truth"; in reading the second pair of lines, therefore, we are forced to stress "altars," "hazards," "moment," "truth." *Altars,* a consecration; *hazards,* a gamble; *truth,* eternal; *moment,* ephemeral: the collision of noumena with phenomena extends the tension of the dusk of dawn, and the pun on *altars* suggests the extraordinary lability of the moment of consecration, a lability the poem will continue to exploit. The opening quatrain employs the present tense even as it undoes the present tense: it does not signify a present, it throws a present tens-ion over a tenseless moment of flux.

This systematic temporal confusion enables the poem to dodge its most important cultural questions—namely, if the dissemination of high culture to the masses is an end devoutly to be wished, how can dissemination avoid trivialization, dissolution, and "kitschification"? If the Tolsonian avant-garde is driven by the desire to create the taste by which it is to be enjoyed, how (to borrow a phrase from Lillian Robinson) do we know when we've won, and how do we go about "winning"? What, in other words, is the cultural position of the avant-garde artist who finally has transformed the masses or been transformed by them?

It is, of course, in the face of serious cultural questions such as these that ideology does its most useful work; and Tolson was fortunate to have as a professional friend and supporter John Ciardi, for it was Ciardi's conception of high culture that provided Tolson with a palliative answer. In 1958, Ciardi wrote a piece for the *Saturday Review* entitled "Dialogue with the Audience," in which a Citizen asks a Poet, "Who *are* you modern poets for? Is there no such thing as an audience?" Ciardi's Poet responds by distinguishing between two kinds of audience, "horizontal" and "vertical." I quote the column at some length, not only because Tolson himself quoted it so often but also because neither Tolson nor, curiously, his critics found it at all remarkable—that is, worthy of scrutiny:

> "The horizontal audience consists of everybody who is alive at this moment. The vertical audience consists of everyone, vertically through time, who will ever read a given poem. . . ."

> "The point is that the horizontal audience always outnumbers the vertical at any one moment, but that the vertical audience for good poetry always outnumbers the horizontal in time-enough. And not only for the greatest poets. Andrew Marvell is certainly a minor poet, but given time enough, more people certainly will have read 'To His Coy Mistress' than will ever have subscribed to *Time, Life,* and *Fortune.* Compared to what a good poem can do, Luce is a piker at getting circulation."

> "Impressive, if true," says the Citizen, "but how does any given poet get his divine sense of the vertical audience?"

> *"By his own ideal projection of his own best sense of himself. It's as simple as that,"* says the Poet. "He may be wrong, but he has nothing else to go by. And there is one thing more—all good poets are difficult when their work is new. And their work always becomes less difficult as their total shape becomes more and more visible. As that shape impresses itself upon time, one begins to know how to relate the parts to their total." (my emphasis)

Notable here are at least three features: the useful confusion as to who outnumbers whom; the implicit claim that "vertical" audiences always form and that worthy marginal poets therefore always eventually become central; and, not least among these, the deft elimination of specificity and agency in the last two sentences, which leave us ultimately with the incomprehensible image of a "shape" that "impresses itself upon time."

That such an argument would have great appeal for Tolson should be obvious. But despite Ciardi's confident implication that the avant-garde always eventually becomes the cultural center, Tolson's poem, by confining itself to the image of an avant-garde already nearly a century old, has (perhaps unwittingly) left ambiguous that avant-garde's contemporary cultural position. And this ambiguity, like the deliberate confusion of times, is woven into the poem's very fabric: Nkomo's citation of Robert Frost at Kennedy's inaugura-

tion, for example, is immediately followed by his extraordinary reference to Cézanne as a "Toussaint L'Ouverture of Esthetics" acclaimed only by his fellow artists:

> ". . . Remember, yes, remember . . .
> Zola, Renoir, Degas, Gauguin, Van Gogh, and
> Rodin
> hailed Cézanne;
> but *vox populi* and red-tapedom
> remained as silent as spectators in a court
> when the crier repeats three times, 'Oyez!'"

What, then, is the relation of the two allusions—oppositional or appositional? If the former, then Frost is an example of the popular recognition and acclaim Cézanne never achieved; if the latter, Frost becomes an image of how the state can defuse the power of a Toussaint L'Ouverture by falsely embracing him, by giving him an "official" role. The Curator actually does entertain the latter possibility—not in **"Pi"** but in **"Omega":**

> Now and then a State,
> when iron fists and hobnails
> explode alarms at the citadel's gate,
> dons the ill-fitting robes of the Medici
> and initiates Project CX,
> to propagandize a rubber-stamped Pyramid of Art
> and to glorify the Cheops at the apex.

Is this the light in which to read the Frost tableau, as a modern version of the hostile silence of vox populi and red-tapedom with which Cézanne was supposedly received—a version wherein "hostile silence" has now become Marcuse's "repressive tolerance"? The question should trouble much of the rest of the poem as well: for we may not be sure, after all, what the Curator means by writing, in **"Delta,"** that the "world-self of the make- / believe becomes the swimming pool of a class, / a balsam apple / of the soul." Does "swimming pool" here potentiate or subvert the image of art as a "balsam apple / of the soul"? Is this swimming pool, in other words, a comfort and refreshment for the sweltering multitudes, or has the work of art been made into a mere commodity, a suburban status symbol?

Even some of the poem's allusions, which seem on the surface unproblematic, recapitulate this ambiguity. Take, for example, this fairly straight-forward stanza from **"Epsilon":**

> Again
> by the waters of Babylon we sit down and weep,
> for the pomp and power
> of the bulls of Bashan
> serve Belshazzarian tables to artists and poets who
> serve the hour,
> torn between two masters,

> God and Caesar—
> this (for Conscience)
> the Chomolungma of disasters.

Clearly enough, this passage laments the power of large-scale market forces, cast here as Psalm 22's bulls of Bashan, to lure artists into lucrative positions that compromise or adulterate artistic commitments. But then the Curator's allusion to "Belshazzarian tables" is troubling, for Belshazzar's feast in Daniel 5.1-4 is immediately followed by the appearance of the writing on the wall in 5.5. We may be weeping because the bulls of Bashan have bought off the artists, or we may be weeping because we are as yet unaware that a Daniel is about to arrive, to signify on the oppressors. But perhaps (to carry the ambiguity further yet) there is no Daniel here at all. Will, then, the prophet in exile arrive, to refuse riches and rewards, speak the truth, overthrow the king, and usher in the new, benevolent administration of Darius the Mede? Or are the artists and poets, their mouths stuffed full of Belshazzar's food, unable to speak?

I suggest the poem deliberately invites and ignores such questions, chiefly to keep alive and plausible its primary cultural myth: the myth of an avant-garde that, despite the opposition of critics, capitalists, and philistines, has survived to become part of "the heritage of Art," which, as **"Omicron"** has it, "nurtures everywhere / the winged and wingless man" and which allows the Curator to write, near poem's end, "I envision the Harlem Gallery of my people." To this end, the poem maintains its cultural contradictions as sedulously as it refrains from any reference to post-Depression marginal artists, and both strategies, mutually supporting, serve to help the poem avoid confronting directly its relation to the audience, and the avant-garde, of its own time.

For where, in a poem that refers so often to jazz greats like King Oliver, are Charlie Parker, Thelonious Monk, John Coltrane? Where, in a poem whose temporal range extends to the Kennedy administration, are Jackson Pollock, Robert Motherwell, Willem de Kooning? The youngest artist in the poem, William Gropper, was born in 1897; Louis Armstrong, its youngest musician, in 1900. Thus, of all the figures in the Curator's anthology, only Satchmo is younger than Tolson. On one level, the omission of more recent experimental artists may be a part of Tolson's reaction to his own self-conscious belatedness, an attempt to conjure the image of the avant-garde as it appeared in the heyday of the Harlem Renaissance; but more significantly, it points also to **Harlem Gallery**'s profound refusal to contemplate its own conflicted and ambiguous position—not only in relation to the mass audience that it seeks to disturb and instruct but also in relation to its fellow travelers on the margins of cultural production.

And this is where Hideho's parable comes in.

II

We are in the Zulu Club, in section **"Phi,"** and we have just heard a telling exchange between Dr. Nkomo and Shadrach Martial Kilroy, president of Afroamerican Freedom, Inc.; Kilroy has claimed that "a specter haunts the Great White World— / the specter of *Homo Aethiopicus,* the pigmented Banquo's ghost." Nkomo's response is at once cynical and definitive; casting the African American's polyglot heritage as a handicap, Nkomo gets the last word on Kilroy: "you / are a people in whose veins / poly-breeds / and / plural strains / mingle and run— / an Albert Ryder of many schools, and *none*." More than this: he creates the space for Heights's incipient performance, as Hideho nods the Curator to the bar and confides to him that the "bunkum session on the Negro / . . . has sparked an inspiration."

The Curator, interestingly, is more antagonistic to Heights here than at any other point in the poem:

> "You poets come too soon or too late,
> Hideho Heights,
> with too little,
> to save the Old Ship of State.
> Remember to remember
> a tribal anthem
> is the yankee-doodle-diddle of a tittle."

But his antagonism is entirely self-defeating: "To Hideho Heights, / . . . I was a half-white egghead with maggots on the brain. / I ate my crow / . . . My clichés at the bar / were bones in the maw of the tomb." Given that the Curator will reveal himself, in the poem's penultimate section, to be an octoroon, "half-white egghead" is severe language indeed. But it may be language appropriate to his racial anxieties at this point, for the Curator has, of course, been implicated in Nkomo's critique of the African American. Surely, whatever the basis for the Curator's resistance to Heights, the problematics of "race" are in the forefront here, as they have not been elsewhere in the poem; and it is into this powerfully charged field of racial politics that Hideho casts his version of a beast fable. Challenging the Curator to "[f]ollow the spoor of the symbols—if you have the wit," he tells the "strange but true" tale of the shark and sea turtle, in which black America, imaged as the sea turtle, is first the shark's dinner and then the image of a triumphant resistance to assimilation:

> "the sea-turtle gnaws
> . . . and gnaws . . . and gnaws . . .
> his way in a way that appalls—
> *his* way to freedom,
> beyond the vomiting dark,

beyond the stomach walls
of the shark."

Lest we (or the Curator) miss the point, the Zulu Club's bartender, a Jamaican veteran of World War II, delivers himself of a profoundly emotional response:

"God knows, Hideho, you got the low-down
on the black turtle and the white shark
in the Deep South."
Then,
describing a pectoral girdle,
his lower lip curled,
and he blurted—like an orgasm:
"And perhaps in many a South of the Great White
World!"
He fumed, he sweated, he paced behind the bar.

. . .

"I was in the bomb-hell at Dunkirk. I was a British
tar.
In Parliament, *white* Churchill quoted one day,
'If we must die, let us not die like hogs . . . '
The words of a poet, my compatriot—*black*
Claude
McKay."

Colonialism as a labor resource in world war: the British swallow the bartender. Quotation and radical recontextualization: Churchill swallows—and fails to acknowledge—McKay's sonnet on the race riots of 1919. Hideho's tale is brought to climax ("blurted—like an orgasm") by the bartender's foregrounding of racial strife against the backdrop of two world wars; and in the revelation vouchsafed by the climax lies a vision in which the spectacle of Claude McKay's words in Churchill's mouth carries with it none of the ambiguous hope or promise of the spectacle of Robert Frost on the steps of the Capitol. For this is a discourse in which "the instinctive drive of the weak to survive" speaks to the politics of separatism in the language of the parable; it is a discourse in which all amalgamation and assimilation is de facto repressive tolerance and therefore cultural genocide. Hideho Heights and the Jamaican bartender, between them, have dared to suggest an answer to the question *Harlem Gallery* has sought so scrupulously to avoid, and though that answer be couched in a parable, the suggestion is clear: in the melting pot we will be eaten.

Unless, that is, we eat our way out, and "in a way that appalls." Perhaps it appalls even Tolson: for it is surely no accident that *Harlem Gallery* follows this scene with the Curator's memory of the night when, having dragged home

a dead-drunk Heights, he found in Heights's apartment "in the modern idiom; / a poem called *E. & O.E.*" Of all things, Tolson's own poem. Outflanked on the issue of "race," the Curator changes the joke and slips the yoke, unmasking Hideho as a kind of modernist "wannabe," a former Parisian "bistro habitué, / an expatriate poet of the Black Venus / in the Age of Whoopee." Hideho's pose, on the streets and in the Zulu Club, may be convincing to the masses, but the Curator alone is privy to the bard's internal contradictions:

He didn't know
I knew
about the split identity
of the People's Poet—
the bifacial nature of his poetry:
the racial ballad in the public domain
and the private poem in the modern vein.

Thence follows the Curator's long epilogic lament on Heights, a moving vatic cry addressed alternately to White Boy and Black Boy and confronting what seem by now twin issues, "race" and culture. The epilogue contains *Harlem Gallery*'s most often cited passages; and among these, one stanza in particular has been taken as the poem's summation. It is nestled in the opening of section **"Chi,"** just before the Curator relates his discovery of *E. & O.E.:*

Poor Boy Blue,
the Great White World
and the Black Bourgeoisie
have shoved the Negro artist into
the white and not-white dichotomy,
the Afroamerican dilemma in the Arts—
the dialectic of
to be or not to be
a Negro.

In *Harlem Gallery,* the African American dilemma is not over whether to be a Negro; it is not even over whether to be a black separatist—for, as we find, even a good separatist-balladeer like Hideho Heights, when he gets into the privacy of his apartment, becomes a modernist despite himself.
—*Michael Bérubé*

There is no mistaking the Curator's tone: however antagonistic he may be to Heights's "bifacial nature," he is genuinely saddened at the ambiguous and conflicted position of the black poet who aspires to little magazines and contemporary anthologies, to an ultimately academic context of re-

ception. But though this stanza may be the Curator's conclusion on Heights's tenuous cultural position, and though
the stanza may even be "moving," I want to suggest also
that there is something fundamentally *wrong* with such a
conclusion—that this ending may be thoroughly elegiac and
yet thoroughly false.

For in what sense has Hideho Heights been caught in a
"white and not-white dichotomy"? What, after all, *is* "the
dialectic of / to be or not to be / a Negro"? If the Curator
suggests, as he intends to, that Hideho shrinks from the task
of transforming audiences, succumbing instead to the polarized horizons of expectation in two different literary
worlds, then the Curator is also suggesting that modernist
poetry is the realm of white folks and that "the Great White
World / and the Black Bourgeoisie" demand African American poets who are sufficiently primitive and technically incompetent—in a word, folk poets only. The dichotomy here,
recall, is based on "the racial ballad in the public domain /
and the private poem in the modern vein": the Curator's pejorative key words are not merely *ballad* and *public* but also
racial; and they are as closely associated, and as heavily
ideologically weighted, as are their counterparts, *poem, private,* and *modern.* This much is clear. But then the Curator's
characterization of the conflict as the dilemma of "to be or
not to be / a Negro" must intend "Negro" in the most bitter, cynical tone imaginable—a tone that implies that poets
who choose to be "Negroes first" are simply conforming to
a stereotypical "racial" role, precisely the role expected of
them by their worst audiences. Indeed, we would do well
to remember here that Hideho is no mere panderer to his
black audience: as we hear in *Harlem Vignettes,* **Harlem
Gallery***'s* lengthy metapoem, "To the Black Bourgeoisie, /
Hideho was a crab louse / in the public region of
Afroamerica." In **Harlem Gallery***'s* terms, that is, Hideho
is politically correct; the question the Curator poses, therefore, has nothing to do with whether "racial ballads" can
have the oppositional force of an avant-garde and everything
to do with whether a contemporary audience, white or black,
elitist or populist, will allow an African American poet to
be a modernist.

This is why, I think, the parable is the pivot point that
swings us into **Harlem Gallery***'s* climactic unmasking of
Hideho Heights; likewise, this is why, in reading over *E. &
O.E.,* the Curator juxtaposes the hesitancy and diffidence of
Heights's private poem to the militant confidence of
Heights's public stand:

> Yet,
> depressed like ondoyant glass,
> Hideho Heights,
> the *Coeur de Lion* of the Negro mass,
> in *E. & O.E.* rationalized:
> "Why place an empty pail

> before a well
> of dry bones?
> Why go to Nineveh to tell
> the ailing that they ail?"

And as if this "preface" to Heights's work weren't enough,
the Curator then recalls, in a metamemory, one of Heights's
triumphant returns to the Zulu Club—this one after a jail
term for an obscure assault on the "Uncle Tom" leader of
the "Ethiopian Tabernacle":

> "A man's conscience is home-bred.
> To see an artist or a leader do
> Uncle Tom's asinine splits
> is an ask-your-mama shame!"
> The Jamaican bartender had staked off his claim:
> "The drinks are on the house, Poet Defender!"
> A sportsman with ruffled grouse
> on the wing over dogs, the poet had continued:
> "Integrity is an underpin—
> the marble lions that support
> the alabaster fountain in
> the Alhambra."

In construing Heights's modernist poem as a contradiction
of his celebration of racial "integrity," then, the Curator is
able not only to suggest the historical inevitability of modernism but to argue as well that the poetics of the sea turtle,
the stance of black separatism, will divide an artist between
two masters, two polarized discourses, each of which claims
a territory unto itself and authority over its inhabitants. And
the implication here is, obviously, that such self-division is
self-destruction.

The choice with which the poem leaves us is thus a deliberately false one: in **Harlem Gallery,** the African American
dilemma is not over whether to be a Negro; it is not even
over whether to be a black separatist—for, as we find, even
a good separatist-balladeer like Hideho Heights, when he
gets into the privacy of his apartment, becomes a modernist despite himself. But although I want to make clear the
ground on which the poem leaves us with a false dilemma,
I want also to recall here that the poem contains within it a
real dilemma—one that, as I argue in the context of the
poem's narrative and historical "time," it remains unwilling or unable to acknowledge. This "real" dilemma is,
unsurprisingly, a function of the poem's real conflict:
whether the African American artist should attempt to create his or her own audience or play to the audiences that
already exist. This is the conflict "resolved" by **Harlem Gallery,** both through Heights's fall and (equally) through the
poem's refusal to contemplate the cultural question consequent on its adoption of the ideology of assimilation—the
question of the avant-garde's position when it is no longer
(for whatever reason) *avant* of the *garde.* We may also see

the poem's conclusion as a symptom of this refusal, inso-far as the Curator's epilogue in **"Psi"** follows Heights's un-masking in **"Chi,"** not with a discussion of what it means for a member of a truly marginal group (such as an Afri-can American poet) to adopt the aesthetics and ideologies of an already institutionalized modernist "avant-garde," but instead with an eleven-page discussion of "race" that de-clares "race" a fiction perpetrated by whites for the oppres-sion of nonwhites. The Curator's answer in **"Psi"** ("Just as the Chinese lack / an ideogram for 'to be,' / our lexicon has no definition / for an ethnic amalgam like Black Boy and me") may be a good answer—but only because the Curator has deliberately asked the wrong question.

In other words, to uphold the cultural ideal of cultural amal-gamation (in Nkomo's phrase, the "homogenized milk of multiculture") embodied in the person and function of the Curator, *Harlem Gallery* needs not only to avoid confront-ing explicitly its own contemporary cultural position, and its own possible present or future audience, but also to delegitimize the separatist cultural position of Hideho Heights. But beyond its will to assimilation, into a postmodern conception either of the irreducibility of "mar-ginality" or of the political conditions for an acceptable em-brace of pluralism, the poem cannot and will not go, trusting instead, in the terms of John Ciardi at his vaguest, that its ideal projection of itself will become a shape that impresses itself upon time.

III

This, then, is where our task begins: in retrieving the dis-course of Hideho Heights. For if *Harlem Gallery* implies that Hideho's ballads are somehow culturally and histori-cally inappropriate, then Heights is being cast as a kind of Paul Laurence Dunbar, and the Curator's unmasking of him in **"Chi"** is a call to African American poets to throw off Dunbar's mask. But it is possible, after all, to see the poem's argument not as an unmasking but as a remasking, an ex-change of masks—Dunbar's for Tolson's. If, in other words, we see the poem's conflict not synchronically but diachronically, as part of an explicitly historical problem-atic, then the conflict's resolution suggests that underneath one mask there is only another mask—the mask of high modernism.

And Tolson warrants such a re-vision; indeed, he himself initiated it, in his astonishing revisionary account of how he enticed Allen Tate to write the preface to *Libretto*. The year before he died, he told the story to Dudley Randall, and it was nearly twenty years before Robert Farnsworth's research proved the tale untrue. Here is how it originally appeared in *Negro Digest*:

Tolson related that after completing *Libretto for the*

Republic of Liberia he asked Tate to write a pref-ace for it, and Tate replied that he wasn't interested in the propaganda of Negro poets. Tolson spent a year studying modern poetic techniques and *rewrit-ing the poem so that it said the same things in a different way and then sent it to Tate.* Tate wrote a preface in which he said, "For the first time, it seems to me, a Negro poet has assimilated the full poetic language of his time. . . ." (my emphasis)

Some critics have been embarrassed by this anecdote, and all the more embarrassed at the thought that it might be true; for on one reading, it presents Tolson (or presents Tolson presenting himself) as a toady in blackface, "Yes-massa"ing the Great White Critic. But to my mind the story is rather appetizing—a modern (modernist) Brer Rabbit story if true, and even more provocative as a tall tale. For it suggests that, even if only retrospectively, Tolson saw his adoption of modernist technique as a guerilla strategy, a means of let-ting revolutionary discourse sound in the ears of conserva-tive whites by masking that discourse in a no longer revolutionary poetics. Tolson seeks to emerge therefore nei-ther as Tate's subaltern nor as Eliot's but as an African American literary version of the maroon, the escaped slave living on the frontier, imperialism's margin, raiding the nearest plantation periodically for supplies and planning the long-term offensive in the meantime. And in the image of Tolson as maroon, we find it altogether appropriate that he has been marooned in turn: unread, or, if read at all, read not as maroon but as another form of "primitive"—the ma-rooned colonial duped into conversion by the missionaries of modernism.

And surely Tolson himself did not imagine that a dissolu-tion of his social and racial politics would follow necessar-ily upon his attempt to "modernize" himself. For him there is no contradiction, because technique, apparently, is mask: "My work is certainly difficult in metaphors, symbols and juxtaposed ideas," he wrote in a 1961 letter; but "there the similarity between me and Eliot separates. That is only tech-nique, and any artist must use the technique of his time. . . . However, when you look at my ideas and Eliot's, we're as far apart as hell and heaven." Tolson's formulation is not theoretically sophisticated: in casting himself against Eliot, Tolson winds up asserting a necessary historical homocentricity of "technique" and strictly opposing it to a content of "ideas." But surely the point here is not to con-vict Tolson of theoretical missteps; rather, the point is that, in his conception of his role, technique is only technique, form is only form—and all forms, by implication, are masks.

What seems most intriguing about his position, in this ma-roon light, is that Tolson appears less as a belated modern-ist than as an unacknowledged precursor: for in the work of the preeminent black critics of the present, we find the argument that black criticism and theory must grapple with the problematics of poststructuralism in order to do justice to the signifyin(g) difference of the black text. Specifically, we find in the work of Henry Louis Gates and Houston Baker a recognizably Tolsonian position: and to charges that they are unduly influenced by Derrida and Foucault, they respond, justifiably and sometimes persuasively, that their appropriations of theories are necessarily transformations of theory—and that, besides, their critical method *is only technique, and any artist must use the technique of his (or her) time.*

Where once Tolson had committed himself to the proposition that the black oppositional poet must take up and take on modernism, Baker and Gates argue that black oppositional critics cannot do without poststructuralism. And yet, as though Melvin Tolson's posthumous career has not yet been sufficiently tangled, Tolson has proved "marginal" to every critical schema articulated to date, even that of so iconoclastic a critic as Houston Baker himself. In fact, in Baker's *Modernism and the Harlem Renaissance,* Tolson appears only in the first introductory paragraph, his name invoked by one of Baker's former interlocutors (xiii). For Baker wants to enact a wholesale change of terms for the discussion of African American modernism, and if he succeeds he effectively pulls the rug out from under what Tolson conceived African American modernism to be. Of course, it may turn out to be possible nonetheless to speak of Tolson in Baker's vocabulary—in the language of the "mastery of form" and "deformation of mastery"—but at present it is undeniable that Baker seeks to disengage African American modernism from precisely the "modernism" with which Tolson was engaged:

> I would suggest that judgments on Afro-American "modernity" and the "Harlem Renaissance" that begin with notions of British, Anglo-American, and Irish "modernism" as "successful" objects, projects, and processes to be emulated by Afro-Americans are misguided. . . . Further, it seems to me that the very *histories* that are assumed in the chronologies of British, Anglo-American, and Irish modernisms are radically opposed to any adequate and accurate account of the history of Afro-American modernism, especially the *discursive* history of such modernism.

Baker's, we might say, is a modernism against Modernism, a modernism that disallows the category of "crossover artists": in his formulation, Anglo-American and African American modernisms are "radically opposed." However, if Baker's vocabulary does succeed in transforming our understanding of African American modernism, then his relation to Tolson becomes still more tangled and ironic, for it is Baker who once declared that Tolson's "game is not

worth the candle," and it is Baker, more so than Gates, who would object strenuously to the notion that he is a postmodern variation of Tolson. Yet just as Gates and Baker seek both to translate and transform poststructuralism, so too did Tolson once transform the terms of modernist poetics—with, as Gates would say, a signifyin(g) black difference. Moreover, just as any account of American poststructuralism would be incomplete without reference to Gates and Baker, so too, I think, would any account of the fate of African American modernism be inadequate without a thorough reading of Tolson—whether in Baker's terms or anyone else's. And the port, as the Curator would say, is eminently "worth the cruise." Both a rope-a-dope and an allaesthetic mask, *Harlem Gallery* is a cultural performance that manages finally to speak even beyond its own Curator, signifyin(g) ultimately not only on Eliot but also—and more significantly—on the critics who would take Tolson as nothing more than Eliot's epigone.

Such a claim may be revisionary indeed; but this is part of my point. For what is finally at issue in Tolson's career, and in his attempt to negotiate possible Anglo-American and African American modernisms, is the relation of his ideological "commitments" to the historical and discursive conditions of revisionism. How we see Tolson's engagement with modernism, that is, depends on how we can reimagine his commitments, resee him, revise him. Here too the parallel with Baker is instructive. For although Baker has shown that he can be (at times) as uncritically immersed in poststructuralism's self-representations as Tolson was (at times) in modernism's, still, neither Baker nor Tolson closes off the possibility of a critical reassessment of the ideologies he inhabits—whether this reassessment be ours or theirs. Both writers challenge us with questions about marginality, modernism, and the roles and responsibilities of academic criticism; the only salient difference between them is that we have not, so far, asked ourselves to confront these questions in the way Tolson presents them. My confrontation, at its furthest reach, produces an apparent paradox: the grounds on which Tolson avoids engaging postmodernity must provide for us the means by which he engages postmodernity—which is to say that his commitment to modernism must provoke our commitment to revisionism.

I suggest therefore that *Harlem Gallery* is best read not as an example of Tolson's uncritical absorption in modernism's self-representations but as a scrupulous, self-critical defense of Tolson's attempt to imagine an African American modernism. What we must remember in such a reading, however, is that no thoroughgoing, insightful negotiation of modernism from *within* modernism is without its self-limitations and blinding commitments—and *Harlem Gallery* is no exception. (Hence the relative freedom from self-contradiction, by contrast, of Baker's revision of African American modernism, which is enabled by the various postmodern vocabularies that allow Baker to fashion a new African American literary history as something like a "discursive formation.") But, in a final paradox, I want to argue that it is the very depth of Tolson's commitments, the extent of his immersion in the idea of the avant-garde, that makes available for us the critical and self-critical interventions that constitute productive revisionism. Tolson's importance, in this framework, depends on his susceptibility to revision; but what my framework allows us to see—and what thereby becomes perhaps most remarkable about Tolson's trajectory—is that through the ballad of Hideho Heights and through his impromptu folktale to Dudley Randall, Tolson began that process of productive revision himself. It is the task to which he continues to call us.

Melvin B. Tolson Jr. (essay date Summer 1990)

SOURCE: "The Poetry of Melvin B. Tolson (1898-1966)," in *World Literature Today,* Vol. 64, No. 3, Summer, 1990, pp. 395-400.

[*In the following essay, Tolson discusses his father's career and major works.*]

"Black Crispus Attucks taught / Us how to die / Before white Patrick Henry's bugle breath / Uttered the vertical / Transmitting cry: / 'Yea give me liberty or give me death.'" These words still reverberate in this sixty-sixth year of the celebration by African Americans of "Black History Month." They express the importance that the struggle against socioeconomic and cultural racism held for Melvin B. Tolson in his lifetime and in the work he left to what he called "the vertical audience," that of the ages. This poet, orator, teacher of English and American literatures, grammarian, small-town mayor, theater founder and director, debate coach was born on 6 February 1898 in Moberly, Missouri, the son and nephew of Methodist preachers. The family moved frequently in Missouri and Iowa to the different churches his studiously intellectual but autodidact father pastored.

Tolson often said that in his earliest youth he was dedicated to the palette. However, he was permanently deterred from this path by his mother's encounter with a bohemianly attired painter who, attracted by the boy's ability, spoke of taking him to Paris! Thomas Whitbread refers to this encounter in his poetic tribute "In Praise of M. B. Tolson," written after Tolson's death in 1966. Subsequently turning to literature, Tolson said that his first poem, **"The Wreck of the *Titanic*,"** was published about 1912, when the family lived in Oskaloosa, Iowa. A favorite teacher encouraged him as early as 1915 or 1916, when the family resided in

Mason City, Iowa. The earliest copies of the poet's work were discovered by Robert Farnsworth, who has done the most extensive research on Tolson's life, having published a definitive biography in 1984. He discovered two short stories and two poems written by the then class poet for the *Lincolnian,* the yearbook of Lincoln High School in Kansas City, Missouri. Tolson was attending high school there while the family lived near his father's church in Independence. These short stories and poems appear in the 1917 and 1918 editions of the yearbook, in which his future career is predicted to be that of "Poet and Playwriter" (*sic*). The feature poem dedicated to his graduating class of 1918 is grandiloquently entitled **"The Past, Present and Future"** and is already distinctively "Tolsonian" in imaginative thrust and language.

> Fair muses, from Olympia's wind-kissed height,
> Inspire our souls with (thy) eternal flame
> That we may sing of this sad hour aright,
> A song full worthy of our Mater's name.
> In sooth, it pains our hearts to break the ties
> That grip us to our friends in warm embrace.
> However Time, who like a meteor flies,
> Has hurled us hence, this tearful time to face.

Later lines, such as "Our hearts beat fast, our eyes flame with desire! / Our souls long for the battlesmoke of strife!" are also typical of the action-filled language and oratorical tone of the later poetry. Although heralded as "the Dunbar to be" of the class and claiming to have tried poems in Negro dialect, Tolson here reminds us of the Dunbar of "The Unsung Heroes" and "Misapprehension" rather than the more familiar creator of delightful poetry like "Soliloquy of a Turkey" or "A Negro Love Song."

The five stanzas of eight iambic-pentameter lines in the *Lincolnian* show a relative ease in the manipulation of *a b a b* rhymes and may be said to substantiate Tolson's own oft-repeated opinion that "poets are made though technique must be taught." It is obvious, despite the clichés and infelicities of form, that the poet of *Harlem Gallery: Book I, The Curator* of 1965 is already present almost fifty years earlier. The poetic direction is already set toward the rich imagery and allusive language of the later period.

In his junior year at Lincoln University, outside Philadelphia, Tolson married Ruth Southall of Charlottesville, Virginia. After graduation in 1923, a son was born and the family moved to Marshall, Texas, on the edge of the oilfield district, where Tolson had a job as English teacher at Wiley College, a small Methodist Episcopal school. Two more sons and a daughter were born during these years. Coincidentally, about a mile away in the same town was a second small black college, Bishop, supported by the Baptist Church. The total student population of the two colleges might occasionally have reached one thousand, though rarely.

In the pantheon of black colleges of this pre-civil-rights era Wiley College was regarded with something like envy and awe by the Negro population of the South. Its prestige was unrivaled west of the Mississippi, and Tolson quickly grew to be one of the intellectual stars of this environment. For the next few years he expended the enormous store of energy in his five-foot-six-inch, 130-pound frame in several directions. He coached the junior-varsity football team, expounding for many years afterward on the strategies he devised to defeat the larger, better-fed varsity players. He played hard, competitive tennis with faculty and students, again proclaiming the advantages of strategy. He trained competitive orators and coached championship debate teams, among whose opponents were the University of Oklahoma (an interracial "first"), Oxford University, and the University of Southern California. He directed the college theater group and helped found the black intercollegiate Southern Association of Dramatic and Speech Arts, for whose festival contests he and his students wrote and presented plays. His students called him "the Little Master" and told and retold (sometimes apocryphal) stories, admiring his debater thrusts of intelligence in discussions—often on the open campus—with students and other professors and his disregard for the clothing amenities associated with being a college professor in those more formal days. Among his finest debaters was James Leonard Farmer, founder of the Congress of Racial Equality (CORE), whose photograph while being carried bodily out of the courthouse of Plaquemines Parish in Louisiana by policemen remains one of the most memorable of the civil-rights movement. Farmer speaks glowingly of Tolson in his autobiography *Lay Bare the Heart* and in the television documentary "Marshall, Texas; Marshall, Texas," in which he is interviewed by the correspondent and commentator Bill Moyers, a native of the town.

Debate remained a vital part of Tolson's teaching life until falling into swift discontinuance just before World War II, about the time the subjects that had furnished the substance of its adversarial roles became too immediately relevant to be "debated." In the midst of this and other activities, Tolson had worked on his Master of Arts degree at Columbia University but finished his thesis only on the eve of Hitler's invasion of France. The subject of his thesis was **"The Harlem Group of Negro Writers,"** and the degree was awarded in 1940. He knew personally some of the Harlem Renaissance figures and, while at Columbia, was inspired to write a sonnet about Harlem. A roommate, according to Tolson, ridiculed the idea of fitting Harlem into a sonnet, and this comment made him think of composing a longer work in the years that followed.

He was back teaching at Wiley College in the early thirties and busy at work on his poetry about Harlem. To encompass the vastness of the community, he finally decided on a framework inspired by *Spoon River Anthology*. Edgar Lee Masters had used the device of a stroll through a graveyard and the epitaphs on headstones to introduce his poetic population. Tolson combined his own early interest in painting and the prominence of this art during the Harlem Renaissance to create another device that would allow a similar scope of poetic presentation. The resulting collection of some 340 poems, *A Gallery of Harlem Portraits,* unsuccessfully made the rounds of publishing houses for several years, after which time Tolson abandoned further attempts, putting the manuscript in a trunk. Some forty years later, in 1979, the publication of approximately half of the "portraits" was finally brought about by Robert Farnsworth. Because of a similarity in titles when Tolson took up the theme again (in *Harlem Gallery: Book I, The Curator* of 1965), there is often confusion of the two on the part of readers and oral commentators of Tolson's work.

The poet himself speaks of the influence of Masters, Browning, and Whitman on *A Gallery of Harlem Portraits*. Another, more obvious influence, which is perhaps taken for granted in African American poetry of the period, is the blues.

> Troubled waters, troubled waters,
> Done begin to roll.
> Troubled waters, troubled waters,
> Gittin' deep an' col'.
> Lawd, don't let dem troubled waters
> Drown ma weary soul.
>
> The New Year comes, the Old Year goes.
> What's down the road nobody knows.
> I play my suit with a poker face,
> But Father Time he holds the ace.

Most of the "portraits" contain blues inserts, both original and traditional. Tolson recalled several times sitting up late at night with Sterling Brown, the poet, the two drinking and delightedly competing at the invention of blues lyrics—never, unfortunately for us, written down or otherwise recorded.

In the same vein, Tolson was renowned as a raconteur, the veracity of whose minutest details sometimes took second place to dramatic effect. Although a few instances of his speaking or being interviewed exist, he would not allow his sons to record the oral history which he recounted so enthusiastically and entertainingly (the body tape recorder was still a thing of the future). These accounts were a gold mine of experiences on debate tours and travels to dramatic festivals in the segregated South and North, as well as encounters with famous, infamous, and ordinary people. We meet many of these events and people, however, in *A Gallery of Harlem Portraits* and in subsequent works published during his lifetime: *Rendezvous with America, Libretto for the Republic of Liberia,* and *Harlem Gallery.*

The "portraits" range through all the classes, colors, and past and present careers imaginable in the Harlem of the twenties and thirties.

> Dusky Bards,
> Heirs of eons of Comedy and Tragedy.
> Pass along the streets and alleys of Harlem
> Singing ballads of the Dark World: . . .
> . . . .
> Radicals, prizefighters, actors and deacons,
> Beggars, politicians, professors and redcaps,
> Bulldikers, Babbitts, racketeers and jig-chasers,
> Harlots, crapshooters, workers and pink-chasers
> Artists, dicties, Pullman porters and messiahs . . .
> The Curator has hung the likenesses of all
> In *"A Gallery of Harlem Portraits."*

Between these two stanzas from the introductory poem **"Harlem"** are eight assorted stanzas of blues lyrics which comment on the relations between men and women, blacks and whites, the powerful and the powerless. Although he espoused the antibourgeois attitude of the artist that has pervaded Western civilization since the late nineteenth century in France, Tolson had not yet done the extensive study or held the hours-long discussions he was to have with his friend and colleague Oliver W. Cox, who came to Wiley in 1938, or the author-editor V. F. Calverton. Nevertheless, in a book-length study of the 1965 *Harlem Gallery* Mariann Russell shows that the earlier "portraits" attribute poverty to the same socio-economic conditions as does the later work, and they too call on the "underdogs of the world to unite."

While he was composing *Portraits,* Tolson was also writing prose. By the summer of 1937 he had written two plays. One, a musical comedy-drama titled *The Moses of Beale Street,* was done in collaboration with Edward Boatner, the famous arranger of spirituals, who also taught at Wiley. The two were partly inspired by the continued success of the miracle play *The Green Pastures,* though they placed many of their scenes in Hell rather than Heaven. An agent agreed to represent them, and Tolson left the manuscript, later lost, with his collaborator while he returned to begin the school year in Marshall.

In May 1938 he began contributing a weekly column to the *Washington Tribune,* an African American newspaper in the District of Columbia. Farnsworth selected one hundred from the seven years' worth of columns and secured their publication in a 1982 volume whose title, *Caviar and Cabbage,* echoed that of the column. There are also records of one-act and three-act plays, one of which was a dramatization of *Black No More,* a novel by Walter White of the NAACP, which was finally performed at a 1952 convention of the Association.

After beginning the newspaper column, Tolson started work on a novel called *Dark Symphony,* of which some ninety-six pages remain. However, at the suggestion of poet Frank Marshall Davis, he entered a 126-line poem in the poetry contest sponsored by the 1940 American Negro Exposition in Chicago. He gave the title **"Dark Symphony"** to the poem, which was awarded first prize by the jury composed of Davis, Arna Bontemps, and Langston Hughes. The opening lines of my essay quote the opening lines of the poem, which is Tolson's most popular work. The first seventeen lines were even used as the frontispiece for the 1976 Schlitz Brewing Company's "Famous Black Americans Historical Calendar." I am sure the poet would have been delighted!

"Dark Symphony" is divided into sections bearing the names of musical notations.

Allegro Moderato

Black Crispus Attucks taught
Us how to die. . . .

Lento Grave

The centuries-old pathos in our voices
Saddens the great white world. . . .

Andante Sostenuto

They tell us to forget
The Golgotha we tread. . . .

Tempo Primo

The New Negro strides upon the continent
In seven-league boots. . . .

Larghetto

None in the Land can say
To us black men Today. . . .

Tempo di Marcia

Out of abysses of Illiteracy,
Through labyrinths of Lies,

Across waste lands of Disease . . .
We advance! . . . .

The musical notations characterize in varying degrees the tone of each of the sections of the poem. In **"Dark Symphony"** Tolson also returns to the cultivation of patterns of rhyme, a practice he had abandoned in *Gallery* except in the blues lyrics. He alternates rhyme with blank-verse sections. This poem is the longest that he had written to this time and is an example of the increasing lengthiness of the major poems he will write hereafter.

"Dark Symphony" appeared in the September 1941 issue of *Atlantic Monthly* and was read by Mary Lou Chamberlain, who later left *Atlantic* and became a member of the editorial board of Dodd, Mead. She suggested Tolson submit a manuscript for publication, the composition of which resulted in **Rendezvous with America**. Other shorter and longer poems were written for the book. One of the shortest is **"My Soul and I,"** dedicated to Tolson's wife and containing only twelve lines. It is a quietly lyrical love poem, one of the very few he ever wrote, in a vein that is counter to his natural intellectual exuberance. The longest poem in the volume, **"Tapestries of Time,"** in eight sections, contains 369 lines in strophes of varying lengths and rhyme schemes. Furthermore, the collection contains several experiments in form: rhyming lines of only two syllables (**"A Song for Myself"**); a pantoum, a Malay fixed-form poem adapted by Baudelaire (**"The Furlough"**); a section of twelve sonnets. There are vignettes based on his work with black and white sharecroppers who wanted to form a union in Harrison County, scenes of life in the pre-civil-rights South, materials from African history and folklore, references to contemporary events, and reflections on the role of the artist in society. All these are themes that recur throughout his prose and poetry.

In 1947 Tolson left Wiley College for Langston University in Langston, Oklahoma, at the invitation of another of his fine debaters, Hobart Jarrett, then chairman of the English Department, and at the urging of his family. He was forty-nine years old and had just been named Poet Laureate of the Republic of Liberia, West Africa. The original sponsors of Liberia, the American Colonization Society, had also founded Lincoln University, of which his friend and schoolmate Horace Mann Bond had recently become president. The Poet Laureate was to compose a celebratory poem for the centennial of the founding of Liberia. As the poem he originally planned grew in length and complexity, Tolson was obliged to compose another, shorter poem that arrived in time for the celebration.

DO

Liberia?

No micro-footnote in a bunioned book
Homed by a pedant
With a gelded look:
You are
The ladder of survival dawn men saw
In the quicksilver sparrow that slips
The eagle's claw!

Seven strophes at the beginning of this book-length ode of 770 lines ask the meaning of Liberia. In seven lines each of roughly similar appearance we are told what Liberia is not, then what it is. The irregularly metered lines rhyme *a b a b* and are centered on the page, a practice which comes to dominate completely the final work of Tolson's career, **Harlem Gallery**. In the **Libretto** this visual structure alternates with other, different patterns as well as with non-rhymed sections. The divisions of the ode bear the names of the diatonic musical scale.

Sometime before beginning the composition of the ode, Tolson had encountered modern poetry and the New Criticism of Eliot, Pound, Ransom, Tate, Brooks, et alia. His own natural bent toward the intellectual, toward the attempt—like Paul Valéry—to render poetic creation as willed an activity as possible, was instantly attracted by the new techniques, though not by the ethos of their practitioners. For him, as for other artists, inspiration was a "given" with whose materials the poet consciously and conscientiously labored to produce a work of art. Techniques could be adapted to the expression of any ideology. Tolson felt the artist as artist made the greatest contribution to his people by creating the finest art object to express their liberation. As he was to say years later during a 1966 writers' conference at Fisk University: "A man has his biology, his sociology, and his psychology—and then he becomes a poet! . . . I'm a black poet, an African-American poet, a Negro poet. I'm no accident."

By the time of his work on the **Libretto** Tolson had begun to limit his extracurricular activities. There were occasional dramatic productions, no athletic activities, fewer though still frequent public addresses (such as those traveling with Roscoe Dunjee, founder-publisher of the Oklahoma City *Black Dispatch*, championing the cause of Ada Lois Sipuel Fisher), and no regular news columns: the emphasis was now principally on the writing of poetry. His reading and study of modern verse and criticism had become even more voracious as he taught himself the newer techniques and adapted them to his own talents. Thus the **Libretto**, though obviously influenced by the modernism of the period, is unlike the poetry of any of his contemporaries. It has lost none of its exultant belief in the final triumph of the "little people" and the achievement of political and socio-economic justice. Like Aimé Césaire, whose *Cahier d'un retour au pays natal* masterfully utilizes the techniques of surrealism,

Tolson remains a poet in blackness. He was fully aware of the difficulties this text presented and supplied pages of notes at the end of the book. In conversations with me he stated that he knew he was "dicing with Fate" in trying to force entrance into the "canon," but he was certain that, like Stendhal, he would be vindicated in time. He felt that he could do it and relished the challenge; so it had to be done!

Libretto underwent constant revision, and Allen Tate finally provided a very complimentary preface. At the same time, Tolson was busy writing other poetry, which appeared in print before the publication of *Libretto* in 1953. (Duke Ellington was the Composer Laureate of Liberia for the same centennial, for which he produced the provocative "Liberian Suite.") The last section of the final **"DO"** presents "The Futurafrique, the chef-d'oeuvre of Liberian Motors," "The United Nations Limited" (a train), "The Bula Matadi" (a luxurious ocean liner), "Le Premier des Noirs, of Pan-African Airways." The ode closes on this vision of Liberia:

> The Parliament of African Peoples signets forever
>   the Recessional of Europe and
>   trumpets the abolition of itself:
>   and no nation uses *Felis leo* or
>   *Aquila heliaca* as the emblem of
>   *blut und boden;* and the hyenas
>   whine no more among the bar-
>   ren bones of the seventeen sun-
>   set sultans of Songhai; and the
>   deserts that gave up the ghost
>   to green pastures chant in the
>   ears and teeth of the Dog, in
>   Rosh Hoshana of the Afric
>   calends: *"Honi soit qui mal y pense!"*

Nine years passed between the publication of *Rendezvous with America* and *Libretto for the Republic of Liberia*. Twelve years would elapse before the publication of Tolson's third and final collection of verse, *Harlem Gallery: Book I, The Curator*. Despite the time and labor required for the composition of the 340 poems of *A Gallery of Harlem Portraits,* he had not, when he decided to come back to the idea, reexamined the original manuscript merely to rework it. In the earlier work there is only a one-line mention of the Curator, but he becomes the principal character of the 1965 *Harlem Gallery*. Furthermore, by the time of the composition of the latter work Tolson's original idea had expanded to include the whole history of the diaspora of African Americans. He now planned to write five volumes, with books 2-5 to be titled respectively *Egypt Land, The Red Sea, The Wilderness* and *The Promised Land*. However, operations for cancer and deteriorating health during and after the writing of *The Curator* prevented any further work. Progress on this volume was indeed facilitated by the re-

fusal of his wife to consent to his running for a fifth term as mayor of Langston City!

Alpha

> The Harlem Gallery, an Afric pepper bird,
>   awakes me at a people's dusk of dawn,
> The age alters its image, a dog's hind leg,
>   and hazards the moment of truth in pawn.
>   The Lord of the House of Flies,
>   jaundice-eyed, synapses purled,
>   wries before the tumultuous canvas,
>   'The Second of May'—
>   by Goya:
>   the dagger of Madrid
>   vs.
>   the scimitar of Murat.
>   In Africa, in Asia, on the Day
> of Barricades, alarm birds bedevil the Great White
>   World,
> a Buridan's ass—not Balaam's—between no oats
>   and
>   hay.

Harlem Gallery: Book I, The Curator opens with these lines, which immediately allude to the Africa of the last line of *Libretto* and to W. E. B. DuBois, the premier African-American scholar. Tolson himself felt this work—with sections entitled **"Alpha"** through **"Omega"**—to be technically a finer artistic achievement than *Libretto*. He was always attempting to write a "great" line and to reduce to an absolute minimum the "stuffing" that writers (and musicians) must often use to get from one to another.

The preface was written by Karl Shapiro, purposely asked because he represented a "school" of poetry different from that of Allen Tate. Shapiro used a topic sentence "Tolson writes in Negro," which he went on to develop but which elicited often stormy comment in the years that followed. It is also a statement that Tate (in the *Libretto* preface) could never have made in admiration. A few years later Jan DeGaetani and the Atlanta Symphony Orchestra premiered T. J. Anderson's "Variations on a Theme by M. B. Tolson," which used materials from both *Libretto* and *Harlem Gallery* (a recording is available on Nonesuch Records).

The five projected volumes were to trace the odyssey of black Americans from Africa to the twentieth-century New World, "from chattel to Esquire," words which close the first volume. The point of view is not that of the artist, as in the original *Portraits,* but that of the Curator, who talks and meditates encyclopedically on race, art, artists, and the Gallery. We learn of the difficulties he has in dealing with "the bulls of Bashan," the moneyed Gallery supporters led by Mr. Guy Delaporte III, president of Bola Boa Enterprises, Inc.

There are conversations with artists and friends, many of them similar to characters and names in *Gallery of Harlem Portraits* or combinations of characters from that work and real life.

After five sections dedicated to the ideas and observations of the Curator, we meet John Laugart (in **"Zeta"**), a "half-blind painter, / spoon-shaped like an aged parrot-fish." He lives in "a catacomb Harlem flat / (grotesquely vivisected like microscoped maggots) / where the caricature of a rat / weathercocked in squeals / to be or not to be / and a snaggle-toothed toilet / grumbled its obscenity." Laugart has painted a masterpiece, *Black Bourgeoisie,* "a synthesis / (savage-sanative) / of Daumier and Gropper and Picasso," which the Curator is certain "will wring from [the Regents'] babbitted souls a Jeremian cry!" The Curator hangs the work anyway, and "Before the *bête noire* of [the painting], Mr. Guy Delaporte III takes his stand / a wounded Cape buffalo defying everything and Everyman!" Later "[Laugart] was robbed and murdered in his flat, / and the only witness was a Hamletian rat."

In Aunt Grindle's Elite Chitterling Shop (**"Eta"**) we meet the Curator's alter ego, Dr. Obi Nkomo, native African Africanist versed in the knowledge and culture of the West, who uses irony to comment on and often challenge the Curator's opinions. It is obvious that the poet sympathizes with them both and uses Nkomo to gain a perspective different from that of the Curator. Often, as a skillful debater, Tolson places the reader in a dilemmatic position before contrasting ideas of the Curator and the "signifying" Nkomo. The latter is also the vehicle for Tolson to incorporate African materials like those he has previously used in prose and poetry.

The name Hideho Heights (**"Lambda"**) combines the famous yell of Cab Calloway with the surname of one of the most cunningly effective of Tolson's debaters, Henry Heights, third member—with Farmer and Jarrett—of the team that defeated the national champions of the University of Southern California in 1935. Hideho was "the vagabond bard of Lenox Avenue, / whose satyric legends adhered like beggar's-lice," whose "voice like a / ferry horn in a river of fog" challenged the Curator: "In the beginning was the Word, / . . . not the Brush!" He comes to the Gallery from a jam session at the Daddy-O Club, "plays the dozens" with his friend, and reads him his poem on Louis "Satchmo" Armstrong, written in a popular jazzy-blues vein. Later, at the Zulu Club (a name Tolson had given to his own basement playroom-bar adorned with African photographs), Hideho reads "The Birth of John Henry," another "racial ballad in the public domain": "The night John Henry is born an ax / of lightning splits the sky, / and a hammer of thunder pounds the earth, / and the eagles and panthers cry!"

Hideho is unaware that one night when he woke up in his own bed after a drunken evening, it was the Curator who had put him to bed, discovering Hideho's secret, "the private poem in the modern vein." Tolson entitles this poem **"E&O.E,"** the name of one he himself had written. It had appeared in *Poetry Magazine* in September 1951, winning the Bess Hokim Prize that year. Tolson uses the Curator's discovery to problematize the relationship of folk poetry and the more difficult variety.

The following are a few of the more important characters of *Harlem Gallery:* Snakehips Briskie ("MU"), dancer, who "Convulsively, unexampledly / . . . began to coil, to writhe / like a prismatic-hued python / in the throes of copulation"; Black Diamond, "heir presumptive to the Lenox Policy Racket"; Shadrach Martial Kilroy, "president of Afroamerican Freedom"; Hedda Starks, alias Black Orchid ("RHO"), "a striptease has-been / of the brassy-pit-band era," but who had possessed a "barbarian bump and sophisticated grind / (every bump butted by the growl of a horn)"; Mister Starks, "from Onward, Mississippi— / via Paris, Texas, via Broken Bow, Oklahoma," whose mother named him "Mister" "Since every Negro male in Dixie was / either a *boy* or an *uncle*." (Starks was pianist-composer of the "Black Orchid Suite" and poet of the manuscript *Harlem Vignettes*.) There are also dozens of "walk-on" characters who people the Harlem of this volume, and space-time allusions are not limited to the Renaissance era.

After a brief, rare "writer's block," Tolson was able to "end" the volume. In **"PSI"** he has the Curator address first "Black Boy" and then "White Boy" on the subject of racial lies, myths, and stereotypes. **"OMEGA"** addresses them both at once, proclaiming the existence of flowers of hope that bloom in the ghetto despite the flowers of death in the white metropolis: "In the black ghetto / the white heather / and the white almond grow, / but the hyacinth / and the asphodel blow / in the white metropolis!" Then he calls on the Seven Sages of ancient Greece ("O Cleobulus, / O Thales, Solon, Periander, Bias, Chilo, / O Pittacus") to "unriddle the phoenix riddle of this." The poem closes on this tribute to the Gallery and to African Americans:

> Our public may possess in Art
> a Mantegna figure's arctic rigidity;
> yet—I hazard—yet,
> this allegro of the Harlem Gallery
> is not a chippy fire,
> for here, in focus, are paintings that chronicle
> a people's New World odyssey
> from chattel to Esquire!

Aldon L. Nielsen (essay date Summer 1992)

SOURCE: "Melvin B. Tolson and the Deterritorialization of Modernism," in *African American Review*, Vol. 26, No. 2, Summer, 1992, pp. 241-55.

[*In the following essay, Nielsen states that Tolson's works "are an assault upon Anglo-American modernism's territorial designs, but they have been little read."*]

"In 1932 I was a Negro poet writing Anglo-Saxon sonnets as a graduate student in an Eastern University"—these are the words that Melvin B. Tolson chose to describe himself as he had been at the outset of his odyssey as an artist, a description which, while recalling the formal beginnings of other modernist poets such as William Carlos Williams, resonates yet more profoundly with Frederick Douglass's recollections of his first interlinear strides towards freedom and a style of his own. But the interlinear tracings of both Douglass and Tolson soon began to diverge radically from their models. Not merely glosses, or even really copying, the writing between the lines of Frederick Douglass and Melvin B. Tolson is a repetition elsewhere of the model which eventually displaces the model; it is a *rewriting* which comes to read itself as prior to the lines of the master. Both Douglass and Tolson run the risk of being flogged for marring the highly prized lines of Master Thomas, and yet each in the end has succeeded in writing "other lines" which challenge the territorial claims of the master text of Western hegemony. Each sought an opening within the dominant text of his time, and placed into that space radical representations of African-American aesthetics whose eventual effect is to assert their own primacy over the stylings of the master class. Tolson's later style, far from being a mask adopted simply to gain entry to the master's house, is a means by which Anglo-American claims to the ground of modernism are set aside.

Certainly Tolson has been flogged for his later style, and the terms of the critical argument over his corpus seem to have been set by the authors of the prefaces to his two last books, Allen Tate and Karl Shapiro. Just as Shapiro's preface was a response as much to Tate's as to Tolson's verses, critics who have come at Tolson afterwards, Black and White alike, have raged and ranged between the Scylla and Charybdis of Shapiro's two most provocative praises of Tolson's poems: that they were "outpounding Pound," and that in them "Tolson writes and thinks in Negro." Indeed, many of Tolson's earliest reviewers and critics seem to have been as exercised, either favorably or negatively, by Shapiro as by Tolson. This is certainly the case in Sarah Webster Fabio's 1966 essay "Who Speaks Negro?" and Josephine Jacobsen, reviewing *Harlem Gallery* for the *Baltimore Evening Sun*, spends roughly half of her print space arguing with Shapiro. Just as it has proved nearly impossible to speak of Tolson's late books without speaking of their prefaces, few have found it possible to speak of the develop-

ment of Tolson's style without expressing suspicion, sometimes severe, about its origins and its racial politics.

In characterizing the reactions of Langston Hughes to Tolson's belated public attention, Arnold Rampersad writes that, "*suddenly,* having overhauled his craft according to the most complex tenets of high modernism, and having renounced the militant pro-Marxism of his first volume, **Rendezvous with America,** Tolson was now sporting laurels of a quality never before conceded by white critics to a black writer" (my emphasis). The "suddenness" of Tolson's stylistic transformation is of course belied by those poems published between the appearance of **Rendezvous with America** and **Libretto for the Republic of Liberia,** as well as by the documentary evidence in the hundreds of drafts collected among Tolson's papers at the Library of Congress. But Hughes's feelings, at least as they are reported by Rampersad, also unfairly associate Tolson's alterations of poetic mode with a betrayal of his earlier politics. This conclusion demands a belief that radical politics require a certain form of poetics, a belief which, according to Rampersad, Hughes held.

> While the *Libretto* and *Harlem Gallery* are clearly indebted to Pound, Eliot, and Tate, they *sound* like none of these poets, and Tolson's late poems differ substantially in form and tone from the work of the one White poet they most resemble in diction, Hart Crane.
> —*Aldon L. Nielsen*

Hughes wrote to his friend Arna Bontemps at the time of the publication of Tolson's *Libretto,* recalling that Tolson had said he would "write so many foreign words and footnotes that they would *have* to pay him some mind!" and attributing, as others have, the most mundane of motivations to Tolson while simultaneously failing to consider Tolson's ironic humor about his public reception. Further, though, as Rampersad represents the shape of this betrayal, Tolson, "the poet laureate of an African country[,] had written the most hyper-European, unpopulist poem ever penned by a black writer. Did it not matter that very few of the American Friends of Liberia, and even fewer Liberians themselves, could understand the poem . . . ?" (For the remainder of this article I will follow Rampersad's usage of *populist* in its contemporary rather than its historical sense.) Elsewhere Rampersad refers to Tolson's poetic transformation as "gentrification."

It is the confluence of racial, political, and aesthetic questions, perhaps inevitable in America, which underscores the peculiarity of these charges against Tolson. No one seems to take Tolson to task in this fashion for his use of White models in his earlier verse. Though the influences of Sandburg and Masters are readily apparent in those early poems, few would accuse Tolson of having deliberately adopted those models to curry favor with the White literary establishment; fewer still would see in his use of Masters as a model a betrayal of potential Black audiences. And yet one might argue that Tolson sounds *more* like his White models in the early than in the late poems. While the *Libretto* and *Harlem Gallery* are clearly indebted to Pound, Eliot, and Tate, they *sound* like none of these poets, and Tolson's late poems differ substantially in form and tone from the work of the one White poet they most resemble in diction, Hart Crane. Still, the suspicion of Tolson's poetics persists.

The charge that Tolson severed himself from Black readers is made still more strange when it is made by White critics. In an early review of *Harlem Gallery* Laurence Lieberman reported the results of an experiment:

> It may well be that my problem in reading this book is that I am not Negro. Well, I have just spent a year teaching at the college in St. Thomas. The student body here is about ninety percent Negro, and nearly every Negro land I can think of is represented, including Africa and the states. Though English is the mother tongue for nearly all of the students, there is so much variety of accent and dialect, I have to struggle to understand what they are saying in class (as indeed they must struggle to understand each other). Africa is the land of *their* racial heritage, quite as much as it is Tolson's. I have tried to get the students—and some of them are promising poets—to become interested in reading Tolson's book. They do not understand him. He simply does not speak their language.

The tortured progress of Lieberman's logic in this passage will be familiar to inveterate readers of White criticism of Black writings. The reviewer begins by momentarily conceding to a racialist argument, that perhaps the fact of Whiteness is in and of itself a block against his understanding of a Black poem. But then, by producing evidence of uninterested or confused Black readers, he dismisses both the racialist argument *and* Tolson's poem. Despite the opening concession, the White teacher retains a position of primacy over both the poem and the students. "Hey, I tried, but you just weren't Black enough," seems to be an apt paraphrase. One could easily imagine a Black professor undertaking a similar experiment, attempting to interest a class of White students in the verse of Wallace Stevens, Hart Crane, or Gertrude Stein. Perhaps such a professor would, faced with failure, assert that these poets simply do not speak the students' language. But would our imaginary professor be likely to accuse the poets in question of being less authentic, less White, or less in touch with their traditions than the students?

This is exactly what Lieberman, despite a few complimentary things he has to say about Tolson's poem, goes on to do:

> The Trinidadians and British Guianese I have met in St. Thomas have a more seminal dispute with Western Culture than any American Negro I have ever read, including Tolson and Baldwin. The Negroes of Trinidad and British Guiana have had Western Culture shoveled down their throats by the United Kingdom at closer range than the American Negroes. Some of the more outspoken among them dismiss the entire civilization arising from the Greeks as barbaric, and favor an Egypt-oriented definition of our cultural heritage. However absurd their claim, they at least offer a possibility for a new major direction and tradition for the modern world. Tolson does not offer this, so far as I can see.

Lieberman is playing a game here which no Black writer can possibly win. He simultaneously berates Tolson for failing to find a Black readership in his classroom, and sets himself up to judge who among Black writers does the most to break with the traditions of Western Culture, traditions about which they make "absurd claims."

That some African-American critics played similar games with his work was something that pained Melvin Tolson. Among his papers is a telling note in which he speaks of himself in the third person, remarking that the Poet Laureate of Liberia "was warned to stop using complex words that did nothing but give delirium tremens to poetry readers of the *Black Gazette* or *Ebony* and *The Negro World*." On the reverse side of this note Tolson has written starkly: "Negro critics beat poets of color / Keep step in the coffle." And in a letter to Allen Tate, Tolson observes that, "if the vanguard white poet is isolated, his Negro fellow is annihilated between the walls of biracialism." It is a mark of Tolson's determination that he refused to keep step in the coffle; it is a disservice to this poet to claim that he effected his successes by cozying up to the masters.

It is understandable, however, that Tolson's readers feel that he wished to be recognized for having brought modernist techniques to African-American verse. On June 1, 1949, pretending an oversight, Tolson appends this postscript to a letter to Tate: "I forgot to mention, Mr. Tate, that I believe the LIBRETTO marks a 'fork in the road,' a change in direction, for what is called Negro Poetry. Between me and you, it's long overdue!" It is this sort of remark that has earned for Tolson some animosity from later readers. And when, in a letter dated March 15 of the following year, Tolson refers to Tate's preface to the *Libretto* as the Negro's "Literary emancipation proclamation," most readers will share a level of exasperation. Who, we must ask, is being freed from whom, by what means, and for what future literary sharecropping? But a reading of Tolson which sees him only as a literary chameleon trying to assimilate with all deliberate speed is achieved at the price of ignoring the full complexity of Tolson's own, often playful remarks, and at the greater cost of not sufficiently reading what Tolson has in fact written.

In the unpublished novel *All Aboard!* one of Tolson's characters makes a comment to a mother which might easily have been directed later to Tate and Shapiro:

> "Mrs. Graves," he said mockingly, "after you've spent your hard-earned bucks on your only son, how d'you expect him to talk?" He shook his forefinger at her. "Didn't Toussaint L'Overture Graves study the same books white boys study?"

The advent of someone like Tolson should come as no surprise to American readers. But, as the name of Tolson's earnest scholar Toussaint L'Overture Graves indicates, while he studied the same books as the White boys, he studied them differently and to different ends. The outcome of his studies portends something rather different than what many of his critics have imagined. What Tolson came to attempt was a decolonizing of American letters, a task which he saw as linking him to Whitman.

Melvin Tolson's *Libretto for the Republic of Liberia* and *Harlem Gallery* are poems which, like the longer works of Pound and Eliot, have designs upon their audiences."
—*Aldon L. Nielsen*

In attempting to decolonize American [literature]," Tolson notes, "Whitman was compelled to emphasize and glorify the Americanism of his art." Tolson is a decolonizer after Whitman and Toussaint L'Overture; he will emphasize and glorify the *African*-Americanism of his art, and he does it on the plain of the master's colony, on the site of the colonized master text of modernism. Tolson even goes so far as to suggest a modern revision of Whitman, a poet of whom Tolson says in one note, "There was no other with his ethnic empathy." Tolson offers an amendment towards the updating of his precursor: "The bronze god was Paul Robeson, the All-American of all time. Yes, if old Walt Whitman, America's greatest poet, had seen that, he would have included Paul Robeson in America's greatest epic, *Leaves of Grass*."

Melvin Tolson's *Libretto for the Republic of Liberia* and *Harlem Gallery* are poems which, like the longer works of Pound and Eliot, have designs upon their audiences. But they are works which both constitute a considerably different audience than that addressed by those White modernists and which constitute that audience on a different ground. Efforts to portray Tolson as a poet who betrayed his populist instincts to achieve the elite readership of academic modernism require that we ignore the nature of his poetry and the breadth of Tolson's own remarks. While it is true that Tolson took some comfort from John Ciardi's New Critical distinction between "vertical" and "horizontal" audiences, looking to possible future readers for fuller vindication, and while he was able to make jokes out of his understanding of the primary book-buying public, writing in one note, "My poetry is of the proletariat, by the proletariat, and for the bourgeoisie," it is also true that Tolson's works, far from being addressed only to experts, question the territory of modernist expertise and present knowledge as a link between poet and populace, a link which the populace should strive after as strongly as the poet:

> Is it too much to ask
> of homo sapiens the sweat of Hellas
> in order to enjoy Sophocles and Ar-
> istophanes . . .
> Even Elvis Presley and Bojangles
> and Patanjali
> require of their devotees the rigor
> of four dimensions.

If the words of the modernist bard do not occupy quite the same relationship to the public as do the proverbs of folk wisdom, they might still fill a similar function:

> The value of a proverb
> the elite never know:
> it is the people
> who reap and sow
> as the words list or blow.

Marked in his notes as a "thing to remember" is the assertion that "Negro artists [are not] alienated in Aframerica like white artists"; rather, "the pessimism of the white man throws into new relief the new Demi-urge in Negro life and Africa." In Tolson's view the African-American writer had no choice but to be a race man: "Racial bias forced him into race consciousness." Though he thinks of the poet as being in a cultural vanguard, he argues against the Eliotic position on culture: "If Mr. Eliot had read Dr. Oliver Cox's 'Race, Caste and Perhaps Class,' he would not have written his 'Class and the Elite.'" Indeed, Tolson saw his work as offering a way out of what he saw as Eliot's dead end. He placed himself in a more pluralist modernism with writers such as Williams, Hughes, and Crane, *contra* Eliot: "'The Bridge' is a way out of the pessimism of 'The Waste Land.' The **'Libretto'** is a vista out of the mysticism of the 'Four Quartets.'"

Far from being an elitist, Tolson was a tireless propagandist among the people for his brand of modernism—as a teacher, a popular public speaker, a columnist, and a poet. Michael Bérubé has recently provided an apt appraisal of the type of populist aesthetic found in *Harlem Gallery:*

> On this count the poem is unambiguous. To do anything less than disseminate modernism to the masses is to give in to cultural forces which would patronize and condescend to "the people" by giving them the kind of art which, in Clement Greenberg's words, "predigests art for the spectator and spares him effort, provides him with a shortcut to the pleasure of art that detours what is necessarily difficult in genuine art."

In his regular columns in the *Washington Tribune,* which ran from 1937 through 1944, Tolson constantly suggested readings to his audience, generally couching these suggestions in the most contemporary terms: "If you want to get the lowdown on the ancient Greeks, read Sappho, the Minnie-the-Moocher of her day." He plugged Margaret Anderson's magazine *Common Ground,* giving the address for potential subscribers, and, in the tradition of Walt Whitman and Ezra Pound, he plugged his own poems as well:

> Of course, I want you to read **"Rendezvous with America."** . . . I just received word that the *Atlantic Monthly* is bringing out my poem, **"Babylon."** Some of you read **"Dark Symphony."** Well, I hope you like this last piece. It has an interesting history.

It is true that Tolson quite consciously wrote more simply in his journalism than in his verse, but it is also true that he genuinely hoped that many of the people in his *Washington Tribune* audience would be among the readers of his verse. If some White writers and their works were alienated from their people, "The mouths of white books choke with dust," Tolson notes. Tolson sees himself much in the role of an organic intellectual, as Antonio Gramsci has defined that term.

Odd as it may at first seem, this is in part an explanation for some of the esoterism in Tolson's works. In his effort to rearticulate modernism as a populist American aesthetic with African roots, Melvin Tolson reconfigured the audience for modern art, revising and reappropriating Eliot's objective correlative. It is this movement which explains an otherwise perverse sounding note among Tolson's papers.

He writes: "I have hidden my identity as a Negro poet in words . . . / thus am I more militantly a Negro." The eye is drawn so strongly to the word *hidden* in this remark that its sense seems hopelessly contradictory. How might one be more militantly Negro by in any way hiding an identity as a Negro poet? What Tolson's possibly unrescuable comment appears in the fuller context of his works to portend is a militant alignment with a history of African and African-American signifying practices, what Tolson sometimes refers to as "Deepitalki." Michael Bérubé is half-right when he describes Tolson's approach: ". . . Tolson saw his adoption of modernist technique as a guerilla strategy, a means of letting revolutionary discourse sound in the ears of conservative whites by masking that discourse in a no longer revolutionary poetics." The poet did see his work as a guerilla strategy, but he did not see conservative Whites as his *only,* or even *primary,* audience. Nor did he see modernist poetics as no longer revolutionary. To the contrary, he came to see modernist poetics as having been already arrived at by African aesthetics, thus rendering the African-American tradition primary rather than merely imitative.

At one point in his development, Tolson separated himself from Eliot, Tate, and other Anglo-American modernists on the grounds of content. In a speech at Kentucky State College, Tolson told his listeners:

> Imitation must be in technique *only.* We have a rich heritage of folk lore and history. We are part of America. We are part of the world. Our native symbols must be lifted into the universal. Yes, we must study the techniques of Robert Lowell, Dylan Thomas, Carlos Williams, Ezra Pound, Karl Shapiro, W. H. Auden. The great revolution has not been in science but in poetry.

Yet, Tolson's rearticulation of modernism led him eventually to assert African progenitors in the realm of technique. Tolson could claim that his esoteric modernism made him more militantly Negro because he claimed that the aesthetic had roots in African and African-American poetics. His audience was not composed entirely of conservative Whites. He writes in one place, "*I talk with old slaves* / (Deepi-Talki)."

Melvin Tolson was an inveterate collector of African proverbs and African talk. Among his papers are page after page upon which he has patiently copied out proverbs unearthed in his reading. He notes of these proverbs and poems, "Sometimes the Africans go esoteric on us," and he traces the tradition of African esoterism into African-American song and speech. "Esoterica," he notes, "meanings of spirituals like symbolism today in poetry. / Exs: 'Go Down Moses' / 'Steal Away to Jesus' / *I talk with old slaves.*" It is also the rearticulation of modernism as African which surfaces in remarks Tolson made to his audience at the Library of Congress when he was invited to read there late in his life:

> You know, poets like to do a great amount of double talking. We think very often that the modernists gave us that concept of poetry, which is untrue. Because I can go back into the Negro work songs, the spirituals and jazz, and show you that double talk of poetry. And I can even [clicking his fingers for emphasis] *go to Africa, as I shall do tonight, and show you that double talk of poetry,* especially in metaphors and symbols. So I'm doing some double talk here.

Having found in the African proverbs a source he could cite to justify the seemingly esoteric diction of his rearticulated modernism, a source which antedates *and,* in his view, influences his more immediate modernist models, Tolson goes on to elaborate a theory of rhythmic signifying rooted in African-American tradition, a theory related to Frost's ideas about sentence sound, and a theory whose source Tolson suggests in an aside may already have found its roundabout way into the American canon:

> Now it is said that you have to watch these poets, because with their beat they're always trying to make you suspend your intellect. And then he's got you in charge. You know how Edgar Allan Poe could do that, [clicking his fingers for emphasis] *sometimes saying nothing, but that beat would get you. . . .* I don't know, he might have got it from the old Negro preacher.
>
> My students often come to me and say: "Well, I went to hear old Reverend So-and-so when I went home during the holidays. And you know the man didn't say *anything,* and everybody was just rocking, . . . rocking."
>
> I said, "You need a course that you haven't got in college yet." [Steps away from the podium and stamps out a rhythm with his feet to demonstrate.] What did that old preacher do? He set up a rhythmic pattern, just like the poet.

Those who would oppose Tolson's modernism to an oral, vernacular tradition, clearly favoring the latter, make at least two mistakes. First, they neglect to consider fully the implications of the fact that the oral tradition is represented by poets *in writing.* Second, they present a grossly reduced vernacular for our consideration. Tolson's turning to the heritage of African proverb and the traditions of pulpit performance is part of an aesthetic that celebrates and continues the richness of verbal signifying practice among the people. In *Blues People,* Amiri Baraka's seminal study of African-American vernacular music, Baraka claims for Black language practice an aesthetic reminiscent of Emily Dickinson's:

> In language, the African tradition aims at circumlocution rather than at exact definition. The direct statement is considered crude and unimaginative; the veiling of all contents in ever-changing paraphrase is considered the criterion of intelligence and personality. In music, the same tendency towards obliquity and ellipsis is noticeable.

Similarly, Tolson had written in his notes that "the direction of a poet is indirection. To speak in military terms, the prosifier says, 'Forward! March!' but the poet says,' Oblique! March!"

In *Understanding the New Black Poetry,* Stephen Henderson identifies among the features of a Black aesthetic in language virtuoso naming and enumerating, metaphysical imagery, compressed and cryptic imagery, and hyperbolic imagery. (Coincidentally, Tolson once began to make notes for a talk on "Hyperbole in Negro Poetry.") These are but a few of the "innumerable forms" of Black linguistic elegance Henderson posits in opposition to those who would reduce "Black" linguistic style to a very narrow register. For Henderson, as for Tolson and Baraka, "there is this tradition of beautiful talk," and that tradition will not be confined within any critic's closed notions of a "street" language. "Don Lee, for example, can use the word 'neoteric' without batting an eye and send us scurrying to our dictionaries. The word is not 'Black' but the casual, virtuoso way that he drops it on us—like 'Deal with that'—*is an elegant Black linguistic gesture.*" Melvin B. Tolson finds in the vernacular of the African-American preacher *and* his flock the same thing he finds in the language arts of Africa, a highly allusive, hyperbolic, compressed metaphoricity, and what Houston Baker has termed "virtuoso mastery of form."

In *Harlem Gallery* Tolson presents this as a sustaining feature of Black life: "Metaphors and symbols in Spirituals and Blues / have been the Negro's manna in the Great White World." Speaking to his newspaper readers in Washington, D.C., Tolson said, "There is mastery in old John Milton's *Paradise Lost.* But no greater mastery than you'll find in one of God's old trombones. At his best, the old preacher had the poetry of word and motion—if you get what I mean." Having schooled himself in the techniques of Anglo-American modernism, Tolson proceeded in the last years of his life to reverse the roles of master and student. Having inscribed his lines, as it were, between the lines of modernism's master text, he was now suggesting that the master text had in fact copied itself out of the text of African traditions. The sea-turtle had eaten his way out of the great white shark, had eaten "*his* way to freedom / beyond the vomiting dark." It comes as no surprise that such audacious signifying has provoked consternation in some readers:

> We chewed this quid a second time,
> for Black Boy often adds
> the dimension of ethnic irony
> to Empson's classic seven.

II

> Thus, the Negro scholar in our day
> Is born to be a genealogist.

When in 1965 interviewer M. W. King asked Melvin Tolson about his having "out-pounded Pound," Tolson immediately responded, "Well, I did go to the Africans instead of the Chinese." Pound too had gone to the Africans, but he had gone with Frobenius as his guide, thus replicating some of the errors of that source, and his own biases prevented his pursuing fuller studies of the development of African civilizations. Tolson had, by the time of his interview with King, been going to the Africans for decades, partly at least to fulfil the role of genealogist: to fill in the ahistorical nothingness to which European art, philosophy, and history had consigned Africa, and to reveal the fuller genealogy of modernism, which includes African sources. In the 1965 interview he remarks that "Gertrude Stein's judgment that the Negro suffers from Nothingness revealed her profound ignorance of African cultures," then reads into the record just a few of the hundreds of African proverbs he had collected when preparing to write his *Libretto for the Republic of Liberia*. Having read some of the same proverbs to his audience at the Library of Congress, he challenges them: "Now you ask the modern poets to make metaphors as good, proverbs as good." Bringing his genealogy around to America, he introduces his poem to old Satchmo, Louis Armstrong, repeating Stein's notorious remark and admonishing his listeners, "Now you listen to this and see if there's any truth to that; and you've *heard* the African proverbs." Coming back to Stein in *Harlem Gallery* Tolson provides a literal genealogy:

> The Toothpick, Funky Five, and
> Tippling Tom!
> Ma Rainey, Countess Willie V., and
> Aunt Harriet!
> Speckled Red, Skinny Head Pete,
> and Stormy Weather!
> Listen, Black Boy.
> Did the High Priestess at 27 rue de
> Fleurus
> assert, "The Negro suffers from

nothingness"?

This artful list Tolson terms the "real *ancients* of the jazz world," and it is meant as self-evident refutation for an audience that recognizes any of these names.

Throughout his career Tolson collected information about African culture, particularly information which belied the myth of an Africa without a history, or which unsettled the myths of European primacy. From Mommsen he collected the observation that "it was through Africa that [Christianity] became a world religion," and on the same sheet of paper, while reading Du Bois, Tolson is reminded that Moses married a Black woman. From Franz Boas he copied out the assertion that "any one who is familiar with the history of Africa before its subjugation by the Europeans knows the industrial skill, the artistic genius, the political ability of the Negro. In every region from West Africa through the Sudan to South Africa we have proof of it." On draft pages of the *Libretto* he notes, "Culture of 14th Century Africa equal to Europe's," and in the final version of the poem he transforms his historical researches into lyric genealogy:

> Solomon in all his glory had no Ox-
> ord.
> Alfred the Great no University of
> Sankoré:
> Footloose professors, chimney
> sweeps of the skull,
> From Europe and Asia; youths,
> souls in one skin,
> Under white scholars like El-Akit,
> under
> Black humanists like Bagayogo.

Of Bagayogo he had also written in "The Negro Scholar": "When Anglo-Saxons laud the Venerable Bede, / Let Africans remember Bagayogo."

The Kingdom of Benin was of special interest to Tolson. In the margin of his working drafts of the *Libretto,* he notes that "Professor Van Luschan considered the craftsmanship of Benin workers equal to the best ever produced by Cellini." Beyond seeing the arts of Benin as having equaled European accomplishments, he sees them as having been the source of much that is modernism: "The listening ear can hear / among the moderns, blue / tomtoms of Benin." In his working draft for the *Libretto,* he had already claimed for Benin an influence upon the revolutionary reconceptualizing of space by modernist artists such as Braque and Picasso: "Benin, whose ivory and / bronze statues gave lyricism and / Space reality to modernistic art. . . ." By the time he completed the *Libretto* he had upped the ante, contemporizing the claim in one direction, while giving it greater specificity in another.

The Bula Matadi, diesel-engined,
fourfold-decked,
swan sleek, glides like an ice-
ballet skater out of the Bight of
Benin, the lily lyricism of whose
ivory and gold figurines larked
space oneness on the shelf ice
of avant-garde Art. . . .

Thus Africa is "No waste land yet"—neither the dark continent portrayed by Eliot, Conrad, Stein, and Crane nor the waste land that Eliot's Europe had become—but out of Africa had come much of the most provocative aesthetics of the modern. Tolson finds:

The ground the Negro Scholar
stands upon
Is fecund with the challenge and
tradition

That Ghana knew, and Melle, and
Ethiopia,
And Songhai: civilizations black
men built
Before the Cambridge wits, the Ox-
ford dons
Gave to the Renaissance a diadem.

Robert M. Farnsworth, in his biography of Melvin B. Tolson, argues that "Tolson clearly saw himself in the vanguard of an army of black cultural soldiers who would make the African past a centerpiece of the world's future. . . ." This could only be accomplished, however, by displacing White hegemony not only over modernist aesthetics, but also over the idea of America and its history. In adapting African musical traditions to the Western scale and tempered instruments, African Americans forever altered both the music of Africa and the music of the West. In his plans to create a Harlem anthology which would serve a similar function to the Greek Anthology, Tolson had to look at both Harlem and the Western classical traditions differently. In writing *Libretto for the Republic of Liberia,* which is organized in sections following the Western musical scale, Tolson, who had already begun to rearticulate modernism as virtuoso African-American form, undertook a confrontation with American history on a transformed ground, displacing White experience from its position of centrality and refiguring both the Middle Passage and the Pilgrim story.

His earlier poem **"Rendezvous with America"** had begun this process by placing the experiences of the Middle Passage on an equal level with the mythic progenitors of White America: "Time unhinged the gates / Of Plymouth Rock and Jamestown and Ellis Island." **"Rendezvous with America,"** having unhinged accepted historical primacies, adopts a questioning rhetorical strategy:

America?
America is the Black Man's country,
The Red Man's, the Yellow Man's,
The Brown Man's, the White Man's.

In this enumeration the White Man's claim to proprietorship comes last, and thus **"Rendezvous with America"** sets the pattern for the *Libretto* in both form and rhetorical stance.

The *Libretto* does not stop at its allusion to the fact that Africans preceded the pilgrims in the New World ("'. . . the Negroes have been in this country longer, on the average, than their white neighbors; they first came to this country on a ship called the Jesus one year before the Mayflower'"), it portrays the founding of Liberia as an altered return to a site of civilization which precedes the American:

Before Liberia was Songhai was: be-
fore
America set the raw founding on
Africa's
Doorstep, before the Genoese diced
west,
Burnt warriors and watermen of
Songhai
Tore into bizarreries the uniforms of
Portugal
And sewed an imperial quilt of
tribes.

At the opening of his *Libretto* Tolson recalls the form of his own earlier poem while simultaneously seeming to offer answers to Countée Cullen's questioning refrain in "Heritage," "What is Africa to me?" *and* distancing himself again from Eliot's "Waste Land":

Liberia?
No micro-footnote in a bunioned
book
Horned by a pedant
With a gelded look:
You are
The ladder of survival dawn men
saw

Liberia is not the ahistorical blank of Eliot's Africa; neither is it the impotent tribal dirge of the Eliotic modern. It is rather the fecund soil upon which African and American histories rerendezvous, the territory upon which both histories are to be reconstituted. Middle Passage and colonizing pilgrimage cross here in a reconstruction that undoes canonical versions of American heritage.

Where his earlier poem had claimed for African Americans a rendezvous with America at Plymouth Rock, in the *Libretto* Tolson figures forth a Black pilgrimage, one which retraces the Middle Passage to rewrite a redemptive history on the territory of a new, African-Americanized Africa. Tolson, writing to an unidentified correspondent, said this of his intentions:

> In the fifth section, I picture the brig *Elizabeth* taking Elizah Johnson and his Black Pilgrim Fathers to West Africa. The dilemma again: the White Pilgrims sail west, but the Black Pilgrims sail east! Using a new stanzaic form—
>
> This is the Middle Passage: here
> Gehenna hatchways vomit up
> The living and the dead.
>
> This is the Middle Passage: here
> The sharks grow fattest and the stench
> Goads God to hold his nose!
>
> I tried to pack into these lines the tragedies of thousands of blacks lost on their [way] to America. Later, I picture the Black Pilgrims landing on Providence Island. I hope I've captured the heroism of it! At least nobody has tried to do it before in verse.

One can not help but think here again of Tolson's story, in *Harlem Gallery,* of the sea-turtle eating its way through the devouring shark to freedom. The same waves that wash over the bones of many thousands gone during the Middle Passage now reverse the myth of English pilgrimage and carry African Americans to their Providence Island, where they will build an Africa made different by the American sojourn. The Black pilgrim fathers will establish Liberia as a city on a hill, as "A moment of the conscience of mankind!" Reversing the colonial expropriation of African resources, Liberia is to make possible the defense of freedom on African soil against racist, European adventures which threaten all the world:

> *The rubber from Liberia shall arm*
>
> *Free peoples and her airport hinterlands*
> *Let loose the winging grapes of wrath*
> *upon*
> *The Desert Fox's cocained nietzcheans*
> *A goose-step from the Gateway of the East!*

A new world music is to sound for a "Futurafrique" in which the "Parliament of African Peoples signets forever the *Recessional of Europe.*"

The ethos of this new New World is summed up in Tolson's citation of the words of Jehudi Ashmun, the White pilgrim who overturned the founding mythos of America by sailing to a lost colony of freed slaves in West Africa:

> "My Negro Kinsmen,
> America is my mother,
> Liberia is my wife,
> And Africa is my brother."

No elitist betrayal of populist poetics, the *Libretto* draws upon many of the most ready-to-hand mythic figurations to point the way to the Futurafrique's realization of the American democratic promise in African lives on African soil:

> The Parliament of African Peoples
> plants the winged
> *lex scripta* of its New Order on
> Roberts Avenue, in Bunker Hill,
> Liberia . . .

Here will be realized the Whitmanian democratic vistas "with leaves of grass and great audiences. . . ." If the Parliament of African Peoples also "trumpets the abolition of itself," it is more a sign of Tolson's lingering Marxism, his hope for an eventual withering away of oppressive state apparatus, than of any doubt about his, or Africa's, project. The Parliament will abolish itself eventually because, as American mythology claimed for its institutions, the "Parliament of African Peoples decrees the Zu'lhijyah of Everyman," and in eternizing "*Afrika sikelel' iAfrika. . . ,*" the *Libretto* simply sounds the notes of self-saving determination which are today a rallying cry for the liberation movements in South Africa: "Africa save Africa."

Tolson's *Libretto for the Republic of Liberia,* in the process of redirecting America's founding myths and redeploying the sources of modernist influences, also displaces the hegemonic view of African-American intellectual development as secondary and imitative by erecting as its own framework the trope of African-American pilgrimage to literacy and educational independence. Following in the tradition of Frederick Douglass, W. E. B. Du Bois, Mary McLeod Bethune, and other writers, Tolson was, in the *Libretto,* memorializing the liberatory impetus of Black educational institutions. In addition to placing in his poem allusions to the legendary centers of African learning such as Timbuktoo, which rival and precede many Anglo-American centers for the dissemination of White intellectual hegemony, Tolson has created in the *Libretto* a poem whose very being is a commemorative to Tolson's African-American *alma mater,* as well as to African learning and philosophy generally.

Tolson's status as the only American artist to have been named Poet Laureate of another nation, Liberia, is more often noted with surprise and credited to Tolson's own cleverness than reckoned for what it most immediately is—tribute to the institutions which have contributed most to the ongoing cultural cross fertilization of African and African-American life. Few White American intellectuals are at all familiar with the histories of what we have come to call Historically Black Colleges and Universities; fewer still know that two of the most important African-American poets, Melvin B. Tolson and Langston Hughes, both studied at Lincoln University; fewer yet are aware of Lincoln's place of primacy as the oldest such institution in North America; and I doubt that any of Tolson's earliest White critics knew of Lincoln's connection with the history of Liberia before learning about it from Tolson.

Writing to Dr. Horace Mann Bond, a former classmate of his at Lincoln who subsequently became president of the university, Tolson promises, "In my *Notes* to the poem (it requires them) I am seeing that Lincoln University shall come to the attention of the superintellectuals of the English-speaking worlds." I believe we are justified in reading more than a little irony in Tolson's reference to Anglo-American superintellectuals. Little of the history he was contending with in his *Libretto* was known to these "super-intellectuals," many of whom blithely assumed that Africa and its diaspora had no history to speak of.

The *Libretto*'s notes were required at least in part to alert readers to the documentary evidence of this history; it was then up to the readers themselves to contend with the implicit ironies. In one of these notes, Tolson informs us that

> Lincoln University, the oldest Negro institution of its kind in the world, was founded as Ashmun Institute. The memory of the white pilgrim survives in old Ashmun Hall and in the Greek and Latin inscriptions cut in stones sacred to Lincoln men. The annual Lincoln-Liberian dinner is traditional, and two of the graduates have been ministers to Liberia.

Both the annual dinner and the contributions of Lincoln alumni to American-Liberian diplomacy mark originary links between the school and the African nation.

The American Colonization Society, formed in 1816, was not, as its name might imply, a society for the furtherance of American imperial desire, but a society organized to work for the repatriation of Africans to their native continent. As such, it was simultaneously a colonizing and decolonizing undertaking. It was their lost colony that Jehudi Ashmun and

his wife sailed to join, along with a number of freed African Americans, in 1822. Established by that same American Colonization Society for the purpose of training future Liberian leaders, Ashmun Institute was subsequently rechristened Lincoln University. (As it happens, Tolson had been a student at Lincoln High School in Kansas City and had published juvenilia in the *Lincolnian* in 1917 and 1918.) What Tolson found in all this was a powerfully fecund metaphorical site on which the boundaries between colonizer and colonized, primary and secondary, and original and imitation were so fluid as to become less than boundaries, undoing the traditional typology of the story of America's progress.

For Tolson, Middle Passage and Pilgrimage are terrible mirror images of one another, reflecting historical horrors and redemptive human possibility. There is a city on a hill in Africa which is both precedent and descendent to the New Canaan in America. The Atlantic becomes a profoundly signifying divider, like the "*paseq*" which Tolson inscribes in his *Libretto,* drawn from his copy of holy scripture, and which he calls the "most mysterious sign in the literature." It is an unsounded textual sign floating an oral and oracular tradition. It is an interruption that denies the boundary lines we would draw between scripture and speech, between *ecriture* and lecture, an unspeakable parting of the scriptural seas. Tolson places these powerful signs in play, displacing the priority of the master text between whose lines he inscribes.

This was not a symptom of arcane obfuscation, but an opening of textual possibilities that others might follow. Tolson teased his students often by telling them that the White Man put everything he didn't want Black people to know in the library. Like William Carlos Williams, Tolson's texts broke through the library walls, releasing knowledge and language from their prison house. They are an assault upon Anglo-American modernism's territorial designs, but they have been little read.

> Behind the curtain, aeon after aeon,
> he who doubts the white book's
> colophon
> is truth's, if not Laodicean, wears
> the black flower T of doomed
> Laocoon.

These lines, looking back to Hawthorne's "black flower of civilized society, a prison," though they indicate Tolson's cognizance of the difficulties his text would encounter in the Great White World, are not where he chose to end. He ends instead at the point where the scale completes its ascent to the originary note, where pilgrimage and Middle Passage join, where

> The Parliament of African peoples
>   pinnacles *Novus*
>   *Homo* in the Ashmun Interna-
>   tional House, where, free and
>   joyful again, all mankind unites,
>   without heralds of earth and
>   water . . .

He concludes, *"Honi soit qui mal y pense!"* He ends, as he will end *Harlem Gallery,* chronicling "a people's New World odyssey."

The texts of Melvin B. Tolson have not been read much, but they have been read to great effect. They have worked their influence on both sides of that permeable but impassable *paseq* of American culture, the endlessly reinscribed line described by W. E. B. Du Bois as the problem of the twentieth century, the color bar. The White poet William Carlos Williams, after reading a section of Tolson's *Libretto* in *Poetry* magazine, immediately replicated Tolson's audacious act by writing Tolson's poem into book 4 of *Paterson,* and by inscribing his own reading between the lines of Tolson's text. And the works of Melvin B. Tolson have had incalculable effects among African and African-American thinkers, both aesthetically and politically.

There is at least one thing which two West African writers and activists had in common with Lyndon Baines Johnson. Johnson signed a note to Tolson thanking him for the autographed copy of his book which Tolson had presented to the White House library during a visit to the executive mansion. Years earlier, at the request of Horace Mann Bond, Tolson had inscribed special copies of *Libretto for the Republic of Liberia* for two African populists whose interest in reading his work may have been more immediate. One of these was Nnamdi Azikiwe, a former Lincoln student who went on to serve as President of Nigeria, and who authored the book *Renascent Africa.* The other, also a Lincoln University graduate, was the first post-colonial leader of Ghana, Kwame Nkrumah. In the years 1943-45, while he was a student at Lincoln, this young, radical African scholar held a number of important meetings with an African-Caribbean scholar, a dedicated reader of poetry, who was in the United States doing the difficult work of cultural and political organizing against capitalist hegemony, meetings for the discussion of a topic Tolson would certainly find interesting, "the value and techniques of illegal work" in decolonizing Africa and securing a modern African territory. This African-Caribbean revolutionary scholar with whom the African revolutionary scholar met on the grounds of this oldest of African-American intellectual institutions was C. L. R. James. Thus was the intellectual triangle trade which Tolson tropes in his poetry embodied and enacted. It remains to be seen how the world shall construe its reading.

FURTHER READING

Criticism

Bérubé, Michael. "Avant-Gardes and De-Author-izations: *Harlem Gallery* and the Cultural Contradictions of Modernism." *Callaloo No. 38* 12, No. 1 (Winter 1989): 192-215.
> Discusses Tolson's *Harlem Gallery* and its relationship to modernism.

Farnsworth, Robert M. "Tribute to Tolson." *New Letters* 46, No. 3 (Spring 1980): 125-27.
> Reviews Dan McCall's *The Man Says Yes* and explains how the novel is loosely based on Tolson's life.

Fussiner, Howard R. "A Mature Voice Speaks." *Phylon* XV, No. 1 (1954): 96-7.
> A review in which Fussiner praises Tolson's *Libretto for the Republic of Liberia.*

Hillyer, Robert. "Among the New Volumes of Verse." *The New York Times Book Review* (10 December 1944): 29.
> Asserts that, "On the whole, [Tolson's] *Rendezvous With America* is an admirable collection."

Mootry, Maria K. "'The Step of Iron Feet': Creative Practice in the War Sonnets of Melvin B. Tolson and Gwendolyn Brooks." *Obsidian II: Black Literature in Review* II, No. 3 (Winter 1987): 69-87.
> Discusses both Tolson's and Gwendolyn Brooks's first collections and asserts that "the authors' series of war sonnets serve as models for the genesis and evolution of their respective ideas about creative practice in relation to social issues."

Smith, Gary. "A Hamlet Rives Us: The Sonnets of Melvin B. Tolson." *CLA Journal* XXIX, No. 3 (March 1986): 261-75.
> Asserts that "as Tolson's sonnets ably demonstrate, his best work is a fusion of art, philosophy, and socio-politics."

Thompson, Dolphin G. "Tolson's Gallery Brings Poetry Home." *Phylon* XXVI, No. 4 (1965): 408-10.
> A review in which Thompson asserts that Tolson's "new book, *Harlem Gallery: Book I, The Curator,* justifies every honor given him and should be the basis for the highest awards the literary world can give."

Walcott, Ronald. "Ellison, Gordone, Tolson: Some Notes on the Blues, Style and Space." *Black World* XXII, No. 2 (December 1972): 4-29.
> Discusses Tolson's *Harlem Gallery.*

Werner, Craig. "Blues for T. S. Eliot and Langston Hughes: The Afro-Modernist Aesthetic of *Harlem Gallery*." *Black American Literature Forum* 24, No. 3 (Fall 1990): 453-72.

Discusses the tools Tolson uses to communicate with his audience in *Harlem Gallery*.

Additional coverage of Tolson's life and career is contained in the following sources published by Gale: *Black Literature Criticism; Black Writers,* **Vol. 1;** *Dictionary of Literary Biography,* **Vols. 48 and 76; and** *DISCovering Authors Modules: Multicultural Authors* **and** *Poets*.

Eudora Welty
1909-

American short story writer and novelist.

The following entry presents an overview of Welty's career. For further information on her life and works, see *CLC,* Volumes 1, 2, 5, 14, 22, and 33.

INTRODUCTION

Eudora Welty has long been respected by her fellow writers, but it was not until the publication of her *Collected Stories of Eudora Welty* (1980) that she received serious critical attention. Early in her career Welty was dismissed by reviewers as a regionalist, since most of her stories are set in Mississippi. However, upon close examination of her work, critics began to see the universal themes in Welty's fiction and the skill with which she evokes a sense of place.

Biographical Information

Welty was born in 1909 and grew up in Jackson, Mississippi. She was the oldest of three children and the only girl. Her father, Christian Welty, grew up in Ohio in a very reserved family of Swiss heritage. Her mother, Chestina Andrews, grew up in the mountains of West Virginia and never felt at home in Mississippi. In contrast to her husband's background, Chestina Andrews grew up in a spirited and gregarious family, and Welty's visits with her grandmother and five uncles in West Virginia were memorable for her. Later Welty would tell of these experiences in her *One Writer's Beginnings* (1984) and fictionally as part of *The Optimist's Daughter* (1972). Welty was surrounded with books as a child. Her father kept an extensive library, and her mother often read aloud to her. After completing public school in Jackson, Welty attended Mississippi State College for Women from 1925 to 1927. She went on to receive her B.A. from the University of Wisconsin in 1929. Welty then attended Columbia University Graduate School of Business in New York from 1930-1931 to study advertising. She was forced to return home to Jackson in 1931 when her father died suddenly. In the early 1930s Welty held a variety of odd jobs with local newspapers and a radio station until she got a position as a publicity agent for the Works Progress Administration (WPA). The job took her throughout the state of Mississippi, which helped inspire her as an artist. Welty began taking photographs of a variety of images and people she encountered in the state. Although she was unsuccessful at finding a publisher for the collection at the time, the photographs were later published in 1971 as *One Time, One Place: Mississippi in the Depres-*

sion; A Snapshot Album (1971). Her job at the WPA also inspired Welty to begin writing about the Depression era. Her first short story, "Death of a Traveling Salesman," was published in *Manuscript* in 1936. Her first collection, titled *A Curtain of Green* (1941), followed in 1941. Welty has continued to live and write from her family home in Jackson, Mississippi, including novels and essays in addition to her short stories. Her novel *The Optimist's Daughter* won the Pulitzer Prize in 1972.

Major Works

Very few of Welty's works are written in the first-person narrative. She prefers a conversational style with a multitude of voices. The best example of this is her novel *Losing Battles* (1970), which is set during the Depression. The story revolves around the family of Granny Vaughn, which gathers in Banner, Mississippi, to celebrate Granny's 90th birthday. The novel is a collection of different family members' tales as they get together for this reunion. Past and present merge as each character tells their story. One of the major characters, the schoolteacher Julia Mortimer, is not even alive in the present of the narrative. She dies shortly before the reunion, but her presence is strongly felt throughout the novel. Welty does not normally use her direct experience in her fiction, and she feels that a reader does not need every biographical detail about a writer to understand his work. However, elements of her life are reflected in portions of her writing. *The Optimist's Daughter* is her most autobiographical work of fiction, and there are many parallel scenes between the novel and personal scenes described in her memoir *One Writer's Beginnings*. The memoir is based on a series of lectures Welty gave at Harvard University about the development of her life as a writer. It is not a straight autobiography or a manual on the techniques of writing; it is simply a personal look at her journey of developing her talents as a writer. There are three sections, "Listening," "Learning to See," and "Finding a Voice." Each section shares personal memories and how, as a writer, Welty absorbed and filtered her experiences.

Critical Reception

Since most of her work is set in Mississippi, Welty was dismissed as a regionalist early in her career. Reviewers eventually recognized the depth and universal themes present in her fiction, however. Maureen Howard asserts, "Eudora Welty is not a regionalist: She is a Southern writer who has lived all her life in Jackson, Miss. It is not surprising that she draws strength from this setting for most of the stories, but it is a mark of her great skill that her perceptions of courthouse towns, poor shacks and farms, the discarded levee are so various and unlimiting." In fact it is her ability to convey her strong sense of place that has caused many reviewers to laud her work. Some critics assert that the appeal of Welty's fiction and her ability to overcome the label of regionalist derives from the fact that she writes from two perspectives. From living in the state almost her entire life, Welty knows Mississippi and its people so intimately that she is able to vividly convey them in her fiction. The fact that her parents were not Southerners, however, gave her the opportunity to view her subject as an outsider. Welty is often praised for her use of dialect and the conversational style of her writing. In describing the varied voices in *Losing Battles*, Paul Bailey said, "Such talk—varied, spontaneous, recognizably absurd—is a pleasure to read because it is always revealing of character." Many critics comment on the folklore influence on her work, especially in *The Golden Apples* (1949) and *The Robber Bridegroom* (1942).

PRINCIPAL WORKS

A Curtain of Green (short stories) 1941
The Robber Bridegroom (novella) 1942
The Wide Net, and Other Stories (short stories) 1943
Delta Wedding (novel) 1946

The Golden Apples (short stories) 1949
Short Stories (essay) 1949
Selected Stories (short stories) 1953
The Ponder Heart (short stories) 1954
The Bride of Innisfallen, and Other Stories (short stories) 1955
Place in Fiction (lectures) 1957
The Shoe Bird (juvenilia) 1964
Thirteen Stories (short stories) 1965
A Sweet Devouring (nonfiction) 1969
A Flock of Guinea Hens Seen from a Car (poem) 1970
Losing Battles (novel) 1970
One Time, One Place: Mississippi in the Depression; A Snapshot Album (photographs) 1971
The Optimist's Daughter (novel) 1972
The Eye of the Story (essays and reviews) 1978
Moon Lake and Other Stories (short stories) 1980
The Collected Stories of Eudora Welty (short stories) 1980
One Writer's Beginnings (lectures) 1984
Eudora Welty Photographs (photographs) 1989

CRITICISM

Maureen Howard (review date 2 November 1980)

SOURCE: "A Collection of Discoveries," in *The New York Times Book Review,* November 2, 1980, pp. 1, 31, 32.

[*In the following review, Howard discusses Welty's* Collected Stories, *and how her range developed throughout her career.*]

In reading **The Collected Stories of Eudora Welty,** there is a particular pleasure in following her performance over the years. Her range is remarkable—her way of telling us that stories are as different as human faces, that beyond the common features of plot and narrative, there are discoveries to be made each time. In **"A Memory"** (which seems to be about her childhood), she writes, "To watch everything about me I regarded grimly and possessively as a *need.*" Now, with all the stories gathered together, we can see with what vigilance she has continued to watch the world around her. She has transformed that early obsession into the vision of a magnificent American artist.

Eudora Welty is not a regionalist: She is a Southern writer who has lived nearly all of her life in Jackson, Miss. It is not surprising that she draws strength from this setting for most of the stories, but it is a mark of her great skill that her perceptions of courthouse towns, poor shacks and farms, the discarded levee are so various and unlimiting. The Delta, the backwoods cabin or fussy middle-class home is rendered in each story, used only as necessary. And the talk, the beguiling Mississippi talk that lends such energy to her work is completely under her control. It is not the South we find in her stories, it is Eudora Welty's South, a region that feeds her imagination, and a place we come to trust. She is a Southerner as Chekhov was a Russian, because place provides them with reality—a reality as difficult, mysterious and impermanent as life.

> **It is not the South we find in her stories, it is Eudora Welty's South, a region that feeds her imagination, and a place we come to trust. She is a Southerner as Chekhov was a Russian, because place provides them with reality—a reality as difficult, mysterious and impermanent as life.**
> —*Maureen Howard*

From the first volume included here, *A Curtain of Green and Other Stories,* we can see the demands that Miss Welty put upon herself as a writer. Each tale finds its own pace and its own design. The characters are so fully realized that the imprint of their life is upon the page. **"Lily Daw and the Three Ladies"** is a farce. A poor simpleton's fate is determined as much by circumstance as the cockeyed morality of the self-approving ladies who take care of her. **"Petrified Man,"** one of the most famous of the early stories, is all gossip. Written as idle beauty-parlor chatter, it reveals the thrill that the dull get from glamorous lives, though that glamour be infamous, corrupt. Such talk may be outrageously funny to overhear but it levels all events— murder, rape, betrayal—to perverse entertainment. Then there is **"A Worn Path,"** the story of an old Negro woman whose endurance is superhuman. It is possible to believe in her because Miss Welty casts Phoenix's mythic journey in an easy folklore that admits magical encounters and the woman's heroic determination. These early stories are filled with dreamers, deaf-mutes, wanderers, the old—people who live outside of society. We are told what in their fantasies, or in fact, sets them apart, but we are made to wonder about the real world that cannot contain them.

There is so much virtuosity in *The Collected Stories,* such a testing of the form, we cannot help but see that the writing was always fresh to her and of great interest. That is the mark of genius. Like Katherine Anne Porter, whom she admired, Eudora Welty has never had the time or patience for repeats. The game of the storyteller, and it is a serious one, is always to find the right emphasis, the right tone. Thus, I am dazzled by a talent that can ventriloquize the petulant whining tale of **"Why I Live at the P.O."** so brilliantly, but I am genuinely impressed that after such success Miss Welty did not write another monologue for some 25 years. Then, on the night of Medgar Evers's death, she wrote **"Where Is the Voice Coming From?"** the loud-mouthed soliloquy of a killer.

The two stories may seem alike in method: They are wonderfully different in intent. We never asked to hear the complaint of the postmistress against her family, but Miss Welty has staged a humiliating spectacle of self-exposure. We become a willing audience. The assassin's voice, we want to hear. We want to hear him to believe him and to confirm what we think we know about bigots and nasty hicks. Our interest is almost prurient, our anger predictable, but Eudora Welty's response to the murder is more profound. Her story is a deflection of common rage to an artistic honesty. "Whoever the murderer is," Miss Welty writes in her preface, "I know him: not his identity, but his coming about, in this time and place. That is, I ought to have learned by now, from here, what such a man, intent on such a deed, had going on in his mind."

Now this is the statement of a writer ultimately responsible to her material, not a writer who takes the occasion of a public event to provide material. She knows what we cannot imagine, the killer's satisfaction and the petty details of his hatred. In a few pages she creates a mind shot through with clichés ("Ain't it about time us taxpayers starts to calling the moves?"), but it is only tinged with the crazed isolation of the psychotic. He is not fantastic, not a cartoon response to our liberal concerns. The killer is real—a man with a sharp-tongued wife, a man who does not own his own automobile. All is understood (It always is in Miss Welty's work) but that does not mean that this wretched man is forgiven.

There are the formal stories, only a few, which make use of history. And again, it is impressive that each time she ventures into new territory. **"First Love"** is set "in extraordinary times, in a season of dreams." A deaf boot-boy falls in love with words he cannot hear, most particularly with the words of Aaron Burr as he enchants his fellow conspirator. The place is the Mississippi territory in the days before one of the greatest courtroom encounters in American history. Burr awaits trial for treason: His long nights of talk are magic to the boy who begins to see clearly what others hear, Burr's brilliance and charm. The story is held strictly to the deaf boy's vision, a narrower view of a historic moment than we are accustomed to, but locked in the boy's silence we finally see beyond Burr's courtroom rhetoric: The tone, as the boy can now observe through Burr's gestures and expression, is elegant and false. He learns, as from first love, that his heart can be broken by words, but he will never be content again with silence. The year is 1807. Aaron Burr might enter here as the lead in a costume piece, a romantic scoundrel held to his set role in history, if Miss Welty did not make the moment both extraordinary and credible by giving it to us through the deaf boy's eyes.

In **"A Still Moment"** it would seem that history operates as a background for parable. We are someplace in the early 19th century on the Old Natchez Trace. A preacher, a murderer, a student (Audubon) converge at the author's bidding. But the parable is not easily construed. Good and evil have blurred edges, like the reasons for lonely journeys, like the mysterious pull of one's vocation. For Audubon read naturalist, journalist—neither is fully accurate—a student, yet a master of his craft. He is a real man confounded by the detailed beauty of nature, by living things and by the difficulties of his journey—not John James Audubon (1785-1851), a symbolic figure:

> He knew that the best he could make would be, after it was apart from his hand, a dead thing and not a live thing, never the essence, only a sum of parts; and that it would always meet with a stranger's sight, and never be one with the beauty in any other man's head in the world. As he had seen the bird most purely at its moment of death, in some fatal way, in his care for looking outward, he saw his long labor most revealingly at the point where it met its limit.

Audubon's words might stand as Miss Welty's graceful statement of the pressure she feels as a writer to bring life out of words insofar as she is able. In **"A Still Moment"** she abandons her parable intentionally. It is a schematic view and in the telling of an honest story it will simply not serve. The historic incident here gives way to a personal moment—Audubon's meeting with his limits becomes Miss Welty's confrontation with herself.

There is one group of tales that interlock, those in *The Golden Apples*. Seen in the midst of *The Collected Stories*, they seem a central performance, theme and variation played out in one place. Morgana is a Southern town of Miss Welty's making. Like Joyce's *Dubliners*, the stories glance off each other—stories of love, ambition, marriage, set side by side without the narrative line of a novel. But unlike Joyce's characters who never intersect, the inhabitants of Morgana turn up again and again. We come to know them— parents and children, teachers and servants—and to expect them in separate scenes held together by a lush colloquial speech and a richness of little plots. As a book, *The Golden Apples* is most like a one-woman show of photographs where a style is discernible in the use of light and detail. The effect is cumulative: Here is the artist's world.

"June Recital" is the most remarkable of the Morgana stories, suffused with tenderness yet never sentimental. A sick boy, home in bed, peeks out his window to the empty house next door to watch strange happenings. The town lies beyond, laden with its history, with voices, dreams, stories. All views are partial, but the story of **"June Recital"** is, in the end complete, a gathering of experience. In "The Art of Fiction," Henry James describes a talent much like Miss Welty's—"The power to judge the unseen from the seen, to trace the implication of things. . . ."

The childhood myths of Morgana are destroyed by mature vision and by time, just as a movie theater and a commercial block have obliterated the pastoral scene. At the end, two lone figures stand in the rain, a community of two under the shelter of a public tree, ". . . listening to the magical percussion, the world beating in their ears. They heard through falling rain the running of the horse and bear, the stroke of the leopard, the dragon's crusty slither, and the glimmer and the trumpet of the swan."

The implication is that the stories of Morgana will be buried in the greater myths of the world, swept into the awesome passage of time.

Guessing the unseen from the seen is strong in a later story, **"No Place for You, My Love."** It is about an affair that never happens. A man and a woman try to escape the heat of New Orleans and presumably their personal histories. In a roadhouse they dance together, but the dance only lends their bodies a necessary formality: There is no release. Something is warped in their denial, their inability to translate attitude into feeling, something shameful that will forever set the incident apart. They have been on a dangerous excursion and dared nothing. But we have seen their failure and Miss Welty knows it is all we need to know. There are other stories in the last volume which are raucous, sprawling. She will try anything and get it right. **"Kin"** is a disorderly panorama that echoes the noise and movement of family life, jumpy, flickering, as unplotted as home movies; there is the opera buffa of **"Going to Naples"**; and finally **"The Demonstrators,"** a report from the troubled South that manages to be written with both passion and balance.

Her work is filled with characters who do not hear, literally or figuratively, with people who talk and do not listen. Their stories bear the sadness and the folly inherent in ignorance and self-absorption. Eudora Welty's writing is an act of generosity—for the partial and incomplete vision of her characters is pieced out and made whole for us: In such completeness there is care and intimacy, something like mature love. The richness of such talent resists a summing up. We can place her with her models, Chekhov and Katherine Anne Porter: She is always honest, always just. And she is vastly entertaining. The stories are magnificent. Her youthful need to watch became a life devoted to observation. There is a superb vigilance in Eudora Welty, a present tense: each work is responsive to its time: history, especially in the South, must not reflect romantic distortions. It is only by the rigorous observation which we find in her *Collected*

Stories that the present is verified and the past kept useful and alive.

Eudora Welty with Jo Brans (interview date Summer 1981)

SOURCE: "Struggling against the Plaid: An Interview with Eudora Welty," reprinted in *Listen to the Voices: Conversations with Contemporary Writers,* Jo Brans, Southern Methodist University Press, 1988. (Originally printed in *Southwest Review,* Vol. 66, No. 3, Summer, 1981, pp. 255-66.)

[In the following interview, Welty discusses her approach to writing and some of her characterizations.]

Eudora Welty is the author of five collections of short stories, a book of photographs, a volume of essays, and five novels. For her novel *The Ponder Heart* she received the American Academy of Arts and Letters Howells Medal in 1955, and for *The Optimist's Daughter* she was awarded the 1973 Pulitzer Prize. Among the most honored of American writers, she has also received the National Institute of Arts and Letters Gold Medal for the Novel, the Presidential Medal of Freedom, and in 1979 the National Medal for Literature for lifetime achievement.

Jo Brans is a member of the English faculty at Southern Methodist University. Brans interviewed Eudora Welty when she visited Dallas in November, 1980, to speak at SMU's sixth annual literary festival.

[Brans:] One thing that especially impressed me in the conversation yesterday was that you said you wrote because you loved language and you love using language. I know you are a photographer, and you've painted too.

[Welty:] Well, I was never a true or serious painter, just a childhood painter.

How does writing compare in your mind with those other art forms?

Oh, it's in the front. The others are just playthings. I didn't have any talent for photographs. I was strictly amateurish. I think the book I did [*One Time, One Place*] has a value in being a record, just because it was taken in the 1930s. And I was in the position of being perfectly accepted wherever I went, and everything was unselfconscious on the part of both the people and myself. There was no posing, and neither was there any pulling back or anything like that. Our relationship was perfectly free and open, so that I was able to get photographs of things really as they were. I think to-

day it has a sort of historical value, which has nothing to do with any kind of professional expertise in taking pictures, which I knew I didn't have. But I am a professional writer. That is my work and my life, and I take it extremely seriously. It isn't just the love of language, or love of the written word, though that is certainly foremost, but the wish to use this language and written word in order to make something, which is what writing is. It's a tool. It's the tool, not the end result. So I guess that would be how you could describe what I'm trying to do.

To create a reality with words. Why is dialogue, spoken language, so important to you—say in **Losing Battles?**

I tried to see if I could do a whole novel completely without going inside the minds of my characters, which is the way I do in most of my writing. I didn't tell how anyone thought—I tried to show it by speech and action. I was deliberately trying to see if I could convey the same thing by speech and outward appearance, as I used to do by going inside people's minds.

It seems to me that in your writing you're hardly ever autobiographical. I've heard you say that you're working out of your feelings, but not your own experiences. Are there any stories that are autobiographical?

I don't deliberately avoid being autobiographical; it's just that when I'm writing a story I have to invent the things that best show my feelings about my own experience or about life, and I think most of us wouldn't be able to take our own experience and make a dramatic situation out of that without some aid. And I do much better with invented characters who can better carry out, act out, my feelings. I don't think you can describe emotion you have not felt. You know, you have to know what it's like—what it is to feel a certain thing—or your description or your use of these emotions will be artificial and shallow. So I certainly understand what my characters are feeling, but I try to show it in a way that is interesting dramatically.

And I don't lead a very dramatic life myself, outwardly. So it's not that I'm concealing myself, it's just that I'm using whatever—a lot of the details come out of my own life, things that I've observed. There was a scene in my novel, *The Optimist's Daughter,* about a three-year-old child in West Virginia, a whole section in there that I suppose you could call autobiographical, but actually it was my own memories of being at my grandmother's, on the farm, and all the things that the child felt—the rivers and the mountains and all those things. Nothing like that could be made up, you see. If you've never been in the mountains you wouldn't know how to say what it was like to be in the mountains. But it was not me as the character. It was my feelings, my memories, my experiences, but it was that character that was feeling them, not me. The character was not me. So, that's an example.

You sort of projected your feelings into this creation.

Yes, and use them to describe this character. I didn't use all that I had, I used just what would help me to explain the character.

How do those characters come to your mind? Do they just spring full-blown into your mind? Or do you work them out. . . ?

Well, it's just part of the whole process of making a story. I mean, they are all one with the plot and the atmosphere of the story and the weather and the location. They don't exist apart from the story—they're not even in the world outside the story. You can't take a character out of this story and put it into another.

It doesn't work?

Well, they wouldn't live. So the characters are all integral parts of the story in which they occur. Of course you use many sources to make a character—occupation, memory, knowledge, dreams, newspaper articles, many things. You may get little bits here and little bits there, because the character is a sort of magnet and attracts different kinds of observations. Not just any, you know; it's just what applies to the character. So how can you tell where they come from, any more than you can tell where anything comes from— where a tune comes from to a composer.

Do you have any set pattern of working? That is, do the characters occur to you first, or a trick of plot, or some idea that you want to express? Is there any particular order that seems to be the same?

It's different with every story. It just depends. Sometimes the story begins with the idea of a character and then you invent a plot which will bring this out. Take that one story that's used lots of times in schools called **"The Worn Path."** That character called up the story. Such a person as that would take a trip like this to do something. That's a good simple case.

*What I love about **"A Worn Path"** is not so much the endurance of the walker as the windmill or whatever you call it at the end. For me that was the beauty of the story, that all of a sudden old Phoenix does move above the . . . just the endurance . . .*

I love that, too.

And walking all the way back down the path with the wind-

mill. *I have a clear picture of that. It made the trip into town worth the coming.*

Absolutely.

In one of your essays you talk about Faulkner, and you say that Faulkner has this sense of blood guilt about the Indians and then about the blacks. In your own work you don't have that.

Well, it's not my theme. You know his work encompassed so much and so many books and so many generations and so much history, that that was an integral part of it. I don't write historically or anything. Most of the things that I write about can be translated into personal relationships. I've never gone into such things as guilt over the Indians or—it just hasn't been my subject. My stories, I think, reflect the racial relationships—guilt is just one aspect of that. Certainly I think any writer is aware of the complicated relationship between the races. It comes out in so many even domestic situations.

Very few of your stories deal directly with blacks, though. And those that do, I've wondered if the blackness is a necessary part of the character. For example, old Phoenix. Why is she black?

It's not a deliberate thing, like, "I am now going to write about the black race." I write about all people. I think my characters are about half and half black and white.

Really?

I would guess. Considering the novels and everything. I think it's the same challenge to a writer. It doesn't matter about color of skin or their age or anything else. Then again, I never have thought about **"The Worn Path"** as being anything but what it was; but one thing may be that when I wrote that story, what started me writing it was the sight of a figure like Phoenix Jackson. I never got close to her, just saw her crossing a distant field early one afternoon in the fall. Just her figure. I couldn't see her up close, but you could tell it was an old woman going somewhere, and I thought, she is bent on an errand. And I know it isn't for herself. It was just the look of her figure.

It's not true, then, what I read—that you were the lady old Phoenix asked to tie her shoe.

Oh, no. I was out with a painter who was painting his landscape and so we were sitting under a tree. I was reading, and I watched her cross the landscape in the half-distance, and when I got home I wrote that story that she had made me think of. She was a black woman. But then I suppose it would be more likely to be a black woman who would be in such desperate need and live so remotely away from help and who would have so far to go. I don't think that story would be the same story with a white person. The white person could have the same character, of course, and do the same thing, but it wouldn't have the same urgency about it.

Well, old Phoenix does fox white people. You know, she takes the nickel from the hunter, then asks the lady to tie her shoe.

It wasn't because they were white, though. Those are two different things altogether. It was the desperate need for the money and for the child that she needed that nickel—she knew it was a sin, too. But asking the lady to tie her shoe—she knew who would be nice to her. She picked a nice person, because she was a nice person, and she picked one. Those are two entirely different motives, taking the nickel from this really nasty white man and asking a favor of a nice lady. She knew in both cases.

She had a wonderful graciousness.

She knew how to treat both.

One of my students went to your reading Sunday night, and she came in with a paper on it. She had misunderstood the title of the story called "Livvie," and she referred to it as "Living," which showed she understood the story anyway.

That's very cute. I'm glad to hear that.

A misprision, I guess, but a nice one. What I'm saying is, I know sometimes I fix interpretations on the things I've read.

Well, I do too. We all do that. And I don't feel a thing bad about it, because a story writer hopes to suggest all kinds of possibilities. Even though it may not have been in the writer's mind, if something in the story suggests it, I think it's legitimate. You know, it doesn't have to be exact. The only way I think to err is to be completely out of tone or out of the scope of the story or its intention. No, it doesn't bother me one bit if someone interprets something in a different way, if I think the story can just as well suggest that as not, because you try to make it full of suggestions, not just one.

As a teacher I'm very sensitive to this whole question, because students frequently say, at the end of the discussion of the story where you really are trying to get at all the things that make the story possible, "Now do you think that Eudora Welty really intended all of that?" And of course there's no defense for a teacher, and all I can say is, "How do I know?"

That's all we say when we read anybody's work.

How can I know what she intended? But if we find it here in the story, the story belongs to us when we're reading it.

Exactly. The only thing that I know bogs a lot of students down, because I get letters all the time, is in the case of that dread subject, symbols. You know, if they get to thinking, This equals this, and this equals that, the whole story is destroyed. Symbols are important, I think, but only if they're organic—you know, occur in the course of the story, are not dragged in to equal something.

No, no. It takes all the life out to do that.

Of course. And symbols aren't equivalents.

—not algebraic equations!

I know it. But, you know, some students get the idea, and it's very troubling to them. And what I hate about it is it might discourage them from ever enjoying reading stories, if they think they're supposed to make an algebraic interpretation, as you said.

In connection with "Livvie," let me ask you something that's really off the wall, probably: was there any thought in your mind at all of reflecting Faulkner's As I Lay Dying? *Just the name of the character Cash, and then the fact that Livvie . . .*

No, that was a coincidence. No indeed—I mean, I wouldn't—you're not aware of any other person's work when you write your own. At the time I wrote that story I didn't know about Faulkner's Cash. When did he write *As I Lay Dying?*

I think about 1930.

You know, Faulkner was out of print when I was growing up.

For a long time, right.

It was about 1940.

When Malcolm Cowley did The Portable Faulkner.

Everything I have of Faulkner's I've bought through searching in secondhand bookstores in order to read them. He wasn't in the libraries. He wasn't to be had—at least in Mississippi. I don't think he was to be had anywhere. He was out of print, for a long time.

That's right. I had forgotten that. That's important.

Well, I guess I hadn't read him until I had been writing for some time. But, at any rate, the presence of Faulkner's writing in Mississippi—I was glad he was there, and I loved his work, but he wasn't hovering over my work. Because when you're writing, you're just thinking about your story, not how would Faulkner do it, how would Chekhov do it, how would Katherine Anne Porter do it?

I wasn't really asking you that. I know that's not true.

Well, a lot of people do wonder, just because he lived there, and of course it is a formidable thing.

His shadow.

I wish that he could have helped me.

What I was thinking was just that sometimes I feel that you've taken some of the same themes. I suppose that was inevitable.

Because we get them out of the same well.

But that, in your mind, is more or less unconscious. And you give them a comic twist. In **Losing Battles,** *for example, all the Beecham kin decide at one point that Gloria might be a Beecham, and that her father might be one of the Beecham brothers, and they seem to be delighted with the whole idea.*

Yes, they're thrilled. That makes her okay.

Right. Even though by Mississippi law at the time that would make the marriage incest. But that's kind of a Faulknerian— I'm thinking of The Sound and the Fury, *where Quentin says he'd rather have slept with his sister Caddy himself than have an outsider—incest would be better. I always think of Faulkner in connection with that idea, because I got my first gasp of shock from him.*

Well, I didn't mean anything serious and tragic at all. I just meant it to show what the Beechams were like. That is, to be a Beecham made everything all right. That was what I was showing.

You have commented that Faulkner's comedy may have more of the South—more of the real life of the South in it than his tragedy.

I think it has everything.

And it seems to me that your writing is basically comic. There is almost always that sense of harmony and reconciliation at the end.

Yes, I think it's a part of tragic things. It intrudes, as it does in life, in even the most tragic situations. Not comedy—I would say humor does. Yes, I like writing comedy. It's very difficult and it's much harder, because one false step—and I've made many of them. . . . That's why I have to work very hard on the comic theme, because it's so much more difficult to do. One false step and the whole thing comes down in a wreck around you.

When I think of comedy, I don't so much think always of humor, as I think of the something at the end that suggests that the world will continue—that life will continue. A kind of optimism for the species. You always suggest this, usually with a synthesis of opposing elements. I love that line in **Losing Battles**—*in Miss Julia's letter—"The side that loses gets to the truth first."*

Oh, yes, that's when she was in her desperate state.

Had she thought of herself at that point as having lost?

Oh, I'm sure. She did.

She did lose?

Well, look at all the people around her. All her class, all the people she'd taught, they didn't know a thing, except the thing that mattered most to them, which I think is most valuable—that is, their love for one another and dependence upon one another, and their family, and their pride, and all of that. But nothing Miss Julia had tried to teach them had ever taken root. Nothing.

In your mind is she like Miss Eckhart in **The Golden Apple?**

She filled a function in the story perhaps that would be kind of similar, in that she was a person unlike the world in which she lived, trying to teach and help somebody. But Miss Eckhart was a very mysterious character. Julia Mortimer was much more straightforward and dedicated and thinking of the people as somebody she wanted to help. Miss Eckhart was a very strange person.

I hope you know that in some ways these questions are meant to serve as checks for me if I need checks in reading your books, and apparently I do. I thought I saw this pattern in several of your things—Miss Eckhart, Julia Mortimer, those characters in the same mold. That is, they represent a discipline. Could I ask you what your sense is of the differences between male and female characters in your stories? I keep thinking about that line from "Livvie" that I mentioned yesterday, "I'd rather a man be anything than a woman be mean." And also, in **Delta Wedding,** *say, the women are obviously making demands on the men.*

Well, men and women are different. I don't mean they're not equally important. But they're different. That's the wonderful thing about life. No, in those different stories I'm not writing about them as men versus women. In the Delta it's very much of a matriarchy, especially in those years in the twenties that I was writing about, and really ever since the Civil War when the men were all gone and the women began to take over everything. You know, they really did. I've met families up there where the women just ruled the roost, and I've made that happen in the book because I thought, that's the way it was in those days in the South. I've never lived in the Delta, and I was too young to have known what was going on in anything in the twenties, but I know that that's a fact. Indeed it's true of many sections of that country after the Civil War changed the pattern of life there. So I've just had that taken for granted—it was part of the story. That was something the men were up against. I think that in many of my stories I do have a force, like Miss Julia Mortimer or Miss Eckhart, but those two are so poles apart in their characters that I can't see much connection.

There's a real passion in Miss Eckhart.

There certainly is. Well, it's a passion for getting some people out of their element. She herself was trapped, you know, with her terrible old mother. And then no telling what kind of strange Germanic background, which I didn't know anything about and could only indicate. I mean we don't know—they had tantrums in that house, and flaming quarrels.

Well, there's that one quarrel that surfaces when the girls are there. She hits her mother, doesn't she, or—?

Or something. I think her mother hits her. But anyway, I wanted to indicate that they were passionate people. And Miss Julia was passionate too. Most of my good characters are. Virgie Rainey had it too, and Miss Eckhart saw it, that Virgie had that power to feel and project her feelings, and she wanted her to realize all of this.

Do you think Virgie does?

I think at the end of the story she is saying good-bye to the life there in Morgana. I think she's got it in her to do something else.

Remember that line about Virgie's sewing? Virgie is cutting out a plaid dress, trying to match up the rows, and Miss Katie says, "There's nothing Virgie Rainey likes like struggling against a good hard plaid." I'm thinking of the struggle in **Losing Battles** *too—Jack and Gloria, who in a way have come from separate worlds. Although Gloria resists it, she's very much the child of Miss Julia Mortimer. She was brought up to be the teacher. And Jack is very much*

the hope and promise of the Renfro clan, and yet I felt reading the book that even though they've been apart most of the time they've been married, they've already impressed their worlds on each other. Is that what you intended?

Yes, indeed. I certainly did. That's exactly correct. And why Gloria—I think every instinct in her wants them to go and live to themselves, as they put it there.

Yes, in that little house.

It's going to be mighty hard to do. But she knows where she stands all right, and she's not intimidated at all. And Jack, of course, is just oblivious to the fact that there could be anything wrong with his staying there and having the best of both.

He wants her to love Granny. Granny is just so unlovable.

Granny doesn't want to. "She didn't say anything, she nodded. She would love you."

I thought Granny was just as mean as she could be.

Well, she's living in her own world, too.

And she wants to be a hundred instead of ninety.

She thinks she is a hundred.

But the most amazing thing is that Jack is willing to love Miss Julia Mortimer.

Yes. He's willing to.

Nobody else in his family is.

No. He is. I really love Jack.

When I asked you in the panel yesterday which of your characters you thought spoke for you, I kind of expected you to say Jack.

Oh, I was thinking about stories yesterday, I wasn't thinking about the novel. Well, Jack is really the reason I went on and made a novel out of this. Because when I first began it, it was a short story which was to end when Jack came home. The story was about why he happened to go to the pen. All that crazy story about the fight. And he was to come home and wonder why they thought anything was wrong. You know: "What's happened?" Well, as soon as he walks in the door I think, "No, I want to go on with him." I had to start all over and write a novel. Yes, he's willing to love Miss Julia. In fact, he says in there, "I love her. I feel like I love her. I've heard her story." I think that's very direct and penetrating: because he's heard her story, he knows what's happened to her.

And she has a reality for him even though he "never laid eyes on her."

And the people who have gone to school to her didn't really see her. Jack is really a good person, even though he is all the other things.

I don't see anything bad in Jack.

No, except that he allows himself to be used by everybody.

But that comes out of his goodness.

It comes out of his goodness and it's so typical also, I think, of just such situations. Haven't you known people like this? We all have. Yes, I really like Jack. He's a much better person than Gloria.

Well, she's a little have-not. Don't you see her in that way? A have-not, so that she's clutching.

An orphan.

I find it hard to express things in any terms other than the story. I really do. Some people can, but I can't. I never think that way. I only think in terms of the story. Of this story.
—Eudora Welty

And that's what Miss Julia represents too. But when Jack says, "I've heard her story," he's really—

They're all living on stories. They tell each other the stories of everybody. And he heard her story. They were blinded to her by having gone to school to her. They just took her as their bane. They're struggling against her. But he heard her story.

Now Virgie Rainey—she struggles against herself. Isn't Virgie essentially a wanderer, who really wants to wander, but for years she makes herself stay there in Morgana?

I guess so. I use that term rather loosely because it also means planets, and I have got a number of characters that I try to suggest can move outside this tiny little town in the Delta, though it's not a cut-and-dried kind of thing. It's not A, B, C, D. But I wanted to suggest it.

They could make it in a larger world.

Yes. That there was a larger world. Whether they could make it or be broken like Eugene MacLain is something else. They know something else is out there. It's just an awareness of the spaciousness and mystery of—really, of living, and that was just a kind of symbol of it, a disguise. I do feel that there are very mysterious things in life, and I would like just to suggest their presence—an awareness of them.

Is the sense of mystery and magic related to your use of mythology?

I think it is. Exactly, that's what it is. Because I use anything I can to suggest it.

And myths then seem to suggest something timeless?

Yes, or something . . .

Perpetually reborn or re-created?

I think so. Something perhaps bigger than ordinary life allows people to be sometimes. I find it hard to express things in any terms other than the story. I really do. Some people can, but I can't. I never think that way. I only think in terms of the story. Of this story.

Paul Bailey (review date 4 June 1982)

SOURCE: "Gloriously ordinary," in *TLS*, No. 4131, June 4, 1982, p. 608.

[*In the following review, Bailey discusses Welty's* Losing Battles *and states that "The prevailing tone is one of glorious ordinariness, but one that never sinks into the terminally cute. . . ."*]

The belated publication in Britain of this exceptionally beautiful novel, which first came out in the United States in 1970, is both welcome and timely, coming as it does so after the appearance here of its author's *Collected Stories*. These two books alone are evidence enough that Eudora Welty is a writer of considerable distinction.

"What I do in writing of any character is to try to enter into the mind, heart, and skin of a human being who is not myself", is how she accounts for her method of working. "Whether this happens to be a man or a woman, old or young, with skin black or white, the primary challenge lies in making the jump itself." That "jump" is achieved with a seeming lack of effort in *Losing Battles* as the various members of Granny Vaughn's copious family gather to celebrate the nimble old lady's ninetieth birthday. No sooner have they arrived at the farm in Banner, Mississippi, than they start talking, and in a manner that is immediately compelling. The majority of Granny's descendants and their spouses are natural raconteurs, in the best tradition of the Old South, and the great originality of *Losing Battles* derives from its being composed of the tales told by these people as they while away a long, hot Sunday in early August sometime in the 1930s—the work of fiction thus produced is at once a novel and a collection of short stories.

Even when her characters' tongues are venomous, her concerned detachment is informing the reader that there is more to the speakers than their temporary state of viciousness would indicate.
—*Paul Bailey*

The dialogue invented by Eudora Welty in this long and delicate book is often cunningly arbitrary. Conversational *culs-de-sac* are explored and then deserted. The Beechams and the Renfros repeat themselves constantly, but each repetition brings with it a variation or two, almost imperceptible. Such talk—varied, spontaneous, recognizably absurd—is a pleasure to read because it is always revealing of character. It is funny, too, but not in a wanton or gratuitous way. In the following example a cyclone is being discussed:

> 'It picked the Methodist Church up all in one piece and carried it through the air and set it down right next to the Baptist Church! Thank the Lord nobody was worshipping in either one,' said Aunt Beck.

> 'I never heard of such a thing,' said Mrs Moody.

> 'Now you have. And those Methodists had to tear their own church down stick by stick so they could carry it back and put it together again on the side of the road where it belonged,' said Miss Beulah. 'A good many Baptists helped 'em.'

> 'I'll tell you something as contrary as people are. Cyclones,' said Mr Renfro.

> 'It's a wonder we all wasn't carried off, killed with the horses and cows, and skinned alive like the chickens,' said Uncle Curtis. 'Just got up and found each other, glad we was all still in the land of the living.'

At the heart of *Losing Battles* is the story, recounted by sundry characters, of Miss Julia Mortimer, the dedicated school teacher who has fought a losing battle against ignorance and

illiteracy. Julia never actually *appears* in the narrative because she dies shortly before the family reunion for Granny, but hers is perhaps the most vivid presence in the entire novel. Welty displays remarkable skill as she resurrects this difficult woman through the voices of Julia's former students, only one of whom—Judge Moody—remembers her without resentment. Yet the more Granny's kin abuse the dead teacher, the more respect and admiration the reader feels for the object of their scorn. This is the triumph of an art that determinedly refuses to cast its own judgment, that registers—with an honourable disinterest—the judgments of the human beings it celebrates. Condemnation, it suggests, is practised by men and women, but not by novelists.

For Eudora Welty's art is, essentially, in accord with the complicated business of living. Like her beloved Chekhov, she eschews the big scenes—they are subjects for discussion; they happen off-stage. Even when her characters' tongues are venomous, her concerned detachment is informing the reader that there is more to the speakers than their temporary state of viciousness would indicate. The principal events of *Losing Battles* are of a trivial kind that is rare in the literature that has come out of the American South—there is no rape, and only a hint of possible, distant incest. The prevailing tone is one of glorious ordinariness, but one that never sinks into the terminally cute—*pace Our Town*, and the jottings of Brautigan, Saroyan and Vonnegut. The humanity that is everywhere demonstrated in *Losing Battles* does not cuddle itself, does not invite approbation. It simply and necessarily informs what is probably the quietest masterpiece to be written in America since the death of Willa Cather.

Nancy B. Sederberg (review date Fall 1983)

SOURCE: "Welty's 'Death of a Traveling Salesman,'" in *The Explicator*, Vol. 42, No. 1, Fall, 1983, pp. 52-4.

[*In the following review, Sederberg analyzes the different symbolic associations of the name Bowman in Welty's "Death of a Traveling Salesman."*]

The name R. J. Bowman in Eudora Welty's **"Death of a Traveling Salesman"** evokes meanings beyond those suggested either by Welty herself or prior critics. In a recent reminiscence, **"Looking Back at the First Story,"** Welty recalls a real-life prototype for Bowman, Mr. Archie Johnson, a neighbor who in the 1930's traveled remote Mississippi roads as a Highway Department inspector and land buyer. On a literal level, the name Bowman is probably a transposition of his given name, Archie, into an equivalent surname, Bowman. Yet Welty is aware of the symbolic associations of names as well, as evidenced by her changing the antagonist's name from Rafe in the *Manuscript* version to Sonny in the book. She comments:

> I had got sensitive to the importance of proper names, and this change is justified: "Sonny" is omnipresent in boys' names in Mississippi and is not dropped just because the boys grow up and marry; "Sonny" helped make the relationship of the man and the woman one that Bowman could mistake at the beginning; and at the same time it harked back to the fire-bringer. . . . Prometheus [who] was in my mind almost at the instant I heard Mr. Johnson tell about the farmer borrowing fire.

Likewise, William M. Jones asserts that the name Bowman is an allusion to Hercules, the archetypal archer of antiquity. He then proceeds to analyze how the weak Bowman functions as a sort of anti-Hercules figure, foil to the strong Herculean Sonny, doer of muscular deeds and bringer of fire and potency. According to Jones, in rejecting the mythical symbolism of Sonny and his earth-mother-wife, Bowman refuses to undergo the necessary process of individuation described by Jung and hence degenerates into psychic debility and death. And so he does.

Yet, two complementary bow-man associations also seem applicable. The first is to another ancient archer—Cupid. This reference appears particularly apt as Bowman's troubles are, both metaphorically and physically, of the heart. To strain an allusion, one might say that his heart veritably *quivers* like a bow (it leaps and expands like a rocket and a colt, falls gently and scatters like an acrobat and ashes) out of its lonely need to achieve communion with his hosts and humanity. The bow imagery is reinforced by the tableau of the mule turning its target-like eyes into his. But Bowman averts his eyes and at the conclusion becomes the hunted, slain by his own self-destructive heart/weapon, rather than a potential wooer.

The second association is suggested by Bowman's strange symbolic gesture as he approaches the threshold of the cabin:

> He stooped and laid his big black hat over the handle on his bag. It was a humble motion, almost a bow, that instantly struck him as absurd and betraying of all his weakness. He looked up at the woman, the wind blowing his hair. He might have continued for a long time in this unfamiliar attitude; he had never been a patient man, but when he was sick he had learned to sink submissively into the pillows, to wait for his medicine. He waited on the woman.

Later, when confronted by Sonny's potent presence, Bowman "knew he should offer explanations and show money—at least appear either penitent or authoritative." Both responses, however, falsely polarize his options. As Robert Heilman notes, "he cannot be either humble or dominant, that is, practice even the one-sided relationships that substitute for genuine mutuality."

The term bow, though, offers a complex continuum of connotations. Most neutrally, bowing is a ritual act of courtesy often offered in greeting (the *Manuscript* text significantly reads "almost a curtsey" for "almost a bow"). Negatively, bowing refers to debasing obeisance, as in "bowing and scraping," or an unwilling act of acquiescence to another's will or authority. It also suggests being bowed down by the burdens of life. In a more positive sense, bowing expresses degrees of acknowledgment and acceptance, compliance and consent, and, finally, reverence for a power superior to oneself. The posture of prayer is, after all, a form of bowing.

The woman before whom Bowman awkwardly bows is also a complex and ambiguous symbol. She is both ancient and youthful to evoke simultaneously the Uroboros or archetypal Great Mothers from Bowman's grandmother back to Rhea as well as an actual procreative mate. She also symbolically links the cycle of birth and death and functions as a guide: a priestess with a lamp before the dark passage of her temple/cabin, which combines elements of a womb and a tomb, or perhaps a medium (the earlier version contains a suggestive reference to Bowman's heart pounding "profoundly, like a medium at a seance"). Far from the weakness and passivity Bowman sees in his unconscious urge to embrace this primordial female principle, it represents a positive acceptance of life-giving sources and an act of faith. One is reminded of a similar gesture in **"A Still Moment"** in which the evangelical preacher, Lorenzo Dow, escapes from the Indians by acquiescing immediately and unhesitatingly to the internal command, "'Incline!'" Though Dow also is too quick to devise his own salvation instead of waiting upon Providence's "less hurried, more divine" protection, he at least is open to the vision which the heron offers. Bowman, in contrast, fails to heed the command, for "he had not known yet how slowly he understood" what the couple represents.

Welty relates her approach in **"Death of a Traveling Salesman"** to a recurrent motif in her fiction: "the journey of errand or search (for some form of the secret of life)," which she asserts also underlies **"A Worn Path,"** **"The Wide Net,"** **"A Still Moment,"** **"The Hitch-Hikers,"** and the entire collection *The Bride of the Innisfallen*. She seems to be suggesting by the multiple associations of the name Bowman that people need to learn how—out of strength not weakness—to bow before mysteries beyond our human control or even knowing.

Eudora Welty with Tom Royals and John Little (interview date 1984)

SOURCE: "A Conversation with Eudora Welty," in *Conversations with Eudora Welty,* edited by Peggy Whitman Prenshaw, University Press of Mississippi, 1984, pp. 252-67.

[*In the following interview, Welty discusses her approach to writing and presents insights into some of her characters and stories.*]

[*Royals:*] *What do you think about the concept of what we're trying to do here, that is to say, to interview a writer and try to arrive at something worthwhile through the medium?*

[Welty:] I don't rightly know. I've always been tenacious in my feeling that we don't need to know a writer's life in order to understand his work and I have really felt very opposed to a lot of biographies that have been written these days, of which the reviewers say they're not any good unless they reveal all sorts of other things about the writer. I know you're not talking about that kind of thing, but it's brought out my inherent feeling that it's good to know something about a writer's background, but only what pertains. I'm willing to tell you anything I can if I think it has that sort of value. You asked me what I thought the value was, and I'm just not sure.

[*Royals:*] *Not sure as to whether knowledge of the writer has a value? The works may stand on their own. Is that what you mean?*

Well, take somebody like Chekhov. It's important to know that he was the grandson of a serf, that he was a doctor, that he had tuberculosis, and that his wife was an actress. All these things matter in understanding his work. But there are a lot of other things, as you know, that don't matter.

[*Royals:*] *The idea of interviewing writers is fairly recent, isn't it?*

I don't know. I think mostly in the past they relied on letters, because, you know, people were great letter writers, and they wrote seriously and fully to their friends, relatives, and so on, so there was a written record of many things about people's lives that just doesn't exist now. Nobody writes letters anymore.

[*Little:*] *But do you think it helps to know about your family life to interpret* **The Optimist's Daughter?**

No, I don't think it's necessary in the least. I think the key fact in my case—I can only speak for myself—is that I have to write out of emotional experience, which is not neces-

sarily out of factual experience. What I do is translate something that's happened to me into dramatic terms. And they don't coincide; well, they almost never coincide. But I couldn't write about any important emotional thing if I hadn't experienced it; that wouldn't even be honest. You have to understand the feelings, and of course, I've got my feelings out of my own experience, but the experience itself is altered, transmuted, made to convey the story. For instance, in **Optimist's Daughter,** I write about the death of a middle-aged woman's elderly father. My own father died at the age of 52 of leukemia. That was entirely different from what happens to the judge; I made him up from whole cloth. But my mother did have operations on her eyes, though not his operation, and my mother did die within my recent experience. So, you can see what happened, it's a transposition, but a complete change, using feelings I understood about the daughter and her parental experience.

[*Little:*] *You can see things in the novel like the recipe, and I know about your mother's use of recipes from reading other background stuff, but neither of us probably knows that this kind of knowledge is essential to interpret the novel.*

I don't think it is. But as a writer who tried to be convincing and honest and detailed, I don't hesitate to pluck detail from everywhere; but real observed detail doesn't mean that the source of it in life has any existence in the imaginary world of my book.

[*Royals:*] *Flannery O'Connor. I've heard people say one needs to know about her Catholic religion to interpret her works.*

I may have said that too, because I know when I did learn something about that, a whole lot of her work opened up for me, and I wish that I had had that benefit in the beginning.

[*Little:*] *When did you learn about her Catholicism?*

Well, I knew she was a Catholic, but I heard her give a lecture at, I think it was Converse College, called "The Catholic Writer," in which she dealt with that relationship directly and it was a revelation to most of the young students and to me too.

[*Royals:*] *Does it open up new views into O'Connor's works?*

Yes, more specific at the time than I can think back to now. But the whole idea of salvation and . . .

[*Little:*] *grace . . .*

Yes, grace and redemption and all of that are so much more

deeply rooted in her fiction, enhancing her stories more than I had realized because I didn't know much about the church itself.

[*Royals:*] *Which of her stories did we study in your class, Eudora?*

We read several—"A Good Man is Hard to Find."

[*Royals:*] *That's the one. I read that and thought it was a tremendous story and knew nothing about her Catholicism, or . . .*

Me too, Tom. That's exactly how I read it. And it is a tremendous story.

[*Royals:*] *What else would I have gotten out of it if I'd known about the Catholic aspects?*

Don't ask me that, because I can't be specific enough. But we should go back to the scene with the old lady and the criminal and their confrontation, to some kind of state of grace that is achieved, to be aware of the difference that conviction made in a violent story.

[*Little:*] *We read "The River," the story with the Reverend Bevel Summers and the baptism in it, and we talked about the name Bevel.*

Yes, we did. I don't know whether I said that or whether I knew it then. I didn't realize it but Bevel is a common name over in Georgia and so she got it perfectly legitimately. It wasn't just a symbol thrown in. It was complete with antecedents. She would be the first to underscore that!

[*Royals:*] *You said you didn't think it was absolutely necessary to know a writer's background to find out what they're all about. Do you think Flannery O'Connor was an exception to the rule?*

No, I don't really. I expect a lot of people simply know more about Catholicism than I happen to, but I shouldn't say "it's a rule" that you don't need to know about the writer's life. What I said about Chekhov would apply. I do think that we need to know general things, somebody's century, and where they come from and what kind of people; those general things, I think do belong. They pertain.

[*Royals:*] *What profession they are, maybe, and that sort of thing.*

It's important if it's illuminating to a writer's work. I didn't mean writers should be completely anonymous.

[*Little:*] *But do you think it's helpful if the reader knows,*

for example, that "Why I Live at the P.O." grew out of your seeing a woman at a post office with an ironing board?

No, I don't think that's any help at all.

[*Little:*] *It's important, I think, to other writers if they learn more about the process of creativity, how stories evolve, how stories are born.*

But that's a good example of how something like that could be said that's a fact but nothing like the truth, the real truth. I did see a woman like this, but what the story grew out of was something much more than that. I mean, it was a lifelong listening to talk on my own block where I grew up as a child, and that was in my head to write out of all the time. The sight of the lady ironing was the striking of the match that set if off, but I wouldn't have written a story just about seeing somebody with an ironing board in the post office. It's nearly always too simplifying to say that any story, however slight, comes from one thing.

[*Little:*] *Sure. It's like, you hear it said that the germ which produced* Anna Karenina *came from an obituary that Tolstoy saw in the paper about a society woman who committed suicide. It's interesting to know about the spark in understanding how a story gets started or the impulse that triggers it in terms of understanding, I guess, the process or craft. But it doesn't help you to interpret or understand the story itself to know where the writer got the idea.*

I think most stories and especially novels have long fuses that run way back, you know, so long that you don't even know the origin, probably. It started so long ago out of something so deep in you. Something sets it off. But you can't say that from that you can certainly see right off what made the story, because you have lived with it, of course, in the meantime.

[*Little:*] *Did you ever tell a real story or an incident, and from the verbalization of that, realize you've got a story?*

Never. In fact, that isn't the way I work. It reminds me of what I've heard of the author James Stephens in Ireland, though. He was like so many of the Irish, they were great talkers, and they met night after night and talked. And people who knew him said he talked all of his stories away, because he told them all and that was it. Of course, he wrote a lot, too, in spite of the talk. But stories don't exist to me in those two elements, sound and penmanship. Not at all.

[*Little:*] *You mean you make an effort not to tell about something you are working on?*

No. It just never occurred to me. You know, it also reminds me of what a club woman asked me to do once: "Would you just come and tell us one of your stories in your own words?"

[*Royals:*] *That's fantastic.*

Honestly.

[*Royals:*] *Speaking of telling stories, I think that's the difference between a writer and a story teller. A writer writes them. A story teller tells them. I don't see the same thing occurring among writers I know. Jim Whitehead tells stories but mostly he listens and writes.*

Well it's two different gifts.

[*Royals:*] *Right.*

And I think, John, this is not to say that when you're writing dialogue stories, you don't hear them in your head, which I do, and I think most writers do; they can be tested. But when you're writing a story, you're constructing something. You really are making something using dialogue, and using what the ear tells you to help you out. When you're telling a story, it's just different. It's just different.

[*Royals:*] *Did you ever ask anybody to read drafts of your stories?*

I couldn't work that way, Tom. I have to get a thing as well made as I can do it before I let anyone see it.

[*Royals:*] *And then that is the publisher.*

Yes—or editor. I like my friends to see them, and I have shown things to friends, but they've been completed sections of something, for instance in **Losing Battles**.

[*Royals:*] *Didn't you ever do that? Most writers, when they're beginning, go and ask teachers or somebody for suggestions.*

I never have. Perhaps it's shyness. Wanting to get something right and not trusting myself until I get it as well as I can, and probably pride. I don't want anyone to see it if it's not the best I can do.

[*Royals:*] *Do you feel like the magic of it might be taken away or the spirit let out or something like that?*

I don't know . . . I don't mean to sound . . . I think I am superstitious, not pretentious. I am superstitious that something would go—its possibilities would go—if you . . . told it before you wrote it. It would take off the bloom before you ever got to write it down. For me. Different people work different ways.

[*Little:*] *I guess it varies among writers. Do you remember telling us about one of your earlier stories that you'd sent to the* Southern Review? *When they rejected it, you burned it and then they wrote back and accepted it. Then you had to sit down and rewrite it from memory?*

That was **"Petrified Man."**

[*Royals:*] *It was?*

Yes, I had sent it all over to every magazine in the U.S.A., I guess, and everybody had sent it back. The *Southern Review* liked it but had faults to find which were certainly legitimate. You know it was a very wild kind of story. They had published me pretty regularly, but they said they didn't think this one was quite right and sent it back. So after that, I burned it up. Then the *Southern Review* wrote and said "We would like to see it again," and so I did write that over from memory. But that was a "by ear" story.

[*Royals:*] *A what?*

By ear. I could just listen to it, and, click, could play it back as if it were on a tape. You couldn't do an interior story that way, at least I couldn't.

[*Little:*] *Do you feel that when you played it back you got everything exactly as you had it the first time?*

As far as I know. It was pretty easy to do. I could probably write that again from scratch if I burned it up because that kind of thing is just like hearing a song—once heard—you could sing it again.

> I write of my fellow Southerners out of a conviction that I know what they are like inside, as well as outside. They're my credentials.
>
> —*Eudora Welty*

[*Royals:*] *How much of your work do you get from current events?*

I should say I get more general information than particular information. Things stay in my head a long time, maybe years, before I use them, and by the time they would ever surface in one of my stories in some general way, the news story might be old hat, politically.

[*Little:*] *Are you ever bothered by your fame in Jackson, or is it usually the telephone and strangers that bother you?*

Jackson is very understanding of me. I'm very proud of it—

my relationship with my hometown. Oddly enough, it's since the recent television interviews that came out this year on public television that I have had an absolute inundation of letters and manuscripts and people wanting interviews. I must have about ten of those requests a week, and I'm so behind in correspondence as a result of that. These letters have been very—many of the letters have been just plain—they don't ask or want anything. An entirely different audience from my book audience. Although it is pleasing to me, I must be hundreds of letters behind with answering.

[*Little:*] *I want to follow up on something you said at the March 1978 writers' conference in North Dakota. You said during a panel discussion that you didn't think your stories had the ability to change society. What sort of response would you expect a Southern white person to get from your writing? What kind of understanding would you shoot for?*

Well, for any reader I always hope that my story justifies itself as a revelation of character, and I would hope for recognition of the common humanity there. I would hope that readers might look in there and see themselves, as I was trying to look in there and see the Southern character. I write of my fellow Southerners out of a conviction that I know what they are like inside, as well as outside. They're my credentials.

[*Little:*] *Do you think that is true for both your stories, "The Demonstrators" and "Where is the Voice Coming From?"*

Well, for any story, I hope, and in **"Where is the Voice Coming From?"** about the murder of Medgar Evers—I was definitely hoping to say, "This is what I think these characters are like on the inside. This is what is going through the mind of that murderer," and I would hope that story could be recognized as such by the readers.

[*Little:*] *All right. The readers should recognize that they have inside themselves something like the murderer in* **"Where is the Voice Coming From?"** *had inside himself?*

Well, not literally—but I felt able to suggest they might have—in those bad times in particular. The different members of the human race are not very different potentially, you know—I mean we're all able to recognize the elements of good and evil in human behavior—we comprehend good and evil, we're familiar with violence in our world. And that particular element of evil was running all through the South at that time. And I feel that anybody who read that story would recognize things they had seen or heard or might even have said, in some version, or imagined or feared themselves.

[*Little:*] *When* **"The Demonstrators"** *came out, you said it*

was not primarily a civil rights story. Would you comment on that?

Well, all of it was a reflection of society at the time it happened. Every story in effect does that. And I was trying for it in both those stories and in several others that I have underway here in the house that will be in my next book. They all reflect the way we were deeply troubled in that society and within ourselves at what was going on in the sixties. They reflect the effect of change sweeping all over the South—of course, over the rest of the country too, but I was writing about where I was living and the complexity of those changes. I think a lot of my work then suggested that it's not just a matter of cut and dried right and wrong—"We're right—You're wrong," "We're black, you're white." You know, I wanted to show the complexity of it all.

[*Little:*] *Ok, let me ask you a technical question. There is a great deal of light imagery in "The Demonstrators." There is moonlight, electric lights, sockets left out of bulbs on the theatre sign that spells "Broadway." There are also lots of shadows. Was this imagery designed to show the obscurity and confusion that people see in things?*

I think it was, John. I never had looked at it in that calculated way, but I saw it like that, was guided by my imaginary scene. I go by that, as a rule. In a story I'm writing now, I'm using light to suggest the shadowy nature of what we know and what we can see and observe. I try in all stories to use the whole physical world to assist me. I think I probably do that instinctively.

[*Little:*] *Ok. That is something I noticed in "The Demonstrators."*

It's odd that I'm doing the same thing now in what I'm writing but very consciously as opposed to unconsciously in **"The Demonstrators."**

[*Little:*] *What are you writing on now?*

I can't talk about that for the same reason I've already told you. I can't discuss things in progress.

[*Little:*] *Yeah. Sure. With "The Demonstrators," there was Eva Duckett, the Fairbrothers, Alonzo Duckett and Horatio Duckett. One owns a newspaper, one is a preacher, and one is married to the mill owner. Are they sisters and brothers? Are they of the same family?*

Sure. Sure they would be. Because in a small town like that you know how it is.

[*Little:*] *Uh huh. Are you making a point with that?*

Yes. I was. I was absolutely.

[*Little:*] *What exactly is that point?*

Well, it was an observation of the way a small town society in the South is often in the control or the grip, whether benevolent or malevolent, of the solid, powerful family. It makes it all the harder for any change to penetrate a town like that. Some may be good people and some not so good, and they may be in themselves helpless to bring about change. They may be victims too.

[*Little:*] *At the end of "The Demonstrators," Dr. Strickland says to Eva Duckett, "If I had what Herman has, I'd go out in the backyard and shoot myself." Is Dr. Strickland showing a more compassionate, human side than what is usually visible in a powerful person?*

He is showing the vulnerability of all of them.

[*Little:*] *And with Marcia Pope, are you saying that she may be the only one who has the strength to come through it all?*

Well, she—I meant she was tenacious to the kinds of things in her teaching and her understanding in a removed, elderly way that was maybe not as affected as the day to day things. She was trying to hold on, to keep the principles. I guess that's what I intended to say about Marcia Pope. She remained impervious.

[*Royals:*] *It comes off, and I wonder if you did a technical thing that made it come off that well. The first and last paragraphs of the story deal with Marcia Pope. So the action was bracketed by Marcia Pope. How much thought did you give to that technique?*

Well, that's important to me, Tom. I like the form of something like that. That is a loose form but yet I feel that it has its own strictness.

[*Royals:*] *I agree.*

I've sort of developed new forms for my more recent stories. They're not nearly as compact in one way as they used to be, but they're more compact in another. That is, they have density of another kind than the plot itself. I want there to be a "felt" form running through that the reader will get. You know, it's like what you said about Miss Marcia Pope, a "felt" connection between things that has its own intensity, its own development.

[*Royals:*] *I think your compactness and density come from the economy of your prose. You just don't waste words.*

Thank you.

[*Royals:*] *In North Dakota when I introduced you at the writers' conference, I said that you were honest in your writing and also an honest person. I might add to that "cautious." Maybe caution has to do with honesty. I've learned here this morning that you're getting ready to publish a new book containing several stories about the sixties. Do you think that you're just now publishing a book about the sixties because of your caution and your desire to be honest— the desire to give such difficult and complete material plenty of time to mature in your mind?*

That might be. Time is an important ingredient in understanding a situation. But the practical reason why I haven't produced more stories of any kind is that they've turned twice into novels. *Losing Battles* was to have been a story. (They weren't all to have been about the sixties.) *The Optimist's Daughter* turned into a novel. Now I still have some others that I'm working on and I'm praying that they won't turn into novels.

[*Little:*] *Before we leave "The Demonstrators," I want to know what the term "I bid that" means in the story. Twosie, the sister, says to Dr. Strickland, who is about to remove the necklace from the fatally wounded woman, "I bid that." Is bid a verb?*

[*Royals:*] *B-I-D. As in "I bid that."*

[*Little:*] *I made that? Is that what it means?*

No, no, no. She bids to have it.

[*Royals:*] *I put in a bid for that? Would that be closer?*

Yes, I bid that. That is to say, I want it to be mine.

[*Little:*] *Wow, she's anticipating the death and wants the necklace.*

Oh, yes. She wants it.

[*Little:*] *For her own, I see.*

She wants to get her name on it. You may not have heard that before. That was an expression when I was a child. You know, somebody would bring back a stack of sandwiches; "I bid the ham."

[*Royals:*] *You say so much so fast, and I think you're pretty literal about it in your fiction.*

Well, I try to be.

[*Royals:*] *We need to talk about "The Demonstrators" some more. Did anybody ever ask you who the demonstrators are in that story?*

I can't remember that I've been asked that.

[*Royals:*] *When John told me he was teaching the story, I hadn't read it yet. I said "What's it all about?" He said, "**The Demonstrators.**" And I asked, "Who are the demonstrators in the story?" and he said "That's a darn good question."*

It is a good question, though I think every character in it is a demonstrator. In fact, I wanted to suggest that. Even the birds at the end when they—

[*Royals:*] *Clothes on the clothesline even?*

Yes, everything is to show. Everything, everybody's showing something.

[*Royals:*] *It's a visual story?*

A visual story. It is a visual story.

[*Royals:*] *And that's where the demonstrators come in.*

Well, I have some real, literal demonstrators who came in off-stage. But also, everybody was showing something to anybody, including the victim . . . those birds at the end, the flickers that showed the red seal on the back of their heads. Everything was showing themselves. Everybody was showing themselves.

[*Royals:*] *You mentioned that the literal demonstrators were off-stage.*

They were.

[*Royals:*] *You write about them in the newspaper, and the guy who . . .*

[*Little:*] *And Dr. Strickland sees this picture about a guy burning his draft card, and the front pages of the newspaper . . .*

[*Royals:*] *Yeah. But they're really giving the energy to the story. I thought the story might be about the effect the demonstrators have had on that town.*

Well, it was in a way, I think. But also, the demonstrators, who falsified their position, soon exemplified what already existed there. The society.

[*Royals:*] *You know, I've heard that great tennis players and great baseball players have 20-20 vision, or 20-10 vision*

and that things really look slower to them than they do to people without really good eyesight. I've begun to think that your vision is probably like that of a great athlete. Maybe you see the world more slowly and in more detail than many people do. How is your eyesight?

That's very generous of you to say that. I thought I'd just seen it longer than most people by now. I don't know. I have got a visual mind. Most people do have, I think. I observe closely because I'm interested. I want to see, but I don't think I have any special gift. I remember reading that Goya had trained himself as an artist to see action, and when he drew a falling horse everyone said the figure was completely grotesque, but that was before the invention of photography, which proved that Goya's eyes saw everything absolutely right, the way a falling horse looked in mid air. Isn't that extraordinary?

[*Royals:*] *That is.*

[*Little:*] *Well, when you read a story like "Petrified Man," you know you must have awful good ears. Would essential ingredients of a writer be good ears and good eyes?*

I believe that. I think that they're the tools of your trade. They're not only the tools of your trade; they're probably what made you a writer to begin with, if you did like to look and to listen. You can't tell which came first. At least in my case. I think everything begins with a given, you know, like a proposition to prove. You set out with a given and then you follow that through, and there are all kinds of givens you can start with, that we give ourselves to begin with.

[*Little:*] *Is that like in the form of an idea? In the form of a theme?*

Sure. Sure, and intention and the whole germ—no, not the germ of a story—the nucleus, whatever one starts from. The whole beginning of a story, which unfolds in it.

[*Little:*] *OK. You don't start with an incident or character. They're included, but you start with an idea?*

There has to be an idea. What is alive in it is this idea. But what gives me the idea is always people. In general, human life gives me the idea; the character, the situation.

[*Little:*] *How articulate, how fixed is that idea when you start? Is it something that happens as the story develops?*

No, I think it's the very heart of it, this idea.

[*Little:*] *And that's there to begin with.*

It's alive in the story.

[*Little:*] *Can you say the theme?*

It develops. Well, I never know what any of these different terms mean. They're all in the story in embryo form, I guess you could call it, before you ever begin writing. Of course, they develop as you go, but it's all toward the fulfillment of the story's whole that you had to begin with. Working without that, I think your characters would be rattling around in a vacuum. With me.

[*Royals:*] *What we're talking about mostly is you start with the character.*

I just mean the way ideas come to me is through people from the living world, not from the abstract, but from the living world. I don't say, "I'm going to sit down and write a story about Greed." But if I'd grown up with somebody that I thought was a terribly greedy old man, and had come to see what that does to a human being, then I might write a story to show what it does to a human being, but I'm not making up an abstract character to illustrate a moral judgment. That wouldn't interest me in the least. Neither do I think I could make it come alive.

[*Royals:*] *What kind of emotional distance and separation do you feel you have to keep from your work?*

I don't know, Tom. I'm sure there's been a variation of those distances in my work, depending on the story and depending on what I'm trying to do. Some subjects I'm much closer to personally than others. I think the closer you are, the more difficult the work is. I'm sure it depends on the story in my case.

[*Royals:*] *I've read books or stories by people who were too emotionally involved. That seems to show . . . but I'm not talking about passion or having creativity or energy.*

Well, getting too close is the easiest thing in the world to have happen, you know, and that is the danger. When it interferes with your impersonality. You have to show—impersonality is not the word.

[*Royals:*] *Objectivity?*

Objectivity. That's exactly it. You can't let anything interfere with that.

[*Royals:*] *I think you do a good job of letting those characters be their own people. You don't even impose your own political beliefs on them.*

I try not to.

[*Royals:*] *In "Where is the Voice Coming From?" was it* difficult for you to create that character and not feel some contempt for him because he was a murderer?

Oh, yes, sure. In fact I did feel it, but I was trying to. Since I wrote it on the night it happened, I was terribly emotionally involved in the writing, but I think that gave me a kind of steely feeling about it, you know, the need for understanding a murderer, which I couldn't have done maybe if I'd thought it over for a period of time. In retrospect, I would have lost my daring, picked the story up with tongs or something.

[*Royals:*] *So, it was a kind of anger, almost anger, you steeled yourself . . .*

It was, it was . . .

[*Royals:*] *. . . not to get soppy about the situation.*

I made myself do it.

[*Royals:*] *I don't believe that could be done by a lesser writer.*

Well I don't know if it was done by this writer or not.

[*Royals:*] *I think it was very successful.*

Thank you. It was hard to do and I was still . . . I stayed in the same mood for a long time afterwards as if I really hadn't finished the story, you know, I should have done more with it. Too late. It was pushing—I was writing ***Losing Battles*** at the time, it just pushed right through it.

[*Little:*] *How many stories have you written in one sitting? I remember your saying "**Powerhouse**" was done in one sitting.*

I did. Almost never have I done anything else in one sitting.

[*Little:*] *This one and "**Powerhouse**" and . . .*

And both of those were completely outside my usual orbit. In both cases I was writing about something that I couldn't personally have known too much about.

[*Little:*] *The amazing thing about "**Powerhouse**" is that it seems that you did know exactly what you were writing about.*

I know it. I knew about my feelings. Well, I knew it, sure I knew that man's music from way back, but not technically. Sure, I knew it. And it was the experience of seeing the man alive . . .

[*Royals:*] *The man you are referring to is the jazz musician, Fats Waller, right?*

Sure.

[*Royals:*] *You know, we were talking about believability of characters. I think the jazz musician in "**Powerhouse**" was a little hard to believe in everything he said. I never knew for sure whether he was putting us on or not.*

Yes, well, I tried to make that a little ambiguous that way, I intended it to show he was really improvising the whole thing. I meant it to be that way.

[*Little:*] *Which is what the story is about. And all his band members don't even know he is improvising the whole thing, right?*

Yes. That's right.

[*Royals:*] *The more you read that story, the more you do realize it is about improvising. I went into it knowing it was about improvising, but I still kept asking, "Is that true?" And then I'd remember that this is a story about improvising.*

Yes, but all the same I wanted the improvising to be kind of mysterious. Powerhouse is an artist. He improvises, they fall in with it—I think it is mysterious. Another consequence is, Tom, I was not in a position to revise that story, because how could I do it? You know, I didn't know enough to have started it to begin with.

[*Royals:*] *Well, I don't think . . .*

So I never did. I knew that it was either that or nothing. So that was it. It could have been helped as a story but not by the author.

[*Little:*] *One last question. Are there any rules beginning writers should follow?*

No. God knows writing is the most independent and individual thing you can do.

Eric Homberger (review date 20 July 1984)

SOURCE: A review of *One Writer's Beginnings*, in *TLS*, No. 4242, July 20, 1984, p. 806.

[*In the following review, Homberger states that Welty's "One Writer's Beginnings is a reminder that the imagination can be as nourished by Jackson, Mississippi, as by Henry James's London, Kafka's Prague or Kundera's Brno."*]

When in 1965, during the civil rights movement, Eudora Welty wrote that "Entering the hearts and minds of our own people is no harder now than it ever was", the most common response was a subdued sense of shock at a writer so little carried away by the dramatic struggles taking place around her.

The argument that Welty's work fails to register the great traumas of the age is a way of placing her "interest" as Southern, and therefore as regional. No myth-maker like Faulkner, her work stands or falls on the sense of place, the particular character of Mississippi. She understands her people with uncanny precision. Her brief story on the murder of Medgar Evers in 1963, **"Where Is the Voice Coming From?"**, was a fine gesture of imaginative insight. When the killer was finally caught, Welty remarks in the preface to her collected stories, it was necessary to revise certain details in her wholly invented characterization, because they had been disturbingly close to the truth.

Looking back on the 1960s, Welty recently commented on the scale of the changes which came in the wake of the civil rights movement: I think we've been through an experience which was more profound than we'd guessed, both black and white. Now we are both more open in a way that—well, I had not experienced it because it had never happened. Now, seeing how much more there was to communication than the wish, and the desire, and the heart, I feel I have more to learn now than I had to learn then.

The learning process continues. Mississippi is no longer the Demon incarnate; young college students find cocaine a better high than civil rights; and there aren't all that many unregistered black voters in the South any more. But of the rich literature of the South in this period, Welty's stories and novels look the most likely to survive.

> The argument that Welty's work fails to register the great traumas of the age is a way of placing her "interest" as Southern, and therefore as regional. No myth-maker like Faulkner, her work stands or falls on the sense of place, the particular character of Mississippi. She understands her people with uncanny precision.
> —*Eric Homberger*

As the appreciation of her achievement deepens, and as her stories find more and more readers, the world which permeates her writing seems remote, even historical. She was born in 1909 in Jackson, Mississippi, the sleepiest state capital in the United States, her parents having come to Jackson at the start of their married life from Ohio and West Virginia. Long family trips north from Mississippi to visit her relations (it took a week to drive each way in the 1920s) gave Welty a sense of an "outside" world which she recalls vividly in the Harvard lectures which have now been published as *One Writer's Beginnings:*

> Towns little or big had beginnings and ends, they reached to an edge and stopped, where the country began again as though the hadn't happened. They were intact and to themselves. You could see a town lying ahead in its whole, as definitely formed as a plate on a table. And your road entered and ran straight through the heart of it; you could see it all, laid out for your passage through. Towns, like people, had clear identities and your imagination could go out to meet them. You saw houses, yards, fields, and people busy in them, the people that had a life where they were. You could hear their bank clocks, striking, you could smell their bakeries. You would know those towns again, recognize the salient detail, see so close up. Nothing was blurred, and in passing along Main Street, slowed down from twenty-five to twenty miles an hour, you didn't miss anything on either side.

In a review of Welty's *Delta Wedding* in 1946, Isaac Rosenfeld argued that "the serious American writer cannot but be alienated from American society, close though he may be to it, and much though he may wish to belong". Rosenfeld could not understand how a Southern writer could "really and truly feel at home in his home." Welty was perhaps too polite, too much the Southern lady, to ask the same question of Rosenfeld's (and Saul Bellow's) Chicago. Received opinion has, for the most part, agreed with Rosenfeld, and it was Bellow, not Welty, who won the Nobel Prize. Taking Welty seriously would mean questioning the massive investment in modernism and alienation in American culture. *One Writer's Beginnings* is a reminder that the imagination can be as nourished by Jackson, Mississippi, as by Henry James's London, Kafka's Prague or, Kundera's Brno.

Eudora Welty with Barbara Lazear Ascher (interview date Autumn 1984)

SOURCE: "A Visit with Eudora Welty," in *The Yale Review*, Vol. 74, No. 1, Autumn, 1984, pp. 147-53.

[*In the following interview, Welty discusses how she develops her characters and what she thinks about writing.*]

She's worn a pretty hat for the occasion, an occasion she says she has dreaded ever since she decided to make an exception to her rule, no interviews. Her smile is shy, her voice soft and hesitant: "You look like a Virginia girl." She reaches for my bag, but I protest—after all, she is seventy-five. Her hair is white. She is slight and walks with slow care in a shiny new pair of loafers. Her azure knit dress is the color of her eyes. The next day, when we have settled into pants and comfortable shoes, she tells me, "I would have worn pants to the airport, but I thought, 'She'll think I'm some sort of hick!'"

She eases herself behind the wheel of her car. She's tired. "I've been on the go ever since the first of the year. And this weekend I signed 400 of those Harvard books for a limited edition. Are you going to use a tape recorder? I always think I sound as if I don't know what I'm talking about on tape. You'll have to excuse me if I don't hear you. I don't hear as well as I used to."

The book to which she refers is her autobiographical *One Writer's Beginnings*. It was developed from the Norton lectures she gave at Harvard and was, she says, "the hardest thing I've ever had to do. First there were the lectures. I don't know why they wanted me. I'm no scholar and I hate to lecture. I much prefer conversation—a back-and-forth exchange. I've always had to teach to supplement my income, but I think if I had to do it again, I'd do something completely different. Not different from writing. Different from teaching. I think I'd do something mechanical, something with my hands."

"Such as plumbing?"

"Such as painting chairs. You paint a chair in the morning, and there it is in the afternoon."

In talking more of the book, she says, "It was amazing to discover that nothing is ever lost. Thomas Mann was right, the memory is a well. In writing this book each memory uncovered another. It was probably important for me to remember these things, but it was very hard. I kept thinking, 'If only I'd known then what I know now.' Or, 'If only I'd said . . .' And I'm so sorry I never had the chance to tell my father how I felt about him. We were a very reserved family. But passionate."

Given the reserve, it is no surprise that in *One Writer's Beginnings* part of her self remains in shadow. She tells, for example, of her father's death and the blood transfusion that was a desperate attempt to avert it, but what is left unwritten is how she felt. "I originally had it in the book," she says, "but I took it out. I thought it would be too self-indulgent. What I remember is that there were venetian blinds in back of me, that the heat of the sun was coming through the slats and onto my back. I suppose that was my creeping horror. That's what a person remembers—the physical sensation. I'd never seen anyone die before. Have you?"

She often asks such questions. "Don't you?" "Can you imagine?" "Don't you find that to be true?" It is her attempt to bring you into the circle, to include you. It goes beyond Southern hospitality and seems to be a complete turning over of the self to another's sensibilities. "Are you warm enough?" "Are you hungry yet?" "Land! You shouldn't have spent so much money on that book. I would have given you a copy." "I worry about you."

It is not possible to capture on paper the rich melody of her accent, but there are certain words that, once you have heard her pronounce them, seem unmistakably hers. "Buzzard" and "sinister" are two of these. As we drove along the Natchez Trace, the setting of many of her tales, two birds were spotted weighing down branches atop a dead tree. "Buzzids," she shuddered, "I hate buzzids. I always knew, when I was coming home on a train, when we had entered Mississippi because you would see buzzids out the window." She notes the cypress swamp beneath their perch: "Isn't it sinista?"

Because the Natchez Trace is what we think of as Eudora Welty country, it is jarring for me to leave it behind and drive into Jackson, a city of 300,000. Jackson's population is up 297,000 since Eudora Welty's parents settled there as a young married couple—her father from an Ohio farm and her mother from the mountains of West Virginia. The grand homes that once graced State Street have given way to Cooke's Prosthetics and Cash-in-a-Flash Pawn Shop. The architecture is that of any town in commercial, suburban America. "I used to play in all these yards," she says, pointing to parking lots. "And that is where the insane asylum used to be. Imagine—it said 'Insane Asylum' on the gates. That's what they were talking about in *The Sound and the Fury* when they said they were going to send Benjy to Jackson. In those days Jackson meant the loony bin."

Her own street, back from State, is quiet and slightly elevated. Her father chose the site in part to ease her mother's homesickness, but "my mother never could see the hill." Her childhood home, a 1920s Tudor designed by her father, is solid and graceful. "I feel awfully selfish living here alone, and I can't afford to keep it up the way I should, but I can't imagine moving. And it's home." The lawn is full of pine needles and is dominated by a huge oak tree. "The builder told my parents to chop down that tree, but they said, 'Never chop down an oak tree.' They were country people. I guess that was something country people say. Well, they were right. That's the only one left—all the pine have died."

We enter through a vestibule. "My father was a Yankee. He thought *all* houses should have vestibules." There is a living room to the left and a library to the right. Between is a solid mahogany staircase. Books are everywhere—they've overrun bookshelves and have moved to tables and desks. There are books by friends—Walker Percy, Reynolds Price, Elizabeth Bowen, Katherine Anne Porter, Elizabeth Spencer, William Jay Smith, and Robert Penn Warren. There are the diaries of Virginia Woolf and a new biography of Ford Madox Ford ("Can you imagine that he held a chair for Turgenev?" she asks). There are Seamus Heaney, Barbara Pym, Chekhov, and all of Henry Green, one of her favorites. On the mantel is a Snowden photograph of V. S. Pritchett, looking spry and amused—she's cut it from a magazine and mounted it. A similar photo is on her desk— "for inspiration." The desk is in the bedroom, where she has always worked. "When there were five of us here it was the only place I *could* work," she says, referring to the days when her parents and brothers also occupied this house.

A writer has to have a strong moral sense. You couldn't write if you yourself didn't have it and know what you were doing. But that's very different from wanting to moralize in your story. Your own moral sense tells you what's true and false and how people would behave. And you know what is just and unjust, but you don't point them out, in my view. I don't think it works in fiction because fiction is dramatic. It's not a platform.

—Eudora Welty

She is generous in her praise and encouragement of other writers. "Anne Tyler was a whiz from the time she was seventeen!" she exclaims. She laughs as she recalls that "Reynolds Price had Anne for one of his first students. He thought, 'Teaching is going to be great!' He thought *all* his students were going to be like Anne." She thinks the title of Tyler's latest novel, *Dinner at the Homesick Restaurant,* is "inspired," and that the last sentence is a tour de force. "If I had written that sentence, I'd be happy all my life!"

When asked about another prize-winning writer whose works she has reviewed, she says, "I wanted so much to like her book, but I found some of it impossibly precious. I did not put my misgivings in the review because it was the first book by a young writer and I couldn't hurt somebody like that. She was a bit self-indulgent, which is perfectly natural for someone of that much talent. I tried to point out the parts that I thought were marvelous."

Although she enjoys talking of writers and books, she warms most to speaking of the act of writing itself. "I love the function of writing—what it is *doing*." (She offers to pour us some Jack Daniels—"what Katherine Anne Porter called 'swish likka.' Just a jigger. This is powerful stuff. Whenever Red Warren is coming he calls and says, 'Eudora, get out the Black Jack, I'm comin' to town.'") "Elizabeth Bowen, in her marvelous notes on writing a novel in *Collected Impressions,* pointed out that dialogue is really a form of action. Because it advances the plot, it's not just chatter. She was so succinct in what she said. I think television may have ruined that for us. If you watch serials and talk shows, you would probably think that one-liners were the answer to conversation. That is what has hurt Broadway so: dialogue has been sacrificed for the one-liner. That's putting it too extremely, but the building of a conversation is designed to gradually reveal something.

"Elizabeth was a marvelous writer about writing and very helpful to me. So was E. M. Forster's *Aspects of the Novel.* I don't think that can ever be outdated. It's important to read these books, but you can't teach a person how to write. That has to come directly from inside the writer.

"What I try to show in fiction are the truths of human relationships. But you have to make up the lies of fiction to reveal these truths—people interacting, things beginning one way and changing to reveal something else. You *show* a truth. You don't tell it. It has to be done of itself."

She feels the same way about moralizing in fiction. "A writer has to have a strong moral sense. You couldn't write if you yourself didn't have it and know what you were doing. But that's very different from wanting to moralize in your story. Your own moral sense tells you what's true and false and how people would behave. And you know what is just and unjust, but you don't point them out, in my view. I don't think it works in fiction because fiction is dramatic. It's not a platform.

"That worried me in the sixties because I was asked so many times by strangers why I didn't come out for civil rights, something I'd worked for for years. They would call me in the middle of the night, mostly from New Jersey and New York City. They would say, 'Eudora Welty, what are you doing down there sitting on your *ass?*' I just told them that I knew what I could write and what I couldn't. That I was doing the best I could in my own field. I would be so shaken up that I couldn't sleep the rest of the night."

Glasses emptied, we depart for dinner at Bill's Burger House: burgers by day, native redfish by night. She is welcomed more like a football captain of a local, undefeated team than a literary eminence. Bill grabs her hand and tells me with Greek-accented gusto, "Everybody love this charming lady." And for the final flourish, "God Bless America!"

A pretty young woman approaches our table. "Miss Welty, you honored us by gracing our wedding tea. I just wanted to say hello." After she leaves I'm told whom she married. The parents and grandparents are identified, as are the members of the family who are Yankees. I begin to understand what she meant when she told me that she agreed with Walker Percy's response, "Because we lost," when reporters asked him why the South had so many fine writers. "Since we never really industrialized—reconstruction saw to that—the pace is slower," she explains. "People don't move around as much. You know who a person's mother is. We're more introspective, interested in the psychology of people."

The next morning when we meet she shares the mail with me, mail that keeps her awake at night because "I feel so guilty that I never have time to answer it." This morning's includes a letter form a sixteen-year-old, Christine from Georgia who writes, "I really loved **'Why I Live at the P.O.'** because it is so true to life. My brother and sister are always trying to get me in trouble." Then she asks whether the narrator of the story "will come back home, and do you think her parents will take her in if she does?"

"Of course." The answer is as natural as though we were speaking of a flesh-and-blood neighbor. "These people *live* by dramatizing themselves. She'll come home, they'll take her in, and it will start all over again."

There are letters asking for explanations. "I think that bears a lot on the fact that young people—students and children—are not taught and don't understand the difference between fiction and nonfiction. I recently heard about a student who, having found my name in a directory, said to his teacher, 'It says here that Miss Welty lives on Pinehurst. I thought she lived at the post office.' Well, after all," she says, pretending this is perfectly understandable, "**'Why I Live at the P.O.'** *was* written in the first person.

"[Students] are not taught. They don't *experience* what a story does. They just try to *figure it out.* I think that television has something to do with that. People don't believe events. I remember when man landed on the moon, I called my cleaning woman in to watch it on television. 'You should see this,' I told her. And she said, 'Now Miss Eudora, you know that ain't true.'"

She tells of a phone call received shortly after publication of *The Ponder Heart.* "The phone rang and a voice said, 'Miss Welty?' 'Yes?' 'This is Officer Ponder.' He was a policeman. 'I'm standing on the corner of State and Manship. I understand you've written a history of my family.' I explained to him, 'Mr. Ponder, that was a story. I love my characters. But they are not real.' Ponder. Isn't that a wonderful name? So he said, 'Oh. Well. If you ever need me I'm here at the corner of State and Manship.'"

That her characters have names similar to or the same as her neighbors' is no accident. "It must always be a name that people really name their children." Even when that name is chosen for mythological significance. "Of course I knew what that meant when I named Phoenix Jackson, but it was also a name that was common among old black women. White owners often gave their slaves mythological names, so we have lots of Homers and Ulysses and Parthenias. Also, poor people in the South tend to give their children beautiful names. They think, 'Well, at least I can give her a pretty name.' And they do."

Asked about Old Man Fate Rainey in *The Golden Apples,* she says, "The South is full of Fates. It turns out to be short for Lafayette who was a real hero down here." And Miss Ice Cream Rainey? "I learned that in Wales they give people names like Tree-Chopper Jones to distinguish him from the other Jones. My dancing-school teacher was called Miss Ice Cream McNair because her husband owned the ice cream parlor. Of course we never called her that to her face."

In a sense these names are found poetry. From obituaries, the telephone book, memory, bus rides, and conversation come Old Mrs. Sad-Talking Morgan, Miss Billy Texas Spights, Mr. Fatty Bowles, Stella-Rondo, Homer Champion, Miss Snowdie MacLain. All characters existing in the nimbus of Welty's love.

"I loved all my schoolteachers. And I loved everybody in *The Golden Apples.* The good ones and the bad, the happy ones and the sad ones. I loved them all." I bring up Phoenix Jackson again, the old black lady in **"A Worn Path"** who makes death-defying trips to town for her grandson's medicine. "I worried about her so much," I say. "I still do," she murmurs.

Of course there is the famous exception—the character she created out of anger rather than love the night that Medgar Evers was shot. The similarity was so striking between the arrested suspect and the imagined murderer, the narrator of **"Where Is the Voice Coming From?",** that changes had to be made before the story appeared in *The New Yorker.* "There was concern that it would be like convicting him before the trial. Of course I didn't know him. I just knew the type of person who might do that and I got inside his head." The title was chosen because she "really did not know where the voice was coming from that was telling the story.

"It's so queer. Your material guides you and enlightens you along the way. That's how you find out what you're after. It *is* a mystery. When I'm not writing, I can't imagine writing. And when I'm writing, it doesn't occur to me to wonder. Sometimes I feel like a completely split personality. I think the really true self is probably the one that is writing. But the other self is trying to protect me. Sometimes I think, 'While I'm out at the jitney will be a good time for me to retype this.' That is, that my daily life will leave me alone to do my work." She pauses to consider this, then laughs shyly, "They're really going to think I've lost my marbles if you print that."

She speaks of other aspects of the work. "Your ears should be like magnets. I used to be able to hear people in back and in front of me and on the street. I don't hear as much as I used to. It's so *maddening* not to overhear remarks. I hate that. When you're working on a story it's always with you. You hear somebody say something and you know that is what one character is going to say to another." Her friends delight in bringing her snatches of dialogue. Reynolds Price recently came bearing what she considers a treasure. "Reynolds was coming here from the airport in a taxi. He said that the driver told him that the reason the reservoir keeps flooding is because 'That dam is done eat out by crawfish.' Isn't that marvelous! 'Done eat out by crawfish.' Eager to contribute, I tell her something I overheard earlier in the day. "Maybe you could use it," I jest. "Or it could use me," is her serious response.

"The fictional eye sees in, through, and around what is really there," she writes in her new book. As she and I stood staring into the silent gloom on the cypress swamp in the Natchez Trace, I asked her, "How would you describe that color?" I was referring to the water's strange shade of beige beneath the darker brown of tree shadows. "Oh, sort of blue. Like an ink wash." Blue? Ink wash? What was she talking about? And suddenly there it was. She had seen the color of the air.

Lee Smith (review date Spring 1985)

SOURCE: "Eudora Welty's Beginnings," in *The Southern Literary Journal,* Vol. XVII, No. 2, Spring, 1985, pp. 120-26.

[*In the following review, Smith discusses what Welty teaches about the sensibility of the writer in her* One Writer's Beginnings.]

One Writer's Beginnings is a crucial book for the serious Eudora Welty scholar; for the reader who has been charmed and beguiled and moved over the years by her wonderful stories and novels; and for the beginning or not-so-beginning writer who has any interest in where it all comes from, anyway: fiction, I mean, and what in the world it has to do with life. The book originated in a set of three lectures delivered at Harvard University in April, 1983, to inaugurate the William E. Massey lecture series, and it remains so organized. The individual essays are entitled **"Listening,"** **"Learning to See,"** and **"Finding a Voice,"** with a generous selection of Miss Welty's family photographs sandwiched in. For an explicit discussion of fiction-writing techniques, readers must go elsewhere; these essays concern the development of a writer's *sensibility* rather than her craft—that inner ear, that special slant of vision, that heightened awareness of the world which distinguishes art from pedestrian fiction and which distinguishes Miss Welty's fiction particularly—her embrace of the gross world in all its lovely and awful specific detail. How did this come about?

First, **"Listening."** Born in 1909 to life insurance executive Christian Webb Welty (1879-1931) and Chestina Andrews Welty (1883-1966), a passionate ex-schoolteacher from West Virginia, Miss Welty was "overprotected" (perhaps because of the first-born brother who died in infancy), greatly cherished, and greatly loved. The house at 741 North Congress Street in Jackson was full of books. "Neither of my parents had come from homes that could afford to buy many books, but though it must have been something of a strain on his salary, as the youngest officer in a young insurance company, my father was all the while carefully selecting and ordering away for what he and Mother thought we children should grow up with. They bought first for the future." Miss Welty "learned from the age of two or three that any room in our house, at any time of day, was there to read in, or be read to. My mother read to me . . . in the big bedroom in the mornings . . . in the diningroom on winter afternoons in front of the coal fire . . . in the kitchen while she sat churning, and the churning sobbed along with *any* story."

Mrs. Welty read "Dickens in the spirit in which she would have eloped with him." Consequently, Miss Welty tells us that ". . . there has never been a line read that I didn't *hear*. As my eyes followed the sentence, a voice was saying it silently to me. It isn't my mother's voice, or the voice of any person I can identify, certainly not my own. It is human, but inward, and it is inwardly that I listen to it. It is to me the voice of the story or the poem itself." Along with the reading of stories went the "striking of clocks"; Mr. Welty, who "loved all instruments that would instruct and fascinate," came from an Ohio family of Swiss origins, and ". . . all of us have been time-minded all our lives." Thus the future writer learned "so penetratingly, and almost first of all, about chronology."

And Miss Welty grew up hearing stories—from the sewing lady, from her mother's friends. ("What I loved . . . was that everything happened in *scenes*.") The happy result was that "long before I wrote stories, I listened for stories. Listening for them is something more acute than listening *to* them. "And she took note of the other sounds—the parents whis-

tling an early morning duet, "The Merry Widow"; the hymns in Sunday School; the majestic cadence of the King James version of the Bible.

Miss Welty's brother Edward was born when she was three, her brother Walter three years later. Along with Edward came Miss Welty's sense of humor. "We both became comics, making each other laugh. We set each other off, as we did for life, from the minute we learned to talk."

The Weltys' summer trips to visit the two families in Ohio and West Virginia, undertaken in a five-passenger Oakland touring car, were essential to "learning to see." Mrs. Welty never quite got over having left the Andrews mountaintop home near Clay, West Virginia, in order to marry the young lumber company employee from Ohio; her five banjo-playing younger brothers never quite got over it, either—on the wedding day, Moses, the youngest, had gone out and "cried on the ground." Miss Welty's mother and her grandmother wrote letters back and forth every day of their lives. A different sort of life went on at Grandpa Welty's farm in southern Ohio. Compared to the boisterous Andrews clan, the Welty's were "scarce in the way of uncles and cousins and kin of an older generation." Nobody talked much. Grandma Welty—his second wife—had "each work day in the week set firmly aside for a single task." If "in the house it was solid stillness" (the organ was not played), in the huge, wonderful barn, "all you touched was warm." Although Mr. Welty had spent a sober childhood, by all indications, he was devoted to his father.

But it was the mountaintop—the wild, beautiful Andrews homestead—which would prove to be more important to the writer-to-be, for it gave Miss Welty her first sensation of "fierce independence." "Indeed it was my chief inheritance from my mother, who was braver. Yet, while she knew that independent spirit so well, it was what she so agonizingly tried to protect me from, in effect to warn me against. It was what we shared, it made the strongest bond between us and the strongest tension. To grow up is to fight for it, to grow old is to lose it after having possessed it. For her, too, it was most deeply connected to the mountains." And each summer trip "made its particular revelation," offering, finally, when the time came, *plot:* "When I did begin to write, the short story was a shape that had already formed itself and stood waiting in the back of my mind. Nor is it surprising to me that when I made my first attempt at a novel, I entered its world . . . as a child riding there on a train."

Now let me digress here a minute. Last spring, Miss Welty, Robert Penn Warren, and his wife, the writer Eleanor Clark, received honorary degrees from Wake Forest University, and I went to a party given in their honor, after the event. Miss Welty, looking tired but lovely, had been given a special seat on the veranda (there *was* a veranda) and a glass of special bourbon, which I'm sure she needed, as she was besieged by admiring fans and hangers-on—including me, completely mute the way I sometimes get in the presence of anybody I really respect. Everybody was asking questions about *One Writer's Beginnings,* which had just been published. One lady wanted to know whether or not Miss Welty considered herself a "real Southerner," since both her parents came from the North. At first Miss Welty seemed surprised by the question, and then she said *of course* she did, that she was *born* in Jackson, and she has lived there all her life. Miss Clark said *she* was reminded of a story often told by a friend of hers, a wonderful story involving a summer house and a cat who had had kittens in the oven. "But *nobody*," Miss Clark concluded, "considered them *biscuits.*" The question-and-answer period resolved itself into general merriment.

Now I think there's some truth to be found here. And the third essay in *One Writer's Beginnings* is about this truth: how, in order to *write* what you see and what you hear, you have to be outside it, too. For the writer is ever the outsider, and the traveler. The writer is the girl in the summer dress at the window of the party—there but not there, seeing and hearing it all, in it but not of it, appreciating the *petits four* and the cut of a dinner jacket and the way the light comes shining in diamonds down from the chandelier, but knowing too the dark behind her, at the open window, feeling all the time the chill in the summer air. The first two essays also include this critical sense of being the observer.

In **"Listening,"** Miss Welty tells an anecdote about a time when she was "taken out of school and put to bed for several months for an ailment the doctor described as 'fast-beating heart.' "Those nights, she was put to bed in a dark corner of her parents' room, the light carefully shaded with a piece of the daily paper, while they rocked in their rockers in a lighted part of the room and discussed their busy day. She can't remember what they talked about—it's not important, anyhow. "It was the murmur of their voices, the back-and-forth, the unnoticed stretching away of time between my bedtime and theirs, that made me bask there at my distance. What I felt was not that I was excluded from them but that I was included, in—and because of—what I could hear of their voices and what I could see of their faces in the cone of yellow light under the brown-scorched shade . . . I suppose I was exercising as early as then the turn of mind, the nature of temperament, of a privileged observer; and owing to the way I became so, it turned out that I became the loving kind." And in **"Learning to See,"** those trips "were stories"; because you've got to travel, you can't stay in the same place and see anything, or hear anything, you have to go and come back in order to notice what was there all along. As much as it is about anything, *One Writer's Beginnings* is about traveling.

At Mississippi State College for Women, we learn in **"Finding a Voice,"** Miss Welty escaped the "life in a crowd" of the dormitory and walked to a fountain on campus to find some precious quiet in order to read a book of poems by William Alexander Percy which included a poem "written from New York City, entitled, 'Home.'"

> I have a need of silence and of stars.
> Too much is said too loudly. I am dazed.
> The silken sound of whirled infinity
> Is lost in voices shouting to be heard. . . .

She "said the poem" to herself, surrounded by Mississippi "silence and stars," but "This did not impinge upon my longing. In the beautiful spring night, I was dedicated to *wanting* a beautiful spring night. To be *transported* was what I wanted." Later, at the University of Wisconsin, she was "smote" by Yeats' "Song of Wandering Aengus"; and it was there, too, that she learned the word for this—"The word is passion." To feel this, and then to bring it back to bear on whatever life we know; this is what writing is about. It's a scary, risky business.

In an earlier essay, **"Place in Fiction"** (from *The Eye of the Story: Selected Essays and Reviews*), Miss Welty wrote: "The truth is, fiction depends for its life on place. Location is the crossroads of circumstance, the proving ground of 'What happened? Who's here? Who's coming?'—and that is the heart's field." But, she goes on to say, place can*not* give theme. "It can present theme, show it to the last detail—but place is forever illustrative: it is a picture of what man has done and imagined, it is his visible past, result. Human life is fiction's only theme."

It is Miss Welty's characters who come, then, to mind—all round, all visible, all *talking,* from Edna Earle to Sister to old Mr. Marblehall to Fay—the whole host of them, peopling pages and pages. In **"Finding a Voice,"** Miss Welty writes that characters "take on life sometimes by luck," but that she suspects it is "when you can write most entirely out of yourself, inside the skin, heart, mind, and soul of a person who is not yourself, that a character becomes in his own right another human being. . . ." Passion—the ability to be transported—is what enables you to write "entirely out of yourself."

She discusses the origin of Miss Eckhardt, the piano teacher in *The Golden Apples,* a character "miles away from that of anybody" she actually knew, including herself. And yet Miss Eckhardt "derived from what I already knew for myself, even felt I had always known. What I have put into her is passion for my own life work, my own art. Exposing yourself to risk is a truth Miss Eckhardt and I had in common." A character on the page, then, becomes a visible form of what is mute and inchoate in the personality. "Not in Miss

Eckhardt as she stands solidly and almost opaquely in the surround of her story," Miss Welty writes, "but in the making of her character out of my most inward and most deeply feeling self, I would say I have found my voice in my fiction." Earlier, in **"Place in Fiction,"** she wrote that "writing of what you know has nothing to do with security: what is more dangerous? How can you go out on a limb if you do not know your own tree? No art ever came out of not risking your neck. And risk—experiment—is a considerable part of the joy of doing, which is the lone, simple reason all writers of serious fiction are willing to work as hard as they do."

So passion makes the risk possible, and the risk is justified by the "joy of doing"—a view of writing which not all writers share with Miss Welty. For the self is the source of the art, as she makes clear; but many of us are fleeing into fiction, *away from* life—our memories are minefields.

It's instructive to read *The Optimist's Daughter* just before, or just after, you read *One Writer's Beginnings*. The parallels, the resemblances, the echoes are striking: the books in the house, the spunky mother from West Virginia whose death (reciting poetry in her blindness) so closely resembles Mrs. Welty's; the parents' courtship; the descriptions of "up home"; the "optimistic" father.

Here's the big difference: Fay. Laurel's father's second wife in *The Optimist's Daughter* ("without any powers of passion or imagination in herself") is one of "the great interrelated family of those who never know the meaning of what has happened to them." Fay is just awful. But Fay makes it fiction: she's the source of the conflict which is the theme of the novel—the past versus the future, change versus stasis—and the presence of conflict makes the difference between fiction and memoir. Fay is a blunderer, like the offensive handyman Mr. Cheek with his "familiar ways and blundering hammer"; like the grandmother's pigeons who "convinced (Laurel) that they could not escape each other and could not themselves be escaped from"; like, finally, the bird caught in the house after Laurel's father's funeral. Laurel cannot hide from the bird forever, although she hides from it for all of one night. At last she must catch it and set it free, as she must leave her mother's cherished breadboard for whatever uses the covetous Fay may find for it, realizing that "Memory lived . . . in the freed hands . . . and in the heart that can empty but fill again . . . in the patterns restored by dreams."

For the reader to go along pointing out what is *real* and *not real* in *The Optimist's Daughter* means nothing, then, finally—Fay and Laurel are equally real, and it's the heart's own truth which has made the novel. *The Optimist's Daughter* does, however, illustrate what Miss Welty says in **"Finding a Voice":** "Writing a story or a novel is one

way of discovering *sequence* in experience, of stumbling upon cause and effect in the happenings of a writer's own life. This has been the case with me. Connections slowly emerge. Like distant landmarks you are approaching, cause and effect begin to align themselves, draw closer together. . . ." This is that "joy of doing" which Miss Welty alluded to in a different way in an earlier essay (**"Katherine Anne Porter: The Eye of the Story"**) when she wrote about the "strong natural curiosity which readers feel to varying degree and which writers feel to the most compelling degree as to how any one story ever gets told. The only way a writer can satisfy his own curiosity is to write it . . . And how different this already makes it from telling it! Suspense, pleasure, curiosity, all are bound up in the making of the written story." *We* are always changing, too, Miss Welty reminds us towards the end of **"Finding a Voice."** "As we discover, we remember; remembering, we discover; and most intensely do we experience this when our separate journeys converge. Our living experience at those meeting points is one of the charged dramatic fields of fiction." For this is the point of *"confluence"*—that place where passion meets life, and recognizes it, and the story is born, and born, over and over again.

Daniel Aaron (review date 2 May 1985)

SOURCE: "Clytie's Legs," in *London Review of Books*, Vol. 7, No. 8, May 2, 1985, pp. 15-6.

[*In the following review, Aaron discusses several of Welty's works and asserts that "it is by design, by her calculated disclosures, that this storyteller makes herself and her writing powerful and free."*]

Eudora Welty's fictional territory stretches as far as the Northern States of her native America, and to Europe too, but its heartland is Jackson, Mississippi and its environs, a country more accessible and neighbourly than Faulkner's Yoknapatawpha. The dust and heat are the same, the people comparably rooted and earthy. Yet Faulkner's South, for all of its authentic particularity, is a space larger than life in which a magnified cast of performers carry out fated acts. His stores, work-places, forests, houses, monuments, jails and churches are the setting for a sprawling historical spectacle that violently unfolds to the accompaniment of rhetorical music.

Jefferson, Mississippi is the centre, Faulkner once said, of a 'cosmos' inhabited by people whom he could move around 'like God'. Eudora Welty's people live mostly in, or near, small free-floating towns like Morgana, with its water tank and courthouse and its 'Confederate soldier on a shaft' that resembles 'a chewed-on candle, as if old gnashing teeth had made him'. They go their own ways and are not haunted by history. You can find them in a scruffy beauty parlour (scene of **'The Petrified Man'**) where Leota says to her 'ten o'clock shampoo-and-set customer: "Reach in my purse and git me a cigarette without no powder in it if you kin, Mrs Fletcher, honey . . . I don't like no perfumed cigarettes."' They frequent drugstores, depots, old ladies' homes, woods and river bottoms, and congregate at funerals. Some are quiet and withdrawn; some chatter incessantly. They eat Milky Ways and hamburgers, drink Coca-Cola and Memphis whisky, and bear the names Stella-Rondo, Missouri, Woodrow Spights Powerhouse, Edna Earle, Wanda Fay and Mrs Marblehall—the last a club woman, member of the Daughters of the Confederacy, who will sing on request 'O Trees of the Evening'—'in a voice that dizzies other ladies like an organ note, and amuses men like a halloo down the well'.

> **Because Eudora Welty shies away from lofty and portentous themes, her characters are less likely than Faulkner's to be snatched into a metaphysical empyrean. She doesn't, as Henry James would say, 'cultivate the high pitch and beat the big drum'.**
> **—Daniel Aaron**

Because Eudora Welty shies away from lofty and portentous themes, her characters are less likely than Faulkner's to be snatched into a metaphysical empyrean. She doesn't, as Henry James would say, 'cultivate the high pitch and beat the big drum'. What interests her is not so much their existential dilemmas as their physical and moral landscape, the enclosing objects, in which she allows herself virtually to disappear: their domestic lives, conversations, clothes and kitchens, the food they eat, the flowers they grow, the cars they drive. The process by which she invests herself in otherness is something akin to the effect produced by the 'mysterious contraption', the stereopticon, in her story, **'Kin'**.

In that story, the narrator recalls the Sundays she spent as a child in the house of Uncle Felix, and how she and her uncle, after the heavy mid-day dinners, would pore over the 'picture cities' in the stereopticon slides. As they studied the strollers on checkered pavements, islands in the sea, volcanoes, the Sphinx, these scenes, she says, were 'brought forward each time so close that it seemed to me the tracings from the beautiful faces of a strange coin were being laid against my brain.' And as she watches Uncle Felix 'with his giant size and absorption . . . looking his fill', it appears to her 'as though, while he held the stereopticon to his eyes, *we* did not see *him.*' Nor do we see her, the individual Eudora Welty; the author with a Jackson habitation and a

legal identity. What we see are a series of fictional slides of people and places and occasions, all transmuted from personal experience, and standing—as she says in one of her interviews—for what your life has meant to you'.

The more self-centred and confiding writers become, the less likely we are to know them. Although insistingly, sometimes touchingly, and more often tiresomely *there,* they hide themselves in their own ink. Whereas writers more sparing in their self-revelations, while unable to obliterate the thumb print of their uniqueness, their special tone and voice, can be tacitly revelatory. Their selfness is buried in the bodies of the worlds they create.

'I do not comprehend all that I am,' St Augustine wrote, and he followed this declaration with the question: 'Is the mind, therefore, too limited to possess itself?' Eudora Welty conveys self-possession by self-dispersal, not by consciously, or even unconsciously, concocting an instantly recognisable 'personality'. Rather she defines and displays herself in the act of seeping into other minds and bodies. This is not a vampirish invasion but a kind of Keatsian entering-into, passive and affectionate, inspired by curiosity, wonder and love—rarely by hate. She may be likened, at least in this respect, to the Whitman who chronicles the incubating self nurtured by the sensuous world:

> There was a child went forth every day,
> And the first object he looked upon and received
> with wonder or pity or love or dread, that object
> he became.

The 'old drunkard staggering home' from a tavern outhouse in Whitman's poem, the schoolmistress and quarrelsome boys, the 'barefoot negro boy and girl', the changes he notes in city and country, have their counterparts in the Mississippi depicted in Eudora Welty's recent account of her literary 'coming forth'.

Made up of three lectures delivered at Harvard in 1983, *One Writer's Beginnings* is a meditation on the making of a secular and earth-bound writer. It includes some facts about herself undivulged in her reported 'conversations' over the past four decades, but adheres tenaciously to the dictum: 'a writer's life belongs to the writer.' Biographical information unrelated to her work, and some that is, are none of the public's business. Hence *One Writer's Beginnings* confines itself to her literary genesis, to the influence of family, school and travel on a sponge-like consciousness—how she listened and learned to see and finally found 'a voice'. In these glowing recollections the town and society of Jackson spring back to life like castle dwellers in the fairy-tale who, frozen to stone for aeons, resume their activities after the enchanter's spell is broken. The accounts of little girls dressed in taffeta and clutching five cent coins in 'hot white

gloves', the trips to the Carnegie Library, the summer expeditions—long voyages, really—in the family car to visit
her mother's and father's people in West Virginia and Ohio,
furnish 'hints, pointers, suggestions' to the future storyteller.

Respectful of solid things, integrated and bolstered by parental supports, she knows her 'home', her 'Place'. She has
studied and internalised local space, acquired standards,
models, canons of order and discipline from her family and
from literature, music, and photography. Thus accoutred,
she can reach those points of 'confluence' (a powerful word
for her) where real and visionary rivers pour into each other.
In Emily Dickinson's lexicon, 'Circumference' was the line
dividing knowable earth from the Eternity of Blank; the
transmundane could only be guessed at from cryptic mes-
sages of birds, or slants of light and other disturbing visita-
tions. With Eudora Welty, reality and illusion merge without
divine condescension or malediction. Dream is palpable, reality ductile to the cherished minorities of her stories, the
ones responsive to 'the old stab of wonder', quick to catch
the signals unheralded by thunderstorms and lightning: a
rain-soaked letter, the appearance of a solitary heron, a key
falling on a wooden floor, a touch of the wrist.

If the magical moments in Eudora Welty's fiction derive
from 'the living world', which forms, she says, 'the vital
component' of her 'inner life', they are nonetheless separate and secret. 'You must never betray pure joy,' the
American girl in **'The Bride of the Innisfallen'** thinks to
herself—'the kind you were born and began with—neither
by hiding it or by parading it. And still you must tell it.'
Eudora Welty tells it by communicating the feelings of ecstasy or insight that her adventurous characters experience
but can't convey.

The ability to absorb and retain what has been seen and
heard, to become many persons without losing hold of the
underlying self, is a gift and an art, but perhaps even more
a matter of discipline. From her earliest years, Eudora Welty
frames and chronologises, corrects her perspective through
books, one of her conduits to the trans-Jackson world. Many
of her childhood memories point to the nascent writer. In
one, the seven-year-old reader lies on the floor deep in the
conglomerate richness of the ten-volume set, *Our Wonder
World*. In another, she lists the contents of her father's library drawer: a kaleidoscope, a gyroscope, 'an assortment
of puzzles composed of metal rings and intersecting links
and keys chained together'. The barometer hanging on the
dining-room wall of the Welty house also deserves mention,
because, thanks to her self-described 'strong meteorologi-
cal sensitivity', storms, floods, high winds and heat precipitate or complement the action in many of her stories. So
does the camera. It taught her to coalesce *One Time, One
Place* (the title of the 'Snapshot Album' of Mississippi photographs she took during the Depression) without violating

the dignity of her subjects, and to re-read objectively the
history of the faces revealed by the dumb camera's unblink-
ing eye.

But these instruments are primarily aids to register rather
than to encompass the ephemeral. Photography, she acknowledges, can train the writer 'to click the shutter at the
crucial moment'. It teaches 'that every feeling waits upon
its gesture,' but the camera is finally only a tool. To reach
the hidden dimensions beyond its scope, the writer must fall
back on the artifice of words, however unstable their meanings, words ostensibly clear or neutral but twistable into the
ambiguous and sinister. In the story **'Circe'** the enchantress
remembers her greeting to Odysseus and his crew: '"Welcome!" I said—the most dangerous word in the world.'
Colours seem to have special connotations for her: black,
blue, green, red (fairy-tale colours), and particularly 'gold'
and 'golden', and their equivalents, 'corn-coloured', 'yellow', 'honey'. These colours resonate with magic and expectation: they are hues of the self, for what the self puts
into words is what it has sucked up from the 'thick', as she
would say, of its background.

The ultimate mystery of a personality or object, however,
lies beyond mannerisms of speech or physical identifications
like the shape of a nose or the colour of eyes or hair. It can
never be divined by the word alone, only approximated. The
cascade of similes pouring through her pages might be taken
as a tacit concession of the impossibility of 'making reality
real', of impaling it on a phrase, because reality is not contained in a single vision. But, through simile and metaphor,
she nonetheless keeps shaving closer to the Thing-in-Itself,
a perpetual grasping at the indefinable. 'Nothing is.' Everything suggests something else. And yet she trusts the
veracity of images, luxuriates in the plenitude of analogy.

Her style is the style of a storyteller who wishes 'to set a
distance' between herself and what she is observing. This
feeling may signify Weltyan reserve as well as a belief in
artistic detachment, but it does not lead her to blur her fictive outlines or to prettify unpretty things. She is not at all
squeamish about mud, stains, blood, river slime, dirty necks,
dandruff, sweat. Her speakers have their own idiosyncratic
vernacular, and her prevailing narrative voice, devoid of af-
fectation or strain, is equal to recording varieties of
behaviour from the refined to the gross. She can evoke the
truly vulgar, be unexpectedly shocking. Her exercises in the
grotesque may seem less bleak or threatening (and more
credible, too) than Nathanael West's or Flannery
O'Connor's, but they are blackish enough, downward in
their humour, and occasionally brutal. Who can forget
Clytie, drowned in a rain barrel, 'with her poor ladylike
black stockinged legs up-ended and hung apart like apart
of tongs'.

Hawthorne, T. S. Eliot said, had 'the firmness, the true coldness, the hard coldness of the genuine artist'. Eliot's observation applies equally well to Hawthorne's admirer, Eudora Welty, although others who have noted this similarity scant her differences from Hawthorne in style and temperament. She is not an allegorist, and her settings, even the myth-pervaded Morgana of *The Golden Apples* and the Natchez Trace of *The Robber Bridegroom,* are recognisably Mississippian and have little in common with his self-styled 'fairy precincts'. His voice and accents sound in the words of his characters; their thoughts are filtered through his own. Her stories buzz with the conversations of individualised persons whose talk seems to have been taken down by some hovering amanuensis.

Her style is the style of a storyteller who wishes 'to set a distance' between herself and what she is observing. This feeling may signify Weltyan reserve as well as a belief in artistic detachment, but it does not lead her to blur her fictive outlines or to prettify unpretty things. She is not at all squeamish about mud, stains, blood, river slime, dirty necks, dandruff, sweat.

—*Daniel Aaron*

Both these writers accommodate depravity in their moral systems, distrust the antinomian impulse, are not mystical about mystery. Their fantasies exhale from things. Neither is indulgent toward the 'good', nor ready to abrogate the laws of consequence. Both are secret observers, Hawthorne often furtive and voyeuristic, Eudora Welty the tactful and sympathising spy. Both care for what Henry James called the 'deeper psychology' in their probes into human relations, their contemplations of blinkered and partial lives. Each spells out the penalties awaiting those who get lost in their private visions.

Relishing the babble of life, Eudora Welty neither loses her 'abiding respect for the unknown' nor relaxes her attentiveness to the obsessions and hallucinations of her eccentric or dim-witted or half-mad characters. They are often more alive, possess more 'self', than their safe-and-sane detractors and patronisers, although she knows that dreamers risk a loss of self once their orbitings bypass the human community. Uncle Daniel in *The Ponder Heart,* insulated from the actual by his fantasies, drifts off to cuckoo-land. Circe, the unchanging daughter of the gods, is fated to repeat her gyrations, because she is unable to grieve or to feel sympathy.

Pain in Eudora Welty's stories is often, if not necessarily, a catalyst for insight. Her most fully realised characters are

likely to be 'wanderers', adventurers, who expose themselves, in Hawthorne's phrase, to 'fearful risks', and, whether doomed or not, wring a 'strange felicity' from their unlicensed excursions. Usually these brief encounters with the elemental are comprehended only dimly if at all by the participants, and they do not emerge from them unscathed or uninstructed. 'No place for you, my love' is about a man and a woman, strangers to each other, who find themselves stranded in New Orleans on a hot summer evening, ride into the country in a rented car toward some possible intimacy, and joylessly return to their starting points: yet both have felt something momentous and irrecoverable. After spending the afternoon improperly with a Tennessee coffee salesman, Ruby Fisher in **'A Piece of News'** reads a paragraph in the newspaper he has left behind of another Ruby Fisher who 'has had the misfortune to be shot in the leg by her husband this week'. Given a sudden glimpse into her secret self, she fantasises her own death at the hands of her husband in a state of shame and bliss. In **'Death of a Travelling Salesman',** the feverish salesman in the presence of a 'mysterious quiet, cool danger' lacks the 'simple words' that would have allowed him 'to communicate some strange thing—something which seemed always to have just escaped him'. But for Ellen Fairchild in *Delta Wedding* 'one moment told you the great things, one moment was enough for you to know the greatest thing.' These radiant events are less 'epiphanies' (for Eudora Welty a pretentious term which is without Joycean reverberations) than eruptions of self-awareness.

The climactic moment in *The Optimist's Daughter*—in form, a long story, she says, 'even though it undertakes the scope of a novel'—occurs when Laurel McKelva Hand finds her dead mother's breadboard in a kitchen cupboard. A middle-aged war widow, she returns to her Mississippi birthplace in time to watch her recently remarried father die, and to confront Wanda Fay, his obnoxious wife. Toward this young woman (a 'ball of fluff', as Helen McNeil calls her in a fine introduction to the novel, but hard as nails) Eudora Welty shows an unexpected hatred. The 'scored and grimy' breadboard Laurel rescues as she prepares to leave the 'desecrated' family house for good is to Wanda Fay 'the last thing anybody needs'. To Laurel it is a correlative of her supplanted mother, of her husband, killed in the Pacific war, who lovingly made it, and of the 'whole solid past' she has not yet managed to resolve or put behind her. Wanda Fay, that piece of perdurable grit, is the key element in the confluence of events that emancipate Laurel from her daughterly obsessions. 'For there is hate as well as love,' Laurel reflects, 'in the coming together and continuing of our lives.

On numerous occasions Eudora Welty has defined the difference between the autobiographical and the personal. Perhaps *The Optimist's Daughter* is the fullest demonstration of that distinction, for it virtually replicates many of the memories she sets down in *One Writer's Beginnings*. Her father, she tells us, energetically practised optimism. Her mother, born like Laurel's in the West Virginia mountains, never felt quite at home in the Mississippi flatlands. Doubtless Eudora Welty's biographers will have much to say about these and other similarities, but, as she has declared many times, Becky and Judge McKelva are not Mrs and Mr Welty, nor is Laura—angry and wounded by her father's absurd second marriage, guilty about her mother, and still grieving for her lost husband—modeled on Eudora Welty calm and sure of herself in Jackson. What is autobiographically factual in the novel, then, is of less consequence (a point made by Helen McNeil and by Eudora Welty herself) than 'the kernel of privately felt experience out of which the narrative developed'. Her characters have expropriated her emotions, and she is dramatising a literary problem and resolving it. Wanda Fay, all appetite, a scary portent of the future, has no memories and is penned in with her appalling self. Laurel, buoyed by memory, can flow into others; she redeems and is redeemed by it.

'A sheltered life,' Eudora Welty remarked, 'can be a daring one as well.' The word 'sheltered' connotes something quite different from 'insulated', 'isolated', 'beleaguered', 'secluded'. Some writers have found all they required in a circumscribed society without feeling tyrannised by the familiar, but a refusal, as she has said, 'to move mentally or spiritually or physically out of the familiar' can signify 'spiritual timidity or poverty or decay'. An 'open mind and receptive heart' make her fictional terrain a Chekhovian rather than a Bloomsbury enclave. She was sheltered, if you will, by family influence inimical to class snobbery or venomous racialism. Her circle of friends and teachers may have been wanting in sophistication, but it was understanding enough to encourage a questing intelligence. The community in which she grew up was sufficiently open-ended and diverse to satisfy a writer not content with the mere paraphernalia of local colour. Her real subject is natural violence and fallible people, the fools and cranks and misfits, the shy and the bold, the dreamers and the literal-minded, with whom she sympathetically and humorously identifies.

Apparently nothing was lost on the child exposed to the gossiping of her elders, and delighted by the strains of comedy in Jane Austen, Dickens, Edward Lear, Twain, and Ring Lardner. These very different writers must have alerted her to the comic possibilities of her own Mississippi microcosm and coloured her benign aspect of the human menagerie. But her affection for the common lot is touched—to paraphrase her out of context—with a grave if seldom belittling irony, and her sympathy for the rebellious, the injured, and the passionate is unsentimental and controlled. Emotion which in softer sensibilities is likely to spill over she restrains in the trammels of form.

Her justly admired story **'A Worn Path'** could easily have turned maudlin and gone soft; directness, irony and humour preserve it and keep it taut. Phoenix Jackson is a frail black woman with a faltering memory and eyes 'blue with age'. She makes a tasking expedition from her place 'away back', as she puts it, 'off the old Natchez Trace' to the city where she goes to get some soothing throat medicine for her grandson who has swallowed lye. She tells the hospital attendant, after momentarily forgetting why she has undertaken the quest:

> My little grandson, he sit up there in the house all
> wrapped up, waiting by himself. We is the only two
> left in the world. He suffer and it don't seem to put
> him back at all. He got a sweet look. He is going
> to last. He wear a little patch and peep out holding
> his mouth open like a little bird.

The story is dredged of tearfulness, because Phoenix herself is too indomitable to be pathetic. Undeterred by her filmy sight, she deals cheerfully and resolutely with her trials—thorny bushes, a barbed wire fence, a log, a scarecrow, a dog, a tumble in a ditch, not to mention mirages of her own making. Her gestures are 'fierce' and soldierly. Likened by the author to 'a festival figure in some parade', she moves 'in a little strutting way' and is as much at home in the pinewoods as the 'foxes, owls, beetles, jack rabbits, coons and wild animals' she importunes to stay out of her path. There is something of the trickster in her, too, for although she is civil rather than obsequious in coping with white people, she exploits their solicitude and complacency. She is even ready to slide into her apron pocket a shining nickel dropped by a young white hunter, or to extract another five cents from the hospital nurse in order to buy a paper windmill for her waiting grandson. But she accepts this donation 'stiffly', and it is her 'fixed and ceremonial stiffness' of body and spirit that prevents this story from melting into pathos.

Stephen Dedalus, in one of his aesthetic harangues, describes a process by which the artist's personality 'finally refines itself out of existence' through the dissolvent of his imagination. Once this mystery, a purification of life, is accomplished, the artist, Stephen says, is left 'like the God of creation . . . within or beyond his handiwork . . . indifferent, paring his fingernails'. In contrast to this rather grandiloquent affirmation is Eudora Welty's more modest and human aim: to be 'invisible' but not 'effaced'. She is to be looked for, not in blatant self-advertising confidences, hints and nudges, but in the metaphorical clues she drops, which are the exposures of a disciplined sensibility. From them we can deduce a history of a life. One might say her writing, spun out like the web of a 'noiseless patient spider', is not about but of herself. At bottom, the beauty and astonishment of her fiction, as Emerson might say, is 'all design'.

For it is by design, by her calculated disclosures, that this storyteller makes herself and her writing powerful and free.

Harriet Pollack (essay date Fall 1986)

SOURCE: "Words Between Strangers: On Welty, Her Style, and Her Audience," *Mississippi Quarterly,* Vol. XXXIX, No. 4, Fall, 1986, pp. 481-505.

[*In the following essay, Pollack analyzes Welty's relationship with her readers.*]

Eudora Welty often speaks of her storytelling in terms that suggest it is a strategy for dealing with separateness. She identifies the source of her work as "attentiveness and *care* for the world . . . and a wish to connect with it," and she tells us that her "continuing passion" is "to part a curtain . . . that falls between people." But paradoxically, while Welty expresses her desire for "connection," she nonetheless prefers what she calls obstruction as the means to this end. "The fine story writers seem to be . . . obstructionists," she notes in **"The Reading and Writing of Short Stories,"** and she finds the "quondam obstruction"—the sheer opaque curtain that veils the meaning of a work—to be "the source of the deepest pleasure we receive from a writer." I find this paradoxical combination of her thematic concern for "connection" and her preference for technical obstruction surprising and provocative, even though Welty's commentators have long discussed it and even though obstruction is commonplace in contemporary fiction. Welty's stated purpose— she writes of successful fiction as "love accomplished"—seems to be contradicted by a reader's experience of the technique she often chooses: a richly articulate style that holds back initially as if she were reluctant to give her fiction to her audience.

One result of this tension between message and technique is fiction before which—as Ruth Vande Kieft has remarked—"the welcome mat [is] clearly out . . . while the sign on the gate post [reads] 'Keep Out.'" This is not the case with all, but with many of Welty's fictions: **"Powerhouse," "A Wide Net,"** *The Golden Apples,* the stories of *The Bride of the Innisfallen* and others. These are fictions which may delight readers of various levels of sophistication and training and yet leave them intrigued, feeling as if perhaps they have missed something in their understanding. And these are fictions that, once they have delighted and puzzled, invite us to ask questions about Welty's style. Some of these questions are larger than how she uses point of view, plot, genre. We might ask, for example, precisely how love and obstruction can become the terms of one artistic equation and what role Welty's style plays in her relationship with her audience—or in other words, how much and exactly what Welty expects of her reader.

The question that occurs to me as I pursue this sort of speculation is whether Welty's style is at times a strategy for winning the struggle that can occur between writer and reader when a text is read, interpreted, and in some sense completed. The hotly debated critical question of who controls the meaning of a text—writer or reader—seems relevant here. Important reader-response critics such as Stanley Fish, Norman Holland, Wolfgang Iser and Jonathan Culler, among many others, have each illuminated the reading process as they see it. Fish and Holland, in their efforts to describe the reader's too-often ignored role in the creation of meaning, have assigned the primary position in this process to the reader and have granted him a remarkable degree of autonomy from the text. Stanley Fish, for example, has denied that a text has meaning independent of the reader's relationship to it. He asserts that a text is not "a thing-in-itself, but an *event,* something that *happens* . . . with the participation of the reader," and that the constraints that determine meaning do not "inhere in language but in situations," that is, in a reader's situations. And Norman Holland has proposed that interpretation is the imposition of the reader's particular "identity theme," the characteristic pattern of understanding that has more to do with the reader's psychology and obsessive interests than with the text itself. These theories that give the reader control over meaning might reasonably unsettle any writer who has worked to polish and perfect a text, and yet they suggest an undeniable circumstance, that texts, as they are consumed and interpreted, do shade off into ideas that exist in readers' minds. Only there is a book completed.

In contrast to Fish and Holland's theories, Wolfgang Iser's formulation of the reading process admits the reader's role, and yet describes a less autonomous, but perhaps ideal reader who is out-going in his textual encounters and therefore careful to respond to the text itself. Iser paints what seems to me the portrait not of every reader in every reading encounter but of what a sensitive reader strives to be. Iser sees reading as a fluid process of self-correction that involves reaction, rereading, and revision as the reader provides a sequence of changing conceptual frameworks for the fiction. "We look forward, we look back, we decide, we change our decisions, we form expectations, we are shocked by their nonfulfillment, we question, we muse, we accept, we reject." Meaning is built gradually: "smaller units progressively merge into bigger ones so that meaning gathers meaning in a kind of snowballing process." Understanding of a text is a carefully constructed product of considerable interaction. Interpretations vary as each reader selects meaning from the potential text and completes it uniquely in response to sensitivities shaped by his education, his social, psychological, and philosophical backgrounds, and his historical place. But meaning does not rest wholly in the imagination of the reader; it resides in the coming together of the reader and the text. The process of reading a text provides the author's blueprint for making meaning with it; the reader builds meaning in part by responding to literary expectations which the text evokes.

In Jonathan Culler's terms, the text bids the reader to draw on his "literary competence." This competence, which is a knowledge of implicit but well-recognized literary conventions, allows a reader to recognize a story pattern, plot type, or genre, to identify a technique of point of view or an allusion and, on the basis of expectations cued by the text, to predict a kind of meaning to be made. In a successful reading, these conventions are the shared knowledge of the author and reader. Otherwise we have the case of the inexperienced student reader of **"The Wide Net"** who is perplexed when William Wallace, searching for the remains of his wife Hazel, wanders into the pleasures of a golden day. This none too hypothetical reader, perhaps unfamiliar with the conventions of the heroic epic, cannot predict that the wandering of a hero may prove to be his track, the path by which he will arrive where he is going. In Culler's view, conventional literary expectations make reading and writing possible. These

> the author can write against, certainly, ... may attempt to subvert, but [they are] none the less the context within which his activity takes place, as surely as the failure to keep a promise is made possible by the institution of promising. Choices between words, between sentences, between different modes of presentation, will be made on the basis of their effects; and the notion of effect presupposes modes of reading which are not random or haphazard. Even if an author does not think of readers, he is himself a reader of his own work and will not be satisfied with it unless he can read it as producing effects.

Here, Culler is able to grant the reader his place in the literary process while affirming that the author's text guides his expectations.

My own reaction to the work of these four critics is to recognize that they have highlighted an obvious but somehow long-neglected variable in the meaning-making process: readers and their responses. Yet when Fish and Holland picture the reader's process as largely independent of an author's control, I cannot help feeling that their correcting visions are misleading, although their strong emphasis on the reader's role is certainly predictable when the goal is to establish his place. One result of their influential discourse has been to make literary discussion of the author and his intentions unfashionable. But because I view reading as an

encounter with minds and worlds, times and cultures distinct from my own, I find myself wanting to reverse this trend away from the author who is other. One particular value of the reader-response critical model, if we put it into such reverse, would be to bring attention unexpectedly back to the writer. In other words, reader-response theory, having raised the issues of who controls meaning and of how it is negotiated by author and reader, both invites us and enables us to ask how an author attempts to direct his readers' somewhat unpredictable responses. For this reason, Iser's and Culler's work is more useful to me as I consider reading as an encounter, taking place sometimes over long distances of time and space, yet yielding an interaction and perhaps even an intimacy. In reading, as in a conversation, two minds can meet. And the one who speaks first, the author, tries to establish expectations to which a reader can predictably respond, albeit somewhat differently from every other reader. Together, through their shared knowledge of literary convention, over their different and mutual interests as well as their historical and cultural perspectives, the author and reader produce the individual literary performance.

The reader-response debate may seem far afield from Welty's own critical vocabulary, but it is relevant to a consideration of her style. A writer such as Welty, who I will argue hopes above all to be met in her fiction, might reasonably be concerned that the shared literary performance of author and reader should not ignore the guidelines that her written text imposes. Welty's concern with the question of who controls meaning in the reading process is clearest in her essay **"How I Write,"** which was first published in 1955 and later revised for inclusion in *The Eye of the Story*. In the first published version, Welty discussed the faults of a type of reader who sees the writing of a story as only "his own process in reverse":

> The analyst, should the story come under his eye, may miss the gentle shock and this pleasure too, for he's picked up the story at once by the heels (as if it had swallowed a button) and is examining the writing as his own process in reverse, as though a story (or any system of feeling) could be more accessible to understanding for being hung upside down.

Apparently, Welty was giving careful thought to the writing and reading processes, to their difference and to their relationship, years before the reader-response critics became vocal in the 1970's. I take Welty as my subject here because she has explicitly shown her awareness of the reading process and the risks that an author faces when giving fiction over to a reader, but also because I believe she has developed a stylistic trait that is her personal strategy for guiding her reader towards meaning. My goal is to identify this particular trait while defining all that Welty hopes for from the writer-reader relation, its hazards notwithstanding. Ultimately, I would like to suggest why when asked by Joanna Maclay in 1980 "how [her] notion of the potential reader" affected what she did "to make [her] meaning clear," Welty answered by quoting a line of Henry Green's: "Prose should be a long intimacy between strangers."

My argument is that Welty's style demonstrates, and in its way seems designed to demonstrate, the primacy of the text in the reading process. Her fiction repeatedly elicits expectations that it promptly defies. Yet the mistaken expectations that a reader develops as he follows the experience provided by her language are a part of her directions to the text's meaning. The effect is to invite the reader to return to the story again and again, to urge him to read it closely and attentively. Areas of obstruction—for example, unusual uses of point of view, of plot, genre, and allusion—are themselves clues in Welty's fiction; and once a reader has identified which of his expectations are frustrated, he is usually on his way to understanding the fiction at hand, having found its center. Seen in this light, Welty's use of obstruction could be a technique for shaping a responsive reader through her control of the textual experience. By composing texts that require attentiveness and yield best to rereading, she might invite a reader to practice self-correction and to follow more closely her lead through the reading process. How she achieves this by manipulating the reader's expectations (of the sort that Iser and Culler stress) will, I hope, become clear in this essay.

Evidence of Welty's interest in the encounter of author and audience, and in the potential struggle between them for control of meaning, is available in several of her fictions that inherently explore problems in audience reception (for example, **"Keela, the Outcast Indian Maiden,"** or *Losing Battles*). One of the earliest of these and, in my view, one of her more "obstructed" short stories is **"Powerhouse,"** an opaque parable (in Welty's words) about "the traveling artist . . . in the alien world" and portrays his interaction with audiences of varying degrees of receptivity. At second glance this story can reveal Welty's perception of the fragility and achievement of the writer-reader relationship, as well as the technical process by which she herself manages and creates that encounter. For the sake of what this story reveals about these issues, I take it as my point of reference and departure.

When we first meet him, Powerhouse is performing for a white audience that has come to marvel at a grotesque "Negro man," to see not the artist behind the mask but the mask they have urged onto him. To them, the black jazz musician looks "Asiatic, monkey, Jewish, Babylonian, Peruvian, fanatic, devil." Powerhouse, stomping and smooching, improvises, however, with the stereotypes that his audience at-

tributes to "people on a stage—and people of a darker race." In his performances, he tries to work this imposed identity until it becomes a medium for expressing his private self. But this particular audience on this particularly rainy night in Alligator, Mississippi, is not ready to receive the man behind his mask. Instead of sympathetically receiving his performance, instead of sharing his effort and his eventual achievement, they "feel ashamed for" the jazzman who seems to them to give everything, and who, holding nothing in reserve, seems to expose himself before their unsympathetic eyes. They are curious, enthusiastic, but not in tune with him.

Attempting to give himself to these alienating spectators, Powerhouse feels displaced and begins to retreat behind the mask that reflects his audience's expectations for a "vast and obscene jazzman." He plays "Pagan Love Song," a sad song that he touches and that touches him back, confirming his estranged mood. Like Welty herself, Powerhouse is an artist who needs to place himself by recognizing his emotions, and to touch home with them in his work. And so he plunges into a depth of self by inventing the suicide of his wife, Gypsy, a story that he tells at first with his "wandering fingers," that is, in a musical exchange perhaps accompanied by stage whispers. The story he improvises creates a reason for his blues: a fictional telegram signed "Uranus Knockwood" that announces the news "Your wife is dead."

Powerhouse's audience for this narrative performance is—in addition to the reader—the band itself, whose members vary in their capacities for sympathy and receptivity. They are implicitly different models of the reader. The far section of the band is "all studious, wearing glasses, every one," and "don't count." These technicians are figuratively and literally too far away to hear the jazzman's story. "Only those playing around Powerhouse are the real ones," the co-creating audience of Valentine, Little Brother, and perhaps Scoot. Of this group, Valentine and Little Brother readily receive, participate in, and protect Powerhouse's invention; Valentine immediately picks up the theme that Powerhouse establishes and begins to improvise on it: "'You say you got a telegram.'" But Scoot, who is a "disbelieving maniac," is not so cooperative; he asks a series of challenging, although participating, questions: "'Gypsy? Why how come her to die, didn't you just phone her up in the night last night long distance?'" Such questions are inappropriate because they take the fiction literally, and so resist Powerhouse's fiction-making project and his purposes. They are combative as well and force Powerhouse to move his story in new directions; they challenge his control of the performance instead of inviting him to proceed with it. For a time, however, Scoot's questions serve Powerhouse well enough. For although Scoot asks Powerhouse to justify his creation rather than to expand it, his questions nevertheless give Powerhouse the opportunity to elaborate; the drummer's bantering questions establish the beat to create against, a function appropriate to his musical instrument.

Leaving the dance hall at intermission with his three accompanists, Powerhouse—now between sets in Negrotown's World Cafe—finds a large audience ready to respond to him as he develops the theme of Gypsy's death in a solely narrative performance that discloses themes of loneliness, disappointment, anger, and defiance. Powerhouse asks first to hear Bessie Smith's "Empty Bed Blues," but the juke box plays instead "Sent For You Yesterday and Here You Come Today," and Powerhouse imagines Gypsy wanting him. She listens for his footsteps and hears those of a stranger passing by. Powerhouse does not come. And she, defiant in her separateness, angrily kills herself by busting her brains all over the world.

> "Listen how it is. My wife gets missing me. Gypsy. She goes to the window. She looks out and sees you know what. Street. Sign saying Hotel. People walking. Somebody looks up. Old man. She looks down, out the window. Well? . . . *Ssssst! Plooey!* What do she do? Jump out and bust her brains all over the world."

Splattering Gypsy in a fantasy that investigates solitude, separateness, and death but is not itself sorrowful, the improvisation transforms Powerhouse's mood of lonely anxiety. As his mood changes, he elaborates on that comic, mythic nemesis, Uranus Knockwood, the father of all misfortune, the man who "takes our wives when we are gone," and who finds Gypsy when she dies:

> "That no-good pussyfooted crooning creeper, that creeper that follow around after me, coming up like weeds behind me, following around after me everything I do and messing around on the trail I leave. Bets my numbers, sings my songs, gets close to my agent like a Betsy-bug; when I going out he just coming in. I got him now! I got my eye on him."

For Powerhouse, Knockwood personifies affliction; he is the troublesome carrier of misfortune who brings disappointment, failure, and anxiety.

During this performance, Valentine and Little Brother encourage and protect Powerhouse's creation. Gradually, a larger audience has formed around the small group and its collaborative members recognize Knockwood immediately. "'Middle-size man.' 'Wears a hat.' 'That's him.' Everybody in the room moans with pleasure." Powerhouse's creation of Knockwood—the man who brings the Blues—becomes for this sympathetic audience a means of chasing those blues away. A waitress, in full sympathy with Powerhouse, calls out, "'I hates that Mr. Knockwoods.'" And she is also the

one who asks him, "'All that the truth?'" Her admiring question, like Scoot's belligerent inquiries, once more raises the problem of the truth of fiction. The musician, performing for this flirtatious, provoking "Little-Bit," at first offers to show his telegram. He is halted for a moment by the protective cry of Little Brother, who does not want the energy building for the next set to be lost, and who fears that if Powerhouse reveals his art, he may sacrifice its power. But Powerhouse, who is now playing primarily for the waitress, explains it anyhow:

> "No, babe, it ain't the truth. . . . Truth is something worse, I ain't said what, yet. It's something hasn't come to me, but I ain't saying it won't. And when it does, then want me to tell you?"

The truth that has not yet come to Powerhouse is something worse and something better than the story of Gypsy's death. That truth is on its way; it is the transfiguration that his story generates once it is successfully received and completed by this audience.

Powerhouse has told a story about loneliness and with it he has produced a sense of belonging. This familiar pattern of the blues performance is analyzed by Ralph Ellison in his essay "Richard Wright's Blues": it fingers a wound, and yet through the joy of expressing, surviving, and successfully sharing a painful emotion with a sympathetic audience, transforms it into something nearly or clearly celebratory. And so Powerhouse, singing the blues, has transcended his isolation and "come out the other side." Heading back to the dance, he creates a telegram of reply that puts the four of them "in a wonderful humor." He will wire the offending Knockwood: "'What in the hell you talking about? Don't make any difference: I gotcha.'" Members of the small group agree, "'You got him now,'" and feel that transformation, the surge of power generated by the fiction. They see that Powerhouse has investigated a death no one believes in—though all know it to be real and haunting—and somehow located through it his own life and strength. With his story, he has mastered his experience; he has transformed his disconcerting present into a future of his choice and created joy by fabricating a tragedy. The truth of his tale is the emotion that it has reflected and transformed.

As Powerhouse prepares to re-enter the white dance hall, Scoot, in crazy obtuseness, asks if Powerhouse isn't going to call home and learn how Gypsy really is. Then "there is a measure of silence." Scoot, "one crazy drummer that's going to get his neck broken some day," endangers the success of Powerhouse's art by failing to receive it. But because Powerhouse has the audience he needs in Valentine and Little Brother, Scoot's belligerence will not harm the evening's culminating musical performance.

In the final section of the story, we see that Powerhouse's successful narrative performance has recharged his creativity. Back in the dance hall and in the audience, we watch Powerhouse approach his piano as if "he saw it for the first time in his life." Then he

> tested it for strength, hit it down in the bass, played an octave with his elbow, lifted the top, looked inside, and leaned against it with all his might. He sat down and played it for a few minutes with outrageous force and got it under his power—a bass deep and coarse as a sea net—then produced something glimmering and fragile, and smiled.

In this scene Powerhouse moves from his theme "I got a telegram my wife is dead" to the number "Somebody Loves Me." He has cast off his loneliness for a certainty that someone loves him—a certainty based on his interaction with the audience at the World Cafe—and he calls and shouts, "'I wonder who?'" Grimacing, he challenges his white audience with the line "Maybe . . . Maybe . . . Maybe it's you!" And with this furious invitation, he also addresses the reader. In a blunt confrontation between author and audience, Powerhouse and Welty may seem to merge, to ask, "What kind of reader are you?" Are you like the white audience, alien, gawking at an entertainer whose creative efforts you block rather than receive? Or like the far section of the band— "studious, wearing glasses," not really with it? Or perhaps you are like Scoot, attentive, but asking all the wrong questions? Or could it be that you are like Valentine and Little Brother, participating in sympathy with the artist?

In short, the question that Welty asks in this last line of **"Powerhouse"** is whether we love her in her story. This question is unexpected because Welty herself has hindered her reader's first approach to intimacy. In a fiction that dramatizes a performer's relationship with several essentially unreceptive audiences, Welty has chosen to complicate her own author-audience relationship by adopting the technique of obstruction. Although my summary has smoothed the story over and temporarily set aside the questions that color a reader's first encounter with it, the story itself unfolds against expectations that it creates but fails to fulfill.

"Powerhouse" is likely to astonish a reader in three ways: (1) in its turn away from the question of whether Gypsy is really dead, (2) in its merging of Powerhouse's narrative invention with his musical creation, and (3) in its unannounced shifts in point of view. I have named and will discuss these narrative surprises while fully aware that the precise steps of every reader's encounter with the story will be different and reflect his or her readerly skills. I am not prescribing here readerly errors necessarily encountered by all readers of this text, but attempting to describe the process of revising expectations that Welty's text calls for, a

process I will be somewhat overly deliberate about, slowing it down so that it can be discussed.

When a reader first meets Powerhouse's statement "'I got a telegram my wife is dead,'" he may wonder why Powerhouse, who should be mourning, is on stage. If he concentrates on Powerhouse's startling announcement, he may be too preoccupied to notice that the jazzman's story is told in a musical exchange:

> "You know what happened to me?" says Powerhouse.
>
> Valentine hums a response, dreaming at the bass.
>
> "I got a telegram my wife is dead," says Powerhouse, *with wandering fingers.*
>
> "Uh-huh?"
>
> His mouth gathers and forms a barbarous O *while his fingers walk up straight, unwillingly, three octaves.*
>
> "Gypsy? Why how come her to die, didn't you just phone her up in the night last night long distance?"
>
> "Telegram say—here the words: Your wife is dead." *He puts 4/4 over the 3/4.*
>
> "Not but four words?" *This is the drummer,* an unpopular boy named Scoot, a disbelieving maniac. . . .
>
> Little Brother, *the clarinet player, who cannot now speak, glares and tilts back. . . .*
>
> "What the hell was she up to?" Powerhouse shudders. *"Tell me, tell me, tell me." He makes triplets, and begins a new chorus. He holds three fingers up.*
>
> "You say you got a telegram." *This is Valentine, patient and sleepy, beginning again.*
>
> *Powerhouse is elaborate.* "Yas, the time I go out, go way downstairs along a long cor-ri-dor to where they puts us: coming back along the cor-ri-dor: steps out and hands me a telegram: Your wife is dead."
>
> "Gypsy?" *The drummer like a spider over his drums.* (italics mine)

This passage introduces both the theme of Gypsy's death and the suspicion that Gypsy is not dead. A first-time reader meets it wondering how to understand Powerhouse's narrative-within-a-narrative. The temporarily obstructed reader, trying to make sense of Powerhouse's tale, may or may not notice and respond to the suggestive phrases that I have italicized. When a reader does focus on these lines, unexpected questions about the unconventionality of this passage arise. "Literary competence," the reader's conventional expectation, is leading the way here, and underlining the importance of Welty's unconventionality. When Powerhouse speaks with wandering fingers, is he literally speaking through his musical performance? His 4/4 over 3/4 and his triplets, not coincidentally, are the rhythms he develops in Gypsy's story. And when Scoot and Little Brother speak, are they speaking in turn as their performances allow and instruments direct? When Valentine begins again, is he beginning a variation on a musical theme? If a reader is attentive and recognizes the correspondence between Powerhouse's fiction and his music, what should he make of music that poses as narrative? Is Powerhouse's story perhaps the narrator's interpretation of his music as she listens intently to hear the performers' "least word, especially what they say to one another, in another language?" How many readers attend the text closely enough to ask these sorts of questions, and at what point in their reading process?

A reader's confusion about Powerhouse's narrative is explicitly invited to turn to skepticism when Scoot asks, "'Gypsy? Why how come her to die?'" Then a reader may be trapped for a time in Scoot's overly literal questions. Wanting to know if Gypsy is really dead, the reader asks a question that the story brushes aside. As his expectations for a literal truth are frustrated, he soon realizes that his is the wrong question, that he has been misdirected by his false expectation, and by Welty, who set up that expectation. His surprise, his obstructed expectation, may then unfold the fiction by leading him to ask why Powerhouse told the tale of Gypsy's death. Gradually, the answer to this question appears if the reader has been willing to follow Welty's text: Powerhouse's music and his story are two interactive elements in one composition on the theme of loneliness which itself is a joyful, creative means to counter it. Like Powerhouse, that person of joy who transforms the black devil stereotypes of his audience into a medium for self-expression, Welty maneuvers the expectations of her readers until they help her to create something of her own.

Welty leads her reader by indirect means to ask about the source of Powerhouse's art, about the truth of his fiction, about his need for an audience. She maneuvers the reader's own reactions—which are structured by the text, as Iser and Culler have suggested—until they create the meaning of the story, a meaning that exists in those reactions rather than in the text per se. She guides the reader with an experiment in point of view. The story's first, second, and fifth sections are told by a hypothetical someone in the audience at the dance. The third and fourth sections, however, seem to be related by a more privileged narrator who moves with Powerhouse through the rainy night. Or perhaps these sections represent the fantasy of the narrator in the audience, whose imagination responds to Powerhouse's art. Whatever the cause, the effect of the shift is clear. By shifting the point of view closer to Powerhouse, Welty moves the reader from the audience's view of him as a marvelous, but "vast and obscene" jazzman, to perception of the man behind that grotesque mask, the man who "seems lost—down in the song, yelling up like somebody in a whirlpool—not guiding [the band]—hailing them only." The shift moves the reader from the audience that views Powerhouse as alien, monstrous, "Asiatic, monkey, . . . devil," to membership in the elite who travel with Powerhouse and know his emotions and artistic strategies. In these sections of the story, the reader's privileged vision exceeds and frames that of the original narrator. The unexpected narrative shift reduces the distance between narrator and subject, and thus urges the reader into sympathy with Powerhouse and his creative need. This new relationship causes the reader to revise his first assessment and perhaps to realize that the meaning of the story was not disclosed in Powerhouse's fiction about Gypsy's death, but at the end of the first section when the narrator spoke cryptically of listening in order to learn "what it is"—that is, "what it is" that makes a performance great. In its way, the story has taught the reader himself to be a part of this thing, for if he has met the challenge of Welty's obstruction, he has become, like Little Brother and Valentine, part of an attentive, involved, cooperative, and loving audience.

Welty's style, then, urges a reader to attend the text, to be a reader responding to a writer. Her "obstructions," paradoxically, are a measure of her apprehension for successful interaction with her audience. Her misgivings about her readers' powers of receptivity, expressed here in fictional form, have also made themselves felt in her interviews and critical essays. I turn to these now to define more precisely Welty's attitude towards the reading encounter.

> **Convinced that meaning is not excavated from a fiction like precious metals from rubble, but is an experience one has while reading, Welty has mocked the critical impulse to explanation, saying, "I was once asked to tell one of my stories in my own words."**
> —*Harriet Pollack*

In her interviews and essays Welty has been warmly responsive to her best readers, and quick to say that—because of the help of such early supporters as Ford Madox Ford, Katherine Anne Porter, Robert Penn Warren, and her agent Diarmuid Russell—her work "has always landed safely and among friends." She has appreciated critical attention, named insights it has given her, and even remained tolerant of interpretations that seemed to her "far-flung" by remembering that a writer hopes to suggest all kinds of possibilities. As early as in **"How I Write,"** she realized that a reader's commentary on a story "may go deeper than its object and more times around; it may pick up a story and waltz with it so that it's never the same," allowing that the waltz might be desirable, since the richness of fictional meaning is made over time and in more than one mind.

But Welty has also shown periodic and healthy exasperation with wrong-headed readers, an exasperation with their failure to meet her in her fictions. Then Welty seems to feel as if a portion of her audience is like Marion, the campfire girl in her story **"A Visit of Charity,"** who set out to meet someone new but retreated when faced with the shock of encounter. In an interview with Henry Mitchell, Welty joked about ordering stationery printed with a ready response for misguided correspondents: "You Just Can't Get There From Here." A reader familiar with her occasionally disturbed reactions to requests that interpretations be confirmed might guess she had a reply to some of those letters in mind. Another such correcting reply is her essay entitled **"Is Phoenix Jackson's Grandson Really Dead?"** in which she responded to the "unrivaled favorite" question of her public, and quietly explained that their inquiry, like those that Scoot had made, was not relevant to "the truth of the story." Earlier, in her essay **"The Reading and Writing of Short Stories,"** she had confessed to being "baffled" by rigid analyses of her stories. "When I see them analyzed—most usually 'reduced to elements'—sometimes I think, 'This is none of me.' Not that I am too proud to like being reduced, especially; but that I could not remember starting with those elements—with anything that I could so label." And in an interview with Charles Bunting, she expressed surprise that some of her readers had failed to respect her as an authority on her fictions:

> I've had students write to me and say, "I'm writing a thesis to prove that *The Golden Apples* is a novel. Please send me...." ... So I write back and say that it isn't a novel, I'm sorry. They go right ahead, of course. It doesn't matter with a thesis, I guess.

These comments all suggest Welty's mistrust of those readers who fail to meet her in her fiction. In **"How I Write"** she described this reader as suffering from too independent an imagination, which was also a failure of imagination. Perhaps resembling the technicians of Powerhouse's band, "studious and wearing glasses," he can seem "blind . . . ingrown and tedious" in his analyses because he thinks that "he is 'supposed' to see in a story . . . a sort of plant-from-seed development, rising in the end to a perfect Christmas tree of symmetry. . . ." Unlike "the reader of more willing imagi-

nation . . . [who] may find the branchings not what he's expecting," this reader, she went on to comment in **"Words Into Fiction,"** errs by replacing her "mystery" with his order:

> . . . a body of criticism stands ready to provide [a] solution, which is a kind of translation of fiction into another language. It offers us close analysis, like a headphone we can clamp on at the U.N. when they are speaking the Arabian tongue. . . .

> A year or so of one writer's life has gone into the writing of a novel. . . . Does this not suggest that . . . words have been found for which there may be no other words?

This sort of approach to fiction, as Welty put it in a remark about Faulkner's critics, is "to tree it." She dislikes the desire to explain and restate fiction that "outside its own terms, which never were explanatory, no longer exists." Convinced that meaning is not excavated from a fiction like precious metals from rubble, but is an experience one has while reading, Welty has mocked the critical impulse to explanation, saying, "I was once asked to tell one of my stories in my own words." Unlike the critics who perturb her with their explications, she believes "great fiction . . . abounds in what makes for confusion. . . . It is very seldom neat, is given to sprawling and escaping from bounds, is capable of contradicting itself, and is not impervious to humor. There is absolutely everything in great fiction but a clear answer." "To make a work of the imagination out to be something in another category, that can be learned in capsule terms, as an algebraic, or mathematical formula, is," she argues, "not honest." Like Little Brother who feared that Powerhouse might lose his performance if he explained it, she does not trust explication. Instead, like her friend Ida M'Toy, she wants to be listened to with the whole attention, to have her "true words" remembered, and to warn us: "'Let her keep it straight, darling.'"

Welty's strategy, then, for shaping and educating the reader who substitutes his own words and meaning for hers is to temporarily hinder his progress through the work. Because he looks only "for his own process in reverse," and so is in some danger of never finding Welty in her own story, she delays his appropriation of it. Her style demands that he gain perspective on his own first impressions, and coerces him to become more familiar with the limited range of possibility that is the text. Welty wants her words, the order she has created, to be held; one important effect of her style is to keep the reader close to those words while he is temporarily uncertain how to convert them into any of his own. Welty would perhaps like her stories to be too complex for analysis; and interpretations of her fictions are, in fact, rarely able to recreate the process by which a reader understands them, although that process is, after all, where the pleasure of an encounter with her fiction rests.

When Welty writes criticism herself, her key words—mystery, passion, and love—are of the affective sort that make analysts nervous. But Welty is not speaking in vague generalizations when she discusses successful fiction as "love accomplished." Instead, she is outlining her expectations for her audience. What she wants from her reader is to have him find her and thereby know her. However, Welty is an author who thinks autobiographical revelations are largely irrelevant in a writer-reader exchange. Instead, the writer's project—at one level—is to transmute his or her essential, as opposed to merely real, self into fiction. When Welty praises other authors, she frequently writes of their presence in the text. For instance, Henry Green "is there at the center of what he writes, but in effect his identity has turned into the fiction. And while you the reader know nothing of Mr. Henry Green's life, as he has taken good care to see to, in the long run a life's confidence is what you feel you have been given." When Welty tells us that this writer lives in his work, that his fiction "should be read instead of some account of his life," she is expressing an oblique but genuine concern that her own fiction be an encounter.

In this reading encounter, Welty expects to move her readers towards an intuition of what Wayne Booth has called "the implied author," what I have called her essential self, a construct that readers infer from the "real" author's conscious and unconscious literary choices. These choices are what Welty refers to when she writes that it is "through the shaping of the work in the hands of the artist that you most nearly come to know what can be known, on the page, of . . . [him] as apart from the others." "The events of a story," she tells us, "may have much or little to do with the writer's own life; but the story *pattern* is the nearest thing to a mirror image of his mind and heart." "It's our perception of this ordering"—and here I find myself thinking of Welty's own ordering for obstruction—"that gives us our nearest understanding" of an author.

Welty expresses both what she hopes for and fears from interaction with her reader with a word that, in her comments and criticism, she repeatedly borrows from her photographer's vocabulary: "exposure." In her preface to *One Time, One Place,* she speaks of having first recognized her narrative goal of exposure—to record the divulging gesture, to disclose the inner secret concealed in the concrete and objective by framing it—while working with a camera. She "learned quickly enough when to click the shutter, but what [she became] aware of more slowly was a story-writer's truth: the thing to wait on, to reach there in time for, is the moment in which people reveal themselves." Welty seeks the perfect fictional exposure that will capture and convey her feeling and identity in words as a camera

arrests a telling sign with the click of a shutter. Welty has argued that fiction, "whatever its subject, is the history itself of [the author's] life's experience in feeling," and should therefore be read with love. But like the young girl in her story **"A Memory"** whose experience of first love contained discoveries of separateness and vulnerability, Welty understands the complexity of the reading process perfectly well enough to dread the hazards of encounter. Consequently, she is somewhat anxious as she exposes her essential, rather than merely actual, self to her audience. She writes of her need for "exposure to the world," but also of "the terrible sense of exposure" that she feels when she suddenly sees her "words with the eyes of the cold public." She writes of exposure as a process that "begins in intuition and has its end in showing the heart that expected, while it dreads that exposure."

The challenge of exposing an essential self in fiction rests in manipulating the external realities of words and readers to bring it into being, and certainly the project is full of risk. The most unreliable factor is the reader: the author's attempt to create and communicate herself will fail if the reader does not receive her. Like Welty's character Clytie who peers into others' faces while looking for the one that is familiar—her own—Welty sets out to meet the reader in part to find herself. It is up to the reader to reflect back to her, mirror-like, the intelligence that glances off her fiction. For this reason, the reader who first misses Welty's intention, then recomposes her text along his own lines, and finally returns to her a stranger's face, is troublesome. Still, Welty relies on this audience because she can only judge her success at constructing herself in her fiction on the basis of its reception. Her essential self is the product of her fiction's reception— the presence that her careful readers come to know as imaginative and intelligent, observant and witty, sympathetic and sharp, quite vulnerable and yet experimental and daring.

Like Powerhouse, Welty risks giving all she has to an audience that perhaps will know no better than to feel ashamed for her self-exposure. She takes this risk with feelings of vulnerability offset by the self-confidence of an artist who understands her medium and knows quite a few ways to manage the reading encounter. "Exposing yourself to risk is a truth Miss Eckhart and I had in common," Welty remarks in a self-revealing line that draws a comparison between her own passion for her life's work and Miss Eckhart's "love of her art and . . . love of giving it." The risk involved here is in the "giving it," as when Miss Eckhart gave to Virgie Rainey who, like some headstrong reader, was fortunately taking even though she appeared to reject. At the end of *One Writer's Beginnings,* the autobiographical essay in which this line appears, Welty remarks, "I am a writer who came of a sheltered life. A sheltered life can be a daring life as well. For all serious daring starts from within." In these lines, I hear Welty noting the connectedness of as well as the distance between what I have called her real and essential selves. And I hear her rediscovering for herself and for us too the daring of imaginative wandering, of artistic experimentation, and of the risk she has taken when giving her fiction over to us, her readers.

Thinking about the range, publication history, and achievement of Welty's fiction, it seems possible that Welty's concern to reach her audience has affected the shape of her career. The very diversity of Welty's fiction reflects her address of different audiences and, perhaps implicitly, her exploration of the idea of audience itself. In the year when Welty discussed the potential chasm between writer and reader in **"How I Write"**—1955—she was already an author who had addressed a variety of audiences, a variety climaxed by the great distance between her easily accessible, democratic *The Ponder Heart* and her obscure, elitist *The Bride of the Innisfallen,* books that were published back-to-back in 1954 and 1955. And then, in 1955, there began a period which lasted for fifteen years and ended when she published *The Optimist's Daughter* and *Losing Battles* in rapid succession in 1969 and 1970. This period, sometimes inaccurately called a gap in her career, was a time when Welty wrote more than she published and experimented by reaching out to new audiences. It seems possible to me that these years reflect a productive reaction to her reader's initial failure to meet her in *The Bride of the Innisfallen,* a failure measurable through the cool response of her reviewers. Did Welty reconsider her address of her audience while postponing exposure as usual?

There is some evidence to support this possibility. First, during these years, Welty's publications addressed several new audiences in new ways. She published essays that clarified her attitude toward criticism, a children's book, *The Shoe Bird,* as well as two stories responding to the Civil-Rights crisis in Mississippi which developed private themes through less private subject matter than she had taken before. What she did not publish, but instead worked on over a period of ten years, was her central fictional project, *Losing Battles.* This project was quite different from *The Bride of the Innisfallen* and problematic to Welty for the same reason that the novel is highly accessible to readers; that is, it is built almost entirely on dialogue and action. Welty commented that because she felt she had "been writing too much by way of description, of introspection on the part of [her] characters, [she] tried to see if [she] could make everything shown." Then, before completing *Losing Battles* and offering it to her readers, she wrote her very personal *The Optimist's Daughter* and quickly published both books. Welty herself has pointed out that during these years she was nursing her failing mother and teaching for a year at Millsaps College—two events that of course changed her usual writing habits. Constrained, she took notes and wrote scenes for *Losing Battles,* tucking "them in a box, with no

opportunity to go back and revise, but writing a scene anew instead of revising it, so that the work prolonged itself." "I . . . kept thinking of more and more scenes. . . . There were extra incidents, which told the same thing in different terms, different scenes, different characters." "I must have thrown away at least as much as I kept in the book. . . . I would write the scene out just to let [the characters] loose on something—my private show." Of course, speculation that this change in habit and project grew up partially in response to thoughts and feelings about meeting her readers is just that, speculation. But during these years, Welty did not offer more of her very personal, or obstructed fiction to her audience through publication. Instead, she grew in new ways and produced *Losing Battles.*

At the climax of this novel Jack Renfro is able to love Julia Mortimer and so to admit her to his family circle: "'I reckon I even love her,' said Jack, 'I heard her story.'" The familial model of author-audience interaction that this novel conveys is not at all beside the point. In her essay on Jane Austen, Welty pictures Austen "reading . . . chapters aloud to her own lively, vocative family, on whose shrewd intuition, practiced estimation of conduct, and seasoned judgment of character she relied almost as well as on her own." In that image, Welty imagines a perfect family circle as the ideal author-audience relationship. Jane Austen, Welty wrote, "must have enjoyed absolute confidence in an understanding reception of her work. [Her] novels still have a bloom of shared pleasure. And the felicity they have for us must partly lie in the confidence they take for granted between the author and her readers."

If Welty has a model of her own to offer to current theorizing about the writer-reader relationship, it is this confidential family. And the function of her sometimes obstructing style is to transform the willing stranger into a member of this inner circle. Welty's narrative obstacles can thus be understood as leading one to read for the sake of encounter rather than appropriation. It is the very process of unraveling difficulties that binds the successful reader to Welty with the thread of fiction; they come to share knowledge inaccessible to others who have not been so attentive, or sympathetic. As the division between reader and audience gradually dissolves, the reader is directed to complete the fiction along the lines that Welty imagined. Her obstruction of her reader's expectations more than reflects, it enacts her characteristic theme of love and separateness; it leads the reader to experience isolation and to discover communion.

In the interview I mentioned earlier, Joanna Maclay asked Eudora Welty "how [her] notion of the potential reader" affected what she did "to make [her] meaning clear." And Welty, who at first answered, "I don't know," ended by quoting Henry Green's remark: "Prose should be a long intimacy between strangers. . . ." In the context of my discussion of Welty's **"Powerhouse"** and her view of reading, I hope that this response has come into focus as a photograph does when rising to exposure in a developer's tray, or as Welty's fictions can in the reading process. Welty, it seems, was writing about and with knowledge of the issues of the reader-response debate two decades before it gained attention, and by adding Welty's voice to the others quoted in this article, I add the writer's point of view.

Suzanne Marrs (essay date October 1986)

SOURCE: "The Metaphor of Race in Eudora Welty's Fiction," in *The Southern Review,* Vol. 22, No. 4, October, 1986, pp. 697-707.

[*In the following essay, Marrs discusses certain aspects of African-American culture that Welty portrays in* Delta Wedding *and* The Golden Apples *including: "separateness despite intimate contact, a consequent and paradoxical freedom from white conventions, and a once common belief in ghosts and magic potions."*]

During the 1930s and early 1940s Eudora Welty was almost as busy with her camera as with her typewriter. She photographed scenes and faces, tried to sell a book of her pictures, and gave a one-woman photographic show in New York City. A primary subject of these photographs was black life in Mississippi: a fortune teller in exotic costume, bottle trees designed to ward off evil spirits, a slave apron with a whole mythology stitched upon it, a black state fair parade, a "Colored Entrance" to a movie theater, black women wearing evening dresses or men's hats for their Saturday afternoon of shopping were all subjects for Welty the photographer. We might logically expect, therefore, black life to be an important element in Welty's fiction, and indeed it is. Although Welty's fictional world is not typically black—it is the white world she knew much more intimately—black characters appear as protagonists in four of her earliest stories. That fact has been widely discussed. Almost unnoticed, however, are the numerous black characters in *Delta Wedding* and *The Golden Apples*. The exclusion from white society, the folk beliefs, and the freedom from white social convention so often depicted in Welty's photographs of blacks are especially crucial in these works. Set in the Mississippi Delta where cotton was king and where large numbers of black field hands and household servants toiled, both works rely upon a supporting cast of black characters who are at once real and emblematic, telling us of "each other's wonder, each other's human plight."

In *Delta Wedding* the institutionalized and artificial separation of black and white serves to dramatize the less obvi-

ous but wholly inevitable separateness of each human being, a separateness which coexists with intimacy. The plantation-owning Fairchilds deal with their servants in a congenial fashion, white and black children play together, and Ellen Fairchild sees to the health and well-being of black servants. But these surface relationships mask a very deep separation. When the black matriarch Partheny is subject to spells of mindlessness, for instance, the Fairchilds are sympathetic, but they never see the tragic import of the spells. Partheny, whose seizures resemble those experienced by Jackson midwife Ida M'Toy, describes her latest spell to Ellen Fairchild:

> "I were mindless, Miss Ellen. I were out of my house. I were looking in de river. I were standing on Yazoo bridge wid dis foot lifted. I were mindless, didn't know my name or name of my sons. Hand stop me. Mr. Troy Flavin he were by my side, gallopin' on de bridge. He laugh at me good—old Partheny! Don't you jump in dat river, make good white folks fish you out! No, sir, no, sir, I ain't goin' to do dat! Guides me home."

Partheny's "mindlessness" takes a particularly appalling form—she loses all sense of her identity. Mindlessness for Aunt Shannon Fairchild takes the form of senility, not of blackouts; she is able to "talk conversationally with Uncle Denis and Aunt Rowena and Great-Uncle George, who had all died no telling how long ago, that she thought were at the table with her." The white woman retreats into the past. Partheny doesn't know her own name or the names of her sons. She recalls no past. In fact, Partheny scarcely has a past of her own. Her life has been focused upon the Fairchilds. Her contact with the family has been close and affectionate: she attended Ellen Fairchild at the birth of daughter Shelley, was the nurse to several of Ellen's children, and assists in the final preparations for Dabney's wedding to Troy Flavin; Ellen Fairchild, similarly, has ministered to the ailing Partheny, provided her with Shellmound Plantation's old wicker furniture, and refused to criticize Partheny's appropriation of insignificant Fairchild possessions. But no other family members even think about Partheny except as she plays a role in family activities. They take her for granted, never questioning that her life should be devoted to them, never realizing that she has been denied a separate past of her own. Though they are more sensitive than Troy, the overseer who laughs as he stops Partheny from jumping into the Yazoo River, the Fairchilds' empathy for their servants is limited.

The expeditious and dispassionate way Troy deals with a fight in which Root M'Hook has cut two other black field hands more explicitly emphasizes Welty's theme of human separateness. Troy, of course, is not the stereotypical sadistic overseer, but Troy sees blacks only as workers, not as human beings. Troy's reaction to the fight is thus to deal only with the facts—he shoots and disarms M'Hook, but he never explores the reason for the blacks' violent confrontation. What role has Pinchy's religious fervor, her "coming through," played in their fight? The field hands suggest it precipitated the violence. How? Troy doesn't inquire, and Shelley Fairchild, who sees and disapproves of the way Troy handles this matter, is not interested in its cause. No one else in the family even hears of the incident. Having an overseer distances them from the blacks. Moreover, neither Troy nor Shelley responds as George had years before to a fight between two black boys. He stopped their knife fight, embraced them when they cried, asked their names, and sent them off unpunished. George cared and continues to care; he tries to break through barriers that separate him even from those outside the family. But George, who repeatedly defies convention, and Ellen, who goes to the "mindless" Partheny, are the only white adults capable of such actions.

Perhaps the novel's clearest representative of separation is Aunt Studney, an emblematic character even though her name, the mysterious sack she carries, and her unusual mannerisms were those of an actual woman (as Welty told the author in a conversation of November 1, 1985). She is as oblivious to the whites as they are to her—"Ain't studyin' you," she tells them. In a sense she mirrors their detachment; the white characters find her attitude to be eccentric, perhaps frightening, often amusing, but they do not see their own attitude toward her in similar terms. And though the Fairchilds study each other carefully, their study does not narrow the distance between them. Though they look "with shining eyes upon their kin," though "their abundance of love" comes forth in jests and teasing, there is much about each other that they do not or cannot or will not know. Welty's focus in *Delta Wedding* is thus upon separateness within the cohesive family. Dabney and Shelley have similar fears and concerns, though one is more emotional, the other more intellectual, but they never realize their common plight. Ellen struggles to understand her two daughters. George and Robbie love but are separated. These characters in some ways are as cut off from one another as Aunt Studney is from them all.

Despite the Fairchilds' distance from one another, the barriers between black and white provide them with occasions to assert family solidarity, occasions which George, to his family's dismay, refuses to act upon. Though she has moments when she wants to be like George, when she does not care if she is a Fairchild, Dabney recalls being shocked by George's behavior during the knife fight, for that fight is "something that the other Fairchilds would have passed by and scorned to notice." George's noticing tells Dabney that he loves "the *world*. . . . Not them! Not them in particular." Dabney wants, at least at times she wants, that sense of belonging, that assertion of group solidarity which comes

when others are excluded. Racial barriers, it thus seems, both encourage the illusion of absolute unity and represent the inevitable separateness of individuals.

The significance of black characters, however, extends beyond the notion of separateness. Welty suggests that both Partheny and Aunt Studney recognize and accept the mysterious power of love and the fact of their own mortality. Their white counterparts, on the other hand, typically repress such knowledge. Dabney loves and immerses herself in that love, though "timid of the element itself," but Shelley fears such an immersion. And no one, Ellen realizes, save George and herself, sees "death on its way." The novel suggests, moreover, that these mysteries must be confronted intuitively; they cannot be explained or dealt with logically.

Patterns of imagery in the novel clearly link Partheny and Aunt Studney with a knowledge of love as well as death. Partheny in her mindless condition has almost plunged from the bridge into the Yazoo, literally the River of Death, and Partheny recognizes, without fear or horror, her near brush with death. But the Yazoo is as much an emblem of love as of death. It is the river into which George, clearly enchanted with his wife, once chased Robbie, and Partheny seems to have a special understanding of such passionate relationships. Knowing in some unaccountable way that George and Robbie have separated, she attempts to remedy that situation, sending George a magical patticake that will bring Robbie back to him. She tells Shelley: "You take dis little patticake to Mr. George Fairchild, was at dis knee at de Grove, and tell him mind he eat it tonight at midnight, by himse'f, and go to bed. Got a little white dove blood in it, dove heart, blood of a snake—things. I just tell you enough in it so you trus' dis patticake." In her knowledge of both love and death, Partheny is linked to Ellen Fairchild. Ellen thinks that George alone of his family sees "death on its way," but her recognition signifies her own knowledge of human mortality as well. And Ellen, whose love for her husband Battle, for her children, and for her brother-in-law George permeates the novel, is primarily responsible for the reconciliation of George and Robbie, the reconciliation Partheny had hoped to bring about.

Perhaps even more importantly, Ellen acts in the intuitive fashion that characterizes Partheny. Partheny's faith in the magical patticake serves as an emblem of Ellen's intuition. That intuition is seen most clearly in Ellen's prophetic dreams.

> Ellen herself had always rather trusted her dreams. It was her weakness, she knew, and it was right for the children as they grew up to deride her, and so she usually told them to the youngest. However, she dreamed the location of mistakes in the accounts and the payroll that her husband—not a born busi-

ness man—had let pass, and discovered how Mr. Bascom had cheated them and stolen so much; and she dreamed whether any of the connection needed her in their various places, the Grove, Inverness, or the tenants down the river, and they always did when she got there. She dreamed of things the children and Negroes lost and of where they were, and often when she looked she did find them, or parts of them, in the dreamed-of places. She was too busy when she was awake to know if a thing was lost or not—she had to dream it.

The novel shows us that Ellen's dreams are valid guides—Laura finds the garnet pin where Ellen has dreamed it will be. But most of the white characters tend not to rely on dreams, not to act on the basis of intuition. Shelley seeks to understand her life by thinking, by analyzing, though this approach leaves her helpless to understand the passion George and Robbie feel—she will not deliver Partheny's patticake to George. Neither does rational Shelley comprehend the meaning of death: "'River of Death' to Shelley meant not the ultimate flow of doom, but the more personal vision of the moment's chatter ceasing, the feelings of the day disencumbered, floating now into recognition. . . ." Though the mystery of death never crosses her mind, Dabney is more open to passion. She loves Troy and describes her love as a river: "In catching sight of love she had seen both banks of a river and the river rushing between—she saw everything but the way down." Yet even Dabney has trouble seeing "the way down," has trouble trusting her intuition as a guide through uncharted territory. George, however, does not have this difficulty. He can fully accept mystery. He can, Ellen realizes with "the darker instinct of a woman," meet "a fate whose dealing out to him he would not contest," whether that fate be death or a seemingly inappropriate love. Thus, only Ellen, who nurses Partheny, and George, who grew up at Partheny's knee, trust their intuition absolutely.

Laura McRaven, the nine-year-old motherless girl, seems most destined to share the wisdom of George and Ellen. Laura, who has loved and lost her mother, is further initiated into the mysteries of love and death on her visit to the Fairchilds, and the enigmatic black woman Aunt Studney, as Carol Moore noted in this journal, plays a crucial role in that initiation. Laura and her cousin Roy journey by boat to Dabney's future home, Marmion, only to meet Aunt Studney carrying her mysterious sack. Aunt Studney, who lives beyond The Deadening, will not let the children look inside her sack. Though the location of Studney's home makes her seem an emblem of mortality, Roy believes her sack is the place "where Mama gets all her babies." And when Laura is plunged into the Yazoo River, these associations with both life and death are reiterated: "As though Aunt Studney's sack had opened after all, like a whale's

mouth, Laura opening her eyes head down saw its insides all around her—dark water and fearful fishes." Laura, whose only previous "swims" have been in Jackson's Pythian Castle with the protection of water wings, is immersed in the river which has repeatedly been associated with the mysteries of love and death and which is now linked to Studney's sack. She placidly accepts this experience, and at the end of the novel she holds her arms "out to the radiant night." She is not disoriented by the unknown and unknowable. Laura, still a child of course, cannot achieve the kind of awareness that George and Ellen know; but Laura, who so much wants to belong to the Fairchild family, will be able to face life's transience and the consequent urgency to love, and she will not have to use the extended family as a shelter from those enigmas. Her decision to return to her father and to Jackson signifies as much.

Black characters in *The Golden Apples* are not so prominent as they are in *Delta Wedding,* but they are essential to the book's thematic development. Most basically, white attitudes toward blacks in these interrelated stories of Morgana, Mississippi, exemplify the white community's need to insulate itself and to believe in its self-sufficiency. When Miss Eckhart is attacked by a "crazy Negro" who pulls her down and threatens to kill her, the people of Morgana expect her to move away. They do not want to face the ugly memory of her rape, though Miss Eckhart herself seems to consider "one thing not so much more terrifying than another." White Morgana will not confront inevitable threats to community solidarity. These white citizens want a world they can control, and they certainly expect to be in control of blacks. They want blacks to be like Plez Morgan, "a real trustworthy nigger," the "real old kind, that knows everybody since time was." Plez is part of the community and assists in its protective deception of Miss Snowdie MacLain when her wandering husband comes home. Probably he does so out of affection for Snowdie; perhaps he also knows better than to intervene in white affairs. Whatever the case, Plez is a man the white community can patronize and cherish, but that community prefers to ignore black violence. The "crazy Negro" who attacks Miss Eckhart jeopardizes the community's illusion of control, an illusion which helps it to deny individual separateness and vulnerability.

Black violence is not the only black threat to community solidarity in *The Golden Apples.* More importantly, blacks are associated, often paired with white characters who are imaginative and unconventional wanderers. In **"A Shower of Gold,"** Plez Morgan is the only person who sees King MacLain when he reappears one Halloween day, and it is Plez who constructs the story of King's return, even recounting an event that he could not have seen: "Plez said though he couldn't swear to seeing from the Presbyterian Church exactly what Mr. King was doing, he knows as good as seeing it that he looked through the blinds." Plez, the man who believes in ghosts and who toys with the idea that he has seen a ghost on Miss Snowdie MacLain's front porch, tells this story. Although Plez helps the community conceal King's visit from Miss Snowdie and although he serves white people faithfully, Plez can never be the social equal of whites. He thus is outside the restraints of Morgana society: King has broken free; Plez has been excluded. And like Plez, King is a man of imagination. King envisions the possibilities of life and leaves Morgana in quest of them. Plez's imagination wanders freely in realms of supernatural and natural events, unfettered by white rationalism. As a result, superstition seems an emblem of imagination in **"A Shower of Gold."**

In **"Moon Lake"** superstition does not play so central a role, but again black characters are free in mind, much freer than their white counterparts. They confront the realities of their world and accept its mysteries. Among the white girl campers at Moon Lake, the orphan Easter lives most intensely. When she sleeps, her hand is open to the night, to the unknown, to the mysterious. But Easter cannot swim and seeks to avoid Moon Lake where there is a chance of "getting sucked under, of being bitten, and of dying three miles away from home" and where Miss Moody sometimes goes out in a boat with "a late date from town." The lake holds out the possibilities of danger and romance—Easter's openness to experience is thus incomplete until she climbs to a diving board, is tickled on the foot, and makes a near fatal plunge into the lake. That initiation experience, which occurs in a series of humorous scenes with serious import, links Easter with the story's black characters and marks her as a wanderer. In the first place, the black boy Exum causes Easter to fall into the lake. Exum plays outdoors in the midday heat as the white girls are forbidden to do; he fishes in Moon Lake, swearing that he can catch an electric eel; and he wears a hat reminiscent of King MacLain's. Exum's freedom, his contact with realities from which the girls are sheltered (the heat, the mysterious lake), his blackness, all make him the appropriate character to prompt Easter's dive. It is not Exum, however, but the white Loch Morrison who then saves Easter. Nevertheless, Loch seems almost black to the girls in the camp. He swims in Moon Lake when all other white characters are indoors. He wears a bathing costume which looks "black and formal as a minstrel suit." And he lives "apart like the cook," a black servant. His rescue of Easter is thus metaphorically significant, for his experiences extend beyond the world of white Morgana with its organized camps and willful ignorance of life's mystery. Ironically, even in acting for the community as its lifeguard, Loch seems to defy its will. Miss Lizzie Stark associates his lifesaving endeavors with sexual passion, an emotion that respectable Morgana fears but that neither Loch nor Easter seems destined to repress. Finally, once Easter has been rescued and revived, Twosie is the camp employee assigned to watch over her. It is Twosie who has heard an ominous warning in a bird's call and has asked, "Know why, in de sky, he say 'Spirit? Spirit?' And den he dive *boom* and say 'GHOST'?" And it is Twosie who tells the girls "Yawl sho ain't got yo' eyes opem good, yawl. Yawl don't know what's out here in woods wid you." Twosie's superstitious nature and her suggestion that the white girls are blind to reality make her the appropriate attendant for Easter. In a comic fashion, she shares the acceptance of mystery and recognition of danger that typify the story's black characters and that now fully typify Easter.

In **"Music from Spain,"** Eugene MacLain has traveled far from Morgana and Moon Lake only to lead a very routine life in San Francisco. Three black characters, however, provide him with images of a freer life, a life as free as his father's and a life that Eugene, consequently, both desires and fears. Eugene's first encounter with a black occurs early in the story. Waiting for a stoplight to change, Eugene stands by an unusual woman: "There was such strange beauty about her that he did not realize for a few moments that she was birth-marked and would be considered disfigured by most people—by himself, ordinarily. She was a Negro or a Polynesian and marked as a butterfly is, over all her visible skin." As Eugene gazes at the woman, he senses "an almost palpable aura of a disgrace or sadness that had to be as ever-present as the skin is, of hiding and flaunting together." Eugene associates this black woman with both the freedom of the butterfly and an ever-present sadness. Welty here again suggests that her black characters are at once free from the confines of white society and oppressed by that society. The woman's "hiding and flaunting" are true to the general experience of blacks, and they are also true to the experience of Welty's wanderers, to the experience of those characters who are unwilling or unable to live according to a formula, who will not or cannot ignore the realities of time, loss, and loneliness, and who seek to live more intensely than convention would permit. Appropriately, then, Eugene believes the strangely beautiful Negress would make a fine mistress for the Spanish guitarist with red fingernails, but he does not think of her as his own mistress. Eugene allots beauty, sadness, defiance of convention to the Spaniard and protects himself.

Eugene's second encounter with blacks comes as he and the Spaniard take a streetcar. The conductor on the car is "a big fat Negro woman who yelled out all the street names with joy." When Eugene sees that the Spaniard is smiling at this woman and at other blacks on the car, he is upset: "Negroes would think he comprehended all their nigger-business." Eugene doesn't comprehend the joy, the plans for a two AM rendezvous at the Cat, the freedom of these characters. Even as he tries to break free from his structured life, Eugene retreats. The Spaniard, however, does understand this "nigger-business" and does share in its joys.

> **Throughout her fiction Welty has succeeded in "making moments double upon themselves, and in the doubling double again." Nowhere is this more true than in *Delta Wedding* and *The Golden Apples*. Events involving black characters in these works are typically double, and the works are rich and complex as a result.**
> **—*Suzanne Marrs***

Finally, Eugene looks into a basement as he and the Spaniard walk through San Francisco. There he sees "a big colored woman plying the keys," and he thinks she must be a long way from home. He associates her with the old Negro in Morgana who in times of trouble has always walked into the Morgana store and asked the proprietor to play "Rocks in My Bed Number Two." Blacks, Eugene knows quite well, created the blues, a musical form which defines the black experience. Significantly, though, Eugene cannot hear the woman playing. Eugene himself has good reason to understand the blues; the death of his daughter Fan has been a devastating blow to him, but he and his wife Emma are unable to talk honestly, openly with each other about Fan's death. Not even music can help them to transform and transcend sorrow. Eugene cannot hear the blues, and he will ultimately return to Morgana as a broken and bitter man.

In **"The Wanderers"** blacks continue to be those characters who are at once most realistic and most imaginative. Juba, Mrs. Stark's maid who comes to help Virgie pack before leaving, is able to deal with realities Virgie still seeks to avoid, and Juba does so in the form of ghost stories. She tells Virgie, "I seen more ghosts than live peoples, round here. Black and white. I seen plenty both. Miss Virgie, some is given to see, some try but is not given. I seen that Mrs. Morrison from 'cross the road in long white nightgown, no head atall, in her driveway Saddy. Reckanize her freckle arms. You ever see her? I seen her here. She die in pain?" Juba may not consciously know that Mrs. Morrison has suffered from white Morgana's life of Rook parties, speakings, and recitals, but Juba does know that despair drove Mrs. Morrison to suicide. Her vision of the ghost reflects that knowledge just as her vision of Katie Rainey "lyin' up big on a stuff davenport like a store window, three four *us* fannin' her" suggests the serenity Katie Rainey had achieved. But Virgie is not ready even now to confront Mrs. Morrison's pain or her mother's death. She turns on Juba and accuses the absent Minerva of having stolen silver-headed Katie's yellow hair switch and the Raineys' baby clothes. In these petty and meaningless thefts, Virgie sees the loss of her past. She lashes out and sends Juba away. Juba, however, understands the emotion behind this outburst

and returns to tell the sobbing Virgie: "That's right. Cry. Cry. Cry."

At least partially because of Juba, Virgie comes to recognize that her mother is gone and that in human transience lies life's one "irreducible urgency." Her departure from Morgana is not a retreat, but the beginning of a quest. At age forty, having wasted years of her own life and having lost her entire family to death, Virgie recognizes what the piano teacher Miss Eckhart had offered her so long ago. Seven miles from Morgana in the town of MacLain, she sits on a stile in front of the courthouse, thinks of Miss Eckhart with love, not hate, and knows the meaning of "*the* Beethoven" and of the picture on Miss Eckhart's studio wall: "Every time Perseus struck off the Medusa's head, there was the beat of time, and the melody. Endless the Medusa, and Perseus endless." Virgie has absorbed the hero, the victim, and the music. No longer does she avoid facing the realities of time, loss, separateness. No longer does she lash out at those who call these realities to mind. When a woman carrying a red hen sits next to her, Virgie thinks of this woman as "the old black thief," perhaps recalling her verbal attack on Minerva but certainly identifying herself with this woman's resolve to survive, to wrest from time all that she can. Virgie accepts the companionship of the woman, and together they hear "the magical percussion, the world beating in their ears." They hear "through falling rain the running of the horse and bear, the stroke of the leopard, the dragon's crusty slither, and the glimmer and the trumpet of the swan." The world of myth, of art, of intuition, of superstition leads to knowledge—a knowledge of love and death which Virgie finally and completely accepts. And her new awareness is marked by the presence of the old black woman, a character who might have seemed a stereotypical chicken-stealing darky to most of Morgana's white citizens, but who for Welty and Virgie is an emblem of courageous striving.

Three realities of black existence in the South are thus crucial to Eudora Welty's achievement in *Delta Wedding* and *The Golden Apples*. Separateness despite intimate contact, a consequent and paradoxical freedom from white conventions, and a once common belief in ghosts and magic potions—these aspects of black culture Welty vividly conveys. But she also uses these aspects of black life to develop her major themes, themes which extend to all life. Welty's accurate depiction of black life is a metaphoric one as well, suggesting the inescapable nature of human isolation, the courage and triumph and pain involved in an independent existence, the limitations of reason, and the validity of intuition. Throughout her fiction Welty has succeeded in "making moments double upon themselves, and in the doubling double again." Nowhere is this more true than in *Delta Wedding* and *The Golden Apples*. Events involving black characters in these works are typically double, and the works are rich and complex as a result.

Barbara Harrell Carson (essay date Spring 1988)

SOURCE: "Eudora Welty's Dance with Darkness: *The Robber Bridegroom*," in *The Southern Literary Journal*, Vol. XX, No. 2, Spring, 1988, pp. 51-68.

[*In the following essay, Harrell Carson discusses the integration of fairy tale and history in Welty's* The Robber Bridegroom.]

The nature and purpose of the relationship between fairy tale and reality in Eudora Welty's *The Robber Bridegroom* has been discussed since the earliest reviews. In what is probably the most perceptive long critical analysis of the work, Michael Kreyling has seen in the mixture of fairy tale and history an expression of the tension between pastoral dream and capitalistic reality in America. It is possible, however, to view the work in a larger metaphysical scheme—one which suggests that the moral weight of the tale comes down on the side of recognizing and accepting the unity of contraries in life, not in choosing one pole of a pair of opposites (such as pastoralism over capitalism) at the expense of the other. In this reading, we can see in the collision of fairy tale and history the tension between the human impulse to simplify life, on the one hand, and, on the other, life's insistent complexity.

Indeed, the folk fairy tale that Welty incorporated into her story is grounded on the child's need for simplicity. As Bruno Bettelheim writes:

> The figures in fairy tales are not ambivalent—not good and bad at the same time, as we are in reality. But since polarization dominates the child's mind, it also dominates fairy tales. A person is either good or bad, nothing in between. One brother is stupid, the other is clever. One sister is virtuous and industrious. . . .

The child cannot handle the grandmother's crabby moments, so she sees the mean grandmother as the wolf, the nice one as the object of Red Ridinghood's charitable visit. She avoids direct confrontation with her own double nature in stories such as **"Sister and Brother,"** in which her undisciplined self, projected as her brother-companion, is turned into a fawn. In *The Robber Bridegroom,* the characters attempt to sustain the child's simple vision of human nature, while life works inexorably to introduce them to its doubleness. In this way, Welty's novel is about the lesson needed to move us from the child's world to the adult's, from a fairy tale vision of life to a philosophically, psychologically, and historically corrected outlook.

The ontology of this corrected vision is based on the old principles of *concordia discors* and *coincidentia oppositorum*. Reality is not an either/or matter, but is created by the dynamic tension of co-existing opposites. The challenge of life is thus not choosing between opposites—joy or sorrow, true or false, beginnings or endings, life or death—but coming to see a whole in which both poles are as inseparably united, as interdependent as the two poles of a magnet.

In Welty's *The Robber Bridegroom* Clement Musgrove's journey from his blissful home in Kentucky into the Mississippi wilderness is itself a trip from fairy tale to reality. Anthony Steven's analysis of the expulsion from the Garden of Eden applies to Clement's move: the loss of paradise, Steven says, is "a parable of the emergence of ego-consciousness, and the replacement of harmonious unity with the conflicts born of awareness of opposing categories of experience (e.g., good and evil, love and hate, pleasure and pain)." However, Welty's characters will learn a lesson opposite Adam and Eve's. While life in Eden was possible only in the presence of one of the paired opposites (good, love, pleasure) and while Judeo-Christian teachings urge a similar either/or morality in life outside of Eden, in the world Welty presents life can only be lived fully with the acknowledgement of the harmony to be found in the co-existence of the contraries.

In *The Robber Bridegroom* nature itself bears witness to the cosmic reality of *concordia discors,* contrasting vividly with the human desire to see everything in either/or terms. When Jamie Lockhart (the gallant who is also the robber) leaves Clement Musgrove's house after he has failed to recognize in Clement's daughter Rosamond the girl who attracted him in the woods, he enters a natural world whose complexity adumbrates the reality that he avoids. He rides "in the confusion of the moonlight, under the twining branches of trees. . . ." The next day when Rosamond, who has likewise failed to recognize in Jamie the bandit she found so charming, sets out to find her highwayman, she enters the same forest, that old literary symbol for a mind on the threshold of self-knowledge—and, hence, knowledge of the reality into which the self fits. Although she does not realize it at the time, the perceptual confusion she experiences as she penetrates the forest (mistaking the gentle for the cruel, the animal for the human, the predator for the defenseless) hints of the overlapping and intertwining nature of reality:

> On and on she went, deeper and deeper into the forest, and its sound was all around. She heard something behind her, but it was only a woodpecker

pecking with his ivory bill. She thought there was a savage there, but it was a deer which was looking so hard at her. Once she thought she heard a baby crying, but it was a wildcat down in the cane.

By the end of the tale she will have learned that other categories that she had also thought to be mutually exclusive are, after all, not so clearcut.

Jamie Lockhart experiences a similar illumination. He is *The Robber Bridegroom's* best exemplar both of the impulse to simplify one's sense of self and one's responses to others, as well as of the need to move toward acceptance of the self's polar reality. Jamie's first conversations with Clement reveal his desire for a life without complications. When Clement confesses his own perpetual guilt before his second wife Salome, Jamie replies: "Guilt is a burdensome thing to carry about in the heart. . . . I would never bother with it." To this Clement replies: "Then you are a man of action, . . . a man of the times, a pioneer and a free agent. There is no one to come to you saying 'I want' what you do not want." Things will change for Jamie in the course of Welty's story. But at its start, he has tried neatly to partition his life, seeing himself as alternately the bandit or the gentleman, never admitting that his reality includes simultaneously both identities. When, at their first formal meeting, he fails to recognize Rosamond as the same beautiful girl he met in the woods, it is not only because she is now ragged and dirty, but also because "it was either love or business that traveled on his mind, never both at once, and this night it was business." However, when Clement offers his daughter as a reward if Jamie captures the bandit who stole her clothes, Jamie is repulsed—in spite of the attraction of the dowry that is an unspoken part of the deal—because this "man of enterprise" actually incarnates (without being aware of it) human *concordia discors,* combining within self the contradictory qualities of the romantic and the materialist. Welty writes that "in his heart" Jamie "carried nothing less than a dream of true love—something of gossamer and roses, though on this topic he never held conversation with himself, or let the information pass to a soul. . . ." Later, when his robber band chides him for staying with Rosamond during the daytime (he had always before confined romance to night and devoted the day to banditry), he halfway draws his dirk in self-defensive protest: "For he thought he had it all divisioned off into time and place, and that many things were for later and for further away, and that now the world had just begun."

Jamie's challenge is to bring into conversation the two sides of himself, accepting his complex reality. Ironically, the innocent Clement voices most clearly the truth of this polarity, when Rosamond visits him after her "marriage" to Jamie. He says:

> 'If being a bandit were his breadth and scope, I should find him and kill him for sure. . . . But since in addition he loves my daughter, he must be not the one man, but two, and I should be afraid of killing the second. For all things are double, and this should keep us from taking liberties with the outside world, and acting too quickly to finish things off.'

It is strangely appropriate in a world where apparent opposites meet that kind-hearted Clement shares this awareness of doubleness with the villains of the piece. In fact, while the innocent planter has only abstract insight into the mingled identity of Rosamond's robber lover, the evil Salome and the Little Harp have specific evidence that Jamie Lockhart and the outlaw are one. At their first meeting, Salome sees the berry stains behind Jamie Lockhart's ear; Little Harp sees Jamie with only a partially stained face after Jamie, interrupted as he began to disguise himself, runs to aid Goat's sister, whom Little Harp had decided to kill instead of marry. Little Harp gloats: "Aha, but I know who you are too. . . . Your name is Jamie Lockhart and you are the bandit in the woods, for you have your two faces on together and I see you both."

Salome and Little Harp on the one hand and Clement on the other demonstrate two responses to an awareness of human complexity. Clement shows that an appreciation of the full instead of the partial human being can lead to compassion and to patience with life's unfolding. He shows, too, that understanding of the doubleness of others can illuminate dark areas of one's own life. His speech about Jamie's doubleness includes this startling bit of self-examination:

> 'All things are divided in half—night and day, the soul and body, and sorrow and joy and youth and age, and sometimes I wonder if even my own wife has not been the one person all the time, and I loved her beauty so at the beginning that it is only now that the ugliness has struck through to beset me like a madness.'

The trick in human relationships that Clement has not applied to his own wife and that Jamie and Rosamond must discover is to see the different "sides" of personalities simultaneously and not sequentially.

For Salome and Little Harp, however, knowledge of Jamie's dual self leads neither to compassion nor to self-knowledge. For them it is the basis for their powerplay over Rosamond and Jamie. Salome's and Little Harp's relations to others have their own kind of simplicity: they use them. That Rosamond and Jamie—both of whom deny one side of their identity—are such easy victims implies the vulnerability that accompanies attempted retreats to a simple identity. Paradoxically, however, that very vulnerability contains the seeds for human growth: only when they are forced to confront their duplex identities can Rosamond and Jamie experience life's fullness of sorrow and joy.

On the other hand, Salome and Little Harp illustrate the self-destruction that accompanies inviolate one-sidedness. If Clement is right that Salome is really the other side of his first wife Amalie (their names are practically anagrams), ugly now and hardened since the murder of their son by Indians, Salome has denied so totally the gentle, loving side of her self that she has become stonelike. At one point Welty writes: ". . . Rosamond did not think the trickery went so deep in her stepmother that it did not come to an end, but made her solid like an image of stone in the garden. . . ." Salome's singlemindedness leads to her capture by the Indians: ". . . her eye, from thinking of golden glitter, had possibly gotten too bright to see the dark that was close around her now." Her coldly determined self-sufficiency leads to her destruction. When Goat, who has come to free her from the Indians, asks why she is crying, she screams: "I am not crying! . . . Be gone! I need no one!" And so he leaves her. Brought before the Indians, she claims the power to command the sun. "Shaking both fists in the smoky air," she proclaims, "No one is to have power over me! . . . No man, and none of the elements. I am by myself in the world!" And she dances to her death, alone, ordering the sun to retire.

Little Harp also demonstrates that nothing is potentially so destructive as single vision—viewing self or other through a single lens. Having reduced himself merely to the violent outlaw—the shadow self of Jamie Lockhart's bandit persona—Little Harp dies when he declares the death of both Big Harp and the bandit Jamie Lockhart. (His plan was to keep the reward offered for Big Harp's head when it was mistaken for Jamie's). Little Harp, like Salome, asserts that he alone is in control: ". . . the Little Harp rules now. And for the proof of everything, I'm killing you now with my own two hands." Instead, of course, Jamie kills him. Only in death does Little Harp reveal the other, feeling side of himself he had denied in life: "The Little Harp, with a wound in his heart, heaved a deep sigh and a tear came out of his eye, for he hated to give up his life as badly as the deer in the woods."

However, while Little Harp's death, like Salome's, implies the deadness even in life of those who develop and recognize only one part of the self, the central significance of Little Harp's murder seems to lie in its symbolizing the death of Jamie's bandit self. Yet even this is not as simple as it first appears. We recognize as clearly as Jamie did that Little Harp represents the violent, outlaw side of Rosamond's handsome lover. While we, like Rosamond, actually see in action only the dashing Lochinvar/Robin

Hood side of Jamie, Welty is careful to remind us of the more somber business of his profession. The first intimation takes the comic form of Mike Fink's obvious fear of Jamie: whoever can bring a tremor to that he-bull, he-rattle-snake, he-alligator of a flatboatman must be some sort of a he-terror himself. When Mike Fink's ominously croaking raven sits easily on Jamie's finger "as though there it belonged," we assume Jamie is at home, too, with Mike Fink's grimmer activities. (Fink has, after all, just had a hearty go at beating Jamie and Clement to death with a floorboard.) Less laughter accompanies the next clue to the reality of Jamie's life as an outlaw, one he himself furnishes when he broadly hints to Clement—almost as if he wished to give himself away—about the parallels between the Indians robbing Clement and Jamie's own banditry. Further inside the nested boxes of *The Robber Bridegroom* are even darker reminders of the non-fairytale quality of robbers' lives. When Jamie first encounters Little Harp and tries to kill him, he instinctively recognizes their shared identity. Welty writes:

> He half pulled out his little dirk to kill the Little Harp then and there. But his little dirk, not unstained with blood, held back and would not touch the feeble creature. Something seemed to speak to Jamie that said, 'This is to be your burden, and so you might as well take it.'

So the Little Harp moves into Jamie's hideout, raping and killing the Indian girl in the same house where Jamie lives with Rosamond, whom he had abducted, too (though, in a fairy tale layer of the story, with her loving compliance). In the death of the Indian girl we are about as far as we can get from lighthearted innocence and from gay, soaring dreams without nightmares. And Jamie's character is here revealed as far from the fairy tale Prince Charming. To Jamie's outlaw band, Little Harp declares, ". . . your chief belongs to me! . . . He is bound over to me body and soul. . . ." Although Jamie throws him out, he knows that "he'll be back with me tomorrow." Even Rosamond comes close to acknowledging the real life of her lover when she admits to Salome that Jamie still brings home to her fine dresses and petticoats—obviously from other women he has accosted and possibly raped.

As the book moves away from its dark center, Jamie resolves comically the problems that have been generated by his keeping the two parts of his self in isolation. However, the solution is not actually the death of his robber side, as the death of Little Harp may seem at first to imply. To think that the robber in Jamie dies completely is to miss the whole point of the theme of doubleness, of the necessary and valuable reality of human psychological polarity. It is also to miss a good joke. Jamie becomes a rich merchant, the perfect way to be both a gentleman and a highwayman. As

Welty tells us: ". . . the outward transfer from bandit to merchant had been almost too easy to count it a change at all, and he was enjoying all the same success he had ever had." Thus the death of Little Harp signals, not the death of Jamie's robber self, but his acceptance of integration of the two poles of self into one whole. New Orleans is the perfect setting for this integration, since it too brings into concord apparent opposites: "Beauty and vice and every delight possible to the soul and body stood hospitably, and usually together, in every doorway and beneath every palmetto by day and lighted torch by night. A shutter opened and a flower bloomed." Here, Jamie—now a man of feeling as well as a man of action, and no longer quite so free of the wants of others—lives the wisdom he has come to, his heroic vision: "But now in his heart Jamie knew that he was a hero and had always been one, only with the power to look both ways and to see a thing from all sides." In Welty's moral scheme the willingness to take this Janus-like perspective is itself heroic.

Jamie is not the only character with two faces in *The Robber Bridegroom*. Almost everyone has either a double identity or a personality made up of contradictory elements, making it difficult for us easily to pass judgment on or finish anyone off. The "evil" characters seem evil precisely because—and to the extent that—they refuse to acknowledge their complexity, a refusal that reduces them to one-dimensional fairy tale villains in their evaluations of themselves and in their relationship to others. But Welty insists that the reader see virtue even in the villains. So the Little Harp turns out in his death to have human feelings; so Salome and Amalie are two halves of an unrecognized whole. The loud-mouthed, murderous Mike Fink of the first part of the tale is also the timorous, ghost-bedeviled mail rider of the conclusion (and even in the opening scene he has such a queasy stomach that he covers his eyes and feels rather than looks at the ruin he thinks he has brought Clement and Jamie, a comic introduction to Welty's idea that all people are double). Later, we see the stupid Goat moved to tears by Rosamond's song and the pitiless Indians feeling pity for Clement. We end up feeling strangely ambivalent even about Salome, whose defiance of all in heaven or on earth demands a kind of admiration as well as scorn.

However, next to Jamie, the character whose doubleness is most fully developed is Rosamond. She is both the spoiled daughter of a rich planter and the self-sacrificing lover of the bandit of the woods. While she has the fairy tale attributes of Gretel, Cinderella, and Snow White (her name, Rose of the World, is close to the generic naming of fairy tales), she is unlike them in being far from the one-sided, virtuous, long-suffering, passive maiden of fairy tales. She is "a great liar" from whose mouth lies fall as naturally as jewels from the lips of fairy princesses. She is also as sexually awakened as Snow White is innocent of all conscious

sexuality. Rosamond has had fantasies of abduction and is coolly self-possessed when she is accosted by the outlaw Jamie (". . . Rosamond . . . had sometimes imagined such a thing happening, and knew what to say"). In fact, it seems to be Rosamond who entices Jamie in their first encounter. "Well, then I suppose I must give you the dress . . . but not a thing further." When Jamie takes even her petticoats, she spends no time worrying about the precarious state of her virtue, but instead wonders "how ever she might look without a stitch on her." And when Jamie offers her a choice between being killed and going home naked, she shows no stupid fairy tale preference for honor over life, asserting, "Why, sir, life is sweet . . . and before I would die on the point of your sword, I would go home naked any day." Returned home, she acquiesces in Salome's orders that she work like a scullery maid, finding in her subservience freedom from others' pleasures and plans for her—a neat instance of *coincidentia oppositorum* in personal relations. The next day, she returns to the forest of her own free will, giving Jamie the opportunity to take what he had left her the day before—a step that will lead to the very unfairytale-like predicament of her pregnancy.

After she begins to live with her robber lover, her psychological state also bears witness to the real-life adult's need for the state of tension created by the simultaneity of apparent contraries. In the robber's cottage, she is perfectly happy, we are told, except that "she had never seen her lover's face. But then the heart cannot live without something to sorrow and be curious over." So even the happiness of love is incomplete without sorrow, which passes in the world of the simple as totally alien to love.

Rosamond's doubleness is even more complexly present in her difference from and similarity to Salome. At first the two seem absolute opposites. An early description establishes their contrast: "For if Rosamond was as beautiful as the day, Salome was as ugly as the night. . . ." But as in the case of the yin-yang principle, Salome and Rosamond share points of contact and dynamic exchange. Like so many opposites in Welty's fiction, these two begin to reveal their similarities, especially after Rosamond is initiated into love, that business so likely to introduce us to life's complicated reality. It is probably not so much ironic as appropriate in a world where opposites meet that the place where Jamie first made love to Rosamond is the same place where Clement had married Salome: ". . . there under the meeting trees at the edge." When Rosamond tells her father and stepmother of her marriage to the bandit, Salome senses her kinship with Rosamond: ". . . at that moment the stepmother gave Rosamond a look of true friendship, as if Rosamond too had got her man by unholy means." And when Salome voices the doubts that Rosamond feels about her lover's identity, "Salome drew so close to Rosamond that they could look down the well and see one shadow, and whispered in her ear. . . ." She is as surely Rosamond's shadow self as the Little Harp is Jamie's. Thus it is fitting that Salome die when Rosamond moves toward integration of the parts of her self, just as Little Harp does when Jamie starts on a similar path.

The attitude toward life conveyed by *The Robber Bridegroom* is as double as Jamie's and Rosamond's identities are. It parallels the splicing of the fairy tale tone to the real horrors of murder, rape, and other savage doings that fill the story. In *The Robber Bridegroom* Welty has given us a story about which we could write precisely what she wrote about Chekhov's stories:

> Yet—Chekhov goes on to say—'Life is terrible and marvelous, and so, however terrible a story you tell in Russia, however you embroider it with nests of robbers, long knives and such marvels, it always finds an echo of reality in the soul of the listener. . . . [Real life] was of itself so marvelous and terrible that the fantastic stories of legend and fairy tale were pale and blended with life.'

Terrible and marvelous—that is the estimation of life Welty gives us in *The Robber Bridegroom*. ("Life is sweet," Rosamond has said, even as she is being robbed; her name, "rose of the world," implies in the old image of flower and thorns both the beauty and pain of life.) It is a perspective very like the Buddhist outlook described by Joseph Campbell in *Myths to Live By:*

> 'All life,' said the Buddha, 'is sorrowful'; and so, indeed, it is. Life consuming life: that is the essence of its being, which is forever a becoming. 'The world,' said the Buddha, 'is an ever-burning fire.' And so it is. And that is what one has to affirm, with a yea! a dance! a knowing, solemn, stately dance of the mystic bliss beyond pain that is at the heart of every mythic rite.

The Robber Bridegroom is one of Welty's dances, acknowledging this insight—not stately so much as spritely, a laugh and a hurrah in the face of horror. And the horror is very much acknowledged, even in this tale so widely read as light-hearted entertainment. The undertone of horror accompanying the wonder of life is introduced early in the story. The first paragraph ends with the declaration, "the way home through the wilderness was beset with dangers," creating a sense of the threats that surround and (if we remember the symbolism of the wilderness) live within the human psyche. The theme of human cruelty to other humans is introduced in the first chapter. The first two innkeepers Clement encounters have lost ears for horse stealing and cock-fighting. While their cropped ears seem funny at the outset, deeper inside the tale we realize that the mutilation

of the criminals is but a societally sanctioned version of the mutilation of the Indian girl by Little Harp. Then, after the slapstick attempt by Mike Fink to kill Clement and Jamie, we are chilled with the almost sickening tale of the treatment of Clement's party by their Indian captors. Humiliation, torture, murder have left Clement with "less than nothing." Not a funny story, it is hard for readers to bear because we know that every act of cruelty detailed by Clement has been perpetrated by one human on another, again and again, around the world, throughout history.

> **The desire to push beyond the view of life as *simplex,* into knowledge of its real multiplicity Welty identified as the motivation behind the plot in *The Robber Bridegroom*. The truth in the story, she wrote, lies in the need "to find out what we all wish to find out, exactly who we are, and who the other fellow is, and what we are doing here all together."**
> **—*Barbara Harrell Carson***

Indeed, for all the rollicking gaiety of its surface, *The Robber Bridegroom* presents one of Welty's darkest visions of reality, a darkness intensified by Clement's perception of a cosmic horror in which humans appear as "little mice" in a life seen as "a maze without end." Psychological forces are as mysterious as the powers of nature. Clement cannot even remember why he came into the wilderness; all he knows is that "there was a great tug at the whole world, to go down over the edge, . . . and our hearts and our own lonely will may have had nothing to do with it." Just as frightening as the mystery of causality is the uncontrollable domino effect of human actions (yet another expression of the tangled nature of reality). Jamie determines to rescue Rosamond, saying, ". . . when I went off and left her, I had no idea what a big thing would come of it." In spite of this recognition, however, human will is ineffectual in fighting life's horror. It is not Jamie who rescues Rosamond, but the stupid Goat. And when Clement, uncharacteristically moved from passivity, determines to rescue his daughter himself, he ends up wrestling all night with a monster that turns out to be a willow tree. If this were not a comedy, protected by its fairy tale wrappings, a character like Clement would surely be driven mad by the cruel, senseless, and overpowering forces of life that assail him. Hearing that the gentleman he trusted to rescue his daughter is the bandit who stole her clothes, her honor, and her heart, he forgets his own wisdom about life's doubleness and retreats into the forest (the appropriate place for encounters with horrors within and without), demanding exactness from a world that will not furnish it:

> 'What exactly is this now? . . . Wrath and love burn

only like campfires. And even the appearance of a hero is no longer a single and majestic event like that of a star in the heavens, but a wandering fire soon lost. A journey is forever lonely and parallel to death, but the two watch each other, the traveler and the bandit, through the trees. Like will-o-the-wisps the little blazes burn on the rafts all night, unsteady beside the shore. Where are they even so soon as tomorrow? Massacre is hard to tell from the performance of other rites, in the great silence where the wanderer is coming. Murder is as soundless as a spout of blood, as regular and rhythmic as sleep. Many find a skull and a little branching of bones between two floors of leaves. In the sky is the perpetual wheel of buzzards. A circle of bandits counts out the gold, with bending shoulders more slaves mount the block and go down, a planter makes a gesture of abundance with his riding whip, a flatboatman falls back from the tavern door to the river below with scarcely time for a splash, a rope descends from a tree and curls into a noose. And all around again are the Indians.

'Yet no one can laugh or cry so savagely in this wilderness as to be heard by the nearest traveler or remembered next year. A fiddle played in a finished hut in a clearing is as vagrant as the swamp breeze. What will the seasons be, when we are lost and dead? The dreadful heat and cold—no more than the shooting star.'

Love and wrath, massacres and mysteries, bandits and slaveowners, music and a swamp breeze—all become equal in insignificance before the rolling seasons, and the only solace seems to be a recognition of the transience and insignificance of everything. Clement could be the prophet of Ecclesiastes crying out on the vanity of life. As he watches Salome going to her death, he looks at the faces of the surrounding Indians and thinks: "The savages have only come the sooner to their end; we will come to ours too. Why have I built my house, and added to it? The planter will go after the hunter, and the merchant after the planter, all having their day."

The monstrous, self-devouring quality of life is captured in Clement's musings, but clearly this is only the dark center of Welty's tale. For while Clement's thoughts imply the question, "If this is what life is like, why go on?", go on he does. And he can go on, and Rosamond and Jamie can too, because they glimpse something of the whole of Welty's insight. Her story unites a confrontation with the monstrousness of life with a recognition of its wonder, a vision that transforms wandering in a maze into a dance. This evaluation of life is very similar to that reflected in the Hindu legend about the God Shiva. Confronted by a demon

demanding that Shiva hand over his wife, the world-goddess Parvati, Shiva hit the earth with lightning and created a new demon which he commanded to eat the first. The first demon threw himself on Shiva's mercy and was forgiven. Bound by the god's original order, the second demon asked, "What shall I eat now?" To which Shiva replied, "Well, let's see: why not eat yourself." And so the demon began, eating its own feet, belly, chest, neck. Joseph Campbell, who tells the story charmingly, continues:

> And the god, thereupon, was enchanted. For here at last was a perfect image of the monstrous thing that is life, which lives on itself. And to that sunlike mask, which was now all that was left of that lionlike vision of hunger, Shiva said, exulting, 'I shall call you Face of Glory, Kirttimukha, and you shall shine above the doors to all my temples. No one who refuses to honor and worship you will come ever to knowledge of me.'

> The obvious lesson of all of which is that the first step to the knowledge of the highest divine symbol of the wonder and mystery of life and its glory in that character: the realization that this is just how it is and that it cannot and will not be changed. . . . So if you really want to help this world, what you will have to teach is how to live in it. And that no one can do who has not himself learned how to live in it the joyful sorrow and sorrowful joy of the knowledge of life as it is.

It is in the teaching of how to live in such a world that Welty's tale offers help for travellers in life's wilderness, alive as it is with Indians, outlaws, and wild animals. She has no secret to make the threats go away, but she knows what will help us live with the horrors surrounding us. Surely part of her "program" is the recognition of the doubleness of life that the book reveals, an awareness of its marvelous as well as its terrible side.

The second part of Welty's strategy for survival is the old one: to have someone to love may make the world seem less terrifying, even if it does nothing to change objective reality. Clement suggests the power of love when he laments: "My wife will build a tower to overlook the boundaries of her land, while I ride its woods and know it to be a maze without end, because my love is lost in it." It is the lost love that makes the world seem a maze.

However, Welty makes clear that the mere physical presence of the loved one is not enough for sustained solace. Even though Rosamond lies by Jamie's side, "she would look out the window and see a cloud put up a mask over the secret face of the moon, and she would hear the pitiful cries of the night creatures. Then it was enough to make her afraid, as if the whole world were circled by a band of Indian savages. . . ." And her fear all wells from the fact that in spite of her study of Jamie's face "she did not know the language it was written in." For love to alleviate the night terrors of existence, it must be love of a whole self by a whole self. That full achievement of this lies beyond human achievement is life's eternal tragedy. However, the closer we approach it, the more effective will be love's protection. Rosamond and Jamie have consummated their love, but each recognizes only half of the other's identity. It is this that makes theirs a false marriage, not just the drunken priest who performed the ceremony.

The desire to push beyond the view of life as *simplex,* into knowledge of its real multiplicity Welty identified as the motivation behind the plot in ***The Robber Bridegroom.*** The truth in the story, she wrote, lies in the need "to find out what we all wish to find out, exactly who we are, and who the other fellow is, and what we are doing here all together." Yet, oddly enough, in the same essay Welty says that in washing off Jamie's disguise Rosamond is making "the classic mistake." So which is it? Is the desire to know others a way to mitigate the pain of life or is it an unforgivable trespass? To an extent, Welty's answer is a perverse Yes—it is both.

More precisely, the novel suggests that there are right and wrong reasons for trying to fathom another's identity. The story opens with the wrong one. Mike Fink threatens to reveal the other part of Jamie's identity in order to have power over him. In silencing Mike Fink, Jamie makes an important distinction: "Say who I am forever, but dare to say *what* I am, and that will be the last breath of any man." Later Clement asks Jamie's name so he can express his gratitude, but he does not ask "*what* you may be." The problem with having handy names or labels for the multiple parts of a human identity is that they can fool us into thinking that we have psychological understanding or "control" of the other person, that we have reduced the mystery of his or her full selfhood.

While it is natural to want protection from the reduction of self symbolized by the threats of Mike Fink and Little Harp to reveal what Jamie is, Welty reiterates in her essays and stories the view that the most pitiful life is one that has been made invulnerable. Certainly the outcome of ***The Robber Bridegroom*** seems to justify Rosamond's attempt to discover Jamie's identity. As a consequence of her act, Jamie's dual selves are integrated, and he and Rosamond are truly married. However, the initial consequence of Rosamond's penetration of Jamie's disguise is the rupture of their relationship, because she has asked for a label, not for an introduction to Jamie's fuller self.

The cause of Rosamond's growing need to know Jamie's identity is significant. As long as their life together is blissful (that is, as long as it has fairy tale perfection), she can accept the mystery. However, with the arrival of Little Harp in their cabin and the death of the Indian girl, the simple happiness she and Jamie shared is threatened. The threat comes from the insidious invasion of her own awareness of Jamie's shadow self—a self she cannot accept and that she, in the form of the psychologically projected Indian maiden, finds terrifying:

> . . . she was torn as she had never been before with an anguish to know his name and his true appearance. For the coming of death and danger had only driven her into her own heart, and it was no matter what he had told her, she could wait no longer to learn the identity of her true love.

Multiplex reality has displaced fairy tale simplicity; Rosamond has entered the world we inhabit. Unfortunately, her reaction to her discovery that her bandit is also Jamie Lockhart does not lead her immediately away from isolation into union with another. Instead of seeing and accepting the sad and joyous human mystery, she retreats to simplistic labelling, and Jamie responds in kind:

> 'You are Jamie Lockhart!' she said.
> 'And you are Clement Musgrove's silly daughter!' said he.
> 'Good-by,' he said. 'For you did not trust me, and did not love me,
> for you wanted only to know who I am. Now I cannot stay in the house with you.'

We recall that Jamie was willing for Mike Fink to declare *who* he was, but not *what* he was. By seeking merely his name, Rosamond has chosen the least important part of Jamie's identity (one available even to his enemies), condemning herself to superficial knowledge of Jamie.

And yet Rosamond's impulse is not entirely wrong. Jamie, in hiding part of himself from the one who loves him, is endangering their love. Rosamond sounds at least partially right when she cries, after Jamie has left her:

> 'My husband was a robber and not a bridegroom. . . . He brought me his love under a mask, and kept all the truth hidden from me, and never called anything by its true name, even his name or mine, and what I would have given him he liked better to steal.'

What she learns, however, is that "names were nothing and united no knots." She has to move past the stage where she can assert: ". . . I already know everything and can learn nothing new." Goat's reply to that declaration ("Do not be so sad as all that . . .") is not the *non-sequitur* it seems. Few states are sadder than thinking we have figured out all life's mysteries—especially the mysteries about other people. To get beyond the labels of "Jamie Lockhart" or "robber" or "Clement's silly daughter"—to appreciate the complex humanity on the other side of the name—that is when the universal search for "who we are and who the other fellow is" might pay off.

In Welty's story as in folk fairy tales, the woman is the one who pushes for integration. The message that Rosamond sends Jamie "out of the future"—from their twins to be born next week—makes very real the power of the female suasion to unification. Rosamond's role is much like that ascribed by Bettelheim to the women in other tales who suspect they are married to beastly bridegrooms:

> . . . one very significant feature of the animal-groom cycle . . . [is that] the groom is absent during the night; he is believed to be animal during the day and to become human only in bed; in short, he keeps his day and night existences separate from each other: . . . he wishes to keep his sex life separated from all else he is doing. The female . . . is unwilling to accept the separation and isolation of purely sexual aspects of life from the rest of it. She tries to force their unification. But once Psyche embarks on trying to wed the aspects of sex, love, and life into a unity, she does not falter, and in the end she wins.

Like Psyche, Rosamond does not falter. She does her penance for asking the wrong questions about her lover's identity. Following Jamie's path along the tangled wilderness of the Natchez Trace, she is "tattered and torn, and tired from sleeping in hollow trees and keeping awake in the woods." The imagery here implies both enlightenment and acceptance of the unity of apparent opposites (in this case, the human unity with the natural world).

In the last chapter we feel the book's emerging from its dark inner core (where we watched the death of the Indian girl, the robber band, Little Harp, and Salome), its returning to the realm of fairy tale. Mike Fink joins Rosamond now as he did Jamie in the beginning. (But even he is chastened and improved, shaken from his blustering self-importance by his encounters with what he takes to be Jamie's ghost.) The idyllic life Jamie and Rosamond establish in New Orleans is our best hint that a fairy tale version of reality dominates as the novella ends. Yet even in this conclusion Welty reminds us of the doubleness of reality that Rosamond and Jamie fail to see—in spite of their personal integration (or, perhaps, because of the protection it offers from life's darker side). Describing their life to her father, Rosamond sketches a happy-ever-after world, complete with beautiful twins, a stately house, a boat, servants, and rich friends. For the moment their eyes are not on the wilderness that still surrounds them or the Indians that inhabit it. And yet Welty's concluding references to Rosamond and Jamie's "hundred slaves" and to the pirates' galleons they sail out to watch, as well as to Clement's return to the wilderness, remind us that evil is closer than they may be aware—"with us, within us," as Welty has declared. Thus, while Jamie and Rosamond have returned to life in a fairy tale, the reader carries away the corrected vision of a reality in which darkness and light, hope and despair, joy and sorrow, beginnings and endings are dynamically united in the terrible and marvelous cosmic dance.

Floyd C. Watkins (essay date Spring 1988)

SOURCE: "Death and the Mountains in *The Optimist's Daughter*," in *Essays in Literature*, Vol. 15, No. 1, Spring, 1988, pp. 77-85.

[*In the following essay, Watkins discusses the importance of mountains in Welty's life and in her novel* The Optimist's Daughter.]

The pervasive relationship between character and place in fiction is especially important and subtle in the fiction of Eudora Welty. Place derives not only from natural geographical characteristics but also from human history and the events that have happened there. In one of several lectures and essays on the subject, Welty comments on the endurance of life in place, which transcends time, locality, and changes in the terrain:

> Whatever is significant and whatever is tragic in its story live as long as the place does, though they are unseen, and the new life will be built upon these things—regardless of commerce and the way of rivers and roads, and other vagrancies.

It follows that the old life, then, goes into the place and emerges in a new life of new personages, who in turn become a part of the complexity of the place which continues to grow along with the addition of new events to old.

Central to the understanding of Welty's fiction is this union of place and person; her works, therefore, must be interpreted according to the way the psyche or the soul is affected by place and the events and culture of a place. Most of Welty's works have been set in her own state of Mississippi, which seems generally and perhaps erroneously to be regarded politically and culturally as one of the most homogeneous states in the country. Welty's fiction, however, is certainly not homogeneous. the people and the culture differ greatly from one book to another. There are stories about the Mississippi Delta in *Delta Wedding;* about the hill country of northern Mississippi in **"A Piece of News"** and *Losing Battles;* about the early American history and culture of Natchez in *The Robber Bridegroom* and some of the short stories; about the black Mississippians in such stories as **"Powerhouse," "Keela, the Outcast Indian Maiden,"** and **"A Worn Path"**; and about the life of many small towns around Jackson and in southern Mississippi in *The Golden Apples, The Ponder Heart,* and other works.

Welty has not turned often and significantly to settings outside Mississippi except in one novel *The Optimist's Daughter*—which is also her only fiction based extensively on her own life and that of her family. This novel is so personal to her that she has restricted the use of the manuscript even by scholars. It is the only story of the visits of Welty and her mother during the summers of Welty's childhood to the ancestral home on Blue Knob, the mountain above the Elk River in Clay, West Virginia.

The West Virginia mountains are different from the flatlands of Mississippi, and out of that difference grows much of the style and the meaning of *The Optimist's Daughter.* Chestina (or Chessy) Andrews Welty (Eudora's mother) refused ever to be convinced that Mississippi was not flat, and similarly Becky McKelva asks in the novel where the mountain is in Mount Salus. Becky, Welty says in an interview, "has her deepest roots in another place, that's the thing that most changed her life—a feeling of being out of place, in a place to which she has never really resigned herself. . . ." Further, Welty admits, "I did draw on some of the childhood and early married experiences of my own mother. That's the only thing that is 'factual'; and the character of Becky, the mother, is not the character of my mother, but it draws upon it." Usually Welty is an author of humor and subtle high comedy rather than the creator of dark tragedies like those written by her fellow Mississippian from the northern part of the state. The sickness and death of Judge McKelva in New Orleans, the wake over him with the serious mourning of his daughter (Laurel) and the antic buffoonery of his younger wife (Fay), and the actions of the community of Mount Salus during his funeral maintain a comic view of life in the larger sense of the term until after the funeral. When the wife, Fay, leaves to visit her home in Texas, and Laurel goes into her mother's sewing room to ponder her life and the lives of her parents, the novel turns to recollections of life in West Virginia, to darker memories, and to contemplations of the tragic moments of those who are dying and those who must stand by and watch the agonies and loneliness of the deathbed.

Becky's strong will, strength, and independence are admirable qualities, but they are also responsible for her tragic flaw: she uses that strength to fight inevitable death and to accuse all those who surround her in her moment of death. Whatever temperament and character she derived from the mountains intensifies her resentment, her hostility, her accusations, her anger at mortality and at herself and at those who cannot enable her to avoid death and who cannot go with her into that dark night. In *One Writer's Beginnings* Welty reveals how she herself gained from the mountains particular virtues like her mother's. In explaining her indebtedness to the mountains, she provides a strong clue to the meaning of the novel. When Welty visited her mother's childhood home, she, like Becky, gained particular virtues attributable to the West Virginia heights:

> It took the mountain top, it seems to me now, to give me the sensation of independence. It was as if I'd discovered something I'd never tested before my short life. Or rediscovered it—for I associated it with the taste of the water that came out of the well, accompanied with the ring of that long metal sleeve against the sides of the living mountain, as from deep down it was wound up to view brimming and streaming long drops behind it like bright stars on a ribbon. . . . The coldness, the far, unseen, unheard springs of what was in my mouth now, the iron strength of its flavor that drew my cheeks in, its fern-laced smell, all said mountain mountain mountain as I swallowed. Every swallow was making me a part of being here, sealing me in place.

Both Eudora Welty and Becky McKelva derive strength from the West Virginia mountains of their mothers' younger years. Laurel enters the past through her memories as they are stimulated when she goes through the twenty-six pigeonholes of her mother's desk after her death. Here she had stored all things "according to their time and place" except for the letters from the Judge. This is the process of discovery, not only of her mother but also of herself. The inner sanctum, the little sewing room where Laurel had "slept in infancy," is a source for whatever understandings she will ever attain. Here at the desk Laurel looks through the mementos of her mother and father's courtship and marriage. These items transport her back to the familial past, and she contemplates that time of family life which is so often a void in the mind of a child and the stories told to a child. Perhaps more than anything else the account of Laurel's memories of her mother's past helps us to arrive at the ultimate theme of the novel. Welty's return to her own childhood and then to her own mother's home and even her mother's childhood in a faraway country is an indication of continuity and, paradoxically, also of change:

> Laurel had been taken "up home" to West Virginia since a summer before she remembered. The house was built on top of what might as well have been already the highest roof in the world. . . . From a

rocking chair could be seen the river where it rounded the foot of the mountain. . . . This point of the river was called Queen's Shoals.

In *The Optimist's Daughter* Welty conveys the remoteness and isolation of the family and of the imagination by stressing the altitude. She removes the novel and Becky from the ordinary world and emphasizes the arduousness of their ordeals when it is necessary for them to enter the outer world.

As a child Laurel herself heard the solitary sounds of the mountain wilderness primeval in West Virginia and asked her grandmother about their mysteries. Early in the morning a sound traveled from one stillness to another, "a blow, then . . . its echo, then another blow, then the echo, then a shouting." The boys, her uncles, interpret literally: "It's just an old man chopping wood." The mother is mysterious and religious: "He's praying." The grandmother, perhaps with the loneliness of older age, says that it is "an old hermit . . . without a soul in the world." Decades later after the mother's death, Laurel, alone in her mother's sewing room, is still contemplating the possibilities of various meanings.

The image of the old man chopping wood and of the distinct sound on the mountain is further developed by the image of the bell on the mountain. "In sight of the door there was an iron bell mounted on a post. If anything were ever to happen, Grandma only needed to ring this bell." Its sound conveys isolation and need from the lonely one to those who are being summoned. This image recalls Laurel's first arrival in West Virginia. She and her mother descended from the train, which left them "by themselves on a steep rock . . . and its own iron bell on a post with its rope hanging down." There is a "mist," which mysteriously obstructs vision but not sound. A pull on the bell, "and close to them appeared a gray boat with two of the boys at the oars. At their very feet had been the river. The boat came breasting out of the mist, and in they stepped. All new things in life were meant to come like that." Not only is it a sudden and (to Laurel) surprising appearance; it is almost a manifestation. Becky and Laurel's having only a large rock for a railroad station and then crossing the river in fog creates great mystery in the mind of a small child.

Becky's mountain home is described with a style appropriate to the pastoral mountains. The beauty comes from images, such as "bird dogs . . . streaking the upslanted pasture through the sweet long grass," the blue valley beneath the mountain, and pigeons which "came down to her feet and walked on the mountain." Again, especially for the child, there is the suggestion of a visitation. The pigeons are both beautiful and repulsive, puzzling and ugly in their relationships with each other, "sticking their beaks down each other's throats, gagging each other, eating out of each other's craws, swallowing down all over again what had

been swallowed before." Their community may suggest love, but it also ambivalently suggests a repulsive and excessive dependence: "they could not escape each other." Their feeding and digestion is fearful and ugly to the child, but the grandmother explains simply that it is just hunger.

Life in the mountains may occasionally be beautiful and even awesome, but it is also fraught with labors and trials, especially in the time before the new methods of rapid transportation. The greatest trial of Becky's days, certainly those before marriage, came with the illness and then the death of her father.

> Becky had gone with her father, who was suffering pain, on a raft propelled by a neighbor, down the river at night when it was filled with ice, to reach a railroad, to wave a lantern at a snow train that would stop and take them on, to reach a hospital.

In Baltimore, she tells the doctors (her father was delirious) what he had said: "If you let them tie me down, I'll die." She can do no more, go no farther. "Baltimore was as far a place as you could go with those you loved, and it was where they left you."

Eudora Welty has taken this story directly from the pages of her family history. The only printed account I have been able to find of the death of Edward (Ned) Raboteau Andrews (the grandfather of Eudora Welty) was recorded on the second page of the Clay County *Star* of March 30, 1899. Most of the story in the fiction appears in only one sentence in the newspaper: "His daughter, Miss Chessie, accompanied him."

After recalling Becky's strength on the journey, Laurel remembers the deathbed conversation between her mother and her father, and then she again recollects West Virginia. She recalls how Becky asked for "spiritual guidance." The young Presbyterian minister, Dr. Bolt, was called to her side, and she rejected him and his attempts to offer solace. She told him, apparently as an indication of his ignorance of her needs and his inability to comfort her or counsel her, "I'd like better than anything you can tell me just to see the mountain one more time." The crowning glory of the mountain which she describes to him is the white strawberry, an actual kind of wild plant, an image, and a beautiful if eerie symbol. It

> grows completely in the wild, . . . very likely . . . in only one spot in the world. . . . I doubt if you'd see them growing after you got there. . . . You could line your hat with leaves and try to walk off with a hatful: that would be how little you knew about those berries. Once you've let them so much as

touch each other, you've already done enough to finish 'em. . . . Nothing you ever ate in your life was anything like as delicate, as fragrant, as those wild white strawberries.

The strawberries are the last image in the passage about the glories and the meanings of the mountains. They are the ultimate in beauty, in physical taste, in rarity, in delicacy. Metaphorically, they are the incarnation of the wonders of the mountain and the beauties and the strengths of Becky the child. They are also a gift of God, a greater gift than anything said to Becky by the young preacher.

Strawberries like those Becky describes actually grew at what is called the Point, the hill which starts the rise to the Andrews farm above the junction of what is now West Virginia Route 4 and Route 16. Mrs. Lois Andrews Cleland, daughter of Carl (one of the Andrews "boys" and later Mayor of Charleston, West Virginia), is the only person I have talked to who has actually seen these strawberries. Carl Andrews took his children to see them some time before Miss Welty wrote about them in *The Optimist's Daughter.* Mrs. Cleland quotes him as saying that just to smell the white strawberries is much more delightful than eating the usual red ones. As the climactic image about the Andrews farm and the mountains of Clay, West Virginia, the strawberries are a supreme beauty with profound meanings. They constitute the final part of the narrative about Becky's West Virginia childhood.

Becky fails to overcome time and death. But the strawberries represent false hopes for long life and at least near-immortality. Welty suggests theological and religious implications by having Becky tell her story on her deathbed to a minister who cannot overcome his insensitivity or understand such wonder. The basic crux of the emotional conditions and the harsh conflicts of the novel are revealed in Laurel's contemplations of the deathbed scene of her mother. Child of the mountains, Becky McKelva was not tolerant of the lowlands. After all the years in Mississippi, at crucial moments her spirit sought strength in the mountains. The desperate accusations and imprecations she hurls at her daughter and her husband on her deathbed are anticipated throughout her life; she never lost her soul's citizenship in the mountains and became naturalized in the place of her home after marriage.

The Optimist's Daughter is conspicuous among Welty's works for its symbolic use of high place. "The high place," Leonard Lutwack says in *The Role of Place in Literature,* "inspires feelings of elation, domination, transcendence; it is the traditional home of poetry." Mountains or high places, furthermore, do not exist without low places between them or on which they stand. There are no mountains without valleys. Mountain literature, then, is the scene of changes, con-

trast, variety. Level places without mountains or valleys, produce monotony, even weakness. Lutwack's study of place in literature provides insight into the West Virginia scenes of *The Optimist's Daughter:* "Scaling heights," he writes, "is a test of character, and the conflict of adversaries is accentuated when it occurs in a high place." On the other hand, "The promise of greatness in a high place . . . may turn into disaster, for under Mount Etna yawns the volcano." The specific and important truth must be slightly rephrased for *The Optimist's Daughter.* Coming out of the mountains by necessity (the trip to Baltimore) or by choice (the chance for a happy marriage in Jackson) signifies risk, hope, danger, and even death. The crossings of a desert or of prairies surrounded by hostile Indians or peoples have the same omens. But the forebodings and dangers are not the same in mountains as on flat crosscountry trips. The twists and turns and rises and falls, the very surprises of the mountains in the many forms which they may take, add great complexities even if they do not increase substantially the risks. Dangers in the mountains and valleys tend to be sudden; in the prairies, they are prolonged, as they intensify in suffering and simultaneously in monotony. Flat places are not, as Lutwack says, necessarily "safe, restful, reassuring." They may be too dry, too rocky, and too far to cross without water. The beauties of the mountains of the Andrews farm, known as Blue Knob, are striking, but perils and trials also come along with the beauty.

The mother, Becky, does not have a prominent role in the novel until the account of her dying. The ultimate fact of life for all, death, is the great change, the moving into oblivion or another world depending on religion and beliefs. The most inescapable and normal thing in the world, it seems the most horrible. It is the ultimate experience not only in terms of the final disposition of body and soul, but also in terms of the definition of character as it is confronted in the drawing of the last breath.

Becky's trip to Baltimore with her father to his death was a foreshadowing of her own dying. She says as her father had before her, "Don't let them tie me down. . . . If they try to hold me, I'll die." Baltimore was an ultimate test of Becky's strength. She had known no one there, but she "had known herself." She trusts no one at the time of her dying, and with great anger and independence she turns from her husband into herself. Because the Judge can do no more than she herself has done, she calls him a coward, a Lucifer, and a Liar. When the Judge dies years later, his daughter, Laurel, stands by his bedside as his main companion if not comforter. He asks no questions; he listens to Laurel's reading "without much comment." His silence is puzzling and difficult to interpret. He dies without uttering a word, asking no quarter from death.

Mysteriously, in the last moments the Judge has "the smile

of a child who is hiding in the dark while the others hunt him, waiting to be found." Whether he goes into that dark night passively or with quiet strength is not clearly apparent. He dies alone with no relative by his bedside. Dr. Courtland says, "The renegade! I believe he's just plain sneaked out on us." The silence of his deathbed is entirely different from the five-year illness of Becky and her defiant accusations while the Judge attempts to promise, placate, comfort, reassure her.

When the Judge died, Laurel meditates among the mysteries of the sewing room, she had not saved him as she had not saved her mother. She was not by his bedside but on the way to the hospital room. Neither had Becky saved her father. "But Becky was the brave one," Laurel remembers, suggesting that no mortal can save another from death. Because of her courage she was most irascible and accusatory when her own time came to die. One characteristic—and only one—is the same in the deaths of the Judge and his wife. He dies in silence, and she, after first blaming herself and others, suffers a stroke and also becomes silent: ("She had died without speaking a word, keeping everything to herself, in exile and humiliation."). Becky had blamed herself for not saving her father, the Judge, for his promises at her deathbed, and Laurel for not saving her: "You could have saved your mother's life. But you stood by and wouldn't intervene. [*How could she*?] I despair for you."

Another complexity of human experience is represented by the Judge's taking his wife's death as a matter of natural process. "He seemed to give the changes his same, kind recognition—to accept them because they had to be only of the time being." Becky had reacted to news of her mother's death in an altogether different way. It is unexpected, and "uncontrollably" Becky cries: "I wasn't there! I wasn't *there!*" Despite her strength and genuine sentiment, she could have done nothing if she had been there, just as the trip to Baltimore had been a heroic but futile confrontation with death. She assumes blame for the death of her mother, because of her own absence at the time of that death. The Judge tells her that she is not to blame, but she anticipates her deathbed accusations of him by bringing up the question of lying. As she will accuse him of being a liar just before she dies, she now says, "You can't make me lie to myself, Clinton!" Becky is strongest at the time of the death of another character, her father; but in her encounter with her own death, strength and independence turn into anger at her own mortality and into the inability of her kin to help her overcome her death or endure it with her. Indeed, the greater the strength of the dying, Miss Welty seems to suggest, the greater the suggestion of weakness of character in the last moments of life.

The Judge's strength and optimism are not good companions by the bedside of the dying; they are, instead, an annoyance. Death often causes conflicts between loved ones. Becky blames the Judge for sufferings imposed by others: "Why do you persist in letting them hurt me?" No well person can respond to a question like that. Within the father and the Judge there are conflicts between an optimistic belief that "all his wife's troubles would turn out all right," and "horror of any sort of private clash," and "his good hope, trust in one another." Conflict seldom, perhaps never, reaches greater depths than when Becky angrily and futilely questions why she married a coward, or greater ambiguity than when she takes "his hand to help him bear it." Bear what? The fact that he is a coward in the face of death, or that his wife thinks he is and calls him one? It is not a pretty picture for either of them.

After Becky calls him a coward, the Judge promises to take her back to the mountains, almost seeming to hope that there is or will be no death. But knowing that there is death and that it is coming to her and that her husband's promises are false optimism or lies, she calls him "Lucifer! . . . *Liar!*" When he refuses "to consider that she was desperate," his attitude is summed up—apparently in Laurel's memories of her mother's anger at his "betrayal on betrayal." Becky's attitude toward death and toward the death-watcher at her bedside establishes the conditions for the deathbed scenes throughout the novel. Her comments are mysterious if not altogether inexplicable, and they do seem to be the climactic statements of the relationships between characters and of the meanings of all the novel. The ultimate interpretations of these mysteries, as nearly as I can understand them, are that the dying hate the privilege that their survivors have of living after the death, that they are angry that it is impossible for the living to accompany the dying into death, that the living may betray the memory and life of the dead after they have died.

Baltimore and Mount Salus are both utterly mortal, and no one can go beyond that. The living and dying must unclasp hands and go their separate ways. It is not logical or theological or indeed even sensible and sane for the dying to expect the living to go along with them. Death, as Emily Dickinson writes, stops kindly for some who do not have time to stop for him, but he is not kindly to others, certainly not kindly to Becky, who struggles mightily against him. The final statements by Becky are not lucid and rational, but that does not make those statements any less real to her or to those who helplessly watch her die. At the ultimate moment death has its sting and its victory even if no one acknowledges its finality.

The strength of place and mountains may be used for defiance as well as for comfort, may increase anger, may add to the intensity of despair. A strong soul may struggle to reject death itself, as Milton's Satan rejects God and even his own fall. Becky herself rather than the Judge may resemble the rebellious Lucifer. Her body comes to death while her strong soul is not ready to stop for it, and she casts about in accusation of others. Ultimately the tragedy of *The Optimist's Daughter* is that the great strength derived from a childhood home in the mountains increases the last despair.

The deaths of the Judge and of Becky have prepared for Laurel's memories of the death of her husband, Phil, and her speculations about what it means to survive the one you love:

> The guilt of outliving those you love is justly to be borne, she thought. Outliving is something we do to them. The fantasies of dying could be no stranger than the fantasies of living. Surviving is perhaps the strangest fantasy of them all.

The precise choice of the world *guilt* is fraught with implications. Guilt results from something the survivor does to the dying. Becky believed that. But it is a *feeling* of guilt, not a moral wrong, not a moral choice. Here is, indeed, the mystery and the culmination of the novel, and it seems to me that it is inexplicable, a statement that defies interpretation. It is as mysterious as the ultimate theological mysteries: how evil came to be, for example, if God is omniscient, omnipotent, and *omni bene volens*. Death is the father of mysteries. How can Laurel be guilty? How can the well-wishing and loving Judge be a coward, a betrayer, a Lucifer? What is death that we are mindful of it and guilty because of it without action and decision? No one knows. Yet, Laurel and Becky accuse, we the living are guilty.

James Walter (essay date Fall 1988)

SOURCE: "Place Dissolved In Grace: Welty's *Losing Battles*," in *The Southern Literary Journal*, Vol. XXI, No. 1, Fall, 1988, pp. 39-53.

[*In the following essay, Walter discusses Welty's* Losing Battles.]

The more one gets to know Eudora Welty's characters and to observe her construction of worlds in words and images, the more difficulty one has in seeing a division between objective and subjective, outward and inward. Her physical locales, though faithful renderings of the world's appearance in convincing visual detail, are always also figures of the thought, emotions, and dreams of her characters and narrators; and usually what wisdom her characters achieve is by way of imaginative awareness of their place as a reflector of their own and time's deepest secrets. Welty's characters typically begin in their stories with attitudes or beliefs settled

in routine or tradition and sometimes hardened by a defensiveness resulting from experience of losing battles with life. Despite their accommodation, however, life turns out for them in much the same way that Judge Moody in *Losing Battles* says it turned out for Miss Mortimer: "What she didn't know till she got to it was what could *happen* to what she was." What can "happen" is hardly ever what was anticipated nor is it ever very securely within human control; rather it unfolds at the prompting of a mysterious shaping spirit alive in particular conjunctions of place, event, and human purpose. The action of this gracious spirit can be read in its dissolution of old and settled perspectives, its opening of minds and hearts to others, and its promotion of new more inclusive communities.

In *Losing Battles,* Welty's characters, almost despite themselves, are being gradually transformed by some dissolving and annealing power in time—a power that might be called grace, because of its gratuitous and generally sanctifying effect. What finally happens to most of the actors in Welty's novel is analogous to what Moody expresses when he says, in responding to a mood sent him in the air, that Miss Mortimer's life-story "could make a stone cry." Somehow, by virtue of a power laboring in the very body of the world, this human transformation comes *out of* the very stone— through inevitable experience that while threatening to harden feeling can also temper a capacity for sympathy.

The main action of Welty's novel, one sees by opening to almost any page, is constant talk among the numerous members of three related families—Vaughn, Beecham, and Renfro—gathered to celebrate a family reunion in the Mississippi hill country during the hard times and drought of summer 1930. Physically unifying and defining the place is its atmosphere: in the oppressive heat of Sunday, day of the reunion, a thick veil of pinkish dust raised from the red clay by any movement of man, beast, or vehicle covers almost everything; on Monday morning, after a night of full moon, a fine gentle rain muddies but also slowly cleans everything, leaving the earth bright for the farmers who must return to labor on it for their livelihood. Emotionally the unity of this world is disclosed in the metaphoric connotations of the dust, moon, and rain. Like the dust that obscures vision, an emotional defensiveness initially confines the family, causing them as a matter of habit to seek safety by joining together against outsiders. The dusty atmosphere figures the condition of their hearts as a result of their frustrations in trying to live off barren soil, their resentment at Jack Renfro's unfair imprisonment and the stain it put on the family name, and their trepidation at human mortality, clear in the condition of Granny Vaughn and in numerous signs attending the reunion. If the dust figures mortality obscuring and covering all that is not vital enough to oppose it, the long-awaited rain, even as it spoils hay left on the ground after cutting, signifies, at the novel's end, a fresh and hopeful spirit in the protagonists as they return to their everyday life and work. The evolution of the novel's world, thus, follows the movement of comedy, from seeming hopelessness in a wasteland state toward affirmation of all that lives; the resolution, assisted by outside help, is in the discovery of the best order of loves and motives within the self, family, and community.

Welty's characters typically begin in their stories with attitudes or beliefs settled in routine or tradition and sometimes hardened by a defensiveness resulting from experience of losing battles with life.
—*James Walter*

This affirmative spirit is already present but concealed within the words and images of the novel's first paragraph:

> When the rooster crowed, the moon had still not left the world but was going down on flushed cheek, one day short of the full. A long thin cloud crossed it slowly, drawing itself out like a name being called. The air changed, as if a mile or so away a wooden door had swung open, and a smell, more of warmth than wet, from a river at low stage, moved upward into the clay hills that stood in darkness.

The general sense of this opening scene is of a new world being announced by the rooster's crowing. The auditory image is followed by a visual one, the moon's "flushed cheek," the first of many images in which nature seems to reflect a human form. Next, the visual leads the auditory in a synaesthetic image: the cloud drawn out "like a name being called" is a visual object which its viewer perceives as speech. The connection between the second and third sentences seems almost causal, as if "hearing" nature's speech awakens the percipient's other senses to smell and feel the life in the very flesh of earth. In its progression, the description of this scene foreshadows the conclusive shape of *Losing Battles* and the effect of its completed story on most of its participants, including the reader.

The novel is narrated by an implied author who seems, at times, to speak as the meditative and prophetic spirit of the place, knowing its people and teaching them somehow before they know it, but eventually being that which is known by its more perceptive inhabitants. A major intention of this author is to show that a remarkable world waits to be seen, and to make the reader see it despite all the obscuring influence of dust, self-love, fear, and passivity. The need to see and be seen, nevertheless, insofar as it compels a search for security in the relative fixedness of visible signs and ob-

jects, is submitted to a critique in this novel. Human realization requires also a certain openness and venturesomeness regarding the unseen, which is often only heard or intuited. The illusoriness of stability sought in the seen world is emphasized near the middle of the novel, just after the family, in a gesture to repress answers to painful questions raised by the newcomer Cleo about Nathan's "play hand" and about "Handsome" Sam Dale, unite in visible solidarity to sing "Gathering Home." Following this attempt by the family to divert the flow of talk, the narrator comments,

> As they sang, the tree over them, Billy Vaughn's Switch, with its ever-spinning leaves all light-points at this hour, looked bright as a river, and the tables might have been a little train of barges it was carrying with it moving slowly downstream. Brother Bethune's gun, still resting against the trunk, was travelling too, and nothing at all was unmovable, or empowered to hold the scene still fixed or stake the reunion there.

Like the Bywy River flowing at the edge of the known world in this novel, the flowing river of time constantly disturbs the stability of the visible and whispers of a mystery that is out of eyesight.

The surprising analogies in this description of "Billy Vaughn's Switch," which is typical of the diction, tone, and style of the lyrical inscriptions throughout the novel, overwhelm the visual sense, inhibit its tyrannizing drive to literalize objects, while stimulating among all the reader's senses a collaboration that intensifies awareness of variety and relation. By compelling the reader to engage in imaginative play with different visual possibilities, it communicates to a deeper human sense, stirring recall of the easily forgotten unity that mysteriously knits the diversity of things.

The imagery of the opening of *Losing Battles* implies the possible rejuvenation of the dry land of its world. The family's hope is represented in the posture of Granny as she sits at the edge of the Renfro porch watching for the reunion to begin and especially for the "joy" of the family, Jack Jordan Renfro, to return from prison. All the family anticipates the resurrection of their fortunes as soon as Jack takes up their battles again; but they look for change according to the old law of "the way we do it in Banner": "Well, Curly skinned Jack's ear, and Jack had to skin Curly's ear, and so on."

It is significant that Mr. Willy Trimble helped Mr. Renfro put on the new roof after Jack's departure for prison and that the old man has since "taken liberties" by "scurrying and frisking around" at will over the family's head. Trimble is an odd figure. Miss Julia Mortimer taught him carpentry so he could make the mailboxes essential to her mail-order nursery, but he has perversely turned his skill to coffin-making. He shows up where least expected—in front of Judge Moody's car forcing him off the road; at Julia Mortimer's when she is dying, to help her from the road into her bed and to respond with a blank look to her last question; and later, as an immovable although unwelcome guest at the main table of the reunion. In school the other children had dubbed him "*Willy Trimble?—Hope Not!*" Brother Bethune calls him "the biggest old joker in Christendom!" He is in a mysterious way a personification of earthly contingency, contrariety, and death, realities the reunion intends to keep at arm's length by its garrulous self-satisfied optimism.

When Jack first arrives home, he patiently indulges his family and enjoys their attention; but when cousin Homer Champion arrives to ridicule him for stopping on his way home to help the wrong man get his car out of a ditch, Jack's vengeance is aroused. The fallen state of the family is fully revealed as goading by Champion perverts their inherited spirit of heroic independence into a refusal to help or accept help from someone who, they believe, has no business being "in our part of the world." Jack may be back within the family circle, but his recent prison experience and his love awakened at first sight of his infant daughter make him a fresh seed unfolding there, preparing a transformation of the family's horizon from within. When Jack graciously offers to help Moody a second time after the Judge swerved his car off the road to avoid hitting Jack's wife and baby, Jack's repudiation of the clan's mechanical system of vengeful justice promises eventual change for all of the family.

The family and the community's habitual tendency to blame others and retaliate, or simply to ignore outsiders, is shown in a humorous variety of ways through the middle of *Losing Battles*. An exaggerated type of the whole community appears in the Broadwees, a tribe of Jack's neighbors who come marching single-file up Banner Road eating watermelons shortly after the Judge's car has reached a precarious perch on Banner Top. The Broadwees possess hardly enough difference among themselves to need first names. Their last name tells everything about them: their absorption by family has so "broadened" their outlook to "we" that personal sight and responsibility largely escape them. Their response to the Moodies' plight is merely to sit down in rows to watch while finishing their watermelon. Their speech is little more than "Boo! Boo! Boo!"—a sound they make in habitual unison against rivals during Banner basketball games and, at the present moment, their only available utterance to express their pleasure in the antics of Lady May.

Like their speech, the watermelons eaten by the Broadwees suggest a great deal about the simple corporate myth they live by. Physical similarities between this fruit, the land it grows on, and the people who eat it are repeatedly stressed throughout the novel, as if some alimentary vein passing through the watermelons connects these people with the soil. For example, we are told that Banner Road runs deep between "banks that were bright as a melon at that instant split open." Later, Mr. Renfro's gesture of splitting watermelons to give to each girl "the bursting red heart to drown her face in" suggests the sensual immediacy of this clan's relation to the natural world, quite different from the imaginative distance imposed by the written letters on the tablets of Moses, with which the melons are compared. The family's initiation of Jack's wife, Gloria, in an attempt to absorb her into their sphere is logically enacted by their concerted effort to force her to eat a hulk of watermelon "shoved down into her face, as big as a man's clayed shoe, swarming with seeds, warm with rain-thin juice."

The melon's color, of course, repeats the pink-to-red tinge of almost everything in the Banner world—its people, the flowers, the dust-filled sky, dust-covered objects, the tender skin of babies, even the well water. But like most natural symbols, the melons radiate multiple and ambiguous significance. On the one hand, they suggest a round and smooth containment, a type of limited, rind-covered life; but on the other hand, their bright meat and myriad seeds, visible when the melons are cracked open, symbolize a hidden power of nourishment and generation in nature. This most abundant fruit of the place contains a hidden life-potential that has its emotional and spiritual analogues in the people of the novel's world. For instance, when Lexie Renfro, the bitter old-maid nurse of Miss Mortimer, arrives at the reunion wearing a hat she borrowed from her patient's closet and bringing food she prepared out of her patient's pantry, these slight reminders of Miss Mortimer become seeds that will yield fruit by the end of the day. Like Jack, but with different meaning, the schoolteacher is a fertile presence in the family's consciousness waiting on something to quicken its growth.

Lexie's hatred of Miss Mortimer and envy of Gloria, a concentration of the family's more reserved feelings, are the activators which more Lexie to begin altering Gloria's oversized dress to the accompaniment of a story she tells detailing her patient's stages of senility. Lexie's aim is to render Gloria totally public and thereby settle her identity according to type in the family myth. At the same time, she attempts to reduce Miss Mortimer to those elements in her personality, sadly exaggerated in old age, which made her seem an ogre beyond the pale of human communion. One effect of Lexie's ventilation of spite is to arouse the ire of Judge Moody, who all along has been listening in an old school chair and getting an education in the ways of these people. When he first speaks, the Judge's motives are no less vindictive than theirs, since he intends to be the agent of their comeuppance. He too had been taught by Miss

Mortimer in her prime, and before disabling his car had been on the way to see her in response to a letter she had sent him a month earlier. The Judge's speaking up at this moment, with support from written "documents" he carries and one provided by Mr. Trimble, initiates what appears to be a radical break from the mode of mythologizing and caricaturing engaged in thus far by most of the representatives of the family. The Judge assumes a demythologizing attitude, telling them, "Your memory's got a dozen holes in it. And some sad mistakes." To a large degree, Moody appears to uncover successfully the thought behind the strange behavior of Miss Mortimer that Lexie had so unsympathetically described.

Lexie's most interesting and, to the family, baffling information had to do with her patient's peculiar demands in her final isolation. When she had called for "her book," Lexie thwarted her by answering, "I don't know which book you mean." The last earthly possession the schoolteacher was able to use was her pencil, with which she wrote rapid letters of indictment against human nature. According to Lexie, she was quiet only when given the pencil: "Like words, just words, was getting to be something good enough to eat. And nothing else was!" In her compulsion she wrote on everything at hand and then crammed it "in the envelope till it won't hold one word more!" On the coverboard of the speller that Mr. Trimble had found, "ungiving," beneath Miss Mortimer's pillow when he placed her in bed, the schoolteacher had etched the combined words M-Y-W-I-L-L. Inside the book, handwriting overlays some of the spelling pages and extends over the margins. It appears that with her last strength Miss Mortimer attacked even the common language, projecting over it according to her own morphology a gloss of her indomitable will. The white space of the margins, which in a text symbolizes the unsaid meaning beyond the words, she assaulted for its intimidating threat to her domineering spirit.

Miss Mortimer, the picture suggests, pitted her life to its end in resolute struggle against all that resisted the sovereignty of her will. Her habitual mode of being was combat—with ignorance; with all that is illogical and unsystematic, particularly the prejudice constitutive of family and community; with nature; and finally with God. As she revealed in the last pitiful question of her life, addressed ironically to the ignorant Mr. Trimble—"What was the trip for?"—she had subordinated her combat's purpose to the sheer exhilaration of engaging it for its own sake. The substance of Miss Mortimer's will, as paraphrased by Judge Moody since the family refuses to be read to, is that they are all "constituted her mourners."

After he reads the will, the Judge's ultimate gesture to try to humble the family, by showing them evidence of a nobility of soul contrasting to their pettiness, is to read to them a letter he had received from Miss Mortimer. The letter includes an illuminating admission: "What I live by is inspiration. I always did—I started out on nothing else but naked inspiration." Recounting her inspired "war with ignorance," Miss Mortimer tells how she managed to turn each defeat, even "on the brink of oblivion" and crawling "along the edge of madness," into a lesson to take her "another mile" ahead. Evidently her inherited Presbyterian belief in Providence had undergone a warp at some stage in her thinking, causing her to posit something like a Darwinian life-process that, through testing creatures in a struggle for survival, provides them in itself a "measure of enjoyment." Experience of loss and failure in her life had for her the single effect of inspiring more heroic determination and effort. Thus, for her, "providence" was only something she had marched boldly to meet in the future, never something to discern in her memory of a past. Even in backing her car when she was younger, she had looked straight ahead, to the jeopardy of whoever happened to be behind her.

Miss Mortimer had proved equal to everything life could throw in her path until the very last when a "puzzler" confronted her: "Something walls me in," she writes, "crowds me around, outwits me, dims my eyesight, loses the pencil I had in my hand." She avows distrust of this unexpected other that exerts its power at concurrent limits of life and of language. In part, the "something" appears to have been her physical frailty as death began to claim her; but the barrier she describes was also mental and spiritual, imposed within the border of her linguistic horizon. Her reliance on a literal exactitude as her mode of understanding human experience incapacitated her for passage or vision beyond the border. An aunt's earlier comment concerning Miss Mortimer's habit of licking her pencil as she furiously wrote suggests the danger in her determination: "I've heard that licking an indelible pencil was one sure way to die." The schoolteacher's effort always to cast words into absolute statement that dispelled mystery, as a way to gain human certitude in time, had only the ironic effect of strengthening the prison-house of her existence. Moreover, because she looked on language and time only as raw material for her shaping will, she neglected to prepare for her own inevitable appropriation by time's sentence. When her final helplessness made her dependent on others, she knew only enough to scorn her fate with vain words: "Is this Heaven, where you lie wide-open to the mercies of others who think they know better than you do what's best—what's true and what isn't? Contradictors, interferers, and prevaricators— are those angels? . . . I think I'm in ignorance, not Heaven."

Her emotional life stifled by her rationalist presuppositions, the schoolteacher had attempted to be the active scourge of the non-rational ties of others. As a result, all her possibly fecund experience of tragic failure and negation, which could have taught her understanding of her human fate and her need for others and for mercy, was reduced by her to a sterile challenge having only the effect of increasing her for her undoing. Although the report of her last moment is given by Mr. Trimble, probably an untrustworthy observer, the spareness of it compels wonder: Did Miss Mortimer go out into the road to seek the communion she had missed, or did she go out for one last battle with backwoods ignorance?

Despite her addiction to writing, Miss Mortimer had actually based her existential outlook on a kind of antinomian orality. Her Emersonian (and Nietzschean?) "inspiration" suggests a conviction of self-reliant presence informing a strong will to contend. Miss Mortimer's writing, then, was only an instrument of her inspiration, a means of extending her conviction of sovereignty over the disorderly and contingent. The attitudes of the family, in contrast, despite its dependence on the spoken word, imply an ultimate reliance on a primary writing. At the reunion there are no isolatoes; all are in a sense copies of each other and conceive of themselves as copies of archetypes made by a first creator. Their orality is simply a confident performance of a ritual according to the script naturalized by tradition. As optimists concerning the continuity of human experience and the integrity of nature under a God whose intentions are conceived as relatively transparent, they each act their parts with a minimum of questioning or wonder; and they expect others to accept instruction and follow suit. Their oral self-display, apart from the pure pleasure of imitation it provides, is rhetorical in purpose, directed to outsiders who are slow to understand their ways. The danger in this outlook is in the tyrannizing potential of the letter, in the cultural idolatry that grows on love of the exterior of signs and forgets the renewable spirit that first called them into being. In *Losing Battles,* there is evidence that the family's pleasurable garrulity is, to a degree, a cover for a more elemental uncertainty and fear of ambiguity; preoccupied as they are with their public ritual, they fail on a more personal level to face and do battle with enemies of the interior world.

Deficiencies in Miss Mortimer and the people of Banner are emphasized in this analysis, perhaps to the point of obscuring virtues, because I think it is important to see clearly why and how, in the early parts of the novel, the combatants are confined, are in a real sense "lost." Despite their good qualities, all the Bannerites *are* initially stymied by psychological and spiritual faults. But to mark their deficiencies is also to make more explicit the re-creative power that, by the story's end, transforms most of them, miraculously. The comic effect of the novel is increased by our seeing that these sinners can be changed.

History's distinctive theme of "something new" is evident in Judge Moody as the completion of the story of Miss Mortimer brings him mysteriously to a clearer view of his own life and to a humble admission: that he "never fully forgave her" for her domineering influence in his life, that he didn't do all his "duty" by her, and that he cherished against her the advice she gave him years ago not to pursue success elsewhere but to remain in Boone County and devote his life to using the power of the courts to educate its stubborn people. The Judge's activated guilt and his deep grief for the poor woman illustrate his improved imagination. His concluding interpretation of Miss Mortimer is perceptive: "She knew exactly who she was. What she didn't know till she got to it was what could *happen* to what she was. Any more than any of us here know." Paradoxically, Moody's sorrowful recognition of contingency and the pathetic finitude of human knowledge does not lead him to despair, but it prepares him for hopeful participation, with less self-consciousness, in the comic resolution of *Losing Battles.*

There are numerous other signs that telling and hearing Miss Mortimer's story, in some ways the story of each one at the reunion, has animated the imaginations of all involved. In a beautifully wrought passage, the lyrical voice of the narrator describes what had been the dust of day as a "deep blue dust that now reached Heaven"; moments later the narrator describes a fine "substance" of moonlight sifting down "upon the world." For the first time this day, as "Silence that was all one big question opened like a tunnel," the participants open together in receptive wonder to an atmospheric memory that feeds their negativity and makes it fruitful.

This power felt by the participants of the reunion is most magnificently displayed by the narrator in the one passage in the novel admitting us fully into the interior of a character, as if this grace of imagination could be demonstrated only in the relatively silent and image-filled place of an individual psyche. The psyche used is the particularly sensitive one of Vaughn Renfro, twelve-year-old brother of Jack and general sufferer of the family's abuse and neglect. If the deceased schoolteacher had made school, book, and writing instruments of mortification, then Vaughn's love of school and especially of "geography" (study of the earth as a script?) suggests the possibility of imagination's rescue of culture's writing from its tendency to kill life by fixing it rigidly in abstract system. In contrast to the narrow and vindictive mythologizing that earlier had diverted the family from truth, the inspired *mythopoesis* that is filtered through Vaughn's consciousness discloses all the obvious, subtle, multiple, and necessary interpenetration of humans with their place and time and the significance they give to each other. What Vaughn perceives as, astride the mule Bet, he listens with ears funneled by an oversized hat he inherited from Grandpa Vaughn, is quite literally a voice myriadly incarnated in many voices "heard" through the world's visible body; the synaesthetic articulation of this voice is similar to that of the "could like a name being called" in the novel's opening paragraph.

> [Vaughn] heard every sound going on, repeating it-self, increasing, as if it were being recollected by loud night talking to itself. At times it might have been the rush of water—the Bywy on the rise in spring; or it might have been the rains catching up after them, to mire them in. Or it might have been that the whole wheel of the sky made the sound as it kept letting fall the soft fire of its turning. . . . It was all-present enough to spill over into voices, as everything, he was ready to believe now, threatened to do, the closer he might come to where something might happen.

Like the cosmos that "defies" Vaughn's honest soul at this moment, this passage gathers, states, intimates, and reso-nates in ways that defy systematic analysis. It tells of a uni-verse that is in its essence an act of communication. It tells of the person's essential privacy and need to share under-standing. It tells that meaning registers chiefly through the intuitions and images held in the heart, and that in any single act of knowing a multitude of mysterious qualities in being escape rational focus to hover at the edge of awareness. It tells of a multitude of emotions aroused in the knower, who needs to visualize, to speak with others, and to write in or-der to gain enough distance from experience and sound not to be absorbed by them. It hints of a grace operative in his-tory and place, which may well be the writing of a divine Author whose book is read best by the innocent eye and the pure heart. And it reveals that, although reading by mortals is at best approximate and therefore inadequate, experience of negation can be fecund. The passage, thus, is a beautiful coda of Welty's obsessive concerns, not only in this novel but in all the fiction she has written.

If at first glance Vaughn's vision appears as a mandala in the Eastern tradition of mysticism, closer inspection uncov-ers its dependency on Western sacred literacy. In imagery, theme, and inspiration this passage and its context corre-spond with Ezekiel's astounding apocalypse of rolling wheels, storm, glimmering light and fiery flashes, roaring waters, compound beings, and battle-like sounds. Just as the prophet received his mission through his empathy with Israel's exilic suffering, so is Vaughn made to experience, in a similar imaginative setting, his connection with a tran-scendent holiness and purpose signified to him through the awesome creation. The further similarity that Vaughn takes *things* in "like a word . . . being swallowed," much as Ezekiel was made to eat the scroll the Lord gave to him, should make clear the continuity between Welty's render-ing of Vaughn's experience and Judaeo-Christian under-standing. The scroll that Ezekiel ate is a symbol of the "firmament" first described in Genesis and later allegorically

interpreted by Augustine to be a scroll of signs stretched over the waters and the earth to raise forgetful human be-ings out of the deep of their separation from God's love. As illustrated in Vaughn's visionary experience, Welty's characteristic technique vis-a-vis traditional symbols is to re-create them in a way that respects their original power to generate fresh perceptions of truth yet avoids their ten-dency to become literal in abstract concept or doctrine.

That this powerful vision is filtered through the conscious-ness of Vaughn elevates him to special status in *Losing Battles.* His fertile gift of imagination is metaphorically in-dicated in the narrator's description of him *feeling* loved ob-jects, such as the Banner school bus, "on his tongue, like a word of his own ready to be spoken, then swallowed back into his throat, going down, inside and inside." It is unimag-inable that any other member of the family would swallow a word; but for Vaughn words are not so much a medium of ritualistic performance as they are mediators of a knowl-edge that joins rational apprehension and interior awareness. The active quality of Vaughn's imagination is evident in his translating an owl's cry he hears as "Who cooks for you? / Who cooks for me?"—questions that ponder the manifold interdependence of man, beast, earth, and provider. Vaughn's difference from the family is clarified as he un-expectedly meets Granny at the door to her room after all the others have fallen asleep; when she, in somnambulistic indiscriminateness, invites him to "Take off your hat . . . And climb in wi' me," he flees the house, telling himself, "She didn't know who I was . . . She didn't care!" Because the family mythos so thoroughly informs Granny's sight, she hardly cares *who* comes to sleep in her bed so long as it is family. Vaughn, however, feeling painfully the family's oppression of the private and personal, runs to the barn where he tumbles to the floor asleep while saying his prayers. The association of Vaughn in this scene with the prophet-like Baptist preacher Grandpa Vaughn, who often filled "the upper regions" of the same barn with prayers in behalf of the family, implies the re-creation in the boy of an archetype of critical consciousness that the family, be-cause of its naturalizing habit, but dimly remembers.

At the conclusion of *Losing Battles,* Jack Renfro attempts to call his white horse Dan, loose from the pasture of Curly Stovall, who had appropriated the horse in Jack's absence as payment for the Renfros' new tin roof. To save pain, the family had lied to Jack that the horse had been "rendered"; thus Jack is elated as he witnesses it in a "few bright min-utes" running "lightly as a blown thistledown" all around Banner. The imagery portraying the horse implies the rev-elation of a spirit in it; its name and color, furthermore, as-sociate it with *Daniel* and *Revelation,* the chief apocalyptic books of the Old and New Testaments. Whatever it stands for, the horse's escape from Curly's lot signifies its oppo-sition to the insecurity which compels the pharisaical storekeeper to cut off other men's shirt-tails for display in his store, gestures calculated to win glory from a seeing world. In contrast, Jack draws the reader's admiration as the novel ends because he has kept faith in an ideal of honor that is personal yet still binds him to others in gracious justice and charity.

The description of Jack's pursuit of Dan includes a pun suggesting Welty's pursuit of elusive truth in her fiction. Gloria tells Jack, "Dan is fickle. And now he's Curly's horse and he's let you know it. Oh, Jack, I know you'd rather he was rendered!" "No," Jack replies, "I rather he's alive and fickle than all mine and sold for his hide and tallow." Truth of the sort Welty reveals in this novel, of human life whose self-made terms of placement are being continuously dissolved by a re-creating grace, is also fickle; any Mortimerian writer's attempt to "render" it with total visual clarity, leaving no margin for the play of words and their connotations—and the play of the reader's active imagination—would indeed "render" this truth to its "hide and tallow." Consequently, throughout her fiction Welty characteristically avoids the hard edges of exact description, relying instead on diction that retains the ambiguity of real experience, on mind-stretching and mixed figures of speech, on hilarious hyperbole and timely silence, and sometimes on an unsettling profusion of visual images that break the tyrannizing control of the reader's eye and thus allow the essence, for a moment, to disclose itself.

In the comic conclusion to *Losing Battles* Jack is shown returning to his farm with his wife and baby behind him on the mule ambiguously named "Bet." He sings a Protestant song of harvest that illustrates once again Welty's amazing ability to combine several levels of meaning in a single action. The song, "Bringing in the sheaves, / Bringing in the sheaves!" in echoing a Biblical hope borne by exiles ("Those that sow in tears shall reap rejoicing . . . shall come back rejoicing, carrying their sheaves"), anticipates a joyous fulfillment ("a Son of Man wielded his sickle over all the earth and reaped the earth's harvest"). The word "sheaves," moreover, which conflates pages with bundles of grain, suggests the novel's own work of discerning a voice in the signifying bodies of earth and of collecting its own sheaves into the credible and significant wholeness of a book whose multiple visual signs mediate that voice. Beyond this volume of temporal writing, Welty suggests, and validating whatever truth it may publish, is that other volume noted in *Revelation,* the "book of the living" whose pages accumulating over the ages are read by their divine author.

It is appropriate, then, that Jack's song echoes the moment in Dante's *Paradiso* when the poet sees, in eternal light,

All things in a single volume bound by Love,

of which the universe is the scattered leaves.

(Canto *XXXIII*)

As its title implies, however, *Losing Battles* is not paradisal or high comedy. Its tone is too naturalistic, evil of an everyday sort remains too visible in its world, some of its petty culprits are still unscathed and at large; and its final celebration—of a married couple with a child returning to work—is too reserved and mundane. Still, its purgatorial comic resolution could have been written only by a poet capable of imagining this world's losing battles as reflecting paradisal light, and the eternal as disclosing something of its form in the letters of its own book that it writes.

Eudora Welty with Sally Wolff (interview date January 1990)

SOURCE: "Some Talk about Autobiography: An Interview with Eudora Welty," in *The Southern Review,* Vol. 26, No. 1, January, 1990, pp. 81-8.

[*In the following interview, conducted in July, 1988, Welty discusses the autobiographical aspects of her novel* The Optimist's Daughter *which correspond to sections of her lectures presented in* One Writer's Beginning.]

The inspiration for this interview came partly as a result of a conference on southern autobiography at Arkansas State in the spring of 1988. In July of that year I visited Eudora Welty at her home in Jackson, Mississippi, where we discussed correspondences between One Writer's Beginnings *and her highly autobiographical novel,* The Optimist's Daughter. *Miss Welty also relates memories and details which reveal more of her personal involvement in this novel.—SW*

[*Wolff:*] *One of the issues raised at the recent conference on southern autobiography is whether there is a distinct body of work that might be thought of as southern autobiography. Do you think certain aspects of southern life and culture might predispose writers to autobiography?*

[Welty:] Yes, I think probably so, don't you? It occurs to me that southerners take certain things for granted—such as certain classes, certain strictures, different backgrounds—people immediately make certain assumptions. Southerners want to place everybody. This was especially true in former times, when someone might say "Oh, so-and-so, his father was so-and-so." It used to be so simple—you might be born on the wrong side of the track. I remember as a child being taught not to make this count. I was warned against it. But it's a way southerners have of locating themselves.

What else in southerners might encourage them to write about themselves?

It's entertaining when it's done well. It helps you get a narrative sense of continuity when there are so many stories through the generations—something that connects people together. I missed that when I lived in other parts of the country. People were friends but had no sense of their ancestors. No one was interested. I did have a good friend—David Daiches—who invited me to visit his family in Edinburgh. The family I met there was so warm and welcoming. His three aunts met me at the door with arms extended. I felt at home with them. In the South we combine a feeling of family and of place. They are twin strands, the sense of family and place. I didn't grow up with this sense of the whole family. As you know from *One Writer's Beginnings,* much of the family was away.

In West Virginia?

Yes.

The feeling of being somewhat isolated from the extended family also comes through in **The Optimist's Daughter** *in Becky and Laurel's memories about West Virginia.*

Yes, I used it in the work in general. I used the point of view of the child coming to something new. I did the same thing in *Delta Wedding* where the child's perspective is a narrative device to lead the reader into something new. In lots of stories it's the stranger to the family that provides this perspective. Maybe that is my point of view.

The rejection of Flags in the Dust *seems to have turned Faulkner inward, down into himself, after which he began writing* The Sound and the Fury. *I'm thinking about that introduction to the book in which he says, "One day I seemed to shut a door between me and all publishers' addresses and booklists . . . and set out to make myself a beautiful and tragic little girl." That book seems autobiographical to me, so much a reminiscence of and a lament for lost childhood. Can you say that some set of events or some factor led you to turn to autobiography?*

Well, in *One Writer's Beginnings* a particular event did. I was asked, as you know, to give the series of lectures at Harvard, and I thought, "I can't possibly say anything they don't already know." But Dan Aaron, my good friend, came to see me and said, "Yes, there is something you know that they do not—what books were in your grandfather's library." I thought, "That's intriguing to think about it that way." If it hadn't been for Dan the book wouldn't have happened. I wrote a great deal more material than I used. I threw away four times what I kept. I may not have chosen well, but I had to choose. One memory calls up another.

Like Thomas Mann says, memory is like a well: the deeper you go, the more you recover. It's probably a good thing the book had to be compressed or I might have gone on forever. I'm not used to writing anything but fiction. I didn't make up anything in *One Writer's Beginnings*. I couldn't help but use my experience in knowing, for instance, what makes a scene—the dramatic sense. I think of things in scenes—trips in the car, being on the ferry boat, my mother and father arguing about their different attitudes about drowning—it was better than making a simple statement. I remember things that way—in scenes, as little wholes.

Would you say, then, that the autobiographer uses the same tools in writing autobiography that the fiction writer does?

My own bent is to use those tools. I would want certain things to be brought out in act, in deed, and in what can be observed. It's natural for me to do it that way. A poet would do it differently, I suppose, as would a railroad engineer.

Could you say that any other factors in particular led you to write autobiographically, especially in **The Optimist's Daughter***?*

I did use things about my mother, as I have said. In *The Optimist's Daughter* I was trying to understand certain things, some of which are reflected in the character of my mother. All that was true. But my mother did not marry a southerner the way Becky does. So much of what I wrote about was not my mother. And that is true for the other characters.

I could not imagine that there was a "Fay" anywhere in your family.

There is no Fay in any of my life, except as she exists in the world.

Fay has always seemed highly symbolic to me.

Yes, I think she is.

What other aspects of the novel might you say were particularly autobiographical?

There are things I never realized growing up that I began to realize. I used certain things that I had been familiar with. You do this when you write any character. My mother had eye trouble, but she didn't have a detached retina. I did know someone who had a detached retina, though. I nursed my mother through cataract surgery, and some of the details I used for the judge. She had sandbags, for instance, and she couldn't move her head. It's not literal, though. If it were it would be a damn difficult task to write the literal truth. It was hard to do in *One Writer's Beginnings,* to give an account of family illness. I don't think I could have done that in a novel.

Would you say, then, that writing autobiography is more difficult than writing fiction?

When I was writing **The Optimist's Daughter,** I never gave a thought to myself—my self did not enter into the novel. It's much easier for me to write fiction. I try to put myself into the characters and see how they felt. Any nonfiction is so different from fiction. A book review, for instance, is completely different from using your imagination in a story.

In an earlier interview, you said that in **One Writer's Beginnings** *you wrote for the first time about yourself and that the experience was enlightening. Could you elaborate about what this writing experience taught you?*

Well, I'd like to think about that for awhile. I will say that it came about without my realizing it at the time. Writing about anything teaches you—it teaches you the recognition of things in your life that you remember, but you might not have recognized their portent. It's like you have an electric shock—and you can say that's when I recognized so-and-so. Writing is a way to come to terms with whatever you've done or not done—what your life has meant to you—good or bad. One thing leads to another subjectively, and you could probably go on forever.

Do you have that same experience writing fiction?

Yes. That same feeling comes from writing fiction. In the course of writing a scene of interplay between two characters, you build to a confrontation that needs to take place—and you realize that's why you were diddling with it and fooling with it in the first place—there was something in there. It's like a belated understanding. I seem to come to understanding belatedly.

Lately I read a statement by Sarah Orne Jewett that all the materials you need to be an artist you know by the time you are ten years old. Would you agree?

How could you ever prove it, though? But yes, I think I know what she means, don't you? Your capacity for realizing the other people in the world, your physical world, even if you can't define them, you know what they are.

And memories of childhood are an important source for the artist.

Yes, they are a fund.

I'm interested in the remark you made earlier that when you were writing **The Optimist's Daughter** *you did not envision yourself in the novel. Laurel has characteristics which are both similar to and unlike yours, doesn't she?*

Yes. In a wider sense, I would say it was my own inquiring mind that corresponds to the girl's in the novel, to the effort to understand your roots and the decision in the end that you can't be held back by the past. I used things that would be useful in the novel. The war was very important, for instance. My friend in World War II married into—well, when someone was lost—like Phil is—I knew what that feeling was like. How could I not have? That was a war people believed in. We still had the belief in World War II that war could be ended by licking the Nazis. The difference in attitude toward war now is striking. Some of my friends put on a production at the New Stage of the songs of Irving Berlin. The young girls were giggling at songs like "Over There!" and the director stopped them and said, "When those songs were written, they *meant* that." It was a bad war. The boys we knew were involved and we were with them. These young people in the theater couldn't conceive of fighting for a cause. This applies to Phil. The part in the novel about the kamikaze happened to my brother Walter. He was in the Navy at Okinawa, and later he was asked, "How close have you come to a kamikaze?" and he said, "Close enough to shake hands with." So I put that in the story. Who could ever make up a thing like that?

No one could. Was Phil made up?

Phil is an amalgamation of a lot of boys I knew. My other brother, the middle child, has some of his characteristics—those double-jointed thumbs, and he was an architect. Phil has not got his character, though. Although he did make a breadboard. But no one ever acted badly about it.

No one ever acted the way Fay does?

Not in my family: but I've seen a-many, a-many. And anyone who's ever had anyone in the hospital will recognize the people who sit in the waiting rooms and eat and drink and talk. I wouldn't want anyone to think that I was using their *sick* in the novel, but these things come back to me, like air, and I use them.

Everybody told me I was absolutely right with the hospital scenes. I heard people say some of those things, like "I'm not gonna let him die wanting water." It's the inadequacy of their comprehension, or maybe they can't express it. They say, "What is *yours* doing? *Mine* is doing OK."

Mr. Dalzell's line, "Don't let the fire go out, son!" is tragic and funny at the same time.

I love Mr. Dalzell. The fire, of course, is life too. He talks in terms of the things he knows—country things. He and the judge were so different, but I thought it would be good to have them in the same room together. They each had a sense of honor and would have respected each other. He was a gentleman—like Fay's old grandfather—these are affinities among characters that don't have anything to do with their circumstances.

Let me go back to Laurel for a moment. I was surprised to read in one of your interviews that you identify most with your character Miss Eckhart rather than with Laurel.

It's not that I shared any of my life with Miss Eckhart. She was devoted to her art. I could identify with Laurel in wanting to know about family and relationships, in living through World War II when my friends and brothers were fighting, and also in my sense that Laurel had left home and had a life elsewhere that had something to do with the arts. I wouldn't have thought of making her a writer. The fact that she was in the arts allied her with Phil, who is also a maker, and in the end she goes back to that life, but without leaving anything behind. She knows the future is to be valued. I sympathize with all these attitudes. I am not Laurel. But I have the feeling of the close-knit family—do you remember the scene where they're holding each other's hands? I've gone through that feeling a lot though my own father died when I was just out of college.

Miss Eckhart and Laurel are alike, then, in their dedication to their art?

Miss Eckhart is a teacher, though—I've never seen myself as a teacher. Both Miss Eckhart and Laurel had belief in the individual—in what an artist does. In her own way—you know, I really hadn't thought of it until now—Laurel was as isolated in the town as Miss Eckhart was. Laurel was protected and pampered by the town, but when it came down to it no one could share in her deepest feelings about life and responsibility. We don't ordinarily talk about things like that in the South, or maybe anywhere.

Laurel's privacy and isolation are reflected in the narration, too. We do not see into Laurel's thoughts until the very end of the book.

She is subservient to what she endures going on around her, and then she is activated by this. She has a muted position. It's not her place to yell and scream. She's kept a lot of things inside her. In the part about New Orleans, when she and Fay are in those cheap rooms where you can hear through the walls—I wanted that to be foreboding.

It is, especially when Fay sees the bride and groom skeletons at the carnival.

I took that part from real life. I took a picture one time at

Mardi Gras in New Orleans of a man and woman dressed as skeletons, and she was holding a bouquet of white lilies. And I saw the man with the Spanish moss; he was dressed entirely in Spanish moss. It was all over his hair, like he had a permanent of long curls, and he was dressed in a whole suit of Spanish moss.

In one of the early versions of **The Optimist's Daughter** *you wrote out some scenes depicting Phil and Laurel courting, and in one scene Phil's mother asks Laurel how far apart their children will be spaced. Why did you decide to delete this material?*

That's a good middlewestern touch in the kitchen, isn't it? I remember writing the courtship scene, but maybe I left it out because it didn't fit my purpose as well. I wanted the relationship of Phil and Laurel to be taken for granted for my purposes in the novel. It gave it a more proper depth and allowed me to concentrate on the scene in which Phil says, "I wanted it! I wanted it!" It's really a short novel, and I still think of it as a long short story. You have to get the proportions right. You have to keep in mind the good of the whole story. That is true for writing short stories, too; you have to get the balance right. Dozens of possible scenes show the same point, and I have to choose as in *One Writer's Beginnings*. I just have to feel my way to it.

Did you save the material for **One Writer's Beginnings** *that you did not use?*

I saved the notebooks I wrote it from. I did write those as lectures, and I did have the deadline of timing—length was one thing I had to go by because they were lectures. I probably threw away some of it that didn't show an event as well. I can remember things in stories—the choice I made for stories—more than in that book.

You said earlier that in the end of **The Optimist's Daughter,** *Laurel learns to move to the future. She packs up the family home, and she leaves for the North. Would you say that autobiographical writing allows you to imagine your own life choices in another way? Is this a freeing experience?*

It can be. The end of the novel embodied Laurel's whole experience. It had to be settled and then done with as far as her practical life is concerned. She would never forget any of the past, though. Miss Adele was very sensitive to what was going on with Laurel. I like my character Miss Adele. Laurel could not be the only one who felt things, who was aware. That just worked out as I was writing it. I'm glad it happened.

Do you recall any other changes that emerged from the experience of writing **The Optimist's Daughter?**

The publisher might have wanted to go ahead and print the novel as it was published in the *New Yorker*. But I wanted a waiting period to let things settle to see how I felt about it. I wanted to let a little time pass. I always change things. I don't know exactly what changes I made in the different versions; it all seems the one thing to me now.

There are some provocative changes; one is the change from the New Yorker *title—"An Only Child." Would you comment on that change?*

I wanted to have something about the eyes. I first wanted to call it "Poor Eyes," but that was voted down. Bill Maxwell and Diarmuid Russell didn't like it. Bill did like *The Optimist's Daughter*. He said it gave a nice "chill of apprehension." But I've never been very good at titles. After the book came out I had letters that had the title wrong: "I so much enjoyed *The Optimistic Daughter*." Another one said *The Optometrist's Daughter*. That's a good one, don't you think? The Optometrist's Daughter? Because of the eyes?

Yes, that's good. Is there a sense in which "An Only Child" is an autobiographical title, even though you are not an only child?

Yes, I dramatized the sense of being an only child. If Laurel had had brothers, like I had, she wouldn't have had the trouble she did. I was not an only child but the only girl—that is difference enough to understand the feeling that you are by yourself.

By yourself in confronting the deaths of so many family members?

Yes.

That reminds me of Mrs. Chisom's summation of Laurel's predicament: "So you ain't got father, mother, brother, sister, husband, chick nor child." I like that: "chick nor child."

Isn't Chisom a good name for them? And I like the sound of Wanda Fay. I love that.

Jan Nordby Gretlund (essay date Fall 1992)

SOURCE: "Welty's *Losing Battles*," in *The Explicator*, Vol. 51, No. 1, Fall, 1992, pp. 49-50.

[*In the following review, Nordby Gretlund discusses the scene in Welty's* Losing Battles *in which Granny invites Vaughn to get in bed with her, and asserts that the scene is* a case of mistaken identity, not a revelation of a dark side of the family.]

It is my impression that there is an intense search among critics for censure by Welty of the farmers in her novel *Losing Battles*. I think that the subconscious rejection of her blatant celebration of the Beecham-Renfros stems from an unsatisfied urge among Welty's admirers to locate passages in her fiction that deal with the dark, or even evil, side of humanity. Several critics are obviously of the conviction that only the presence of unexplained evil will give her fiction its full depth, so they cast about for the negative aspects of Welty's characters. And whereas the dark side of man is definitely present in her fiction, critics are not always locating it in the right places. As a typical case in point I can refer to the many surprising interpretations of the following scene.

It is late in the evening after the reunion. Granny Vaughn has retired to her bed, and Vaughn, Jack's brother, who is twelve, is making his way through the passage of the house to the loft, to bed down after a long day's hard work:

> Then all of a sudden there came through the passage a current of air. A door swung open in Vaughn's face and there was Granny, tiny in her bed in full lamplight. For a moment the black bearskin on the floor by the bed shone red-haired, live enough to spring at him. After the moonlight and the outdoors, the room was as yellow and close as if he and Granny were embedded together in a bar of yellow soap. "Take off your hat," Granny's mouth said. "And climb in wi' me." He fled out of her dazzled sight. "She didn't know who I was," he told himself, running. And then, "She didn't care!"

The rest of the scene is simply a description of the confused boy's flight to the loft.

In an early essay, originally broadcast by Voice of America in 1973, Seymour Gross commented that the night scene is "the literal and symbolic dark time of the novel." He continues: "Granny, anguished by the end of the reunion, pleads with Vaughn, neither knowing nor caring who he is, to get into bed with her." Gross's idea about this scene has been perpetuated by Larry J. Reynolds in an equally influential essay of 1978. Reynolds wrote, "Vaughn Renfro's painful and nightmarish vision as he encounters Granny in bed further discloses a reality neither lighthearted, comic, nor charming. . . . Granny is ready to ask someone to share her bed, not knowing nor caring who it is, because she does know that that person represents relief from the loneliness she feels." As Reynolds goes on, it becomes obvious that he is relieved "that the truth about Granny Vaughn's family has been completely revealed." Most critics follow Gross and Reynolds in this reading. As Elizabeth Evans phrases it: "Vaughn is distressed when Granny awakens and, *not knowing who he is,* invites him to her bed [my italics]."

But is this really an important scene that completely reveals the dark side of this family? As Elin Harkema, who is an old woman, has pointed out to me, the truth is that Granny believes she knows the person she is inviting into her bed very well. To understand this we have to remember an earlier sentence in the novel, about Vaughn's riding Bet, the mule, through the night "dosed with moonlight," wondering what Jack's return will mean to him. Welty continues: "Grandpa Vaughn's hat came down low and made his ears stick out like funnels." In other words, Vaughn is wearing Grandpa Vaughn's hat, and a little later he carries well water in it. It is probably her late husband that Granny thinks she sees that night. Remember what she said: "Take off your hat. . . . And climb in wi' me."

Granny Vaughn is ninety years old. Her eyesight is failing, she is asleep after a tiring day, and she is awakened by a thud when her door swings open. Is it any wonder that when she looks up against the glare of the lamplight and against moonlight "the thickness of China" and sees the outline of her husband's hat in her doorway, she is "dazzled" enough to believe for a second that her husband is still with her? It is no wonder that the boy is puzzled by Granny's invitation, but is there any reason why we should be puzzled or shocked?

Sally Wolff (essay date Fall 1992)

SOURCE: "'Among Those Missing': Phil Hand's Disappearance from *The Optimist's Daughter,*" in *Southern Literary Journal,* Vol. 25, No. 1, Fall, 1992, pp. 74-88.

[*In the following essay, Wolff discusses how the character of Philip Hand, from Welty's* The Optimist's Daughter, *was changed as the author revised the work.*]

Eudora Welty published **The Optimist's Daughter** first as a short story in the *New Yorker* in 1969 and subsequently as a novel in 1972. Radically revising the character of Philip Hand during successive interim versions of the story, initially omitting and then adding, Welty finally excised most material that elaborates his character and brief marriage to Laurel. In the novel, little description of Phil remains except for a paragraph about his origins on an Ohio farm and a brief reminiscence about their wedding day, altogether amounting to no more than four pages of text. During the process of achieving the final version, Welty deleted some twenty pages of romantic scenes depicting the meeting, courtship, and marriage of Phil and Laurel.

Not included in the original story, Phil Hand evolved into a strong physical presence in the interim versions. The Philip Hand in the resulting novel, however, is dead, disembodied, arising only in Laurel's reverie on the night of her father's funeral. In the novel, though gone, Philip Hand makes his voice heard:

> the past had been raised up, and *he* looked at her, Phil himself—here waiting, all the time, Lazarus. He looked at her out of eyes wild with the craving for his unlived life, with mouth open like a funnel's. . . . 'Laurel! Laurel! Laurel!' Phil's voice cried. She wept for what happened to life. 'I wanted it!' Phil cried. His voice rose with the wind in the night and went around the house and around the house. It became a roar. 'I wanted it!'

In the novel version, left bodiless and graveless in his World War II death, Phil exists in Laurel's mind, not as a whole man, not even as a memory of a whole, but as a remembered image, a remembered voice. Phil is only a cry of despair that reverberates in Laurel's mind with an excruciating anguish not found elsewhere in Eudora Welty's fiction. His anguish naturally becomes Laurel's cry, too, of lost opportunity for life and love. As the physicality of Phil disappears, the text about him does also. Almost simultaneously creating and erasing, Welty alters Phil from the resplendent young bridegroom of the early sketches to a shadow and an absence. Her final rendering of him is the deathly, ghostly sound, occurring in Laurel's dream, as she slumps forward in her chair. Welty has commented upon the decision to alter the presentation of Phil:

> I wanted the relationship of Phil and Laurel to be taken for granted for my purpose in the novel. It gave it a more proper depth and allowed me to concentrate on the scene in which Phil says, 'I wanted it!' It's really a short novel, and I still think of it as a long short story. You have to get the proportions right. You have to keep in mind the good of the whole story.

By deliberately excising Phil, Welty dramatically restructures the story into a novel that focuses not upon the happy days enjoyed by Laurel and Phil, but upon the end of those days and his disappearance. As the literal presence of Phil diminishes, he metaphorically looms larger, and as the descriptions of his everyday life with Laurel and their domestic bliss are made more sketchy, Phil becomes more fully identified. The excisions profoundly transform **"The Optimist's Daughter"** from a story about love to a novel about tragedy and death. Initially pictured an only child, Laurel evolves into a character who knew love, was courted, married, and widowed—a woman whose untold love story ended almost before it began. Only Phil's memory emerges as the sustaining power of the novel's final pages.

In early drafts Phil does not appear, but Laurel is immediately introduced as a widow. Draft one, sentence one reads: "Laurel Hand, born Laurel McKelva." Welty pictured Laurel's marriage before she created a husband for her. In fact, Welty recently stated that "Phil was always there in my mind, even before I decided to write about him." Laurel's absent husband is mentioned only once in several early drafts of the story, as Mrs. Chisom queries Laurel about him. In draft one, for example, we find only one reference to Laurel's husband:

> "You had a bad luck with *your* husband, too?" Mrs. Chisom asked Laurel.
> "He was lost over North Africa."
> "So you ain't got father, mother, brother, sister, husband, chick nor child." Mrs. Chisom poked Laurel as if to send her from the room.
> "Not a soul to call on, that's you."

Though blunt and intrusive, Mrs. Chisom has struck at the heart of Laurel's lonely predicament. Like Everyman, Laurel has no "soul to call on" and must rely only upon her memory. The title for draft one of the story, "An Only Child," is particularly apt, in this context, emphasizing Laurel's aloneness and reflecting Welty's autobiographical tendency to incorporate into this work her experience as the only girl in a family with two brothers, a configuration that gave her the "feeling that you are by yourself."

In draft two of "An Only Child," the mention of Laurel's husband is made more vague rather than more detailed: he "died in the war." Here he is dead even without the African location, without any location. She subsequently changes the scene of Phil's death, a third time, to the Battle of Leyte (Gulf), but in the final version he dies in an unspecified location in the Pacific, an early indication of the eventual placelessness, gravelessness, and anonymity Welty later accords his wartime death. Further alterations occur in Phil's war assignments. Initially serving as a fighter pilot, Phil later dies as a communications officer aboard a mine sweeper in the Navy.

Not until the third draft of the story does Welty first sketch a full character resembling Phil Hand, yet he remains unnamed. This character, a friend who lives in Chicago, will comfort Laurel:

> —a friend who was not to be turned away like another Major Bullock, a friend who with healthy Middlewestern impatience would *answer* her. . . .

The character of Phil Hand, Welty says, derives partly from

her brothers and partly from the memories of friends lost in World War II. Her compositional technique is evinced in the combining of aspects of real people and places with the imagined to create a fictional whole. She specifically refers to "Those who fought in the Italian campaign started out over North Africa. . . . I had a friend who fought in the Italian campaign. But my brother fought in Okinawa, and I put that in, too." Her brother's character informs Phil's characteristics the most vividly:

> Phil is an amalgamation of a lot of boys I knew. My other brother, the middle child, has some of his characteristics—those double-jointed thumbs, and he was an architect. Phil has not got his character, though. Although he did make a breadboard. But no one ever acted badly about it.

Some twenty pages of fragments describe Phil and Laurel together during early courtship days and suggest that Welty gathered together the material about this "Chicago friend" from different places or drafts. Suzanne Marrs points out in *The Welty Collection* that this material contains Welty's note to herself to "Omit this part for now," and that these fragments indicate her possible intention "to return to this character before publishing her story as a book."

What seems clear, at least, is that Welty once considered a greater emphasis on the early love relationship between Phil and Laurel than she finally chose for either story or novel. "Sometimes you have to know what happened to character, even if you do not use it," Welty says. Her decision to exclude the sketches of Phil as a courting lover and young husband results in an intensified conclusion for the novel, one with more mystery and pathos.

Among these revisions and drafts, available in the Mississippi State Archives, the portraits of Philip Hand do exist as Welty originally conceived them. Particularly vivid are several romantic scenes that capture the spontaneous attraction between Laurel and Phil, a quality that survives in subsequent versions, until finally it is radically reduced. Here Welty finally names Laurel's friend "Phil," and describes the couple in the kitchen of Phil's mother, on the occasion of Laurel's first visit to his family home. We hear again the theme of the "only child" as Phil's mother pleads for more than one grandchild.

> His family in their Middlewestern way had seemed to her pleasantly fond and wholesomely unacquainted with one another. In the occasion of their first visit, she had heard Phil's mother ask him at the table if he liked ice cream. In exactly the same voice she had asked Laurel, over dishwashing, how soon, how many, and how wide apart would the children be? When Laurel dropped a pie plate, Mrs.

Hand had [implored] [explained], "Please, not an *only* child!" . . . She laughed at the thought of her own mother making any of these remarks.

Though his Midwestern mother's directness is given voice here, Phil still has no voice of his own. Laurel's point of view governs this kitchen scene, and as Phil's mother questions her directly about children, Welty establishes a contrast between her manner and Laurel's Southern decorum. "That's a good middlewestern touch in the kitchen, isn't it," Welty now muses about her early draft. The question of the children implies marriage and sex, surprising the shy Laurel, who drops the pie plate she is holding. "Southerners," Welty says, "would not have asked the question, though it is a perfectly good question to ask." Despite these familial differences, Laurel's attraction to Phil grows. She enjoys his independence of mind and love of privacy—two qualities Laurel also possesses:

> Part of Philip's arrest on her mind was his complete silence about his family. Nobody ever sat at a board and drew with a pencil who was not in love with privacy, she supposed. Phil seemed a prodigy of independence, and yet he was deprived—she had first thought him shallow; he seemed not even very much to tolerate the human species.

Draft three continues Welty's definition of Phil Hand, yet the descriptions are still sketchy, and like his name, synecdochal. His gentleness and love of birds are clear:

> He was an Ohio boy, had loved birds; he stole away from life class to watch birds instead, filled his sketchbook with them, knew all about their nesting, migrations—had shown Laurel the birds of the lake, of the Northern cold.

The meeting between Laurel and Phil, she writes: "had been spontaneous—they had begun by dancing well together." Yet after the publication of the *New Yorker* story, the meeting place changes to the steps of the Chicago Art Institute. The predominant characteristics of both meetings are consistent: the attraction between these two people is spontaneous and strong, mutual, immediate, and undeniable.

> She and Philip first walked toward each other by chance in front of the Art Institute. Each knew who the other was, there had been a friend in common. It was a cold, dark Sunday afternoon in the middle of March; the lake was indigo. They walked into the museum together and walked up the staircase, enclosed by the Sunday throng, shoulder to shoulder. As they climbed, a Monet on the floor above (it was a loan exhibition) shed light halfway down the staircase towards them, out of a lady's open

parasol. They were stopped at the same moment with a foot on the same step. Then up they sped. For the rest of the afternoon, they walked miles without ever leaving the museum and never stopped talking. They were aware of an attraction as if it had been some amazing resemblance growing between them, which called clamorous attention to itself and reverberated to their footsteps. In front of a Bonnard lithograph six inches square, which contained the expansiveness of a woman standing with her arm down—curved to place a bowl in front of a man seated at a table, they came to another halt, and exchanged addresses and phone numbers. Both wrote with Venus drawing pencils, and both pencils raced, as though two lives would depend upon their quickness.

Welty characterizes the marriage of Laurel and Phil as one of magical ease—"They would live in Chicago where they had met . . . at the Art Institute . . . [They hurried] each night to get back to the apartment, that dark into which the two used to walk [,] swaying with happiness." The "manual training" Phil received in high school enables him to solve the domestic, electrical, and carpentry problems around the house.

> He was amused that she had come to marriage unprepared for life with anybody who knew how to make things work. He re-routed the wiring in their apartment to give them their bed light. He made a four-legged stool for her to stand on to put up her curtains and hang her wash. He said it was just like the stool he'd made in manual training class the seventh grade in Logan's Bridge, Ohio.

Eventually he makes the breadboard, a touching gift of his handiwork for his mother-in-law.

The compatibility between Laurel and Phil derives partly from their common art; the idea of designing has metaphorical significance for both Laurel and Phil. An architect, Phil imagines and sketches houses—domestic structures—while Laurel, first a painter, later opts for design—she becomes a decorator of interior spaces. This change in Laurel's career, from painter to interior designer, is a significant one, suggesting that she is a shaper of interior landscapes.

Quickly, however, the first indications come that Laurel has lost Phil.

> Laurel thought we loved each other! To love is not to dismiss. It was not even a very long time ago. But memory was a reckless power, as independent of wish as the power of loving. [Phil was the only ghost in her life, she thought]. The reminder of loss

was still a part of her conscious effort to live, but was familiar now, almost in the nature of comfort. Losing your love was like being given a compass, though too late for the journey.

Welty likens love to memory, since both are "reckless" powers now ranging out of control, "independent" of the wish of the individual. She likens the loss of love to a compass—found "too late" to chart the waters together. Laurel makes the "conscious effort to live" after Phil's death, only to meet perpetual loneliness as a penance. His accustomed absence—in Derridean terms, the presence of an absence—takes on the familiarity of "a comfort."

Laurel's memories of Phil in these unpublished sketches now begin to move, "press forward," and erupt in her mind, unbeckoned, beyond her conscious control, and requiring her full attention. She ruminates about this selective, uncontrollable quality of memory, which Welty later calls "the somnambulist." Phil, the most repressed memory she has, emerges from the deep recesses of her mind:

> Of all those who moved in her mind, he was the retiring one. Those closest to us in time seem quickest to vanish, and those who lay deep back begin to press forward, making voices heard. [In the long period of sleeplessness of the war and after the war [he was lost], [she was in effect staying awake]. . . .

Laurel's sleeplessness carries forward the more general motif in the novel of sightlessness, hindsight, and the personification of memory as somnambulist. Laurel's father and mother each die blind or nearly blind. The loss of sight ironically creates deepened hindsight in both Judge McKelva and his daughter, each of whom achieves a heightened understanding of love. In this context, Welty's title change of draft four, from "An Only Child" to "Poor Eyes," is understandable. She has commented further upon that change in title:

> I wanted to have something about the eyes. I first wanted to call it "Poor Eyes," but that was voted down. Bill Maxwell and Diarmuid Russell didn't like it. Bill did like **The Optimist's Daughter.** He said it gave a nice "chill of apprehension." But I've never been very good at titles. After the book came out I had letters that had the title wrong: "I so much enjoyed *The Optimistic Daughter.*" Another said *The Optometrist's Daughter.* That's a good one, don't you think? The Optometrist's Daughter? Because of the eyes?

Welty's title also reflects her own propensity to learn through hindsight: "I seem to come to understanding belatedly," she says, and in **One Writer's Beginnings** she applies this sense of understanding to her parents' lives.

It seems to me, writing of my parents now in my seventies, that I see continuities in their lives that weren't visible to me when they were living. Even at the times that have left me my most vivid memories of them, there were connections between them that escape me. Could it be because I can better see their lives—or any lives I know—today because I am a fiction writer?

Sleeplessness and hindsight seem most closely related in Welty's image of memory as "the somnambulist," the wakeful sleeper.

The revisions also carefully trace Phil's wartime activities and death. During the war, Phil's letter home warns of the proximity of the perilous Kamikaze planes and presages his imminent death.

> He had written on a V-mail letter not to her but to her father, and she, being at home, had opened it—the only letter not her own she had ever opened [and done as if to show she was married]—read aloud the absurdly reduced laconic words that the suicide flyers had been up to now approaching the carrier 'close enough to shake hands with me.'

The autobiographical underpinnings of these scenes become clear in Welty's statements:

> My friend in World War II married into—well, when someone was lost like Phil is—I knew what that feeling was like. How could I not have? . . . It was a bad war. The boys we knew were involved in this, and we were with them. These young people (today) . . . couldn't conceive of fighting for a cause. This applies to Phil. The part in the novel about the *kamikaze* happened to Walter. He was in the Navy *Okinawa,* and later he was asked, 'How close have you come to a *kamikaze*' and he said, 'Close enough to shake hands with.' So I put that in the story. Who could ever make up a thing like that?"

The inevitable moment soon arrives, in these dramatic but fragmented sketches, in which Laurel receives the news of Phil's death.

> That night there came knocking—first on the front room door of this apartment and then, down the hall, at her bedroom door: [S]he was writing him a letter, half drawing it the way they wrote to each other. She put her head out the front door—She recognized the knocker in a moment. It was the neighborhood Taxi, that was all;

"Wrong door." she said, pert-voiced, a young matron in the north.

He came on in. "You got a place to sit down, lady? You got a death message." He handed her a telegram. [from Washington.]

"But you were just the taxi driver!" He put on his cap, with a badge lettered "TAXI[.]" and clumped off down the stairs. Still standing in her doorway with her telegram, she heard the taxi proving itself, creaking off into the snow.

This scene is redolent with implication. Laurel receives the news of Phil's death as she is in the bedroom writing him a letter. But she is "half-drawing" this letter, "the way they always wrote to each other," another testament to their shared artistry and affection. Laurel is unaware that as she composes the letter, Phil is dead.

The ironically off-handed method by which the devastating death letter reaches Laurel, by way of "just the taxi driver," has echoes in other Welty stories of the injustice of accident. In **"A Piece of News,"** for example, Ruby Fisher reads a shocking news story that she believes to be pronouncing her own death. The news article startles her, as for Laurel, because the outside world violates the private sphere abruptly; the newspaper and the taxi driver alter lives with cruel anonymity. Miss Larkin in **"A Curtain of Green"** similarly loses her husband to accident, her loss lasting a lifetime. Laurel can control neither the shock of Phil's death, nor the abruptly inadequate and inappropriate manner in which the news arrives.

Disappearing while flying over the Pacific, Phil is, as military euphemism would have it, "among the missing." But Laurel's imagination dwells upon the gruesome fate of her lover's body:

> But of what had happened to him and his plane, there had been no living witness, [there was no trace]. He was among those missing, and that was the end of it. He was bones on the Pacific floor. Or his drowned body had washed up on some strip of sand and birds he would have loved and known had eaten him. And because there was nothing of him left, her [his] memory of Phil was intact; satisfied. Everything changes. [His memory was intact, yet vast (.) (F)or her it was Chicago].

Phil is physically gone, his body violently destroyed. "Bodiless and graveless," as Welty describes him later in the novel, Phil's association with birds becomes even more ironic because this careful watcher and lover of birds—who "filled his sketchbook" with birds, "knew all about their . . .

nesting, migrations," had shown these birds to Laurel—has now literally been eaten by them.

Phil's death by drowning also has significant ramifications in the larger context of the novel. Death by water is a common end for Welty characters. Clytic drowns in a rainbarrel; Hazel Jamison in **"The Wide Net"** threatens to drown herself, and since she is presumed drowned, the community drags the river for her body. Grady's father has drowned in the Pearl River (in **"The Wide Net"**), and tears come to Grady's eyes when he imagines his drowned father's visage:

> Without warning he saw something . . . perhaps the image in the river seemed to be his father, the drowned man—with arms open, eyes open, mouth open . . . Grady stared and blinked, again something wrinkled up his face.

Written thirty years before *The Optimist's Daughter,* this passage closely resembles the drowned visage of Phil as it appears to Laurel in the novel—mouth open, eyes open, voice crying out, as the survivor weeps for love and for the dead.

For Welty, the drowned face is the face of death in its most horrifying form—eyes that are open but cannot see, arms open wide that cannot embrace, and a mouth that is open but has no breath or voice. Although Judge McKelva does not literally drown, Welty insists on a parallel:

> He made what seemed to her a response at last, yet a mysterious response. His whole pillowless head went dusky, as if he laid it under the surface of dark, pouring water and held it there.

In Welty's photographs and stories, the human face is the clearest image of life, and so bereft of all expression and voice, the drowned face becomes her most profound image of the finality of death.

The association of water with death and memory occurs in all versions of *The Optimist's Daughter,* perhaps because water, with its fluid properties, resembles the onset and then the "flood" of memory, that can "roll its wave" over Laurel "unbidden." In the first complete draft of the novel, for example, water evokes Laurel's memory of Phil as she washes her hands.

> 'the way to cool off the soonest is to let water run over the veins in your wrists.' Philip Hand's voice returned in the running water and spoke from her memory unbidden. She stood there, letting the water cool her, and the tears brimmed her eyes.

Memory arises against her will. Phil is disembodied here, as well—no image appears; Laurel simply hears his voice. But the moment is not one of horror as in the final pages of the novel. Instead the voice soothes her soul, just as the running water cools her body. Water and grief commingle again as Laurel weeps at her father's funeral. As she stands at the gravesite, grief deafens her, and she does not hear the funeral sermon.

> Dr. Bolt assumed position and pronounced the words. Again Laurel failed to hear what came from his lips. She might not even have heard the high school band. Sounds from the highway rolled in upon her with the rise and fall of eternal ocean waves. They were as deafening as grief. Windshields flashed into her eyes like lights through tears.

The psychological significance of the journey that the judge embarks upon is here suggested by Welty's powerfully descriptive language. Sounds from the interstate achieve the deafening pitch of "eternal ocean waves." "The ancient porter," unloading Judge McKelva's coffin from the train, is a modern-day Charon, the mythic boatman who ferries the souls of the dead down the river of eternal woe. Sound carries meaning: "There was a dead boom like the rolling in of an ocean wave. The hearse door had been slammed shut." Laurel's father is poised for his journey down the river of oblivion. The bridge over the Mississippi River, shrouded in nightfall, that Laurel sees from the Judge's hospital room window shortly before his death, further symbolizes his impending passage into the world beyond. The metaphor of the wave now takes on even more texture and resonance in describing her marriage to Phil.

> As far as Laurel had ever known, there had not happened a single blunder in their short life together. But with Phil's death, the knowledge that nothing had protected him had rolled its wave in on her, over her head, and when its savagery was spent had left her stranded.

Like Phil's bones, washed ashore, Laurel is emotionally "stranded" without him. Her memory of him is "vast," like the Pacific Ocean in which he drowns, and her soul expires along with Phil's: "If Phil had lived and I had lived!"

But Laurel cannot renew Phil's life nor save it. Saving one's life is at first a joking matter between the two lovers:

> 'You saved my life,' she'd said when Phil replaced the broken sash cord so that the little kitchen window could be raised. 'Well, that time it was easy,' he said, and, both laughing, they sat down to the table with a blessing of a fresh breeze from the lake.

Even to the sound of a distant band concert—and he'd whistled along with it, as though to say a proper husband could produce music just by loving it, skim it right off the lake.

Overseas, in wartime battles of fire and water, Phil is vulnerable to the *kamikaze,* and neither she nor anyone can protect him from death: "She'd had to learn it again, and now from Philip Hand again. Who knew better than she now that protecting was the feeblest act of love."

The theme of protection and vulnerability continues to wind suggestively through the later novel. Laurel's mother Becky cannot protect her own father from death, nor can Laurel save her father from destruction. Welty cites in *One Writer's Beginnings* the roots of this idea in her parents' lives. Her father saves her mother's life once, but ultimately she cannot save him when he needs a blood transfusion:

> This time, *she* would save *his* life, as he'd saved hers so long ago, when she was dying of septicemia. What he'd done for her in giving her the champagne, she would be able to do for him now in giving her own blood.

The medical procedure fails, and Welty's father dies: "My mother . . . never stopped blaming herself. She saw this as her failure to save his life." The complexity of these lessons results in the fictional Laurel's understanding that "protecting was the feeblest act of love."

In revising *The Optimist's Daughter,* Welty excised most passages that elaborate the character of Philip Hand and his early married days with Laurel. The little description of Phil's character remaining in the novel, a brief account of his wedding day, does not substitute for the excision of sketches portraying happy love. These excisions emphasize the horror of Phil's demise and the tragedy of his loss. Commenting upon her decision to deemphasize their romance, Welty said that:

> There wasn't time for any of it. I played Laurel down from the beginning—she's the eyes. But when I started developing it more, I decided to concentrate on Phil's death rather than on the earlier material. . . . Laurel's romance wants to come out, too. She's been trying to bring it forth. Her own has been kept waiting. Finally it burgeons out, especially in the context of the records she goes through, and the storm, and the crisis.

Not included in her original story, Phil Hand evolves into a character during Welty's compositional process. After the radical excisions, the Philip Hand of the final draft, dead and disembodied, arises in Laurel's purgatorial memory, like the ghost of Hamlet, returned from the grave to inflame the survivor with grief. The novel now relentlessly and powerfully apprehends the image of the dead Philip Hand.

> She had gone on living with the old perfection undisturbing. Now, by her own hands, the past had been raised up, and *he* looked at her, Phil himself— here waiting, all the time, Lazarus. He looked at her out of eyes wild with the craving for his unlived life, with mouth open like a funnel's . . . 'Laurel! Laurel! Laurel!' Phil's voice cried. She wept for what happened to life. 'I wanted it!' Phil cried. His voice rose with the wind in the night and went around the house and around the house. It became a roar. 'I wanted it!'

Here at last is the remembered voice of the husband silenced by death, "raised up" like Lazarus by Laurel's "hands." His voice rises with the wind in a deep and profound cry for life that becomes Laurel's expression, too, of her own missed opportunity: "I wanted it!" Phil's voice, the tornadic "roar" whirling around the house, becomes the second metaphor for the sound, like the eternal ocean waves, of deafening grief.

Removing the early sketches, reducing Phil to a voice enveloping Laurel, Welty achieves the emotional pitch and imagistic clarity that is the genius of *The Optimist's Daughter*. Phil's spirit merges with the bird that rushes through Laurel's house, as images of water shift to those of flight and sound. The next scene introduces a small, brown chimney sweep who enters the house with a disturbing, "pounding" wingbeat. Once inside the house, the bird "frantically" strikes itself against the window. Laurel catches and releases the bird, which flies away with a gently palpable wind. The bird, like Phil, appears bodiless as it recedes:

> Something struck her face—not feathers; it was a blow of wind. The bird was away. In the air it was nothing but a pair of wings—she saw no body any more, no tail, just a tilting crescent being drawn back into the sky.

The final image of the disappearing bird symbolically incorporates both Phil's physical absence and his presence. Avid birdwatcher, sketcher of birds, eaten by them on the Pacific sands, Phil assumes here the corporeality of the chimney swift, as the housekeeper, Missouri, warns with her folk wisdom, "Bird in the house means death." As Laurel carries the bird out of the house, she has "full knowledge" of its body and spirit "vibrating through the ribs of the baskets, the beat of its wings or of its heart." The violent winds of the past are transformed here into a feather-like brush of wind of a chimney swift's wing. Her night of agony is over;

even the house is still "like a ship that has tossed all night and come to harbor." Laurel's waves of emotion subside. The catharsis is at hand: the exhalation of the breath, the calming of the wind and water.

In the final moments of the ultimate chapter comes the heartrending apotheosis of Philip Hand and Laurel's own salvation, as Welty draws together the disparate symbols of bird, war-plane, and wind into the single image of the "tilting crescent," spent in memory. Mrs. Chisom was mistaken: Laurel has indeed had "a soul to call on," and that soul, like memory, "is like a well; the deeper you go, the more you recover." Thus transfigured, Phil abides imperviously in Laurel's memory of him. With Phil forever among the missing, no body to recover, no grave to tend, Laurel has only memory by which to apprehend and enshrine the disappearing man.

Eben E. Bass (essay date Spring 1993)

SOURCE: "The Languages of *Losing Battles,*" in *Studies in American Fiction*, Vol. 21, No. 1, Spring, 1993, pp. 67-82.

[*In the following essay, Bass analyzes the female characters' use of written and spoken language in Welty's* Losing Battles *and states "Though the feminine language modes of* Losing Battles *are 'opposites,' they serve a common goal: querying and challenging male-authored decrees."*]

Although they serve a common end, written and spoken language complement and compete with each other in Eudora Welty's *Losing Battles*. Teaching, writing, and books are the province of Julia Mortimer, who dies on the morning of Granny Vaughn's reunion. Lexie Renfro had presumed to be Julia's successor, but she "fell down on Virgil" and could not finish her training at Normal. Gloria Short, Julia's chosen heir, also denies that role when she marries Jack Renfro, her pupil. Julia's opposite, Granny Vaughn, commands a different province, spoken language and its transmission of family history. These two feminine modes of expression differ in that written language (books, letters) conceptualizes, moves toward abstractions; whereas oral language deals with the concrete, the experiential. In a process marked by both modes, the pulpit oratory of the late Grandpa Vaughn diminishes into that of Brother Bethune speaking (to Granny's disparagement) from the family reunion pulpit.

When Grandpa Vaughn's patriarchal voice is replaced by Brother Bethune's, his Baptist conception of authority (infant baptism can't save souls from sin) is reduced to local mythology, a shift from the oracular to the anecdotal. Both feminine voice modes thus mark a decline in male authority. Beulah rules her family, not her husband Ralph; and their idolized son Jack's impulsiveness gives rise to demonstrable instances of male folly. Rather than looking inside Curly Stovall's open safe for the missing gold ring, for example, Jack carries away the whole safe: "but he's a man! Done it the man's way," as Aunt Nanny says. Even the account of Grandpa Vaughn's daddy, builder of Damascus Church, implies criticism: "he'd preach in the church on Sunday and the rest of the week he could stand on his own front porch and have it to look at"—six days, not one, to admire his creation. Whether through Julia's book language (meant to lead Banner beyond parochialism) or Granny Vaughn's oral history (to perpetuate family values), male authority is questioned: not out of malice or subversion, but rather in an undercurrent of irony, sometimes funny, sometimes sad.

Battles and banners are seminal images in *Losing Battles;* they mark the main conflict of the novel between local and absolute. Thus Curly Stovall's store and Gloria's Banner School face each other across the road that runs through town "as if in the course of continuing battle." Jack's noisy fight with Curly in the store over the missing gold ring disrupts Gloria's efforts across the road to teach her class the poem about Columbus and the gray Azores. She teaches an ideal of outreach; Jack and Curly's rivalry becomes a comic brawl. Other contenders are "two ancient, discolored sawdust piles [left from Dearman's sawmill business] . . . like the *Monitor* and the *Merrimack* in the history book." Aside from its pictures, the book conceptualizes Civil War issues in the abstraction of printed words, whereas the actual sawdust piles not only look like the ironclad ships, but are the debilitated physical remnants of the Reconstruction itself. The issues of the War become localized in concrete images.

Written words rather than images signifying combat appear in the letter from Julia that Judge Moody reads to the reunion (to the family's displeasure, who want it "told" to them); Julia wrote, "I've fought a hard war with ignorance. Except in those cases that you can count on your fingers, I lost every battle." Moody himself is one "success" who stayed in Boone County, but he never forgave Julia for compelling him to stay there. As a judge he remains her judgment on Banner's ignorance—"the very pocket." Lexie, Ralph Renfro's old maid sister who wanted to teach school and who dampens the spirit of the reunion, likewise remarks to Ralph: "these children of yours are the least prepared to be *corrected* of any I ever ran up against. How they'll conduct themselves on the Day of Judgment I find hard to imagine." Thus written language is broadly judgmental, whereas oral tradition fosters impulse and concern for localism.

Both battle and banner converge in the emblem of Jack's "torn sleeve that flowed free from his shoulder like some

old flag carried home from far-off battle." The sleeve marks Jack's arrival at the reunion; like the sawdust piles that image the ironclad vessels, it too speaks of the South's history of lost battles. And from the beam in Curly's store hang local "shirt-tails of every description . . . like so many fading banners of welcome." To these trophies of Curly's other victories in battle, Jack's shirttail is added after Curly knocks him senseless in the fight at the end of the novel. The shirt-tails are like feudal banners captured from claimants to Curly's male fiefdom, his store, which indeed once belonged to Jack's father. But the contending oral and written languages, which are female-dominated, underlie the novel, the surface of which deals with matters like Jack's and Curly's rival claims to a ramshackle truck and a horse: prizes in a male world. Gloria, the short-time teacher, sees the truck for its real worth, a man's "play-pretty" that really wouldn't take her and Jack anywhere.

Granny Vaughn's full name, mentioned but once in *Losing Battles,* relates to the oral consciousness of her family; as proclaimed by Brother Bethune in his reunion speech, "Miss Thurzah Elvira Jordan . . . [was] known far and wide in the realms of the Baptists for the reach of her voice as a young lady." Her name comes from "Tirzah" in Canticles: "thou art beautiful, O my love, as Tirzah, comely as Jerusalem, terrible as an army with banners." Granny's sermon-bred family know about Thurzah and Banner as these are epitomized by their spirited vocal matriarch and by the name of their community.

Though married, with a child, and reunited with Jack, Gloria yet assumes the role of a school teacher when she orders the rest of the men at the reunion not to join her and Jack for his vengeful encounter with Judge Moody. She, Jack and Lady May will do it alone, she says, as she "lifted her old teacher's satchel . . . and hung the strap over her shoulder." To complete Gloria's role, Beulah praises her daughter-in-law's self-containment and assurance in terms of written language: "once you've hidden her Bible . . . and wished her writing tablet out of sight, you wouldn't find a trace of her. . . . You can't reach her." Although Julia wanted people to open their minds and hearts to others "so they could be read like books," Gloria finally rejects Julia's council and decides, "people don't want to be read like books."

As much as he loves Gloria, Jack still senses a missing part: "you know all the books. But about what's at home, there's still a little bit left for you to find out." He means her sense of family, or lack of it: she is an orphan, and much of the talk at the reunion deals with who her parents were. Mistrusting books and writing and favoring oral history instead, the Beechams and Renfros never write letters, whereas "*I'm not afraid of pencil and paper,*" says Gloria. While Jack served time in Parchman, she wrote to tell him that they had become parents, but he never wrote back—remiss, "like a man," as the women folk would say. Earlier, when he was her student, Gloria sent Jack home as punishment for fighting Curly, and she demanded a written excuse from his mother, but Beulah characteristically refused to write anything. Forceful and articulate at the reunion, however, Beulah *tells* much about the fight with Curly which ended in Jack's sentence to the pen.

Vaughn, Jack's put-upon younger brother (now twelve, the age when Jack had to quit school) nevertheless is the "best speller"; his toehold on literacy recalls Julia's triumph when Gloria "spelled down" the legislature. Humorously related to the family's conflicts over written language is the name of the youngest surviving uncle, Noah Webster (of the dictionary) Beecham; a sad instance is Julia's spelling book, where she lettered her will in pin pricks, her pencil having been taken away from her by Lexie. Despite its initial promise, literacy would appear to be a lost cause, though there are occasional cycles of hope—if marked by nothing more than spelling skills.

Spoken words in *Losing Battles* contend with the enemy just as do those written or read from a book by school teachers. Granny Vaughn was famous for her voice when she was young: "talked back to General Grant. Remembers the conversation," says Aunt Beck. When Grant shot a cannon ball into Captain Jordan's five-foot-square chimney, Granny, then a child, ran out and scolded him for it to his face. Grant is not only the enemy Northerner, but also the male aggressor, who is put down by a young girl.

The family uses spoken language as a way of sharing. Aunt Beck complains about the newest sister-in-law: "can't she [Cleo] wait till Brother Bethune gets here for dinner and tells it [the family history] to us all at the table?" Though his dictionary name belies him, Noah Webster, speaking to Gloria, describes the spoken tradition best: "long after you're an old lady without much further stretch to go, sitting back in the same rocking chair Granny's got her little self in now, you'll be hearing it told to Lady May and all her hovering brood. How we brought Jack Renfro back safe from the pen!" As if by folk magic, an act of will, the family perpetuates its values in oral tradition with Jack as its central figure. Thus when he is about to lower the Buick into place, Beulah says that her son will show better judgment than Samson did, but that is more her expectation than her conviction. For all his heroics, Jack is bedeviled by bad luck and his own likeable folly; beneath the admiration of his mother and his young wife lies the question of his right reasoning.

Whereas Julia forbade Gloria to marry Jack (she thought they were first cousins), Gloria defied her and did so anyway. Julia said any child born of the marriage would be deaf and dumb—symbolic affronts to oral history—but to prove her mentor wrong, Gloria planned to take Lady May to see

Julia as soon as the little girl could talk. During the night after the reunion a heavy rain falls on the Renfro house: "then the new roof resounded with all the noise of battle," in the course of which Lady May "put her voice into the fray, and spoke to it the first sentence of her life: 'What you huntin', man?'" As if by nature the child vocalizes the matriarchal battle-challenge inherited from Granny Vaughn, who shamed General Grant.

In contrast, Judge Moody, the first of Julia's proteges (as Gloria is the last), has little use for spoken language. He has come at Julia's written request, to affirm the law forbidding marriage of cousins, a law Julia was instrumental in getting passed. At Banner Top he scolds the family for talking to death the dilemma of the Buick perched above the roadside. Amusingly, though, his court sessions have to be held in the cramped quarters of a Sunday school room because the court house and its written records were burned (by varmints, as Granny says) after Jack's trial. And in his comic predicament at Granny's reunion, Moody sits like a pupil in the school chair, to be lessoned in the reunion's oral history.

Writing takes another comic form in the character of Miss Ora Stovall, Banner correspondent for the *Vindicator*. "Watch out, Freewill! Banner's going to beat you this week!" she says, planning her account of the reunion, the Buick's misfortunes, and Julia's funeral. Though written, Miss Ora's newspaper column will have much the flavor of spoken language: gossip, "human interest," provincialism, a "story" told like a folk tale. Even her name is almost "Oral," just as Lexie, who wanted to but couldn't be a school teacher, is a diminished "lexicon."

After the reunion, with everyone else in the Renfro house asleep, Vaughn, wearing Grandpa Vaughn's old hat, rides Bet the mule and hears "loud night talking to itself. . . . No matter how good at hollering back a boy might grow up to be, hollering back would never make the wheel [of the sky] stop." Earlier, when Jack and Gloria prepare to sleep on the bare porch, "Jack in his gown came running out . . . and before she [Gloria] could get her hand over his mouth he had given his holler." These vocal outbursts come from the old tradition of the travelers' holler to signal others as they made their way through the Mississippi wilderness. Willy Trimble also has a network of "hollers" whereby aged, infirm people can let each other know that they are still alive every morning, but Julia refused to take part in it; instead, she wrote desperate letters which jaded Lexie might or might not post in the mail box.

Gloria's Bible, as expected, functions pedagogically as a book; other Bibles, though on printed pages, give rise to spoken folk myth. When Brother Bethune climbs up Banner Top and stumbles next to Jack and Gloria, he drops his tuning fork and his Bible. "Bound in thin black leather skinned to the red of a school eraser, [it] looked as if it had come to his door every Sunday by being thrown at it, rolled up like the Ludlow Sunday newspaper." In the pulpit, however, Bethune orally transposes a printed book (his Bible is worn almost to an abstraction) into local legend and experience.

Because he doesn't measure up to her late husband, Granny Vaughn doesn't want Brother Bethune to preach at the re-union, and as matriarch she forbids his use of the Vaughn Bible. It is her repository for sacred family emblems, a closed book on the past containing Grandpa's eyeglasses, a lock of her daughter Ellen's hair, Ellen's wedding ring, the post card from Sam Dale. Out of respect for her mother, Beulah orders the Renfro Bible fetched instead, but Bethune doesn't really read from it either: "he threw open the Bible . . . as if to show he could start on any page it wanted him to." His funny, inept applications show how local, oral history has its own way with things, but to the ears of the re-union, especially those of the women, his sayings are absurd. Grandpa's patriarchal authority has been replaced by a poor diminished thing.

For an ungainly starter to Granny's reunion, Brother Bethune praises the old home, the happy family and "what exactly in the Book it looks like to me this minute [is] Belshazzar's Feast. Miss Beulah may have even out-pro-vided it!" Beulah, offended by Bethune's foolishness, says Grandpa Vaughn would have said the blessing, given the family history, and its lesson, before even looking at the table. Much of Bethune's message, in fact, is interspersed with women's voices correcting his lapses, the worst being his forgetting that Grandpa Vaughn is dead.

Inept as it seems to Beulah, however, the Belshazzar trope says more than what appears on its comic surface. The bib-lical narrative in which none of Belshazzar's court is able to interpret the writing on the palace wall dwindles in *Losing Battles* to the family's aversion to written language. To be sure, there are Uncle Nathan's signs (painted left-handed), which speak to minimum literacy; but they do not require reading by a prophet, can be read by all. They are practically oral-visual in the sense of a cartoon caption or a speaker's ballooned words in a comic strip, the modicum of Banner literacy. Also, "the part of the hand" seen writ-ing on Belshazzar's wall presages the ghost of Nathan Beecham's missing right hand (and oddly connects with the heaven-pointing, bodiless hand seen at the top of Dearman's monument in the cemetery).

The most pervasive biblical emblem in *Losing Battles* (and one with oral force) comes from God's order to the prophet Nathan (the name of one of Beulah's brothers) to "build me a house to dwell in" because, ever since the Israelites came up out of Egypt, God's house has been a tent and a taber-

nacle; the permanent house must be built of cedar as a sign that the Israelites will no longer be wanderers. Therefore Great Grandfather Vaughn, newly arrived in the wilderness, "raised that house out of his own oaks, pines, and cedars, and then he raised the church"; also, he "hewed them pews out of solid cedar, and the pulpit is all one tree." Thus the one-tree pulpit makes patriarchal declamation the center of Damascus Church. Lying in the Renfro yard is the trunk of an old cedar tree where on the morning of the reunion Gloria patiently waits for Jack. Later, after his arrival, they sit on the log together. They were married in Damascus Church by Grandpa Vaughn, in front of the cedar pulpit.

Cedar takes on a comic role in the "tall old cedar tree [that] was stubbornly growing out of the end and standing over" Banner Top. Because of Lady May and Gloria's absurd con-frontation in the road with Judge Moody, his car veers up the embankment. "The Buick had skinned past the trunk, the tree had creaked back into place," so that "now the old cedar stood guard just behind the left rear fender."

But since its staying power seems an impediment, with comic male ineptness Mr. Renfro blasts away the cedar so that the Buick can be pulled back down to the road. His dy-namiting is noisy enough for the Last Judgment, mingling with the thunder of the night storm following the reunion. By just a few roots, the tree hangs upside down over the edge of Banner Top. A delayed, unintended second explo-sion (Mr. Renfro used old dynamite) dislodges the last of the cedar's roots; it falls down the bank. When the rope breaks that holds the Buick over the edge, Jack and Gloria fall into the cedar tree (it still has some staying power), then land safely on their feet next to the Buick, which stands on its nose.

Cedar is also the intended lining for the rough pine coffin Willy Trimble carries in his wagon. When Mrs. Moody sees this receptacle, she refuses to ride with it to get to the re-union. Willy planned to get cedar boards "from Dearman's time" to put within the coffin; he hoped it would be used for Julia. Since he couldn't master books, she taught him woodworking when he was her student at Banner School, but the coffin doesn't suit the literate mourners at Julia's wake. And at Julia's burial owls fly out of the old cedar tree behind her grave, suggesting the flight of literacy and knowledge.

The emblem sequence thus forms a paradigm of decline: the cedar log in the Renfro yard, the old tree dislodged at Ban-ner Top, the lining for the rejected coffin, and the ancient tree at the head of Julia's grave. In each instance, the cedar's biblical, patriarchal force diminishes from its original, the permanent house for God to dwell in, Damascus Church, where the Word is spoken from the one-tree pulpit. The dwindling of that male voice has been remarked by the Banner women's speaking, as it also has been by Julia, single-handed defender of books, whose "church" is the school-house.

The most telling sign of female dominance in *Losing Battles* relates to the relationship between Beulah and her favorite brother Sam Dale, cemented by his emasculation as a child by a spark from the fireplace, and Beulah's failure to find a timely cure for the injury. Beulah holds herself to blame for this harm done to the best of her brothers, a pain made even worse by his dying in the World War. Her inwardly turned anger reinforces the power of her speech, which dominates the many voices of the reunion. She is Granny's vocal heir.

Less effectually, Brother Bethune adapts parable to local legend. When first meeting Jack, he "pivoted on his gun and fixed him with his loving gimlet eye. 'It's the Prodigal Son.'" Jack escaped from the penitentiary at Parchman one day before his release in order to be on time for Granny's birthday, but he was not away from home wasting his inheritance or eating pig fodder. As comic overtone, the Renfro pig will be fed leavings from the reunion, and it accompanies some wild pigs who gobble up Mrs. Moody's chocolate layer cake when the cake falls out of the Buick. To complete the parable, Beulah even calls their pig an "old sinner," as if to lay Jack the Prodigal's misalleged sins on the scapegoat animal.

In another skewed parable, Jack in his well-meaning folly is said to have become a Samaritan because he pushed Judge Moody's car out of the ditch, but when Mrs. Moody signals for help to get her car down from Banner Top, neither Uncle Homer driving his chicken van nor the "hungry Methodists headed home for dinner" stop as Samaritans to aid the distressed Moodys (who are, and indeed look like, Presbyterians). The Samaritan in Luke helped a victim despised and passed by by others, but the affluent Moodys are scarcely victims who have been robbed and beaten. The Bible parable is turned inside out; in addition to their hunger, the Methodists most likely "pass by on the other side" because they feel inferior to Presbyterians. Mrs. Moody's vocal distress dominates this whole sequence, during which she trades on her need for some male Samaritan help, but neither Homer Champion nor Rev. Dollarhide, consummate politician and hymn-prone preacher, offers any help.

Like the lyrics in Shakespeare's plays, old-time hymns also provide vocal irony for the events of *Losing Battles*. Before their church dismisses, the Baptist-rival Methodists sing "Shall We Gather at the River," a skewed appraisal of the political fish fry Curly plans for that very Sunday afternoon at the river's edge. A little later, the Methodists are heard singing "Throw Out the Life Line," to anticipate the absurd human chain begun by Jack to save the Buick on the rainy

Monday after the reunion. The chain involves everyone except Miss Lexie and Miss Ora, who are parodies of the two language modes, oral and written; the others hang onto the rope from which the unfortunate car is suspended over the edge of Banner Top. Although no one is "sinking today" (in the hymn's phrase), everyone (Baptists and the rest) gets a thorough soaking in the steady rain.

Granny's reunion ends when Uncle Nathan, left-handed, plays a different hymn tune on his cornet: "Let the Lower Lights Be Burning"—"Some poor fainting, struggling seaman, You may rescue, you may save." A self-styled evangelist, Nathan "becomes" the old-time prophet as his way of repenting for his murder of Dearman, exploiter of timber and of people. After his solo, Nathan takes a coal tar torch and burns out the caterpillar nets in the trees around the Renfro house. "We've lost him, I know, to the Book of Revelation," says Beulah, the family's spokeswoman. Revelation mentions locusts and scorpions being emitted from the "bottomless pit," and Nahum says that the sinners of Nineveh will be devoured by fire as if they were canker-worms.

If one reads Welty's subtext, biblical Nathan finds his obverse in Nathan Beecham: whereas the former chastises King David for sending Uriah to certain death in battle so that David could possess his captain's beautiful wife Bathsheba, Nathan Beecham kills Dearman the timber exploiter and expropriator of the Renfro house and store. As hinted by Granny, Dearman had impregnated Rachel Sojourner, who was admired especially by Nathan, and whom Sam Dale later promised to marry. Thus Nathan felt justified in the revenge he took for his brother who was "sent into battle," who died, although not in action, and who was lost to his adulterous and pregnant wife-to-be. Biblical Nathan chastises the king with a parable; whereas his Beecham namesake kills Dearman, then cuts off his own right hand, to follow biblical injunction, and to follow the quirky mission of planting along the roadways his left-handed signs about repentance. Nathan's full story, finally revealed at the reunion, has been known and concealed by Granny and Beulah; his method of penance, as we shall see, was ordained by Julia. Thus his role is circumscribed by both female language modes.

Women's folk art in the form of patchwork quilts also adds biblical overtones to *Losing Battles*. "The Delectable Mountains" patterned quilt is Granny's favorite gift on the day of her reunion birthday. It displays the "called-for number of sheep," which would be ninety and nine. The parable search for the missing hundredth becomes the search for Gloria Short's mother, who by way of extended oral reminiscence turns out to be Rachel Sojourner (her name means "homeless ewe"). Rachel abandoned her baby and died shortly later of pneumonia; her grave, marked by a lamb no longer "very snowy," is about to slide into the Bywy River.

In a biblical allusion not spoken by a character, but in keeping with the characters' perceptions, Julia's funeral procession crosses Banner Bridge, which could at any moment collapse under the load. "Behind the hearse the line seemed to narrow itself, grow thinner and longer, as if now it had to pass through the eye of a needle." That line of Julia's admirers, people of rank, book knowledge, and substance, should indeed be concerned about "passing through the eye." Whether Julia herself will enter the Kingdom is problematic; the only churchman present at her grave site to aid that endeavor, a Catholic priest, speaks in Latin. Julia chose him for the role because he once learned algebra from her, but his speaking a strange tongue and wearing "skirts" elicits Miss Ora's critical "what does *he* call *him*self?" Brother Bethune, the only available Protestant clergyman, absentmindedly thought he was to perform a marriage at Damascus Church and did not appear for the grave ceremony at all. Thus Julia, sponsor of books and writing, is spared the gravesite oratory of Banner; by her choice, Latin, algebra, and the skirted priest become its foreign substitutes.

When Jack and Gloria arrive at the cemetery, barely in time for Julia's burial, "the original grasshopper [on Sam Dale's grave] was repeated here too, repeated everywhere and a hundred times over, grave-sitting or grave-hopping in the stubble." The army of graves that Jack and Gloria pass on their way to Julia's burial swarms with grasshoppers, numerous and apocalyptic as Nahum's prophecy to Nineveh. Though these Banner graves comprise "an army of tablets," the cemetery stands too close to the Bywy River, into which Rachel Sojourner's lamb will soon slide, the same river in which Ellen and Euclid Beecham drowned after the accident at Banner Bridge. As the narrator observes, a "long and colorless tree" submerged in the Bywy at Deepening Bend (seen as Jack and Gloria pause at Rachel's grave) looks like a fern pressed in a book. This is the very spot in the river where Ellen's drowned body was found. Welty's elegiac simile echoes Granny's use of her Bible as keeper of *memento mori*: the "fern" tree pressed in a figurative book, for Ellen's drowning, is like the lock of hair and wedding ring of Ellen, or the post card from Sam Dale, that are kept in the Vaughn Bible. A "book" is a closed receptacle, unlike spoken words, which are open and responsive. And the "army of tablets" in the graveyard are those surfaces on which are recorded brief, written words about the deceased, concealing more than they reveal: tablets as factual and abstract as Gloria the school teacher's writing tablet.

The tallest monument in Banner cemetery is for Dearman, "on its top the moss-ringed finger that pointed straight up from its hand in a chiseled cuff above the words 'At Rest,'" A monumental equivalent to Nathan's artificial hand, but with a difference; the index finger has a ring of moss, whereas Nathan's hand (a gift from his brother) has a seal ring on the ring finger, ironically echoing the gold wedding ring over which Jack and Curly fought. After a disembodied hand writes mysterious words on the wall at Belshazzar's feast, the king dies; Nathan killed Dearman and severed his own hand in repentance, his prosthesis mock-imitated by the hand on the monument.

One can tell where Nathan Beecham has traveled by the signs painted left-handed that he leaves behind. Just when Jack tries to be amorous with Gloria on Banner Top, she bumps her head on something hard, Nathan's sign "Destruction is at Hand." Thus one dimension of Nathan's warning relates to Banner Top's fame as a Lovers' Leap; another is to its being the legendary jumping-off place for Indians who didn't want to be repatriated. The same sign also plays its joke as a humiliating perch for the Buick. Another of Nathan's signs, freshly painted, appears in the ditch where Moody says he got stuck on Sunday: "Where Will YOU Spend Eternity?" Though these clumsy mottoes express abstract concepts, Welty puts them to humorous, concrete uses, much as she does with other folk emblems in the novel. Unlike the mysterious handwriting on Belshazzar's palace wall, Nathan's signs "speak" clearly to local experience. But curiously enough, Nathan's role as wandering evangelist began with Julia, who conceptualized or abstracted his role and in effect sent him away from his community. "Nathan, even when there's nothing left to hope for, you can start again from there, and go on your way and *be good*." Despite the signs' intent, however, in Julia's pedagogy they achieve bare literacy.

Though not very church-minded or good, Curly Stovall adds a further evangelical note to the dilemma of the Buick, perched as it is on Nathan's "Destruction" sign. "Who told you you could run that pleasure car up yonder and leave it, lady? That's a spot just waiting to give trouble. Full of temptations of all kinds." At her age, Mrs. Moody doesn't need to be warned about the amorous dangers of Lovers' Leap (indeed Jack's sister Etoyle mistakenly calls her the Judge's "mother"), but Welty keeps up the humorous byplay when in all innocence the younger sister Elvie approaches, singing, "yield not to temptation for yielding is sin."

Losing Battles features an amusing, non-ecumenical meeting of Protestant sects. Mrs. Moody (herself once a school teacher and now the Judge's judge) feels embarrassed about her husband's muddy knees; he appears, ill-kempt and unshaven, as one of Julia's pallbearers. "People from Ludlow, and Presbyterians from everywhere, will wonder what you've been doing down on your knees," she says. After all, Presbyterians don't kneel. They do, however, believe in Divine intervention. "Like it sprung right out of the ground! Providence sent that. My husband only had to turn his back," Mrs. Moody remarks when she sees Curly arriving in his truck, which she hopes will tow the Buick down to the road. Mrs. Moody also presumes Divine intention (predestination?) when she says, "if that car hasn't fallen to its destruction before much else happens, it wasn't intended to fall." "How much longer do you think Providence is prepared to go on operating on our behalf?" the Judge asks her. "Oscar, instead of tempting Providence, you'd better to head on down this road" to the store with a telephone, replies Mrs. Moody. But the store is closed on Sunday, and Miss Pet Hanks, the phone operator, won't be able to take the vocal distress call. Characteristically, the Judge fails to get "on line" in this oral community.

Before the Buick climbed to Banner Top on reunion day, Elvie's sister Etoyle sat in the cedar tree watching for the approach of Judge Moody. "A puff of dust showed along the next ridge over, as though a match had been laid to a string in Freewill whose other end was here at Banner Top. 'That's him. He's coming the long way round.'" Supposedly coming of his own free will, Moody is nevertheless compelled to do so by Julia's letter, a summons from a woman ten years older than he to whom he had other ties than romantic ones. She is still his teacher, he, her "pupil." So much for the dilemma of Calvinism, free will versus predestination. Culturally, Southern Presbyterians presumed to a higher social scale than did the evangelical sects; the fact that Gloria came from the Ludlow Presbyterian Orphan Asylum makes her think better of herself than of what is deemed to be her mother's family, the Sojourners, "lower than Aycock," who are nominally Methodists.

Further contention exists between the evangelical sects themselves. In the cyclone, the Methodist church was picked up bodily and set down next to the Baptist church, whereupon the Methodists took it apart piecemeal, put it back together "on the side of the road where it belonged. . . . A good many Baptists helped them." The banks of the road separating the two churches look, in the rain, like the parting of the Red Sea (the biblical "red" literally becoming the red banks of the road approaching Banner). And the funny procession of school bus, truck, Buick, and mules passing down Banner Road comprises the escaping "Israelites," with rival churches, singers versus orators, on opposite sides of the parted Sea. Welty even provides her vocalizing Baptists with total immersion in the rain, along with the Presbyterian Moodys and Methodist Stovalls—Curly and Ora—all equally immersed, "baptized."

As we learn from the oral history of the family, Euclid Beecham, a Methodist circuit rider, became husband to Ellen; parents of Granny Vaughn's many grandchildren, they died in the bridge accident. But before the marriage, Grandpa Vaughn had made Euclid into a Baptist. The couple were married by Grandpa in the Damascus church made of cedar. When Euclid and Ellen fled from the family by night in their buggy, Granny Vaughn rushed out and tried to stop them, but she was almost crushed between the buggy shaft and a tree, the remains of that tree being the cedar log which is Gloria's seat at the reunion. The log with its tragic story, its comic other self at Banner Top, and its sad counterpart at Julia's grave, thus hark back to the cedars of Damascus Baptist Church. Each has its staying power, though a lessening one: the cedar that once stopped Granny is now only a log; the Banner Top cedar stays the Buick (for a time) and even when uprooted, for the moment it eases Jack and Gloria's fall; the old cedar heading Julia's grave is the uncertain barrier between it and the fatal river.

Built of cedar, "Damascus was a firm-cornered, narrow church resting on four snowy limestone rocks." The church cornerstones recall the stone step to Banner School, under which Julia asked to be buried. But the male supervisors—"the *bad* boys of Banner School"—turned down her request. They said that the whole building would fall if the stone were moved: Grandfather Renfro began the schoolhouse with that stone, and "he meant it to stay. He didn't mean it to come out for anybody." Dr. Carruthers and Judge Moody are Julia's only successes who stayed in Boone County, the Judge even regretting having done so. Julia expected all her students to resist learning, but the treachery of the successes who don't return and the "bad boys'" refusal of her burial request show what she was up against with men. Remaining a mistrustful old maid was her form of protest.

After stating her burial instructions (which are ignored), Julia's will concludes, "and then, you fools—mourn me." But Brother Bethune, finally in key with the Bible (he does after all carry a tuning fork) says, "whosoever shall say, thou fool, shall be in danger of hell fire!"—a corollary to the commandment, "Thou shalt not kill." Judge Moody, chief defender of Julia Mortimer, authority figure and defender of learning, is thus put down by Brother Bethune, inept and "foolish" though he is, when Bethune speaks "in the flat tones of inspiration. 'We're going to forgive you.'" Taking up that spirit, partly out of humor, partly out of tolerance for an intolerant man, the entire reunion (except for Jack) joins in the forgiveness. The dominating male authority figure gives in to the diminished one.

Bethune's vocal "inspiration" short-circuits from Julia's written inspiration in an unlikely juncture that links the two disparate parts of the novel. In her last testimony Julia wrote that when all else failed, she finally depended on inspiration. Also "inspired" is the busload of school teachers who decide to take Gloria with them to Julia's wake. Even Lexie said to Julia, "you used to be my inspiration."

Another unlikely juncture in *Losing Battles* connects gender to church affiliation and politics. Although snakes and politicians are said to be the only flourishing creatures in Boone County, the poorest in all Mississippi, both accommodate themselves to its mythological church heritage. Brother Bethune, childless and alone, is the champion snake killer who deals in his own way with the first creature. The second makes marriages of convenience. As candidate for the office of justice of the peace, Uncle Homer (by marriage to Mr. Renfro's sister) counts on Baptist votes from the Renfros and Beechams. The opposing candidate Curly Stovall, a Methodist, will nevertheless get the best of Jack his rival by marrying Jack's sister to end their contention over the gold ring and to take Renfro-Beecham votes away from Homer. Thus matriarchy lies behind male power politics.

Used for quite different causes, Homer's and Curly's political campaign posters contrast with Uncle Nathan's apocalyptic signs, but both function in similar ways: they "speak" like cartoon captions. Though abstract and conceptual so far as individual words go, the campaign posters (like Nathan's signs) have a visual/oral impact that denotes Banner's literacy level, poised as it is between speaking and writing. Uncle Homer's "qualifications were listed in indentation like a poem on a tombstone:"

Experienced	
	Courteous
Lifelong Baptist	
	Married
Reliable	
	Just Leave It To Homer

"Poem on a tombstone" is an epitaph. More hopeful in a crude design that suggests sunrise and Resurrection, Curly's poster shows him wearing a hat, and "coming out from the crown on rays were the different words 'Courteous,' 'Banner-Born,' 'Methodist,' 'Deserving,' and 'Easy to Find.'" Other than place of birth, the claims are dubious, but as a radiant halo they speak confidently to Curly's winning the election. His victory will come about because of a marriage of contraries: Methodist to Baptist, Jack's enemy to Jack's sister Ella Fay—just as Jack's marriage to Gloria joins the written and oral traditions. Though the campaign posters contain words, the word arrangements speak as emblem-designs with specific, given meanings for Welty's narrative. Homer's epitaph will be no match for Curly's halo. An epitaph is a "closed book" on one's life that proposes to have "read" one to the end, just as the finality of being "read" by a school teacher causes Julia's former students their apprehension of being "ended" by her.

Thus the language of writing and print is a centrifugal force in *Losing Battles,* moving outward toward the abstract or conceptual (the summary epitaph) and away from the concrete center. Julia, the advocate of recorded language, sends forth her emissaries, but they fail to return to her until the time of her funeral. That is the tragedy of her message written to Judge Moody on the blank fly leaves torn from her Bible. Rather than choosing a Scriptural text, she writes her own Apocrypha, just as she asked to be buried under the schoolhouse step rather than among Christian families. (She ends up, however, in a borrowed grave in Banner Cemetery). In contrast, spoken language is the centripital force that gathers together the extended family of Granny Vaughn. Since writing and printed language move outward to the abstract, the words in Julia's letter are "too hard" for the listening reunion. Spoken language draws in close to make the emblematic concrete, familial, as in the humorously (mis)applied parables of the Samaritan and of the Prodigal, or in the diminished staying power of the cedar trees.

Judge Moody may say that Banner, the very pocket of ignorance in its oral history, is too self-forgiving; but for Beulah, Banner is "the very heart" of Boone County. Trained as a school teacher and emissary of books and writing, Gloria wants Jack to leave his closely-centered family, but he resists. Despite this year's spoiled hay crop, he ends up singing "Bringing in the Sheaves." Still, Gloria will probably demand a last word, just as Ella Fay will likely give Curly his comeuppance once they are married. After all, Gloria spelled down the (all-male) legislature, Granny defied General Grant, and Julia defied male-sanctioned burial customs. Gloria and Mrs. Moody, both former school teachers, exert their common sense against Jack and his father's hare-brained schemes for rescuing the Buick. Though the feminine language modes of *Losing Battles* are "opposites," they serve a common goal: querying and challenging male-authored decrees.

Gary M. Ciuba (essay date Fall 1993)

SOURCE: "Time and Confluence: Self and Structure in Welty's *One Writer's Beginnings*," in *The Southern Literary Journal*, Vol. XXVI, No. 1, Fall, 1993, pp. 78-93.

[*In the following essay, Ciuba discusses Welty's* One Writer's Beginnings, *asserting that Welty's "narrative confluence abolishes distances and divisions in time, links generations, connects seemingly disparate events into the pattern of a lifetime."*]

The first picture in the photo album that forms part of *One Writer's Beginnings* shows the young Eudora Welty in a telling moment: the delighted child is clenching her father's pocket watch, dangling its fob before the camera. "Life doesn't hold still," she later comments about her own photographs. "A good snapshot stopped a moment from running away." Like her own art that seeks the revealing gesture in the fleeting scene, the emblematic photo of the one-year-old halts Eudora Welty forever in the paradoxical position of keeping time—of marking its passage and holding it as a possession. *One Writer's Beginnings* is written precisely at the point of such temporal convergence. It reveals the confluence of past and present as the design of Welty's life and art by making such intersection the structural principle behind her lifestory as an artist.

In writing her autobiography at such a junction, Welty turns what seems like a necessity of the genre into a statement of her self. Augustine's description of memory as the "present of things past" defines the dual temporal perspective basic to autobiography. But as if following Ben Franklin's annals of the self-made man, a long tradition in American autobiography has arranged memory into chronology and emphasized the past over the present. *One Writer's Beginnings* duly acknowledges the custom of organizing a retrospect by hours and years. The pocket watch held by the infant Eudora in the photo keeps the conventional passage of time echoing throughout Welty's memoirs. As a child, she recalls growing up to the sound of a grandfather clock, cuckoo clock, and bedroom clock. As a college student, she felt the tolling of the chapel clock shake her bed at Mississippi State College for Women. And when Welty later got her first paid job in communications, she worked for a radio station in the base of the clocktower at Lamar Life. Published when she was seventy-five, Welty's reminiscences frankly confess the steady and straight-forward progress of time. She knows that the past—when infants had calling cards, the night sky over Jackson was nothing but blackness, and gargoyles graced her father's office building—is past. She even uses a loosely linear structure to plan the three sections of *One Writer's Beginnings*. "**Listening**" attends to her childhood years in Jackson; "**Learning to See**" reviews a journey in 1917 or 1918 to visit her maternal and paternal grandparents; and "**Finding a Voice**" speaks of her years in college and her first works as a serious writer.

But if the whole triptych shows how Welty gained the ears, eyes, and tongue of a storyteller, her fragmented and wayward memories ultimately reject the external organization of clocks and calendars. Her roundabout narrative flows with the casual immediacy of the raconteuring that Twain described as basic to his own *Autobiography:* "Start it at no particular time of your life; wander at your free will all over your life; talk only about the thing which interests you for the moment; drop it the moment its interest threatens to pale, and turn your talk upon the new and more interesting thing that has intruded itself into your mind meantime." Twain hoped that such formless form might provide the model for all future autobiographies. Originally delivered as a series of lectures at Harvard, *One Writer's Beginnings* shifts and drifts along the most vital currents of the Southern oral tradition. Welty omits sizable portions of her life and travels

through her past without being restricted by fidelity to historical sequence. The problem with organizing her memories according to the rigid succession of years is the same as the problem with the rigorous windows that the narrator of Welty's quasi-autobiographical "**A Memory**" wants to impose on the transiency and turbulence of her girlhood. Both devices overlook Welty's discovery that greater than any perspective is "a single, entire human being who will never be confined in any frame."

Published when she was seventy-five, Welty's reminiscences frankly confess the steady and straight-forward progress of time. She knows that the past—when infants had calling cards, the night sky over Jackson was nothing but blackness, and gargoyles graced her father's office building—is past.
—*Gary M. Ciuba*

The structure of *One Writer's Beginnings* repeatedly violates chronological framework to portray the integral, elusive self as the confluence of past and present. "It is our inward journey that leads us through time," Welty explains, "forward or back, seldom in a straight line, most often spiraling." Her allegiance to the dynamics of inner time typifies the increased appreciation of subjectivity in modern and postmodern autobiographies. Paul John Eakin sees traditional examples of the genre as encouraging the reader to believe that "the play we witness is a historical one, a largely faithful and unmediated reconstruction of events that took place long ago." But Welty rejects such documentary drama for what Eakin calls the play "of the autobiographical act itself, in which the materials of the past are shaped by memory and imagination to serve the needs of present consciousness." *One Writer's Beginnings* makes the process of recollection as revealing as the recollections themselves. Welty does not remember and then write, as if her life were a finished pageant that simply needed to be chronicled by an objective and anonymous observer. Rather, Welty writes as she remembers. She follows the dictum of veteran autobiographer Wallace Fowlie, "Living belongs to the past. Writing is the present." Living out the writing, Welty shows how personal and family history are always flowing together in the consciousness of the storyteller.

Welty defined the subjective temporality of *One Writer's Beginnings* in her 1973 essay "**Some Notes on Time in Fiction.**" Although clock time "has an arbitrary, bullying power over daily affairs," fiction wrests from time such authority by subjecting it to plot. The story can accelerate, reverse, prolong, or contract time. "It can set a fragment of the past within a frame of the present and cause them to exist simultaneously." Such freedom, Welty claims, "bears a not too curious resemblance to our own interior clock; it is so by design. Fiction penetrates chronological time to reach our deeper version of time that's given to us by the way we think and feel." *One Writer's Beginnings* is autobiography as fiction—not because it explores the problematic relation between memory and imagination like Mary McCarthy's *Memories of A Catholic Girlhood* but because it records the same irregular, internalized time that flows through all of Welty's stories and novels.

Yet despite its highly individual course, the structure of *One Writer's Beginnings* is not haphazard. Welty shuns what is merely amorphous, much as does the designing narrator of **"A Memory."** Hence, her reminiscences are ordered by the same insight that guides her fiction. Writing stories and novels, Welty asserts, has given her a "sense of where to look for the threads, how to follow, how to connect, find in the thick of the tangle what clear line persists." Her memoirs pursue a strand of discovering affinities and continuities between apparent disconnections. "The events in our lives happen in a sequence in time," she recognizes, "but in their significance to ourselves they find their own order, a timetable not necessarily—perhaps not possibly—chronological." Welty's distinctive rearrangement of the years does not keep events fixed to the standard autobiographical timeline but allows them to flow together or be forgotten according to their importance to her. Her ostensibly erratic play of recollection conveys the free and fluid exploration of her lifetime as one memory leads back or ahead to others, connected with it, commenting on it, the whole forming out of lives and generations a "continuous thread of revelation." If *One Writer's Beginnings* does not follow a straight line, it does pursue what Lewis Simpson has called the "southern aesthetic of memory" to discover the plot strands of Welty's life.

At the end of *One Writer's Beginnings,* Welty finally names the temporal design that has organized the stream of recollections from the start. As if the preceding hundred pages were a prelude, she writes, "I'm prepared now to use the wonderful word *confluence,* which of itself exists as a reality and a symbol in one. It is the only kind of symbol that for me as a writer has any weight, testifying to the pattern, one of the chief patterns, of human experience." *Confluence* provides an image for both the content and the flow of Welty's memories, for the self formed by the various tributaries of her past and for the formal structure of Welty's autobiographical essays. *One Writer's Beginnings* pursues this primal pattern by showing the connections between apparently different times in Welty's life as well as the intersections between obviously different lives and Welty's own time. All of these crossings coexist in memory, "the greatest confluence of all."

The title of Welty's memoirs explains this fundamental confluence. Since memory finds a meaningful conjunction between now and then, Welty traces her present identity as a writer back to the very beginnings of her life. In the first paragraph of an autobiography that dispenses with the ordering of clock time, she tells of being formed in and by clock time. "In our house on North Congress Street in Jackson, Mississippi, where I was born, the oldest of three children, in 1909," she begins **"Listening"** with her typical rootedness in time and place, "we grew up to the striking of clocks." But even as Welty recalls their tolling throughout her house, she displaces the supremacy of linear ticktock. Since the author is not just the remembered child but also the remembering adult, this memory of time's sound does not exist by itself but immediately flows into other tenses. It leads her to speculate about the significance of her ancestral past and then to anticipate its consequence in the future, her present time as autobiographer. Welty writes by confluence, not by chronology. She first wonders whether her father's Swiss heritage may have predisposed the Weltys to being "time-minded all our lives." When Welty returns to her father's family in part two, she seems to circle back to the very beginning of her book and of her life as well, but on her first page she does not take the traditional opportunity to retell these distant origins. Instead, Welty interprets her memory of hearing time by its later reverberation in her career: "This was good at least for a future fiction writer, being able to learn so penetratingly, and almost first of all, about chronology." If the novel cannot begin until the clock starts, as Welty observes in **"Some Notes on Time in Fiction,"** she already heard in childhood the mechanism animating every short story and her life story as well. Although Welty concedes that she made these clocks her own without even realizing it, she grants, "it would be there when I needed it." For her as for Faulkner, "Memory believes before knowing remembers."

From the first paragraph of **"Listening,"** time is ticking, but its typical sequence is undermined because incidents from various points in Welty's life are always "subject to confluence" in memory. Welty views past events from the perspective of the present and joins these episodes with others unrelated in time to disclose the larger pattern of how she began as a writer. In writing her memoirs Welty rewrites her life so that she reveals not just how the past seemed to her but how it seems to her now as autobiographer. As she recalls listening to songs, sermons, conversations, monologues, lessons in school, her own and her mother's reading, Welty shows how she heard her way to becoming a writer. All the earmarks of her fiction—her attention to dialogue and narrative voice, her pleasure in the sounds of words and cadences of sentences, her sense of story and dramatic scenes—begin in her youth. The child crafted the writer, but Welty the writer also crafts the child. She brings all the author's resources, which she began to discover in her early years, to capture her photographs of the artist as a young woman. Eudora is one of Welty's own best characters. And as her narrative skill in the present shapes her account of the past, the events in her life often follow the pattern of a short story.

Welty recalls discovering a classic epiphany about confluence while home from grammar school for several months due to a fast-beating heart. The memory charges a conversation between her mother and father with an erotic subtext to show how Welty the writer was born of a girl who loved to listen and who made listening into a virtual act of love. As the young Eudora lay at night in her parents' bed while they sat in rockers by a shaded lamp, she listened to their voices, hearing the murmur but not the actual words of their conversation. The daughter was privy to the subtle balancing of opposites in her parents, the "design for patterning and formulating complementarities" that Peggy Whitman Prenshaw shows is basic to Welty's fiction. Connecting early and later selves, Welty explains that her girlhood detachment disclosed what she afterwards turned into the necessary preparation to tell any story: she must find a frame, get a perspective, determine her distance. However, the adult writer never became a mere voyeur in her fictional world because her early stance as private observer was balanced by discovering another home truth.

Welty conflates not only her younger and older selves but also herself and her parents. In the bedroom, she was participating in a primal scene of linguistic intercourse. The child-writer sensed "the chief secret there was—the two of them, father and mother, sitting there as one." The daughter heard in her parents' tête-à-tête the flowing together of their lives, and she felt like a deeply responding part of their marital union. "I was conscious of this secret and of my fast-beating heart in step together," she writes, as if the quickened rhythm of her body were joining in such heartfelt lovemaking through language. Welty understands that this combination of childhood inclusion and aloofness gave her the eyes by which she would see her stories. "I suppose I was exercising as early as then the turn of mind, the nature of temperament, of a privileged observer; and owing to the way I became so, it turned out that I became the loving kind."

The second part of *One Writer's Beginnings* makes clear that its author had her beginnings not only in Chestina Andrews and Christian Welty but also in all the ancestors that preceded them. Whereas **"Listening"** turned its ear to her parents, **"Learning to See"** surveys a trip when Eudora was eight or nine to visit her grandparents in West Virginia and Ohio. What she learned to see on this journey was her own identity as a part of a community in time. The journey motif gives the section a more linear structure than that of its predecessor. However, part two is not so much a travel log as a free-flowing excursion into time past that connects events widely-separated over many years to show that Welty is the confluence of family history.

Although autobiography implicitly seems to announce that "I am I," Welty cannot define herself in narcissistic isolation but only through her kinfolk. Her abiding attachments confirm Susan Friedman's argument that women autobiographers often view themselves not simply in opposition to a world of others but also in relation to it. Elizabeth Fox-Genovese refines this feminist reading of lives that become texts by emphasizing the specific social and historical conditions that shape a woman's self-representation. She shows how this position between individualism and community is especially typical of the autobiographies of Southern women. Yet for Welty, the central community is neither Friedman's sisterhood nor Fox-Genovese's culture of race, class, and region. It is the family. Welty does not become a self by leaving her forebears behind but by taking them with her. Hence, she recounts not just her emergence from the abandoned world of childhood but also her continued rediscovery of bonds with the still present and interdependent past.

The West Virginia homestead of the Andrews family was a site for such temporal confluence. Its stories connected people of different times into generations. Welty's grandfather, the high-spirited Ned Andrews, loved to provoke his wife with tall tales, and since he died early, his sons knew him by oral tradition rather than by actual experience. Welty turns the home that Ned built into a memory house, for each place in it serves as the beginning of a narrative about the past. "Here in the center of the Andrews kitchen" was the long table where Ned prepared to transcribe music for the family band or to defend his cases at Clay Courthouse. "It was in the quilted bed in the front room of this house" where Ned suffered with an infected appendix and called upon Welty's mother, only a young girl at the time, to plunge a knife into his side. "It was from that door" that the fifteen-year-old Chessie left with her father to travel by raft and train to the Baltimore hospital where he died. "It was from this house" that soon afterwards Chessie set out to teach, reciting poems from McGuffey's Readers along her way to the one-room school. The Andrews home locates Welty not just in the hills so beloved by her mother but in the storied past. As each memory of the house leads to a more distant memory about her mother's beginnings, Welty's family history dramatizes the consanguinity that she describes in **"Some Notes on Time in Fiction"**: "Remembering is done through the blood, it is a bequeathment, it takes account of what happens before a man is born as if he were there taking part." Part two of *One Writer's Beginnings* traces the bloodlines of Welty's ancestry and of her art.

Since Welty's narrative is governed by the personal time of

its writer as she remembers rather than by close adherence to chronology, she interrupts this sequence on the Andrews home with a recollection from almost fifty years later: her elderly mother, helpless in bed and nearly blind, reciting with unabated ardor the same verses that she had memorized years ago from the primers of her students. Welty remembers, "She was teaching me one more, almost her last, lesson: emotions do not grow old. I knew that I would feel as she did," and the autobiographer makes that moment near the end of her mother's life circle ahead to her own life of seven decades by adding, "and I do." Welty neither recalls her mother's West Virginia origins as a prelude to her own beginnings in part one nor records the debilities that preceded her mother's death in 1966 as the finale to part three. Instead, her memory works by confluence. It reduces the original order of events and the half century that separates them to accidents of time, and it then rearranges these episodes according to the interpretive sequence of the artist's consciousness. Linking Chessie's girlhood with her passionate old age, Welty combines both of these memories with her own present as a writer at age seventy-five. The same enduring vitality makes the apparently discrete times of mother and daughter flow together.

Welty tasted the very wellsprings that nourished the independent spirit of her mother's family during her girlhood summer on the mountain. Then she became one of the folk of the West Virginia hills. Welty recalls that as she drank of the family well and of her homeland, the water's metallic flavor and ferny smell "all said mountain mountain mountain as I swallowed." Welty's deep draught grounded her in the locale that she had imbibed. "Every swallow was making me a part of being here, sealing me in place, with my bare feet planted on the mountain and sprinkled with my rapturous spills. What I felt I'd come here to do was something on my own." Inspired by such communion with the genius loci, the child tried to embody this newfound self-determination by taking a different course from the path along which her mother and uncles dawdled. However, the bold wayfaring led not to a triumph of autonomy but to a discovery of communal identity. Welty was initiated into the vast company of Southern women that Shirley Abbott names the "daughters of time." After the errant adventurer fell and was presented with torn dress to her grandmother, Eudora Carden brushed aside her grandchild's hair and peered into her eyes. What the gentle lady discerned in her namesake was the peculiar confluence of their lives as mountain women. "Hadn't we come right to the point of our both being named Eudora?" Welty wonders. And Eudora Carden saw that well-given bond in the context of a wider kinship when she looked from her granddaughter to her daughter and then back again. "I learned on our trip what that look meant," Welty explains in **"Learning to See"**: "it was matching family faces."

In name and features generations converged. And as Welty juxtaposes memories, heedless of temporal order, she repeatedly makes the same kind of match. She writes her sense of self—communal, historical, regional—into the structure of her autobiography by selecting, omitting, and connecting so that widely different times in her life and family come face to face and show their similar identities. As Welty remembers her childhood trip into matrilineal history, her past of sixty-five years ago turns into her mother's past and finally into her grandmother's past. Welty follows her mountaintop meeting with Eudora Carden by recording the story of her maternal great grandparents, Eudora Ayres and William Carden, who came to West Virginia before it was a state. She finally ends the account of her visit to the high country with a memory that is evoked not by chronology but the logic of association. Once again Welty recalls her mother feebled by age, this time in her wheelchair as she tries to pick out "The West Virginia Hills" on the piano, fingering keys that she could not even see. The song that Chessie had once sung while washing supper dishes for her family was now the anthem of her independence in old age. "'A mountaineer,' she announced to me proudly, as though she had never told me this before and now I had better remember it, 'always will be *free*.'" The conflux of Welty's memories illustrates how the independence that Eudora first tasted on the mountain as a girl lasted throughout her mother's lifetime and has now become a personal inheritance that must not be forgotten. All the folk of the West Virginia hills wear this same proud countenance.

If Welty's journey to her mother's kindred was a discovery of liberating connections with the past, her summer visit to her father's family in Ohio was a frustrating search for confluence. The Andrews' household remembered by talking, but the Weltys denied memory by silence. Although Welty traces her father's roots back to three brothers from Switzerland, who came to America before the Revolutionary War, she recalls that her father never told her a single family story. Indeed, his Ohio home was so empty and silent that his daughter could not even imagine Christian as a child there. At the heart of Welty's disconnection from her father's past was Allie Welty, the grandmother who died when her son was still a boy. Unlike the uncles' banjos that delighted Eudora with ballads and hymns in West Virginia, Allie's organ in the Ohio parlor was never played or approached. The stilled instrument was a way of not remembering her just as Welty's middle name was an accidental way of misremembering her. Much as she bore the first name of her grandmother Carden, Eudora had been given the middle name of Alice after her paternal grandmother. But it was later discovered that her kinswoman's name was Almira. "Her name had been remembered wrong. I imagined what that would have done to her," Welty writes. "It seemed to me to have made her an orphan. That was worse to me than if I had been able to imagine dying."

Eudora Alice Welty should have been the name of the dead grandmother's ongoing connection with her family, but instead it became the sign of her absence and abandonment. The word did not work as Welty had long expected it. From childhood the writer believed in the real presence embodied in speech. In **"Listening"** Welty recalled feeling the rondure of *moon* as a six-year-old, and she remembered how when she saw the Book of Kells as an adult, she sensed that the illumination was "a part of the word's beauty and holiness that had been there from the start." In Welty's beginning was the sacred, potent word; she even quotes the first line of John's gospel when she witnesses to how the King James Bible has resounded in her prose. But when her mistaken middle name recorded how even language had not kept hold of the past, the future novelist glimpsed a dereliction more terrible than death. Almira Welty lived not in the spoken present of a story but only in her unsaying—in oblivious silence and misnomer. The closest that Eudora Welty could come to her half-forgotten ancestor was the poignant vision of a childlike inversion: her grandmother had not died to the family but the family had died to her. In the Ohio parlor, there was no matching of names, faces, and lives as in her hillcountry rendezvous with Eudora Carden—no confluence.

Although the young Welty heard in Ohio the aesthetics of loss, this disconnection finally leads the mature writer back to a connection with her father's past. Through memory and imagination the daughter attunes herself to the deprivation of his childhood. Welty recalls that as a girl, she occasionally heard in her father's quiet home a music box, playing a tune from a faraway time, but she only comes to understand the melody in retrospect. "Now I look back, or listen back, in the same desire to imagine, and it seems possible that the sound of that sparse music, so faint and unearthly to my childhood ears, was the sound he'd had to speak to him in all that country silence among so many elders where he was the only child." Welty understands that "sound of unspeakable loneliness" better because she discovered after her father's death a worn giftbook from his youth. Besides various consolations from relatives and friends, it contained a message that his mother had written on the day of her death. "It had been given him to keep and he had kept it," Welty affirms. Her recollections of her childhood visit to Ohio conclude with the discovery of this memento as an adult because the keepsake makes sense of the lasting sadness that Welty heard when she was young. Welty's present rounds about her past and then curves back farther to her father's past. Like the music box, the memory books of Christian Welty and, to some extent, of Eudora Welty keep the same time of old bereavement.

Welty's trips to the homes of her mother and father schooled the child of memory in the continuity of the present with the past, the continuation of the past in the future. They made her feel the temporal confluence that she would later define in **"Some Notes on Time in Fiction"** by quoting Faulkner: the past is "a part of every man, every woman, and every moment. All of his and her ancestry, background, is all a part of himself and herself at any moment. And so a man, a character in a story at any moment in action, is not just himself as he is then, he is all that made him. If Welty's focus on her precursors seems to deflect attention from herself, it actually reflects her sense of self more profoundly than any supposedly more candid confessions. To be Eudora Welty is to live in the context of a particular history and in concert with her family.

In **"Finding A Voice"** Welty tells how her childhood expedition in part two formed part of a longer journey toward becoming a writer. She makes the two essays flow into each other by beginning the last section of *One Writer's Beginnings* with another trip. As the near ten-year-old traveled by rail with her father, her awareness of passing through the passing world reinforced the sense of place and transiency that would later define her stories and novels. The girl who rode through her life in time anticipates the writer whose characters would repeat the same transit in her fiction. Having discovered her point of view in a ready-made frame of the window, the young Eudora watched whole towns leap before her gaze and then disappear. And what she could not spy beyond the pasture or over the hill, she invented. Even before she was ten, Welty was seeing as she would from first novel to last. Laura McRaven's reverie on the train at the beginning of *Delta Wedding* as well as Laurel McKelva Hand's dream of the train ride to Mount Salus at the end of *The Optimist's Daughter* grew from precisely such play of the mind over the terrain. Weltyland, despite its celebrated depiction of the Southern locale, is a highly subjective country for the child who first sees as much as for the adult who later remembers and recreates it in her fiction.

As Welty reviews her childhood train ride, it becomes a circuitous passage that reconnects her with the origins of her life and art in her parents. On the journey, Christian Welty saw the vanishing scenery by memory rather than through fantasy, for he had passed its landmarks during the course of many trips. But his daughter never learned exactly how customary was this route until years later. Throughout *One Writer's Beginnings* Welty continually calls attention to what she did not know and to when she later found it out. She does not present herself as the eternally omniscient narrator of her own life who reads back into the past what she only discovered in the future. Rather, Welty shows how she has learned the whole of her own story only in time. Memory discovers the confluence hidden in personal history. Welty remembers learning after her father's death that he used to travel the thousands of miles from Mississippi to West Virginia by train to court Chestina Andrews. And when he could not afford the trip, the couple wrote daily letters. Kept over the years by Welty's mother in an attic trunk, these pages "brought my parents before me for the first time as young, as inexperienced, consumed with the strength of their hopes and desires, as *living* on these letters." The writer read her beginnings in the fervent writings of her parents. Welty's initial memory of a childhood train ride leads her to recall a later discovery of an earlier time, a revelation of her parents' passion before she was ever born. Their letters, which once bridged space, now bridge all of these overlapping times—especially those sent by her father. "Annihilating those miles between them—the miles I came along to travel with him, that first time on the train," they were "so ardent, so direct and tender in expression, so urgent, that they seemed to bare, along with his love, the rest of his whole life to me." Retrospect turns into prospect as Welty recovers a proleptic image of her father's life journey.

Since Welty's memory makes the recent and distant past into contemporaries, *One Writer's Beginnings* holds all of these times together—the memoirist as imagining young daughter and discovering adult, Christian Welty as parent and future husband. By seeing her father as a fiancé, a role that she could never have envisioned when only a girl herself, the much older writer at last understood how Christian Welty must have seen the landscape on her childhood train ride. She arrived at the truth of the past only by way of what was then the future. And as an artist, the daughter of Christian Welty eventually came to share his passionate vision. Welty recalls a final confluence with her father when she began writing seriously in her twenties, for then she found the world as revealing as the countryside that he had passed on the train. Conflating tenses, superimposing her later discovery on her girlhood recollections, Welty explains that she achieved this new perspective "because (as with my father now) *memory* had become attached to seeing, love had added itself to discovery," and she felt the desire to connect herself to the outside world. Welty's father knew the train route not just by heart but with his heart—with the tender recollections of all the journeys before his marriage. Writing repeats the same interior progress for Welty because it involves not just vision but re-vision, not just insight but intimacy.

When Welty concludes her memoirs with the publication of her early fiction, she shows how her stories join in confluence with her life story. These first works not only mark the end to her beginnings as a writer but also record the same time of her life, the same search for pattern, as do her autobiographical essays. "Writing a story or a novel is one way of discovering *sequence* in experience," she explains, "of stumbling upon cause and effect in the happenings of a writer's own life." Fiction finds the proximity between origin and distant end, and then it connects events "too indefinite of outline in themselves" into "a larger shape." Welty brings that form into focus by an image from the railroad trips that cross so much of her life and art. As when a train rounding a curve throws its light back on what could not be seen, the storywriter beholds "a mountain of meaning rising behind you on the way you've come, is rising there still, proven now through retrospect." *One Writer's Beginnings* discloses just such a looming, backward view as does all of Welty's writing from the beginning.

The revelations of once-obscured design make Welty's autobiography so continuous with her fiction that the story of how she came to collect *The Golden Apples* is also the summary story of how she structures each of the essays in *One Writer's Beginnings*. As she was writing her tales of Morgana, Mississippi, Welty did not know that they would form a cycle, but she noticed afterwards that they were about the same characters—sometimes under different names or at different parts of their lives. "They touched on every side," she realized, joined unwittingly from their creation "by the strongest ties—identities, kinships, relationships, or affinities already known or remembered or foreshadowed." *One Writer's Beginnings* composes Welty's life as if it were just such a suite of stories. It manifests the hidden continuities and contiguities that hold together her own identity in time, the characters of her family, and the course of her career. Like the individual pieces in *The Golden Apples,* all of her memories touch on every side. "In writing, as in life," Welty observes, "the connections of all sorts of relationships and kinds lie in wait of discovery, and give out their signals to the Geiger counter of the charged imagination, once it is drawn into the right field." If writing and life share such buried correlations, these networks of associations find their natural confluence when Welty writes her life.

In the final pages of *One Writer's Beginnings,* Welty dramatizes her vision of such latent connections throughout time when she quotes the beginning of the last chapter from *The Optimist's Daughter.* Her novelistic autobiography and autobiographical novel fittingly converge in a passage about convergence. Having dreamed about a train ride over a long bridge with her dead husband, Laurel awakens to realize that it was actually a memory of the trip years ago when she and Phil traveled from Chicago to Mount Salus, where they were to be married. The story that she told herself while asleep was a revelation of confluence. As Laurel and her fiancé looked down from the transcendent perspective of the bridge, they saw not just the commingling of the Ohio and Mississippi Rivers but the coming together of the whole world: below them, trees advancing from the horizon, and above them, birds meeting in a V and descending along the common course of the waters. "And they themselves were a part of the confluence," for while Laurel sat by the window, Phil touched her arm, and the two rode together toward their mutual act of faith. As if this immense panorama might localize the time of their conjoined lives, Laurel believed that they were going to live forever as one. But when her husband died in the war a year later, she separated herself from the underlying connections at the center of life and of Welty's writings. After remembering her earlier vision of unity, Laurel realizes that "Phil could still tell her of her life. For her life, any life, she had to believe, was nothing but the continuity of its love." Just as Laurel believes that the great rivers will still flow together at Cairo although she will not see them when she flies back to Chicago, the optimist's daughter places her faith in such confluence.

Welty writes her memoirs at the same point of intersection. Like Laurel in beholding the central design of life as the pattern of the heart, at the end of *One Writer's Beginnings* Welty sees the successiveness of time suddenly freed by an embracing simultaneity. The past is not behind her but beside her. And to remember is to renew membership in this enduring commonality: "I glimpse our whole family life as if it were freed of that clock time which spaces us apart so inhibitingly, divides young and old, keeps our living through the same experiences at separate distances." Flowing by linked associations rather than governed by chronology, Welty's memoirs duplicate exactly such temporal coincidence. Her narrative confluence abolishes distances and divisions in time, links generations, connects seemingly disparate events into the pattern of a lifetime. "The memory is a living thing—it too is in transit," Welty writes, always aware of the progress through time. "But during its moment, all that is remembered joins, and lives—the old and the young, the past and the present, the living and the dead." Memory suspends tenses to create a meeting place for what can never or no longer meet in time. In *One Writer's Beginnings* Welty can be always with herself and her family at the start of her own life story. Like the one-year-old in the photograph, the writer can hold time in her hands.

Alexandr Vaschenko (essay date Fall 1993)

SOURCE: "That Which 'The Whole World Knows': Functions of Folklore in Eudora Welty's Stories," in *The Southern Quarterly*, Vol. XXXII, No. 1, Fall, 1993, pp. 9-15.

[*In the following essay, Vaschenko discusses the folklore elements present in Welty's short fiction.*]

When it is approached, the subject defined appears to be a part of the general mystery that the stories of Eudora Welty present for any attentive reader. Yet the literary and the folk do intertwine in such an unprecedented way in her narration that this constitutes a challenge for any critical mind.

This approach to the short stories and novellas of Welty reveals some of their complexity of form and meaning, for

the genres of folklore employed are as various as the means to employ them. Indeed, the field to be covered quite unexpectedly may turn out to be so vast that it cannot be encompassed here. Yet what may be called the most pronounced ways to bring the folk elements into narration, as manifested in Welty's shorter fiction, will be discussed here at length. I should like to approach my subject from the point of view of the aesthetic function performed by concrete folklore elements.

In the American tradition, folklore is understood in a broad sense to include almost all of the manifestations of folk life, not just verbal art. From that point of view, we should begin with the mythological dimension, especially if mythology is thought of in terms of a body of concrete myths and the specific ways to tell them. This level manifests itself in Welty's fiction by way of the symbolic chains exemplified mainly by ancient Greek and Celtic images. These two different mythologies certainly combine in bringing forth the purport of the stories in *The Golden Apples.* Although both traditions can be traced back to written sources, rather than to oral, these are undoubtedly based on folk models. Because of them the general atmosphere of the stories in *The Golden Apples* becomes one of life as wonder, mystery and fantasy, which is characteristic of Celtic folklore and, to a large extent, ancient Greek mythology.

Even though the images of Psyche, Circe, Perseus, Medusa, the Shower of Gold, the Golden Apples and many others may persist in the works of Eudora Welty, they lose considerably their orality, assuming a function that is purely literary in nature. For this reason, folklore in Welty moves toward the more concrete and exceptional uses of folklore proper.

All classifications work poorly with Welty's stories, and not all of the writer's stories are to be regarded as good cases for the study of folk elements as the first and foremost features in making their structure and meaning. Most obvious and easy to deal with is the case when the subject matter as a whole is borrowed or reset from a folk source, but that is, characteristically, the least common with Welty. *The Robber Bridegroom,* being a creative remodeling of the Brothers Grimm fairy tale, may be an exception that proves the rule. Yet at least two groups of stories which are very different from each other show that they are designed with the idea that the literary and the folk should complement each other. And each group of stories employs folk elements that are different and uses them for different reasons.

The first group comes somewhat early in Welty's career and thematically is grouped around the Natchez Trace, that is, most of the stories in *The Wide Net and Other Stories* (1943) and *The Robber Bridegroom.* These works are grouped not only thematically but stylistically, because of the special goal the author wished to achieve.

Being closely connected with specific and striking landscape features, these stories are oriented toward imitation of the folk genre called "local legends," hovering between these and historical anecdotes, with concrete historical names involved. This presupposes that the time is also legendary. In **"First Love,"** for example, the narrator begins, "Whatever happened, it happened in extraordinary times, in a season of dreams." The real time, if one bothers to investigate, is the period between the 1790s and the 1810s. *The Robber Bridegroom,* as the author specifies in *The Eye of the Story,* is "set in the Natchez country of the late eighteenth century, in the declining days of Spanish rule."

The outcome of this combination, of the legendary time and place in these works, is that the writer implants the Natchez Trace in our consciousness as an aesthetic symbol and spiritual landmark of universal scope, performing, on one level, a task not unlike Miguel Angel Asturias in the *Leyendas de Guatemala,* E. Pauline Johnson in the *Legends of Vancouver,* or a number of writers in the Russian tradition, be it Shergin with his tales about the northern seamen, the pomors or Bajov with his legends of the Ural mountains. After reading these Welty stories, one is truly convinced that there appears such a place as the Natchez Trace in the imaginary—as well as geographic—map of the world and that there is no America without the Natchez Trace. One could not have achieved this goal through folklore alone, for it would be confined only to the local vicinity, having stayed limited to the folk knowledge of the early settlers. Only by giving birth to this folk material as a literary reality could it be made widely appreciated and universally significant.

Welty has written, "The line between history and fairy tale is not always clear." In *The Robber Bridegroom,* where the fairy tale quality is so clearly manifested, one must notice also the hidden presence of such genres as the tall tale and the ballad, especially with the appearance of such figures as Mike Fink and Jimmy Lockhart. Besides, one can notice that two different times are combined in the narrative: the unspecified time of the fairy tale and mythic time. These times merge, for as we proceed from the beginning to the end of the narrative, the surrounding wilderness becomes civilized. One structural peculiarity is also present, for we experience every now and again some gap in explanation and are to take the striking and the grotesque for granted. In folklore this is natural, as the stanzas of the ballad leap from one piece of narration to another, but here it becomes a device to enhance the analytical and mystical qualities of the narrative.

This legendary atmosphere becomes clearly manifested through the structure of the language and the imagery em-

ployed, the peculiar rhythm and syntax, as can be seen especially in the opening lines of many of these stories. These just slightly modify but clearly make use of the folk formulas for the beginning of the story.

> Whatever happened, it happened in extraordinary times, in a season of dreams, and in Natchez it was the bitterest winter of them all. (**"First Love"**)

> Lorenzo Dow rode the Old Natchez Trace at top speed upon a race horse, and the cry of the itinerant Man of God, "I must have souls and souls I must have" rang in his own windy ears. (**"A Still Moment"**)

> Solomon carried Livvie twenty-one miles away from her home when he married her. He carried her away up the old Natchez Trace into the deep country to live in his house. She was sixteen—only a girl, then. . . . He told her himself that it had been a long time and a day she did not know about, since that road was a traveled road with people coming and going. He was good to her, but he kept her in the house. (**"Livvie"**)

These are clearly marked folktale-like opening lines, but in the same passages Welty brings into the narrative the literary preoccupation with the details of the immediate and individual perception, constantly breaking the folk pattern, in order to complicate the general idea of the story. It continues to be one of the author's chief artistic devices in all of the Natchez Trace stories.

Beginning with these early stories, another type of narrative structure began to develop in Welty's stories—one structure among all the diversity of her stories. Yet it is unmistakably present in stories like **"Lily Daw and the Three Ladies," "Petrified Man," "Why I Live at the P.O.," "Old Mr. Marblehall,"** as well as in several stories in *The Golden Apples* and some of the later ones. In these stories, the narrator (the protagonist) represents somebody who is an intricate part of a community who is usually telling about somebody who is at odds with community views, or vice versa. Again, we can see the striking structural difference when we read the opening lines in these stories:

> Mrs. Watts and Mrs. Carson were both in the post office in Victory when the letter came from the Ellisville Institute for the Feeble Minded of Mississippi. . . . Mrs. Watts held it taut between her pink hands, and Mrs. Carson underscored each line slowly with her thimbled finger. Everybody else at the post office wondered what was up now. (**"Lily Daw and the Three Ladies"**)

Reach in my purse and get me a cigarette without no powder in it if you kin, Mr. Fletcher, honey, said Leota to her ten o'clock shampoo and set customer. I don't like no perfumed cigarettes. (**"Petrified Man"**)

Old Mr. Marblehall never did anything, never got married, until he was sixty. You can see him out taking a walk. Watch and you'll see how preciously old people come to think they are made. (**"Old Mr. Marblehall"**)

That was Miss Snowdie Maclain. She comes after her butter, won't let me run over with it from just across the road. Her husband walked out of the house one day and left his hat on the banks of the Big Black River—that could have started something, too. (**"Shower of Gold"**)

Let us make a special note of the place of action: the post office, the beauty shop, the neighborhood or, equally, it may be the house of the dead, as in **"Wanderers."** The diversity of these will look similar only in one respect: these are the places and the occasions where and when the people gather to chat, exchange news and gossip. So the reader is brought at once on the scene of the traditional speech events, so to speak. Here the folk elements, as employed in the narrative flow, represent not the local but the regional way of life, linking it with the universal. The South in general is the place, be it Morgana, Victory or any other small town. And this time it is the different folk genres that are being structured. To portray the South preeminently as a way of life which is most characteristic yet universal, Welty turns to what with some risk may be called a folk genre, small town gossip. Yet the risk happens to be not so great after all, when one outlines its peculiar qualities.

In the *Encyclopedia of Southern Culture* one may come across many broad characteristics of southern life, such as laying an emphasis on "leisure time, the strong continuity between generations of many families, the interest in family background and genealogy and the love of storytelling"; or that "southern regional identity will partially determine the aspects of a person's life that are worth telling stories about, but these narratives also relate to American culture and to universal human concerns"; or that "the personal experience narrative acts as a means of reincorporating the mystical event into everyday reality, a structuring of an unstructured incident so that it can be shared with and perhaps inspire others." The latter quotation describes the genre of the "Personal Experience Narratives," the "Family Narratives," the "Oral History Narratives" and, one may add, just "Gossiping-or Sitting-on-the-Porch Narratives."

We can find examples of all these in the Welty short fic-

tion under discussion here, but for the sake of brevity, we should concentrate on small town gossip narrative. As I understand it, gossip is viewed as a complex phenomenon. Not only is it entertainment, but it is a way of being, of sharing and expressing certain community views and values. Gossip involves taking sides, employing many speech events, such as metaphors, understatements and the like—including a great deal of improvisation, acting, impersonation, etc.—in other words, folklore characteristics. And out of the many great southern writers, Welty seems to be the most aware of the creative potential in this element of folk life and folk expression—which she uses to its full measure. Each time she uses it, the small town gossip element may be presented differently, yet it is manifested on many levels.

A comparison between Faulkner's narration and Welty's will illustrate this point. In Faulkner, however different his characters may be in social, cultural or racial terms, be it Benjy Compson, Ike McCaslin or Gavin Stevens—or even Lucas Beauchamp—their voices are, in the long run, the same written-speech voice, the epic literary biblical voice of the author coming through in long monologues incorporated into the narrative.

It is very different with Welty. First, she seems to avoid the depiction of extraordinary events as her subject matter. She sticks to the apparently insignificant. Second, her narrators, while gossiping, often serve the role of counterposition between the visually present or told about and what is actually meant by the author.

What, then, does this small town gossip technique actually amount to when applied to Welty's narrative composition? First of all, it means the adoption of a loose structure of gossip storytelling. When reading these stories, we experience constant digressions from what appears to be the main issue or subject. Instead, we come across interruption or running-ahead-of-time information, the inclusion of less important or what appears to be seemingly unrelated matters, all kinds of odd motifs which are seemingly at war with the main idea of the story. The plot itself seems to wander about freely, coming and going as it pleases. Before the reader has time to account for what is going on in the story, the "gossip technique" has reached the level of the reader's psychology, bringing forth the aftermath of the oral mental processes of a small community, so that the reader—now actually the listener and participant—becomes the wanderer among those others meant in the closing story of *The Golden Apples*. Little by little we also come to understand that all this is done to both challenge our intellectual analytical activity and to give us the opportunity to formulate our own view on the matter. On the more abstract level, it brings forward the philosophical concept of life as a complex phenomenon, where some kind of mystical and wonderful pattern is making its way through all of the haphazard and chaotic manifestations of the story. This technique also helps to avoid the narrowness of certain conventional literary techniques, but it nevertheless complicates the position of the reader. There are many variations to this technique in Welty's stories, with or without the oral speech patterns involved, with just a community point of view present.

Secondly, the gossip technique, when employed as the means of telling a story, involves the characteristic logistics of phrase structure. One immediate aspect of this is that the phrase and the sentence acquire an immense multitude of meanings. It simultaneously characterizes the 'events of the fabula, the community point of view and, by extension, its values *and* the philosophy of the narrator and narration—even when they may be expressing different points of view.

> In *One Writer's Beginnings* Welty states that her self-education began with listening—that is, mastering the oral characteristics of the language and the world around her. This statement holds true for many southern writers whose distinguished oral quality is too often obscured by their openly literary means.
> —*Alexandr Vaschenko*

Another verbal and narrative outcome of the gossip technique is that the written phrase structurally tends to become oral. This means that the relationship between the narrator and the reader becomes close to the relationship between the storyteller and the listener. And more: the story itself acquires the touch of "just a story for entertainment," told for the mere purpose of passing the time, for amusement. It is only eventually that it proves to reveal the whole of its meaning through small trifles and everyday details. These "trifles," however, involve a leisurely time and thought and actually point to the freedom of self-expression, as well as the freedom, the variability of the events depicted, freedom of interpretation of the causes and effects, of the detail and the whole.

Thus, on a general level, gossiping is implanted in the reader's perception as a local way of life which is preserved only through this style of living and storytelling and by means of this proves to possess universal appeal.

Given all this, we might conclude that there are two groups of stories in Welty's short fiction classified according to the use of folk styles. First, when the meaning of the story is extracted from the plot itself, from what is told, so to speak (as in the Natchez Trace stories, organized according to the

poetics of certain folk genres). Second, when the meaning is derived in spite of the plot or from the way the story is told. In the Natchez Trace stories, the author is the narrator and the discourse is clearly of a "narrative" type. In the "gossip technique" stories, a line of imaginary storytellers appears, and the story is told rather than narrated. Both are, to an extent, folk structured but according to different aesthetic systems.

From this we can see that quite often the events narrated and the voice of the narrator, the "point of view," make a peculiar combination. Contrast between the two is more pronounced in the second group, for the events being narrated are everyday occurrences, while the mode of the narration is oral. The event and the telling about it are simultaneous but counterpositioned, unlike in the Natchez Trace stories, where the narrator is blended into the narrated, as in the romantic legendary tradition. In the "gossip technique" stories, the actions of a hero undermine the community views, paradoxically enough, as in **"The Shower of Gold."**

In *One Writer's Beginnings* Welty states that her self-education began with listening—that is, mastering the oral characteristics of the language and the world around her. This statement holds true for many southern writers whose distinguished oral quality is too often obscured by their openly literary means. The fictional world of Eudora Welty shows eloquently the multitude of consequences coming out of this orality. If the reader is a symbolic wanderer and the community is ambivalent about its values—and the world, too, possessing the quality of a fairy tale in all that is bitter and sweet—then it means we have to look deeper into these categories, redefining that which "the whole world knows": community values, immediate reality, the meaning of the self, the fairy tale and storytelling itself.

In Eudora Welty's fiction we indeed come across the making of a metaphor for the South, which is oral in quality. The technique and the framing of the story that she employs has proved to be so rich and productive that it has been developed in stories by Peter Taylor, Elizabeth Spencer and perhaps others. In other words, it is by listening that these writers have developed their craft, which is so unique in the literary world, and succeeded in building up a metaphor which is invariably a combining of the oral with the literary and is, at the same time, endlessly confirming *and* questioning that which "the whole world knows."

Carol Shields (review date 12 August 1994)

SOURCE: "Wafts of the South," in *TLS,* No. 4767, August 12, 1994, pp. 20-1.

[In the following review, Shields discusses three books: a biography of Eudora Welty, a collection of her book reviews, and her novel The Optimist's Daughter.*]*

Eudora Welty was born in 1909 in Jackson, Mississippi, where she still lives. This stern rootedness has always compounded the wonderment in Miss Welty's admirers, for there is, first, her long list of writing accomplishments to contemplate, and then an accompanying respect for her serene, unwriterly willingness to stay put. She is, in a sense, a curiosity in American literary history, a writer who stayed home, who has lived, in fact, in the same house she moved to with her family when she was a girl of sixteen.

Her five novels, her dozens of short stories and essays, and her fine memoir *One Writer's Beginnings,* all found their sense and shape in an upstairs bedroom of the Welty house on Pinehurst Street. The mention of this upstairs bedroom may call to mind Emily Dickinson (another writer who kept to her room), but the comparison fails from the start; Eudora Welty's writing has always turned outward to embrace the society she was born into, and her life, moreover, has been characterized by a rare richness of friendship. Old friends, familiar surroundings, conversation, books, occasional travel, the pleasures of the post, the sustaining power of routine in a small and knowable city; these seem the steady forces that have nurtured her gift—a gift which is often described as being uniquely Southern.

> **Eudora Welty's writing has always turned outward to embrace the society she was born into, and her life, moreover, has been characterized by a rare richness of friendship.**
>
> —*Carol Shields*

Most serious readers of fiction are acquainted with the work of William Faulkner, and are on speaking terms with Walker Percy or Toni Morrison, and so have overcome their apprehensions about the universe of critters, grits and Grandaddy-catching frogs-down-by-the-swamp. Southern writing—whatever that phrase embodies—is lyrically seductive and, at its best, brings fresh narrative news from another frontier.

North Americans love their regional pigeon-holes. The sheer immensity of continental space drives writers, and critics, into the consolation of shared corners, hunkering down with their geographical fellows, becoming New England writers, Western writers, writers of the Great Plains, even attaching themselves to smaller subdivisions: Montana writers, North Carolina writers (of which there seem a disproportionate number), San Francisco writers, Marin County writers, and,

of course, that pressing throng of writers from the South, including writers from the "deep South". We almost never speak of *Northern writers,* perhaps because this largest-by-far category is simply "the other" against which "the rest" are poised and compared.

There's more than self-interest behind these clusterings. The tug of landscape plays a part, certainly, and the reliability of an accessible human network, but there are also the comforts of related syntax and, finally, a strong comradely resistance to the monolith of New York publishing, with its perceived appetites and *modus operandi.*

Such territorial groupings, not nearly cohesive enough to be called "schools", shatter quickly under analysis. Every theory of regional writing produces its contrary example, and, in fact, writers, even those eager enough to support local presses or literary magazines, are the first to resist identification by geographical category. Eudora Welty, reviewing Marguerite Steedman's novel *But You'll Be Back,* in 1942, objects to the jacket copy which advertises the book's characters as being "Normal Southern" people; This is "a jolting phrase", she writes, and she hopes it "does not indicate that hereafter southern people are to be subdivided after having already been divided from the rest of the country".

Two years later, reviewing a novel by the mostly forgotten Harry Harrison Kroll, Miss Welty says, "This is a distinctly Southern Book, in that every word springs straight up from Southern earth." Kroll's attachment to a recognizable terrain seems as far as Eudora Welty is willing to go in isolating qualities of "Southernness". Interestingly, it is only in these two early reviews that the "Southern question" is raised; her later reviews avoid the subject almost entirely. It may be that she despaired of defining so slippery an essence as regionalism; perhaps the breadth of her reading— she was discovering South American fiction as early as the 1940s—made her sceptical of arbitrary enclosures.

The University Press of Mississippi has now published Eudora Welty's complete collected book reviews, sixty-seven, written between the years 1942 and 1984, most of them for the *New York Times Book Review:* Pearl Amelia McHaney can be thanked for bringing this graceful collection together. The availability of Welty's critical work locates the author historically, enlarging our understanding of the evolving Welty aesthetic, and creating a sort of subjunctive biography which will be especially enlightening for those who believe that the books we read form a part of our consciousness, and sometimes the best part.

For close to fifty years Eudora Welty has been reading books and setting down her impressions, always with sensitivity and with an exceptional openness, even a kind of gaiety—something that appears to have gone out of book-reviewing. The collection can be seen as a random slice of publishers' offerings in the middle years of our century, and random it certainly is. Welty must have been more than once surprised by what she was given for review: there are wobbly first novels here, histories, essays, letters and journals, mysteries, children's fiction, fairy-tales, art books, even a how-to book for window-box gardeners. But along the way came such writers as S. J. Perelman, William Sansom, Faulkner, Rose Macaulay, Isak Dinesen, J. D. Salinger, V. S. Pritchett, Patrick White, E. M. Forster, whose work she adores, Elizabeth Bowen, a close friend, and Virginia Woolf, about whom she writes brilliantly.

The simplicity of Eudora Welty's opening sentences are a rebuke to those reviewers who stand on their heads to be clever. "This is a book of twenty-one short stories"; "These are stories and sketches collected from writings over a period of several years"; or "This is a disarming book, and a pleasure to read". Her strategy is classical. She provides a brief description of the work, followed by a careful, balanced analysis, and her strength lies in identifying—sharply, wittily, often metaphorically—the centre of a writer's power, or else a debilitating weakness. Of Colette she says, "She writes indeed of love", but "not with her love". Of Sylvia Townsend Warner: "Miss Warner is careful never to lose herself beyond a point where wit will not bring her back." Of a convoluted paragraph in Annie Dillard's *Pilgrim at Tinker Creek* she writes, "I honestly do not know what she is talking about at such times".

She shows an early appreciation of Henry Green and Elizabeth Bowen, and her particular enthusiasms may send readers back to the delights of Perelman, or scurrying after a second-hand copy of *Marianne Thornton: A domestic biography* by E. M. Forster. These critical pieces, written between Welty's novels and short stories, will stand as "a graceful and imperturbable monument to interruption", which is the phrase she herself uses to describe Virginia Woolf's journalism.

She is less than sympathetic in her review of Arthur Mizener's biography of Ford Madox Ford, *The Saddest Story*. Mizener, she says, makes the mistake of alternating his clumsy "coarse-grained" comments with Ford's carefully cadenced prose, and the result is "like being carried in a train along the southern coast of France—long tunnel, blinding view of the sea, and over again". This, unhappily, is the problem faced by Paul Binding in his critical memoir, *The Still Moment: Eudora Welty, Portrait of a Writer*. It may be that literary studies like *The Still Moment* are doomed to be clumsy and mechanistic, since traditional critical methods have demanded comment—those endless tunnels—followed by concrete evidence in the form of a quoted passage. Eudora Welty's luminous and highly textured language

presses again and again against the darkness of Binding's vague, awkward, hesitantly offered commentary. "Since her early years she had wanted to be a writer, and had indeed written things." *Things?* Or, speaking of a photograph Eudora Welty had taken, he writes, "This picture also brings home to me, more than its fellows, both the strength—and eternity, if you prefer—of a moment and its helplessness in the inexorable forward march of Time." After quoting a passage from **Delta Wedding,** he sums up with: "This passage brings us a fresh realization of the disturbing coexistences of ordinary life, and of the extreme difficulty (and danger) of simplifying things [those things again] with ready moral judgments."

This is a valuable book none the less. Between his dutiful paragraphs of exegesis, Binding assembles an affectionate and penetrating portrait. Eudora Welty, he reminds us, is a Southerner by birth, but her parents came from more northerly states and were able to provide their daughter with an outsider's eye. Welty herself was educated in the North, first at the University of Wisconsin, then Columbia where she studied advertising. The Depression drew her back to Mississippi, and there she found work with the WPA (Works Progress Administration), travelling to every corner of the state, conducting person-to-person interviews and taking, for her own pleasure, photographs of her fellow Mississippians. This field-work, undertaken with youthful ardour, was to form the rich material of her fiction. Binding underlines the importance of Welty's fortunate apprenticeship. The photographs, which she developed herself, deepened her sense of the human image rooted in its landscape, and her interviews animated these images, so that her fiction vibrates with the lively orality so often associated with "Southern" writing.

Wisely, Binding refuses to be throttled by a precise definition of what Southern writing is. For, despite innumerable studies devoted to its analysis, and hundreds of college courses designed around its contours, Southern writing is, in the end, almost what anyone wants it to be—writing about the South, or writing set in the South, writing by writers born in the South, who have passed through the South, who have Southern antecedents or who express themselves through the use of Southern locutions. (A certain amount of confusion exists about whether the word Southern should be capitalized, though the "S" in South is almost always in upper case.)

There are those who feel that there can be no Southern writing since there is no longer a stable South; the old agricultural South is fast becoming suburbanized; Southerners now watch the same television programmes as other Americans, and avail themselves of the same fast-food and consumer products. Race and gender may be the webs that hold us together now, not the accidents of geography. Some insist that Southern writing cannot be defined, but only felt; that it falls on the ear with a detectable but indescribable Southern slant; that it's romantically inflated, a forced garden, writing that is slightly out of control with an unreliable traffic director. For Reynolds Price, it contains, almost always, the consciousness of race. For others, it holds the memory imprint of the colonized or defeated. It is lush, Gothic, rural, claustrophobic, informed by a humour that lies broad in the brain, drawing its narratives from folk stories, from anecdotes, from tall tales, from language that bends easily to metaphor. It is less about the arabesque of the unfolded self than about the way families and communities work.

John Barth, who is sometimes, but not always, classified as a Southern writer, claims that the most important narrative question for the writer is not "What happened?" but "Who am I?" On the other hand, a narrative question closer to the Southern sense of story-telling might be "Who are we?" or, taking it a centimetre closer to the essence of what a story is, "How are we who we are?" Two of Eudora Welty's novels have been reissued by Virago, and each finds its narrative energy in the conundrum of community.

The Optimist's Daughter is often considered Eudora Welty's most lasting achievement. Published in 1972, it won a Pulitzer Prize, but in today's political climate it feels a little hollow and somehow unsure of itself. Its spareness and its use of vernacular materials point towards an awakening of the liberated self, but the denouement of the novel leaves more questions unanswered than addressed.

Welty's heroine is Laurel, a childless widow in her forties, who travels from Chicago to her family home in the South where she faces her father's illness and death, and where she must confront the egregious Wanda Fay, a heartless, selfish, silly woman, the wife her father married in his old age. Wanda Fay is unique in Eudora Welty's fiction, a vessel of pure evil who remains unredeemed by the author. The novel poses a timeless question: how can we love the parents who have ultimately failed us? Laurel's mother, we are told, ended her life in madness, her father with a foolish alliance, and in the period following his funeral, Laurel disengages herself from the pain of family distress by absorbing into her consciousness all that was good and worthy. But she never thinks to ask herself what it is that has deprived Wanda Fay of a heart, what circumstances have squeezed the woman dry—was it poverty, a failure of acceptance in her own family? Both are hinted at. In the end, Wanda Fay brings more comedy than tragedy to the pages of this puzzling novel, and Laurel returns to the North, carrying with her what may be the seeds of her own heartlessness. The book invites a perplexing double reading: Mr Cheek, a seasonal handyman, in telling Laurel that she resembles her dead mother, can be seen as the messenger of evil or else an astute prophet; the bird that flies into the family house may presage misfortune or the beginning of a necessary cleansing.

The quality of Southernness may be difficult to bottle, but it comes wafting off every page of *Losing Battles.* It's not just that the characters are called Aunt Beck, Brother Bethune, or Miss Beulah. It's that each of them is provided with an oral gift matched by an aural receptivity. The book is all talk, a whole Sunday of talk that stretches into Monday morning. The time is the 1930s, in the old segregated South; the occasion is the ninetieth birthday of Granny Vaughn; the mood is comic and tender. The chatter goes on and on, passing from gossip to banter to declaration to confession, about buttered biscuits, family bibles, about the fear of entrapment and of death, about fluctuations in faith, about how hot the weather's got; and each of these conversations secures a cultural moment. The novel sprawls in a dozen directions, but always letting in the noise of life.

It is good to have these novels in print. Eudora Welty, besides producing her own fine body of work, has been a major influence on America's Anne Tyler, on Canada's Alice Munro, and on many other writers, men as well as women, who have faced the daunting task of making literature out of the humble clay of home.

FURTHER READING

Bibliographies

Prestianni, Vincent. "From Porter to O'Connor: Modern Southern Writers of Fiction. Seven Bibliographies of Bibliographies." *Bulletin of Bibliography* 48, No. 3 (September 1991): 137-51.

> Provides a bibliography for other bibliographies about Welty and other Southern writers.

Criticism

Butterworth, Nancy K. "From Civil War to Civil Rights: Race Relations in Welty's 'A Worn Path.'" *Eudora Welty: Eye of the Storyteller,* edited by Dawn Trouard, pp. 165-72. Kent, OH: The Kent State University Press, 1989.

> Discusses the place of race relation's in Welty's "A Worn Path" by analyzing the character of Phoenix.

Caldwell, Price. "Sexual Politics in Welty's 'Moon Lake' and 'Petrified Man.'" *Studies in American Fiction* 18, No. 2 (Autumn 1990): 171-81.

> Discusses Welty's short stories "Petrified Man" and "Moon Lake" stating that "These stories portray the comedy of human beings trying to impose their interpretations on nature."

Clerc, Charles. "Anatomy of Welty's 'Where is the Voice Coming From?'" *Studies in Short Fiction* 23, No. 4 (Fall 1986): 389-400.

Analyzes Welty's short story "Where is the Voice Coming From?"

Eichelberger, Julia. "From Medusa to Sibyl: Welty's Art as Cultural Critique." *Mississippi Quarterly* 46, No. 2 (Spring 1993): 299-304.

Reviews Peter Schmidt's *The Heart of the Story: Eudora Welty's Short Fiction.*

Evans, Elizabeth. "Eudora Welty and The Dutiful Daughter." *Eudora Welty: Eye of the Storyteller,* edited by Dawn Trouard, pp. 57-68. Kent, OH: The Kent State University Press, 1989.

Discusses the heavy price daughters pay for being dutiful in three of Welty's works.

Flower, Dean. "Eudora Welty Come from Away." *The Hudson Review* XXXVIII, No. 3 (Autumn 1985): 473-480.

Analyzes Welty's position on the question of roaming or staying home.

Marrs, Suzanne. "'The Treasure Most Dearly Regarded': Memory and Imagination in *Delta Wedding.*" *The Southern Literary Journal* XXV, No. 2 (Spring 1993): 79-91.

Asserts that "The emergence of distant memories from the unconscious mind and the very conscious examination of an era not her own are crucial to Welty's achievement in *Delta Wedding,* for perspective in time seems at once to provide her with vivid images, to prompt a metaphoric use of those images, and to grant her the freedom to alter and combine images in the service of her story's metaphoric patterns."

Mortimer, Gail L. "'The Way to Get There': Journeys and Destinations in the Stories of Eudora Welty." *The Southern Literary Journal* XIX, No. 2 (Spring 1987): 61-9.

Asserts that the journey is more important than the destination in Welty's fiction.

Peterman, Gina D. "*A Curtain of Green:* Eudora Welty's Auspicious Beginning." *Mississippi Quarterly* 46, No. 1 (Winter 1992): 91-114.

Discusses the history of Welty's first short-story collection *A Curtain of Green.*

Pitavy-Souques, Daniele. "On Suffering and Joy: Aspects of Storytelling in Welty's Short Fiction." *Eudora Welty: Eye of the Storyteller,* edited by Dawn Trouard, pp. 142-50. Kent, OH: The Kent State University Press, 1989.

Discusses the way Welty presents suffering in her stories.

Polk, Noel. "Going to Naples and Other Places in Eudora Welty's Fiction." *Eudora Welty: Eye of the Storyteller,* edited by Dawn Trouard, pp. 153-64. Kent, OH: The Kent State University Press, 1989.

Asserts that "Welty never exploits place, hers or anybody else's, for its own sake, but rather hopes, in writing about it, to *see* it anew, for the first time every time."

Romines, Ann. "How Not to Tell a Story: Eudora Welty's First-Person Tales." *Eudora Welty: Eye of the Storyteller,* edited by Dawn Trouard, pp. 94-104. Kent, OH: The Kent State University Press, 1989.

Discusses Welty's stories in which she uses first-person narration.

Saunders, James Robert. "'A Worn Path': The Eternal Quest of Welty's Phoenix Jackson." *The Southern Literary Journal* XXV, No. 1 (Fall 1992): 62-73.

Discusses the importance of Phoenix Jackson's journey in Welty's "A Worn Path."

Schmidt, Peter. *The Heart of the Story: Eudora Welty's Short Fiction.* Jackson, MS: University Press of Mississippi, 1991, 312 p.

Provides a study of Welty's short stories and attempts to show "how through a sibylline sleight-of-hand Welty's art merges disguise and revelation into one motion."

Vande Kieft, Ruth Marguerite. *Eudora Welty.* Boston: Twayne Publishers, 1987, 209 p.

Provides a close reading of Eudora Welty's fiction.

Additional coverage of Welty's life and career is contained in the following sources published by Gale: *Concise Dictionary of American Literary Biography, 1941-1968; Contemporary Authors,* **Vol. 9-12R;** *Contemporary Authors Biographical Series,* **Vol. 1;** *Contemporary Authors New Revision Series,* **Vol. 32;** *Dictionary of Literary Biography,* **Vols. 2, 102, 143;** *Dictionary of Literary Biography Yearbook,* **Vol. 87;** *DISCovering Authors; DISCovering Authors: British; DISCovering Authors: Canadian; DISCovering Authors Modules: Most Studied* **and** *Novelists; Major Twentieth-Century Writers; Short Story Criticism,* **Vol. 1; and** *World Literature Criticism.*

□ Contemporary Literary Criticism

Indexes

Literary Criticism Series
Cumulative Author Index
Cumulative Topic Index
Cumulative Nationality Index
Title Index, Volume 105

How to Use This Index

The main references

Camus, Albert
1913-1960 ...... **CLC 1, 2, 4, 9, 11, 14,
32, 69; DA; DAB; DAC; DAM DRAM,
MST, NOV; DC2; SSC 9; WLC**

list all author entries in the following Gale Literary Criticism series:

BLC = *Black Literature Criticism*
CLC = *Contemporary Literary Criticism*
CLR = *Children's Literature Review*
CMLC = *Classical and Medieval Literature Criticism*
DA = *DISCovering Authors*
DAB = *DISCovering Authors: British*
DAC = *DISCovering Authors: Canadian*
DAM = *DISCovering Authors Modules*
  DRAM = *dramatists;* **MST** = *most-studied*
  authors; **MULT** = *multicultural authors;* **NOV** =
  novelists; **POET** = *poets;* **POP** = *popular/genre*
  writers; **DC** = *Drama Criticism*
HLC = *Hispanic Literature Criticism*
LC = *Literature Criticism from 1400 to 1800*
NCLC = *Nineteenth-Century Literature Criticism*
PC = *Poetry Criticism*
SSC = *Short Story Criticism*
TCLC = *Twentieth-Century Literary Criticism*
WLC = *World Literature Criticism, 1500 to the Present*

The cross-references

See also CA 89-92; DLB 72; MTCW

list all author entries in the following Gale biographical and literary sources:

AAYA = *Authors & Artists for Young Adults*
AITN = *Authors in the News*
BEST = *Bestsellers*
BW = *Black Writers*
CA = *Contemporary Authors*
CAAS = *Contemporary Authors Autobiography Series*
CABS = *Contemporary Authors Bibliographical Series*
CANR = *Contemporary Authors New Revision Series*
CAP = *Contemporary Authors Permanent Series*
CDALB = *Concise Dictionary of American Literary Biography*
CDBLB = *Concise Dictionary of British Literary Biography*

DLB = *Dictionary of Literary Biography*
DLBD = *Dictionary of Literary Biography Documentary Series*
DLBY = *Dictionary of Literary Biography Yearbook*
HW = *Hispanic Writers*
JRDA = *Junior DISCovering Authors*
MAICYA = *Major Authors and Illustrators for Children and Young Adults*
MTCW = *Major 20th-Century Writers*
NNAL = *Native North American Literature*
SAAS = *Something about the Author Autobiography Series*
SATA = *Something about the Author*
YABC = *Yesterday's Authors of Books for Children*

Literary Criticism Series
Cumulative Author Index

Aleixandre, Vicente 1898-1984 ... CLC 9, 36;
    DAM POET; PC 15
    See also CA 85-88; 114; CANR 26; DLB 108;
    HW; MTCW
Alepoudelis, Odysseus
    See Elytis, Odysseus
Aleshkovsky, Joseph 1929-
    See Aleshkovsky, Yuz
    See also CA 121; 128
Aleshkovsky, Yuz .... CLC 44
    See also Aleshkovsky, Joseph
Alexander, Lloyd (Chudley) 1924- ... CLC 35
    See also AAYA 1; CA 1-4R; CANR 1, 24, 38,
    55; CLR 1, 5; DLB 52; JRDA; MAICYA;
    MTCW; SAAS 19; SATA 3, 49, 81
Alexie, Sherman (Joseph, Jr.) 1966- CLC 96;
    DAM MULT
    See also CA 138; DLB 175; NNAL
Alfau, Felipe 1902- .... CLC 66
    See also CA 137
Alger, Horatio, Jr. 1832-1899 .... NCLC 8
    See also DLB 42; SATA 16
Algren, Nelson 1909-1981 .... CLC 4, 10, 33
    See also CA 13-16R; 103; CANR 20, 61;
    CDALB 1941-1968; DLB 9; DLBY 81, 82;
    MTCW
Ali, Ahmed 1910- .... CLC 69
    See also CA 25-28R; CANR 15, 34
Alighieri, Dante 1265-1321 ...... CMLC 3, 18;
    WLCS
Allan, John B.
    See Westlake, Donald E(dwin)
Allan, Sidney
    See Hartmann, Sadakichi
Allan, Sydney
    See Hartmann, Sadakichi
Allen, Edward 1948- .... CLC 59
Allen, Paula Gunn 1939- .... CLC 84; DAM
    MULT
    See also CA 112; 143; DLB 175; NNAL
Allen, Roland
    See Ayckbourn, Alan
Allen, Sarah A.
    See Hopkins, Pauline Elizabeth
Allen, Sidney H.
    See Hartmann, Sadakichi
Allen, Woody 1935- CLC 16, 52; DAM POP
    See also AAYA 10; CA 33-36R; CANR 27, 38;
    DLB 44; MTCW
Allende, Isabel 1942- . CLC 39, 57, 97; DAM
    MULT, NOV; HLC; WLCS
    See also AAYA 18; CA 125; 130; CANR 51;
    DLB 145; HW; INT 130; MTCW
Alleyn, Ellen
    See Rossetti, Christina (Georgina)
Allingham, Margery (Louise) 1904-1966CLC
    19
    See also CA 5-8R; 25-28R; CANR 4, 58; DLB
    77; MTCW
Allingham, William 1824-1889 ...... NCLC 25
    See also DLB 35
Allison, Dorothy E. 1949- .... CLC 78
    See also CA 140
Allston, Washington 1779-1843 .... NCLC 2
    See also DLB 1
Almedingen, E. M. .... CLC 12
    See also Almedingen, Martha Edith von
    See also SATA 3
Almedingen, Martha Edith von 1898-1971
    See Almedingen, E. M.
    See also CA 1-4R; CANR 1
Almqvist, Carl Jonas Love 1793-1866 N C L C
    42

Alonso, Damaso 1898-1990 .... CLC 14
    See also CA 110; 131; 130; DLB 108; HW
Alov
    See Gogol, Nikolai (Vasilyevich)
Alta 1942- .... CLC 19
    See also CA 57-60
Alter, Robert B(ernard) 1935- .... CLC 34
    See also CA 49-52; CANR 1, 47
Alther, Lisa 1944- .... CLC 7, 41
    See also CA 65-68; CANR 12, 30, 51; MTCW
Altman, Robert 1925- .... CLC 16
    See also CA 73-76; CANR 43
Alvarez, A(lfred) 1929- .... CLC 5, 13
    See also CA 1-4R; CANR 3, 33; DLB 14, 40
Alvarez, Alejandro Rodriguez 1903-1965
    See Casona, Alejandro
    See also CA 131; 93-96; HW
Alvarez, Julia 1950- .... CLC 93
    See also CA 147
Alvaro, Corrado 1896-1956 .... TCLC 60
Amado, Jorge 1912-CLC 13, 40; DAM MULT,
    NOV; HLC
    See also CA 77-80; CANR 35; DLB 113;
    MTCW
Ambler, Eric 1909- .... CLC 4, 6, 9
    See also CA 9-12R; CANR 7, 38; DLB 77;
    MTCW
Amichai, Yehuda 1924- .... CLC 9, 22, 57
    See also CA 85-88; CANR 46, 60; MTCW
Amichai, Yehudah
    See Amichai, Yehuda
Amiel, Henri Frederic 1821-1881 .... NCLC 4
Amis, Kingsley (William) 1922-1995CLC 1, 2,
    3, 5, 8, 13, 40, 44; DA; DAB; DAC; DAM
    MST, NOV
    See also AITN 2; CA 9-12R; 150; CANR 8, 28,
    54; CDBLB 1945-1960; DLB 15, 27, 100,
    139; DLBY 96; INT CANR-8; MTCW
Amis, Martin (Louis) 1949- CLC 4, 9, 38, 62,
    101
    See also BEST 90:3; CA 65-68; CANR 8, 27,
    54; DLB 14; INT CANR-27
Ammons, A(rchie) R(andolph) 1926-CLC 2, 3,
    5, 8, 9, 25, 57; DAM POET; PC 16
    See also AITN 1; CA 9-12R; CANR 6, 36, 51;
    DLB 5, 165; MTCW
Amo, Tauraatua i
    See Adams, Henry (Brooks)
Anand, Mulk Raj 1905- .. CLC 23, 93; DAM
    NOV
    See also CA 65-68; CANR 32; MTCW
Anatol
    See Schnitzler, Arthur
Anaximander c. 610B.C.-c. 546B.C.CMLC 22
Anaya, Rudolfo A(lfonso) 1937- ..... CLC 23;
    DAM MULT, NOV; HLC
    See also AAYA 20; CA 45-48; CAAS 4; CANR
    1, 32, 51; DLB 82; HW 1; MTCW
Andersen, Hans Christian 1805-1875NCLC 7;
    DA; DAB; DAC; DAM MST, POP; SSC
    6; WLC
    See also CLR 6; MAICYA; YABC 1
Anderson, C. Farley
    See Mencken, H(enry) L(ouis); Nathan, George
    Jean
Anderson, Jessica (Margaret) Queale 1916-
    CLC 37
    See also CA 9-12R; CANR 4, 62
Anderson, Jon (Victor) 1940- .. CLC 9; DAM
    POET
    See also CA 25-28R; CANR 20
Anderson, Lindsay (Gordon) 1923-1994C L C
    20

See also CA 125; 128; 146
Anderson, Maxwell 1888-1959TCLC 2; DAM
    DRAM
    See also CA 105; 152; DLB 7
Anderson, Poul (William) 1926- .... CLC 15
    See also AAYA 5; CA 1-4R; CAAS 2; CANR
    2, 15, 34; DLB 8; INT CANR-15; MTCW;
    SATA 90; SATA-Brief 39
Anderson, Robert (Woodruff) 1917-CLC 23;
    DAM DRAM
    See also AITN 1; CA 21-24R; CANR 32; DLB
    7
Anderson, Sherwood 1876-1941 TCLC 1, 10,
    24; DA; DAB; DAC; DAM MST, NOV;
    SSC 1; WLC
    See also CA 104; 121; CANR 61; CDALB
    1917-1929; DLB 4, 9, 86; DLBD 1; MTCW
Andier, Pierre
    See Desnos, Robert
Andouard
    See Giraudoux, (Hippolyte) Jean
Andrade, Carlos Drummond de .... CLC 18
    See also Drummond de Andrade, Carlos
Andrade, Mario de 1893-1945 .... TCLC 43
Andreae, Johann V(alentin) 1586-1654LC 32
    See also DLB 164
Andreas-Salome, Lou 1861-1937 ... TCLC 56
    See also DLB 66
Andress, Lesley
    See Sanders, Lawrence
Andrewes, Lancelot 1555-1626 .... LC 5
    See also DLB 151, 172
Andrews, Cicily Fairfield
    See West, Rebecca
Andrews, Elton V.
    See Pohl, Frederik
Andreyev, Leonid (Nikolaevich) 1871-1919
    TCLC 3
    See also CA 104
Andric, Ivo 1892-1975 .... CLC 8
    See also CA 81-84; 57-60; CANR 43, 60; DLB
    147; MTCW
Androvar
    See Prado (Calvo), Pedro
Angelique, Pierre
    See Bataille, Georges
Angell, Roger 1920- .... CLC 26
    See also CA 57-60; CANR 13, 44; DLB 171
Angelou, Maya 1928-CLC 12, 35, 64, 77; BLC;
    DA; DAB; DAC; DAM MST, MULT,
    POET, POP; WLCS
    See also AAYA 7, 20; BW 2; CA 65-68; CANR
    19, 42; DLB 38; MTCW; SATA 49
Annensky, Innokenty (Fyodorovich) 1856-1909
    TCLC 14
    See also CA 110; 155
Annunzio, Gabriele d'
    See D'Annunzio, Gabriele
Anodos
    See Coleridge, Mary E(lizabeth)
Anon, Charles Robert
    See Pessoa, Fernando (Antonio Nogueira)
Anouilh, Jean (Marie Lucien Pierre) 1910-1987
    CLC 1, 3, 8, 13, 40, 50; DAM DRAM
    See also CA 17-20R; 123; CANR 32; MTCW
Anthony, Florence
    See Ai
Anthony, John
    See Ciardi, John (Anthony)
Anthony, Peter
    See Shaffer, Anthony (Joshua); Shaffer, Peter
    (Levin)
Anthony, Piers 1934- .... CLC 35; DAM POP

See also AAYA 11; CA 21-24R; CANR 28, 56; DLB 8; MTCW; SAAS 22; SATA 84

Antoine, Marc
See Proust, (Valentin-Louis-George-Eugene-) Marcel

Antoninus, Brother
See Everson, William (Oliver)

Antonioni, Michelangelo 1912- .... **CLC 20**
See also CA 73-76; CANR 45

Antschel, Paul 1920-1970
See Celan, Paul
See also CA 85-88; CANR 33, 61; MTCW

Anwar, Chairil 1922-1949 .... **TCLC 22**
See also CA 121

Apollinaire, Guillaume 1880-1918**TCLC 3, 8, 51; DAM POET; PC 7**
See also Kostrowitzki, Wilhelm Apollinaris de
See also CA 152

Appelfeld, Aharon 1932- .... **CLC 23, 47**
See also CA 112; 133

Apple, Max (Isaac) 1941- .... **CLC 9, 33**
See also CA 81-84; CANR 19, 54; DLB 130

Appleman, Philip (Dean) 1926- .... **CLC 51**
See also CA 13-16R; CAAS 18; CANR 6, 29, 56

Appleton, Lawrence
See Lovecraft, H(oward) P(hillips)

Apteryx
See Eliot, T(homas) S(tearns)

Apuleius, (Lucius Madaurensis) 125(?)-175(?) **CMLC 1**

Aquin, Hubert 1929-1977 .... **CLC 15**
See also CA 105; DLB 53

Aragon, Louis 1897-1982.. **CLC 3, 22; DAM NOV, POET**
See also CA 69-72; 108; CANR 28; DLB 72; MTCW

Arany, Janos 1817-1882 .... **NCLC 34**

Arbuthnot, John 1667-1735 .... **LC 1**
See also DLB 101

Archer, Herbert Winslow
See Mencken, H(enry) L(ouis)

Archer, Jeffrey (Howard) 1940- ..... **CLC 28; DAM POP**
See also AAYA 16; BEST 89:3; CA 77-80; CANR 22, 52; INT CANR-22

Archer, Jules 1915- .... **CLC 12**
See also CA 9-12R; CANR 6; SAAS 5; SATA 4, 85

Archer, Lee
See Ellison, Harlan (Jay)

Arden, John 1930-**CLC 6, 13, 15; DAM DRAM**
See also CA 13-16R; CAAS 4; CANR 31; DLB 13; MTCW

Arenas, Reinaldo 1943-1990 . **CLC 41; DAM MULT; HLC**
See also CA 124; 128; 133; DLB 145; HW

Arendt, Hannah 1906-1975 .... **CLC 66, 98**
See also CA 17-20R; 61-64; CANR 26, 60; MTCW

Aretino, Pietro 1492-1556 .... **LC 12**

Arghezi, Tudor .... **CLC 80**
See also Theodorescu, Ion N.

Arguedas, Jose Maria 1911-1969 **CLC 10, 18**
See also CA 89-92; DLB 113; HW

Argueta, Manlio 1936- .... **CLC 31**
See also CA 131; DLB 145; HW

Ariosto, Ludovico 1474-1533 .... **LC 6**

Aristides
See Epstein, Joseph

Aristophanes 450B.C.-385B.C.**CMLC 4; DA; DAB; DAC; DAM DRAM, MST; DC 2; WLCS**

See also DLB 176

Arlt, Roberto (Godofredo Christophersen) 1900-1942**TCLC 29; DAM MULT; HLC**
See also CA 123; 131; HW

Armah, Ayi Kwei 1939-**CLC 5, 33; BLC; DAM MULT, POET**
See also BW 1; CA 61-64; CANR 21; DLB 117; MTCW

Armatrading, Joan 1950- .... **CLC 17**
See also CA 114

Arnette, Robert
See Silverberg, Robert

Arnim, Achim von (Ludwig Joachim von Arnim) 1781-1831 ...... **NCLC 5; SSC 29**
See also DLB 90

Arnim, Bettina von 1785-1859 .... **NCLC 38**
See also DLB 90

Arnold, Matthew 1822-1888**NCLC 6, 29; DA; DAB; DAC; DAM MST, POET; PC 5; WLC**
See also CDBLB 1832-1890; DLB 32, 57

Arnold, Thomas 1795-1842 .... **NCLC 18**
See also DLB 55

Arnow, Harriette (Louisa) Simpson 1908-1986 **CLC 2, 7, 18**
See also CA 9-12R; 118; CANR 14; DLB 6; MTCW; SATA 42; SATA-Obit 47

Arp, Hans
See Arp, Jean

Arp, Jean 1887-1966 .... **CLC 5**
See also CA 81-84; 25-28R; CANR 42

Arrabal
See Arrabal, Fernando

Arrabal, Fernando 1932- .... **CLC 2, 9, 18, 58**
See also CA 9-12R; CANR 15

Arrick, Fran .... **CLC 30**
See also Gaberman, Judie Angell

Artaud, Antonin (Marie Joseph) 1896-1948 **TCLC 3, 36; DAM DRAM**
See also CA 104; 149

Arthur, Ruth M(abel) 1905-1979 ...... **CLC 12**
See also CA 9-12R; 85-88; CANR 4; SATA 7, 26

Artsybashev, Mikhail (Petrovich) 1878-1927 **TCLC 31**

Arundel, Honor (Morfydd) 1919-1973**CLC 17**
See also CA 21-22; 41-44R; CAP 2; CLR 35; SATA 4; SATA-Obit 24

Arzner, Dorothy 1897-1979 .... **CLC 98**

Asch, Sholem 1880-1957 .... **TCLC 3**
See also CA 105

Ash, Shalom
See Asch, Sholem

Ashbery, John (Lawrence) 1927-**CLC 2, 3, 4, 6, 9, 13, 15, 25, 41, 77; DAM POET**
See also CA 5-8R; CANR 9, 37; DLB 5, 165; DLBY 81; INT CANR-9; MTCW

Ashdown, Clifford
See Freeman, R(ichard) Austin

Ashe, Gordon
See Creasey, John

Ashton-Warner, Sylvia (Constance) 1908-1984 **CLC 19**
See also CA 69-72; 112; CANR 29; MTCW

Asimov, Isaac 1920-1992 **CLC 1, 3, 9, 19, 26, 76, 92; DAM POP**
See also AAYA 13; BEST 90:2; CA 1-4R; 137; CANR 2, 19, 36, 60; CLR 12; DLB 8; DLBY 92; INT CANR-19; JRDA; MAICYA; MTCW; SATA 1, 26, 74

Assis, Joaquim Maria Machado de
See Machado de Assis, Joaquim Maria

Astley, Thea (Beatrice May) 1925- ... **CLC 41**

See also CA 65-68; CANR 11, 43

Aston, James
See White, T(erence) H(anbury)

Asturias, Miguel Angel 1899-1974 **CLC 3, 8, 13; DAM MULT, NOV; HLC**
See also CA 25-28; 49-52; CANR 32; CAP 2; DLB 113; HW; MTCW

Atares, Carlos Saura
See Saura (Atares), Carlos

Atheling, William
See Pound, Ezra (Weston Loomis)

Atheling, William, Jr.
See Blish, James (Benjamin)

Atherton, Gertrude (Franklin Horn) 1857-1948 **TCLC 2**
See also CA 104; 155; DLB 9, 78

Atherton, Lucius
See Masters, Edgar Lee

Atkins, Jack
See Harris, Mark

Atkinson, Kate .... **CLC 99**

Attaway, William (Alexander) 1911-1986 **CLC 92; BLC; DAM MULT**
See also BW 2; CA 143; DLB 76

Atticus
See Fleming, Ian (Lancaster)

Atwood, Margaret (Eleanor) 1939-**CLC 2, 3, 4, 8, 13, 15, 25, 44, 84; DA; DAB; DAC; DAM MST, NOV, POET; PC 8; SSC 2; WLC**
See also AAYA 12; BEST 89:2; CA 49-52; CANR 3, 24, 33, 59; DLB 53; INT CANR-24; MTCW; SATA 50

Aubigny, Pierre d'
See Mencken, H(enry) L(ouis)

Aubin, Penelope 1685-1731(?) .... **LC 9**
See also DLB 39

Auchincloss, Louis (Stanton) 1917-**CLC 4, 6, 9, 18, 45; DAM NOV; SSC 22**
See also CA 1-4R; CANR 6, 29, 55; DLB 2; DLBY 80; INT CANR-29; MTCW

Auden, W(ystan) H(ugh) 1907-1973**CLC 1, 2, 3, 4, 6, 9, 11, 14, 43; DA; DAB; DAC; DAM DRAM, MST, POET; PC 1; WLC**
See also AAYA 18; CA 9-12R; 45-48; CANR 5, 61; CDBLB 1914-1945; DLB 10, 20; MTCW

Audiberti, Jacques 1900-1965**CLC 38; DAM DRAM**
See also CA 25-28R

Audubon, John James 1785-1851 .. **NCLC 47**

Auel, Jean M(arie) 1936-**CLC 31; DAM POP**
See also AAYA 7; BEST 90:4; CA 103; CANR 21; INT CANR-21; SATA 91

Auerbach, Erich 1892-1957 .... **TCLC 43** `
See also CA 118; 155

Augier, Emile 1820-1889 .... **NCLC 31**

August, John
See De Voto, Bernard (Augustine)

Augustine, St. 354-430 .... **CMLC 6; DAB**

Aurelius
See Bourne, Randolph S(illiman)

Aurobindo, Sri 1872-1950 .... **TCLC 63**

Austen, Jane 1775-1817 **NCLC 1, 13, 19, 33, 51; DA; DAB; DAC; DAM MST, NOV; WLC**
See also AAYA 19; CDBLB 1789-1832; DLB 116

Auster, Paul 1947- .... **CLC 47**
See also CA 69-72; CANR 23, 52

Austin, Frank
See Faust, Frederick (Schiller)

Austin, Mary (Hunter) 1868-1934 . **TCLC 25**

See also CA 109; DLB 9, 78

Autran Dourado, Waldomiro
See Dourado, (Waldomiro Freitas) Autran

Averroes 1126-1198 .... **CMLC 7**
See also DLB 115

Avicenna 980-1037 .... **CMLC 16**
See also DLB 115

Avison, Margaret 1918- **CLC 2, 4, 97; DAC; DAM POET**
See also CA 17-20R; DLB 53; MTCW

Axton, David
See Koontz, Dean R(ay)

Ayckbourn, Alan 1939- **CLC 5, 8, 18, 33, 74; DAB; DAM DRAM**
See also CA 21-24R; CANR 31, 59; DLB 13; MTCW

Aydy, Catherine
See Tennant, Emma (Christina)

Ayme, Marcel (Andre) 1902-1967 .... **CLC 11**
See also CA 89-92; CLR 25; DLB 72; SATA 91

Ayrton, Michael 1921-1975 .... **CLC 7**
See also CA 5-8R; 61-64; CANR 9, 21

Azorin .... **CLC 11**
See also Martinez Ruiz, Jose

Azuela, Mariano 1873-1952 . **TCLC 3; DAM MULT; HLC**
See also CA 104; 131; HW; MTCW

Baastad, Babbis Friis
See Friis-Baastad, Babbis Ellinor

Bab
See Gilbert, W(illiam) S(chwenck)

Babbis, Eleanor
See Friis-Baastad, Babbis Ellinor

Babel, Isaac
See Babel, Isaak (Emmanuilovich)

Babel, Isaak (Emmanuilovich) 1894-1941(?)
TCLC 2, 13; SSC 16
See also CA 104; 155

Babits, Mihaly 1883-1941 .... **TCLC 14**
See also CA 114

Babur 1483-1530 .... **LC 18**

Bacchelli, Riccardo 1891-1985 .... **CLC 19**
See also CA 29-32R; 117

Bach, Richard (David) 1936- **CLC 14; DAM NOV, POP**
See also AITN 1; BEST 89:2; CA 9-12R; CANR 18; MTCW; SATA 13

Bachman, Richard
See King, Stephen (Edwin)

Bachmann, Ingeborg 1926-1973 .... **CLC 69**
See also CA 93-96; 45-48; DLB 85

Bacon, Francis 1561-1626 .... **LC 18, 32**
See also CDBLB Before 1660; DLB 151

Bacon, Roger 1214(?)-1292 .... **CMLC 14**
See also DLB 115

Bacovia, George .... **TCLC 24**
See also Vasiliu, Gheorghe

Badanes, Jerome 1937- .... **CLC 59**

Bagehot, Walter 1826-1877 .... **NCLC 10**
See also DLB 55

Bagnold, Enid 1889-1981 .... **CLC 25; DAM DRAM**
See also CA 5-8R; 103; CANR 5, 40; DLB 13, 160; MAICYA; SATA 1, 25

Bagritsky, Eduard 1895-1934 .... **TCLC 60**

Bagrjana, Elisaveta
See Belcheva, Elisaveta

Bagryana, Elisaveta .... **CLC 10**
See also Belcheva, Elisaveta
See also DLB 147

Bailey, Paul 1937- .... **CLC 45**
See also CA 21-24R; CANR 16, 62; DLB 14

Baillie, Joanna 1762-1851 .... **NCLC 2**

See also DLB 93

Bainbridge, Beryl (Margaret) 1933- **CLC 4, 5, 8, 10, 14, 18, 22, 62; DAM NOV**
See also CA 21-24R; CANR 24, 55; DLB 14; MTCW

Baker, Elliott 1922- .... **CLC 8**
See also CA 45-48; CANR 2

Baker, Jean H. .... **TCLC 3, 10**
See also Russell, George William

Baker, Nicholson 1957- **CLC 61; DAM POP**
See also CA 135

Baker, Ray Stannard 1870-1946 .... **TCLC 47**
See also CA 118

Baker, Russell (Wayne) 1925- .... **CLC 31**
See also BEST 89:4; CA 57-60; CANR 11, 41, 59; MTCW

Bakhtin, M.
See Bakhtin, Mikhail Mikhailovich

Bakhtin, M. M.
See Bakhtin, Mikhail Mikhailovich

Bakhtin, Mikhail
See Bakhtin, Mikhail Mikhailovich

Bakhtin, Mikhail Mikhailovich 1895-1975
CLC 83
See also CA 128; 113

Bakshi, Ralph 1938(?)- .... **CLC 26**
See also CA 112; 138

Bakunin, Mikhail (Alexandrovich) 1814-1876
NCLC 25, 58

Baldwin, James (Arthur) 1924-1987 **CLC 1, 2, 3, 4, 5, 8, 13, 15, 17, 42, 50, 67, 90; BLC; DA; DAB; DAC; DAM MST, MULT, NOV, POP; DC 1; SSC 10; WLC**
See also AAYA 4; BW 1; CA 1-4R; 124; CABS 1; CANR 3, 24; CDALB 1941-1968; DLB 2, 7, 33; DLBY 87; MTCW; SATA 9; SATA-Obit 54

Ballard, J(ames) G(raham) 1930- **CLC 3, 6, 14, 36; DAM NOV, POP; SSC 1**
See also AAYA 3; CA 5-8R; CANR 15, 39; DLB 14; MTCW; SATA 93

Balmont, Konstantin (Dmitriyevich) 1867-1943
TCLC 11
See also CA 109; 155

Balzac, Honore de 1799-1850 **NCLC 5, 35, 53; DA; DAB; DAC; DAM MST, NOV; SSC 5; WLC**
See also DLB 119

Bambara, Toni Cade 1939-1995 **CLC 19, 88; BLC; DA; DAC; DAM MST, MULT; WLCS**
See also AAYA 5; BW 2; CA 29-32R; 150; CANR 24, 49; DLB 38; MTCW

Bamdad, A.
See Shamlu, Ahmad

Banat, D. R.
See Bradbury, Ray (Douglas)

Bancroft, Laura
See Baum, L(yman) Frank

Banim, John 1798-1842 .... **NCLC 13**
See also DLB 116, 158, 159

Banim, Michael 1796-1874 .... **NCLC 13**
See also DLB 158, 159

Banjo, The
See Paterson, A(ndrew) B(arton)

Banks, Iain
See Banks, Iain M(enzies)

Banks, Iain M(enzies) 1954- .... **CLC 34**
See also CA 123; 128; CANR 61; INT 128

Banks, Lynne Reid .... **CLC 23**
See also Reid Banks, Lynne
See also AAYA 6

Banks, Russell 1940- .... **CLC 37, 72**

See also CA 65-68; CAAS 15; CANR 19, 52; DLB 130

Banville, John 1945- .... **CLC 46**
See also CA 117; 128; DLB 14; INT 128

Banville, Theodore (Faullain) de 1832-1891
NCLC 9

Baraka, Amiri 1934- **CLC 1, 2, 3, 5, 10, 14, 33; BLC; DA; DAC; DAM MST, MULT, POET, POP; DC 6; PC 4; WLCS**
See also Jones, LeRoi
See also BW 2; CA 21-24R; CABS 3; CANR 27, 38, 61; CDALB 1941-1968; DLB 5, 7, 16, 38; DLBD 8; MTCW

Barbauld, Anna Laetitia 1743-1825 **NCLC 50**
See also DLB 107, 109, 142, 158

Barbellion, W. N. P. .... **TCLC 24**
See also Cummings, Bruce F(rederick)

Barbera, Jack (Vincent) 1945- .... **CLC 44**
See also CA 110; CANR 45

Barbey d'Aurevilly, Jules Amedee 1808-1889
NCLC 1; SSC 17
See also DLB 119

Barbusse, Henri 1873-1935 .... **TCLC 5**
See also CA 105; 154; DLB 65

Barclay, Bill
See Moorcock, Michael (John)

Barclay, William Ewert
See Moorcock, Michael (John)

Barea, Arturo 1897-1957 .... **TCLC 14**
See also CA 111

Barfoot, Joan 1946- .... **CLC 18**
See also CA 105

Baring, Maurice 1874-1945 .... **TCLC 8**
See also CA 105; DLB 34

Barker, Clive 1952- .... **CLC 52; DAM POP**
See also AAYA 10; BEST 90:3; CA 121; 129; INT 129; MTCW

Barker, George Granville 1913-1991 **CLC 8, 48; DAM POET**
See also CA 9-12R; 135; CANR 7, 38; DLB 20; MTCW

Barker, Harley Granville
See Granville-Barker, Harley
See also DLB 10

Barker, Howard 1946- .... **CLC 37**
See also CA 102; DLB 13

Barker, Pat(ricia) 1943- .... **CLC 32, 94**
See also CA 117; 122; CANR 50; INT 122

Barlow, Joel 1754-1812 .... **NCLC 23**
See also DLB 37

Barnard, Mary (Ethel) 1909- .... **CLC 48**
See also CA 21-22; CAP 2

Barnes, Djuna 1892-1982 **CLC 3, 4, 8, 11, 29; SSC 3**
See also CA 9-12R; 107; CANR 16, 55; DLB 4, 9, 45; MTCW

Barnes, Julian (Patrick) 1946- **CLC 42; DAB**
See also CA 102; CANR 19, 54; DLBY 93

Barnes, Peter 1931- .... **CLC 5, 56**
See also CA 65-68; CAAS 12; CANR 33, 34; DLB 13; MTCW

Baroja (y Nessi), Pio 1872-1956 **TCLC 8; HLC**
See also CA 104

Baron, David
See Pinter, Harold

Baron Corvo
See Rolfe, Frederick (William Serafino Austin Lewis Mary)

Barondess, Sue K(aufman) 1926-1977 **CLC 8**
See also Kaufman, Sue
See also CA 1-4R; 69-72; CANR 1

Baron de Teive
See Pessoa, Fernando (Antonio Nogueira)

Barres, Maurice 1862-1923 .... **TCLC 47**
See also DLB 123

Barreto, Afonso Henrique de Lima
See Lima Barreto, Afonso Henrique de

Barrett, (Roger) Syd 1946- .... **CLC 35**

Barrett, William (Christopher) 1913-1992
CLC 27
See also CA 13-16R; 139; CANR 11; INT
CANR-11

Barrie, J(ames) M(atthew) 1860-1937 **T C L C**
2; DAB; DAM DRAM
See also CA 104; 136; CDBLB 1890-1914;
CLR 16; DLB 10, 141, 156; MAICYA;
YABC 1

Barrington, Michael
See Moorcock, Michael (John)

Barrol, Grady
See Bograd, Larry

Barry, Mike
See Malzberg, Barry N(athaniel)

Barry, Philip 1896-1949 .... **TCLC 11**
See also CA 109; DLB 7

Bart, Andre Schwarz
See Schwarz-Bart, Andre

Barth, John (Simmons) 1930-**CLC 1, 2, 3, 5, 7,**
9, 10, 14, 27, 51, 89; DAM NOV; SSC 10
See also AITN 1, 2; CA 1-4R; CABS 1; CANR
5, 23, 49; DLB 2; MTCW

Barthelme, Donald 1931-1989**CLC 1, 2, 3, 5, 6,**
8, 13, 23, 46, 59; DAM NOV; SSC 2
See also CA 21-24R; 129; CANR 20, 58; DLB
2; DLBY 80, 89; MTCW; SATA 7; SATA-
Obit 62

Barthelme, Frederick 1943- .... **CLC 36**
See also CA 114; 122; DLBY 85; INT 122

Barthes, Roland (Gerard) 1915-1980**CLC 24,**
83
See also CA 130; 97-100; MTCW

Barzun, Jacques (Martin) 1907- .... **CLC 51**
See also CA 61-64; CANR 22

Bashevis, Isaac
See Singer, Isaac Bashevis

Bashkirtseff, Marie 1859-1884 ...... **NCLC 27**

Basho
See Matsuo Basho

Bass, Kingsley B., Jr.
See Bullins, Ed

Bass, Rick 1958- .... **CLC 79**
See also CA 126; CANR 53

Bassani, Giorgio 1916- .... **CLC 9**
See also CA 65-68; CANR 33; DLB 128, 177;
MTCW

Bastos, Augusto (Antonio) Roa
See Roa Bastos, Augusto (Antonio)

Bataille, Georges 1897-1962 .... **CLC 29**
See also CA 101; 89-92

Bates, H(erbert) E(rnest) 1905-1974**CLC 46;**
DAB; DAM POP; SSC 10
See also CA 93-96; 45-48; CANR 34; DLB 162;
MTCW

Bauchart
See Camus, Albert

Baudelaire, Charles 1821-1867 . **NCLC 6, 29,**
55; DA; DAB; DAC; DAM MST, POET;
PC 1; SSC 18; WLC

Baudrillard, Jean 1929- .... **CLC 60**

Baum, L(yman) Frank 1856-1919 ... **TCLC 7**
See also CA 108; 133; CLR 15; DLB 22; JRDA;
MAICYA; MTCW; SATA 18

Baum, Louis F.
See Baum, L(yman) Frank

Baumbach, Jonathan 1933- .... **CLC 6, 23**
See also CA 13-16R; CAAS 5; CANR 12;

DLBY 80; INT CANR-12; MTCW

Bausch, Richard (Carl) 1945- .... **CLC 51**
See also CA 101; CAAS 14; CANR 43, 61; DLB
130

Baxter, Charles 1947-**CLC 45, 78; DAM POP**
See also CA 57-60; CANR 40; DLB 130

Baxter, George Owen
See Faust, Frederick (Schiller)

Baxter, James K(eir) 1926-1972 .... **CLC 14**
See also CA 77-80

Baxter, John
See Hunt, E(verette) Howard, (Jr.)

Bayer, Sylvia
See Glassco, John

Baynton, Barbara 1857-1929 .... **TCLC 57**

Beagle, Peter S(oyer) 1939- .... **CLC 7, 104**
See also CA 9-12R; CANR 4, 51; DLBY 80;
INT CANR-4; SATA 60

Bean, Normal
See Burroughs, Edgar Rice

Beard, Charles A(ustin) 1874-1948 **TCLC 15**
See also CA 115; DLB 17; SATA 18

Beardsley, Aubrey 1872-1898 .... **NCLC 6**

Beattie, Ann 1947-**CLC 8, 13, 18, 40, 63; DAM**
NOV, POP; SSC 11
See also BEST 90:2; CA 81-84; CANR 53;
DLBY 82; MTCW

Beattie, James 1735-1803 .... **NCLC 25**
See also DLB 109

Beauchamp, Kathleen Mansfield 1888-1923
See Mansfield, Katherine
See also CA 104; 134; DA; DAC; DAM MST

Beaumarchais, Pierre-Augustin Caron de 1732-
1799 .... **DC 4**
See also DAM DRAM

Beaumont, Francis 1584(?)-1616**LC 33; DC 6**
See also CDBLB Before 1660; DLB 58, 121

Beauvoir, Simone (Lucie Ernestine Marie
Bertrand) de 1908-1986**CLC 1, 2, 4, 8, 14,**
31, 44, 50, 71; DA; DAB; DAC; DAM MST,
NOV; WLC
See also CA 9-12R; 118; CANR 28, 61; DLB
72; DLBY 86; MTCW

Becker, Carl (Lotus) 1873-1945 ..... **TCLC 63**
See also CA 157; DLB 17

Becker, Jurek 1937-1997 .... **CLC 7, 19**
See also CA 85-88; 157; CANR 60; DLB 75

Becker, Walter 1950- .... **CLC 26**

Beckett, Samuel (Barclay) 1906-1989 **CLC 1,**
2, 3, 4, 6, 9, 10, 11, 14, 18, 29, 57, 59, 83;
DA; DAB; DAC; DAM DRAM, MST,
NOV; SSC 16; WLC
See also CA 5-8R; 130; CANR 33, 61; CDBLB
1945-1960; DLB 13, 15; DLBY 90; MTCW

Beckford, William 1760-1844 .... **NCLC 16**
See also DLB 39

Beckman, Gunnel 1910- .... **CLC 26**
See also CA 33-36R; CANR 15; CLR 25;
MAICYA; SAAS 9; SATA 6

Becque, Henri 1837-1899 .... **NCLC 3**

Beddoes, Thomas Lovell 1803-1849 **NCLC 3**
See also DLB 96

Bede c. 673-735 .... **CMLC 20**
See also DLB 146

Bedford, Donald F.
See Fearing, Kenneth (Flexner)

Beecher, Catharine Esther 1800-1878 **N C L C**
30
See also DLB 1

Beecher, John 1904-1980 .... **CLC 6**
See also AITN 1; CA 5-8R; 105; CANR 8

Beer, Johann 1655-1700 .... **LC 5**
See also DLB 168

Beer, Patricia 1924- .... **CLC 58**
See also CA 61-64; CANR 13, 46; DLB 40

Beerbohm, Max
See Beerbohm, (Henry) Max(imilian)

Beerbohm, (Henry) Max(imilian) 1872-1956
TCLC 1, 24
See also CA 104; 154; DLB 34, 100

Beer-Hofmann, Richard 1866-1945**TCLC 60**
See also CA 160; DLB 81

Begiebing, Robert J(ohn) 1946- .... **CLC 70**
See also CA 122; CANR 40

Behan, Brendan 1923-1964 **CLC 1, 8, 11, 15,**
79; DAM DRAM
See also CA 73-76; CANR 33; CDBLB 1945-
1960; DLB 13; MTCW

Behn, Aphra 1640(?)-1689**LC 1, 30; DA; DAB;**
DAC; DAM DRAM, MST, NOV, POET;
DC 4; PC 13; WLC
See also DLB 39, 80, 131

Behrman, S(amuel) N(athaniel) 1893-1973
CLC 40
See also CA 13-16; 45-48; CAP 1; DLB 7, 44

Belasco, David 1853-1931 .... **TCLC 3**
See also CA 104; DLB 7

Belcheva, Elisaveta 1893- .... **CLC 10**
See also Bagryana, Elisaveta

Beldone, Phil "Cheech"
See Ellison, Harlan (Jay)

Beleno
See Azuela, Mariano

Belinski, Vissarion Grigoryevich 1811-1848
NCLC 5

Belitt, Ben 1911- .... **CLC 22**
See also CA 13-16R; CAAS 4; CANR 7; DLB
5

Bell, Gertrude 1868-1926 .... **TCLC 67**
See also DLB 174

Bell, James Madison 1826-1902 ... **TCLC 43;**
BLC; DAM MULT
See also BW 1; CA 122; 124; DLB 50

Bell, Madison Smartt 1957- ...... **CLC 41, 102**
See also CA 111; CANR 28, 54

Bell, Marvin (Hartley) 1937-**CLC 8, 31; DAM**
POET
See also CA 21-24R; CAAS 14; CANR 59; DLB
5; MTCW

Bell, W. L. D.
See Mencken, H(enry) L(ouis)

Bellamy, Atwood C.
See Mencken, H(enry) L(ouis)

Bellamy, Edward 1850-1898 .... **NCLC 4**
See also DLB 12

Bellin, Edward J.
See Kuttner, Henry

Belloc, (Joseph) Hilaire (Pierre Sebastien Rene
Swanton) 1870-1953 **TCLC 7, 18; DAM**
POET
See also CA 106; 152; DLB 19, 100, 141, 174;
YABC 1

Belloc, Joseph Peter Rene Hilaire
See Belloc, (Joseph) Hilaire (Pierre Sebastien
Rene Swanton)

Belloc, Joseph Pierre Hilaire
See Belloc, (Joseph) Hilaire (Pierre Sebastien
Rene Swanton)

Belloc, M. A.
See Lowndes, Marie Adelaide (Belloc)

Bellow, Saul 1915-**CLC 1, 2, 3, 6, 8, 10, 13, 15,**
25, 33, 34, 63, 79; DA; DAB; DAC; DAM
MST, NOV, POP; SSC 14; WLC
See also AITN 2; BEST 89:3; CA 5-8R; CABS
1; CANR 29, 53; CDALB 1941-1968; DLB
2, 28; DLBD 3; DLBY 82; MTCW

Belser, Reimond Karel Maria de 1929-
  See Ruyslinck, Ward
  See also CA 152
Bely, Andrey .... TCLC 7; PC 11
  See also Bugayev, Boris Nikolayevich
Benary, Margot
  See Benary-Isbert, Margot
Benary-Isbert, Margot 1889-1979 .... CLC 12
  See also CA 5-8R; 89-92; CANR 4; CLR 12;
    MAICYA; SATA 2; SATA-Obit 21
Benavente (y Martinez), Jacinto 1866-1954
    TCLC 3; DAM DRAM, MULT
  See also CA 106; 131; HW; MTCW
Benchley, Peter (Bradford) 1940- CLC 4, 8;
    DAM NOV, POP
  See also AAYA 14; AITN 2; CA 17-20R; CANR
    12, 35; MTCW; SATA 3, 89
Benchley, Robert (Charles) 1889-1945 T C L C
    1, 55
  See also CA 105; 153; DLB 11
Benda, Julien 1867-1956 .... TCLC 60
  See also CA 120; 154
Benedict, Ruth (Fulton) 1887-1948 TCLC 60
  See also CA 158
Benedikt, Michael 1935- .... CLC 4, 14
  See also CA 13-16R; CANR 7; DLB 5
Benet, Juan 1927- .... CLC 28
  See also CA 143
Benet, Stephen Vincent 1898-1943 . TCLC 7;
    DAM POET; SSC 10
  See also CA 104; 152; DLB 4, 48, 102; YABC
    1
Benet, William Rose 1886-1950 .... TCLC 28;
    DAM POET
  See also CA 118; 152; DLB 45
Benford, Gregory (Albert) 1941- ...... CLC 52
  See also CA 69-72; CAAS 27; CANR 12, 24,
    49; DLBY 82
Bengtsson, Frans (Gunnar) 1894-1954 T C L C
    48
Benjamin, David
  See Slavitt, David R(ytman)
Benjamin, Lois
  See Gould, Lois
Benjamin, Walter 1892-1940 .... TCLC 39
Benn, Gottfried 1886-1956 .... TCLC 3
  See also CA 106; 153; DLB 56
Bennett, Alan 1934- CLC 45, 77; DAB; DAM
    MST
  See also CA 103; CANR 35, 55; MTCW
Bennett, (Enoch) Arnold 1867-1931 TCLC 5,
    20
  See also CA 106; 155; CDBLB 1890-1914;
    DLB 10, 34, 98, 135
Bennett, Elizabeth
  See Mitchell, Margaret (Munnerlyn)
Bennett, George Harold 1930-
  See Bennett, Hal
  See also BW 1; CA 97-100
Bennett, Hal .... CLC 5
  See also Bennett, George Harold
  See also DLB 33
Bennett, Jay 1912- .... CLC 35
  See also AAYA 10; CA 69-72; CANR 11, 42;
    JRDA; SAAS 4; SATA 41, 87; SATA-Brief
    27
Bennett, Louise (Simone) 1919- CLC 28; BLC;
    DAM MULT
  See also BW 2; CA 151; DLB 117
Benson, E(dward) F(rederic) 1867-1940
    TCLC 27
  See also CA 114; 157; DLB 135, 153
Benson, Jackson J. 1930- .... CLC 34

See also CA 25-28R; DLB 111
Benson, Sally 1900-1972 .... CLC 17
  See also CA 19-20; 37-40R; CAP 1; SATA 1,
    35; SATA-Obit 27
Benson, Stella 1892-1933 .... TCLC 17
  See also CA 117; 155; DLB 36, 162
Bentham, Jeremy 1748-1832 .... NCLC 38
  See also DLB 107, 158
Bentley, E(dmund) C(lerihew) 1875-1956
    TCLC 12
  See also CA 108; DLB 70
Bentley, Eric (Russell) 1916- .... CLC 24
  See also CA 5-8R; CANR 6; INT CANR-6
Beranger, Pierre Jean de 1780-1857 NCLC 34
Berdyaev, Nicolas
  See Berdyaev, Nikolai (Aleksandrovich)
Berdyaev, Nikolai (Aleksandrovich) 1874-1948
    TCLC 67
  See also CA 120; 157
Berdyayev, Nikolai (Aleksandrovich)
  See Berdyaev, Nikolai (Aleksandrovich)
Berendt, John (Lawrence) 1939- ...... CLC 86
  See also CA 146
Berger, Colonel
  See Malraux, (Georges-)Andre
Berger, John (Peter) 1926- .... CLC 2, 19
  See also CA 81-84; CANR 51; DLB 14
Berger, Melvin H. 1927- .... CLC 12
  See also CA 5-8R; CANR 4; CLR 32; SAAS 2;
    SATA 5, 88
Berger, Thomas (Louis) 1924- CLC 3, 5, 8, 11,
    18, 38; DAM NOV
  See also CA 1-4R; CANR 5, 28, 51; DLB 2;
    DLBY 80; INT CANR-28; MTCW
Bergman, (Ernst) Ingmar 1918- CLC 16, 72
  See also CA 81-84; CANR 33
Bergson, Henri 1859-1941 .... TCLC 32
Bergstein, Eleanor 1938- .... CLC 4
  See also CA 53-56; CANR 5
Berkoff, Steven 1937- .... CLC 56
  See also CA 104
Bermant, Chaim (Icyk) 1929- .... CLC 40
  See also CA 57-60; CANR 6, 31, 57
Bern, Victoria
  See Fisher, M(ary) F(rances) K(ennedy)
Bernanos, (Paul Louis) Georges 1888-1948
    TCLC 3
  See also CA 104; 130; DLB 72
Bernard, April 1956- .... CLC 59
  See also CA 131
Berne, Victoria
  See Fisher, M(ary) F(rances) K(ennedy)
Bernhard, Thomas 1931-1989 CLC 3, 32, 61
  See also CA 85-88; 127; CANR 32, 57; DLB
    85, 124; MTCW
Bernhardt, Sarah (Henriette Rosine) 1844-1923
    TCLC 75
  See also CA 157
Berriault, Gina 1926- .... CLC 54
  See also CA 116; 129; DLB 130
Berrigan, Daniel 1921- .... CLC 4
  See also CA 33-36R; CAAS 1; CANR 11, 43;
    DLB 5
Berrigan, Edmund Joseph Michael, Jr. 1934-
    1983
  See Berrigan, Ted
  See also CA 61-64; 110; CANR 14
Berrigan, Ted .... CLC 37
  See also Berrigan, Edmund Joseph Michael, Jr.
  See also DLB 5, 169
Berry, Charles Edward Anderson 1931-
  See Berry, Chuck
  See also CA 115

Berry, Chuck .... CLC 17
  See also Berry, Charles Edward Anderson
Berry, Jonas
  See Ashbery, John (Lawrence)
Berry, Wendell (Erdman) 1934- CLC 4, 6, 8,
    27, 46; DAM POET
  See also AITN 1; CA 73-76; CANR 50; DLB 5,
    6
Berryman, John 1914-1972 CLC 1, 2, 3, 4, 6, 8,
    10, 13, 25, 62; DAM POET
  See also CA 13-16; 33-36R; CABS 2; CANR
    35; CAP 1; CDALB 1941-1968; DLB 48;
    MTCW
Bertolucci, Bernardo 1940- .... CLC 16
  See also CA 106
Berton, Pierre (Francis De Marigny) 1920-
    CLC 104
  See also CA 1-4R; CANR 2, 56; DLB 68
Bertrand, Aloysius 1807-1841 .... NCLC 31
Bertran de Born c. 1140-1215 .... CMLC 5
Besant, Annie (Wood) 1847-1933 .... TCLC 9
  See also CA 105
Bessie, Alvah 1904-1985 .... CLC 23
  See also CA 5-8R; 116; CANR 2; DLB 26
Bethlen, T. D.
  See Silverberg, Robert
Beti, Mongo ...... CLC 27; BLC; DAM MULT
  See also Biyidi, Alexandre
Betjeman, John 1906-1984 CLC 2, 6, 10, 34,
    43; DAB; DAM MST, POET
  See also CA 9-12R; 112; CANR 33, 56; CDBLB
    1945-1960; DLB 20; DLB Y 84; MTCW
Bettelheim, Bruno 1903-1990 .... CLC 79
  See also CA 81-84; 131; CANR 23, 61; MTCW
Betti, Ugo 1892-1953 .... TCLC 5
  See also CA 104; 155
Betts, Doris (Waugh) 1932- ...... CLC 3, 6, 28
  See also CA 13-16R; CANR 9; DLBY 82; INT
    CANR-9
Bevan, Alistair
  See Roberts, Keith (John Kingston)
Bialik, Chaim Nachman 1873-1934 TCLC 25
Bickerstaff, Isaac
  See Swift, Jonathan
Bidart, Frank 1939- .... CLC 33
  See also CA 140
Bienek, Horst 1930- .... CLC 7, 11
  See also CA 73-76; DLB 75
Bierce, Ambrose (Gwinett) 1842-1914(?)
    TCLC 1, 7, 44; DA; DAC; DAM MST; SSC
    9; WLC
  See also CA 104; 139; CDALB 1865-1917;
    DLB 11, 12, 23, 71, 74
Biggers, Earl Derr 1884-1933 .... TCLC 65
  See also CA 108; 153
Billings, Josh
  See Shaw, Henry Wheeler
Billington, (Lady) Rachel (Mary) 1942- C L C
    43
  See also AITN 2; CA 33-36R; CANR 44
Binyon, T(imothy) J(ohn) 1936- .... CLC 34
  See also CA 111; CANR 28
Bioy Casares, Adolfo 1914- CLC 4, 8, 13, 88;
    DAM MULT; HLC; SSC 17
  See also CA 29-32R; CANR 19, 43; DLB 113;
    HW; MTCW
Bird, Cordwainer
  See Ellison, Harlan (Jay)
Bird, Robert Montgomery 1806-1854 NCLC 1
Birney, (Alfred) Earle 1904- CLC 1, 4, 6, 11;
    DAC; DAM MST, POET
  See also CA 1-4R; CANR 5, 20; DLB 88;
    MTCW

See also CA 104; 129; CANR 60; CDALB
 1929-1941; DLBD 6; MTCW

Chang, Eileen 1920- .... **SSC 28**

Chang, Jung 1952- .... **CLC 71**
 See also CA 142

Channing, William Ellery 1780-1842 **N C L C
 17**
 See also DLB 1, 59

Chaplin, Charles Spencer 1889-1977 **CLC 16**
 See also Chaplin, Charlie
 See also CA 81-84; 73-76

Chaplin, Charlie
 See Chaplin, Charles Spencer
 See also DLB 44

Chapman, George 1559(?)-1634 **LC 22; DAM
 DRAM**
 See also DLB 62, 121

Chapman, Graham 1941-1989 .... **CLC 21**
 See also Monty Python
 See also CA 116; 129; CANR 35

Chapman, John Jay 1862-1933 .... **TCLC 7**
 See also CA 104

Chapman, Lee
 See Bradley, Marion Zimmer

Chapman, Walker
 See Silverberg, Robert

Chappell, Fred (Davis) 1936- ..... **CLC 40, 78**
 See also CA 5-8R; CAAS 4; CANR 8, 33; DLB
 6, 105

Char, Rene(-Emile) 1907-1988 **CLC 9, 11, 14,
 55; DAM POET**
 See also CA 13-16R; 124; CANR 32; MTCW

Charby, Jay
 See Ellison, Harlan (Jay)

Chardin, Pierre Teilhard de
 See Teilhard de Chardin, (Marie Joseph) Pierre

Charles I 1600-1649 .... **LC 13**

Charyn, Jerome 1937- .... **CLC 5, 8, 18**
 See also CA 5-8R; CAAS 1; CANR 7, 61;
 DLBY 83; MTCW

Chase, Mary (Coyle) 1907-1981 ....**DC 1**
 See also CA 77-80; 105; SATA 17; SATA-Obit
 29

Chase, Mary Ellen 1887-1973 .... **CLC 2**
 See also CA 13-16; 41-44R; CAP 1; SATA 10

Chase, Nicholas
 See Hyde, Anthony

Chateaubriand, Francois Rene de 1768-1848
 NCLC 3
 See also DLB 119

Chatterje, Sarat Chandra 1876-1936(?)
 See Chatterji, Saratchandra
 See also CA 109

Chatterji, Bankim Chandra 1838-1894 **NCLC
 19**

Chatterji, Saratchandra .... **TCLC 13**
 See also Chatterje, Sarat Chandra

Chatterton, Thomas 1752-1770 .**LC 3; DAM
 POET**
 See also DLB 109

Chatwin, (Charles) Bruce 1940-1989 **CLC 28,
 57, 59; DAM POP**
 See also AAYA 4; BEST 90:1; CA 85-88; 127

Chaucer, Daniel
 See Ford, Ford Madox

Chaucer, Geoffrey 1340(?)-1400 **LC 17; DA;
 DAB; DAC; DAM MST, POET; PC 19;
 WLCS**
 See also CDBLB Before 1660; DLB 146

Chaviaras, Strates 1935-
 See Haviaras, Stratis
 See also CA 105

Chayefsky, Paddy .... **CLC 23**

See also Chayefsky, Sidney
 See also DLB 7, 44; DLBY 81

Chayefsky, Sidney 1923-1981
 See Chayefsky, Paddy
 See also CA 9-12R; 104; CANR 18; DAM
 DRAM

Chedid, Andree 1920- .... **CLC 47**
 See also CA 145

Cheever, John 1912-1982 **CLC 3, 7, 8, 11, 15,
 25, 64; DA; DAB; DAC; DAM MST, NOV,
 POP; SSC 1; WLC**
 See also CA 5-8R; 106; CABS 1; CANR 5, 27;
 CDALB 1941-1968; DLB 2, 102; DLBY 80,
 82; INT CANR-5; MTCW

Cheever, Susan 1943- .... **CLC 18, 48**
 See also CA 103; CANR 27, 51; DLBY 82; INT
 CANR-27

Chekhonte, Antosha
 See Chekhov, Anton (Pavlovich)

Chekhov, Anton (Pavlovich) 1860-1904 **TCLC
 3, 10, 31, 55; DA; DAB; DAC; DAM
 DRAM, MST; SSC 2, 28; WLC**
 See also CA 104; 124; SATA 90

Chernyshevsky, Nikolay Gavrilovich 1828-1889
 NCLC 1

Cherry, Carolyn Janice 1942-
 See Cherryh, C. J.
 See also CA 65-68; CANR 10

Cherryh, C. J. .... **CLC 35**
 See also Cherry, Carolyn Janice
 See also DLBY 80; SATA 93

Chesnutt, Charles W(addell) 1858-1932
 TCLC 5, 39; BLC; DAM MULT; SSC 7
 See also BW 1; CA 106; 125; DLB 12, 50, 78;
 MTCW

Chester, Alfred 1929(?)-1971 .... **CLC 49**
 See also CA 33-36R; DLB 130

Chesterton, G(ilbert) K(eith) 1874-1936
 TCLC 1, 6, 64; DAM NOV, POET; SSC 1
 See also CA 104; 132; CDBLB 1914-1945;
 DLB 10, 19, 34, 70, 98, 149, 178; MTCW;
 SATA 27

Chiang Pin-chin 1904-1986
 See Ding Ling
 See also CA 118

Ch'ien Chung-shu 1910- .... **CLC 22**
 See also CA 130; MTCW

Child, L. Maria
 See Child, Lydia Maria

Child, Lydia Maria 1802-1880 .... **NCLC 6**
 See also DLB 1, 74; SATA 67

Child, Mrs.
 See Child, Lydia Maria

Child, Philip 1898-1978 .... **CLC 19, 68**
 See also CA 13-14; CAP 1; SATA 47

Childers, (Robert) Erskine 1870-1922 **T C L C
 65**
 See also CA 113; 153; DLB 70

Childress, Alice 1920-1994 **CLC 12, 15, 86, 96;
 BLC; DAM DRAM, MULT, NOV; DC 4**
 See also AAYA 8; BW 2; CA 45-48; 146; CANR
 3, 27, 50; CLR 14; DLB 7, 38; JRDA;
 MAICYA; MTCW; SATA 7, 48, 81

Chin, Frank (Chew, Jr.) 1940- ....**DC 7**
 See also CA 33-36R; DAM MULT

Chislett, (Margaret) Anne 1943- ...... **CLC 34**
 See also CA 151

Chitty, Thomas Willes 1926- .... **CLC 11**
 See also Hinde, Thomas
 See also CA 5-8R

Chivers, Thomas Holley 1809-1858 **NCLC 49**
 See also DLB 3

Chomette, Rene Lucien 1898-1981

See Clair, Rene
 See also CA 103

Chopin, Kate **TCLC 5, 14; DA; DAB; SSC 8;
 WLCS**
 See also Chopin, Katherine
 See also CDALB 1865-1917; DLB 12, 78

Chopin, Katherine 1851-1904
 See Chopin, Kate
 See also CA 104; 122; DAC; DAM MST, NOV

Chretien de Troyes c. 12th cent. -.. **CMLC 10**

Christie
 See Ichikawa, Kon

Christie, Agatha (Mary Clarissa) 1890-1976
 **CLC 1, 6, 8, 12, 39, 48; DAB; DAC; DAM
 NOV**
 See also AAYA 9; AITN 1, 2; CA 17-20R; 61-
 64; CANR 10, 37; CDBLB 1914-1945; DLB
 13, 77; MTCW; SATA 36

Christie, (Ann) Philippa
 See Pearce, Philippa
 See also CA 5-8R; CANR 4

Christine de Pizan 1365(?)-1431(?) .... **LC 9**

Chubb, Elmer
 See Masters, Edgar Lee

Chulkov, Mikhail Dmitrievich 1743-1792 **LC 2**
 See also DLB 150

Churchill, Caryl 1938- ..... **CLC 31, 55; DC 5**
 See also CA 102; CANR 22, 46; DLB 13;
 MTCW

Churchill, Charles 1731-1764 .... **LC 3**
 See also DLB 109

Chute, Carolyn 1947- .... **CLC 39**
 See also CA 123

Ciardi, John (Anthony) 1916-1986 .**CLC 10,
 40, 44; DAM POET**
 See also CA 5-8R; 118; CAAS 2; CANR 5, 33;
 CLR 19; DLB 5; DLBY 86; INT CANR-5;
 MAICYA; MTCW; SATA 1, 65; SATA-Obit
 46

Cicero, Marcus Tullius 106B.C.-43B.C.
 CMLC 3

Cimino, Michael 1943- .... **CLC 16**
 See also CA 105

Cioran, E(mil) M. 1911-1995 .... **CLC 64**
 See also CA 25-28R; 149

Cisneros, Sandra 1954- **CLC 69; DAM MULT;
 HLC**
 See also AAYA 9; CA 131; DLB 122, 152; HW

Cixous, Helene 1937- .... **CLC 92**
 See also CA 126; CANR 55; DLB 83; MTCW

Clair, Rene .... **CLC 20**
 See also Chomette, Rene Lucien

Clampitt, Amy 1920-1994 ..... **CLC 32; PC 19**
 See also CA 110; 146; CANR 29; DLB 105

Clancy, Thomas L., Jr. 1947-
 See Clancy, Tom
 See also CA 125; 131; CANR 62; INT 131;
 MTCW

Clancy, Tom .... **CLC 45; DAM NOV, POP**
 See also Clancy, Thomas L., Jr.
 See also AAYA 9; BEST 89:1, 90:1

Clare, John 1793-1864 **NCLC 9; DAB; DAM
 POET**
 See also DLB 55, 96

Clarin
 See Alas (y Urena), Leopoldo (Enrique Garcia)

Clark, Al C.
 See Goines, Donald

Clark, (Robert) Brian 1932- .... **CLC 29**
 See also CA 41-44R

Clark, Curt
 See Westlake, Donald E(dwin)

Clark, Eleanor 1913-1996 .... **CLC 5, 19**

See also CA 9-12R; 151; CANR 41; DLB 6

Clark, J. P.
See Clark, John Pepper
See also DLB 117

Clark, John Pepper 1935- ......**CLC 38; BLC; DAM DRAM, MULT; DC 5**
See also Clark, J. P.
See also BW 1; CA 65-68; CANR 16

Clark, M. R.
See Clark, Mavis Thorpe

Clark, Mavis Thorpe 1909- ....**CLC 12**
See also CA 57-60; CANR 8, 37; CLR 30; MAICYA; SAAS 5; SATA 8, 74

Clark, Walter Van Tilburg 1909-1971**CLC 28**
See also CA 9-12R; 33-36R; DLB 9; SATA 8

Clarke, Arthur C(harles) 1917-**CLC 1, 4, 13, 18, 35; DAM POP; SSC 3**
See also AAYA 4; CA 1-4R; CANR 2, 28, 55; JRDA; MAICYA; MTCW; SATA 13, 70

Clarke, Austin 1896-1974 ....**CLC 6, 9; DAM POET**
See also CA 29-32; 49-52; CAP 2; DLB 10, 20

Clarke, Austin C(hesterfield) 1934-**CLC 8, 53; BLC; DAC; DAM MULT**
See also BW 1; CA 25-28R; CAAS 16; CANR 14, 32; DLB 53, 125

Clarke, Gillian 1937- ....**CLC 61**
See also CA 106; DLB 40

Clarke, Marcus (Andrew Hislop) 1846-1881
NCLC 19

Clarke, Shirley 1925- ....**CLC 16**

Clash, The
See Headon, (Nicky) Topper; Jones, Mick; Simonon, Paul; Strummer, Joe

Claudel, Paul (Louis Charles Marie) 1868-1955
TCLC 2, 10
See also CA 104

Clavell, James (duMaresq) 1925-1994**CLC 6, 25, 87; DAM NOV, POP**
See also CA 25-28R; 146; CANR 26, 48; MTCW

Cleaver, (Leroy) Eldridge 1935- .....**CLC 30; BLC; DAM MULT**
See also BW 1; CA 21-24R; CANR 16

Cleese, John (Marwood) 1939- ....**CLC 21**
See also Monty Python
See also CA 112; 116; CANR 35; MTCW

Cleishbotham, Jebediah
See Scott, Walter

Cleland, John 1710-1789 ....**LC 2**
See also DLB 39

Clemens, Samuel Langhorne 1835-1910
See Twain, Mark
See also CA 104; 135; CDALB 1865-1917; DA; DAB; DAC; DAM MST, NOV; DLB 11, 12, 23, 64, 74; JRDA; MAICYA; YABC 2

Cleophil
See Congreve, William

Clerihew, E.
See Bentley, E(dmund) C(lerihew)

Clerk, N. W.
See Lewis, C(live) S(taples)

Cliff, Jimmy ....**CLC 21**
See also Chambers, James

Clifton, (Thelma) Lucille 1936- **CLC 19, 66; BLC; DAM MULT, POET; PC 17**
See also BW 2; CA 49-52; CANR 2, 24, 42; CLR 5; DLB 5, 41; MAICYA; MTCW; SATA 20, 69

Clinton, Dirk
See Silverberg, Robert

Clough, Arthur Hugh 1819-1861 ...**NCLC 27**
See also DLB 32

Clutha, Janet Paterson Frame 1924-
See Frame, Janet
See also CA 1-4R; CANR 2, 36; MTCW

Clyne, Terence
See Blatty, William Peter

Cobalt, Martin
See Mayne, William (James Carter)

Cobbett, William 1763-1835 ....**NCLC 49**
See also DLB 43, 107, 158

Coburn, D(onald) L(ee) 1938- ....**CLC 10**
See also CA 89-92

Cocteau, Jean (Maurice Eugene Clement) 1889-1963**CLC 1, 8, 15, 16, 43; DA; DAB; DAC; DAM DRAM, MST, NOV; WLC**
See also CA 25-28; CANR 40; CAP 2; DLB 65; MTCW

Codrescu, Andrei 1946-**CLC 46; DAM POET**
See also CA 33-36R; CAAS 19; CANR 13, 34, 53

Coe, Max
See Bourne, Randolph S(illiman)

Coe, Tucker
See Westlake, Donald E(dwin)

Coetzee, J(ohn) M(ichael) 1940- **CLC 23, 33, 66; DAM NOV**
See also CA 77-80; CANR 41, 54; MTCW

Coffey, Brian
See Koontz, Dean R(ay)

Cohan, George M(ichael) 1878-1942**TCLC 60**
See also CA 157

Cohen, Arthur A(llen) 1928-1986 .**CLC 7, 31**
See also CA 1-4R; 120; CANR 1, 17, 42; DLB 28

Cohen, Leonard (Norman) 1934- **CLC 3, 38; DAC; DAM MST**
See also CA 21-24R; CANR 14; DLB 53; MTCW

Cohen, Matt 1942- ....**CLC 19; DAC**
See also CA 61-64; CAAS 18; CANR 40; DLB 53

Cohen-Solal, Annie 19(?)- ....**CLC 50**

Colegate, Isabel 1931- ....**CLC 36**
See also CA 17-20R; CANR 8, 22; DLB 14; INT CANR-22; MTCW

Coleman, Emmett
See Reed, Ishmael

Coleridge, M. E.
See Coleridge, Mary E(lizabeth)

Coleridge, Mary E(lizabeth) 1861-1907**TCLC 73**
See also CA 116; DLB 19, 98

Coleridge, Samuel Taylor 1772-1834**NCLC 9, 54; DA; DAB; DAC; DAM MST, POET; PC 11; WLC**
See also CDBLB 1789-1832; DLB 93, 107

Coleridge, Sara 1802-1852 ....**NCLC 31**

Coles, Don 1928- ....**CLC 46**
See also CA 115; CANR 38

Colette, (Sidonie-Gabrielle) 1873-1954**TCLC 1, 5, 16; DAM NOV; SSC 10**
See also CA 104; 131; DLB 65; MTCW

Collett, (Jacobine) Camilla (Wergeland) 1813-1895 ....**NCLC 22**

Collier, Christopher 1930- ....**CLC 30**
See also AAYA 13; CA 33-36R; CANR 13, 33; JRDA; MAICYA; SATA 16, 70

Collier, James L(incoln) 1928-**CLC 30; DAM POP**
See also AAYA 13; CA 9-12R; CANR 4, 33, 60; CLR 3; JRDA; MAICYA; SAAS 21; SATA 8, 70

Collier, Jeremy 1650-1726 ....**LC 6**

Collier, John 1901-1980 ....**SSC 19**

See also CA 65-68; 97-100; CANR 10; DLB 77

Collingwood, R(obin) G(eorge) 1889(?)-1943
TCLC 67
See also CA 117; 155

Collins, Hunt
See Hunter, Evan

Collins, Linda 1931- ....**CLC 44**
See also CA 125

Collins, (William) Wilkie 1824-1889**NCLC 1, 18**
See also CDBLB 1832-1890; DLB 18, 70, 159

Collins, William 1721-1759 .**LC 4, 40; DAM POET**
See also DLB 109

Collodi, Carlo 1826-1890 ....**NCLC 54**
See also Lorenzini, Carlo
See also CLR 5

Colman, George
See Glassco, John

Colt, Winchester Remington
See Hubbard, L(afayette) Ron(ald)

Colter, Cyrus 1910- ....**CLC 58**
See also BW 1; CA 65-68; CANR 10; DLB 33

Colton, James
See Hansen, Joseph

Colum, Padraic 1881-1972 ....**CLC 28**
See also CA 73-76; 33-36R; CANR 35; CLR 36; MAICYA; MTCW; SATA 15

Colvin, James
See Moorcock, Michael (John)

Colwin, Laurie (E.) 1944-1992**CLC 5, 13, 23, 84**
See also CA 89-92; 139; CANR 20, 46; DLBY 80; MTCW

Comfort, Alex(ander) 1920-**CLC 7; DAM POP**
See also CA 1-4R; CANR 1, 45

Comfort, Montgomery
See Campbell, (John) Ramsey

Compton-Burnett, I(vy) 1884(?)-1969**CLC 1, 3, 10, 15, 34; DAM NOV**
See also CA 1-4R; 25-28R; CANR 4; DLB 36; MTCW

Comstock, Anthony 1844-1915 ......**TCLC 13**
See also CA 110

Comte, Auguste 1798-1857 ....**NCLC 54**

Conan Doyle, Arthur
See Doyle, Arthur Conan

Conde, Maryse 1937- ......**CLC 52, 92; DAM MULT**
See also Boucolon, Maryse
See also BW 2

Condillac, Etienne Bonnot de 1714-1780 **LC 26**

Condon, Richard (Thomas) 1915-1996**CLC 4, 6, 8, 10, 45, 100; DAM NOV**
See also BEST 90:3; CA 1-4R; 151; CAAS 1; CANR 2, 23; INT CANR-23; MTCW

Confucius 551B.C.-479B.C. .. **CMLC 19; DA; DAB; DAC; DAM MST; WLCS**

Congreve, William 1670-1729 **LC 5, 21; DA; DAB; DAC; DAM DRAM, MST, POET; DC 2; WLC**
See also CDBLB 1660-1789; DLB 39, 84

Connell, Evan S(helby), Jr. 1924-**CLC 4, 6, 45; DAM NOV**
See also AAYA 7; CA 1-4R; CAAS 2; CANR 2, 39; DLB 2; DLBY 81; MTCW

Connelly, Marc(us Cook) 1890-1980 ..**CLC 7**
See also CA 85-88; 102; CANR 30; DLB 7; DLBY 80; SATA-Obit 25

Connor, Ralph ....**TCLC 31**
See also Gordon, Charles William

TCLC 6
See also CA 104; DLB 74

Davis, Richard Harding 1864-1916 **TCLC 24**
See also CA 114; DLB 12, 23, 78, 79; DLBD 13

Davison, Frank Dalby 1893-1970 ..... **CLC 15**
See also CA 116

Davison, Lawrence H.
See Lawrence, D(avid) H(erbert Richards)

Davison, Peter (Hubert) 1928- .... **CLC 28**
See also CA 9-12R; CAAS 4; CANR 3, 43; DLB 5

Davys, Mary 1674-1732 .... **LC 1**
See also DLB 39

Dawson, Fielding 1930- .... **CLC 6**
See also CA 85-88; DLB 130

Dawson, Peter
See Faust, Frederick (Schiller)

Day, Clarence (Shepard, Jr.) 1874-1935
TCLC 25
See also CA 108; DLB 11

Day, Thomas 1748-1789 .... **LC 1**
See also DLB 39; YABC 1

Day Lewis, C(ecil) 1904-1972 . **CLC 1, 6, 10;**
DAM POET; PC 11
See also Blake, Nicholas
See also CA 13-16; 33-36R; CANR 34; CAP 1; DLB 15, 20; MTCW

Dazai, Osamu .... **TCLC 11**
See also Tsushima, Shuji
See also DLB 182

de Andrade, Carlos Drummond
See Drummond de Andrade, Carlos

Deane, Norman
See Creasey, John

de Beauvoir, Simone (Lucie Ernestine Marie Bertrand)
See Beauvoir, Simone (Lucie Ernestine Marie Bertrand) de

de Beer, P.
See Bosman, Herman Charles

de Brissac, Malcolm
See Dickinson, Peter (Malcolm)

de Chardin, Pierre Teilhard
See Teilhard de Chardin, (Marie Joseph) Pierre

Dee, John 1527-1608 .... **LC 20**

Deer, Sandra 1940- .... **CLC 45**

De Ferrari, Gabriella 1941- .... **CLC 65**
See also CA 146

Defoe, Daniel 1660(?)-1731 **LC 1; DA; DAB;**
DAC; DAM MST, NOV; WLC
See also CDBLB 1660-1789; DLB 39, 95, 101; JRDA; MAICYA; SATA 22

de Gourmont, Remy(-Marie-Charles)
See Gourmont, Remy (-Marie-Charles) de

de Hartog, Jan 1914- .... **CLC 19**
See also CA 1-4R; CANR 1

de Hostos, E. M.
See Hostos (y Bonilla), Eugenio Maria de

de Hostos, Eugenio M.
See Hostos (y Bonilla), Eugenio Maria de

Deighton, Len .... **CLC 4, 7, 22, 46**
See also Deighton, Leonard Cyril
See also AAYA 6; BEST 89:2; CDBLB 1960 to Present; DLB 87

Deighton, Leonard Cyril 1929-
See Deighton, Len
See also CA 9-12R; CANR 19, 33; DAM NOV, POP; MTCW

Dekker, Thomas 1572(?)-1632 .. **LC 22; DAM DRAM**
See also CDBLB Before 1660; DLB 62, 172

Delafield, E. M. 1890-1943 .... **TCLC 61**

See also Dashwood, Edmee Elizabeth Monica de la Pasture
See also DLB 34

de la Mare, Walter (John) 1873-1956 **TCLC 4,**
53; DAB; DAC; DAM MST, POET; SSC
14; WLC
See also CDBLB 1914-1945; CLR 23; DLB 162; SATA 16

Delaney, Franey
See O'Hara, John (Henry)

Delaney, Shelagh 1939- **CLC 29; DAM DRAM**
See also CA 17-20R; CANR 30; CDBLB 1960 to Present; DLB 13; MTCW

Delany, Mary (Granville Pendarves) 1700-1788
LC 12

Delany, Samuel R(ay, Jr.) 1942- **CLC 8, 14, 38;**
BLC; DAM MULT
See also BW 2; CA 81-84; CANR 27, 43; DLB 8, 33; MTCW

De La Ramee, (Marie) Louise 1839-1908
See Ouida
See also SATA 20

de la Roche, Mazo 1879-1961 .... **CLC 14**
See also CA 85-88; CANR 30; DLB 68; SATA 64

De La Salle, Innocent
See Hartmann, Sadakichi

Delbanco, Nicholas (Franklin) 1942- **CLC 6,**
13
See also CA 17-20R; CAAS 2; CANR 29, 55; DLB 6

del Castillo, Michel 1933- .... **CLC 38**
See also CA 109

Deledda, Grazia (Cosima) 1875(?)-1936
TCLC 23
See also CA 123

Delibes, Miguel .... **CLC 8, 18**
See also Delibes Setien, Miguel

Delibes Setien, Miguel 1920-
See Delibes, Miguel
See also CA 45-48; CANR 1, 32; HW; MTCW

DeLillo, Don 1936- **CLC 8, 10, 13, 27, 39, 54,**
76; DAM NOV, POP
See also BEST 89:1; CA 81-84; CANR 21; DLB 6, 173; MTCW

de Lisser, H. G.
See De Lisser, H(erbert) G(eorge)
See also DLB 117

De Lisser, H(erbert) G(eorge) 1878-1944
TCLC 12
See also de Lisser, H. G.
See also BW 2; CA 109; 152

Deloria, Vine (Victor), Jr. 1933- .... **CLC 21;**
DAM MULT
See also CA 53-56; CANR 5, 20, 48; DLB 175; MTCW; NNAL; SATA 21

Del Vecchio, John M(ichael) 1947- ... **CLC 29**
See also CA 110; DLBD 9

de Man, Paul (Adolph Michel) 1919-1983
CLC 55
See also CA 128; 111; CANR 61; DLB 67; MTCW

De Marinis, Rick 1934- .... **CLC 54**
See also CA 57-60; CAAS 24; CANR 9, 25, 50

Dembry, R. Emmet
See Murfree, Mary Noailles

Demby, William 1922- . **CLC 53; BLC; DAM**
MULT
See also BW 1; CA 81-84; DLB 33

de Menton, Francisco
See Chin, Frank (Chew, Jr.)

Demijohn, Thom
See Disch, Thomas M(ichael)

de Montherlant, Henry (Milon)
See Montherlant, Henry (Milon) de

Demosthenes 384B.C.-322B.C. ...... **CMLC 13**
See also DLB 176

de Natale, Francine
See Malzberg, Barry N(athaniel)

Denby, Edwin (Orr) 1903-1983 .... **CLC 48**
See also CA 138; 110

Denis, Julio
See Cortazar, Julio

Denmark, Harrison
See Zelazny, Roger (Joseph)

Dennis, John 1658-1734 .... **LC 11**
See also DLB 101

Dennis, Nigel (Forbes) 1912-1989 .... **CLC 8**
See also CA 25-28R; 129; DLB 13, 15; MTCW

Dent, Lester 1904(?)-1959 .... **TCLC 72**
See also CA 112

De Palma, Brian (Russell) 1940- .... **CLC 20**
See also CA 109

De Quincey, Thomas 1785-1859 ...... **NCLC 4**
See also CDBLB 1789-1832; DLB 110; 144

Deren, Eleanora 1908(?)-1961
See Deren, Maya
See also CA 111

Deren, Maya 1917-1961 .... **CLC 16, 102**
See also Deren, Eleanora

Derleth, August (William) 1909-1971 **CLC 31**
See also CA 1-4R; 29-32R; CANR 4; DLB 9; SATA 5

Der Nister 1884-1950 .... **TCLC 56**

de Routisie, Albert
See Aragon, Louis

Derrida, Jacques 1930- .... **CLC 24, 87**
See also CA 124; 127

Derry Down Derry
See Lear, Edward

Dersonnes, Jacques
See Simenon, Georges (Jacques Christian)

Desai, Anita 1937- **CLC 19, 37, 97; DAB; DAM**
NOV
See also CA 81-84; CANR 33, 53; MTCW; SATA 63

de Saint-Luc, Jean
See Glassco, John

de Saint Roman, Arnaud
See Aragon, Louis

Descartes, Rene 1596-1650 .... **LC 20, 35**

De Sica, Vittorio 1901(?)-1974 .... **CLC 20**
See also CA 117

Desnos, Robert 1900-1945 .... **TCLC 22**
See also CA 121; 151

Destouches, Louis-Ferdinand 1894-1961 **C L C**
9, 15
See also Celine, Louis-Ferdinand
See also CA 85-88; CANR 28; MTCW

de Tolignac, Gaston
See Griffith, D(avid Lewelyn) W(ark)

Deutsch, Babette 1895-1982 .... **CLC 18**
See also CA 1-4R; 108; CANR 4; DLB 45; SATA 1; SATA-Obit 33

Devenant, William 1606-1649 .... **LC 13**

Devkota, Laxmiprasad 1909-1959 . **TCLC 23**
See also CA 123

De Voto, Bernard (Augustine) 1897-1955
TCLC 29
See also CA 113; 160; DLB 9

De Vries, Peter 1910-1993 **CLC 1, 2, 3, 7, 10,**
28, 46; DAM NOV
See also CA 17-20R; 142; CANR 41; DLB 6; DLBY 82; MTCW

Dexter, John
See Bradley, Marion Zimmer

Dexter, Martin
See Faust, Frederick (Schiller)

Dexter, Pete 1943- ... **CLC 34, 55; DAM POP**
See also BEST 89:2; CA 127; 131; INT 131; MTCW

Diamano, Silmang
See Senghor, Leopold Sedar

Diamond, Neil 1941- .... **CLC 30**
See also CA 108

Diaz del Castillo, Bernal 1496-1584 .... **LC 31**

di Bassetto, Corno
See Shaw, George Bernard

Dick, Philip K(indred) 1928-1982**CLC 10, 30, 72; DAM NOV, POP**
See also CA 49-52; 106; CANR 2, 16; DLB 8; MTCW

Dickens, Charles (John Huffam) 1812-1870
NCLC 3, 8, 18, 26, 37, 50; DA; DAB; DAC; DAM MST, NOV; SSC 17; WLC
See also CDBLB 1832-1890; DLB 21, 55, 70, 159, 166; JRDA; MAICYA; SATA 15

Dickey, James (Lafayette) 1923-1997 **CLC 1, 2, 4, 7, 10, 15, 47; DAM NOV, POET, POP**
See also AITN 1, 2; CA 9-12R; 156; CABS 2; CANR 10, 48, 61; CDALB 1968-1988; DLB 5; DLBD 7; DLBY 82, 93, 96; INT CANR-10; MTCW

Dickey, William 1928-1994 .... **CLC 3, 28**
See also CA 9-12R; 145; CANR 24; DLB 5

Dickinson, Charles 1951- .... **CLC 49**
See also CA 128

Dickinson, Emily (Elizabeth) 1830-1886
NCLC 21; DA; DAB; DAC; DAM MST, POET; PC 1; WLC
See also AAYA 22; CDALB 1865-1917; DLB 1; SATA 29

Dickinson, Peter (Malcolm) 1927-**CLC 12, 35**
See also AAYA 9; CA 41-44R; CANR 31, 58; CLR 29; DLB 87, 161; JRDA; MAICYA; SATA 5, 62, 95

Dickson, Carr
See Carr, John Dickson

Dickson, Carter
See Carr, John Dickson

Diderot, Denis 1713-1784 .... **LC 26**

Didion, Joan 1934-**CLC 1, 3, 8, 14, 32; DAM NOV**
See also AITN 1; CA 5-8R; CANR 14, 52; CDALB 1968-1988; DLB 2, 173; DLBY 81, 86; MTCW

Dietrich, Robert
See Hunt, E(verette) Howard, (Jr.)

Dillard, Annie 1945- **CLC 9, 60; DAM NOV**
See also AAYA 6; CA 49-52; CANR 3, 43, 62; DLBY 80; MTCW; SATA 10

Dillard, R(ichard) H(enry) W(ilde) 1937-
CLC 5
See also CA 21-24R; CAAS 7; CANR 10; DLB 5

Dillon, Eilis 1920-1994 .... **CLC 17**
See also CA 9-12R; 147; CAAS 3; CANR 4, 38; CLR 26; MAICYA; SATA 2, 74; SATA-Obit 83

Dimont, Penelope
See Mortimer, Penelope (Ruth)

Dinesen, Isak .... **CLC 10, 29, 95; SSC 7**
See also Blixen, Karen (Christentze Dinesen)

Ding Ling .... **CLC 68**
See also Chiang Pin-chin

Disch, Thomas M(ichael) 1940- .... **CLC 7, 36**
See also AAYA 17; CA 21-24R; CAAS 4; CANR 17, 36, 54; CLR 18; DLB 8; MAICYA; MTCW; SAAS 15; SATA 92

Disch, Tom
See Disch, Thomas M(ichael)

d'Isly, Georges
See Simenon, Georges (Jacques Christian)

Disraeli, Benjamin 1804-1881 .... **NCLC 2, 39**
See also DLB 21, 55

Ditcum, Steve
See Crumb, R(obert)

Dixon, Paige
See Corcoran, Barbara

Dixon, Stephen 1936- .... **CLC 52; SSC 16**
See also CA 89-92; CANR 17, 40, 54; DLB 130

Doak, Annie
See Dillard, Annie

Dobell, Sydney Thompson 1824-1874 **NCLC 43**
See also DLB 32

Doblin, Alfred .... **TCLC 13**
See also Doeblin, Alfred

Dobrolyubov, Nikolai Alexandrovich 1836-1861
NCLC 5

Dobyns, Stephen 1941- .... **CLC 37**
See also CA 45-48; CANR 2, 18

Doctorow, E(dgar) L(aurence) 1931- **CLC 6, 11, 15, 18, 37, 44, 65; DAM NOV, POP**
See also AAYA 22; AITN 2; BEST 89:3; CA 45-48; CANR 2, 33, 51; CDALB 1968-1988; DLB 2, 28, 173; DLBY 80; MTCW

Dodgson, Charles Lutwidge 1832-1898
See Carroll, Lewis
See also CLR 2; DA; DAB; DAC; DAM MST, NOV, POET; MAICYA; YABC 2

Dodson, Owen (Vincent) 1914-1983 **CLC 79; BLC; DAM MULT**
See also BW 1; CA 65-68; 110; CANR 24; DLB 76

Doeblin, Alfred 1878-1957 .... **TCLC 13**
See also Doblin, Alfred
See also CA 110; 141; DLB 66

Doerr, Harriet 1910- .... **CLC 34**
See also CA 117; 122; CANR 47; INT 122

Domecq, H(onorio) Bustos
See Bioy Casares, Adolfo; Borges, Jorge Luis

Domini, Rey
See Lorde, Audre (Geraldine)

Dominique
See Proust, (Valentin-Louis-George-Eugene-) Marcel

Don, A
See Stephen, Leslie

Donaldson, Stephen R. 1947- **CLC 46; DAM POP**
See also CA 89-92; CANR 13, 55; INT CANR-13

Donleavy, J(ames) P(atrick) 1926-**CLC 1, 4, 6, 10, 45**
See also AITN 2; CA 9-12R; CANR 24, 49, 62; DLB 6, 173; INT CANR-24; MTCW

Donne, John 1572-1631**LC 10, 24; DA; DAB; DAC; DAM MST, POET; PC 1**
See also CDBLB Before 1660; DLB 121, 151

Donnell, David 1939(?)- .... **CLC 34**

Donoghue, P. S.
See Hunt, E(verette) Howard, (Jr.)

Donoso (Yanez), Jose 1924-1996**CLC 4, 8, 11, 32, 99; DAM MULT; HLC**
See also CA 81-84; 155; CANR 32; DLB 113; HW; MTCW

Donovan, John 1928-1992 .... **CLC 35**
See also AAYA 20; CA 97-100; 137; CLR 3; MAICYA; SATA 72; SATA-Brief 29

Don Roberto
See Cunninghame Graham, R(obert) B(ontine)

Doolittle, Hilda 1886-1961**CLC 3, 8, 14, 31, 34, 73; DA; DAC; DAM MST, POET; PC 5; WLC**
See also H. D.
See also CA 97-100; CANR 35; DLB 4, 45; MTCW

Dorfman, Ariel 1942- ...... **CLC 48, 77; DAM MULT; HLC**
See also CA 124; 130; HW; INT 130

Dorn, Edward (Merton) 1929- ... **CLC 10, 18**
See also CA 93-96; CANR 42; DLB 5; INT 93-96

Dorsan, Luc
See Simenon, Georges (Jacques Christian)

Dorsange, Jean
See Simenon, Georges (Jacques Christian)

Dos Passos, John (Roderigo) 1896-1970 **CLC 1, 4, 8, 11, 15, 25, 34, 82; DA; DAB; DAC; DAM MST, NOV; WLC**
See also CA 1-4R; 29-32R; CANR 3; CDALB 1929-1941; DLB 4, 9; DLBD 1, 15; DLBY 96; MTCW

Dossage, Jean
See Simenon, Georges (Jacques Christian)

Dostoevsky, Fedor Mikhailovich 1821-1881
NCLC 2, 7, 21, 33, 43; DA; DAB; DAC; DAM MST, NOV; SSC 2; WLC

Doughty, Charles M(ontagu) 1843-1926
TCLC 27
See also CA 115; DLB 19, 57, 174

Douglas, Ellen .... **CLC 73**
See also Haxton, Josephine Ayres; Williamson, Ellen Douglas

Douglas, Gavin 1475(?)-1522 .... **LC 20**

Douglas, Keith (Castellain) 1920-1944**TCLC 40**
See also CA 160; DLB 27

Douglas, Leonard
See Bradbury, Ray (Douglas)

Douglas, Michael
See Crichton, (John) Michael

Douglas, Norman 1868-1952 .... **TCLC 68**

Douglass, Frederick 1817(?)-1895**NCLC 7, 55; BLC; DA; DAC; DAM MST, MULT; WLC**
See also CDALB 1640-1865; DLB 1, 43, 50, 79; SATA 29

Dourado, (Waldomiro Freitas) Autran 1926-
CLC 23, 60
See also CA 25-28R; CANR 34

Dourado, Waldomiro Autran
See Dourado, (Waldomiro Freitas) Autran

Dove, Rita (Frances) 1952-**CLC 50, 81; DAM MULT, POET; PC 6**
See also BW 2; CA 109; CAAS 19; CANR 27, 42; DLB 120

Dowell, Coleman 1925-1985 .... **CLC 60**
See also CA 25-28R; 117; CANR 10; DLB 130

Dowson, Ernest (Christopher) 1867-1900
TCLC 4
See also CA 105; 150; DLB 19, 135

Doyle, A. Conan
See Doyle, Arthur Conan

Doyle, Arthur Conan 1859-1930**TCLC 7; DA; DAB; DAC; DAM MST, NOV; SSC 12; WLC**
See also AAYA 14; CA 104; 122; CDBLB 1890-1914; DLB 18, 70, 156, 178; MTCW; SATA 24

Doyle, Conan
See Doyle, Arthur Conan

Doyle, John
See Graves, Robert (von Ranke)

Doyle, Roddy 1958(?)- .... **CLC 81**

See also AAYA 14; CA 143

Doyle, Sir A. Conan
See Doyle, Arthur Conan

Doyle, Sir Arthur Conan
See Doyle, Arthur Conan

Dr. A
See Asimov, Isaac; Silverstein, Alvin

Drabble, Margaret 1939-CLC **2, 3, 5, 8, 10, 22, 53; DAB; DAC; DAM MST, NOV, POP**
See also CA 13-16R; CANR 18, 35; CDBLB 1960 to Present; DLB 14, 155; MTCW; SATA 48

Drapier, M. B.
See Swift, Jonathan

Drayham, James
See Mencken, H(enry) L(ouis)

Drayton, Michael 1563-1631 .... LC **8**

Dreadstone, Carl
See Campbell, (John) Ramsey

Dreiser, Theodore(Herman Albert) 1871-1945 TCLC **10, 18, 35; DA; DAC; DAM MST, NOV; WLC**
See also CA 106; 132; CDALB 1865-1917; DLB 9, 12, 102, 137; DLBD 1; MTCW

Drexler, Rosalyn 1926- .... CLC **2, 6**
See also CA 81-84

Dreyer, Carl Theodor 1889-1968 ...... CLC **16**
See also CA 116

Drieu la Rochelle, Pierre(-Eugene) 1893-1945 TCLC **21**
See also CA 117; DLB 72

Drinkwater, John 1882-1937 .... TCLC **57**
See also CA 109; 149; DLB 10, 19, 149

Drop Shot
See Cable, George Washington

Droste-Hulshoff, Annette Freiin von 1797-1848 NCLC **3**
See also DLB 133

Drummond, Walter
See Silverberg, Robert

Drummond, William Henry 1854-1907 T C L C **25**
See also CA 160; DLB 92

Drummond de Andrade, Carlos 1902-1987 CLC **18**
See also Andrade, Carlos Drummond de
See also CA 132; 123

Drury, Allen (Stuart) 1918- .... CLC **37**
See also CA 57-60; CANR 18, 52; INT CANR-18

Dryden, John 1631-1700 LC **3, 21; DA; DAB; DAC; DAM DRAM, MST, POET; DC 3; WLC**
See also CDBLB 1660-1789; DLB 80, 101, 131

Duberman, Martin 1930- .... CLC **8**
See also CA 1-4R; CANR 2

Dubie, Norman (Evans) 1945- .... CLC **36**
See also CA 69-72; CANR 12; DLB 120

Du Bois, W(illiam) E(dward) B(urghardt) 1868-1963 CLC **1, 2, 13, 64, 96; BLC; DA; DAC; DAM MST, MULT, NOV; WLC**
See also BW 1; CA 85-88; CANR 34; CDALB 1865-1917; DLB 47, 50, 91; MTCW; SATA 42

Dubus, Andre 1936- CLC **13, 36, 97; SSC 15**
See also CA 21-24R; CANR 17; DLB 130; INT CANR-17

Duca Minimo
See D'Annunzio, Gabriele

Ducharme, Rejean 1941- .... CLC **74**
See also DLB 60

Duclos, Charles Pinot 1704-1772 .... LC **1**

Dudek, Louis 1918- .... CLC **11, 19**

See also CA 45-48; CAAS 14; CANR 1; DLB 88

Duerrenmatt, Friedrich 1921-1990 CLC **1, 4, 8, 11, 15, 43, 102; DAM DRAM**
See also CA 17-20R; CANR 33; DLB 69, 124; MTCW

Duffy, Bruce (?)- .... CLC **50**

Duffy, Maureen 1933- .... CLC **37**
See also CA 25-28R; CANR 33; DLB 14; MTCW

Dugan, Alan 1923- .... CLC **2, 6**
See also CA 81-84; DLB 5

du Gard, Roger Martin
See Martin du Gard, Roger

Duhamel, Georges 1884-1966 .... CLC **8**
See also CA 81-84; 25-28R; CANR 35; DLB 65; MTCW

Dujardin, Edouard (Emile Louis) 1861-1949 TCLC **13**
See also CA 109; DLB 123

Dulles, John Foster 1888-1959 .... TCLC **72**
See also CA 115; 149

Dumas, Alexandre (Davy de la Pailleterie) 1802-1870 .. NCLC **11; DA; DAB; DAC; DAM MST, NOV; WLC**
See also DLB 119; SATA 18

Dumas, Alexandre 1824-1895 NCLC **9; DC 1**
See also AAYA 22

Dumas, Claudine
See Malzberg, Barry N(athaniel)

Dumas, Henry L. 1934-1968 .... CLC **6, 62**
See also BW 1; CA 85-88; DLB 41

du Maurier, Daphne 1907-1989 CLC **6, 11, 59; DAB; DAC; DAM MST, POP; SSC 18**
See also CA 5-8R; 128; CANR 6, 55; MTCW; SATA 27; SATA-Obit 60

Dunbar, Paul Laurence 1872-1906 . TCLC **2, 12; BLC; DA; DAC; DAM MST, MULT, POET; PC 5; SSC 8; WLC**
See also BW 1; CA 104; 124; CDALB 1865-1917; DLB 50, 54, 78; SATA 34

Dunbar, William 1460(?)-1530(?) .... LC **20**
See also DLB 132, 146

Duncan, Dora Angela
See Duncan, Isadora

Duncan, Isadora 1877(?)-1927 .... TCLC **68**
See also CA 118; 149

Duncan, Lois 1934- .... CLC **26**
See also AAYA 4; CA 1-4R; CANR 2, 23, 36; CLR 29; JRDA; MAICYA; SAAS 2; SATA 1, 36, 75

Duncan, Robert (Edward) 1919-1988 CLC **1, 2, 4, 7, 15, 41, 55; DAM POET; PC 2**
See also CA 9-12R; 124; CANR 28, 62; DLB 5, 16; MTCW

Duncan, Sara Jeannette 1861-1922 TCLC **60**
See also CA 157; DLB 92

Dunlap, William 1766-1839 .... NCLC **2**
See also DLB 30, 37, 59

Dunn, Douglas (Eaglesham) 1942- CLC **6, 40**
See also CA 45-48; CANR 2, 33; DLB 40; MTCW

Dunn, Katherine (Karen) 1945- .... CLC **71**
See also CA 33-36R

Dunn, Stephen 1939- .... CLC **36**
See also CA 33-36R; CANR 12, 48, 53; DLB 105

Dunne, Finley Peter 1867-1936 ...... TCLC **28**
See also CA 108; DLB 11, 23

Dunne, John Gregory 1932- .... CLC **28**
See also CA 25-28R; CANR 14, 50; DLBY 80

Dunsany, Edward John Moreton Drax Plunkett 1878-1957

See Dunsany, Lord
See also CA 104; 148; DLB 10

Dunsany, Lord .... TCLC **2, 59**
See also Dunsany, Edward John Moreton Drax Plunkett
See also DLB 77, 153, 156

du Perry, Jean
See Simenon, Georges (Jacques Christian)

Durang, Christopher (Ferdinand) 1949-C L C **27, 38**
See also CA 105; CANR 50

Duras, Marguerite 1914-1996 CLC **3, 6, 11, 20, 34, 40, 68, 100**
See also CA 25-28R; 151; CANR 50; DLB 83; MTCW

Durban, (Rosa) Pam 1947- .... CLC **39**
See also CA 123

Durcan, Paul 1944-CLC **43, 70; DAM POET**
See also CA 134

Durkheim, Emile 1858-1917 .... TCLC **55**

Durrell, Lawrence (George) 1912-1990 C L C **1, 4, 6, 8, 13, 27, 41; DAM NOV**
See also CA 9-12R; 132; CANR 40; CDBLB 1945-1960; DLB 15, 27; DLBY 90; MTCW

Durrenmatt, Friedrich
See Duerrenmatt, Friedrich

Dutt, Toru 1856-1877 .... NCLC **29**

Dwight, Timothy 1752-1817 .... NCLC **13**
See also DLB 37

Dworkin, Andrea 1946- .... CLC **43**
See also CA 77-80; CAAS 21; CANR 16, 39; INT CANR-16; MTCW

Dwyer, Deanna
See Koontz, Dean R(ay)

Dwyer, K. R.
See Koontz, Dean R(ay)

Dye, Richard
See De Voto, Bernard (Augustine)

Dylan, Bob 1941- .... CLC **3, 4, 6, 12, 77**
See also CA 41-44R; DLB 16

Eagleton, Terence (Francis) 1943-
See Eagleton, Terry
See also CA 57-60; CANR 7, 23; MTCW

Eagleton, Terry .... CLC **63**
See also Eagleton, Terence (Francis)

Early, Jack
See Scoppettone, Sandra

East, Michael
See West, Morris L(anglo)

Eastaway, Edward
See Thomas, (Philip) Edward

Eastlake, William (Derry) 1917-1997 CLC **8**
See also CA 5-8R; 158; CAAS 1; CANR 5; DLB 6; INT CANR-5

Eastman, Charles A(lexander) 1858-1939 TCLC **55; DAM MULT**
See also DLB 175; NNAL; YABC 1

Eberhart, Richard (Ghormley) 1904- CLC **3, 11, 19, 56; DAM POET**
See also CA 1-4R; CANR 2; CDALB 1941-1968; DLB 48; MTCW

Eberstadt, Fernanda 1960- .... CLC **39**
See also CA 136

Echegaray (y Eizaguirre), Jose (Maria Waldo) 1832-1916 .... TCLC **4**
See also CA 104; CANR 32; HW; MTCW

Echeverria, (Jose) Esteban (Antonino) 1805-1851 .... NCLC **18**

Echo
See Proust, (Valentin-Louis-George-Eugene-) Marcel

Eckert, Allan W. 1931- .... CLC **17**
See also AAYA 18; CA 13-16R; CANR 14, 45;

Epstein, Leslie 1938- .... **CLC 27**
See also CA 73-76; CAAS 12; CANR 23

Equiano, Olaudah 1745(?)-1797**LC 16; BLC; DAM MULT**
See also DLB 37, 50

ER .... **TCLC 33**
See also CA 160; DLB 85

Erasmus, Desiderius 1469(?)-1536 ...... **LC 16**

Erdman, Paul E(mil) 1932- .... **CLC 25**
See also AITN 1; CA 61-64; CANR 13, 43

Erdrich, Louise 1954- ..... **CLC 39, 54; DAM MULT, NOV, POP**
See also AAYA 10; BEST 89:1; CA 114; CANR 41, 62; DLB 152, 175; MTCW; NNAL; SATA 94

Erenburg, Ilya (Grigoryevich)
See Ehrenburg, Ilya (Grigoryevich)

Erickson, Stephen Michael 1950-
See Erickson, Steve
See also CA 129

Erickson, Steve 1950- .... **CLC 64**
See also Erickson, Stephen Michael
See also CANR 60

Ericson, Walter
See Fast, Howard (Melvin)

Eriksson, Buntel
See Bergman, (Ernst) Ingmar

Ernaux, Annie 1940- .... **CLC 88**
See also CA 147

Eschenbach, Wolfram von
See Wolfram von Eschenbach

Eseki, Bruno
See Mphahlele, Ezekiel

Esenin, Sergei (Alexandrovich) 1895-1925 **TCLC 4**
See also CA 104

Eshleman, Clayton 1935- .... **CLC 7**
See also CA 33-36R; CAAS 6; DLB 5

Espriella, Don Manuel Alvarez
See Southey, Robert

Espriu, Salvador 1913-1985 .... **CLC 9**
See also CA 154; 115; DLB 134

Espronceda, Jose de 1808-1842 ..... **NCLC 39**

Esse, James
See Stephens, James

Esterbrook, Tom
See Hubbard, L(afayette) Ron(ald)

Estleman, Loren D. 1952-**CLC 48; DAM NOV, POP**
See also CA 85-88; CANR 27; INT CANR-27; MTCW

Eugenides, Jeffrey 1960(?)- .... **CLC 81**
See also CA 144

Euripides c. 485B.C.-406B.C.**CMLC 23; DA; DAB; DAC; DAM DRAM, MST; DC 4; WLCS**
See also DLB 176

Evan, Evin
See Faust, Frederick (Schiller)

Evans, Evan
See Faust, Frederick (Schiller)

Evans, Marian
See Eliot, George

Evans, Mary Ann
See Eliot, George

Evarts, Esther
See Benson, Sally

Everett, Percival L. 1956- .... **CLC 57**
See also BW 2; CA 129

Everson, R(onald) G(ilmour) 1903- . **CLC 27**
See also CA 17-20R; DLB 88

Everson, William (Oliver) 1912-1994 **CLC 1, 5, 14**

See also CA 9-12R; 145; CANR 20; DLB 5, 16; MTCW

Evtushenko, Evgenii Aleksandrovich
See Yevtushenko, Yevgeny (Alexandrovich)

Ewart, Gavin (Buchanan) 1916-1995**CLC 13, 46**
See also CA 89-92; 150; CANR 17, 46; DLB 40; MTCW

Ewers, Hanns Heinz 1871-1943 ..... **TCLC 12**
See also CA 109; 149

Ewing, Frederick R.
See Sturgeon, Theodore (Hamilton)

Exley, Frederick (Earl) 1929-1992 **CLC 6, 11**
See also AITN 2; CA 81-84; 138; DLB 143; DLBY 81

Eynhardt, Guillermo
See Quiroga, Horacio (Sylvestre)

Ezekiel, Nissim 1924- .... **CLC 61**
See also CA 61-64

Ezekiel, Tish O'Dowd 1943- .... **CLC 34**
See also CA 129

Fadeyev, A.
See Bulgya, Alexander Alexandrovich

Fadeyev, Alexander .... **TCLC 53**
See also Bulgya, Alexander Alexandrovich

Fagen, Donald 1948- .... **CLC 26**

Fainzilberg, Ilya Arnoldovich 1897-1937
See Ilf, Ilya
See also CA 120

Fair, Ronald L. 1932- .... **CLC 18**
See also BW 1; CA 69-72; CANR 25; DLB 33

Fairbairn, Roger
See Carr, John Dickson

Fairbairns, Zoe (Ann) 1948- .... **CLC 32**
See also CA 103; CANR 21

Falco, Gian
See Papini, Giovanni

Falconer, James
See Kirkup, James

Falconer, Kenneth
See Kornbluth, C(yril) M.

Falkland, Samuel
See Heijermans, Herman

Fallaci, Oriana 1930- .... **CLC 11**
See also CA 77-80; CANR 15, 58; MTCW

Faludy, George 1913- .... **CLC 42**
See also CA 21-24R

Faludy, Gyoergy
See Faludy, George

Fanon, Frantz 1925-1961**CLC 74; BLC; DAM MULT**
See also BW 1; CA 116; 89-92

Fanshawe, Ann 1625-1680 .... **LC 11**

Fante, John (Thomas) 1911-1983 ..... **CLC 60**
See also CA 69-72; 109; CANR 23; DLB 130; DLBY 83

Farah, Nuruddin 1945- **CLC 53; BLC; DAM MULT**
See also BW 2; CA 106; DLB 125

Fargue, Leon-Paul 1876(?)-1947 ... **TCLC 11**
See also CA 109

Farigoule, Louis
See Romains, Jules

Farina, Richard 1936(?)-1966 .... **CLC 9**
See also CA 81-84; 25-28R

Farley, Walter (Lorimer) 1915-1989 **CLC 17**
See also CA 17-20R; CANR 8, 29; DLB 22; JRDA; MAICYA; SATA 2, 43

Farmer, Philip Jose 1918- .... **CLC 1, 19**
See also CA 1-4R; CANR 4, 35; DLB 8; MTCW; SATA 93

Farquhar, George 1677-1707 ...**LC 21; DAM DRAM**

See also DLB 84

Farrell, J(ames) G(ordon) 1935-1979 **CLC 6**
See also CA 73-76; 89-92; CANR 36; DLB 14; MTCW

Farrell, James T(homas) 1904-1979**CLC 1, 4, 8, 11, 66; SSC 28**
See also CA 5-8R; 89-92; CANR 9, 61; DLB 4, 9, 86; DLBD 2; MTCW

Farren, Richard J.
See Betjeman, John

Farren, Richard M.
See Betjeman, John

Fassbinder, Rainer Werner 1946-1982**CLC 20**
See also CA 93-96; 106; CANR 31

Fast, Howard (Melvin) 1914- **CLC 23; DAM NOV**
See also AAYA 16; CA 1-4R; CAAS 18; CANR 1, 33, 54; DLB 9; INT CANR-33; SATA 7

Faulcon, Robert
See Holdstock, Robert P.

Faulkner, William (Cuthbert) 1897-1962**CLC 1, 3, 6, 8, 9, 11, 14, 18, 28, 52, 68; DA; DAB; DAC; DAM MST, NOV; SSC 1; WLC**
See also AAYA 7; CA 81-84; CANR 33; CDALB 1929-1941; DLB 9, 11, 44, 102; DLBD 2; DLBY 86; MTCW

Fauset, Jessie Redmon 1884(?)-1961**CLC 19, 54; BLC; DAM MULT**
See also BW 1; CA 109; DLB 51

Faust, Frederick (Schiller) 1892-1944(?) **TCLC 49; DAM POP**
See also CA 108; 152

Faust, Irvin 1924- .... **CLC 8**
See also CA 33-36R; CANR 28; DLB 2, 28; DLBY 80

Fawkes, Guy
See Benchley, Robert (Charles)

Fearing, Kenneth (Flexner) 1902-1961 . **C L C 51**
See also CA 93-96; CANR 59; DLB 9

Fecamps, Elise
See Creasey, John

Federman, Raymond 1928- .... **CLC 6, 47**
See also CA 17-20R; CAAS 8; CANR 10, 43; DLBY 80

Federspiel, J(uerg) F. 1931- .... **CLC 42**
See also CA 146

Feiffer, Jules (Ralph) 1929- ..... **CLC 2, 8, 64; DAM DRAM**
See also AAYA 3; CA 17-20R; CANR 30, 59; DLB 7, 44; INT CANR-30; MTCW; SATA 8, 61

Feige, Hermann Albert Otto Maximilian
See Traven, B.

Feinberg, David B. 1956-1994 .... **CLC 59**
See also CA 135; 147

Feinstein, Elaine 1930- .... **CLC 36**
See also CA 69-72; CAAS 1; CANR 31; DLB 14, 40; MTCW

Feldman, Irving (Mordecai) 1928- ..... **CLC 7**
See also CA 1-4R; CANR 1; DLB 169

Felix-Tchicaya, Gerald
See Tchicaya, Gerald Felix

Fellini, Federico 1920-1993 .... **CLC 16, 85**
See also CA 65-68; 143; CANR 33

Felsen, Henry Gregor 1916- .... **CLC 17**
See also CA 1-4R; CANR 1; SAAS 2; SATA 1

Fenton, James Martin 1949- .... **CLC 32**
See also CA 102; DLB 40

Ferber, Edna 1887-1968 .... **CLC 18, 93**
See also AITN 1; CA 5-8R; 25-28R; DLB 9, 28, 86; MTCW; SATA 7

Ferguson, Helen

See Kavan, Anna
Ferguson, Samuel 1810-1886 .... **NCLC 33**
See also DLB 32
Fergusson, Robert 1750-1774 .... **LC 29**
See also DLB 109
Ferling, Lawrence
See Ferlinghetti, Lawrence (Monsanto)
Ferlinghetti, Lawrence (Monsanto) 1919(?)-
CLC 2, 6, 10, 27; DAM POET; PC 1
See also CA 5-8R; CANR 3, 41; CDALB 1941-
1968; DLB 5, 16; MTCW
Fernandez, Vicente Garcia Huidobro
See Huidobro Fernandez, Vicente Garcia
Ferrer, Gabriel (Francisco Victor) Miro
See Miro (Ferrer), Gabriel (Francisco Victor)
Ferrier, Susan (Edmonstone) 1782-1854
NCLC 8
See also DLB 116
Ferrigno, Robert 1948(?)- .... **CLC 65**
See also CA 140
Ferron, Jacques 1921-1985 .... **CLC 94; DAC**
See also CA 117; 129; DLB 60
Feuchtwanger, Lion 1884-1958 .... **TCLC 3**
See also CA 104; DLB 66
Feuillet, Octave 1821-1890 .... **NCLC 45**
Feydeau, Georges (Leon Jules Marie) 1862-
1921 .... **TCLC 22; DAM DRAM**
See also CA 113; 152
Fichte, Johann Gottlieb 1762-1814 **NCLC 62**
See also DLB 90
Ficino, Marsilio 1433-1499 .... **LC 12**
Fiedeler, Hans
See Doeblin, Alfred
Fiedler, Leslie A(aron) 1917- . **CLC 4, 13, 24**
See also CA 9-12R; CANR 7; DLB 28, 67;
MTCW
Field, Andrew 1938- .... **CLC 44**
See also CA 97-100; CANR 25
Field, Eugene 1850-1895 .... **NCLC 3**
See also DLB 23, 42, 140; DLBD 13; MAICYA;
SATA 16
Field, Gans T.
See Wellman, Manly Wade
Field, Michael .... **TCLC 43**
Field, Peter
See Hobson, Laura Z(ametkin)
Fielding, Henry 1707-1754 **LC 1; DA; DAB;**
DAC; DAM DRAM, MST, NOV; WLC
See also CDBLB 1660-1789; DLB 39, 84, 101
Fielding, Sarah 1710-1768 .... **LC 1**
See also DLB 39
Fierstein, Harvey (Forbes) 1954- ... **CLC 33;**
DAM DRAM, POP
See also CA 123; 129
Figes, Eva 1932- .... **CLC 31**
See also CA 53-56; CANR 4, 44; DLB 14
Finch, Robert (Duer Claydon) 1900- **CLC 18**
See also CA 57-60; CANR 9, 24, 49; DLB 88
Findley, Timothy 1930- . **CLC 27, 102; DAC;**
DAM MST
See also CA 25-28R; CANR 12, 42; DLB 53
Fink, William
See Mencken, H(enry) L(ouis)
Firbank, Louis 1942-
See Reed, Lou
See also CA 117
Firbank, (Arthur Annesley) Ronald 1886-1926
TCLC 1
See also CA 104; DLB 36
Fisher, M(ary) F(rances) K(ennedy) 1908-1992
CLC 76, 87
See also CA 77-80; 138; CANR 44
Fisher, Roy 1930- .... **CLC 25**

See also CA 81-84; CAAS 10; CANR 16; DLB
40
Fisher, Rudolph 1897-1934 . **TCLC 11; BLC;**
DAM MULT; SSC 25
See also BW 1; CA 107; 124; DLB 51, 102
Fisher, Vardis (Alvero) 1895-1968 ...... **CLC 7**
See also CA 5-8R; 25-28R; DLB 9
Fiske, Tarleton
See Bloch, Robert (Albert)
Fitch, Clarke
See Sinclair, Upton (Beall)
Fitch, John IV
See Cormier, Robert (Edmund)
Fitzgerald, Captain Hugh
See Baum, L(yman) Frank
FitzGerald, Edward 1809-1883 .... **NCLC 9**
See also DLB 32
Fitzgerald, F(rancis) Scott (Key) 1896-1940
TCLC 1, 6, 14, 28, 55; DA; DAB; DAC;
DAM MST, NOV; SSC 6; WLC
See also AITN 1; CA 110; 123; CDALB 1917-
1929; DLB 4, 9, 86; DLBD 1, 15, 16; DLBY
81, 96; MTCW
Fitzgerald, Penelope 1916- ... **CLC 19, 51, 61**
See also CA 85-88; CAAS 10; CANR 56; DLB
14
Fitzgerald, Robert (Stuart) 1910-1985**CLC 39**
See also CA 1-4R; 114; CANR 1; DLBY 80
FitzGerald, Robert D(avid) 1902-1987**CLC 19**
See also CA 17-20R
Fitzgerald, Zelda (Sayre) 1900-1948**TCLC 52**
See also CA 117; 126; DLBY 84
Flanagan, Thomas (James Bonner) 1923-
CLC 25, 52
See also CA 108; CANR 55; DLBY 80; INT
108; MTCW
Flaubert, Gustave 1821-1880**NCLC 2, 10, 19,**
62; DA; DAB; DAC; DAM MST, NOV;
SSC 11; WLC
See also DLB 119
Flecker, Herman Elroy
See Flecker, (Herman) James Elroy
Flecker, (Herman) James Elroy 1884-1915
TCLC 43
See also CA 109; 150; DLB 10, 19
Fleming, Ian (Lancaster) 1908-1964 . **CLC 3,**
30; DAM POP
See also CA 5-8R; CANR 59; CDBLB 1945-
1960; DLB 87; MTCW; SATA 9
Fleming, Thomas (James) 1927- .... **CLC 37**
See also CA 5-8R; CANR 10; INT CANR-10;
SATA 8
Fletcher, John 1579-1625 .... **LC 33; DC 6**
See also CDBLB Before 1660; DLB 58
Fletcher, John Gould 1886-1950 .... **TCLC 35**
See also CA 107; DLB 4, 45
Fleur, Paul
See Pohl, Frederik
Flooglebuckle, Al
See Spiegelman, Art
Flying Officer X
See Bates, H(erbert) E(rnest)
Fo, Dario 1926- .... **CLC 32; DAM DRAM**
See also CA 116; 128; MTCW
Fogarty, Jonathan Titulescu Esq.
See Farrell, James T(homas)
Folke, Will
See Bloch, Robert (Albert)
Follett, Ken(neth Martin) 1949- ..... **CLC 18;**
DAM NOV, POP
See also AAYA 6; BEST 89:4; CA 81-84; CANR
13, 33, 54; DLB 87; DLBY 81; INT CANR-
33; MTCW

Fontane, Theodor 1819-1898 .... **NCLC 26**
See also DLB 129
Foote, Horton 1916-**CLC 51, 91; DAM DRAM**
See also CA 73-76; CANR 34, 51; DLB 26; INT
CANR-34
Foote, Shelby 1916-**CLC 75; DAM NOV, POP**
See also CA 5-8R; CANR 3, 45; DLB 2, 17
Forbes, Esther 1891-1967 .... **CLC 12**
See also AAYA 17; CA 13-14; 25-28R; CAP 1;
CLR 27; DLB 22; JRDA; MAICYA; SATA 2
Forche, Carolyn (Louise) 1950- **CLC 25, 83,**
86; DAM POET; PC 10
See also CA 109; 117; CANR 50; DLB 5; INT
117
Ford, Elbur
See Hibbert, Eleanor Alice Burford
Ford, Ford Madox 1873-1939**TCLC 1, 15, 39,**
57; DAM NOV
See also CA 104; 132; CDBLB 1914-1945;
DLB 162; MTCW
Ford, Henry 1863-1947 .... **TCLC 73**
See also CA 115; 148
Ford, John 1895-1973 .... **CLC 16**
See also CA 45-48
Ford, Richard .... **CLC 99**
Ford, Richard 1944- .... **CLC 46**
See also CA 69-72; CANR 11, 47
Ford, Webster
See Masters, Edgar Lee
Foreman, Richard 1937- .... **CLC 50**
See also CA 65-68; CANR 32
Forester, C(ecil) S(cott) 1899-1966 ... **CLC 35**
See also CA 73-76; 25-28R; SATA 13
Forez
See Mauriac, Francois (Charles)
Forman, James Douglas 1932- .... **CLC 21**
See also AAYA 17; CA 9-12R; CANR 4, 19,
42; JRDA; MAICYA; SATA 8, 70
Fornes, Maria Irene 1930- .... **CLC 39, 61**
See also CA 25-28R; CANR 28; DLB 7; HW;
INT CANR-28; MTCW
Forrest, Leon 1937- .... **CLC 4**
See also BW 2; CA 89-92; CAAS 7; CANR 25,
52; DLB 33
Forster, E(dward) M(organ) 1879-1970 **C L C**
1, 2, 3, 4, 9, 10, 13, 15, 22, 45, 77; DA; DAB;
DAC; DAM MST, NOV; SSC 27; WLC
See also AAYA 2; CA 13-14; 25-28R; CANR
45; CAP 1; CDBLB 1914-1945; DLB 34, 98,
162, 178; DLBD 10; MTCW; SATA 57
Forster, John 1812-1876 .... **NCLC 11**
See also DLB 144, 184
Forsyth, Frederick 1938-**CLC 2, 5, 36; DAM**
NOV, POP
See also BEST 89:4; CA 85-88; CANR 38, 62;
DLB 87; MTCW
Forten, Charlotte L. .... **TCLC 16; BLC**
See also Grimke, Charlotte L(ottie) Forten
See also DLB 50
Foscolo, Ugo 1778-1827 .... **NCLC 8**
Fosse, Bob .... **CLC 20**
See also Fosse, Robert Louis
Fosse, Robert Louis 1927-1987
See Fosse, Bob
See also CA 110; 123
Foster, Stephen Collins 1826-1864 **NCLC 26**
Foucault, Michel 1926-1984 . **CLC 31, 34, 69**
See also CA 105; 113; CANR 34; MTCW
Fouque, Friedrich (Heinrich Karl) de la Motte
1777-1843 .... **NCLC 2**
See also DLB 90
Fourier, Charles 1772-1837 .... **NCLC 51**
Fournier, Henri Alban 1886-1914

See Alain-Fournier
See also CA 104
Fournier, Pierre 1916- .... **CLC 11**
See also Gascar, Pierre
See also CA 89-92; CANR 16, 40
Fowles, John 1926-**CLC 1, 2, 3, 4, 6, 9, 10, 15, 33, 87; DAB; DAC; DAM MST**
See also CA 5-8R; CANR 25; CDBLB 1960 to Present; DLB 14, 139; MTCW; SATA 22
Fox, Paula 1923- .... **CLC 2, 8**
See also AAYA 3; CA 73-76; CANR 20, 36, 62; CLR 1, 44; DLB 52; JRDA; MAICYA; MTCW; SATA 17, 60
Fox, William Price (Jr.) 1926- .... **CLC 22**
See also CA 17-20R; CAAS 19; CANR 11; DLB 2; DLBY 81
Foxe, John 1516(?)-1587 .... **LC 14**
Frame, Janet 1924-**CLC 2, 3, 6, 22, 66, 96; SSC 29**
See also Clutha, Janet Paterson Frame
France, Anatole .... **TCLC 9**
See also Thibault, Jacques Anatole Francois
See also DLB 123
Francis, Claude 19(?)- .... **CLC 50**
Francis, Dick 1920-**CLC 2, 22, 42, 102; DAM POP**
See also AAYA 5, 21; BEST 89:3; CA 5-8R; CANR 9, 42; CDBLB 1960 to Present; DLB 87; INT CANR-9; MTCW
Francis, Robert (Churchill) 1901-1987 **C L C 15**
See also CA 1-4R; 123; CANR 1
Frank, Anne(lies Marie) 1929-1945**TCLC 17; DA; DAB; DAC; DAM MST; WLC**
See also AAYA 12; CA 113; 133; MTCW; SATA 87; SATA-Brief 42
Frank, Elizabeth 1945- .... **CLC 39**
See also CA 121; 126; INT 126
Frankl, Viktor E(mil) 1905- .... **CLC 93**
See also CA 65-68
Franklin, Benjamin
See Hasek, Jaroslav (Matej Frantisek)
Franklin, Benjamin 1706-1790 .. **LC 25; DA; DAB; DAC; DAM MST; WLCS**
See also CDALB 1640-1865; DLB 24, 43, 73
Franklin, (Stella Maraia Sarah) Miles 1879-1954 .... **TCLC 7**
See also CA 104
Fraser, (Lady) Antonia (Pakenham) 1932-**CLC 32**
See also CA 85-88; CANR 44; MTCW; SATA-Brief 32
Fraser, George MacDonald 1925- ...... **CLC 7**
See also CA 45-48; CANR 2, 48
Fraser, Sylvia 1935- .... **CLC 64**
See also CA 45-48; CANR 1, 16, 60
Frayn, Michael 1933-**CLC 3, 7, 31, 47; DAM DRAM, NOV**
See also CA 5-8R; CANR 30; DLB 13, 14; MTCW
Fraze, Candida (Merrill) 1945- .... **CLC 50**
See also CA 126
Frazer, J(ames) G(eorge) 1854-1941**TCLC 32**
See also CA 118
Frazer, Robert Caine
See Creasey, John
Frazer, Sir James George
See Frazer, J(ames) G(eorge)
Frazier, Ian 1951- .... **CLC 46**
See also CA 130; CANR 54
Frederic, Harold 1856-1898 .... **NCLC 10**
See also DLB 12, 23; DLBD 13
Frederick, John

See Faust, Frederick (Schiller)
Frederick the Great 1712-1786 .... **LC 14**
Fredro, Aleksander 1793-1876 .... **NCLC 8**
Freeling, Nicolas 1927- .... **CLC 38**
See also CA 49-52; CAAS 12; CANR 1, 17, 50; DLB 87
Freeman, Douglas Southall 1886-1953**T C L C 11**
See also CA 109; DLB 17
Freeman, Judith 1946- .... **CLC 55**
See also CA 148
Freeman, Mary Eleanor Wilkins 1852-1930 **TCLC 9; SSC 1**
See also CA 106; DLB 12, 78
Freeman, R(ichard) Austin 1862-1943**T C L C 21**
See also CA 113; DLB 70
French, Albert 1943- .... **CLC 86**
French, Marilyn 1929-**CLC 10, 18, 60; DAM DRAM, NOV, POP**
See also CA 69-72; CANR 3, 31; INT CANR-31; MTCW
French, Paul
See Asimov, Isaac
Freneau, Philip Morin 1752-1832 ... **NCLC 1**
See also DLB 37, 43
Freud, Sigmund 1856-1939 .... **TCLC 52**
See also CA 115; 133; MTCW
Friedan, Betty (Naomi) 1921- .... **CLC 74**
See also CA 65-68; CANR 18, 45; MTCW
Friedlander, Saul 1932- .... **CLC 90**
See also CA 117; 130
Friedman, B(ernard) H(arper) 1926- **CLC 7**
See also CA 1-4R; CANR 3, 48
Friedman, Bruce Jay 1930- ...... **CLC 3, 5, 56**
See also CA 9-12R; CANR 25, 52; DLB 2, 28; INT CANR-25
Friel, Brian 1929- .... **CLC 5, 42, 59**
See also CA 21-24R; CANR 33; DLB 13; MTCW
Friis-Baastad, Babbis Ellinor 1921-1970**C L C 12**
See also CA 17-20R; 134; SATA 7
Frisch, Max (Rudolf) 1911-1991**CLC 3, 9, 14, 18, 32, 44; DAM DRAM, NOV**
See also CA 85-88; 134; CANR 32; DLB 69, 124; MTCW
Fromentin, Eugene (Samuel Auguste) 1820-1876 .... **NCLC 10**
See also DLB 123
Frost, Frederick
See Faust, Frederick (Schiller)
Frost, Robert (Lee) 1874-1963**CLC 1, 3, 4, 9, 10, 13, 15, 26, 34, 44; DA; DAB; DAC; DAM MST, POET; PC 1; WLC**
See also AAYA 21; CA 89-92; CANR 33; CDALB 1917-1929; DLB 54; DLBD 7; MTCW; SATA 14
Froude, James Anthony 1818-1894**NCLC 43**
See also DLB 18, 57, 144
Froy, Herald
See Waterhouse, Keith (Spencer)
Fry, Christopher 1907- **CLC 2, 10, 14; DAM DRAM**
See also CA 17-20R; CAAS 23; CANR 9, 30; DLB 13; MTCW; SATA 66
Frye, (Herman) Northrop 1912-1991**CLC 24, 70**
See also CA 5-8R; 133; CANR 8, 37; DLB 67, 68; MTCW
Fuchs, Daniel 1909-1993 .... **CLC 8, 22**
See also CA 81-84; 142; CAAS 5; CANR 40; DLB 9, 26, 28; DLBY 93

Fuchs, Daniel 1934- .... **CLC 34**
See also CA 37-40R; CANR 14, 48
Fuentes, Carlos 1928-**CLC 3, 8, 10, 13, 22, 41, 60; DA; DAB; DAC; DAM MST, MULT, NOV; HLC; SSC 24; WLC**
See also AAYA 4; AITN 2; CA 69-72; CANR 10, 32; DLB 113; HW; MTCW
Fuentes, Gregorio Lopez y
See Lopez y Fuentes, Gregorio
Fugard, (Harold) Athol 1932-**CLC 5, 9, 14, 25, 40, 80; DAM DRAM; DC 3**
See also AAYA 17; CA 85-88; CANR 32, 54; MTCW
Fugard, Sheila 1932- .... **CLC 48**
See also CA 125
Fuller, Charles (H., Jr.) 1939-**CLC 25; BLC; DAM DRAM, MULT; DC 1**
See also BW 2; CA 108; 112; DLB 38; INT 112; MTCW
Fuller, John (Leopold) 1937- .... **CLC 62**
See also CA 21-24R; CANR 9, 44; DLB 40
Fuller, Margaret .... **NCLC 5, 50**
See also Ossoli, Sarah Margaret (Fuller marchesa d')
Fuller, Roy (Broadbent) 1912-1991**CLC 4, 28**
See also CA 5-8R; 135; CAAS 10; CANR 53; DLB 15, 20; SATA 87
Fulton, Alice 1952- .... **CLC 52**
See also CA 116; CANR 57
Furphy, Joseph 1843-1912 .... **TCLC 25**
Fussell, Paul 1924- .... **CLC 74**
See also BEST 90:1; CA 17-20R; CANR 8, 21, 35; INT CANR-21; MTCW
Futabatei, Shimei 1864-1909 .... **TCLC 44**
See also DLB 180
Futrelle, Jacques 1875-1912 .... **TCLC 19**
See also CA 113; 155
Gaboriau, Emile 1835-1873 .... **NCLC 14**
Gadda, Carlo Emilio 1893-1973 .... **CLC 11**
See also CA 89-92; DLB 177
Gaddis, William 1922- **CLC 1, 3, 6, 8, 10, 19, 43, 86**
See also CA 17-20R; CANR 21, 48; DLB 2; MTCW
Gage, Walter
See Inge, William (Motter)
Gaines, Ernest J(ames) 1933- **CLC 3, 11, 18, 86; BLC; DAM MULT**
See also AAYA 18; AITN 1; BW 2; CA 9-12R; CANR 6, 24, 42; CDALB 1968-1988; DLB 2, 33, 152; DLBY 80; MTCW; SATA 86
Gaitskill, Mary 1954- .... **CLC 69**
See also CA 128; CANR 61
Galdos, Benito Perez
See Perez Galdos, Benito
Gale, Zona 1874-1938**TCLC 7; DAM DRAM**
See also CA 105; 153; DLB 9, 78
Galeano, Eduardo (Hughes) 1940- ... **CLC 72**
See also CA 29-32R; CANR 13, 32; HW
Galiano, Juan Valera y Alcala
See Valera y Alcala-Galiano, Juan
Gallagher, Tess 1943- ...... **CLC 18, 63; DAM POET; PC 9**
See also CA 106; DLB 120
Gallant, Mavis 1922- ... **CLC 7, 18, 38; DAC; DAM MST; SSC 5**
See also CA 69-72; CANR 29; DLB 53; MTCW
Gallant, Roy A(rthur) 1924- .... **CLC 17**
See also CA 5-8R; CANR 4, 29, 54; CLR 30; MAICYA; SATA 4, 68
Gallico, Paul (William) 1897-1976 ..... **CLC 2**
See also AITN 1; CA 5-8R; 69-72; CANR 23; DLB 9, 171; MAICYA; SATA 13

Gallo, Max Louis 1932- .... **CLC 95**
See also CA 85-88
Gallois, Lucien
See Desnos, Robert
Gallup, Ralph
See Whitemore, Hugh (John)
Galsworthy, John 1867-1933**TCLC 1, 45; DA;**
DAB; DAC; DAM DRAM, MST, NOV;
SSC 22; WLC 2
See also CA 104; 141; CDBLB 1890-1914;
DLB 10, 34, 98, 162; DLBD 16
Galt, John 1779-1839 .... **NCLC 1**
See also DLB 99, 116, 159
Galvin, James 1951- .... **CLC 38**
See also CA 108; CANR 26
Gamboa, Federico 1864-1939 .... **TCLC 36**
Gandhi, M. K.
See Gandhi, Mohandas Karamchand
Gandhi, Mahatma
See Gandhi, Mohandas Karamchand
Gandhi, Mohandas Karamchand 1869-1948
TCLC 59; DAM MULT
See also CA 121; 132; MTCW
Gann, Ernest Kellogg 1910-1991 ...... **CLC 23**
See also AITN 1; CA 1-4R; 136; CANR 1
Garcia, Cristina 1958- .... **CLC 76**
See also CA 141
Garcia Lorca, Federico 1898-1936**TCLC 1, 7,**
49; DA; DAB; DAC; DAM DRAM, MST,
MULT, POET; DC 2; HLC; PC 3; WLC
See also CA 104; 131; DLB 108; HW; MTCW
Garcia Marquez, Gabriel (Jose) 1928-**CLC 2,**
3, 8, 10, 15, 27, 47, 55, 68; DA; DAB; DAC;
DAM MST, MULT, NOV, POP; HLC; SSC
8; WLC
See also AAYA 3; BEST 89:1, 90:4; CA 33-
36R; CANR 10, 28, 50; DLB 113; HW;
MTCW
Gard, Janice
See Latham, Jean Lee
Gard, Roger Martin du
See Martin du Gard, Roger
Gardam, Jane 1928- .... **CLC 43**
See also CA 49-52; CANR 2, 18, 33, 54; CLR
12; DLB 14, 161; MAICYA; MTCW; SAAS
9; SATA 39, 76; SATA-Brief 28
Gardner, Herb(ert) 1934- .... **CLC 44**
See also CA 149
Gardner, John (Champlin), Jr. 1933-1982
CLC 2, 3, 5, 7, 8, 10, 18, 28, 34; DAM NOV,
POP; SSC 7
See also AITN 1; CA 65-68; 107; CANR 33;
DLB 2; DLBY 82; MTCW; SATA 40; SATA-
Obit 31
Gardner, John (Edmund) 1926-**CLC 30; DAM**
POP
See also CA 103; CANR 15; MTCW
Gardner, Miriam
See Bradley, Marion Zimmer
Gardner, Noel
See Kuttner, Henry
Gardons, S. S.
See Snodgrass, W(illiam) D(e Witt)
Garfield, Leon 1921-1996 .... **CLC 12**
See also AAYA 8; CA 17-20R; 152; CANR 38,
41; CLR 21; DLB 161; JRDA; MAICYA;
SATA 1, 32, 76; SATA-Obit 90
Garland, (Hannibal) Hamlin 1860-1940
TCLC 3; SSC 18
See also CA 104; DLB 12, 71, 78
Garneau, (Hector de) Saint-Denys 1912-1943
TCLC 13
See also CA 111; DLB 88

Garner, Alan 1934-**CLC 17; DAB; DAM POP**
See also AAYA 18; CA 73-76; CANR 15; CLR
20; DLB 161; MAICYA; MTCW; SATA 18,
69
Garner, Hugh 1913-1979 .... **CLC 13**
See also CA 69-72; CANR 31; DLB 68
Garnett, David 1892-1981 .... **CLC 3**
See also CA 5-8R; 103; CANR 17; DLB 34
Garos, Stephanie
See Katz, Steve
Garrett, George (Palmer) 1929-**CLC 3, 11, 51**
See also CA 1-4R; CAAS 5; CANR 1, 42; DLB
2, 5, 130, 152; DLBY 83
Garrick, David 1717-1779 ....**LC 15; DAM**
DRAM
See also DLB 84
Garrigue, Jean 1914-1972 .... **CLC 2, 8**
See also CA 5-8R; 37-40R; CANR 20
Garrison, Frederick
See Sinclair, Upton (Beall)
Garth, Will
See Hamilton, Edmond; Kuttner, Henry
Garvey, Marcus (Moziah, Jr.) 1887-1940
TCLC 41; BLC; DAM MULT
See also BW 1; CA 120; 124
Gary, Romain .... **CLC 25**
See Kacew, Romain
See also DLB 83
Gascar, Pierre .... **CLC 11**
See also Fournier, Pierre
Gascoyne, David (Emery) 1916- .... **CLC 45**
See also CA 65-68; CANR 10, 28, 54; DLB 20;
MTCW
Gaskell, Elizabeth Cleghorn 1810-1865**NCLC**
5; DAB; DAM MST; SSC 25
See also CDBLB 1832-1890; DLB 21, 144, 159
Gass, William H(oward) 1924-**CLC 1, 2, 8, 11,**
15, 39; SSC 12
See also CA 17-20R; CANR 30; DLB 2; MTCW
Gasset, Jose Ortega y
See Ortega y Gasset, Jose
Gates, Henry Louis, Jr. 1950- **CLC 65; DAM**
MULT
See also BW 2; CA 109; CANR 25, 53; DLB
67
Gautier, Theophile 1811-1872 .. **NCLC 1, 59;**
DAM POET; PC 18; SSC 20
See also DLB 119
Gawsworth, John
See Bates, H(erbert) E(rnest)
Gay, Oliver
See Gogarty, Oliver St. John
Gaye, Marvin (Penze) 1939-1984 ..... **CLC 26**
See also CA 112
Gebler, Carlo (Ernest) 1954- .... **CLC 39**
See also CA 119; 133
Gee, Maggie (Mary) 1948- .... **CLC 57**
See also CA 130
Gee, Maurice (Gough) 1931- .... **CLC 29**
See also CA 97-100; SATA 46
Gelbart, Larry (Simon) 1923- .... **CLC 21, 61**
See also CA 73-76; CANR 45
Gelber, Jack 1932- .... **CLC 1, 6, 14, 79**
See also CA 1-4R; CANR 2; DLB 7
Gellhorn, Martha (Ellis) 1908- .. **CLC 14, 60**
See also CA 77-80; CANR 44; DLBY 82
Genet, Jean 1910-1986**CLC 1, 2, 5, 10, 14, 44,**
46; DAM DRAM
See also CA 13-16R; CANR 18; DLB 72;
DLBY 86; MTCW
Gent, Peter 1942- .... **CLC 29**
See also AITN 1; CA 89-92; DLBY 82
Gentlewoman in New England, A

See Bradstreet, Anne
Gentlewoman in Those Parts, A
See Bradstreet, Anne
George, Jean Craighead 1919- .... **CLC 35**
See also AAYA 8; CA 5-8R; CANR 25; CLR 1;
DLB 52; JRDA; MAICYA; SATA 2, 68
George, Stefan (Anton) 1868-1933**TCLC 2, 14**
See also CA 104
Georges, Georges Martin
See Simenon, Georges (Jacques Christian)
Gerhardi, William Alexander
See Gerhardie, William Alexander
Gerhardie, William Alexander 1895-1977
CLC 5
See also CA 25-28R; 73-76; CANR 18; DLB
36
Gerstler, Amy 1956- .... **CLC 70**
See also CA 146
Gertler, T. .... **CLC 34**
See also CA 116; 121; INT 121
Ghalib .... **NCLC 39**
See also Ghalib, Hsadullah Khan
Ghalib, Hsadullah Khan 1797-1869
See Ghalib
See also DAM POET
Ghelderode, Michel de 1898-1962**CLC 6, 11;**
DAM DRAM
See also CA 85-88; CANR 40
Ghiselin, Brewster 1903- .... **CLC 23**
See also CA 13-16R; CAAS 10; CANR 13
Ghose, Zulfikar 1935- .... **CLC 42**
See also CA 65-68
Ghosh, Amitav 1956- .... **CLC 44**
See also CA 147
Giacosa, Giuseppe 1847-1906 .... **TCLC 7**
See also CA 104
Gibb, Lee
See Waterhouse, Keith (Spencer)
Gibbon, Lewis Grassic .... **TCLC 4**
See also Mitchell, James Leslie
Gibbons, Kaye 1960-**CLC 50, 88; DAM POP**
See also CA 151
Gibran, Kahlil 1883-1931 . **TCLC 1, 9; DAM**
POET, POP; PC 9
See also CA 104; 150
Gibran, Khalil
See Gibran, Kahlil
Gibson, William 1914- .. **CLC 23; DA; DAB;**
DAC; DAM DRAM, MST
See also CA 9-12R; CANR 9, 42; DLB 7; SATA
66
Gibson, William (Ford) 1948- ... **CLC 39, 63;**
DAM POP
See also AAYA 12; CA 126; 133; CANR 52
Gide, Andre (Paul Guillaume) 1869-1951
TCLC 5, 12, 36; DA; DAB; DAC; DAM
MST, NOV; SSC 13; WLC
See also CA 104; 124; DLB 65; MTCW
Gifford, Barry (Colby) 1946- .... **CLC 34**
See also CA 65-68; CANR 9, 30, 40
Gilbert, Frank
See De Voto, Bernard (Augustine)
Gilbert, W(illiam) S(chwenck) 1836-1911
TCLC 3; DAM DRAM, POET
See also CA 104; SATA 36
Gilbreth, Frank B., Jr. 1911- .... **CLC 17**
See also CA 9-12R; SATA 2
Gilchrist, Ellen 1935-**CLC 34, 48; DAM POP;**
SSC 14
See also CA 113; 116; CANR 41, 61; DLB 130;
MTCW
Giles, Molly 1942- .... **CLC 39**
See also CA 126

Gill, Patrick
   See Creasey, John
Gilliam, Terry (Vance) 1940- .... **CLC 21**
   See also Monty Python
   See also AAYA 19; CA 108; 113; CANR 35;
      INT 113
Gillian, Jerry
   See Gilliam, Terry (Vance)
Gilliatt, Penelope (Ann Douglass) 1932-1993
      CLC 2, 10, 13, 53
   See also AITN 2; CA 13-16R; 141; CANR 49;
      DLB 14
Gilman, Charlotte (Anna) Perkins (Stetson)
      1860-1935 .... **TCLC 9, 37; SSC 13**
   See also CA 106; 150
Gilmour, David 1949- .... **CLC 35**
   See also CA 138, 147
Gilpin, William 1724-1804 .... **NCLC 30**
Gilray, J. D.
   See Mencken, H(enry) L(ouis)
Gilroy, Frank D(aniel) 1925- .... **CLC 2**
   See also CA 81-84; CANR 32; DLB 7
Gilstrap, John 1957(?)- .... **CLC 99**
   See also CA 160
Ginsberg, Allen 1926-1997 **CLC 1, 2, 3, 4, 6, 13,**
      36, 69; DA; DAB; DAC; DAM MST,
      POET; PC 4; WLC 3
   See also CA 1-4R; 157; CANR 2, 41;
      CDALB 1941-1968; DLB 5, 16, 169; MTCW
Ginzburg, Natalia 1916-1991 **CLC 5, 11, 54, 70**
   See also CA 85-88; 135; CANR 33; DLB 177;
      MTCW
Giono, Jean 1895-1970 .... **CLC 4, 11**
   See also CA 45-48; 29-32R; CANR 2, 35; DLB
      72; MTCW
Giovanni, Nikki 1943- **CLC 2, 4, 19, 64; BLC;**
      DA; DAB; DAC; DAM MST, MULT,
      POET; PC 19; WLCS
   See also AAYA 22; AITN 1; BW 2; CA 29-32R;
      CAAS 6; CANR 18, 41, 60; CLR 6; DLB 5,
      41; INT CANR-18; MAICYA; MTCW; SATA
      24
Giovene, Andrea 1904- .... **CLC 7**
   See also CA 85-88
Gippius, Zinaida (Nikolayevna) 1869-1945
   See Hippius, Zinaida
   See also CA 106
Giraudoux, (Hippolyte) Jean 1882-1944
      TCLC 2, 7; DAM DRAM
   See also CA 104; DLB 65
Gironella, Jose Maria 1917- .... **CLC 11**
   See also CA 101
Gissing, George (Robert) 1857-1903 **TCLC 3,**
      24, 47
   See also CA 105; DLB 18, 135, 184
Giurlani, Aldo
   See Palazzeschi, Aldo
Gladkov, Fyodor (Vasilyevich) 1883-1958
      TCLC 27
Glanville, Brian (Lester) 1931- .... **CLC 6**
   See also CA 5-8R; CAAS 9; CANR 3; DLB 15,
      139; SATA 42
Glasgow, Ellen (Anderson Gholson) 1873(?)-
      1945 .... **TCLC 2, 7**
   See also CA 104; DLB 9, 12
Glaspell, Susan 1882(?)-1948 .... **TCLC 55**
   See also CA 110; 154; DLB 7, 9, 78; YABC 2
Glassco, John 1909-1981 .... **CLC 9**
   See also CA 13-16R; 102; CANR 15; DLB 68
Glasscock, Amnesia
   See Steinbeck, John (Ernst)
Glasser, Ronald J. 1940(?)- .... **CLC 37**
Glassman, Joyce

   See Johnson, Joyce
Glendinning, Victoria 1937- .... **CLC 50**
   See also CA 120; 127; CANR 59; DLB 155
Glissant, Edouard 1928- . **CLC 10, 68; DAM**
      MULT
   See also CA 153
Gloag, Julian 1930- .... **CLC 40**
   See also AITN 1; CA 65-68; CANR 10
Glowacki, Aleksander
   See Prus, Boleslaw
Gluck, Louise (Elisabeth) 1943- **CLC 7, 22, 44,**
      81; DAM POET; PC 16
   See also CA 33-36R; CANR 40; DLB 5
Glyn, Elinor 1864-1943 .... **TCLC 72**
   See also DLB 153
Gobineau, Joseph Arthur (Comte) de 1816-
      1882 .... **NCLC 17**
   See also DLB 123
Godard, Jean-Luc 1930- .... **CLC 20**
   See also CA 93-96
Godden, (Margaret) Rumer 1907- ... **CLC 53**
   See also AAYA 6; CA 5-8R; CANR 4, 27, 36,
      55; CLR 20; DLB 161; MAICYA; SAAS 12;
      SATA 3, 36
Godoy Alcayaga, Lucila 1889-1957
   See Mistral, Gabriela
   See also BW 2; CA 104; 131; DAM MULT;
      HW; MTCW
Godwin, Gail (Kathleen) 1937- **CLC 5, 8, 22,**
      31, 69; DAM POP
   See also CA 29-32R; CANR 15, 43; DLB 6;
      INT CANR-15; MTCW
Godwin, William 1756-1836 .... **NCLC 14**
   See also CDBLB 1789-1832; DLB 39, 104, 142,
      158, 163
Goebbels, Josef
   See Goebbels, (Paul) Joseph
Goebbels, (Paul) Joseph 1897-1945 **TCLC 68**
   See also CA 115; 148
Goebbels, Joseph Paul
   See Goebbels, (Paul) Joseph
Goethe, Johann Wolfgang von 1749-1832
      NCLC 4, 22, 34; DA; DAB; DAC; DAM
      DRAM, MST, POET; PC 5; WLC 3
   See also DLB 94
Gogarty, Oliver St. John 1878-1957 **TCLC 15**
   See also CA 109; 150; DLB 15, 19
Gogol, Nikolai (Vasilyevich) 1809-1852 **NCLC**
      5, 15, 31; DA; DAB; DAC; DAM DRAM,
      MST; DC 1; SSC 4, 29; WLC
Goines, Donald 1937(?)-1974 **CLC 80; BLC;**
      DAM MULT, POP
   See also AITN 1; BW 1; CA 124; 114; DLB 33
Gold, Herbert 1924- .... **CLC 4, 7, 14, 42**
   See also CA 9-12R; CANR 17, 45; DLB 2;
      DLBY 81
Goldbarth, Albert 1948- .... **CLC 5, 38**
   See also CA 53-56; CANR 6, 40; DLB 120
Goldberg, Anatol 1910-1982 .... **CLC 34**
   See also CA 131; 117
Goldemberg, Isaac 1945- .... **CLC 52**
   See also CA 69-72; CAAS 12; CANR 11, 32;
      HW
Golding, William (Gerald) 1911-1993 **CLC 1,**
      2, 3, 8, 10, 17, 27, 58, 81; DA; DAB; DAC;
      DAM MST, NOV; WLC
   See also AAYA 5; CA 5-8R; 141; CANR 13,
      33, 54; CDBLB 1945-1960; DLB 15, 100;
      MTCW
Goldman, Emma 1869-1940 .... **TCLC 13**
   See also CA 110; 150
Goldman, Francisco 1955- .... **CLC 76**
Goldman, William (W.) 1931- .... **CLC 1, 48**

   See also CA 9-12R; CANR 29; DLB 44
Goldmann, Lucien 1913-1970 .... **CLC 24**
   See also CA 25-28; CAP 2
Goldoni, Carlo 1707-1793 **LC 4; DAM DRAM**
Goldsberry, Steven 1949- .... **CLC 34**
   See also CA 131
Goldsmith, Oliver 1728-1774 **LC 2; DA; DAB;**
      DAC; DAM DRAM, MST, NOV, POET;
      WLC
   See also CDBLB 1660-1789; DLB 39, 89, 104,
      109, 142; SATA 26
Goldsmith, Peter
   See Priestley, J(ohn) B(oynton)
Gombrowicz, Witold 1904-1969 **CLC 4, 7, 11,**
      49; DAM DRAM
   See also CA 19-20; 25-28R; CAP 2
Gomez de la Serna, Ramon 1888-1963 **CLC 9**
   See also CA 153; 116; HW
Goncharov, Ivan Alexandrovich 1812-1891
      NCLC 1, 63
Goncourt, Edmond (Louis Antoine Huot) de
      1822-1896 .... **NCLC 7**
   See also DLB 123
Goncourt, Jules (Alfred Huot) de 1830-1870
      NCLC 7
   See also DLB 123
Gontier, Fernande 19(?)- .... **CLC 50**
Gonzalez Martinez, Enrique 1871-1952
      TCLC 72
   See also HW
Goodman, Paul 1911-1972 ...... **CLC 1, 2, 4, 7**
   See also CA 19-20; 37-40R; CANR 34; CAP 2;
      DLB 130; MTCW
Gordimer, Nadine 1923- **CLC 3, 5, 7, 10, 18, 33,**
      51, 70; DA; DAB; DAC; DAM MST, NOV;
      SSC 17; WLCS
   See also CA 5-8R; CANR 3, 28, 56; INT CANR-
      28; MTCW
Gordon, Adam Lindsay 1833-1870 **NCLC 21**
Gordon, Caroline 1895-1981 **CLC 6, 13, 29, 83;**
      SSC 15
   See also CA 11-12; 103; CANR 36; CAP 1;
      DLB 4, 9, 102; DLBY 81; MTCW
Gordon, Charles William 1860-1937
   See Connor, Ralph
   See also CA 109
Gordon, Mary (Catherine) 1949- **CLC 13, 22**
   See also CA 102; CANR 44; DLB 6; DLBY
      81; INT 102; MTCW
Gordon, N. J.
   See Bosman, Herman Charles
Gordon, Sol 1923- .... **CLC 26**
   See also CA 53-56; CANR 4; SATA 11
Gordone, Charles 1925-1995 **CLC 1, 4; DAM**
      DRAM
   See also BW 1; CA 93-96; 150; CANR 55; DLB
      7; INT 93-96; MTCW
Gore, Catherine 1800-1861 .... **NCLC 65**
   See also DLB 116
Gorenko, Anna Andreevna
   See Akhmatova, Anna
Gorky, Maxim **TCLC 8; DAB; SSC 28; WLC**
   See also Peshkov, Alexei Maximovich
Goryan, Sirak
   See Saroyan, William
Gosse, Edmund (William) 1849-1928 **TCLC 28**
   See also CA 117; DLB 57, 144, 184
Gotlieb, Phyllis Fay (Bloom) 1926- .. **CLC 18**
   See also CA 13-16R; CANR 7; DLB 88
Gottesman, S. D.
   See Kornbluth, C(yril) M.; Pohl, Frederik
Gottfried von Strassburg fl. c. 1210- **CMLC**
      10

See also DLB 138

Gould, Lois .... **CLC 4, 10**
See also CA 77-80; CANR 29; MTCW

Gourmont, Remy (-Marie-Charles) de 1858-1915 .... **TCLC 17**
See also CA 109; 150

Govier, Katherine 1948- .... **CLC 51**
See also CA 101; CANR 18, 40

Goyen, (Charles) William 1915-1983**CLC 5, 8, 14, 40**
See also AITN 2; CA 5-8R; 110; CANR 6; DLB 2; DLBY 83; INT CANR-6

Goytisolo, Juan 1931- . **CLC 5, 10, 23; DAM MULT; HLC**
See also CA 85-88; CANR 32, 61; HW; MTCW

Gozzano, Guido 1883-1916 .... **PC 10**
See also CA 154; DLB 114

Gozzi, (Conte) Carlo 1720-1806 .... **NCLC 23**

Grabbe, Christian Dietrich 1801-1836**N C L C 2**
See also DLB 133

Grace, Patricia 1937- .... **CLC 56**

Gracian y Morales, Baltasar 1601-1658**LC 15**

Gracq, Julien .... **CLC 11, 48**
See also Poirier, Louis
See also DLB 83

Grade, Chaim 1910-1982 .... **CLC 10**
See also CA 93-96; 107

Graduate of Oxford, A
See Ruskin, John

Grafton, Garth
See Duncan, Sara Jeannette

Graham, John
See Phillips, David Graham

Graham, Jorie 1951- .... **CLC 48**
See also CA 111; DLB 120

Graham, R(obert) B(ontine) Cunninghame
See Cunninghame Graham, R(obert) B(ontine)
See also DLB 98, 135, 174

Graham, Robert
See Haldeman, Joe (William)

Graham, Tom
See Lewis, (Harry) Sinclair

Graham, W(illiam) S(ydney) 1918-1986**C L C 29**
See also CA 73-76; 118; DLB 20

Graham, Winston (Mawdsley) 1910- **CLC 23**
See also CA 49-52; CANR 2, 22, 45; DLB 77

Grahame, Kenneth 1859-1932**TCLC 64; DAB**
See also CA 108; 136; CLR 5; DLB 34, 141, 178; MAICYA; YABC 1

Grant, Skeeter
See Spiegelman, Art

Granville-Barker, Harley 1877-1946**TCLC 2; DAM DRAM**
See also Barker, Harley Granville
See also CA 104

Grass, Guenter (Wilhelm) 1927-**CLC 1, 2, 4, 6, 11, 15, 22, 32, 49, 88; DA; DAB; DAC; DAM MST, NOV; WLC**
See also CA 13-16R; CANR 20; DLB 75, 124; MTCW

Gratton, Thomas
See Hulme, T(homas) E(rnest)

Grau, Shirley Ann 1929- .. **CLC 4, 9; SSC 15**
See also CA 89-92; CANR 22; DLB 2; INT CANR-22; MTCW

Gravel, Fern
See Hall, James Norman

Graver, Elizabeth 1964- .... **CLC 70**
See also CA 135

Graves, Richard Perceval 1945- .... **CLC 44**
See also CA 65-68; CANR 9, 26, 51

Graves, Robert (von Ranke) 1895-1985 **C L C 1, 2, 6, 11, 39, 44, 45; DAB; DAC; DAM MST, POET; PC 6**
See also CA 5-8R; 117; CANR 5, 36; CDBLB 1914-1945; DLB 20, 100; DLBY 85; MTCW; SATA 45

Graves, Valerie
See Bradley, Marion Zimmer

Gray, Alasdair (James) 1934- .... **CLC 41**
See also CA 126; CANR 47; INT 126; MTCW

Gray, Amlin 1946- .... **CLC 29**
See also CA 138

Gray, Francine du Plessix 1930- ..... **CLC 22; DAM NOV**
See also BEST 90:3; CA 61-64; CAAS 2; CANR 11, 33; INT CANR-11; MTCW

Gray, John (Henry) 1866-1934 ...... **TCLC 19**
See also CA 119

Gray, Simon (James Holliday) 1936- **CLC 9, 14, 36**
See also AITN 1; CA 21-24R; CAAS 3; CANR 32; DLB 13; MTCW

Gray, Spalding 1941-**CLC 49; DAM POP; DC 7**
See also CA 128

Gray, Thomas 1716-1771**LC 4, 40; DA; DAB; DAC; DAM MST; PC 2; WLC**
See also CDBLB 1660-1789; DLB 109

Grayson, David
See Baker, Ray Stannard

Grayson, Richard (A.) 1951- .... **CLC 38**
See also CA 85-88; CANR 14, 31, 57

Greeley, Andrew M(oran) 1928- ..... **CLC 28; DAM POP**
See also CA 5-8R; CAAS 7; CANR 7, 43; MTCW

Green, Anna Katharine 1846-1935 **TCLC 63**
See also CA 112; 159

Green, Brian
See Card, Orson Scott

Green, Hannah
See Greenberg, Joanne (Goldenberg)

Green, Hannah 1927(?)-1996 .... **CLC 3**
See also CA 73-76; CANR 59

Green, Henry 1905-1973 .... **CLC 2, 13, 97**
See also Yorke, Henry Vincent
See also DLB 15

Green, Julian (Hartridge) 1900-
See Green, Julien
See also CA 21-24R; CANR 33; DLB 4, 72; MTCW

Green, Julien .... **CLC 3, 11, 77**
See also Green, Julian (Hartridge)

Green, Paul (Eliot) 1894-1981**CLC 25; DAM DRAM**
See also AITN 1; CA 5-8R; 103; CANR 3; DLB 7, 9; DLBY 81

Greenberg, Ivan 1908-1973
See Rahv, Philip
See also CA 85-88

Greenberg, Joanne (Goldenberg) 1932- **C L C 7, 30**
See also AAYA 12; CA 5-8R; CANR 14, 32; SATA 25

Greenberg, Richard 1959(?)- .... **CLC 57**
See also CA 138

Greene, Bette 1934- .... **CLC 30**
See also AAYA 7; CA 53-56; CANR 4; CLR 2; JRDA; MAICYA; SAAS 16; SATA 8

Greene, Gael .... **CLC 8**
See also CA 13-16R; CANR 10

Greene, Graham (Henry) 1904-1991**CLC 1, 3, 6, 9, 14, 18, 27, 37, 70, 72; DA; DAB; DAC; DAM MST, NOV; SSC 29; WLC**
See also AITN 2; CA 13-16R; 133; CANR 35, 61; CDBLB 1945-1960; DLB 13, 15, 77, 100, 162; DLBY 91; MTCW; SATA 20

Greer, Richard
See Silverberg, Robert

Gregor, Arthur 1923- .... **CLC 9**
See also CA 25-28R; CAAS 10; CANR 11; SATA 36

Gregor, Lee
See Pohl, Frederik

Gregory, Isabella Augusta (Persse) 1852-1932 **TCLC 1**
See also CA 104; DLB 10

Gregory, J. Dennis
See Williams, John A(lfred)

Grendon, Stephen
See Derleth, August (William)

Grenville, Kate 1950- .... **CLC 61**
See also CA 118; CANR 53

Grenville, Pelham
See Wodehouse, P(elham) G(renville)

Greve, Felix Paul (Berthold Friedrich) 1879-1948
See Grove, Frederick Philip
See also CA 104; 141; DAC; DAM MST

Grey, Zane 1872-1939 .. **TCLC 6; DAM POP**
See also CA 104; 132; DLB 9; MTCW

Grieg, (Johan) Nordahl (Brun) 1902-1943 **TCLC 10**
See also CA 107

Grieve, C(hristopher) M(urray) 1892-1978 **CLC 11, 19; DAM POET**
See also MacDiarmid, Hugh; Pteleon
See also CA 5-8R; 85-88; CANR 33; MTCW

Griffin, Gerald 1803-1840 .... **NCLC 7**
See also DLB 159

Griffin, John Howard 1920-1980 ..... **CLC 68**
See also AITN 1; CA 1-4R; 101; CANR 2

Griffin, Peter 1942- .... **CLC 39**
See also CA 136

Griffith, D(avid Lewelyn) W(ark) 1875(?)-1948 **TCLC 68**
See also CA 119; 150

Griffith, Lawrence
See Griffith, D(avid Lewelyn) W(ark)

Griffiths, Trevor 1935- .... **CLC 13, 52**
See also CA 97-100; CANR 45; DLB 13

Grigson, Geoffrey (Edward Harvey) 1905-1985 **CLC 7, 39**
See also CA 25-28R; 118; CANR 20, 33; DLB 27; MTCW

Grillparzer, Franz 1791-1872 .... **NCLC 1**
See also DLB 133

Grimble, Reverend Charles James
See Eliot, T(homas) S(tearns)

Grimke, Charlotte L(ottie) Forten 1837(?)-1914
See Forten, Charlotte L.
See also BW 1; CA 117; 124; DAM MULT, POET

Grimm, Jacob Ludwig Karl 1785-1863**NCLC 3**
See also DLB 90; MAICYA; SATA 22

Grimm, Wilhelm Karl 1786-1859 .... **NCLC 3**
See also DLB 90; MAICYA; SATA 22

Grimmelshausen, Johann Jakob Christoffel von 1621-1676 .... **LC 6**
See also DLB 168

Grindel, Eugene 1895-1952
See Eluard, Paul
See also CA 104

Grisham, John 1955- .... **CLC 84; DAM POP**
See also AAYA 14; CA 138; CANR 47

1960 to Present; DLB 40; DLBY 95; MTCW
Hearn, (Patricio) Lafcadio (Tessima Carlos)
1850-1904 .... **TCLC 9**
See also CA 105; DLB 12, 78
Hearne, Vicki 1946- .... **CLC 56**
See also CA 139
Hearon, Shelby 1931- .... **CLC 63**
See also AITN 2; CA 25-28R; CANR 18, 48
Heat-Moon, William Least .... **CLC 29**
See also Trogdon, William (Lewis)
See also AAYA 9
Hebbel, Friedrich 1813-1863**NCLC 43; DAM**
DRAM
See also DLB 129
Hebert, Anne 1916-**CLC 4, 13, 29; DAC; DAM**
MST, POET
See also CA 85-88; DLB 68; MTCW
Hecht, Anthony (Evan) 1923- **CLC 8, 13, 19;**
DAM POET
See also CA 9-12R; CANR 6; DLB 5, 169
Hecht, Ben 1894-1964 .... **CLC 8**
See also CA 85-88; DLB 7, 9, 25, 26, 28, 86
Hedayat, Sadeq 1903-1951 .... **TCLC 21**
See also CA 120
Hegel, Georg Wilhelm Friedrich 1770-1831
NCLC 46
See also DLB 90
Heidegger, Martin 1889-1976 .... **CLC 24**
See also CA 81-84; 65-68; CANR 34; MTCW
Heidenstam, (Carl Gustaf) Verner von 1859-
1940 .... **TCLC 5**
See also CA 104
Heifner, Jack 1946- .... **CLC 11**
See also CA 105; CANR 47
Heijermans, Herman 1864-1924 .... **TCLC 24**
See also CA 123
Heilbrun, Carolyn G(old) 1926- .... **CLC 25**
See also CA 45-48; CANR 1, 28, 58
Heine, Heinrich 1797-1856 .... **NCLC 4, 54**
See also DLB 90
Heinemann, Larry (Curtiss) 1944- ... **CLC 50**
See also CA 110; CAAS 21; CANR 31; DLBD
9; INT CANR-31
Heiney, Donald (William) 1921-1993
See Harris, MacDonald
See also CA 1-4R; 142; CANR 3, 58
Heinlein, Robert A(nson) 1907-1988**CLC 1, 3,**
8, 14, 26, 55; DAM POP
See also AAYA 17; CA 1-4R; 125; CANR 1,
20, 53; DLB 8; JRDA; MAICYA; MTCW;
SATA 9, 69; SATA-Obit 56
Helforth, John
See Doolittle, Hilda
Hellenhofferu, Vojtech Kapristian z
See Hasek, Jaroslav (Matej Frantisek)
Heller, Joseph 1923-**CLC 1, 3, 5, 8, 11, 36, 63;**
DA; DAB; DAC; DAM MST, NOV, POP;
WLC
See also AITN 1; CA 5-8R; CABS 1; CANR 8,
42; DLB 2, 28; DLBY 80; INT CANR-8;
MTCW
Hellman, Lillian (Florence) 1906-1984**CLC 2,**
4, 8, 14, 18, 34, 44, 52; DAM DRAM; DC 1
See also AITN 1, 2; CA 13-16R; 112; CANR
33; DLB 7; DLBY 84; MTCW
Helprin, Mark 1947-**CLC 7, 10, 22, 32; DAM**
NOV, POP
See also CA 81-84; CANR 47; DLBY 85;
MTCW
Helvetius, Claude-Adrien 1715-1771 .. **LC 26**
Helyar, Jane Penelope Josephine 1933-
See Poole, Josephine
See also CA 21-24R; CANR 10, 26; SATA 82

Hemans, Felicia 1793-1835 .... **NCLC 29**
See also DLB 96
Hemingway, Ernest (Miller) 1899-1961 **C L C**
1, 3, 6, 8, 10, 13, 19, 30, 34, 39, 41, 44, 50,
61, 80; DA; DAB; DAC; DAM MST, NOV;
SSC 25; WLC
See also AAYA 19; CA 77-80; CANR 34;
CDALB 1917-1929; DLB 4, 9, 102; DLBD
1, 15, 16; DLBY 81, 87, 96; MTCW
Hempel, Amy 1951- .... **CLC 39**
See also CA 118; 137
Henderson, F. C.
See Mencken, H(enry) L(ouis)
Henderson, Sylvia
See Ashton-Warner, Sylvia (Constance)
Henderson, Zenna (Chlarson) 1917-1983**S S C**
29
See also CA 1-4R; 133; CANR 1; DLB 8; SATA
5
Henley, Beth .... **CLC 23; DC 6**
See also Henley, Elizabeth Becker
See also CABS 3; DLBY 86
Henley, Elizabeth Becker 1952-
See Henley, Beth
See also CA 107; CANR 32; DAM DRAM,
MST; MTCW
Henley, William Ernest 1849-1903 .. **TCLC 8**
See also CA 105; DLB 19
Hennissart, Martha
See Lathen, Emma
See also CA 85-88
Henry, O. .... **TCLC 1, 19; SSC 5; WLC**
See also Porter, William Sydney
Henry, Patrick 1736-1799 .... **LC 25**
Henryson, Robert 1430(?)-1506(?) ...... **LC 20**
See also DLB 146
Henry VIII 1491-1547 .... **LC 10**
Henschke, Alfred
See Klabund
Hentoff, Nat(han Irving) 1925- .... **CLC 26**
See also AAYA 4; CA 1-4R; CAAS 6; CANR
5, 25; CLR 1; INT CANR-25; JRDA;
MAICYA; SATA 42, 69; SATA-Brief 27
Heppenstall, (John) Rayner 1911-1981 **C L C**
10
See also CA 1-4R; 103; CANR 29
Heraclitus c. 540B.C.-c. 450B.C. .. **CMLC 22**
See also DLB 176
Herbert, Frank (Patrick) 1920-1986 **CLC 12,**
23, 35, 44, 85; DAM POP
See also AAYA 21; CA 53-56; 118; CANR 5,
43; DLB 8; INT CANR-5; MTCW; SATA 9,
37; SATA-Obit 47
Herbert, George 1593-1633 ..... **LC 24; DAB;**
DAM POET; PC 4
See also CDBLB Before 1660; DLB 126
Herbert, Zbigniew 1924- .. **CLC 9, 43; DAM**
POET
See also CA 89-92; CANR 36; MTCW
Herbst, Josephine (Frey) 1897-1969 **CLC 34**
See also CA 5-8R; 25-28R; DLB 9
Hergesheimer, Joseph 1880-1954 .. **TCLC 11**
See also CA 109; DLB 102, 9
Herlihy, James Leo 1927-1993 .... **CLC 6**
See also CA 1-4R; 143; CANR 2
Hermogenes fl. c. 175- .... **CMLC 6**
Hernandez, Jose 1834-1886 .... **NCLC 17**
Herodotus c. 484B.C.-429B.C. ...... **CMLC 17**
See also DLB 176
Herrick, Robert 1591-1674**LC 13; DA; DAB;**
DAC; DAM MST, POP; PC 9
See also DLB 126
Herring, Guilles

See Somerville, Edith
Herriot, James 1916-1995**CLC 12; DAM POP**
See also Wight, James Alfred
See also AAYA 1; CA 148; CANR 40; SATA
86
Herrmann, Dorothy 1941- .... **CLC 44**
See also CA 107
Herrmann, Taffy
See Herrmann, Dorothy
Hersey, John (Richard) 1914-1993**CLC 1, 2, 7,**
9, 40, 81, 97; DAM POP
See also CA 17-20R; 140; CANR 33; DLB 6;
MTCW; SATA 25; SATA-Obit 76
Herzen, Aleksandr Ivanovich 1812-1870
NCLC 10, 61
Herzl, Theodor 1860-1904 .... **TCLC 36**
Herzog, Werner 1942- .... **CLC 16**
See also CA 89-92
Hesiod c. 8th cent. B.C.- .... **CMLC 5**
See also DLB 176
Hesse, Hermann 1877-1962**CLC 1, 2, 3, 6, 11,**
17, 25, 69; DA; DAB; DAC; DAM MST,
NOV; SSC 9; WLC
See also CA 17-18; CAP 2; DLB 66; MTCW;
SATA 50
Hewes, Cady
See De Voto, Bernard (Augustine)
Heyen, William 1940- .... **CLC 13, 18**
See also CA 33-36R; CAAS 9; DLB 5
Heyerdahl, Thor 1914- .... **CLC 26**
See also CA 5-8R; CANR 5, 22; MTCW; SATA
2, 52
Heym, Georg (Theodor Franz Arthur) 1887-
1912 .... **TCLC 9**
See also CA 106
Heym, Stefan 1913- .... **CLC 41**
See also CA 9-12R; CANR 4; DLB 69
Heyse, Paul (Johann Ludwig von) 1830-1914
TCLC 8
See also CA 104; DLB 129
Heyward, (Edwin) DuBose 1885-1940 **T C L C**
59
See also CA 108; 157; DLB 7, 9, 45; SATA 21
Hibbert, Eleanor Alice Burford 1906-1993
CLC 7; DAM POP
See also BEST 90:4; CA 17-20R; 140; CANR
9, 28, 59; SATA 2; SATA-Obit 74
Hichens, Robert S. 1864-1950 .... **TCLC 64**
See also DLB 153
Higgins, George V(incent) 1939-**CLC 4, 7, 10,**
18
See also CA 77-80; CAAS 5; CANR 17, 51;
DLB 2; DLBY 81; INT CANR-17; MTCW
Higginson, Thomas Wentworth 1823-1911
TCLC 36
See also DLB 1, 64
Highet, Helen
See MacInnes, Helen (Clark)
Highsmith, (Mary) Patricia 1921-1995**CLC 2,**
4, 14, 42, 102; DAM NOV, POP
See also CA 1-4R; 147; CANR 1, 20, 48, 62;
MTCW
Highwater, Jamake (Mamake) 1942(?)- **C L C**
12
See also AAYA 7; CA 65-68; CAAS 7; CANR
10, 34; CLR 17; DLB 52; DLBY 85; JRDA;
MAICYA; SATA 32, 69; SATA-Brief 30
Highway, Tomson 1951-**CLC 92; DAC; DAM**
MULT
See also CA 151; NNAL
Higuchi, Ichiyo 1872-1896 .... **NCLC 49**
Hijuelos, Oscar 1951- **CLC 65; DAM MULT,**
POP; HLC

Horovitz, Israel (Arthur) 1939-**CLC 56; DAM DRAM**
See also CA 33-36R; CANR 46, 59; DLB 7
Horvath, Odon von
See Horvath, Oedoen von
See also DLB 85, 124
Horvath, Oedoen von 1901-1938 ... **TCLC 45**
See also Horvath, Odon von
See also CA 118
Horwitz, Julius 1920-1986 .... **CLC 14**
See also CA 9-12R; 119; CANR 12
Hospital, Janette Turner 1942- .... **CLC 42**
See also CA 108; CANR 48
Hostos, E. M. de
See Hostos (y Bonilla), Eugenio Maria de
Hostos, Eugenio M. de
See Hostos (y Bonilla), Eugenio Maria de
Hostos, Eugenio Maria
See Hostos (y Bonilla), Eugenio Maria de
Hostos (y Bonilla), Eugenio Maria de 1839-1903 .... **TCLC 24**
See also CA 123; 131; HW
Houdini
See Lovecraft, H(oward) P(hillips)
Hougan, Carolyn 1943- .... **CLC 34**
See also CA 139
Household, Geoffrey (Edward West) 1900-1988 **CLC 11**
See also CA 77-80; 126; CANR 58; DLB 87; SATA 14; SATA-Obit 59
Housman, A(lfred) E(dward) 1859-1936 **TCLC 1, 10; DA; DAB; DAC; DAM MST, POET; PC 2; WLCS**
See also CA 104; 125; DLB 19; MTCW
Housman, Laurence 1865-1959 .... **TCLC 7**
See also CA 106; 155; DLB 10; SATA 25
Howard, Elizabeth Jane 1923- ..... **CLC 7, 29**
See also CA 5-8R; CANR 8, 62
Howard, Maureen 1930- .... **CLC 5, 14, 46**
See also CA 53-56; CANR 31; DLBY 83; INT CANR-31; MTCW
Howard, Richard 1929- .... **CLC 7, 10, 47**
See also AITN 1; CA 85-88; CANR 25; DLB 5; INT CANR-25
Howard, Robert E(rvin) 1906-1936 **TCLC 8**
See also CA 105; 157
Howard, Warren F.
See Pohl, Frederik
Howe, Fanny 1940- .... **CLC 47**
See also CA 117; CAAS 27; SATA-Brief 52
Howe, Irving 1920-1993 .... **CLC 85**
See also CA 9-12R; 141; CANR 21, 50; DLB 67; MTCW
Howe, Julia Ward 1819-1910 .... **TCLC 21**
See also CA 117; DLB 1
Howe, Susan 1937- .... **CLC 72**
See also CA 160; DLB 120
Howe, Tina 1937- .... **CLC 48**
See also CA 109
Howell, James 1594(?)-1666 .... **LC 13**
See also DLB 151
Howells, W. D.
See Howells, William Dean
Howells, William D.
See Howells, William Dean
Howells, William Dean 1837-1920**TCLC 7, 17, 41**
See also CA 104; 134; CDALB 1865-1917; DLB 12, 64, 74, 79
Howes, Barbara 1914-1996 .... **CLC 15**
See also CA 9-12R; 151; CAAS 3; CANR 53; SATA 5
Hrabal, Bohumil 1914-1997 .... **CLC 13, 67**

See also CA 106; 156; CAAS 12; CANR 57
Hsun, Lu
See Lu Hsun
Hubbard, L(afayette) Ron(ald) 1911-1986 **CLC 43; DAM POP**
See also CA 77-80; 118; CANR 52
Huch, Ricarda (Octavia) 1864-1947**TCLC 13**
See also CA 111; DLB 66
Huddle, David 1942- .... **CLC 49**
See also CA 57-60; CAAS 20; DLB 130
Hudson, Jeffrey
See Crichton, (John) Michael
Hudson, W(illiam) H(enry) 1841-1922**T C L C 29**
See also CA 115; DLB 98, 153, 174; SATA 35
Hueffer, Ford Madox
See Ford, Ford Madox
Hughart, Barry 1934- .... **CLC 39**
See also CA 137
Hughes, Colin
See Creasey, John
Hughes, David (John) 1930- .... **CLC 48**
See also CA 116; 129; DLB 14
Hughes, Edward James
See Hughes, Ted
See also DAM MST, POET
Hughes, (James) Langston 1902-1967**CLC 1, 5, 10, 15, 35, 44; BLC; DA; DAB; DAC; DAM DRAM, MST, MULT, POET; DC 3; PC 1; SSC 6; WLC**
See also AAYA 12; BW 1; CA 1-4R; 25-28R; CANR 1, 34; CDALB 1929-1941; CLR 17; DLB 4, 7, 48, 51, 86; JRDA; MAICYA; MTCW; SATA 4, 33
Hughes, Richard (Arthur Warren) 1900-1976 **CLC 1, 11; DAM NOV**
See also CA 5-8R; 65-68; CANR 4; DLB 15, 161; MTCW; SATA 8; SATA-Obit 25
Hughes, Ted 1930- **CLC 2, 4, 9, 14, 37; DAB; DAC; PC 7**
See also Hughes, Edward James
See also CA 1-4R; CANR 1, 33; CLR 3; DLB 40, 161; MAICYA; MTCW; SATA 49; SATA-Brief 27
Hugo, Richard F(ranklin) 1923-1982 **CLC 6, 18, 32; DAM POET**
See also CA 49-52; 108; CANR 3; DLB 5
Hugo, Victor (Marie) 1802-1885**NCLC 3, 10, 21; DA; DAB; DAC; DAM DRAM, MST, NOV, POET; PC 17; WLC**
See also DLB 119; SATA 47
Huidobro, Vicente
See Huidobro Fernandez, Vicente Garcia
Huidobro Fernandez, Vicente Garcia 1893-1948 .... **TCLC 31**
See also CA 131; HW
Hulme, Keri 1947- .... **CLC 39**
See also CA 125; INT 125
Hulme, T(homas) E(rnest) 1883-1917 **T C L C 21**
See also CA 117; DLB 19
Hume, David 1711-1776 .... **LC 7**
See also DLB 104
Humphrey, William 1924-1997 .... **CLC 45**
See also CA 77-80; 160; DLB 6
Humphreys, Emyr Owen 1919- .... **CLC 47**
See also CA 5-8R; CANR 3, 24; DLB 15
Humphreys, Josephine 1945- ..... **CLC 34, 57**
See also CA 121; 127; INT 127
Huneker, James Gibbons 1857-1921**TCLC 65**
See also DLB 71
Hungerford, Pixie
See Brinsmead, H(esba) F(ay)

Hunt, E(verette) Howard, (Jr.) 1918-. **CLC 3**
See also AITN 1; CA 45-48; CANR 2, 47
Hunt, Kyle
See Creasey, John
Hunt, (James Henry) Leigh 1784-1859**N C L C 1; DAM POET**
Hunt, Marsha 1946- .... **CLC 70**
See also BW 2; CA 143
Hunt, Violet 1866-1942 .... **TCLC 53**
See also DLB 162
Hunter, E. Waldo
See Sturgeon, Theodore (Hamilton)
Hunter, Evan 1926-. **CLC 11, 31; DAM POP**
See also CA 5-8R; CANR 5, 38, 62; DLBY 82; INT CANR-5; MTCW; SATA 25
Hunter, Kristin (Eggleston) 1931- .... **CLC 35**
See also AITN 1; BW 1; CA 13-16R; CANR 13; CLR 3; DLB 33; INT CANR-13; MAICYA; SAAS 10; SATA 12
Hunter, Mollie 1922- .... **CLC 21**
See also McIlwraith, Maureen Mollie Hunter
See also AAYA 13; CANR 37; CLR 25; DLB 161; JRDA; MAICYA; SAAS 7; SATA 54
Hunter, Robert (?)-1734 .... **LC 7**
Hurston, Zora Neale 1903-1960**CLC 7, 30, 61; BLC; DA; DAC; DAM MST, MULT, NOV; SSC 4; WLCS**
See also AAYA 15; BW 1; CA 85-88; CANR 61; DLB 51, 86; MTCW
Huston, John (Marcellus) 1906-1987 **CLC 20**
See also CA 73-76; 123; CANR 34; DLB 26
Hustvedt, Siri 1955- .... **CLC 76**
See also CA 137
Hutten, Ulrich von 1488-1523 .... **LC 16**
See also DLB 179
Huxley, Aldous (Leonard) 1894-1963 **CLC 1, 3, 4, 5, 8, 11, 18, 35, 79; DA; DAB; DAC; DAM MST, NOV; WLC**
See also AAYA 11; CA 85-88; CANR 44; CDBLB 1914-1945; DLB 36, 100, 162; MTCW; SATA 63
Huysmans, Charles Marie Georges 1848-1907
See Huysmans, Joris-Karl
See also CA 104
Huysmans, Joris-Karl .... **TCLC 7, 69**
See also Huysmans, Charles Marie Georges
See also DLB 123
Hwang, David Henry 1957-... **CLC 55; DAM DRAM; DC 4**
See also CA 127; 132; INT 132
Hyde, Anthony 1946- .... **CLC 42**
See also CA 136
Hyde, Margaret O(ldroyd) 1917- ..... **CLC 21**
See also CA 1-4R; CANR 1, 36; CLR 23; JRDA; MAICYA; SAAS 8; SATA 1, 42, 76
Hynes, James 1956(?)- .... **CLC 65**
Ian, Janis 1951- .... **CLC 21**
See also CA 105
Ibanez, Vicente Blasco
See Blasco Ibanez, Vicente
Ibarguengoitia, Jorge 1928-1983 ..... **CLC 37**
See also CA 124; 113; HW
Ibsen, Henrik (Johan) 1828-1906 **TCLC 2, 8, 16, 37, 52; DA; DAB; DAC; DAM DRAM, MST; DC 2; WLC**
See also CA 104; 141
Ibuse Masuji 1898-1993 .... **CLC 22**
See also CA 127; 141; DLB 180
Ichikawa, Kon 1915- .... **CLC 20**
See also CA 121
Idle, Eric 1943-.................................... **CLC 21**
See also Monty Python
See also CA 116; CANR 35

Ignatow, David 1914- .... **CLC 4, 7, 14, 40**
  See also CA 9-12R; CAAS 3; CANR 31, 57;
  DLB 5
Ihimaera, Witi 1944- .... **CLC 46**
  See also CA 77-80
Ilf, Ilya .... **TCLC 21**
  See also Fainzilberg, Ilya Arnoldovich
Illyes, Gyula 1902-1983 .... **PC 16**
  See also CA 114; 109
Immermann, Karl (Lebrecht) 1796-1840
  NCLC 4, 49
  See also DLB 133
Inchbald, Elizabeth 1753-1821 ...... **NCLC 62**
  See also DLB 39, 89
Inclan, Ramon (Maria) del Valle
  See Valle-Inclan, Ramon (Maria) del
Infante, G(uillermo) Cabrera
  See Cabrera Infante, G(uillermo)
Ingalls, Rachel (Holmes) 1940- .... **CLC 42**
  See also CA 123; 127
Ingamells, Rex 1913-1955 .... **TCLC 35**
Inge, William (Motter) 1913-1973 . **CLC 1, 8,**
  19; DAM DRAM
  See also CA 9-12R; CDALB 1941-1968; DLB
  7; MTCW
Ingelow, Jean 1820-1897 .... **NCLC 39**
  See also DLB 35, 163; SATA 33
Ingram, Willis J.
  See Harris, Mark
Innaurato, Albert (F.) 1948(?)- .. **CLC 21, 60**
  See also CA 115; 122; INT 122
Innes, Michael
  See Stewart, J(ohn) I(nnes) M(ackintosh)
Ionesco, Eugene 1909-1994 **CLC 1, 4, 6, 9, 11,**
  15, 41, 86; DA; DAB; DAC; DAM DRAM,
  MST; WLC
  See also CA 9-12R; 144; CANR 55; MTCW;
  SATA 7; SATA-Obit 79
Iqbal, Muhammad 1873-1938 .... **TCLC 28**
Ireland, Patrick
  See O'Doherty, Brian
Iron, Ralph
  See Schreiner, Olive (Emilie Albertina)
Irving, John (Winslow) 1942- **CLC 13, 23, 38;**
  DAM NOV, POP
  See also AAYA 8; BEST 89:3; CA 25-28R;
  CANR 28; DLB 6; DLBY 82; MTCW
Irving, Washington 1783-1859 . **NCLC 2, 19;**
  DA; DAB; DAM MST; SSC 2; WLC
  See also CDALB 1640-1865; DLB 3, 11, 30,
  59, 73, 74; YABC 2
Irwin, P. K.
  See Page, P(atricia) K(athleen)
Isaacs, Susan 1943- .... **CLC 32; DAM POP**
  See also BEST 89:1; CA 89-92; CANR 20, 41;
  INT CANR-20; MTCW
Isherwood, Christopher (William Bradshaw)
  1904-1986 .... **CLC 1, 9, 11, 14, 44; DAM**
  DRAM, NOV
  See also CA 13-16R; 117; CANR 35; DLB 15;
  DLBY 86; MTCW
Ishiguro, Kazuo 1954- **CLC 27, 56, 59; DAM**
  NOV
  See also BEST 90:2; CA 120; CANR 49;
  MTCW
Ishikawa, Hakuhin
  See Ishikawa, Takuboku
Ishikawa, Takuboku 1886(?)-1912 **TCLC 15;**
  DAM POET; PC 10
  See also CA 113; 153
Iskander, Fazil 1929- .... **CLC 47**
  See also CA 102
Isler, Alan (David) 1934- .... **CLC 91**

See also CA 156
Ivan IV 1530-1584 .... **LC 17**
Ivanov, Vyacheslav Ivanovich 1866-1949
  TCLC 33
  See also CA 122
Ivask, Ivar Vidrik 1927-1992 .... **CLC 14**
  See also CA 37-40R; 139; CANR 24
Ives, Morgan
  See Bradley, Marion Zimmer
J. R. S.
  See Gogarty, Oliver St. John
Jabran, Kahlil
  See Gibran, Kahlil
Jabran, Khalil
  See Gibran, Kahlil
Jackson, Daniel
  See Wingrove, David (John)
Jackson, Jesse 1908-1983 .... **CLC 12**
  See also BW 1; CA 25-28R; 109; CANR 27;
  CLR 28; MAICYA; SATA 2, 29; SATA-Obit
  48
Jackson, Laura (Riding) 1901-1991
  See Riding, Laura
  See also CA 65-68; 135; CANR 28; DLB 48
Jackson, Sam
  See Trumbo, Dalton
Jackson, Sara
  See Wingrove, David (John)
Jackson, Shirley 1919-1965 . **CLC 11, 60, 87;**
  DA; DAC; DAM MST; SSC 9; WLC
  See also AAYA 9; CA 1-4R; 25-28R; CANR 4,
  52; CDALB 1941-1968; DLB 6; SATA 2
Jacob, (Cyprien-)Max 1876-1944 .... **TCLC 6**
  See also CA 104
Jacobs, Jim 1942- .... **CLC 12**
  See also CA 97-100; INT 97-100
Jacobs, W(illiam) W(ymark) 1863-1943
  TCLC 22
  See also CA 121; DLB 135
Jacobsen, Jens Peter 1847-1885 .... **NCLC 34**
Jacobsen, Josephine 1908- .... **CLC 48, 102**
  See also CA 33-36R; CAAS 18; CANR 23, 48
Jacobson, Dan 1929- .... **CLC 4, 14**
  See also CA 1-4R; CANR 2, 25; DLB 14;
  MTCW
Jacqueline
  See Carpentier (y Valmont), Alejo
Jagger, Mick 1944- .... **CLC 17**
Jakes, John (William) 1932- .. **CLC 29; DAM**
  NOV, POP
  See also BEST 89:4; CA 57-60; CANR 10, 43;
  DLBY 83; INT CANR-10; MTCW; SATA 62
James, Andrew
  See Kirkup, James
James, C(yril) L(ionel) R(obert) 1901-1989
  CLC 33
  See also BW 2; CA 117; 125; 128; CANR 62;
  DLB 125; MTCW
James, Daniel (Lewis) 1911-1988
  See Santiago, Danny
  See also CA 125
James, Dynely
  See Mayne, William (James Carter)
James, Henry Sr. 1811-1882 .... **NCLC 53**
James, Henry 1843-1916 **TCLC 2, 11, 24, 40,**
  47, 64; DA; DAB; DAC; DAM MST, NOV;
  SSC 8; WLC
  See also CA 104; 132; CDALB 1865-1917;
  DLB 12, 71, 74; DLBD 13; MTCW
James, M. R.
  See James, Montague (Rhodes)
  See also DLB 156
James, Montague (Rhodes) 1862-1936 **T C L C**

6; SSC 16
  See also CA 104
James, P. D. .... **CLC 18, 46**
  See also White, Phyllis Dorothy James
  See also BEST 90:2; CDBLB 1960 to Present;
  DLB 87
James, Philip
  See Moorcock, Michael (John)
James, William 1842-1910 .... **TCLC 15, 32**
  See also CA 109
James I 1394-1437 .... **LC 20**
Jameson, Anna 1794-1860 .... **NCLC 43**
  See also DLB 99, 166
Jami, Nur al-Din 'Abd al-Rahman 1414-1492
  LC 9
Jammes, Francis 1868-1938 .... **TCLC 75**
Jandl, Ernst 1925- .... **CLC 34**
Janowitz, Tama 1957- .. **CLC 43; DAM POP**
  See also CA 106; CANR 52
Japrisot, Sebastien 1931- .... **CLC 90**
Jarrell, Randall 1914-1965 **CLC 1, 2, 6, 9, 13,**
  49; DAM POET
  See also CA 5-8R; 25-28R; CABS 2; CANR 6,
  34; CDALB 1941-1968; CLR 6; DLB 48, 52;
  MAICYA; MTCW; SATA 7
Jarry, Alfred 1873-1907 .. **TCLC 2, 14; DAM**
  DRAM; SSC 20
  See also CA 104; 153
Jarvis, E. K.
  See Bloch, Robert (Albert); Ellison, Harlan
  (Jay); Silverberg, Robert
Jeake, Samuel, Jr.
  See Aiken, Conrad (Potter)
Jean Paul 1763-1825 .... **NCLC 7**
Jefferies, (John) Richard 1848-1887 **NCLC 47**
  See also DLB 98, 141; SATA 16
Jeffers, (John) Robinson 1887-1962 **CLC 2, 3,**
  11, 15, 54; DA; DAC; DAM MST, POET;
  PC 17; WLC
  See also CA 85-88; CANR 35; CDALB 1917-
  1929; DLB 45; MTCW
Jefferson, Janet
  See Mencken, H(enry) L(ouis)
Jefferson, Thomas 1743-1826 .... **NCLC 11**
  See also CDALB 1640-1865; DLB 31
Jeffrey, Francis 1773-1850 .... **NCLC 33**
  See also DLB 107
Jelakowitch, Ivan
  See Heijermans, Herman
Jellicoe, (Patricia) Ann 1927- .... **CLC 27**
  See also CA 85-88; DLB 13
Jen, Gish .... **CLC 70**
  See also Jen, Lillian
Jen, Lillian 1956(?)-
  See Jen, Gish
  See also CA 135
Jenkins, (John) Robin 1912- .... **CLC 52**
  See also CA 1-4R; CANR 1; DLB 14
Jennings, Elizabeth (Joan) 1926- . **CLC 5, 14**
  See also CA 61-64; CAAS 5; CANR 8, 39; DLB
  27; MTCW; SATA 66
Jennings, Waylon 1937- .... **CLC 21**
Jensen, Johannes V. 1873-1950 ...... **TCLC 41**
Jensen, Laura (Linnea) 1948- .... **CLC 37**
  See also CA 103
Jerome, Jerome K(lapka) 1859-1927 **TCLC 23**
  See also CA 119; DLB 10, 34, 135
Jerrold, Douglas William 1803-1857 **NCLC 2**
  See also DLB 158, 159
Jewett, (Theodora) Sarah Orne 1849-1909
  TCLC 1, 22; SSC 6
  See also CA 108; 127; DLB 12, 74; SATA 15
Jewsbury, Geraldine (Endsor) 1812-1880

26; DLB 33

Killigrew, Anne 1660-1685 .... **LC 4**
See also DLB 131

Kim
See Simenon, Georges (Jacques Christian)

Kincaid, Jamaica 1949- .. **CLC 43, 68; BLC; DAM MULT, NOV**
See also AAYA 13; BW 2; CA 125; CANR 47, 59; DLB 157

King, Francis (Henry) 1923-**CLC 8, 53; DAM NOV**
See also CA 1-4R; CANR 1, 33; DLB 15, 139; MTCW

King, Martin Luther, Jr. 1929-1968 **CLC 83; BLC; DA; DAB; DAC; DAM MST, MULT; WLCS**
See also BW 2; CA 25-28; CANR 27, 44; CAP 2; MTCW; SATA 14

King, Stephen (Edwin) 1947-**CLC 12, 26, 37, 61; DAM NOV, POP; SSC 17**
See also AAYA 1, 17; BEST 90:1; CA 61-64; CANR 1, 30, 52; DLB 143; DLBY 80; JRDA; MTCW; SATA 9, 55

King, Steve
See King, Stephen (Edwin)

King, Thomas 1943- ... **CLC 89; DAC; DAM MULT**
See also CA 144; DLB 175; NNAL

Kingman, Lee .... **CLC 17**
See also Natti, (Mary) Lee
See also SAAS 3; SATA 1, 67

Kingsley, Charles 1819-1875 .... **NCLC 35**
See also DLB 21, 32, 163; YABC 2

Kingsley, Sidney 1906-1995 .... **CLC 44**
See also CA 85-88; 147; DLB 7

Kingsolver, Barbara 1955-**CLC 55, 81; DAM POP**
See also AAYA 15; CA 129; 134; CANR 60; INT 134

Kingston, Maxine (Ting Ting) Hong 1940-
CLC 12, 19, 58; DAM MULT, NOV; WLCS
See also AAYA 8; CA 69-72; CANR 13, 38; DLB 173; DLBY 80; INT CANR-13; MTCW; SATA 53

Kinnell, Galway 1927- **CLC 1, 2, 3, 5, 13, 29**
See also CA 9-12R; CANR 10, 34; DLB 5; DLBY 87; INT CANR-34; MTCW

Kinsella, Thomas 1928- .... **CLC 4, 19**
See also CA 17-20R; CANR 15; DLB 27; MTCW

Kinsella, W(illiam) P(atrick) 1935- . **CLC 27, 43; DAC; DAM NOV, POP**
See also AAYA 7; CA 97-100; CAAS 7; CANR 21, 35; INT CANR-21; MTCW

Kipling, (Joseph) Rudyard 1865-1936 **T C L C 8, 17; DA; DAB; DAC; DAM MST, POET; PC 3; SSC 5; WLC**
See also CA 105; 120; CANR 33; CDBLB 1890-1914; CLR 39; DLB 19, 34, 141, 156; MAICYA; MTCW; YABC 2

Kirkup, James 1918- .... **CLC 1**
See also CA 1-4R; CAAS 4; CANR 2; DLB 27; SATA 12

Kirkwood, James 1930(?)-1989 .... **CLC 9**
See also AITN 2; CA 1-4R; 128; CANR 6, 40

Kirshner, Sidney
See Kingsley, Sidney

Kis, Danilo 1935-1989 .... **CLC 57**
See also CA 109; 118; 129; CANR 61; DLB 181; MTCW

Kivi, Aleksis 1834-1872 .... **NCLC 30**

Kizer, Carolyn (Ashley) 1925-**CLC 15, 39, 80;**

DAM POET
See also CA 65-68; CAAS 5; CANR 24; DLB 5, 169

Klabund 1890-1928 .... **TCLC 44**
See also DLB 66

Klappert, Peter 1942- .... **CLC 57**
See also CA 33-36R; DLB 5

Klein, A(braham) M(oses) 1909-1972**CLC 19; DAB; DAC; DAM MST**
See also CA 101; 37-40R; DLB 68

Klein, Norma 1938-1989 .... **CLC 30**
See also AAYA 2; CA 41-44R; 128; CANR 15, 37; CLR 2, 19; INT CANR-15; JRDA; MAICYA; SAAS 1; SATA 7, 57

Klein, T(heodore) E(ibon) D(onald) 1947-
CLC 34
See also CA 119; CANR 44

Kleist, Heinrich von 1777-1811 **NCLC 2, 37; DAM DRAM; SSC 22**
See also DLB 90

Klima, Ivan 1931- .... **CLC 56; DAM NOV**
See also CA 25-28R; CANR 17, 50

Klimentov, Andrei Platonovich 1899-1951
See Platonov, Andrei
See also CA 108

Klinger, Friedrich Maximilian von 1752-1831
NCLC 1
See also DLB 94

Klingsor the Magician
See Hartmann, Sadakichi

Klopstock, Friedrich Gottlieb 1724-1803
NCLC 11
See also DLB 97

Knapp, Caroline 1959- .... **CLC 99**
See also CA 154

Knebel, Fletcher 1911-1993 .... **CLC 14**
See also AITN 1; CA 1-4R; 140; CAAS 3; CANR 1, 36; SATA 36; SATA-Obit 75

Knickerbocker, Diedrich
See Irving, Washington

Knight, Etheridge 1931-1991 **CLC 40; BLC; DAM POET; PC 14**
See also BW 1; CA 21-24R; 133; CANR 23; DLB 41

Knight, Sarah Kemble 1666-1727 .... **LC 7**
See also DLB 24

Knister, Raymond 1899-1932 .... **TCLC 56**
See also DLB 68

Knowles, John 1926- . **CLC 1, 4, 10, 26; DA; DAC; DAM MST, NOV**
See also AAYA 10; CA 17-20R; CANR 40; CDALB 1968-1988; DLB 6; MTCW; SATA 8, 89

Knox, Calvin M.
See Silverberg, Robert

Knox, John c. 1505-1572 .... **LC 37**
See also DLB 132

Knye, Cassandra
See Disch, Thomas M(ichael)

Koch, C(hristopher) J(ohn) 1932- .... **CLC 42**
See also CA 127

Koch, Christopher
See Koch, C(hristopher) J(ohn)

Koch, Kenneth 1925- ..... **CLC 5, 8, 44; DAM POET**
See also CA 1-4R; CANR 6, 36, 57; DLB 5; INT CANR-36; SATA 65

Kochanowski, Jan 1530-1584 .... **LC 10**

Kock, Charles Paul de 1794-1871 . **NCLC 16**

Koda Shigeyuki 1867-1947
See Rohan, Koda
See also CA 121

Koestler, Arthur 1905-1983**CLC 1, 3, 6, 8, 15,**

33
See also CA 1-4R; 109; CANR 1, 33; CDBLB 1945-1960; DLBY 83; MTCW

Kogawa, Joy Nozomi 1935- .. **CLC 78; DAC; DAM MST, MULT**
See also CA 101; CANR 19, 62

Kohout, Pavel 1928- .... **CLC 13**
See also CA 45-48; CANR 3

Koizumi, Yakumo
See Hearn, (Patricio) Lafcadio (Tessima Carlos)

Kolmar, Gertrud 1894-1943 .... **TCLC 40**

Komunyakaa, Yusef 1947- .... **CLC 86, 94**
See also CA 147; DLB 120

Konrad, George
See Konrad, Gyoergy

Konrad, Gyoergy 1933- .... **CLC 4, 10, 73**
See also CA 85-88

Konwicki, Tadeusz 1926- .... **CLC 8, 28, 54**
See also CA 101; CAAS 9; CANR 39, 59; MTCW

Koontz, Dean R(ay) 1945- ..... **CLC 78; DAM NOV, POP**
See also AAYA 9; BEST 89:3, 90:2; CA 108; CANR 19, 36, 52; MTCW; SATA 92

Kopit, Arthur (Lee) 1937-**CLC 1, 18, 33; DAM DRAM**
See also AITN 1; CA 81-84; CABS 3; DLB 7; MTCW

Kops, Bernard 1926- .... **CLC 4**
See also CA 5-8R; DLB 13

Kornbluth, C(yril) M. 1923-1958 .... **TCLC 8**
See also CA 105; 160; DLB 8

Korolenko, V. G.
See Korolenko, Vladimir Galaktionovich

Korolenko, Vladimir
See Korolenko, Vladimir Galaktionovich

Korolenko, Vladimir G.
See Korolenko, Vladimir Galaktionovich

Korolenko, Vladimir Galaktionovich 1853-
1921 .... **TCLC 22**
See also CA 121

Korzybski, Alfred (Habdank Skarbek) 1879-
1950 .... **TCLC 61**
See also CA 123; 160

Kosinski, Jerzy (Nikodem) 1933-1991**CLC 1, 2, 3, 6, 10, 15, 53, 70; DAM NOV**
See also CA 17-20R; 134; CANR 9, 46; DLB 2; DLBY 82; MTCW

Kostelanetz, Richard (Cory) 1940- .. **CLC 28**
See also CA 13-16R; CAAS 8; CANR 38

Kostrowitzki, Wilhelm Apollinaris de 1880-
1918
See Apollinaire, Guillaume
See also CA 104

Kotlowitz, Robert 1924- .... **CLC 4**
See also CA 33-36R; CANR 36

Kotzebue, August (Friedrich Ferdinand) von
1761-1819 .... **NCLC 25**
See also DLB 94

Kotzwinkle, William 1938- ..... **CLC 5, 14, 35**
See also CA 45-48; CANR 3, 44; CLR 6; DLB 173; MAICYA; SATA 24, 70

Kowna, Stancy
See Szymborska, Wislawa

Kozol, Jonathan 1936- .... **CLC 17**
See also CA 61-64; CANR 16, 45

Kozoll, Michael 1940(?)- .... **CLC 35**

Kramer, Kathryn 19(?)- .... **CLC 34**

Kramer, Larry 1935- .... **CLC 42; DAM POP**
See also CA 124; 126; CANR 60

Krasicki, Ignacy 1735-1801 .... **NCLC 8**

Krasinski, Zygmunt 1812-1859 .... **NCLC 4**

Kraus, Karl 1874-1936 .... **TCLC 5**

See also CA 104; DLB 118

Kreve (Mickevicius), Vincas 1882-1954T C L C **27**

Kristeva, Julia 1941- .... **CLC 77**
See also CA 154

Kristofferson, Kris 1936- .... **CLC 26**
See also CA 104

Krizanc, John 1956- .... **CLC 57**

Krleza, Miroslav 1893-1981 .... **CLC 8**
See also CA 97-100; 105; CANR 50; DLB 147

Kroetsch, Robert 1927- CLC **5, 23, 57; DAC; DAM POET**
See also CA 17-20R; CANR 8, 38; DLB 53; MTCW

Kroetz, Franz
See Kroetz, Franz Xaver

Kroetz, Franz Xaver 1946- .... **CLC 41**
See also CA 130

Kroker, Arthur 1945- .... **CLC 77**

Kropotkin, Peter (Aleksieevich) 1842-1921 **TCLC 36**
See also CA 119

Krotkov, Yuri 1917- .... **CLC 19**
See also CA 102

Krumb
See Crumb, R(obert)

Krumgold, Joseph (Quincy) 1908-1980 C L C **12**
See also CA 9-12R; 101; CANR 7; MAICYA; SATA 1, 48; SATA-Obit 23

Krumwitz
See Crumb, R(obert)

Krutch, Joseph Wood 1893-1970 ...... **CLC 24**
See also CA 1-4R; 25-28R; CANR 4; DLB 63

Krutzch, Gus
See Eliot, T(homas) S(tearns)

Krylov, Ivan Andreevich 1768(?)-1844N C L C **1**
See also DLB 150

Kubin, Alfred (Leopold Isidor) 1877-1959 **TCLC 23**
See also CA 112; 149; DLB 81

Kubrick, Stanley 1928- .... **CLC 16**
See also CA 81-84; CANR 33; DLB 26

Kumin, Maxine (Winokur) 1925- CLC **5, 13, 28; DAM POET; PC 15**
See also AITN 2; CA 1-4R; CAAS 8; CANR 1, 21; DLB 5; MTCW; SATA 12

Kundera, Milan 1929- . CLC **4, 9, 19, 32, 68; DAM NOV; SSC 24**
See also AAYA 2; CA 85-88; CANR 19, 52; MTCW

Kunene, Mazisi (Raymond) 1930- .... **CLC 85**
See also BW 1; CA 125; DLB 117

Kunitz, Stanley (Jasspon) 1905-CLC **6, 11, 14; PC 19**
See also CA 41-44R; CANR 26, 57; DLB 48; INT CANR-26; MTCW

Kunze, Reiner 1933- .... **CLC 10**
See also CA 93-96; DLB 75

Kuprin, Aleksandr Ivanovich 1870-1938 **TCLC 5**
See also CA 104

Kureishi, Hanif 1954(?)- .... **CLC 64**
See also CA 139

Kurosawa, Akira 1910-CLC **16; DAM MULT**
See also AAYA 11; CA 101; CANR 46

Kushner, Tony 1957(?)-CLC **81; DAM DRAM**
See also CA 144

Kuttner, Henry 1915-1958 .... **TCLC 10**
See also Vance, Jack
See also CA 107; 157; DLB 8

Kuzma, Greg 1944- .... **CLC 7**

See also CA 33-36R

Kuzmin, Mikhail 1872(?)-1936 ...... **TCLC 40**

Kyd, Thomas 1558-1594LC **22; DAM DRAM; DC 3**
See also DLB 62

Kyprianos, Iossif
See Samarakis, Antonis

La Bruyere, Jean de 1645-1696 .... **LC 17**

Lacan, Jacques (Marie Emile) 1901-1981 **CLC 75**
See also CA 121; 104

Laclos, Pierre Ambroise Francois Choderlos de 1741-1803 .... **NCLC 4**

La Colere, Francois
See Aragon, Louis

Lacolere, Francois
See Aragon, Louis

La Deshabilleuse
See Simenon, Georges (Jacques Christian)

Lady Gregory
See Gregory, Isabella Augusta (Persse)

Lady of Quality, A
See Bagnold, Enid

La Fayette, Marie (Madelaine Pioche de la Vergne Comtes 1634-1693 .... **LC 2**

Lafayette, Rene
See Hubbard, L(afayette) Ron(ald)

Laforgue, Jules 1860-1887NCLC **5, 53; PC 14; SSC 20**

Lagerkvist, Paer (Fabian) 1891-1974 CLC **7, 10, 13, 54; DAM DRAM, NOV**
See also Lagerkvist, Par
See also CA 85-88; 49-52; MTCW

Lagerkvist, Par .... **SSC 12**
See also Lagerkvist, Paer (Fabian)

Lagerloef, Selma (Ottiliana Lovisa) 1858-1940 **TCLC 4, 36**
See also Lagerlof, Selma (Ottiliana Lovisa)
See also CA 108; SATA 15

Lagerlof, Selma (Ottiliana Lovisa)
See Lagerloef, Selma (Ottiliana Lovisa)
See also CLR 7; SATA 15

La Guma, (Justin) Alex(ander) 1925-1985 **CLC 19; DAM NOV**
See also BW 1; CA 49-52; 118; CANR 25; DLB 117; MTCW

Laidlaw, A. K.
See Grieve, C(hristopher) M(urray)

Lainez, Manuel Mujica
See Mujica Lainez, Manuel
See also HW

Laing, R(onald) D(avid) 1927-1989 .. **CLC 95**
See also CA 107; 129; CANR 34; MTCW

Lamartine, Alphonse (Marie Louis Prat) de 1790-1869NCLC **11; DAM POET; PC 16**

Lamb, Charles 1775-1834 ..... NCLC **10; DA; DAB; DAC; DAM MST; WLC**
See also CDBLB 1789-1832; DLB 93, 107, 163; SATA 17

Lamb, Lady Caroline 1785-1828 ... NCLC **38**
See also DLB 116

Lamming, George (William) 1927- CLC **2, 4, 66; BLC; DAM MULT**
See also BW 2; CA 85-88; CANR 26; DLB 125; MTCW

L'Amour, Louis (Dearborn) 1908-1988 C L C **25, 55; DAM NOV, POP**
See also AAYA 16; AITN 2; BEST 89:2; CA 1-4R; 125; CANR 3, 25, 40; DLBY 80; MTCW

Lampedusa, Giuseppe (Tomasi) di 1896-1957 **TCLC 13**
See also Tomasi di Lampedusa, Giuseppe
See also DLB 177

Lampman, Archibald 1861-1899 ... **NCLC 25**
See also DLB 92

Lancaster, Bruce 1896-1963 .... **CLC 36**
See also CA 9-10; CAP 1; SATA 9

Lanchester, John .... **CLC 99**

Landau, Mark Alexandrovich
See Aldanov, Mark (Alexandrovich)

Landau-Aldanov, Mark Alexandrovich
See Aldanov, Mark (Alexandrovich)

Landis, Jerry
See Simon, Paul (Frederick)

Landis, John 1950- .... **CLC 26**
See also CA 112; 122

Landolfi, Tommaso 1908-1979 .... CLC **11, 49**
See also CA 127; 117; DLB 177

Landon, Letitia Elizabeth 1802-1838 N C L C **15**
See also DLB 96

Landor, Walter Savage 1775-1864 **NCLC 14**
See also DLB 93, 107

Landwirth, Heinz 1927-
See Lind, Jakov
See also CA 9-12R; CANR 7

Lane, Patrick 1939- ... CLC **25; DAM POET**
See also CA 97-100; CANR 54; DLB 53; INT 97-100

Lang, Andrew 1844-1912 .... **TCLC 16**
See also CA 114; 137; DLB 98, 141, 184; MAICYA; SATA 16

Lang, Fritz 1890-1976 .... CLC **20, 103**
See also CA 77-80; 69-72; CANR 30

Lange, John
See Crichton, (John) Michael

Langer, Elinor 1939- .... **CLC 34**
See also CA 121

Langland, William 1330(?)-1400(?)... LC **19; DA; DAB; DAC; DAM MST, POET**
See also DLB 146

Langstaff, Launcelot
See Irving, Washington

Lanier, Sidney 1842-1881 ..... NCLC **6; DAM POET**
See also DLB 64; DLBD 13; MAICYA; SATA 18

Lanyer, Aemilia 1569-1645 .... LC **10, 30**
See also DLB 121

Lao Tzu .... **CMLC 7**

Lapine, James (Elliot) 1949- .... **CLC 39**
See also CA 123; 130; CANR 54; INT 130

Larbaud, Valery (Nicolas) 1881-1957TCLC **9**
See also CA 106; 152

Lardner, Ring
See Lardner, Ring(gold) W(ilmer)

Lardner, Ring W., Jr.
See Lardner, Ring(gold) W(ilmer)

Lardner, Ring(gold) W(ilmer) 1885-1933 **TCLC 2, 14**
See also CA 104; 131; CDALB 1917-1929; DLB 11, 25, 86; DLBD 16; MTCW

Laredo, Betty
See Codrescu, Andrei

Larkin, Maia
See Wojciechowska, Maia (Teresa)

Larkin, Philip (Arthur) 1922-1985CLC **3, 5, 8, 9, 13, 18, 33, 39, 64; DAB; DAM MST, POET**
See also CA 5-8R; 117; CANR 24, 62; CDBLB 1960 to Present; DLB 27; MTCW

Larra (y Sanchez de Castro), Mariano Jose de 1809-1837 .... **NCLC 17**

Larsen, Eric 1941- .... **CLC 55**
See also CA 132

Larsen, Nella 1891-1964CLC **37; BLC; DAM**

Litwos
See Sienkiewicz, Henryk (Adam Alexander Pius)

Liu E 1857-1909 .... **TCLC 15**
See also CA 115

Lively, Penelope (Margaret) 1933- .. **CLC 32, 50; DAM NOV**
See also CA 41-44R; CANR 29; CLR 7; DLB 14, 161; JRDA; MAICYA; MTCW; SATA 7, 60

Livesay, Dorothy (Kathleen) 1909-**CLC 4, 15, 79; DAC; DAM MST, POET**
See also AITN 2; CA 25-28R; CAAS 8; CANR 36; DLB 68; MTCW

Livy c. 59B.C.-c. 17 .... **CMLC 11**

Lizardi, Jose Joaquin Fernandez de 1776-1827 **NCLC 30**

Llewellyn, Richard
See Llewellyn Lloyd, Richard Dafydd Vivian
See also DLB 15

Llewellyn Lloyd, Richard Dafydd Vivian 1906-1983 .... **CLC 7, 80**
See also Llewellyn, Richard
See also CA 53-56; 111; CANR 7; SATA 11; SATA-Obit 37

Llosa, (Jorge) Mario (Pedro) Vargas
See Vargas Llosa, (Jorge) Mario (Pedro)

Lloyd Webber, Andrew 1948-
See Webber, Andrew Lloyd
See also AAYA 1; CA 116; 149; DAM DRAM; SATA 56

Llull, Ramon c. 1235-c. 1316 .... **CMLC 12**

Locke, Alain (Le Roy) 1886-1954 .. **TCLC 43**
See also BW 1; CA 106; 124; DLB 51

Locke, John 1632-1704 .... **LC 7, 35**
See also DLB 101

Locke-Elliott, Sumner
See Elliott, Sumner Locke

Lockhart, John Gibson 1794-1854 .. **NCLC 6**
See also DLB 110, 116, 144

Lodge, David (John) 1935- .... **CLC 36; DAM POP**
See also BEST 90:1; CA 17-20R; CANR 19, 53; DLB 14; INT CANR-19; MTCW

Loennbohm, Armas Eino Leopold 1878-1926
See Leino, Eino
See also CA 123

Loewinsohn, Ron(ald William) 1937-**CLC 52**
See also CA 25-28R

Logan, Jake
See Smith, Martin Cruz

Logan, John (Burton) 1923-1987 .... **CLC 5**
See also CA 77-80; 124; CANR 45; DLB 5

Lo Kuan-chung 1330(?)-1400(?) ....**LC 12**

Lombard, Nap
See Johnson, Pamela Hansford

London, Jack . **TCLC 9, 15, 39; SSC 4; WLC**
See also London, John Griffith
See also AAYA 13; AITN 2; CDALB 1865-1917; DLB 8, 12, 78; SATA 18

London, John Griffith 1876-1916
See London, Jack
See also CA 110; 119; DA; DAB; DAC; DAM MST, NOV; JRDA; MAICYA; MTCW

Long, Emmett
See Leonard, Elmore (John, Jr.)

Longbaugh, Harry
See Goldman, William (W.)

Longfellow, Henry Wadsworth 1807-1882 **NCLC 2, 45; DA; DAB; DAC; DAM MST, POET; WLCS**
See also CDALB 1640-1865; DLB 1, 59; SATA 19

Longley, Michael 1939- .... **CLC 29**
See also CA 102; DLB 40

Longus fl. c. 2nd cent. - .... **CMLC 7**

Longway, A. Hugh
See Lang, Andrew

Lonnrot, Elias 1802-1884 .... **NCLC 53**

Lopate, Phillip 1943- .... **CLC 29**
See also CA 97-100; DLBY 80; INT 97-100

Lopez Portillo (y Pacheco), Jose 1920-**CLC 46**
See also CA 129; HW

Lopez y Fuentes, Gregorio 1897(?)-1966**CLC 32**
See also CA 131; HW

Lorca, Federico Garcia
See Garcia Lorca, Federico

Lord, Bette Bao 1938- .... **CLC 23**
See also BEST 90:3; CA 107; CANR 41; INT 107; SATA 58

Lord Auch
See Bataille, Georges

Lord Byron
See Byron, George Gordon (Noel)

Lorde, Audre (Geraldine) 1934-1992**CLC 18, 71; BLC; DAM MULT, POET; PC 12**
See also BW 1; CA 25-28R; 142; CANR 16, 26, 46; DLB 41; MTCW

Lord Houghton
See Milnes, Richard Monckton

Lord Jeffrey
See Jeffrey, Francis

Lorenzini, Carlo 1826-1890
See Collodi, Carlo
See also MAICYA; SATA 29

Lorenzo, Heberto Padilla
See Padilla (Lorenzo), Heberto

Loris
See Hofmannsthal, Hugo von

Loti, Pierre... **TCLC 11**
See also Viaud, (Louis Marie) Julien
See also DLB 123

Louie, David Wong 1954- .... **CLC 70**
See also CA 139

Louis, Father M.
See Merton, Thomas

Lovecraft, H(oward) P(hillips) 1890-1937 **TCLC 4, 22; DAM POP; SSC 3**
See also AAYA 14; CA 104; 133; MTCW

Lovelace, Earl 1935- .... **CLC 51**
See also BW 2; CA 77-80; CANR 41; DLB 125; MTCW

Lovelace, Richard 1618-1657 .... **LC 24**
See also DLB 131

Lowell, Amy 1874-1925 .... **TCLC 1, 8; DAM POET; PC 13**
See also CA 104; 151; DLB 54, 140

Lowell, James Russell 1819-1891 .... **NCLC 2**
See also CDALB 1640-1865; DLB 1, 11, 64, 79

Lowell, Robert (Traill Spence, Jr.) 1917-1977 **CLC 1, 2, 3, 4, 5, 8, 9, 11, 15, 37; DA; DAB; DAC; DAM MST, NOV; PC 3; WLC**
See also CA 9-12R; 73-76; CABS 2; CANR 26, 60; DLB 5, 169; MTCW

Lowndes, Marie Adelaide (Belloc) 1868-1947 **TCLC 12**
See also CA 107; DLB 70

Lowry, (Clarence) Malcolm 1909-1957**TCLC 6, 40**
See also CA 105; 131; CANR 62; CDBLB 1945-1960; DLB 15; MTCW

Lowry, Mina Gertrude 1882-1966
See Loy, Mina
See also CA 113

Loxsmith, John
See Brunner, John (Kilian Houston)

Loy, Mina .... **CLC 28; DAM POET; PC 16**
See also Lowry, Mina Gertrude
See also DLB 4, 54

Loyson-Bridet
See Schwob, (Mayer Andre) Marcel

Lucas, Craig 1951- .... **CLC 64**
See also CA 137

Lucas, E(dward) V(errall) 1868-1938 **T C L C 73**
See also DLB 98, 149, 153; SATA 20

Lucas, George 1944- .... **CLC 16**
See also AAYA 1; CA 77-80; CANR 30; SATA 56

Lucas, Hans
See Godard, Jean-Luc

Lucas, Victoria
See Plath, Sylvia

Ludlam, Charles 1943-1987 .... **CLC 46, 50**
See also CA 85-88; 122

Ludlum, Robert 1927-**CLC 22, 43; DAM NOV, POP**
See also AAYA 10; BEST 89:1, 90:3; CA 33-36R; CANR 25, 41; DLBY 82; MTCW

Ludwig, Ken .... **CLC 60**

Ludwig, Otto 1813-1865 .... **NCLC 4**
See also DLB 129

Lugones, Leopoldo 1874-1938 .... **TCLC 15**
See also CA 116; 131; HW

Lu Hsun 1881-1936 .... **TCLC 3; SSC 20**
See also Shu-Jen, Chou

Lukacs, George .... **CLC 24**
See also Lukacs, Gyorgy (Szegeny von)

Lukacs, Gyorgy (Szegeny von) 1885-1971
See Lukacs, George
See also CA 101; 29-32R; CANR 62

Luke, Peter (Ambrose Cyprian) 1919-1995 **CLC 38**
See also CA 81-84; 147; DLB 13

Lunar, Dennis
See Mungo, Raymond

Lurie, Alison 1926- .... **CLC 4, 5, 18, 39**
See also CA 1-4R; CANR 2, 17, 50; DLB 2; MTCW; SATA 46

Lustig, Arnost 1926- .... **CLC 56**
See also AAYA 3; CA 69-72; CANR 47; SATA 56

Luther, Martin 1483-1546 .... **LC 9, 37**
See also DLB 179

Luxemburg, Rosa 1870(?)-1919 ..... **TCLC 63**
See also CA 118

Luzi, Mario 1914- .... **CLC 13**
See also CA 61-64; CANR 9; DLB 128

Lyly, John 1554(?)-1606 ....**DC 7**
See also DAM DRAM; DLB 62, 167

L'Ymagier
See Gourmont, Remy (-Marie-Charles) de

Lynch, B. Suarez
See Bioy Casares, Adolfo; Borges, Jorge Luis

Lynch, David (K.) 1946- .... **CLC 66**
See also CA 124; 129

Lynch, James
See Andreyev, Leonid (Nikolaevich)

Lynch Davis, B.
See Bioy Casares, Adolfo; Borges, Jorge Luis

Lyndsay, Sir David 1490-1555 .... **LC 20**

Lynn, Kenneth S(chuyler) 1923- .... **CLC 50**
See also CA 1-4R; CANR 3, 27

Lynx
See West, Rebecca

Lyons, Marcus
See Blish, James (Benjamin)

WLCS
See also CA 104; 133; CDALB 1865-1917; DLB 54; MTCW
Masters, Hilary 1928- .... **CLC 48**
See also CA 25-28R; CANR 13, 47
Mastrosimone, William 19(?)- .... **CLC 36**
Mathe, Albert
See Camus, Albert
Mather, Cotton 1663-1728 .... **LC 38**
See also CDALB 1640-1865; DLB 24, 30, 140
Mather, Increase 1639-1723 .... **LC 38**
See also DLB 24
Matheson, Richard Burton 1926- ..... **CLC 37**
See also CA 97-100; DLB 8, 44; INT 97-100
Mathews, Harry 1930- .... **CLC 6, 52**
See also CA 21-24R; CAAS 6; CANR 18, 40
Mathews, John Joseph 1894-1979 .. **CLC 84; DAM MULT**
See also CA 19-20; 142; CANR 45; CAP 2; DLB 175; NNAL
Mathias, Roland (Glyn) 1915- .... **CLC 45**
See also CA 97-100; CANR 19, 41; DLB 27
Matsuo Basho 1644-1694 .... **PC 3**
See also DAM POET
Mattheson, Rodney
See Creasey, John
Matthews, Greg 1949- .... **CLC 45**
See also CA 135
Matthews, William 1942- .... **CLC 40**
See also CA 29-32R; CAAS 18; CANR 12, 57; DLB 5
Matthias, John (Edward) 1941- .... **CLC 9**
See also CA 33-36R; CANR 56
Matthiessen, Peter 1927-**CLC 5, 7, 11, 32, 64; DAM NOV**
See also AAYA 6; BEST 90:4; CA 9-12R; CANR 21, 50; DLB 6, 173; MTCW; SATA 27
Maturin, Charles Robert 1780(?)-1824**NCLC 6**
See also DLB 178
Matute (Ausejo), Ana Maria 1925- .. **CLC 11**
See also CA 89-92; MTCW
Maugham, W. S.
See Maugham, W(illiam) Somerset
Maugham, W(illiam) Somerset 1874-1965
CLC 1, 11, 15, 67, 93; DA; DAB; DAC; DAM DRAM, MST, NOV; SSC 8; WLC
See also CA 5-8R; 25-28R; CANR 40; CDBLB 1914-1945; DLB 10, 36, 77, 100, 162; MTCW; SATA 54
Maugham, William Somerset
See Maugham, W(illiam) Somerset
Maupassant, (Henri Rene Albert) Guy de 1850-1893**NCLC 1, 42; DA; DAB; DAC; DAM MST; SSC 1; WLC**
See also DLB 123
Maupin, Armistead 1944-**CLC 95; DAM POP**
See also CA 125; 130; CANR 58; INT 130
Maurhut, Richard
See Traven, B.
Mauriac, Claude 1914-1996 .... **CLC 9**
See also CA 89-92; 152; DLB 83
Mauriac, Francois (Charles) 1885-1970 **C L C 4, 9, 56; SSC 24**
See also CA 25-28; CAP 2; DLB 65; MTCW
Mavor, Osborne Henry 1888-1951
See Bridie, James
See also CA 104
Maxwell, William (Keepers, Jr.) 1908-**CLC 19**
See also CA 93-96; CANR 54; DLBY 80; INT 93-96
May, Elaine 1932- .... **CLC 16**

See also CA 124; 142; DLB 44
Mayakovski, Vladimir (Vladimirovich) 1893-1930 .... **TCLC 4, 18**
See also CA 104; 158
Mayhew, Henry 1812-1887 .... **NCLC 31**
See also DLB 18, 55
Mayle, Peter 1939(?)- .... **CLC 89**
See also CA 139
Maynard, Joyce 1953- .... **CLC 23**
See also CA 111; 129
Mayne, William (James Carter) 1928-**CLC 12**
See also AAYA 20; CA 9-12R; CANR 37; CLR 25; JRDA; MAICYA; SAAS 11; SATA 6, 68
Mayo, Jim
See L'Amour, Louis (Dearborn)
Maysles, Albert 1926- .... **CLC 16**
See also CA 29-32R
Maysles, David 1932- .... **CLC 16**
Mazer, Norma Fox 1931- .... **CLC 26**
See also AAYA 5; CA 69-72; CANR 12, 32; CLR 23; JRDA; MAICYA; SAAS 1; SATA 24, 67
Mazzini, Guiseppe 1805-1872 .... **NCLC 34**
McAuley, James Phillip 1917-1976 .. **CLC 45**
See also CA 97-100
McBain, Ed
See Hunter, Evan
McBrien, William Augustine 1930-.. **CLC 44**
See also CA 107
McCaffrey, Anne (Inez) 1926-**CLC 17; DAM NOV, POP**
See also AAYA 6; AITN 2; BEST 89:2; CA 25-28R; CANR 15, 35, 55; DLB 8; JRDA; MAICYA; MTCW; SAAS 11; SATA 8, 70
McCall, Nathan 1955(?)- .... **CLC 86**
See also CA 146
McCann, Arthur
See Campbell, John W(ood, Jr.)
McCann, Edson
See Pohl, Frederik
McCarthy, Charles, Jr. 1933-
See McCarthy, Cormac
See also CANR 42; DAM POP
McCarthy, Cormac 1933-**CLC 4, 57, 59, 101**
See also McCarthy, Charles, Jr.
See also DLB 6, 143
McCarthy, Mary (Therese) 1912-1989**CLC 1, 3, 5, 14, 24, 39, 59; SSC 24**
See also CA 5-8R; 129; CANR 16, 50; DLB 2; DLBY 81; INT CANR-16; MTCW
McCartney, (James) Paul 1942- **CLC 12, 35**
See also CA 146
McCauley, Stephen (D.) 1955- .... **CLC 50**
See also CA 141
McClure, Michael (Thomas) 1932-**CLC 6, 10**
See also CA 21-24R; CANR 17, 46; DLB 16
McCorkle, Jill (Collins) 1958- .... **CLC 51**
See also CA 121; DLBY 87
McCourt, James 1941- .... **CLC 5**
See also CA 57-60
McCoy, Horace (Stanley) 1897-1955**TCLC 28**
See also CA 108; 155; DLB 9
McCrae, John 1872-1918 .... **TCLC 12**
See also CA 109; DLB 92
McCreigh, James
See Pohl, Frederik
McCullers, (Lula) Carson (Smith) 1917-1967
CLC 1, 4, 10, 12, 48, 100; DA; DAB; DAC; DAM MST, NOV; SSC 9, 24; WLC
See also AAYA 21; CA 5-8R; 25-28R; CABS 1, 3; CANR 18; CDALB 1941-1968; DLB 2, 7, 173; MTCW; SATA 27
McCulloch, John Tyler

See Burroughs, Edgar Rice
McCullough, Colleen 1938(?)-**CLC 27; DAM NOV, POP**
See also CA 81-84; CANR 17, 46; MTCW
McDermott, Alice 1953- .... **CLC 90**
See also CA 109; CANR 40
McElroy, Joseph 1930- .... **CLC 5, 47**
See also CA 17-20R
McEwan, Ian (Russell) 1948- .... **CLC 13, 66; DAM NOV**
See also BEST 90:4; CA 61-64; CANR 14, 41; DLB 14; MTCW
McFadden, David 1940- .... **CLC 48**
See also CA 104; DLB 60; INT 104
McFarland, Dennis 1950- .... **CLC 65**
McGahern, John 1934-**CLC 5, 9, 48; SSC 17**
See also CA 17-20R; CANR 29; DLB 14; MTCW
McGinley, Patrick (Anthony) 1937- . **CLC 41**
See also CA 120; 127; CANR 56; INT 127
McGinley, Phyllis 1905-1978 .... **CLC 14**
See also CA 9-12R; 77-80; CANR 19; DLB 11, 48; SATA 2, 44; SATA-Obit 24
McGinniss, Joe 1942- .... **CLC 32**
See also AITN 2; BEST 89:2; CA 25-28R; CANR 26; INT CANR-26
McGivern, Maureen Daly
See Daly, Maureen
McGrath, Patrick 1950- .... **CLC 55**
See also CA 136
McGrath, Thomas (Matthew) 1916-1990**CLC 28, 59; DAM POET**
See also CA 9-12R; 132; CANR 6, 33; MTCW; SATA 41; SATA-Obit 66
McGuane, Thomas (Francis III) 1939-**CLC 3, 7, 18, 45**
See also AITN 2; CA 49-52; CANR 5, 24, 49; DLB 2; DLBY 80; INT CANR-24; MTCW
McGuckian, Medbh 1950- ..... **CLC 48; DAM POET**
See also CA 143; DLB 40
McHale, Tom 1942(?)-1982 .... **CLC 3, 5**
See also AITN 1; CA 77-80; 106
McIlvanney, William 1936- .... **CLC 42**
See also CA 25-28R; CANR 61; DLB 14
McIlwraith, Maureen Mollie Hunter
See Hunter, Mollie
See also SATA 2
McInerney, Jay 1955- ... **CLC 34; DAM POP**
See also AAYA 18; CA 116; 123; CANR 45; INT 123
McIntyre, Vonda N(eel) 1948- .... **CLC 18**
See also CA 81-84; CANR 17, 34; MTCW
McKay, ClaudeTCLC 7, 41; BLC; DAB; PC 2
See also McKay, Festus Claudius
See also DLB 4, 45, 51, 117
McKay, Festus Claudius 1889-1948
See McKay, Claude
See also BW 1; CA 104; 124; DA; DAC; DAM MST, MULT, NOV, POET; MTCW; WLC
McKuen, Rod 1933- .... **CLC 1, 3**
See also AITN 1; CA 41-44R; CANR 40
McLoughlin, R. B.
See Mencken, H(enry) L(ouis)
McLuhan, (Herbert) Marshall 1911-1980
CLC 37, 83
See also CA 9-12R; 102; CANR 12, 34, 61; DLB 88; INT CANR-12; MTCW
McMillan, Terry (L.) 1951-**CLC 50, 61; DAM MULT, NOV, POP**
See also AAYA 21; BW 2; CA 140; CANR 60
McMurtry, Larry (Jeff) 1936-**CLC 2, 3, 7, 11, 27, 44; DAM NOV, POP**

Morren, Theophil
    See Hofmannsthal, Hugo von
Morris, Bill 1952- .... CLC 76
Morris, Julian
    See West, Morris L(anglo)
Morris, Steveland Judkins 1950(?)-
    See Wonder, Stevie
    See also CA 111
Morris, William 1834-1896 .... NCLC 4
    See also CDBLB 1832-1890; DLB 18, 35, 57,
    156, 178, 184
Morris, Wright 1910- ...... CLC 1, 3, 7, 18, 37
    See also CA 9-12R; CANR 21; DLB 2; DLBY
    81; MTCW
Morrison, Arthur 1863-1945 .... TCLC 72
    See also CA 120; 157; DLB 70, 135
Morrison, Chloe Anthony Wofford
    See Morrison, Toni
Morrison, James Douglas 1943-1971
    See Morrison, Jim
    See also CA 73-76; CANR 40
Morrison, Jim .... CLC 17
    See also Morrison, James Douglas
Morrison, Toni 1931-CLC 4, 10, 22, 55, 81, 87;
    BLC; DA; DAB; DAC; DAM MST, MULT,
    NOV, POP
    See also AAYA 1, 22; BW 2; CA 29-32R;
    CANR 27, 42; CDALB 1968-1988; DLB 6,
    33, 143; DLBY 81; MTCW; SATA 57
Morrison, Van 1945- .... CLC 21
    See also CA 116
Morrissy, Mary 1958- .... CLC 99
Mortimer, John (Clifford) 1923-CLC 28, 43;
    DAM DRAM, POP
    See also CA 13-16R; CANR 21; CDBLB 1960
    to Present; DLB 13; INT CANR-21; MTCW
Mortimer, Penelope (Ruth) 1918- .... CLC 5
    See also CA 57-60; CANR 45
Morton, Anthony
    See Creasey, John
Mosca, Gaetano 1858-1941 .... TCLC 75
Mosher, Howard Frank 1943- .... CLC 62
    See also CA 139
Mosley, Nicholas 1923- .... CLC 43, 70
    See also CA 69-72; CANR 41, 60; DLB 14
Mosley, Walter 1952- CLC 97; DAM MULT,
    POP
    See also AAYA 17; BW 2; CA 142; CANR 57
Moss, Howard 1922-1987 CLC 7, 14, 45, 50;
    DAM POET
    See also CA 1-4R; 123; CANR 1, 44; DLB 5
Mossgiel, Rab
    See Burns, Robert
Motion, Andrew (Peter) 1952- .... CLC 47
    See also CA 146; DLB 40
Motley, Willard (Francis) 1909-1965 CLC 18
    See also BW 1; CA 117; 106; DLB 76, 143
Motoori, Norinaga 1730-1801 .... NCLC 45
Mott, Michael (Charles Alston) 1930-CLC 15,
    34
    See also CA 5-8R; CAAS 7; CANR 7, 29
Mountain Wolf Woman 1884-1960 .. CLC 92
    See also CA 144; NNAL
Moure, Erin 1955- .... CLC 88
    See also CA 113; DLB 60
Mowat, Farley (McGill) 1921-CLC 26; DAC;
    DAM MST
    See also AAYA 1; CA 1-4R; CANR 4, 24, 42;
    CLR 20; DLB 68; INT CANAR-24; JRDA;
    MAICYA; MTCW; SATA 3, 55
Moyers, Bill 1934- .... CLC 74
    See also AITN 2; CA 61-64; CANR 31, 52
Mphahlele, Es'kia

See Mphahlele, Ezekiel
    See also DLB 125
Mphahlele, Ezekiel 1919-CLC 25; BLC; DAM
    MULT
    See also Mphahlele, Es'kia
    See also BW 2; CA 81-84; CANR 26
Mqhayi, S(amuel) E(dward) K(rune Loliwe)
    1875-1945TCLC 25; BLC; DAM MULT
    See also CA 153
Mrozek, Slawomir 1930- .... CLC 3, 13
    See also CA 13-16R; CAAS 10; CANR 29;
    MTCW
Mrs. Belloc-Lowndes
    See Lowndes, Marie Adelaide (Belloc)
Mtwa, Percy (?)- .... CLC 47
Mueller, Lisel 1924- .... CLC 13, 51
    See also CA 93-96; DLB 105
Muir, Edwin 1887-1959 .... TCLC 2
    See also CA 104; DLB 20, 100
Muir, John 1838-1914 .... TCLC 28
Mujica Lainez, Manuel 1910-1984 ... CLC 31
    See also Lainez, Manuel Mujica
    See also CA 81-84; 112; CANR 32; HW
Mukherjee, Bharati 1940-CLC 53; DAM NOV
    See also BEST 89:2; CA 107; CANR 45; DLB
    60; MTCW
Muldoon, Paul 1951-CLC 32, 72; DAM POET
    See also CA 113; 129; CANR 52; DLB 40; INT
    129
Mulisch, Harry 1927- .... CLC 42
    See also CA 9-12R; CANR 6, 26, 56
Mull, Martin 1943- .... CLC 17
    See also CA 105
Mulock, Dinah Maria
    See Craik, Dinah Maria (Mulock)
Munford, Robert 1737(?)-1783 .... LC 5
    See also DLB 31
Mungo, Raymond 1946- .... CLC 72
    See also CA 49-52; CANR 2
Munro, Alice 1931- .... CLC 6, 10, 19, 50, 95;
    DAC; DAM MST, NOV; SSC 3; WLCS
    See also AITN 2; CA 33-36R; CANR 33, 53;
    DLB 53; MTCW; SATA 29
Munro, H(ector) H(ugh) 1870-1916
    See Saki
    See also CA 104; 130; CDBLB 1890-1914; DA;
    DAB; DAC; DAM MST, NOV; DLB 34, 162;
    MTCW; WLC
Murasaki, Lady .... CMLC 1
Murdoch, (Jean) Iris 1919-CLC 1, 2, 3, 4, 6, 8,
    11, 15, 22, 31, 51; DAB; DAC; DAM MST,
    NOV
    See also CA 13-16R; CANR 8, 43; CDBLB
    1960 to Present; DLB 14; INT CANR-8;
    MTCW
Murfree, Mary Noailles 1850-1922 ... SSC 22
    See also CA 122; DLB 12, 74
Murnau, Friedrich Wilhelm
    See Plumpe, Friedrich Wilhelm
Murphy, Richard 1927- .... CLC 41
    See also CA 29-32R; DLB 40
Murphy, Sylvia 1937- .... CLC 34
    See also CA 121
Murphy, Thomas (Bernard) 1935- ... CLC 51
    See also CA 101
Murray, Albert L. 1916- .... CLC 73
    See also BW 2; CA 49-52; CANR 26, 52; DLB
    38
Murray, Judith Sargent 1751-1820NCLC 63
    See also DLB 37
Murray, Les(lie) A(llan) 1938-CLC 40; DAM
    POET
    See also CA 21-24R; CANR 11, 27, 56

Murry, J. Middleton
    See Murry, John Middleton
Murry, John Middleton 1889-1957 TCLC 16
    See also CA 118; DLB 149
Musgrave, Susan 1951- .... CLC 13, 54
    See also CA 69-72; CANR 45
Musil, Robert (Edler von) 1880-1942 T C L C
    12, 68; SSC 18
    See also CA 109; CANR 55; DLB 81, 124
Muske, Carol 1945- .... CLC 90
    See also Muske-Dukes, Carol (Anne)
Muske-Dukes, Carol (Anne) 1945-
    See Muske, Carol
    See also CA 65-68; CANR 32
Musset, (Louis Charles) Alfred de 1810-1857
    NCLC 7
My Brother's Brother
    See Chekhov, Anton (Pavlovich)
Myers, L(eopold) H(amilton) 1881-1944
    TCLC 59
    See also CA 157; DLB 15
Myers, Walter Dean 1937- ..... CLC 35; BLC;
    DAM MULT, NOV
    See also AAYA 4; BW 2; CA 33-36R; CANR
    20, 42; CLR 4, 16, 35; DLB 33; INT CANR-
    20; JRDA; MAICYA; SAAS 2; SATA 41, 71;
    SATA-Brief 27
Myers, Walter M.
    See Myers, Walter Dean
Myles, Symon
    See Follett, Ken(neth Martin)
Nabokov, Vladimir (Vladimirovich) 1899-1977
    CLC 1, 2, 3, 6, 8, 11, 15, 23, 44, 46, 64;
    DA; DAB; DAC; DAM MST, NOV; SSC
    11; WLC
    See also CA 5-8R; 69-72; CANR 20; CDALB
    1941-1968; DLB 2; DLBD 3; DLBY 80, 91;
    MTCW
Nagai Kafu 1879-1959 .... TCLC 51
    See also Nagai Sokichi
    See also DLB 180
Nagai Sokichi 1879-1959
    See Nagai Kafu
    See also CA 117
Nagy, Laszlo 1925-1978 .... CLC 7
    See also CA 129; 112
Naipaul, Shiva(dhar Srinivasa) 1945-1985
    CLC 32, 39; DAM NOV
    See also CA 110; 112; 116; CANR 33; DLB
    157; DLBY 85; MTCW
Naipaul, V(idiadhar) S(urajprasad) 1932-
    CLC 4, 7, 9, 13, 18, 37, 105; DAB; DAC;
    DAM MST, NOV
    See also CA 1-4R; CANR 1, 33, 51; CDBLB
    1960 to Present; DLB 125; DLBY 85;
    MTCW
Nakos, Lilika 1899(?)- .... CLC 29
Narayan, R(asipuram) K(rishnaswami) 1906-
    CLC 7, 28, 47; DAM NOV; SSC 25
    See also CA 81-84; CANR 33, 61; MTCW;
    SATA 62
Nash, (Fredric) Ogden 1902-1971 . CLC 23;
    DAM POET
    See also CA 13-14; 29-32R; CANR 34, 61; CAP
    1; DLB 11; MAICYA; MTCW; SATA 2, 46
Nathan, Daniel
    See Dannay, Frederic
Nathan, George Jean 1882-1958 .... TCLC 18
    See also Hatteras, Owen
    See also CA 114; DLB 137
Natsume, Kinnosuke 1867-1916
    See Natsume, Soseki
    See also CA 104

See also O Nuallain, Brian

O'Brien, Richard 1942- .... **CLC 17**
See also CA 124

O'Brien, (William) Tim(othy) 1946- . **CLC 7, 19, 40, 103; DAM POP**
See also AAYA 16; CA 85-88; CANR 40, 58; DLB 152; DLBD 9; DLBY 80

Obstfelder, Sigbjoern 1866-1900 ... **TCLC 23**
See also CA 123

O'Casey, Sean 1880-1964 **CLC 1, 5, 9, 11, 15, 88; DAB; DAC; DAM DRAM, MST; WLCS**
See also CA 89-92; CANR 62; CDBLB 1914-1945; DLB 10; MTCW

O'Cathasaigh, Sean
See O'Casey, Sean

Ochs, Phil 1940-1976 .... **CLC 17**
See also CA 65-68

O'Connor, Edwin (Greene) 1918-1968 **CLC 14**
See also CA 93-96; 25-28R

O'Connor, (Mary) Flannery 1925-1964 **C L C 1, 2, 3, 6, 10, 13, 15, 21, 66, 104; DA; DAB; DAC; DAM MST, NOV; SSC 1, 23; WLC**
See also AAYA 7; CA 1-4R; CANR 3, 41; CDALB 1941-1968; DLB 2, 152; DLBD 12; DLBY 80; MTCW

O'Connor, Frank .... **CLC 23; SSC 5**
See also O'Donovan, Michael John
See also DLB 162

O'Dell, Scott 1898-1989 .... **CLC 30**
See also AAYA 3; CA 61-64; 129; CANR 12, 30; CLR 1, 16; DLB 52; JRDA; MAICYA; SATA 12, 60

Odets, Clifford 1906-1963 **CLC 2, 28, 98; DAM DRAM; DC 6**
See also CA 85-88; CANR 62; DLB 7, 26; MTCW

O'Doherty, Brian 1934- .... **CLC 76**
See also CA 105

O'Donnell, K. M.
See Malzberg, Barry N(athaniel)

O'Donnell, Lawrence
See Kuttner, Henry

O'Donovan, Michael John 1903-1966 **CLC 14**
See also O'Connor, Frank
See also CA 93-96

Oe, Kenzaburo 1935- **CLC 10, 36, 86; DAM NOV; SSC 20**
See also CA 97-100; CANR 36, 50; DLB 182; DLBY 94; MTCW

O'Faolain, Julia 1932- .... **CLC 6, 19, 47**
See also CA 81-84; CAAS 2; CANR 12, 61; DLB 14; MTCW

O'Faolain, Sean 1900-1991 **CLC 1, 7, 14, 32, 70; SSC 13**
See also CA 61-64; 134; CANR 12; DLB 15, 162; MTCW

O'Flaherty, Liam 1896-1984 **CLC 5, 34; SSC 6**
See also CA 101; 113; CANR 35; DLB 36, 162; DLBY 84; MTCW

Ogilvy, Gavin
See Barrie, J(ames) M(atthew)

O'Grady, Standish (James) 1846-1928 **T C L C 5**
See also CA 104; 157

O'Grady, Timothy 1951- .... **CLC 59**
See also CA 138

O'Hara, Frank 1926-1966 . **CLC 2, 5, 13, 78; DAM POET**
See also CA 9-12R; 25-28R; CANR 33; DLB 5, 16; MTCW

O'Hara, John (Henry) 1905-1970 **CLC 1, 2, 3, 6, 11, 42; DAM NOV; SSC 15**

See also CA 5-8R; 25-28R; CANR 31, 60; CDALB 1929-1941; DLB 9, 86; DLBD 2; MTCW

O Hehir, Diana 1922- .... **CLC 41**
See also CA 93-96

Okigbo, Christopher (Ifenayichukwu) 1932-1967 .... **CLC 25, 84; BLC; DAM MULT, POET; PC 7**
See also BW 1; CA 77-80; DLB 125; MTCW

Okri, Ben 1959- .... **CLC 87**
See also BW 2; CA 130; 138; DLB 157; INT 138

Olds, Sharon 1942- .... **CLC 32, 39, 85; DAM POET**
See also CA 101; CANR 18, 41; DLB 120

Oldstyle, Jonathan
See Irving, Washington

Olesha, Yuri (Karlovich) 1899-1960 .. **CLC 8**
See also CA 85-88

Oliphant, Laurence 1829(?)-1888 .. **NCLC 47**
See also DLB 18, 166

Oliphant, Margaret (Oliphant Wilson) 1828-1897 .... **NCLC 11, 61; SSC 25**
See also DLB 18, 159

Oliver, Mary 1935- .... **CLC 19, 34, 98**
See also CA 21-24R; CANR 9, 43; DLB 5

Olivier, Laurence (Kerr) 1907-1989 . **CLC 20**
See also CA 111; 150; 129

Olsen, Tillie 1913- **CLC 4, 13; DA; DAB; DAC; DAM MST; SSC 11**
See also CA 1-4R; CANR 1, 43; DLB 28; DLBY 80; MTCW

Olson, Charles (John) 1910-1970 **CLC 1, 2, 5, 6, 9, 11, 29; DAM POET; PC 19**
See also CA 13-16; 25-28R; CABS 2; CANR 35, 61; CAP 1; DLB 5, 16; MTCW

Olson, Toby 1937- .... **CLC 28**
See also CA 65-68; CANR 9, 31

Olyesha, Yuri
See Olesha, Yuri (Karlovich)

Ondaatje, (Philip) Michael 1943- **CLC 14, 29, 51, 76; DAB; DAC; DAM MST**
See also CA 77-80; CANR 42; DLB 60

Oneal, Elizabeth 1934-
See Oneal, Zibby
See also CA 106; CANR 28; MAICYA; SATA 30, 82

Oneal, Zibby .... **CLC 30**
See also Oneal, Elizabeth
See also AAYA 5; CLR 13; JRDA

O'Neill, Eugene (Gladstone) 1888-1953 **TCLC 1, 6, 27, 49; DA; DAB; DAC; DAM DRAM, MST; WLC**
See also AITN 1; CA 110; 132; CDALB 1929-1941; DLB 7; MTCW

Onetti, Juan Carlos 1909-1994 ... **CLC 7, 10; DAM MULT, NOV; SSC 23**
See also CA 85-88; 145; CANR 32; DLB 113; HW; MTCW

O Nuallain, Brian 1911-1966
See O'Brien, Flann
See also CA 21-22; 25-28R; CAP 2

Opie, Amelia 1769-1853 .... **NCLC 65**
See also DLB 116, 159

Oppen, George 1908-1984 ...... **CLC 7, 13, 34**
See also CA 13-16R; 113; CANR 8; DLB 5, 165

Oppenheim, E(dward) Phillips 1866-1946 **TCLC 45**
See also CA 111; DLB 70

Origen c. 185-c. 254 .... **CMLC 19**

Orlovitz, Gil 1918-1973 .... **CLC 22**
See also CA 77-80; 45-48; DLB 2, 5

Orris
See Ingelow, Jean

Ortega y Gasset, Jose 1883-1955 .... **TCLC 9; DAM MULT; HLC**
See also CA 106; 130; HW; MTCW

Ortese, Anna Maria 1914- .... **CLC 89**
See also DLB 177

Ortiz, Simon J(oseph) 1941- .. **CLC 45; DAM MULT, POET; PC 17**
See also CA 134; DLB 120, 175; NNAL

Orton, Joe .... **CLC 4, 13, 43; DC 3**
See also Orton, John Kingsley
See also CDBLB 1960 to Present; DLB 13

Orton, John Kingsley 1933-1967
See Orton, Joe
See also CA 85-88; CANR 35; DAM DRAM; MTCW

Orwell, George . **TCLC 2, 6, 15, 31, 51; DAB; WLC**
See also Blair, Eric (Arthur)
See also CDBLB 1945-1960; DLB 15, 98

Osborne, David
See Silverberg, Robert

Osborne, George
See Silverberg, Robert

Osborne, John (James) 1929-1994 **CLC 1, 2, 5, 11, 45; DA; DAB; DAC; DAM DRAM, MST; WLC**
See also CA 13-16R; 147; CANR 21, 56; CDBLB 1945-1960; DLB 13; MTCW

Osborne, Lawrence 1958- .... **CLC 50**

Oshima, Nagisa 1932- .... **CLC 20**
See also CA 116; 121

Oskison, John Milton 1874-1947 .. **TCLC 35; DAM MULT**
See also CA 144; DLB 175; NNAL

Ossoli, Sarah Margaret (Fuller marchesa d') 1810-1850
See Fuller, Margaret
See also SATA 25

Ostrovsky, Alexander 1823-1886 **NCLC 30, 57**

Otero, Blas de 1916-1979 .... **CLC 11**
See also CA 89-92; DLB 134

Otto, Whitney 1955- .... **CLC 70**
See also CA 140

Ouida .... **TCLC 43**
See also De La Ramee, (Marie) Louise
See also DLB 18, 156

Ousmane, Sembene 1923- .... **CLC 66; BLC**
See also BW 1; CA 117; 125; MTCW

Ovid 43B.C.-18(?) **CMLC 7; DAM POET; PC 2**

Owen, Hugh
See Faust, Frederick (Schiller)

Owen, Wilfred (Edward Salter) 1893-1918 **TCLC 5, 27; DA; DAB; DAC; DAM MST, POET; PC 19; WLC**
See also CA 104; 141; CDBLB 1914-1945; DLB 20

Owens, Rochelle 1936- .... **CLC 8**
See also CA 17-20R; CAAS 2; CANR 39

Oz, Amos 1939- **CLC 5, 8, 11, 27, 33, 54; DAM NOV**
See also CA 53-56; CANR 27, 47; MTCW

Ozick, Cynthia 1928- **CLC 3, 7, 28, 62; DAM NOV, POP; SSC 15**
See also BEST 90:1; CA 17-20R; CANR 23, 58; DLB 28, 152; DLBY 82; INT CANR-23; MTCW

Ozu, Yasujiro 1903-1963 .... **CLC 16**
See also CA 112

Pacheco, C.
See Pessoa, Fernando (Antonio Nogueira)

See Pound, Ezra (Weston Loomis)
Pohl, Frederik 1919- .... **CLC 18; SSC 25**
  See also CA 61-64; CAAS 1; CANR 11, 37;
    DLB 8; INT CANR-11; MTCW; SATA 24
Poirier, Louis 1910-
  See Gracq, Julien
  See also CA 122; 126
Poitier, Sidney 1927- .... **CLC 26**
  See also BW 1; CA 117
Polanski, Roman 1933- .... **CLC 16**
  See also CA 77-80
Poliakoff, Stephen 1952- .... **CLC 38**
  See also CA 106; DLB 13
Police, The
  See Copeland, Stewart (Armstrong); Summers,
    Andrew James; Sumner, Gordon Matthew
Polidori, John William 1795-1821 . **NCLC 51**
  See also DLB 116
Pollitt, Katha 1949- .... **CLC 28**
  See also CA 120; 122; MTCW
Pollock, (Mary) Sharon 1936- **CLC 50; DAC;
    DAM DRAM, MST**
  See also CA 141; DLB 60
Polo, Marco 1254-1324 .... **CMLC 15**
Polonsky, Abraham (Lincoln) 1910- **CLC 92**
  See also CA 104; DLB 26; INT 104
Polybius c. 200B.C.-c. 118B.C. ...... **CMLC 17**
  See also DLB 176
Pomerance, Bernard 1940- .... **CLC 13; DAM
    DRAM**
  See also CA 101; CANR 49
Ponge, Francis (Jean Gaston Alfred) 1899-1988
    CLC 6, 18; DAM POET
  See also CA 85-88; 126; CANR 40
Pontoppidan, Henrik 1857-1943 .... **TCLC 29**
Poole, Josephine .... **CLC 17**
  See also Helyar, Jane Penelope Josephine
  See also SAAS 2; SATA 5
Popa, Vasko 1922-1991 .... **CLC 19**
  See also CA 112; 148; DLB 181
Pope, Alexander 1688-1744 **LC 3; DA; DAB;
    DAC; DAM MST, POET; WLC**
  See also CDBLB 1660-1789; DLB 95, 101
Porter, Connie (Rose) 1959(?)- .... **CLC 70**
  See also BW 2; CA 142; SATA 81
Porter, Gene(va Grace) Stratton 1863(?)-1924
    TCLC 21
  See also CA 112
Porter, Katherine Anne 1890-1980 **CLC 1, 3, 7,
    10, 13, 15, 27, 101; DA; DAB; DAC; DAM
    MST, NOV; SSC 4**
  See also AITN 2; CA 1-4R; 101; CANR 1; DLB
    4, 9, 102; DLBD 12; DLBY 80; MTCW;
    SATA 39; SATA-Obit 23
Porter, Peter (Neville Frederick) 1929- **CLC 5,
    13, 33**
  See also CA 85-88; DLB 40
Porter, William Sydney 1862-1910
  See Henry, O.
  See also CA 104; 131; CDALB 1865-1917; DA;
    DAB; DAC; DAM MST; DLB 12, 78, 79;
    MTCW; YABC 2
Portillo (y Pacheco), Jose Lopez
  See Lopez Portillo (y Pacheco), Jose
Post, Melville Davisson 1869-1930 **TCLC 39**
  See also CA 110
Potok, Chaim 1929- . **CLC 2, 7, 14, 26; DAM
    NOV**
  See also AAYA 15; AITN 1, 2; CA 17-20R;
    CANR 19, 35; DLB 28, 152; INT CANR-
    19; MTCW; SATA 33
Potter, (Helen) Beatrix 1866-1943
  See Webb, (Martha) Beatrice (Potter)

See also MAICYA
Potter, Dennis (Christopher George) 1935-1994
    CLC 58, 86
  See also CA 107; 145; CANR 33, 61; MTCW
Pound, Ezra (Weston Loomis) 1885-1972**CLC
    1, 2, 3, 4, 5, 7, 10, 13, 18, 34, 48, 50; DA;
    DAB; DAC; DAM MST, POET; PC 4;
    WLC**
  See also CA 5-8R; 37-40R; CANR 40; CDALB
    1917-1929; DLB 4, 45, 63; DLBD 15;
    MTCW
Povod, Reinaldo 1959-1994 .... **CLC 44**
  See also CA 136; 146
Powell, Adam Clayton, Jr. 1908-1972**CLC 89;
    BLC; DAM MULT**
  See also BW 1; CA 102; 33-36R
Powell, Anthony (Dymoke) 1905- **CLC 1, 3, 7,
    9, 10, 31**
  See also CA 1-4R; CANR 1, 32, 62; CDBLB
    1945-1960; DLB 15; MTCW
Powell, Dawn 1897-1965 .... **CLC 66**
  See also CA 5-8R
Powell, Padgett 1952- .... **CLC 34**
  See also CA 126
Power, Susan 1961- .... **CLC 91**
Powers, J(ames) F(arl) 1917- **CLC 1, 4, 8, 57;
    SSC 4**
  See also CA 1-4R; CANR 2, 61; DLB 130;
    MTCW
Powers, John J(ames) 1945-
  See Powers, John R.
  See also CA 69-72
Powers, John R. .... **CLC 66**
  See also Powers, John J(ames)
Powers, Richard (S.) 1957- .... **CLC 93**
  See also CA 148
Pownall, David 1938- .... **CLC 10**
  See also CA 89-92; CAAS 18; CANR 49; DLB
    14
Powys, John Cowper 1872-1963**CLC 7, 9, 15,
    46**
  See also CA 85-88; DLB 15; MTCW
Powys, T(heodore) F(rancis) 1875-1953
    TCLC 9
  See also CA 106; DLB 36, 162
Prado (Calvo), Pedro 1886-1952 ... **TCLC 75**
  See also CA 131; HW
Prager, Emily 1952- .... **CLC 56**
Pratt, E(dwin) J(ohn) 1883(?)-1964 **CLC 19;
    DAC; DAM POET**
  See also CA 141; 93-96; DLB 92
Premchand .... **TCLC 21**
  See also Srivastava, Dhanpat Rai
Preussler, Otfried 1923- .... **CLC 17**
  See also CA 77-80; SATA 24
Prevert, Jacques (Henri Marie) 1900-1977
    CLC 15
  See also CA 77-80; 69-72; CANR 29, 61;
    MTCW; SATA-Obit 30
Prevost, Abbe (Antoine Francois) 1697-1763
    LC 1
Price, (Edward) Reynolds 1933- **CLC 3, 6, 13,
    43, 50, 63; DAM NOV; SSC 22**
  See also CA 1-4R; CANR 1, 37, 57; DLB 2;
    INT CANR-37
Price, Richard 1949- .... **CLC 6, 12**
  See also CA 49-52; CANR 3; DLBY 81
Prichard, Katharine Susannah 1883-1969
    CLC 46
  See also CA 11-12; CANR 33; CAP 1; MTCW;
    SATA 66
Priestley, J(ohn) B(oynton) 1894-1984**CLC 2,
    5, 9, 34; DAM DRAM, NOV**

See also CA 9-12R; 113; CANR 33; CDBLB
    1914-1945; DLB 10, 34, 77, 100, 139; DLBY
    84; MTCW
Prince 1958(?)- .... **CLC 35**
Prince, F(rank) T(empleton) 1912- .. **CLC 22**
  See also CA 101; CANR 43; DLB 20
Prince Kropotkin
  See Kropotkin, Peter (Alekseievich)
Prior, Matthew 1664-1721 .... **LC 4**
  See also DLB 95
Prishvin, Mikhail 1873-1954 .... **TCLC 75**
Pritchard, William H(arrison) 1932- **CLC 34**
  See also CA 65-68; CANR 23; DLB 111
Pritchett, V(ictor) S(awdon) 1900-1997 **C L C
    5, 13, 15, 41; DAM NOV; SSC 14**
  See also CA 61-64; 157; CANR 31; DLB 15,
    139; MTCW
Private 19022
  See Manning, Frederic
Probst, Mark 1925- .... **CLC 59**
  See also CA 130
Prokosch, Frederic 1908-1989 ...... **CLC 4, 48**
  See also CA 73-76; 128; DLB 48
Prophet, The
  See Dreiser, Theodore (Herman Albert)
Prose, Francine 1947- .... **CLC 45**
  See also CA 109; 112; CANR 46
Proudhon
  See Cunha, Euclides (Rodrigues Pimenta) da
Proulx, E. Annie 1935- .... **CLC 81**
**Proust, (Valentin-Louis-George-Eugene-)
    Marcel** 1871-1922 **TCLC 7, 13, 33; DA;
    DAB; DAC; DAM MST, NOV; WLC**
  See also CA 104; 120; DLB 65; MTCW
Prowler, Harley
  See Masters, Edgar Lee
Prus, Boleslaw 1845-1912 .... **TCLC 48**
Pryor, Richard (Franklin Lenox Thomas) 1940-
    CLC 26
  See also CA 122
Przybyszewski, Stanislaw 1868-1927**TCLC 36**
  See also CA 160; DLB 66
Pteleon
  See Grieve, C(hristopher) M(urray)
  See also DAM POET
Puckett, Lute
  See Masters, Edgar Lee
Puig, Manuel 1932-1990**CLC 3, 5, 10, 28, 65;
    DAM MULT; HLC**
  See also CA 45-48; CANR 2, 32; DLB 113; HW;
    MTCW
Pulitzer, Joseph 1847-1911 .... **TCLC 76**
  See also CA 114; DLB 23
Purdy, Al(fred Wellington) 1918- **CLC 3, 6, 14,
    50; DAC; DAM MST, POET**
  See also CA 81-84; CAAS 17; CANR 42; DLB
    88
Purdy, James (Amos) 1923- **CLC 2, 4, 10, 28,
    52**
  See also CA 33-36R; CAAS 1; CANR 19, 51;
    DLB 2; INT CANR-19; MTCW
Pure, Simon
  See Swinnerton, Frank Arthur
Pushkin, Alexander (Sergeyevich) 1799-1837
    **NCLC 3, 27; DA; DAB; DAC; DAM
    DRAM, MST, POET; PC 10; SSC 27;
    WLC**
  See also SATA 61
P'u Sung-ling 1640-1715 .... **LC 3**
Putnam, Arthur Lee
  See Alger, Horatio, Jr.
Puzo, Mario 1920-**CLC 1, 2, 6, 36; DAM NOV,
    POP**

See also CA 65-68; CANR 4, 42; DLB 6;
MTCW
Pygge, Edward
See Barnes, Julian (Patrick)
Pyle, Ernest Taylor 1900-1945
See Pyle, Ernie
See also CA 115; 160
Pyle, Ernie 1900-1945 .... **TCLC 75**
See also Pyle, Ernest Taylor
See also DLB 29
Pym, Barbara (Mary Crampton) 1913-1980
CLC 13, 19, 37
See also CA 13-14; 97-100; CANR 13, 34; CAP
1; DLB 14; DLBY 87; MTCW
Pynchon, Thomas (Ruggles, Jr.) 1937-**CLC 2,
3, 6, 9, 11, 18, 33, 62, 72; DA; DAB; DAC;
DAM MST, NOV, POP; SSC 14; WLC**
See also BEST 90:2; CA 17-20R; CANR 22,
46; DLB 2, 173; MTCW
Pythagoras c. 570B.C.-c. 500B.C.. **CMLC 22**
See also DLB 176
Qian Zhongshu
See Ch'ien Chung-shu
Qroll
See Dagerman, Stig (Halvard)
Quarrington, Paul (Lewis) 1953- ..... **CLC 65**
See also CA 129; CANR 62
Quasimodo, Salvatore 1901-1968 ..... **CLC 10**
See also CA 13-16; 25-28R; CAP 1; DLB 114;
MTCW
Quay, Stephen 1947- .... **CLC 95**
Quay, The Brothers
See Quay, Stephen; Quay, Timothy
Quay, Timothy 1947- .... **CLC 95**
Queen, Ellery, ... **CLC 3, 11**
See also Dannay, Frederic; Davidson, Avram;
Lee, Manfred B(ennington); Marlowe,
Stephen; Sturgeon, Theodore (Hamilton);
Vance, John Holbrook
Queen, Ellery, Jr.
See Dannay, Frederic; Lee, Manfred
B(ennington)
Queneau, Raymond 1903-1976 **CLC 2, 5, 10,
42**
See also CA 77-80; 69-72; CANR 32; DLB 72;
MTCW
Quevedo, Francisco de 1580-1645 .... **LC 23**
Quiller-Couch, Arthur Thomas 1863-1944
TCLC 53
See also CA 118; DLB 135, 153
Quin, Ann (Marie) 1936-1973 .... **CLC 6**
See also CA 9-12R; 45-48; DLB 14
Quinn, Martin
See Smith, Martin Cruz
Quinn, Peter 1947- .... **CLC 91**
Quinn, Simon
See Smith, Martin Cruz
Quiroga, Horacio (Sylvestre) 1878-1937
TCLC 20; DAM MULT; HLC
See also CA 117; 131; HW; MTCW
Quoirez, Francoise 1935- .... **CLC 9**
See also Sagan, Francoise
See also CA 49-52; CANR 6, 39; MTCW
Raabe, Wilhelm 1831-1910 .... **TCLC 45**
See also DLB 129
Rabe, David (William) 1940-... **CLC 4, 8, 33;
DAM DRAM**
See also CA 85-88; CABS 3; CANR 59; DLB 7
Rabelais, Francois 1483-1553**LC 5; DA; DAB;
DAC; DAM MST; WLC**
Rabinovitch, Sholem 1859-1916
See Aleichem, Sholom
See also CA 104

Rachilde 1860-1953 .... **TCLC 67**
See also DLB 123
Racine, Jean 1639-1699 . **LC 28; DAB; DAM
MST**
Radcliffe, Ann (Ward) 1764-1823**NCLC 6, 55**
See also DLB 39, 178
Radiguet, Raymond 1903-1923 ...... **TCLC 29**
See also DLB 65
Radnoti, Miklos 1909-1944 .... **TCLC 16**
See also CA 118
Rado, James 1939- .... **CLC 17**
See also CA 105
Radvanyi, Netty 1900-1983
See Seghers, Anna
See also CA 85-88; 110
Rae, Ben
See Griffiths, Trevor
Raeburn, John (Hay) 1941- .... **CLC 34**
See also CA 57-60
Ragni, Gerome 1942-1991 .... **CLC 17**
See also CA 105; 134
Rahv, Philip 1908-1973 .... **CLC 24**
See also Greenberg, Ivan
See also DLB 137
Raine, Craig 1944- .... **CLC 32, 103**
See also CA 108; CANR 29, 51; DLB 40
Raine, Kathleen (Jessie) 1908- ...... **CLC 7, 45**
See also CA 85-88; CANR 46; DLB 20; MTCW
Rainis, Janis 1865-1929 .... **TCLC 29**
Rakosi, Carl .... **CLC 47**
See also Rawley, Callman
See also CAAS 5
Raleigh, Richard
See Lovecraft, H(oward) P(hillips)
Raleigh, Sir Walter 1554(?)-1618 . **LC 31, 39**
See also CDBLB Before 1660; DLB 172
Rallentando, H. P.
See Sayers, Dorothy L(eigh)
Ramal, Walter
See de la Mare, Walter (John)
Ramon, Juan
See Jimenez (Mantecon), Juan Ramon
Ramos, Graciliano 1892-1953 .... **TCLC 32**
Rampersad, Arnold 1941- .... **CLC 44**
See also BW 2; CA 127; 133; DLB 111; INT
133
Rampling, Anne
See Rice, Anne
Ramsay, Allan 1684(?)-1758 .... **LC 29**
See also DLB 95
Ramuz, Charles-Ferdinand 1878-1947**T C L C
33**
Rand, Ayn 1905-1982**CLC 3, 30, 44, 79; DA;
DAC; DAM MST, NOV, POP; WLC**
See also AAYA 10; CA 13-16R; 105; CANR
27; MTCW
Randall, Dudley (Felker) 1914-**CLC 1; BLC;
DAM MULT**
See also BW 1; CA 25-28R; CANR 23; DLB
41
Randall, Robert
See Silverberg, Robert
Ranger, Ken
See Creasey, John
Ransom, John Crowe 1888-1974**CLC 2, 4, 5,
11, 24; DAM POET**
See also CA 5-8R; 49-52; CANR 6, 34; DLB
45, 63; MTCW
Rao, Raja 1909-...... **CLC 25, 56; DAM NOV**
See also CA 73-76; CANR 51; MTCW
Raphael, Frederic (Michael) 1931-**CLC 2, 14**
See also CA 1-4R; CANR 1; DLB 14
Ratcliffe, James P.

See Mencken, H(enry) L(ouis)
Rathbone, Julian 1935- .... **CLC 41**
See also CA 101; CANR 34
Rattigan, Terence (Mervyn) 1911-1977**CLC 7;
DAM DRAM**
See also CA 85-88; 73-76; CDBLB 1945-1960;
DLB 13; MTCW
Ratushinskaya, Irina 1954- .... **CLC 54**
See also CA 129
Raven, Simon (Arthur Noel) 1927- .. **CLC 14**
See also CA 81-84
Rawley, Callman 1903-
See Rakosi, Carl
See also CA 21-24R; CANR 12, 32
Rawlings, Marjorie Kinnan 1896-1953**T CLC
4**
See also AAYA 20; CA 104; 137; DLB 9, 22,
102; JRDA; MAICYA; YABC 1
Ray, Satyajit 1921-1992 .. **CLC 16, 76; DAM
MULT**
See also CA 114; 137
Read, Herbert Edward 1893-1968 ..... **CLC 4**
See also CA 85-88; 25-28R; DLB 20, 149
Read, Piers Paul 1941- .... **CLC 4, 10, 25**
See also CA 21-24R; CANR 38; DLB 14; SATA
21
Reade, Charles 1814-1884 .... **NCLC 2**
See also DLB 21
Reade, Hamish
See Gray, Simon (James Holliday)
Reading, Peter 1946- .... **CLC 47**
See also CA 103; CANR 46; DLB 40
Reaney, James 1926- .. **CLC 13; DAC; DAM
MST**
See also CA 41-44R; CAAS 15; CANR 42; DLB
68; SATA 43
Rebreanu, Liviu 1885-1944 .... **TCLC 28**
Rechy, John (Francisco) 1934- **CLC 1, 7, 14,
18; DAM MULT; HLC**
See also CA 5-8R; CAAS 4; CANR 6, 32; DLB
122; DLBY 82; HW; INT CANR-6
Redcam, Tom 1870-1933 .... **TCLC 25**
Reddin, Keith .... **CLC 67**
Redgrove, Peter (William) 1932-.. **CLC 6, 41**
See also CA 1-4R; CANR 3, 39; DLB 40
Redmon, Anne .... **CLC 22**
See also Nightingale, Anne Redmon
See also DLBY 86
Reed, Eliot
See Ambler, Eric
Reed, Ishmael 1938-**CLC 2, 3, 5, 6, 13, 32, 60;
BLC; DAM MULT**
See also BW 2; CA 21-24R; CANR 25, 48; DLB
2, 5, 33, 169; DLBD 8; MTCW
Reed, John (Silas) 1887-1920 .... **TCLC 9**
See also CA 106
Reed, Lou .... **CLC 21**
See also Firbank, Louis
Reeve, Clara 1729-1807 .... **NCLC 19**
See also DLB 39
Reich, Wilhelm 1897-1957 .... **TCLC 57**
Reid, Christopher (John) 1949- .... **CLC 33**
See also CA 140; DLB 40
Reid, Desmond
See Moorcock, Michael (John)
Reid Banks, Lynne 1929-
See Banks, Lynne Reid
See also CA 1-4R; CANR 6, 22, 38; CLR 24;
JRDA; MAICYA; SATA 22, 75
Reilly, William K.
See Creasey, John
Reiner, Max
See Caldwell, (Janet Miriam) Taylor (Holland)

Robinson, Lloyd
  See Silverberg, Robert
Robinson, Marilynne 1944- .... **CLC 25**
  See also CA 116
Robinson, Smokey .... **CLC 21**
  See also Robinson, William, Jr.
Robinson, William, Jr. 1940-
  See Robinson, Smokey
  See also CA 116
Robison, Mary 1949- .... **CLC 42, 98**
  See also CA 113; 116; DLB 130; INT 116
Rod, Edouard 1857-1910 .... **TCLC 52**
Roddenberry, Eugene Wesley 1921-1991
  See Roddenberry, Gene
  See also CA 110; 135; CANR 37; SATA 45;
    SATA-Obit 69
Roddenberry, Gene .... **CLC 17**
  See also Roddenberry, Eugene Wesley
  See also AAYA 5; SATA-Obit 69
Rodgers, Mary 1931- .... **CLC 12**
  See also CA 49-52; CANR 8, 55; CLR 20; INT
    CANR-8; JRDA; MAICYA; SATA 8
Rodgers, W(illiam) R(obert) 1909-1969**CLC 7**
  See also CA 85-88; DLB 20
Rodman, Eric
  See Silverberg, Robert
Rodman, Howard 1920(?)-1985 .... **CLC 65**
  See also CA 118
Rodman, Maia
  See Wojciechowska, Maia (Teresa)
Rodriguez, Claudio 1934- .... **CLC 10**
  See also DLB 134
Roelvaag, O(le) E(dvart) 1876-1931**TCLC 17**
  See also CA 117; DLB 9
Roethke, Theodore (Huebner) 1908-1963**CLC**
  1, 3, 8, 11, 19, 46, 101; DAM POET; PC 15
  See also CA 81-84; CABS 2; CDALB 1941-
    1968; DLB 5; MTCW
Rogers, Thomas Hunton 1927- .... **CLC 57**
  See also CA 89-92; INT 89-92
Rogers, Will(iam Penn Adair) 1879-1935
  TCLC 8, 71; DAM MULT
  See also CA 105; 144; DLB 11; NNAL
Rogin, Gilbert 1929- .... **CLC 18**
  See also CA 65-68; CANR 15
Rohan, Koda .... **TCLC 22**
  See also Koda Shigeyuki
Rohlfs, Anna Katharine Green
  See Green, Anna Katharine
Rohmer, Eric .... **CLC 16**
  See also Scherer, Jean-Marie Maurice
Rohmer, Sax .... **TCLC 28**
  See also Ward, Arthur Henry Sarsfield
  See also DLB 70
Roiphe, Anne (Richardson) 1935- .. **CLC 3, 9**
  See also CA 89-92; CANR 45; DLBY 80; INT
    89-92
Rojas, Fernando de 1465-1541 .... **LC 23**
Rolfe, Frederick (William Serafino Austin
  Lewis Mary) 1860-1913 .... **TCLC 12**
  See also CA 107; DLB 34, 156
Rolland, Romain 1866-1944 .... **TCLC 23**
  See also CA 118; DLB 65
Rolle, Richard c. 1300-c. 1349 ...... **CMLC 21**
  See also DLB 146
Rolvaag, O(le) E(dvart)
  See Roelvaag, O(le) E(dvart)
Romain Arnaud, Saint
  See Aragon, Louis
Romains, Jules 1885-1972 .... **CLC 7**
  See also CA 85-88; CANR 34; DLB 65; MTCW
Romero, Jose Ruben 1890-1952 .... **TCLC 14**
  See also CA 114; 131; HW

Ronsard, Pierre de 1524-1585 ... **LC 6; PC 11**
Rooke, Leon 1934- .. **CLC 25, 34; DAM POP**
  See also CA 25-28R; CANR 23, 53
Roosevelt, Theodore 1858-1919 ..... **TCLC 69**
  See also CA 115; DLB 47
Roper, William 1498-1578 .... **LC 10**
Roquelaure, A. N.
  See Rice, Anne
Rosa, Joao Guimaraes 1908-1967 .... **CLC 23**
  See also CA 89-92; DLB 113
Rose, Wendy 1948-**CLC 85; DAM MULT; PC**
  13
  See also CA 53-56; CANR 5, 51; DLB 175;
    NNAL; SATA 12
Rosen, R. D.
  See Rosen, Richard (Dean)
Rosen, Richard (Dean) 1949- .... **CLC 39**
  See also CA 77-80; CANR 62; INT CANR-30
Rosenberg, Isaac 1890-1918 .... **TCLC 12**
  See also CA 107; DLB 20
Rosenblatt, Joe .... **CLC 15**
  See also Rosenblatt, Joseph
Rosenblatt, Joseph 1933-
  See Rosenblatt, Joe
  See also CA 89-92; INT 89-92
Rosenfeld, Samuel 1896-1963
  See Tzara, Tristan
  See also CA 89-92
Rosenstock, Sami
  See Tzara, Tristan
Rosenstock, Samuel
  See Tzara, Tristan
Rosenthal, M(acha) L(ouis) 1917-1996. **C L C**
  28
  See also CA 1-4R; 152; CAAS 6; CANR 4, 51;
    DLB 5; SATA 59
Ross, Barnaby
  See Dannay, Frederic
Ross, Bernard L.
  See Follett, Ken(neth Martin)
Ross, J. H.
  See Lawrence, T(homas) E(dward)
Ross, Martin
  See Martin, Violet Florence
  See also DLB 135
Ross, (James) Sinclair 1908- **CLC 13; DAC;**
  DAM MST; SSC 24
  See also CA 73-76; DLB 88
Rossetti, Christina (Georgina) 1830-1894
  NCLC 2, 50; DA; DAB; DAC; DAM MST,
  POET; PC 7; WLC
  See also DLB 35, 163; MAICYA; SATA 20
Rossetti, Dante Gabriel 1828-1882.**NCLC 4;**
  DA; DAB; DAC; DAM MST, POET; WLC
  See also CDBLB 1832-1890; DLB 35
Rossner, Judith (Perelman) 1935-**CLC 6, 9, 29**
  See also AITN 2; BEST 90:3; CA 17-20R;
    CANR 18, 51; DLB 6; INT CANR-18;
    MTCW
Rostand, Edmond (Eugene Alexis) 1868-1918
  TCLC 6, 37; DA; DAB; DAC; DAM
  DRAM, MST
  See also CA 104; 126; MTCW
Roth, Henry 1906-1995 ..... **CLC 2, 6, 11, 104**
  See also CA 11-12; 149; CANR 38; CAP 1;
    DLB 28; MTCW
Roth, Philip (Milton) 1933-**CLC 1, 2, 3, 4, 6, 9,**
  15, 22, 31, 47, 66, 86; DA; DAB; DAC;
  DAM MST, NOV, POP; SSC 26; WLC
  See also BEST 90:3; CA 1-4R; CANR 1, 22,
    36, 55; CDALB 1968-1988; DLB 2, 28, 173;
    DLBY 82; MTCW
Rothenberg, Jerome 1931- .... **CLC 6, 57**

  See also CA 45-48; CANR 1; DLB 5
Roumain, Jacques (Jean Baptiste) 1907-1944
  TCLC 19; BLC; DAM MULT
  See also BW 1; CA 117; 125
Rourke, Constance (Mayfield) 1885-1941
  TCLC 12
  See also CA 107; YABC 1
Rousseau, Jean-Baptiste 1671-1741 ...... **LC 9**
Rousseau, Jean-Jacques 1712-1778**LC 14, 36;**
  DA; DAB; DAC; DAM MST; WLC
Roussel, Raymond 1877-1933 .... **TCLC 20**
  See also CA 117
Rovit, Earl (Herbert) 1927- .... **CLC 7**
  See also CA 5-8R; CANR 12
Rowe, Nicholas 1674-1718 .... **LC 8**
  See also DLB 84
Rowley, Ames Dorrance
  See Lovecraft, H(oward) P(hillips)
Rowson, Susanna Haswell 1762(?)-1824
  NCLC 5
  See also DLB 37
Roy, Gabrielle 1909-1983 **CLC 10, 14; DAB;**
  DAC; DAM MST
  See also CA 53-56; 110; CANR 5, 61; DLB 68;
    MTCW
Rozewicz, Tadeusz 1921- .. **CLC 9, 23; DAM**
  POET
  See also CA 108; CANR 36; MTCW
Ruark, Gibbons 1941- .... **CLC 3**
  See also CA 33-36R; CAAS 23; CANR 14, 31,
    57; DLB 120
Rubens, Bernice (Ruth) 1923- .... **CLC 19, 31**
  See also CA 25-28R; CANR 33; DLB 14;
    MTCW
Rubin, Harold
  See Robbins, Harold
Rudkin, (James) David 1936- .... **CLC 14**
  See also CA 89-92; DLB 13
Rudnik, Raphael 1933- .... **CLC 7**
  See also CA 29-32R
Ruffian, M.
  See Hasek, Jaroslav (Matej Frantisek)
Ruiz, Jose Martinez .... **CLC 11**
  See also Martinez Ruiz, Jose
Rukeyser, Muriel 1913-1980**CLC 6, 10, 15, 27;**
  DAM POET; PC 12
  See also CA 5-8R; 93-96; CANR 26, 60; DLB
    48; MTCW; SATA-Obit 22
Rule, Jane (Vance) 1931- .... **CLC 27**
  See also CA 25-28R; CAAS 18; CANR 12; DLB
    60
Rulfo, Juan 1918-1986 ...... **CLC 8, 80; DAM**
  MULT; HLC; SSC 25
  See also CA 85-88; 118; CANR 26; DLB 113;
    HW; MTCW
Rumi, Jalal al-Din 1297-1373 .... **CMLC 20**
Runeberg, Johan 1804-1877 .... **NCLC 41**
Runyon, (Alfred) Damon 1884(?)-1946**T C L C**
  10
  See also CA 107; DLB 11, 86, 171
Rush, Norman 1933- .... **CLC 44**
  See also CA 121; 126; INT 126
Rushdie, (Ahmed) Salman 1947-**CLC 23, 31,**
  55, 100; DAB; DAC; DAM MST, NOV,
  POP; WLCS
  See also BEST 89:3; CA 108; 111; CANR 33,
    56; INT 111; MTCW
Rushforth, Peter (Scott) 1945- .... **CLC 19**
  See also CA 101
Ruskin, John 1819-1900 .... **TCLC 63**
  See also CA 114; 129; CDBLB 1832-1890;
    DLB 55, 163; SATA 24
Russ, Joanna 1937- .... **CLC 15**

See also CA 25-28R; CANR 11, 31; DLB 8; MTCW

Russell, George William 1867-1935
See Baker, Jean H.
See also CA 104; 153; CDBLB 1890-1914; DAM POET

Russell, (Henry) Ken(neth Alfred) 1927-**C L C 16**
See also CA 105

Russell, Willy 1947- .... **CLC 60**

Rutherford, Mark .... **TCLC 25**
See also White, William Hale
See also DLB 18

Ruyslinck, Ward 1929- .... **CLC 14**
See also Belser, Reimond Karel Maria de

Ryan, Cornelius (John) 1920-1974 ..... **CLC 7**
See also CA 69-72; 53-56; CANR 38

Ryan, Michael 1946- .... **CLC 65**
See also CA 49-52; DLBY 82

Ryan, Tim
See Dent, Lester

Rybakov, Anatoli (Naumovich) 1911-**CLC 23, 53**
See also CA 126; 135; SATA 79

Ryder, Jonathan
See Ludlum, Robert

Ryga, George 1932-1987**CLC 14; DAC; DAM MST**
See also CA 101; 124; CANR 43; DLB 60

S. H.
See Hartmann, Sadakichi

S. S.
See Sassoon, Siegfried (Lorraine)

Saba, Umberto 1883-1957 .... **TCLC 33**
See also CA 144; DLB 114

Sabatini, Rafael 1875-1950 .... **TCLC 47**

Sabato, Ernesto (R.) 1911-**CLC 10, 23; DAM MULT; HLC**
See also CA 97-100; CANR 32; DLB 145; HW; MTCW

Sacastru, Martin
See Bioy Casares, Adolfo

Sacher-Masoch, Leopold von 1836(?)-1895 **NCLC 31**

Sachs, Marilyn (Stickle) 1927- .... **CLC 35**
See also AAYA 2; CA 17-20R; CANR 13, 47; CLR 2; JRDA; MAICYA; SAAS 2; SATA 3, 68

Sachs, Nelly 1891-1970 .... **CLC 14, 98**
See also CA 17-18; 25-28R; CAP 2

Sackler, Howard (Oliver) 1929-1982 **CLC 14**
See also CA 61-64; 108; CANR 30; DLB 7

Sacks, Oliver (Wolf) 1933- .... **CLC 67**
See also CA 53-56; CANR 28, 50; INT CANR-28; MTCW

Sadakichi
See Hartmann, Sadakichi

Sade, Donatien Alphonse Francois Comte 1740-1814 .... **NCLC 47**

Sadoff, Ira 1945- .... **CLC 9**
See also CA 53-56; CANR 5, 21; DLB 120

Saetone
See Camus, Albert

Safire, William 1929- .... **CLC 10**
See also CA 17-20R; CANR 31, 54

Sagan, Carl (Edward) 1934-1996 ..... **CLC 30**
See also AAYA 2; CA 25-28R; 155; CANR 11, 36; MTCW; SATA 58; SATA-Obit 94

Sagan, Francoise .... **CLC 3, 6, 9, 17, 36**
See also Quoirez, Francoise
See also DLB 83

Sahgal, Nayantara (Pandit) 1927- .... **CLC 41**
See also CA 9-12R; CANR 11

Saint, H(arry) F. 1941- .... **CLC 50**
See also CA 127

St. Aubin de Teran, Lisa 1953-
See Teran, Lisa St. Aubin de
See also CA 118; 126; INT 126

Saint Birgitta of Sweden c. 1303-1373**C M L C 24**

Sainte-Beuve, Charles Augustin 1804-1869 **NCLC 5**

Saint-Exupery, Antoine (Jean Baptiste Marie Roger) de 1900-1944**TCLC 2, 56; DAM NOV; WLC**
See also CA 108; 132; CLR 10; DLB 72; MAICYA; MTCW; SATA 20

St. John, David
See Hunt, E(verette) Howard, (Jr.)

Saint-John Perse
See Leger, (Marie-Rene Auguste) Alexis Saint-Leger

Saintsbury, George (Edward Bateman) 1845-1933 .... **TCLC 31**
See also CA 160; DLB 57, 149

Sait Faik .... **TCLC 23**
See also Abasiyanik, Sait Faik

Saki .... **TCLC 3; SSC 12**
See also Munro, H(ector) H(ugh)

Sala, George Augustus .... **NCLC 46**

Salama, Hannu 1936- .... **CLC 18**

Salamanca, J(ack) R(ichard) 1922-**CLC 4, 15**
See also CA 25-28R

Sale, J. Kirkpatrick
See Sale, Kirkpatrick

Sale, Kirkpatrick 1937- .... **CLC 68**
See also CA 13-16R; CANR 10

Salinas, Luis Omar 1937- ...... **CLC 90; DAM MULT; HLC**
See also CA 131; DLB 82; HW

Salinas (y Serrano), Pedro 1891(?)-1951 **TCLC 17**
See also CA 117; DLB 134

Salinger, J(erome) D(avid) 1919-**CLC 1, 3, 8, 12, 55, 56; DA; DAB; DAC; DAM MST, NOV, POP; SSC 2, 28; WLC**
See also AAYA 2; CA 5-8R; CANR 39; CDALB 1941-1968; CLR 18; DLB 2, 102, 173; MAICYA; MTCW; SATA 67

Salisbury, John
See Caute, David

Salter, James 1925- .... **CLC 7, 52, 59**
See also CA 73-76; DLB 130

Saltus, Edgar (Everton) 1855-1921 . **TCLC 8**
See also CA 105

Saltykov, Mikhail Evgrafovich 1826-1889 **NCLC 16**

Samarakis, Antonis 1919- .... **CLC 5**
See also CA 25-28R; CAAS 16; CANR 36

Sanchez, Florencio 1875-1910 .... **TCLC 37**
See also CA 153; HW

Sanchez, Luis Rafael 1936- .... **CLC 23**
See also CA 128; DLB 145; HW

Sanchez, Sonia 1934- ..... **CLC 5; BLC; DAM MULT; PC 9**
See also BW 2; CA 33-36R; CANR 24, 49; CLR 18; DLB 41; DLBD 8; MAICYA; MTCW; SATA 22

Sand, George 1804-1876**NCLC 2, 42, 57; DA; DAB; DAC; DAM MST, NOV; WLC**
See also DLB 119

Sandburg, Carl (August) 1878-1967**CLC 1, 4, 10, 15, 35; DA; DAB; DAC; DAM MST, POET; PC 2; WLC**
See also CA 5-8R; 25-28R; CANR 35; CDALB 1865-1917; DLB 17, 54; MAICYA; MTCW;

SATA 8

Sandburg, Charles
See Sandburg, Carl (August)

Sandburg, Charles A.
See Sandburg, Carl (August)

Sanders, (James) Ed(ward) 1939- .... **CLC 53**
See also CA 13-16R; CAAS 21; CANR 13, 44; DLB 16

Sanders, Lawrence 1920-**CLC 41; DAM POP**
See also BEST 89:4; CA 81-84; CANR 33, 62; MTCW

Sanders, Noah
See Blount, Roy (Alton), Jr.

Sanders, Winston P.
See Anderson, Poul (William)

Sandoz, Mari(e Susette) 1896-1966 .. **CLC 28**
See also CA 1-4R; 25-28R; CANR 17; DLB 9; MTCW; SATA 5

Saner, Reg(inald Anthony) 1931- .... **CLC 9**
See also CA 65-68

Sannazaro, Jacopo 1456(?)-1530 .... **LC 8**

Sansom, William 1912-1976 **CLC 2, 6; DAM NOV; SSC 21**
See also CA 5-8R; 65-68; CANR 42; DLB 139; MTCW

Santayana, George 1863-1952 .... **TCLC 40**
See also CA 115; DLB 54, 71; DLBD 13

Santiago, Danny .... **CLC 33**
See also James, Daniel (Lewis)
See also DLB 122

Santmyer, Helen Hoover 1895-1986 . **CLC 33**
See also CA 1-4R; 118; CANR 15, 33; DLBY 84; MTCW

Santoka, Taneda 1882-1940 .... **TCLC 72**

Santos, Bienvenido N(uqui) 1911-1996 . **C L C 22; DAM MULT**
See also CA 101; 151; CANR 19, 46

Sapper .... **TCLC 44**
See also McNeile, Herman Cyril

Sapphire 1950- .... **CLC 99**

Sappho fl. 6th cent. B.C.- ...... **CMLC 3; DAM POET; PC 5**
See also DLB 176

Sarduy, Severo 1937-1993 .... **CLC 6, 97**
See also CA 89-92; 142; CANR 58; DLB 113; HW

Sargeson, Frank 1903-1982 .... **CLC 31**
See also CA 25-28R; 106; CANR 38

Sarmiento, Felix Ruben Garcia
See Dario, Ruben

Saroyan, William 1908-1981**CLC 1, 8, 10, 29, 34, 56; DA; DAB; DAC; DAM DRAM, MST, NOV; SSC 21; WLC**
See also CA 5-8R; 103; CANR 30; DLB 7, 9, 86; DLBY 81; MTCW; SATA 23; SATA-Obit 24

Sarraute, Nathalie 1900-**CLC 1, 2, 4, 8, 10, 31, 80**
See also CA 9-12R; CANR 23; DLB 83; MTCW

Sarton, (Eleanor) May 1912-1995**CLC 4, 14, 49, 91; DAM POET**
See also CA 1-4R; 149; CANR 1, 34, 55; DLB 48; DLBY 81; INT CANR-34; MTCW; SATA 36; SATA-Obit 86

Sartre, Jean-Paul 1905-1980**CLC 1, 4, 7, 9, 13, 18, 24, 44, 50, 52; DA; DAB; DAC; DAM DRAM, MST, NOV; DC 3; WLC**
See also CA 9-12R; 97-100; CANR 21; DLB 72; MTCW

Sassoon, Siegfried (Lorraine) 1886-1967**C L C 36; DAB; DAM MST, NOV, POET; PC 12**
See also CA 104; 25-28R; CANR 36; DLB 20; MTCW

Satterfield, Charles
　See Pohl, Frederik
Saul, John (W. III) 1942-**CLC 46; DAM NOV, POP**
　See also AAYA 10; BEST 90:4; CA 81-84; CANR 16, 40
Saunders, Caleb
　See Heinlein, Robert A(nson)
Saura (Atares), Carlos 1932- .... **CLC 20**
　See also CA 114; 131; HW
Sauser-Hall, Frederic 1887-1961 ...... **CLC 18**
　See also Cendrars, Blaise
　See also CA 102; 93-96; CANR 36, 62; MTCW
Saussure, Ferdinand de 1857-1913 **TCLC 49**
Savage, Catharine
　See Brosman, Catharine Savage
Savage, Thomas 1915- .... **CLC 40**
　See also CA 126; 132; CAAS 15; INT 132
Savan, Glenn 19(?)- .... **CLC 50**
Sayers, Dorothy L(eigh) 1893-1957 **TCLC 2, 15; DAM POP**
　See also CA 104; 119; CANR 60; CDBLB 1914-1945; DLB 10, 36, 77, 100; MTCW
Sayers, Valerie 1952- .... **CLC 50**
　See also CA 134; CANR 61
Sayles, John (Thomas) 1950- . **CLC 7, 10, 14**
　See also CA 57-60; CANR 41; DLB 44
Scammell, Michael 1935- .... **CLC 34**
　See also CA 156
Scannell, Vernon 1922- .... **CLC 49**
　See also CA 5-8R; CANR 8, 24, 57; DLB 27; SATA 59
Scarlett, Susan
　See Streatfeild, (Mary) Noel
Schaeffer, Susan Fromberg 1941- **CLC 6, 11, 22**
　See also CA 49-52; CANR 18; DLB 28; MTCW; SATA 22
Schary, Jill
　See Robinson, Jill
Schell, Jonathan 1943- .... **CLC 35**
　See also CA 73-76; CANR 12
Schelling, Friedrich Wilhelm Joseph von 1775-1854 .... **NCLC 30**
　See also DLB 90
Schendel, Arthur van 1874-1946 ... **TCLC 56**
Scherer, Jean-Marie Maurice 1920-
　See Rohmer, Eric
　See also CA 110
Schevill, James (Erwin) 1920- .... **CLC 7**
　See also CA 5-8R; CAAS 12
Schiller, Friedrich 1759-1805**NCLC 39; DAM DRAM**
　See also DLB 94
Schisgal, Murray (Joseph) 1926- .... **CLC 6**
　See also CA 21-24R; CANR 48
Schlee, Ann 1934- .... **CLC 35**
　See also CA 101; CANR 29; SATA 44; SATA-Brief 36
Schlegel, August Wilhelm von 1767-1845 **NCLC 15**
　See also DLB 94
Schlegel, Friedrich 1772-1829 .... **NCLC 45**
　See also DLB 90
Schlegel, Johann Elias (von) 1719(?)-1749**LC 5**
Schlesinger, Arthur M(eier), Jr. 1917-**CLC 84**
　See also AITN 1; CA 1-4R; CANR 1, 28, 58; DLB 17; INT CANR-28; MTCW; SATA 61
Schmidt, Arno (Otto) 1914-1979 ...... **CLC 56**
　See also CA 128; 109; DLB 69
Schmitz, Aron Hector 1861-1928
　See Svevo, Italo

　See also CA 104; 122; MTCW
Schnackenberg, Gjertrud 1953- .... **CLC 40**
　See also CA 116; DLB 120
Schneider, Leonard Alfred 1925-1966
　See Bruce, Lenny
　See also CA 89-92
Schnitzler, Arthur 1862-1931**TCLC 4; SSC 15**
　See also CA 104; DLB 81, 118
Schoenberg, Arnold 1874-1951 ...... **TCLC 75**
　See also CA 109
Schonberg, Arnold
　See Schoenberg, Arnold
Schopenhauer, Arthur 1788-1860 . **NCLC 51**
　See also DLB 90
Schor, Sandra (M.) 1932(?)-1990 ...... **CLC 65**
　See also CA 132
Schorer, Mark 1908-1977 .... **CLC 9**
　See also CA 5-8R; 73-76; CANR 7; DLB 103
Schrader, Paul (Joseph) 1946- .... **CLC 26**
　See also CA 37-40R; CANR 41; DLB 44
Schreiner, Olive (Emilie Albertina) 1855-1920 **TCLC 9**
　See also CA 105; DLB 18, 156
Schulberg, Budd (Wilson) 1914- ... **CLC 7, 48**
　See also CA 25-28R; CANR 19; DLB 6, 26, 28; DLBY 81
Schulz, Bruno 1892-1942**TCLC 5, 51; SSC 13**
　See also CA 115; 123
Schulz, Charles M(onroe) 1922- .... **CLC 12**
　See also CA 9-12R; CANR 6; INT CANR-6; SATA 10
Schumacher, E(rnst) F(riedrich) 1911-1977 **CLC 80**
　See also CA 81-84; 73-76; CANR 34
Schuyler, James Marcus 1923-1991**CLC 5, 23; DAM POET**
　See also CA 101; 134; DLB 5, 169; INT 101
Schwartz, Delmore (David) 1913-1966**CLC 2, 4, 10, 45, 87; PC 8**
　See also CA 17-18; 25-28R; CANR 35; CAP 2; DLB 28, 48; MTCW
Schwartz, Ernst
　See Ozu, Yasujiro
Schwartz, John Burnham 1965- .... **CLC 59**
　See also CA 132
Schwartz, Lynne Sharon 1939- .... **CLC 31**
　See also CA 103; CANR 44
Schwartz, Muriel A.
　See Eliot, T(homas) S(tearns)
Schwarz-Bart, Andre 1928- .... **CLC 2, 4**
　See also CA 89-92
Schwarz-Bart, Simone 1938- .... **CLC 7**
　See also BW 2; CA 97-100
Schwob, (Mayer Andre) Marcel 1867-1905 **TCLC 20**
　See also CA 117; DLB 123
Sciascia, Leonardo 1921-1989 . **CLC 8, 9, 41**
　See also CA 85-88; 130; CANR 35; DLB 177; MTCW
Scoppettone, Sandra 1936- .... **CLC 26**
　See also AAYA 11; CA 5-8R; CANR 41; SATA 9, 92
Scorsese, Martin 1942- .... **CLC 20, 89**
　See also CA 110; 114; CANR 46
Scotland, Jay
　See Jakes, John (William)
Scott, Duncan Campbell 1862-1947**TCLC 6; DAC**
　See also CA 104; 153; DLB 92
Scott, Evelyn 1893-1963 .... **CLC 43**
　See also CA 104; 112; DLB 9, 48
Scott, F(rancis) R(eginald) 1899-1985**CLC 22**
　See also CA 101; 114; DLB 88; INT 101

Scott, Frank
　See Scott, F(rancis) R(eginald)
Scott, Joanna 1960- .... **CLC 50**
　See also CA 126; CANR 53
Scott, Paul (Mark) 1920-1978 .... **CLC 9, 60**
　See also CA 81-84; 77-80; CANR 33; DLB 14; MTCW
Scott, Walter 1771-1832**NCLC 15; DA; DAB; DAC; DAM MST, NOV, POET; PC 13; WLC**
　See also AAYA 22; CDBLB 1789-1832; DLB 93, 107, 116, 144, 159; YABC 2
Scribe, (Augustin) Eugene 1791-1861 **NCLC 16; DAM DRAM; DC 5**
Scrum, R.
　See Crumb, R(obert)
Scudery, Madeleine de 1607-1701 .... **LC 2**
Scum
　See Crumb, R(obert)
Scumbag, Little Bobby
　See Crumb, R(obert)
Seabrook, John
　See Hubbard, L(afayette) Ron(ald)
Sealy, I. Allan 1951- .... **CLC 55**
Search, Alexander
　See Pessoa, Fernando (Antonio Nogueira)
Sebastian, Lee
　See Silverberg, Robert
Sebastian Owl
　See Thompson, Hunter S(tockton)
Sebestyen, Ouida 1924- .... **CLC 30**
　See also AAYA 8; CA 107; CANR 40; CLR 17; JRDA; MAICYA; SAAS 10; SATA 39
Secundus, H. Scriblerus
　See Fielding, Henry
Sedges, John
　See Buck, Pearl S(ydenstricker)
Sedgwick, Catharine Maria 1789-1867**NCLC 19**
　See also DLB 1, 74
Seelye, John 1931- .... **CLC 7**
Seferiades, Giorgos Stylianou 1900-1971
　See Seferis, George
　See also CA 5-8R; 33-36R; CANR 5, 36; MTCW
Seferis, George .... **CLC 5, 11**
　See also Seferiades, Giorgos Stylianou
Segal, Erich (Wolf) 1937- . **CLC 3, 10; DAM POP**
　See also BEST 89:1; CA 25-28R; CANR 20, 36; DLBY 86; INT CANR-20; MTCW
Seger, Bob 1945- .... **CLC 35**
Seghers, Anna .... **CLC 7**
　See also Radvanyi, Netty
　See also DLB 69
Seidel, Frederick (Lewis) 1936- .... **CLC 18**
　See also CA 13-16R; CANR 8; DLBY 84
Seifert, Jaroslav 1901-1986 .. **CLC 34, 44, 93**
　See also CA 127; MTCW
Sei Shonagon c. 966-1017(?) .... **CMLC 6**
Selby, Hubert, Jr. 1928-**CLC 1, 2, 4, 8; SSC 20**
　See also CA 13-16R; CANR 33; DLB 2
Selzer, Richard 1928- .... **CLC 74**
　See also CA 65-68; CANR 14
Sembene, Ousmane
　See Ousmane, Sembene
Senancour, Etienne Pivert de 1770-1846 **NCLC 16**
　See also DLB 119
Sender, Ramon (Jose) 1902-1982**CLC 8; DAM MULT; HLC**
　See also CA 5-8R; 105; CANR 8; HW; MTCW
Seneca, Lucius Annaeus 4B.C.-65 . **CMLC 6;**

DAM DRAM; DC 5

Senghor, Leopold Sedar 1906-**CLC 54; BLC; DAM MULT, POET**
See also BW 2; CA 116; 125; CANR 47; MTCW

Serling, (Edward) Rod(man) 1924-1975 **C L C 30**
See also AAYA 14; AITN 1; CA 65-68; 57-60; DLB 26

Serna, Ramon Gomez de la
See Gomez de la Serna, Ramon

Serpieres
See Guillevic, (Eugene)

Service, Robert
See Service, Robert W(illiam)
See also DAB; DLB 92

Service, Robert W(illiam) 1874(?)-1958**TCLC 15; DA; DAC; DAM MST, POET; WLC**
See also Service, Robert
See also CA 115; 140; SATA 20

Seth, Vikram 1952-**CLC 43, 90; DAM MULT**
See also CA 121; 127; CANR 50; DLB 120; INT 127

Seton, Cynthia Propper 1926-1982 .. **CLC 27**
See also CA 5-8R; 108; CANR 7

Seton, Ernest (Evan) Thompson 1860-1946 **TCLC 31**
See also CA 109; DLB 92; DLBD 13; JRDA; SATA 18

Seton-Thompson, Ernest
See Seton, Ernest (Evan) Thompson

Settle, Mary Lee 1918- .... **CLC 19, 61**
See also CA 89-92; CAAS 1; CANR 44; DLB 6; INT 89-92

Seuphor, Michel
See Arp, Jean

Sevigne, Marie (de Rabutin-Chantal) Marquise de 1626-1696 .... **LC 11**

Sewall, Samuel 1652-1730 .... **LC 38**
See also DLB 24

Sexton, Anne (Harvey) 1928-1974**CLC 2, 4, 6, 8, 10, 15, 53; DA; DAB; DAC; DAM MST, POET; PC 2; WLC**
See also CA 1-4R; 53-56; CABS 2; CANR 3, 36; CDALB 1941-1968; DLB 5, 169; MTCW; SATA 10

Shaara, Michael (Joseph, Jr.) 1929-1988**C L C 15; DAM POP**
See also AITN 1; CA 102; 125; CANR 52; DLBY 83

Shackleton, C. C.
See Aldiss, Brian W(ilson)

Shacochis, Bob .... **CLC 39**
See also Shacochis, Robert G.

Shacochis, Robert G. 1951-
See Shacochis, Bob
See also CA 119; 124; INT 124

Shaffer, Anthony (Joshua) 1926- .... **CLC 19; DAM DRAM**
See also CA 110; 116; DLB 13

Shaffer, Peter (Levin) 1926-**CLC 5, 14, 18, 37, 60; DAB; DAM DRAM, MST; DC 7**
See also CA 25-28R; CANR 25, 47; CDBLB 1960 to Present; DLB 13; MTCW

Shakey, Bernard
See Young, Neil

Shalamov, Varlam (Tikhonovich) 1907(?)-1982 **CLC 18**
See also CA 129; 105

Shamlu, Ahmad 1925- .... **CLC 10**

Shammas, Anton 1951- .... **CLC 55**

Shange, Ntozake 1948-**CLC 8, 25, 38, 74; BLC; DAM DRAM, MULT; DC 3**
See also AAYA 9; BW 2; CA 85-88; CABS 3;

CANR 27, 48; DLB 38; MTCW

Shanley, John Patrick 1950- .... **CLC 75**
See also CA 128; 133

Shapcott, Thomas W(illiam) 1935- ... **CLC 38**
See also CA 69-72; CANR 49

Shapiro, Jane .... **CLC 76**

Shapiro, Karl (Jay) 1913- ... **CLC 4, 8, 15, 53**
See also CA 1-4R; CAAS 6; CANR 1, 36; DLB 48; MTCW

Sharp, William 1855-1905 .... **TCLC 39**
See also CA 160; DLB 156

Sharpe, Thomas Ridley 1928-
See Sharpe, Tom
See also CA 114; 122; INT 122

Sharpe, Tom .... **CLC 36**
See also Sharpe, Thomas Ridley
See also DLB 14

Shaw, Bernard .... **TCLC 45**
See also Shaw, George Bernard
See also BW 1

Shaw, G. Bernard
See Shaw, George Bernard

Shaw, George Bernard 1856-1950**TCLC 3, 9, 21; DA; DAB; DAC; DAM DRAM, MST; WLC**
See also Shaw, Bernard
See also CA 104; 128; CDBLB 1914-1945; DLB 10, 57; MTCW

Shaw, Henry Wheeler 1818-1885 .. **NCLC 15**
See also DLB 11

Shaw, Irwin 1913-1984 **CLC 7, 23, 34; DAM DRAM, POP**
See also AITN 1; CA 13-16R; 112; CANR 21; CDALB 1941-1968; DLB 6, 102; DLBY 84; MTCW

Shaw, Robert 1927-1978 .... **CLC 5**
See also AITN 1; CA 1-4R; 81-84; CANR 4; DLB 13, 14

Shaw, T. E.
See Lawrence, T(homas) E(dward)

Shawn, Wallace 1943- .... **CLC 41**
See also CA 112

Shea, Lisa 1953- .... **CLC 86**
See also CA 147

Sheed, Wilfrid (John Joseph) 1930-**CLC 2, 4, 10, 53**
See also CA 65-68; CANR 30; DLB 6; MTCW

Sheldon, Alice Hastings Bradley 1915(?)-1987
See Tiptree, James, Jr.
See also CA 108; 122; CANR 34; INT 108; MTCW

Sheldon, John
See Bloch, Robert (Albert)

Shelley, Mary Wollstonecraft (Godwin) 1797-1851**NCLC 14, 59; DA; DAB; DAC; DAM MST, NOV; WLC**
See also AAYA 20; CDBLB 1789-1832; DLB 110, 116, 159, 178; SATA 29

Shelley, Percy Bysshe 1792-1822 . **NCLC 18; DA; DAB; DAC; DAM MST, POET; PC 14; WLC**
See also CDBLB 1789-1832; DLB 96, 110, 158

Shepard, Jim 1956- .... **CLC 36**
See also CA 137; CANR 59; SATA 90

Shepard, Lucius 1947- .... **CLC 34**
See also CA 128; 141

Shepard, Sam 1943- **CLC 4, 6, 17, 34, 41, 44; DAM DRAM; DC 5**
See also AAYA 1; CA 69-72; CABS 3; CANR 22; DLB 7; MTCW

Shepherd, Michael
See Ludlum, Robert

Sherburne, Zoa (Morin) 1912- .... **CLC 30**

See also AAYA 13; CA 1-4R; CANR 3, 37; MAICYA; SAAS 18; SATA 3

Sheridan, Frances 1724-1766 .... **LC 7**
See also DLB 39, 84

Sheridan, Richard Brinsley 1751-1816**NCLC 5; DA; DAB; DAC; DAM DRAM, MST; DC 1; WLC**
See also CDBLB 1660-1789; DLB 89

Sherman, Jonathan Marc .... **CLC 55**

Sherman, Martin 1941(?)- .... **CLC 19**
See also CA 116; 123

Sherwin, Judith Johnson 1936- .... **CLC 7, 15**
See also CA 25-28R; CANR 34

Sherwood, Frances 1940- .... **CLC 81**
See also CA 146

Sherwood, Robert E(mmet) 1896-1955**T C L C 3; DAM DRAM**
See also CA 104; 153; DLB 7, 26

Shestov, Lev 1866-1938 .... **TCLC 56**

Shevchenko, Taras 1814-1861 .... **NCLC 54**

Shiel, M(atthew) P(hipps) 1865-1947**TCLC 8**
See also Holmes, Gordon
See also CA 106; 160; DLB 153

Shields, Carol 1935- .... **CLC 91; DAC**
See also CA 81-84; CANR 51

Shields, David 1956- .... **CLC 97**
See also CA 124; CANR 48

Shiga, Naoya 1883-1971 ...... **CLC 33; SSC 23**
See also CA 101; 33-36R; DLB 180

Shilts, Randy 1951-1994 .... **CLC 85**
See also AAYA 19; CA 115; 127; 144; CANR 45; INT 127

Shimazaki, Haruki 1872-1943
See Shimazaki Toson
See also CA 105; 134

Shimazaki Toson 1872-1943 .... **TCLC 5**
See also Shimazaki, Haruki
See also DLB 180

Sholokhov, Mikhail (Aleksandrovich) 1905-1984 .... **CLC 7, 15**
See also CA 101; 112; MTCW; SATA-Obit 36

Shone, Patric
See Hanley, James

Shreve, Susan Richards 1939- .... **CLC 23**
See also CA 49-52; CAAS 5; CANR 5, 38; MAICYA; SATA 46, 95; SATA-Brief 41

Shue, Larry 1946-1985**CLC 52; DAM DRAM**
See also CA 145; 117

Shu-Jen, Chou 1881-1936
See Lu Hsun
See also CA 104

Shulman, Alix Kates 1932- .... **CLC 2, 10**
See also CA 29-32R; CANR 43; SATA 7

Shuster, Joe 1914- .... **CLC 21**

Shute, Nevil .... **CLC 30**
See also Norway, Nevil Shute

Shuttle, Penelope (Diane) 1947- .... **CLC 7**
See also CA 93-96; CANR 39; DLB 14, 40

Sidney, Mary 1561-1621 .... **LC 19, 39**

Sidney, Sir Philip 1554-1586 **LC 19, 39; DA; DAB; DAC; DAM MST, POET**
See also CDBLB Before 1660; DLB 167

Siegel, Jerome 1914-1996 .... **CLC 21**
See also CA 116; 151

Siegel, Jerry
See Siegel, Jerome

Sienkiewicz, Henryk (Adam Alexander Pius) 1846-1916 .... **TCLC 3**
See also CA 104; 134

Sierra, Gregorio Martinez
See Martinez Sierra, Gregorio

Sierra, Maria (de la O'LeJarraga) Martinez
See Martinez Sierra, Maria (de la O'LeJarraga)

See Smith, Martin Cruz
Smith, Martin Cruz 1942- ..... **CLC 25; DAM MULT, POP**
See also BEST 89:4; CA 85-88; CANR 6, 23, 43; INT CANR-23; NNAL
Smith, Mary-Ann Tirone 1944- .... **CLC 39**
See also CA 118; 136
Smith, Patti 1946- .... **CLC 12**
See also CA 93-96
Smith, Pauline (Urmson) 1882-1959 **TCLC 25**
Smith, Rosamond
See Oates, Joyce Carol
Smith, Sheila Kaye
See Kaye-Smith, Sheila
Smith, Stevie .... **CLC 3, 8, 25, 44; PC 12**
See also Smith, Florence Margaret
See also DLB 20
Smith, Wilbur (Addison) 1933- .... **CLC 33**
See also CA 13-16R; CANR 7, 46; MTCW
Smith, William Jay 1918- .... **CLC 6**
See also CA 5-8R; CANR 44; DLB 5; MAICYA; SAAS 22; SATA 2, 68
Smith, Woodrow Wilson
See Kuttner, Henry
Smolenskin, Peretz 1842-1885 .... **NCLC 30**
Smollett, Tobias (George) 1721-1771 .... **LC 2**
See also CDBLB 1660-1789; DLB 39, 104
Snodgrass, W(illiam) D(e Witt) 1926- **CLC 2, 6, 10, 18, 68; DAM POET**
See also CA 1-4R; CANR 6, 36; DLB 5; MTCW
Snow, C(harles) P(ercy) 1905-1980 **CLC 1, 4, 6, 9, 13, 19; DAM NOV**
See also CA 5-8R; 101; CANR 28; CDBLB 1945-1960; DLB 15, 77; MTCW
Snow, Frances Compton
See Adams, Henry (Brooks)
Snyder, Gary (Sherman) 1930- **CLC 1, 2, 5, 9, 32; DAM POET**
See also CA 17-20R; CANR 30, 60; DLB 5, 16, 165
Snyder, Zilpha Keatley 1927- .... **CLC 17**
See also AAYA 15; CA 9-12R; CANR 38; CLR 31; JRDA; MAICYA; SAAS 2; SATA 1, 28, 75
Soares, Bernardo
See Pessoa, Fernando (Antonio Nogueira)
Sobh, A.
See Shamlu, Ahmad
Sobol, Joshua .... **CLC 60**
Soderberg, Hjalmar 1869-1941 ..... **TCLC 39**
Sodergran, Edith (Irene)
See Soedergran, Edith (Irene)
Soedergran, Edith (Irene) 1892-1923 **T C L C 31**
Softly, Edgar
See Lovecraft, H(oward) P(hillips)
Softly, Edward
See Lovecraft, H(oward) P(hillips)
Sokolov, Raymond 1941- .... **CLC 7**
See also CA 85-88
Solo, Jay
See Ellison, Harlan (Jay)
Sologub, Fyodor .... **TCLC 9**
See also Teternikov, Fyodor Kuzmich
Solomons, Ikey Esquir
See Thackeray, William Makepeace
Solomos, Dionysios 1798-1857 .... **NCLC 15**
Solwoska, Mara
See French, Marilyn
Solzhenitsyn, Aleksandr I(sayevich) 1918- **CLC 1, 2, 4, 7, 9, 10, 18, 26, 34, 78; DA; DAB; DAC; DAM MST, NOV; WLC**
See also AITN 1; CA 69-72; CANR 40; MTCW

Somers, Jane
See Lessing, Doris (May)
Somerville, Edith 1858-1949 .... **TCLC 51**
See also DLB 135
Somerville & Ross
See Martin, Violet Florence; Somerville, Edith
Sommer, Scott 1951- .... **CLC 25**
See also CA 106
Sondheim, Stephen (Joshua) 1930- . **CLC 30, 39; DAM DRAM**
See also AAYA 11; CA 103; CANR 47
Sontag, Susan 1933- **CLC 1, 2, 10, 13, 31, 105; DAM POP**
See also CA 17-20R; CANR 25, 51; DLB 2, 67; MTCW
Sophocles 496(?)B.C.-406(?)B.C. ... **CMLC 2; DA; DAB; DAC; DAM DRAM, MST; DC 1; WLCS**
See also DLB 176
Sordello 1189-1269 .... **CMLC 15**
Sorel, Julia
See Drexler, Rosalyn
Sorrentino, Gilbert 1929- **CLC 3, 7, 14, 22, 40**
See also CA 77-80; CANR 14, 33; DLB 5, 173; DLBY 80; INT CANR-14
Soto, Gary 1952- **CLC 32, 80; DAM MULT; HLC**
See also AAYA 10; CA 119; 125; CANR 50; CLR 38; DLB 82; HW; INT 125; JRDA; SATA 80
Soupault, Philippe 1897-1990 .... **CLC 68**
See also CA 116; 147; 131
Souster, (Holmes) Raymond 1921- **CLC 5, 14; DAC; DAM POET**
See also CA 13-16R; CAAS 14; CANR 13, 29, 53; DLB 88; SATA 63
Southern, Terry 1924(?)-1995 .... **CLC 7**
See also CA 1-4R; 150; CANR 1, 55; DLB 2
Southey, Robert 1774-1843 .... **NCLC 8**
See also DLB 93, 107, 142; SATA 54
Southworth, Emma Dorothy Eliza Nevitte 1819-1899 .... **NCLC 26**
Souza, Ernest
See Scott, Evelyn
Soyinka, Wole 1934- **CLC 3, 5, 14, 36, 44; BLC; DA; DAB; DAC; DAM DRAM, MST, MULT; DC 2; WLC**
See also BW 2; CA 13-16R; CANR 27, 39; DLB 125; MTCW
Spackman, W(illiam) M(ode) 1905-1990 **C L C 46**
See also CA 81-84; 132
Spacks, Barry (Bernard) 1931- .... **CLC 14**
See also CA 154; CANR 33; DLB 105
Spanidou, Irini 1946- .... **CLC 44**
Spark, Muriel (Sarah) 1918- **CLC 2, 3, 5, 8, 13, 18, 40, 94; DAB; DAC; DAM MST, NOV; SSC 10**
See also CA 5-8R; CANR 12, 36; CDBLB 1945-1960; DLB 15, 139; INT CANR-12; MTCW
Spaulding, Douglas
See Bradbury, Ray (Douglas)
Spaulding, Leonard
See Bradbury, Ray (Douglas)
Spence, J. A. D.
See Eliot, T(homas) S(tearns)
Spencer, Elizabeth 1921- .... **CLC 22**
See also CA 13-16R; CANR 32; DLB 6; MTCW; SATA 14
Spencer, Leonard G.
See Silverberg, Robert
Spencer, Scott 1945- .... **CLC 30**
See also CA 113; CANR 51; DLBY 86

Spender, Stephen (Harold) 1909-1995 **CLC 1, 2, 5, 10, 41, 91; DAM POET**
See also CA 9-12R; 149; CANR 31, 54; CDBLB 1945-1960; DLB 20; MTCW
Spengler, Oswald (Arnold Gottfried) 1880-1936 **TCLC 25**
See also CA 118
Spenser, Edmund 1552(?)-1599 **LC 5, 39; DA; DAB; DAC; DAM MST, POET; PC 8; WLC**
See also CDBLB Before 1660; DLB 167
Spicer, Jack 1925-1965 **CLC 8, 18, 72; DAM POET**
See also CA 85-88; DLB 5, 16
Spiegelman, Art 1948- .... **CLC 76**
See also AAYA 10; CA 125; CANR 41, 55
Spielberg, Peter 1929- .... **CLC 6**
See also CA 5-8R; CANR 4, 48; DLBY 81
Spielberg, Steven 1947- .... **CLC 20**
See also AAYA 8; CA 77-80; CANR 32; SATA 32
Spillane, Frank Morrison 1918-
See Spillane, Mickey
See also CA 25-28R; CANR 28; MTCW; SATA 66
Spillane, Mickey .... **CLC 3, 13**
See also Spillane, Frank Morrison
Spinoza, Benedictus de 1632-1677 .... **LC 9**
Spinrad, Norman (Richard) 1940- ... **CLC 46**
See also CA 37-40R; CAAS 19; CANR 20; DLB 8; INT CANR-20
Spitteler, Carl (Friedrich Georg) 1845-1924 **TCLC 12**
See also CA 109; DLB 129
Spivack, Kathleen (Romola Drucker) 1938- **CLC 6**
See also CA 49-52
Spoto, Donald 1941- .... **CLC 39**
See also CA 65-68; CANR 11, 57
Springsteen, Bruce (F.) 1949- .... **CLC 17**
See also CA 111
Spurling, Hilary 1940- .... **CLC 34**
See also CA 104; CANR 25, 52
Spyker, John Howland
See Elman, Richard
Squires, (James) Radcliffe 1917-1993 **CLC 51**
See also CA 1-4R; 140; CANR 6, 21
Srivastava, Dhanpat Rai 1880(?)-1936
See Premchand
See also CA 118
Stacy, Donald
See Pohl, Frederik
Stael, Germaine de
See Stael-Holstein, Anne Louise Germaine Necker Baronn
See also DLB 119
Stael-Holstein, Anne Louise Germaine Necker Baronn 1766-1817 .... **NCLC 3**
See also Stael, Germaine de
Stafford, Jean 1915-1979 **CLC 4, 7, 19, 68; SSC 26**
See also CA 1-4R; 85-88; CANR 3; DLB 2, 173; MTCW; SATA-Obit 22
Stafford, William (Edgar) 1914-1993 **CLC 4, 7, 29; DAM POET**
See also CA 5-8R; 142; CAAS 3; CANR 5, 22; DLB 5; INT CANR-22
Stagnelius, Eric Johan 1793-1823 . **NCLC 61**
Staines, Trevor
See Brunner, John (Kilian Houston)
Stairs, Gordon
See Austin, Mary (Hunter)
Stannard, Martin 1947- .... **CLC 44**

See Chekhov, Anton (Pavlovich)

Tchicaya, Gerald Felix 1931-1988 .. **CLC 101**
  See also CA 129; 125

Tchicaya U Tam'si
  See Tchicaya, Gerald Felix

Teasdale, Sara 1884-1933 .... **TCLC 4**
  See also CA 104; DLB 45; SATA 32

Tegner, Esaias 1782-1846 .... **NCLC 2**

Teilhard de Chardin, (Marie Joseph) Pierre
  1881-1955 .... **TCLC 9**
  See also CA 105

Temple, Ann
  See Mortimer, Penelope (Ruth)

Tennant, Emma (Christina) 1937-**CLC 13, 52**
  See also CA 65-68; CAAS 9; CANR 10, 38,
  59; DLB 14

Tenneshaw, S. M.
  See Silverberg, Robert

Tennyson, Alfred 1809-1892 ... **NCLC 30, 65;**
  DA; DAB; DAC; DAM MST, POET; PC
  6; WLC
  See also CDBLB 1832-1890; DLB 32

Teran, Lisa St. Aubin de .... **CLC 36**
  See also St. Aubin de Teran, Lisa

Terence 195(?)B.C.-159B.C. **CMLC 14; DC 7**

Teresa de Jesus, St. 1515-1582 .... **LC 18**

Terkel, Louis 1912-
  See Terkel, Studs
  See also CA 57-60; CANR 18, 45; MTCW

Terkel, Studs .... **CLC 38**
  See also Terkel, Louis
  See also AITN 1

Terry, C. V.
  See Slaughter, Frank G(ill)

Terry, Megan 1932- .... **CLC 19**
  See also CA 77-80; CABS 3; CANR 43; DLB 7

Tertz, Abram
  See Sinyavsky, Andrei (Donatevich)

Tesich, Steve 1943(?)-1996 .... **CLC 40, 69**
  See also CA 105; 152; DLBY 83

Teternikov, Fyodor Kuzmich 1863-1927
  See Sologub, Fyodor
  See also CA 104

Tevis, Walter 1928-1984 .... **CLC 42**
  See also CA 113

Tey, Josephine .... **TCLC 14**
  See also Mackintosh, Elizabeth
  See also DLB 77

Thackeray, William Makepeace 1811-1863
  NCLC 5, 14, 22, 43; DA; DAB; DAC; DAM
  MST, NOV; WLC
  See also CDBLB 1832-1890; DLB 21, 55, 159,
  163; SATA 23

Thakura, Ravindranatha
  See Tagore, Rabindranath

Tharoor, Shashi 1956- .... **CLC 70**
  See also CA 141

Thelwell, Michael Miles 1939- .... **CLC 22**
  See also BW 2; CA 101

Theobald, Lewis, Jr.
  See Lovecraft, H(oward) P(hillips)

Theodorescu, Ion N. 1880-1967
  See Arghezi, Tudor
  See also CA 116

Theriault, Yves 1915-1983 .... **CLC 79; DAC;**
  DAM MST
  See also CA 102; DLB 88

Theroux, Alexander (Louis) 1939- **CLC 2, 25**
  See also CA 85-88; CANR 20

Theroux, Paul (Edward) 1941- **CLC 5, 8, 11,**
  15, 28, 46; DAM POP
  See also BEST 89:4; CA 33-36R; CANR 20,
  45; DLB 2; MTCW; SATA 44

Thesen, Sharon 1946- .... **CLC 56**

Thevenin, Denis
  See Duhamel, Georges

Thibault, Jacques Anatole Francois 1844-1924
  See France, Anatole
  See also CA 106; 127; DAM NOV; MTCW

Thiele, Colin (Milton) 1920- .... **CLC 17**
  See also CA 29-32R; CANR 12, 28, 53; CLR
  27; MAICYA; SAAS 2; SATA 14, 72

Thomas, Audrey (Callahan) 1935-**CLC 7, 13,**
  37; SSC 20
  See also AITN 2; CA 21-24R; CAAS 19; CANR
  36, 58; DLB 60; MTCW

Thomas, D(onald) M(ichael) 1935- . **CLC 13,**
  22, 31
  See also CA 61-64; CAAS 11; CANR 17, 45;
  CDBLB 1960 to Present; DLB 40; INT
  CANR-17; MTCW

Thomas, Dylan (Marlais) 1914-1953**TCLC 1,**
  8, 45; DA; DAB; DAC; DAM DRAM,
  MST, POET; PC 2; SSC 3; WLC
  See also CA 104; 120; CDBLB 1945-1960;
  DLB 13, 20, 139; MTCW; SATA 60

Thomas, (Philip) Edward 1878-1917 . **T C L C**
  10; DAM POET
  See also CA 106; 153; DLB 19

Thomas, Joyce Carol 1938- .... **CLC 35**
  See also AAYA 12; BW 2; CA 113; 116; CANR
  48; CLR 19; DLB 33; INT 116; JRDA;
  MAICYA; MTCW; SAAS 7; SATA 40, 78

Thomas, Lewis 1913-1993 .... **CLC 35**
  See also CA 85-88; 143; CANR 38, 60; MTCW

Thomas, Paul
  See Mann, (Paul) Thomas

Thomas, Piri 1928- .... **CLC 17**
  See also CA 73-76; HW

Thomas, R(onald) S(tuart) 1913- **CLC 6, 13,**
  48; DAB; DAM POET
  See also CA 89-92; CAAS 4; CANR 30;
  CDBLB 1960 to Present; DLB 27; MTCW

Thomas, Ross (Elmore) 1926-1995 ... **CLC 39**
  See also CA 33-36R; 150; CANR 22

Thompson, Francis Clegg
  See Mencken, H(enry) L(ouis)

Thompson, Francis Joseph 1859-1907**TCLC 4**
  See also CA 104; CDBLB 1890-1914; DLB 19

Thompson, Hunter S(tockton) 1939-. **CLC 9,**
  17, 40, 104; DAM POP
  See also BEST 89:1; CA 17-20R; CANR 23,
  46; MTCW

Thompson, James Myers
  See Thompson, Jim (Myers)

Thompson, Jim (Myers) 1906-1977(?)**CLC 69**
  See also CA 140

Thompson, Judith .... **CLC 39**

Thomson, James 1700-1748 ... **LC 16, 29, 40;**
  DAM POET
  See also DLB 95

Thomson, James 1834-1882 **NCLC 18; DAM**
  POET
  See also DLB 35

Thoreau, Henry David 1817-1862**NCLC 7, 21,**
  61; DA; DAB; DAC; DAM MST; WLC
  See also CDALB 1640-1865; DLB 1

Thornton, Hall
  See Silverberg, Robert

Thucydides c. 455B.C.-399B.C. .... **CMLC 17**
  See also DLB 176

Thurber, James (Grover) 1894-1961 . **CLC 5,**
  11, 25; DA; DAB; DAC; DAM DRAM,
  MST, NOV; SSC 1
  See also CA 73-76; CANR 17, 39; CDALB
  1929-1941; DLB 4, 11, 22, 102; MAICYA;

MTCW; SATA 13

Thurman, Wallace (Henry) 1902-1934**T C L C**
  6; BLC; DAM MULT
  See also BW 1; CA 104; 124; DLB 51

Ticheburn, Cheviot
  See Ainsworth, William Harrison

Tieck, (Johann) Ludwig 1773-1853 **NCLC 5,**
  46
  See also DLB 90

Tiger, Derry
  See Ellison, Harlan (Jay)

Tilghman, Christopher 1948(?)- .... **CLC 65**
  See also CA 159

Tillinghast, Richard (Williford) 1940-**CLC 29**
  See also CA 29-32R; CAAS 23; CANR 26, 51

Timrod, Henry 1828-1867 .... **NCLC 25**
  See also DLB 3

Tindall, Gillian 1938- .... **CLC 7**
  See also CA 21-24R; CANR 11

Tiptree, James, Jr. .... **CLC 48, 50**
  See also Sheldon, Alice Hastings Bradley
  See also DLB 8

Titmarsh, Michael Angelo
  See Thackeray, William Makepeace

Tocqueville, Alexis (Charles Henri Maurice
  Clerel Comte) 1805-1859 ... **NCLC 7, 63**

Tolkien, J(ohn) R(onald) R(euel) 1892-1973
  CLC 1, 2, 3, 8, 12, 38; DA; DAB; DAC;
  DAM MST, NOV, POP; WLC
  See also AAYA 10; AITN 1; CA 17-18; 45-48;
  CANR 36; CAP 2; CDBLB 1914-1945; DLB
  15, 160; JRDA; MAICYA; MTCW; SATA 2,
  32; SATA-Obit 24

Toller, Ernst 1893-1939 .... **TCLC 10**
  See also CA 107; DLB 124

Tolson, M. B.
  See Tolson, Melvin B(eaunorus)

Tolson, Melvin B(eaunorus) 1898(?)-1966
  CLC 36, 105; BLC; DAM MULT, POET
  See also BW 1; CA 124; 89-92; DLB 48, 76

Tolstoi, Aleksei Nikolaevich
  See Tolstoy, Alexey Nikolaevich

Tolstoy, Alexey Nikolaevich 1882-1945**T C L C**
  18
  See also CA 107; 158

Tolstoy, Count Leo
  See Tolstoy, Leo (Nikolaevich)

Tolstoy, Leo (Nikolaevich) 1828-1910**TCLC 4,**
  11, 17, 28, 44; DA; DAB; DAC; DAM MST,
  NOV; SSC 9; WLC
  See also CA 104; 123; SATA 26

Tomasi di Lampedusa, Giuseppe 1896-1957
  See Lampedusa, Giuseppe (Tomasi) di
  See also CA 111

Tomlin, Lily .... **CLC 17**
  See also Tomlin, Mary Jean

Tomlin, Mary Jean 1939(?)-
  See Tomlin, Lily
  See also CA 117

Tomlinson, (Alfred) Charles 1927-**CLC 2, 4, 6,**
  13, 45; DAM POET; PC 17
  See also CA 5-8R; CANR 33; DLB 40

Tomlinson, H(enry) M(ajor) 1873-1958**TCLC**
  71
  See also CA 118; DLB 36, 100

Tonson, Jacob
  See Bennett, (Enoch) Arnold

Toole, John Kennedy 1937-1969 **CLC 19, 64**
  See also CA 104; DLBY 81

Toomer, Jean 1894-1967 .... **CLC 1, 4, 13, 22;**
  BLC; DAM MULT; PC 7; SSC 1; WLCS
  See also BW 1; CA 85-88; CDALB 1917-1929;
  DLB 45, 51; MTCW

Torley, Luke
　See Blish, James (Benjamin)
Tornimparte, Alessandra
　See Ginzburg, Natalia
Torre, Raoul della
　See Mencken, H(enry) L(ouis)
Torrey, E(dwin) Fuller 1937- .... **CLC 34**
　See also CA 119
Torsvan, Ben Traven
　See Traven, B.
Torsvan, Benno Traven
　See Traven, B.
Torsvan, Berick Traven
　See Traven, B.
Torsvan, Berwick Traven
　See Traven, B.
Torsvan, Bruno Traven
　See Traven, B.
Torsvan, Traven
　See Traven, B.
Tournier, Michel (Edouard) 1924-**CLC 6, 23,**
　36, 95
　See also CA 49-52; CANR 3, 36; DLB 83;
　MTCW; SATA 23
Tournimparte, Alessandra
　See Ginzburg, Natalia
Towers, Ivar
　See Kornbluth, C(yril) M.
Towne, Robert (Burton) 1936(?)- ..... **CLC 87**
　See also CA 108; DLB 44
Townsend, Sue 1946- .... **CLC 61; DAB; DAC**
　See also CA 119; 127; INT 127; MTCW; SATA
　55, 93; SATA-Brief 48
Townshend, Peter (Dennis Blandford) 1945-
　CLC 17, 42
　See also CA 107
Tozzi, Federigo 1883-1920 .... **TCLC 31**
　See also CA 160
Traill, Catharine Parr 1802-1899 .. **NCLC 31**
　See also DLB 99
Trakl, Georg 1887-1914 .... **TCLC 5; PC 20**
　See also CA 104
Transtroemer, Tomas (Goesta) 1931-**CLC 52,**
　65; DAM POET
　See also CA 117; 129; CAAS 17
Transtromer, Tomas Gosta
　See Transtroemer, Tomas (Goesta)
Traven, B. (?)-1969 .... **CLC 8, 11**
　See also CA 19-20; 25-28R; CAP 2; DLB 9,
　56; MTCW
Treitel, Jonathan 1959- .... **CLC 70**
Tremain, Rose 1943- .... **CLC 42**
　See also CA 97-100; CANR 44; DLB 14
Tremblay, Michel 1942- **CLC 29, 102; DAC;**
　DAM MST
　See also CA 116; 128; DLB 60; MTCW
Trevanian .... **CLC 29**
　See also Whitaker, Rod(ney)
Trevor, Glen
　See Hilton, James
Trevor, William 1928- . **CLC 7, 9, 14, 25, 71;**
　SSC 21
　See also Cox, William Trevor
　See also DLB 14, 139
Trifonov, Yuri (Valentinovich) 1925-1981
　CLC 45
　See also CA 126; 103; MTCW
Trilling, Lionel 1905-1975 ...... **CLC 9, 11, 24**
　See also CA 9-12R; 61-64; CANR 10; DLB 28,
　63; INT CANR-10; MTCW
Trimball, W. H.
　See Mencken, H(enry) L(ouis)
Tristan

See Gomez de la Serna, Ramon
Tristram
　See Housman, A(lfred) E(dward)
Trogdon, William (Lewis) 1939-
　See Heat-Moon, William Least
　See also CA 115; 119; CANR 47; INT 119
Trollope, Anthony 1815-1882**NCLC 6, 33; DA;**
　DAB; DAC; DAM MST, NOV; SSC 28;
　WLC
　See also CDBLB 1832-1890; DLB 21, 57, 159;
　SATA 22
Trollope, Frances 1779-1863 .... **NCLC 30**
　See also DLB 21, 166
Trotsky, Leon 1879-1940 .... **TCLC 22**
　See also CA 118
Trotter (Cockburn), Catharine 1679-1749**L C**
　8
　See also DLB 84
Trout, Kilgore
　See Farmer, Philip Jose
Trow, George W. S. 1943- .... **CLC 52**
　See also CA 126
Troyat, Henri 1911- .... **CLC 23**
　See also CA 45-48; CANR 2, 33; MTCW
Trudeau, G(arretson) B(eekman) 1948-
　See Trudeau, Garry B.
　See also CA 81-84; CANR 31; SATA 35
Trudeau, Garry B. .... **CLC 12**
　See also Trudeau, G(arretson) B(eekman)
　See also AAYA 10; AITN 2
Truffaut, Francois 1932-1984 .. **CLC 20, 101**
　See also CA 81-84; 113; CANR 34
Trumbo, Dalton 1905-1976 .... **CLC 19**
　See also CA 21-24R; 69-72; CANR 10; DLB
　26
Trumbull, John 1750-1831 .... **NCLC 30**
　See also DLB 31
Trundlett, Helen B.
　See Eliot, T(homas) S(tearns)
Tryon, Thomas 1926-1991 . **CLC 3, 11; DAM**
　POP
　See also AITN 1; CA 29-32R; 135; CANR 32;
　MTCW
Tryon, Tom
　See Tryon, Thomas
Ts'ao Hsueh-ch'in 1715(?)-1763 .... **LC 1**
Tsushima, Shuji 1909-1948
　See Dazai, Osamu
　See also CA 107
Tsvetaeva (Efron), Marina (Ivanovna) 1892-
　1941 .... **TCLC 7, 35; PC 14**
　See also CA 104; 128; MTCW
Tuck, Lily 1938- .... **CLC 70**
　See also CA 139
Tu Fu 712-770 .... **PC 9**
　See also DAM MULT
Tunis, John R(oberts) 1889-1975 ...... **CLC 12**
　See also CA 61-64; CANR 62; DLB 22, 171;
　JRDA; MAICYA; SATA 37; SATA-Brief 30
Tuohy, Frank .... **CLC 37**
　See also Tuohy, John Francis
　See also DLB 14, 139
Tuohy, John Francis 1925-
　See Tuohy, Frank
　See also CA 5-8R; CANR 3, 47
Turco, Lewis (Putnam) 1934- ...... **CLC 11, 63**
　See also CA 13-16R; CAAS 22; CANR 24, 51;
　DLBY 84
Turgenev, Ivan 1818-1883 .... **NCLC 21; DA;**
　DAB; DAC; DAM MST, NOV; DC 7; SSC
　7; WLC
Turgot, Anne-Robert-Jacques 1727-1781 **L C**
　26

Turner, Frederick 1943- .... **CLC 48**
　See also CA 73-76; CAAS 10; CANR 12, 30,
　56; DLB 40
Tutu, Desmond M(pilo) 1931- **CLC 80; BLC;**
　DAM MULT
　See also BW 1; CA 125
Tutuola, Amos 1920-1997**CLC 5, 14, 29; BLC;**
　DAM MULT
　See also BW 2; CA 9-12R; 159; CANR 27; DLB
　125; MTCW
Twain, Mark **TCLC 6, 12, 19, 36, 48, 59; SSC**
　26; WLC
　See also Clemens, Samuel Langhorne
　See also AAYA 20; DLB 11, 12, 23, 64, 74
Tyler, Anne 1941- . **CLC 7, 11, 18, 28, 44, 59,**
　103; DAM NOV, POP
　See also AAYA 18; BEST 89:1; CA 9-12R;
　CANR 11, 33, 53; DLB 6, 143; DLBY 82;
　MTCW; SATA 7, 90
Tyler, Royall 1757-1826 .... **NCLC 3**
　See also DLB 37
Tynan, Katharine 1861-1931 .... **TCLC 3**
　See also CA 104; DLB 153
Tyutchev, Fyodor 1803-1873 .... **NCLC 34**
Tzara, Tristan 1896-1963 ...... **CLC 47; DAM**
　POET
　See also Rosenfeld, Samuel; Rosenstock, Sami;
　Rosenstock, Samuel
　See also CA 153
Uhry, Alfred 1936- ... **CLC 55; DAM DRAM,**
　POP
　See also CA 127; 133; INT 133
Ulf, Haerved
　See Strindberg, (Johan) August
Ulf, Harved
　See Strindberg, (Johan) August
Ulibarri, Sabine R(eyes) 1919-**CLC 83; DAM**
　MULT
　See also CA 131; DLB 82; HW
Unamuno (y Jugo), Miguel de 1864-1936
　TCLC 2, 9; DAM MULT, NOV; HLC; SSC
　11
　See also CA 104; 131; DLB 108; HW; MTCW
Undercliffe, Errol
　See Campbell, (John) Ramsey
Underwood, Miles
　See Glassco, John
Undset, Sigrid 1882-1949**TCLC 3; DA; DAB;**
　DAC; DAM MST, NOV; WLC
　See also CA 104; 129; MTCW
Ungaretti, Giuseppe 1888-1970**CLC 7, 11, 15**
　See also CA 19-20; 25-28R; CAP 2; DLB 114
Unger, Douglas 1952- .... **CLC 34**
　See also CA 130
Unsworth, Barry (Forster) 1930- ..... **CLC 76**
　See also CA 25-28R; CANR 30, 54
Updike, John (Hoyer) 1932-**CLC 1, 2, 3, 5, 7,**
　9, 13, 15, 23, 34, 43, 70; DA; DAB; DAC;
　DAM MST, NOV, POET, POP; SSC 13, 27;
　WLC
　See also CA 1-4R; CABS 1; CANR 4, 33, 51;
　CDALB 1968-1988; DLB 2, 5, 143; DLBD
　3; DLBY 80, 82; MTCW
Upshaw, Margaret Mitchell
　See Mitchell, Margaret (Munnerlyn)
Upton, Mark
　See Sanders, Lawrence
Urdang, Constance (Henriette) 1922-**CLC 47**
　See also CA 21-24R; CANR 9, 24
Uriel, Henry
　See Faust, Frederick (Schiller)
Uris, Leon (Marcus) 1924- **CLC 7, 32; DAM**
　NOV, POP

See also AITN 1, 2; BEST 89:2; CA 1-4R;
    CANR 1, 40; MTCW; SATA 49
Urmuz
    See Codrescu, Andrei
Urquhart, Jane 1949- .... **CLC 90; DAC**
    See also CA 113; CANR 32
Ustinov, Peter (Alexander) 1921- .... **CLC 1**
    See also AITN 1; CA 13-16R; CANR 25, 51;
    DLB 13
U Tam'si, Gerald Felix Tchicaya
    See Tchicaya, Gerald Felix
U Tam'si, Tchicaya
    See Tchicaya, Gerald Felix
Vaculik, Ludvik 1926- .... **CLC 7**
    See also CA 53-56
Vaihinger, Hans 1852-1933 .... **TCLC 71**
    See also CA 116
Valdez, Luis (Miguel) 1940- .. **CLC 84; DAM
    MULT; HLC**
    See also CA 101; CANR 32; DLB 122; HW
Valenzuela, Luisa 1938- **CLC 31, 104; DAM
    MULT; SSC 14**
    See also CA 101; CANR 32; DLB 113; HW
Valera y Alcala-Galiano, Juan 1824-1905
    TCLC 10
    See also CA 106
Valery, (Ambroise) Paul (Toussaint Jules) 1871-
    1945 ..... **TCLC 4, 15; DAM POET; PC 9**
    See also CA 104; 122; MTCW
Valle-Inclan, Ramon (Maria) del 1866-1936
    TCLC 5; DAM MULT; HLC
    See also CA 106; 153; DLB 134
Vallejo, Antonio Buero
    See Buero Vallejo, Antonio
Vallejo, Cesar (Abraham) 1892-1938**TCLC 3,
    56; DAM MULT; HLC**
    See also CA 105; 153; HW
Vallette, Marguerite Eymery
    See Rachilde
Valle Y Pena, Ramon del
    See Valle-Inclan, Ramon (Maria) del
Van Ash, Cay 1918- .... **CLC 34**
Vanbrugh, Sir John 1664-1726 **LC 21; DAM
    DRAM**
    See also DLB 80
Van Campen, Karl
    See Campbell, John W(ood, Jr.)
Vance, Gerald
    See Silverberg, Robert
Vance, Jack .... **CLC 35**
    See also Kuttner, Henry; Vance, John Holbrook
    See also DLB 8
Vance, John Holbrook 1916-
    See Queen, Ellery; Vance, Jack
    See also CA 29-32R; CANR 17; MTCW
**Van Den Bogarde, Derek Jules Gaspard Ulric
    Niven** 1921-
    See Bogarde, Dirk
    See also CA 77-80
Vandenburgh, Jane .... **CLC 59**
Vanderhaeghe, Guy 1951- .... **CLC 41**
    See also CA 113
van der Post, Laurens (Jan) 1906-1996**CLC 5**
    See also CA 5-8R; 155; CANR 35
van de Wetering, Janwillem 1931- ... **CLC 47**
    See also CA 49-52; CANR 4, 62
Van Dine, S. S. .... **TCLC 23**
    See also Wright, Willard Huntington
Van Doren, Carl (Clinton) 1885-1950 **T C L C
    18**
    See also CA 111
Van Doren, Mark 1894-1972 .... **CLC 6, 10**
    See also CA 1-4R; 37-40R; CANR 3; DLB 45;

MTCW
Van Druten, John (William) 1901-1957**TCLC
    2**
    See also CA 104; DLB 10
Van Duyn, Mona (Jane) 1921- **CLC 3, 7, 63;
    DAM POET**
    See also CA 9-12R; CANR 7, 38, 60; DLB 5
Van Dyne, Edith
    See Baum, L(yman) Frank
van Itallie, Jean-Claude 1936- .... **CLC 3**
    See also CA 45-48; CAAS 2; CANR 1, 48; DLB
    7
van Ostaijen, Paul 1896-1928 .... **TCLC 33**
Van Peebles, Melvin 1932- **CLC 2, 20; DAM
    MULT**
    See also BW 2; CA 85-88; CANR 27
Vansittart, Peter 1920- .... **CLC 42**
    See also CA 1-4R; CANR 3, 49
Van Vechten, Carl 1880-1964 .... **CLC 33**
    See also CA 89-92; DLB 4, 9, 51
Van Vogt, A(lfred) E(lton) 1912- .... **CLC 1**
    See also CA 21-24R; CANR 28; DLB 8; SATA
    14
Varda, Agnes 1928- .... **CLC 16**
    See also CA 116; 122
Vargas Llosa, (Jorge) Mario (Pedro) 1936-
    **CLC 3, 6, 9, 10, 15, 31, 42, 85; DA; DAB;
    DAC; DAM MST, MULT, NOV; HLC**
    See also CA 73-76; CANR 18, 32, 42; DLB 145;
    HW; MTCW
Vasiliu, Gheorghe 1881-1957
    See Bacovia, George
    See also CA 123
Vassa, Gustavus
    See Equiano, Olaudah
Vassilikos, Vassilis 1933- .... **CLC 4, 8**
    See also CA 81-84
Vaughan, Henry 1621-1695 .... **LC 27**
    See also DLB 131
Vaughn, Stephanie .... **CLC 62**
Vazov, Ivan (Minchov) 1850-1921 . **TCLC 25**
    See also CA 121; DLB 147
Veblen, Thorstein (Bunde) 1857-1929 **T C L C
    31**
    See also CA 115
Vega, Lope de 1562-1635 .... **LC 23**
Venison, Alfred
    See Pound, Ezra (Weston Loomis)
Verdi, Marie de
    See Mencken, H(enry) L(ouis)
Verdu, Matilde
    See Cela, Camilo Jose
Verga, Giovanni (Carmelo) 1840-1922**T C L C
    3; SSC 21**
    See also CA 104; 123
Vergil 70B.C.-19B.C. ... **CMLC 9; DA; DAB;
    DAC; DAM MST, POET; PC 12; WLCS**
Verhaeren, Emile (Adolphe Gustave) 1855-1916
    TCLC 12
    See also CA 109
Verlaine, Paul (Marie) 1844-1896**NCLC 2, 51;
    DAM POET; PC 2**
Verne, Jules (Gabriel) 1828-1905**TCLC 6, 52**
    See also AAYA 16; CA 110; 131; DLB 123;
    JRDA; MAICYA; SATA 21
Very, Jones 1813-1880 .... **NCLC 9**
    See also DLB 1
Vesaas, Tarjei 1897-1970 .... **CLC 48**
    See also CA 29-32R
Vialis, Gaston
    See Simenon, Georges (Jacques Christian)
Vian, Boris 1920-1959 .... **TCLC 9**
    See also CA 106; DLB 72

Viaud, (Louis Marie) Julien 1850-1923
    See Loti, Pierre
    See also CA 107
Vicar, Henry
    See Felsen, Henry Gregor
Vicker, Angus
    See Felsen, Henry Gregor
Vidal, Gore 1925-**CLC 2, 4, 6, 8, 10, 22, 33, 72;
    DAM NOV, POP**
    See also AITN 1; BEST 90:2; CA 5-8R; CANR
    13, 45; DLB 6, 152; INT CANR-13; MTCW
Viereck, Peter (Robert Edwin) 1916- . **CLC 4**
    See also CA 1-4R; CANR 1, 47; DLB 5
Vigny, Alfred (Victor) de 1797-1863**NCLC 7;
    DAM POET**
    See also DLB 119
Vilakazi, Benedict Wallet 1906-1947**TCLC 37**
**Villiers de l'Isle Adam, Jean Marie Mathias
    Philippe Auguste Comte** 1838-1889
    NCLC 3; SSC 14
    See also DLB 123
Villon, Francois 1431-1463(?) .... **PC 13**
Vinci, Leonardo da 1452-1519 .... **LC 12**
Vine, Barbara .... **CLC 50**
    See also Rendell, Ruth (Barbara)
    See also BEST 90:4
Vinge, Joan D(ennison) 1948-**CLC 30; SSC 24**
    See also CA 93-96; SATA 36
Violis, G.
    See Simenon, Georges (Jacques Christian)
Visconti, Luchino 1906-1976 .... **CLC 16**
    See also CA 81-84; 65-68; CANR 39
Vittorini, Elio 1908-1966 .... **CLC 6, 9, 14**
    See also CA 133; 25-28R
Vizenor, Gerald Robert 1934-**CLC 103; DAM
    MULT**
    See also CA 13-16R; CAAS 22; CANR 5, 21,
    44; DLB 175; NNAL
Vizinczey, Stephen 1933- .... **CLC 40**
    See also CA 128; INT 128
Vliet, R(ussell) G(ordon) 1929-1984 **CLC 22**
    See also CA 37-40R; 112; CANR 18
Vogau, Boris Andreyevich 1894-1937(?)
    See Pilnyak, Boris
    See also CA 123
Vogel, Paula A(nne) 1951- .... **CLC 76**
    See also CA 108
Voight, Ellen Bryant 1943- .... **CLC 54**
    See also CA 69-72; CANR 11, 29, 55; DLB 120
Voigt, Cynthia 1942- .... **CLC 30**
    See also AAYA 3; CA 106; CANR 18, 37, 40;
    CLR 13; INT CANR-18; JRDA; MAICYA;
    SATA 48, 79; SATA-Brief 33
Voinovich, Vladimir (Nikolaevich) 1932-**C L C
    10, 49**
    See also CA 81-84; CAAS 12; CANR 33;
    MTCW
Vollmann, William T. 1959-... **CLC 89; DAM
    NOV, POP**
    See also CA 134
Voloshinov, V. N.
    See Bakhtin, Mikhail Mikhailovich
Voltaire 1694-1778 . **LC 14; DA; DAB; DAC;
    DAM DRAM, MST; SSC 12; WLC**
von Daeniken, Erich 1935- .... **CLC 30**
    See also AITN 1; CA 37-40R; CANR 17, 44
von Daniken, Erich
    See von Daeniken, Erich
von Heidenstam, (Carl Gustaf) Verner
    See Heidenstam, (Carl Gustaf) Verner von
von Heyse, Paul (Johann Ludwig)
    See Heyse, Paul (Johann Ludwig von)
von Hofmannsthal, Hugo

See Hofmannsthal, Hugo von
von Horvath, Odon
See Horvath, Oedoen von
von Horvath, Oedoen
See Horvath, Oedoen von
von Liliencron, (Friedrich Adolf Axel) Detlev
See Liliencron, (Friedrich Adolf Axel) Detlev von
Vonnegut, Kurt, Jr. 1922-**CLC 1, 2, 3, 4, 5, 8, 12, 22, 40, 60; DA; DAB; DAC; DAM MST, NOV, POP; SSC 8; WLC**
See also AAYA 6; AITN 1; BEST 90:4; CA 1-4R; CANR 1, 25, 49; CDALB 1968-1988; DLB 2, 8, 152; DLBD 3; DLBY 80; MTCW
Von Rachen, Kurt
See Hubbard, L(afayette) Ron(ald)
von Rezzori (d'Arezzo), Gregor
See Rezzori (d'Arezzo), Gregor von
von Sternberg, Josef
See Sternberg, Josef von
Vorster, Gordon 1924- .... **CLC 34**
See also CA 133
Vosce, Trudie
See Ozick, Cynthia
Voznesensky, Andrei (Andreievich) 1933-
CLC 1, 15, 57; DAM POET
See also CA 89-92; CANR 37; MTCW
Waddington, Miriam 1917- .... **CLC 28**
See also CA 21-24R; CANR 12, 30; DLB 68
Wagman, Fredrica 1937- .... **CLC 7**
See also CA 97-100; INT 97-100
Wagner, Linda W.
See Wagner-Martin, Linda (C.)
Wagner, Linda Welshimer
See Wagner-Martin, Linda (C.)
Wagner, Richard 1813-1883 .... **NCLC 9**
See also DLB 129
Wagner-Martin, Linda (C.) 1936- .... **CLC 50**
See also CA 159
Wagoner, David (Russell) 1926- **CLC 3, 5, 15**
See also CA 1-4R; CAAS 3; CANR 2; DLB 5; SATA 14
Wah, Fred(erick James) 1939- .... **CLC 44**
See also CA 107; 141; DLB 60
Wahloo, Per 1926-1975 .... **CLC 7**
See also CA 61-64
Wahloo, Peter
See Wahloo, Per
Wain, John (Barrington) 1925-1994 . **CLC 2, 11, 15, 46**
See also CA 5-8R; 145; CAAS 4; CANR 23, 54; CDBLB 1960 to Present; DLB 15, 27, 139, 155; MTCW
Wajda, Andrzej 1926- .... **CLC 16**
See also CA 102
Wakefield, Dan 1932- .... **CLC 7**
See also CA 21-24R; CAAS 7
Wakoski, Diane 1937- **CLC 2, 4, 7, 9, 11, 40; DAM POET; PC 15**
See also CA 13-16R; CAAS 1; CANR 9, 60; DLB 5; INT CANR-9
Wakoski-Sherbell, Diane
See Wakoski, Diane
Walcott, Derek (Alton) 1930-**CLC 2, 4, 9, 14, 25, 42, 67, 76; BLC; DAB; DAC; DAM MST, MULT, POET; DC 7**
See also BW 2; CA 89-92; CANR 26, 47; DLB 117; DLBY 81; MTCW
Waldman, Anne 1945- .... **CLC 7**
See also CA 37-40R; CAAS 17; CANR 34; DLB 16
Waldo, E. Hunter
See Sturgeon, Theodore (Hamilton)

Waldo, Edward Hamilton
See Sturgeon, Theodore (Hamilton)
Walker, Alice (Malsenior) 1944-**CLC 5, 6, 9, 19, 27, 46, 58, 103; BLC; DA; DAB; DAC; DAM MST, MULT, NOV, POET, POP; SSC 5; WLCS**
See also AAYA 3; BEST 89:4; BW 2; CA 37-40R; CANR 9, 27, 49; CDALB 1968-1988; DLB 6, 33, 143; INT CANR-27; MTCW; SATA 31
Walker, David Harry 1911-1992 .... **CLC 14**
See also CA 1-4R; 137; CANR 1; SATA 8; SATA-Obit 71
Walker, Edward Joseph 1934-
See Walker, Ted
See also CA 21-24R; CANR 12, 28, 53
Walker, George F. 1947- . **CLC 44, 61; DAB; DAC; DAM MST**
See also CA 103; CANR 21, 43, 59; DLB 60
Walker, Joseph A. 1935- .... **CLC 19; DAM DRAM, MST**
See also BW 1; CA 89-92; CANR 26; DLB 38
Walker, Margaret (Abigail) 1915- **CLC 1, 6; BLC; DAM MULT; PC 20**
See also BW 2; CA 73-76; CANR 26, 54; DLB 76, 152; MTCW
Walker, Ted .... **CLC 13**
See also Walker, Edward Joseph
See also DLB 40
Wallace, David Foster 1962- .... **CLC 50**
See also CA 132; CANR 59
Wallace, Dexter
See Masters, Edgar Lee
Wallace, (Richard Horatio) Edgar 1875-1932
TCLC 57
See also CA 115; DLB 70
Wallace, Irving 1916-1990 **CLC 7, 13; DAM NOV, POP**
See also AITN 1; CA 1-4R; 132; CAAS 1; CANR 1, 27; INT CANR-27; MTCW
Wallant, Edward Lewis 1926-1962**CLC 5, 10**
See also CA 1-4R; CANR 22; DLB 2, 28, 143; MTCW
Walley, Byron
See Card, Orson Scott
Walpole, Horace 1717-1797 .... **LC 2**
See also DLB 39, 104
Walpole, Hugh (Seymour) 1884-1941**TCLC 5**
See also CA 104; DLB 34
Walser, Martin 1927- .... **CLC 27**
See also CA 57-60; CANR 8, 46; DLB 75, 124
Walser, Robert 1878-1956 **TCLC 18; SSC 20**
See also CA 118; DLB 66
Walsh, Jill Paton .... **CLC 35**
See also Paton Walsh, Gillian
See also AAYA 11; CLR 2; DLB 161; SAAS 3
Walter, Villiam Christian
See Andersen, Hans Christian
Wambaugh, Joseph (Aloysius, Jr.) 1937-**CLC 3, 18; DAM NOV, POP**
See also AITN 1; BEST 89:3; CA 33-36R; CANR 42; DLB 6; DLBY 83; MTCW
Wang Wei 699(?)-761(?) .... **PC 18**
Ward, Arthur Henry Sarsfield 1883-1959
See Rohmer, Sax
See also CA 108
Ward, Douglas Turner 1930- .... **CLC 19**
See also BW 1; CA 81-84; CANR 27; DLB 7, 38
Ward, Mary Augusta
See Ward, Mrs. Humphry
Ward, Mrs. Humphry 1851-1920 .. **TCLC 55**
See also DLB 18

Ward, Peter
See Faust, Frederick (Schiller)
Warhol, Andy 1928(?)-1987 .... **CLC 20**
See also AAYA 12; BEST 89:4; CA 89-92; 121; CANR 34
Warner, Francis (Robert le Plastrier) 1937-
CLC 14
See also CA 53-56; CANR 11
Warner, Marina 1946- .... **CLC 59**
See also CA 65-68; CANR 21, 55
Warner, Rex (Ernest) 1905-1986 ...... **CLC 45**
See also CA 89-92; 119; DLB 15
Warner, Susan (Bogert) 1819-1885 **NCLC 31**
See also DLB 3, 42
Warner, Sylvia (Constance) Ashton
See Ashton-Warner, Sylvia (Constance)
Warner, Sylvia Townsend 1893-1978 **CLC 7, 19; SSC 23**
See also CA 61-64; 77-80; CANR 16, 60; DLB 34, 139; MTCW
Warren, Mercy Otis 1728-1814 ..... **NCLC 13**
See also DLB 31
Warren, Robert Penn 1905-1989**CLC 1, 4, 6, 8, 10, 13, 18, 39, 53, 59; DA; DAB; DAC; DAM MST, NOV, POET; SSC 4; WLC**
See also AITN 1; CA 13-16R; 129; CANR 10, 47; CDALB 1968-1988; DLB 2, 48, 152; DLBY 80, 89; INT CANR-10; MTCW; SATA 46; SATA-Obit 63
Warshofsky, Isaac
See Singer, Isaac Bashevis
Warton, Thomas 1728-1790 ..... **LC 15; DAM POET**
See also DLB 104, 109
Waruk, Kona
See Harris, (Theodore) Wilson
Warung, Price 1855-1911 .... **TCLC 45**
Warwick, Jarvis
See Garner, Hugh
Washington, Alex
See Harris, Mark
Washington, Booker T(aliaferro) 1856-1915
TCLC 10; BLC; DAM MULT
See also BW 1; CA 114; 125; SATA 28
Washington, George 1732-1799 .... **LC 25**
See also DLB 31
Wassermann, (Karl) Jakob 1873-1934 **T C L C 6**
See also CA 104; DLB 66
Wasserstein, Wendy 1950- ... **CLC 32, 59, 90; DAM DRAM; DC 4**
See also CA 121; 129; CABS 3; CANR 53; INT 129; SATA 94
Waterhouse, Keith (Spencer) 1929- . **CLC 47**
See also CA 5-8R; CANR 38; DLB 13, 15; MTCW
Waters, Frank (Joseph) 1902-1995 .. **CLC 88**
See also CA 5-8R; 149; CAAS 13; CANR 3, 18; DLBY 86
Waters, Roger 1944- .... **CLC 35**
Watkins, Frances Ellen
See Harper, Frances Ellen Watkins
Watkins, Gerrold
See Malzberg, Barry N(athaniel)
Watkins, Gloria 1955(?)-
See hooks, bell
See also BW 2; CA 143
Watkins, Paul 1964- .... **CLC 55**
See also CA 132; CANR 62
Watkins, Vernon Phillips 1906-1967 **CLC 43**
See also CA 9-10; 25-28R; CAP 1; DLB 20
Watson, Irving S.
See Mencken, H(enry) L(ouis)

Watson, John H.
See Farmer, Philip Jose
Watson, Richard F.
See Silverberg, Robert
Waugh, Auberon (Alexander) 1939- .. **CLC 7**
See also CA 45-48; CANR 6, 22; DLB 14
Waugh, Evelyn (Arthur St. John) 1903-1966
CLC 1, 3, 8, 13, 19, 27, 44; DA; DAB; DAC; DAM MST, NOV, POP; WLC
See also CA 85-88; 25-28R; CANR 22; CDBLB 1914-1945; DLB 15, 162; MTCW
Waugh, Harriet 1944- .... **CLC 6**
See also CA 85-88; CANR 22
Ways, C. R.
See Blount, Roy (Alton), Jr.
Waystaff, Simon
See Swift, Jonathan
Webb, (Martha) Beatrice (Potter) 1858-1943 **TCLC 22**
See also Potter, (Helen) Beatrix
See also CA 117
Webb, Charles (Richard) 1939- .... **CLC 7**
See also CA 25-28R
Webb, James H(enry), Jr. 1946- .... **CLC 22**
See also CA 81-84
Webb, Mary (Gladys Meredith) 1881-1927 **TCLC 24**
See also CA 123; DLB 34
Webb, Mrs. Sidney
See Webb, (Martha) Beatrice (Potter)
Webb, Phyllis 1927- .... **CLC 18**
See also CA 104; CANR 23; DLB 53
Webb, Sidney (James) 1859-1947 .. **TCLC 22**
See also CA 117
Webber, Andrew Lloyd .... **CLC 21**
See also Lloyd Webber, Andrew
Weber, Lenora Mattingly 1895-1971 **CLC 12**
See also CA 19-20; 29-32R; CAP 1; SATA 2; SATA-Obit 26
Weber, Max 1864-1920 .... **TCLC 69**
See also CA 109
Webster, John 1579(?)-1634(?) ... **LC 33; DA; DAB; DAC; DAM DRAM, MST; DC 2; WLC**
See also CDBLB Before 1660; DLB 58
Webster, Noah 1758-1843 .... **NCLC 30**
Wedekind, (Benjamin) Frank(lin) 1864-1918 **TCLC 7; DAM DRAM**
See also CA 104; 153; DLB 118
Weidman, Jerome 1913- .... **CLC 7**
See also AITN 2; CA 1-4R; CANR 1; DLB 28
Weil, Simone (Adolphine) 1909-1943 **TCLC 23**
See also CA 117; 159
Weinstein, Nathan
See West, Nathanael
Weinstein, Nathan von Wallenstein
See West, Nathanael
Weir, Peter (Lindsay) 1944- .... **CLC 20**
See also CA 113; 123
Weiss, Peter (Ulrich) 1916-1982 **CLC 3, 15, 51; DAM DRAM**
See also CA 45-48; 106; CANR 3; DLB 69, 124
Weiss, Theodore (Russell) 1916- **CLC 3, 8, 14**
See also CA 9-12R; CAAS 2; CANR 46; DLB 5
Welch, (Maurice) Denton 1915-1948 **TCLC 22**
See also CA 121; 148
Welch, James 1940- ..... **CLC 6, 14, 52; DAM MULT, POP**
See also CA 85-88; CANR 42; DLB 175; NNAL
Weldon, Fay 1933- . **CLC 6, 9, 11, 19, 36, 59; DAM POP**
See also CA 21-24R; CANR 16, 46; CDBLB

1960 to Present; DLB 14; INT CANR-16; MTCW
Wellek, Rene 1903-1995 .... **CLC 28**
See also CA 5-8R; 150; CAAS 7; CANR 8; DLB 63; INT CANR-8
Weller, Michael 1942- .... **CLC 10, 53**
See also CA 85-88
Weller, Paul 1958- .... **CLC 26**
Wellershoff, Dieter 1925- .... **CLC 46**
See also CA 89-92; CANR 16, 37
Welles, (George) Orson 1915-1985 **CLC 20, 80**
See also CA 93-96; 117
Wellman, Mac 1945- .... **CLC 65**
Wellman, Manly Wade 1903-1986 .... **CLC 49**
See also CA 1-4R; 118; CANR 6, 16, 44; SATA 6; SATA-Obit 47
Wells, Carolyn 1869(?)-1942 .... **TCLC 35**
See also CA 113; DLB 11
Wells, H(erbert) G(eorge) 1866-1946 **TCLC 6, 12, 19; DA; DAB; DAC; DAM MST, NOV; SSC 6; WLC**
See also AAYA 18; CA 110; 121; CDBLB 1914-1945; DLB 34, 70, 156, 178; MTCW; SATA 20
Wells, Rosemary 1943- .... **CLC 12**
See also AAYA 13; CA 85-88; CANR 48; CLR 16; MAICYA; SAAS 1; SATA 18, 69
Welty, Eudora 1909- **CLC 1, 2, 5, 14, 22, 33, 105; DA; DAB; DAC; DAM MST, NOV; SSC 1, 27; WLC**
See also CA 9-12R; CABS 1; CANR 32; CDALB 1941-1968; DLB 2, 102, 143; DLBD 12; DLBY 87; MTCW
Wen I-to 1899-1946 .... **TCLC 28**
Wentworth, Robert
See Hamilton, Edmond
Werfel, Franz (V.) 1890-1945 .... **TCLC 8**
See also CA 104; DLB 81, 124
Wergeland, Henrik Arnold 1808-1845 **NCLC 5**
Wersba, Barbara 1932- .... **CLC 30**
See also AAYA 2; CA 29-32R; CANR 16, 38; CLR 3; DLB 52; JRDA; MAICYA; SAAS 2; SATA 1, 58
Wertmueller, Lina 1928- .... **CLC 16**
See also CA 97-100; CANR 39
Wescott, Glenway 1901-1987 .... **CLC 13**
See also CA 13-16R; 121; CANR 23; DLB 4, 9, 102
Wesker, Arnold 1932- .... **CLC 3, 5, 42; DAB; DAM DRAM**
See also CA 1-4R; CAAS 7; CANR 1, 33; CDBLB 1960 to Present; DLB 13; MTCW
Wesley, Richard (Errol) 1945- .... **CLC 7**
See also BW 1; CA 57-60; CANR 27; DLB 38
Wessel, Johan Herman 1742-1785 .... **LC 7**
West, Anthony (Panther) 1914-1987 **CLC 50**
See also CA 45-48; 124; CANR 3, 19; DLB 15
West, C. P.
See Wodehouse, P(elham) G(renville)
West, (Mary) Jessamyn 1902-1984 **CLC 7, 17**
See also CA 9-12R; 112; CANR 27; DLB 6; DLBY 84; MTCW; SATA-Obit 37
West, Morris L(anglo) 1916- .... **CLC 6, 33**
See also CA 5-8R; CANR 24, 49; MTCW
West, Nathanael 1903-1940 **TCLC 1, 14, 44; SSC 16**
See also CA 104; 125; CDALB 1929-1941; DLB 4, 9, 28; MTCW
West, Owen
See Koontz, Dean R(ay)
West, Paul 1930- .... **CLC 7, 14, 96**
See also CA 13-16R; CAAS 7; CANR 22, 53;

DLB 14; INT CANR-22
West, Rebecca 1892-1983 .... **CLC 7, 9, 31, 50**
See also CA 5-8R; 109; CANR 19; DLB 36; DLBY 83; MTCW
Westall, Robert (Atkinson) 1929-1993 **CLC 17**
See also AAYA 12; CA 69-72; 141; CANR 18; CLR 13; JRDA; MAICYA; SAAS 2; SATA 23, 69; SATA-Obit 75
Westlake, Donald E(dwin) 1933- **CLC 7, 33; DAM POP**
See also CA 17-20R; CAAS 13; CANR 16, 44; INT CANR-16
Westmacott, Mary
See Christie, Agatha (Mary Clarissa)
Weston, Allen
See Norton, Andre
Wetcheek, J. L.
See Feuchtwanger, Lion
Wetering, Janwillem van de
See van de Wetering, Janwillem
Wetherell, Elizabeth
See Warner, Susan (Bogert)
Whale, James 1889-1957 .... **TCLC 63**
Whalen, Philip 1923- .... **CLC 6, 29**
See also CA 9-12R; CANR 5, 39; DLB 16
Wharton, Edith (Newbold Jones) 1862-1937 **TCLC 3, 9, 27, 53; DA; DAB; DAC; DAM MST, NOV; SSC 6; WLC**
See also CA 104; 132; CDALB 1865-1917; DLB 4, 9, 12, 78; DLBD 13; MTCW
Wharton, James
See Mencken, H(enry) L(ouis)
Wharton, William (a pseudonym) **CLC 18, 37**
See also CA 93-96; DLBY 80; INT 93-96
Wheatley (Peters), Phillis 1754(?)-1784 **LC 3; BLC; DA; DAC; DAM MST, MULT, POET; PC 3; WLC**
See also CDALB 1640-1865; DLB 31, 50
Wheelock, John Hall 1886-1978 .... **CLC 14**
See also CA 13-16R; 77-80; CANR 14; DLB 45
White, E(lwyn) B(rooks) 1899-1985 **CLC 10, 34, 39; DAM POP**
See also AITN 2; CA 13-16R; 116; CANR 16, 37; CLR 1, 21; DLB 11, 22; MAICYA; MTCW; SATA 2, 29; SATA-Obit 44
White, Edmund (Valentine III) 1940- **CLC 27; DAM POP**
See also AAYA 7; CA 45-48; CANR 3, 19, 36, 62; MTCW
White, Patrick (Victor Martindale) 1912-1990 **CLC 3, 4, 5, 7, 9, 18, 65, 69**
See also CA 81-84; 132; CANR 43; MTCW
White, Phyllis Dorothy James 1920-
See James, P. D.
See also CA 21-24R; CANR 17, 43; DAM POP; MTCW
White, T(erence) H(anbury) 1906-1964 **CLC 30**
See also AAYA 22; CA 73-76; CANR 37; DLB 160; JRDA; MAICYA; SATA 12
White, Terence de Vere 1912-1994 ... **CLC 49**
See also CA 49-52; 145; CANR 3
White, Walter F(rancis) 1893-1955 **TCLC 15**
See also White, Walter
See also BW 1; CA 115; 124; DLB 51
White, William Hale 1831-1913
See Rutherford, Mark
See also CA 121
Whitehead, E(dward) A(nthony) 1933- **CLC 5**
See also CA 65-68; CANR 58
Whitemore, Hugh (John) 1936- .... **CLC 37**
See also CA 132; INT 132

Whitman, Sarah Helen (Power) 1803-1878
  NCLC 19
  See also DLB 1
Whitman, Walt(er) 1819-1892 . **NCLC 4, 31;
  DA; DAB; DAC; DAM MST, POET; PC
  3; WLC**
  See also CDALB 1640-1865; DLB 3, 64; SATA
  20
Whitney, Phyllis A(yame) 1903- ..... **CLC 42;
  DAM POP**
  See also AITN 2; BEST 90:3; CA 1-4R; CANR
  3, 25, 38, 60; JRDA; MAICYA; SATA 1, 30
Whittemore, (Edward) Reed (Jr.) 1919-**CLC 4**
  See also CA 9-12R; CAAS 8; CANR 4; DLB 5
Whittier, John Greenleaf 1807-1892**NCLC 8,
  59**
  See also DLB 1
Whittlebot, Hernia
  See Coward, Noel (Peirce)
Wicker, Thomas Grey 1926-
  See Wicker, Tom
  See also CA 65-68; CANR 21, 46
Wicker, Tom .... **CLC 7**
  See also Wicker, Thomas Grey
Wideman, John Edgar 1941- **CLC 5, 34, 36,
  67; BLC; DAM MULT**
  See also BW 2; CA 85-88; CANR 14, 42; DLB
  33, 143
Wiebe, Rudy (Henry) 1934- .. **CLC 6, 11, 14;
  DAC; DAM MST**
  See also CA 37-40R; CANR 42; DLB 60
Wieland, Christoph Martin 1733-1813**NCLC
  17**
  See also DLB 97
Wiene, Robert 1881-1938 .... **TCLC 56**
Wieners, John 1934- .... **CLC 7**
  See also CA 13-16R; DLB 16
Wiesel, Elie(zer) 1928- **CLC 3, 5, 11, 37; DA;
  DAB; DAC; DAM MST, NOV; WLCS 2**
  See also AAYA 7; AITN 1; CA 5-8R; CAAS 4;
  CANR 8, 40; DLB 83; DLBY 87; INT
  CANR-8; MTCW; SATA 56
Wiggins, Marianne 1947- .... **CLC 57**
  See also BEST 89:3; CA 130; CANR 60
Wight, James Alfred 1916-
  See Herriot, James
  See also CA 77-80; SATA 55; SATA-Brief 44
Wilbur, Richard (Purdy) 1921-**CLC 3, 6, 9, 14,
  53; DA; DAB; DAC; DAM MST, POET**
  See also CA 1-4R; CABS 2; CANR 2, 29; DLB
  5, 169; INT CANR-29; MTCW; SATA 9
Wild, Peter 1940- .... **CLC 14**
  See also CA 37-40R; DLB 5
Wilde, Oscar (Fingal O'Flahertie Wills)
  1854(?)-1900**TCLC 1, 8, 23, 41; DA; DAB;
  DAC; DAM DRAM, MST, NOV; SSC 11;
  WLC**
  See also CA 104; 119; CDBLB 1890-1914;
  DLB 10, 19, 34, 57, 141, 156; SATA 24
Wilder, Billy .... **CLC 20**
  See also Wilder, Samuel
  See also DLB 26
Wilder, Samuel 1906-
  See Wilder, Billy
  See also CA 89-92
Wilder, Thornton (Niven) 1897-1975**CLC 1, 5,
  6, 10, 15, 35, 82; DA; DAB; DAC; DAM
  DRAM, MST, NOV; DC 1; WLC**
  See also AITN 2; CA 13-16R; 61-64; CANR
  40; DLB 4, 7, 9; MTCW
Wilding, Michael 1942- .... **CLC 73**
  See also CA 104; CANR 24, 49
Wiley, Richard 1944- .... **CLC 44**

See also CA 121; 129
Wilhelm, Kate .... **CLC 7**
  See also Wilhelm, Katie Gertrude
  See also AAYA 20; CAAS 5; DLB 8; INT
  CANR-17
Wilhelm, Katie Gertrude 1928-
  See Wilhelm, Kate
  See also CA 37-40R; CANR 17, 36, 60; MTCW
Wilkins, Mary
  See Freeman, Mary Eleanor Wilkins
Willard, Nancy 1936- .... **CLC 7, 37**
  See also CA 89-92; CANR 10, 39; CLR 5; DLB
  5, 52; MAICYA; MTCW; SATA 37, 71;
  SATA-Brief 30
Williams, C(harles) K(enneth) 1936-**CLC 33,
  56; DAM POET**
  See also CA 37-40R; CAAS 26; CANR 57; DLB
  5
Williams, Charles
  See Collier, James L(incoln)
Williams, Charles (Walter Stansby) 1886-1945
  TCLC 1, 11
  See also CA 104; DLB 100, 153
Williams, (George) Emlyn 1905-1987**CLC 15;
  DAM DRAM**
  See also CA 104; 123; CANR 36; DLB 10, 77;
  MTCW
Williams, Hugo 1942- .... **CLC 42**
  See also CA 17-20R; CANR 45; DLB 40
Williams, J. Walker
  See Wodehouse, P(elham) G(renville)
Williams, John A(lfred) 1925- ..... **CLC 5, 13;
  BLC; DAM MULT**
  See also BW 2; CA 53-56; CAAS 3; CANR 6,
  26, 51; DLB 2, 33; INT CANR-6
Williams, Jonathan (Chamberlain) 1929-
  CLC 13
  See also CA 9-12R; CAAS 12; CANR 8; DLB
  5
Williams, Joy 1944- .... **CLC 31**
  See also CA 41-44R; CANR 22, 48
Williams, Norman 1952- .... **CLC 39**
  See also CA 118
Williams, Sherley Anne 1944-**CLC 89; BLC;
  DAM MULT, POET**
  See also BW 2; CA 73-76; CANR 25; DLB 41;
  INT CANR-25; SATA 78
Williams, Shirley
  See Williams, Sherley Anne
Williams, Tennessee 1911-1983**CLC 1, 2, 5, 7,
  8, 11, 15, 19, 30, 39, 45, 71; DA; DAB;
  DAC; DAM DRAM, MST; DC 4; WLC**
  See also AITN 1, 2; CA 5-8R; 108; CABS 3;
  CANR 31; CDALB 1941-1968; DLB 7;
  DLBD 4; DLBY 83; MTCW
Williams, Thomas (Alonzo) 1926-1990**CLC 14**
  See also CA 1-4R; 132; CANR 2
Williams, William C.
  See Williams, William Carlos
Williams, William Carlos 1883-1963**CLC 1, 2,
  5, 9, 13, 22, 42, 67; DA; DAB; DAC; DAM
  MST, POET; PC 7**
  See also CA 89-92; CANR 34; CDALB 1917-
  1929; DLB 4, 16, 54, 86; MTCW
Williamson, David (Keith) 1942- ...... **CLC 56**
  See also CA 103; CANR 41
Williamson, Ellen Douglas 1905-1984
  See Douglas, Ellen
  See also CA 17-20R; 114; CANR 39
Williamson, Jack .... **CLC 29**
  See also Williamson, John Stewart
  See also CAAS 8; DLB 8
Williamson, John Stewart 1908-

See Williamson, Jack
  See also CA 17-20R; CANR 23
Willie, Frederick
  See Lovecraft, H(oward) P(hillips)
Willingham, Calder (Baynard, Jr.) 1922-1995
  CLC 5, 51
  See also CA 5-8R; 147; CANR 3; DLB 2, 44;
  MTCW
Willis, Charles
  See Clarke, Arthur C(harles)
Willy
  See Colette, (Sidonie-Gabrielle)
Willy, Colette
  See Colette, (Sidonie-Gabrielle)
Wilson, A(ndrew) N(orman) 1950- ... **CLC 33**
  See also CA 112; 122; DLB 14, 155
Wilson, Angus (Frank Johnstone) 1913-1991
  CLC 2, 3, 5, 25, 34; SSC 21
  See also CA 5-8R; 134; CANR 21; DLB 15,
  139, 155; MTCW
Wilson, August 1945- **CLC 39, 50, 63; BLC;
  DA; DAB; DAC; DAM DRAM, MST,
  MULT; DC 2; WLCS**
  See also AAYA 16; BW 2; CA 115; 122; CANR
  42, 54; MTCW
Wilson, Brian 1942- .... **CLC 12**
Wilson, Colin 1931- .... **CLC 3, 14**
  See also CA 1-4R; CAAS 5; CANR 1, 22, 33;
  DLB 14; MTCW
Wilson, Dirk
  See Pohl, Frederik
Wilson, Edmund 1895-1972**CLC 1, 2, 3, 8, 24**
  See also CA 1-4R; 37-40R; CANR 1, 46; DLB
  63; MTCW
Wilson, Ethel Davis (Bryant) 1888(?)-1980
  CLC 13; DAC; DAM POET
  See also CA 102; DLB 68; MTCW
Wilson, John 1785-1854 .... **NCLC 5**
Wilson, John (Anthony) Burgess 1917-1993
  See Burgess, Anthony
  See also CA 1-4R; 143; CANR 2, 46; DAC;
  DAM NOV; MTCW
Wilson, Lanford 1937- **CLC 7, 14, 36; DAM
  DRAM**
  See also CA 17-20R; CABS 3; CANR 45; DLB
  7
Wilson, Robert M. 1944- .... **CLC 7, 9**
  See also CA 49-52; CANR 2, 41; MTCW
Wilson, Robert McLiam 1964- .... **CLC 59**
  See also CA 132
Wilson, Sloan 1920- .... **CLC 32**
  See also CA 1-4R; CANR 1, 44
Wilson, Snoo 1948- .... **CLC 33**
  See also CA 69-72
Wilson, William S(mith) 1932- .... **CLC 49**
  See also CA 81-84
Wilson, Woodrow 1856-1924 .... **TCLC 73**
  See also DLB 47
Winchilsea, Anne (Kingsmill) Finch Counte
  1661-1720 .... **LC 3**
Windham, Basil
  See Wodehouse, P(elham) G(renville)
Wingrove, David (John) 1954- .... **CLC 68**
  See also CA 133
Wintergreen, Jane
  See Duncan, Sara Jeannette
Winters, Janet Lewis .... **CLC 41**
  See also Lewis, Janet
  See also DLBY 87
Winters, (Arthur) Yvor 1900-1968 **CLC 4, 8,
  32**
  See also CA 11-12; 25-28R; CAP 1; DLB 48;
  MTCW

Winterson, Jeanette 1959-CLC 64; DAM POP
  See also CA 136; CANR 58
Winthrop, John 1588-1649 .... LC 31
  See also DLB 24, 30
Wiseman, Frederick 1930- .... CLC 20
  See also CA 159
Wister, Owen 1860-1938 .... TCLC 21
  See also CA 108; DLB 9, 78; SATA 62
Witkacy
  See Witkiewicz, Stanislaw Ignacy
Witkiewicz, Stanislaw Ignacy 1885-1939
  TCLC 8
  See also CA 105
Wittgenstein, Ludwig (Josef Johann) 1889-1951
  TCLC 59
  See also CA 113
Wittig, Monique 1935(?)- .... CLC 22
  See also CA 116; 135; DLB 83
Wittlin, Jozef 1896-1976 .... CLC 25
  See also CA 49-52; 65-68; CANR 3
Wodehouse, P(elham) G(renville) 1881-1975
  CLC 1, 2, 5, 10, 22; DAB; DAC; DAM
  NOV; SSC 2
  See also AITN 2; CA 45-48; 57-60; CANR 3,
  33; CDBLB 1914-1945; DLB 34, 162;
  MTCW; SATA 22
Woiwode, L.
  See Woiwode, Larry (Alfred)
Woiwode, Larry (Alfred) 1941- .... CLC 6, 10
  See also CA 73-76; CANR 16; DLB 6; INT
  CANR-16
Wojciechowska, Maia (Teresa) 1927-CLC 26
  See also AAYA 8; CA 9-12R; CANR 4, 41; CLR
  1; JRDA; MAICYA; SAAS 1; SATA 1, 28,
  83
Wolf, Christa 1929- .... CLC 14, 29, 58
  See also CA 85-88; CANR 45; DLB 75; MTCW
Wolfe, Gene (Rodman) 1931- CLC 25; DAM
  POP
  See also CA 57-60; CAAS 9; CANR 6, 32, 60;
  DLB 8
Wolfe, George C. 1954- .... CLC 49
  See also CA 149
Wolfe, Thomas (Clayton) 1900-1938TCLC 4,
  13, 29, 61; DA; DAB; DAC; DAM MST,
  NOV; WLC
  See also CA 104; 132; CDALB 1929-1941;
  DLB 9, 102; DLBD 2, 16; DLBY 85; MTCW
Wolfe, Thomas Kennerly, Jr. 1931-
  See Wolfe, Tom
  See also CA 13-16R; CANR 9, 33; DAM POP;
  INT CANR-9; MTCW
Wolfe, Tom .... CLC 1, 2, 9, 15, 35, 51
  See also Wolfe, Thomas Kennerly, Jr.
  See also AAYA 8; AITN 2; BEST 89:1; DLB
  152
Wolff, Geoffrey (Ansell) 1937- .... CLC 41
  See also CA 29-32R; CANR 29, 43
Wolff, Sonia
  See Levitin, Sonia (Wolff)
Wolff, Tobias (Jonathan Ansell) 1945- . C L C
  39, 64
  See also AAYA 16; BEST 90:2; CA 114; 117;
  CAAS 22; CANR 54; DLB 130; INT 117
Wolfram von Eschenbach c. 1170-c. 1220
  CMLC 5
  See also DLB 138
Wolitzer, Hilma 1930- .... CLC 17
  See also CA 65-68; CANR 18, 40; INT CANR-
  18; SATA 31
Wollstonecraft, Mary 1759-1797 .... LC 5
  See also CDBLB 1789-1832; DLB 39, 104, 158
Wonder, Stevie .... CLC 12

See also Morris, Steveland Judkins
Wong, Jade Snow 1922- .... CLC 17
  See also CA 109
Woodberry, George Edward 1855-1930
  TCLC 73
  See also DLB 71, 103
Woodcott, Keith
  See Brunner, John (Kilian Houston)
Woodruff, Robert W.
  See Mencken, H(enry) L(ouis)
Woolf, (Adeline) Virginia 1882-1941TCLC 1,
  5, 20, 43, 56; DA; DAB; DAC; DAM MST,
  NOV; SSC 7; WLC
  See also CA 104; 130; CDBLB 1914-1945;
  DLB 36, 100, 162; DLBD 10; MTCW
Woollcott, Alexander (Humphreys) 1887-1943
  TCLC 5
  See also CA 105; DLB 29
Woolrich, Cornell 1903-1968 .... CLC 77
  See also Hopley-Woolrich, Cornell George
Wordsworth, Dorothy 1771-1855 .. NCLC 25
  See also DLB 107
Wordsworth, William 1770-1850.. NCLC 12,
  38; DA; DAB; DAC; DAM MST, POET;
  PC 4; WLC
  See also CDBLB 1789-1832; DLB 93, 107
Wouk, Herman 1915-CLC 1, 9, 38; DAM NOV,
  POP
  See also CA 5-8R; CANR 6, 33; DLBY 82; INT
  CANR-6; MTCW
Wright, Charles (Penzel, Jr.) 1935-CLC 6, 13,
  28
  See also CA 29-32R; CAAS 7; CANR 23, 36,
  62; DLB 165; DLBY 82; MTCW
Wright, Charles Stevenson 1932- ... CLC 49;
  BLC 3; DAM MULT, POET
  See also BW 1; CA 9-12R; CANR 26; DLB 33
Wright, Jack R.
  See Harris, Mark
Wright, James (Arlington) 1927-1980CLC 3,
  5, 10, 28; DAM POET
  See also AITN 2; CA 49-52; 97-100; CANR 4,
  34; DLB 5, 169; MTCW
Wright, Judith (Arandell) 1915- CLC 11, 53;
  PC 14
  See also CA 13-16R; CANR 31; MTCW; SATA
  14
Wright, L(aurali) R. 1939- .... CLC 44
  See also CA 138
Wright, Richard (Nathaniel) 1908-1960 C L C
  1, 3, 4, 9, 14, 21, 48, 74; BLC; DA; DAB;
  DAC; DAM MST, MULT, NOV; SSC 2;
  WLC
  See also AAYA 5; BW 1; CA 108; CDALB
  1929-1941; DLB 76, 102; DLBD 2; MTCW
Wright, Richard B(ruce) 1937- .... CLC 6
  See also CA 85-88; DLB 53
Wright, Rick 1945- .... CLC 35
Wright, Rowland
  See Wells, Carolyn
Wright, Stephen Caldwell 1946- .... CLC 33
  See also BW 2
Wright, Willard Huntington 1888-1939
  See Van Dine, S. S.
  See also CA 115; DLBD 16
Wright, William 1930- .... CLC 44
  See also CA 53-56; CANR 7, 23
Wroth, LadyMary 1587-1653(?) .... LC 30
  See also DLB 121
Wu Ch'eng-en 1500(?)-1582(?) .... LC 7
Wu Ching-tzu 1701-1754 .... LC 2
Wurlitzer, Rudolph 1938(?)- .... CLC 2, 4, 15
  See also CA 85-88; DLB 173

Wycherley, William 1641-1715LC 8, 21; DAM
  DRAM
  See also CDBLB 1660-1789; DLB 80
Wylie, Elinor (Morton Hoyt) 1885-1928
  TCLC 8
  See also CA 105; DLB 9, 45
Wylie, Philip (Gordon) 1902-1971 ... CLC 43
  See also CA 21-22; 33-36R; CAP 2; DLB 9
Wyndham, John .... CLC 19
  See also Harris, John (Wyndham Parkes Lucas)
  Beynon
Wyss, Johann David Von 1743-1818NCLC 10
  See also JRDA; MAICYA; SATA 29; SATA-
  Brief 27
Xenophon c. 430B.C.-c. 354B.C. ... CMLC 17
  See also DLB 176
Yakumo Koizumi
  See Hearn, (Patricio) Lafcadio (Tessima Carlos)
Yanez, Jose Donoso
  See Donoso (Yanez), Jose
Yanovsky, Basile S.
  See Yanovsky, V(assily) S(emenovich)
Yanovsky, V(assily) S(emenovich) 1906-1989
  CLC 2, 18
  See also CA 97-100; 129
Yates, Richard 1926-1992 .... CLC 7, 8, 23
  See also CA 5-8R; 139; CANR 10, 43; DLB 2;
  DLBY 81, 92; INT CANR-10
Yeats, W. B.
  See Yeats, William Butler
Yeats, William Butler 1865-1939TCLC 1, 11,
  18, 31; DA; DAB; DAC; DAM DRAM,
  MST, POET; PC 20; WLC
  See also CA 104; 127; CANR 45; CDBLB
  1890-1914; DLB 10, 19, 98, 156; MTCW
Yehoshua, A(braham) B. 1936- .. CLC 13, 31
  See also CA 33-36R; CANR 43
Yep, Laurence Michael 1948-............ CLC 35
  See also AAYA 5; CA 49-52; CANR 1, 46; CLR
  3, 17; DLB 52; JRDA; MAICYA; SATA 7,
  69
Yerby, Frank G(arvin) 1916-1991 .CLC 1, 7,
  22; BLC; DAM MULT
  See also BW 1; CA 9-12R; 136; CANR 16, 52;
  DLB 76; INT CANR-16; MTCW
Yesenin, Sergei Alexandrovich
  See Esenin, Sergei (Alexandrovich)
Yevtushenko, Yevgeny (Alexandrovich) 1933-
  CLC 1, 3, 13, 26, 51; DAM POET
  See also CA 81-84; CANR 33, 54; MTCW
Yezierska, Anzia 1885(?)-1970 .... CLC 46
  See also CA 126; 89-92; DLB 28; MTCW
Yglesias, Helen 1915- ....CLC 7, 22
  See also CA 37-40R; CAAS 20; CANR 15; INT
  CANR-15; MTCW
Yokomitsu Riichi 1898-1947 .... TCLC 47
Yonge, Charlotte (Mary) 1823-1901TCLC 48
  See also CA 109; DLB 18, 163; SATA 17
York, Jeremy
  See Creasey, John
York, Simon
  See Heinlein, Robert A(nson)
Yorke, Henry Vincent 1905-1974...... CLC 13
  See also Green, Henry
  See also CA 85-88; 49-52
Yosano Akiko 1878-1942 .... TCLC 59; PC 11
Yoshimoto, Banana .... CLC 84
  See also Yoshimoto, Mahoko
Yoshimoto, Mahoko 1964-
  See Yoshimoto, Banana
  See also CA 144
Young, Al(bert James) 1939- .CLC 19; BLC;
  DAM MULT

Literary Criticism Series
Cumulative Topic Index

This index lists all topic entries in Gale's *Classical and Medieval Literature Criticism, Contemporary Literary Criticism, Literature Criticism from 1400 to 1800, Nineteenth-Century Literature Criticism,* and *Twentieth-Century Literary Criticism.*

Age of Johnson LC 15: 1-87
Johnson's London, 3-15
aesthetics of neoclassicism, 15-36
"age of prose and reason," 36-45
clubmen and bluestockings, 45-56
printing technology, 56-62
periodicals: "a map of busy life," 62-74
transition, 74-86

Age of Spenser LC 39: 1-70
Overviews, 2-21
Literary Style, 22-34
Poets and the Crown, 34-70

AIDS in Literature CLC 81: 365-416

Alcohol and Literature TCLC 70: 1-58
overview, 2-8
fiction, 8-48
poetry and drama, 48-58

American Abolitionism NCLC 44: 1-73
overviews, 2-26
abolitionist ideals, 26-46
the literature of abolitionism, 46-72

American Black Humor Fiction TCLC 54: 1-85
characteristics of black humor, 2-13
origins and development, 13-38
black humor distinguished from related literary trends, 38-60
black humor and society, 60-75
black humor reconsidered, 75-83

American Civil War in Literature NCLC 32: 1-109
overviews, 2-20
regional perspectives, 20-54
fiction popular during the war, 54-79
the historical novel, 79-108

American Frontier in Literature NCLC

28: 1-103
definitions, 2-12
development, 12-17
nonfiction writing about the frontier, 17-30
frontier fiction, 30-45
frontier protagonists, 45-66
portrayals of Native Americans, 66-86
feminist readings, 86-98
twentieth-century reaction against frontier literature, 98-100

American Humor Writing NCLC 52: 1-59
overviews, 2-12
the Old Southwest, 12-42
broader impacts, 42-5
women humorists, 45-58

American Popular Song, Golden Age of TCLC 42: 1-49
background and major figures, 2-34
the lyrics of popular songs, 34-47

American Proletarian Literature TCLC 54: 86-175
overviews, 87-95
American proletarian literature and the American Communist Party, 95-111
ideology and literary merit, 111-7
novels, 117-36
Gastonia, 136-48
drama, 148-54
journalism, 154-9
proletarian literature in the United States, 159-74

American Romanticism NCLC 44: 74-138
overviews, 74-84
sociopolitical influences, 84-104
Romanticism and the American frontier, 104-15
thematic concerns, 115-37

American Western Literature TCLC 46:

1-100
definition and development of American Western literature, 2-7
characteristics of the Western novel, 8-23
Westerns as history and fiction, 23-34
critical reception of American Western literature, 34-41
the Western hero, 41-73
women in Western fiction, 73-91
later Western fiction, 91-9

Art and Literature TCLC 54: 176-248
overviews, 176-93
definitions, 193-219
influence of visual arts on literature, 219-31
spatial form in literature, 231-47

Arthurian Literature CMLC 10: 1-127
historical context and literary beginnings, 2-27
development of the legend through Malory, 27-64
development of the legend from Malory to the Victorian Age, 65-81
themes and motifs, 81-95
principal characters, 95-125

Arthurian Revival NCLC 36: 1-77
overviews, 2-12
Tennyson and his influence, 12-43
other leading figures, 43-73
the Arthurian legend in the visual arts, 73-6

Australian Literature TCLC 50: 1-94
origins and development, 2-21
characteristics of Australian literature, 21-33
historical and critical perspectives, 33-41
poetry, 41-58
fiction, 58-76

Topic Index

Topic Index

Topic Index

Contemporary Literary Criticism
Cumulative Nationality Index

　　　　　　　　CONTEMPORARY LITERARY CRITICISM

Nationality Index

CLC-105 Title Index